We the People

AN INTRODUCTION TO AMERICAN POLITICS

We the People

AN INTRODUCTION TO AMERICAN POLITICS

Benjamin Ginsberg
THE JOHNS HOPKINS UNIVERSITY

Theodore J. Lowi
CORNELL UNIVERSITY

Margaret Weir
THE BROOKINGS INSTITUTION

W · W · NORTON & COMPANY
NEW YORK · LONDON

TO

Sandy, Cindy, and Alex Ginsberg
Angele, Anna, and Jason Lowi
Nicholas Ziegler

PRINTED IN THE UNITED STATES OF AMERICA

First Edition

The text of this book is composed in Sabon
with the display set in Garamond 3.
Composition by New England Typographic Service
Manufacturing by Quebecor/Hawkins
Book design by Jack Meserole

Cover illustrations, clockwise from upper left: Charles Steiner/SYGMA;
University Archives. The Bancroft Library. University of California, Berkeley;
Rob Crandall/The Image Works; Fred Ward/Black Star
Further acknowledgments and copyrights appear on p. A71,
which constitutes a continuation of the copyright page.

Library of Congress Cataloging-in-Publication Data

Ginsberg, Benjamin.
We the people: an introduction to American politics / Benjamin Ginsberg, Theodore J. Lowi, Margaret Weir.
p. cm.
Includes bibliographical references and index.
ISBN 0-393-97027-2
1. United States—Politics and government. I. Lowi, Theodore J. II. Weir, Margaret, 1952– . III. Title.
JK271.G65 1997b
320.473—dc21 96-39782

W. W. Norton & Company, Inc., 500 Fifth Avenue, New York, N.Y. 10110
http://www.wwnorton.com
W. W. Norton & Company, Ltd., 10 Coptic Street, London WC1A 1PU

1 2 3 4 5 6 7 8 9 0

Contents

PART II

★

Foundations

PART III

✶

Politics

6

Public Opinion 186

7

The Media 226

8

Political Parties 260

9

Campaigns and Elections 300

10

Groups and Interests 346

PART IV
★
Institutions

11

Congress 390

13

Bureaucracy in a Democracy 490

Appendix

Preface

We the People is a milestone in a collaboration that began between Theodore J. Lowi and Benjamin Ginsberg almost twenty years ago. The first result of that collaboration, *American Government: Freedom and Power,* was first published in 1990. With its most recent edition, we and the publishers feel warranted in expressing satisfaction that its historical/institutional method has been confirmed, not only by its reception among the teachers who have adopted it and the students who have read it, but also by the extent to which it has been imitated by so many other introductory texts.

But unlike political leaders, textbooks should not try to be all things to all people. Endurance is most often ensured by recognition of one's limitations. Lowi and Ginsberg increasingly came to feel that *American Government* needed a sibling to address a number of themes and problems that have become much more central to American politics since *American Government* was conceived in the early 1980s. For a good text should be both timeless and timely. It should present principles whose value goes beyond the immediate events of the day. At the same time, however, it should present students with the principles they need to help elevate their understanding of contemporary events.

We viewed this process as a challenge rather than as a chore. The first step Lowi and Ginsberg took to meet the challenge of developing a new text was to invite a third author to join the enterprise: Margaret Weir, a senior fellow in the Governmental Studies Program at the Brookings Institution, and an expert on social policy in the United States and Europe. Weir brings with her a strong background in urban politics as well as the benefit of several years of teaching experience at Harvard.

From the start, the three of us agreed that this younger sibling would be titled *We the People* and would focus on four sets of issues. The first of these is the question of who is and who is not part of the American political community. This question has been the source of enormous conflict throughout American history and has become salient once again as events at home and throughout the world have brightened the light of democracy, exposing for everyone to see the unreasonable restrictions on who are "we the people," how should "we the people" be defined, and what powers, rights, and obligations "we the people" should have. Although the United States has so far experienced comparatively little conflict over the basic institutions and practices of government, and although our institutions have evolved in a roughly democratic direction, the struggle over the scope and inclusiveness of the American political process has often been a bitter one, and neither the struggle nor the bitterness is over.

The original American political community consisted of a rather limited group of white male property holders. Over the ensuing two centuries, "we the people" became a larger and more inclusive body as a result of such forces as the abolitionist movement, the women's suffrage movement, and the Civil Rights movement. This expansion of the political community was marked by enormous conflicts involving questions of race, gender, social class, and religious identity. Today, these conflicts continue in the form of struggles over such issues as affirmative action, welfare reform, abortion, the gender gap, the political mobilization of religious groups, and the rise and fall of minority voting districts. These themes are raised in Chapter 2 of *We the People* and are explored further throughout the book.

But regardless of our country's spotty record, one American feature has been and remains the envy of the entire world: Expansion of our political community *has* taken place, and it has happened without having to create new institutions, rules, or procedures. Our democracy is no crustacean that has to shed its structure as it grows.

The second set of issues that we focus on concerns American political values. The American nation is defined not only by its form of government but also by a set of shared beliefs and values, the most basic of which are liberty, equality, and democracy. Although these can be located in antiquity, Americans gave them new vitality and credibility in our founding documents—the Declaration of Independence and the Constitution, which transformed ancient and abstract principles into operating structures and rules for the new Republic. Although the path has deviated and wrong turns have been taken, the general direction of America has been one worthy of pride—a pride we authors share with virtually all of the American people. But our job as authors is to recognize the gap between ideals and realities and to treat the gap honestly so that our students come to understand that a good citizen is a critical citizen, one whose obedience is not unconditional. Liberty, equality, and democracy are concepts that link all the chapters of our book. They are also criteria against which to measure and to judge all aspects of governmental and political performance.

A third set of issues comes down to the key structural element of the American Constitution: the relationship between the national government and the state and local governments. For more than a century of American history under the Constitution, this relationship was resolved in favor of state and local government. About sixty years ago, this relationship was resolved in favor of national power. In recent years, however, widespread appeals for devolution of power back toward the states have reopened old questions, reviving debates that confounded the Founders. In *We the People* we examine the vitality of democratic government at the state and local levels, comparing it to the national level, in order to determine for ourselves as well as for our students not only what powers are at stake but where the balance between the levels might best be struck. We find enormous variation among the states in governmental structure, administrative capability, and political patterns. As welfare reforms and other programs give the states more latitude to develop and implement their own policies, we can expect some surprising developments that will in themselves be great lessons in the art and science of government. We are confident that students will have a much better understanding of the nature of government after they have worked with our text, because they will have been given the experience of *many* governments, all within the American scheme of values.

Fourth and finally, *We the People* addresses a pedagogical question: Why should Americans be engaged with government and politics at all? For the entire first century and more of American history under the Constitution, Americans were relatively heavily involved in political life, as activists or as active spectators. Politics was a kind of entertainment, a defining aspect of community life. Politics in America was interesting even to those who had not yet been made full members of the political community. As the size of all governments, especially the national government, began to grow after World War I, Americans by all appearances still took their politics seriously, and the scope of their interest seemed to expand from campaigns and elections into public policy issues keeping pace with the expansion of government and of government programs.

During the 1960s and 1970s, American students were heavily engaged with politics, many seeing it, quite realistically, as a matter of life and death. Even during the early 1980s, when *American Government: Freedom and Power* was being planned, it was our assumption that political engagement needed guidance—but that it was *there* to be guided. It hardly seemed necessary to explain to students why they should take politics seriously, as observers as well as activists.

But the involvement of the American people in political life has been declining, and students have been increasingly willing to ask why they should be interested in politics at all. We are deeply troubled by this trend and have committed this book to its reversal. Our chapters are introduced by discussions that show where students fit into the materials to be addressed by that chapter and why they should take a personal, indeed selfish, interest in the outcomes of government. For example, our discussion of the media opens with the issues of press freedom faced by college newspapers. Our chapter on civil rights begins with an evaluation of affirmative action programs in college admissions. The opening pages of our discussion of federalism deals with interstate differences that affect college students. Our hope is to make politics interesting to students by demonstrating that their interests are at stake—that their forebears were correct in viewing politics as a matter of life and death.

Acknowledgments

Our students at Cornell and Johns Hopkins and Harvard have been an essential factor in the writing of this book. They have been our most immediate intellectual community, a hospitable one indeed. Another part of our community, perhaps a large suburb, is the discipline of political science itself. Our debt to the scholarship of our colleagues is scientifically measurable, probably to several decimal points, in the footnotes of each chapter. Despite many complaints that the field is too scientific or not scientific enough, political science is alive and well in the United States. It is an aspect of democracy itself, and it has grown and changed in response to the developments in government and politics that we have chronicled in our book. If we did a "time line" on the history of political science, it would show a close association with developments in "the American state." Sometimes the discipline has been out of phase and critical; at other times, it has been in phase and perhaps apologetic. But political science has never been at a loss for relevant literature, and without it, our job would have been impossible.

We are especially pleased to acknowledge our debt to the many colleagues who had a direct and active role in criticism and preparation of the manuscript. Our thanks go to

Sarah Binder, Brookings Institution
Kathleen Gille, Office of Representative David Bonior
Rodney Hero, University of Colorado at Boulder
Robert Katzmann, Brookings Institution
Kathleen Knight, University of Houston
Robin Kolodny, Temple University
Nancy Kral, Tomball College
Robert C. Lieberman, Columbia University
David A. Marcum, University of Wyoming
Laura R. Winsky Mattei, State University of New York at Buffalo
Marilyn S. Mertens, Midwestern State University
Barbara Suhay, Henry Ford Community College
Carolyn Wong, Stanford University, and
Julian Zelizer, State University of New York at Albany

We owe a special debt to Robert J. Spitzer of the State University of New York at Cortland for preparing the "We the People" essays and to Michael Harvey of the University of Wisconsin at Milwaukee for preparing the "American Political Culture" essays. By linking concepts to historical events and contemporary debates, these essays help to make this a more lively and interesting book and thus one that students will be more likely to read and remember.

We are also grateful for the talents and hard work of several research assistants, whose contributions can never be adequately compensated. Douglas Harris, formerly of Johns Hopkins and now at Colgate University, put an enormous amount of thought and time into many of the figures and tables as well as many of the study aids that appear in the text. At Cornell, Hollie Heath, Brenda Holzinger, and Dennis Merryfield gave significant help to the book. Betty Waaler of the College of William and Mary also provided valuable research assistance.

We would like to give special thanks to Jacqueline Pastore at Cornell University, who not only prepared portions of the manuscript but also helped to hold the entire project together. We especially thank her for her hard work and dedication.

Perhaps above all, we wish to thank those at W. W. Norton who kept the production and all the loose ends of the book coherent and in focus. Steve Dunn has helped to define the overall scope of the book and offered many suggestions for specific discussions. Traci Nagle guided us in refining our arguments and our prose. Stephanie Price and Sarah Caldwell both devoted an enormous amount of their time to the book. Neil Ryder Hoos creatively located most of the photos that illustrate the text. Ruth Dworkin has been efficient and dedicated in managing the details of production. Finally, we thank Roby Harrington, the head of Norton's college department and our long-time friend and supporter.

We are more than happy, however, to absolve all these contributors from any flaws, errors, and misjudgments that will inevitably be discovered. We wish the book could be free of all production errors, grammatical errors, misspellings, misquotes, missed citations, etc. From that standpoint, a book ought to try to be perfect. But substantively we have not tried to write a flawless book; we have not tried to write a book to please everyone. We have again tried to write an effective book, a book that cannot be taken lightly. Our goal was not to make every reader a political scientist or a political activist. Our goal was to restore politics as a subject matter of vigorous and enjoyable discourse, recapturing it from the bondage of the thirty-second sound bite and the thirty-page technical briefing. Every person can be knowledgeable because everything about politics is accessible. One does not have to be a television anchorperson to profit from political events. One does not have to be a philosopher to argue about the requisites of democracy, a lawyer to dispute constitutional interpretations, an economist to debate a public policy. We would be very proud if our book contributes in a small way to the restoration of the ancient art of political controversy.

BENJAMIN GINSBERG
THEODORE J. LOWI
MARGARET WEIR

SEPTEMBER 1996

PART I

American Political Life

1

American Political Culture

SINCE THE TIME of the nation's founding, Americans have been sharply divided about the proper size and role of the government. During the debates over the ratification of the Constitution, the Federalists (as the supporters of the new scheme of government called themselves) argued that a powerful and active government was needed to promote commerce, prevent political strife, and protect America's international interests. The Antifederalists (as opponents of the proposed Constitution came to be called) replied that a government with the power to achieve these results would also have the power to oppress its citizens. The Antifederalists argued that it was better to forgo the potential benefits of a powerful government in order to avoid the threat such a government would pose.

After the Constitution's ratification, the debate over the power of government continued. In fact, it gave birth to America's two-party system during George Washington's presidency. The Hamiltonian Federalists, who are the indirect ancestors of modern-day Republicans, introduced an ambitious economic program designed to give America a powerful central government. The Jeffersonian Democratic Republicans, the direct forebears of modern-day Democrats, organized in opposition to this program, arguing for a weaker and decentralized national government.

Conflict over the power and role of the national government remains at the heart of American politics today. Contemporary Democrats assert that the United States needs a powerful and active national government, capable of assuming a wide array of regulatory responsibilities and with the capacity to provide a broad range of social services. Contemporary Republicans, on the other hand, argue that many current governmental functions should be eliminated or turned over to the states. This difference in outlook is related to the differences in the constituencies the two parties seek to represent. The Republican Party tends to speak for wealthier Americans, who often see themselves as paying for governmental programs that benefit others. The Democratic Party, on the other hand, tends to speak for the recipients of social services and the beneficiaries of regulatory programs.

Not only do Americans argue with one another about government, but many are *themselves* ambivalent about the government's proper role. In 1994, Americans gave the Republicans a majority in Congress in part because Republican candidates promised to cut federal taxes and government spending. Once cuts were proposed, however, many individuals who supported the principle of smaller government organized furiously to protect the programs they favored. Most saw no contradiction. As Republican pollster Frank Luntz warned congressional Republicans, while the "public does not want to pay higher taxes," people also "do not want to see their services cut."[1] Among the most bizarre examples of this phenomenon is the case of James Nichols, one of the men accused of involvement in the bombing of the Oklahoma City federal office building in April 1995. Nichols reportedly was outspoken in his hatred of the federal government and often boasted that he refused to pay federal taxes. Yet his antigovernment sentiments did not keep Nichols from accepting $89,950 in federal farm subsidies between 1986 and 1992.[2]

Despite such disagreements and qualms, government has become a powerful and pervasive force in the United States. In 1789, 1889, and even as recently as 1929, America's national government was limited in size, scope, and influence; most of the important functions of government were provided by the states. In 1933, however, the influence of the government began to expand to meet the crises created by the stock market crash of 1929, the Great Depression, and the run on banks of 1933. Congress passed legislation that brought the government into the businesses of home mortgages, farm mortgages, credit, and relief of personal distress. Whereas in 1933 people had tried to withdraw their money from the banks only to find that their savings had been wiped out, sixty years later most Americans are confident that although many savings and loan institutions may be insolvent, their money is still safe because it is guaranteed by the national government. Today, the national government is an enormous institution with programs and policies reaching into every corner of American life. It oversees the nation's economy; it is the nation's largest employer; it provides citizens with a host of services; it controls the world's most formidable military establishment; and it regulates a wide range of social and commercial activities in which Americans engage.

Indeed, Americans are completely surrounded by government programs and government controls. Citizens are so dependent upon government today that much of what they have come to take for granted—as, somehow, part of the natural environment—is in fact created by government. For example, a college student who drives her car to school may think that she is engaged in a purely private activity. Yet the simple act of driving an automobile is heavily dependent upon a multitude of government initiatives and is surrounded by a host of governmental rules. The roads upon which the student drives were constructed by a local government, probably with the assistance of some fraction of the more than $20 billion in federal highway funds spent each year. The roads are maintained by municipal, county, and state governments. During the winter, snow is removed from the roads by local governments. Traffic is regulated by local governments. Road signs are placed and maintained by local and state governments. The student holds a driver's license issued by her state government, which has also registered her vehicle and inspected it for safety and compliance with emissions standards. The vehicle itself has been manufactured to meet safety and emissions standards set by the federal government. The contract under which the student purchased the automobile as well as the loan she signed if she borrowed money for the purchase were both governed by commercial sales and banking regulations established by the state and federal governments. The list goes on.

It might be possible for this student to drive to school without all this government assistance and regulation. In principle, roads might be privately owned, traffic unregulated, and neither drivers nor their autos required to meet any standards. Perhaps our student could still reach her destination in such an environment. Certainly, her driving experience would be markedly different from the current one.

The example of this driver could be applied in endless other situations. Government plays a role in everyone's activities and, by the same token, regulates almost everything we do. Figure 1.1 is a diagram of some of the governmental services received by and controls exerted upon any recent college

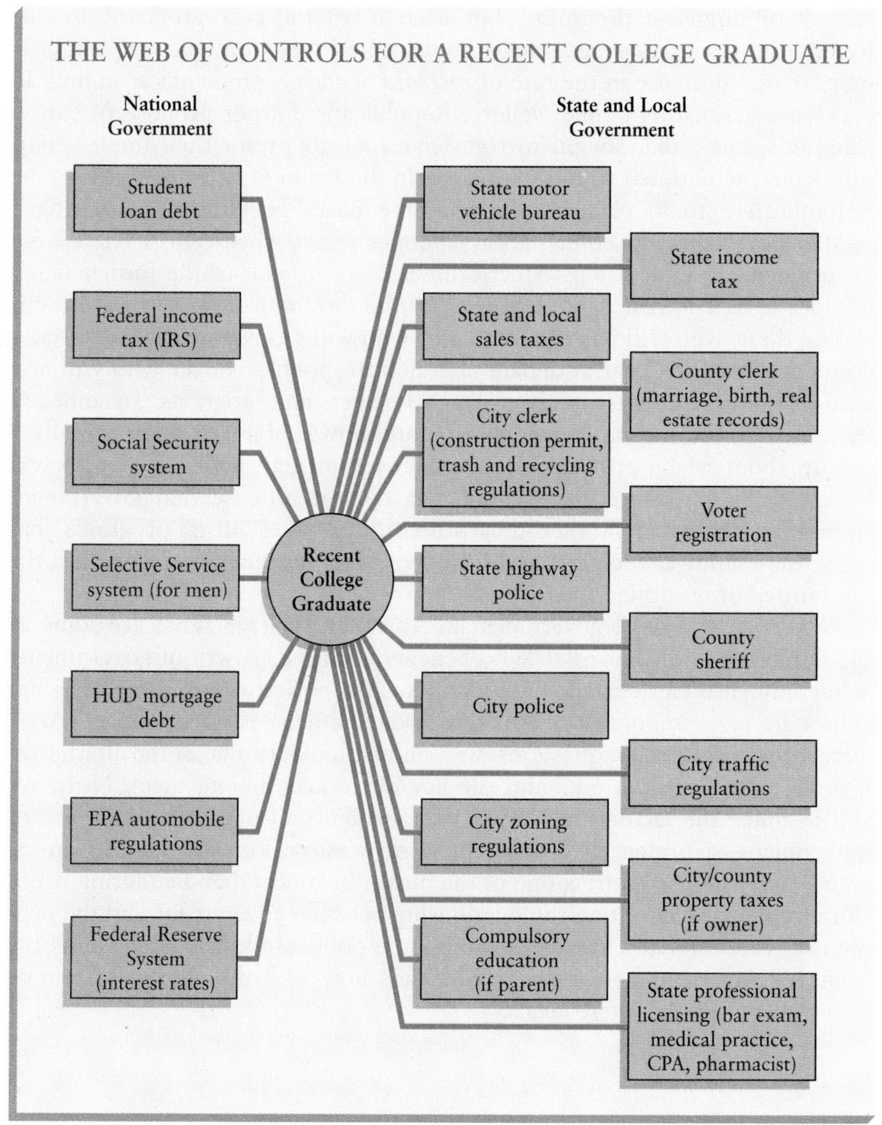

FIGURE 1.1
Government is a pervasive force in the lives of all Americans, especially at the state and local level. Think of the many ways in which government affects your life every day.

graduate. Some of these governmental activities are federal, while others are the province of state and local governments.

Most Americans want to keep the benefits they receive from government. Though they may resent it in principle, in practice even most conservatives have reconciled themselves to an activist state. Many self-styled "conservatives" differ more with their "liberal" counterparts over the proper character of government than over its ultimate desirability. Ronald Reagan, the most conservative American president in more than half a century, began his successful 1980 presidential campaign not by promising to curtail government activity but by vowing "to restore to the federal government the capacity to do the people's work." In a similar vein, after their victory in the 1994 congressional elections, Republicans pledged to slash government spending on a variety of domestic programs. But even if all the cuts proposed by the Republican Congress were actually implemented they would accomplish little more than a decrease in the rate of *increase* of the government's spending. In many areas, such as public welfare, Republicans did not propose to cancel programs, but rather sought to transfer responsibility for their implementation from the national to the state level. In the realm of national defense, the Republicans actually pledged to *increase* the federal government's spending.

The real debate in contemporary politics is not whether to have a large government or a small one. Americans decided in favor of the former many decades ago. The real fight is over what the government should do, how it should do it, who will pay the costs, and who will receive the benefits of government. Thus, the central debate in American politics is over who will and who will not have access to governmental powers and programs. To some extent, the current argument over the size and power of government is really a debate about which groups will receive governmental services and who will be asked to pay the costs. Republicans do not propose that government should be eliminated. Rather, they primarily propose cutting programs that serve and empower the poor and members of minority groups, to reduce the tax burden of wealthier voters.

What is the role of government in American society? What are some of the implications of that role? Who benefits from the growth of government? What influence can citizens have upon such a powerful government? What values are most important to America's political debate and system of governance? To answer these questions, we will first look at some of the alternative forms government can take and the key differences among them. Next, we will examine the factors that led to the emergence of one particular form of government—representative democracy—in western Europe and the United States. We will also address one of the most fundamental and enduring problem of democratic politics: the relationship between government and the people it governs. Finally, we will examine the political ideals that serve as the basis for American government and assess how well the current system of government upholds these ideals.

★ Government

Government is the term generally used to describe the formal institutions through which a land and its people are ruled. To govern is to rule. A government may be as simple as a tribal council that meets occasionally to advise the chief, or as complex as the vast establishments, with their forms, rules, and bureaucracies, found in the United States and the countries of Europe. A more complex government is sometimes referred to as "the state."

FORMS OF GOVERNMENT

Governments vary in their structure, in their size, and in the way they operate. Two questions are of special importance in determining how governments differ: Who governs? And how much government control is permitted?

In May 1989, demonstrators gathered in Beijing's Tiananmen Square to protest against the totalitarian Chinese government. The protesters chose an American symbol, the Statue of Liberty, as a model for their "Goddess of Democracy." The demonstrations lasted several weeks, but eventually they were brutally suppressed by the Chinese authorities and many of the protesters were sent to prison.

In some nations, governing is done by a single individual—a king or dictator, for example. This state of affairs is called **autocracy.** Where a small group—perhaps landowners, military officers, or wealthy merchants—control most of the governing decisions, that government is said to be an **oligarchy.** If more people participate, and if the populace is deemed to have some influence over decision making, that government is tending toward **democracy.**

Governments also vary considerably in terms of how they govern. In the United States and a small number of other nations, governments are limited as to what they are permitted to control (substantive limits), as well as how they go about it (procedural limits). Governments that are so limited are called **constitutional governments,** or liberal governments. In other nations, including many in Europe as well as in South America, Asia, and Africa, though the law imposes few real limits, the government is nevertheless kept in check by other political and social institutions that the government is unable to control but must come to terms with—such as autonomous territories, an organized church, organized business groups, or organized labor unions. Such governments are generally called **authoritarian.** In a third group of nations, including the Soviet Union under Joseph Stalin, Nazi Germany, and perhaps prewar Japan and Italy, governments not only are free of legal limits but also seek to eliminate those organized social groups that might challenge or limit the government's authority. These governments typically attempt to

CONSTITUTIONAL, AUTHORITARIAN, AND TOTALITARIAN GOVERNMENTS

Most Western democracies have constitutions that actually define the limits and scope of governmental power. But the mere existence of a constitution does not, by itself, define a regime as constitutional. Some governments have constitutions that they ignore. At least until recently, this was the case in such eastern European nations as Romania and Bulgaria. In the true constitutional setting, the actual processes of government follow the forms prescribed by the constitution, and groups in society have sufficient freedom and power to oppose efforts by the government to overstep these limits. The governments in the United States and western Europe provide the best examples.

Authoritarian governments must sometimes be responsive to a small number of powerful social groups and institutions such as the army, but such governments recognize no formal obligations to consult their citizens or to respect limits on their actions. Examples of authoritarian governments in the recent past include Spain under the leadership of General Francisco Franco and Portugal under Prime Minister Antonio Salazar.

Totalitarian governments can be distinguished from both democratic and authoritarian governments by the lack of any distinction between the government and other important social institutions. Indeed, totalitarian governments generally seek to destroy all other social institutions—for example, churches, labor unions, and political parties—that may function as rival sources of power. Examples of totalitarian governments include the Third Reich in Germany under Adolf Hitler in the 1930s and 1940s and the government of the Soviet Union under Joseph Stalin between the 1930s and 1950s.

In recent years, a number of authoritarian regimes in eastern Europe, including the Soviet Union and its satellite states, faced severe economic hardship and popular discontent. After 1989, most of these regimes, including those in Czechoslovakia, Poland, Hungary, East Germany, and the Soviet Union itself, collapsed and were replaced by new governments.

BOX 1.1

dominate or control every sphere of political, economic, and social life and, as a result, are called **totalitarian** (see Box 1.1).

Americans have the good fortune to live in a nation in which limits are placed on what governments can do and how they can do it. But such constitutional democracies are relatively rare in today's world; it is estimated that only twenty or so of the world's nearly two hundred governments could be included in this category. And constitutional democracies were unheard of before the modern era. Prior to the eighteenth and nineteenth centuries, governments seldom sought—and rarely received—the support of their ordinary subjects. The available evidence strongly suggests that the ordinary people had little love for the government or for the social order. After all, they had no stake in it. They equated government with the police officer, the bailiff, and the tax collector.[3]

Beginning in the seventeenth century, in a handful of Western nations, two important changes began to take place in the character and conduct of government. First, governments began to acknowledge formal limits upon their power. Second, a small number of governments began to provide the ordinary citizen with a formal voice in public affairs—through the vote. Obviously, the desirability of limits on government and the expansion of popular influence were at the heart of the American Revolution in 1776. "No taxation without representation," as we shall see in Chapter 3, was hotly debated from the beginning of the Revolution through the founding in 1789. But even before the Revolution, a tradition of limiting government and expanding participation in the political process had developed throughout western Europe. Thus, to understand how the relationship between rulers and the ruled was transformed, we must broaden our focus to take into account events in Europe as well as in America. We will have to divide the transformation into its two separate parts. The first is the effort to put limits on government. The second is the effort to expand the influence of the people through politics.

Limiting Government

The key force behind the imposition of limits on government power was a new social class, the bourgeoisie. Bourgeoisie is a French word for freeman of the city, or *bourg*. Being part of the bourgeoisie later became associated with being "middle class" and with being in commerce or industry. In order to gain a share of control of government, joining or even displacing the kings, aristocrats, and gentry who had dominated government for centuries, the bourgeoisie sought to change existing institutions—especially parliaments—into instruments of real political participation. Parliaments had existed for centuries, but were generally aristocratic institutions. The bourgeoisie embraced parliaments as means by which they could exert the weight of their superior numbers and growing economic advantage against their aristocratic rivals. At the same time, the bourgeoisie sought to place restraints on the capacity of governments to threaten these economic and political interests by placing formal or constitutional limits on governmental power. The three bourgeois (also called liberal) philosophers with the strongest influence on American thinking were John Locke, Adam Smith, and John Stuart Mill (see Box 1.2).

Although motivated primarily by the need to protect and defend their own interests, the bourgeoisie advanced many of the principles that became the central underpinnings of individual liberty for all citizens—freedom of speech, freedom of assembly, freedom of conscience, and freedom from arbitrary search and seizure. It is important to note here that the bourgeoisie generally did not favor democracy as we know it. They were advocates of electoral and representative institutions, but they favored property requirements and other restrictions so as to limit participation to the middle classes. Yet once these institutions of politics and the protection of the right to engage in politics were established, it was difficult to limit them to the bourgeoisie. Time after time, principles first advanced to justify a selfish interest tend to take on a life of their own and to be extended to those for whom the principles were not at first designed.

THE PHILOSOPHICAL BASIS OF LIMITED GOVERNMENT

Three liberal philosophers had a particularly strong influence on American political thought: John Locke (1632–1704), Adam Smith (1723–90), and John Stuart Mill (1806–73). These three thinkers espoused the liberal philosophy that placed limits on government.

John Locke (below, left) argued for limited government because of his belief that, just as a person had a right to his own body, he had a right to his own labor and the fruits of that labor. From that he argued that people formed a government to protect their property, lives, and liberty, and that this government could not properly act to harm or take away that which it had been created to protect. According to Locke in his *Second Treatise on Government* (1690), government could only properly function with the consent of the governed through their representatives; if the government acted improperly, it would have broken its contract with society and would no longer be a legitimate government. The people would have the right to revolt and the right to form a new government.

Adam Smith (below, center) supported a severely limited government as a protection for the economic freedom of the individual. In his *Wealth of Nations* (1776), he argued for private enterprise as the most efficient means of production, leading to the growth of national wealth and income. He believed that freedom for individual economic and social advancement was only possible in a competitive free market, unhindered by government intervention. Nonetheless, he argued that government must protect the economic freedoms—free trade, free choice of individuals to do what they want, to live where they wish, and to invest and spend as they see fit—by ensuring that the market remains competitive and honest through such governmental actions as the regulation of standard weights and measures, the prevention of the formation of monopolies, and the defense of the community.

John Stuart Mill (below, right) believed that government should be limited so as not to interfere with the self-development of the individual. In order for individuals to fully develop their faculties, Mill believed, they need as large a sphere of freedom as possible, including freedom of thought and discussion. In *On Liberty* (1859), Mill argued that any restrictions on individuals ought to be based on recognized principles rather than on the preferences of the majority. He believed that social control should be exercised only to prevent harm to others. He maintained that when thoughts are suppressed, if they are right, individuals are deprived of truth; if the ideas are wrong, they are deprived of that better understanding of truth that comes out of conflict with error.

BOX 1.2

Access to Government: The Expansion of Participation

The expansion of participation from the bourgeoisie to ever-larger segments of society took two paths. In some nations, popular participation was expanded by the crown or the aristocracy, which ironically saw common people as potential political allies against the bourgeoisie. Thus in nineteenth-century Prussia, for example, it was the emperor and his great minister Otto von Bismarck who expanded popular participation in order to build political support among the lower orders.

In other nations, participation expanded because competing segments of the bourgeoisie sought to gain political advantage by reaching out and mobilizing the support of working- and lower-class groups who craved the opportunity to take part in politics—"lining up the unwashed," as one American historian put it.[4] To be sure, excluded groups often agitated for greater participation. But seldom was such agitation, by itself, enough to secure the right to participate. Usually, expansion of voting rights resulted from a combination of pressure from below and help from above.

This process began in America with the formation of the Jeffersonian Republicans in the late 1790s. The Jeffersonians, led by Thomas Jefferson and other southern planters, hoped to dislodge the Federalists, led by New England merchants, who had been in control of the government since 1787. The Jeffersonians organized political clubs throughout the nation and began mobilizing popular support. Where the suffrage was restricted by such measures as property requirements or poll taxes, the Jeffersonians sought to end limitations in order to enfranchise more of their potential supporters.

At first, the Federalists reacted to Jefferson's strategy with dismay. Fearing Jefferson as the leader of a vulgar and dangerous democratic party, the Federalist majority in Congress adopted the Alien and Sedition Acts of 1798, which, among other things, declared any opposition to or criticism of the

In George Caleb Bingham's painting, *The Verdict of the People* (1853-54), a jubilant crowd celebrates the outcome of the political process. While the nineteenth century was marked by high levels of political participation, voting was primarily the domain of white men.

Residents of rural Wilcox County, Alabama, lining up to vote in 1966. Prior to the passage of the Voting Rights Act of 1965, Wilcox County had no registered black voters.

government to be a crime. Alexander Hamilton and other Federalist leaders went so far as to urge that opposition groups be eliminated by force, if necessary. The failure of the Federalists to suppress their Republican opposition was, in large measure, due to the fact that the Federalists lacked the military and political means to do so. Their inability to crush the opposition eventually led to acceptance of the principle of the "loyal opposition"—the idea that opposing those in power was not a form of disloyalty to the government. The Federalists found that they had no choice but to compete with the Jeffersonians at their own game and seek to mobilize popular support for their candidates.

This pattern of suffrage expansion by groups hoping to derive some political advantage has been typical in American history. After the Civil War, one of the chief reasons that Republicans moved to enfranchise newly freed slaves was to use the support of the former slaves to maintain Republican control over the defeated Southern states. Similarly, in the early twentieth century, upper-middle-class "Progressives" advocated women's suffrage because they believed that women were likely to support the reforms espoused by the Progressive movement.

Likewise, liberal Democrats in the 1960s strongly supported voting rights for African Americans in the South. Clearly, there were compelling moral reasons for this support: How could America call itself a democratic nation when millions of citizens were deprived of a basic democratic right? At the same time, though, Democratic liberals hoped that this expansion of voting rights would increase their own political power, since most African Americans were presumed to be liberal and Democratic in their political orientation. This strategy was at least partially successful. The mobilization of millions of black voters helped to give the Democratic Party's liberal wing much greater power within the party. However, this strategy also gave the Republicans an opportunity to win the support of white voters in the South.

During roughly the same period of American history, Democrats succeeded in securing the adoption of a constitutional amendment lowering the voting age from twenty-one to eighteen. Democrats believed at the time that most young people would support their party. Today, however, many young people support the Republican Party. Once again, a principle turned out to have unanticipated consequences.

Influencing the Government through Participation: Politics

Expansion of participation means that more and more people have a legal right to take part in politics. Politics is an important term. In its broadest sense, "politics" refers to conflicts over the character, membership, and policies of any organization to which people belong. As Harold Lasswell, a famous political scientist, once put it, politics is the struggle over "who gets what, when, how."[5] Although politics is a phenomenon that can be found in any organization, our concern in this book is more narrow. Here, **politics** will be used to refer only to conflicts and struggles over the leadership, structure, and policies of governments. The goal of politics, as we define it, is to have a share or a say in the composition of the government's leadership, how the government is organized, or what its policies are going to be. Having a share is called **power** or influence.

Politics can take many forms, including everything from sending letters to government officials through voting, lobbying legislators on behalf of particular programs, and participating in protest marches and even violent demonstrations. A system of government that gives citizens a regular opportunity to elect the top government officials is usually called a **representative democracy** or **republic.** A regime that permits citizens to vote directly on laws and policies is often called a **direct democracy**. At the national level, America is a representative democracy in which citizens select government officials but do not vote on legislation. Some states, however, have provisions for direct legislation through popular referendum. For example, California voters in 1995 decided to bar undocumented immigrants from receiving some state services.

Groups and organized interests obviously do not vote (although their members do), but they certainly do participate in politics. Their political activities usually consist of such endeavors as providing funds for candidates, lobbying, and trying to influence public opinion. The pattern of struggles among interests is called group politics, or **pluralism.** Americans have always been ambivalent about pluralist politics. Although the right of groups to press their views is the essence of liberty, Americans often fear that organized groups may sometimes exert too much influence, advancing special interests at the expense of larger public interests. We will return to this problem in Chapter 10.

Sometimes, of course, politics does not take place through formal channels at all, but instead involves direct action. **Direct action politics** can include either violent politics or civil disobedience, both of which attempt to shock rulers into behaving more responsibly. Direct action can also be a form of revolutionary politics, which rejects the system entirely and attempts to replace it with a new ruling group and a new set of rules. In recent years in the

United States, groups ranging from animal-rights activists through right-to-life advocates have used direct action and even violence to underline their demands. Direct political action is protected by the U.S. Constitution; violence is not. The framers knew that the right to protest is essential to the maintenance of political freedom, even where the ballot box is available.

★ American Political Culture: Conflict and Consensus

Underlying and framing political struggles in the United States are agreements and disagreements over basic political values and philosophies. Although former president George Bush once dismissed philosophical questions as "that vision thing," philosophical positions and values shape citizens' views of the world and define their sense of what is right and wrong, just and unjust, possible and impossible. If Americans shared no philosophical principles or values, they would have difficulty communicating, much less agreeing upon a common system of government and politics. On the other hand, sharing broad values does not guarantee political consensus. We can agree on principles but disagree over their application.

In fact, differing perspectives can help us understand the patterns of conflict and consensus that have marked the development of American politics. Perhaps the dominant interpretation of U.S. history is that of a success story: as the nation developed, different groups gradually gained equal influence in politics and policy. In this story, the American consensus around a set of basic political ideals provided the framework for the political inclusion of all groups. But today this story of progress is questioned from two different sides, highlighting the continuing significance of conflict. Some critics claim that measures such as affirmative action have not promoted political inclusion and instead have condoned reverse discrimination and a segmented society. Far from fulfilling American ideals, they argue, these policies represent a movement away from our most fundamental values. An opposing perspective questions the progress that has been made in promoting equality. Pointing to the disproportionately high rates of poverty among minorities and continuing evidence of discrimination against women and minorities, this side questions whether Americans are serious about equality. Much of the debate over the role of government has been over what government should do and how far it should go to redress the inequalities within our society and political system.

Even though Americans have disagreed over the meaning of such political ideals as equality, they still agree on the importance of these ideals. Within these conflicts, we can identify shared values, beliefs, and attitudes that form our **political culture** and serve to hold the United States and its people together. These values date back to the time of the founding of the union.

What Are Americans' Core Political Values?

The essential documents of the American founding—the Declaration of Independence and the Constitution—enunciated a set of political principles about the purposes of the new republic. In contrast with many other democracies, in the United States these political ideals did not just remain words on dusty documents. Americans actively embraced the principles of the Founders and made them central to the national identity. Let us look more closely at three of these ideals: liberty, equality, and democracy.

Liberty No ideal is more central to American values than liberty. The Declaration of Independence defined three inalienable rights: "Life, Liberty and the pursuit of Happiness." The Preamble of the Constitution likewise identified the need to secure "the Blessings of Liberty" as one of the key reasons for drawing up the Constitution. The Bill of Rights above all preserves individual liberties and rights. For Americans, liberty has come to mean many of the freedoms guaranteed in the Bill of Rights: freedom of speech and writing, the right to assemble freely, and the right to practice religious beliefs without interference from the government. The idea of freedom is also tied to support for free enterprise and the right to enjoy the fruits of one's labor. Free competition and unfettered movement of goods are essential aspects of freedom.[6] As this list makes clear, the dedication to liberty in the United States has been linked throughout history with the idea of limited government.

Patrick Henry delivering his famous "Give me liberty, or give me death" speech. Since the Founding, liberty has been central to the political values of Americans.

Equality The Declaration of Independence declares as its first "self-evident" truth that "all men are created equal." As central as it is to the American political creed, however, equality has been a less well defined ideal than liberty because people interpret "equality" in different ways. Few Americans have wholeheartedly embraced full equality of results, but most Americans share the ideal of equality of opportunity—that is, the notion that each person should be given a fair chance to go as far as his or her talents will allow. Yet it is hard for Americans to reach agreement about what constitutes equality of opportunity. Must *past* inequalities be remedied in order to ensure equal opportunity in the *present?* Should inequalities in the legal, political, and economic spheres be given the same weight? In contrast to liberty, which requires limits on the role of government, equality implies an *obligation* of the government to the people.[7]

Democracy As we saw earlier, the essence of democracy is the participation of the people in choosing their rulers and the people's ability to influence what those rulers do. In a democracy, political power ultimately comes from the people. Forms of participation in a democracy vary greatly, but voting is a key element of the representative democracy that the Founders established. Ideally, democracy envisions an engaged citizenry prepared to exercise its power over rulers.

Does the System Uphold American Political Values?

Clearly, the ideals of liberty, equality, and democracy are open to diverse interpretations. Moreover, the ideals can easily conflict with one another in practice. When we examine American history, we can see that there have been large gaps between these ideals and the practice of American politics. We can also see that some ideals are prized more than others at different historical moments. But it is also clear that as Americans have engaged in political conflict about who should participate in politics and how political institutions should be organized, they have called upon these ideals to justify their actions. Now let's re-examine these ideals, noting key historical conflicts and current controversies about what they should mean in practice.

Liberty The central historical conflict regarding liberty in the United States was the enslavement of blacks. The facts of slavery and the differential treatment of the races has cast a long shadow over all of American history. In fact, scholars today note that the American definition of freedom has been formed in relation to the concept of slavery. The right to control one's labor and the right to receive rewards for that labor have been central elements of our definition of freedom precisely because these freedoms were denied to slaves.[8]

Concerns about the meaning of liberty also arise in connection with government regulation of economic and social activity. Economic regulations imposed to ensure public health and safety are often decried by the affected businesses as infringements on their freedom. For example, in 1994, the Occupational Safety and Health Administration (OSHA) of the national government prepared to issue regulations intended to protect workers from repetitive stress injuries. Such injuries, which affect 700,000 workers a year, are caused by long hours on the assembly line or at the computer. OSHA's regulations would have required employers to provide specified work breaks and proper furniture and other equipment. Although such regulations might have been welcomed by workers, employers viewed them as intrusive and extremely costly. In the face of strong opposition from employers, OSHA backed down and decided not to issue the regulations.[9]

Social regulations prompt similar disputes. Some citizens believe that government should enforce certain standards of behavior or instill particular values in citizens. Examples of such activity abound: welfare rules that once denied benefits to women who were found with a "man in the house," the practice of saying prayers in school, laws that require parents to pay child support for their children even if those children no longer live with them, and laws that require citizens to wear seatbelts are just a few examples. Deciding the proper scope of economic and social regulation is a topic of great concern and much conflict among Americans today.

Equality Because equality is such an elusive concept, many conflicts have arisen over what it should mean in practice. Americans have engaged in three kinds of controversies about the public role in addressing inequality. The first is determining what constitutes equality of access to public institutions. In 1896, the Supreme Court ruled in *Plessy v. Ferguson* that "separate but equal" accommodations for blacks and whites were constitutional. In 1954, in a major legal victory for the Civil Rights movement, the Supreme Court overturned the separate but equal doctrine in *Brown v. Board of Education.* Today, new questions have been raised about what constitutes equal access to public institutions. Some argue that the unequal financing of public schools in cities, suburbs, and rural districts is a violation of the right to equal education. To date these claims have not been supported by the courts, which have rejected the notion that the unequal economic impacts of public policy outcomes are a constitutional matter.[10] Lawsuits arguing a right to "economic equal protection" stalled in 1973 when the Supreme Court ruled that a Texas school-financing law did not violate the Constitution even though the law affected rich and poor students differently.[11]

A second debate concerns the public role in ensuring equality of opportunity in private life. Although Americans generally agree that discrimination should not be tolerated, people disagree over what should be done to ensure equality of opportunity (see Table 1.1). Controversies about affirmative action programs reflect these disputes. Supporters of affirmative action claim that such programs are necessary to compensate for past discrimination in order to obtain true equality of opportunity today. Opponents maintain that affirmative action amounts to reverse discrimination and that a society that espouses true equality should not acknowledge gender or racial differences. The question of the public responsibility for private inequalities is central to gender issues. The traditional view, still held by many today, sees the special responsibilities of women in the family as something that falls outside the range of public concern. Indeed, from this perspective, women's role within families is essential to the functioning of a democratic society. In the past twenty years, especially, these traditional views have come under fire, as advocates for women have argued that women occupy a subordinate place within the family and that such private inequalities are a topic of public concern.[12]

TABLE 1.1

AMERICAN ATTITUDES ABOUT POLITICAL EQUALITY, 1992

Statement	Percentage who agree
Our society should do whatever is necessary to make sure that everyone has an equal opportunity to succeed.	95
We have gone too far in pushing equal rights in this country.	53
One of the big problems in this country is that we don't give everyone an equal chance.	71
It is not really that big a problem if some people have more of a chance in life than others.	38
The country would be better off if we worried less about how equal people are.	54
If people were treated more equally in this country, we would have many fewer problems.	84

SOURCE: Based on data from the American National Election Studies conducted by the University of Michigan, Center for Political Studies, and provided by the Inter-University Consortium for Political and Social Research, Ann Arbor, Michigan.

Equality, particularly equal opportunity and equal pay for equal work, has been a primary concern of the women's movement. Here, women's advocates march to the White House to urge the president not to weaken affirmative action programs.

A third debate about equality concerns differences in income and wealth. Unlike in other countries, income inequality has not been an enduring topic of political controversy in the United States, which currently has the largest gap in income and wealth between rich and poor citizens of any developed nation. But Americans have generally tolerated great differences among rich and poor citizens, in part because of a pervasive belief that mobility is possible and that economic success is the product of individual effort.[13] At times, however, concern about economic inequalities emerges, often around the issue of fair taxation. Some analysts today warn that the growing division between rich and poor may invigorate a politics of class and polarize political debate along income lines.[14]

Democracy Despite Americans' deep attachment to the *ideal* of democracy, many questions can be raised about our *practice* of democracy. The first is the restricted definition of the political community during much of American history. The United States was not a full democracy until the 1960s, when African Americans were at last guaranteed the right to vote. Property restrictions on the right to vote were eliminated by 1828; in 1870, the Fifteenth Amendment to the Constitution granted African Americans the vote, although later exclusionary practices denied them that right; in 1920, the Nineteenth Amendment guaranteed women the right to vote; and in 1965, the Voting Rights Act finally secured the right of African Americans to vote.

Just securing the right to vote does not end concerns about democracy, however. The organization of electoral institutions can have a significant impact on access to elections and on who can get elected. During the first two decades of the twentieth century, states and cities enacted many reforms that made it harder to vote, including strict registration requirements and scheduling of elections. The aim was to rid politics of corruption but the consequence was to reduce participation. Other institutional decisions affect which candidates stand the best chance of getting elected (see Chapter 9).

A further consideration about democracy concerns the relationship between economic power and political power. Money has always played an important role in elections and governing in the United States. Many argue that the pervasive influence of money in American electoral campaigns today undermines democracy. With the decline of locally based political parties that depended on party loyalists to turn out the vote, and the rise of political action committees, political consultants, and expensive media campaigns, money has become the central fact of life in American politics. Money often determines who runs for office; it can exert a heavy influence on who wins; and, some argue, money affects what politicians do once they are in office.[15]

A final consideration that must be raised about democracy is the engagement of the citizenry. Low turnout for elections and a pervasive sense of apathy and cynicism characterize American politics today. Many people say that it does not matter if they participate because their votes will not make any difference. This disillusionment and sense of ineffectiveness undermines the vitality of democracy and reduces the accountability of the rulers to the ruled.

 Values and Government

Many of the most important dilemmas of American political life involve conflicts among fundamental political values as those values are put into opera-

Martin Luther King, Jr., the civil rights leader, shakes the hand of President Lyndon B. Johnson following the signing of the Voting Rights Act of 1965, a milestone in assuring political equality for African Americans.

tion. For example, Americans strongly value both liberty and equality, but often programs designed to promote one may impose restraints upon the other. Thus, affirmative action programs or statutes designed to prevent discrimination against the handicapped, such as the Americans with Disabilities Act, may promote equality but may also infringe upon the liberty of employers to hire whomever they wish. In a similar vein, democratic political processes may sometimes produce results that can challenge both liberty and equality. After all, Adolf Hitler and the Nazis came to power in Germany in the 1930s largely through democratic means. Even in America, political extremists who oppose both liberty and equality have been elected to office. As recently as 1991, a white supremacist, David Duke, was very nearly elected governor of Louisiana.

Conversely, in the name of equality or liberty, courts often hand down verdicts that undo decisions of democratically elected legislatures and even decisions reached in popular referenda. The 1995 referendum in California that was mentioned earlier—which would have forbidden the state from providing a number of social services to undocumented immigrants—was invalidated by the state courts later that year. Principles that seem incontrovertible in the abstract become more problematic in operation. In the process of resolving conflicts among core beliefs, America's political principles change and evolve. Even core values should be understood as works in progress rather than immutable facts.

In principle, conflicts among liberty, equality, and democracy can be reconciled. In practice, however, over time, democracy poses a fundamental threat to liberty. This is so because, over time, democracy promotes strong government, often to promote equality, and, over time, strong government inevitably threatens liberty. And with issues of social policy such as affirmative action, what some see as guaranteeing equality, others view as an infringement of liberty. But, as we shall see, in the United States, the institutions of democratic government have been critical in guaranteeing both liberty and equality.

FOR FURTHER READING

Bendix, Reinhard. *Nation-Building and Citizenship.* New York: Wiley, 1964.

Dahl, Robert. *Democracy and Its Critics.* New Haven, CT: Yale University Press, 1989.

Hochschild, Jennifer L. *Facing Up to the American Dream: Race, Class, and the Soul of the Nation.* Princeton, NJ: Princeton University Press, 1995.

Huntington, Samuel P. *American Politics: The Promise of Disharmony.* Cambridge, MA: Harvard University Press, 1981.

Lasswell, Harold. *Politics: Who Gets What, When, How.* New York: Meridian Books, 1958.

McClosky, Herbert, and John Zaller. *The American Ethos: Public Attitudes toward Capitalism and Democracy.* Cambridge, MA: Harvard University Press, 1984.

Norton, Anne. *Republic of Signs: Liberal Theory and American Political Culture.* Chicago: University of Chicago Press, 1993.

Putnam, Robert. *Making Democracy Work: Civic Traditions in Modern Italy.* Princeton, NJ: Princeton University Press, 1993.

Skocpol, Theda. *States and Social Revolutions.* New York: Cambridge University Press, 1979.

de Tocqueville, Alexis. *Democracy in America.* Trans. Phillips Bradley. New York: Knopf, Vintage Books, 1945; orig. published 1835.

STUDY OUTLINE

1. The debate begun by the Federalists and the Antifederalists over the power and role of the national government continued after the ratification of the Constitution, gave birth to America's two-party system, and remains at the heart of American politics today.
2. Most Americans want to keep the benefits of government. The real debate in American politics is over what the government should do, how it should do it, who will pay the costs, and who will receive the benefits.

GOVERNMENT

1. Governments vary in their structure, in their size, and in the way they operate.
2. Beginning in the seventeenth century, two important changes began to take place in the governance of some Western nations: governments began to acknowledge formal limits on their power, and governments began to give citizens a formal voice in politics through the vote.
3. Political participation can take many forms: the vote, group activities, and even direct action, such as violence or civil disobedience.

AMERICAN POLITICAL CULTURE: CONFLICT AND CONSENSUS

1. Three important political values in American politics are liberty, equality, and democracy.

DOES THE SYSTEM UPHOLD AMERICAN POLITICAL VALUES?

1. At times in American history there have been large gaps between the ideals embodied in Americans' core values and the practice of American government.
2. Many of the important dilemmas of American politics revolve around conflicts over fundamental political values. One such conflict involves the ideals of liberty and democracy. Over time, democracy promotes stronger, more active government, which over time may threaten liberty.

PRACTICE QUIZ

1. Which of the following was (were) affected by the debate over the proper role of the national government in America?
   a. the ratification debate
   b. America's two-party system
   c. modern debates between Democrats and Republicans
   d. all of the above
2. The famous political scientist Harold Lasswell defined politics as the struggle over
   a. who gets elected.
   b. who gets what, when, how.
   c. who protests.
   d. who gets to vote.
3. What is the basic difference between autocracy and oligarchy?
   a. the extent to which the average citizen has a say in government affairs
   b. the means of collecting taxes and conscripting soldiers
   c. the number of people who control governing decisions
   d. They are fundamentally the same thing.
4. The bourgeoisie championed
   a. democracy.
   b. "taxation without representation."
   c. limitations on government power.
   d. societal revolution.
5. Which of the following was not done, at least in part, to secure political advantage for political forces in society?
   a. the expansion of voting rights for African Americans
   b. the lowering of the voting age to eighteen
   c. the Jeffersonians' efforts to enhance the political power of merchants in nineteenth-century America
   d. the expansion of voting rights in nineteenth-century Prussia
6. In which of the following do citizens have the most direct control over public decision making?
   a. referendums
   b. representative democracy
   c. oligarchy
   d. pluralism

7. Which of the following is not related to the American conception of "liberty"?
   a. freedom of speech
   b. free enterprise
   c. freedom of religion
   d. All of the above are related to liberty.

8. Why has income inequality not been a major controversy in American politics?
   a. The U.S. does not really have a large income gap between the rich and the poor.
   b. Coercive techniques have been used to deny expression of these concerns.
   c. Many Americans believe that mobility is possible.
   d. The government has made large expenditures to eradicate such inequality.

9. Which of the following does not represent a current discrepancy between the ideal and practice of democracy in America?
   a. the use of property restrictions for voting in three remaining states
   b. the influence of money in electoral politics
   c. the low voter turnout in American elections
   d. All of the above represent discrepancies between the ideal and practice of democracy in modern America.

10. What is the most dire potential consequence of citizens viewing their government as a servant?
    a. Citizens will allow the government to grow to the point where they can no longer control it.
    b. Citizens could be served more efficiently by the private sector.
    c. The ideals of democracy and equality will eventually conflict.
    d. Citizens will no longer be able to do things for themselves.

CRITICAL THINKING QUESTIONS

1. What type of government does the United States have? Is it the most democratic government possible? Do citizens make the decisions of government or do they merely influence them? Describe the ways in which citizens in America participate in politics.

2. Think of some examples that demonstrate the gaps between the ideals of America's core political values and the practice of American politics. Describe how such gaps were reconciled in the past. Identify one current gap between Americans' values and their political practices. How might this discrepancy be reconciled?

KEY TERMS

authoritarian government a system of rule in which the government recognizes no formal limits but may nevertheless be restrained by the power of other social institutions. (p. 7)

autocracy a form of government in which a single individual—a king, queen, or dictator—rules. (p. 7)

constitutional government a system of rule in which formal and effective limits are placed on the powers of the government. (p. 7)

democracy a system of rule that permits citizens to play a significant part in the governmental process, usually through the election of key public officials. (p. 7)

direct-action politics a form of politics, such as civil disobedience or revolutionary action, that takes place outside formal channels. (p. 13)

direct democracy a system of rule that permits citizens to vote directly on laws and policies. (p. 13)

government institutions and procedures through which a territory and its people are ruled. (p. 6)

oligarchy a form of government in which a small group—landowners, military officers, or wealthy merchants—controls most of the governing decisions. (p. 7)

pluralism the theory that all interests are and should be free to compete for influence in the government. The outcome of this competition is compromise and moderation. (p. 13)

political culture broadly shared values, beliefs, and attitudes about how the government should function. American political culture emphasizes the values of liberty, equality, and democracy. (p. 14)

politics conflict over the leadership, structure, and policies of governments. (p. 13)

power influence over a government's leadership, organization, or policies. (p. 13)

representative democracy/republic a system of government in which the populace selects representatives, who play a significant role in governmental decision making. (p. 13)

totalitarian government a system of rule in which the government recognizes no formal limits on its power and seeks to absorb or eliminate other social institutions that might challenge it. (p. 8)

2

The Politics of Race, Class, Gender, and Religion

★ Expanding the American Political Community

How have racial and ethnic differences, gender, class, and religious affiliation affected the right to participate in the political process throughout America's history?

How successfully have social groups such as white ethnics, African Americans, Latinos, Asian Americans, women, and religious groups realized the right to full political participation?

What tactics did these groups employ to gain full access to the political process?

★ Contemporary Conflicts

Does having the right to political participation ensure equal representation within the political system?

Does having the right to political participation ensure having political power?

Does political participation matter?

What is the role of the government in upholding the values of liberty, equality, and democracy?

FOR MUCH OF ITS HISTORY, the University of Maryland did not admit black students. To compensate for this discrimination, the university in 1979 set up a scholarship program open only to black students. Ten years later a Hispanic student sued the university on the grounds that the scholarship program was discriminatory. Other students also expressed concerns that the scholarships were unfair. As one student put it, "I had nothing to do with what happened 400 years ago. Why should I have to pay the price?" But university administrators and many African American students saw the issue differently. One African American student defended the scholarships, noting the country's history of racial discrimination: "I would love to be judged solely based on my merit, but there is a history in this country that does not allow that." In 1994, a federal court ruled the scholarships unconstitutional. The court did not declare all minority scholarships unconstitutional, but it stipulated that such scholarships must be narrowly tailored to address past discrimination in order to be legal. Because the Maryland program offered scholarships to middle-class African Americans, many from out of state, it did not pass this test in the eyes of the court.[1]

In 1996, a federal appeals court cast further doubt on the future of affirmative action in university admissions. The court struck down a University of Texas law school admissions policy that gave preference to black and Hispanic applicants. The school had sought to justify its policy on the grounds that racial diversity was beneficial to the school, but the court ruled that any attention to race was a violation of the Constitution's guarantee of equal protection unless specific past discrimination could be proven.[2]

In 1991, after Brown University eliminated its women's gymnastics and volleyball teams, the women sued. They claimed that the university's decisions violated Title IX of the Education Amendments of 1972, which prohibits sex discrimination at schools that receive federal funds. In March 1995, a federal judge ruled in favor of the women, stating that the university had discriminated against female students. This was not the first time that female students had won legal battles over university athletic programs: courts have ordered Indiana University of Pennsylvania to reinstate its women's gymnastics and swimming teams, and Colorado State University received notice that it must revive its women's softball team. Although many female athletes and their supporters view these rulings as important victories, in some cases male students have had to pay a price. As university budgets shrink, reestablishing women's athletic teams can mean cutting back on programs for men. Brown University, defending its decision, argued that strict proportionality between men and women was not fair; the university "spent over $100,000 in expert witnesses to prove that men were more interested in sports than women."[3]

COLLEGE FRESHMEN BACK ADMISSIONS FOR RACE, BUT NOT AFFIRMATIVE ACTION

A 1995 survey of 240,082 students revealed that a large majority supports the use of race as a criterion for college admissions, but fewer are committed to the principle of "affirmative action." Seventy percent of the respondents said that the race of an applicant should be given some special consideration for admissions. On the other hand, about 50 percent thought that "affirmative action" in admissions should be eliminated. This discrepancy reveals both the ambiguity of Americans' views on the topic as well as the political significance of the term "affirmative action."

SOURCE: Tamara Henry, "Freshmen Back Admissions for Race, Not Affirmative Action," *USA Today,* January 8, 1996, p. A1. Data from the UCLA Higher Education Research Institute.

These stories offer a window on some of the most contentious political issues in America today. They show how social differences, such as race and gender, can become important political issues that are recognized and fought over in policy decisions. These stories also show the role that the national government currently plays in forming policies that impose equality for the benefit of groups previously denied full equality.

Cultural divisions, such as religious identity, can provoke similar controversies. Students at the University of Virginia challenged the university in court when it refused to subsidize the publication of a religious magazine, even though the university funded many other student publications. The Supreme Court's 1995 decision in *Rosenberger v. Rector and Visitors of the University of Virginia* directed the university to provide funding for the magazine.[4] The decision signaled an important shift in the relationship between church and state by sanctioning the funding of religion with public funds.

The social and cultural issues at the heart of these legal cases point to the most fundamental divisions in contemporary American politics. These disputes about racial and gender discrimination reveal that Americans hold conflicting perspectives about how to reconcile their core national values—liberty, equality, and democracy—with their history of social discrimination and political exclusion. What some people, such as the African American student at the University of Maryland quoted above, see as guaranteeing equal access, others, such as the Hispanic student who sued, view as an infringement of liberty. Such differing perspectives can help us understand the patterns of conflict and consensus that have marked the development of American politics. These episodes also reveal that because of conflicts within American society over these values, the national government and other political institutions play a key role in defining and implementing measures to ensure equality and liberty.

As we saw in the preceding chapter, certain social groups throughout American history have struggled to achieve political equality through the right to vote. In many cases, political equality was usually achieved because those who already held political power were willing to grant groups lacking political power the rights to vote and to participate in the political process in other ways. But the struggles to gain these rights were important, too. We will now look at these struggles in more detail.

This chapter describes the forms of participation and the kinds of access to the political system that groups of different social backgrounds and cultural beliefs fought for and have subsequently enjoyed. We will examine the effect of racial and ethnic differences, gender, class, and religious affiliation on political participation and access. In the last section we will discuss the enduring political and policy conflicts produced by these social and cultural conflicts and assess the success of the struggle to achieve equality. As we will see, despite the ideals of equality, liberty, and democracy enunciated in the Constitution, many groups have been denied political equality and the right to participate because of their race, economic status, gender, or religion. We will also see that the civil liberties of many members of these groups were greatly threatened at many points in American history. But the struggles that these groups waged for freedom and equality eventually succeeded. These successes often brought new conflicts in their wake, as all participants in America's democratic system struggle to define liberty and equality.

Expanding the American Political Community

- How have racial and ethnic differences, gender, class, and religious affiliation affected the right to participate in the political process throughout America's history?
- How successfully have social groups such as white ethnics, African Americans, Latinos, Asian Americans, women, and religious groups realized the right to full political participation?
- What tactics did these groups employ to gain full access to the political process?

Groups with distinctive social and cultural identities have often played pivotal roles in changing American politics. Conflicts over their inclusion have tested Americans' understanding of equality, liberty, and democracy. Establishing access to the political system for these groups has expanded the definition of the political community and has often provoked important institutional changes as well. Moreover, the ongoing participation of such groups has often transformed politics, altering political coalitions and changing political debates. This section will examine the experiences of four kinds of cultural and social groups in American politics: racial and ethnic, gender, class, and religious. It asks to what extent members of these particular groups have recognized common interests and have sought to act politically on those interests. We will pay particular attention to the forms of mobilization these groups used to build political strength and what strategies they employed to gain access to the political system. The story of their fight for political equality and fundamental liberties is a tribute to the creativity and persistence of these groups, but also to the resilience of the American political system.[5]

ETHNICITY AND RACE

Ethnic and racial identities are the most politically significant social identities in the United States. This great diversity has distinguished the United States from most European nations, which for most of modern history have been much more ethnically and racially homogenous. As we examine the process of political inclusion of different groups, we shall see that American politics encouraged racial and ethnic identification even as it has excluded many groups on the basis of race or national origin.

White Ethnics The term "white ethnic" encompasses a wide range of groups who for most of American history did not identify as a single group. In fact, some of these groups—Italians, for example—were not always identified as "white" when they entered this country.

European immigration was the central fact of American life from the colonial period until the 1920s, when Congress sharply cut off immigration. In peak years nearly a million new immigrants entered the country. The colonists came overwhelmingly from the British Isles, particularly from England; a smattering were German or Dutch. The first post-colonial wave of immigration came in the 1840s, when the Irish began to outnumber all other immigrants; Germans and Scandinavians came in the greatest numbers between 1880 and 1890. Finally, between 1890 and 1910, a huge wave of immigration from eastern and central Europe brought Italians, Slavs, and eastern European Jews to the country.[6] The results of these waves of European immigration are reflected in America today: as Figure 2.1 indicates, whites (largely of European origin) comprise 73 percent of the total U.S. population.

FIGURE 2.1

ESTIMATED POPULATION OF THE UNITED STATES BY RACE AND ETHNICITY, 1996

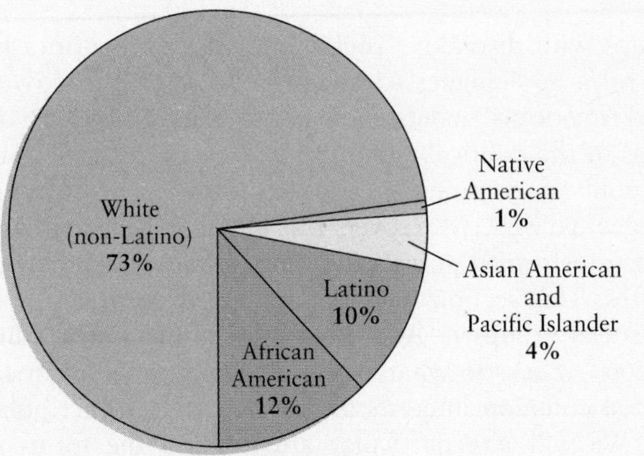

SOURCE: U.S. Bureau of the Census, "Population Projections of the United States by Age, Sex, Race, and Hispanic Origin: 1993 to 2050," *Current Population Reports*, Series P25–1104 (Washington, DC: Government Printing Office, 1993), pp. 18–19.

Many native-born Americans saw immigrants as a threat to their jobs, their way of life, the political system, and American culture and values as a whole.

Although the American story is often told as one of assimilation, in fact American politics acknowledged and encouraged the maintenance of ethnic identities in two ways. First, **nativist** anti-immigrant movements highlighted the differences between the newcomers and other Americans. And second, the openness of the political system encouraged politicians to recognize ethnic groups and to mobilize them—as a group—into politics.

The nativist movement had three strands.[7] The first was an anti-Catholic drive, which took hold beginning in the 1840s, when Irish immigrants began to appear in great numbers. Opponents of immigration formed the Know-Nothing Party (officially named the American Party) in the 1850s, seeking to enact laws that would restrict the civil and political rights of immigrants. A second strand was anti-radicalism. Many of those opposed to immigrants saw them as a source of labor radicalism and political unrest; indeed, many immigrants, especially those from Germany and eastern Europe, brought with them a tradition of socialism and labor activism. The third strand of the nativist movement was racial. In the 1880s and 1890s, a huge wave of new immigrants arrived from eastern and southern Europe. Darker of skin than earlier immigrants from northern Europe, they were attacked as "races of... the very lowest stage of degradation.[8] Opponents of immigration first sought to raise the requirements for naturalization and then moved to restrict entry altogether. They eventually succeeded, from 1917 to 1924, with a series of immigration laws that greatly reduced the number of immigrants entering the country and raised the barriers to naturalization by instituting literacy tests and other restrictions. These immigration restrictions reflected a new racial consciousness. They established a quota system, based on national origins, that greatly favored northern Europeans, who were thought to be more assimilable than southern or eastern Europeans.

For most of American history, citizenship and political equality came to white ethnics without a struggle. Immigrant groups did mobilize against nativism and efforts to restrict immigration, but despite the sometimes virulent

The Bureau of Naturalization provided English language classes for recent immigrants in order to prepare them for citizenship. Most white immigrants were eligible for citizenship after five years in the United States.

anti-immigrant sentiment and the eventual restrictions imposed on immigration, the political rights of white immigrants were never in serious peril. They were eligible to become naturalized citizens after five years of residence; rates of naturalization varied from 45.6 percent of all foreign-born residents in 1910 to 67.9 percent by 1950.[9] Many of America's big cities were governed by **political machines,** which were party organizations that controlled local politics by nominating candidates for office and mobilizing voters to elect those candidates. These machines realized that the votes of the newly arrived immigrants could help particular candidates win office and, consequently, saw to it that immigrants quickly became citizens. In New York, the most important political machine, called Tammany Hall, filled out citizenship applications for immigrants and paid the necessary application fees. In the two weeks before elections in New York, Philadelphia, and Baltimore, naturalization rates increased sharply.[10] In addition, many states and territories allowed noncitizens to vote and enjoy other rights of citizenship.

Once immigrants became citizens, their ethnic identifications remained important political guideposts. In cities, political machines appealed to voters along ethnic lines and parceled out patronage on the basis of ethnic group membership. Precinct captains spoke the language of the immigrants and acted as a link to the broader world. Thus, although ethnic neighborhoods were insulated, they were not isolated. Ethnic concerns entered politics around such issues as the prohibition of alcohol, Sunday-closing laws (a way to preserve Sunday as a day for religious observance by prohibiting businesses from opening on Sunday), and language instruction in the public schools.

Even after white ethnic groups had become assimilated into a broader American culture—which itself was altered by their inclusion—ethnic appeals remained prominent in political life. This was particularly true in big cities, where the practice of ticket balancing ensured that slates of candidates bore a range of ethnic names. For example, in New York City in 1961, a Republican slate of Lefkowitz, Gilhooley, and Fino faced a Democratic lineup of Wagner, Screvane, and Beame.[11] The presence of Irish (Irish-German in the case of Wagner), Italian, and Jewish names on both tickets reflected the need to cover ethnic bases. In recent years, however, the political significance of ethnic identities has begun to fade. Even in New York City, where ethnicity was once a central concern in politics, white ethnic groups no longer fall into predictable voting blocs.

African Americans For African Americans, the central fact of political life has been a denial of full citizenship rights for most of American history. By accepting the institution of slavery, the Founders embraced a system fundamentally at odds with the "Blessings of Liberty" promised in the Constitution. Their decision set the stage for two centuries of African American struggles to achieve full citizenship. In the course of these battles, African Americans built organizations and devised political strategies that transformed American politics.

The vast majority of enslaved blacks had few means for organizing to assert themselves. Their hopes for achieving full citizenship rights initially seemed fulfilled when three constitutional amendments were adopted after the Civil War: the Thirteenth Amendment abolished slavery; the Fourteenth Amendment guaranteed equal protection under the law; and the Fifteenth Amendment guaranteed voting rights for blacks. Protected by the presence of

The Shackle Broken by the Genius of Freedom (1874) celebrates the benefits of emancipation. The center top panel shows the house of representatives of South Carolina, the only former slave state to elect a majority of blacks to its legislature.

federal troops, African American men were able to exercise their political rights immediately after the war. During Reconstruction, blacks were elected to many political offices: two black senators were elected from Mississippi and a total of fourteen African Americans were elected to the House of Representatives between 1869 and 1877. African Americans also held many state-level political offices. As voters and public officials, black citizens found a home in the Republican Party, which had secured the ratification of the three constitutional amendments guaranteeing black rights. After the war, the Republican Party continued to reach out to black voters as a means to build party strength in the South.[12]

This political equality was short-lived, however. The national government withdrew its troops from the South and turned its back on African Americans in 1877. In the Compromise of 1877, southern Democrats agreed to allow the Republican candidate, Rutherford B. Hayes, to become president after a disputed election. In exchange, northern Republicans dropped their support for the civil liberties and political participation of African Americans. After that, southern states erected a tight system of social, political, and economic inequality that made a mockery of the promises in the Constitution. These years marked the beginning of a long process in which African Americans built organizations and devised strategies for asserting their constitutional rights.

W.E.B. DuBois, a founder of the NAACP and a prominent American thinker throughout the twentieth century.

Four broad strategies emerged to guide the African American quest for equality. The first approach, promoted by Booker T. Washington, head of the Tuskegee Institute in Alabama, rejected the struggle for political rights. Instead, it urged blacks toward self-help through such means as moral uplift and vocational training.[13] A second strategy sought to win political rights through political pressure and litigation. This approach was championed by the National Association for the Advancement of Colored People (NAACP), established by a group of black and white reformers in 1909. Among the NAACP's founders was W. E. B. DuBois, one of the most influential and creative thinkers on racial issues of the twentieth century. Because the northern black vote was so small in the early decades of the twentieth century, the organization primarily relied on the courts to press for black political rights. After the 1920s, the NAACP built a strong membership base, with some strength in the South, which would be critical when the Civil Rights movement gained momentum in the 1950s.

The great migration of blacks to the North beginning around World War I enlivened two other strategies, both of which had deep roots in the black community. The first strategy focused on **black nationalism.** Support for separatism and emigration back to Africa arose soon after the Civil War, but the nationalist movement reached a zenith in the urban North in the 1920s. Marcus Garvey's Universal Negro Improvement Association attracted millions of supporters with its messages of economic independence and emigration back to Africa.[14] The other approach that began to gain ground was a protest strategy. Although protest organizations had existed in the nineteenth century, the continuing migration of blacks to the North made protest an increasingly useful tool. Black labor leader A. Philip Randolph forced the federal government to address racial discrimination in hiring practices during World War II by threatening a massive march on Washington. The federal

The Woolworth lunch counter sit-in in Greensboro, North Carolina, started a wave of sit-ins throughout the South.

government also grew more attentive to blacks as their voting strength increased as a result of the northward migration. By the 1940s, the black vote had swung away from Republicans, but the Democratic hold on black votes was by no means absolute.

These four strands—self-improvement, political pressure and legal strategies, black nationalism, and protest—all played a part in the modern Civil Rights movement, which took off in the 1950s. The movement drew on an organizational base and network of communication rooted in black churches, the NAACP, and black colleges.

The nonviolent protest tactics adopted by local clergy members, including Rev. Martin Luther King, Jr., eventually spread across the South and brought national attention to the movement. The clergy organized into a group called the Southern Christian Leadership Conference (SCLC). Students also played a key role. The most important student organization was the Student Nonviolent Coordinating Committee (SNCC). In 1960, four black students sat down at the lunch counter of the Greensboro, North Carolina, Woolworth's, which like most southern establishments did not serve African Americans. Their sit-in was the first of many. Through a combination of protest, legal action, and political pressure, the Civil Rights movement compelled a reluctant federal government to enforce black civil and political rights. The 1964 Civil Rights Act and the 1965 Voting Rights Act were the great legislative victories of the movement; the end of legal segregation and the beginning of black political power were the results.[15]

Martin Luther King, Jr., addressed the crowd during the 1963 March on Washington, where he delivered his famous "I have a dream" speech.

Significant though they were, the victories of the Civil Rights movement did not substantially alter the living conditions of poor African Americans in the North. There, frustrations stemming from discrimination, poor housing, inferior education, and low-wage jobs boiled over in urban riots during the

THE AMERICAN AGONY OVER ABOLITION

No issue in the nation's history so deeply divided Americans as that of the abolition of slavery. The importation and subjugation of Africans kidnapped from their native lands was a practice virtually as old as the country itself: the first slaves brought to what became the United States arrived in 1619, a year before the Plymouth colony was established in Massachusetts. White southerners built their agricultural economy (especially cotton production) on a large slave labor force. By 1840, for example, nearly half of the populations of Alabama and Louisiana consisted of black slaves. Even so, only about a quarter of southern white families owned slaves.

The subjugation of blacks through slavery was so much a part of the southern culture that efforts to restrict or abolish slavery were met with fierce resistance. Despite the manifest cruelties of the slave system, southerners referred to the system by the quaint term "peculiar institution." The label meant little to slavery's opponents, however, and an abolitionist movement grew and spread among northerners in the 1830s (although abolitionist sentiment could be traced back to the pre-Revolutionary era). The movement was most closely identified with the writing of William Lloyd Garrison. Slavery had been all but eliminated in the North by this time, but few northerners favored outright abolition. In fact, most whites held attitudes toward blacks that would be considered racist today.

Slavery was important to the South for economic reasons, but the heart of the controversy was moral, not economic. One abolitionist labeled slavery "the blight of this nation, the curse of the North and the curse of the South"; "man cannot, consistently with reason, religion, and the eternal and immutable principles of justice, be the property of man."[1] Southerners responded in increasingly strident terms that not only was slavery not evil, but it was actually beneficial to blacks: "The negro slaves of the South are the happiest, and, in some sense, the freest people in the world," crowed one defender of slavery.[2] According to one historian, "Never before had the justification of human bondage been presented with so much moral fervor."[3]

1960s. Such poor conditions created fertile ground for the messages of nationalism and self-help. The most powerful advocate of these ideas was Malcolm X, who was a member of the Nation of Islam until the year before his assassination in 1965. Malcolm X expressed the frustration of many poor urban blacks: "I don't see any American dream, I see an American nightmare."[16] The ideas of protest, self-help, and black cultural pride were also taken up by the Black Panther Party, which established a presence in many cities in the late 1960s.

The victories of the Civil Rights movement made blacks full citizens and stimulated a tremendous growth in the number of black public officials at all levels of government, as blacks exercised their newfound political rights. Yet despite these successes, racial segregation remains a fact of life in the United States, and new problems have emerged. Most troubling is the persistence of black urban poverty, now coupled with deep social and economic isolation.[17] These conditions raise new questions about African American political participation. One question concerns black political cohesion: Will blacks continue to vote as a bloc given the sharp economic differences that now divide a large black middle class from an equally large group of deeply impoverished African Americans? A second question concerns the benefits of participation:

The abolitionist movement spread primarily through local organizations in the North. Antislavery groups coalesced in New York, Ohio, New Hampshire, Pennsylvania, New Jersey, and Michigan. In addition to forming antislavery societies, the movement spawned two political parties: the Liberty Party, a staunchly antislavery party, and the Free Soil Party, a larger but more moderate third party that sought primarily to restrict the spread of slavery into new western territories. Garrison noted his dismay at the Free Soil Party's more modest and pragmatic approach: "It is a party for keeping Free Soil and not for setting men free."

Some opponents of slavery took matters into their own hands, aiding in the escape of runaway slaves along the Underground Railroad. Even today, private homes and churches, scattered throughout the northeast, that were used to hide blacks on their trips to Canada, attest to the involvement of local citizenry. In the South, a similar, if contrary, fervor prompted mobs to break into post offices in order to seize and destroy antislavery literature.

The emotional power of the slavery issue was such that it ruptured the Democratic Party, splitting it into "slave" and "free" factions. It destroyed the other major party of the time, the Whig Party. And it gave rise to a new party, the Republican Party, which would become the last minor political party to become a major political party in the United States. Most important, however, the slavery question precipitated the nation's most bloody conflict, the Civil War. From the ashes of the Civil War came the Thirteenth, Fourteenth, and Fifteenth Amendments, which would redefine civil rights from that day to this.

SOURCE: Merton L. Dillon, *The Abolitionists* (Dekalb, IL: Northern Illinois University Press, 1974).

[1] John M. Blum et al., *The National Experience* (New York: Harcourt, Brace, and World, 1968), p. 266.

[2] Ibid.

[3] Ibid., p. 267.

How can political participation improve the lives of African Americans, especially of the poor?

Public opinion and voting evidence indicate that African Americans continue to vote as a bloc despite their economic differences.[18] Surveys of black voters show that blacks across the income spectrum believe that their fates are linked because of their race. This sense of shared experience and a common fate has united blacks at the polls and in politics.[19] Since the 1960s, blacks have overwhelmingly chosen Democratic candidates and black candidates have sought election under the Democratic banner. In recent years, however, a small number of black Republicans has been elected to the House of Representatives. Evidence that affluent black Americans are less likely than poorer African Americans to support traditional policies that assist the poor suggests that this trend could continue in the future. However, Republican hostility to affirmative action and other programs of racial preference is likely to sharply check any large-scale black migration to the Republican Party.

At the same time, however, the black community and its political leadership has been considerably frustrated about the benefits of loyalty to the Democratic Party. Some analysts argue that the structure of party competition makes it difficult for African Americans to win policy benefits through

The Million Man March of 1995, which drew hundreds of thousands of black men to Washington for a show of unity and a renewal of commitment to their families and communities.

political participation. Because Republicans have not sought to win the black vote and Democrats take it for granted, neither party is willing to support bold measures to address the mounting problems of poor African Americans.

Thus, concerns about strategy and organization remain very much on the African American political agenda. In the face of unfavorable political and legal outcomes, interest in self-help has resurged, as evidenced by the gathering of hundreds of thousands of black men in Washington in 1995 for the Million Man March. Yet many black Americans continue to search for new ways to induce the government to address their distinctive concerns. These questions and problems now confront a new generation of African Americans.

Latinos The labels "Latino" and "Hispanic" encompass a wide range of groups with diverse national origins and distinctive cultural identities. The experiences of these groups in the American political system have often been very different from one another as well. Mexican Americans, Puerto Ricans, Cubans, and Central Americans have used varying strategies and organizational forms to gain access to American politics. As we will see, their struggles for political equality often differed according to when they entered the United States, in what region of the country they lived, and how racial considerations affected white views of whether they could become full citizens.

Mexican Americans are the largest group of Latinos in the United States today; their population is estimated at 14.6 million (see Table 2.1). The Mexican American experience with political equality has been diverse and changing, because the experiences of Mexican Americans range from a people conquered in the middle of the nineteenth century to immigrants who arrived yesterday. The first Mexican Americans did not immigrate to the United States; the United States came to them when the Americans annexed Texas in 1845 and defeated Mexico in 1848. The land that today makes up the states of New Mexico, California, Nevada, Utah, Colorado, Arizona, and Texas, all once part of Mexico, was added to American territory in those years.

The early political experiences of Mexican Americans were shaped by race and by region. In 1898, Mexican Americans were given formal political rights, including the right to vote. In many places, however, and especially in Texas, Mexican Americans were segregated and prevented from voting through such means as the white primary and the poll tax.[20] Region made a difference too. In contrast to the northeastern and midwestern cities to which most European ethnics immigrated, the Southwest did not have a tradition of ethnic mobilization associated with machine politics. Particularly after the political reforms enacted in the first decades of the twentieth century, city politics in the Southwest was dominated by a small group of Anglo elites. In the countryside, when Mexican Americans participated in politics, it was often as part of a political organization dominated by a large white landowner, or *patron*.

The earliest Mexican American independent political organizations, the League of United Latin American Citizens (LULAC) and the GI Forum, worked to stem discrimination against Mexican Americans in the years after World War II. By the late 1950s, the first Mexican American was elected to Congress, and four others followed in the 1960s. In the late 1960s a new kind of Mexican American political movement was born. Inspired by the black Civil Rights movement, Mexican American students launched boycotts of high school classes in East Los Angeles, Denver, and San Antonio. Students in colleges and universities across California joined in as well. Among their demands were bilingual education, an end to discrimination, and more cul-

TABLE 2.1

LATINOS IN THE UNITED STATES, 1993

	Estimated population	Percentage of total U.S. population
Mexican	14,628,000	5.6
Puerto Rican	2,402,000	0.9
Cuban	1,071,000	0.4
Total Latino	22,752,000	8.9

SOURCE: Patricia A. Montgomery, "The Hispanic Population in the United States: March 1993," *Current Population Reports,* P20-475 (Washington, DC: U.S. Government Printing Office, 1994).

tural recognition. In Crystal City, Texas, which had been dominated by Anglo politicians despite a population that was overwhelmingly Mexican American, the newly formed La Raza Unida Party took over the city government.[21]

The "Chicano" movement of the 1960s consciously modeled itself after the African American Civil Rights movement, adopting a more racially defined political strategy than earlier Mexican American politicians had used. Since that time, Mexican American political strategy has developed along two tracks. One is a traditional ethnic-group path of voter registration and voting along ethnic lines. The second is a legal strategy using the various civil rights laws designed to ensure fair access to the political system. The Mexican American Legal Defense Fund (MALDEF) has played a key role in designing and pursuing the latter strategy. The two strategies are often used to reinforce one another, but at times they come into conflict.

Like that of the Mexicans, the Puerto Rican experience of the United States began with the experience of conquest. Puerto Rico became an unincorporated territory of the United States in 1898, after the Spanish-American War. In 1917, Puerto Ricans were made American citizens, although their island did not become a state. In the 1950s, Puerto Ricans began migrating to the mainland in large numbers, settling mainly in cities on the eastern seaboard—New York in particular.

Although they migrated to cities that had active traditions of ethnic group political participation, Puerto Ricans did not become politically mobilized until the late 1960s. In New York State, the requirement that voters be literate in English barred the majority of Puerto Ricans from registering in the 1950s.[22] By the 1960s, Puerto Ricans had become more politically mobilized and voted predominantly for Democratic candidates. Nevertheless, as one of the poorest ethnic groups in the United States, Puerto Ricans tend to have relatively low rates of political participation.

The Cuban experience with American politics has been quite different from those of Mexicans and Puerto Ricans. The vast majority of Cuban immigrants have come to the United States since the early 1960s as refugees from communist Cuba. In contrast to Puerto Rican and Mexican immigrants, many of the Cubans who came to the United States were middle class. Because they were granted refugee status, they also received federal government assistance in their settlement process. A central feature of Cuban American politics is a resolute anticommunism, which has led Cuban Americans to favor the Republican Party. Cuban political participation has also been shaped by the great concentration of Cubans in southern Florida. This concentration has allowed Cubans to become a major political force in Miami, and in Florida more broadly. The first Cuban American was elected to Congress from Florida in 1989.

Although Mexican Americans, Puerto Ricans, and Cubans make up the majority of Latinos in the United States, in the last decade substantial numbers of Spanish-speaking immigrants and refugees from the Caribbean, Central America, and South America have entered the country. During the 1980s, 23 percent of all legal immigrants to the United States came from these other Latin American countries.[23] These groups have altered the ethnic composition of Latinos in many cities, but they have not yet begun participating in politics in significant numbers.

A Latino voter registration drive in Texas. Increasing rates of naturalization and voter registration will make the Latino vote a powerful force in American Politics.

The experience of Latinos in winning political equality stands between those of African Americans and white immigrants. In some regions of the country, restrictions on participation limited political equality until the 1960s. Even though Latinos have secured formal political equality, as a group Latinos have a relatively low level of political mobilization. Many analysts have called the Hispanic vote "the sleeping giant" because it has not yet realized its potential influence. Two important reasons for the low mobilization levels among Latinos are the low rates of voter registration and low rates of naturalization. Only two-thirds of voting-age Latinos are American citizens. Mexican immigrants have the lowest rate of naturalization of all immigrant groups: only 13 percent of legal Mexican immigrants who came to the United States between 1970 and 1979 had become citizens in 1989. (For comparison, the rate for Vietnamese immigrants was 75 percent and for other Asians, 60 percent.[24]) In recent years, Hispanic political organizations have launched campaigns to encourage Latino immigrants to become citizens. They have also sought to register those who *are* citizens to vote, so that they can exercise the rights that come with political equality.

Asian Americans As with Latinos, Asian Americans are a diverse group with many different national backgrounds. The majority of Asian immigrants have come to the United States in the past thirty years, but people from China began arriving on the West Coast in the 1850s.

The early Asian experience in the United States was shaped by a series of naturalization laws dating back to 1790, the first of which declared that only white aliens were eligible for citizenship. Chinese immigrants had begun arriving in California in the 1850s, drawn by the boom of the Gold Rush, but they were immediately met with hostility. The virulent antagonism toward

Chinese immigrants in California led Congress to declare Chinese immigrants ineligible for citizenship in 1870. Racial and cultural differences accounted for some of the white hostility toward the Chinese; many whites believed that the Chinese were "unassimilable" and uninterested in American democracy. But economic competition also fueled antagonism; white workers viewed Chinese laborers as a source of cheap labor that would drive down the wages of all workers. The Workingmen's Party of San Francisco stirred up some of the most vicious anti-Chinese rhetoric and actions, including mob attacks that left many Chinese dead. The Chinese found few allies to defend them in 1882 when the first Chinese Exclusion Act easily passed Congress. This new law suspended the entry of Chinese laborers.

At the time of the Exclusion Act, the Chinese community was composed predominantly of single male laborers, with few women and children. The few Chinese children in San Francisco were initially denied entry to the public schools; only after parents of American-born Chinese children pressed legal action were the children allowed to attend public school. Even then, however, they were segregated into a separate Chinese school. American-born Chinese children could not be denied citizenship, however; this right was confirmed by the Supreme Court in 1898, when it ruled in *United States v. Wong Kim Ark* that anyone born in the United States was entitled to full citizenship.[25] Still, new Chinese immigrants were barred from the United States until 1943, after China had become a key wartime ally and Congress repealed the Chinese Exclusion Act and permitted Chinese residents to become citizens. As discrimination eased, Chinese Americans ventured out of Chinatowns to take jobs in a variety of wartime industries.[26]

The early Japanese experience in the United States mirrored that of the Chinese. When Japanese immigration to California began to increase in the early 1900s, it set off a wave of hysteria. Whites formed the Asiatic Exclusion

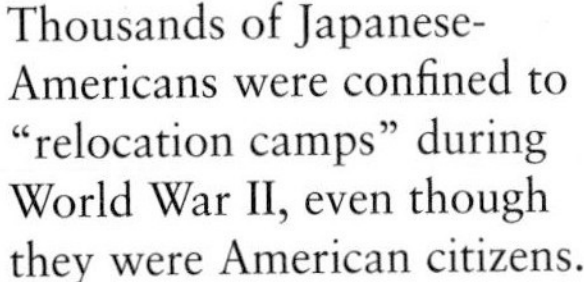

Thousands of Japanese-Americans were confined to "relocation camps" during World War II, even though they were American citizens.

ASIAN AMERICANS IN THE UNITED STATES, 1990

	Estimated population	Percentage of total U.S. population
Chinese	1,649,000	0.7
Filipino	1,420,000	0.6
Japanese	866,000	0.3
Korean	797,000	0.3

SOURCE: U.S. Bureau of the Census, *Asian and Pacific Islanders in the United States,* Series 1990 CP-3-5 (August 1993).

TABLE 2.2

League, demanding that immigration be stopped. Fears of the "Yellow Peril" were explicitly racial.

With the advent of World War II and the bombing of Pearl Harbor by the Japanese government in 1941, anti-Japanese sentiment once again flourished, particularly on the West Coast. Several months later Congress passed a law that authorized the military to exclude any person it deemed to be a threat from designated areas. Under this law, more than 110,000 Japanese people—two-thirds of them American citizens—were rounded up and sent to "relocation camps." There they were kept for up to three years, deprived of their property, their jobs, and their freedom.

After the war, Japanese Americans began to challenge the laws that restricted their rights in the United States. In 1952 the McCarran-Walter Act finally rescinded the 1790 law allowing only white aliens to become citizens. A later generation of Japanese Americans revived the issue of reparations for those who had been interned during World War II. In 1988 they succeeded in winning passage of a federal law that issued a formal apology and promised a payment of $20,000 to each of the survivors of the camps.

Asian immigration climbed rapidly after the 1965 Immigration Act, which lifted discriminatory quotas on Asian immigration. During the 1980s, 37 percent of new immigrants arrived from a wide range of Asian countries, including the Philippines, China, Korea, and Vietnam. Many Cambodians and Vietnamese entered the country as refugees during these years as well.[27] Asian Americans are widely dispersed throughout the United States, but nearly 40 percent live in California.[28]

The very diversity of national backgrounds among Asian Americans has impeded the development of group-based political power. As Table 2.2 shows, no one national group dominates among the Asian American population. In California, Asian American political activists have had some success in mobilizing around particular issues. For example, in 1988 Asian American opposition blocked the nomination of a candidate for state treasurer because he had opposed reparations for the Japanese interned in camps during World War II. Asian Americans have also exerted pressure on the University of California at Berkeley to review admission policies that appeared to discriminate against Asians.[29] In particular cities where there are concentrations of Asians from the same national background, Asian Americans have gained political representation. Yet even under these circumstances there are often several competing factions that represent different interpretations of Asian American interests.[30] The geographical dispersion of Asian Americans and their diverse backgrounds and experiences raise questions about whether Asian Americans will form a cohesive political group mobilized around issues of common interest.

Native Americans Today there are approximately two million Native Americans in the United States. When Europeans first came to North America, the "American Indian" population was estimated at three to seven million. Spread across the continent, they represented several hundred distinct cultural groups or tribes. For the first century after the Founding, the experience of Native Americans with the American government was like that between warring nations. It was a war that the United States government won. For the next hundred years, the relationship was that of a conquered people and their conquerors. Not until the 1960s did a movement representing all tribes assert the rights of Native Americans within the American political system.

The political status of Native Americans was left unclear in the Constitution. But by the early 1800s, the courts had defined each of the Indian tribes as a nation. As members of an Indian nation, Native Americans were declared noncitizens of the United States. By 1900, however, in response to increasing demands for land as Americans moved westward, most Native Americans had been confined to reservations on unwanted lands held in trust for the tribes by the federal government. The political status of Native Americans changed in 1924, when congressional legislation granted citizenship to those who had been born in the United States. A variety of changes in federal policy toward Native Americans during the 1930s paved the way for a later resurgence of their political power. Most important was the federal decision to encourage Native Americans on reservations to establish local self-government.[31]

The Native Americans who occupied Alcatraz Island in 1969 claimed it as Indian property. Their dramatic action brought national attention to the American Indian Movement.

During World War II, many Native Americans left the reservations to work in wartime industries. After the war, the federal government began to encourage Native Americans to move to cities. Once in the cities, Native Americans from different tribes began to see their interests in common and to create a single Native American identity. In the past they had thought of themselves as members of particular tribes, not as a single group. Central among the issues that helped to drive the resurgence of Native American political power was the need to protect the reservations. Although the federal government had guaranteed the land to them by treaty, Native Americans faced constant efforts to take the land away from them. In addition, deep poverty and contact with government institutions that had little respect for Native American culture fueled their mobilization.

The Native American political movement gathered force in the 1960s, as Native Americans began to use protest, litigation, and assertion of tribal rights to improve their situation. In 1968, Dennis Banks co-founded the American Indian Movement (AIM), the most prominent Native American protest organization. AIM won national attention in 1969 when two hundred of its members, representing twenty different tribes, took over the famous prison island of Alcatraz in San Francisco Bay, claiming it for Native

Americans. In 1971, AIM members took over the town of Wounded Knee, South Dakota, the site of the last major battle between Native Americans and the U.S. Army, in which a Sioux village had been massacred. The federal government responded to the rise in Indian activism with the Indian Self-Determination and Education Assistance Act, which began to give Indians more control over their own land.[32]

In recent years, Native Americans have used their increasing autonomy to promote economic development on reservations, where deep poverty remains widespread. The biggest moneymaker for reservations has been casino gambling. The Supreme Court paved the way for casino gambling in a 1987 ruling that Indian tribes, as sovereign nations, are exempt from most state gambling regulations. An estimated ninety tribes have opened casinos, which bring in a total income of over $1 billion. Gambling has brought the greatest economic success the tribes have ever seen. They have been able to use the money from gambling to build housing and schools and to establish a base from which to diversify into other forms of economic development. Rather than leasing their lands to non-Indian companies, many tribes are now setting up their own businesses.[33]

Class

If asked what economic class they belong to, most Americans reply that they are in the middle class. The relative weakness of class in the United States stems in part from the American ideals of equality and individual liberty. But it is also a product of the American political system. For it is not just values but also the experiences—both positive and negative—of workers with the American political system that have prevented class from becoming a significant category of political action in the United States.

A glance at American history shows that there were times when class organization was very important. In the early years of the Republic, workers—mainly skilled artisans—formed political parties in more than sixty cities and towns. They demanded the ten-hour day, free public schooling, and democratic political reforms. After the Civil War, the Knights of Labor became the first mass organization of the working class. In the 1880s, local elections featured Knights of Labor political tickets in more than two hundred state and local elections. Fueling this political activity was deep discontent with the emergence of big corporations, the factory system, and the degradation of work in general. In addition, deep economic depressions in the 1870s threw people out of work in unprecedented numbers. These conditions lay behind the massive labor strikes in the late nineteenth century. In fact, it is often forgotten that the United States has the most violent labor history of any industrialized nation.

If we look at the demands these workers made, we see that they were very much in tune with the key values of a thriving democracy. In fact, workers often drew on these values to support their positions. For example, workers assailed the emergence of the large corporation as anti-democratic. They defended a shorter working day and adequate wages as essential for workers to exercise the rights and responsibilities of citizenship. They argued that workers needed time to spend with their families and to attend public lectures.

The 1886 convention of the Knights of Labor. The organization accepted large numbers of black and female workers as members.

Labor organizations at this time had quite a broad notion of who was a member of the working class; for example, anyone except a capitalist or a lawyer could become a member of the Knights of Labor.[34]

Despite all this working-class activity, workers' parties never managed to last in the United States, and national politics did not organize along class lines. The American Federation of Labor (AFL), the largest labor union to survive into the twentieth century, turned its back on politics. Instead of formally aligning with a political party, the union remained aloof from politics and instead practiced "business unionism"—the AFL would fight for workers' rights but it would not enter the political arena to do so.

The closest Americans have come to having a class-based politics in this century was during the New Deal of the 1930s. President Franklin Roosevelt changed American politics with legislation that assisted workers and their families: work relief, the Social Security Act, and the right to organize labor unions, for instance. Roosevelt used explicit class imagery to retain the political support of working-class voters and spoke of the need to equalize the distribution of wealth in the United States. His policies cemented working-class support for the Democratic Party, and the Republican Party became increasingly identified with business interests. These divisions were by no means absolute, however. The Democratic Party had plenty of supporters in the business community. Furthermore, the southern attachment to the Democratic Party had little to do with class; it was based more on the Democratic Party's refusal to challenge the political and economic inequality of blacks in the South. This loose class alignment characterized American politics until the 1960s, when racial and cultural divisions, along with a growing distrust of all politicians, began to diminish the expression of class in politics.

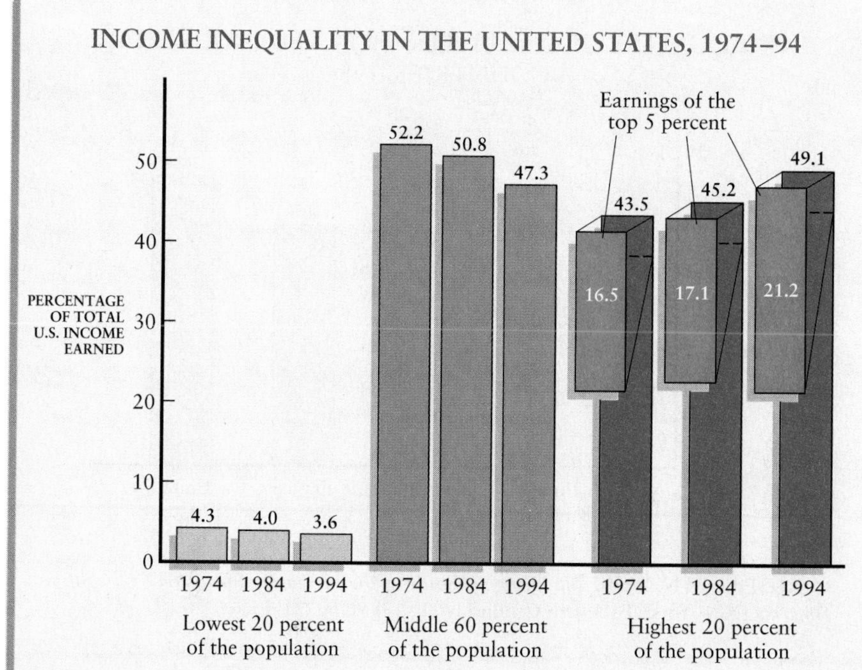

SOURCE: U.S. Bureau of the Census, "Income, Poverty, and Valuation of Noncash Benefits: 1994," *Current Population Reports*, Series P60–189 (Washington, DC: Government Printing Office, 1996), p. xii.

FIGURE 2.2
Over the last two decades, America's lower and middle classes have been growing relatively poorer, while the upper classes have been growing wealthier. In 1994, the top 5 percent of the population took home more than 20 percent of the income in the United States.

What are the prospects of reviving a class orientation in politics today? If we simply look at what Americans say about class, it does not look promising. Polls show that 93 percent of all Americans identify themselves as middle class; only 1 percent say they are in the upper class.[35] Nonetheless, some analysts argue that trends in the distribution of income and wealth over the past two decades have laid the groundwork for class politics. Since 1970, while incomes in the United States have remained stagnant, inequality has grown (see Figure 2.2). In fact, the United States has the greatest inequality in income and wealth of any industrial nation (see Figure 2.3).[36] In recent years, Democratic candidates have sought to highlight these realities to revive a politics of class. But, aware of the weakness of class identity in the United States, they embrace only a loose definition of class. For example, in recent years, Democrats have attacked the Reagan and Bush tax policies as unfair to middle-class Americans. Republicans reject these arguments, however, saying that their policies create economic growth, which benefits all Americans. Thus, Republicans claim, there is a shared interest across classes, not opposing interests. Republicans also charge that class appeals are un-American. For example, President George Bush defended himself against Democratic attacks by remarking that class is "for European democracies or something else—it isn't for the United States of America. We are not going to be divided by class."[37]

The recent Democratic efforts reveal the difficulty of trying to organize politics around class. Since most people feel they are in the middle class,

INEQUALITY OF WEALTH IN SELECTED INDUSTRIAL COUNTRIES, 1986

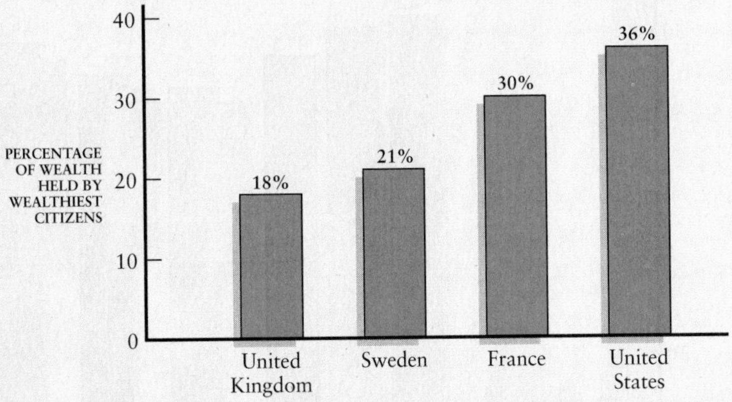

SOURCE: Edward N. Wolff, *Top Heavy: A Study of the Increasing Inequality of Wealth in America* (New York: Twentieth Century Fund, 1995), pp. 21-25.

FIGURE 2.3

In the United States, the wealthiest 1 percent of the population holds 36 percent of the country's wealth—a higher proportion than in any other industrialized country.

Democrats face the challenge of deciding how and where to draw the line between the middle class and the rich. Moreover, the impact of the new inequality has been especially felt by the poor; assisting them requires taxing the upper end of the middle class. Yet upper-middle-class taxpayers participate the most and are the most vocal in American politics. They mounted such vigorous opposition to the Clinton income tax increase in 1993 that most Americans ended up thinking that their taxes had been raised, when in fact the increase only affected those at the very top of the income distribution.

Democrats also face another problem: To win support from voters on the lower half of the income spectrum, Democrats have to show that they can enact policies that will reduce economic inequality. In an uncertain economic environment and with an electorate deeply mistrustful of politicians, this is a tall order. Nonetheless, widespread public concern about jobs and income suggests that politicians will continue to invoke the themes of class.

GENDER

Until 1920, electoral politics was a decidedly masculine world. Not only were women barred from voting in national politics, but electoral politics was closely tied to such male social institutions as lodges, bars, and clubs. Yet the exclusion of women from this political world did not prevent them from engaging in public life. Instead, women carved out a "separate sphere" for their public activities. Emphasizing female stewardship over the moral realm, women became important voices in social reform well before they won the right to vote.[38]

Women played leading roles in two key groundswells of social reform: the abolitionist movement prior to the Civil War and the movement against political corruption and urban social squalor beginning in the 1880s. Some women pressed for the right to vote immediately after the Civil War, when male ex-slaves won the franchise. Politicians in both parties rejected women's suffrage as disruptive and unrealistic. Barred from voting, women found other means of participating in public life. For one thing, they formed their own clubs; as the nineteenth century ended, the General Federation of Women's Clubs boasted 495 affiliates throughout the country. These clubs provided female fellowship, but they also sought to bring women's distinctive perspectives into the public sphere. Women, they believed, had a special mission to bring morality into public life. Thus, women fought to prohibit alcohol consumption through the Woman's Christian Temperance Union; worked in urban charity organizations; sought to abolish child labor and to establish laws protecting public health; and led movements to reform education and schools in cities across the country.

At the same time, women began organizing to win the right to vote. Women formally started to press for the vote in 1867 when a state referendum to give women the vote in Kansas failed. Scattered efforts over the next decades took organizational form when the National American Woman Suffrage Association (NAWSA) formed in 1890. Many states granted women the right to vote before the national government did; Western states with less-entrenched political systems opened politics to women earliest. When Wyoming became a state in 1890, it was the first state to grant full suffrage to women. Colorado, Utah, and Idaho all followed suit in the next several years. Suffrage organizations grew—NAWSA claimed two million members by 1917—and staged mass meetings, parades, petitions, and protests.

Suffragettes on the sidewalk in front of the White House in 1920. That year, after decades of political mobilization and state-level victories, women won a constitutional amendment guaranteeing the right to vote.

NAWSA organized state-by-state efforts to win the right to vote. A more militant group, the National Woman's Party, staged pickets and got arrested in front of the White House to protest President Wilson's opposition to a constitutional amendment granting women the right to vote. Finally in 1920, the Nineteenth Amendment was ratified, guaranteeing women the right to vote.

The consequences of gaining the vote proved disappointing, however, especially to feminists, who wanted equality between men and women. The earliest advocates of women's rights had favored equality in all spheres of life. By contrast, the mainstream of the suffrage movement stressed "women's special sphere"—the realm of morality, social reform, and family. Politics proved somewhat more amenable to the latter vision because it accorded better with widely held cultural beliefs. The idea of a separate women's sphere also built on institutions and initiatives that had begun before women had the vote. For example, Democrats responded to the women's vote by establishing the Women's Bureau within the Labor Department. Once granted the franchise, however, women did not vote as a group, and many of them did not vote at all. Thus, hopes that women would achieve equality through the vote or that their votes would make some distinctive impact on politics diminished. In this context, the National Woman's Party's legislation for an Equal Rights Amendment stood little chance of success when it was submitted to Congress in 1923. Even legislation premised on women's "special sphere"—such as maternal and child health care reform—was abandoned by the end of the 1920s. Not until the 1960s did a broad movement for women's equality reemerge. The initial impetus for its revival was growing concern about inequality in the world of work.

Three federal government actions laid the groundwork for a new feminist movement. Prodded by the Women's Bureau of the Labor Department, President John Kennedy set up a President's Commission on the Status of Women in 1961. The commission had a broad mandate to investigate the status of women. The group's final report, issued in 1963, detailed the range of inequalities that continued to face women. Investigators had found that one-third of two thousand employers surveyed admitted to keeping separate wage scales for men and women. They also found many instances of double pay scales in surveys of labor contracts and job-hiring orders. Many of these differences had been longstanding: during World War II, the Women's Bureau had documented widespread differences between the pay given to men and women in the war industries. In one instance, they found that male trainees received ten cents more per hour than the women who were training them were paid.[39] But the impact of the commission did not end with the report. It prompted states to set up their own commissions, creating a network armed with new information about women's unequal status.[40] Complementing the activity generated by the commission were two new laws promising women equal treatment. The first was the Equal Pay Act of 1963, which outlawed wage discrimination against women. The second was Title VII of the Civil Rights Act of 1964, which outlawed discrimination in employment. Unexpectedly, it was a conservative Democratic representative, Howard W. Smith, who added "sex" to Title VII as a category of prohibited discrimination. He did this to make the act look silly and to divide liberals. Despite derisive references to "Ladies' Day in the House," the provision remained in the act.

Representative Pat Schroeder addressing a pro-choice rally organized by the National Organization for Women. Since *Roe v. Wade*, many women's organizations have devoted much of their energy to keeping abortion a legal choice.

Galvanized by the new lines of communication set up in the early 1960s and armed with new legal tools, women formed a set of organizations dedicated to fight for equality for women in many different spheres. Among the new organizations were the National Organization for Women (NOW), the Women's Equity Action League (WEAL), and the National Women's Political Caucus (NWPC). NOW used protest tactics to combat the unequal treatment of women. It picketed the Equal Employment Opportunity Commission for refusing to ban sex-segregated employment ads and filed charges against the *New York Times* for publishing such ads. WEAL focused on legal action around a wide range of sex discrimination issues, including lawsuits against law and medical schools for discriminatory admissions policies. The NWPC promoted the election of female candidates and the appointment of women to political office.

By the early 1970s, legislative successes were bolstered by important legal victories, the most stunning of which was the 1973 legalization of abortion in *Roe v. Wade*. The movement next turned its efforts to passing an Equal Rights Amendment (ERA), which the National Woman's Party had regularly proposed since 1923. Buoyed by the strength of the new women's movement, success appeared within reach. Congress approved the amendment in 1972 and sent it to the states for ratification. But the ERA fell three states short of the thirty-eight needed for ratification and, by 1982, it was dead.

Why did the ERA fail? In the years after Congress passed the ERA, two developments had changed the political climate. One was the emergence of a politically sophisticated anti-ERA movement, spearheaded by conservative activist Phyllis Schlafly. Schlafly and her well-financed organization mounted campaigns in state after state, ultimately derailing the early momentum that the ERA had built. Second, a disconnection had developed between the women's movement, as represented by its key organizations, and many

American women. Most women did not identify the ERA as an essential piece of legislation, and the concerns of the feminist organizations supporting it seemed increasingly remote from the lives of ordinary women.[41]

The failure of the ERA was a defeat for the feminist organizations, but it by no means marked the end of gender politics. Three developments indicate the ongoing significance of gender issues in American politics. First is the emergence of a **gender gap**—a distinctive pattern of male and female voting decisions—in electoral politics. Although proponents of women's suffrage had expected women to make a distinctive impact on politics as soon as they won the vote, not until the 1980s did voting patterns reveal a clear difference between male and female votes. In 1980, men voted heavily for Republican candidate Ronald Reagan; women divided their votes between Reagan and the incumbent Democratic president, Jimmy Carter. Since that election, gender differences have emerged in congressional and state elections, as well. Women tend to vote in higher numbers for Democratic candidates, while Republicans win more male votes. Behind these voting patterns are differing assessments of key policy issues. For one thing, more women than men take liberal positions on political issues; women are more likely than men to oppose military activities and support social spending. For example, 54 percent of women approved of the U.S. decision to send troops to Saudi Arabia in 1991, compared to 78 percent of men. On social spending, these trends reverse: 69 percent of women favor increased spending on Social Security, compared to 57 percent of men; 83 percent of women favor improving the nation's health care, compared to 76 percent of men; 72 percent of women advocate more spending on programs for the homeless, compared to 63 percent of men.[42] It is important to note that these differences do not mean that all women vote more liberally than all men. In fact, the voting differences between women who are homemakers and women who are in the workforce are almost as large as the differences between men and women. The sharpest differences are found between married men and single women, with single women tending to take the most liberal positions.[43]

These gender differences were evident in the 1994 election that brought a Republican Congress to power (see Figure 2.4). Republican candidates ran particularly well among men, and although women tended to vote Democratic, their turnout rates were lower than in earlier years.[44] Journalists portrayed the election results as the emergence of a new political phenomenon: the "angry white male" vote. Politicians are well aware of these divisions and take them into account in their electoral strategies. President Clinton, for example, has sought to appeal to working women, an important Democratic constituency.

The second key development in gender politics in recent years is the growing number of women in political office (see Figure 2.5). Journalists dubbed 1992 the "Year of the Woman" because so many women were elected to Congress: women doubled their numbers in the House and tripled them in the Senate. By 1995 women held 10.3 percent of the seats in the House of Representatives and 8 percent in the Senate; 20.1 percent of state legislators are women.[45] Organizations supporting female candidates have worked to encourage more women to run for office and have supported them financially. In addition to the bipartisan National Women's Political Caucus, the Women's Campaign Fund and EMILY's List provide pro-choice Democratic

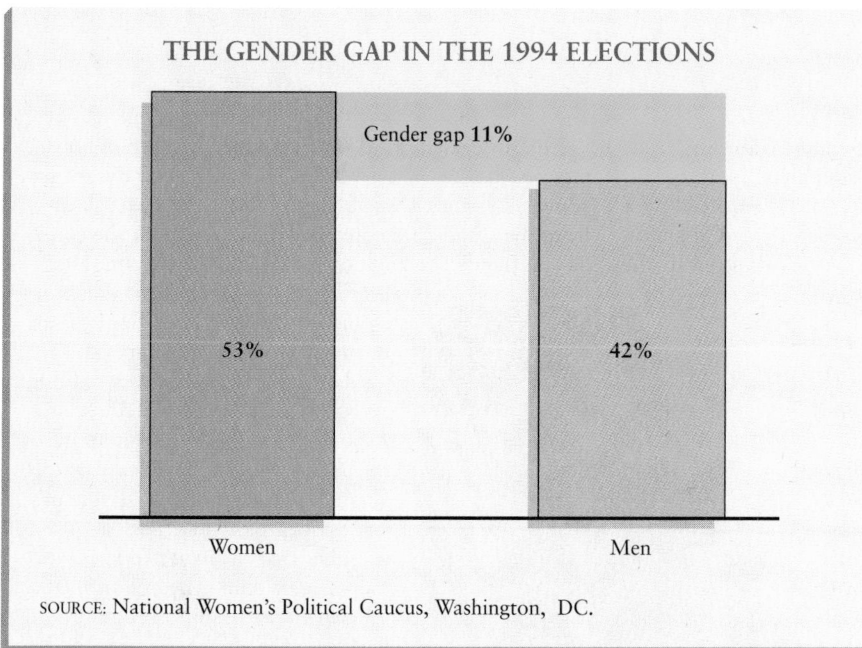

FIGURE 2.4
Substantially more women than men voted for a Democratic candidate for the House of Representatives in 1994; this difference is referred to as the "gender gap."

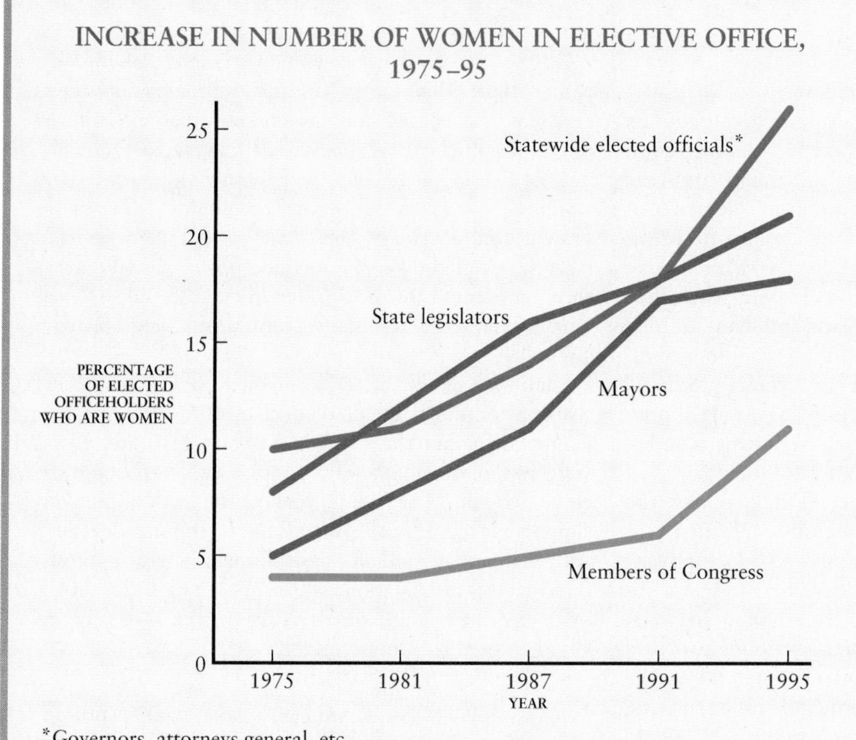

FIGURE 2.5

Shannon Faulkner

In August 1995, after a two-and-a-half-year legal struggle, the Citadel, a state-supported military college in Charleston, South Carolina, was forced by a federal judge to admit a young woman named Shannon Faulkner. Faulkner had originally been admitted to the Citadel in 1993, but when the school discovered that she was a woman (she had had references to her sex deleted from her high school transcript), it rescinded her admission. Faulkner sued on the grounds that the school's male-only policy was unconstitutional. But Faulkner's trailblazing effort came to a stunning end: exhausted by the arduous legal battle and in poor physical shape, Faulkner collapsed from heat stroke within the first hours of training, spent four days in the infirmary, and then announced her withdrawal from the school.

The Citadel, which until 1995 was one of only two male-only, state-supported military colleges in the nation (the other was Virginia Military Institute) prides itself on instilling discipline and loyalty in its cadets—qualities obviously essential to making good soldiers. The Citadel does so by subjecting first-year cadets to a relentless barrage of criticism, lack of privacy, and enforced conformism, all meant to break down their individuality. For those cadets who survive to "Recognition Day" at the end of the year, when they shake hands with their tormentors and can address older students by their first names, the psychological effect can be overwhelming, as a 1989 Citadel graduate, now a lawyer, testified: "I have never experienced anything like that; the feeling of accomplishment is unbelievable. The Citadel made me what I am today."[1]

According to supporters of the all-male policy, the presence of women will erode the intensity of the first-year experience. Faulkner would have enjoyed more privacy than male first-year cadets: a lock on her door, for instance, and private rather than communal showers. Other standards would have differed too: instead of a shaved head, she would have had her hair cut to the standards required for women in the U.S. military. And, in a procedure known as "gender norming," she would not have been subject to the same standards of physical performance as men. In defending their all-male policy, Citadel officials argued that Faulkner had the opportunity to pursue an equivalent education without being admitted to their school. She could have gotten a degree from the Citadel's nonmilitary night school or she could have attended a military instruction program established by the Citadel at a nearby women's college, Converse College. But Faulkner and her supporters argued that these alternatives did not represent a truly "equal" education. As long as women were not allowed to be cadets, the essence of the Citadel's education, a woman's Citadel degree would not carry the prestige that a man's does. Nor, they said, would a degree from the women's leadership program at Converse College have anything like the value of a Citadel degree.

Faulkner and her supporters forced the Citadel to do what West Point and the other national military academies had already done: admit women on a basis of equality. Rather than celebrate the Citadel's all-male tradition as a source of strength, Faulkner and many others believed it was a source of weakness that made sexist soldiers, not good soldiers. One of Faulkner's lawyers, who watched as cadets boisterously celebrated her withdrawal announcement, said, "I was reminded again of how the Citadel takes these young boys . . . and teaches them antifeminism and teaches them the old-boy network. That's the real illness, not this young woman's stress."[2]

Shannon Faulkner gave up her fight, but other women continued the challenge. In 1996, the Supreme Court ruled that the Virginia Military Institute, also a state-supported, male-only school, could no longer exclude women. The ruling spelled the end of publicly supported single-sex institutions of higher learning. Although many students and alumni remained bitterly opposed to coeducation, the school had little choice. Two days after the Court's decision, the board of the Citadel voted to admit women.

[1] Quoted in Jim Schlosser, "Alumni Believe Citadel Worth It," *Greensboro News & Record,* October 16, 1995, p. A1.

[2] Quoted in Debbi Wilgoren, "The Citadel Reasserts Its All-Male Tradition," *Washington Post,* August 20, 1995, p. A3.

women with early campaign financing, which is critical to establishing electoral momentum (the acronym of the latter group stands for Early Money Is Like Yeast). Recent research has shown that the key to increasing the numbers of women in political office is to encourage more women to run for election. Women are disadvantaged as candidates not because they are women but because male candidates are more likely to have the advantage of incumbency.[46] Although women in public office by no means take uniform positions on policy issues, surveys show that, on the whole, women legislators are more supportive of women's rights, health care spending, and children's and family issues.[47]

The third way in which women affect politics today is through the continuing salience of policy issues of special concern to women. Before the women's movement, many issues of deep concern to women were simply not on the political agenda. Today, however, issues such as abortion, sexual harassment, and comparable worth, and the concerns of families and children are often central to political debate. In 1991 the issue of sexual harassment burst into public consciousness when University of Oklahoma law professor Anita Hill accused Supreme Court nominee Clarence Thomas of sexual harassment. As Figure 2.6 shows, the number of sexual harassment complaints rose sharply after the hearings. The spectacle of the hearings—in which an all-male Senate Judiciary Committee harshly questioned Hill—also galvanized many women politically. In the words of pollster Celinda Lake, "Anita Hill has become a metaphor for something a lot broader than sexual harassment. She has become a symbol for a system that's failed, that's become distorted and out of touch."[48] The salience of sexual harassment and abortion

Anita Hill testifying before the Senate Judiciary Committee. Her charges against Supreme Court nominee Clarence Thomas catapulted the issue of sexual harassment into public consciousness.

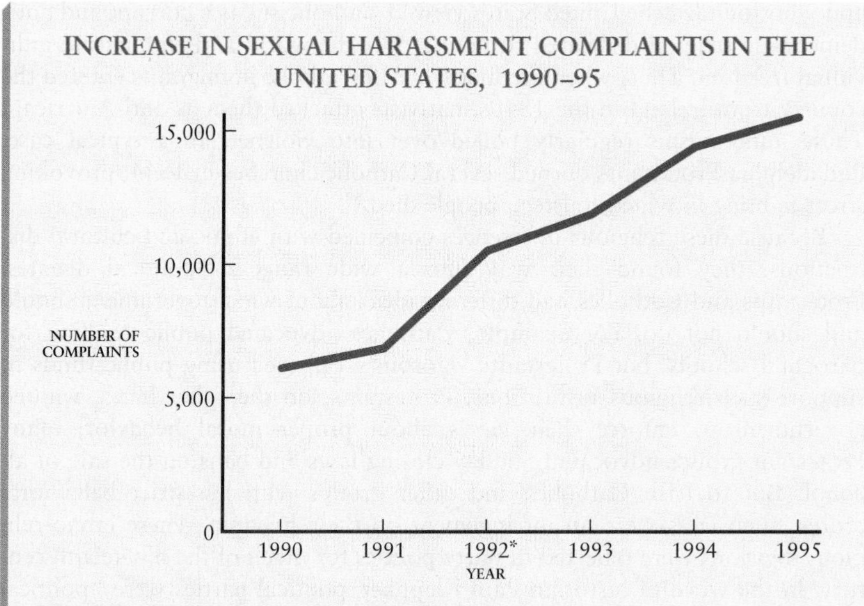

FIGURE 2.6

The number of sexual harassment complaints reported to the Equal Employment Opportunity Commission has increased dramatically since the early 1990s.

as political issues contributed to the electoral gains of female candidates in 1992.

Since the 1960s the women's movement has helped to transform the place of women in society and the economy, it has brought unprecedented numbers of women into public office, and it has altered the national political agenda. Although women's opinions diverge widely on many political issues, the emergence of a gender gap in voting and the growing numbers of women in political office ensure that gender issues will continue to influence American politics.

RELIGION

Religion has always played an important role in American politics and public life. Religious freedom was a central tenet of the new nation. The people who first settled the American colonies sought the freedom to practice their religious beliefs. The central role that religion played in their lives made it likely that religious beliefs would spill over into politics and debates about how to organize public life. Thus, despite the formal separation of church and state established by the Constitution, religious groups have regularly entered the political arena, often provoking heated debate about the proper role of government in enforcing moral values and in protecting the personal freedoms of those with different values.

Political scientist Samuel P. Huntington has noted that Protestant religious ideas were an important source for many Americans' core political values, such as democracy and liberty.[49] Another element central to this Protestantism was anti-Catholicism: the Protestants who settled in North America and who founded the United States viewed Catholicism as a corrupt and antidemocratic religion dedicated to taking over the world and eliminating individual freedom. Thus, when the first wave of Catholic immigrants entered the country from Ireland in the 1840s, nativists attacked them as anti-American. These antagonisms regularly boiled over into violence. In a typical case, Philadelphia Protestants burned several Catholic churches in 1844, provoking street fighting in which fourteen people died.[50]

Because these religious differences coincided with ethnic and cultural distinctions, they found their way into a wide range of political debates. Protestants and Catholics had different ideas about what government should and should not do. For example, Catholics advocated public funding for parochial schools, but Protestants vigorously opposed using public funds to support such religious institutions. Protestants, on the other hand, wanted government to enforce their views about proper moral behavior; many Protestant groups advocated Sunday closing laws and bans on the sale of alcohol. But to Irish Catholics and other groups with less-strict behavioral mores, such laws were an infringement on their freedom. These ethno-religious divisions were reflected in party politics for much of the nineteenth century. In the word of historian Paul Kleppner, political parties were "political churches" before the 1890s: the Whig Party and later the Republican Party attracted the votes of Protestant groups that supported public moralism, whereas the Democratic Party won votes among Catholics. This party divi-

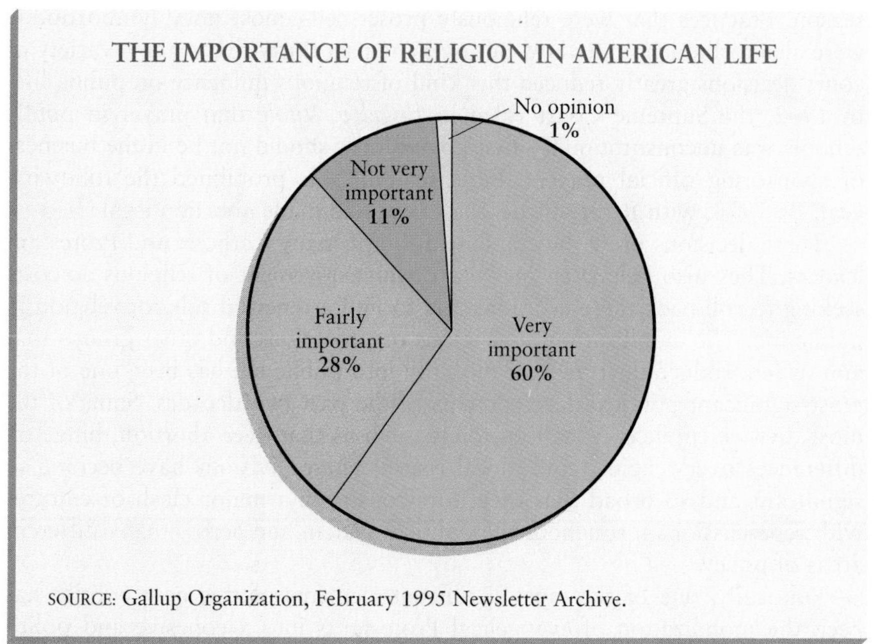

FIGURE 2.7

The Americans surveyed in this poll were asked, "How important is religion in your own life?"

sion ended in the 1890s, when Republicans moderated their attachment to the Protestant moral agenda.

Yet religion continues to play an important role in American life (see Figure 2.7). For some people, religious groups provide an organizational infrastructure for participating in politics around issues of special group concern. Black churches, for example, were instrumental in the Civil Rights movement, and black religious leaders continue to play important roles in national and local politics. Jews have also been active as a group in politics, but less through religious bodies than through a variety of social action agencies. Such agencies include the American Jewish Congress, the Anti-Defamation League, and the American Jewish Committee.

For white Catholics and mainline Protestants, church organizations are not as central in organizing political participation but, in both cases, the church leadership takes strong stands on public issues. For example, the Catholic Church has been an outspoken opponent of abortion. The Catholic bishops also issue pastoral letters in which they take stands on other public issues. On issues of economic inequality and social policy, the Catholic Church often takes more liberal stands, supporting government activism. Leaders of mainline Protestant churches, including Episcopalians, Lutherans, and Methodists, maintain a strong presence in Washington, with offices in the large Methodist Building right behind Congress on Capitol Hill. For the most part, the leaders of these groups take liberal stands on issues of foreign and domestic policy, although they refrain from outright lobbying in order to maintain their tax-exempt status.

For most of American history, religious values have been woven deeply into the fabric of public life. Public school students began the day with prayers or Bible reading; city halls displayed crèches during the Christmas season. Practices that were religiously proscribed—most notably abortion—were also forbidden under law. But over the past thirty-five years, a variety of court decisions greatly reduced this kind of religious influence on public life. In 1962, the Supreme Court ruled in *Engel v. Vitale* that prayer in public schools was unconstitutional—that government should not be in the business of sponsoring official prayers. Bible reading was prohibited the following year. By 1973, with *Roe v. Wade,* the Court had made abortion legal.[51]

These decisions drew the condemnation of many Catholic and Protestant leaders. They also helped to spawn a countermovement of religious activists seeking to roll back these decisions and to find a renewed role for religion in public life. The mobilization of religious organizations and other groups that aim to reintroduce their view of morality into public life has been one of the most significant political developments of the past two decades. Some of the most divisive conflicts in politics today, such as that over abortion, hinge on differences over religious and moral issues. These divisions have become so significant and so broad that they now constitute a major clash of cultures with repercussions throughout the political system and across many different areas of policy.

Jerry Falwell, founder of the Moral Majority.

Politically, one of the most significant elements of this new politics has been the mobilization of evangelical Protestants into a cohesive and politically shrewd organization aligned with the Republican Party. Evangelical Christians traditionally shunned politics; those who voted tended to cast ballots for Democrats, reflecting the heavy representation of southerners among evangelicals. But in the 1970s evangelical leaders such as television preachers Jerry Falwell and Pat Robertson began expressing growing concerns about what they regarded as a breakdown of traditional moral values. As evidence of such a breakdown, they pointed to growing rates of out-of-wedlock birth, divorce and drug use, as well as the gay rights movement. They believed that the legal decisions about school prayer and abortion were part of a larger movement to remove traditional values from the public sphere. What finally galvanized the movement politically, however, was a decision by the Carter administration in 1978 to deny tax exemptions for Christian academies. These academies were predominantly white, private schools formed in the wake of the desegregation of public schools. The Moral Majority—the first broad political organization of evangelical Christians—grew out of the effort to protect the Christian academies.[52]

Formed in 1979, the Moral Majority and its leader, Jerry Falwell, strove to bring a broad, conservative moral agenda into politics. The group first showed its political muscle in the 1980 election, when it aligned with the Republican Party, eventually backing Ronald Reagan for president. Over the next few years, evangelicals strengthened their movement by registering voters and mobilizing them with sophisticated, state-of-the-art political techniques. Their success was evident in the 1984 election, when 80 percent of evangelical Christians voted for Reagan. The 1988 election was a turning point in the political development of the Christian Right. Televangelist Pat Robertson ran for president and, although his candidacy was unsuccessful, his effort laid the groundwork for future political strength. Robertson's supporters gained control of some state Republican parties and won positions of power in others. With this new organizational base and sharply honed politi-

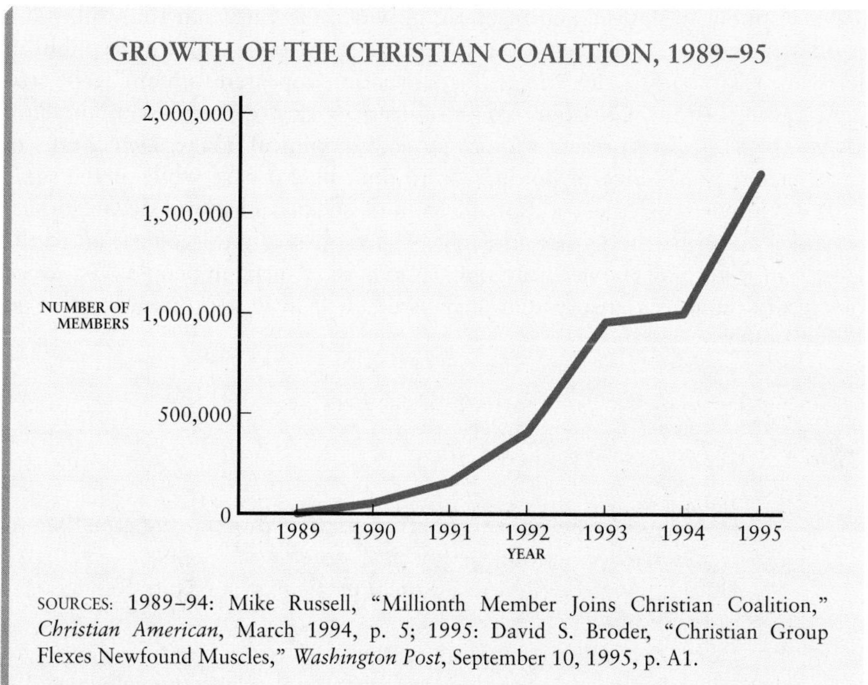

SOURCES: 1989–94: Mike Russell, "Millionth Member Joins Christian Coalition," *Christian American*, March 1994, p. 5; 1995: David S. Broder, "Christian Group Flexes Newfound Muscles," *Washington Post*, September 10, 1995, p. A1.

FIGURE 2.8

cal skills, Robertson formed a new organization, the Christian Coalition. This organization has become one of the most important groups in American politics today because of its ability to reach and mobilize a large grassroots base. Its recent success in mobilizing voters can be seen in Figure 2.8. It is now part of a growing number of loosely connected organizations dedicated to similar goals.[53]

The rise of the Christian Coalition has raised important challenges for both political parties. Republicans, who have benefited enormously from their alliance with this new political base, face the dilemma of retaining the support of the Christian Right without losing more moderate voters. The

Pat Buchanan's speech at 1992 Republican national convention and his cultural conservatism proved divisive for the Republican Party.

1992 Republican national convention, in which the Christian Right played a prominent role, was widely viewed as a negative event for the Republican Party as a whole. The rhetoric at the convention appeared to many to be strident and intolerant. Christian Coalition leaders learned their lesson and subsequently worked to present a more moderate political image. Democrats, in turn, face the challenge of holding on to their liberal base while at the same time acknowledging the widespread fears of social and moral decay so successfully raised by the Christian Right. The sophisticated organization of the Christian Right and the deep divisions among the American people on a range of cultural concerns ensure that such issues will have a prominent place in future politics.

Contemporary Conflicts

- Does having the right to political participation ensure equal representation within the political system?
- Does having the right to political participation ensure having political power?
- Does political participation matter?
- What is the role of the government in upholding the values of liberty, equality, and democracy?

Since the 1960s, changes in civil rights and immigration laws have created a more inclusive citizenship. But as the American political system has struggled to define this new inclusiveness in practice—to determine what it means for political institutions and policies—new questions have emerged abut social diversity and the values of liberty, equality, and democracy. Since the Founding, Americans have been preoccupied with the question of how democracy can guarantee and maintain political liberty and equality. In the practice of democracy, these ideals often come into conflict; some groups feel that their freedoms are limited in order to advance the equality of others. Even though the basic rights to vote and participate politically were won by all citizens in the 1960s, many questions remain about the meaning of equality and liberty for groups that once were excluded: Does having the right to vote mean that a group has equal political power? Should American democracy strive to grant all groups an equal voice? Concerns have also arisen about the health of American democracy. As government seems more remote from the average citizen, participation has dropped off. How can the commitments to liberty and equality be maintained in a political system that no longer engages many Americans?

In this section we examine contemporary conflicts over the proper role of political institutions and policy. These conflicts include questions about how groups can gain access to the political system and what role the government should play beyond ensuring political equality. We shall see that conflicts about the scope and meaning of liberty, equality, and democracy are very much a part of these debates.

Who Participates, and How?

Political participation makes the ideals of liberty and equality come alive. Two issues regarding participation have significant implications for American political ideals today. The first asks whether the established forms of participation ensure fair representation for minorities, and whether representation yields power. As we shall see in Chapter 9, African Americans in the South found that simply being allowed to vote did not ensure influence over the outcome of elections. Moreover, access to the political system did not result in influence over policy. One problem was that many state legislatures drew voting districts that scattered blacks across districts so that their voting power was diluted. The 1982 amendments to the Voting Rights Act were intended to solve this problem and improve chances of minority candidates by encouraging the creation of **minority districts.** Opponents of this strategy charged that such districts violated established American traditions by recognizing group rights over the rights of individuals. Supporters replied that such districts were the best way to improve minority representation. In the early 1990s, several Supreme Court decisions cast doubt on the future of such districts by ruling that race cannot be a primary factor in drawing district boundaries.[54]

A "freedom marcher" in 1965. Although the Voting Rights Act of 1965 strengthened the right of African Americans to vote, some have questioned whether this right translated into political power.

The turn away from minority districting has provoked interest in other forms of representation that allow minority voices to be heard. A variety of alternative electoral arrangements have been used in many states and localities. Among such arrangements are cumulative voting (used in Peoria, Illinois), in which candidates run in larger districts from which more than one representative is elected. In this system, voters have more than one vote, allowing them to spread their votes across several candidates or to express an intense preference by casting all of their votes for one candidate. Another electoral form that allows more minority representation is proportional representation. In this system, ballots are cast for parties' slates of candidates; seats are awarded based on the percentage of the vote each slate receives. In contrast to the U.S. "winner-take-all" system, **proportional representation** gives minority voices of all types a chance of winning some power. Such modifications to America's electoral institutions could have a variety of negative repercussions that would make them undesirable, but the changes themselves would not fundamentally challenge American notions of political equality. Indeed, they may fit within those notions more easily than drawing districts according to race.

More threatening to maintaining the national ideals of liberty and equality is a second issue regarding political participation. Increasingly, Americans are questioning whether political participation matters at all. There is growing evidence that Americans are less engaged in their communities and in the nation's political life than they were in the past. This public apathy and political detachment have deeply negative implications for the system of democracy, since it is through public engagement—and often political conflict—that a nation's ideals are reinvigorated.

Those who worry about the health of American democracy point to declining participation in politics and weakening civic engagement. As we note in Chapter 9, voter participation remains low and is skewed toward the upper-middle class. In the 1994 midterm elections that brought about the "Republican revolution" in Congress, only 44.6 percent of the voting-age population cast ballots. Among those who did vote, the upper-middle class was overrepresented. Participation in nonelectoral forms of public activity has also been declining. For example, one study showed that in 1993 only 13 percent of Americans reported attending a public meeting on town or school affairs, down from 22 percent in 1973. Along with this diminishing political participation has come a drop in the number of Americans who belong to such groups as parent-teacher associations, labor unions, and the League of Women Voters.[55] These facts indicate a disengagement from public and community life that reduces opportunities for individuals and groups to interact around broader public goals.

Some people argue that the behavior of American elites—the upper-middle class and the corporate community—has been a driving factor in the unraveling of American democracy. Many American elites no longer participate in broad public institutions; instead, they send their children to private schools, obtain their medical care from generous private insurance plans, and hire private police to ensure their security. This "secession of the rich" has had damaging consequences for American democracy because these groups no longer have a stake in what happens to the public sector. Their main interest is to keep taxes low and to protect themselves from public problems.[56] Another sign of elite withdrawal is the declining commitment of American businesses to local communities. In the past, mayors and other local politicians could depend on the business community to take a leading role in the civic life of their cities. In the last twenty years, however, as local businesses have been subsumed by national and international conglomerates, businesses have lost their attachment to particular places and are much less dependable contributors to the local welfare.

Thus, the biggest problem in American political life is not that new groups are participating and making unusual demands on the political system, or even that such groups are asserting new identities that threaten established values. The real problem may be that large numbers of Americans have given up on public engagement altogether.

WHAT IS THE ROLE OF GOVERNMENT?

Two questions, each with significant implications for what government does, cut across all of American history. The first asks whether government should act to promote particular moral values and norms of behavior. The second question considers whether the government has special responsibilities toward racial minorities and women because of their history of political exclusion and their vulnerability to continuing discrimination. Today such questions are among the most salient in politics. The arguments that Americans as a nation have about these issues reveal the continuing relevance of the ideals of liberty and equality, but they also expose the great difficulty of reconciling these ideals in practice.

Should government act as a moral authority and encourage (or even enforce) particular kinds of behavior? Or should it explicitly condone a wide range of behaviors? In some domains these questions directly pit different views of the world against one another. For example, members of the Christian Coalition view abortion and homosexuality as morally unacceptable and believe government should not permit either. By contrast, many Americans believe that such issues are matters of individual choice and privacy; to them, government should protect personal liberties such as the right to privacy and freedom of choice. Other issues provoke less direct confrontation of views, but still elicit little agreement about what government should do. For example, many Americans are concerned about the breakup of families and the growing levels of out-of-wedlock birth, but there is little consensus about what government can or should do to change such trends. Both sets of issues present challenges to Americans' political values by pitting individual liberty against moral authority.

The tensions between individual liberty and political and social equality are evident in debates about what policies government should adopt toward racial minorities and women. Conflicts over affirmative action have become the flashpoint for this debate. **Affirmative action** is the name given to a variety of government policies that range from actively promoting equality of opportunity to policies that move toward equality of result. Opponents charge that affirmative action programs cut against the deeply held American values of individual achievement and opportunity. Supporters contend that such special policies are necessary to promote equality for some groups, such as African Americans, with bitter histories of exclusion and discrimination based on race. Thus, debates about affirmative action directly pit two important American political values—equality and individual liberty—against each other.

American political culture has supplied a core set of values that has helped to knit together a culturally diverse nation. But the scope and meaning of these values has shifted over the course of history. In the past, these values were applied selectively, as some people were excluded from the definition of the American political community. Today, a more inclusive definition has evolved. Nonetheless, greater inclusion poses still more difficult questions about the meaning of liberty, equality, and democracy in practice. The answers given to these questions today will shape the meaning of the American dream for future generations.

★ Summary

Some of the most contentious political issues in the United States today concern conflicts that stem from social differences such as race and gender. Such struggles reveal the important role that the national government plays in forming and enforcing policies that aim to ensure equality for all groups. Government efforts at guaranteeing equality may create new problems, however, because they often entail restricting the liberties of some citizens. It is through such conflicts that Americans put the core ideals of liberty, equality, and democracy into practice.

The first section of this chapter examined the efforts of groups who had been denied political equality to gain access to the American political system.

Throughout much of the country's history, racial and ethnic differences were used as a basis to deny some groups full political equality. White ethnics experienced discrimination, but their rights to political equality were never in serious doubt. For African Americans, the struggle to eliminate slavery and the quest for full political equality after slavery was abolished have constituted the most far-reaching political struggles in all of American history. Gender differences have also had an important impact on American politics. It took decades of mobilization and a constitutional amendment (the Nineteenth Amendment, passed in 1920) to grant women the right to vote. For women and racial minorities alike, efforts to achieve political equality did not stop with winning the right to vote. Groups continued to struggle to win political office and to make their voices heard in the political arena.

Class and religion are two other important bases of social difference that were examined in this chapter. Class has never been as important in the American context as it has been elsewhere in the world because Americans believe in individual mobility. Religion, on the other hand, has always played a role in public life in the United States, where religious freedom was a central tenet of the Founders. Today, the mobilization of religious groups has had an important impact on politics.

The last section of the chapter examined contemporary conflicts among liberty, equality, and democracy. One of the most difficult questions Americans face is determining what role the government should play beyond ensuring formal political equality. In addition, many political analysts now worry about the vitality of American democracy. As participation in civic life declines, it will be increasingly difficult to adapt the ideals of liberty, equality and democracy to new challenges confronting the nation.

FOR FURTHER READING

Dawson, Michael C. *Behind the Mule: Race and Class in African-American Politics.* Princeton, NJ: Princeton University Press, 1994.

de la Garza, Rodolfo O., Louis DeSipio, F. Chris Garcia, John A. Garcia, and Angelo Falcon. *Latino Voices: Mexican, Puerto Rican, and Cuban Perspectives on American Politics.* Boulder, CO: Westview, 1992.

Edsall, Thomas B., and Mary D. Edsall. *Chain Reaction: The Impact of Race, Rights, and Taxes on American Politics.* New York: Norton, 1992.

Hero, Rodney E. *Latinos and the U.S. Political System: Two-Tiered Pluralism.* Philadelphia: Temple University Press, 1992.

Klein, Ethel. *Gender Politics.* Cambridge, MA: Harvard University Press, 1984.

McClain, Paula D., and Joseph Stewart, Jr. *"Can We All Get Along?" Racial and Ethnic Minorities in American Politics.* Boulder, CO: Westview, 1995.

Mansbridge, Jane J. *Why We Lost the ERA.* Chicago: University of Chicago Press, 1986.

Sonenshein, Raphael J. *Politics in Black and White: Race and Power in Los Angeles.* Princeton, NJ: Princeton University Press, 1993.

Takaki, Ronald T. *A Different Mirror: A History of Multicultural America.* Boston: Little, Brown, 1993.

Tate, Katherine. *From Protest to Politics: The New Black Voters in American Elections.* Cambridge, MA: Harvard University Press, 1993.

Verba, Sidney, Kay Lehman Schlozman, and Henry E. Brady. *Voice and Equality: Civic Voluntarism in American Politics.* Cambridge, MA: Harvard University Press, 1996.

STUDY OUTLINE

Expanding the American Political Community

1. Americans hold conflicting perspectives about how to reconcile our core national values of liberty, equality, and democracy with our history of social discrimination and political exclusion.
2. Racial and ethnic identities are the most politically significant social identities in the United States.
3. Although the American story is often told as one of group assimilation, in fact American politics acknowledged and encouraged ethnic identities in two ways: (1) Nativist anti-immigrant movements emphasized the differences between new immigrants and other Americans; and (2) The political system provided an incentive for politicians to recognize ethnic groups and mobilize them into politics.
4. For African Americans, the central fact of political life has been a denial of full citizenship rights for most of American history.
5. Four strategies of mobilization emerged to guide African Americans' quest for equality: self-improvement, political pressure and legal strategies, black nationalism, and protest.
6. The labels "Latino" or "Hispanic" encompass a wide range of groups with diverse national origins, distinctive cultural identities, and disparate political experiences in America.
7. In recent years, Latino political organizations have attempted to mobilize members of their community. This effort, if successful, would tap a "sleeping giant" of political influence.
8. The diversity of national backgrounds among Asian Americans has impeded the development of group-based political power. Furthermore, the geographical dispersion of Asian Americans and their diverse experiences raise questions about whether Asian Americans will ever form a cohesive political bloc.
9. For much of their history, the relationship of Native Americans to the U.S. government has been that of a warring, then a conquered, people.
10. In the 1960s, using protest, litigation, and the assertion of tribal rights, the Native American political movement gained strength, which helped tribes achieve self-government and economic development.
11. The relative weakness of class in the United States stems from the ideals of equality and liberty, as well as from the positive and negative experiences of workers within the American political system.
12. The closest Americans have come to having a class-based politics in this century was during the New Deal.
13. Because most Americans consider themselves to be middle class, mobilizing citizens on class-based appeals is difficult.
14. Although women were barred from electoral politics for much of American history, they were important voices in social reform movements, such as the abolitionist movement and the movements against political corruption and urban squalor.
15. Although women gained the vote in 1920, their political power was still thwarted for decades. Not until the 1960s did a broad movement for women's equality emerge.
16. The ongoing significance of gender issues in American politics is indicated by three trends: the gender gap, the increase in the number of women holding public office, and the continued importance of political issues of special concern to women.
17. Religion has always played an important role in American politics. Despite the formal separation of church and state, religious groups have regularly entered the political arena.
18. A significant element of modern religious politics has been the mobilization of evangelical Protestants into a cohesive and politically active organization aligned with the Republican Party.

Contemporary Conflicts

1. One question posed by the recent inclusion of some groups in American politics is whether the right to vote means that a group has equal political power.
2. One significant problem in American political life is that a large number of Americans have given up on participating in politics.

PRACTICE QUIZ

1. Which of the following have been the most politically significant social identities in American politics?
   a. class
   b. race and ethnicity
   c. gender
   d. religion

2. Nativist movements against European immigration were marked by
   a. anti-Catholicism.
   b. anti-radicalism.
   c. racism.
   d. all of the above

3. Which of the following statements best describes the impact of Reconstruction on African American political involvement?
   a. It was immediate, but short-lived.
   b. It sustained African American dominance.
   c. It actually hurt African American participation.
   d. It had little impact.

4. Which of the following African American leaders was *most* associated with the strategy of self-improvement?
   a. Booker T. Washington
   b. Marcus Garvey
   c. W. E. B. DuBois
   d. Malcolm X

5. Which of the following helps to explain the relatively low level of Latino political participation?
   a. low rates of voter registration
   b. low rates of naturalization
   c. both a and b
   d. neither a nor b

6. What has impeded the group power of Asian Americans?
   a. the corruption of group leaders
   b. a lack of economic resources
   c. organized attempts to keep Asian Americans from participating
   d. heterogeneity

7. In which of the following eras was class *least* salient in American politics?
   a. the early years of the republic
   b. after the Civil War
   c. during the New Deal
   d. in the 1980s

8. What percentage of Americans identify themselves as upper class?
   a. 1 percent
   b. 5 percent
   c. 10 percent
   d. 18 percent

9. Which of the following helps to explain the ongoing significance of gender issues in American politics?
   a. the similarity of male and female voting trends
   b. the increase in the number of women holding public office
   c. the decline of party politics
   d. the increasing professionalization of state legislatures

10. Which of the following structural changes might increase the political power of minorities in American politics?
    a. instituting a "winner-take-all" system
    b. using a cumulative voting system
    c. further expansion of voting rights
    d. raising the barriers to interest-group lobbying

CRITICAL THINKING QUESTIONS

1. Trace the development of the "American political community." Describe the evolution of this community in terms of the opportunities for various groups for participation and inclusion in political affairs. Describe one group's struggle for inclusion. What were the obstacles the group's members faced? What strategies did they use to overcome those obstacles? To what extent have they succeeded in their quest for participation and inclusion? How did they succeed?

2. Describe the ways in which the ideals of liberty and equality have come into conflict in terms of the politics of ethnicity, class, gender, and religion. Looking at various laws, court cases, social movements, and political behaviors, describe how liberty has, at times, prevented equality. Might the quest for equality pre-empt liberty?

KEY TERMS

affirmative action government policies or programs that seek to redress past injustices against specified groups by making special efforts to provide members of these groups with access to educational and employment opportunities. (p. 61)

black nationalism a movement that supported total separatism for African Americans, supporting goals that ranged from economic independence to emigration back to Africa. (p. 32)

gender gap a distinctive pattern of male and female voting that became important in the 1980s. (p. 50)

minority district a gerrymandered voting district that improves the chances of minority candidates by making selected minority groups the majority within the district. (p. 59)

nativism a nineteenth-century anti-immigrant movement based on fears of immigrants' Catholicism, potential political radicalism, and race. Nativism also refers to a general antagonism toward immigration. (p. 29)

political machines local party organizations that control urban politics by mobilizing voters to elect the machines' candidates. (p. 30)

proportional representation a multiple-member district system that allows each political party representation in proportion to its percentage of the total vote. By contrast, the "winner-take-all" system of elections awards the seat to the one candidate who wins the most votes. (p. 59)

PART II

Foundations

3

The Founding and the Constitution

- ★ The First Founding: Interests and Conflicts
  - What conflicts were apparent and what interests prevailed during the American Revolution and the drafting of the Articles of Confederation?
- ★ The Second Founding: From Compromise to Constitution
  - Why were the Articles of Confederation unable to hold the nation together?
  - In what ways is the United States Constitution a marriage of interest and principle?
  - How did the framers of the Constitution reconcile their competing interests and principles?
- ★ The Constitution
  - What principles does the Constitution embody?
  - What were the intents of the framers of the Constitution regarding the legislative, executive, and judicial branches?
  - What limits on the national government's power are embodied in the Constitution?
- ★ The Fight for Ratification
  - What different interests did the Federalists and the Antifederalists represent in the fight over ratification?
  - Over what key principles did the Federalists and the Antifederalists disagree?
- ★ The Changing Constitution
  - Why is the Constitution difficult to amend?
  - What purposes do the amendments to the Constitution serve?
- ★ Reflections on Liberty, Equality, and Democracy
  - Did the framers value liberty, equality, and democracy? Why or why not?

"NO TAXATION WITHOUT REPRESENTATION" were words that stirred a generation of Americans long before they even dreamed of calling themselves Americans rather than English. Reacting to new English attempts to extract tax revenues to pay for the troops that were being sent to defend the colonial frontier, protests erupted throughout the colonies against the infamous Stamp Act of 1765. This act created revenue stamps and required that they be affixed to all printed and legal documents, including newspapers, pamphlets, advertisements, notes and bonds, leases, deeds, and licenses. To show their displeasure with the act, the colonists conducted mass meetings, parades, bonfires, and other demonstrations throughout the spring and summer of 1765. In Boston, for example, a stamp agent was hanged and burned in effigy. Later, the home of the lieutenant-governor was sacked, leading to his resignation and that of all of his colonial commission and stamp agents. By November 1765, business proceeded and newspapers were published without the stamp; in March 1766, Parliament repealed the detested law. Through their protest, the nonimportation agreements that the colonists subsequently adopted, and the Stamp Act Congress that met in October 1765, the colonists took the first steps that ultimately would lead to war and a new nation.

The people of every nation tend to glorify their own history and especially their nation's creation. Americans are no exception. To most contemporary Americans, the Revolutionary period represents a heroic struggle by a determined and united group of colonists against British oppression. The Boston Tea Party, the battles of Lexington and Concord, the winter at Valley Forge—these are the events that are emphasized in American history. Similarly, the American Constitution—the document establishing the system of government that ultimately emerged from this struggle—is often seen as an inspired, if not divine, work, expressing timeless principles of democratic government. These views are by no means false. During the founding era, Americans did struggle against misrule. Moreover, the American Constitution did establish the foundations for more than two hundred years of democratic government.

To really understand the character of the American founding and the meaning of the American Constitution, however, it is essential to look beyond the myths and rhetoric and to explore the conflicting interests and forces at work during the Revolutionary and constitutional periods. Thus, we will first assess the political backdrop of the American Revolution, and then we will examine the Constitution that ultimately emerged as the basis for America's government.

In addition to looking at what happened during the founding period, we will also examine what did *not* happen. The story of the Founding and the Constitution is generally presented to students as a fait accompli: the Constitution, which established the best of all possible forms of government, was adopted without much difficulty and its critics and doubters were quickly proven wrong. In reality, though, the constitutional period was precisely the era in American history when *nothing* was a given. Nothing was simple. The proposed new system of government faced considerable opposition. The objections raised by opponents of the proposed constitution—who called themselves Antifederalists—were profound and important. The Antifederalists thought that the state governments would be able to represent the people much better than the national government could. They also were concerned that the officials of a large and powerful government would inevitably abuse their authority. The Antifederalists understood the basic problem of freedom and power and feared that the powers given to the national government to do good would sooner or later be turned to evil purposes.

One noted authority has asserted that the Federalists won the great debate over the Constitution because their ideas were better.[1] The jury, however, may still be out on whether the Constitution's opponents were proven wrong. The Federalists presented some very powerful ideas, and the Constitution they wrote became so well established as to seem part of the natural political environment today. Nevertheless, the issues raised by the Antifederalists should be pondered by every student of American politics, because they provide an essential perspective from which to view and evaluate the American system of government.

The story of the founding is not so much the morality tale that is usually presented to students as it is a study of political choices. And because Americans continue to make choices about the constitutional framework, the debates of the founding period are as relevant today as they were then. During the 1980s, proponents of adding an "equal rights amendment" to the Constitution raised important questions about equal representation. In the 1990s, both friends and foes of a proposed "balanced budget amendment" are forced to confront questions of tyranny and governmental power. If we limit the government's power, are we striking a blow for liberty or merely limiting the government's capacity to serve its citizens? The great questions Americans confronted at the close of the eighteenth century are not so different from those we face at the end of the twentieth.

The founding era was also the period during which Americans first confronted the great question of who was to be included and who was to be excluded from full citizenship. The answer given by the Founders—all white men were entitled to full citizenship rights—was an extremely democratic position for its time. America was one of the few nations that extended citizenship so broadly. Yet the founding generation did not resolve the question once and for all. Over the ensuing two hundred years, as we shall see, the question of who is and who is not a full citizen of the United States has been debated many times and has never been completely resolved.

The First Founding: Interests and Conflicts

> ➤ What conflicts were apparent and what interests prevailed during the American Revolution and the drafting of the Articles of Confederation?

Competing ideals and principles often reflect competing interests, and so it was in Revolutionary America. The American Revolution and the American Constitution were outgrowths and expressions of a struggle among economic and political forces within the colonies. Five sectors of society had interests that were important in colonial politics: (1) the New England merchants; (2) the southern planters; (3) the "royalists"—holders of royal lands, offices, and patents (licenses to engage in a profession or business activity); (4) shopkeepers, artisans, and laborers; and (5) small farmers. Throughout the eighteenth century, these groups were in conflict over issues of taxation, trade, and commerce. For the most part, however, the southern planters, the New England merchants, and the royal office and patent holders—groups that together made up the colonial elite—were able to maintain a political alliance that held in check the more radical forces representing shopkeepers, laborers, and small farmers. After 1750, however, by seriously threatening the interests of New England merchants and southern planters, British tax and trade policies split the colonial elite, permitting radical forces to expand their political influence, and set into motion a chain of events that culminated in the American Revolution.[2]

BRITISH TAXES AND COLONIAL INTERESTS

Beginning in the 1750s, the debts and other financial problems faced by the British government forced it to search for new revenue sources. This search rather quickly led to the Crown's North American colonies, which, on the whole, paid remarkably little in taxes to their parent country. The British government reasoned that a sizable fraction of its debt was, in fact, attributable to the expenses it had incurred in defense of the colonies during the recent French and Indian wars, as well as to the continuing protection that British forces were giving the colonists from Indian attacks and that the British navy was providing for colonial shipping. Thus, during the 1760s, England sought to impose new, though relatively modest, taxes upon the colonists.

Like most governments of the period, the British regime had limited ways in which to collect revenues. The income tax, which in the twentieth century has become the single most important source of governmental revenues, had not yet been developed. For the most part, in the mid–eighteenth century, governments relied on tariffs, duties, and other taxes on commerce, and it was to such taxes, including the Stamp Act, that the British turned during the 1760s.

The Stamp Act and other taxes on commerce, such as the Sugar Act of 1764, which taxed sugar, molasses, and other commodities, most heavily affected the two groups in colonial society whose commercial interests and activities were most extensive—the New England merchants and southern planters. Under the famous slogan "no taxation without representation," the merchants and planters together sought to organize opposition to these new taxes. In the course of the struggle against British tax measures, the planters and merchants broke with their royalist allies and turned to their former adversaries—the shopkeepers, small farmers, laborers, and artisans—for help. With the assistance of these groups, the merchants and planters organized demonstrations and a boycott of British goods that ultimately forced the Crown to rescind most of its new taxes.

From the perspective of the merchants and planters, however, the British government's decision to eliminate most of the hated taxes represented a victorious end to their struggle with the mother country. They were anxious to end the unrest they had helped to arouse, and they supported the British government's efforts to restore order. Indeed, most respectable Bostonians supported the actions of the British soldiers involved in the Boston Massacre. In their subsequent trial, the soldiers were defended by John Adams, a pillar of Boston society and a future president of the United States. Adams asserted that the soldiers' actions were entirely justified, provoked by "a motley rabble of saucy boys, Negroes and mulattos, Irish teagues and outlandish Jack tars." All but two of the soldiers were acquitted.[3]

Despite the efforts of the British government and the better-to-do strata of colonial society, it proved difficult to bring an end to the political strife. The more radical forces representing shopkeepers, artisans, laborers, and small farmers, who had been mobilized and energized by the struggle over taxes, continued to agitate for political and social change within the colonies. These radicals, led by individuals like Samuel Adams, a cousin of John Adams, asserted that British power supported an unjust political and social structure within the colonies, and began to advocate an end to British rule.[4]

Political Strife and the Radicalizing of the Colonists

The political strife within the colonies was the background for the events of 1773–74. In 1773, the British government granted the politically powerful East India Company a monopoly on the export of tea from Britain, eliminating a lucrative form of trade for colonial merchants. To add to the injury, the East India Company sought to sell the tea directly in the colonies instead of working through the colonial merchants. Tea was an extremely important commodity in the 1770s, and these British actions posed a mortal threat to the New England merchants. Together with their southern allies, the merchants once again called upon their radical adversaries for support. The most dramatic result was the Boston Tea Party of 1773, led by Samuel Adams.

This event was of decisive importance in American history. The merchants had hoped to force the British government to rescind the Tea Act, but they did not support any demands beyond this one. They certainly did not seek independence from Britain. Samuel Adams and the other radicals, however, hoped to provoke the British government to take actions that would alienate its colonial supporters and pave the way for a rebellion. This was precisely the purpose of the Boston Tea Party, and it succeeded. By dumping the East India Company's tea into Boston Harbor, Adams and his followers goaded the British into enacting a number of harsh reprisals. Within five months after the incident in Boston, the House of Commons passed a series of acts that closed the port of Boston to commerce, changed the provincial government of

In many ways, the British helped provoke the Boston Tea Party by providing the ailing East India Company with a monopoly on the tea trade with the American colonies. But the colonists feared British monopolies would hurt colonial merchants' business; they protested by throwing the East India Company's tea into Boston Harbor.

Massachusetts, provided for the removal of accused persons to England for trial, and most important, restricted movement to the West—further alienating the southern planters who depended upon access to new western lands. These acts of retaliation confirmed the worst criticisms of England and helped radicalize Americans. Radicals like Samuel Adams and Christopher Gadsden of South Carolina had been agitating for more violent measures to deal with England. But ultimately they needed Britain's political repression to create widespread support for independence.

Thus, the Boston Tea Party set into motion a cycle of provocation and retaliation that in 1774 resulted in the convening of the First Continental Congress—an assembly of delegates from all parts of the country—that called for a total boycott of British goods and, under the prodding of the radicals, began to consider the possibility of independence from British rule. The eventual result was the Declaration of Independence.

THE DECLARATION OF INDEPENDENCE

In 1776, the Second Continental Congress appointed a committee consisting of Thomas Jefferson of Virginia, Benjamin Franklin of Pennsylvania, Roger Sherman of Connecticut, John Adams of Massachusetts, and Robert Livingston of New York to draft a statement of American independence from British rule. The Declaration of Independence, written by Jefferson and adopted by the Second Continental Congress, was an extraordinary document both in philosophical and political terms. Philosophically, the Declaration was remarkable for its assertion that certain rights, called "unalienable rights"—including life, liberty, and the pursuit of happiness—could not be abridged by governments. In the world of 1776, a world in which some kings still claimed to rule by divine right, this was a dramatic statement. Politically, the Declaration was remarkable because, despite the differences of interest that divided the colonists along economic, regional, and philosophical lines, the Declaration identified and focused on problems, grievances, aspirations, and principles that might unify the various colonial groups. The Declaration was an attempt to identify and articulate a history and set of principles that might help to forge national unity.[5]

THE ARTICLES OF CONFEDERATION

Having declared their independence, the colonies needed to establish a governmental structure. In November of 1777, the Continental Congress adopted the **Articles of Confederation and Perpetual Union**—the United States's first written constitution. Although it was not ratified by all the states until 1781, it was the country's operative constitution for almost twelve years, until March 1789.

The Articles of Confederation was a constitution concerned primarily with limiting the powers of the central government. The central government, first of all, was based entirely in a Congress. Since it was not intended to be a powerful government, it was given no executive branch. Execution of its laws was to be left to the individual states. Second, the Congress had little power. Its members were not much more than delegates or messengers from the state legislatures. They were chosen by the state legislatures, their salaries were paid out of the state treasuries, and they were subject to immediate recall by state authorities. In addition, each state, regardless of its size, had only a single vote.

The Congress was given the power to declare war and make peace, to make treaties and alliances, to coin or borrow money, and to regulate trade with the Native Americans. It could also appoint the senior officers of the United States army. But it could not levy taxes or regulate commerce among the states. Moreover, the army officers it appointed had no army to serve in because the nation's armed forces were composed of the state militias. Probably the most unfortunate part of the Articles of Confederation was that the central government could not prevent one state from discriminating against other states in the quest for foreign commerce.

In brief, the relationship between the Congress and the states under the Articles of Confederation was much like the contemporary relationship between the United Nations and its member states, a relationship in which virtually all governmental powers are retained by the states. It was properly called a "confederation" because, as provided under Article II, "each state retains its sovereignty, freedom and independence, and every Power, Jurisdiction and right, which is not by this confederation expressly delegated to the United States, in Congress assembled." Not only was there no executive, there also was no judicial authority and no other means of enforcing the Congress's will. If there was to be any enforcement at all, it would be done for the Congress by the states.[6]

The Second Founding: From Compromise to Constitution

- Why were the Articles of Confederation unable to hold the nation together?
- In what ways is the United States Constitution a marriage of interest and principle?
- How did the framers of the Constitution reconcile their competing interests and principles?

The Declaration of Independence and the Articles of Confederation were not sufficient to hold the new nation together as an independent and effective nation-state. From almost the moment of armistice with the British in 1783, moves were afoot to reform and strengthen the Articles of Confederation.

International Standing and Balance of Power

There was a special concern for the country's international position. Competition among the states for foreign commerce allowed the European powers to play the states off against one another, which created confusion on both sides of the Atlantic. At one point during the winter of 1786–87, John

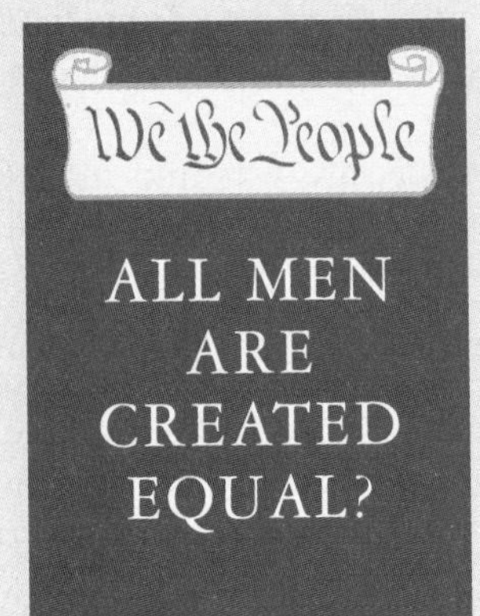

"We hold these truths to be self-evident, that all men are created equal, that they are endowed by their Creator with certain unalienable Rights, that among these are Life, Liberty and the pursuit of Happiness." These noble sentiments, so beautifully expressed in the Declaration of Independence, proclaimed to the world Americas devotion to liberty and equality. Yet Americans by no means agreed that liberty and equality did or should apply to all.

To be sure, America lacked the aristocratic class to be found in European nations. As the French writer Hector St. John de Crèvecoeur wrote in 1782, Europe was controlled by "great lords who possess everything, and a herd of people who have nothing." By contrast, America had no "aristocratical families, no courts, no kings, no bishops." Even so, some American revolutionary leaders favored a society where family status and inherited wealth set the few apart from the many. And most agreed that blacks and women were not entitled to the equality of condition expressed in many early documents.

Nearly a quarter of early America's population was bound in servitude through the institutions of slavery and indentured servitude. With rare exceptions, blacks were treated as nothing more than the property of their owners. America's women were normally barred from voting, and were denied equal rights under the law. Even setting these obvious inequities aside—after all, American attitudes toward women and blacks were not so different from those of most Europeans—debate raged in America over the proper scope of popular sovereignty and social equality.

The institution of slavery was hotly debated during the writing of the Declaration of Independence; in fact, a reference to slavery as an evil was removed from a draft of the document at the insistence of southern representatives. Yet Virginia Methodists condemned slavery in 1784. That same year, Connecticut, Massachusetts, Pennsylvania, and Rhode Island all abolished slavery (although relatively few slaves lived in the North). Within twenty years, every state north of Delaware had done the same. Many southern blacks took matters into their own hands. For example, over 5,000 slaves left South Carolina with the British army before the Revolutionary

Adams of Massachusetts, a leader in the independence struggle, was sent to negotiate a new treaty with the British, one that would cover disputes left over from the war. The British government responded that, since the United States under the Articles of Confederation was unable to enforce existing treaties, it would negotiate with each of the thirteen states separately.

At the same time, well-to-do Americans—in particular the New England merchants and southern planters—were troubled by the influence that "radical" forces exercised in the Continental Congress and in the governments of several of the states. The colonists' victory in the Revolutionary War had not only meant the end of British rule, but also significantly changed the balance of political power within the new states. As a result of the Revolution, one key segment of the colonial elite—the royal land, office, and patent holders—was stripped of its economic and political privileges. In fact, many of these individuals, along with tens of thousands of other colonists who considered themselves loyal British subjects, left for Canada after the British surrender. And while the pre-Revolutionary elite was weakened, the pre-Revolutionary radicals were now better organized than ever before and were the controlling forces in such states as Pennsylvania and Rhode Island, where they pursued

War came to an end. Other blacks were able to translate Revolutionary War service into a promise of freedom. In 1800, two blacks plotted a large-scale slave uprising in Richmond, Virginia. Although thwarted, it presaged many future uprisings. And the linkage between American democratic values and the repudiation of slavery eventually became overwhelming.

The prevailing attitude toward women was summarized by a prominent Boston minister, who advised, "Wives submit your selves to your own Husbands, in subjection to them." Prominent women questioned their legal and familial inferiority, as when in 1776 Abigail Adams urged her husband, John, a member of the Continental Congress, to "remember the Ladies, and be more generous to them than your ancestors." John failed to heed his wife's plea. A legal principle called "coverture" limited a wife's legal rights, including the rights to sue, to make wills and contracts, and even to own property. Another early feminist, Judith Sargent Murray, wrote an essay called "On the Equality of the Sexes," in which she argued for "mutual esteem, mutual friendship, [and] mutual confidence" between husbands and wives. Such beliefs gained wide currency among more well educated women.

By the 1790s, some Christian ministers began to extol the role of women as moral educators. This changing attitude opened the door to educational opportunities for women through religious academies, which by the early 1800s began to produce ever-increasing numbers of women teachers, who in turn spread the cause of women's rights.

The disparity between the high-sounding sentiments of the Declaration of Independence and actual practices in early America was great. Yet Americans were haunted by this contradiction, and the country ultimately abandoned the practices rather than turn their backs on the principles.

SOURCE: Jack P. Greene, ed., *Colonies to Nation, 1763–1789* (New York: Norton, 1975).

economic and political policies that struck terror into the hearts of the pre-Revolutionary political establishment. In Rhode Island, for example, between 1783 and 1785, a legislature dominated by representatives of small farmers, artisans, and shopkeepers had instituted economic policies, including drastic currency inflation, that frightened business and property owners throughout the country. Of course, the central government under the Articles of Confederation was powerless to intervene.

The Annapolis Convention

The continuation of international weakness and domestic economic turmoil led many Americans to consider whether their newly adopted form of government might not already require revision. In the fall of 1786, many state leaders accepted an invitation from the Virginia legislature for a conference of representatives of all the states. Delegates from five states actually attended. This conference, held in Annapolis, Maryland, was the first step toward the second founding. The one positive thing that came out of the Annapolis Convention was a carefully worded resolution calling on the Congress to send commissioners to Philadelphia at a later time "to devise such further provisions as shall appear to them necessary to render the Constitution of the Federal Government adequate to the exigencies of the Union."[7] This resolution was drafted by Alexander Hamilton, a thirty-four-year-old New York lawyer who had played a significant role in the Revolution as George Washington's secretary and who would play a still more significant role in framing the Constitution and forming the new government in the 1790s. But the resolution did not necessarily imply any desire to do more than improve and reform the Articles of Confederation.

In the winter of 1787, the Massachusetts legislature levied heavy taxes that hit the poor particularly hard. Daniel Shays led a makeshift army against the federal arsenal at Springfield in protest. Shays's group was easily routed, but they did get the legislature to grant some of their demands.

Shays's Rebellion

It is quite possible that the Constitutional Convention of 1787 in Philadelphia would never have taken place at all except for a single event that occurred during the winter following the Annapolis Convention: Shays's Rebellion.

Daniel Shays, a former army captain, led a mob of farmers in a rebellion against the government of Massachusetts. The purpose of the rebellion was to prevent foreclosures on their debt-ridden land by keeping the county courts of western Massachusetts from sitting until after the next election. The state militia dispersed the mob, but for several days Shays and his followers terrified the state government by attempting to capture the federal arsenal at Springfield, provoking an appeal to the Congress to help restore order. Within a few days, the state government regained control and captured fourteen of the rebels (all were eventually pardoned). In 1787, a newly elected Massachusetts legislature granted some of the farmers' demands.

Although the incident ended peacefully, its effects lingered and spread. Washington summed it up: "I am mortified beyond expression that in the moment of our acknowledged independence we should by our conduct verify the predictions of our transatlantic foe, and render ourselves ridiculous and contemptible in the eyes of all Europe."[8]

The Congress under the Confederation had been unable to act decisively in a time of crisis. This provided critics of the Articles of Confederation with precisely the evidence they needed to push Hamilton's Annapolis resolution through the Congress. Thus, the states were asked to send representatives to Philadelphia to discuss constitutional revision. Delegates were eventually sent by every state except Rhode Island.

The Constitutional Convention

Delegates selected by the state governments convened in Philadelphia in May 1787, with political strife, international embarrassment, national weakness, and local rebellion fixed in their minds. Recognizing that these issues were symptoms of fundamental flaws in the Articles of Confederation, the delegates soon abandoned the plan to revise the Articles and committed themselves to a second founding—a second, and ultimately successful, attempt to create a legitimate and effective national system of government. This effort occupied the convention for the next five months.

A Marriage of Interest and Principle Scholars have for years disagreed about the motives of the Founders in Philadelphia. Among the most controversial views of the framers' motives is the "economic interpretation" put forward by historian Charles Beard and his disciples.[9] According to Beard's account, America's founders were a collection of securities speculators and property owners whose only aim was personal enrichment. From this perspective, the Constitution's lofty principles were little more than sophisticated masks behind which the most venal interests sought to enrich themselves.

Contrary to Beard's approach is the view that the framers of the Constitution *were* concerned with philosophical and ethical principles. Indeed, the framers sought to devise a system of government consistent with the dominant philosophical and moral principles of the day. But, in fact, these two views belong together; the Founders' interests were reinforced by their principles. The convention that drafted the American Constitution was chiefly organized by the New England merchants and southern planters. Although the delegates representing these groups did not all hope to profit personally from an increase in the value of their securities, as Beard would have it, they did hope to benefit in the broadest political and economic sense by breaking the power of their radical foes and establishing a system of government more compatible with their long-term economic and political interests. Thus, the framers sought to create a new government capable of promoting commerce and protecting property from radical state legislatures. At the same time, they hoped to fashion a government less susceptible than the existing state and national regimes to populist forces hostile to the interests of the commercial and propertied classes.

The Great Compromise The proponents of a new government fired their opening shot on May 29, 1787, when Edmund Randolph of Virginia offered a resolution that proposed corrections and enlargements in the Articles of Confederation. The proposal, which showed the strong influence of James Madison, was not a simple motion. It provided for virtually every aspect of a new government. Randolph later admitted it was intended to be an alternative draft constitution, and it did in fact serve as the framework for what ultimately became the Constitution. (There is no verbatim record of the debates, but Madison was present during virtually all of the deliberations and kept full notes on them.[10])

The portion of Randolph's motion that became most controversial was called the **Virginia Plan.** This plan provided for a system of representation in the national legislature based upon the population of each state or the proportion of each state's revenue contribution to the national government, or both. (Randolph also proposed a second branch of the legislature, but it was to be elected by the members of the first branch.) Since the states varied enormously in size and wealth, the Virginia Plan was thought to be heavily biased in favor of the large states.

While the convention was debating the Virginia Plan, additional delegates were arriving in Philadelphia and were beginning to mount opposition to it. Their resolution, introduced by William Paterson of New Jersey and known as the **New Jersey Plan,** did not oppose the Virginia plan point for point. Instead, it concentrated on specific weaknesses in the Articles of Confederation, in the spirit of revision rather than radical replacement of that document. Supporters of the New Jersey Plan did not seriously question the convention's commitment to replacing the Articles. But their opposition to the Virginia Plan's scheme of representation was sufficient to send its proposals back to committee for reworking into a common document. In particular, delegates from the less populous states, which included Delaware, New Jersey, Connecticut, and New York, asserted that the more populous states, such as Virginia, Pennsylvania, North Carolina, Massachusetts, and Georgia, would dominate the new government if representation were determined by population. The smaller states argued that each state should be equally represented in the new regime regardless of that state's population.

The issue of representation was one that threatened to wreck the entire constitutional enterprise. Delegates conferred, factions maneuvered, and tempers flared. James Wilson of Pennsylvania told the small-state delegates that if they wanted to disrupt the union they should go ahead. The separation could, he said, "never happen on better grounds." Small-state delegates were equally blunt. Gunning Bedford of Delaware declared that the small states might look elsewhere for friends if they were forced. "The large states," he said, "dare not dissolve the confederation. If they do the small ones will find some foreign ally of more honor and good faith, who will take them by the hand and do them justice." These sentiments were widely shared. The union, as Oliver Ellsworth of Connecticut put it, was "on the verge of dissolution, scarcely held together by the strength of a hair."

The outcome of this debate was the Connecticut Compromise, also known as the **Great Compromise.** Under the terms of this compromise, in the first branch of Congress—the House of Representatives—the representatives would be apportioned according to the number of inhabitants in each state. This, of course, was what delegates from the large states had sought. But in the second branch—the Senate—each state would have an equal vote regardless of its size; this provision addressed the concerns of the small states. This compromise was not immediately satisfactory to all the delegates. Indeed, two of the most vocal members of the small-state faction, John Lansing and Robert Yates of New York, were so incensed by the concession that their colleagues had made to the large-state forces that they stormed out of the convention. In the end, however, both sets of forces preferred compromise to the breakup of the Union, and the plan was accepted.

The Question of Slavery: The "Three-Fifths" Compromise The story so far is too neat, too easy, and too anticlimactic. If it were left here, it would only contribute to American mythology. After all, the notion of a bicameral (two-chambered) legislature was very much in the air in 1787. Some of the states had had bicameral legislatures for years. The Philadelphia delegates might well have gone straight to the adoption of two chambers based on two different principles of representation even without the dramatic interplay of conflict and compromise. But a far more fundamental issue had to be confronted before the Great Compromise could take place: the issue of slavery.

Many of the conflicts that emerged during the Constitutional Convention were reflections of the fundamental differences between the slave and the nonslave states—differences that pitted the southern planters and New

England merchants against one another. This was the first premonition of a conflict that would almost destroy the Republic in later years. In the midst of debate over large versus small states, Madison observed,

> The great danger to our general government is the great southern and northern interests of the continent, being opposed to each other. Look to the votes in Congress, and most of them stand divided by the geography of the country, not according to the size of the states.[11]

More than 90 percent of the country's slaves resided in five states—Georgia, Maryland, North Carolina, South Carolina, and Virginia—where they accounted for 30 percent of the total population. In some places, slaves outnumbered nonslaves by as much as ten to one. If the Constitution were to embody any principle of national supremacy, some basic decisions would have to be made about the place of slavery in the general scheme. Madison hit on this point on several occasions as different aspects of the Constitution were being discussed. For example, he observed,

> It seemed now to be pretty well understood that the real difference of interests lay, not between the large and small but between the northern and southern states. The institution of slavery and its consequences formed the line of discrimination. There were five states on the South, eight on the northern side of this line. Should a proportional representation take place it was true, the northern side would still outnumber the other: but not in the same degree, at this time; and every day would tend towards an equilibrium.[12]

Northerners and Southerners eventually reached agreement through the **Three-fifths Compromise.** The seats in the House of Representatives would be apportioned according to a "population" in which five slaves would count

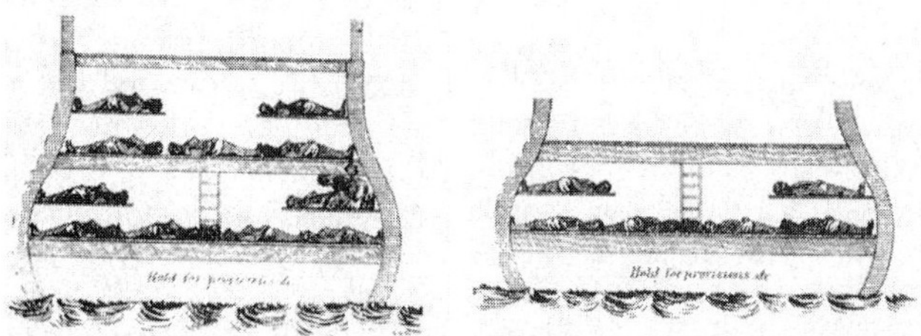

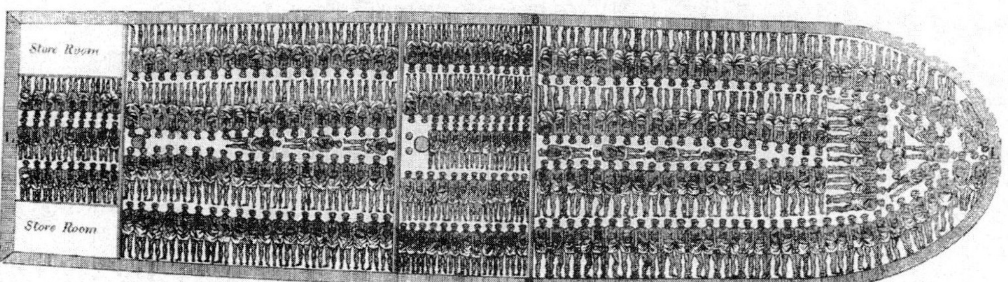

These cross-sectional views of a slave ship show the crowded conditions that Africans endured on the passage to America. The Constitution explicitly prevented Congress from banning the slave trade until at least 1808. Even though the trade was banned on January 1 of that year, illegal traffic in slaves continued.

as three free persons. The slaves would not be allowed to vote, of course, but the number of representatives would be apportioned accordingly.

The issue of slavery was the most difficult one faced by the framers and nearly destroyed the Union. Although some delegates believed slavery to be morally wrong, an evil and oppressive institution that made a mockery of the ideals and values espoused in the Constitution, morality was not the issue that caused the framers to support or oppose the Three-fifths Compromise. Whatever they thought of the institution of slavery, most delegates from the northern states opposed counting slaves in the distribution of congressional seats. Wilson of Pennsylvania, for example, argued that if slaves were citizens they should be treated and counted like other citizens. If, on the other hand, they were property, then why should not other forms of property be counted toward the apportionment of representatives? But southern delegates made it clear that if the northerners refused to give in, they would never agree to the new government. William R. Davie of North Carolina heatedly said that it was time "to speak out." He asserted that the people of North Carolina would never enter the Union if slaves were not counted as part of the basis for representation. Without such agreement, he asserted ominously, "the business was at an end." Even southerners like Edmund Randolph of Virginia, who conceded that slavery was immoral, insisted upon including slaves in the allocation of congressional seats. This conflict between the southern and northern delegates was so divisive that many came to question the possibility of creating and maintaining a union of the two. Pierce Butler of South Carolina declared that the North and South were as different as Russia and Turkey. Eventually, the North and South compromised on the issue of slavery and representation. Indeed, northerners even agreed to permit a continuation of the odious slave trade to keep the South in the union. But, in due course, Butler proved to be correct, and a bloody war was fought when the disparate interests of the North and the South could no longer be reconciled.

The Constitution

- What principles does the Constitution embody?
- What were the intents of the framers of the Constitution regarding the legislative, executive, and judicial branches?
- What limits on the national government's power are embodied in the Constitution?

The political significance of the Great Compromise and the Three-fifths Compromise was to reinforce the unity of the mercantile and planter forces that sought to create a new government. The Great Compromise reassured those who feared that the importance of their own local or regional influence would be reduced by the new governmental framework. The Three-fifths Compromise temporarily defused the rivalry between the merchants and planters. Their unity secured, members of the alliance supporting the estab-

Delegates to the Constitutional Convention gather to sign their names to the Constitution on September 17, 1787.

lishment of a new government moved to fashion a constitutional framework consistent with their economic and political interests.

In particular, the framers sought a new government that, first, would be strong enough to promote commerce and protect property from radical state legislatures such as Rhode Island's. This became the constitutional basis for national control over commerce and finance, as well as for the establishment of national judicial supremacy and the effort to construct a strong presidency. Second, the framers sought to prevent what they saw as the threat posed by the "excessive democracy" of the state and national governments under the Articles of Confederation. This led to such constitutional principles as **bicameralism** (division of the Congress into two chambers), **checks and balances,** staggered terms in office, and indirect election (selection of the president by an **electoral college** rather than by voters directly). Third, the framers, lacking the power to force the states or the public at large to accept the new form of government, sought to identify principles that would help to secure support. This became the basis of the constitutional provision for direct popular election of representatives and, subsequently, for the addition of the Bill of Rights to the Constitution. Finally, the framers wanted to be certain that the government they created did not pose even more of a threat to its citizens' liberties and property rights than did the radical state legislatures they feared and despised. To prevent the new government from abusing its power, the framers incorporated principles such as the separation of powers and federalism into the Constitution. Let us assess the major provisions of the Constitution's seven articles (listed in Box 3.1) to see how each relates to these objectives.

The Legislative Branch

The Constitution provided in Article I, Sections 1–7, for a Congress consisting of two chambers—a House of Representatives and a Senate. Members of the House of Representatives were given two-year terms in office and were to be elected directly by the people. Members of the Senate were to be appointed by the state legislatures (this was changed in 1913 by the Seventeenth

THE SEVEN ARTICLES OF THE CONSTITUTION

1. **The Legislative Branch**
   House: two-year terms, elected directly by the people.
   Senate: six-year terms (staggered so that only one-third of the Senate changes in any given election), appointed by state legislature (changed in 1913 to direct election).
   Expressed powers of the national government: collecting taxes, borrowing money, regulating commerce, declaring war, and maintaining an army and a navy; all other power belongs to the states, unless deemed otherwise by the elastic ("necessary and proper") clause.
   Exclusive powers of the national government: states are expressly forbidden to issue their own paper money, tax imports and exports, regulate trade outside their own borders, and impair the obligation of contracts; these powers are the exclusive domain of the national government.
2. **The Executive Branch**
   Presidency: four-year terms (limited in 1951 to a maximum of two terms), elected indirectly by the electoral college.
   Powers: can recognize other countries, negotiate treaties, grant reprieves and pardons, convene Congress in special sessions, and veto congressional enactments.
3. **The Judicial Branch**
   Supreme Court: lifetime terms, appointed by the president with the approval of the Senate.
   Powers: include resolving conflicts between federal and state laws, determining whether power belongs to the national government or the states, and settling controversies between citizens of different states.
4. **National Unity and Power**
   Reciprocity among states: establishes that each state must give "full faith and credit" to official acts of other states, and guarantees citizens of any state the "privileges and immunities" of every other state.
5. **Amending the Constitution**
   Procedure: requires approval by two-thirds of Congress and adoption by three-fourths of the states.
6. **National Supremacy**
   The Constitution and national law are the supreme law of the land and cannot be overruled by state law.
7. **Ratification**
   The Constitution became effective when approved by nine states.

BOX 3.1

Amendment, which instituted direct election of senators) for six-year terms. These terms were staggered so that the appointments of one-third of the senators would expire every two years. The Constitution assigned somewhat different tasks to the House and Senate. Though the approval of each body was required for the enactment of a law, the Senate alone was given the power to ratify treaties and approve presidential appointments. The House, on the other hand, was given the sole power to originate revenue bills.

The character of the legislative branch was directly related to the framers' major goals. The House of Representatives was designed to be directly responsible to the people in order to encourage popular consent for the new Constitution and to help enhance the power of the new government. At the same time, to guard against "excessive democracy," the power of the House of Representatives was checked by the Senate, whose members were to be appointed by the states for long terms rather than be elected directly by the people. The purpose of this provision, according to Alexander Hamilton, was to avoid, "an unqualified complaisance to every sudden breeze of passion, or to every transient impulse which the people may receive."[13] Staggered terms of service in the Senate, moreover, were intended to make that body even more resistant to popular pressure. Since only one-third of the senators would be selected at any given time, the composition of the institution would be protected from changes in popular preferences transmitted by the state legislatures. This would prevent what James Madison called "mutability in the public councils arising from a rapid succession of new members."[14] Thus, the structure of the legislative branch was designed to contribute to governmental power, to promote popular consent for the new government, and at the same time to place limits on the popular political currents that many of the framers saw as a radical threat to the economic and social order.

The issues of power and consent were important throughout the Constitution. Section 8 of Article I specifically listed the powers of Congress, which include the authority to collect taxes, to borrow money, to regulate commerce, to declare war, and to maintain an army and navy. By granting Congress these powers, the framers indicated very clearly that they intended the new government to be far more influential than its predecessor. At the same time, by defining the new government's most important powers as belonging to Congress, the framers sought to promote popular acceptance of this critical change by reassuring citizens that their views would be fully represented whenever the government exercised its new powers.

As a further guarantee to the people that the new government would pose no threat to them, the Constitution implied that any powers not listed were not granted at all. This is the doctrine of **expressed power.** The Constitution grants only those powers specifically expressed in its text. But the framers intended to create an active and powerful government, and so they included the **necessary and proper clause,** sometimes known as the **"elastic clause,"** which signified that the enumerated powers were meant to be a source of strength to the national government, not a limitation on it. Each power could be used with the utmost vigor, but no new powers could be seized upon by the national government without a constitutional amendment. In the absence of such an amendment, any power not enumerated was conceived to be "reserved" to the states (or the people).

The Executive Branch

The Constitution provided for the establishment of the presidency in Article II. As Alexander Hamilton commented, the presidential article aimed toward "energy in the Executive." It did so in an effort to overcome the natural tendency toward stalemate that was built into the bicameral legislature as well

AMERICAN POLITICAL CULTURE

The Founding in American Culture

In 1923, transport workers in San Pedro Harbor, California, went on strike. The police, cooperating with the workers' employers, arrested hundreds of strikers and detained them in overcrowded jails. At a protest rally for the striking workers and their families, the famous writer Upton Sinclair spoke against the repression of the workers. He began by reading the Bill of Rights. But before he could finish reciting the First Amendment guarantee of "the right of the people peaceably to assemble," the police arrested him. The complaint brought against Sinclair charged him with "discussing, arguing, orating and debating certain thoughts and theories, which . . . were detrimental and in opposition to the orderly conduct of affairs of business, affecting the rights of private property."[1]

The faith Americans have in the Constitution is remarkable, especially when we consider episodes like the arrest of Upton Sinclair for reading the First Amendment in public. How can words on parchment restrain a government from undertaking whatever actions it deems necessary or convenient?

The American faith that the Constitution protects people against tyrannical government is a mixture of reverence, naiveté, and wisdom. It derives in part from a widespread American reverence that the Founders were more like demigods than mortals—that they were wiser, more far-seeing, and more concerned with the good of the nation than the petty politicians of today. "Miracle at Philadelphia," the title of one popular history of the Constitutional Convention, conveys this common impulse to elevate the accomplishments of the Founders above the normal political realm.[2]

Such an attitude, as our look at the Founding reveals, is somewhat naive. The Founders were a disparate group of individuals with many different interests. Many different groups contended for control over the shape of the Constitution. (And many others—women, blacks, and the poor—had no voice in the process at all.) The drafting of the Constitution proceeded not as a majestic exercise in disinterested political wisdom, but as a process of compromise. To treat the Founders as a single, homogeneous group distorts the nature of what they accomplished: a series of brilliant political compromises, rather than the clear articulation of political ideals.

To point this out is not to say that Americans should strip their culture of reverence for the Founding. The American Constitution survives as an amazingly successful expression of political wisdom, of the human effort to balance power and freedom in a lasting political order. And idealizing the Founding is itself an act of wisdom, for it makes it harder for subsequent politicians to turn away from the ideals associated with the Founding. The ideals of representative government, the rule of law, constitutionalism, and the liberties listed in the Bill of Rights serve as effective ongoing checks on the United States government.

In 1838, a young Abraham Lincoln urged his listeners at the Springfield Young Men's Lyceum to "let reverence for the laws" and the Constitution "become the *political religion* of the nation; and let the old and the young, the rich and the poor, the grave and the gay, of all sexes and tongues, and colors and conditions, sacrifice unceasingly upon its altars."[3] Drawing on the ideals of the Founding rather than the reality of its compromise with slavery, and referring specifically to Americans "of all colors and conditions," Lincoln used the Constitution as the basis for an argument against slavery that would become his, and his era's, greatest cause. Such is the noblest end that constitutionalism can achieve.

[1] Quoted in Michael Kammen, *A Machine That Would Go of Itself: The Constitution in American Culture* (New York: Vintage, 1987), p. xv.

[2] Catherine Drinker Bowen, *Miracle at Philadelphia: The Story of the Constitutional Convention, May to September, 1787* (Boston: Little, Brown, 1966).

[3] *The Collected Works of Abraham Lincoln*, ed. Roy P. Basler (New Brunswick, NJ: Rutgers University Press, 1953), vol. 1, p. 112. Emphasis in the original.

as into the separation of powers among the three branches. The Constitution afforded the president a measure of independence from the people and from the other branches of government—particularly the Congress.

In line with the framers' goal of increased power to the national government, the president was granted the unconditional power to accept ambassadors from other countries; this amounted to the power to "recognize" other countries. The president was also given the power to negotiate treaties, although their acceptance required the approval of the Senate. The president was given the unconditional right to grant reprieves and pardons, except in cases of impeachment. And the president was provided with the power to appoint major departmental personnel, to convene Congress in special session, and to veto congressional enactments. (The veto power is formidable, but it is not absolute, since Congress can override it by a two-thirds vote.)

The framers hoped to create a presidency that would make the federal government rather than the states the agency capable of timely and decisive action to deal with public issues and problems. This was the meaning of the "energy" that Hamilton hoped to impart to the executive branch.[15] At the same time, however, the framers sought to help the president withstand excessively democratic pressures by creating a system of indirect rather than direct election through a separate electoral college.

The Judicial Branch

In establishing the judicial branch in Article III, the Constitution reflected the framers' preoccupations with nationalizing governmental power and checking radical democratic impulses while guarding against potential interference with liberty and property from the new national government itself.

Under the provisions of Article III, the framers created a court that was to be literally a supreme court of the United States, and not merely the highest court of the national government. The most important expression of this intention was granting the Supreme Court the power to resolve any conflicts that might emerge between federal and state laws. In particular, the Supreme Court was given the right to determine whether a power was exclusive to the national government, concurrent with the states, or exclusive to the states. In addition, the Supreme Court was assigned jurisdiction over controversies between citizens of different states. The long-term significance of this provision was that as the country developed a national economy, it came to rely increasingly on the federal judiciary, rather than on the state courts, for the resolution of disputes.

Judges were given lifetime appointments in order to protect them from popular politics and from interference by the other branches. This, however, did not mean that the judiciary would remain totally impartial to political considerations, or to the other branches, for the president was to appoint the judges, and the Senate to approve the appointments. Congress would also have the power to create inferior (lower) courts, to change the jurisdiction of the federal courts, to add or subtract federal judges, and even to change the size of the Supreme Court.

No direct mention is made in the Constitution of **judicial review**—the power of the courts to render the final decision when there is a conflict of interpretation of the Constitution or of laws between the courts and Congress, the courts and the executive branch, or the courts and the states. The Supreme Court eventually assumed the power of judicial review. Its assumption of this power, as we shall see in Chapter 14, was not based on the Constitution itself but on the politics of later decades and the membership of the Court.

NATIONAL UNITY AND POWER

Various provisions in the Constitution addressed the framers' concern with national unity and power, including Article IV's provisions for comity (reciprocity) among states and among citizens of all states. Each state was prohibited from discriminating against the citizens of other states in favor of its own citizens, with the Supreme Court charged with deciding in each case whether a state had discriminated against goods or people from another state. The Constitution restricted the power of the states in favor of ensuring enough power to the national government to give the country a free-flowing national economy.

The framers' concern with national supremacy was also expressed in Article VI, in the **supremacy clause,** which provided that national laws and treaties "shall be the supreme law of the land." This meant that all laws made under the "authority of the United States" would be superior to all laws adopted by any state or any other subdivision, and the states would be expected to respect all treaties made under that authority. The supremacy clause also bound the officials of all state and local as well as federal governments to take an oath of office to support the national Constitution. This meant that every action taken by the United States Congress would have to be applied within each state as though the action were in fact state law.

AMENDING THE CONSTITUTION

The Constitution established procedures for its own revision in Article V. Its provisions are so difficult that Americans have availed themselves of the amending process only seventeen times since 1791, when the first ten amendments were adopted. Many other amendments have been proposed in Congress, but fewer than forty of them have even come close to fulfilling the Constitution's requirement of a two-thirds vote in Congress, and only a fraction have gotten anywhere near adoption by three-fourths of the states. Article V also provides that the Constitution can be amended by a constitutional convention. Occasionally, proponents of particular measures, such as a balanced-budget amendment, have called for a constitutional convention to consider their proposals. Whatever the purpose for which it was called, however, such a convention would presumably have the authority to revise America's entire system of government.

RATIFYING THE CONSTITUTION

The rules for the ratification of the Constitution were set forth in Article VII. Nine of the thirteen states would have to ratify, or agree upon, the terms in order for the Constitution to pass.

Constitutional Limits on the National Government's Power

As we have indicated, although the framers sought to create a powerful national government, they also wanted to guard against possible misuse of that power. To that end, the framers incorporated two key principles into the Constitution—the **separation of powers** and **federalism.** A third set of limitations, in the form of the **Bill of Rights,** was added to the Constitution to help secure its ratification when opponents of the document charged that it paid insufficient attention to citizens' rights.

The Separation of Powers No principle of politics was more widely shared at the time of the 1787 founding than the principle that power must be used to balance power. The French political theorist Montesquieu (1689–1755) believed that this balance was an indispensable defense against tyranny, and his writings, especially his major work, *The Spirit of the Laws,* "were taken as political gospel" at the Philadelphia Convention.[16] The principle of the separation of powers is not stated explicitly in the Constitution, but it is clearly built on Articles I, II, and III, which provide for the following:

1. Three separate and distinct branches of government (see Figure 3.1).
2. Different methods of selecting the top personnel, so that each branch is responsible to a different constituency. This is supposed to produce a "mixed regime," in which the personnel of each department will de-

THE SEPARATION OF POWERS

Executive	Legislative	Judicial
Enforces laws	Passes federal laws	Reviews lower court decisions
Commander in chief of armed forces	Controls federal appropriations	Decides constitutionality of laws
Makes foreign treaties	Approves treaties and presidential appointments	Decides cases involving disputes between states
Proposes laws	Regulates interstate commerce	
Appoints Supreme Court justices and federal court judges	Establishes lower court system	
Pardons those convicted in federal court		

FIGURE 3.1
The Constitution provides for the separation of powers to ensure that no one branch of American government holds too much power.

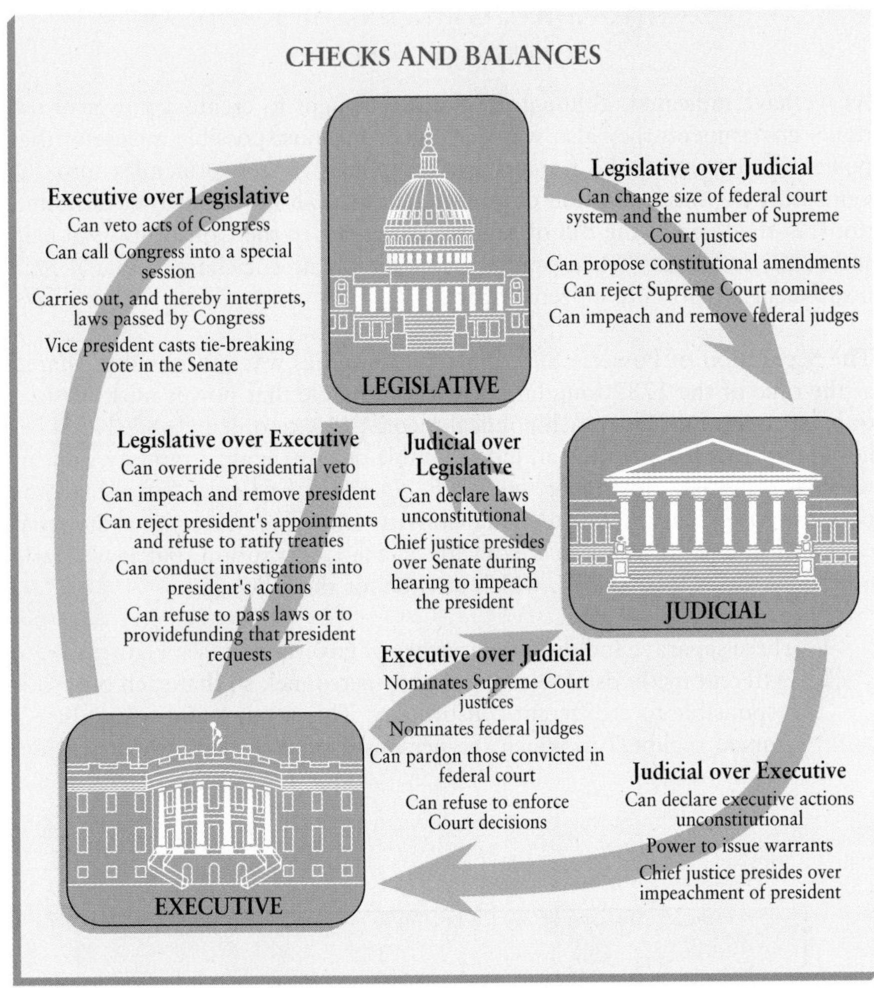

FIGURE 3.2

velop very different interests and outlooks on how to govern, and different groups in society will be assured some access to governmental decision making; and

3. **Checks and balances**—a system under which each of the branches is given some power over the others. Familiar examples are the presidential veto power over legislation, the power of the Senate to approve presidential appointments, and judicial review of acts of Congress (see Figure 3.2).

One clever formulation of the separation of powers is that of a system not of separated powers but of "separated institutions sharing power,"[17] and thus diminishing the chance that power will be misused.

Federalism Compared to the confederation principle of the Articles of Confederation, federalism was a step toward greater centralization of power. The delegates agreed that they needed to place more power at the national level, without completely undermining the power of the state governments. Thus, they devised a system of two sovereigns—the states and the nation—with the hope that competition between the two would be an effective limitation on the power of both.

The Bill of Rights Late in the Philadelphia Convention, a motion was made to include a bill of rights in the Constitution. After a brief debate in which hardly a word was said in its favor and only one speech was made against it, the motion was almost unanimously turned down. Most delegates sincerely believed that since the federal government was already limited to its expressed powers, further protection of citizens was not needed. The delegates argued that the states should adopt bills of rights because their greater powers needed greater limitations. But almost immediately after the Constitution was ratified, there was a movement to adopt a national bill of rights. This is why the Bill of Rights, adopted in 1791, comprises the first ten amendments to the Constitution rather than being part of the body of it. We will have a good deal more to say about the Bill of Rights in Chapter 5.

The Fight for Ratification

- What different interests did the Federalist and the Antifederalists represent in the fight over ratification?
- Over what key principles did the Federalists and the Antifederalists disagree?

The first hurdle faced by the new Constitution was ratification by state conventions of delegates elected by the people of each state. This struggle for ratification was carried out in thirteen separate campaigns. Each involved different people, moved at a different pace, and was influenced by local as well as national considerations. Two sides faced off throughout the states, however; the two sides called themselves Federalists and Antifederalists (see Table 3.1). The **Federalists** (who more accurately should have called themselves "Nationalists" but who took their name to appear to follow in the revolutionary tradition) supported the Constitution and preferred a strong national government. The **Antifederalists** opposed the Constitution and preferred a federal system of government that was decentralized; they took on their name by default, in reaction to their better-organized opponents. The Federalists were united in their support of the Constitution, while the Antifederalists were divided as to what they believed the alternative to the Constitution should be.

James Madison, the "father" of the Constitution, was a prominent Federalist.

During the struggle over ratification of the Constitution, Americans argued about great political issues and principles. How much power should the national government be given? What safeguards were most likely to prevent the abuse of power? What institutional arrangements could best ensure adequate representation for all Americans? Was tyranny to be feared more from the many or from the few?

FEDERALISTS VS. ANTIFEDERALISTS

	Federalists	Antifederalists
Who were they?	Property owners, creditors, merchants	Small farmers, frontiersmen, debtors, shopkeepers
What did they believe?	Believed that elites were best fit to govern; feared "excessive democracy"	Believed that government should be closer to the people; feared concentration of power in hands of the elites
What system of government did they favor?	Favored strong national government; believed in "filtration" so that only elites would obtain governmental power	Favored rentention of power by state governments and protection of individual rights
Who were their leaders?	Alexander Hamilton James Madison George Washington	Patrick Henry George Mason Elbridge Gerry George Clinton

TABLE 3.1

In political life, as we observed earlier, principles—even great principles—are seldom completely divorced from some set of interests. In 1787, Americans were divided along economic, regional, and political lines. These divisions inevitably influenced their attitudes toward the profound political questions of the day. Many well-to-do merchants and planters favored the creation of a stronger central government that would have the capacity to protect property, promote commerce, and keep some of the more radical state legislatures in check. At the same time, many powerful state leaders, such as Governor George Clinton of New York, feared that strengthening the national government would reduce their own influence and status. Each of these interests, of course, justified its position with an appeal to principle.

George Clinton, a prominent Antifederalist, feared that a single government ruling a large population would be too quick to deprive the people of their liberties.

Principles are often important weapons in political warfare, and seeing how and by whom they are wielded can illuminate their otherwise obscure implications. In our own time, dry academic discussions of topics such as "free trade" become easier to grasp once it is noted that free trade and open markets are generally favored by low-cost producers, while protectionism is the goal of firms whose costs of production are higher than the international norm.

Even if a principle is invented and initially brandished to serve an interest, however, once it has been articulated it can take on a life of its own and prove to have implications that transcend the narrow interests it was created to serve. Some opponents of the Constitution, for example, who criticized the absence of a bill of rights in the initial document, did so simply with the hope of blocking the document's ratification. Yet, the Bill of Rights that was later added to the Constitution has proven for two centuries to be a bulwark of civil liberty in the United States.

Similarly, closer to our own time, support for the extension of voting rights and for massive legislative redistricting under the rubric of "one person, one vote" during the 1960s came mainly from liberal Democrats who were hoping to strengthen their own political base, since the groups that would benefit most from these initiatives were overwhelmingly Democratic. The principles of equal access to the ballot and one person, one vote, however, have a moral and political validity that is independent of the political interests that propelled these ideas into the political arena.

These examples show us that truly great political principles surmount the interests that initially set them forth. The first step in understanding a political principle is understanding why and by whom it is espoused. The second step is understanding the full implications of the principle itself—implications that may go far beyond the interests that launched it. Thus, even though the great political principles about which Americans argued in 1787 *did* reflect competing interests, they also represented views of society, government, and politics that surmount interest, and so must be understood in their own terms. Whatever the underlying clash of interests that may have guided them, the Federalists and Antifederalists presented important alternative visions of America.

Federalists vs. Antifederalists

During the ratification struggle, thousands of essays, speeches, pamphlets, and letters were presented in support of and in opposition to the proposed Constitution. The best-known pieces supporting ratification of the Constitution were the eighty-five essays written, under the name of "Publius," by Alexander Hamilton, James Madison, and John Jay between the fall of 1787 and the spring of 1788. These **Federalist Papers,** as they are collectively known today, defended the principles of the Constitution and sought to dispel fears of a national authority. The Antifederalists published essays of their own, arguing that the new Constitution betrayed the Revolution and was a step toward monarchy. Among the best of the Antifederalist works were the essays, usually attributed to New York Supreme Court justice Robert Yates, that were written under the name of "Brutus" and published in the *New York Journal* at the same time the Federalist Papers appeared. The Antifederalist view was also ably presented in the pamphlets and letters written by a former delegate to the Continental Congress and future U.S. senator, Richard Henry Lee of Virginia, using the pen name "The Federal Farmer." These essays highlight the major differences of opinion between Federalists and Antifederalists. Federalists appealed to basic principles of government in support of their nationalist vision. Antifederalists cited equally fundamental precepts to support their vision of a looser confederacy of small republics.

Representation One major area of contention between the two sides was the question of representation. The Antifederalists asserted that representatives must be "a true picture of the people, . . . [possessing] the knowledge of their circumstances and their wants."[18] This could only be achieved, argued

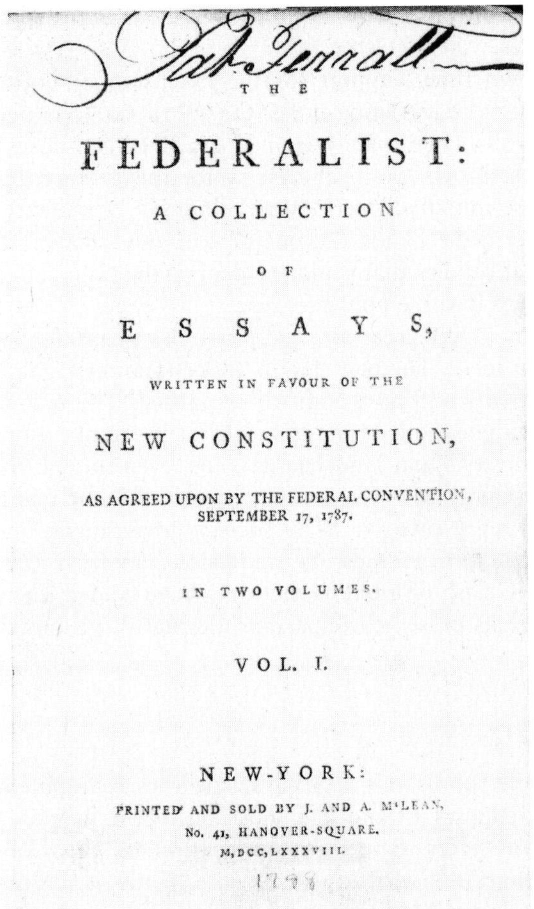

Pat. Farrall

THE

FEDERALIST:

A COLLECTION

OF

ESSAYS,

WRITTEN IN FAVOUR OF THE

NEW CONSTITUTION,

AS AGREED UPON BY THE FEDERAL CONVENTION, SEPTEMBER 17, 1787.

IN TWO VOLUMES.

VOL. I.

NEW-YORK:

PRINTED AND SOLD BY J. AND A. M'LEAN, No. 41, HANOVER-SQUARE. M,DCC,LXXXVIII.

One of the legacies of the debate over ratification of the Constitution is the Federalist Papers, a collection of essays originally published in New York newspapers between October 1787 and July 1788.

the Antifederalists, in small, relatively homogeneous republics such as the existing states. In their view, the size and extent of the entire nation precluded the construction of a truly representative form of government. As Brutus put it, "Is it practicable for a country so large and so numerous . . . to elect a representation that will speak their sentiments? . . . It certainly is not."[19]

Federalists, for their part, saw no reason that representatives should be precisely like those they represented. In the Federalist view, one of the great advantages of representative government over direct democracy was precisely the possibility that the people would choose as their representatives individuals possessing ability, experience, and talent superior to their own. In Madison's words, rather than serve as a mirror or reflection of society, representatives must be "[those] who possess [the] most wisdom to discern, and [the] most virtue to pursue, the common good of the society."[20]

Although the terms of discussion have changed, this debate over representation continues today. Some argue that representatives must be very close in life experience, race, and ethnic background to their constituents to truly understand the needs and interests of those constituents. This argument is made by contemporary proponents of giving the states more control over social programs. This argument is also made by proponents of "minority districts"—legislative districts whose boundaries are drawn so as to guarantee that minorities will be able to elect their own representative to Congress. Opponents of this practice, which we will explore further in Chapter 9, have argued in court that it is discriminatory and unnecessary; blacks, they say, can be represented by whites and vice versa. Who is correct? It would appear that this question can never be answered to everyone's complete satisfaction.

Tyranny of the Majority A second important issue dividing Federalists and Antifederalists was the threat of **tyranny**—unjust rule by the group in power. Both opponents and defenders of the Constitution frequently affirmed their fear of tyrannical rule. Each side, however, had a different view of the most likely source of tyranny and, hence, of the way in which the threat was to be forestalled.

From the Antifederalist perspective, the great danger was the tendency of all governments—including republican governments—to become gradually more and more "aristocratic" in character, wherein the small number of individuals in positions of authority would use their stations to gain more and more power over the general citizenry. In essence, the few would use their power to tyrannize the many. For this reason, Antifederalists were sharply critical of those features of the Constitution that divorced governmental institutions from direct responsibility to the people—institutions such as the Senate, the executive, and the federal judiciary. The latter, appointed for life, presented a particular threat: "I wonder if the world ever saw . . . a court of justice invested with such immense powers, and yet placed in a situation so little responsible," protested Brutus.[21]

The Federalists, too, recognized the threat of tyranny, but they believed that the danger particularly associated with republican governments was not aristocracy, but instead, majority tyranny. The Federalists were concerned that a popular majority, "united and actuated by some common impulse of passion, or of interest, adverse to the rights of other citizens," would endeavor to "trample on the rules of justice."[22] From the Federalist perspective, it was precisely those features of the Constitution attacked as potential sources of tyranny by the Antifederalists that actually offered the best hope of averting the threat of oppression. The size and extent of the nation, for instance, was for the Federalists a bulwark against tyranny. In Madison's famous formulation,

> The smaller the society the fewer will probably be the distinct parties and interests, the more frequently will a majority be found of the same party; and the smaller the number of individuals composing a majority, and the smaller the compass within which they are placed, the more easily will they concert and execute their plans of oppression. Extend the sphere and you take in a greater variety of parties and interests; you make it less probable that a majority of the whole will have a common motive to invade the rights of other citizens; or if such a common motive exists, it will be more difficult for all who feel it to discover their own strength and to act in unison with each other."[23]

Echoes of this debate continue today. Many Americans believe that those in authority sooner or later forget the needs of the people they serve. This belief fuels contemporary demands for congressional term limits as well as governmental ethics legislation. Others, however, believe that such restrictions hobble the government's ability to act and potentially deprive the public of the services of its most talented and experienced leaders. At the same time, as we shall see in Chapter 9, the fear of "majority tyranny" expressed by the Federalists and of the power of mass participation underlies the less-than-energetic effort that many American politicians have made on behalf of fuller popular participation in our nation's political life.

This Antifederalist tract published in 1788 by Mercy Otis Warren of Massachusetts warned of government tyranny and oppression of the rights and liberties of the people.

Governmental Power A third major difference between Federalists and Antifederalists was the issue of governmental power. Both the opponents and proponents of the Constitution agreed on the principle of **limited government.** They differed, however, on the fundamentally important question of how to place limits on governmental action. Antifederalists favored limiting and enumerating the powers granted to the national government in relation both to the states and to the people at large. To them, the powers given the national government ought to be "confined to certain defined national objects."[24] Otherwise, the national government would "swallow up all the power of the state governments."[25] Antifederalists bitterly attacked the supremacy clause and the necessary and proper clause of the Constitution as unlimited and dangerous grants of power to the national government.[26]

Antifederalists also demanded that a bill of rights be added to the Constitution to place limits upon the government's exercise of power over the citizenry. Federalists favored the construction of a government with broad powers. They wanted a government that had the capacity to defend the nation against foreign foes, guard against domestic strife and insurrection, promote commerce, and expand the nation's economy. Antifederalists shared some of these goals but still feared governmental power. Hamilton pointed out, however, that these goals could not be achieved without allowing the government to exercise the necessary power. Federalists acknowledged that every power could be abused but argued that the way to prevent misuse of power was not by depriving the government of the powers needed to achieve national goals. Instead, they argued that the threat of abuse of power would be mitigated by the Constitution's internal checks and controls. As Madison put it, "the power surrendered by the people is first divided between two distinct governments, and then the portion allotted to each subdivided among distinct and separate departments. Hence, a double security arises to the rights of the people. The different governments will control each other, at the same time that each will be controlled by itself."[27] The Federalists' concern with avoiding unwarranted limits on governmental power led them to oppose a bill of rights, which they saw as nothing more than a set of unnecessary restrictions on the government.

The Federalists acknowledged that abuse of power remained a possibility, but felt that the risk had to be taken because of the goals to be achieved. "The very idea of power included a possibility of doing harm," said the Federalist John Rutledge during the South Carolina ratification debates. "If the gentleman would show the power that could do no harm," Rutledge continued, "he would at once discover it to be a power that could do no good."[28] This aspect of the debate between the Federalists and the Anti-

New York was the scene of a great celebration following the ratification of the Constitution. The federal ship *Hamilton* leads this parade.

federalists, perhaps more than any other, continues to reverberate through American politics. Should the nation limit the federal government's power to tax and spend? Should Congress limit the capacity of federal agencies to issue new regulations? Should the government endeavor to create new rights for minorities, the disabled, and others? What is the proper balance between promoting equality and protecting liberty? Though the details have changed, these are the same great questions that have been debated since the time of the founding.

Reflections on the Founding

The final product of the Constitutional Convention would have to be considered an extraordinary victory for the groups that had most forcefully called for the creation of a new system of government to replace the Articles of Confederation. Antifederalist criticisms forced the Constitution's proponents to accept the addition of a bill of rights designed to limit the powers of the national government. In general, however, it was the Federalist vision of America that triumphed. The Constitution adopted in 1789 created the framework for a powerful national government that for more than two hundred years has defended the nation's interests, promoted its commerce, and maintained national unity. In one notable instance, the national government fought and won a bloody war to prevent the nation from breaking apart. And despite this powerful government, the system of internal checks and balances has functioned reasonably well, as the Federalists predicted, to prevent the national government from tyrannizing its citizens.

Although they were defeated in 1789, the Antifederalists present us with an important picture of a road not taken and of an America that might have been. Would the country have been worse off if it had been governed by a confederacy of small republics linked by a national administration with severely limited powers? Were the Antifederalists correct in predicting that a government given great power in the hope that it might do good would, through "insensible progress," inevitably turn to evil purposes? Two hundred years of government under the federal Constitution are not necessarily enough to definitively answer these questions. Time must tell.

The Changing Constitution

- Why is the Constitution difficult to amend?
- What purposes do the amendments to the Constitution serve?

The Constitution has endured for two centuries as the framework of government. But it has not endured without change. Without change, the Constitution might have become merely a sacred text, stored under glass.

AMENDMENTS: MANY ARE CALLED, FEW ARE CHOSEN

The need for change was recognized by the framers of the Constitution, and the provisions for amendment incorporated into Article V were thought to be "an easy, regular and Constitutional way" to make changes, which would occasionally be necessary because members of Congress "may abuse their power and refuse their consent on that very account . . . to admit to amendments to correct the source of the abuse."[29] Madison made a more balanced defense of the amendment procedure in Article V: "It guards equally against that extreme facility, which would render the Constitution too mutable; and that extreme difficulty, which might perpetuate its discovered faults."[30]

Experience since 1789 raises questions even about Madison's more modest claims. The Constitution has proven to be extremely difficult to amend. In the history of efforts to amend the Constitution, the most appropriate characterization is "many are called, few are chosen." Between 1789 and 1993, 9,746 amendments were formally offered in Congress. Of these, Congress officially proposed only 29, and 27 of these were eventually ratified by the states. But the record is even more severe than that. Since 1791, when the first 10 amendments, the Bill of Rights, were added, only 17 amendments have been adopted. And two of them—Prohibition and its repeal—cancel each other out, so that for all practical purposes, only 15 amendments have been added to the Constitution since 1791. Despite vast changes in American society and its economy, only 12 amendments have been adopted since the Civil War amendments in 1868.

Four methods of amendment are provided for in Article V:

1. Passage in House and Senate by two-thirds vote; then ratification by majority vote of the legislatures of three-fourths (thirty-eight) of the states.
2. Passage in House and Senate by two-thirds vote; then ratification by conventions called for the purpose in three-fourths of the states.

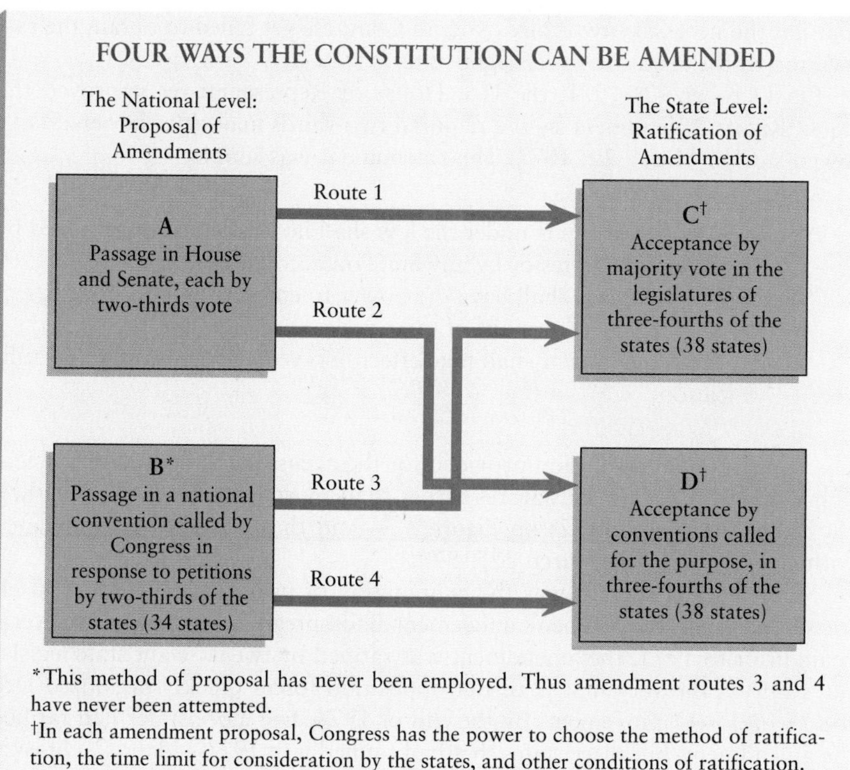

*This method of proposal has never been employed. Thus amendment routes 3 and 4 have never been attempted.

†In each amendment proposal, Congress has the power to choose the method of ratification, the time limit for consideration by the states, and other conditions of ratification.

FIGURE 3.3

3. Passage in a national convention called by Congress in response to petitions by two-thirds of the states; ratification by majority vote of the legislatures of three-fourths of the states.
4. Passage in a national convention, as in (3); then ratification by conventions called for the purpose in three-fourths of the states.

(Figure 3.3 illustrates each of these possible methods.) Since no amendment has ever been proposed by national convention, however, methods (3) and (4) have never been employed. And method (2) has only been employed once (the Twenty-first Amendment, which repealed the Eighteenth, or Prohibition, Amendment). Thus, method (1) has been used for all the others.

Now it should be clear why it has been so difficult to amend the Constitution. The requirement of a two-thirds vote in the House and the Senate means that any proposal for an amendment in Congress can be killed by only 34 senators *or* 136 members of the House. What is more, if the necessary two-thirds vote is obtained, the amendment can still be killed by the refusal or inability of only thirteen state legislatures to ratify it. Since each state has an equal vote regardless of its population, the thirteen holdout states may represent a very small fraction of the total American population.

THE CASE OF THE EQUAL RIGHTS AMENDMENT

The Equal Rights Amendment (ERA) is a case study of a proposed amendment that almost succeeded. In fact, the ERA is one of the very few proposals

Phyllis Schlafly, leader of the group Stop ERA, argued that the ERA was unnecessary and even harmful to women.

Gloria Steinem, one of the founders of the National Organization for Women (NOW), helped organize state-by-state campaigns to persuade state legislatures to pass the ERA.

that got the necessary two-thirds vote in Congress yet failed to obtain the ratification of the requisite thirty-eight states.

On October 12, 1971, the U.S. House of Representatives approved the Equal Rights Amendment by the required two-thirds majority; the Senate followed suit on March 22, 1972. The amendment was simple:

> Sec. 1. Equality of rights under the law shall not be denied or abridged by the United States or by any State on account of sex.
> Sec. 2. The Congress shall have the power to enforce, by appropriate legislation, the provisions of this article.
> Sec. 3. This amendment shall take effect two years after the date of ratification.

The congressional resolution provided for the accustomed method of ratification through the state legislatures rather than by state conventions—method (1) rather than method (2) on Figure 3.3—and that it had to be completed within seven years, by March 22, 1979.

Since the amendment was the culmination of nearly a half-century of efforts, and since the women's movement had spread its struggle for several years prior to 1971, the amendment was ratified by twenty-eight state legislatures during the very first year. But opposition forces quickly organized into the "Stop ERA" movement. By the end of 1974, five more states had ratified the amendment, but three states that had ratified it in 1973—Idaho, Nebraska, and Tennessee—had afterwards voted to rescind their ratification. This posed an unprecedented problem: whether a state legislature had the right to rescind its approval. The Supreme Court refused to deal with this question, insisting that it was a political question to be settled by Congress. If the ERA had been ratified by the thirty-eight-state minimum, Congress would have had to decide whether to respect the rescissions or to count them as ratifications.

This point was rendered moot by events. By the end of 1978, thirty-five state legislatures had ratified the ERA—counting the three rescinding legislatures as ratifiers. But even counting them, the three additional state ratifications necessary to reach thirty-eight became increasingly difficult to get. In each of the remaining fifteen states, the amendment had already been rejected at least once. The only hope of the ERA forces was that the 1978 elections would change the composition of some of those state legislatures. Pinning their hopes on that, the ERA forces turned back to Congress and succeeded in getting an extension of the ratification deadline to June 30, 1982. This was an especially significant victory, because it was the first time Congress had extended the time limit since it began placing time restrictions on ratification in 1917. But this victory in Washington failed to impress any of the fifteen hold-out legislatures. June 30, 1982, came and went, and the ERA was, for the time being at least, laid to rest. It was beaten by the efforts of the "Stop ERA" group and by the emergence of conservatism generally, which had culminated in Ronald Reagan's election as president.[31]

Which Were Chosen? An Analysis of the Twenty-Seven

There is more to the amending difficulties than the politics of campaigning and voting. It would appear that only a limited number of changes needed by society can actually be made through the Constitution. Although we shall see that the ERA fits the pattern of successful amendments, most efforts to amend the Constitution have failed because they were simply attempts to use the Constitution as an alternative to legislation for dealing directly with a public problem. A review of the successful amendments will provide two insights: First, it will give us some understanding of the conditions underlying successful amendments; and second, it will reveal a great deal about what constitutionalism means.

The purpose of the ten amendments in the Bill of Rights was basically structural, to give each of the three branches clearer and more restricted boundaries. The First Amendment clarified the jurisdiction of Congress. Although the powers of Congress under Article I, Section 8, would not have justified laws regulating religion, speech, and the like, the First Amendment made this limitation explicit: "Congress shall make no law. . . . " The Second, Third, and Fourth amendments similarly spelled out specific limits on the executive branch. This was seen as a necessity given the abuses of executive power Americans had endured under British rule.

The Fifth, Sixth, Seventh, and Eighth amendments contain some of the most important safeguards for individual citizens against the arbitrary exercise of government power. And these amendments sought to accomplish their goal by defining the judicial branch more concretely and clearly than had been done in Article III of the Constitution. Table 3.2 analyzes the ten amendments included in the Bill of Rights.

Five of the seventeen amendments adopted since 1791 are directly concerned with the expansion of the electorate and, thus, political equality (see Table 3.3). The Founders were unable to establish a national electorate with uniform voting qualifications. They decided to evade it by providing in the

TABLE 3.2

THE BILL OF RIGHTS: ANALYSIS OF ITS PROVISIONS

Amendment	Purpose
I	*Limits on Congress:* Congress is not to make any law establishing a religion or abridging speech, press, assembly, or petition freedoms.
II, III, IV	*Limits on Executive:* The executive branch is not to infringe on the right of people to keep arms (II), is not to arbitrarily take houses for a militia (III), and is not to engage in the search or seizure of evidence without a court warrant swearing to belief in the probable existence of a crime (IV).
V, VI, VII, VIII	*Limits on Courts:* The courts are not to hold trials for serious offenses without provision for a grand jury (V), a petit (trial) jury (VII), a speedy trial (VI), presentation of charges, confrontation of hostile witnesses (VI), immunity from testimony against oneself (V), and immunity from trial more than once for the same offense (V). Neither bail nor punishment can be excessive (VIII), and no property can be taken without just compensation (V).
IX, X	*Limits on National Government:* All rights not enumerated are reserved to the states or the people.

AMENDING THE CONSTITUTION TO EXPAND THE ELECTORATE

Amendment	Purpose	Year proposed	Year adopted
XV	Extended voting rights to all races	1869	1870
XIX	Extended voting rights to women	1919	1920
XXIII	Extended voting rights to residents of the District of Columbia	1960	1961
XXIV	Extended voting rights to all classes by abolition of poll taxes	1962	1964
XXVI	Extended voting rights to citizens aged 18 and over	1971	1971*

*The Twenty-sixth Amendment holds the record for speed of adoption. It was proposed on March 23, 1971, and adopted on July 5, 1971.

TABLE 3.3

final draft of Article I, Section 2, that eligibility to vote in a national election would be the same as "the Qualification requisite for Elector of the most numerous branch of the state Legislature." Article I, Section 4, added that Congress could alter state regulations as to the "Times, Places, and Manner of holding Elections for Senators and Representatives." Nevertheless, this meant that any important *expansion* of the American electorate would almost certainly require a constitutional amendment.

Six more amendments are also electoral in nature, although they are not concerned directly with voting rights and the expansion of the electorate (see Table 3.4). These six amendments are concerned with the elective offices themselves (the Twentieth, Twenty-second, and Twenty-fifth) or with the relationship between elective offices and the electorate (the Twelfth, Fourteenth, and Seventeenth). One could conclude that one effect was the enhancement of democracy.

Another five amendments have sought to expand or to delimit the powers of the national and state governments (see Table 3.5).[32] The Eleventh Amendment protected the states from suits by private individuals and took away from the federal courts any power to take suits by private individuals of one state (or a foreign country) against another state. The other three amendments in Table 3.5 are obviously designed to reduce state power (Thirteenth), to reduce state power and expand national power (Fourteenth), and to expand national power (Sixteenth). The Twenty-seventh put a limit on Congress's ability to raise its own salary.

The one missing amendment underscores the meaning of the rest: the Eighteenth, or Prohibition, Amendment. This is the only instance in which the country tried to *legislate* by constitutional amendment. In other words, it is the only amendment that was designed to deal directly with some substantive social problem. And it was the only amendment ever to have been repealed. Two other amendments—the Thirteenth, which abolished slavery, and the Sixteenth, which established the power to levy an income tax—can be said to have had the effect of legislation. But the purpose of the Thirteenth was to restrict the power of the states by forever forbidding them to treat any

TABLE 3.4

AMENDING THE CONSTITUTION TO CHANGE THE RELATIONSHIP BETWEEN ELECTED OFFICES AND THE ELECTORATE

Amendment	Purpose	Year proposed	Year adopted
XII	Provided separate ballot for vice president in the electoral college	1803	1804
XIV	(Part 1) Provided a national definition of citizenship*	1866	1868
XVII	Provided direct election of senators	1912	1913
XX	Eliminated "lame duck" session of Congress	1932	1933
XXII	Limited presidential term	1947	1951
XXV	Provided presidential succession in case of disability	1965	1967

*In defining *citizenship,* the Fourteenth Amendment actually provided the constitutional basis for expanding the electorate to include all races, women, and residents of the District of Columbia. Only the "eighteen-year-olds' amendment" should have been necessary, since it changed the definition of citizenship. The fact that additional amendments were required following the Fourteenth suggests that voting is not considered an inherent right of U.S. citizenship. Instead it is viewed as a privilege.

human being as property. As for the Sixteenth, it is certainly true that income tax legislation followed immediately; nevertheless, the amendment concerns itself strictly with establishing the power of Congress to enact such legislation. The legislation came later; and if down the line a majority in Congress

TABLE 3.5

AMENDING THE CONSTITUTION TO EXPAND OR LIMIT THE POWER OF GOVERNMENT

Amendment	Purpose	Year proposed	Year adopted
XI	Limited jurisdiction of federal courts over suits involving the states	1794	1798
XIII	Eliminated slavery and eliminated the right of states to allow property in persons	1865*	1865
XIV	(Part 2) Applied due process of Bill of Rights to the states	1866	1868
XVI	Established national power to tax incomes	1909	1913
XXVII	Limited Congress's power to raise its own salary	1789	1992

*The Thirteenth Amendment was proposed January 31, 1865, and adopted less than a year later, on December 18, 1865.

had wanted to abolish the income tax, they could also have done this by legislation rather than through the arduous path of a constitutional amendment repealing the income tax.

All of this points to the principle underlying the twenty-five existing amendments: All are concerned with the structure or composition of government. This is consistent with the dictionary, which defines *constitution* as the makeup or composition of something. And it is consistent with the concept of a constitution as "higher law," because the whole point and purpose of a higher law is to establish a framework within which government and the process of making ordinary law can take place. Even those who would have preferred more changes in the Constitution would have to agree that there is great wisdom in this principle. A constitution ought to enable legislation and public policies to take place, but it should not determine what that legislation or those public policies ought to be.

For those whose hopes for change center on the Constitution, it must be emphasized that the amendment route to social change is, and always will be, extremely limited. Through a constitution it is possible to establish a working structure of government; and through a constitution it is possible to establish basic rights of citizens by placing limitations on the powers of that government. Once these things have been accomplished, the real problem is how to extend rights to those people who do not already enjoy them. Of course, the Constitution cannot enforce itself. But it can and does have a real influence on everyday life because a right or an obligation set forth in the Constitution can become a cause of action in the hands of an otherwise powerless person.

Private property is an excellent example. Property is one of the most fundamental and well-established rights in the United States; but it is well established not because it is recognized in so many words in the Constitution, but because legislatures and courts have made it a crime for anyone, including the government, to trespass or to take away property without compensation.

A constitution is good if it produces the cause of action that leads to good legislation, good case law, and appropriate police behavior. A constitution cannot eliminate power. But its principles can be a citizen's dependable defense against the abuse of power.

Reflections on Liberty, Equality, and Democracy

> ➤ Did the framers value liberty, equality, and democracy? Why or why not?

The Constitution's framers placed individual liberty ahead of all other political values. Their concern for liberty led many of the framers to distrust both democracy and equality. They feared that democracy could degenerate into a majority tyranny in which the populace, perhaps led by a rabble-rousing demagogue, would trample on liberty. As to equality, the framers were products of their time and place; our contemporary ideas of racial and gender equality would have been foreign to them. The framers were concerned primarily about another manifestation of equality: They feared that those with-

In *Liberty Displaying the Arts and Sciences* by Samuel Jennings, Lady Liberty offers the promise of learning to a group of blacks. Americans idealized the principle of liberty, even though the young nation did not offer liberty to all of its people.

out property or position might be driven by what some called a "leveling spirit" to infringe upon liberty in the name of greater economic or social equality. Indeed, the framers believed that this leveling spirit was most likely to produce demagoguery and majority tyranny. As a result, the basic structure of the Constitution—separated powers, internal checks and balances, and federalism—was designed to safeguard liberty, and the Bill of Rights created further safeguards for liberty. At the same time, however, many of the Constitution's other key provisions, such as indirect election of senators and the president, as well as the appointment of judges for life, were designed to limit democracy and, hence, the threat of majority tyranny.

By championing liberty, however, the framers virtually guaranteed that democracy and even a measure of equality would sooner or later evolve in the United States. For liberty inevitably leads to the growth of political activity and the expansion of political participation. In James Madison's famous phrase, "Liberty is to faction as air is to fire."[33] Where they have liberty, more and more people, groups, and interests will almost inevitably engage in politics and gradually overcome whatever restrictions might have been placed upon participation. This is precisely what happened in the early years of the American Republic. During the Jeffersonian period, political parties formed. During the Jacksonian period, many state suffrage restrictions were removed and popular participation greatly expanded. Over time, liberty is conducive to democracy.

Liberty does not guarantee that everyone will be equal. It does, however, reduce the threat of inequality in one very important way. Historically, the greatest inequalities of wealth, power, and privilege have arisen where governments have used their power to allocate status and opportunity among individuals or groups. From the aristocracies of the early modern period to the *nomenklatura* of twentieth-century despotisms, the most extreme cases of inequality are associated with the most tyrannical regimes. In the United States, however, by promoting a democratic politics, over time liberty unleashed forces that militated against inequality. As a result, over the past two hundred years, groups that have learned to use the political process have achieved important economic and social gains.

When the framers chose liberty as the basis for a constitution, it wasn't such a bad place to start.

Summary

Political conflicts between the colonies and England, and among competing groups within the colonies, led to the first founding as expressed by the Declaration of Independence. The first constitution, the Articles of Confederation, was adopted one year later (1777). Under this document, the states retained their sovereignty and the central government had few powers and no means of enforcing its will. The national government's weakness led to the Constitution of 1787, the second founding.

The Constitution's framers sought, first, to fashion a new government sufficiently powerful to promote commerce and protect property from radical state legislatures. Second, the framers sought to bring an end to the "excessive democracy" of the state and national governments under the Articles of Confederation. Third, the framers introduced mechanisms that helped secure popular consent for the new government. Finally, the framers made certain that their new government would not itself pose a threat to liberty and property.

The struggle for the ratification of the Constitution pitted the Antifederalists, who thought the proposed new government would be too powerful, against the Federalists, who supported the Constitution and were able to secure its ratification after a nationwide political debate.

This chapter also sought to gain an appreciation of constitutionalism itself. In addition to describing how the Constitution is formally amended, we analyzed the twenty-seven amendments in order to determine what they had in common, contrasting them with the hundreds of amendments that were offered but never adopted. We found that with the exception of the two Prohibition amendments, all amendments were oriented toward some change in the framework or structure of government. The Prohibition Amendment was the only adopted amendment that sought to legislate by constitutional means.

FOR FURTHER READING

Beard, Charles. *An Economic Interpretation of the Constitution of the United States*. New York: Macmillan, 1913.

Cohler, Anne M. *Montesquieu's Politics and the Spirit of American Constitutionalism*. Lawrence: University Press of Kansas, 1988.

Farrand, Max, ed. *The Records of the Federal Convention of 1787*. 4 vols. New Haven, CT: Yale University Press, 1966.

Hamilton, Alexander, James Madison, and John Jay. *The Federalist Papers*. Edited by Isaac Kramnick. New York: Viking, 1987.

Jensen, Merrill. *The Articles of Confederation*. Madison: University of Wisconsin Press, 1963.

Lipset, Seymour M. *The First New Nation: The United States in Historical and Comparative Perspective.* New York: Basic Books, 1963.

McDonald, Forrest. *The Formation of the American Republic.* New York: Penguin, 1967.

Main, Jackson Turner. *The Social Structure of Revolutionary America.* Princeton, NJ: Princeton University Press, 1965.

Rossiter, Clinton. *1787: Grand Convention.* New York: Macmillan, 1966.

Storing, Herbert, ed. *The Complete Anti-Federalist.* 7 vols. Chicago: University of Chicago Press, 1981.

Wills, Gary. *Explaining America.* New York: Penguin, 1982.

Wood, Gordon S. *The Creation of the American Republic.* New York: Norton, 1982.

STUDY OUTLINE

The First Founding: Interests and Conflicts

1. In an effort to alleviate financial problems, including considerable debt, the British government sought to raise revenue by taxing its North American colonies. This energized New England merchants and southern planters, who then organized colonial resistance.
2. Colonial resistance set into motion a cycle of provocation and reaction that resulted in the First Continental Congress and eventually the Declaration of Independence.
3. The Declaration of Independence was an attempt to identify and articulate a history and set of principles that might help to forge national unity.
4. The colonies established the Articles of Confederation and Perpetual Union. Under the Articles, the central government was based entirely in Congress, yet Congress had little power.

The Second Founding: From Compromise to Constitution

1. Concern over America's precarious position in the international community coupled with domestic concern that "radical forces" had too much influence in Congress and in state governments led to the Annapolis Convention in 1786.
2. Shays's Rebellion in Massachusetts provided critics of the Articles of Confederation with the evidence they needed to push for constitutional revision.
3. Recognizing fundamental flaws in the Articles, the delegates to the Philadelphia Convention abandoned the plan to revise the Articles and committed themselves to a second founding.
4. Conflict between large and small states over the issue of representation in Congress led to the Great Compromise, which created a bicameral legislature based on two different principles of representation.
5. The Three-fifths Compromise addressed the question of slavery by apportioning the seats in the House of Representatives according to a population in which five slaves would count as three persons.

The Constitution

1. The new government was to be strong enough to defend the nation's interests internationally, promote commerce and protect property, and prevent the threat posed by "excessive democracy."
2. The House of Representatives was designed to be directly responsible to the people in order to encourage popular consent for the Constitution. The Senate was designed to guard against the potential for excessive democracy in the House.
3. The Constitution grants Congress important and influential powers, but any power not specifically enumerated in its text is reserved specifically to the states.
4. The framers hoped to create a presidency with energy—one that would be capable of timely and decisive action to deal with public issues and problems.
5. The establishment of the Supreme Court reflected the framers' preoccupations with nationalizing governmental power and checking radical democratic impulses while guarding against potential interference with liberty and property from the new national government itself.
6. Various provisions in the Constitution addressed the framers' concern with national unity and power. Such provisions included clauses promoting reciprocity among states.
7. Procedures for amending the Constitution are provided in Article V. These procedures are so difficult that amendments are quite rare in American history.
8. To guard against possible misuse of national government power, the framers incorporated the principles of the separation of powers and federalism, as well as a Bill of Rights, in the Constitution.
9. The separation of powers was based on the principle that power must be used to balance power.

10. Although the framers' move to federalism was a step toward greater centralization of national government power, they retained state power by devising a system of two sovereigns.
11. The Bill of Rights was adopted as the first ten amendments to the Constitution in 1791.

THE FIGHT FOR RATIFICATION

1. The struggle for ratification was carried out in thirteen separate campaigns—one in each state.
2. The Federalists supported the Constitution and a stronger national government. The Antifederalists, on the other hand, preferred a more decentralized system of government and fought against ratification.
3. The principles about which Americans argued at the founding reflected competing interests.
4. Federalists and Antifederalists had differing views regarding issues such as representation and the prevention of tyranny.
5. Antifederalist criticisms helped to shape the Constitution and the national government, but it was the Federalist vision of America that triumphed.

THE CHANGING CONSTITUTION

1. Provisions for amending the Constitution, incorporated into Article V, have proven to be difficult criteria to meet. Relatively few amendments have been made to the Constitution.
2. Most of the amendments to the Constitution deal with the structure or composition of the government.

REFLECTIONS ON LIBERTY, EQUALITY, AND DEMOCRACY

1. The Constitution's framers placed individual liberty ahead of all other political values. But by emphasizing liberty, the framers virtually guaranteed that democracy and equality would evolve in the United States.

PRACTICE QUIZ

1. In the Revolutionary struggles, which of the following groups was allied with the New England merchants?
   a. artisans
   b. southern planters
   c. western speculators
   d. laborers
2. How did the British attempt to raise revenue in the North American colonies?
   a. income tax
   b. taxes on commerce
   c. expropriation and government sale of land
   d. government asset sales
3. The first governing document in the United States was
   a. the Declaration of Independence.
   b. the Articles of Confederation and Perpetual Union.
   c. the Constitution.
   d. none of the above.
4. Which state's proposal embodied a principle of representing states in the Congress according to their size and wealth?
   a. Connecticut
   b. Maryland
   c. New Jersey
   d. Virginia
5. Where was the execution of laws conducted under the Articles of Confederation?
   a. the presidency
   b. the Congress
   c. the states
   d. the expanding federal bureaucracy
6. Which of the following was *not* a reason that the Articles of Confederation seemed too weak?
   a. the lack of a single voice in international affairs
   b. the power of radical forces in the Congress
   c. the impending "tyranny of the states"
   d. the power of radical forces in several states
7. What mechanism was instituted in the Congress to guard against "excessive democracy"?
   a. bicameralism
   b. staggered Senate terms
   c. appointment of senators for long terms
   d. all of the above
8. Which of the following best describes the Supreme Court as understood by the Founders?
   a. the highest court of the national government
   b. arbiter of disputes within the Congress
   c. a figurehead commission of elders
   d. a supreme court of the nation and its states
9. Which of the following were the Antifederalists most concerned with?
   a. interstate commerce
   b. the protection of property
   c. the distinction between principles and interests
   d. the potential for tyranny in the central government
10. The draft constitution that was introduced at the start of the Constitutional Convention was authored by
    a. Edmund Randolph.
    b. Thomas Jefferson.
    c. James Madison.
    d. George Clinton.

CRITICAL THINKING QUESTIONS

1. In many ways, the framers of the Constitution created a central government much stronger than the government created by the Articles of Confederation. Still, the framers seem to have taken great care to limit the power of the central government in various ways. Describe the ways in which the central government under the Constitution was stronger than the central government under the Articles. Describe the ways in which the framers limited the national government's power under the Constitution. Why might the framers have placed such limits on the government they had just created?
2. Recount and explain the ideological, geographical, social, and political conflicts both at the time of the American Revolution and at the time of the writing of the United States Constitution. What experiences and interests informed the forces involved in each of these conflicts? How did the framers resolve these conflicts? Were there any conflicts left unresolved?

KEY TERMS

Antifederalists those who favored strong state governments and a weak national government and who were opponents of the constitution proposed at the American Constitutional Convention of 1787. (p. 91)

Articles of Confederation America's first written constitution, adopted by the Continental Congress in 1777 and which served as the basis for America's national government until 1789. (p. 74)

bicameral having a legislative assembly composed of two chambers or houses. (p. 83)

Bill of Rights the first ten amendments to the U.S. Constitution, ratified in 1791; they ensure certain rights and liberties to the people. (p. 89)

checks and balances mechanisms through which each branch of government is able to participate in and influence the activities of the other branches. Major examples include the presidential veto power over congressional legislation, the power of the Senate to approve presidential appointments, and judicial review of congressional enactments. (p. 83)

elastic clause Article I, Section 8, of the Constitution (also known as the necessary and proper clause), which enumerates the powers of Congress and provides Congress with the authority to make all laws "necessary and proper" to carry them out. (p. 85)

electoral college the presidential electors from each state who meet after the popular election to cast ballots for president and vice president. (p. 83)

expressed powers specific powers granted to Congress under Article I, Section 8, of the Constitution. (p. 85)

federalism a system of government in which power is divided, by a constitution, between a central government and regional governments. (p. 89)

Federalist Papers a series of essays written by James Madison, Alexander Hamilton, and John Jay supporting the ratification of the Constitution. (p. 93)

Federalists those who favored a strong national government and supported the constitution proposed at the American Constitutional Convention of 1787. (p. 91)

Great Compromise the agreement reached at the Constitutional Convention of 1787 that gave each state an equal number of senators regardless of its population, but linked representation in the House of Representatives to population. (p. 80)

judicial review the power of the courts to declare actions of the legislative and executive branches invalid or unconstitutional. The Supreme Court asserted this power in *Marbury v. Madison*. (p. 87)

limited government a government whose powers are defined and limited by a constitution. (p. 96)

New Jersey Plan a framework for the Constitution, introduced by William Paterson, which called for equal state representation in the national legislature regardless of population. (p. 79)

separation of powers the division of governmental power among several institutions that must cooperate in decision making. (p. 89)

supremacy clause Article VI of the Constitution, which states that laws passed by the national government and all treaties are the supreme law of the land and superior to all laws adopted by any state or any subdivision. (p. 88)

Three-Fifths Compromise the agreement reached at the Constitutional Convention of 1787 that stipulated that for purposes of the apportionment of congressional seats, every slave would be counted as three-fifths of a person. (p. 81)

tyranny oppressive and unjust government that employs cruel and unjust use of power and authority. (p. 95)

Virginia Plan a framework for the Constitution, introduced by Edmund Randolph, which called for representation in the national legislature based upon the population of each state. (p. 79)

4

Federalism

★ The Federal Framework

How does federalism limit the power of the national government?

What is the influence of federalism on governance?

How strong a role have the states traditionally had in the federal framework?

★ Who Does What? The Changing Federal Framework

Why did the balance of responsibility shift toward the national government in the 1930s?

What means does the national government use to control the actions of the states?

How has the relationship between the national government and the states evolved over the last several decades?

What methods have been employed to give more control back to the states?

If you live in Huntington, West Virginia, you might decide to spend a Saturday night cruising in a friend's new car; in Fargo, North Dakota, the same weekend plans would get you a ticket. And if you decide to take your car out to the highway, in Montana during the day you could go as fast as you like, but if you live in New York State, you would risk getting a speeding ticket if you drove over 65 miles per hour.

Driving is just one of the many areas in which where you live affects what you can do and what the government does. If you lose your job in New Hampshire, the highest level of unemployment insurance benefits you can get is $196 per week; in neighboring Massachusetts, you could receive as much as $487 per week. By giving the states power to set benefit levels on such social policies as unemployment insurance and welfare, the American system of federalism allows substantial inequalities to exist across the country. Likewise, what kinds of classes are offered in high schools, the taxes citizens pay for public schools, and the tuition you pay if you attend a state university or college are all affected by where you live. In fact, most of the rules and regulations that Americans face in their daily lives are set by state and local governments.[1]

State and local governments play such important roles in the lives of American citizens because the United States is a federal system in which other levels of government are assigned considerable responsibility. The enduring significance of state and local governments reflects the Founders' mistrust of centralized power and the long-standing preference of Americans for local self-government as the best form of democracy. Such local self-government has meant that personal liberty has varied substantially from state to state. As we saw in Chapter 2, before the 1960s, southern states used their powers of local self-rule to deny basic freedoms to their black citizens. In the two hundred years since the Founding, struggles to realize the ideas of liberty and equality for all citizens have expanded the power of the federal government and reduced the powers of the states. Especially since the New Deal in the 1930s, the national government has played a much more prominent role in protecting liberty and promoting equality. In recent years, however, citizens have become more mistrustful of government, and especially of the national government. Once again we are facing questions about whether the national government is too powerful and whether the institutions of government in Washington should step aside and let the states take on more responsibility. This is an old debate in American politics; it traces back to the Founding, when the Federalists argued in favor of a stronger national government and the Antifederalists opposed them.

The debate about "who should do what" remains one of the most important discussions in American politics. Much is at stake in how authority is divided up among the different levels of government. The debate about how responsibilities should be sorted out among levels of government is often informed by conflicting principles and differing evaluations about what each level of government is best suited to do. For example, many people believe that the United States needs national goals and standards to ensure equal opportunities for citizens across the nation; others contend that state and local governments can do a better job at most things because they are closer to the people. For this reason the states have been called "laboratories of democracy": they can experiment with different policies to find measures that best meet the needs and desires of their citizens.

But decisions about who should do what are also highly political. Groups that want government to do more to promote equality frequently prefer a stronger national role. After all, it was the national government that first implemented the civil rights policies in the 1960s and guaranteed civil liberties in all states. Groups that want less government, on the other hand, often favor shifting power to the states or localities. Many conservatives oppose a strong national role because they believe that nationwide regulations infringe on individual liberties. Furthermore, different interest groups argue for placing policy responsibilities at the level of government that they find easiest to influence. And politicians in national, state, and local governments often have quite different views about which level of government should be expected to do what.

Thus, both political principles and interests influence decisions about how power and responsibility should be sorted out across the levels of government. At various points in history, Americans have given different answers to questions about the appropriate role of national, state, and local governments. National power increased as the national government initiated new social and regulatory policies during the New Deal of the 1930s and the Great Society of the 1960s. But in the 1970s and 1980s, states began to claim more authority over these policies. The effort to increase state responsibility and reduce the national role received a boost when the Republicans took over Congress in 1995. With the support of a growing number of Republican governors, congressional Republicans advocated a strategy of **devolution,** in which the national government would grant the states more authority over a range of policies.

This chapter is divided into two sections. In the first section, we will examine the development of the principle of federalism as interpreted by the Supreme Court. Then we will look at how the federal framework has changed in recent years, and finally we will examine the growth of the national government's role, as well as recent efforts to shift more power back to the states.

The Federal Framework

- ➤ How does federalism limit the power of the national government?
- ➤ What is the influence of federalism on governance?
- ➤ How strong a role have the states traditionally had in the federal framework?

The Constitution has had its most fundamental influence on American life through federalism. **Federalism** can be defined with misleading ease and simplicity as the division of powers and functions between the national government and the state governments. With federalism, the framers sought to limit the national government by creating a second layer of state governments. American federalism recognized two sovereigns in the original Constitution and reinforced the principle in the Bill of Rights by granting a few **"expressed powers"** to the national government and reserving all the rest to the states. Tracing the influence of federalism is not so simple, but we can make the task easier by breaking it down into three distinct forms.

First, federalism sought to limit national power by creating two sovereigns—the national government and the state governments. This system was called **dual federalism**. At the time of the nation's founding, the states had already existed as former colonies and, for nearly thirteen years, as virtually autonomous units under the Articles of Confederation. The Constitution imposed a stronger national government upon the states. But even after the ratification of the Constitution, the states continued to be more important than the national government. For nearly a century and a half, virtually all of the fundamental policies governing the lives of American citizens were made by the state legislatures, not by Congress.

The novelty of this arrangement can be appreciated by noting that each of the major European countries at that time had a *unitary* government: a single national government with national ministries; a national police force; and a single, national code of laws for crimes, commerce, public works, education, and all other areas.

Second, that same federalism specifically restrained the power of the national government over the economy. The Constitution gave the Congress the responsibility to regulate interstate commerce. However, the Supreme Court defined "interstate commerce" in narrow terms that prevented Congress from regulating local economic conditions. The federalist structure of strong states and a weak national government prevailed until 1937, when the Supreme

Court redefined "interstate commerce" to permit the national government to regulate local economic conditions.

Third, since federalism freed the states to make so many important policies according to the wishes of their own citizens, states were also free to be different from one another. Federalism allowed a great deal of variation from state to state in the rights enjoyed by citizens, in the roles played by governments, and in definitions of crime and its punishment. During the past half-century, Americans have moved toward greater national uniformity in state laws and in the rights enjoyed by citizens. Nevertheless, as we shall see, federalism continues even today to permit significant differences among the states.

Each of these consequences of federalism will be considered in its turn. The first two—the creating of two sovereigns and the restraining of the economic power of the national government—will be treated in this chapter, along with an assessment of their continuing influence. The third, even though it is an aspect of federalism, will be an important part of the next chapter, because it relates to the framework of individual rights and liberties.

RESTRAINING NATIONAL POWER WITH DUAL FEDERALISM, 1789–1937

As we have noted, the Constitution created two layers of government: the national government and the state governments. The consequences of this dual federalism are fundamental to the American system of government in theory and in practice; they have meant that states have done most of the fundamental governing. For evidence, look at Table 4.1. It lists the major types of public policies by which Americans were governed for the first century and a half under the Constitution. We call it the "traditional system" because it prevailed for three-quarters of American history and because it closely approximates the intentions of the framers of the Constitution.

In 1815, President James Madison called for a federally funded program of "internal improvements," which during the first half of the nineteenth century was one of the few policy roles for the national government. By improving transportation through the construction of roads and canals, the government fostered the growth of the market economy.

TABLE 4.1

THE FEDERAL SYSTEM: SPECIALIZATION OF GOVERNMENTAL FUNCTIONS IN THE TRADITIONAL SYSTEM (1800–1933)

National government policies (domestic)	State government policies	Local government policies
Internal improvements	Property laws (including slavery)	Adaptation of state laws to local conditions ("variances")
Subsidies	Estate and inheritance laws	Public works
Tariffs	Commerce laws	Contracts for public works
Public lands disposal	Banking and credit laws	Licensing of public accommodations
Patents	Corporate laws	Assessible improvements
Currency	Insurance laws	Basic public services
	Family laws	
	Morality laws	
	Public health laws	
	Education laws	
	General penal laws	
	Eminent domain laws	
	Construction codes	
	Land-use laws	
	Water and mineral laws	
	Criminal procedure laws	
	Electoral and political parties laws	
	Local government laws	
	Civil service laws	
	Occupations and professions laws	

Under the traditional system, the national government was quite small by comparison both to the state governments and to the governments of other Western nations. Not only was it smaller than most governments of that time, it was actually very narrowly specialized in the functions it performed. The national government built or sponsored the construction of roads, canals, and bridges (internal improvements). It provided cash subsidies to shippers and shipbuilders and distributed free or low-priced public land to encourage western settlement and business ventures. It placed relatively heavy taxes on imported goods (tariffs), not only to raise revenues but to protect "infant industries" from competition from the more advanced European enterprises. It protected patents and provided for a common currency, also to encourage and facilitate enterprises and to expand markets.

What do these functions of the national government reveal? First, virtually all its functions were aimed at assisting commerce. It is quite appropriate to refer to the traditional American system as a "commercial republic." Second, virtually none of the national government's policies directly coerced citizens. The emphasis of governmental programs was on assistance, promo-

One of the many areas in which state laws govern is in determining the minimum age for drivers. Gail and Russell Bowen, whose seventeen-year-old daughter died in a car wreck, testify before the Kentucky state senate in favor of a graduated licensing program for young drivers.

tion, and encouragement—the allocation of land or capital where they were insufficiently available for economic development.

Meanwhile, state legislatures were actively involved in economic regulation during the nineteenth century. In the United States, then and now, private property exists only in state laws and state court decisions regarding property, trespass, and real estate. American capitalism took its form from state property and trespass laws, as well as from state laws and court decisions regarding contracts, markets, credit, banking, incorporation, and insurance. Laws concerning slavery were a subdivision of property law in states where slavery existed. The practice of important professions, such as law and medicine, was and is illegal, except as provided for by state law. Marriage, divorce, and the birth or adoption of a child have always been regulated by state law. To educate or not to educate a child has been a decision governed more by state laws than by parents, and not at all by national law. It is important to note also that virtually all the criminal laws—regarding everything from trespass to murder—have been state laws. Most of the criminal laws adopted by Congress are concerned with the District of Columbia and other federal territories.

All this (and more, as shown in the middle column of Table 4.1) demonstrates without any question that most of the fundamental governing in the United States was done by the states. The contrast between national and state policies, as shown by Table 4.1, demonstrates the difference in the power vested in each. The list of items in the middle column could actually have been made longer. Moreover, each item on the list is a category of law that fills many volumes of statutes and court decisions.

This contrast between national and state governments is all the more impressive because it is basically what the framers of the Constitution intended. Since the 1930s, the national government has expanded into local and intrastate matters, far beyond what anyone would have foreseen in 1790, 1890, or even in the 1920s. But this significant expansion of the national government did not alter the basic framework. The national government has become much larger, but the states have continued to be central to the American system of government.

Here lies probably the most important point of all: The fundamental impact of federalism on the way the United States is governed comes not from any particular provision of the Constitution but from the framework itself, which has determined the flow of government functions and, through that, the political development of the country. By allowing state governments to do most of the fundamental governing, the Constitution saved the national government from many policy decisions that might have proven too divisive for a large and very young country. There is no doubt that if the Constitution had provided for a unitary rather than a federal system, the war over slavery would have come in 1789 or 1809 rather than in 1860; and if it had come that early, the South might very well have seceded and established a separate and permanent slaveholding nation.

In helping the national government remain small and aloof from the most divisive issues of the day, federalism contributed significantly to the political stability of the nation, even as the social, economic, and political systems of many of the states and regions of the country were undergoing tremendous, profound, and sometimes violent, change.[2] As we shall see, some important aspects of federalism have changed, but the federal framework has survived two centuries and a devastating civil war.

Federalism as a Limitation on the National Government's Power

Having created the national government, and recognizing the potential for abuse of power, the states sought through federalism to constrain the national government. The "traditional system" of a weak national government prevailed for over a century despite economic forces favoring its expansion and despite Supreme Court cases giving a pro-national interpretation to Article I, Section 8, of the Constitution.

That article delegates to Congress the power "to regulate commerce with foreign nations, and among the several States and with the Indian tribes." This **commerce clause** was consistently interpreted *in favor* of national power by the Supreme Court for most of the nineteenth century. The first and most important case favoring national power over the economy was *McCulloch v. Maryland*.[3] This case involved the question of whether Congress had the power to charter a national bank, since such an explicit grant of power was nowhere to be found in Article I, Section 8. Chief Justice John Marshall answered that the power could be "implied" from other powers that were expressly delegated to Congress, such as the "powers to lay and collect taxes; to borrow money; to regulate commerce; and to declare and conduct a war."

The constitutional authority for what is known as the **implied powers doctrine** is a clause in Article I, Section 8, that enables Congress "to make all laws which shall be necessary and proper for carrying into Execution the foregoing powers." By allowing Congress to use this **necessary and proper**

clause to interpret its delegated powers expansively, the Supreme Court created the potential for an unprecedented increase in national government power. Marshall also concluded that whenever a state law conflicted with a federal law (as in the case of *McCulloch v. Maryland*), the state law would be deemed invalid since the Constitution states that "the laws of the United States . . . 'shall be the supreme law of the land.' " Both parts of this great case are "pro-national," yet Congress did not immediately seek to expand the policies of the national government.

Another major case, *Gibbons v. Ogden* in 1824, reinforced this nationalistic interpretation of the Constitution. The important but relatively narrow issue was whether the state of New York could grant a monopoly to Robert Fulton's steamboat company to operate an exclusive service between New York and New Jersey. Chief Justice Marshall argued that New York State did not have the power to grant this particular monopoly. In order to reach this decision, it was necessary for Marshall to define what Article I, Section 8, meant by "commerce among the several states." He insisted that the definition was "comprehensive," extending to "every species of commercial intercourse." He did say that this comprehensiveness was limited "to that commerce which concerns more states than one," giving rise to what later came to be called "interstate commerce." *Gibbons* is important because it established the supremacy of the national government in all matters affecting interstate commerce.[4] But what would remain uncertain during several decades of constitutional discourse was the precise meaning of interstate commerce.

Article I, Section 8, backed by the implied powers decision in *McCulloch* and by the broad definition of "interstate commerce" in *Gibbons*, was a source of power for the national government as long as Congress sought to facilitate commerce through subsidies, services, and land grants. But later in the nineteenth century, when the national government sought to use those powers to *regulate* the economy rather than merely to promote economic development, federalism and the concept of interstate commerce began to operate as restraints on, rather than sources of, national power.

Any effort of the national government to regulate commerce in such areas as fraud, the production of impure goods, the use of child labor, or the existence of dangerous working conditions or long hours was declared unconstitutional by the Supreme Court as a violation of the concept of interstate commerce. Such legislation meant that the federal government was entering the factory and the workplace—local areas—and was attempting to regulate goods that had not passed into commerce. To enter these local workplaces was to exercise police power—the power reserved to the states for the protection of the health, safety, and morals of their citizens. No one questioned the power of the national government to regulate businesses that intrinsically involved interstate commerce, such as railroads, gas pipelines, and waterway transportation. But well into the twentieth century, the Supreme Court used the concept of interstate commerce as a barrier against most efforts by Congress to regulate local conditions.

This aspect of federalism was alive and well during an epoch of tremendous economic development, the period between the Civil War and the 1930s. It gave the American economy a freedom from federal government control that closely approximated the ideal of free enterprise. The economy

AMERICAN POLITICAL CULTURE

Federalism and Welfare Reform

Why were two of the Senate's staunchest conservative Republicans, Alfonse D'Amato of New York and Phil Gramm of Texas, shouting angrily at each other at a Republican welfare reform conference in June 1995? The answer has to do with the difficulty of putting federalism into practice. In principle, conservatives tend to agree on the virtue of federalism: Wherever possible, let the states, rather than the national government, govern. In the case of welfare reform, this principle has inspired Republican calls to transform the patchwork of federal antipoverty programs and regulations into block grants that would allow states to decide how to spend the money. But when it comes to specific legislation that would alter and limit patterns of revenue flow from the national government to the states, even stalwart conservatives can disagree about how to write federalism into law. Such has been the case with proposals to reform the largest government antipoverty program, Medicaid, which cost U.S. taxpayers about $160 billion in 1994. As tighter limits were put on Medicaid spending, the tug-of-war between the states threatened to tear apart the conservative congressional coalition that agreed on so much in 1995.

Federal Medicaid funds are allocated to states according to a complex formula. Wealthier states such as Massachusetts or California get a dollar in federal funds for every dollar they spend on health care, while poorer states such as Mississippi or Texas get four dollars for every one they spend. This formula is meant to encourage less-wealthy states to spend more on health care for the poor. Ultimately, each state can decide how much it wants to spend on Medicaid, and state-by-state Medicaid spending does, in fact, vary dramatically. Currently, for example, New York spends $4,852 per person annually in Medicaid (in combined state and federal spending), while Utah spends $953. Because New York and some other states spend so much, they receive much more federal money than other states.

As long as federal spending rises—and Medicaid spending has been rising at a rate of 10 percent a year—these state-by-state disparities do not cause much conflict. States can decide to raise or lower their spending levels, and know that federal funds will change accordingly. But congressional Republicans, committed to balancing the national budget, want to freeze Medicaid spending at 1994 levels for five years. The trouble with a freeze, from the point of view of the states, is that it does not take into account changes in their own spending, economic conditions, or population changes. If 1994 spending levels are locked in for five years, then New York is assured of receiving far more federal Medicaid funds than a state like Texas, regardless of how much either chooses to spend over those years, and regardless of the projected growth in Texas's population and the projected decline in New York's. On the other hand, New York also knows that, no matter how much it increases health care spending (and New York's state constitution requires its government to provide health care for all its residents), it will not receive a single additional dollar in federal funds. Thus Senators D'Amato of New York and Gramm of Texas, while both committed in the abstract to the principle of federalism, are loath to agree to any formula for dividing up federal funds that they see as unfavorable to their own states.

Early in the 1995 push for welfare reform, Republican governors wholeheartedly endorsed the idea of block grants as a way of reclaiming the power to govern from the national government. But as the realities of spending freezes and inflexible allocations set in, and as it became clearer that Republican welfare reform proposals would entail a massive cost shift to the states, more and more Republican governors found that their ideological commitment to federalism was not as strong as their nonideological commitment to defending their state's interests. In the clash of principles at the heart of welfare reform, defending one's dollars may emerge as the mightiest principle of all.

In 1916, the national government passed the Keating-Owen Child Labor Act, which excluded from interstate commerce goods manufactured by children under fourteen. The act was ruled unconstitutional by the Supreme Court on the grounds that the regulation of interstate commerce could not extend to the conditions of labor. The regulation of child labor remained in the hands of state governments until the 1930s.

was never entirely free, of course; in fact, entrepreneurs themselves did not want complete freedom from government. They needed law and order. They needed a stable currency. They needed courts and police to enforce contracts and prevent trespass. They needed roads, canals, and railroads. But federalism, as interpreted by the Supreme Court for seventy years after the Civil War, made it possible for business to have its cake and eat it, too. Entrepreneurs enjoyed the benefits of national policies facilitating commerce and were protected by the courts from policies regulating commerce.[5]

All this changed after 1937, when the Supreme Court threw out the old distinction between interstate and intrastate commerce, converting the commerce clause from a source of limitations to a source of power for the national government. The Court began to refuse to review appeals challenging acts of Congress protecting the rights of employees to organize and engage in collective bargaining, regulating the amount of farmland in cultivation, extending low-interest credit to small businesses and farmers, and restricting the activities of corporations dealing in the stock market, and many other laws that contributed to the construction of the "welfare state."[6]

THE CONTINUING INFLUENCE OF FEDERALISM: STATE AND LOCAL GOVERNMENT TODAY

State Government One way in which the framers sought to preserve a strong role for the states was through the Tenth Amendment to the Constitution. The Tenth Amendment states that the powers that the Constitution does not delegate to the national government or prohibit to the states are "reserved to the States respectively, or to the people." The Antifederalists, who feared that a strong central government would encroach on individual liberty, repeatedly pressed for such an amendment as a way of limiting national power. Federalists agreed to the amendment because they did not think it would do much harm, given the powers the Constitution already granted to the national government.

The Tenth Amendment is also called the **reserved powers** amendment because it aims to reserve powers to the states. But as we have seen, the Constitution also contained the seeds of a very expansive national government—in the commerce clause. For much of the nineteenth century, federal power remained limited. The Tenth Amendment was used to bolster arguments about **states' rights,** which in their extreme version claimed that the states did not have to submit to national laws when they believed the national government had exceeded its authority. These arguments in favor of states' rights were voiced less often after the Civil War. But the Supreme Court continued to use the Tenth Amendment to strike down laws that it thought exceeded national power, including a Civil Rights Act passed in 1875.

In the early twentieth century, however, the Tenth Amendment appeared to lose its force. Reformers began to press for national regulations to limit the power of large corporations and to preserve the health and welfare of citizens. The Supreme Court approved of some of these laws but it struck others down, including a law combatting child labor. The Court stated that the law violated the Tenth Amendment because only states should have the power to regulate conditions of employment. By the late 1930s, however, the Supreme Court had approved such an expansion of federal power in the "First Constitutional Revolution" that the Tenth Amendment appeared irrelevant. In fact, in 1941, Justice Harlan Fiske Stone declared that the Tenth Amendment was simply a "truism," that it had no real meaning.[7]

Yet the idea that some powers should be reserved to the states did not go away. Indeed, in the 1950s, southern opponents of the Civil Rights movement revived the idea of states' rights. In 1956, ninety-six southern members of Congress issued a "Southern Manifesto" in which they declared that southern states were not constitutionally bound by Supreme Court decisions outlawing racial segregation. They believed that states' rights should override individual rights to liberty and formal equality. With the triumph of the Civil Rights movement, the slogan of "states' rights" became tarnished by its association with racial inequality.

Recent years have seen a revival of interest in the Tenth Amendment and important Supreme Court decisions limiting federal power. Much of the interest in the Tenth Amendment stems from conservatives who believe that a strong federal government encroaches on individual liberties. They believe such freedoms are better protected by returning more power to the states. In 1995, Republican presidential candidate Bob Dole carried a copy of the Tenth Amendment in his pocket as he campaigned, pulling it out to read at rallies.[8] The Supreme Court's ruling in *United States v. Lopez* in 1995 fueled further interest in the Tenth Amendment. In that case, the Court, stating that Congress had exceeded its authority under the commerce clause, struck down a federal law that barred handguns near schools. This was the first time since the New Deal that the Court had limited congressional powers in this way. The Court further limited the power of the federal government over the states in a 1996 ruling that prevented Native Americans from the Seminole tribe from suing the state of Florida in federal court. A 1988 law had given

Republican Party leaders have contended that the national government has grown too powerful at the expense of the states and argue that the Tenth Amendment should restrict the growth of national power.

Indian tribes the right to sue a state in federal court if the state did not negotiate in good faith over issues related to gambling casinos on tribal land. The Supreme Court's ruling appeared to signal a much broader limitation on national power by raising new questions about whether individuals can sue a state if it fails to uphold federal law. [9] It remains to be seen whether these rulings signal a move toward a much more restricted federal government in future Supreme Court decisions, or whether they will simply serve as a reminder that federal power is not infinite.[10]

The expansion of the power of the national government has not left the states powerless. The state governments continue to make most of the fundamental laws; the national government did not expand at the expense of the states. The growth of the national government has been an addition, not a redistribution of power from the states. No better demonstration of the continuing influence of the federal framework can be offered than the fact that the middle column of Table 4.1 is still a fairly accurate characterization of state government today.

Local Government and the Constitution Local government occupies a peculiar but very important place in the American system. In fact, the status of American local government is probably unique in world experience. First, it must be pointed out that local government has no status in the American Constitution. The policies listed in the rightmost column of Table 4.1 are there because *state* legislatures created local governments, and *state* constitutions and laws permitted local governments to take on some of the responsibilities of the state governments. Most states amended their own constitutions to give their larger cities **home rule**—a guarantee of noninterference in various areas of local affairs. But local governments enjoy no such recognition in the Constitution. Local governments have always been mere conveniences of the states.[11]

86,743 GOVERNMENTS IN THE UNITED STATES

Type	Number
National	1
State	50
County	3,043
Municipal	19,296
Townships	16,666
School districts	14,556
Other special districts	33,131

SOURCE: *Statistical Abstract of the United States, 1993* (Washington, DC: Government Printing Office, 1993).

TABLE 4.2

Local governments became administratively important in the early years of the Republic because the states possessed little administrative capability. They relied on local governments—cities and counties—to implement the laws of the state. Local government was an alternative to a statewide bureaucracy (see Table 4.2).

Who Does What? The Changing Federal Framework

- Why did the balance of responsibility shift toward the national government in the 1930s?
- What means does the national government use to control the actions of the states?
- How has the relationship between the national government and the states evolved over the last several decades?
- What methods have been employed to give more control back to the states?

Questions about how to divide responsibilities between the states and the national government first arose more than two hundred years ago, when the framers wrote the Constitution to create a stronger union. But they did not solve the issue of who should do what. There is no "right" answer to that question; each generation of Americans has provided its own answer. In recent years, Americans have grown distrustful of the federal government and have supported giving more responsibility to the states.[12] Even so, they still want the federal government to set standards and promote equality.

Political debates about the division of responsibility often take sides: some people argue for a strong federal role to set national standards, while others say the states should do more. These two goals are not necessarily at odds.

The key is to find the right balance. During the first 150 years of American history, that balance favored state power. But the balance began to shift toward Washington in the 1930s. In this section, we will look at how the balance shifted, and then we will consider current efforts to reshape the relationship between the national government and the states.

EXPANSION OF THE NATIONAL GOVERNMENT

The New Deal of the 1930s signaled the rise of a more active national government. The door to increased federal action opened when states proved unable to cope with the demands brought on by the Great Depression. Before the Depression, states and localities took responsibility for addressing the needs of the poor, usually through private charity. But the extent of the need created by the Depression quickly exhausted local and state capacities. By 1932, 25 percent of the workforce was unemployed. The jobless lost their homes and settled into camps all over the country, called "Hoovervilles" after President Herbert Hoover. Elected in 1928, the year before the Depression hit, Hoover steadfastly maintained that there was little the federal government could do to alleviate the misery caused by the Depression. It was a matter for state and local governments, he said.

Yet demands mounted for the federal government to take action. In Congress, some Democrats proposed that the federal government finance public works to aid the economy and put people back to work. Other members of Congress introduced legislation to provide federal grants to the states to assist them in their relief efforts. None of these measures passed while Hoover remained in the White House.

When Franklin D. Roosevelt took office in 1933, he energetically threw the federal government into the business of fighting the Depression. He pro-

A "Hooverville" in Seattle, Washington, in 1933. The residents of this Hooverville elected a mayor and city council to govern their "town."

During the 1950s, the national government funded 90 percent of the cost of building more than 42,500 miles of interstate highways. State governments paid for the remaining 10 percent.

posed a variety of temporary measures to provide federal relief and work programs. Most of the programs he proposed were to be financed by the federal government but administered by the states. In addition to these temporary measures, Roosevelt presided over the creation of several important federal programs designed to provide future economic security for Americans.

FEDERAL GRANTS

For the most part, the new national programs that the Roosevelt administration developed did not directly take power away from the states. Instead, Washington typically redirected states by offering them **grants-in-aid**, whereby Congress appropriates money to state and local governments on the condition that the money be spent for a particular purpose defined by Congress.

The principle of the grant-in-aid can be traced back to the nineteenth-century land grants that the national government made to the states for the improvement of agriculture and farm-related education. Since farms were not in "interstate commerce," it was unclear whether the Constitution permitted the national government to provide direct assistance to agriculture. Grants made to the states, but designated to go to farmers, presented a way of avoiding the question of constitutionality while pursuing what was recognized in Congress as a national goal.

Franklin Roosevelt's New Deal expanded the range of grants-in-aid into social programs, providing grants to the states for financial assistance to poor children in the Aid to Dependent Children program (later renamed Aid to Families with Dependent Children, or AFDC). Congress added new grants after World War II, creating new programs to help states fund activities such as providing school lunches and building highways. Sometimes the national government required state or local governments to match the national contribution dollar-for-dollar, but in some programs, such as the development of the interstate highway system, the congressional grants provided 90 percent of the cost of the program.

These types of federal grants-in-aid are also called **categorical grants**, because the national government determines the purposes, or categories, for which the money can be used. For the most part, the categorical grants created before the 1960s simply helped the states perform their traditional functions.[13] In the 1960s, however, the national role dramatically expanded and the number of categorical grants increased sharply (see Table 4.3). For exam-

TABLE 4.3

THE HISTORICAL TREND OF FEDERAL GRANTS-IN-AID

		Grants-in-aid as a percentage of			
Fiscal year	Amount of grants-in-aid (in billions)	Total federal outlays	Federal domestic programs[1]	State and local expenditures	Gross domestic product
Five-year intervals					
1950	$2.3	5.3%	11.6%	8.2%	0.8%
1955	3.2	4.7	17.2	9.7	0.8
1960	7.0	7.6	20.6	11.5	1.4
1965	10.9	9.2	20.3	15.1	1.6
1970	24.1	12.3	25.3	16.3	2.4
1975	49.8	15.0	23.1	18.5	3.3
Annually					
1980	91.5	15.5	23.3	21.1	3.5
1981	94.8	14.0	21.6	19.5	3.2
1982	88.2	11.8	19.0	16.8	2.8
1983	92.5	11.4	18.6	16.3	2.8
1984	97.6	11.5	19.6	16.3	2.6
1985	105.9	11.2	19.3	16.1	2.7
1986	112.4	11.3	19.8	15.7	2.7
1987	108.5	10.8	19.0	14.0	2.4
1988	115.4	10.8	19.0	14.0	2.4
1989	122.0	10.7	18.7	13.7	2.4
1990	135.4	10.8	17.0	13.9	2.5
1991	154.6	11.7	18.4	14.5	2.7
1992	178.1	12.9	20.5	NA	3.0
1993	193.7	13.8	21.5	NA	3.1
1994	217.3	14.6	22.1	NA	3.3
1995 (estimate)	230.6	15.2	22.7	NA	3.3

NA = Not available.
[1]Excludes outlays for national defense, international affairs, and net interest.
SOURCES: Office of Management and Budget, *Budget of the United States Government, Fiscal Year 1995. Historical Tables* (Washington, DC: Government Printing Office, 1994); Tax Foundation, *Facts & Figures on Government Finance, 1994 Edition* (Washington, DC: Tax Foundation, 1993), pp. 66, 124.

ple, during the Eighty-ninth Congress (1965–66) alone, the number of categorical grant-in-aid programs grew from 221 to 379.[14] The grants authorized during the 1960s announced national purposes much more strongly than did earlier grants. Central to that national purpose was the need to provide opportunities to the poor.

Many of the categorical grants enacted during the 1960s were **project grants**, which require state and local governments to submit proposals to federal agencies. In contrast to the older **formula grants**, which used a formula (composed of such elements as need and state and local capacities) to distribute funds, the new project grants made funding available on a competitive basis. Federal agencies would give grants to the proposals they judged to be the best. In this way, the national government acquired substantial control over which state and local governments got money, how much they got, and how they spent it.

Cooperative Federalism

The growth of categorical grants created a new kind of federalism. If the traditional system of two sovereigns performing highly different functions could be called dual federalism, historians of federalism suggest that the system since the New Deal could be called **cooperative federalism**. The most important student of the history of American federalism, Morton Grozdins, characterized this as a move from "layer-cake federalism" to "marble-cake federalism,"[15] in which intergovernmental cooperation and sharing have blurred a once-clear distinguishing line, making it difficult to say where the national government ends and the state and local governments begin (see Figure 4.1).

For a while in the 1960s, however, it appeared as if the state governments would become increasingly irrelevant to American federalism. Many of the new federal grants bypassed the states and instead sent money directly to local governments and even to local nonprofit organizations. The theme

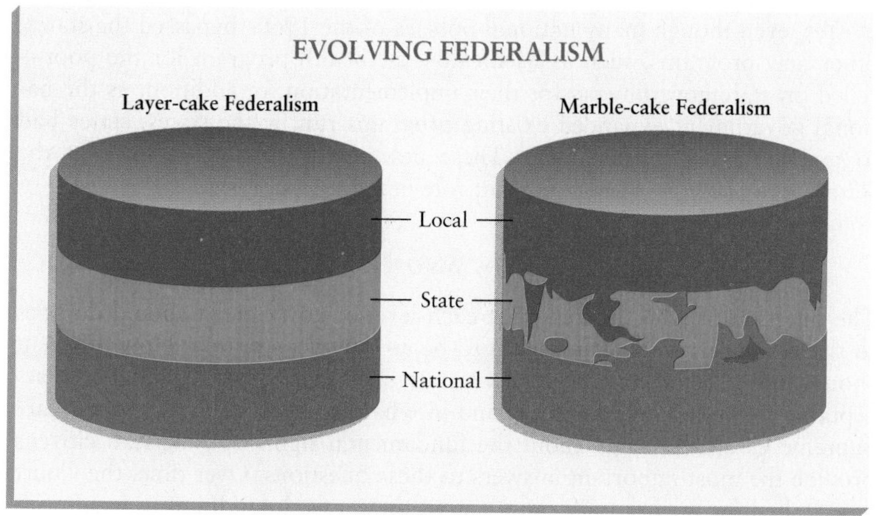

FIGURE 4.1

In marble-cake federalism, national policies, state policies, and local policies overlap in many areas.

Governor George Wallace of Alabama stood in defiance as he turned back Attorney General Nicholas Katzenbach, who was trying to enroll two black students at the University of Alabama at Tuscaloosa in 1963. Wallace, who proclaimed "segregation now, segregation tomorrow, segregation forever," was a vocal advocate of states' rights.

heard repeatedly in Washington was that the states simply could not be trusted to carry out national purposes.[16]

One of the reasons that Washington distrusted the states was because of the way African American citizens were treated in the South. The southern states' forthright defense of segregation, justified on the grounds of states' rights, helped to tarnish the image of the states as the Civil Rights movement took hold. The national officials who planned the War on Poverty in the 1960s pointed to the racial exclusion practiced in the southern states as a reason for bypassing state governments. Political scientist James Sundquist described how the "Alabama syndrome" affected the War on Poverty: "In the drafting of the Economic Opportunity Act, an 'Alabama syndrome' developed. Any suggestion within the poverty task force that the states be given a role in the administration of the act was met with the question, 'Do you want to give that kind of power to [Alabama governor] George Wallace?' "[17]

Yet, even though many national policies of the 1960s bypassed the states, other new programs, such as Medicaid—the health program for the poor—relied on state governments for their implementation. In addition, as the national government expanded existing programs run by the states, states had to take on more responsibility. These new responsibilities meant that the states were playing a very important role in the federal system.

REGULATED FEDERALISM AND NATIONAL STANDARDS

The question of who decides what each level of government should do goes to the very heart of what it means to be an American citizen. How different should things be when one crosses a state line? In what policy areas is it acceptable to have state differences and in what areas should states be similar? Supreme Court decisions about the fundamental rights of American citizens provide the most important answers to these questions. Over time, the Court has pushed for greater uniformity across the states. In addition to legal decisions, the national government uses two other tools to create similarities across the states: grants-in-aid and regulations.

Grants-in-aid, as we have seen, are a little like bribes: Congress gives money to state and local governments if they agree to spend it for the purposes Congress specifies. But as Congress began to enact legislation in new areas, such as environmental policy, it also imposed additional regulations on states and localities. Some political scientists call this a move toward **regulated federalism.**[18] The national government began to set standards of conduct or required the states to set standards that met national guidelines. Figure 4.2 shows how much federal regulation grew, especially during the 1970s. The effect of these national standards is that state and local policies in the areas of environmental protection, social services, and education are more uniform from coast to coast than are other nationally funded policies.

Some national standards require the federal government to take over areas of regulation formerly overseen by state or local governments. Such **preemption** occurs when state and local actions are found to be inconsistent with federal requirements. If this occurs, all regulations in the preempted area must henceforth come from the national government. In many cases, the scope of the federal authority to preempt is decided by the courts. For example, in 1973 the Supreme Court struck down a local ordinance prohibiting

FIGURE 4.2

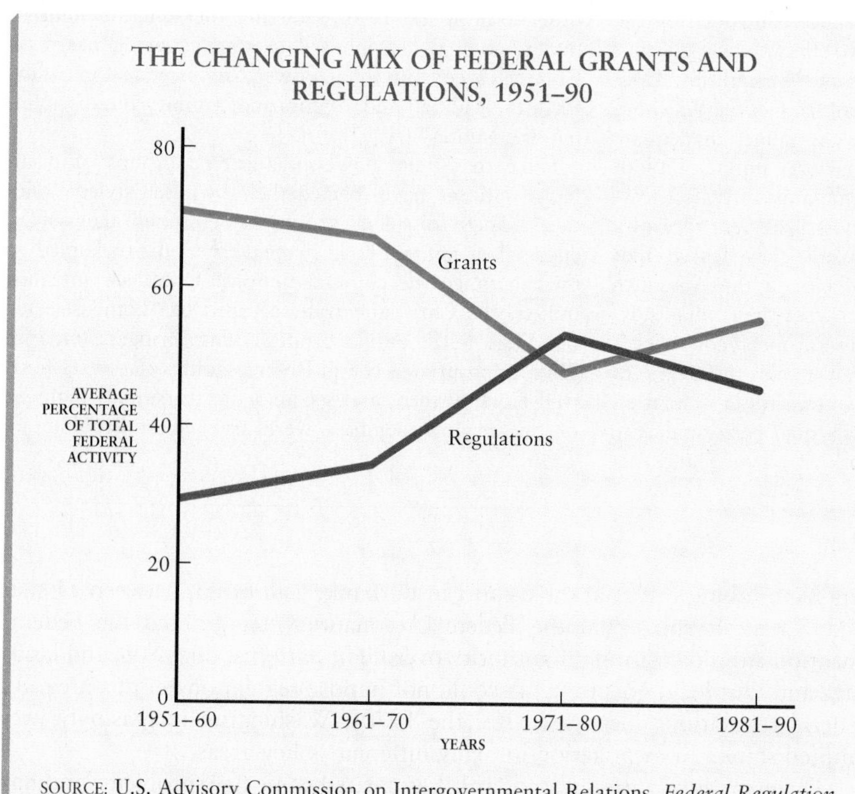

SOURCE: U.S. Advisory Commission on Intergovernmental Relations, *Federal Regulation of State and Local Governments: The Mixed Record of the 1980s* (Washington, DC: Advisory Commission on Intergovernmental Relations, 1993), p. 56.

In American popular culture, militias are synonymous with freedom. In the early history of the United States, the country's defense rested with groups of citizen-soldiers (also called "unorganized" militias), who were generally defined as adult male citizens of fighting age—usually eighteen to forty-five years old—and who were obliged to enroll with the government for military service, serving or training for a few months out of each year. The Revolutionary War was fought in large measure by these citizen-soldiers, who were organized into militias by state governments. America's eventual victory over the British added to the image of militias as the bulwark of American freedom.

Yet even in colonial times, many American leaders realized that full-time, professional armies controlled by the national government were far more effective as a military force than the state-controlled, part-time militias. Even America's supreme military commander, George Washington, complained about the poor discipline, inadequate training, weak motivation, and general unreliability of militias. Washington kept his complaints private, however, because most Americans opposed the very idea of a national professional standing army; they feared that such an army would be tempted to end the American democratic experiment by overthrowing the civilian government, as had happened in many European countries.

Military necessity eventually overrode the fears of standing armies, and the old universal militia system effectively ended with the militias' abysmal performance in the War of 1812, where their lack of training and tendency to run in the face of enemy guns culminated in the British sacking of Washington, D.C. Local militia groups continued to meet and train (in what were called "musters"), but as political historian Stephen Skowronek has noted, "by the 1840s the militia system envisioned in the early days of the republic was a dead letter. Universal military training fell victim to a general lack of interest and administrative incompetence at both the federal and state levels."[1] Instead, America relied for its military needs on select or "organized" militias (small, well-trained volunteer forces that eventually became the National Guard) and standing professional armies filled by enlistment or the draft. Congress revamped the nation's obsolete militia regulations in the early 1900s in order to bring the nation's military, including the militias, under national (as opposed to state) control, based on Congress's constitutional power "to provide for calling forth the Militia" and "organizing, arming, and disciplining, the Militia" (Art. I).

Since that time, however, scattered groups of disaffected citizens have formed their own self-styled "militias." These dissident groups have armed themselves, engaged in military-style maneuvers, and proclaimed as their heritage the colonial militias. One such so-called militia, the Christian Front, planned to "bomb selected buildings, seize public utilities, blast bridges, terrorize Jews, appropriate Federal Reserve gold, assassinate fourteen Congressmen, and set up a dictatorship."[2] Eighteen of the group's members were arrested in Brooklyn in 1940.

jets from taking off from the airport in Burbank, California, between 11 P.M. and 7 A.M. It ruled that the Federal Aeronautics Act granted the Federal Aviation Administration all authority over flight patterns, take-offs, and landings and that local governments could not impose regulations in this area. As federal regulations increased after the 1970s, Washington increasingly preempted state and local action in many different policy areas.

The growth of national standards has created some new problems and has raised questions about how far federal standardization should go. One problem that emerged in the 1980s was the increase in **unfunded mandates**—regulations or new conditions for receiving grants that impose costs on state and

In the early 1990s, similar fringe groups sprang up in many states. By 1995, such militia groups were said to have been organized in as many as 47 states, comprising perhaps 20,000 members. Public concern over the intentions of these groups heightened with the April 19, 1995, bombing of a federal office building in Oklahoma City. Nearly 170 people died in the blast.

Although militia concerns and motivations vary, they share a profound mistrust of governmental authority and a fear that the American government is poised to turn its authority over to a world government, possibly controlled by the United Nations. (Like earlier militia and paramilitary groups, many of today's "militias" also subscribe to anti-Semitic and racist beliefs.) No evidence supports such allegations, but militia fears were nevertheless fanned by the government's botched attempts to capture extremist Randy Weaver in 1992 and to raid the Branch Davidian compound near Waco, Texas, in 1993. Here, militia leaders argued, was proof of the government's bad intentions.

For all of their claims to the militia tradition, the modern self-styled militias differ from colonial militias in two vital respects. First, the modern militias are organized and operate without government consent or control. By the Constitution's definition, as well as according to federal and state laws, a militia can exist only by or under the regulation and control of a state or national government. Second, the modern militias' very reason for existence is their hostility to the existing American government. While colonial militias fought against British rule, they still fought for a government—namely, the fledgling American government.

Some militia representatives claim that they have a constitutionally protected right to engage in rebellion against the government. Yet no such right exists, for the simple reason that if such a right existed, it would amount to nothing less than government suicide. As legal expert Roscoe Pound noted many years ago, "a legal right of the citizen to wage war on the government is something that cannot be admitted. . . . In the urban industrial society of today a general right to bear efficient arms so as to be enabled to resist oppression by the government would mean that gangs could exercise an extra-legal rule which would defeat the whole Bill of Rights."[3]

SOURCE: Robert J. Spitzer, *The Politics of Gun Control* (Chatham, NJ: Chatham House, 1995).

[1]Stephen Skowronek, *Building a New American State* (Cambridge, U.K.: Cambridge University Press, 1982), p. 315.

[2]Philip Jenkins, "Home-Grown Terror," *American Heritage*, September 1995, p. 39.

[3]Quoted in Robert J. Spitzer, *The Politics of Gun Control* (Chatham, NJ: Chatham House, 1995), p. 47.

local governments for which they are not reimbursed by the national government. The growth of unfunded mandates was the product of a Democratic Congress, which wanted to achieve liberal social objectives, and a Republican president, who opposed increased social spending. Between 1983 and 1991, Congress mandated standards in many policy areas, including social services and environmental regulations, without providing additional funds to meet those standards. Altogether, Congress enacted twenty-seven laws that imposed new regulations or required states to expand existing programs.[19] For example, in the late 1980s, Congress ordered the states to extend the coverage provided by Medicaid, the medical insurance program for the poor. The

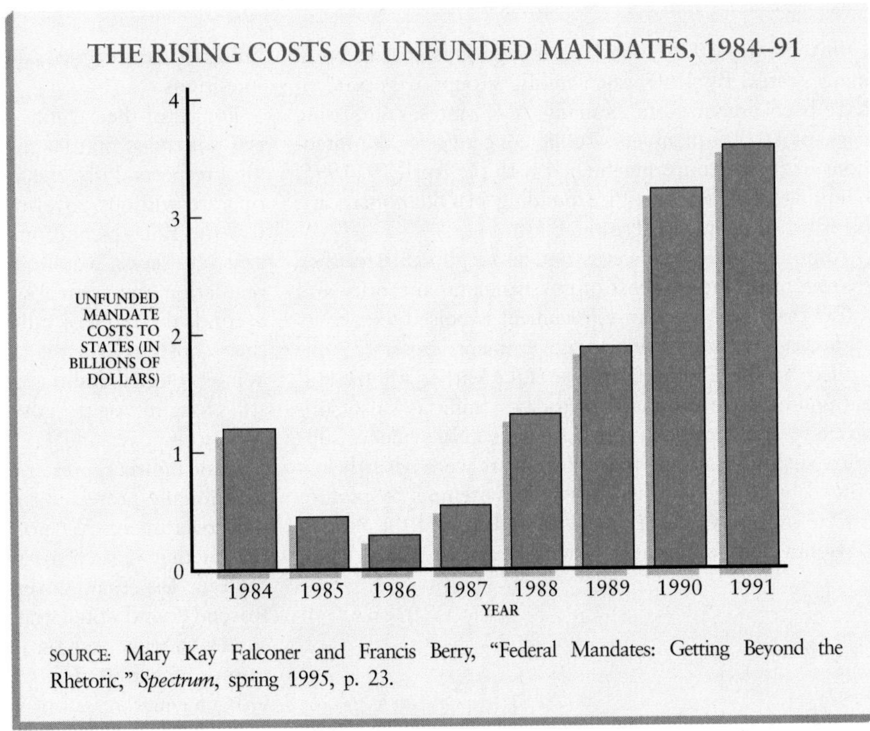

SOURCE: Mary Kay Falconer and Francis Berry, "Federal Mandates: Getting Beyond the Rhetoric," *Spectrum*, spring 1995, p. 23.

FIGURE 4.3

aim was to make the program serve more people, particularly poor children, and to expand services. But Congress did not supply additional funding to help states meet these new requirements; the states had to shoulder the increased financial burden themselves.

States and localities quickly began to protest the cost of unfunded mandates. Although it is very hard to determine the exact cost of federal regulations, the Congressional Budget Office estimated that between 1983 and 1990, new federal regulations cost states and localities between $8.9 and $12.7 billion (see Figure 4.3).[20] States complained that mandates took up so much of their budgets that they were not able to set their own priorities.

These burdens became part of a rallying cry to reduce the power of the federal government—a cry that took center stage when a Republican Congress was elected in 1994. One of the first measures the new Congress passed was an act to limit the cost of unfunded mandates. Under the new law, Congress must estimate the cost of any proposal it believes will run more than $50 million. It must then vote to approve the regulation, acknowledging the expenditure. The effect of this act is likely to be limited; it does not prevent congressional members from passing unfunded mandates, but only makes them think twice before they do. Moreover, the act exempts several areas of regulation. States must still enforce anti-discrimination laws and meet other requirements to receive federal assistance. Only nine of the twenty-seven mandates enacted between 1981 and 1990 would have been covered by the new law.[21]

New Federalism and State Control

In 1970, the mayor of Oakland, California, told Congress that there were twenty-two separate employment and training programs in his city but that few poor residents were being trained for jobs that were available in the local labor market.[22] National programs had proliferated as Congress enacted many small grants, but there was little coordination or adaptation of programs to local needs. Today many governors argue for more control over such national grant programs. They complain that national grants do not allow for enough local flexibility and instead take a "one size fits all" approach.[23] These criticisms point to a fundamental problem in American federalism: How to get the best results for the money spent. Do some divisions of responsibility between states and the federal government work better than others? Since the 1970s, as states have become more capable of administering large-scale programs, the idea of solving administrative problems by devolving more responsibility to the states has become popular.

Proponents of more state authority have looked to **block grants** as a way of reducing federal control. Block grants are federal grants that allow the states considerable leeway in spending federal money. President Nixon led the first push for block grants in the early 1970s, as part of his **New Federalism.** Nixon's block grants consolidated programs in the areas of job training, community development, and social services into three large block grants. These

FIGURE 4.4

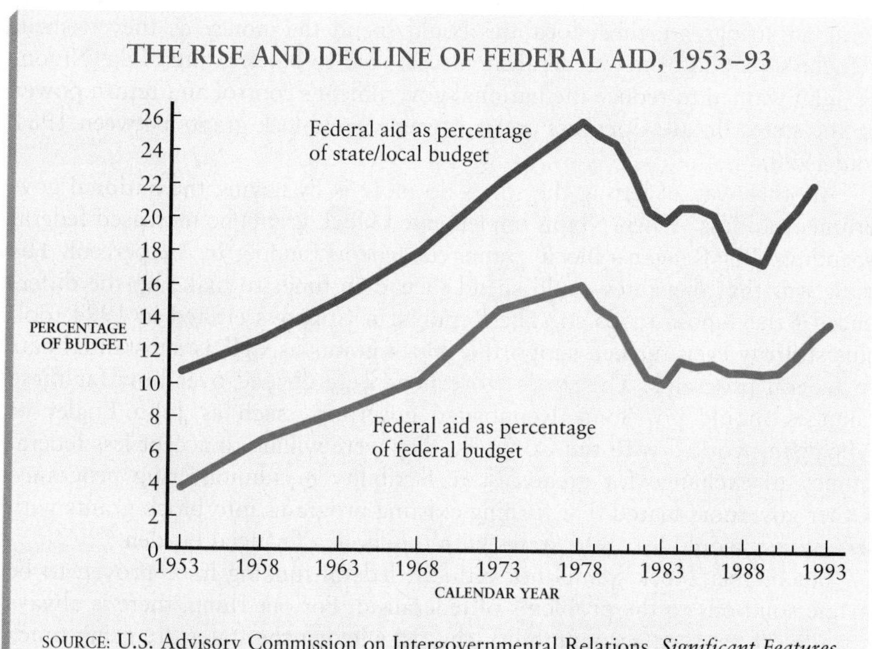

SOURCE: U.S. Advisory Commission on Intergovernmental Relations, *Significant Features of Fiscal Federalism: 1993*, vol. 2 (Washington, DC: U.S. Advisory Committee on Intergovernmental Relations, 1993).

Michigan governor John Engler has been a prominent supporter of block grants, which give state governors more flexibility in administering programs such as welfare.

grants imposed some conditions on states and localities for how the money should be spent, but not the narrow regulations contained in the categorical grants. In addition, Congress approved a fourth block grant called revenue sharing. Revenue sharing provided money to local governments and counties with no strings attached; localities could spend the money as they wished. Reagan's version of new federalism also looked to block grants. Like Nixon, Reagan wanted to reduce the national government's control and return power to the states. In all, Congress created twelve new block grants between 1981 and 1990.[24]

Another way of letting the states do more is by having the national government do less. When Nixon implemented block grants he increased federal spending. But Reagan's block grants cut federal funding by 12 percent. His view was that the states could spend their own funds to make up the difference, if they chose to do so. The Republican Congress elected in 1994 took this strategy even further, supporting block grants as well as substantial cuts in federal programs. The states' governors were divided over how far these changes should go. Some Republican governors, such as John Engler of Michigan, worked with the Congress; they were willing to accept less federal money in exchange for greater state flexibility in administering programs. Other governors feared that turning existing programs into block grants with less money would leave the states with too large a financial burden.[25]

But neither block grants nor reduced federal funding have proven to be magic solutions to the problems of federalism. For one thing, there is always a trade-off between accountability, that is, whether the states are using funds for the purposes intended, and flexibility. Accountability and proper use of funds continue to be troublesome issues. Even after block grants were created, Congress reimposed regulations in order to increase the states' accountability. If the objective is to have accountable and efficient government, it is

FEDERAL AID AS A PERCENTAGE OF GENERAL ANNUAL EXPENDITURE, 1977 AND 1992

City	1977	1992	City	1977	1992
Buffalo	31%	6%	Oakland	39%	6%
Cleveland	29	11	Oklahoma City	39	3
Detroit	31	8	Portland	28	2
Honolulu	30	7	San Antonio	28	3
Louisville	41	8	Tulsa	24	3

SOURCE: Department of Commerce, *Statistical Abstract of the United States, 1994* (Washington, DC: Government Printing Office, 1994), pp. 317–18.

TABLE 4.4

not clear that state bureaucracies are any more efficient or more capable than national agencies. In Mississippi, for example, the state Department of Human Services spent money from the child care block grant for office furniture and designer salt and pepper shakers that cost $37.50 a pair. As one Mississippi state legislator said, "I've seen too many years of good ol' boy politics to know they shouldn't [transfer money to the states] without stricter controls and requirements."[26]

Both liberals and conservatives have charged that block grants are a way for politicians to avoid the big, controversial policy questions. Instead of facing problems head on, these critics say, the federal government uses block grants to kick the problem down to the states.[27]

Reduced federal funding may leave states with problems which they do not have the resources to solve. During the 1980s, many states had to raise taxes in order to make up for some of the cuts in federal funding. (The impact of these cuts can be seen in Table 4.4.) But in the early 1990s, when a recession hit, states had to cut back services because they were short of funds even after raising taxes. How much of a financial burden the states can carry without harming the fundamental services citizens have come to expect from government is a major question now confronting all Americans. One area of state funding that has suffered considerably in the past years is higher education. In 1995, New York's Republican governor, George Pataki, sparked student protests when he sought deep cuts in state funding for the State University of New York and the City University of New York, while proposing to increase tuition by $1,000 a year.[28]

As states are expected to take on greater responsibility, they will become even more important political arenas, where different interests fight to see their vision of the proper role of government implemented.

Cuts in federal funding have had a big impact on universities. These Louisiana State University students are protesting proposed funding cuts.

THE INTERGOVERNMENTAL LOBBY

As states have grown more accountable and effective, they have increased their presence in national politics. One of the ways states influence national policy debates is through lobbying organizations. In the 1960s and 1970s, or-

President Clinton addressing the National Governors' Association conference in 1993. Clinton promised governors that states would have the power to experiment with welfare reform.

ganizations of state and local governments grew dramatically and became a powerful force in national politics. This phenomenon is known as the **intergovernmental lobby**. There are many lobbying organizations representing state and local governments in Washington, D.C., but seven of them are especially important. The "big seven" include three organizations that represent states—the National Governors' Association (NGA), the National Conference of State Legislatures, and the Council of State Governments—and four major organizations representing local governments—the U.S. Conference of Mayors, the National League of Cities, the National Association of Counties, and the International City/County Management Association.

Many of these organizations were formed in the early part of this century to provide a forum for members to meet and share information. The NGA, for example, grew out of a White House meeting called by President Theodore Roosevelt in 1908. After that meeting the nation's governors began to gather for yearly conferences. But the organization was not very effective and it did not try to influence national policy. Like many of the other organizations, the NGA expanded its operations in Washington in the 1960s and 1970s. The NGA did not even have an office in Washington until 1967. But by 1981, it had an office building on Capitol Hill, a staff of seventy people, and a budget of $5.7 million.[29]

Interestingly, much of the money for the expansion of these organizations that lobby the federal government came from the federal government itself. In 1981, more than 58 percent of the NGA's budget came from the federal government; federal funds accounted for half the budget of the National Conference of State Legislatures. During the 1980s, many of the public interest groups representing state and local governments saw their budgets cut in half. The Reagan administration cut their federal funding in order to reduce their pressure as lobbying organizations.[30]

Even with reduced funds, these organizations continue to play a role in policy making. Because they are bipartisan, the organizations of the intergovernmental lobby usually do not take official positions on controversial policy issues. They do, however, try to reach agreement about what kinds of federal policies would be best for states and localities. During the 1980s, governors came together in the NGA to work with Congress to design a welfare reform plan that would allow states flexibility without too much financial responsibility. In the 1990s, however, the debate over welfare reform became too partisan, and the governors were unable to agree on an official NGA position. Instead, individual governors have worked with members of Congress to design policy.

Is There a Right Answer?

Some students of federalism say that states are best at doing some things and the national government is better at doing others. They argue that rather than share responsibility for funding, as many programs now do, each level of government should be fully responsible for the things that it does best.

In 1985, the Robb-Evans Commission, a bipartisan group, proposed a comprehensive approach to the division of responsibility. It argued that the national government should leave all economic development programs to the states and that the national government should take responsibility for programs that serve the poor. The commission built on the ideas of many economists and political scientists who maintain that states and localities should not be in charge of **redistributive programs**, that is, programs that are primarily for the benefit of the poor. These scholars argue that because states and local governments have to compete with one another, they do not have the incentive to spend their money on the needy people in their areas. Instead, they want to keep taxes low and spend money on things that promote economic development.[31]

The incentive that states and localities have to compete with one another is an important one. Businesses can move away from states with high taxes or other policies they may not like. This is what happened in Texarkana, Arkansas, and Texarkana, Texas, which are officially two different cities, although they are separated only by a state line. On the Arkansas side, a state law limits retailers from charging interest rates of more than about 10 percent; on the Texas side there is no such limit. As a result, all new car dealerships, the biggest mall, and most stores are located on the Texas side.[32] Downtown Texarkana, Arkansas, is emptier and shabbier than downtown Texarkana, Texas, even though they are practically the same city.

The Texarkana case is unusual because the two cities are so close together. But businesses often make decisions to move or locate new operations on the basis of such differences. Although most research shows that differences in taxes actually are not a key factor in the decisions of a company to locate its headquarters in a particular place, state officials often believe that they are. As a result, state politicans feel the pressure to keep taxes low and to pay more attention to businesses and well-to-do residents than to the poor.

There is some evidence that states concerned about competition from other states will reduce the amount they spend on the poor. Although states were hailed as the innovators in welfare reform during the 1980s, as state budgets got tighter in the 1990s, they changed from being "laboratories of democracy" to being contestants in a "race to the bottom." This means that if one state cuts welfare, neighboring states will institute similar or deeper cuts, both to reduce the amount they spend on welfare and to prevent recipients from the less-generous states from moving in. Between 1993 and 1995, Wisconsin, Illinois, Indiana, and Michigan all implemented similar restrictions on welfare recipients. New York sought to make cuts that would make its welfare benefits more in line with those of Masssachusetts and Connecticut.

The concerns that drove these reforms were expressed by a New York state legislator: "The concern we have is that unless we make our welfare system and our tax and regulatory system competitive with the states around us, we will have too many disincentives for business to move here. Welfare is a big part of that."[33] There are many good arguments for changing welfare, but fear of competition from other states can distort state policy decisions. For this reason, many analysts have long argued that welfare and other redistributive programs should be financed and regulated by the federal government, not the states.

In recent years, the American public has grown disillusioned with the federal government and has supported efforts to give the states more responsibilities. A 1995 poll found that 55 percent of Americans thought that the states should be able to use block grants as they see fit; only 30 percent said the federal government should set standards. But in some policy areas, including providing welfare benefits, creating minority opportunities, and enforcing air and water quality, Americans continue to favor a strong federal role.[34]

American federalism has never conformed to any ideal standard; it remains a work in progress. The decision about "who does what" has always been one of the main bones of contention among different groups struggling for power. Because questions about federalism concern power as well as principle, defining what states should do and what the federal government should do is the continuing task of American democracy.

★ Summary

In this chapter, we have examined one of the central principles of American government—federalism. The Constitution divides powers between the national government and the states, but over time national power has grown substantially. Many aspects of expanded federal power stem from struggles to realize the ideals of liberty and equality for all citizens.

The aim of federalism in the Constitution was to limit national power by creating two sovereigns—the national government and the state governments. The Founders hoped that this system of dual federalism would ensure the liberty of citizens by preventing the national government from becoming too powerful. But during the 1930s, American citizens used the democratic system to change the balance between federal and state governments. The failure of the states to provide basic economic security for citizens during the Great Depression led to an expansion of the federal government. Most Americans were supportive of this growing federal power because they believed that economic power had become too concentrated in the hands of big corporations and the common person was the loser. Thus, the ideal of equality—in this case, the belief that working people should have a fighting chance to support themselves—overrode fears that a strong federal government would abridge liberties. Expanded federal powers first took the form of grants-in-aid to states. Later, federal regulations became more common.

In recent years, many Americans have come to believe that the pendulum has swung too far in the direction of expanded federal power. A common charge is that the federal government is too big and, as a result, has encroached on fundamental liberties. State and local governments complain that they cannot govern because their powers have been preempted or because they have to use their own funds to fulfill unfunded mandates imposed by the federal government. The move to devolve more powers to the states has been called "new federalism." Advocates of reduced federal power believe that states can protect liberty without creating unacceptable inequalities. Others continue to believe that a strong central government is essential to ensuring basic equalities. They argue that economic competition among the states means that states cannot ensure equality as well as the federal government can. Such questions about how federalism affects the goals of liberty and equality are not easily settled and will remain a continuing task of American democracy.

FOR FURTHER READING

Anton, Thomas. *American Federalism and Public Policy.* Philadelphia: Temple University Press, 1989.

Bensel, Richard. *Sectionalism and American Political Development: 1880–1980.* Madison: University of Wisconsin Press, 1984.

Bowman, Ann O'M., and Richard Kearny. *The Resurgence of the States.* Englewood Cliffs, NJ: Prentice-Hall, 1986.

Dye, Thomas R. *American Federalism: Competition among Governments.* Lexington, MA: Lexington Books, 1990.

Elazar, Daniel. *American Federalism: A View from the States,* 3rd ed. New York: Harper & Row, 1984.

Grodzins, Morton. *The American System.* Chicago: Rand McNally, 1974.

Kelley, E. Wood. *Policy and Politics in the United States: The Limits of Localism.* Philadelphia: Temple University Press, 1987.

Kettl, Donald. *The Regulation of American Federalism.* Baltimore: Johns Hopkins University Press, 1987.

Peterson, Paul E. *The Price of Federalism.* Washington, DC: Brookings, 1995.

STUDY OUTLINE

The Federal Framework

1. In an effort to limit national power, the framers of the Constitution established a system of dual federalism, wherein both the national and state governments would have sovereignty.
2. Federalism and a restrictive definition of "interstate commerce" limited the national government's control over the economy.
3. Federalism allows a great deal of variation between states.
4. Under the traditional system of federalism, the national

government was small and very narrowly specialized in its functions compared with other Western nations. Most of its functions were aimed at promoting commerce.
5. Under the traditional system, states rather than the national government did most of the fundamental governing in the country.
6. The system of federalism limited the expansion of the national government despite economic forces and expansive interpretations of the Constitution in cases such as *McCulloch v. Maryland* and *Gibbons v. Ogden*.
7. For most of U.S. history, the concept of interstate commerce kept the national government from regulating the economy. But in 1937, the Supreme Court converted the commerce clause from a source of limitations to a source of power for the national government.

WHO DOES WHAT? THE CHANGING FEDERAL FRAMEWORK

1. The rise of national government activity after the New Deal did not necessarily mean that states lost power directly. Rather, the national government paid states through grants-in-aid to administer federal programs.
2. Some federal programs bypass the states by sending money directly to local governments or local organizations. The states are most important, however; they are integral to federal programs such as Medicaid.
3. As states became more effective, states and state officials sought more influence in national politics. They often lobbied for more state control over federal spending decisions.

PRACTICE QUIZ

1. Which term describes the sharing of powers between the national government and the state governments?
   a. separation of powers
   b. federalism
   c. checks and balances
   d. shared powers
2. The system of federalism that allowed states to do most of the fundamental governing from 1789 to 1937 was
   a. home rule.
   b. regulated federalism.
   c. dual federalism.
   d. cooperative federalism.
3. Which of the following resulted from the federal system?
   a. It limited the power of the national government in relation to the states.
   b. It restrained the power of the national government over the economy.
   c. It allowed variation among the states.
   d. all of the above
4. Which of the following best describes the role of the national government in the traditional federal system?
   a. "master of the states"
   b. "commercial republic"
   c. "morality police"
   d. "controller of public works"
5. The overall effect of the growth of national policies has been
   a. to weaken state government.
   b. to strengthen state government.
   c. to provide uniform laws in the nation.
   d. to make the states more diverse culturally.
6. Which amendment to the Constitution stated that the powers not delegated to the national government or prohibited to the states were "reserved to the states"?
   a. First Amendment
   b. Fifth Amendment
   c. Tenth Amendment
   d. Twenty-sixth Amendment
7. One of the most powerful tools by which the federal government has attempted to get the states to act in ways that are desired by the federal government is by
   a. providing grants-in-aid.
   b. requiring licensing.
   c. granting home rule.
   d. defending states' rights.
8. The form of regulated federalism that allows the federal government to take over areas of regulation formerly overseen by states or local governments is called
   a. categorical grants.
   b. formula grants.
   c. project grants.
   d. preemption.
9. To what does the term "new federalism" refer?
   a. the national government's regulation of state action through grants-in-aid
   b. the type of federalism relying on categorical grants
   c. efforts to return more policy-making discretion to the states through the use of block grants
   d. the recent emergence of local governments as important political actors
10. The intergovernmental lobby represents the interests of
    a. the intergovernment.
    b. state and local governments.
    c. Congress.
    d. lobbyists.

CRITICAL THINKING QUESTIONS

1. The role of the national government has changed significantly from the Founding era to the present. In what ways and to what extent do you think the framers of the Constitution would recognize modern American federalism? Do you think they would be pleased by the current balance of power between the sovereign national government and the sovereign state governments? In what ways did the system of federalism perform its intended functions? In what ways did it not?
2. Should states be required to implement unfunded mandates? Are Americans better off or worse off as a result of devolution?

KEY TERMS

block grants federal grants-in-aid that allow states considerable discretion in how the funds should be spent. (p. 133)

categorical grants congressional grants given to states and localities on the condition that expenditures be limited to a problem or group specified by law. (p. 126)

commerce clause Article I, Section 8, of the Constitution, which delegates to Congress the power "to regulate commerce with foreign nations, and among the several States and with the Indian tribes." This clause was interpreted by the Supreme Court in favor of national power over the economy. (p. 117)

cooperative federalism a type of federalism existing since the New Deal era in which grants-in-aid have been used strategically to encourage states and localities (without commanding them) to pursue nationally defined goals. Also known as *intergovernmental cooperation*. (p. 127)

devolution a policy to remove a program from one level of government by delegating it or passing it down to a lower level of government, such as from the national government to the state and local governments. (p. 112)

dual federalism the system of government that prevailed in the United States from 1789 to 1937, in which most fundamental governmental powers were shared between the federal and state governments. (p. 113)

expressed powers specific powers granted to Congress under Article I, Section 8, of the Constitution. (p. 113)

federalism a system of government in which power is divided, by a constitution, between a central government and regional governments. (p. 113)

formula grants grants-in-aid in which a formula is used to determine the amount of federal funds a state or local government will receive. (p. 127)

grants-in-aid programs through which Congress provides money to state and local governments on the condition that the funds be employed for purposes defined by the federal government. (p. 125)

home rule power delegated by the state to a local unit of government to manage its own affairs. (p. 122)

implied powers doctrine support for powers derived from the "necessary and proper" clause of Article I, Section 8, of the Constitution. Such powers are not specifically expressed, but are implied through the expansive interpretation of delegated powers. (p. 117)

intergovernmental lobbying efforts by organizations representing state and local governments to influence national government policy making (examples include the National Governors' Association and the U.S. Conference of Mayors). (p. 136)

necessary and proper clause from Article I, Section 8, of the Constitution, it provides Congress with the authority to make all laws "necessary and proper" to carry out its expressed powers. (p. 117)

New Federalism attempts by Presidents Nixon and Reagan to return power to the states through block grants. (p. 133)

preemption the principle that allows the national government to override state or local actions in certain policy areas. (p. 129)

project grants grant programs in which state and local governments submit proposals to federal agencies and for which funding is provided on a competitive basis. (p. 127)

redistributive programs economic policies designed to control the economy through taxing and spending, with the goal of benefiting the poor. (p. 137)

regulated federalism a form of federalism in which Congress imposes legislation on states and localities, requiring them to meet national standards. (p. 129)

reserved powers powers, derived from the Tenth Amendment to the Constitution, that are not specifically delegated to the national government or denied to the states. (p. 121)

states' rights the principle that the states should oppose the increasing authority of the national government. This principle was most popular in the period before the Civil War. (p. 121)

unfunded mandates regulations or conditions for receiving grants that impose costs on state and local governments for which they are not reimbursed by the federal government. (p. 130)

5

The Bill of Rights and Civil Liberties

- ★ **The Bill of Rights: A Charter of Liberties**
  How does the Bill of Rights provide for individual liberties?
  What are the differences between the substantive and procedural restraints contained within the Bill of Rights? What are some examples of each?
- ★ **Nationalizing the Bill of Rights**
  Does the Bill of Rights put limits only on the national government or does it limit state governments as well?
  How and when did the Supreme Court nationalize the Bill of Rights?
- ★ **The First Amendment and Freedom of Religion**
  How does the First Amendment guarantee the non-establishment and free exercise of religion?
  In what way has the free exercise of religion become a recent political issue?
- ★ **The First Amendment and Freedom of Speech and the Press**
  What forms of speech are protected by the First Amendment? What forms are not protected?
- ★ **The Second Amendment and the Right to Bear Arms**
  Is the right to bear arms guaranteed by the Bill of Rights? How is its exercise restricted?
- ★ **Rights of the Criminally Accused**
  What is due process?
  How do the Fourth, Fifth, Sixth, and Eighth amendments provide for the due process of law?
- ★ **The Right to Privacy**
  What is the right to privacy? How has it been derived from the Bill of Rights? What forms does the right to privacy take today?
- ★ **The Future of the Bill of Rights**
  What is the likelihood that the Supreme Court will try to reverse the nationalization of the Bill of Rights?

In 1993, the directors of the Aware Woman Center for Choice, an abortion clinic in Melbourne, Florida, convinced a county trial judge to issue an injunction prohibiting anti-abortion protesters from the group Operation Rescue from demonstrating within thirty-six feet of the clinic. The injunction also banned protesters from coming into contact with women approaching the clinic within three hundred feet of the entrance. This same ban applied to protests at the homes of doctors and other clinic personnel.

In its 1994 decision in the case of *Madsen v. Women's Health Center*, the Supreme Court upheld the thirty-six-foot buffer zone as a reasonable means of protecting access to the clinic. The Court also approved a part of the injunction that imposed limited noise restrictions on the protesters "to insure the health and well-being of the patients at the clinic." But the Court rejected parts of the injunction that sought to ban general marching through the clinic's neighborhood, to ban picketing, and to limit speech and the display of graphic pictures that were disagreeable to the clients and the personnel of the clinic, arguing that these prohibitions violated the protesters' right to free speech as guaranteed by the First Amendment. In a particularly fractured decision, three justices dissented from part of the majority decision, and four justices dissented from other parts. Moreover, some of these dissents were intentionally critical, even suggesting that the Court would not have put such limitations on the freedom of speech of the protesters if the issue had been anything other than that of abortion. In other words, they accused the majority of taking the content of speech into account, and that "content-based . . . restrictions upon speech . . . may be designed and used precisely to suppress the ideas in question rather than to achieve any proper governmental aim."[1]

The dissents in the *Madsen* case reveal a truth far beyond the facts of a divided Court and an intensely critical argument: The Bill of Rights is not easy to use. Its provisions are always in need of interpretation. Furthermore, the burden usually falls on the person (or persons) who contends that his or her rights have been deprived (in this case the anti-abortion protesters) to *prove* that those rights were indeed deprived. Unfortunately, when citizens are divided by a large moral or cultural gulf—as Americans are between pro-life and pro-choice—free speech is often the first victim.

Despite the difficulty of getting protection from the Bill of Rights and the fragility of so many of its provisions, at least the Bill of Rights is available and can make a difference. Few citizens in other countries can make such a claim. In fact, few people in recorded history have enjoyed such protections, including American citizens before the 1960s. For more than 170 years, the Bill of Rights meant little to most Americans. Guaranteeing the liberties articulated in the Bill of Rights to all Americans required a long struggle.

The first task of this chapter is to define the Bill of Rights and establish its relationship to personal liberty. The second task is to trace the development of the Bill of Rights and explore why it took so long for it to become an effective instrument for the protection of personal liberty. The third and final task of this chapter is to assess where the Bill of Rights stands today.

The Bill of Rights: A Charter of Liberties

- How does the Bill of Rights provide for individual liberties?
- What are the differences between the substantive and procedural restraints contained within the Bill of Rights? What are some examples of each?

When the first Congress under the newly ratified Constitution met in late April of 1789 (having been delayed since March 4 by lack of a quorum because of bad winter roads), the most important item of business was the consideration of a proposal to add a bill of rights to the Constitution. Such a proposal by Virginia delegate George Mason had been turned down with little debate in the waning days of the Philadelphia Constitutional Convention in 1787, not because the delegates were against rights, but because, as the Federalists, led by Alexander Hamilton, later argued, it was "not only unnecessary in the proposed Constitution but would even be dangerous."[2] First, according to Hamilton, a bill of rights would be irrelevant to a national government that was given only delegated powers in the first place. To put restraints on "powers which are not granted" could provide a pretext for governments to claim more powers than were in fact granted: "For why declare that things shall not be done which there is no power to do?"[3] Second, the Constitution was to Hamilton and the Federalists a bill of rights in itself, or contained provisions that amounted to a bill of rights without requiring additional amendments (see Table 5.1). For example, Article I, Section 9, included the right of habeas corpus, which prohibits the government from depriving a person of liberty without an open trial before a judge.

Despite the power of Hamilton's arguments, when the Constitution was submitted to the states for ratification, Antifederalists, most of whom had not been delegates in Philadelphia, picked up on the argument of Thomas Jefferson (who also had not been a delegate) that the omission of a bill of rights was a major imperfection of the new Constitution. The Federalists conceded that in order to gain ratification they would have to make an "unwritten but unequivocal pledge" to add a bill of rights that would include a confirmation (in what became the Tenth Amendment) of the understanding that all powers not expressly delegated to the national government or explicitly prohibited to the states were reserved to the states.[4]

"After much discussion and manipulation . . . at the delicate prompting of Washington and under the masterful prodding of Madison," the House of Representatives adopted seventeen amendments; of these, the Senate adopted twelve. Ten of the amendments were ratified by the states on December 15, 1791; from the start these ten were called the Bill of Rights (see Box 5.1).[5]

TABLE 5.1

RIGHTS IN THE ORIGINAL CONSTITUTION (NOT IN THE BILL OF RIGHTS)

Clause	Right established
Article I, Sec. 9	guarantee of *habeas corpus*
Article I, Sec. 9	prohibition of bills of attainder
Article I, Sec. 9	prohibition of *ex post facto* laws
Article I, Sec. 9	prohibition against acceptance of titles of nobility, etc., from any foreign state
Article III	guarantee of trial by jury in state where crime was committed
Article III	treason defined and limited to the life of the person convicted, not to the person's heirs

*See glossary definition of terms.

BOX 5.1

THE BILL OF RIGHTS

Amendment I: Limits on Congress

Congress cannot make any law establishing a religion or abridging freedoms of religious exercise, speech, assembly, or petition.

Amendments II, III, IV: Limits on the Executive

The executive branch cannot infringe on the right of the people to keep arms (II), cannot arbitrarily take houses for militia (III), and cannot search for or seize evidence without a court warrant swearing to the probable existence of a crime (IV).

Amendments V, VI, VII, VIII: Limits on the Judiciary

The courts cannot hold trials for serious offenses without provision for a grand jury (V), a trial jury (VII), a speedy trial (VI), presentation of charges and confrontation by the accused of hostile witnesses (VI), and immunity from testimony against oneself and immunity from trial more than once for the same offense (V). Furthermore, neither bail nor punishment can be excessive (VIII), and no property can be taken without "just compensation" (V).

Amendments IX, X: Limits on the National Government

Any rights not enumerated are reserved to the state or the people (X), but the enumeration of certain rights in the Constitution should not be interpreted to mean that those are the only rights the people have (IX).

The Bill of Rights might well have been entitled the "Bill of Liberties," because the provisions that were incorporated in the Bill of Rights were seen as defining a private sphere of personal liberty, free of governmental restrictions.[6] As Jefferson had put it, a bill of rights "is what people are entitled to against every government on earth. . . ." Note the emphasis—citizen *against* government. **Civil liberties** are protections of citizens from improper government action.

Thus, the Bill of Rights is a series of "thou shalt nots"—restraints imposed upon government (see Table 5.2). Some of these restraints are **substantive liberties,** which put limits on *what* the government shall and shall not have power to do—such as establishing a religion, quartering troops in private homes without consent, or seizing private property without just compensation. Other restraints are **procedural liberties,** which deal with *how* the

TABLE 5.2

The Bill of Rights accentuates the negative.

CIVIL LIBERTIES IN THE BILL OF RIGHTS

Amendment	Example
I	"Congress shall make *no* law . . ."
II	"The right . . . to bear Arms, shall *not* be infringed"
III	"*No* soldier shall . . . be quartered . . ."
IV	"*No* Warrants shall issue, but upon probable cause . . ."
V	"*No* person shall be held to answer for a . . . crime, unless on a presentment or indictment of a Grand Jury . . ."
VIII	"Excessive bail shall *not* be required . . . *nor* cruel and unusual punishments inflicted."

government is supposed to act. These procedural liberties are usually grouped under the general category of **due process of law,** which first appears in the Fifth Amendment provision that "no person shall be . . . deprived of life, liberty, or property, without due process of law." For example, even though the government has the substantive power to declare certain acts to be crimes and to arrest and imprison persons who violate criminal laws, it may not do so without meticulously observing procedures designed to protect the accused person. The best known procedural rule is that an accused person is presumed innocent until proven guilty. This rule does not question the government's power to punish someone for committing a crime; it questions only the way the government determines who committed the crime. Substantive and procedural restraints together identify the realm of civil liberties.

In contrast, **civil rights** as a category refers to the obligations imposed on government to take positive action to protect citizens from any illegal actions of government agencies as well as of other private citizens. Civil rights did not become part of the Constitution until 1868, with the adoption of the Fourteenth Amendment, which sought to provide for each citizen "the equal protection of the laws." The easiest and clearest way to understand the distinction between civil liberties and civil rights is to remember that civil liberties issues arise under the "due process" clause in the original Bill of Rights, while civil rights issues arise under the "equal protection" clause that came into play only after the adoption of the Fourteenth Amendment.

Although we will look first at civil liberties because the struggle for freedom against arbitrary and discriminatory action by governments has the longest history, we should not lose sight of the connection in the real world between civil liberties and civil rights and, generally, between liberty and equality. The history of immigration to America, the American colonial experience, and the American Revolution built deeply into the American character and the American culture a commitment to individual liberty and a fear of government intrusions on that liberty. These sentiments have in turn given Americans a love/hate relationship with their government. The 1990s have been an era of particularly strong antagonism toward government interference into personal liberty. Yet the other side of that love/hate equation is also important, because the individual must recognize that the need to be protected *from* government is forever coupled with the need for an *active and positive* government to protect and to advance each individual's opportunity to enjoy liberty.[7]

Nationalizing the Bill of Rights

- Does the Bill of Rights put limits only on the national government or does it limit state governments as well?
- How and when did the Supreme Court nationalize the Bill of Rights?

The First Amendment provides that "Congress shall make no law. . . . " But this is the only amendment in the Bill of Rights that addresses itself exclusively to the national government. For example, the Second Amendment provides that "the right of the people to keep and bear Arms, shall not be infringed." And the Fifth Amendment says, among other things, that "no person shall . . . be twice put in jeopardy of life or limb" for the same crime. Since the First Amendment is the only part of the Bill of Rights that is explicit in its intention to put limits on Congress and therefore on the national government, a fundamental question inevitably arises: Do the remaining provisions of the Bill of Rights put limits only on the national government, or do they limit the state governments as well?

The Supreme Court first answered this question in 1833 by ruling that the Bill of Rights limited only the national government and not the state governments.[8] But in 1868, when the Fourteenth Amendment was added to the Constitution, the question arose once again. The Fourteenth Amendment reads as if it were meant to impose the Bill of Rights upon the states:

> No *State* shall make or enforce any law which shall abridge the privileges or immunities of citizens of the United States; nor shall any *State* deprive any person of life, liberty, or property, without due process of law; nor deny to any person within its jurisdiction the equal protection of the laws [emphasis added].

This language sounds like an effort to extend the Bill of Rights in its entirety to all citizens, wherever they might reside.[9] Yet this was not the Supreme Court's interpretation of the amendment for nearly a hundred years. Within five years of ratification of the Fourteenth Amendment, the Court was making decisions as though the amendment had never been adopted.[10]

The only change in civil liberties during the first sixty years following the adoption of the Fourteenth Amendment came in 1897, when the Supreme Court held that the due process clause of the Fourteenth Amendment did in fact prohibit states from taking property for a public use without just compensation.[11] However, the Supreme Court had selectively "incorporated" into the Fourteenth Amendment only the property protection provision of the Fifth Amendment and no other clause of the Fifth or any other amendment of the Bill of Rights. In other words, although according to the Fifth Amendment "due process" applied to the taking of life and liberty as well as property, only property was incorporated into the Fourteenth Amendment as a limitation on state power.

No further expansion of civil liberties via the Fourteenth Amendment occurred until 1925, when the Supreme Court held that freedom of speech is "among the fundamental personal rights and 'liberties' protected by the due process clause of the Fourteenth Amendment from impairment by the states."[12] In 1931, the Court added freedom of the press to that short list protected by the Bill of Rights from state action; in 1939, it added freedom of assembly.[13]

But that was as far as the Court was willing to go. As late as 1937, the Supreme Court was still loathe to nationalize civil liberties beyond the First Amendment. The Constitution, as interpreted as late as 1937 by the Supreme Court in *Palko v. Connecticut*, left standing the framework in which the states had the power to determine their own law on a number of fundamental issues. *Palko* established the principle of **selective incorporation**, by which only some of the liberties in the Bill of Rights were applied to the states.[14] It left states with the power to pass laws segregating the races—a power that the thirteen former Confederate states chose to exercise. The constitutional framework also left states with the power to engage in searches and seizures without a warrant, to indict accused persons without a grand jury, to deprive accused persons of trial by jury, to deprive persons of their right not to have to testify against themselves, to deprive accused persons of their right to confront adverse witnesses, and to prosecute accused persons more than once for the same crime.[15] Few states chose to use these kinds of powers, but some states did, and the power to do so was available for any state whose legislative majority or courts so chose.

So, until 1961, only the First Amendment and one clause of the Fifth Amendment had been clearly incorporated into the Fourteenth Amendment as binding on the states as well as on the national government.[16] After that, one by one, most of the important provisions of the Bill of Rights were incorporated into the Fourteenth Amendment and applied to the states. Table 5.3 shows the progress of this revolution in the interpretation of the Constitution. By the end of the 1960s, according to one of the leading works of constitutional history, "the final step in nationalizing the Bill of Rights was taken by Congress. In the Civil Rights Act of 1968, it extended the guarantees of the first eight amendments to Indians living under tribal authority on reservations. Thus, all governments in the United States—federal, state, local, and those of Indian tribes—were restricted by the Bill of Rights."[17]

But the controversy over incorporation lives on. Although many have urged the Supreme Court to take the final step by explicitly declaring as a matter of constitutional law that the *entire* Bill of Rights was incorporated by

TABLE 5.3

INCORPORATION OF THE BILL OF RIGHTS INTO THE FOURTEENTH AMENDMENT

Selected provisions and amendments	Not "incorporated" until	Key case
Eminent domain (V)	1897	*Chicago, Burlington, and Quincy R.R. v. Chicago*
Freedom of speech (I)	1925	*Gitlow v. New York*
Freedom of press (I)	1931	*Near v. Minnesota*
Freedom of assembly (I)	1939	*Hague v. CIO*
Freedom from unnecessary search and seizure (IV)	1949	*Wolf v. Colorado*
Freedom from warrantless search and seizure (IV)("exclusionary rule")	1961	*Mapp v. Ohio*
Freedom from cruel and unusual punishment (VIII)	1962	*Robinson v. California*
Right to counsel in any criminal trial (VI)	1963	*Gideon v. Wainwright*
Right against self-incrimination and forced confessions (V)	1964	*Mallory v. Hogan* *Escobedo v. Illinois*
Right to privacy (III, IV, & V)	1965	*Griswold v. Connecticut*
Right to counsel and to remain silent (VI)	1966	*Miranda v. Arizona*
Right against double jeopardy (V)	1969	*Benton v. Maryland*

the Fourteenth Amendment, the current Supreme Court shows no inclination to do that. Indeed, the current Court might even go in an opposite direction. For, as we shall see, the Court continually reminds everyone that if it has the power to expand the Bill of Rights, it also has the power to contract it.[18]

Since liberty for some requires restraining the liberty of others, the general status of civil liberties can never be considered fixed and permanent. Every provision in the Bill of Rights is subject to interpretation, and in any dispute involving a clause of the Bill of Rights, interpretations will always be shaped by the interpreter's interest in the outcome.

The best way to examine the Bill of Rights today is the simplest way—to take each of the major provisions one at a time. Some of these provisions are settled areas of law, and others are not. Any one of them can be reinterpreted by the Court at any time.

The First Amendment and Freedom of Religion

- How does the First Amendment guarantee the non-establishment and free exercise of religion?
- In what way has the free exercise of religion become a recent political issue?

The Bill of Rights begins by guaranteeing freedom, and the First Amendment provides for that freedom in two distinct clauses: "Congress shall make no law [1] respecting an establishment of religion, or [2] prohibiting the free exercise thereof." The first clause is called the "establishment clause," and the second is called the "free exercise clause."

Separation between Church and State

The **establishment clause** has been interpreted quite strictly to mean that a virtual "wall of separation" exists between church and state. The separation of church and state was especially important to the great numbers of American colonists who had sought refuge from persecution for having rejected membership in state-sponsored churches. The concept of a "wall of separation" was Jefferson's own formulation, and this concept has figured in all of the modern Supreme Court cases arising under the establishment clause.

Despite the absolute sound of the phrase "wall of separation," there is ample room to disagree on how high the wall is or of what materials it is composed. For example, the Court has been consistently strict in cases of school prayer, striking down such practices as Bible reading,[19] nondenominational prayer,[20] and even a moment of silence for meditation.[21] In each of these cases, the Court reasoned that school-sponsored observations, even of an apparently nondenominational character, are highly suggestive of school sponsorship and therefore violate the prohibition against establishment of religion. On the other hand, the Court has been quite permissive (and some

The separation between church and state has never been clearly defined. For example, the Supreme Court allowed for the display of this Nativity scene on the Boston Common because it has a secular purpose—promoting a national holiday.

would say inconsistent) about the public display of religious symbols, such as city-sponsored Nativity scenes in commercial or municipal areas.[22] And although the Court has consistently disapproved of government financial support for religious schools, even when the purpose has been purely educational and secular, the Court has permitted certain direct aid to students of such schools in the form of busing, for example. In 1971, after thirty years of cases involving religious schools, the Court attempted to specify some criteria to guide their decisions and those of lower courts, indicating, for example, in a decision invalidating state payments for the teaching of secular subjects in parochial schools, circumstances under which the Court might allow certain financial assistance. The case was *Lemon v. Kurtzman;* in its decision, the Supreme Court established three criteria to guide future cases, in what came to be called the ***Lemon* test.** The Court held that government aid to religious schools would be accepted as constitutional if (1) it had a secular purpose, (2) its effect was neither to advance nor to inhibit religion, and (3) it did not entangle government and religious institutions in each other's affairs.[23] Although these restrictions make the *Lemon* test a hard test to pass, imaginative authorities are finding ways to do so.

Free Exercise of Religion

The **free exercise clause** protects the right to believe and to practice whatever religion one chooses; it also protects the right to be a nonbeliever. The precedent-setting case involving free exercise is *West Virginia State Board of Education v. Barnette* (1943), which involved the children of a family of Jehovah's Witnesses who refused to salute and pledge allegiance to the American flag on the grounds that their religious faith did not permit it. Three years earlier, the Court had upheld such a requirement and had permitted schools to expel students for refusing to salute the flag. But the entry of the United States into a war to defend democracy coupled with the ugly treatment to which the Jehovah's Witnesses children had been subjected induced the Court to reverse itself and to endorse the free exercise of religion even when it may be offensive to the beliefs of the majority.[24]

Although the Supreme Court has been fairly consistent and strict in protecting the free exercise of religious belief, it has taken pains to distinguish between religious beliefs and actions based on those beliefs. In one case, for example, two Native Americans had been fired from their jobs for smoking peyote, an illegal drug. They claimed that they had been fired from their jobs illegally because smoking peyote was a religious sacrament protected by the free exercise clause. The Court did not agree with their claim,[25] but Congress did: it enacted the Religious Freedom Restoration Act of 1993, forbidding any federal agency or state government from burdening a person's free exercise of religion unless the agency or state government demonstrates that its action "furthers a compelling governmental interest" and "is the least restrictive means of furthering that compelling governmental interest." This act only prolonged the controversy over what kinds of religious exercise are protected by the First Amendment. What about polygamy, a practice allowed in the Mormon faith? What about snake worship? Or the refusal of Amish parents to send their children to school beyond eighth grade because exposing their children to "modern values" would undermine their religious commitment? In this last example, the Court decided in favor of the Amish and endorsed a very strong interpretation of the protection of free exercise.[26]

This Native American holy man performed a "cedar ceremony" outside the Supreme Court prior to the Court's decision against two Native Americans who argued that smoking peyote was a religious sacrament protected by the free exercise clause.

A much more recent case brings both the establishment clause and the free exercise clause back into dispute. This case involved Rachel Bauchman, a Jewish student attending a Salt Lake City public high school whose students were predominantly Mormon. With her parents' approval, Ms. Bauchman complained that the high school choir, of which she was a performing member, was singing too many Christian devotionals and performing too often at local churches. The first response of the authorities to her complaint was to add two Jewish songs to the choir's program; their second response was to permit Rachel to sit in the library during rehearsals while still getting an A for participation. But when these accommodations failed, and after Rachel was told that participation in the choir's graduation ceremony performance was compulsory for her grade, the Bauchman family obtained the services of a First Amendment lawyer.

The U.S district judge in Salt Lake City held in favor of the school, conceding that although Rachel may well have been offended, the lyrics did not violate her constitutional rights. The Bauchman family appealed to the U.S. Court of Appeals in Denver, which immediately issued a restraining order forbidding performance of two popular Christian songs at the graduation ceremony—"Friends" and "The Lord Bless You and Keep You." In keeping with the appeals court ruling, the choir sang two replacement songs but then remained standing for an unauthorized rendition of "Friends." The U.S. Court of Appeals later ruled that the school administration did not violate the court's restraining order by failing to stop the choir from singing "Friends."[27]

It is difficult to predict how the courts will settle such controversies. The Bauchman case is even more complex than most other cases involving the separation between church and state because it directly involves *both* religious clauses of the First Amendment.

The Politics of Freedom of Religion

It is precisely because of issues such as those confronted in the Bauchman case and because of the difficulty of anticipating how the courts will rule that conservative religious groups have been pressing Congress to solve the problem with a constitutional amendment. In recent years, such groups have been promoting a "religious equality amendment" as the only way to soften the absoluteness of the "wall of separation" between church and state and between religious expression and public and community demands. Congress has also passed two acts that softened Supreme Court decisions restricting government-sponsored religious activities. The Religious Freedom Restoration Act was signed and praised by President Bill Clinton as an effort to "protect the exercise of religion from being inappropriately burdened by government action." And in 1995, Congress passed the Equal Access Act to allow school authorities to provide access to public school facilities for religious activities without fear of lawsuits or loss of federal funding. Activities by "student noncurriculum-related clubs during noninstructional time" were defined so as to include prayer services, Bible reading, and other forms of worship.

But conservative groups argued that Supreme Court decisions maintaining church-state separation and revising or clarifying the First Amendment should be entirely reversed by an amendment that would clearly establish the power, indeed the obligation, of local public authorities to permit religious activities in public places. In an attempt to head off the promoters of such an amendment, President Clinton issued an unusual memorandum on July 12, 1995, providing an interpretation of the Religious Freedom Restoration and Equal Access acts that might provide sufficient reassurance to religiously observant people so that they would feel no need to amend the Constitution and

Although the Supreme Court has consistently struck down school-sponsored prayer, students can pray in school as long as the school does not endorse it.

the Bill of Rights. President Clinton's memorandum is phrased much like a Supreme Court opinion and may have a similar kind of influence on the federal courts as well as on people and groups who would either seek access to public places for religious services or would organize and litigate against such access.[28]

The religious movement of the 1980s and the judicial and congressional activities of the 1990s identified or actually created unsettled areas involving the establishment clause and the free exercise clause. Thus, although the principle of a substantial separation of church and state still holds, judicial and congressional actions have knocked some cracks in the wall of separation and have moved the constitutional position toward more religious pluralism and away from an absolute wall. Still, many of the more religiously observant groups in American society are not satisfied. In late July 1996, several religious groups tried once again to revive the school prayer amendment, in an attempt to influence the outcome of the 1996 presidential election.

The First Amendment and Freedom of Speech and the Press

> ➤ What forms of speech are protected by the First Amendment? What forms are not protected?

Freedom of speech and freedom of the press are considered critical for a democracy. For this reason, they were given a prominence in the Bill of Rights equal to that of freedom of religion: "Congress shall make no law . . . abridging the freedom of speech, or of the press. . . ." In 1938, freedom of speech (which in all important respects includes freedom of the press) was given extraordinary constitutional status when the Supreme Court established the "preferred freedoms doctrine" as the judicial test in cases involving certain fundamental constitutional freedoms provided in the First Amendment. Ordinarily, when the constitutionality of a law is in question, the **burden of proof** is on the person making the complaint. But in matters dealing with laws governing these fundamental freedoms, the burden of proof is reversed: the government must convince the court that there is a compelling public need for the restriction being proposed. As the Supreme Court put it, any legislation that attempts to restrict these fundamental freedoms "is to be subjected to a more exacting judicial scrutiny... than are most other types of legislation."[29]

What the Court was saying is that the democratic political process must be protected at almost any cost. This higher standard of judicial review came to be called **strict scrutiny.** Strict scrutiny implies that speech—at least some kinds of speech—will be protected almost absolutely. But as it turns out, only some types of speech are fully protected against restrictions. As we shall see, many forms of speech are less than absolutely protected—even though they are entitled to strict scrutiny. This section will look at these two categories of speech: (1) absolutely protected speech, and (2) conditionally protected speech.

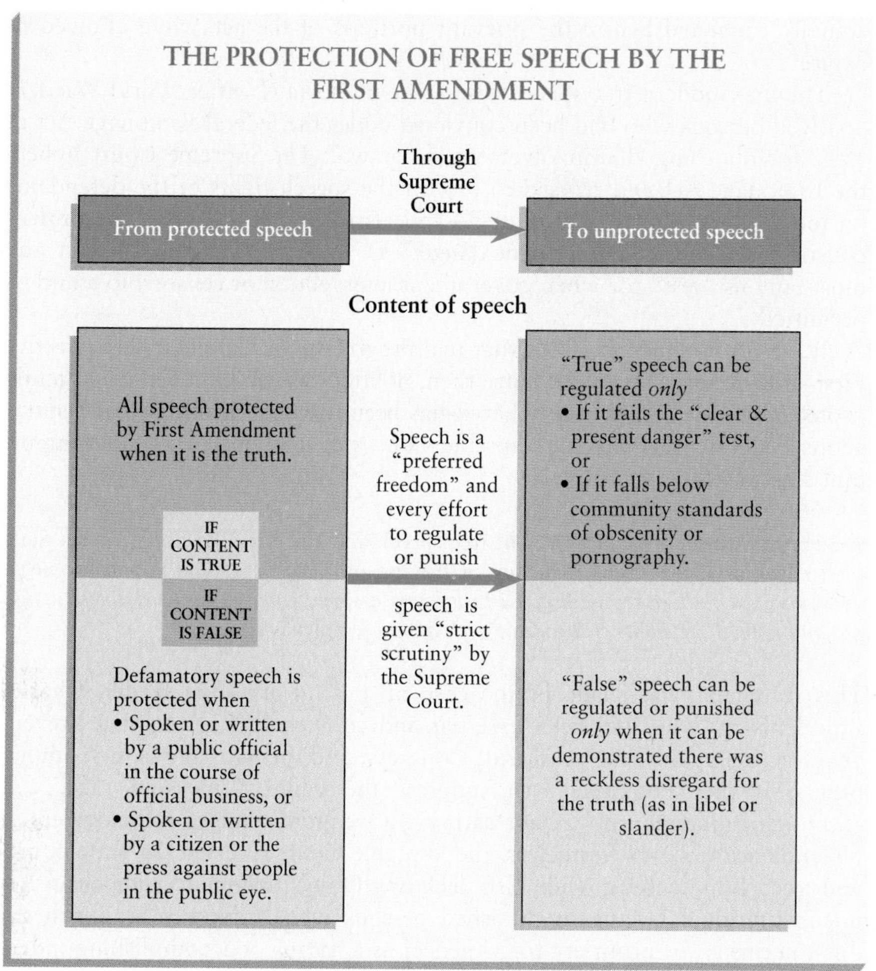

FIGURE 5.1

ABSOLUTELY PROTECTED SPEECH

There is one and only one absolute defense against efforts to place limitations on speech, oral or in print: the truth. The truth is protected even when its expression damages the person to whom it applies. And of all forms of speech, political speech is the most consistently protected.

Political Speech Political speech was the activity of greatest concern to the framers of the Constitution, even though they found it the most difficult provision to observe. Within seven years of the ratification of the Bill of Rights in 1791, Congress adopted the infamous Alien and Sedition Acts, which, among other things, made it a crime to say or publish anything that might tend to defame or bring into disrepute the government of the United States. Quite clearly, the acts' intentions were to criminalize the very conduct given absolute protection by the First Amendment (see also Chapter 8). Fifteen violators—including several newspaper editors—were indicted, and a few were actually convicted before the relevant portions of the acts were allowed to expire.

The first modern free speech case arose immediately after World War I. It involved persons who had been convicted under the federal Espionage Act of 1917 for opposing U.S. involvement in the war. The Supreme Court upheld the Espionage Act and refused to protect the speech rights of the defendants on the grounds that their activities—appeals to draftees to resist the draft—constituted a "clear and present danger" to security.[30] This is the first and most famous "test" for when government intervention or censorship could be permitted.

It was only after the 1920s that real progress toward a genuinely effective First Amendment was made. Since then, political speech has been consistently protected by the courts even when it has been deemed "insulting" or "outrageous." Here is the way the Supreme Court put it in one of its most important statements on the subject:

> The constitutional guarantees of free speech and free press do not permit a State to forbid or proscribe advocacy of the use of force or of law violation *except where such advocacy is directed to inciting or producing imminent lawless action and is likely to incite or produce such action* [emphasis added].[31]

This statement was made in the case of a Ku Klux Klan leader, Charles Brandenburg, who had been arrested and convicted of advocating "revengent" action against the president, Congress, and the Supreme Court, among others, if they continued "to suppress the white, Caucasian race. . . ." Although Brandenburg was not carrying a weapon, some of the members of his audience were. Nevertheless, the Supreme Court reversed the state courts and freed Brandenburg while also declaring Ohio's Criminal Syndicalism Act unconstitutional because it punished persons who "advocate, or teach the duty, necessity, or propriety [of violence] as a means of accomplishing industrial or political reform . . . "; or who publish materials or "voluntarily assemble . . . to teach or advocate the doctrines of criminal syndicalism." The Supreme Court argued that the statute did not distinguish "mere advocacy" from "incitement to imminent lawless action." It would be difficult to go much farther in protecting freedom of speech.

Symbolic Speech, Speech Plus, and the Rights of Assembly and Petition The First Amendment treats the freedoms of assembly and petition as equal to the freedoms of religion and political speech. Freedom of assembly and freedom of petition are closely associated with speech but go beyond it to speech associated with action. Since at least 1931, the Supreme Court has sought to protect actions that are designed to send a political message. (Usually the purpose of a symbolic act is not only to send a direct message but to draw a crowd—to do something spectacular in order to draw spectators to the action and thus strengthen the message.) Thus the Court held unconstitutional a California statute making it a felony to display a red flag "as a sign, symbol or emblem of opposition to organized government."[32] Although today there are limits on how far one can go with actions that symbolically convey a message, the protection of such action is very broad. Thus, although the Court upheld a federal statute making it a crime to burn draft cards to protest the Vietnam War on the grounds that the government had a compelling interest in preserving draft cards as part of the conduct of the war itself, it considered the wearing of black armbands to school a protected form of assembly for symbolic action.

Burning the American flag is a constitutionally protected form of symbolic speech.

A more contemporary example is the burning of the American flag as a symbol of protest. In 1984, at a political rally held during the Republican National Convention in Dallas, Texas, a political protester burned an American flag in violation of a Texas statute that prohibited desecration of a venerated object. In a 5-to-4 decision, the Supreme Court declared the Texas law unconstitutional on the grounds that flag burning was expressive conduct protected by the First Amendment.[33] Congress reacted immediately with a proposal for a constitutional amendment reversing the Court's Texas decision, and when the amendment failed to receive the necessary two-thirds majority in the Senate, Congress passed the Flag Protection Act of 1989. Protesters promptly violated this act and their prosecution moved quickly into the federal district court, which declared the new law unconstitutional. The Supreme Court, in another 5-to-4 decision, affirmed the lower court decision.[34] A renewed effort began in Congress to adopt a constitutional amendment that would reverse the Supreme Court and place this form of expressive conduct outside the realm of protected speech or assembly.

Closer to the original intent of the assembly and petition clause is the category of **"speech plus"**—following speech with physical activity such as picketing, distributing leaflets, and other forms of peaceful demonstration or assembly. Such assemblies are consistently protected by courts under the First Amendment; state and local laws regulating such activities are closely scrutinized and frequently overturned. But the same assembly on private property is quite another matter and can in many circumstances be regulated. For ex-

Anti-abortion demonstrators protest outside the Buffalo, N.Y., GYN Womenservices clinic. The Supreme Court has recognized the right of assembly for antiabortion protesters but has allowed the preservation of a "buffer zone" between demonstrators and abortion clinics.

ample, the directors of a shopping center can lawfully prohibit an assembly protesting a war or supporting a ban on abortion. Assemblies in public areas can also be restricted under some circumstances, especially when the assembly or demonstration jeopardizes the health, safety, or rights of others. This condition was the basis of the Supreme Court's decision to uphold a lower court order that restricted the access abortion protesters had to the entrances of abortion clinics.[35]

One of the most interesting examples of activity protected by the petition provision of the First Amendment is **lobbying**, which involves petitioning members of Congress in support of or against a particular piece of legislation (see Chapter 10). The Federal Regulation of Lobbying Act of 1946 sought to regulate persons who, "directly or indirectly," solicit, collect, or receive money to influence Congress. This is directly aimed at the right to petition Congress—after all, that is what lobbying is all about. But fairly soon after the adoption of the Lobbying Act, the Supreme Court restricted it to efforts to "directly" influence legislation; it held that the statute covered only direct communication with members of Congress and not indirect efforts to influence Congress through broad public appeals. But otherwise, Congress was quite respectful of the First Amendment in the Lobbying Act, because it required only that lobbyists register with Congress and report their lobbying activities to Congress. Anything beyond the requirement of registration and reporting would have been considered a direct violation of the constitutional right of petition.[36] The 1995 efforts of Congress to reform the 1946 act have worked in the very same direction, by strengthening the disclosure provisions. The rationale behind registration requirements is that the light of publicity might force the lobbyists to regulate themselves.

Conditionally Protected Speech

At least four forms of speech fall outside the absolute guarantees of the First Amendment and therefore outside the realm of absolute protection. Since they do enjoy some protection, they qualify as "conditionally protected" types of speech: (1) libel and slander, (2) obscenity and pornography, (3) fighting words, and (4) commercial speech. It should be emphasized once again that these four types of speech still enjoy considerable protection by the courts.

Libel and Slander Some speech is not protected at all. If a written statement is made in "reckless disregard of the truth" and is considered damaging to the victim because it is "malicious, scandalous, and defamatory," it can be punished as **libel.** If an oral statement of such nature is made, it can be punished as **slander.**

Today, most libel suits involve freedom of the press, and the realm of free press is enormous. Historically, newspapers were subject to the law of libel, which provided that newspapers that printed false and malicious stories could be compelled to pay damages to those they defamed. In recent years, however, American courts have greatly narrowed the meaning of libel and made it extremely difficult, particularly for politicians or other public figures, to win a libel case against a newspaper. In the important 1964 case of *New*

York Times v. Sullivan, the Court held that to be deemed libelous a story about a public official not only had to be untrue, but also had to result from "actual malice" or "reckless disregard" for the truth.[37] In other words, the newspaper had to *deliberately* print false and malicious material. In practice, it is nearly impossible to prove that a paper deliberately printed maliciously false information and, as conservatives discovered in the 1980s, it is especially difficult for a politician or other public figure to win a libel case. Libel suits against CBS News by General William Westmoreland and against *Time* magazine by Israeli general Ariel Sharon, suits that were financed by conservative legal foundations that hoped to embarrass the media, were both defeated in court because they failed to show "actual malice." In the 1991 case of *Masson v. New Yorker Magazine,* this tradition was again affirmed when the Court held that fabricated quotations attributed to a public figure were libelous only if the fabricated account "materially changed" the meaning of what the person actually said.[38] Essentially, the print media have been able to publish anything they want about a public figure.

However, in at least one recent case, the Court has opened up the possibility for public officials to file libel suits against the press. In 1985, the Court held that the press was immune from libel only when the printed material was "a matter of public concern." In other words in future cases a newspaper would have to show that the public official was engaged in activities that were indeed *public.* This new principle has made the press more vulnerable to libel suits, but it still leaves an enormous realm of freedom for the press. For example, Reverend Jerry Falwell, the leader of the Moral Majority, lost his libel suit against *Hustler* magazine even though the magazine had published a cartoon of Falwell showing him having drunken intercourse with his mother in an outhouse. A unanimous Supreme Court rejected a jury verdict in favor of damages for "emotional distress" on the grounds that parodies, no matter how outrageous, are protected because "outrageousness" is too subjective a test and thus would interfere with the free flow of ideas protected by the First Amendment.[39]

Rev. Jerry Falwell and his lawyer spoke outside the Supreme Court following the Court's decision against Falwell in his libel suit against *Hustler* magazine.

Obscenity and Pornography If libel and slander cases can be difficult because of the problem of determining the truth of statements and whether those statements are malicious and damaging, cases involving pornography and obscenity can be even more sticky. It is easy to say that pornography and obscenity fall outside the realm of protected speech, but it is impossible to draw a clear line defining exactly where protection ends and unprotected speech begins. Not until 1957 did the Supreme Court confront this problem, and it did so with a definition of obscenity that may have caused more confusion than it cleared up. Justice William Brennan, in writing the Court's opinion, defined obscenity as speech or writing that appeals to the "prurient interest"—that is, books, magazines, films, etc. whose purpose is to excite lust as this appears "to the average person, applying contemporary community standards. . . . " Even so, Brennan added, the work should be judged obscene only when it is "utterly without redeeming social importance."[40] Brennan's definition, instead of clarifying the Court's view, actually caused more confusion. In 1964, Justice Potter Stewart confessed that, although he found pornography impossible to define, "I know it when I see it."[41]

AMERICAN POLITICAL CULTURE

Pornography and the Internet

The Internet was created in the 1960s as a way for scattered military researchers to communicate with each other via computer. It has now grown into a vast electronic gathering place for hundreds of thousands of people. By its very nature, the Internet is not easy to regulate or restrict. Users roam the "Net" from the anonymity and isolation of their own computers, posting whatever they wish, and encountering all kinds of activities and writings: academic forums where researchers from around the world can share ideas and findings; bulletin boards for people who want to talk about any of thousands of topics; diatribes against the government and detailed instructions for making fertilizer-and-fuel-oil bombs; and the rawest kinds of written and visual pornography.

In 1994, Jake Baker, a sophomore at the University of Michigan, wrote a violent sexual fantasy and posted it on the Internet. The story described in vivid detail the capture, rape, torture, and murder of a young woman, a fellow Michigan student whom he identified by name. Others read the posted story; afterwards Mr. Baker and one of his readers in Canada exchanged E-mail about carrying out such an attack. Eventually Mr. Baker was charged with a federal crime: transmitting a threat over state lines by electronic mails. He could have received a prison term of up to five years in jail had he been convicted, but a federal judge dismissed the charge, saying that it would be more appropriate for university officials to discipline Mr. Baker.

Stories such as this have become increasingly familiar in recent years. Are they rare exceptions, or is the Internet dangerously unregulated? How comfortable are we that children can easily access explicit pornographic images and stories over the Internet, or that the anonymity provided by the Internet gives those who wish to the perfect means to befriend and arrange to meet unsuspecting young children? Such concerns have prompted recent calls to regulate the Internet. In the summer of 1995, the Republican majority in the Senate actually passed a bill sponsored by the then–majority leader, Bob Dole, to impose censorship on the Net. Dole proposed outlawing obscenity or sexually explicit material from being posted on computer networks, imposing fines of up to $100,000 on anyone who makes indecent sexual material available to minors via computer, and making the transmission of indecent or harassing messages, such as Jake Baker's, a crime.

Community standards of decency, even within the high-tech "community" of computer networks, are an important value for Republicans. But so is freedom of expression. After Senate Republicans won passage of the bill to regulate the Internet, the Speaker of the House, Newt Gingrich, came out squarely against it: "It is clearly a violation of free speech, and it's a violation of the right of adults to communicate with each other."[1] Gingrich argued that rather than having the government censor the Internet, control should fall to the marketplace, by letting commercial on-line services regulate the material they permit to be posted.

The Internet and its progeny, such as the World Wide Web, are the frontier of modern communication. As technology continues to develop, as costs decline, and as computer literacy spreads, electronic communities and computer communication will surely claim an even greater role in people's lives. And as with all frontier communities, the inhabitants of this community face a challenge in deciding how to police it and what balance of freedom and control to impose upon it. These are political questions, to be settled ultimately by legislatures. But such political questions have their roots in our cultural values. What sort of communities do we wish to live in? How should we choose to balance individual rights against an ordered society?

[1]Edmund L. Andrews, "Gingrich Opposes Smut Rule for Internet," *New York Times*, June 22, 1995, p. A20.

All attempts by the courts to define pornography and obscenity have proved impractical, because each instance required courts to screen thousands of pages of print material and feet of film alleged to be pornographic. The vague and impractical standards that had been developed meant ultimately that almost nothing could be banned on the grounds of pornography and obscenity. An effort was made to strengthen the restrictions in 1973, when the Supreme Court expressed its willingness to define pornography as a work which (1) as a whole, is deemed prurient by the "average person" according to "community standards"; (2) depicts sexual conduct "in a patently offensive way"; and (3) lacks "serious literary, artistic, political, or scientific value." This definition meant that pornography would be determined by local rather than national standards. Thus, a local bookseller might be prosecuted for selling a volume that was a bestseller nationally but that was deemed pornographic locally.[42] This new definition of standards did not help much either, and not long after 1973 the Court began again to review all such community antipornography laws, reversing most of them.

Consequently, today there is a widespread fear that Americans are free to publish any and all variety of intellectual expression, whether there is any "redeeming social value" or not. Yet this area of free speech is far from settled. The search continues for limits to the protection of speech that tends toward the pornographic and obscene. In fact, a surprising new alliance has formed between conservative groups in America and a number of leading feminists. Both mainstream conservatives and the religious Right adamantly believe that virtually nothing of even a barely suggestive and subtle pornographic or obscene nature deserves the protection of the First Amendment. Thus, conservatives are actively supporting state and local antipornography and obscenity legislation and vigorous police enforcement of what they broadly call "standards of decency." Their influence has been felt keenly by top politicians, including 1996 Republican presidential candidate Bob Dole, who publicly condemned the movies and musical output of communications giant Time Warner.[43] Conservatives have joined forces with an impressive number of feminists on the basis of the feminist argument that every pornographic statement is an act of violence against women and should be censored by law. If the Constitution has to be changed or reinterpreted to permit passage of such laws, they support that as well.[44]

The cover that started a controversy.

A second example of the contemporary battle against obscene speech is that against "cyberporn"—pornography on the Internet. Opponents of this form of expression argue that it should be banned because of the easy access children have to the Internet. Wildly different estimates have been made of the extent and availability of cyberporn, and there are equally vast differences of opinion on the effect of cyberporn on the viewer. On July 3, 1995, *Time* magazine focused its cover story on the extent and dangers of cyberporn. Only three weeks later, however, *Time* backed away from its report, admitting that a more careful review of existing studies revealed that pornography could be identified in fewer than .005 percent of all the messages posted on the Internet. This reversal of *Time*'s original position caused a furor among those who were beginning to use the original story to support the case for regulating speech on the Internet. They argued that the low figure of .005 percent does not reveal how often those pornographic files are downloaded. In other words, even a tiny amount of space on the vast Internet can still constitute a threat to social values and social order.[45] The statistics and the dispute over the meaning of the statistics all lead to a more fundamental point: where obscenity and pornography are concerned, Internet technology has simply made the line between free speech and regulated speech impossible to draw. The Supreme Court tried to draw such a line in its 1973 opinion in *Miller v. California,* providing that "contemporary community standards" should be used to determine whether a law restricting pornographic and obscene materials is appropriate. But such a rule can no longer be applied, for the obvious reason that Internet communication is nationwide—and worldwide. It is no longer a matter of what to do about *Playboy* on the shelves of the local newsstand.

Concern over Internet smut, sparked by the original *Time* publicity, might well lead to a crackdown on all Internet communication, which will lead inevitably toward new judicial guidelines. The first sign of such an effort came on June 11, 1996, when a three-judge federal court in Pennsylvania granted a preliminary injunction to stop enforcement of provisions of the Communications Decency Act of 1996 that applied to communications over the Internet deemed to be "indecent" or "patently offensive" to minors. But no one can tell whether the appeals courts or the Supreme Court will accept the constitutionality of such speech regulation or whether they will throw out all regulation in favor of a wide open, free market of ideas, however offensive they may be to some.

Fighting Words Speech can also lose its protected position when it moves toward the sphere of action. "Expressive speech," for example, is protected until it moves from the symbolic realm to the realm of actual conduct—to direct incitement of damaging conduct with the use of so-called **fighting words.** In 1942, the Supreme Court upheld the arrest and conviction of a man who had violated a state law forbidding the use of offensive language in public. He had called the arresting officer a "goddamned racketeer" and "a damn Fascist." When his case reached the Supreme Court, the arrest was upheld on the grounds that the First Amendment provides no protection for such offensive language because such words "are no essential part of any exposition of ideas."[46] This case was reaffirmed in a much more famous and important case during the height of the Cold War, when the Supreme Court held that "there is no substantial public interest in permitting certain kinds of utterances: the lewd and obscene, the profane, the libelous, and the insulting or 'fighting' words—those which by their very utterance inflict injury or tend to incite an immediate breach of the peace."[47]

Since that time, however, the Supreme Court has reversed almost every conviction based on arguments that the speaker had used "fighting words." But again, that does not mean that this is an absolutely settled area. In recent years, the increased activism of minority and women's groups has prompted a movement against words that might be construed as offensive to members of a particular group. This movement has come to be called, derisively, "political correctness." In response to this movement, many organizations have attempted to impose codes of etiquette that acknowledge these enhanced sensitivities. These efforts to formalize the restraints on the use of certain words in public are causing great concern over their possible infringement of freedom of speech. But how should we determine what words are "fighting words" that fall outside the protections of the freedom of speech?

For example, scores of universities have attempted to develop speech codes to suppress utterances deemed to be racial or ethnic slurs. What these universities find, however, is that the codes produce more problems than they solve. The University of Pennsylvania learned this when it first tried to apply its newly written "Harassment Code." Around midnight in January of 1993, Eden Jacobowitz and several other students trying to study yelled from their dorm windows at a noisy group of partying black sorority members: "Shut up, you water buffaloes." Other students also made rude comments, including racial and sexual slurs, but Jacobowitz was the only one who actually came forward and admitted to having yelled. Born in Israel and fluent in Hebrew, Jacobowitz explained that "water buffalo" loosely translated from Hebrew means "rude person." Nevertheless, the University of Pennsylvania brought Jacobowitz before a campus judicial inquiry board and charged him with racial harassment in violation of the new code. The black women at whom he had yelled also brought civil charges of racial harassment against Jacobowitz. Five months after the incident, all charges were dropped—both the civil charges and those brought by the university. After reviewing the matter, Penn officials confessed that the university's harassment code "contained flaws which could not withstand the stress of intense publicity and international attention."[48]

Such concerns are not limited to universities, although universities have probably moved farthest toward efforts to formalize "politically correct" speech guidelines. Similar developments have taken place in large corporations, both public and private, in which many successful complaints and lawsuits have been brought alleging that the words of employers or their supervisors create a "hostile or abusive working environment." These cases arise out of the civil rights laws and are almost entirely concerned with gender discrimination as interpreted and applied by the Equal Employment Opportunity Commission (EEOC). The Supreme Court has upheld these laws and EEOC decisions as valid exercises of federal power, and even Chief Justice William Rehnquist, a conservative, has agreed that "sexual harassment" that creates a "hostile working environment" includes "unwelcome sexual advances, requests for sexual favors, and other *verbal* or physical conduct of a sexual nature" (emphasis added).[49] There is a fundamental free speech issue involved in these regulations of hostile speech. So far, the assumption favoring the regulation of hostile speech in universities and other workplaces is that "some speech must be shut down in the name of free speech because it tends to silence those disparaged by it,"[50] even though a threat of hostile action (usually embodied in "fighting words") is not present. The United States is on something of a collision course between the right to express hostile views and the protection of the sensitivities of minorities and women. The collisions will end up in the courts, but not before a lot more airing in public and balancing efforts by state legislatures and Congress.

In 1993, Teresa Harris won a unanimous Supreme Court decision in her sexual harassment suit against her employer. The Court's decision made it easier for individuals to prove sexual harassment in the workplace.

Whatever the outcome of the effort to be politically correct, the point of these issues is already clear. Some words are fighting words and will not be protected by the First Amendment. Common civility moves most people to seek political correctness, to pay heed to the special sensitivities of others. But the standards for what constitutes fighting words do change. Until the end of the eighteenth century, duels were fought over the slightest offense to a person's honor or dignity. Nineteenth-century Western lore is filled with stories of gunfights precipitated by insults considered ridiculously petty today. Neither courts nor universities will ever succeed in codifying political correctness. But, case by case and situation by situation, some words will always incite some people to violent and lawless retaliation, and some degree of censorship—some departure from First Amendment protection—will be invoked.

Commercial Speech Commercial speech, such as newspaper or television advertisements, does not have full First Amendment protection because it cannot be considered political speech. Initially considered to be entirely outside the protection of the First Amendment, commercial speech has made gains during the twentieth century. Some commercial speech is still unprotected and therefore regulated. For example, the regulation of false and misleading advertising by the Federal Trade Commission is an old and well-established power of the federal government. The Supreme Court long ago approved the constitutionality of laws prohibiting the electronic media from carrying cigarette advertising.[51] The Supreme Court has upheld a state university ban on Tupperware parties in college dormitories.[52] It has also upheld city ordinances prohibiting the posting of all signs on public property (as long as the ban is total, so that there is no hint of censorship).[53] And the Supreme Court, in a heated 5-to-4 decision written by Chief Justice Rehnquist, upheld Puerto Rico's statute restricting casino gambling advertising aimed at residents of Puerto Rico.[54]

However, the gains far outweigh the losses in the effort to expand the protection commercial speech enjoys under the First Amendment. "In part, this reflects the growing appreciation that commercial speech is part of the free flow of information necessary for informed choice and democratic participation."[55] For example, the Supreme Court in 1975 struck down a state statute making it a misdemeanor to sell or circulate newspapers encouraging abortions; the Court ruled that the statute infringed upon constitutionally protected speech and upon the right of the reader to make informed choices.[56] On a similar basis, the Court reversed its own earlier decisions upholding laws that prohibited dentists and other professionals from advertising their services. For the Court, medical service advertising was a matter of health that could be advanced by the free flow of information.[57] In 1983, the Supreme Court struck down a congressional statute that prohibited the unsolicited mailing of advertisements for contraceptives. These instances of commercial speech are significant in themselves, but they are all the more significant because they indicate the breadth and depth of the freedom existing today to direct appeals broadly to a large public, not only to sell goods and services but also to mobilize people for political purposes.

An additional facet of commercial speech involves the question of broadcasting rights: the commercial and political rights of broadcasters must be restricted and regulated because of the technological limits of the airwaves. It is a fairly well established principle that no person or corporation has a right to use the public airwaves without having to get permission in the form of a license. Without the fairly strict regulation of access to radio and television channels, such chaos would result that virtually all the rights of free speech, assembly, and petition would be rendered difficult if not impossible to enjoy. A veritable revolution in the deregulation of the telecommunications industry was passed into law by Congress and signed by the president in early 1996. But one power of the national government was not touched by the new law: The allocation of the limited space on the broadcast spectrum will not be turned over to pure market competition. The national government will continue to regulate the use of the broadcasting channels because that may be the only effective way to keep the various electronic media from interfering with each other, whether deliberately or spontaneously.

The Second Amendment and the Right to Bear Arms

> ➤ Is the right to bear arms guaranteed by the Bill of Rights? How is its exercise restricted?

> A well regulated Militia, being necessary to the security of a free State, the right of the people to keep and bear Arms, shall not be infringed.

The Second Amendment may seem to some to be the product of a long-ago, quaint era, but it is very much alive in spirit and has emerged as one of America's most pressing contemporary public issues.

The point and purpose of the Second Amendment is the provision for militias; they were to be the backing of the government for the maintenance of local public order. "Militia" was understood at the time of the Founding to be a military or police resource for state governments, and militias were specifically distinguished from armies and troops, which came within the sole constitutional jurisdiction of Congress. Under Article I, Section 8, Congress was given the power

> To declare war; . . . To raise and support Armies; . . . To provide and maintain a Navy; . . . To provide for calling forth the Militia to execute the Laws of the Union, suppress Insurrections and repel Invasions; . . . [and] to provide for organizing, arming, and disciplining, the Militia, and for governing such Part of them as may be employed in the Service of the United States, reserving to the States respectively . . . the Authority of training the Militia according to the discipline prescribed by Congress.

Article I, Section 10, made it quite explicit that "no State shall, without the Consent of Congress . . . keep Troops, or Ships of War in time of Peace, . . . or engage in War." The Supreme Court went even further, in the turbulent year of 1939, with the holding that

> the Militia which the States were expected to maintain and train is set in contrast with Troops which they were forbidden to keep without the consent of Congress. The sentiment of the time strongly disfavored standing armies; the common view was that adequate defense of country and laws could be secured through the Militia—civilians primarily, soldiers on occasion.[58]

The right to bear arms seems unquestionable, although states are allowed to regulate the sale of weapons by requiring a waiting period or a background check on the purchaser.

Thus, there seems to be no question that the right of people to bear arms is based upon and associated with participation in a state militia. Nevertheless, individuals do have a constitutional right to bear arms, as is provided in the second half of the amendment. The experience of Americans with colonial military rule pointed the Founders and their supporters to the need of every citizen for some kind of personal self-defense. One of the fundamental requirements of a strong government is that it have a monopoly on the use of force. Broad distribution of guns in the hands of citizens does in fact weaken the government, for better or for worse. When confronted with the issue in those terms, few Americans would be likely to approve of an American government possessing a monopoly of force, with a totally disarmed citizenry. The fundamental right of Americans to own weapons is promoted by one of America's biggest and most influential contemporary interest groups, the National Rifle Association (NRA).

But the line drawn between owning weapons as part of a militia or army, on the one hand, and as individuals, on the other, raises some complex questions, for which neither the NRA nor its adversaries have good answers. For example, can clear boundaries be drawn around technologies, separating weapons for defense of home and hearth from offensive weapons of massive destructive power? Can a distinction be made between arms necessary for participation in a "well regulated militia" and for individual anti-personnel defense, on the one hand, and weapons used as part of an individual's participation in *private* militias not sponsored or regulated by government, on the other? And, given the absoluteness of the Second Amendment—that "the right of the people to keep and bear Arms, shall not be infringed"—does any government have any authority to draw the boundaries alluded to above?

Part of the answer to these questions can be found in the amendment itself. A "well regulated" militia implies that the state governments *do* have power to regulate the arms as well as the arms bearers. And in Article I, Section 8, clauses 15 and 16, the Constitution seems to be unmistakably clear: Congress is given the power of "calling forth the Militia to execute the Laws of the Union, . . ." and the power "to provide for organizing, arming, and disciplining, the Militia, and for governing such Part of them as may be employed in the Service of the United States. . . ." The Constitution then reinforces the power of the States by granting the power to the States to appoint the officers and provide for the training of the militia "according to the discipline prescribed by Congress."

Thus American citizens unquestionably have a right to bear arms, but the exercise of this right can be regulated both by state and by federal law. Within this well-designed domain, however, are no rules for what is wise and what is foolish legislation, or what is appropriate and what is inappropriate regulation. Issues such as these have to be settled in the political process, not by courts—and certainly not by arms, even if Americans do have a right to bear them.[59]

Rights of the Criminally Accused

- What is due process?
- How do the Fourth, Fifth, Sixth, and Eighth amendments provide for the due process of law?

Except for the First Amendment, most of the battle to apply the Bill of Rights to the states was fought over the various protections granted to individuals who are accused of a crime, who are suspects in the commission of a crime, or who are brought before the court as a witness to a crime. The Fourth, Fifth, Sixth, and Eighth amendments, taken together, are the essence of the **due process of law,** even though this fundamental concept does not appear until the very last words of the Fifth Amendment. Even the Supreme Court itself has admitted that "due process of law" cannot be given a precise and final definition or explanation. In lieu of an outright definition, the Court maintains the position it took over a century ago: it prefers to rely on "the gradual process of judicial inclusion and exclusion" to indicate the meaning of "due process."[60]

Because most criminal laws in the United States exist at the state level (see Chapter 14), most of the questions over due process have concerned state laws as applied by state police, state prosecutors, and state courts. In the next sections we will look at specific cases that illuminate the dynamics of this important constitutional issue. The procedural safeguards that we will discuss may seem remote to most law-abiding citizens, but they help define the limits of government action against the personal liberty of every citizen.

In all court matters involving crime, "the state" is the plaintiff, or the party charging an individual with the crime: "*New York v. Jones,*" "*New Jersey v. Smith,*" or "*The People of the State of California v. Orenthal James Simpson.*" The idea of the entire power of a state being arrayed against a defendant is pretty imposing; it seems unequal even if the accused has the resources to hire renowned attorneys for his or her defense—as O. J. Simpson did, for example. Few defendants have the resources that Simpson did, therefore the requirements of due process are an attempt to equalize the playing field between an accused individual and the all-powerful state.

Many Americans believe that "legal technicalities" are responsible for setting many actual criminals free. In many cases, that is absolutely true. In fact, setting defendants free is the very purpose of the requirements that constitute due process. One of America's traditional and most strongly held juridical values is that "it is far worse to convict an innocent man than to let a guilty man go free."[61] In civil suits, verdicts rest upon "the preponderance of the evidence"; in criminal cases, guilt has to be proven "beyond a reasonable doubt"—a far higher standard. The provisions for due process in the Bill of Rights were added in order to improve the probability that the standard of "reasonable doubt" will be respected.

THE FOURTH AMENDMENT AND SEARCHES AND SEIZURES

> The right of the people to be secure in their persons, houses, papers, and effects, against unreasonable searches and seizures, shall not be violated, and no Warrants shall issue, but upon probable cause, supported by Oath or affirmation, and particularly describing the place to be searched, and the persons or things to be seized.

The purpose of the Fourth Amendment is to guarantee the security of citizens against unreasonable (i.e., improper) searches and seizures. In 1990 the Supreme Court summarized its understanding of the Fourth Amendment brilliantly and succinctly: "A search compromises the individual interest in privacy; a seizure deprives the individual of dominion over his or her person or property."[62]

These high school band members were searched for weapons before a football game in Birmingham, Alabama. A reasonable search?

But how are we to define what is reasonable and what is unreasonable? Generally, in the administration of justice in the United States, the decision about whether a search is reasonable is in the hands of judges and courts. First of all, it is the courts that issue a warrant before a search or arrest can be made. If a court has issued a warrant for a search, that search is considered reasonable. But in some circumstances, the time or opportunity may not be available for a court-issued warrant to be obtained. For example, a police officer has the authority to ask a person on the street to give "credible and reliable" identification and to account for his or her presence. But if that person refuses to cooperate and the officer has to take additional steps to get a response, the Fourth Amendment comes into play. The officer must have "probable cause," or reasonable suspicion that the person may be involved in a crime, to detain him or her for further inquiry. Whether such "probable cause" exists is another decision made by a judge or court.

When a crime has occurred and the investigation of it begins, the police often face a thicket of unknowns, and they are always operating on the verge of trampling valuable evidence or violating the rights of suspects and witnesses. The O. J. Simpson case is illustrative. Without eyewitnesses or videotapes to indicate who had committed two murders, the police had to search for clues. In the hysteria following the public revelation of such a scandal involving an extraordinary celebrity, the murder scene was trampled, potentially valuable evidence was mishandled, accounts of events were inconsistent, and expert reports and lab results from samples of blood, clothing, grass, and soil were inconclusive or uncertain. Should a person's fate hang (pardon the pun) on such evidence?

Often the American public expresses frustration when a jury delivers an acquittal in a case involving a prominent suspect or a seemingly solid presentation of evidence. But, as with freedom of speech and the press, if Americans genuinely support the right to a fair trial, they must also support the acquittal of the accused when the police or the courts fail to adhere to due process.

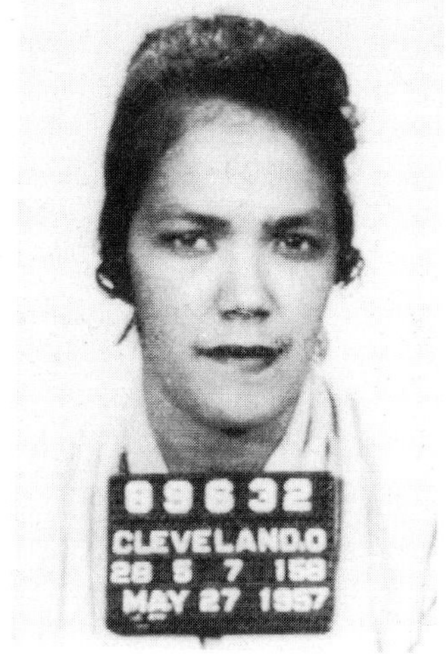

Dollree Mapp's lawsuit against the Cleveland Police Department went to the Supreme Court and nationalized the exclusionary rule.

The 1961 case of *Mapp v. Ohio* illustrates the beauty and the agony of one of the most important procedures that have grown out of the Fourth Amendment—the **exclusionary rule,** which prohibits evidence obtained during an illegal search from being introduced in a trial. Dollree (Dolly) Mapp was "a Cleveland woman of questionable reputation" (by some accounts), the ex-wife of one prominent boxer, and the fiancée of an even more famous one. Acting on a tip that Dolly Mapp was harboring a suspect in a bombing incident, several policemen forcibly entered Ms. Mapp's house claiming they had a warrant to look for the bombing suspect. The police did not find the bombing suspect but did find some materials connected to the local numbers racket (an illegal gambling operation) and a quantity of "obscene materials," in violation of an Ohio law banning possession of such materials. Although the warrant was never produced, the evidence that had been seized was admitted by a court, and Ms. Mapp was charged and convicted for illegal possession of obscene materials.

By the time Ms. Mapp's appeal reached the Supreme Court, the issue of obscene materials had faded into obscurity, and the question before the Court was whether any evidence produced under the circumstances of the search of her home was admissible. The Court's opinion affirmed the exclusionary rule: Under the Fourth Amendment (applied to the states through the Fourteenth Amendment), "all evidence obtained by searches and seizures in violation of the Constitution . . . is inadmissible."[63] This means that even people who are clearly guilty of the crime of which they are accused must not be convicted if the only evidence for their conviction was obtained illegally.

The exclusionary rule is the most severe restraint ever imposed by the Constitution and the courts on the behavior of the police. And that was precisely the basis on which it was defended from its critics. As one author put it, "victims of unreasonable searches are often not in a position to sue the police. Nor are police and prosecutors likely to move against fellow officers who are engaging in unlawful searches."[64] The exclusionary rule is so dramatic a restriction because it rules out precisely the evidence that produces a conviction; it frees those people who are *known* to have committed the crime of which they have been accused. Because it works so dramatically in favor of persons known to have committed a crime, the Court has since softened the application of the rule. In recent years, the federal courts have relied upon a discretionary use of the exclusionary rule, whereby they make a judgment as to the "nature and quality of the intrusion." It is thus difficult to know ahead of time whether a defendant will or will not be protected from an illegal search under the Fourth Amendment.[65]

THE FIFTH AMENDMENT

> No person shall be held to answer for a capital, or otherwise infamous crime, unless on a presentment or indictment of a Grand Jury, except in cases arising in the land or naval forces, or in the Militia, when in actual service in time of War or public danger; nor shall any person be subject for the same offence to be twice put in jeopardy of life or limb; nor shall be compelled in any criminal case to be a witness against himself, nor be deprived of life, liberty, or property, without due process of law; nor shall private property be taken for public use, without just compensation.

Grand Juries The first clause of the Fifth Amendment, the right to a grand jury to determine whether a trial is warranted, is considered "the oldest institution known to the Constitution."[66] Grand juries play an important role in federal criminal cases. However, the provision for a grand jury is the one important civil liberties provision of the Bill of Rights that was not incorporated by the Fourteenth Amendment to apply to state criminal prosecutions. Thus, some states operate without grand juries. In such states, the prosecuting attorney simply files a "bill of information" affirming that there is sufficient evidence available to justify a trial. If the accused person is to be held in custody, the prosecutor must take the available information before a judge to determine that the evidence shows probable cause.

Double Jeopardy "Nor shall any person be subject for the same offence to be twice put in jeopardy of life or limb" is the constitutional protection from **double jeopardy,** or being tried more than once for the same crime. The protection from double jeopardy was at the heart of the *Palko* case in 1937, which, as we saw earlier in this chapter, also established the principle of selective incorporation of the Bill of Rights. In that case, the state of Connecticut had indicted Frank Palko for first-degree murder, but a lower court had found him guilty of only second-degree murder and sentenced him to life in prison. Unhappy with the verdict, the state of Connecticut appealed the conviction to its highest court, won the appeal, got a new trial, and then succeeded in getting Palko convicted of first-degree murder. Palko appealed to the Supreme Court on what seemed an open and shut case of double jeopardy. Yet, although the majority of the Court agreed that this could indeed be considered a case of double jeopardy, they decided that double jeopardy was *not* one of the provisions of the Bill of Rights incorporated in the Fourteenth Amendment as a restriction on the powers of the states. It took more than thirty years for the Court to nationalize the constitutional protection against double jeopardy. Palko was eventually executed for the crime, because he lived in the state of Connecticut rather than in some state whose constitution included a guarantee against double jeopardy.

Self-Incrimination Perhaps the most significant liberty found in the Fifth Amendment, and the one most familiar to many Americans who watch television crime shows, is the guarantee that no citizen "shall be compelled in any criminal case to be a witness against himself. . . ." The most famous case concerning self-incrimination is one of such importance that Chief Justice Earl Warren assessed its results as going "to the very root of our concepts of

American criminal jurisprudence."[67] Twenty-three-year-old Ernesto Miranda was sentenced to between twenty and thirty years in prison for the kidnapping and rape of an eighteen-year-old girl. The girl had identified him in a police lineup, and, after two hours of questioning, Miranda confessed, subsequently signing a statement that his confession had been made voluntarily, without threats or promises of immunity. These confessions were admitted into evidence, served as the basis for Miranda's conviction, and also served as the basis of the appeal of his conviction all the way to the Supreme Court. In one of the most intensely and widely criticized decisions ever handed down by the Supreme Court, Ernesto Miranda's case produced the rules the police must follow before questioning an arrested criminal suspect. The reading of a person's "Miranda rights" (see Figure 5.2) became a standard scene in every police station and on virtually every dramatization of police action on television and in the movies. *Miranda* advanced the civil liberties of accused persons by expanding not only the scope of the Fifth Amendment clause covering coerced confessions and self-incrimination, but also by confirming the right to counsel (discussed later). The Supreme Court under Burger and Rehnquist has considerably softened the *Miranda* restrictions, making the job of the police a little easier, but the ***Miranda* rule** still stands as a protection against egregious police abuses of arrested persons.

Ernesto Miranda was arrested for kidnapping and rape. At first he denied his guilt, but he eventually confessed to the crime. Since he was never told that he was not required to answer police questions, his case was appealed on the grounds that his right against self-incrimination had been violated.

Eminent Domain The other fundamental clause of the Fifth Amendment is the "takings clause," which extends to each citizen a protection against the "taking" of private property "without just compensation." Although this part of the Fifth Amendment is not specifically concerned with protecting persons accused of crimes, it is nevertheless a fundamentally important in-

YOUR MIRANDA RIGHTS

DEFENDANT | LOCATION

SPECIFIC WARNING REGARDING INTERROGATIONS

1. YOU HAVE THE RIGHT TO REMAIN SILENT.
2. ANYTHING YOU SAY CAN AND WILL BE USED AGAINST YOU IN A COURT OF LAW.
3. YOU HAVE THE RIGHT TO TALK TO A LAWYER AND HAVE HIM PRESENT WITH YOU WHILE YOU ARE BEING QUESTIONED.
4. IF YOU CANNOT AFFORD TO HIRE A LAWYER ONE WILL BE APPOINTED TO REPRESENT YOU BEFORE ANY QUESTIONING, IF YOU WISH ONE.

SIGNATURE OF DEFENDANT | DATE

WITNESS | TIME

☐ REFUSED SIGNATURE SAN FRANCISCO POLICE DEPARTMENT PR.9.1.4

FIGURE 5.2

The reading of one's "Miranda rights" is now standard police procedure.

stance where the government and the citizen are adversaries. The power of any government to take private property for a public use is called **eminent domain.** This power is essential to the very concept of sovereignty. The Fifth Amendment neither invents eminent domain nor takes it away; its purpose is to put limits on that inherent power through procedures that require a showing of a public purpose and the provision of fair payment for the taking of someone's property. This provision is now universally observed in all U.S. principalities, but it has not always been meticulously observed.

Take the case of Mr. Berman, who in the 1950s owned and operated a "mom and pop" grocery store in a run-down neighborhood on the southwest side of the District of Columbia. In carrying out a vast urban redevelopment program, the city government of Washington, D.C., took Mr. Berman's property as one of a large number of privately owned lots to be cleared for new housing and business construction. Mr. Berman, and his successors after his death, took the government to court on the grounds that it was an unconstitutional use of eminent domain to take property from one private owner and eventually to turn that property back, in altered form, to another private owner. Berman and his successors lost their case. The Supreme Court's argument was a curious but very important one: the "public interest" can mean virtually anything a legislature says it means. In other words, since the overall slum clearance and redevelopment project was in the public interest, according to the legislature, the eventual transfers of property that were going to take place were justified.[68]

The Sixth Amendment and the Right to Counsel

> In all criminal prosecutions, the accused shall enjoy the right to a speedy and public trial, by an impartial jury of the State and district wherein the crime shall have been committed, which district shall have been ascertained by law, and to be informed of the nature and cause of the accusation; to be confronted with the witnesses against him; to have compulsory process for obtaining witnesses in his favor, and to have the Assistance of Counsel for his defence.

Like the exclusionary rule of the Fourth Amendment and the self-incrimination clause of the Fifth Amendment, the "right to counsel" provision of the Sixth Amendment is notable for freeing defendants who seem to the public to be patently guilty as charged. Other provisions of the Sixth Amendment, such as the right to a speedy trial and the right to confront witnesses before an impartial jury, are less controversial in nature.

Gideon v. Wainwright is the perfect case study because it involved a disreputable person who seemed patently guilty of the crime for which he was convicted. In and out of jails for most of his fifty-one years, Clarence Earl Gideon received a five-year sentence for breaking and entering a pool room in Panama City, Florida. While serving time in jail, Gideon became a fairly well qualified "jailhouse lawyer," made his own appeal on a handwritten, barely literate petition, and eventually won the landmark ruling on the right to counsel in all felony cases.[69]

The right to counsel has been expanded rather than contracted during the past few decades, when the courts have become more conservative. For example, although at first the right to counsel was met by judges assigning

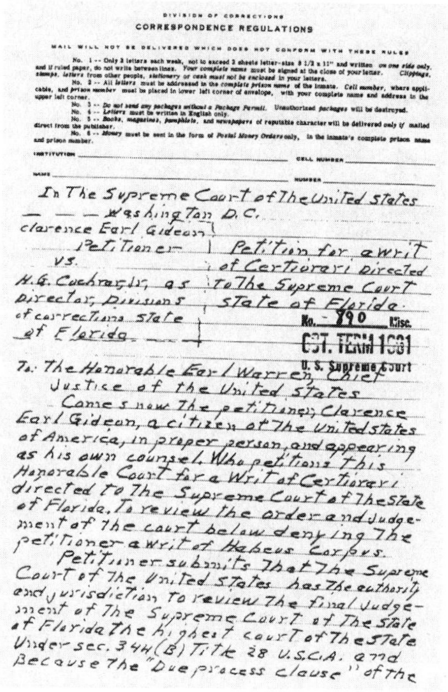
DIVISION OF CORRECTIONS
CORRESPONDENCE REGULATIONS
MAIL WILL NOT BE DELIVERED WHICH DOES NOT CONFORM WITH THESE RULES
No. 1 -- Only 2 letters each week, not to exceed 2 sheets letter-size 8 1/2 x 11" and written *on one side only*, and if ruled paper, do not write between lines. *Your complete name* must be signed at the close of your letter. *Clippings, stamps, letters* from other people, *stationery* or *cash must not be enclosed* in your letters.
No. 2 -- All *letters* must be addressed in the *complete prison name* of the inmate. *Cell number*, where applicable, and *prison number* must be placed in lower left corner of envelope, with your complete name and address in the upper left corner.
No. 3 -- *Do not send any packages without a Package Permit.* Unauthorized *packages* will be destroyed.
No. 4 -- *Letters* must be written in English only.
No. 5 -- *Books, magazines, pamphlets,* and *newspapers* of reputable character will be delivered *only if* mailed direct from the publisher.
No. 6 -- *Money* must be sent in the form of *Postal Money Orders* only, in the inmate's complete prison name and prison number.
INSTITUTION ______ CELL NUMBER ______
NAME ______ NUMBER ______

In The Supreme Court of The United States
— — — Washington D.C.
clarence Earl Gideon
Petitioner | Petition for a writ
vs. | of Certiorari Directed
H.G. Cochran, Jr., as | To The Supreme Court
Director, Divisions | State of Florida.
of corrections State
of Florida
No. 890 Misc.
OCT. TERM 1961
U. S. Supreme Court

To: The Honorable Earl Warren, Chief Justice of the United States
Comes now the petitioner, Clarence Earl Gideon, a citizen of The United states of America, in proper person, and appearing as his own counsel. Who petitions this Honorable Court for a Writ of Certiorari directed to The Supreme Court of The State of Florida. To review the order and Judgement of the court below denying The petitioner a writ of Habeus Corpus.
Petitioner submits That The Supreme Court of The United States has The authority and jurisdiction to review The final Judgement of The Supreme Court of The State of Florida The highest court of The State Under sec. 344(B) Title 28 U.S.C.A. and Because The "Due process clause" of The

Clarence Gideon's petition, which led to the Supreme Court's landmark ruling on the right to counsel.

lawyers from the community as a formal public obligation, most states and cities now have created an office of public defender; these state-employed professional defense lawyers typically provide poor defendants with much better legal representation. And, although a defendant does not have the right to choose any private defense attorney, defendants do have the right to appeal a conviction on the grounds that the counsel provided by the state was deficient. Moreover, the right to counsel extends beyond serious crimes to any trial, with or without jury, that holds the possibility of imprisonment. In other words, the Sixth Amendment provides a right that is seriously intended to be implemented.[70]

The Eighth Amendment and Cruel and Unusual Punishment

The Eighth Amendment prohibits "excessive bail," "excessive fines," and "cruel and unusual punishment." Virtually all the debate over Eighth Amendment issues focuses on the last clause of the amendment: the protection from "cruel and unusual punishment." One of the greatest challenges in interpreting this provision consistently lies in the fact that what is considered "cruel and unusual" varies from culture to culture and from generation to generation. And unfortunately, it also varies by class and race. A sentence of ten years in prison for robbing a liquor store is not considered excessive, yet embezzlement or insider trading involving millions of dollars merits only three years of community service. Are "white collar" crimes less serious than "working class" crimes? Consider the 1995 action by Congress to mandate a five-year minimum sentence for offenses involving five or more grams of

These demonstrators called for the hanging of convicted child-killer Westley Allan Dodd outside the Washington State Penitentiary. Groups supporting and opposing the death penalty commonly gather outside prisons before an execution.

crack cocaine. The same five-year mandatory sentence for *powdered* cocaine, however, kicks in only when the amount involved is *five hundred* grams or more. As one black member of the House put it, "crack cocaine happens to be used by poor people, mostly black people, because it's cheap. Powdered cocaine happens to be used by wealthy white people."[71]

By far the biggest issue of class and race inconsistency as constituting cruel and unusual punishment arises over the death penalty. In 1972, the Supreme Court overturned several state death penalty laws, not because they were cruel and unusual, but because they were being applied in a capricious manner—i.e., blacks were much more likely than whites to be sentenced to death, and the poor more likely than the rich, and men more likely than women.[72] Very soon after that decision, a majority of states revised their capital punishment provisions to meet the Court's standards.[73] Since 1976, the Court has consistently upheld state laws providing for capital punishment, although the Court also continues to review numerous death penalty appeals each year.

The Right to Privacy

> What is the right to privacy? How has it been derived from the Bill of Rights? What forms does the right to privacy take today?

Some of the people all of the time and all of the people some of the time would just like to be left alone, to have their own private domain into which no one—friends, family, government, church, or employer—has the right to enter without permission.

Many Jehovah's Witnesses felt that way in the 1930s. They risked serious punishment in 1940 by telling their children not to salute the flag or say the "Pledge of Allegiance" in school because of their understanding of the First Commandment's prohibition of the worship of "graven images." They lost their appeal, the children were expelled, and the parents were punished.[74] However, as we saw earlier in this chapter, within three years, the Supreme Court concluded that the 1940 decision was "wrongly decided."[75]

These two cases arose under the freedom of religion provisions of the First Amendment, but they were also the first cases to confront the possibility of another right that is not mentioned anywhere in the Constitution or the Bill of Rights: the right to be left alone. As Justice Robert Jackson put it toward the end of his opinion in the 1943 case, "the action of the local authorities in compelling the flag salute and pledge transcends constitutional limitations on their power and *invades* the sphere of intellect and spirit which it is the purpose of the First Amendment to our Constitution to reserve from all official control" (emphasis added).[76] This "sphere" of freedom includes but of course is not limited to the freedom to have religious beliefs.

World War II and McCarthyism distracted government and public attention from these issues. But when the Court began to take a more activist role in the mid-1950s and 1960s, the idea of a "right to privacy" was revived. In 1958, the Supreme Court recognized "privacy in one's association" in its decision to prevent the state of Alabama from using the membership list of the National Association for the Advancement of Colored People in the state's investigations.[77]

The sphere of privacy was drawn in earnest in 1965, when the Court ruled that a Connecticut statute forbidding the use of contraceptives violated the right of marital privacy. Estelle Griswold, the executive director of the Planned Parenthood League of Connecticut, was arrested by the state of Connecticut for providing information, instruction, and medical advice about contraception to married couples. She and her associates were found guilty as accessories to the crime and fined $100 each. The Supreme Court reversed the lower court decisions and declared the Connecticut law unconstitutional because it violated "a right of privacy older than the Bill of Rights—older than our political parties, older than our school system."[78] Justice William O. Douglas, author of the majority decision in the *Griswold* case, argued that this right of privacy is also grounded in the Constitution, because it fits into a "zone of privacy" created by a combination of the Third, Fourth, and Fifth amendments. A concurring opinion, written by Justice Arthur Goldberg, attempted to strengthen Douglas's argument by adding that "the concept of liberty... embraces the right of marital privacy though that right is not mentioned explicitly in the Constitution [and] is supported by numerous decisions of this Court ... and *by the language and history of the Ninth Amendment*" (emphasis added).[79]

The right to privacy was confirmed and extended in 1973 in the most important of all privacy decisions, and one of the most important Supreme Court decisions in American history: *Roe v. Wade*. This decision established a woman's right to have an abortion and prohibited states from making abortion a criminal act.[80] Despite the conservatism of the Nixon appointees to the Court, the Burger Court's decision in *Roe* took a revolutionary step toward establishing the right to privacy. It is important to emphasize that the preference for privacy rights and for their extension to include the rights of women to control their own bodies was not something invented by the Supreme Court in a vacuum. Most states did not regulate abortions in any fashion until the 1840s, at which time only six of the twenty-six existing states had any regulations governing abortion at all. In addition, many states had begun to ease their abortion restrictions well before the 1973 *Roe* decision, although in recent years a number of states have reinstated some restrictions on abortion (see Figure 5.3).

Like any important principle, once privacy was established as an aspect of civil liberties protected by the Bill of Rights through the Fourteenth Amendment, it took on a life of its own. In a number of important decisions, the Supreme Court and the lower federal courts sought to protect rights that could not be found in the text of the Constitution but could be discovered through the study of the philosophic sources of fundamental rights. Through this line of reasoning, the federal courts sought to protect privacy in the form of sexual autonomy, lifestyle choices, sexual preferences, procreational choice, and various forms of intimate association.

Criticism mounted with every extension of this line of reasoning. The federal courts were accused of creating an uncontrollable expansion of demands for new rights. The Supreme Court, critics argued, had displaced the judgments of legislatures and state courts with its own judgment of what was reasonable, without regard to local popular majorities or specific constitutional provisions. This new "judicial activism," as it came to be called in the 1980s, was the basis for a more strongly critical label for the Court: "the imperial judiciary."[81]

The controversy over judicial power has not diminished. In fact it is intensifying under Chief Justice William Rehnquist, an avowed critic of "judicial activism" especially as it relates to privacy and other new rights, such as the right to be represented in districts of numerically equal size[82] and the right not to be required to participate in prayers in school.[83] Under Rehnquist, the Court has been moving in a more conservative, de-nationalizing direction.

One of the Court's conservative trends concerns the burning question of abortion rights. In *Webster v. Reproductive Health Services,* the Court narrowly upheld (by a 5-to-4 majority) the constitutionality of restrictions on the use of public medical facilities for abortion.[84] And in the 1992 case of *Planned Parenthood v. Casey,* another 5-to-4 majority of the Court upheld *Roe* but narrowed its scope, refusing to invalidate a Pennsylvania law that significantly limits freedom of choice. The Court's decision defined the right to an abortion as a "limited or qualified" right subject to regulation by the states as long as the regulation does not constitute an "undue burden."[85] As one constitutional authority concluded from this case, "until there is a Freedom of Choice Act, and/or a U.S. Supreme Court able to wean *Roe* from its respirator, state legislatures will have significant discretion over the access that women will have to legalized abortions."[86]

Another possible conservative trend concerns the privacy rights of homosexuals. One morning in Atlanta, Georgia, in the mid-1980s, Michael Hardwick was arrested by a police officer who discovered him in bed with another man. The officer had come to serve a warrant for Hardwick's arrest for failure to appear in court to answer charges of drinking in public. One of Hardwick's unknowing housemates invited the officer to look in Hardwick's

ABORTION REGULATION AND DEREGULATION

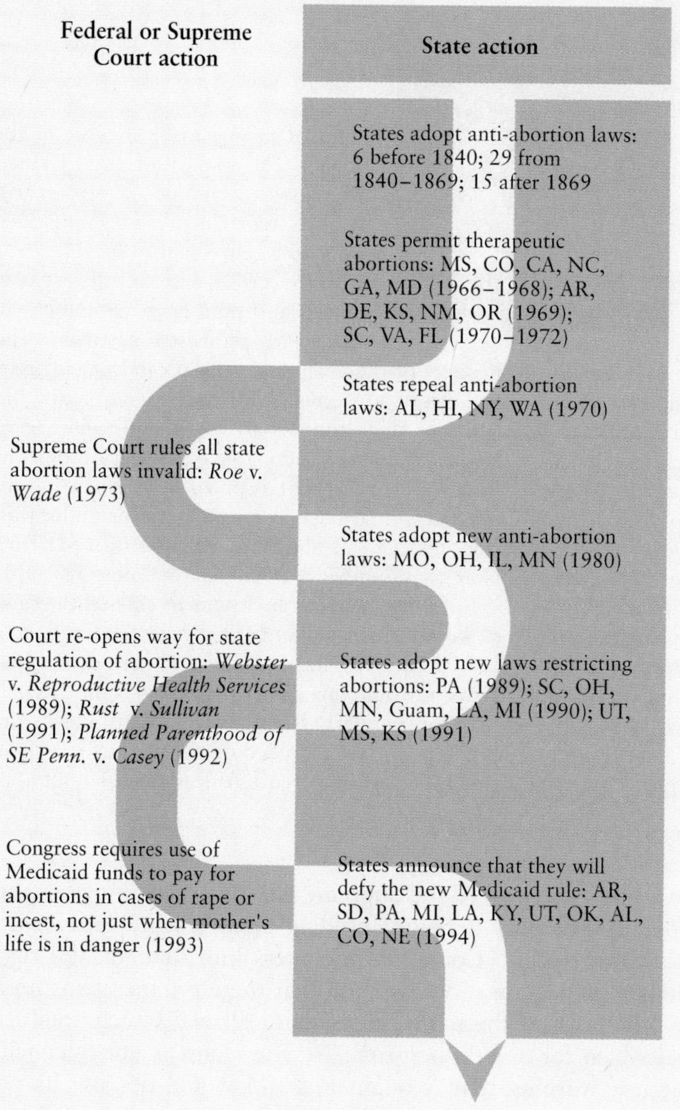

Federal or Supreme Court action	State action
	States adopt anti-abortion laws: 6 before 1840; 29 from 1840–1869; 15 after 1869
	States permit therapeutic abortions: MS, CO, CA, NC, GA, MD (1966–1968); AR, DE, KS, NM, OR (1969); SC, VA, FL (1970–1972)
	States repeal anti-abortion laws: AL, HI, NY, WA (1970)
Supreme Court rules all state abortion laws invalid: *Roe* v. *Wade* (1973)	
	States adopt new anti-abortion laws: MO, OH, IL, MN (1980)
Court re-opens way for state regulation of abortion: *Webster* v. *Reproductive Health Services* (1989); *Rust* v. *Sullivan* (1991); *Planned Parenthood of SE Penn.* v. *Casey* (1992)	States adopt new laws restricting abortions: PA (1989); SC, OH, MN, Guam, LA, MI (1990); UT, MS, KS (1991)
Congress requires use of Medicaid funds to pay for abortions in cases of rape or incest, not just when mother's life is in danger (1993)	States announce that they will defy the new Medicaid rule: AR, SD, PA, MI, LA, KY, UT, OK, AL, CO, NE (1994)

SOURCES: Raymond Tatalovich and Byron Daynes, *The Politics of Abortion* (New York: Praeger, 1981), p. 18. Copyright © by Praeger Publishers. Used with permission. Updated with data from the *New York Times*, July 4–6, 1989, and the *Los Angeles Times*, March 31, 1994.

FIGURE 5.3

room, where he found Hardwick and another man engaging in "consensual sexual behavior." He was then arrested under Georgia's laws against heterosexual and homosexual sodomy. Hardwick filed a lawsuit against the state, challenging the constitutionality of the Georgia law. Hardwick won his case in the federal court of appeals. The state of Georgia, in an unusual move, ap-

ABORTION RIGHTS, PRIVACY, AND CIVIL LIBERTIES

In a time when condoms are distributed in some public schools and when birth control and sex education are freely discussed, it seems difficult to believe that the practice of contraception was once illegal in some states. From the 1940s until 1965, the Supreme Court consistently refused to hear legal challenges to laws that barred individuals—even married couples—from purchasing contraceptives.

In 1965, however, the Court ruled in *Griswold v. Connecticut* that a constitutionally based "right to privacy" barred states from preventing married couples from practicing birth control. Although no such right is actually stated in the Bill of Rights, the Court noted that the idea of personal privacy had been recognized in common law for hundreds of years, and could reasonably be considered to arise from the Third Amendment (prohibiting the quartering of troops in people's homes), the Fifth Amendment (protection against self-incrimination), the Ninth Amendment (providing that citizens had other rights beyond those specified rights in the Constitution), and especially the Fourth Amendment (protecting the right of people to be "secure in their persons"). The implication from *Griswold* that people were entitled to privacy rights, as well as reproductive freedom, opened the door to legalized abortion.

In the 1960s, several states enacted liberalized abortion laws as public attention turned for the first time toward this issue. Leaders of the emerging women's movement, physicians, and others concerned with overpopulation and birth control lent their support to the liberalization of abortion laws. California became one of several states to liberalize its laws, a move that resulted in a profound change in practices. In 1968, the state's first year under the liberalized laws, 5,018 abortions were performed. Three years later, that number had jumped to almost 117,000.

Into this changing environment entered the case of *Roe v. Wade,* which sought to challenge Texas's strict abortion law. After two hearings over a period of almost two years, the Supreme Court struck down the Texas law, and therefore similarly strict laws in other states as well. In its decision, the Court relied on the privacy principle. It also ruled that the Fourteenth Amendment did not apply to fe-

pealed the court's decision to the Supreme Court. The majority of the Court reversed the lower court decision, holding against Mr. Hardwick, on the grounds that "the federal Constitution confers [no] fundamental right upon homosexuals to engage in sodomy," and that therefore there was no basis to invalidate "the laws of the many states that still make such conduct illegal and have done so for a very long time."[87] The Court majority concluded its opinion with a warning that it ought not and would not use its power to "discover new fundamental rights embedded in the Due Process Clause." In other words, the Court under Chief Justice Rehnquist was expressing its determination to restrict quite severely the expansion of the Ninth Amendment and the development of new substantive rights. The four dissenters argued that the case was not about a fundamental right to engage in homosexual sodomy, but was in fact about "the most comprehensive of rights and the right most valued by civilized men, [namely,] the right to be let alone."[88] It is unlikely that many states will adopt new laws against consensual homosexual activity or will vigorously enforce old laws of such a nature already on their books. But it is equally clear that the current Supreme Court will refrain from reviewing such laws and will resist expanding the Ninth Amendment as a source of new substantive rights.

tuses; the amendment's guarantees extended only to "all persons born or naturalized in the United States," and no court case had ever recognized a fetus as a person. In addition, the Court cited scientific and medical evidence to lay down a three-tiered approach to abortions. In the first trimester of pregnancy, when over 90 percent of abortions occur, a woman's right to abortion was to be fully protected. In the second trimester, states could enact restrictions only to protect the health and safety of the pregnant woman. In the third trimester, the government may intervene at the point of fetal viability—that is, when the fetus is capable of living outside of the womb.

By extending the umbrella of privacy, this sweeping ruling dramatically changed abortion practices in America. In addition, it galvanized and nationalized the abortion debate. Groups opposed to abortion, such as the National Right to Life Committee, organized to fight the new liberal standard, while abortion rights groups sought to maintain that protection. In recent years, the legal standard shifted against abortion rights supporters in two key Supreme Court cases. In *Webster v. Reproductive Health Services* (1989), the Court upheld a series of restrictions on abortion practices, but a slim majority of the nine justices still upheld *Roe*. In the 1992 case of *Planned Parenthood of Southeastern Pennsylvania v. Casey,* the Court upheld another series of restrictions, but again, a majority of justices stated strongly that *Roe* should be upheld. With a generation of women now accustomed to having access to abortion, and with over 1.5 million abortions performed in the United States each year, the political pendulum seems to be swinging away from a return to pre-*Roe* days.

SOURCE: Barbara Hinckson Craig and David M. O'Brien, *Abortion and American Politics* (Chatham, NJ: Chatham House, 1993).

The Future of the Bill of Rights

➤ What is the likelihood that the Supreme Court will try to reverse the nationalization of the Bill of Rights?

The next and final question for this chapter is whether the current Supreme Court, with its conservative majority, will try to reverse the nationalization of the Bill of Rights after a period of more than thirty-five years. Although such a move is possible, it is not certain. First of all, the Rehnquist Court has not actually reversed important decisions made by the Warren or Burger courts, but instead has given narrower and more restrictive interpretations of earlier Court decisions. Radical activists such as Justices Rehnquist, Antonin Scalia, and Clarence Thomas, who would prefer to overturn many of the Court's decisions from the 1960s and 1970s, do not yet command a majority on the Court.

Meanwhile, the resurgence of federalism may play itself out in judicial territory. One certain trend in the Court that is likely to continue is its commitment to giving more discretion to the states, returning some of the power to state legislatures that was taken away during the "nationalization" of the Bill of Rights. But what if the state legislatures begin using their regained powers in ways they had used them before the nationalization of the Bill of Rights? What would be the reaction when states pass laws imposing further criminal restrictions on abortion? Permitting more religious practices in the public schools? Spreading the application of capital punishment to new crimes? Imposing stricter sentences on white-collar crimes? Terminating the use of buses to maintain desegregated schools? On the other hand, there have been times when states were dominated by radical Left rather than radical Right tendencies. If that should occur once again, what would a conservative majority on the Court do? Would the Court be equally respectful of state-level democracy then?

★ Summary

The provisions of the Bill of Rights seek to protect citizens from government action. The so-called civil liberties ought to be carefully distinguished from civil rights, which did not become part of the Constitution until the Fourteenth Amendment and its provision for "equal protection of the laws."

During its first century, the Bill of Rights was applicable only to the national government and not to the state governments. The Fourteenth Amendment (1868) seemed to apply the Bill of Rights to the states, but the Supreme Court continued to apply the Bill of Rights as though the Fourteenth Amendment had never been adopted. For sixty years following adoption of the Fourteenth Amendment, only one provision was "incorporated" into the Fourteenth Amendment and applied as a restriction on the state governments: the Fifth Amendment "eminent domain" clause, which was incorporated in 1897. Even as recently as 1961, only the eminent domain clause and the clauses of the First Amendment had been incorporated into the Fourteenth Amendment and applied to the states. After 1961, one by one, most of the provisions of the Bill of Rights were finally incorporated and applied to the states, although a conservative Supreme Court has tried to reverse this trend during the 1980s and 1990s. The status of the First Amendment seems to have been least affected by this conservative trend. Protection of purely political speech remains close to absolute. The categories of conditionally protected speech include "speech-plus," libel and slander, obscenity and pornography, fighting words, and commercial speech. Nevertheless, the realm of free speech in all these areas is still quite broad.

Of the other amendments and clauses in the Bill of Rights, the ones most likely to receive conservative interpretations are illegal search and seizure cases, arising under the Fourth Amendment, and cases involving the Eighth Amendment cruel and unusual punishment clause.

Where the Bill of Rights will go as the American people approach the end of the century is very unclear.

FOR FURTHER READING

Abraham, Henry J. *Freedom and the Court: Civil Rights and Liberties in the United States.* 6th ed. New York: Oxford University Press, 1994.

Bryner, Gary C., and A. Don Sorensen, eds. *The Bill of Rights: A Bicentennial Assessment.* Albany: State University of New York Press, 1993.

Eisenstein, Zillah. *The Female Body and the Law.* Berkeley: University of California Press, 1988.

Friendly, Fred W. *Minnesota Rag: The Dramatic Story of the Landmark Supreme Court Case that Gave New Meaning to Freedom of the Press.* New York: Vintage, 1982.

Glendon, Mary Ann. *Rights Talk: The Impoverishment of Political Discourse.* New York: Free Press, 1991.

Hentoff, Nat. *The First Freedom: The Tumultuous History of Free Speech in America.* New York: Basic Books, 1994.

Levy, Leonard. *Legacy of Suppression: Freedom of Speech and Press in Early American History.* New York: Harper, 1963.

Lewis, Anthony. *Gideon's Trumpet.* New York: Random House, 1964.

Meyer, Michael J., and William A. Parent. *The Constitution of Rights: Human Dignity and American Values.* Ithaca, NY: Cornell University Press, 1992.

Minow, Martha. *Making All the Difference: Inclusion, Exclusion, and American Law.* Ithaca, NY: Cornell University Press, 1990.

Silverstein, Mark. *Constitutional Faiths.* Ithaca, NY: Cornell University Press, 1984.

Stone, Geoffrey R., Richard A. Epstein, and Cass R. Sunstein, eds. *The Bill of Rights in the Modern State.* Chicago: University of Chicago Press, 1992.

STUDY OUTLINE

The Bill of Rights: A Charter of Liberties

1. Despite the insistence of Alexander Hamilton that a bill of rights was both unnecessary and dangerous, adding a list of explicit rights was the most important item of business for the First Congress in 1789.
2. The Bill of Rights would have been more aptly named the "Bill of Liberties," because it is made up of provisions that protect citizens from improper government action.
3. Civil rights did not become part of the Constitution until 1868 with the adoption of the Fourteenth Amendment, which sought to provide for each citizen "the equal protection of the laws."

Nationalizing the Bill of Rights

1. In *Barron v. Baltimore,* the Supreme Court found that the Bill of Rights limited only the national government and not state governments.
2. Although the language of the Fourteenth Amendment seems to indicate that the protections of the Bill of Rights apply to state governments as well as the national government, for the remainder of the nineteenth century the Supreme Court (with only one exception) made decisions as if the Fourteenth Amendment had never been adopted.
3. As of 1961, only the First Amendment and one clause of the Fifth Amendment had been "selectively incorporated" into the Fourteenth Amendment. After 1961, however, most of the provisions of the Bill of Rights were incorporated into the Fourteenth Amendment and applied to the states.

The First Amendment and Freedom of Religion

1. The religious movement of the 1980s, culminating in the judicial and congressional activities of the 1990s, identified or created unsettled areas involving the establishment clause and the free-exercise clause.

The First Amendment and Freedom of Speech and the Press

1. Although freedom of speech and freedom of the press hold an important place in the Bill of Rights, the extent and nature of certain types of expression are subject to constitutional debate.

The Second Amendment and the Right to Bear Arms

1. Constitutionally, the Second Amendment unquestionably protects citizens' rights to bear arms, but this right can be regulated by both state and federal law.

RIGHTS OF THE CRIMINALLY ACCUSED

1. The purpose of due process is to equalize the playing field between the accused individual and the all-powerful state.

THE RIGHT TO PRIVACY

1. In the case of *Griswold v. Connecticut*, the Supreme Court found a right of privacy in the Constitution. This right was confirmed and extended in 1973 in the case of *Roe v. Wade*.

PRACTICE QUIZ

1. From 1789 until the 1960s, the Bill of Rights put limits on
   a. the national government only.
   b. the state government only.
   c. both the national and state governments.
   d. neither the national nor the state governments.

2. The amendment that provided the basis for the modern understanding of the government's obligation to protect civil rights was the
   a. First Amendment.
   b. Ninth Amendment.
   c. Fourteenth Amendment.
   d. Twenty-second Amendment.

3. Which of the following Founders did not support adding a Bill of Rights to the Constitution?
   a. George Mason
   b. Thomas Jefferson
   c. Alexander Hamilton
   d. All of the above supported the Bill of Rights.

4. The process by which some of the liberties in the Bill of Rights were applied to the states (or nationalized) is known as
   a. selective incorporation.
   b. judicial activism.
   c. civil liberties.
   d. establishment.

5. Which of the following provided that all of the protections contained in the Bill of Rights applied to the states as well as the national government?
   a. the Fourteenth Amendment
   b. *Palko v. Connecticut*
   c. *Gitlow v. New York*
   d. none of the above

6. Which of the following protections are not contained in the First Amendment?
   a. the establishment clause
   b. the free exercise clause
   c. freedom of the press
   d. All of the above are First Amendment protections.

7. Which of the following describes a written statement made in "reckless disregard of the truth" that is considered damaging to a victim because it is "malicious, scandalous, and defamatory"?
   a. slander
   b. libel
   c. fighting words
   d. expressive speech

8. Which chief justice oversaw the softening of *Miranda* restrictions?
   a. Earl Warren
   b. Warren Burger
   c. William Rehnquist
   d. Both b and c are correct.

9. In what case was a right to privacy first found in the Constitution?
   a. *Griswold v. Connecticut*
   b. *Roe v. Wade*
   c. *Baker v. Carr*
   d. *Planned Parenthood v. Casey*

10. Which famous case deals with Sixth Amendment issues?
    a. *Miranda v. Arizona*
    b. *Mapp v. Ohio*
    c. *Gideon v. Wainwright*
    d. *Terry v. Ohio*

CRITICAL THINKING QUESTIONS

1. In many ways it seems that the Bill of Rights is an ambiguous document. Choose one protection offered in the Bill of Rights and explain how it has been interpreted in various ways. What does this say about the role of politics and the Constitution in defining the limits of governmental power? What does it say about the power of the Supreme Court in American politics?

2. Recount the history of the constitutional "right to privacy." How has this right affected American politics since the 1960s? How has this right interacted with the other rights in the Bill of Rights? Read the Third, Fourth, Fifth, and Ninth amendments. In your opinion, do American citizens have a right to privacy?

KEY TERMS

burden of proof obligation of the prosecution (the government) in criminal cases to demonstrate the guilt of the defendant "beyond a reasonable doubt"; in civil cases the burden is on the plaintiff to prove his or her case by "a preponderance of the evidence"—a less difficult standard of proof. (p. 154)

civil liberties areas of personal freedom with which governments are constrained from interfering. (p. 146)

civil rights legal or moral claims that citizens are entitled to make upon the government. (p. 147)

double jeopardy the Fifth Amendment right providing that no person can be tried twice for the same crime. (p. 170)

due process of law the right of every citizen against arbitrary action by national or state governments. (p. 167)

eminent domain the right of government to take private property for public use. (p. 172)

establishment clause the First Amendment clause that says that "Congress shall make no law respecting an establishment of religion." This law means that a "wall of separation" exists between church and state. (p. 150)

exclusionary rule the ability of courts to exclude evidence obtained in violation of the Fourth Amendment. (p. 169)

fighting words speech that directly incites damaging conduct. (p. 162)

free exercise clause the First Amendment clause that protects a citizen's right to believe and practice whatever religion he or she chooses. (p. 151)

habeas corpus a court order demanding that an individual in custody be brought into court and shown the cause for detention. *Habeas corpus* is guaranteed by the Constitution and can be suspended only in cases of rebellion or invasion. (p. 145)

***Lemon* test** a rule articulated in *Lemon v. Kurtzman* that government action toward religion is permissible if it is secular in purpose, does not lead to "excessive entanglement" with religion, and neither promotes nor inhibits the practice of religion. (p. 151)

libel a written statement made in "reckless disregard of the truth" that is considered damaging to a victim because it is "malicious, scandalous, and defamatory." (p. 158)

lobbying a strategy by which organized interests seek to influence the passage of legislation by exerting direct pressure on members of the legislature. (p. 158)

***Miranda* rule** the requirement, articulated by the Supreme Court in *Miranda v. Arizona,* that persons under arrest must be informed prior to police interrogation of their rights to remain silent and to have the benefit of legal counsel. (p. 171)

preferred freedoms doctrine see *strict scrutiny.*

procedural liberties restraints on how the government is supposed to act; for example, citizens are guaranteed the due process of law. (p. 146)

selective incorporation the process by which different protections in the Bill of Rights were incorporated into the Fourteenth Amendment, thus guaranteeing citizens protection from state as well as national government. (p. 148)

slander an oral statement, made in "reckless disregard of the truth," which is considered damaging to the victim because it is "malicious, scandalous, and defamatory." (p. 158)

speech-plus speech accompanied by conduct such as sit-ins, picketing, and demonstrations; protection of this form of speech under the First Amendment is conditional, and restrictions imposed by state or local authorities are acceptable if properly balanced by considerations of public order. (p. 157)

strict scrutiny a test, used by the Supreme Court in racial discrimination cases and other cases involving civil liberties and civil rights, which places the burden of proof on the government rather than on the challengers to show that the law in question is constitutional. (p. 154)

substantive liberties restraints on what the government shall and shall not have the power to do. (p. 146)

PART III

★

Politics

6

Public Opinion

★ Political Opinion

In what ways do Americans agree on fundamental values but disagree on fundamental issues?

How are political beliefs formed? What influences individuals' political beliefs?

What do the differences between liberals and conservatives reveal about American political debate?

What influences the way political attitudes are expressed as opinions?

★ Government and the Shaping of Public Opinion

How does the government try to shape public opinion?

How are political issues marketed and managed both by the government and by private groups?

★ Measuring Public Opinion

How can public opinion be measured?

What problems arise from public opinion polling?

★ Public Opinion and Democracy

How responsive is the government to public opinion?

DEMOCRATIC GOVERNMENT assumes an informed, interested public. But many Americans have little political knowledge or interest. In many respects, college students are among the least politically interested and aware of all Americans. A recent national survey of more than 300,000 college freshmen, sponsored by the American Council of Education and conducted by the University of California at Los Angeles, found that less than one-third of the students surveyed thought "keeping up with political affairs" was important. Only 16 percent said that they frequently discussed political issues. Few students had any interest in civic activism. Less than one-fourth, for example, said that it was important to "participate in programs to help clean up the environment." Barely one-third thought that it was important to "help promote racial understanding." Most students seemed far more concerned with grades, school expenses, and job prospects than with political matters.[1]

It is, of course, perfectly reasonable for individuals to focus more intently upon their own immediate concerns than upon national political issues. The former are real and concrete, while the latter seem abstract and distant. Moreover, students can do something about their grades and job prospects, but issues of government and politics often seem utterly beyond their control. As John Muffo, director of academic assessment at Virginia Polytechnic University, said, "There seems to be a growing sense [among students] of, 'Well, there's nothing you can really do about changing politics, so why bother?' "[2]

Nevertheless, if most citizens have no interest in politics and government, how can popular government or the "self-government" so often invoked by the Founders exist? Fortunately, most citizens do have opinions about government and politics and, indeed, may take an interest in the political process when they feel that it affects them. Even apathetic college students can be mobilized to protest, march, and demonstrate to make their opinions known to those in power.

In the spring and fall of 1995, for example, thousands of students at the University of California at Berkeley marched to protest plans by the university's Board of Regents to eliminate affirmative action in the nine-campus University of California system.[3] This was one of the few protests that had taken place on the Berkeley campus since the 1960s, when it was one of the centers of student opposition to the Vietnam War. Public opinion, however, is like the surface of the sea: almost without warning, a calm can give way to powerful storms.

Public opinion is the term used to denote the beliefs and attitudes that people have about issues, events, and personalities. This chapter will examine the role of public opinion in American politics. First, we will look at the processes and institutions that help form the political beliefs of Americans. Second, we will consider the ways in which beliefs are shaped and marketed by governmental institutions as well as by private groups. Third, we will see how opinions are assessed and measured. Finally, we will consider the question of government's responsiveness to citizens' opinions.

Political Opinion

- In what ways do Americans agree on fundamental values but disagree on fundamental issues?
- How are political beliefs formed? What influences individuals' political beliefs?
- What do the differences between liberals and conservatives reveal about American political debate?
- What influences the way political attitudes are expressed as opinions?

When we think of opinion, we often think in terms of differences of opinion. The media are fond of reporting and analyzing political differences between blacks and whites, men and women (the so-called gender gap), the young and old, and so on. Certainly, Americans differ on many issues, and often these differences do seem to be associated with race, religion, gender, age, or other social characteristics. Today, Americans seem sharply divided on truly fundamental questions about the role of government in American society, the proper place of religious and moral values in public life, and how best to deal with racial conflicts.

FUNDAMENTAL VALUES

As we review these differences, however, it is important to remember that Americans also agree on a number of matters. Indeed, most Americans share a common set of values, including a belief in the principles—if not always the actual practice—of liberty, equality, and democracy. **Equality of opportunity** has always been an important theme in American society. Americans believe that all individuals should be allowed to seek personal and material success. Moreover, Americans generally believe that such success should be linked to personal effort and ability, rather than to family "connections" or other forms of special privilege. Similarly, Americans have always voiced strong support for the principle of individual **liberty**. They typically support the notion that governmental interference with individuals' lives and property should be kept to the minimum consistent with the general welfare (although in recent years Americans have grown accustomed to greater levels of governmental intervention than would have been deemed appropriate by the founders of liberal theory). And most Americans also believe in **democracy.** They presume that every person should have the opportunity to take part in the nation's governmental and policy-making processes and to have some "say" in determining how they are governed.[4] Figure 6.1 offers some indication of this American consensus on fundamental values: Ninety-five percent

FIGURE 6.1

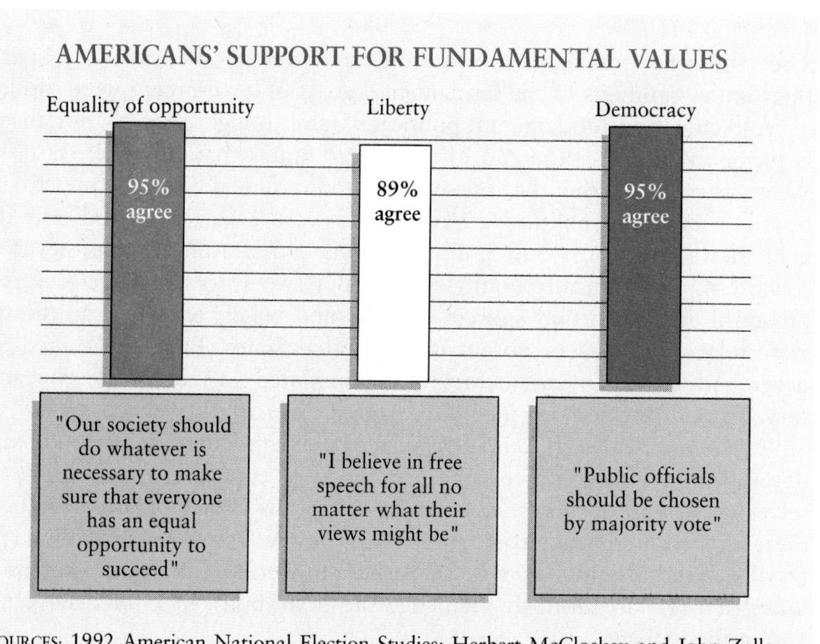

SOURCES: 1992 American National Election Studies; Herbert McCloskey and John Zaller, *The American Ethos: Public Attitudes toward Capitalism and Democracy* (Cambridge, MA: Harvard University Press, 1984), p. 25; and Robert S. Erikson, Norman R. Luttbeg, and Kent L. Tedin, *American Public Opinion: Its Origins, Content, and Impact*, 4th ed. (New York: Macmillan, 1991), p. 108.

of Americans who were polled believed in equal opportunity, 89 percent supported free speech without regard to the views being expressed, and 95 percent expressed support for majority rule.

One indication of the extent to which Americans of all political stripes share these fundamental values is shown by a comparison of the acceptance speeches delivered by Bill Clinton and George Bush upon receiving their parties' presidential nominations in 1992. Clinton and Bush differed on many specific issues and policies. Yet the political visions they presented reveal an underlying similarity. The fundamental emphasis of both candidates was on equality of opportunity. Clinton, in his speech, declared,

> Somewhere at this very moment another child is born in America. . . . Let it be our cause to see that child has the chance to live to the fullest of her God-given capacities. Let it be our cause to see that child grow up strong and secure, braced by her challenges but never struggling alone; with family and friends and a faith that in America, no one is left out; no one is left behind.

And George Bush concluded his acceptance speech by proclaiming,

> And the world changes for which we've sacrificed for a generation have finally come to pass, and with them a rare and unprecedented opportunity to pass the sweet cup of prosperity around our American table. . . . As I travel our land I meet veterans who once worked the turrets of a tank and can now master the keyboards of a high-tech economy.

Thus, however much the two candidates differed on means and specifics, their understandings of the fundamental goals of government were similar.

Agreement on fundamental political values, though certainly not absolute, is probably more widespread in the United States than anywhere else in the Western world. During the course of Western political history, competing economic, social, and political groups put forward a variety of radically divergent views, opinions, and political philosophies. America has never been socially or economically homogeneous. But two forces that were extremely powerful and important sources of ideas and beliefs elsewhere in the world were relatively weak or absent in the United States. First, the United States never had the feudal aristocracy that dominated so much of European history. Second, for reasons including America's prosperity and the early availability of political rights, no Socialist movements comparable to those that developed in nineteenth-century Europe were ever able to establish themselves in the United States. As a result, during the course of American history, there existed neither an aristocracy to assert the virtues of inequality, special privilege, and a rigid class structure, nor a powerful American Communist or Socialist party to seriously challenge the desirability of limited government and individualism.[5]

Obviously, the principles that Americans espouse have not always been put into practice. For two hundred years, Americans were able to believe in the principles of equality of opportunity and individual liberty while denying them in practice to generations of African Americans. Yet it is important to note that the strength of the principles ultimately helped to overcome practices that deviated from those principles. Proponents of slavery and, later, of segregation were defeated in the arena of public opinion because their practices differed so sharply from the fundamental principles accepted by most Americans.

Forms of Disagreement

Agreement on fundamentals by no means implies that Americans do not differ with one another on a wide variety of issues. American political life is characterized by vigorous debate on economic, foreign policy, and social policy issues; race relations; environmental affairs; and a host of other matters. At times, even in America, disagreement on issues becomes so sharp that the proponents of particular points of view have sought to stifle political debate by declaring their opponents' positions to be too repulsive to be legitimately discussed. During the 1950s, for example, some ultra-conservatives sought to outlaw the expression of opinions they deemed to be "communistic." Often this label was applied as a way of discrediting what were essentially liberal views. In the 1990s, some groups have sought to discredit conservatives by accusing them of racism, sexism, and homophobia when their views have not agreed with more liberal sentiments. On a number of university campuses, some African American and feminist groups have advocated the adoption of speech codes outlawing expression seen as insulting to individuals on the basis of their race or gender. In general, however, efforts to regulate the expression of opinion in this way have not been very successful in the United States. Americans believe strongly in free speech and prefer the hidden regulatory hand of the market to the heavier regulatory hand of the law. Many of

Disagreement over abortion rights has been particularly divisive in the United States.

the universities that initially adopted speech codes have been forced to rescind them.[6]

As we shall see later in this chapter, differences of political opinion are often associated with such variables as income, education, and occupation. Similarly, factors such as race, gender, ethnicity, age, religion, and region, which not only influence individuals' interests but also shape their experiences and upbringing, have enormous influence upon their beliefs and opinions. For example, individuals whose incomes differ substantially have different views on the desirability of a number of important economic and social programs. In general, the poor—who are the chief beneficiaries of these programs—support them more strongly than do those whose taxes pay for the programs. Similarly, blacks and whites have different views on questions of civil rights and civil liberties—presumably reflecting differences of interest and historical experience. In recent years, many observers have begun to take note of a number of differences between the views expressed by men and those supported by women, especially on foreign policy questions, where women appear to be much more concerned with the dangers of war, and on social welfare issues, where women show more concern than men for the problems of the poor and the unfortunate. Let us see how such differences develop.

THE FORMATION OF POLITICAL BELIEFS

The attitudes that individuals hold about political issues and personalities tend to be shaped by their underlying political beliefs and values. For example, an individual who has basically negative feelings about government intervention into America's economy and society would probably be predisposed to oppose the development of new health care and social programs. Similarly, someone who distrusts the military would likely be suspicious of any call for the use of American troops. The processes through which these underlying political beliefs and values are formed are collectively called **political socialization.**

The process of political socialization is important. Probably no nation, and certainly no democracy, could survive if its citizens did not share some fundamental beliefs. If Americans had few common values or perspectives, it would be very difficult for them to reach agreement on particular issues. In contemporary America, some elements of the socialization process tend to produce differences in outlook, whereas others promote similarities. Four of the most important **agencies of socialization** that foster differences in political perspectives are the family, membership in social groups, education, and prevailing political conditions. A fifth important agency of socialization tends to promote similarities in political values; this agency is the government.

No inventory of agencies of socialization can fully explain the development of a given individual's basic political beliefs. In addition to the factors that are important for everyone, forces that are unique to each individual play a role in shaping political orientations. For one person, the character of an early encounter with a member of another racial group can have a lasting impact upon that individual's view of the world. For another, a highly salient political event, such as the Vietnam War, can leave an indelible mark upon that person's political consciousness. For a third person, some deep-seated personality characteristic, such as paranoia, for example, may strongly influence the formation of political beliefs. Nevertheless, knowing that we cannot fully explain the development of any given individual's political outlook, let us look at some of the most important agencies of socialization that do affect one's beliefs.

Sources of Attitudinal Difference

The Family Most people acquire their initial orientation to politics from their families. As might be expected, differences in family background tend to produce divergent political outlooks. Although relatively few parents spend much time teaching their children about politics, political conversations occur in most households and children tend to absorb many of their parents' political views, perhaps without realizing it. Studies have suggested, for example, that party preferences are initially acquired at home. Children raised in households in which both parents are Democrats tend to become Democrats themselves, whereas children raised in homes where both parents are Republicans tend to favor the GOP (Grand Old Party, a traditional nickname for the Republican Party).[7] Similarly, children reared in politically liberal households are more likely than not to develop a liberal outlook, whereas children raised in politically conservative settings are prone to see the world through conservative lenses. Obviously, not all children absorb their parents' political views. Two of former president Ronald Reagan's three children, for instance, rejected their parents' conservative values. Moreover, even those children whose views are initially shaped by parental values may change their

Political beliefs begin to be formed at an early age, as children are exposed to their parents' political views.

The reactions of these college students to the announcement of the "not guilty" verdict in the trial of O. J. Simpson reveal the gulf of opinion between whites and blacks about Simpson's guilt.

minds as they mature and experience political life for themselves. Nevertheless, the family is an important initial source of political orientation for everyone.

Social Groups Another important source of divergent political orientations and values are the social groups to which individuals belong. Social groups include those to which individuals belong involuntarily—gender and racial groups, for example—as well as those to which people belong voluntarily—such as political parties, labor unions, and educational and occupational groups. Some social groups have both voluntary and involuntary attributes. For example, individuals are born with a particular social class background, but as a result of their own efforts people move up—or down—the class structure.

Membership in social groups can affect political values in a variety of ways. Membership in a particular group can give individuals important experiences and perspectives that shape their view of political and social life. In American society, for example, the experiences of blacks and whites can differ significantly. Blacks are a minority and have been victims of persecution and discrimination throughout American history. Blacks and whites also have different educational and occupational opportunities, often live in separate communities, and may attend separate schools. Such differences tend to produce distinctive political outlooks. For example, in 1995 blacks and whites had very different reactions to the murder trial of former football star O. J. Simpson, who was accused of killing his ex-wife and a friend of hers. Seventy percent of the white Americans surveyed believed that Simpson was guilty, based on the evidence presented by the police and prosecutors. But an identical 70 percent of the black Americans surveyed immediately after the trial believed that the police had fabricated evidence and had sought to convict

The Million Man March

On a cool, sunny, fall morning in 1995, Calvin Owens and his two teenage sons, having arrived in Washington, D.C., the previous evening after a twenty-seven-hour bus ride from Houston, stood in front of the Lincoln Memorial and looked out over a sea of black men stretching over the length of the Mall. Close to 850,000 people, almost all of them men, had assembled there.[1] Young and old, tall and short, fat and thin, dressed in jeans, work clothes, suits, military uniforms, and dashikis, hair worn short or long or in dreadlocks or shaved: more black men had gathered together in Washington that day than Calvin Owens or his sons had ever seen—indeed, more than any American had ever seen. This was the Million Man March of October 16, 1995.

What was the Million Man March? What did it mean? Organizers of the march proclaimed it as a rally supporting self-reliance, atonement, and the acceptance of personal responsibility, in this case by black men for their families and their communities. Americans are divided over whether it was a watershed in American race relations, a 1990s equivalent of the 1963 March on Washington, or just a one-day spectacle with little impact on individuals or the nation.

The divisions over the march begin with the man who called for and organized it: Louis Farrakhan. Farrakhan, the leader of the Nation of Islam, is regarded by millions of Americans as an anti-Semite and a racist. He denies such charges, but his close association with the march led many of the most prominent black organizations in the United States, among them the NAACP and the Urban League, to avoid endorsing the rally. Colin Powell, the first African American to attain the country's highest military post, chair of the Joint Chiefs of Staff, spoke for many when he said that he supported the aims of the rally but wished someone other than Farrakhan had come up with the idea for it. Farrakhan's exclusionary focus on men and his social conservatism alienated many others. Although many black women supported the event and helped with its organization, many others spoke out against it as chauvinistic. Some whites noted angrily that a similar and similarly publicized gathering of white men would be widely denounced as racist.

Certainly the tone of the rally was vastly different from that of the historic 1963 March on Washington. Whereas Martin Luther King, Jr., in his famous "I Have a Dream" speech, had proclaimed to a multiracial gathering his vision of a future America in which black children and white children could play and live together, Louis Farrakhan pointed to the realities of the present: "There's still two Americas, one black, one white, separate and unequal. . . . We are being torn apart and we cannot gloss it over with nice speeches."[2]

But in a broader perspective, the main themes of the Million Man March were part of a long tradition of American spiritual pilgrimages and gatherings. For this was a spiritual gathering as much as a political one. For the hundreds of thousands of black men (and women) who went to Washington, and for millions of Americans who watched on television, the march provided a sense of unity, power, and pride, as a sign held up in the rally proclaimed: "Black men standing tall, unbent and unbowed."[3] Calvin Owens, who brought his young sons from Houston to be part of the event, explained why he did so: "So they could see for themselves that there are opportunities out here just waiting to be grabbed by them. So they could see for themselves there are other choices. So they could see for themselves that there is hope."[4]

[1]The National Park Service's official estimate after the march was 400,000, but a more careful analysis by Boston University's Remote Sensing Center estimated the crowd at 837,000, with a margin of error of 20 percent. See Richard Lorant, "Boston Experts Revise March Tally Down to 837,000; Park Service May Adjust Its Count," *Washington Times*, October 28, 1995, p. A11.

[2]Quoted in Sam Walker, "March Shows Two Americas in Search of a New Bridge; Prospect of Energized Black Voters Could Change Political Calculus," *Christian Science Monitor*, October 18, 1995, p. 3.

[3]Quoted in Lori Rodriguez, "Show of Unity, Message of Hope; March Gives History Lesson for Local Family," *Houston Chronicle*, October 17, 1995, p. A1.

[4]Quoted in Rodriguez, "Show of Unity."

Simpson of a crime he had not committed; these beliefs were presumably based on blacks' experiences with and perceptions of the criminal justice system.[8]

According to other recent surveys, blacks and whites in the United States differ on a number of issues. For example, among middle-income Americans (defined as those earning between $30,000 and $75,000 per year), 65 percent of black respondents and only 35 percent of white respondents thought racism was a major problem in the United States today. Within this same group of respondents, 63 percent of blacks and only 39 percent of whites thought the federal government should provide more services even at the cost of higher taxes.[9] Other issues show a similar pattern of disagreement, reflecting the differences in experience, background, and interests between blacks and whites in America (see Figure 6.2).

Men and women have important differences of opinion as well. Reflecting differences in social roles, political experience, and occupational patterns, women tend to be less militaristic than men on issues of war and peace, more likely than men to favor measures to protect the environment, and more supportive than men of government social and health care programs (see Table

FIGURE 6.2

African Americans and white Americans have strong differences of opinion on certain issues.

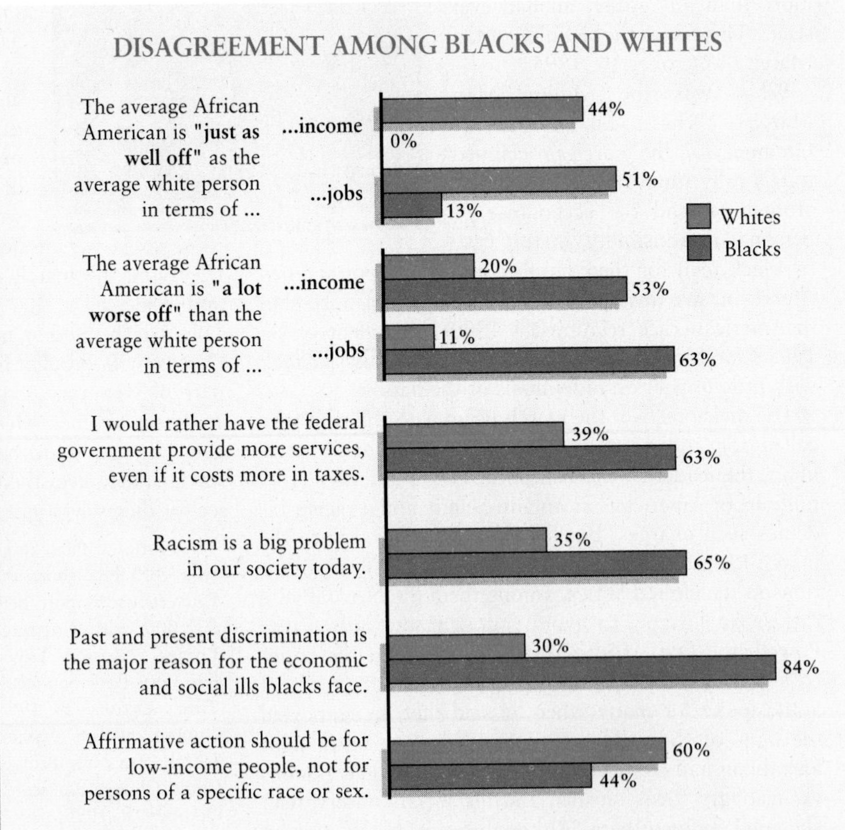

SOURCE: Washington Post/Kaiser Family Foundation/Harvard University survey reported in Kevin Merida, "Worry, Frustration Build for Many in Black Middle Class," *Washington Post*, October 9, 1995, p. A1. © 1995 The Washington Post. Reprinted with permission.

TABLE 6.1

DISAGREEMENTS AMONG MEN AND WOMEN ON ISSUES OF WAR AND PEACE

Government action	Percentage approving of action	
	Men	Women
Presence of U.S. troops in Bosnia	44	38
Bombing of military sites in Iraq	86	80
Ending ban on homosexuals in military	34	51
Military operation against Somali warlord	72	60
Going to war against Iraq	72	53
Sending U.S. troops to Saudi Arabia in response to Iraqi invasion of Kuwait	78	54

SOURCE: Gallup Poll, 1991, 1993, 1995.

6.1). Perhaps because of these differences on issues, women are more likely than men to vote for Democratic candidates.[10] This tendency for men's and women's opinions to differ is called the **gender gap.**

Membership in a social group can affect individuals' political orientations in another way: through the efforts of groups themselves to influence their members. Labor unions, for example, often seek to "educate" their members through meetings, rallies, and literature. These activities are designed to shape union members' understanding of politics and to make them more amenable to supporting the political positions favored by union leaders. Similarly, organization can sharpen the impact of membership in an involuntary group. Women's groups, black groups, religious groups, and the like usually endeavor to structure their members' political views through intensive educational programs. The importance of such group efforts can be seen from the impact of group membership on political opinion. Women who belong to women's organizations, for example, are likely to differ more from men in their political views than women without such group affiliation.[11] Other analysts have found that African Americans who belong to black organizations are likely to differ more from whites in their political orientations than blacks who lack such affiliations.[12]

A third way that membership in social groups can affect political attitudes is through what might be called objective political interests. On many economic issues, for example, the interests of the rich and poor differ significantly. Inevitably, these differences of interest will produce differences of political outlook. James Madison and other framers of the Constitution thought that the inherent gulf between the rich and the poor would always be the most important source of conflict in political life. Certainly today, struggles over tax policy, welfare policy, health care policy, and so forth are fueled by differences of interest between wealthier and poorer Americans. In a similar vein, objective differences of interest between "senior citizens" and younger Americans can lead to very different views on such diverse issues as health care policy, social security, and criminal justice.

It is worth pointing out again that, like the other agencies of socialization, group membership can never fully explain a given individual's political views. One's unique personality and life experiences may produce political views very different from those of the group to which one might nominally belong. This is why some African Americans are conservative Republicans, or why an occasional wealthy industrialist is also a socialist. Group membership is conducive to particular outlooks, but it is not determinative.

Education A third important source of differences in political perspectives comes from a person's education. In some respects, of course, schooling is a great equalizer. As we will see later in this chapter, governments use public education to try to teach all children a common set of civic values. At the same time, however, differences in educational attainment are strongly associated with differences in political outlook. In particular, those who attend college are often exposed to philosophies and modes of thought that will forever distinguish them from their friends and neighbors who do not pursue college diplomas. Table 6.2 outlines some general differences of opinion that are found between college graduates and other Americans.

In recent years, conservatives have charged that liberal college professors indoctrinate their students with liberal ideas. College does seem to have some "liberalizing" effect upon students, but, more significantly, college seems to convince students of the importance of political participation and of their own capacity to have an impact upon politics and policy. Thus, one of the major differences between college graduates and other Americans can be seen in levels of political participation. College graduates vote, write "letters to the

TABLE 6.2

EDUCATION AND PUBLIC OPINION

Issues	Education			
	Drop-out	High school	Some college	College grad.
1. Women and men should have equal roles.	62	74	82	83
2. The Gulf War was worth it.	48	55	57	61
3. The death penalty should be abolished.	23	17	16	25
4. Government should see to it that people have good jobs and an acceptable standard of living.	43	29	26	27
5. Government should improve the social and economic conditions of African Americans.	25	13	20	31
6. Government should provide fewer services to reduce government spending.	25	28	26	42

SOURCE: The American National Election Studies, 1992 data, provided by the Inter-University Consortium for Political and Social Research, University of Michigan.

editor," join campaigns, take part in protests, and, generally, make their voices heard. Does this mean that college graduates are turned into dangerous radicals by liberal professors? Quite the contrary: College seems to convince individuals that it is important to involve themselves in the nation's politics. What perspective could be more conservative?

Political Conditions A fourth set of factors that shape political orientations and values are the conditions under which individuals and groups are recruited into and involved in political life. Although political beliefs are influenced by family background and group membership, the precise content and character of these views is, to a large extent, determined by political circumstances. For example, in the nineteenth century, millions of southern Italian peasants left their homes. Some migrated to cities in northern Italy; others came to cities in the United States. Many of those who moved to northern Italy were recruited by socialist and communist parties and became mainstays of the forces of the Italian Left. At the same time, their cousins and neighbors who migrated to American cities were recruited by urban patronage machines and became mainstays of political conservatism. In both instances, group membership influenced political beliefs. Yet the character of those beliefs varied enormously with the political circumstances in which a given group found itself.

In a similar vein, the views held by members of a particular group can shift drastically over time, as political circumstances change. For example, American white southerners were staunch members of the Democratic Party from the Civil War through the 1960s. As members of this political group, they became key supporters of liberal New Deal and post–New Deal social programs that greatly expanded the size and power of the American national government. Since the 1960s, however, southern whites have shifted in large numbers to the Republican Party. Now they provide a major base of support for efforts to scale back social programs and to sharply reduce the size and power of the national government. The South's move from the Democratic to the Republican camp took place because of white southern opposition to the Democratic Party's racial policies and because of determined Republican efforts to win white southern support. It was not a change in the character of white southerners but a change in the political circumstances in which they found themselves that induced this major shift in political allegiances and outlooks in the South.

The moral of this story is that a group's views cannot be inferred simply from the character of the group. College students are not inherently radical or inherently conservative. Jews are not inherently liberal. Southerners are not inherently conservative. Men are not inherently supportive of the military. Any group's political outlooks and orientations are shaped by the political circumstances in which that group finds itself, and those outlooks can change as circumstances change.

Political Ideology: Liberalism and Conservatism

The set of underlying orientations, ideas, and beliefs through which individuals come to understand and interpret politics is called an **ideology**. Ideologies

PROFILE OF A LIBERAL: JESSE JACKSON

Advocates increasing taxes for corporations and for the wealthy.
Advocates a "Right to Food Policy" to make available a nutritionally balanced diet for all U.S. citizens.
Advocates the establishment of a national health care program for all citizens.
Advocates higher salaries for teachers, more college grants and loans, and a doubling of the federal education budget.
Favors increasing the minimum wage.
Advocates the use of $500 billion in pension funds to finance public works programs, including the construction of a "national railroad."
Favors foreign assistance programs designed to wipe out hunger and starvation throughout the world.
Advocates dramatic expansion of federal social and urban programs.

BOX 6.1

take many different forms. Some people may view politics primarily in religious terms. During the course of European political history, for example, Protestantism and Catholicism were often political ideologies as much as they were religious creeds. Each set of beliefs not only included elements of religious practice but also involved ideas about secular authority and political action. Other people may see politics through racial lenses. Nazism was a political ideology that placed race at the center of political life and sought to interpret politics in terms of racial categories.

In America today, people often describe themselves as liberals or conservatives. Liberalism and conservatism are political ideologies that include beliefs about the role of the government, ideas about public policies, and notions about which groups in society should properly exercise power (see Boxes 6.1 and 6.2). These ideologies can be seen as the end results of the process of political socialization that was discussed in the preceding section.

Today, the term **liberal** has come to imply support for political and social reform, extensive government intervention in the economy, the expansion of federal social services, and more vigorous efforts on behalf of the poor, minorities, and women, as well as greater concern for consumers and the environment. In social and cultural areas, liberals generally support abortion rights, are concerned with the rights of persons accused of crime, support decriminalization of drug use, and oppose state involvement with religious institutions and religious expression. In international affairs, liberal positions are usually seen as including support for arms control, opposition to the development and testing of nuclear weapons, support for aid to poor nations, opposition to the use of American troops to influence the domestic affairs of developing nations, and support for international organizations such as the United Nations.

By contrast, the term **conservative** today is used to describe those who generally support the social and economic status quo and are suspicious of efforts to introduce new political formulae and economic arrangements. Conservatives believe strongly that a large and powerful government poses a threat to citizens' freedom. Thus, in the domestic arena, conservatives generally oppose the expansion of governmental activity, asserting that solutions to social and economic problems can be developed in the private sector. Conservatives particularly oppose efforts to impose government regulation on business, pointing out that such regulation is frequently economically inefficient and costly and can ultimately lower the entire nation's standard of living. As to social and cultural positions, many conservatives oppose abortion, support school prayer, are more concerned for the victims than the perpetrators of crimes, oppose school busing, and support traditional family arrangements. In international affairs, conservatism has come to mean support for the maintenance of American military power.

Often political observers search for logical connections among the various positions identified with liberalism or with conservatism, and they are disappointed or puzzled when they are unable to find a set of coherent philosophical principles that define and unite the several elements of either of these sets of beliefs. On the liberal side, for example, what is the logical connection between opposition to U.S. government intervention in the affairs of foreign nations and calls for greater intervention in America's economy and society? On the conservative side, what is the logical relationship between opposition to governmental regulation of business and support for a ban on abortion? Indeed, the latter would seem to be just the sort of regulation of private conduct that conservatives claim to abhor.

Frequently, the relationships among the various elements of liberalism or the several aspects of conservatism are political rather then logical. One underlying basis of liberal views is that all or most represent criticisms of or attacks on the foreign and domestic policies and cultural values of the business and commercial strata that have been prominent in the United States for the past century. In some measure, the tenets of contemporary conservatism represent this elite's defense of its positions against its enemies, who include organized labor, minority groups, and some intellectuals and professionals.

Box 6.2

PROFILE OF A CONSERVATIVE: PATRICK BUCHANAN

Wants to trim the size of the federal government and to transfer power to state and local governments.
Wants to diminish government regulation of business.
Favors prayer in the public schools.
Opposes gay rights legislation.
Supports programs that would allow children and parents more flexibility in deciding what school to attend.
Supports strict regulation of pornography.
Favors making most abortions illegal.
Would eliminate some environmental regulations.
Supports harsher treatment of criminals.
Opposes affirmative action programs.
Opposes allowing women to serve in military combat units.
Opposes U.S. participation in international organizations.
Opposes the North American Free Trade Agreement (NAFTA).

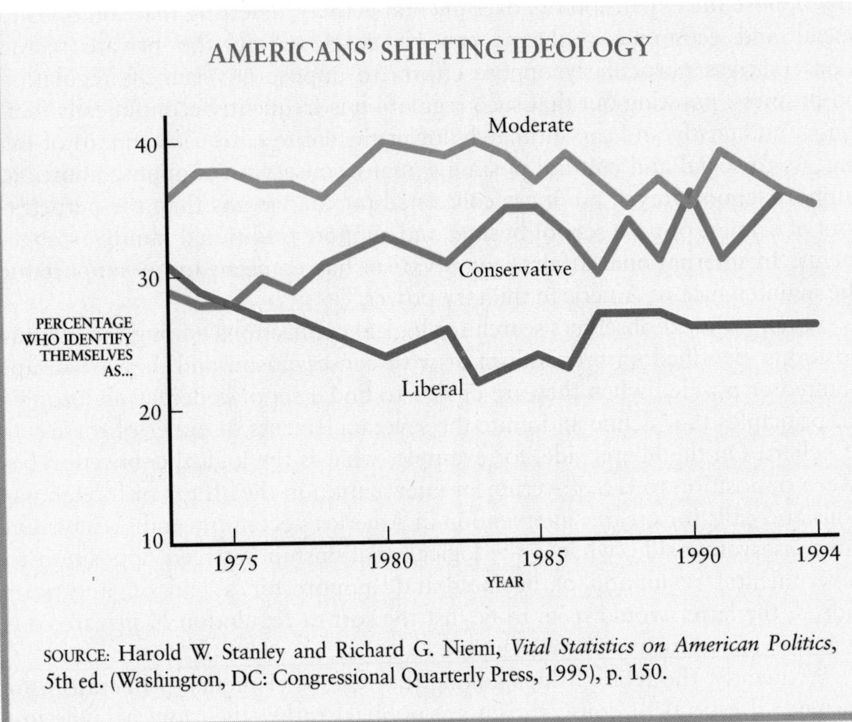

SOURCE: Harold W. Stanley and Richard G. Niemi, *Vital Statistics on American Politics*, 5th ed. (Washington, DC: Congressional Quarterly Press, 1995), p. 150.

FIGURE 6.3

Thus, liberals attack business and commercial elites by advocating more governmental regulation, including consumer protection and environmental regulation, opposing military weapons programs, and supporting expensive social programs. Conservatives counterattack by asserting that governmental regulation of the economy is ruinous and that military weapons are needed in a changing world, and they seek to stigmatize their opponents for showing no concern for the rights of "unborn" Americans.

Of course, it is important to note that many people who call themselves liberals or conservatives accept only part of the liberal or conservative ideology. During the 1980s, many political commentators asserted that Americans were becoming increasingly conservative. Indeed, it was partly in response to this view that the Democrats in 1992 selected a presidential candidate drawn from the party's moderate wing. Although it appears that Americans have adopted more conservative outlooks on some issues, their views in most areas have remained largely unchanged or even have become more liberal in recent years. Thus, many individuals who are liberal on social issues are conservative on economic issues. There is nothing illogical about these mixed positions. They simply indicate the relatively open and fluid character of American political debate. As Figure 6.3 indicates, Americans are often apt to shift their ideological preferences.

From Attitudes to Opinions

An individual's opinions on particular issues, events, and personalities emerge as he or she evaluates these phenomena through the lenses of the attitudes and orientations that, taken together, comprise his or her political ideology. Thus, if a conservative is confronted with a plan to expand federal social programs, he or she is likely to express opposition to the endeavor without spending too much time pondering the specific plan. Similarly, if a liberal is asked to comment on former president Ronald Reagan, he or she is not likely to hesitate long before offering a negative view. Underlying attitudes and ideologies tend to automatically color people's perceptions and opinions about political personalities and events.

Opinions on particular issues, however, are seldom fully shaped by underlying ideologies. Few individuals possess ideologies so cohesive and intensely held that they will automatically shape all their opinions. Indeed, when we occasionally encounter individuals with rigid worldviews, who see everything through a particular political lens, we tend to dismiss them as "ideologues," or lacking common sense.

Although ideologies color our political perspectives, they seldom fully determine our views. This is true for a variety of reasons. First, as noted earlier, most individuals' ideologies contain internal contradictions. Take, for example, a conservative view of the issue of abortion. Should conservatives favor outlawing abortion as an appropriate means of preserving public morality, or should they oppose restrictions on abortion because these represent government intrusions into private life? In this instance, as in many others, ideology can point in different directions.

Second, individuals may have difficulty linking particular issues or personalities to their own underlying beliefs. Some issues defy ideological characterization. Should conservatives support or oppose the proposed elimination of the Department of Commerce? What should liberals think about America's intervention in Haiti? Each of these policies combines a mix of issues and is too complex to be viewed through simple ideological lenses.

Finally, most people have at least some conflicting underlying attitudes. Most conservatives support *some* federal programs—defense, or tax deductions for businesses, for example—and wish to see them, and hence the government, expanded. Many liberals favor American military intervention in other nations for what they deem to be humanitarian purposes, but generally oppose American military intervention in the affairs of other nations.

Thus, most individuals' attitudes on particular issues do not spring automatically from their ideological predispositions. It is true that most people have underlying beliefs that help to shape their attitudes on particular issues. Yet at the same time, most people's general beliefs on most matters allow ample room for their specific opinions to be swayed—sometimes by sober reflection and mature analysis, or sometimes by propaganda and heated political debate in what is sometimes called the "marketplace of ideas."

The Marketplace of Ideas

When individuals attempt to form opinions about particular political issues, events, and personalities, they seldom do so in isolation. Typically, they are confronted—and sometimes bombarded—by the efforts of a host of individuals and groups seeking to persuade them to adopt a particular point of view. Someone trying to decide what to think about Bill Clinton, Bob Dole, Colin Powell, or Newt Gingrich could hardly avoid an avalanche of opinions expressed through the media, in meetings, or in conversations with friends. The **marketplace of ideas** is the interplay of opinions and views that takes place as competing forces attempt to persuade as many people as possible to accept a particular position on a particular event.

The marketplace of ideas has created a common ground in which the discussion of issues is encouraged, based on common understandings. Despite the many and often sharp divisions that exist in the twentieth century—between liberals and conservatives, different income groups, different regional groups—most Americans see the world through similar lenses. This idea market makes it possible for ideas of all sorts to compete for attention and acceptance. Ideas and opinions do not spread spontaneously through the marketplace, however. Just as in the case of products in the marketplace for goods and services, ideas must be vigorously promoted in order to become widely known and accepted.

Government and the Shaping of Public Opinion

- How does the government try to shape public opinion?
- How are political issues marketed and managed both by the government and by private groups?

Public opinion is not some disembodied entity that stands alone and unalterable. Opinion can be molded, shaped, or manipulated. In many areas of the world, governments determine which opinions their citizens may or may not express. People who assert views that their rulers do not approve of may be subject to imprisonment—or worse. Americans and the citizens of the other Western democracies are fortunate to live in nations where freedom of opinion and expression are generally taken for granted.

Even with freedom of opinion, however, not all ideas and opinions flourish. Both private groups and the government itself attempt to influence which opinions take hold in the public imagination. In this section, we will examine how government seeks to shape values that in turn influence public opinion. Then we will discuss the marketing of political issues, both by the government and by private groups.

Enlisting Public Support for Government

All governments attempt to shape or structure citizens' underlying beliefs about the regime, the social and economic structure, and the political process. Governments seek to imbue their citizens with positive feelings toward the established order through the creation of a national ethos, the promotion of property ownership, education, and the opportunity to participate in national politics. Nationalism, property ownership, education, and political participation can be labeled "deadly virtues"; they may be forces for good if they help to create a unified and public-spirited citizenry, or forces for evil if they are merely used as instruments of control.

During World War I, the U.S. government sought to build public support for the war effort that fostered Americans' sense of patriotism.

Nationalism **Nationalism** is the belief that people who occupy the same territory have something important in common that makes them separate from and superior to other people. It is based on myths about the origin and history of the people, their exploits and sufferings as a nation, their heroes, and their mission in the world. Such myths are not necessarily falsehoods. They are simply beliefs that are accepted whether they are true or false.

Nationalism takes root in family, community, and tribal loyalties, but it is strong enough to displace those local ties in favor of the nation. The great virtue of nationalism is precisely that it gives individuals something far larger than themselves with which to identify. It brings out nobility in people, calling on them to sacrifice something of themselves—perhaps even their lives—for their society. Nationalism helps weave the social fabric together.

Nationalism has a darker side, however. Since it encourages pride in one's own country, it can also produce distrust and hatred of others. This tendency is often encouraged by rulers as a means of whipping up support for a war or other international adventures. There will always be conflicts among nations, but these conflicts are much more likely to escalate toward full-scale war when each country is backed by strong national myths. The paramount example of the misuse of nationalism is the case of Nazi Germany, where nationalistic sentiment was perverted to justify aggression and murder on an unprecedented scale.

The search for alternative sources of energy and peaceful uses of nuclear power encouraged the development of nuclear power plants in the 1950s and 1960s. Touted as cleaner, safer, and cheaper than fossil fuels, developers even boasted that nuclear energy would ultimately be so cheap that people could throw their gas and electric meters away. Yet despite the hazards of increasing American reliance on foreign oil, Americans became increasingly suspicious of and hostile to the nuclear power industry.

In the 1960s, several grassroots movements united to oppose the use and spread of nuclear power. Environmentalists and conservationists were among the first to note that nuclear power plants discharged enormous quantities of hot water, which often killed large numbers of fish. Although such thermal pollution could be fixed, the greater fear of the possibly dire consequences from radiation leaks provided an emotional rallying point for nuclear opponents. In economic terms, nuclear power plants proved to be enormously expensive to build and maintain. Worse, they produced large quantities of nuclear waste material, for which no satisfactory disposal plans were developed.

With the energy crisis of 1973–74, more public attention focused on the search for environmentally sound energy alternatives to oil. Even though nuclear power still held promise as an alternative to dependency on foreign oil, suspicions and doubts about nuclear energy only grew. Environmental groups such as the Sierra Club and the Friends of the Earth joined the debate, as did consumer activists such as Ralph Nader. Some scientists who had devoted their lives to nuclear technology began to speak out about such dangers as theft and sabotage of nuclear material. For the first time, this coalition called for a moratorium on nuclear power development. Nader, who organized an anti–nuclear power group called Critical Mass, referred to nuclear power as "technological suicide." The suspicious 1974 death of Karen Silkwood, a worker at the Kerr-McGee nuclear power plant in Oklahoma who had been exposed to high doses of radiation, dramatized safety problems for power plant workers. Further safety problems and scandals were dramatized by the near-meltdown at the Three Mile Island nuclear facility in Pennsylvania in 1979.

Other grassroots groups soon entered the fray. The National Council of Churches voted for a nuclear moratorium. An ad hoc group called the Clamshell Alliance staged a mass protest to oppose the construction of a plant in Seabrook, New Hampshire. In 1979, 65,000 people staged an antinuclear rally in Washington, D.C.

Private Property Property ownership is probably a less universal factor in the manipulation of belief than nationalism, but that makes it no less important. Governments regard widespread property ownership to be a good, conservative force in society because it discourages disorder and revolution. The citizen who owns property has a stake in the existing order—a "piece of the rock"—which he or she will seek to protect.

Many important American leaders have dreamed of creating the ideal polity, or political system, around property ownership. Thomas Jefferson, for example, believed that the American Republic ought to be composed of a population of farmers, each with enough property to appreciate social order and to oppose excessive wealth and power. Although the United States did not become a republic of farmers, this idea was certainly behind the federal government's nineteenth-century policy of giving millions of acres of land from the public treasury to persons who were willing to settle and improve it. **Homesteading,** or squatting, was the name for this method of gaining prop-

Other, similar citizens' groups sprang up around the country, including the Abalone, Catfish, Crabshell, Cactus, and Safe Energy alliances. The cumulative effects of this movement were dramatic. From 1939 to 1971, the national government had spent $52 billion on atomic energy development. Through 1974, utility companies had ordered the construction of 231 nuclear power plants. But from 1974 to 1978, only fifteen plants were ordered. Since 1978 nuclear power plant construction has stopped in the United States.

Opponents of nuclear power relied on a variety of tactics to bring about this change. They held marches and rallies and staged sit-ins. They demanded investigations into safety problems and cost overruns that had previously been kept quiet. They used stronger environmental regulations to file lawsuits and to push the government to control more tightly the operations of existing plants. For example, several groups filed suit against twenty of the thirty-two nuclear power plants operating in 1975 in order to shut them down, arguing that the plants had unsafe cooling systems that could fail and produce a nuclear meltdown. And as consumers who drew energy from companies that operated nuclear power plants saw their energy bills rise, public confidence plummeted. In Indiana, for example, the state Public Service Commission allowed the company that owned the Marble Hill nuclear power plant to recover two-thirds of their initial investment ($1.8 billion) by increasing the rates charged to consumers by 8 percent.

Rural localities have increasingly refused to accept nuclear waste products, further hampering the nuclear power industry. In the early 1990s, local residents in rural Cortland County in upstate New York successfully fought a state-led effort to install a low-level nuclear waste dump in their area. Even though most of those who spearheaded the fight had never been politically active, their tenacious resistance and successful politicking reflected the prevailing national mood: "Not In My Back Yard." But it also reflected a growing public consensus: "Not In *Any* Back Yard."

SOURCE: John L. Campbell, *Collapse of an Industry: Nuclear Power and the Contradictions of U.S. Policy* (Ithaca, NY: Cornell University Press, 1988).

erty ownership. It was justified—indeed encouraged—by the government in large part as a means of giving people a stake in their country.

Even leaders of some of the least-privileged groups in American society have discovered the importance of property ownership, particularly home ownership. As one African American leader put it,

> Fulfillment can never come through housing efforts which afford people no sense of investment, nor ownership with control of, their immediate environment. Renters tend to be far less responsible than home-owners. Black people, in our urban ghettos, are a renter class, and hence the system tends inevitably to make them into irresponsible people.[13]

Mass industrialization has expanded the meaning of property, but its value has not weakened. For most people, property is no longer a plot of land but instead is a mortgage on a house or a stock certificate that indicates ownership of a tiny proportion of some large corporation.

Education In the United States, education is a multi-billion-dollar investment. Few people question the need for the investment because it promises to yield people with high-level skills, problem-solving capacity, and high productivity, along with a significant amount of social mobility. This is not to say that a formal education has helped every American realize the ideal of success. But it does mean that education has made it possible for most Americans to join the work force.

Formal schooling goes beyond skills and training, however. Schools shape values as well. Harry L. Gracey has described school as "academic boot camp." He meant that beginning as early as kindergarten, students learn "to go through the routines and to follow orders with unquestioning obedience, even when these make no sense to them. They learn to tolerate and even to prosper in the bureaucratized environment of school, and this is preparation for their later life."[14] This socialization is usually done at the state and local government levels, where most educational policies in the United States are formulated. The schools themselves are capable of adjusting their curricula to the occupational needs of their region.

Daily recitation of the Pledge of Allegiance is just one example of how the educational system influences Americans' patriotic beliefs.

An example of the use of the school system to orient students toward national needs is the reaction of the United States in the late 1950s to the embarrassment of Sputnik, the Soviet Union's triumphal entry into space. This Soviet triumph convinced many American policy makers that the country's pool of scientific and technical skills was too small. Consequently, within two or three years, mathematics and the sciences were deliberately reorganized throughout the country. They became the "new math" and the "new science" that within half a decade of Sputnik dominated American school curricula.

Since that time, a reaction against the extremes of the new math and new science has occurred. Many local schools have returned to conventional approaches—especially in math. But this change is itself an expression of local efforts to adapt students to national and local needs.

Participation and Cooptation To participate is to share, or to take part in. It is an association with others, usually for the purpose of taking joint action, and is essential for any kind of democratic government. Even representation is not enough unless there is widespread participation in the choice of representatives. Virtually all political leaders endorse some types of participation, particularly voting.

Participation is an instrument of governance because it encourages people to give their consent to being governed. A broad and popularly based process of local consultation, discussion, town meetings, and secret ballots may actually produce a sense of the will of the people. But even when it does not produce a clear sense of that will, the purpose of participation is nonetheless fulfilled because the process itself produces consent. Deeply embedded in people's sense of fair play is the principle that those who play the game must accept the outcome. Those who participate in politics are similarly committed, even if they are consistently on the losing side. Why do politicians plead with everyone to get out and vote? Because voting is the simplest and easiest form of participation by masses of people. Even though it involves minimal participation, it is sufficient to commit all voters to being governed, regardless of who wins. (Voting will be discussed in more detail in Chapter 9.)

There are many examples in recent American history of the use of participation to generate more favorable popular beliefs about the government. It is no coincidence, for example, that youths between the ages of eighteen and twenty-one were given the right to vote in the late 1960s, at a time when they were already participating at almost historic levels. Young people at that time were politically active, but they were not participating in conventional ways, and they were protesting against established authority. Congress and the state legislatures, therefore, ratified the Twenty-sixth Amendment in 1971, giving eighteen-year-olds the right to vote. The vote was used to placate young Americans, to provide them with a conventional channel of participation, and to justify suppressing their disorderly activities. The following testimony by the late senator Jacob Javits of New York is one example of the motivation behind the voting rights amendment:

> We all realize that only a tiny minority of college students on these campuses engaged in unlawful acts. But these deplorable incidents make a point. . . . I am convinced that self-styled student leaders who urged such acts of civil disobedience would find themselves with little or no support if students were given a more meaningful role in the political process. Passage of the [Twenty-sixth Amendment] . . . would give us the means, sort of the famous carrot and the stick, to channel this energy.[15]

The decision to lower the voting age to eighteen is a classic example of **cooptation**—a strategy of bringing an individual into a group by joint action of the members of that group, usually in order to reduce or eliminate the individual's opposition. The most familiar examples of cooptation through participation are the efforts of political leaders to balance their electoral tickets and their political appointments. Political party leaders in city, state, and national campaigns try their best to select candidates for public office who "rep-

Americans between the ages of eighteen and twenty-one were given the right to vote to encourage them to work through the established political system rather than rebel against the system.

resent" each of the important groups in their constituency. This effort involves balancing ethnic, religious, and regional groups, as well as men and women and any other segments of the constituency. African American, Hispanic American, and women's movement leaders study presidential appointments with considerable interest. They do this not so much because an additional black or Hispanic or female representative would give them much more power, but because such appointments are a measure of their current worth in national politics.

Nationalism, property ownership, education, and participation are used by all governments to bolster popular support for leaders and their policies. Through these mechanisms, governments seek to give their citizens a more generally positive orientation toward the political and social order, regardless of their attitudes toward specific programs. Through these techniques, governments hope to convince their citizens voluntarily to obey laws, pay taxes, and serve in the armed forces. Many social scientists believe that if popular support falls below some minimum level, the result could be chaos or even some form of rebellion. This fear was especially manifest during the 1960s and 1970s when diminished levels of popular support did indeed coincide with increases in political violence and unrest.

Marketing Political Issues

Beyond these broad efforts by the government to subtly shape popular attachments to the political regime, both the government and private groups attempt to muster support for different political ideas and programs. Both use public relations to enlist support and shape opinion.

Few ideas spread spontaneously. Usually, whether they are matters of fashion, science, or politics, ideas must be vigorously promoted to become widely known and accepted. For example, the clothing, sports, and entertainment fads that occasionally seem to appear from nowhere and sweep the country before being replaced by some other new trend are almost always the product of careful marketing campaigns by one or another commercial interest, rather than spontaneous phenomena. Like their counterparts in fashion, successful—or at least widely held—political ideas are usually the products of carefully orchestrated campaigns by government or by organized groups and interests, rather than the results of spontaneous popular enthusiasm.

Government Management of Issues All governments attempt, to a greater or lesser extent, to influence, manipulate, or manage their citizens' beliefs. But the extent to which public opinion is actually affected by governmental public relations efforts is probably limited. The government—despite its size and power—is only one source of information and evaluation in the United States. Very often, governmental claims are disputed by the media, by interest groups, and at times by opposing forces within the government itself. Often, too, governmental efforts to manipulate public opinion backfire when the public is made aware of the government's tactics. Thus, in 1971, the United States government's efforts to build popular support for the Vietnam War were hurt when CBS News aired its documentary "The Selling of the

Pentagon," which purported to reveal the extent and character of governmental efforts to sway popular sentiment. In this documentary, CBS demonstrated the techniques, including planted news stories and faked film footage, that the government had used to misrepresent its activities in Vietnam. These revelations, of course, undermined popular trust in all governmental claims.

The Clinton White House initiated more sustained and systematic use of public-opinion polling than any previous administration. During Bill Clinton's first year in office, the Democratic National Committee paid pollster Stanley Greenberg nearly $2 million for national surveys, tracking polls, and focus groups to measure public response to the president's speeches and proposals. When the president delivered a major speech, Greenberg would organize groups of people to watch and register their reactions electronically. The rhetoric used by the president to promote several of his major policies was suggested by poll findings. For example, in the area of health care, Greenberg's surveys indicated that phrases such as "real insurance reform" and "health benefits guaranteed at work" elicited more favorable public responses than "insurance purchasing alliances" and "employer mandates." Some critics charged that many of Clinton's policy initiatives, such as the proposed two-year limit on welfare and the "three strikes and you're out" sentencing rule for repeat criminals, were developed in response to poll data. The administration asserted that it used polls only as a check on its communications strategy.[16]

Of course, as the Clinton administration worked diligently to mobilize popular support, its opponents struggled equally hard to mobilize popular opinion against the White House. As we shall see in Chapter 10, a host of public and private interest groups opposed to President Clinton's programs crafted public relations campaigns designed to generate opposition to him. For example, in 1994, while Clinton campaigned to bolster popular support for his health care reform proposals, groups representing small business and segments of the insurance industry, among others, developed their own pub-

licity campaigns that ultimately convinced many Americans that Clinton's initiative posed a threat to their own health care. These opposition campaigns played an important role in the eventual defeat of the president's proposals.

Often, claims and counterclaims by the government and its opponents are aimed chiefly at elites and opinion makers rather than directly at the public. For example, many of the television ads about the health care debate were aired primarily in and around Washington and New York City, where they were more likely to be seen by persons influential in politics, business, and the media. The presumption behind this strategy was that such individuals are likely to be the key decision makers on most issues. Political, business, and media elites are also seen as "opinion leaders" who have the capacity to sway the views of larger segments of the public. Thus both the president and his foes campaigned especially vigorously in Washington, New York, and a small number of other major metropolitan areas in their 1994 struggle over health care reform.[17]

Private Groups and the Shaping of Public Opinion As the story of the health care debate may suggest, political issues and ideas seldom emerge spontaneously from the grass roots. We have already seen how the government tries to shape public opinion. But the ideas that become prominent in political life are also developed and spread by important economic and political groups searching for issues that will advance their causes. One example is the "right-to-life" issue that has inflamed American politics over the past twenty years.

Rev. Pat Robertson, founder of the Christian Broadcasting Network and the Christian Coalition. Religion is a dominant influence on the political opinions of many Americans.

The notion of right-to-life, whose proponents seek to outlaw abortion and overturn the Supreme Court's *Roe v. Wade* decision, was developed and heavily promoted by conservative politicians who saw the issue of abortion as a means of uniting Catholic and Protestant conservatives and linking both groups to the Republican Party. These politicians convinced Catholic and evangelical Protestant leaders that they shared similar views on the question of abortion, and they worked with religious leaders to focus public attention on the negative issues in the abortion debate. To advance their cause, leaders of the movement sponsored well-publicized Senate hearings, where testimony, photographs, and other exhibits were presented to illustrate the violent effects of abortion procedures. At the same time, publicists for the movement produced leaflets, articles, books, and films such as *The Silent Scream* to highlight the agony and pain ostensibly felt by the unborn when they were being aborted. All this underscored the movement's claim that abortion was nothing more or less than the murder of millions of innocent human beings. Finally, Catholic and evangelical Protestant religious leaders were organized to denounce abortion from their church pulpits and, increasingly, from their electronic pulpits on the Christian Broadcasting Network (CBN) and the various other television forums available for religious programming. Religious leaders also organized demonstrations, pickets, and disruptions at abortion clinics throughout the nation.[18] Abortion rights remain a potent issue; it even influenced the debate over health care reform.

Among President Clinton's most virulent critics have been leaders of the religious Right who were outraged by his support for abortion and gay rights. Conservative religious leaders have attacked the president's programs and mounted biting personal attacks on both Clinton and his wife, Hillary Rodham Clinton. Other conservative groups not associated with the religious Right have also launched sharp assaults against the president. Nationally syndicated talk-show host Rush Limbaugh, for one, is a constant critic of the administration.

Typically, ideas are marketed most effectively by groups with access to financial resources, public or private institutional support, and sufficient skill or education to select, develop, and draft ideas that will attract interest and support. Thus, the development and promotion of conservative themes and ideas in recent years has been greatly facilitated by the millions of dollars that conservative corporations and business organizations such as the Chamber of Commerce and the Public Affairs Council spend each year on public information and what is now called in corporate circles "issues management." In addition, conservative business leaders have contributed millions of dollars to such conservative institutions as the Heritage Foundation, the Hoover Institution, and the American Enterprise Institute.[19] Many of the ideas that helped those on the right influence political debate were first developed and articulated by scholars associated with institutions such as these.

Although they do not usually have access to financial assets that match those available to their conservative opponents, liberal intellectuals and professionals have ample organizational skills, access to the media, and practice in creating, communicating, and using ideas. During the past three decades, the chief vehicle through which liberal intellectuals and professionals have advanced their ideas has been the "public interest group," an institution that relies heavily upon voluntary contributions of time, effort, and interest on the part of its members. Through groups like Common Cause, the National Organization for Women, the Sierra Club, Friends of the Earth, and Physicians for Social Responsibility, intellectuals and professionals have been able to use their organizational skills and educational resources to develop and promote ideas.[20] Often, research conducted in universities and in liberal "think tanks" such as the Brookings Institution provides the ideas upon which liberal politicians rely. For example, the welfare reform plan introduced by the Clinton administration in 1994 originated with the work of former Harvard professor David Ellwood. Ellwood's academic research led him to the conclusion that the nation's welfare system would be improved if services to the poor were expanded in scope but limited in duration. His idea was adopted by the 1992 Clinton campaign, which was searching for a position on welfare that would appeal to both liberal and conservative Democrats. The Ellwood plan seemed perfect: It promised liberals an immediate expansion of welfare benefits, yet it held out to conservatives the idea that welfare recipients would receive benefits only for a limited period of time. The Clinton welfare reform plan even borrowed phrases from Ellwood's book *Poor Support*.[21]

Journalist and author Joe Queenan has correctly observed that although political ideas can erupt spontaneously, they almost never do. Instead, he says,

> issues are usually manufactured by tenured professors and obscure employees of think tanks. . . . It is inconceivable that the American people, all by themselves,

> could independently arrive at the conclusion that the depletion of the ozone layer poses a dire threat to our national well-being, or that an immediate, across-the-board cut in the capital-gains tax is the only thing that stands between us and the economic abyss. The American people do not have that kind of sophistication. *They have to have help.*[22]

Whatever their particular ideology or interest, those groups that can muster the most substantial financial, institutional, educational, and organizational resources—or, as we shall see later, access to government power—are also best able to promote their ideas in the marketplace. Obviously, these resources are most readily available to upper-middle- and upper-class groups. As a result, their ideas and concerns are most likely to be discussed and disseminated by books, films, newspapers, magazines, and the electronic media. As we shall see in the next chapter, upper-income groups dominate the marketplace of ideas, not only as producers and promoters, but also as consumers of ideas. In general, and particularly in the political realm, the print and broadcast media and the publishing industry are most responsive to the tastes and views of the more "upscale" segments of the potential audience.

CONFORMITY

Of course, not all people are equally likely to accept all ideas at all times. Underlying political beliefs and ideologies predispose some individuals to accept, and others to reject, a given idea or opinion. This is one reason that opinions are so diverse in America. Ironically, however, over time the idea market may work to erode such differences. The operation of the idea market in the United States continually exposes individuals to concepts and information originating outside their own region, class, or ethnic community. It is this steady exposure that over time leads members of every social group to acquire at least some of the ideas and perspectives embraced by the others. Given continual exposure to the ideas of other strata, it is virtually impossible for any group to resist some modification of its own beliefs.

For example, we saw earlier in this chapter that factors such as race, gender, and education level seem to produce differences in political perspective. Interestingly, however, among people who report that they spend a great deal of time reading newspapers and watching television news (and thus are most exposed to the national flow of political information and ideas), differences of opinion are reduced rather than increased. For example, blacks who have high levels of exposure to the national news media have political views closer to those of white Americans than do blacks who obtain their information and ideas primarily from media that cater exclusively to black audiences.[23]

Without some measure of inter-group agreement, American politics would be so bitter and contentious that the nation's ability to continue to make decisions democratically would be called into question. For example, if blacks and whites could not agree on some fundamental matters, they could not live together in a democracy. But agreement on fundamental issues has negative as well as positive implications. In his famous nineteenth-century work, *Democracy in America,* Alexis de Tocqueville wrote that freedom of expression could produce enormous pressure for conformity. He called this pressure "tyranny of the majority" and warned that it was one of the worst forms of tyranny because it permitted no escape. Thus, rather than see all differences and conflicts of opinion in America as a problem, a certain measure of difference may be an indication that American politics continues to be healthy and vigorous.

Measuring Public Opinion

- ➤ How can public opinion be measured?
- ➤ What problems arise from public opinion polling?

As recently as fifty years ago, American political leaders gauged public opinion by people's applause or cheers and by the presence of crowds in meeting places. This direct exposure to the people's views did not necessarily produce accurate knowledge of public opinion. It did, however, give political leaders confidence in their public support—and therefore confidence in their ability to govern by consent.

Abraham Lincoln and Stephen Douglas debated each other seven times in the summer and autumn of 1858, two years before they became presidential nominees. Their debates took place before audiences in parched cornfields and courthouse squares. A century later, the presidential debates, although seen by millions, take place before a few reporters and technicians in television studios that might as well be on the moon. The public's response cannot be experienced directly. This distance between leaders and followers is one of the agonizing problems of modern democracy. The media send information to millions of people, but they are not yet as efficient at getting information back to leaders. Is government by consent possible where the scale of communication is so large and impersonal? In order to compensate for the decline

The second Lincoln-Douglas debate, at Freeport, Illinois, attracted a large local crowd as well as the nation's attention to the debate over slavery.

in their ability to experience public opinion for themselves, leaders have turned to science, in particular to the science of opinion polling.

It is no secret that politicians and public officials make extensive use of **public opinion polls** to help them decide whether to run for office, what policies to support, how to vote on important legislation, and what types of appeals to make in their campaigns. President Lyndon Johnson was famous for carrying the latest Gallup and Roper poll results in his pocket, and it is widely believed that he began to withdraw from politics because the polls reported losses in public support. All recent presidents and other major political figures have worked closely with polls and pollsters.

CONSTRUCTING PUBLIC OPINION FROM SURVEYS

The population in which pollsters are interested is usually quite large. To conduct their polls they first choose a **sample** of the total population. The selection of this sample is important. Above all, it must be representative; the views of those in the sample must accurately and proportionately reflect the views of the whole. To a large extent, the validity of the poll's results depends on the sampling procedure used (see Box 6.3).

FIGURE 6.4

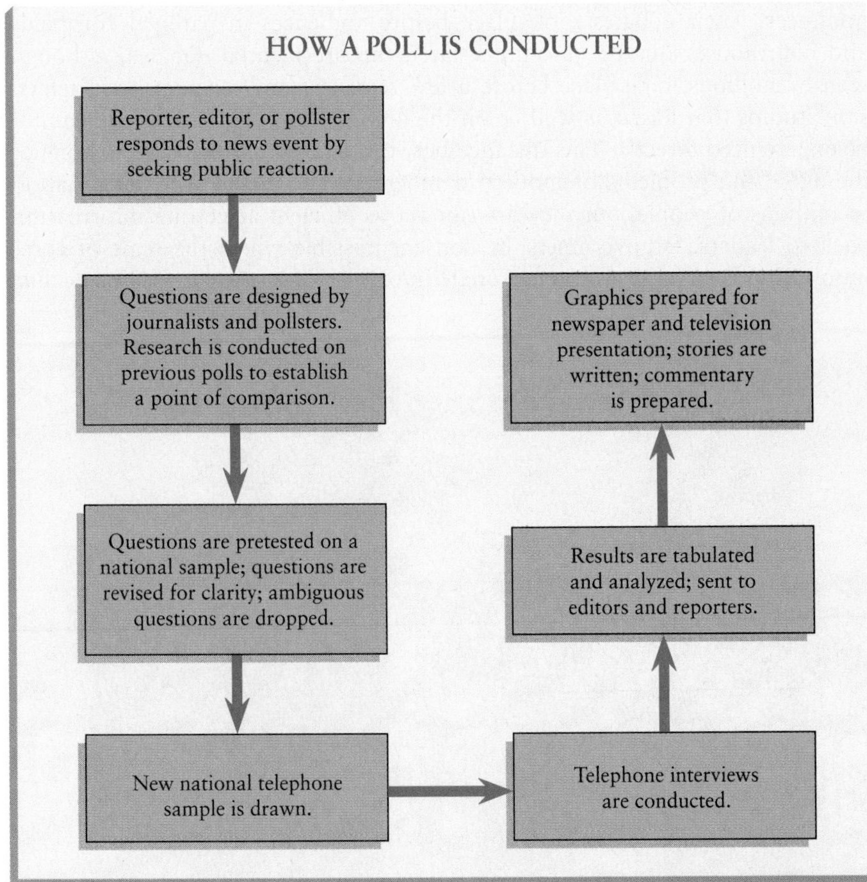

METHODS OF MEASURING PUBLIC OPINION

Interpreting Mass Opinion from Mass Behavior and Mass Attributes

Consumer behavior: predicts that people tend to vote against the party in power during a downslide in the economy

Group demographics: can predict party affiliation and voting by measuring income, race, and type of community (urban or rural)

Getting Public Opinion Directly from the People

Person-to-person: form impressions based on conversations with acquaintances, aides, and associates

Selective polling: form impressions based on interviews with a few representative members of a group or groups

Bellwether districts: form impressions based on an entire community that has a reputation for being a good predictor of the entire nation's attitudes

Constructing Public Opinion from Surveys

Quota sampling: respondents are chosen because they match a general population along several significant dimensions, such as geographic region, sex, age, and race

Probability sampling: respondents are chosen without prior screening, based entirely on a lottery system

Area sampling: respondents are chosen as part of a systematic breakdown of larger homogeneous units into smaller representative areas

Haphazard sampling: respondents are chosen by pure chance with no systematic method

Systematically biased sampling: respondents are chosen with a hidden or undetected bias toward a given demographic group

Box 6.3

The degree of reliability in polling is a function of sample size. The same sample is needed to represent a small population as to represent a large population. The typical size of a sample ranges from 450 to 1,500 respondents. This number, however, reflects a trade-off between cost and degree of precision desired. The degree of accuracy that can be achieved with even a small sample can be seen from the polls' success in predicting election outcomes.

Table 6.3 shows how accurate two of the major national polling organizations have been in predicting the outcomes of presidential elections. In only three instances between 1952 and 1992 did the final October poll of a major pollster predict the wrong outcome; and in all three of those instances—Harris in 1968 and Gallup in 1976, as well as Roper in 1960—the actual election was extremely close and the prediction was off by no more than two percentage points.

Even with reliable sampling procedures, problems can occur. Validity can be adversely affected by poor question format, faulty ordering of questions, inappropriate vocabulary, ambiguity of questions, or questions with built-in biases. Often, seemingly minor differences in the wording of a question can convey vastly different meanings to respondents and thus produce quite different response patterns.

For example, for many years the University of Chicago's National Opinion Research Center has asked respondents whether they think the fed-

TABLE 6.3

TWO POLLSTERS AND THEIR RECORDS (1948–92)

	Harris	Gallup	Actual outcome
1992			
Clinton	44%	44%	43%
Bush	38	37	38
Perot	17	14	19
1988			
Bush	51%	53%	54%
Dukakis	47	42	46
1984			
Reagan	56%	59%	59%
Mondale	44	41	41
1980			
Reagan	48%	47%	51%
Carter	43	44	41
Anderson		8	
1976			
Carter	48%	48%	51%
Ford	45	49	48
1972			
Nixon	59%	62%	61%
McGovern	35	38	38
1968			
Nixon	40%	43%	43%
Humphrey	43	42	43
Wallace	13	15	14
1964			
Johnson	62%	64%	61%
Goldwater	33	36	39
1960			
Kennedy	49%	51%	50%
Nixon	41	49	49
1956			
Eisenhower	NA	60%	58%
Stevenson		41	42
1952			
Eisenhower	47%	51%	55%
Stevenson	42	49	44
1948			
Truman	NA	44.5%	49.6%
Dewey		49.5	45.1

All figures except those for 1948 are rounded. NA = Not asked.

SOURCES: Data from the Gallup Poll, the Harris Survey (New York: Chicago Tribune–New York News Syndicate, various press releases 1964–92).

eral government is spending too much, too little, or about the right amount of money on "assistance for the poor." Answering the question posed this way, about two-thirds of all respondents seem to believe that the government is spending too little. However, the same survey also asks whether the government spends too much, too little, or about the right amount for "welfare." When the word "welfare" is substituted for "assistance for the poor," about half of all respondents indicate that too much is being spent.[24]

In the early days of a political campaign when voters are asked which candidates they do, or do not, support, the answer they give often has little significance, because the choice is not yet important to them. Their preferences may change many times before the actual election. This is part of the explanation for the phenomenon of the post-convention "bounce" in the popularity of presidential candidates, which was observed after the 1992 Democratic and Republican national conventions.[25] Respondents' preferences reflected the amount of attention a candidate had received during the conventions rather than strongly held views.

Salient interests are interests that stand out beyond others, that are of more than ordinary concern to respondents in a survey or to voters in the electorate. Politicans, social scientists, journalists, or pollsters who assume something is important to the public, when in fact it is not, are creating an **illusion of saliency**. This illusion can be created and fostered by polls despite careful controls over sampling, interviewing, and data analysis. In fact, the illusion is strengthened by the credibility that science gives survey results.

The problem of saliency has become especially acute as a result of the proliferation of media polls. The television networks and major national newspapers all make heavy use of opinion polls. Increasingly, polls are being commissioned by local television stations and local and regional newspapers

In probably the most famous instance of pollsters getting it wrong, Gallup predicted that Thomas E. Dewey would defeat Harry S. Truman in the 1948 presidential election. Truman, pictured here, won easily. The Gallup organization subsequently changed its polling methods.

as well.[26] On the positive side, polls allow journalists to make independent assessments of political realities—assessments not influenced by the partisan claims of politicians.

At the same time, however, media polls can allow journalists to make news when none really exists. Polling diminishes journalists' dependence upon news makers. A poll commissioned by a news agency can provide the basis for a good story even when candidates, politicians, and other newsmakers refuse to cooperate by engaging in newsworthy activities. Thus, on days when little or nothing is actually taking place in a political campaign, poll results, especially apparent changes in candidate popularity margins, can provide exciting news. Several times during the 1992 presidential campaign, for example, small changes in the relative standing of the Democratic and Republican candidates produced banner headlines around the country. Stories about what the candidates actually did or said often took second place to reporting the "horse race."

Interestingly, because rapid and dramatic shifts in candidate margins tend to take place when voters' preferences are least fully formed, horse race news is most likely to make the headlines when it is actually least significant.[27] In other words, media interest in poll results is inversely related to the actual salience of voters' opinions and the significance of the polls' findings. However, by influencing perceptions, especially those of major contributors, media polls can influence political realities.

The most noted, but least serious, of polling problems is the **bandwagon effect,** which occurs when polling results influence people to support the candidate marked as the probable victor. Some scholars argue that this bandwagon effect can be offset by an "underdog effect" in favor of the candidate who is trailing in the polls.[28] However, a candidate who demonstrates a lead in the polls usually finds it considerably easier to raise campaign funds than a candidate whose poll standing is poor. With these additional funds, poll leaders can often afford to pay for television time and other campaign activities that will cement their advantage. For example, Bill Clinton's substantial lead in the polls during much of the summer of 1992 helped the Democrats raise far more money than in any previous campaign, primarily from interests hoping to buy access to a future President Clinton. For once, the Democrats were able to outspend the usually better-heeled Republicans. Thus, the *appearance* of a lead, as shown by the polls, helped make Clinton's lead a reality.

PUBLIC OPINION, POLITICAL KNOWLEDGE, AND THE IMPORTANCE OF IGNORANCE

Many people are distressed to find public opinion polls not only unable to discover public opinion, but also unable to avoid producing unintentional distortions of their own. No matter how hard they try, no matter how mature the science of opinion polling becomes, politicians may remain substantially ignorant of public opinion.

Although knowledge is good for its own sake, and knowledge of public opinion may sometimes produce better government, ignorance also has its uses. It can, for example, operate as a restraint on the use of power. Leaders who think they know what the public wants are often autocratic rulers.

Leaders who realize that they are always partially in the dark about the public are likely to be more modest in their claims, less intense in their demands, and more uncertain in their uses of power. Their uncertainty may make them more accountable to their constituencies because they will be more likely to continue searching for consent.

One of the most valuable benefits of survey research is actually "negative knowledge"—knowledge that pierces through irresponsible claims about the breadth of opinion or the solidarity of group or mass support. Because this sort of knowledge reveals the complexity and uncertainty of public opinion, it can help make citizens less gullible, group leaders less strident, and politicians less deceitful. This alone gives public opinion research, despite its great limitations, an important place in the future of American politics.[29]

Public Opinion and Democracy

> How responsive is the government to public opinion?

In democratic nations, leaders should pay heed to public opinion, and the evidence suggests that indeed they do. There are many instances in which public policy and public opinion do not coincide, but in general the government's actions are consistent with citizens' preferences. One recent study, for example, found that between 1935 and 1979, in about two-thirds of all cases, significant changes in public opinion were followed within one year by changes in government policy consistent with the shift in the popular mood.[30] Other studies have come to similar conclusions.

Despite the evidence of broad agreement between opinion and policy, there are always areas of disagreement. For example, the majority of Americans favored stricter governmental control of handguns for years before Congress finally adopted the modest restrictions on firearms purchases embodied in the Brady bill and the Violent Crime Control Act, both passed in 1994. Similarly, most Americans—blacks as well as whites—oppose school busing to achieve racial balance, yet such busing continues to be used in many parts of the nation. Most Americans are far less concerned with the rights of the accused than the federal courts seem to be. Most Americans oppose U.S. military intervention in other nations' affairs, yet such interventions continue to take place and often win public approval after the fact.

Several factors can contribute to a lack of consistency between opinion and governmental policy. First, the nominal majority on a particular issue may not be as intensely committed to its preference as the adherents of the minority viewpoint. An intensely committed minority may often be more willing to commit its time, energy, efforts, and resources to the affirmation of its opinions than an apathetic, even if large, majority. In the case of firearms, for example, although the proponents of gun control are by a wide margin the majority, most do not regard the issue as one of critical importance to themselves and are not willing to commit much effort to advancing their cause. The opponents of gun control, by contrast, are intensely committed, well organized, and well financed, and as a result are usually able to carry the day.

A second important reason that public policy and public opinion may not coincide has to do with the character and structure of the American system of government. The framers of the American Constitution, as we saw in Chapter 3, sought to create a system of government that was based upon popular consent but that did not invariably and automatically translate shifting popular sentiments into public policies. As a result, the American governmental process includes arrangements such as an appointed judiciary that can produce policy decisions that may run contrary to prevailing popular sentiment—at least for a time.

When all is said and done, however, there can be little doubt that in general the actions of the American government do not remain out of line with popular sentiment for very long. One could take these as signs of a vital and thriving democracy.

Summary

Americans disagree on many issues, but they nevertheless share a number of important values, including liberty, equality of opportunity, and democracy. Although factors such as race, education, gender, and social class produce important differences in outlook, Americans probably agree more on fundamental values than do the citizens of most other nations.

Most people acquire their initial orientation to political life from their families. Subsequently, political views are influenced by interests, personal experiences, group memberships, and the conditions under which citizens are first mobilized into politics.

Most governments, including the U.S. government, endeavor to shape their citizens' political beliefs. The most important tools used by governments for opinion management are nationalism, property ownership, education, and participation. In democracies, private groups compete with government to shape opinion.

Public opinion is generally measured by polling. But while polls measure opinion, they also distort it, often imputing salience to issues that citizens care little about or creating the illusion that most people are moderate or centrist in their views.

Over time, the government's policies are strongly affected by public opinion, although there can be lags and divergences, especially when an intense minority confronts a more apathetic majority.

FOR FURTHER READING

Cook, Elizabeth A., Ted G. Jelen, and Clyde Wilcox. *Between Two Absolutes: Public Opinions and the Politics of Abortion*. Boulder, CO: Westview, 1992

Erikson, Robert S., Norman Luttbeg, and Kent Tedin. *American Public Opinion: Its Origins, Content and Impact*. 5th ed. Boston, MA: Allyn and Bacon, 1994.

Gallup, George. *The Pulse of Democracy*. New York: Simon and Schuster, 1940.

Ginsberg, Benjamin. *The Captive Public: How Mass Opinion Promotes State Power*. New York: Basic Books, 1986.

Herbst, Susan. *Numbered Voices: How Opinion Polling Has Shaped American Politics*. Chicago: University of Chicago Press, 1993.

Key, V. O. *Public Opinion and American Democracy*. New York: Knopf, 1961.

Lippman, Walter. *Public Opinion*. New York: Harcourt, Brace, 1922.

Mayer, William G. *The Changing American Mind: How and Why American Public Opinion Changed between 1960 and 1988*. Ann Arbor: University of Michigan Press, 1992.

Neuman, W. Russell. *The Paradox of Mass Politics: Knowledge and Opinion in the American Electorate*. Cambridge, MA: Harvard University Press, 1986.

Page, Benjamin I., and Robert Y. Shapiro. *The Rational Public: Fifty Years of Trends in Americans' Policy Preferences*. Chicago: University of Chicago Press, 1992.

Rinehart, Sue Tolleson. *Gender Consciousness and Politics*. New York: Routledge, 1992.

Schuman, Howard, Charlotte Steeh, and Lawrence Bobo. *Racial Attitudes in America*. Cambridge, MA: Harvard University Press, 1990.

STUDY OUTLINE

Political Opinion

1. Although Americans have many political differences, they share a common set of values, including liberty, equality of opportunity, and democracy.
2. Agreement on fundamental political values is probably more widespread in the United States than anywhere else in the Western world.
3. Often for reasons associated with demographics, Americans do differ widely with one another on a variety of issues.
4. Most people acquire their initial orientation to politics from their families.
5. Membership in both voluntary and involuntary social groups can affect an individual's political values through personal experience, the influence of group leaders, and recognition of political interests.
6. One's level of education is an important factor in shaping political beliefs.
4. Conditions under which individuals and groups are recruited into political life also shape political orientations.
7. Many Americans describe themselves as either liberal or conservative in political orientation.
8. Although ideologies shape political opinions, they seldom fully determine one's views.

Government and the Shaping of Public Opinion

1. Nationalism, property ownership, education, and political participation and cooptation are methods used by the government to enlist public support.
2. Nationalism helps weave the social fabric together.
3. Property ownership is a conservative force in society that discourages disorder and revolution.
4. Education spreads and changes cultural values, including attitudes toward one's personal qualities as well as general political ideologies.
5. Participation and cooptation are used by governments to acquire the consent of the governed.
6. Both the government and private groups attempt to muster support by using public relations to shape opinion.

Measuring Public Opinion

1. In order to construct public opinion from surveys, a polling sample must be large and the views of those in the sample must accurately and proportionately reflect the views of the whole.
2. The inability of polls to discover public opinion or to avoid unintentional distortions of political knowledge allows a certain level of ignorance to function as a restraint on the use of political power.

Public Opinion and Democracy

1. Government policies in the United States are generally consistent with popular preferences. There are, however, always some inconsistencies.
2. Disagreements between opinion and policy come about because on some issues, such as gun control, an intensely committed minority can defeat a more apathetic majority. Moreover, the American system of government is not designed to quickly transform changes in opinion into changes in government programs.

PRACTICE QUIZ

1. Which of the following helps to explain why the United States has such high level of agreement on fundamental political values?
   a. The United States never had a feudal aristocracy.
   b. The United States never had a strong socialist movement.
   c. Both a and b are correct.
   d. Neither a nor b is correct.
2. Variables such as income, education, race, gender, and ethnicity
   a. often create differences of political opinion in America.
   b. have consistently been a challenge to America's core political values.
   c. have little impact on political opinions.
   d. help explain why public opinion polls are so unreliable.
3. Which of the following is an agency of socialization?
   a. the family
   b. social groups
   c. education
   d. all of the above
4. When men and women respond differently to issues of public policy, they are demonstrating an example of
   a. liberalism.
   b. educational differences.
   c. the gender gap.
   d. party politics.
5. Which of the following has never been a political ideology?
   a. liberalism
   b. Nazism
   c. Catholicism
   d. All of the above have been political ideologies.
6. Which of the following is an example of cooptation?
   a. ticket balancing
   b. homesteading
   c. voting
   d. conscription
7. What might explain differences in political attitudes between African Americans and white Americans?
   a. different life experiences
   b. differences in education
   c. both a and b
   d. Neither a nor b is very important in explaining these differences.
8. According to the poll cited in this chapter, with which of the following statements does a higher percentage of white Americans agree, as compared with African Americans?
   a. I would rather have the federal government provide more services, even if it costs more in taxes.
   b. Racism is a big problem in our society today.
   c. The average African American is "just as well off" as the average white person in terms of jobs.
   d. Past and present discrimination is the major reason for the economic and social ills blacks face.
9. Which of the following does not represent an element of the typical "liberal" philosophy?
   a. support for nuclear rather than conventional weapons
   b. support of abortion rights
   c. support of the United Nations
   d. expansion of federal social services
10. Which of the following refers to the impact of other opinions in society on individual opinion formation?
    a. the marketplace of ideas
    b. the central tendency
    c. conservatism
    d. totalitarianism

CRITICAL THINKING QUESTIONS

1. In the American system of government, public opinion seems to be an important factor in political and governmental decision making. In what ways does the public, through opinion, control its political leaders? In what ways do political leaders control public opinion? What are the positive and negative consequences of governing by popular opinion?
2. Describe the differences between liberal and conservative ideologies in American politics. Using one social or demographic group as an example, describe some of the factors that may have shaped the ideological orientation of that particular group. What factors may explain inconsistencies in that group's political ideology or issue positions?

KEY TERMS

agencies of socialization social institutions, including families and schools, that help to shape individuals' basic political beliefs and values. (p. 192)

bandwagon effect a situation wherein reports of voter or delegate opinion can influence the actual outcome of an election or a nominating convention. (p. 220)

conservative today this term refers to those who generally support the social and economic status quo and are suspicious of efforts to introduce new political formulae and economic arrangements. Conservatives believe that a large and powerful government poses a threat to citizens' freedom. (p. 200)

cooptation the strategy of bringing an individual into a group by joint action of the members of that group, usually in order to reduce or eliminate the individual's opposition. (p. 209)

democracy a system of rule that permits citizens to play a significant part in the governmental process, usually through the election of key public officials. (p. 189)

equality of opportunity a widely shared American ideal that all people should have the freedom to use whatever talents and wealth they have to reach their fullest potential. (p. 189)

gender gap a distinctive pattern of male and female voting that became important in the 1980s. (p. 197)

homesteading a national policy that permitted people to gain ownership of property by occupying public or unclaimed lands, living on the land for a specified period of time, and making certain minimal improvements on that land. Also known as *squatting*. (p. 206)

ideology the combined doctrines, assertions, and intentions of a social or political group that justify its behavior. (p. 199)

illusion of saliency the impression conveyed by polls that something is important to the public when actually it is not. (p. 219)

liberal a liberal today generally supports political and social reform; extensive governmental intervention in the economy; the expansion of federal social services; more vigorous efforts on behalf of the poor, minorities, and women; and greater concern for consumers and the environment. (p. 200)

liberty freedom from government control. (p. 189)

marketplace of ideas the public forum in which beliefs and ideas are exchanged and compete. (p. 204)

nationalism the widely held belief that the people who occupy the same territory have something in common, and that they are a single community. (p. 205)

political socialization the induction of individuals into the political culture; learning how to accept authority; learning what is legitimate and what is not. (p. 192)

public opinion citizens' attitudes about political issues, personalities, institutions, and events. (p. 188)

public opinion polls scientific instruments for measuring public opinion. (p. 216)

salient interests attitudes and views that are important to the individual holding them. (p. 219)

sample a small group selected by researchers to represent the most important characteristics of an entire population. (p. 216)

7

The Media

TEXT EDITION
JAVA EDITION
PATHFINDER Personal Edition
WELCOME TO THE NEW PATHFINDER!
PATHFINDER
WHAT'S NEW
HELP
SEARCH
BULLETIN BOARDS
CHAT
AUGUST 1, 9:11 AM
LATEST NEWS
Britain Destroys Orphan'' Human Embryos
Jury Deadlocked in Whitewater Trial
Congress Reaches Health Insurance Accord
CNN & NEWS
ONLINE
Money PERSONAL FINANCE
CNNfn & FORTUNE BUSINESS
People ONLINE
TECHWATCH WITH The Netly News
SPORTS FROM SIonline
HEALTH, FITNESS &
STRONG
Mutual
Funds
Center
THE FORD

★ Organization of the Media

How has the nationalization of the news media contributed to the nationalization of American politics?

How is the media regulated by the government? How does this regulation differ between the broadcast media and the print media?

★ News Coverage

How are media content and news coverage affected by the producers, subjects, and consumers of the news?

★ Media Power in American Politics

How do the media shape public perceptions of events, issues, and institutions?

What are the sources of media power?

★ Media Power and Democracy

Are the media too powerful and thus in need of restriction, or are a free media necessary for democracy?

VIRTUALLY ALL AMERICANS believe in the principle of freedom of the press. Yet it is interesting to see how quickly groups that champion freedom when the press attacks *their enemies* can become advocates of censorship when the press turns and attacks *them*. For many years, for example, Republicans complained about the liberal bias of the national media while Democrats staunchly defended freedom of the press. The advent of an effective conservative media, however, especially the emergence of a host of new right-wing radio talk programs, seems to have changed the perspectives of both partisan camps. In the wake of the April 1995 bombing of the Oklahoma City federal office building by supporters of the radical Right, President Clinton and other Democrats accused conservative media personalities such as G. Gordon Liddy and Rush Limbaugh of encouraging violence through their rhetoric. In response, Republican leaders and conservative columnists accused the Democrats of attempting to undermine freedom of the press.

In recent years, newspapers on many college campuses have come under attack by groups that object to their coverage. Traditionally, of course, school administrators sought to influence the content of student newspapers. Today, because of court decisions protecting college papers from the actions of school authorities, most college administrations maintain a hands-off policy toward the campus press. In a number of recent cases, however, student groups that differ politically with a campus paper have sought to prevent the paper's publication and distribution, often by stealing thousands of copies of the paper before other students could read it.

For example, in April 1993, an African American student group at the University of Pennsylvania absconded with 14,000 copies of the student newspaper, the *Daily Pennsylvanian*, after the paper published columns criticizing affirmative action.[1] At Pennsylvania State University, more than 6,000 copies of a conservative student paper, the *Lionhearted*, were stolen after the paper published a cartoon that offended feminist groups. One Penn State professor reportedly defended the thefts, arguing that they were justified because of the paper's "misogynistic" views.[2] At a number of other campuses, including Brandeis, Dartmouth, the University of Wisconsin, Trenton State University, the University of Illinois, and Southeastern Louisiana University (SLU), thousands of copies of student newspapers have been stolen by groups objecting to the views the papers presented. At SLU, the theft of 2,000 copies of the *Lion's Roar* allegedly was perpetrated by an officer of the school's student government who wanted to prevent his fellow students from reading an article that criticized his organization. All told, nearly 200,000 copies of student newspapers have been stolen on college campuses since 1992.[3]

In the national political arena, no group has yet stooped to theft in dealing with critical newspaper coverage. Nevertheless, attempts to silence or discredit the opposition press have a long history in America. As you will recall from Chapter 5, the infamous Alien and Sedition Acts were enacted by the Federalists in an attempt to silence the Republican press. In recent times, during the 1950s McCarthy era, right-wing politicians used charges of communist infiltration to intimidate the liberal news media. During President Richard Nixon's administration, the White House attacked its critics in the media by threatening to take action to bar the television networks from owning local affiliates, as well as by illegally wiretapping the phones of government officials suspected of leaking information to the press. In the early 1980s, conservative groups financed a series of libel suits against CBS News, *Time* magazine, and other media organizations, in an attempt to discourage them from publicizing material critical of Reagan administration policies.[4]

In 1995, as noted above, liberal forces sought to discredit segments of the conservative media by asserting that criticisms of the government by conservative radio and television broadcasters had created a climate that stimulated acts of violence by right-wing extremists. In the wake of the Oklahoma City bombing, liberal columnist Anthony Lewis wrote, "The drumbeat of right-wing rhetoric in the past few years has been Washington as the enemy. . . . Anyone who thinks such words have had no effect is ignorant of political history."[5] The same point was reiterated by President Clinton in a number of speeches. Just as Senator Joseph McCarthy sought to silence the liberal press by accusing it of abetting communism, so some liberals hoped to silence the conservative media by linking it to right-wing terrorism.

In this chapter we will examine the place of the media in American politics. First, we will look at the organization of the American news media. Second, we will discuss the factors that help to determine "what's news"—that is, the factors that shape media coverage of events and personalities. Third, we will examine the scope of media power in politics. Finally, we will address the question of responsibility: To whom, if anyone, are the media accountable for the use of their formidable power?

Organization of the Media

> ➤ How has the nationalization of the news media contributed to the nationalization of American politics?
> ➤ How is the media regulated by the government? How does this regulation differ between the broadcast media and the print media?

The United States boasts more than one thousand television stations, approximately eighteen hundred daily newspapers, and more than nine thousand radio stations.[6] The great majority of these enterprises are locally owned and operated and present a good deal of news and many features with a distinctly local flavor. For example, for many months, viewers of the Syracuse, New York, evening news were informed that the day's "top story" concerned the proposed construction of a local garbage-burning steam plant. Similarly, in Seattle, Washington, viewers were treated to years of discussion about the construction of a domed athletic stadium, and audiences in Baltimore, Maryland, watched and read about struggles over downtown redevelopment. In all these cases, as in literally thousands of others, the local media focused heavily on a matter of particular local concern, providing local viewers, readers, and listeners with considerable information and viewpoints.

Yet, however much variation the American news media offer in terms of local coverage, there is far less diversity in the reporting of national events and issues. More than three-fourths of the daily newspapers in the United States are owned by large media conglomerates such as the Hearst or Gannett corporations; thus the diversity of coverage and editorial opinion in American newspapers is not as broad as it might seem. Most of the national news that is published by local newspapers is provided by two wire services: the Associated Press and United Press International. More than five hundred of the nation's television stations are affiliated with one of the four networks and carry that network's evening news reports. Dozens of others carry PBS (Public Broadcasting System) news. Several hundred local radio stations also carry network news or National Public Radio news broadcasts. At the same time, although there are only three truly national newspapers, the *Wall Street Journal,* the *Christian Science Monitor,* and *USA Today,* two other papers, the *New York Times* and the *Washington Post,* are read by political leaders and other influential Americans throughout the nation. Such is the influence of these two "elite" newspapers that their news coverage sets the standard for virtually all other news outlets. Stories carried in the *New York Times* or the *Washington Post* influence the content of many other papers as well as of the network news. Note how often this text, like most others, relies upon *New York Times* and *Washington Post* stories as sources for contemporary events.

National news is also carried to millions of Americans by the three major newsmagazines—*Time, Newsweek,* and *U.S. News & World Report.* Thus, even though the number of TV and radio stations and daily newspapers reporting news in the United States is enormous, and local coverage varies

CNN's live coverage of the Persian Gulf War captivated American television viewers and brought the war into their homes.

greatly from place to place, the number of sources of national news is actually quite small—two wire services, four broadcast networks, public radio and television, two elite newspapers, three newsmagazines, and a scattering of other sources such as the national correspondents of a few large local papers and the small independent radio networks. Beginning in the late 1980s, Cable News Network (CNN) became another major news source for Americans. The importance of CNN increased dramatically after its spectacular coverage of the Persian Gulf War. At one point, CNN was able to provide live coverage of American bombing raids on Baghdad, Iraq, after the major networks' correspondents had been forced to flee to bomb shelters. Even the availability of new electronic media on the Internet has failed to expand news sources. Most national news available on the World Wide Web, for example, consists of electronic versions of the conventional print media.

NATIONALIZATION OF THE NEWS

In general, the national news media cover more or less the same sets of events, present similar information, and emphasize similar issues and problems (see Figure 7.1). Indeed, the national news services watch one another quite carefully. It is unlikely that a major story carried by one will not soon find its way into the pages or programming of the others. As a result, in the United States a rather centralized national news has developed, through which a relatively similar picture of events, issues, and problems is presented to the entire nation.[7] The nationalization of the news began at the turn of the century, was accelerated by the development of radio networks in the 1920s and 1930s, and was brought to a peak by the creation of the television networks after the 1950s. This nationalization of news content has very important consequences for American politics.

THE NATIONALIZATION OF THE NEWS

Detroit Free Press

Metro final

On Guard For 165 Years

Friday

REPUBLICAN '96 CONVENTION

Estrogen helps fight Alzheimer's

Women taking hormone are less likely to get disease, study finds

"All the News That's Fit to Print"

The New York Times

Late Edition

NEW YORK, FRIDAY, AUGUST 16, 1996

60 CENTS

Estrogen May Reduce Alzheimer's Risk in Women, Study Says

(c) 1996 by the New York Times Company. Reprinted by permission.

SAINT PAUL

PIONEER PRESS

METRO FINAL

FRIDAY

Estrogen seems to reduce risk of Alzheimer's

One year's dosage gives protection, 10 years may cut incidence by 40%

HEALTH

The Washington Post

FRIDAY, AUGUST 16, 1996

Estrogen May Reduce Chances of Getting Alzheimer's

Long Use of Hormone in Study of 1,124 Menopausal Women Lowers Risk by 30 to 40 Percent

Star Tribune

Minneapolis Edition

NEWSPAPER OF THE TWIN CITIES

Study finds estrogen use among women may delay or reduce risk of Alzheimer's

Health and medicine

The Boston Globe

Drug helps women avert Alzheimer's

FIGURE 7.1

Much of the news that is reported in American newspapers grows out of organizational press releases or wire service reports. For example, on August 16, 1996, newspapers across the country reported that estrogen may play a role in preventing Alzheimer's disease. The similarities between the stories suggested that they were all drawn from one or two wire service reports.

Nationalization of the news has contributed greatly to the nationalization of politics and of political perspectives in the United States. Prior to the development of the national media and the nationalization of news coverage, news traveled very slowly. Every region and city saw national issues and problems primarily through a local lens. Concerns and perspectives varied greatly from region to region, city to city, and village to village. Today, in large measure as a result of the nationalization of the media, residents of all parts of the country share a similar picture of the day's events.[8] They may not agree on everything, but most see the world in similar ways.

The exception to this pattern can be found with those Americans whose chief source of news is something other than the "mainstream" national media. Despite the nationalization and homogenization of the news, some Americans live in **news enclaves**, where alternative news coverage is available. For example, some African Americans rely upon newspapers and radio stations that aim their coverage primarily at black audiences. As a result, these individuals may interpret events differently than white Americans and even other blacks do.[9] The existence of a black-focused media helps to explain why many African Americans and white Americans reacted differently to the 1995 trial of O. J. Simpson in Los Angeles. While national media outlets generally portrayed Simpson as guilty of the murder of his former wife, other

Darryl Cabey was paralyzed by subway gunman Bernhard Goetz 12 years ago. When the Civil Court ruled that he would pay $43 million in damages to Cabey, Goetz filed for bankruptcy. The court has just denied his bid.

SEE PAGE 6

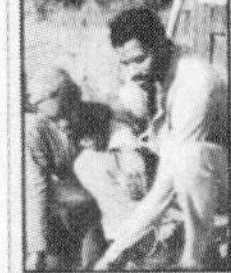

Reading is the central, almost mystical subject of Charles Burnett's *Nightjohn*, which, says Armond White, challenges the racist notion that white folks are keeping great film art to themselves.

SEE PAGE 19

Although some 25 years ago Muhammad Ali was successful in turning a large part of Black opinion against Joe Frazier, Frazier's current jabs at a man with his hands down is sad, says Marion Boykin.

SEE PAGE 32

NEW YORK'S MOST AUTHORITATIVE BLACK WEEKLY NEWSPAPER

THE CITY SUN

SPEAKING TRUTH TO POWER

AUGUST 7 - AUGUST 13, 1996 VOL. 12, NO. 30

75¢

INTERNATIONAL
Nigeria Commentary

NATIONAL
Rebuilding A Slave Ship

VIEWPOINT
Embarrassing Ghanaians?

THE RICH GET RICHER THE POOR GET PUNISHED

See Page 4

President Clinton, shown with Dexter and Coretta Scott King, was able to "overcome" his commitment to the poor.

Slick Willie's Welfare Surprise

File Photo

While much of the mainstream media applauded the welfare reform plan of 1996, African American newspapers such as the *City Sun* had a different view.

media outlets depicted Simpson as a victim of a racist criminal justice system. This latter view came to be echoed by a large number of African Americans.

In a similar vein, some radio stations and print media are aimed exclusively at religious and social conservatives. These individuals are also likely to develop and retain a perception of the news that is quite different from that of "mainstream" America. For example, the rural Midwesterners who rely upon the ultra-conservative People's Radio Network for their news coverage may become concerned about the alleged efforts of the United Nations to subordinate the United States in a world government, a viewpoint unfamiliar to most Americans. Similarly, the story of Michael New, a U.S. Army medic who was court-martialed for refusing to wear a United Nations patch on his uniform when his unit was deployed on a peacekeeping mission to Macedonia, was ignored for months by the national media. However, the story was front-page news for the *Patriot Press* and the *Liberty News*, small, right-wing newspapers that portrayed New as a patriotic hero for refusing to subordinate himself to the U.N. The story became so significant to rural social conservatives that 1996 Republican presidential candidate Pat Buchanan began to refer to it when campaigning in conservative rural areas.[10] Eventually, the mainstream national media began to cover New's trial.

Regulation of the Broadcast Media

In some countries, the government controls media content. In other countries, the government owns the broadcast media (e.g., the BBC in Britain) but it does not tell the media what to say. In the United States, the government neither owns nor controls the communications networks, but it does regulate the broadcast media.

American radio and television are regulated by the Federal Communications Commission (FCC), an independent regulatory agency established in 1934. Radio and TV stations must have FCC licenses that must be renewed every five years. Licensing provides a mechanism for allocating radio and TV frequencies to prevent broadcasts from interfering with and garbling one another. License renewals are almost always granted automatically by the FCC. Indeed, renewal requests are now filed by postcard.

But even though licensing is a routine administrative matter, the federal government has used its licensing power to impose several regulations that can affect the political content of radio and TV broadcasts. The first of these is the **equal time rule,** under which broadcasters must provide candidates for the same political office equal opportunities to communicate their messages to the public. If, for example, a television station sells commercial time to a state's Republican gubernatorial candidate, it may not refuse to sell time to the Democratic candidate for the same position.

The second FCC regulation affecting the content of broadcasts is the **right of rebuttal,** which requires that individuals be given the opportunity to respond to personal attacks. In the 1969 case of *Red Lion Broadcasting Company v. FCC,* for example, the U.S. Supreme Court upheld the FCC's determination that a television station was required to provide a liberal author with an opportunity to respond to an attack from a conservative commentator that the station had aired.[11]

For many years, a third important federal regulation was the **fairness doctrine.** Under this doctrine, broadcasters who aired programs on controversial issues were required to provide time for opposing views. In 1985, however, the FCC stopped enforcing the fairness doctrine on the grounds that there were so many radio and television stations—to say nothing of newspapers and newsmagazines—that in all likelihood many different viewpoints were already being presented without having to require each station to try to present all sides of an argument. Critics of this FCC decision charge that in many media markets the number of competing viewpoints is small. Nevertheless, a

THE MINNESOTA RAG AND PRESS FREEDOM

Few people liked Jay Near. A free-lance reporter who wrote when and where he could find a job, Near eked out a living with stories that were usually scandalous and sometimes malicious. In the 1920s and 1930s, reporters like Near could find many small-time magazines and newspapers for which to write, as long as the stories were sensational enough. But Near brought his own personal hatreds into his writing; he was unapologetically anti-Semitic, anti-Catholic, anti-labor, and anti-black. And he was not reluctant to express his views in his articles, often using the most offensive racial slurs when referring to individuals and groups. In short, Near was the kind of reporter who gave reporting a bad name.

With the help of an associate, Near began to publish his own weekly scandal sheet in the Minneapolis–St. Paul, Minnesota, area. He called his paper the *Saturday Press*. The lifespan of the *Press* consisted of nine issues published in the fall of 1927. Yet even before the first issue hit the streets, local authorities moved to stop publication of this odious rag, not only because it was racist and jingoist, but also because of allegations that Near printed of collusion between organized crime figures and local public officials. Coming during the era of alcohol prohibition in America, when bootlegging and related crimes led to widespread corruption among government officials, these allegations were at least partly true.

Authorities obtained a restraining order barring Near and his associates from publishing any present or future issues of the *Press*. The legal basis for this ruling was a Minnesota state law enacted in 1925 called the Public Nuisance Bill, also known as the "gag law." This law made illegal the production, publication, circulation, or possession of any publication found to be "obscene, lewd and lascivious" or "malicious, scandalous and defamatory." At first the restraining order was applied temporarily, but it was later made permanent. The *Saturday Press* was shut down; moreover, Near was barred from practicing his profession. Despite having little money and even fewer friends, Near appealed his conviction, which was upheld by Minnesota's highest court. Because of his dire financial and legal situation, Near appealed for help to the prominent publisher of the *Chicago Tribune*, Col. Robert R. McCormick. McCormick had no

congressional effort to require the FCC to enforce the fairness doctrine was blocked by the Reagan administration in 1987.

FREEDOM OF THE PRESS

Unlike the broadcast media, the print media are not subject to federal regulation. Indeed, the great principle underlying the federal government's relationship with the press is the doctrine against **prior restraint.** Beginning with the landmark 1931 case of *Near v. Minnesota,* the U.S. Supreme Court has held that, except under the most extraordinary circumstances, the First Amendment of the Constitution prohibits government agencies from seeking to prevent newspapers or magazines from publishing whatever they wish.[12] Indeed, in the case of *New York Times v. U.S.,* the so-called *Pentagon Papers* case, the Supreme Court ruled that the government could not even block publication of secret Defense Department documents furnished to the *New York Times* by a liberal opponent of the Vietnam War who had obtained the documents illegally.[13] In a 1990 case, however, the Supreme Court upheld a lower-particular interest in helping Near, but he realized that the actions taken by the state of Minnesota against Near could also be applied to his newspaper by politicians in Illinois who would have gleefully put McCormick out of business because of his scorching criticisms of many prominent political figures. A new organization, formed to help average people protect their rights—the American Civil Liberties Union (ACLU)—also joined to help Near. The ACLU also realized that if a state could impose such a "prior restraint" on a publication, it could effectively exercise censorship, which would render meaningless the freedom of the press protected by the First Amendment.

At the time the Supreme Court agreed to hear Near's appeal, the right of American citizens to claim free press protection under the First Amendment had not yet been established (free speech had just been extended to all citizens by the Supreme Court in 1925). In a 5-to-4 decision handed down in 1931, the Court ruled in *Near v. Minnesota* that the Minnesota law was unconstitutional. The Court pointed out that the ability of the press to uncover scandal and wrongdoing could only occur by defaming the corrupt. Those who were legitimately wronged in the press have recourse through libel actions, the Court said, but the right to publish itself cannot be protected unless the right to publish scandalous and even defamatory stories is also protected. As Chief Justice Charles Evans Hughes wrote in the majority opinion, "The fact that the liberty of the press may be abused by miscreant purveyors of scandal does not make any the less necessary the immunity of the press from previous restraint in dealing with official misconduct."

Near himself was mostly forgotten after his brief fame. He died in poverty and obscurity in 1936. Yet because of this hate-monger, press freedom was given the special protection it rightly deserved.

The Saturday Press

Vol. 1, No. 4 — Minneapolis, Minn., Oct. 15, 1927 — Price 5 Cents

A Direct Challenge to Police Chief Brunskill

The Chief, in Banning This Paper from News Stands, Definitely Aligns Himself With Gangland, Violates the Law He Is Sworn to Uphold, When He Tries to Suppress This Publication. The Only Paper in the City That Dares Expose the Gang's Deadly Grip on Minneapolis. A Plain Statement of Facts and a Warning of Legal Action.

Possibly there are moments when "a soft answer turneth away wrath" but as against such short periods there are long hours when the English language becomes woefully deficient in expressive words, and I find that deficiency painfully evident right now.

On September 24th, the first issue of the Saturday Press made its appearance. It launched no attack against the police department nor against Chief of Police Frank Brunskill news stands FOR WE HAD BEEN TOLD BY THE GAMBLING SYNDICATE THAT CHIEF OF POLICE BRUNSKILL WAS THE "WEAK SISTER" OF THE SYNDICATE. Think of it—the Chief of Police on whom every citizen must rely for protection of life and property, a member, by the gang's admission, OF THE GAMBLING SYNDICATE! Do you wonder that we made no attempt to place the Saturday Press on the news stands of Minneapolis, where

Respectfully Submitted

There seems to be an impression among gentlemen of peculiar bent that the suppression of our street sales has rendered abortive our attempt to cleanse this city of gang rule. These gents are intellectual single-trackers; twenty - two caliber saps rattling around in a four hundred thousand city. Lest they become too hilarious, I beg to call their attention to the following letter, the original of which was mailed to the Hennepin County Grand Jury on Wednesday of this week.

Read it carefully, "me brave buckos" and see if you can discern a flutter of a white flag. We've just begun to fight!

Minneapolis, Minnesota,

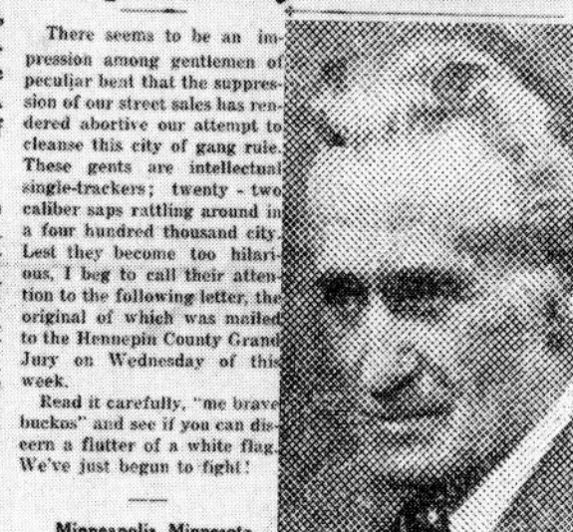

SOURCE: Fred W. Friendly, *Minnesota Rag* (New York: Vintage, 1981).

court order restraining Cable News Network (CNN) from broadcasting tapes of conversations between former Panamanian dictator Manuel Noriega and his lawyer, supposedly recorded by the U.S. government. By a vote of 7 to 2, the Court held that CNN could be restrained from broadcasting the tapes until the trial court in the Noriega case had listened to the tapes and had decided whether their broadcast would violate Noriega's right to a fair trial. This case would seem to weaken the "no prior restraint" doctrine. But whether the same standard will apply to the print media has yet to be tested in the courts. In 1994, the Supreme Court ruled that cable television systems were entitled to essentially the same First Amendment protections as the print media.[14]

Even though newspapers may not be restrained from publishing whatever they want, they may be subject to sanctions after the fact. Historically, newspapers were subject to the law of libel, which provided that newspapers that printed false and malicious stories could be compelled to pay damages to those they defamed. In recent years, however, American courts have greatly narrowed the meaning of libel and made it extremely difficult, particularly for politicians or other public figures, to win a libel case against a newspaper. The most important case on this topic is the 1964 U.S. Supreme Court case of *New York Times v. Sullivan,* in which the Court held that to be deemed libelous a story about a public official not only had to be untrue, but had to result from "actual malice" or "reckless disregard" for the truth.[15] In other words, the newspaper had to deliberately print false and malicious material. In practice, it is nearly impossible to prove that a paper has deliberately printed false and damaging information and, as conservatives discovered in the 1980s, it is very difficult for a politician or other public figure to win a libel case. Libel suits against CBS News by General William Westmoreland and against *Time* magazine by Israeli general Ariel Sharon, both financed by conservative legal foundations that hoped to embarrass the media, were both defeated in court because they failed to show "actual malice." In the 1991 case of *Masson v. New Yorker Magazine,* this tradition was again affirmed when the Court held that fabricated quotations attributed to a public figure were libelous only if the fabricated account "materially changed" the meaning of what the person actually said.[16] For all intents and purposes, the print media can publish anything they want about a public figure.

News Coverage

➤ How are media content and news coverage affected by the producers, subjects, and consumers of the news?

Because of the important role the media can play in national politics, it is vitally important to understand the factors that affect media coverage.[17] What accounts for the media's agenda of issues and topics? What explains the character of coverage—why does a politician receive good or bad press? What factors determine the interpretation or "spin" that a particular story will receive? Although a host of minor factors plays a role, there are three major factors: (1) the journalists or producers of the news; (2) the sources or topics of the news; and (3) the audience for the news.

JOURNALISTS

Media content and news coverage are inevitably affected by the views, ideals, and interests of those who seek out, write, and produce news and other stories. At one time, newspaper publishers exercised a great deal of influence over their papers' news content. Publishers such as William Randolph Hearst and Joseph Pulitzer became political powers through their manipulation of news coverage. Hearst, for example, almost singlehandedly pushed the United States into war with Spain in 1898 through his newspapers' relentless coverage of the alleged brutality employed by Spain in its efforts to suppress a rebellion in Cuba, at that time a Spanish colony. The sinking of the American battleship *Maine* in Havana harbor under mysterious circumstances gave Hearst the ammunition he needed to force a reluctant President McKinley to lead the nation into war. Today, few publishers have that kind of

$50,000 REWARD.—WHO DESTROYED THE MAINE?—$50,000 REWARD.

EDITION FOR GREATER NEW YORK

NEW YORK JOURNAL

AND ADVERTISER.

The Journal will give $50,000 for information, furnished to it exclusively, that will convict the person or persons who sank the Maine.

NEW YORK, THURSDAY, FEBRUARY 17, 1898.—16 PAGES. PRICE ONE CENT

DESTRUCTION OF THE WAR SHIP MAINE WAS THE WORK OF AN ENEMY.

$50,000!

$50,000 REWARD!

For the Detection of the Perpetrator of the Maine Outrage!

Assistant Secretary Roosevelt Convinced the Explosion of the War Ship Was Not an Accident.

The Journal Offers $50,000 Reward for the Conviction of the Criminals Who Sent 258 American Sailors to Their Death. Naval Officers Unanimous That the Ship Was Destroyed on Purpose.

$50,000!

$50,000 REWARD!

For the Detection of the Perpetrator of the Maine Outrage!

NAVAL OFFICERS THINK THE MAINE WAS DESTROYED BY A SPANISH MINE.

Hidden Mine or a Sunken Torpedo Believed to Have Been the Weapon Used Against the American Man-of-War---Officers and Men Tell Thrilling Stories of Being Blown Into the Air Amid a Mass of Shattered Steel and Exploding Shells---Survivors Brought to Key West Scout the Idea of Accident---Spanish Officials Protest Too Much---Our Cabinet Orders a Searching Inquiry---Journal Sends Divers to Havana to Report Upon the Condition of the Wreck.

Was the Vessel Anchored Over a Mine?

BY CAPTAIN E. L. ZALINSKI, U. S. A.

(Captain Zalinski is the inventor of the famous dynamite gun, which would be the principal factor in our coast defence in case of war.)

Assistant Secretary of the Navy Theodore Roosevelt says he is convinced that the destruction of the Maine in Havana Harbor was not an accident.

The Journal offers a reward of $50,000 for exclusive evidence that will convict the person, persons or Government criminally responsible for the destruction of the American battle ship and the death of 258 of its crew.

The suspicion that the Maine was deliberately blown up grows stronger every hour. Not a single fact to the contrary has been produced.

Captain Sigsbee, of the Maine, and Consul-General Lee both urge that public opinion be suspended until they have completed their investigation. They are taking the course of tactful men who are convinced that there has been treachery.

Washington reports very late that Captain Sigsbee had feared some such event as a hidden mine. The English cipher code was used all day yesterday by the naval officers in cabling instead of the usual American code.

The *New York Journal*'s sensationalistic coverage of the sinking of the *Maine* in Havana harbor inflamed the American public and edged the United States toward war with Spain.

power. Most publishers are concerned more with the business operations of their newspapers than with editorial content, although a few continue to impose their interests and tastes on the news.

More important than publishers, for the most part, are the reporters. Those who cover the news for the national media generally have a good deal of discretion or freedom to interpret stories and, as a result, have an opportunity to interject their views and ideals into news stories (see Figure 7.2). For example, the personal friendship and respect that some reporters felt for Franklin Roosevelt or John Kennedy helped to generate more favorable news coverage for these presidents. Likewise, the dislike and distrust felt by many reporters for Richard Nixon was also communicated to the public. In the case of Ronald Reagan, the disdain that many journalists felt for the president was communicated in stories suggesting that he was often asleep or inattentive when important decisions were made. Conservatives have long charged that the liberal biases of journalists result in distorted news coverage.[18] A recent study indicated that 44 percent of journalists consider themselves Democrats, while only 16 percent are Republicans. Another survey has indicated that even among the radio talk-show hosts lambasted by President Clinton, Democrats outnumber Republicans by a wide margin: Of 112 hosts surveyed, 39 percent had voted for Clinton in 1992, and only 23 percent had supported George Bush.[19]

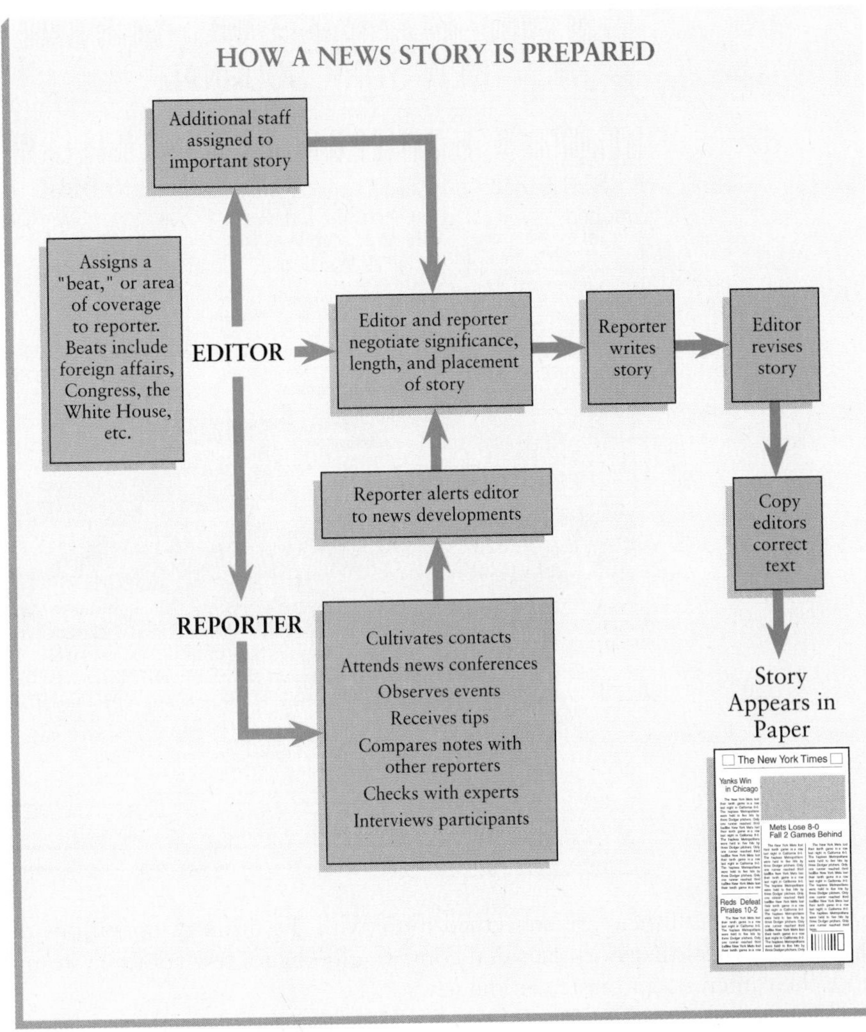

FIGURE 7.2

Most journalists deny that their political outlooks result in biased reporting.[20] Conservatives, however, are quick to point to instances in which the mainstream national media appear to give more weight to liberal than to conservative positions. For example, a recent study by the conservative Media Research Center indicated that of 141 public officials interviewed on health care reform by the major networks, 102 were Democrats who supported reform, and only 39 were Republican opponents of national legislation.[21]

SOURCES OF THE NEWS

News coverage is also influenced by the individuals or groups who are subjects of the news or whose interests and activities are actual or potential news topics. All politicians, for example, seek to shape or manipulate their media images by cultivating good relations with reporters as well as through news leaks and staged news events. Some politicians become extremely adept image makers—or at least skilled at hiring publicists who are skillful image makers.

Furthermore, political candidates often endeavor to tailor their images for specific audiences. For example, to cultivate a favorable image among younger voters during his 1992 campaign, Bill Clinton made several appearances on MTV, and he continued to grant interviews to MTV after his election. His MTV forays came to an end, however, when he was severely criticized for discussing his preferred type of underwear with members of an MTV audience. Apparently undeterred by Clinton's experience, Republican presidential candidate Bob Dole sought to polish his image among younger voters in 1996 by also appearing on MTV. Dole's advisers hoped the seventy-two-year-old candidate could use MTV to reach out to younger voters, but most observers thought Dole appeared out of place on the youth-oriented network.

Government agencies also endeavor to create and shape news. Federal, state, and local agencies provide journalists with thousands of news releases every week, highlighting the efforts and accomplishments of one public program or another. Much of the news reported about the activities of government agencies originates with such news releases. Some government agencies are extremely zealous in their efforts to create positive news. The Clinton administration's energy secretary, Hazel O'Leary, for example, retained a consulting firm to develop a rating system for the Washington reporters who covered her activities. O'Leary hoped to be able to direct the department's public relations efforts toward the reporters most likely to give her agency positive coverage, while restricting the access of reporters whose coverage was deemed less favorable. O'Leary abandoned the effort, however, when her activities were reported in the press.[22]

Entertainment shows have become a popular means for candidates to reach the public. For instance, presidential hopeful Bob Dole appeared on David Letterman's late-night talk show. During the 1996 presidential campaign, candidates also appeared on MTV and on the *Tonight Show,* hosted by Jay Leno.

By using media consultants and "issues managers," many social, economic, and political groups also vigorously promote their ideas and interests through speeches, articles, books, news releases, research reports, and other mechanisms designed to attract favorable media coverage. Typically, competing forces seek to present—and to persuade the media to present—their interests as more general or "public" interests. In recent years, for example, liberals have been very successful in inducing the media to present their environmental, consumer, and political reform proposals as matters of the public interest. Indeed, the advocates of these goals are organized in "public interest" groups (see Chapter 10). Seldom do the national media ever question a public interest group's equation of its goals with the general interest of all.

The capacity of news sources and subjects to influence the news is hardly unlimited. Media consultants and issues managers may shape the news for a time, but it is generally not difficult for the media to penetrate the smoke screens thrown up by news sources if they have a reason to do so. That reason is sometimes supplied by the third and most important factor influencing news content—the audience.

The Power of Consumers

The print and broadcast media are businesses that, in general, seek to show a profit. This means that like any other business, they must cater to the preferences of consumers. This has very important consequences for the content and character of the news media.

Catering to the Upscale Audience In general, and especially in the political realm, the print and broadcast media and the publishing industry are not only responsive to the interests of consumers generally, but they are particularly responsive to the interests and views of the more "upscale" segments of their audience. The preferences of these audience segments have a profound effect upon the content and orientation of the press, of radio and television programming, and of books, especially in the areas of news and public affairs.[23] The influence of the upscale audience is a function of the economics of publishing and broadcasting. Books, especially books dealing with academic or intellectual issues, are purchased almost exclusively by affluent and well-educated consumers. As a result, the publishing industry caters to the tastes of this segment of the market.

For their part, newspapers, magazines, and the broadcast media depend primarily upon advertising revenues for their profits. These revenues, in turn, depend upon the character and size of the audience that they are able to provide to advertisers for their product displays and promotional efforts. From the perspective of most advertisers and especially those whose products are relatively expensive, the most desirable audiences for their ads and commercials consist of younger, upscale consumers. What makes these individuals an especially desirable consumer audience is, of course, their affluence and their spending habits. Although they represent only a small percentage of the population, individuals under the age of fifty whose family income is in the eightieth percentile or better account for nearly 50 percent of the retail dollars spent on consumer goods in the United States. To reach this audience, advertisers are particularly anxious to promote their products in the periodicals and newspapers and on the radio and television broadcasts that are known or believed to attract upscale patronage. Thus, advertisers flock to magazines like the *New Yorker, Fortune, Forbes, Architectural Digest,* and *Time.* Similarly, the pages of elite newspapers like the *New York Times* and the *Washington Post* are usually packed with advertisements for clothing, autos, computer equipment, stereo equipment, furs, jewelry, resorts and vacations, and the entire range of products and services that are such integral parts of the lifestyles of the well-to-do business and professional strata.

Although affluent consumers do watch television programs and read periodicals whose contents are designed simply to amuse or entertain, the one area that most directly appeals to the upscale audience is that of news and public affairs. The affluent—who are also typically well-educated—are the core audience of newsmagazines, journals of opinion, books dealing with public affairs, such newspapers as the *New York Times* and the *Washington Post,* and broadcast news and weekend and evening public affairs programs. Although other segments of the public also read newspapers and watch television news, their level of interest in world events, national political issues, and the like is closely related to their level of education. As a result, upscale Americans are over-represented in the news and public affairs audience. The concentration of these strata in the audience makes news, politics, and public affairs potentially very attractive topics to advertisers, publishers, radio broadcasters, and television executives.

To attract audiences to their news and public affairs offerings, the media and publishing industries employ polls and other market research techniques, including the famous Nielsen and Arbitron rating services, analyses of sales, as well as a good deal of intuition to identify their audience's political interests, tastes, perspectives, and biases. The results of this research—and guesswork—affect the character, style, and content of the programming presented by the networks, as well as the topics of the books published by major houses and the stories and reports presented by the various periodicals. The media seek to present material consistent with the interests or biases of important segments of the audience, and in a way that appeals to, or is at least not offensive to, the tastes or sensitivities of that audience.

Not surprisingly, given their general market power, it is the upper- and middle-class segments of the audience whose interests and tastes especially influence the media's news, public affairs, and political coverage. This is evident from the topics covered, the style of coverage, and in the case of network television, the types of reporters and newscasters who appear on the screen. First, the political and social topics given most extensive attention by the national media are mainly, albeit not exclusively, topics that appeal to the interests of well-educated professionals, executives, and intellectuals. In recent years, these topics have included the nuclear arms race, ecological and environmental matters, budgetary and fiscal questions, regulation of business and the economy, political changes in Russia, Eastern Europe, and South Africa, attacks on Americans and American interests by terrorists, and, of course, the fluctuations of the stock market, interest rates, the value of the dollar, the price of precious metals, and the cost of real estate. Although many of these topics may indeed be of general importance and concern, most are of more

The O. J. Simpson trial received overwhelming media attention. Tabloid newspapers like those pictured here presented pages and pages of articles on the trial each day.

interest to upscale segments of the audience than to lower-middle- or working-class groups.

While these matters of concern to the upscale audience receive extensive media coverage, there are entire categories of events, issues, and phenomena of interest to lower-middle- and working-class Americans that receive scant attention from the national print and broadcast media. For example, trade union news and events are discussed only in the context of major strikes or revelations of corruption. No network or national periodical routinely covers labor organizations. Religious and church affairs receive little coverage. The activities of veterans', fraternal, ethnic, and patriotic organizations are also generally ignored. Certainly, interpretations of economic events tend to reveal a class bias. For example, an increase in airline fares—a cost borne primarily by upper-income travelers—is usually presented as a negative development. Higher prices for commodities heavily used by the poor, such as alcohol and cigarettes, on the other hand, are generally presented as morally justified.

The upscale character of the national media's coverage stands in sharp contrast to the topics discussed by radio and television talk shows and the small number of news tabloids and major daily newspapers that seek to reach a blue-collar audience. These periodicals and programs feature some of the same events described by the national media. But from the perspective of these outlets and their viewers and readers, "public affairs" includes healthy doses of celebrity gossip, crime news, discussions of the occult, and sightings of UFOs. Also featured are ethnic, fraternal, patriotic, and religious affairs and even demolition derbies. Executives, intellectuals, and professionals, as well as the journalists and writers who serve them, may sneer at this blue-collar version of the news, but after all, are the stories of UFOs presented by the decidedly downscale *New York Post* any more peculiar than the stories of the UN told by the imperious *New York Times*?

The Media and Protest While the media respond most to the upscale audience, groups who cannot afford the services of media consultants and issues managers can publicize their views and interests through protest. Frequently, the media are accused of encouraging protest and even violence as a result of the fact that they are instantly available to cover it, providing protesters with the publicity they crave. Clearly, protest and even violence can be important vehicles for attracting the attention and interest of the media, and thus may provide an opportunity for media attention to groups otherwise lacking the financial or organizational resources to broadcast their views. During the 1960s, for example, the media coverage given to civil rights demonstrators and particularly to the violence that southern law enforcement officers in cities such as Selma and Birmingham directed against peaceful black demonstrators at least temporarily increased white sympathy for the civil rights cause. This was, of course, one of the chief aims of Dr. Martin Luther King's strategy of nonviolence.[24] In subsequent years, the media turned their attention to antiwar demonstrations and, more recently, to antiabortion demonstrations, antinuclear demonstrations, and even to acts of international terrorism designed specifically to induce the Western media to publicize the terrorists' causes. But while protest, disorder, and even terrorism can succeed in drawing media attention, these methods ultimately do not allow groups from the bottom of the social ladder to compete effectively in the media.

The chief problem with protest as a media technique is that, in general, the media upon which the protesters depend have considerable discretion in reporting and interpreting the events they cover. For example, should a particular group of protesters be identified as "freedom fighters" or "terrorists"? If a demonstration leads to violence, was this the fault of the protesters or the authorities? The answers to these questions are typically determined by the media, not by the protesters. This means that media interpretation of protest activities is more a reflection of the views of the groups and forces to which the media are responsive—as we have seen, usually segments of the upper-middle class—than a function of the wishes of the protesters themselves. It is

While demonstrating in Birmingham, Alabama, civil rights protesters were sprayed with fire hoses by the order of Police Commissioner Bull Conner. Images like this one were seen around the world and helped increase pressure on the United States to uphold its claims of being a nation of "liberty and justice for all."

worth noting that civil rights protesters received their most favorable media coverage when a segment of the white, upper-middle class saw blacks as potential political allies. After the demise of this alliance, the media focused less on the brutal treatment of peaceful black demonstrators by bigoted law enforcement officials—the typical civil rights story of the 1960s—and focused more on "black militants" when covering black protest activities. In the 1980s and early 1990s, the media generally portrayed African Americans as victims of Republican neglect. Thus, George Bush and his Republican administration, rather than the participants, received much of the blame for such events as the Los Angeles riots, sparked by a videotape of police officers beating an African American motorist.

Thus, the effectiveness of protest as a media strategy depends, in large measure, on the character of national political alignments and coalitions. If protesters are aligned with or potentially useful to more powerful forces, then protest can be an effective mechanism for the communication of the ideas and interests of the lower classes. If, on the other hand, the social forces to which the media are most responsive are not sympathetic to the protesters or their views, then protest is likely to be defined by the print and broadcast media as mindless and purposeless violence. For example, the media have generally treated the white, working-class, "militia" movement as a dangerous and irrational development while continuing to show a measure of sympathy and understanding for upper-middle-class animal-rights activists, even when the latter have engaged in violent and disruptive behavior. And in general, the media have been unsympathetic to antiabortion protesters, who tend to be drawn from the lower-middle class.

Entertainers can easily attract media attention and publicity for their political causes. The pop band the Go-Gos were prominent in the anti-fur campaign.

Typically, upper-class protesters—student demonstrators and the like—have little difficulty securing favorable publicity for themselves and their causes. Upper-class protesters are often more skilled than their lower-class counterparts in the techniques of media manipulation. That is, they typically have a better sense—often as a result of formal courses on the subject—of how to package messages for media consumption. For example, it is important to know what time of day a protest should occur if it is to be carried on the evening news. Similarly, the setting, definition of the issues, character of the rhetoric used, and so on, all help to determine whether a protest will receive favorable media coverage, unfavorable coverage, or no coverage at all. Moreover, upper-middle-class protesters can often produce their own media coverage through "underground" newspapers, college papers, student radio and television stations, and, now, over the Internet. The same resources and skills that generally allow upper-middle-class people to publicize their ideas are usually not left behind when segments of this class choose to engage in disruptive forms of political action.

Media Power in American Politics

- How do the media shape public perceptions of events, issues, and institutions?
- What are the sources of media power?

The content and character of news and public affairs programming—what the media choose to present and how they present it—can have far-reaching political consequences. Media disclosures can greatly enhance—or fatally damage—the careers of public officials. Media coverage can rally support for—or intensify opposition to—national policies. The media can shape and modify, if not fully form, public perceptions of events, issues, and institutions.

Shaping Events

In recent American political history, the media have played a central role in at least three major events. First, the media were critically important factors in the Civil Rights movement of the 1950s and 1960s. Television photos showing peaceful civil rights marchers attacked by club-swinging police helped to generate sympathy among northern whites for the civil rights struggle and greatly increased the pressure on Congress to bring an end to segregation.[25] Second, the media were instrumental in compelling the Nixon administration to negotiate an end to American involvement in the Vietnam War. Beginning in 1967, the national media portrayed the war as misguided and unwinnable and, as a result, helped to turn popular sentiment against continued American involvement.[26] So strong was the effect of the media, in fact, that when Walter Cronkite told television news viewers that the war was unwinnable, Johnson himself was reported to have said, "If I've lost Walter, then it's over. I've lost Mr. Average Citizen."[27]

Media images of the Vietnam War were seen by millions of Americans and helped turn public sentiment against U.S. involvement in the war. In this famous photo, terrified children flee from a Napalm bomb attack.

Finally, the media were central actors in the Watergate affair, which ultimately forced President Richard Nixon, landslide victor in the 1972 presidential election, to resign from office in disgrace. It was the relentless series of investigations launched by the *Washington Post*, the *New York Times*, and the television networks that led to the disclosures of the various abuses of which Nixon was guilty and ultimately forced Nixon to choose between resignation and almost certain impeachment.

The Sources of Media Power

The power of the media stems from several sources. First, the media help to set the agenda for political discussion. Groups and forces that wish to bring their ideas before the public in order to generate support for policy proposals or political candidacies must somehow secure media coverage. If the media are persuaded that an idea is newsworthy, then they may declare it an "issue" that must be confronted or a "problem" to be solved, thus clearing the first hurdle in the policy-making process. On the other hand, if an idea lacks or loses media appeal, its chance of resulting in new programs or policies is diminished. Some ideas seem to surface, gain media support for a time, lose media appeal, and then resurface. Examples include repair of the "infrastructure," a topic that surfaced in the early 1980s, disappeared after 1983, and then re-emerged in the press in the 1992 presidential campaign. Similarly, national health insurance excited media attention in the 1970s, all but disappeared during the 1980s, and became a major topic again after 1992.

A second source of the media's power is their influence as interpreters and evaluators of events and political results. For example, media interpretations may often determine how people perceive an election outcome. In 1968, despite the growing strength of the opposition to his Vietnam War policies, the incumbent president, Lyndon Johnson, won two-thirds of the votes cast in New Hampshire's Democratic presidential primary. His rival, Senator Eugene McCarthy, received less than one-third. The broadcast media, however, declared the outcome to have been a great victory for McCarthy, who was said to have done much better than "expected" (or at least expected by the media). His "defeat" in New Hampshire was one of the factors that persuaded Johnson to withdraw from the 1968 presidential race.

During the 1992 campaign, while being interviewed on *60 Minutes,* Ross Perot ascribed his earlier decision to withdraw from the presidential campaign to his fear of a Republican "dirty tricks" campaign directed against him. Most media commentators reacted to Perot's assertion with incredulity and cited it as evidence that the Texan lacked the emotional stability needed by a president. Following that episode, they reported that Perot's campaign was "losing momentum." Though Perot still received approximately 19 percent of the popular vote, the *60 Minutes* broadcast and the subsequent media reaction probably lost him substantial support in the electorate.

Of course, the influence of media interpretations extends beyond the electoral arena. For example, the national media portrayed the 1967 North Vietnamese Tet offensive as a staggering defeat for American military forces when, in fact, Tet was a crushing defeat for the North Vietnamese. The media's interpretation, however, turned Tet into a decisive political victory for North Vietnam and marked the beginning of the end of American involvement in the Vietnam War.

Finally, the media have a good deal of power to shape popular perceptions of politicians and political leaders. Most citizens will never meet Bill Clinton or Al Gore or Newt Gingrich. Popular perceptions and evaluations of these individuals are often based solely upon their media images. Obviously, through public relations and other techniques, politicians seek to cultivate favorable media images. But the media have a good deal of discretion over how individuals are portrayed or how they are allowed to portray themselves. In 1988, the media savaged Republican vice presidential candidate Dan Quayle for avoiding serving in Vietnam by using family connections to obtain a place in the Indiana National Guard during the 1960s. In 1992, however, the media treated George Bush's charges that Bill Clinton had attempted to evade the draft as an inappropriate effort to divert popular attention from the "real" issues of the campaign.

In the case of political candidates, the media have considerable influence over whether or not a particular individual will receive public attention, whether or not a particular individual will be taken seriously as a viable contender, and whether the public will perceive a candidate's performance favorably. Thus, if the media find a candidate interesting, they may treat him or her as a serious contender even though the facts of the matter seem to suggest otherwise. For example, in 1992, the broadcast media found Ross Perot to be an incredible novelty. Here was a self-made billionaire with oversized ears who was determined to challenge the American political establishment. Some members of the press treated Perot as a potential Mussolini, while others portrayed him as a wealthy Harry Truman. Nevertheless, from the beginning,

AMERICAN POLITICAL CULTURE

Comic Books

After television, the first mass medium that millions of young Americans become truly familiar with is comic books. Comic books come in all guises, from simply written juvenile stories to ambitious and complex narratives such as Harvey Pekar's brooding American Splendor series and Art Spiegelman's brilliant, Pulitzer Prize–winning Maus books. But the comic books with the widest audiences—the true mass media of the comic world—are superhero comics. At first, it might not seem that with their simple, repetitive plots of clashes between superheroes and supervillains, these comic books do much to shape Americans' cultural and political awareness. But precisely because superhero comic books describe endless variations on the battle between good and evil, they cannot entirely evade broader moral questions—in particular, questions about the relationship between the heroes and the society and government within which, or against which, they act. Over the last half-century, while the basic comic book conflict between heroes and villains has remained the same, the political and cultural backdrop has darkened, and faith in government has largely given way to cynicism.

The comic books that popularized the genre more than fifty years ago were staunchly patriotic. Superman was sworn to uphold "truth, justice, and the American way." Batman, the caped crusader, was allied with Gotham City's police department. Captain America, created by the government-sponsored Project Super Soldier during World War II, spent his first years helping American soldiers fight fascism. After Senate investigations in 1954 into the supposed link between the violence and immorality in comics and juvenile delinquency, however, superhero comic books went into decline. As they regained popularity at the end of the 1950s and into the 1960s, they continued to put forward a largely positive view of government. The characters in the X-men, for instance, one of the most popular and durable of the 1960s comic series, at first worked with the FBI.

But in the late 1960s and the early 1970s, superhero comics, mirroring broader changes in American culture, began to treat government less as an ally and more as part of the problem, and even on occasion as the enemy. In the years after the Watergate scandal, Captain America fought against a corrupt White House. The most acclaimed superhero comic of the 1980s, the Dark Knight series, cast the once pro-establishment Batman as "an embittered and misunderstood anti-hero hunted by . . . [a] Big Brotherish government, which has outlawed all superheros except for a subservient version of Superman. . . .[1]

In recent years, overt political messages have tended to recede from comic-book story lines. But an underlying baseline of cynicism and skepticism seems to have been established. One of the more popular comic book series in the 1990s is Team Youngblood, about a band of young superheroes who must battle not only the usual assortment of menacing villains, but also a corrupt White House trying to exploit them. The twenty-eight-year-old creator of Team Youngblood explains how his depiction of the government arose: "I grew up watching the end of the Vietnam War, Watergate, the Iran-Contra affair. Now that the Soviets are gone, the biggest, most terrifying thing out there is the U.S. government."[2]

[1] David Segal, "Pow! Wham! Take That, Uncle Sam; In Today's Comic Book Culture, the Arch-Villain Is the Government," *Washington Post*, December 11, 1994, p. C3.

[2] Quoted in Segal, "Pow! Wham!"

Perot received enormous media attention, which helped make his quixotic candidacy a serious threat to the two major parties.[28]

In a similar vein, the media may declare that a candidate has "momentum," a mythical property that the media confer upon candidates they admire. Momentum has no substantive meaning—it is simply a media prediction that a particular candidate will do even better in the future than in the past. Such media prophecies can become self-fulfilling as contributors and supporters jump on the bandwagon of the candidate possessing this "momentum." In 1992, when Bill Clinton's poll standings surged in the wake of the Democratic National Convention, the media determined that Clinton had enormous momentum. In fact, nothing that happened during the remainder of the race led the media to change its collective judgment. Even when George Bush's poll standing began to improve, many news stories pointed to Bush's inability to gain momentum. While there is no way to ascertain what impact this coverage had on the race, at the very least, Republican contributors and activists must have been discouraged by the constant portrayal of their candidate as lacking—and the opposition as possessing—this magical "momentum."

Of course, what the media confer they can also take away. Soon after his "momentum" carried Bill Clinton to victory in the 1992 election, the new president became the target of fierce attacks by prominent members of the national media. After a series of miscues during his first month in office, previously friendly commentators described Clinton as "incredibly inept," as "stumbling," and as a man with the "common sense of a gnat." Clinton went, according to one prominent journalist, "from *Time's* 'Man of the Year' to punching bag of the week." Some analysts suggested that the media were trying to compensate for their earlier enthusiastic support for Clinton.[29]

Media power to shape images is not absolute. Other image makers compete with and indeed do manipulate the media by planting stories and rumors and staging news events. Some politicians are so adept at communicating with the public and shaping their own images that the media seem to have lit-

Politicians rely on the media in order to get their message heard by the public. News interview programs, such as NBC's *Meet the Press*, have been a traditional venue for media appearances.

tle effect upon them. For example, for six years Ronald Reagan appeared to have the ability to project such a positive image to millions of Americans that media criticism had little or no effect upon his popularity. It was for this reason that the media came to refer to Reagan as the "Teflon-coated" president—criticism never seemed to "stick" to him (although eventually even Reagan's "Teflon coating" chipped and cracked).

In 1991, President Bush's war policy in the Persian Gulf was predicated upon the assumption that if fighting lasted for more than a short period of time, critical news coverage would make it impossible to continue. In this case, its anticipation of the activities of the media shaped the reality of the Bush administration's military strategy. At the same time, the Bush administration imposed severe limits on press coverage of the war to limit the ability of the media to shape public perceptions on the basis of its own agenda. Journalists were not allowed free access to American or allied forces or to any part of the war zone. Instead, reporters and crews were provided with Pentagon reports, news briefings, and guided tours of the battlefield. This permitted the United States government to exercise a great deal of influence over the media's coverage of the war, and helped the government maintain a generally favorable flow of stories throughout the war. Reporters and cameras were even barred from Dover Air Force Base in Delaware, where the bodies of soldiers killed in the Persian Gulf were brought. The government feared the negative impact of news photos showing American casualties.[30]

One of the few news sources not subject to Pentagon control was CNN correspondent Peter Arnett, who broadcast live from the Iraqi capital, Baghdad. The Iraqi government hoped to generate favorable publicity for its own cause in the United States by permitting CNN to broadcast scenes of destruction and photos of casualties produced by American bombing raids. The

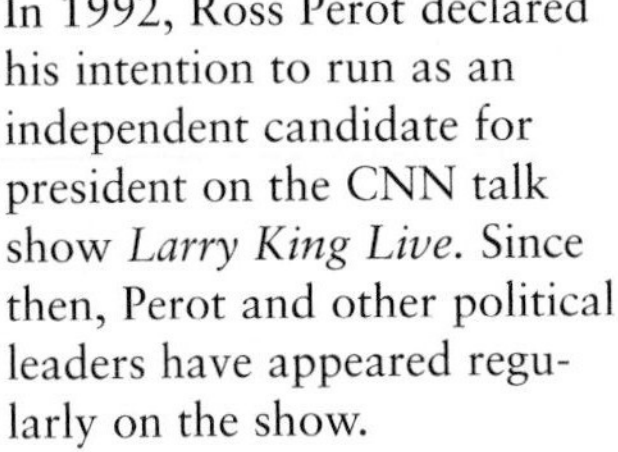
In 1992, Ross Perot declared his intention to run as an independent candidate for president on the CNN talk show *Larry King Live*. Since then, Perot and other political leaders have appeared regularly on the show.

U.S. government was unhappy about Arnett's broadcasts, but could do nothing to stop them.

During the 1992 presidential campaign, candidates developed a number of techniques designed to take control of the image-making process away from journalists and media executives. Among the most important of these techniques were the many town meetings and television talk and entertainment show appearances that all the major candidates made. Frequent exposure on such programs as *Larry King Live* and *Today* gave candidates an opportunity to shape and focus their own media images and to overwhelm any negative image that might be projected by the media. This strategy worked especially well for the independent candidate Ross Perot. By the end of the 1992 campaign, many journalists were depicting Perot as more than a bit of a kook. Nevertheless, Perot's numerous appearances on talk shows, in addition to his lengthy "infomercials," allowed him to maintain some—though not total—control over his media image.

Members of the national news media responded by aggressively investigating and refuting many of the candidates' claims. Each of the major television networks, for example, aired regular critical analyses of the candidates' speeches, television commercials, and talk show appearances. For example, when George Bush appeared in Texas to witness American, Mexican, and Canadian representatives initial the North American Free Trade Agreement (NAFTA), NBC commentators dismissed the trip as election-year politics. CBS also told viewers that the trip was purely political and added a segment featuring a group of American workers who feared that the NAFTA agreement would threaten their jobs. CNN investigated and refuted a Clinton television commercial claiming that Bush's labor secretary, Lynn Martin, had called job growth in Arkansas during Clinton's tenure as governor "enormous." This was a claim that Clinton repeated during the presidential debates. CNN reporter Brooks Jackson revealed that Martin actually had said that Arkansas had low wages and dead-end jobs; she then went on to say, "If you say Arkansas's growth is enormous, if you are working from a low base, it's true."[31]

This type of political coverage serves the public interest by subjecting candidates' claims to scrutiny and refuting errors and distortions. At the same time, such critical coverage serves the interests of the news media by enhancing their own control over political imagery and perceptions and, thus, the power of the media vis-à-vis other political actors and institutions in the United States. We shall examine this topic in the next section, as we consider the development and significance of investigative reporting.

After his election, President Clinton returned to the town meeting and talk show formats that had served him well during the campaign as a way of reaching the public without media intervention. The national media, however, were not prepared to accept the president's efforts to circumvent them and moved to reassert their own political "spin" control. For example, following Clinton's February 10, 1993, nationally televised town meeting on the economy, many major newspapers were sharply critical of the president's responses to questions posed by members of a Michigan studio audience and a group of callers from across the country. Clinton was accused both of giving inadequate answers to questions and of screening participants to exclude hos-

In recent years, candidates for office have sought out new means to reach the public. Town meetings have been a favorite media forum for Bill Clinton, because he, rather than a journalist or moderator, can control their agenda.

tile questioners. Some media commentators challenged the validity of the entire town meeting format, claiming that members of the general public—as distinguished from journalists—were not adequately prepared to confront the president. Commentators called for more events dominated by the media, such as press conferences, and fewer events like town meetings in which the role of the media was reduced.[32]

The Rise of Investigative Reporting

The political power of the news media has greatly increased in recent years through the growing prominence of "investigative reporting"—a form of journalism in which the media adopt an adversarial posture toward the government and public officials.

During the nineteenth century, American newspapers were completely subordinate to the political parties. Newspapers depended upon official patronage—legal notice and party subsidies—for their financial survival and were controlled by party leaders. (A vestige of that era survived into the twentieth century in such newspaper names as the *Springfield Republican* and the *St. Louis Globe-Democrat.*) At the turn of the century, with the development of commercial advertising, newspapers became financially independent. This made possible the emergence of a formally nonpartisan press.

Presidents were the first national officials to see the opportunities in this development. By communicating directly to the electorate through newspapers and magazines, Theodore Roosevelt and Woodrow Wilson established political constituencies for themselves independent of party organizations and strengthened their own power relative to Congress. President Franklin Roosevelt used the radio, most notably in his famous fireside chats, to reach out to voters throughout the nation and to make himself the center of

American politics. FDR was also adept at developing close personal relationships with reporters that enabled him to obtain favorable news coverage despite the fact that in his day a majority of newspaper owners and publishers were staunch conservatives. Following Roosevelt's example, subsequent presidents have all sought to use the media to enhance their popularity and power. For example, through televised news conferences, President John F. Kennedy mobilized public support for his domestic and foreign policy initiatives.

Franklin Delano Roosevelt used radio addresses, called "fireside chats," to reach millions of listeners and build support for his New Deal programs.

During the 1950s and early 1960s, a few members of Congress also made successful use of the media—especially television—to mobilize national support for their causes. Senator Estes Kefauver of Tennessee became a major contender for the presidency and won a place on the 1956 Democratic national ticket as a result of his dramatic televised hearings on organized crime. Senator Joseph McCarthy of Wisconsin made himself a powerful national figure through his well-publicized investigations of alleged communist infiltration of key American institutions. These senators, however, were more exceptional than typical. Through the mid-1960s, the executive branch continued to generate the bulk of news coverage, and the media served as a cornerstone of presidential power.

The Vietnam War shattered this relationship between the press and the presidency. During the early stages of U.S. involvement, American officials in Vietnam who disapproved of the way the war was being conducted leaked information critical of administrative policy to reporters. Publication of this material infuriated the White House, which pressured publishers to block its release—on one occasion, President Kennedy went so far as to ask the *New York Times* to reassign its Saigon correspondent. However, the national print and broadcast media—the network news divisions, the national news weeklies, the *Washington Post,* and the *New York Times*—discovered that there was an audience for critical coverage among segments of the public skeptical

Washington Post reporters Robert Woodward and Carl Bernstein played an important role in uncovering the Watergate conspiracy, which eventually led to the resignation of President Richard M. Nixon.

of administration policy. As the Vietnam conflict dragged on, critical media coverage fanned antiwar sentiment. Moreover, growing opposition to the war among liberals encouraged some members of Congress, most notably Senator J. William Fulbright, chair of the Senate Foreign Relations Committee, to break with the president. In turn, these shifts in popular and congressional sentiment emboldened journalists and publishers to continue to present critical news reports. Through this process, journalists developed a commitment to "investigative reporting," while a constituency emerged that would rally to the defense of the media when it came under White House attack.

This pattern, established during the Vietnam War, endured through the 1970s and into the 1980s. Political forces opposed to presidential policies, many members of Congress, and the national news media began to find that their interests often overlapped. Liberal opponents of the Nixon, Carter, Reagan, and Bush administrations welcomed news accounts critical of the conduct of executive agencies and officials in foreign affairs and in such domestic areas as race relations, the environment, and regulatory policy. In addition, many senators and representatives found it politically advantageous to champion causes favored by the antiwar, consumer, or environmental movements because, by conducting televised hearings on such issues, they were able to mobilize national constituencies, to become national figures, and in a number of instances to become serious contenders for their party's presidential nomination.

For their part, aggressive use of the techniques of investigation, publicity, and exposure allowed the national media to enhance their autonomy and carve out a prominent place for themselves in American government and politics. Increasingly, media coverage has come to influence politicians' careers, the mobilization of political constituencies, and the fate of issues and causes. Inasmuch as members of Congress and groups opposed to presidential policies in the 1970s and 1980s benefited from the growing influence of the press, they were prepared to rush to its defense when it came under attack. This constituency could be counted upon to denounce any move by the White House or its supporters to curb media influence as an illegitimate effort to manage the news, chill free speech, and undermine the First Amendment. It was the emergence of these overlapping interests, more than an ideological bias, that often led to a de facto alliance between liberal political forces and the national news media.

This confluence of interests was in evidence during the 1992 presidential campaign. Most journalists endeavored to be evenhanded in their coverage of the candidates. As we saw above, the media subjected all the major campaigns to regular scrutiny and criticism. However, as several studies have since indicated, during the course of the campaign the media tended to be more critical of George Bush and more supportive of Bill Clinton.[33] This was an almost inevitable outgrowth of the de facto alliance that developed over a number of years between the media and liberal forces. Like any long-standing relationship, this one tends to shape the attitudes and perceptions of the participants. Without any need for overt bias or sinister conspiracy, journalists tend naturally to provide more favorable coverage to liberal politicians and causes.

The linkage between substantial segments of the media and liberal interest groups is by no means absolute. Indeed, over the past several years a conservative media complex has emerged in opposition to the liberal media. This complex includes two major newspapers, the *Wall Street Journal* and the *Washington Times,* several magazines such as the *American Spectator,* and a host of conservative radio and television talk programs. These radio programs, in particular, helped Republicans win the 1994 congressional elections. Conservative religious leaders like Rev. Jerry Falwell and Pat Robertson, leader of the Christian Coalition, have used their television shows to attack President Clinton's programs and to mount biting personal attacks on both Clinton and his wife. For example, a videotape promoted by Falwell accused Clinton of arranging for the murder of an Arkansas investigator who allegedly had evidence of the president's sexual misconduct. Other conservative groups not associated with the religious Right have also launched sharp assaults against the president. Nationally syndicated talk show host Rush Limbaugh is a constant critic of the administration. Floyd Brown, leader of Citizens United, a group with 40 employees and a $3 million annual budget, attacks Clinton on a daily radio show and faxes anti-Clinton news bulletins to more than 1,200 journalists and talk show hosts. One of Brown's bulletins asserted that Deputy White House Counsel Vincent Foster had not shot himself in a Virginia park as reported by the police, but had actually died in a White House "safe house." This allegation was then aired by Rush Limbaugh on his national radio program.

The emergence of this conservative media complex has meant that liberal policies and politicians are virtually certain to come under attack even when the "liberal media" are sympathetic to them. For example, charges that President Clinton and his wife were involved in financial improprieties as partners in the Whitewater Development Corporation, as well as allegations

Radio talk show host Rush Limbaugh is the most popular figure in the conservative media; millions of Americans listen to his program.

that, while governor, Clinton had sexually harassed an Arkansas state employee, Paula Jones, were first publicized by the conservative press. Only after these stories had received a good deal of coverage in the *Washington Times* and the *American Spectator* did the mainstream "liberal" media begin to highlight them. Of course, once the stories broke, the *Washington Post,* the *New York Times,* and the major television networks devoted substantial investigative resources and time to them. In due course, the "liberal" media probably gave the Whitewater and Jones charges just as much play as the "conservative" media, often with just as little regard for hard evidence.[34]

Media Power and Democracy

➤ Are the media too powerful and thus in need of restriction, or are a free media necessary for democracy?

The free media are an institution absolutely essential to democratic government. Ordinary citizens depend upon the media to investigate wrongdoing, to publicize and explain governmental actions, to evaluate programs and politicians, and to bring to light matters that might otherwise be known only to a handful of governmental insiders. In short, without free and active media, popular government would be virtually impossible. Citizens would have few means through which to know or assess the government's actions—other than the claims or pronouncements of the government itself. Moreover, without active—indeed, aggressive—media, citizens would be hard pressed to make informed choices among competing candidates at the polls. Often enough, the media reveal discrepancies between candidates' claims and their actual records, and between the images that candidates seek to project and the underlying realities.

At the same time, the increasing decay of party organizations (see Chapter 8) has made politicians ever more dependent upon favorable media coverage. National political leaders and journalists have had symbiotic relationships, at least since FDR's presidency, but initially politicians were the senior partners. They benefited from media publicity, but they were not totally dependent upon it as long as they could still rely upon party organizations to mobilize votes. Journalists, on the other hand, depended upon their relationships with politicians for access to information and would hesitate to report stories that might antagonize valuable sources for fear of being excluded from the flow of information in retaliation. Thus, for example, reporters did not publicize potentially embarrassing information, widely known in Washington, about the personal lives of such figures as Franklin Roosevelt and John F. Kennedy.

With the decline of party organizations, the balance of power between politicians and journalists has been reversed. Now that politicians have become heavily dependent upon the media to reach their constituents, journalists no longer need fear that their access to information can be restricted in retaliation for negative coverage.

★ What Are Political Parties?

How have political parties developed in the United States?

How are political parties organized? Along what levels are they organized?

★ The Two-Party System in America

How do parties form? What are the historical origins of today's Democratic and Republican parties?

What is the history of party politics in America? How do the Democrats and Republicans compare today?

What has been the historical role of third parties in the United States?

★ Functions of the Parties

What are the most important functions that parties serve?

How do parties help in getting people to vote? What ties do people have to political parties? How do parties influence voters' choices?

★ The Weakening of Party Organization

Why has the importance of parties in the American political system declined?

What have the parties done to maintain their influence within government?

★ Parties and Democracy

Do parties help or hinder democracy?

IN MANY PARTS of the world, college students are associated with the most radical political parties and often spearhead riots, demonstrations, and other forms of political violence. In the Persian Gulf kingdom of Bahrain, for example, thousands of Shiite Muslim students clashed in late 1994 with police as part of a Shiite-supported party's effort to overthrow the Bahraini government. A number of police officers and students were killed.[1] In Bangladesh, a national student party led a general strike against the government. During the course of their protest, student demonstrators had a violent clash with police that led to more than eighty-five casualties.[2] In France, nationwide student demonstrations forced Prime Minister Edouard Balladur to suspend a number of proposed changes in his government's education policies.[3] Other major student protests have recently occurred in Kenya, Portugal, Taiwan, and China; in Sudan, student opponents of the regime are arrested and tortured on a regular basis.[4]

American college students, by contrast, have been politically quiescent for the past twenty-five years. In the 1960s, of course, anti–Vietnam War protests by students helped force changes in American politics. During that period, the Democratic Party appealed for the support of politically active students by sponsoring the Twenty-sixth Amendment, which lowered the voting age to eighteen. The Democrats also gave young people a greater opportunity to take part in party affairs, especially in the nomination of Democratic presidential candidates. State-level party organizations were required to make certain that young people were adequately represented throughout the nominating process, including in the state's delegation to the national party convention.

Unfortunately for the Democrats, many college students today seem to have switched their allegiance to the Republican camp. On many college campuses, student groups affiliated with the GOP, such as the College Republicans and the Young Republicans, are vocal and active while their Democratic counterparts seem moribund. Recently, Democratic student groups sponsored rallies at universities around the country to protest Republican efforts to reduce domestic social spending in education and other areas. President Clinton himself called upon students to "stand up for education, and stand up for the future."[5] Despite the president's efforts, however, the protests were ignored on most college campuses. Some students said they favored cuts in federal spending on education. "I personally believe the deficit is maybe the No. 1 issue that needs to be addressed, and everyone has to bite the bullet," a Georgia State University student said.[6]

Over the course of American history, students have occasionally responded to particular events that affect them, such as the Vietnam War, by participating in radical or protest politics. For the most part, however, students in the United States have been a quiescent or even a conservative political force. One major reason behind the political inertia of American college students is the relationship between education and access in American society. Higher education is probably the most important route of access to economic success and social status in the United States. Although a college or postgraduate degree is not an absolute guarantee of affluence, for the most part, graduates of American colleges and universities can look forward to meaningful careers in which they will have the opportunity to use and profit from their academic credentials. This expectation, as much as anything else, works against political militancy on the part of American college and university students. Why would students participate in radical attacks upon a political and social order that promises to reward them?

In many other parts of the world, by contrast, economic and political conditions are such that college and university graduates find themselves without access to significant career opportunities. For example, some developing countries produce many more university graduates than can be absorbed by the private economy and the civil service. Since they can see so little opportunity in the existing order that is compatible with their education and aspirations, students and graduates in those nations are often susceptible to the appeals of radical parties that advocate fundamental social and economic change. This fact partially explains why many German university students became enthusiastic supporters of the Nazi Party during the 1930s. Because of the collapse of the German economy, students could see no meaningful place for themselves in the existing society and so were more receptive to the appeals of a violent extremist party that promised a new and better society.

In the United States, of course, the students most likely to sympathize with extremist political groups are precisely those who have reason to fear that their access to success will be blocked. To take the most important example, many African American college students believe that racial discrimination will prevent them from reaping the rewards that their credentials and training should bring. It is therefore no mystery that some black college students reject both major political parties and are instead attracted to the doctrines of the Nation of Islam or other groups that call for radical changes in American society.

As these examples suggest, the relationship between political parties and constituent social groups is never simple. Groups that in one social setting are associated with radical parties may, in another place and time, be pillars of conservatism. Groups initially mobilized by one party may shift their allegiance to another as circumstances change. As we will see later in this chapter, during periods of electoral realignment in the United States, enormous blocs of voters have migrated from one party to the other, with major consequences for public policy and political power.

At the same time, the role of parties in political processes is more complex than we sometimes think. In modern history, political parties have been the chief points of contact between governments, on the one side, and groups and forces in society, on the other. In organized political parties, social forces can gain some control over governmental policies and personnel. Simultaneously, governments often seek to organize and influence important groups in society through political parties. All political parties have this dual character: they are instruments through which citizens and governments attempt to influence one another. In some nations, such as the People's Republic of China, the leading political party serves primarily the interests of the government. In others, such as the United States, political parties force the government to concern itself with the needs of its citizens.

The idea of political parties was not always accepted in the United States. In the early years of the Republic, parties were seen as threats to the social order. In his 1796 "Farewell Address," President George Washington warned his countrymen to shun partisan politics:

> Let me warn you in the most solemn manner against the baneful effects of the spirit of party generally. This spirit exists under different shapes in all government, more or less stifled, controlled, or repressed, but in those of the popular form it is seen in its greater rankness and is truly their worst enemy.

Often, those in power viewed the formation of political parties by their opponents as acts of treason that merited severe punishment. Thus, in 1798, the Federalist Party, which controlled the national government, in effect sought to outlaw its Jeffersonian Republican opponents through the infamous Alien and Sedition Acts, which, among other things, made it a crime to publish or say anything that might tend to defame or bring into disrepute either the president or the Congress (see Box 8.1). Under this law, fifteen individuals—including several Republican newspaper editors—were arrested and convicted.[7]

Obviously, over the past two hundred years, Americans' conception of political parties has changed considerably—from subversive organizations to bulwarks of democracy. In this chapter, we will examine the realities underlying these changing conceptions. First, we will look at party organization and

THE ALIEN AND SEDITION ACTS:
A PARTY'S ATTEMPT TO SUPPRESS THE OPPOSITION

In 1798, war seemed likely to break out between the United States and France. The overt purpose of the Alien and Sedition Acts was to protect the government against subversive activities by foreigners in the country—particularly the French. Their covert purpose, however, was to suppress the Republican Party, led by Thomas Jefferson and James Madison, which was rapidly gaining strength in its opposition to the Federalists.

The four pieces of legislation collectively referred to as the Alien and Sedition Acts are (1) the Naturalization Act, passed June 18, 1798; (2) the Act Concerning Aliens, passed June 25, 1798; (3) the Act Respecting Alien Enemies, passed July 6, 1798; and (4) the Act for the Punishment of Certain Crimes (the Sedition Act), passed July 14, 1798.

The Alien Enemies Act never went into effect because it was contingent on the declaration of war. The Alien Act, which gave the president power to order out of the country all aliens he considered a threat to national security, was never enforced. Nonetheless, it is believed to have been responsible for the departure of many French immigrants. Since most naturalized citizens became Republicans, this act may have functioned to diminish the number of potential Republicans. In extending the period of residence required for naturalization from five to fourteen years, the Naturalization Act was an obvious move to weaken the Republican Party.

The Sedition Act had the most serious legal implications. It was designed to suppress critics of the administration by limiting their freedom of speech and of the press. It was used to indict approximately fifteen persons. Although fewer than half of those indicted were ever brought to trial, several prominent Republican journalists were convicted. By 1802 all but the Alien Enemies Act had either expired or been repealed.

BOX 8.1

its place in the American political process. Second, we will evaluate America's two-party system and assess the similarities and differences between the parties. Third, we will discuss the functions of the parties. Finally, we will address the significance and changing role of parties in American politics today and discuss the effects parties have on democracy.

What Are Political Parties?

- How have political parties developed in the United States?
- How are political parties organized? Along what levels are they organized?

Political parties, like interest groups, are organizations seeking influence over government. Ordinarily, they can be distinguished from interest groups on the basis of their orientation. A party seeks to control the entire government by electing its members to office and thereby controlling the government's personnel. Interest groups usually accept government and its personnel as a given and try to influence government policies through them.

Outgrowths of the Electoral Process

Political parties as they are known today developed along with the expansion of suffrage and can be understood only in the context of elections. The two are so intertwined that American parties actually take their structure from the electoral process. The shape of party organization in the United States has followed a simple rule: For every district where an election is held, there should be some kind of party unit. Republicans failed to maintain units in most of the southern counties between 1900 and 1952; Democrats were similarly unsuccessful in many areas of New England. But for most of the history of the United States, two major parties have had enough of an organized presence to oppose each other in elections in most of the nation's towns, cities, and counties. This makes the American party system one of the oldest political institutions in the history of democracy.

Compared with political parties in Europe, parties in the United States have always seemed weak. They have no criteria for party membership—no cards for their members to carry, no obligatory participation in any activity, no notion of exclusiveness. Today, they seem weaker than ever; they inspire less loyalty and are less able to control nominations. Some people are even talking about a "crisis of political parties," as though party politics were being abandoned. But there continues to be at least some substance to party organizations in the United States.

Party Organization

In the United States, party organizations exist at virtually every level of government (see Figure 8.1). These organizations are usually committees made up of a number of active party members. State law and party rules prescribe how such committees are constituted. Usually, committee members are elected at local party meetings—called **caucuses**—or as part of the regular primary election. The best-known examples of these committees are at the national level—the Democratic National Committee and the Republican National Committee.

National Convention At the national level, the party's most important institution is the quadrennial **national convention**. The convention is attended by delegates from each of the states; as a group, they nominate the party's presidential and vice presidential candidates, draft the party's campaign platform for the presidential race, and approve changes in the rules and regulations governing party procedures. Before World War II, presidential nominations occupied most of the time, energy, and effort expended at the national convention. The nomination process required days of negotiation and compromise among state party leaders and often required many ballots before a nominee was selected. In recent years, however, presidential candidates have essentially nominated themselves by winning enough delegate support in pri-

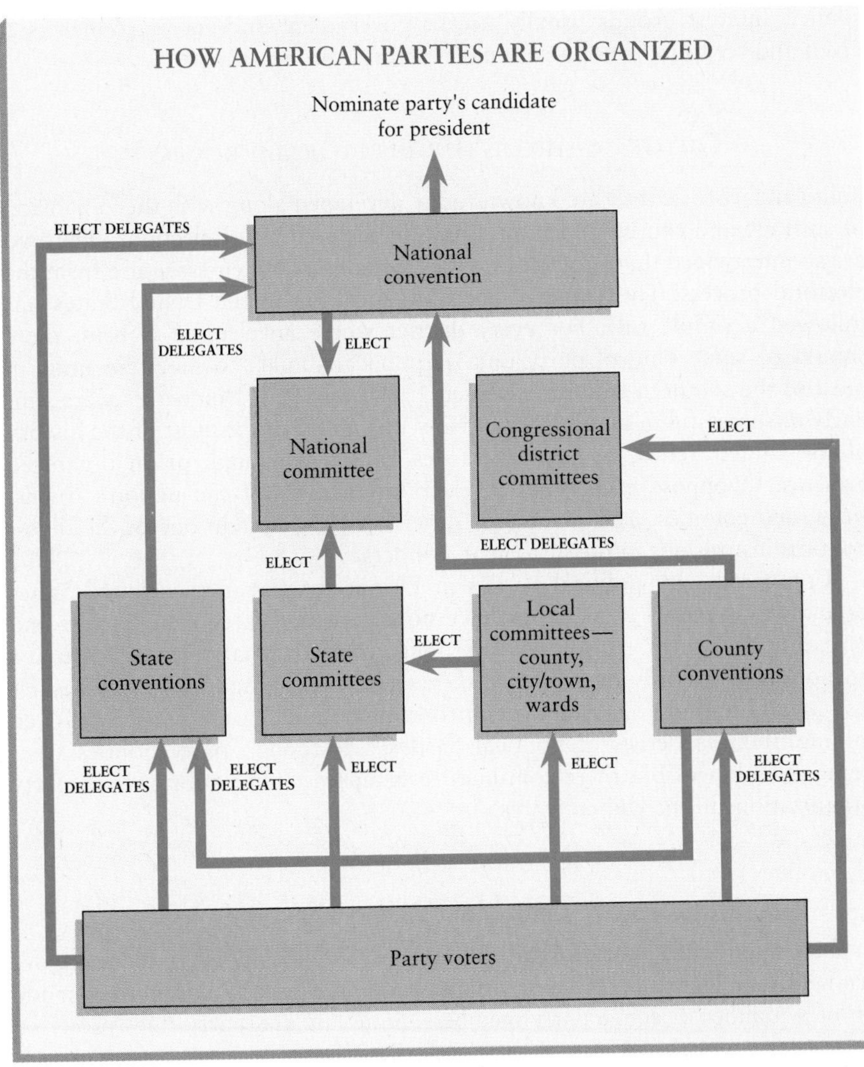

FIGURE 8.1

mary elections to win the official nomination on the first ballot. The actual convention has played little or no role in selecting the candidates.

The convention's other two tasks, determining the party's rules and its platform, remain important. Party rules can determine the relative influence of competing factions within the party and can also increase or decrease the party's chances for electoral success. In 1972, for example, the Democratic National Convention adopted a new set of rules favored by the party's liberal wing. Under these rules, state delegations to the Democratic convention were required to include women and members of minority groups in rough proportion to those groups' representation among the party's membership in that state. Liberals correctly calculated that women and African Americans would generally support liberal ideas and candidates. The rules also called for the use of proportional representation—a voting system liberals thought would give them an advantage by allowing the election of more women and minority delegates. (Although Republican rules do not require proportional representation, some state legislatures have moved to compel both parties to use this system in their presidential primaries.)

The convention also approves the party **platform**. Platforms are often dismissed as documents filled with platitudes that are seldom read by voters. To some extent this criticism is well founded. Not one voter in a thousand so much as glances at the party platform, and even the news media pay little attention to the documents. Furthermore, the parties' presidential candidates make little use of the platforms in their campaigns; usually they prefer to develop and promote their own themes. Nonetheless, the platform can be an important document. The platform should be understood as a contract in which the various party factions attending the convention state their terms for supporting the ticket. For one faction, welfare reform may be a key issue. For another faction, tax reduction may be more important. For a third, the critical issue might be deficit reduction. When one of these "planks" is included in the platform, its promoters are asserting that this is what they want in exchange for their support for the ticket, while other party factions are agreeing that the position seems reasonable and appropriate.

Thus, party platforms should be seen more as internal party documents than as public pledges. In 1992, for example, the Democratic platform went into great detail on environmental issues such as "old-growth forests" and "critical habitats" that mean little to most voters but are very important to environmental groups that form an important part of the Democratic Party's activist coalition. Similarly, the Republicans' 1992 platform advocated the construction of a wall to prevent illegal immigrants from crossing the nation's border with Mexico. This is hardly a matter of much concern to most of the

Enthusiastic delegates at the 1996 Republican National Convention. Although the Republican Party showcased its diversity at its 1996 convention, on average, delegates to the convention tended to be wealthy white men.

THE PROHIBITION PARTY

From colonial crusades against the harmful effects of demon rum to the successful effort to raise the drinking age nationwide from eighteen to twenty-one in the late 1980s, the crusade against alcohol has been one of America's most enduring social and moral crusades. The terrible social consequences of excessive alcohol consumption have been and continue to be widely and deeply felt throughout American society. The persistence of the temperance movement is epitomized by America's third oldest (and oldest third) political party, the Prohibition Party.

The party can be traced back to several separate state parties in Maine, New York, and Pennsylvania that formed in the 1850s. Many of the leaders of these parties were also prominent in the antislavery and women's suffrage movements—issues that also combined moral and social concerns. The resolution of the slavery issue with the Civil War prompted prohibitionists to turn their full attention to temperance. Despite early links with the Republican Party, neither of the major parties took much interest in the temperance cause. Worse, many states repealed prohibition measures after the Civil War, and others ceased enforcement. President Ulysses S. Grant, who was widely popular, embodied the turn toward liquor, as his partiality for strong spirits was widely known.

The first national Prohibition Party convention was held in 1869. Its first presidential nominating convention came three years later. The party's presidential candidate, James Black (a co-founder of the Republican Party in the 1850s), garnered a paltry 5,607 votes, but the party's early efforts revealed a profound and widespread concern for societal decline in morality and the need for a national "spiritual awakening." "A Christian lacking commitment to prohibition," asserted the party, was "no Christian at all."[1] In addition, the party in its formative years advocated such progressive political reforms as women's suffrage, civil service reform, inheritance and income tax legislation, child labor laws, and pensions for the elderly.

The party's high-water mark was reached in 1892, when its presidential candidate received 2.25 percent of the presidential vote. By the end of the decade, however, two forces undercut the party's growth and influence. First, those in the party who wanted it to focus solely on the alcohol issue gained control over those who advocated a more broad and progressive social and political agenda. This shift led to a contraction of the party's base of support. Second, the prohibition movement shifted away from party politics and toward two other groups, the Anti-Saloon League (ASL) and the Women's Christian Temperance Union (WCTU). The great political success of the temperance movement—the adoption of the Eighteenth Amendment to the Constitution in 1919—was the result of a pressure politics approach adopted by the

country's Republicans. But to party loyalists in the southwestern states, as well as to some social conservatives among GOP activists, this is a matter of some significance. By including these planks in their platforms, each party was saying to these activists that they were welcome in the party coalition.

National Committee Between conventions, each national political party is technically headed by its national committee. For the Democrats and Republicans, these are called the Democratic National Committee (DNC) and the Republican National Committee (RNC), respectively. These national committees raise campaign funds, head off factional disputes within the party, and endeavor to enhance the party's media image. The actual work of each national committee is overseen by its chairperson. Other committee members are generally major party contributors or fund raisers and serve in a largely ceremonial capacity.

ASL and the WCTU and applied to both major political parties. The Prohibition Party survived, but it viewed other temperance groups with suspicion because of the willingness of the ASL and the WCTU to bargain and seek compromise with others in the political process. The Prohibition Party considered issue purity to be more important, a fact that guaranteed that the party would remain small.

With the repeal of the prohibition amendment in 1933 (by passage of the Twenty-first Amendment), the Prohibition Party again assumed a prominent role in temperance politics. Yet from that time to the present, it has been a far more conservative and elitist movement, building its appeal on states' rights, distrust of the national government, international isolationism, and economic laissez-faire. Even though the Prohibition Party survives to the present, its narrow modern form all but prevents it from tapping into national grassroots concerns for alcohol abuse and moral crisis that fuel other contemporary political and social movements.

SOURCE: Norman Clark, *Deliver Us from Evil: An Interpretation of American Prohibition* (New York: Norton, 1976).

[1]Jack S. Blocker, Jr., *Retreat From Reform* (Westport, CT: Greenwood, 1976), p. 131.

For whichever party controls the White House, the party's national committee chair is appointed by the president. Typically, this means that that party's national committee becomes little more than an adjunct to the White House staff. For a first-term president, the committee devotes the bulk of its energy to the re-election campaign. The national committee chair of the party not in control of the White House is selected by the committee itself and usually takes a broader view of the party's needs, raising money and performing other activities on behalf of the party's members in Congress and in the state legislatures. Thus, after Bill Clinton took office in 1992, DNC chair David Wilhelm focused his efforts almost exclusively on Clinton's re-election. RNC chair Haley Barbour not only worked to put a Republican in the White House, but also sought to strengthen the Republican Party at the congressional and local levels by recruiting strong candidates and raising money for their campaigns.

Republican National Committee chair Haley Barbour.

Congressional Campaign Committees Each party also forms House and Senate campaign committees to raise funds for House and Senate election campaigns. Their efforts may or may not be coordinated with the activities of the national committees. For the party that controls the White House, the national committee and the congressional campaign committees are often rivals, since both groups are seeking donations from the same people but for different candidates: the national committee seeks funds for the presidential race while the congressional campaign committees approach the same contributors for support for the congressional contests. In recent years, the Republican Party has attempted to coordinate the fund-raising activities of all its committees. Republicans have sought to give the GOP's national institutions the capacity to invest funds in those close congressional, state, and local races where they can do the most good. The Democrats have been slower to coordinate their various committee activities, and this may have placed them at a disadvantage in recent congressional and local races.

State and Local Party Organizations Each of the two major parties has a central committee in each state. The parties traditionally also have county committees and, in some instances, state senate district committees, judicial district committees, and in the case of larger cities, city-wide party committees and local assembly district "ward" committees as well. Congressional districts also may have party committees.

Some cities also have precinct committees. Precincts are not districts from which any representative is elected but instead are legally defined subdivisions of wards that are used to register voters and set up ballot boxes or voting machines. A precinct is typically composed of three hundred to six hundred voters. Well-organized political parties—especially the famous old machines of New York, Chicago, and Boston—provided for "precinct captains" and a fairly tight group of party members around them (see Box 8.2). Precinct captains were usually members of long standing in neighborhood party club-

BOSS RULE IN CHICAGO

During the 1950s and 1960s, Mayor Richard J. Daley was the absolute ruler of the city of Chicago. Politicians, judges, the police and fire departments, and municipal agencies all were subservient to the Daley "machine." The source of machine power was its control of county and municipal elections. Those who supported Daley's political opponents often found that such heresy could be dangerous. Consider the case of one supporter of Republican Benjamin Adamowski, who opposed Daley in the 1957 mayoral election:

> The owner of a small restaurant at Division and Ashland, the heart of the city's Polish neighborhood, put up a big Adamowski sign. The day it went up the precinct captain came around and said, "How come the sign, Harry?" "Ben's a friend of mine," the restaurant owner said. "Ben's a nice guy, Harry, but that's a pretty big sign. I'd appreciate it if you'd take it down." "No, it's staying up."
>
> The next day the captain came back. "Look, I'm the precinct captain. Is there anything wrong, any problem, anything I can help you with?" Harry said no. "Then why don't you take it down. You know how this looks in my job." Harry wouldn't budge. The sign stayed up.
>
> On the third day, the city building inspectors came. The plumbing improvement alone cost Harry $2,100.

SOURCE: Mike Royko, *Boss: Richard J. Daley of Chicago* (New York: Dutton, 1971).

Box 8.2

houses, which were important social centers as well as places for distributing favors to constituents.[8] As the old machines declined, so did this level of party organization. (The causes of party decline will be discussed later in this chapter.) Party organizations are now layerings of committees with overlapping boundaries and interlocking memberships.

In this kind of loosely jointed, multi-layered organization, a strong and centralized political party is exceptional. Nonetheless, many cities and counties and even a few states upon occasion have had such well-organized parties that they were called **machines** and their leaders were called "bosses." Some of the great reform movements in American history were motivated by the excessive powers and abuses of these machines and their bosses. But few, if any, machines are left today, and the current political challenge is strengthening weak parties rather than weakening strong ones.

The Two-Party System in America

- How do parties form? What are the historical origins of today's Democratic and Republican parties?
- What is the history of party politics in America? How do the Democrats and Republicans compare today?
- What has been the historical role of third parties in the United States?

Mayor Richard J. Daley of Chicago, the last of the big-city bosses, controlled an impressive political machine.

Although George Washington, and in fact many leaders of his time, deplored partisan politics, the two-party system emerged early in the history of the new Republic. Beginning with the Federalists and the Jeffersonian Republicans in the late 1780s, two major parties would dominate national politics, although which particular two parties they were would change with the times and issues. This two-party system has culminated in today's Democrats and Republicans.

HISTORICAL ORIGINS

Historically, parties form in one of two ways. The first, which could be called "internal mobilization," occurs when political conflicts break out and government officials and competing factions seek to mobilize popular support. This is precisely what happened during the early years of the American Republic. Competition in the Congress between northeastern mercantile and southern agrarian factions led first the southerners and then the northeasterners to attempt to organize popular followings. The result was the foundation of America's first national parties—the Jeffersonians, whose primary base was in the South, and the Federalists, whose strength was greatest in the New England states.

The second common mode of party organization, which could be called "external mobilization," takes place when a group of politicians outside the established governmental framework develops and organizes popular support to win governmental power. For example, during the 1850s, a group of state politicians who opposed slavery, especially the expansion of slavery in America's territorial possessions, built what became the Republican Party by constructing party organizations and mobilizing popular support in the Northeast and West. The evolution of American political parties is shown in Figure 8.2.

FIGURE 8.2

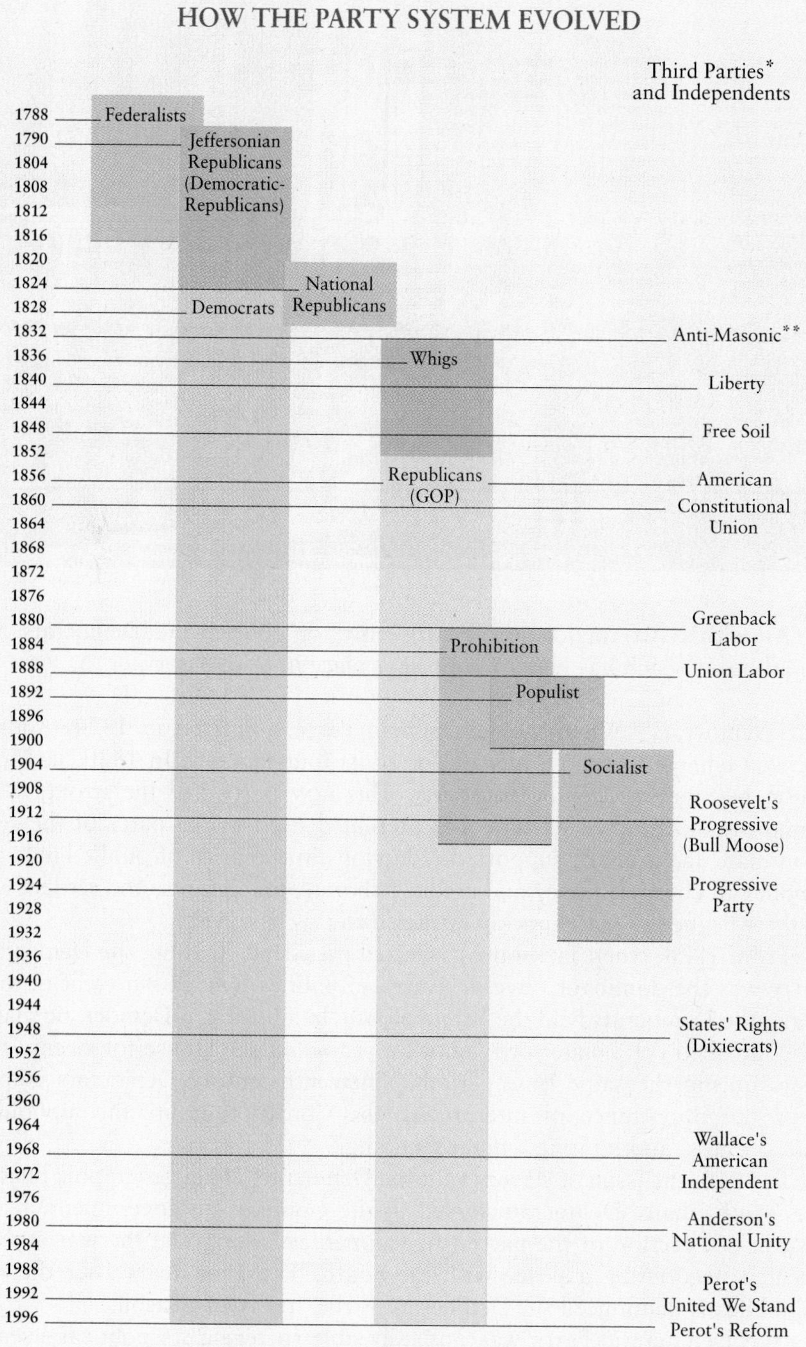

HOW THE PARTY SYSTEM EVOLVED

Third Parties*
and Independents

1788 Federalists
1790 Jeffersonian Republicans (Democratic-Republicans)
1804
1808
1812
1816
1820
1824 National Republicans
1828 Democrats
1832 Anti-Masonic**
1836 Whigs
1840 Liberty
1844
1848 Free Soil
1852
1856 Republicans (GOP) — American
1860 Constitutional Union
1864
1868
1872
1876
1880 Greenback Labor
1884 Prohibition
1888 Union Labor
1892 Populist
1896
1900
1904 Socialist
1908
1912 Roosevelt's Progressive (Bull Moose)
1916
1920
1924 Progressive Party
1928
1932
1936
1940
1944
1948 States' Rights (Dixiecrats)
1952
1956
1960
1964
1968 Wallace's American Independent
1972
1976
1980 Anderson's National Unity
1984
1988
1992 Perot's United We Stand
1996 Perot's Reform

*Or in some cases, fourth party; most of these parties lasted through only one term.

†The Anti-Masonics had the distinction not only of being the first third party, they were also the first party to hold a national nominating convention and the first to announce a party platform.

Andrew Jackson's election to the presidency in 1828 was considered a victory for the common people and for the Democratic Party. Jackson's inauguration celebration on the White House lawn lasted several days. This engraving satirized Jackson's popular following.

America's two major parties are now, of course, the Democrats and Republicans. Each has had an important place in U.S. history.

The Democrats When the Jeffersonian Party splintered in 1824, Andrew Jackson emerged as the leader of one of its four factions. In 1830, Jackson's group became the Democratic Party. This new party had the strongest national organization of its time and presented itself as the party of the common man. Jacksonians supported reductions in the price of public lands and a policy of cheaper money and credit. Laborers, immigrants, and settlers west of the Alleghenies were quickly attracted to this new party.

From 1828, when Jackson was elected president, to 1860, the Democratic Party was the dominant force in American politics. For all but eight of those years, the Democrats held the White House. In addition, a Democratic majority controlled the Senate for twenty-six years and the House for twenty-four years during the same time period. Nineteenth-century Democrats emphasized the importance of interpreting the Constitution literally, upholding states' rights, and limiting federal spending.

In 1860, the issue of slavery split the Democrats along geographic lines. In the South, many Democrats served in the Confederate government. In the North, one faction of the party (the Copperheads) opposed the war and advocated negotiating a peace with the South. Thus, for years after the war, Republicans denounced the Democrats as the "party of treason."

The Democratic Party was not fully able to regain its political strength until the Great Depression. In 1932, Democrat Franklin D. Roosevelt entered the White House. Subsequently, the Democrats won control of Congress as well. Roosevelt's New Deal coalition, composed of Catholics, Jews, blacks, farmers, intellectuals, and members of organized labor, dominated American politics until the 1970s and served as the basis for the party's expansion of federal power and efforts to remedy social problems.

The Democrats were never fully united. In Congress, southern Democrats often aligned with Republicans in the "conservative coalition" rather than with members of their own party. But the Democratic Party remained America's majority party, usually controlling both Congress and the White House, for nearly four decades after 1932. By the 1980s, the Democratic coalition faced serious problems. The once-Solid South often voted for the Republicans, along with many blue-collar northern voters. On the other hand, the Democrats increased their strength among African American voters and women. The Democrats maintained a strong base in the bureaucracies of the federal government and the states, in labor unions, and in the not-for-profit sector of the economy. During the 1980s and 1990s, moderate Democrats were able to take control of the party nominating process and sought to broaden middle-class support for the Democrats. This helped the Democrats elect a president in 1992. In 1994, however, the unpopularity of President Bill Clinton led to the loss of the Democrats' control of both houses of Congress for the first time since 1946.

The Republicans The 1854 Kansas-Nebraska Act overturned the Missouri Compromise of 1820 and the Compromise of 1850, which had barred the expansion of slavery in the American territories. The Kansas-Nebraska Act gave each territory the right to decide whether or not to permit slavery. Opposition to this policy galvanized antislavery groups and led them to create a new party, the Republicans. It drew its membership from existing political groups—former Whigs, Know-Nothings, Free Soilers, and antislavery Democrats. In 1856, the party's first presidential candidate, John C. Fremont, won one-third of the popular vote and carried eleven states.

The early Republican platforms appealed to commercial as well as antislavery interests. The Republicans favored homesteading, internal improvements, the construction of a transcontinental railroad, and protective tariffs,

The 1860 Republican Convention at Chicago, at which Abraham Lincoln received the presidential nomination.

as well as the containment of slavery. In 1858, the Republican Party won control of the House of Representatives; in 1860, the Republican presidential candidate, Abraham Lincoln, was victorious.

For almost seventy-five years after the North's victory in the Civil War, the Republicans were America's dominant political party. Between 1860 and 1932, Republicans occupied the White House for fifty-six years, controlled the Senate for sixty years, and the House for fifty. During these years, the Republicans came to be closely associated with big business. The party of Lincoln became the party of Wall Street.

The Great Depression ended Republican hegemony, however. The voters held President Herbert Hoover responsible for the economic catastrophe, and by 1936, the party's popularity was so low that Republicans won only eighty-nine seats in the House and seventeen in the Senate. The Republican presidential candidate in 1936, Governor Alfred M. Landon of Kansas, carried only two states. The Republicans won only four presidential elections between 1932 and 1980, and they controlled Congress for only four of those years (1947–49 and 1953–55).

The Republican Party has widened its appeal over the last four decades. Groups previously associated with the Democratic Party—particularly blue-collar workers and southern Democrats—have been increasingly attracted to Republican presidential candidates (for example, Dwight D. Eisenhower, Richard Nixon, Ronald Reagan, and George Bush). Yet Republicans generally did not do as well at the state and local levels and, until recently, had little chance of capturing a majority in either the House or Senate. The Watergate scandal of the Nixon administration was a setback in the party's efforts to increase its political power. In 1980, under the leadership of Ronald Reagan, the Republicans began to mount a new bid to become the nation's majority party, but the Iran-Contra scandal damaged Reagan's popularity. Reagan's successor, George Bush, was voted out after one term in office, mainly in response to voters' concerns about the economy. In 1994, the Republican Party finally won a majority in both houses of Congress, in large part because of the unpopularity of President Bill Clinton and the growing strength of the Republican Party in the South.

During the 1990s, conservative religious groups, who had been attracted to the Republican camp by its opposition to abortion and support for school prayer, made a concerted effort to expand their influence within the party. This effort led to conflict between these members of the "religious Right" and more traditional "country-club" Republicans, whose major concerns were matters such as taxes and federal regulation of business. Although this coalition swept the polls in 1994, it remains to be seen whether these two wings of the Republican Party can maintain a united front against the Democrats.[9]

ELECTORAL ALIGNMENTS AND REALIGNMENTS

In the United States, party politics has followed a fascinating pattern (see Figure 8.3). Typically, during the course of American political history, the national electoral arena has been dominated by one party for a period of roughly thirty years. At the conclusion of this period, the dominant party has been supplanted by a new party in what political scientists call a **critical elec-**

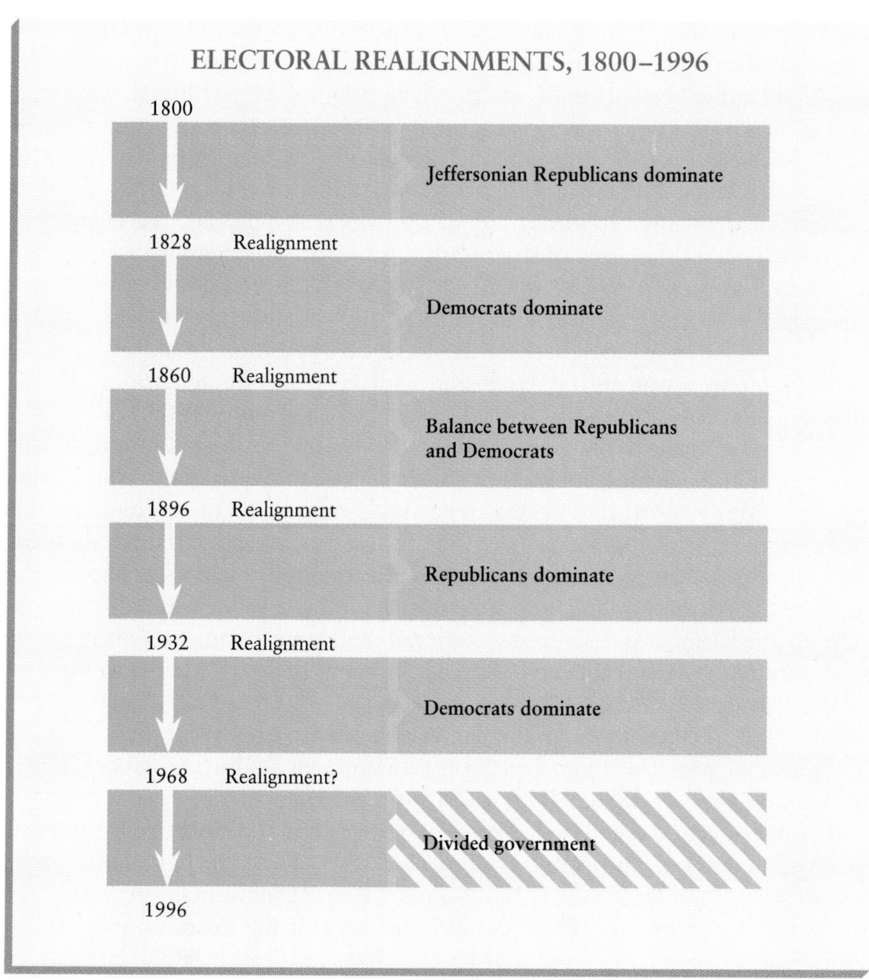

FIGURE 8.3

Political scientists disagree over whether electoral alignments occurred in 1968 and 1996, because no one party clearly dominated the national government after those elections.

toral realignment. The realignment is typically followed by a long period in which the new party is the dominant political force in the United States—not necessarily winning every election but generally maintaining control of the Congress and usually of the White House as well.[10]

Although there are some disputes among scholars about the precise timing of these critical realignments, there is general agreement that at least five have occurred since the founding of the American Republic. The first took place around 1800 when the Jeffersonian Republicans defeated the Federalists and became the dominant force in American politics. The second realignment occurred in about 1828, when the Jacksonian Democrats took control of the White House and the Congress. The third period of realignment centered on 1860. During this period, the newly founded Republican Party led by Abraham Lincoln won power, in the process destroying the Whig Party, which had been one of the nation's two major parties since the 1830s. During the fourth critical period, centered on the election of 1896, the Republicans reasserted their dominance of the national government, which had been weakening since the 1880s. The fifth realignment took place during the period 1932–36 when the Democrats, led by Franklin Delano Roosevelt, took control of the White House and Congress and, despite sporadic interruptions, maintained control of both through the 1960s.

Historically, realignments occur when new issues combined with economic or political crises persuade large numbers of voters to re-examine their traditional partisan loyalties and permanently shift their support from one party to another. For example, during the 1850s, diverse regional, income, and business groups supported one of the two major parties, the Democrats or the Whigs, on the basis of their positions on various economic issues, such as internal improvements, the tariff, monetary policy, and banking. This economic alignment was shattered during the 1850s. The newly formed Republican Party campaigned on the basis of opposition to slavery and, in particular, opposition to the expansion of slavery into the territories. The issues of slavery and sectionalism produced divisions within both the Democratic and the Whig parties, ultimately leading to the dissolution of the latter, and these issues compelled voters to re-examine their partisan allegiances. Many northern voters who had supported the Whigs or the Democrats on the basis of their economic stands shifted their support to the Republicans as slavery replaced tariffs and economic concerns as the central item on the nation's political agenda. Many southern Whigs shifted their support to the Democrats. The new sectional alignment of forces that emerged was solidified by the trauma of the Civil War and persisted almost to the turn of the century.

In 1896, this sectional alignment was at least partially supplanted by an alignment of political forces based on economic and cultural factors. During the economic crises of the 1880s and 1890s, the Democrats forged a coalition consisting of economically hard-pressed midwestern and southern farmers, as well as small-town and rural economic interests. These groups tended to be native-stock, fundamentalist Protestants. The Republicans, on the other hand, put together a coalition comprising most of the business community, industrial workers, and city dwellers. In the election of 1896, Republican candidate William McKinley, emphasizing business, industry, and urban interests, decisively defeated Democrat William Jennings Bryan, who spoke for sectional interests, farmers, and fundamentalism. Republican dominance lasted until 1932.

Such periods of critical realignment in American politics have had extremely important institutional and policy results. Realignments occur when new issue concerns coupled with economic or political crises weaken the established political elite and permit new groups of politicians to create coalitions of forces capable of capturing and holding the reins of governmental power. The construction of new governing coalitions during these realigning periods has effected major changes in American governmental institutions and policies. Each period of realignment represents a turning point in American politics. The choices made by the national electorate during these periods have helped shape the course of American political history for a generation.[11]

Similarities and Differences Today

One of the most familiar observations about American politics is that the two major parties try to be all things to all people and are therefore indistinguishable from each other. Data and experience give some support to this observation. Even in the late 1960s, when American society was unusually polarized, Democratic and Republican candidates stood for some of the same things. The wide range of interests within the Democratic Party today can be represented by liberals such as Richard Gephardt and Tom Harkin, and by conservatives such as Charles Stenholm. The 1992 Democratic presidential ticket featured two moderates, Bill Clinton and Al Gore, who appealed successfully for the votes of many conservative Democrats and moderate Republicans. A similar spectrum exists within the Republican Party, as represented by liberals such as Constance Morella and conservatives such as Newt Gingrich, although in the 1980s and 1990s, liberal Republicans became something of an endangered species.

Parties in the United States are not programmatic or ideological, as they have sometimes been in England or other parts of Europe. But this does not mean there are no differences between them. During the Reagan era, important differences emerged between the positions of Democratic and Republican party leaders on a number of key issues, and these differences are still apparent today. For example, the national leadership of the Republican party supports maintaining high levels of military spending, cuts in social programs, tax relief for middle- and upper-income voters, tax incentives to businesses, and the "social agenda" backed by members of conservative religious denominations. The national Democratic leadership, on the other hand, supports expanded social welfare spending, cuts in military spending, increased regulation of business, and a variety of consumer and environmental programs. In 1990, most Republicans supported President Bush's policies in the Persian Gulf, while most Democrats opposed the use of American military force against Iraq—at least until the president's policies turned out to be successful.

These differences reflect differences in philosophy as well as differences in the core constituencies to which the parties seek to appeal. The Democratic Party at the national level seeks to unite organized labor, the poor, members of racial minorities, and liberal upper-middle-class professionals. The Republicans, by contrast, appeal to business, upper-middle- and upper-class groups in the private sector, and social conservatives.

American Third Parties

Although the United States is said to possess a two-party system, the country has always had more than two parties. Typically, **third parties** in the United States have represented social and economic protests that, for one or another reason, were not given voice by the two major parties.[12] Such parties have had a good deal of influence on ideas and elections in the United States. The Populists, a party centered in the rural areas of the West and Midwest, and the Progressives, spokesmen for the urban middle classes in the late nineteenth and early twentieth centuries, are the most important examples in the past hundred years. More recently, Ross Perot, who ran in 1992 as an independent and in 1996 as the Reform Party's nominee, impressed voters with his folksy style; he garnered almost 19 percent of the votes cast in the 1992 presidential election. Table 8.1 shows a listing of all the parties that offered candidates in one or more states in 1996, as well as independent candidates

TABLE 8.1

In the 1996 presidential election, in addition to the Democratic and Republican nominees, at least nineteen candidates appeared on the ballot in one or more states. Ross Perot came the closest to challenging the major-party candidates with more than 8 percent of the popular vote. The remaining eighteen candidates shared 1.56 percent of the votes cast with numerous write-ins.

PARTIES AND CANDIDATES IN 1996

Candidate	Party	Vote total	Percentage of vote
Bill Clinton	Democratic	45,628,667	49.16%
Bob Dole	Republican	37,869,435	40.80
Ross Perot	Reform	7,874,283	8.48
Ralph Nader	Green	580,627	.63
Harry Browne	Libertarian	470,818	.51
Howard Phillips	U.S. Taxpayers	178,779	.19
John Hagelin	Natural Law	110,194	.12
Monica Moorehead	Workers World	29,118	.03
Marsha Feinland	Peace and Freedom	22,593	.02
James Harris	Socialist Workers	11,513	.01
Charles Collins	Independent	7,234	.00
Dennis Peron	Grassroots	5,503	.00
Mary Hollis	Socialist	3,376	.00
Jerry White	Socialist Equality	2,752	.00
Diane Templin	Independent American	1,875	.00
Earl Dodge	Independent	1,198	.00
Peter Crane	Independent	1,105	.00
Ralph Forbes	Independent	861	.00
John Birrenbach	Independent Grassroots	760	.00
Isabell Masters	Independent	737	.00
Steve Michael	Independent	407	.00
Other candidates	—	5,575	.00
TOTAL		92,807,410	100.0%

*With 99 percent of votes tallied.
SOURCE: *USA Today,* November 8–10, 1996, p. 8A.

who ran. With the exception of Ross Perot, the third-party and independent candidates together polled only 1.5 million votes. They gained no electoral votes for president, and most of them disappeared immediately after the presidential election. The significance of Table 8.1 is that it demonstrates the large number of third parties running candidates and appealing to voters. Although the Republican Party was only the third American political party ever to make itself permanent (by replacing the Whigs), other third parties have enjoyed an influence far beyond their electoral size. This was because large parts of their programs were adopted by one or both of the major parties, who sought to appeal to the voters mobilized by the new party, and so to expand their own electoral strength. The Democratic Party, for example, became a great deal more liberal when it adopted most of the Progressive program early in the twentieth century. Many Socialists felt that President Roosevelt's New Deal had adopted most of their party's program, including old-age pensions, unemployment compensation, an agricultural marketing program, and laws guaranteeing workers the right to organize into unions.

This kind of influence explains the short lives of third parties. Their causes are usually eliminated by the ability of the major parties to absorb their programs and to draw their supporters into the mainstream. There are, of course, additional reasons for the short duration of most third parties. One is the usual limitation of their electoral support to one or two regions. Populist support, for example, was primarily midwestern. The 1948 Progressive Party, with Henry Wallace as its candidate, drew nearly half its votes from the state of New York. The American Independent Party polled nearly 10 million popular votes and 45 electoral votes for George Wallace in 1968—the most electoral votes ever polled by a third-party candidate. But all of Wallace's electoral votes and the majority of his popular vote came from the states of the Deep South.

Americans usually assume that only the candidates nominated by one of the two major parties have any chance of winning an election. Thus, a vote cast for a third-party or independent candidate is often seen as a vote wasted. Voters who would prefer a third-party candidate may feel compelled to vote for the major-party candidate whom they regard as the "lesser of two evils" to avoid wasting their vote in a futile gesture. Third-party candidates must struggle—usually without success—to overcome the perception that they cannot win. Thus, in 1992, many voters who favored Ross Perot gave their votes to George Bush or Bill Clinton on the presumption that Perot was not really electable.

As many scholars have pointed out, third-party prospects are also hampered by America's **single-member-district** plurality election system. In many other nations, several individuals can be elected to represent each legislative district. This is called a system of **multiple-member districts.** With this type of

In 1996, Ross Perot ran for president as the candidate for the Reform Party, but his impact on the race was negligible. Supporters are hoping that the party will be strengthened for the next presidential election, in 2000.

system, the candidates of weaker parties have a better chance of winning at least some seats. For their part, voters are less concerned about wasting ballots and usually more willing to support minor-party candidates.

Reinforcing the effects of the single-member district, plurality voting rules (see Chapter 9) generally have the effect of setting what could be called a high threshold for victory. To win a plurality race, candidates usually must secure many more votes than they would need under most European systems of proportional representation. For example, to win an American plurality election in a single-member district where there are only two candidates, a politician must win more than 50 percent of the votes cast. To win a seat from a European multiple-member district under proportional rules, a candidate may need to win only 15 or 20 percent of the votes cast. This high American threshold discourages minor parties and encourages the various political factions that might otherwise form minor parties to minimize their differences and remain within the major-party coalitions.[13]

It would nevertheless be incorrect to assert (as some scholars have maintained) that America's single-member plurality election system is the major cause of its historical two-party pattern. All that can be said is that American election law depresses the number of parties likely to survive over long periods of time in the United States. There is nothing magical about two. Indeed, the single-member plurality system of election can also discourage second parties. After all, if one party consistently receives a large plurality of the vote, people may eventually come to see their vote *even for the second party* as a wasted effort. This happened to the Republican Party in the Deep South before World War II.

Functions of the Parties

➤ What are the most important functions that parties serve?
➤ How do parties help in getting people to vote? What ties do people have to political parties? How do parties influence voters' choices?

Parties perform a wide variety of functions. They are mainly involved in nominations and elections—providing the candidates for office, getting out the vote, and facilitating mass electoral choice. They also influence the institutions of government—providing the leadership and organization of the various congressional committees.

NOMINATIONS

Article I, Section 4, of the Constitution makes only a few provisions for elections. It delegates to the states the power to set the "times, places, and manner" of holding elections, even for U.S. senators and representatives. It does, however, reserve to Congress the power to make such laws if it chooses to do so. The Constitution has been amended from time to time to expand the right

Parties are responsible for nominating candidates to run for office. Here, the 1996 Republican hopefuls get ready for a public forum prior to the Iowa caucuses.

to participate in elections. Congress has also occasionally passed laws about elections, congressional districting, and campaign practices. But the Constitution and the laws are almost completely silent on nominations, setting only citizenship and age requirements for candidates. The president must be at least thirty-five years of age, a natural-born citizen, and a resident of the United States for fourteen years. A senator must be at least thirty, a U.S. citizen for at least nine years, and a resident of the state he or she represents. A member of the House must be at least twenty-five, a U.S. citizen for seven years, and a resident of the state he or she represents.

Nomination is the process by which a party selects a single candidate to run for each elective office. The nominating process can precede the election by many months, as it does when the many candidates for the presidency are eliminated from consideration through a grueling series of debates and state primaries until there is only one survivor in each party—the party's nominee.

Nomination is the parties' most serious and difficult business. When more than one person aspires to an office, the choice can divide friends and associates. In comparison to such an internal dispute, the electoral campaign against the opposition is almost fun, because there the fight is against the declared adversaries.

Getting Out the Vote

The actual election period begins immediately after the nominations. Historically, this has been a time of glory for the political parties, whose popular base of support is fully displayed at election time. All the paraphernalia of party committees and all the committee members are activated into local party workforces.

In the late nineteenth century, party bosses went to great lengths to keep the party's members faithful—even sponsoring barbecues prior to election day.

The major parties, until recent years at least, have been the principal agents responsible for giving citizens the motivation and incentive actually to vote. By law, in most American states, party workers staff the electoral machinery. Indeed, at one time, the parties even printed the ballots used by voters. Although the parties have played a role in both civic education and legal facilitation of voting, their principal efforts have been aimed at the direct mobilization of voters. One of the most interesting pieces of testimony to the lengths to which parties have been willing to go to induce citizens to vote is a list of Chicago precinct captains' activities in the 1920s and 1930s. Among other matters, these party workers helped constituents obtain food, coal, and money for rent; gave advice in dealing with juvenile and domestic problems; helped constituents to obtain government and private jobs; adjusted taxes; aided with permits, zoning, and building-code problems; served as liaisons with social, relief, and medical agencies; provided legal assistance and help in dealing with government agencies; and in addition handed out Christmas baskets and attended weddings and funerals.[14] Obviously, all these services were provided in the hope of winning voters' support at election time.

Party competition has long been known to be a key factor in stimulating voting. As political scientists Stanley Kelley, Richard Ayres, and William Bowen note, competition gives citizens an incentive to vote and politicians an incentive to get them to vote.[15] The origins of the American national electorate can be traced to the competitive organizing activities of the Jeffersonian Republicans and the Federalists. According to historian David Fischer,

> During the 1790s the Jeffersonians revolutionized electioneering. . . . Their opponents complained bitterly of endless "dinings," "drinkings," and celebrations; of

handbills "industriously posted along every road"; of convoys of vehicles which brought voters to the polls by the carload; of candidates "in perpetual motion."[16]

The Federalists, although initially reluctant, soon learned the techniques of mobilizing voters: "mass meetings, barbecues, stump-speaking, festivals of many kinds, processions and parades, runners and riders, door-to-door canvassing, the distribution of tickets and ballots, . . . free transportation to the polls, outright bribery and corruption of other kinds."[17]

The result of this competition for votes was described by historian Henry Jones Ford in his classic *Rise and Growth of American Politics.*[18] Ford examined the popular clamor against John Adams and Federalist policies in the 1790s that made government a "weak, shakey affair" and appeared to contemporary observers to mark the beginnings of a popular insurrection against the government.[19] Attempts by the Federalists initially to suppress mass discontent, Ford observed, might have "caused an explosion of force which would have blown up the government."[20] What intervened to prevent rebellion was Jefferson's "great unconscious achievement," the creation of an opposition party that served to "open constitutional channels of political agitation."[21] The creation of the Jeffersonian Republican Party diverted opposition to the administration into electoral channels. Party competition gave citizens a sense that their votes were valuable and that it was thus not necessary to take to the streets to have an impact upon political affairs. Whether or not Ford was correct in crediting party competition with an ability to curb civil unrest, it is clear that competition between the parties promoted voting.

In recent decades, as we will see later in this chapter, the importance of

In recent years, the parties have been less active in registering voters and encouraging them to vote. One exception has been Jesse Jackson's efforts to register African American voters for the Democratic Party.

AMERICAN POLITICAL CULTURE

Unlikely Allies in the Fight against "Gangsta Rap"

America's durable two-party system often encourages its citizens to think that all political disputes fall on a single continuum of values and beliefs, a continuum that moves steadily from a liberal, Democratic "Left" to a conservative, Republican "Right." But many political issues defy a simple partisan opposition between Left and Right. For instance, opposition to violence-filled popular music might seem to be an issue solely for conservative Republicans, but in 1995 revulsion against "gangsta rap" forged an unlikely alliance of conservatives, led by William J. Bennett, author of *The Book of Virtues* and Ronald Reagan's former secretary of education, and liberals, led by C. DeLores Tucker, chair of the National Political Congress of Black Women. Together, Bennett and Tucker argue that gangsta rap is teaching millions of young listeners harmful lessons in misogyny and sexual violence.

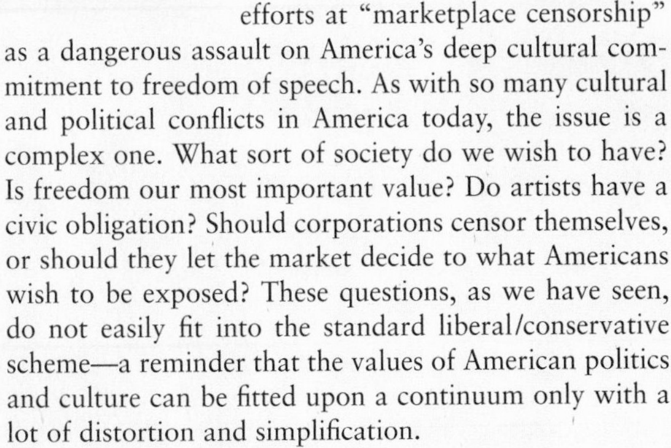

Gangsta rap has arisen in the last several years to become one of the most popular categories of rap music; artists such as Snoop Doggy Dogg and Ice T have become nationally known. Stemming from the lives of its artists, almost all of them urban, African American young men, gangsta rap typically displays a fascination with violence in all its manifestations—violence against rivals, violence against the police and other authority figures, and, most notoriously, sexual aggression and violence against women. Advocates of gangsta rap say it accurately portrays the realities of urban life for millions of African Americans, that it is playful rather than menacing, and that it is merely the latest instance in a long tradition of popular art that some people find offensive.

But those opposed to gangsta rap say that its lyrics are marked by explicit misogyny and routinely speak of rape, torture, and mutilation of women. Bennett and Tucker assert that their opposition to the messages of gangsta rap resists partisanship: ". . . this is not about parties and politics. It is about forestalling America's slide toward decivilization. We come from different parties and different ends of the political spectrum. But we share a deep concern for what these lyrics do to our culture and our children."[1]

Bennett and Tucker, and most opponents of gangsta rap, are not trying to censor it directly. Rather, they are trying to put pressure on those corporations that profit from the promotion and sale of such music, in particular Time Warner, Inc., which owns half of Interscope Records, the major gangsta rap label. By making Time Warner rather than the artists their target, Bennett and Tucker hope to avoid accusations of censorship and to let the marketplace accomplish what no law could: to induce Americans to reject the glorification of violence and misogyny in gangsta rap.

Naturally, the efforts to silence or water down gangsta rap are being resisted by the artists themselves, by companies such as Time Warner, and by many people who see such efforts at "marketplace censorship" as a dangerous assault on America's deep cultural commitment to freedom of speech. As with so many cultural and political conflicts in America today, the issue is a complex one. What sort of society do we wish to have? Is freedom our most important value? Do artists have a civic obligation? Should corporations censor themselves, or should they let the market decide to what Americans wish to be exposed? These questions, as we have seen, do not easily fit into the standard liberal/conservative scheme—a reminder that the values of American politics and culture can be fitted upon a continuum only with a lot of distortion and simplification.

[1] William J. Bennett and C. DeLores Tucker, "Lyrics from the Gutter," *New York Times*, June 2, 1995, p. A29.

party as a political force in the United States has diminished considerably. The decline of party is one of the factors responsible for the relatively low rates of voter turnout that characterize American national elections. To an extent, the federal and state governments have directly assumed some of the burden of voter mobilization once assigned to the parties. Voter registration drives and public funding of electoral campaigns are two obvious ways in which government helps to induce citizens to go to the polls. Another more subtle public mechanism for voter mobilization is the primary election, which can increase voter interest in the electoral process. (We will look at these mechanisms in the next chapter.) It remains to be seen, however, whether government mechanisms of voter mobilization can be as effective as party mechanisms. Of course, a number of private groups, such as the League of Women Voters, church groups, and civil rights groups, have also actively participated in voter registration efforts, but none have been as effective as political parties.

INFLUENCING VOTERS' CHOICES

Parties facilitate mass electoral choice. As Harvard political scientist V. O. Key pointed out long ago, the persistence over time of competition between groups possessing a measure of identity and continuity is virtually a necessary condition for electoral control.[22] Party identity increases the electorate's capacity to recognize its options. Continuity of party division facilitates organization of the electorate on the long-term basis necessary to sustain any popular influence in the governmental process. In the absence of such identity and continuity of party division, the voter is, in Key's words, confronted con-

Since voters are presented with so many options in casting their vote, party identification can strongly influence voters' choices.

stantly by "new faces, new choices," and little basis exists for "effectuation of the popular will."[23]

Even more significant, however, is the fact that party organization is generally an essential ingredient for effective electoral competition by groups lacking substantial economic or institutional resources. Party building has typically been the strategy pursued by groups that must organize the collective energies of large numbers of individuals to counter their opponents' superior material means or institutional standing. Historically, disciplined and coherent party organizations were generally developed first by groups representing the political aspirations of the working classes. Parties, French political scientist Maurice Duverger notes, "are always more developed on the Left than on the Right because they are always more necessary on the Left than on the Right."[24] In the United States, the first mass party was built by the Jeffersonians as a counterweight to the superior social, institutional, and economic resources that could be deployed by the incumbent Federalists. In a subsequent period of American history, the efforts of the Jacksonians to construct a coherent mass party organization were impelled by a similar set of circumstances. Only by organizing the power of numbers could the Jacksonian coalition hope to compete successfully against the superior resources that could be mobilized by its adversaries.

In the United States, the political success of party organizations forced their opponents to copy them in order to meet the challenge. It was, as Duverger points out, "contagion from the Left" that led politicians of the Center and Right to attempt to build strong party organizations.[25] These efforts were sometimes successful. In the United States during the 1830s, the Whig Party, which was led by northeastern business interests, carefully copied the effective organizational techniques devised by the Jacksonians. The Whigs won control of the national government in 1840. But even when groups nearer the top of the social scale responded in kind to organizational efforts by their inferiors, the net effect nonetheless was to give lower-class groups an opportunity to compete on a more equal footing. In the absence of coherent mass organization, middle- and upper-class factions almost inevitably have a substantial competitive edge over their lower-class rivals. Even when both sides organize, the net effect is still to erode the relative advantage of the well-off. Parties of the Right, moreover, were seldom actually able to equal the organizational coherence of the working-class opposition. As Duverger and others have observed, middle- and upper-class parties generally failed to construct organizations as effective as those built by their working-class foes, who typically commanded larger and more easily disciplined forces.

Although political parties continue to be significant, the role of party organizations in electoral politics has clearly declined over the past three decades, as we will see later in this chapter. This decline, and the partial replacement of the party by new forms of electoral technology, is one of the most important developments in twentieth-century American politics.

PARTIES AND THE ELECTORATE

The parties' competitive efforts to attract citizens to the polls and to affect voters' choices are not their only influences on voting. Individual voters tend

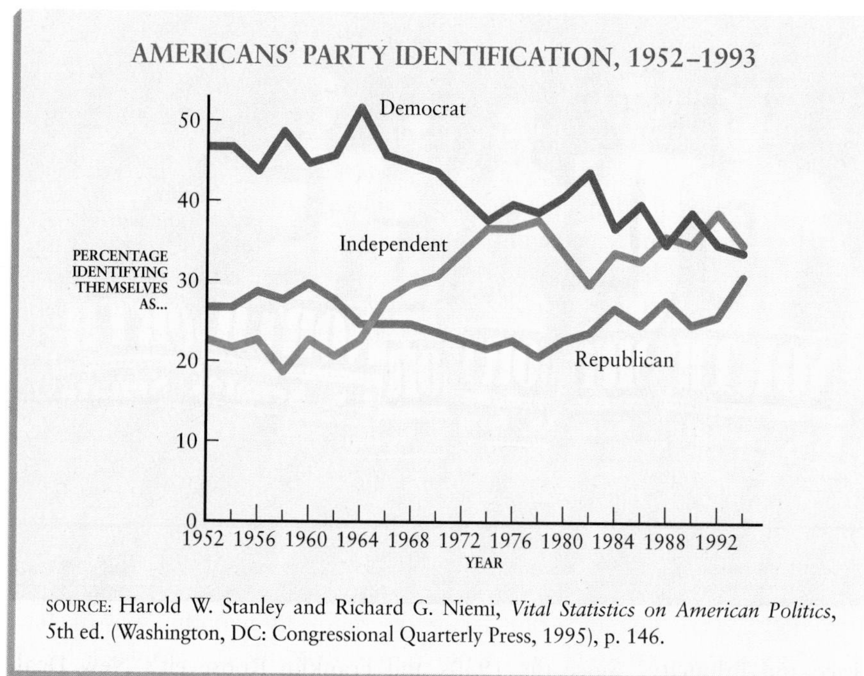

SOURCE: Harold W. Stanley and Richard G. Niemi, *Vital Statistics on American Politics*, 5th ed. (Washington, DC: Congressional Quarterly Press, 1995), p. 146.

FIGURE 8.4

to form psychological ties with political parties, that is, citizens develop a **party identification**. Although the strength of partisan ties in the United States has declined in recent years, most Americans continue to identify with either the Republican Party or the Democratic Party (see Figure 8.4). Party identification gives citizens a stake in election outcomes that goes beyond the particular race at hand. This is why strong party identifiers are more likely than other Americans to go to the polls and, of course, are more likely than others to support the party with which they identify. **Party activists** are drawn from the ranks of the strong identifiers. Activists are those who not only vote but also contribute their time, energy, and effort to party affairs. Activists ring doorbells, stuff envelopes, attend meetings, and contribute money to the party cause. No party could succeed without the thousands of volunteers who undertake the mundane tasks needed to keep the organization going.

Group Affiliations

The Democratic and Republican parties are America's only national parties. They are the only political organizations that draw support from most regions of the country and from Americans of every racial, economic, religious, and ethnic group. The two parties do not draw equal support from members of every social stratum, however. When we refer to the Democratic or Republican "coalition," we mean the groups that generally support one or the other party. In the United States today, a variety of group characteristics are associated with party identification. These include race and ethnicity, gender, religion, class, ideology, and region.

much of the West and Southwest. The area of greatest Democratic Party strength is the Northeast. The Midwest is a battleground, more or less evenly divided between the two parties.

The explanations for these regional variations are complex. Southern Republicanism has come about because conservative white southerners identify the Democratic Party with the Civil Rights movement and with liberal positions on abortion, school prayer, and other social issues. Republican strength in the South and in the West is also related to the weakness of organized labor in these regions, as well as to the dependence of the two regions upon military programs supported by the Republicans. Democratic strength in the Northeast is a function of the continuing influence of organized labor in the large cities of this region, as well as of the region's large population of minority and elderly voters, who benefit from Democratic social programs.

Figure 8.5 indicates the relationship between party identification and a number of social criteria. Race, religion, and income seem to have the greatest influence on Americans' party affiliations. None of these social characteristics are inevitably linked to partisan identification, however. There are black Republicans, southern white Democrats, Jewish Republicans, and even an occasional conservative Democrat. The general party identifications just discussed are broad tendencies that both reflect and reinforce the issue and policy positions the two parties take in the national and local political arenas.

THE PARTIES' INFLUENCE ON NATIONAL GOVERNMENT

The ultimate test of the party system is its relationship to and influence on the institutions of government. Congress, in particular, depends more on the party system than is generally recognized. For one thing, the speakership of the House is essentially a party office. All the members of the House take part in the election of the Speaker. But the actual selection is made by the **majority party,** that is, the party that holds a majority of seats in the House. (The other party is known as the **minority party.**) When the majority party caucus presents a nominee to the entire House, its choice is then invariably ratified in a straight vote along party lines.

The committee system of both houses of Congress is also a product of the two-party system. Although the rules organizing committees and the rules defining the jurisdiction of each are adopted like ordinary legislation by the whole membership, all other features of the committees are shaped by parties. For example, each party is assigned a quota of members for each committee, depending upon the percentage of total seats held by the party. On the rare occasions when an independent or third-party candidate is elected, the leaders of the two parties must agree against whose quota this member's committee assignments will count. Presumably the member will not be able to serve on any committee until the question of quota is settled.

As we shall see in Chapter 11, the assignment of individual members to committees is a party decision. Each party has a "committee on committees" to make such decisions. Permission to transfer to another committee is also a party decision. Moreover, advancement up the committee ladder toward the chair is a party decision. Since the late nineteenth century, most advancements have been automatic—based upon the length of continual service on

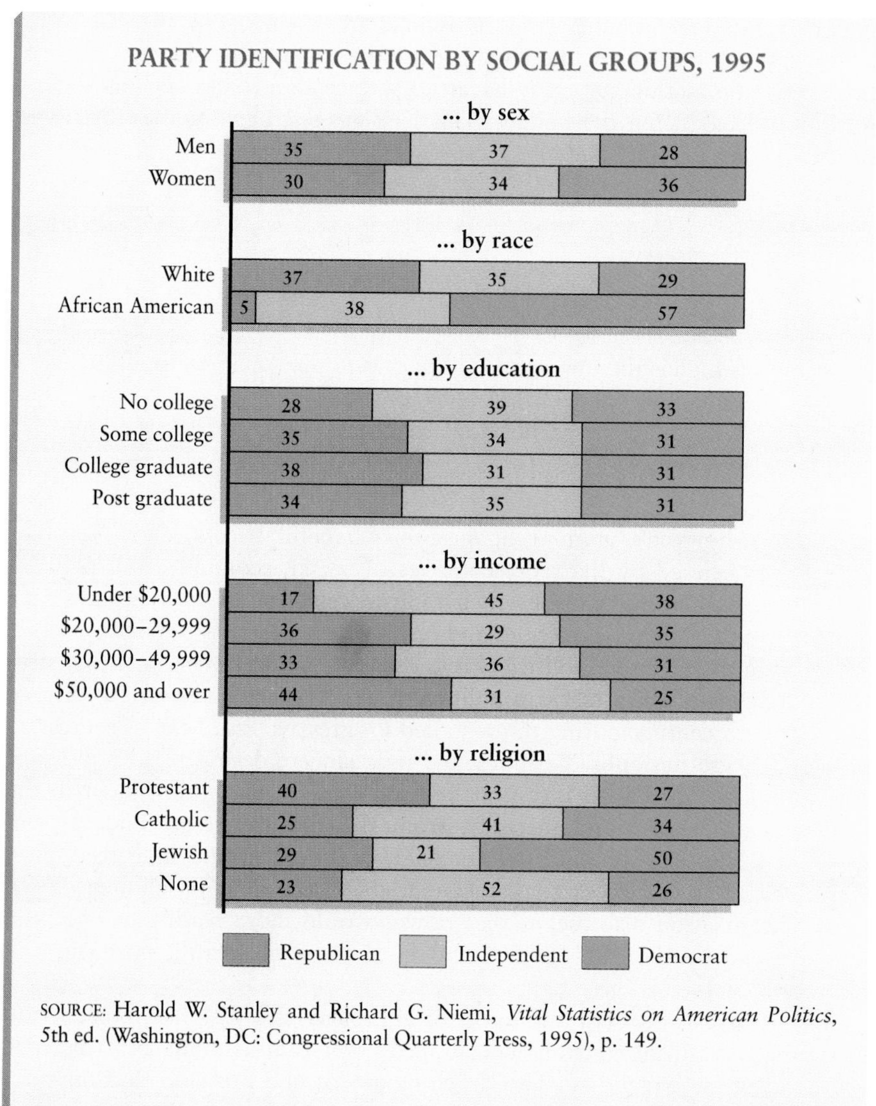

SOURCE: Harold W. Stanley and Richard G. Niemi, *Vital Statistics on American Politics*, 5th ed. (Washington, DC: Congressional Quarterly Press, 1995), p. 149.

FIGURE 8.5

the committee. This seniority system has existed only because of the support of the two parties, however, and either party can depart from it by a simple vote. During the 1970s, both parties reinstituted the practice of reviewing each chair—voting anew every two years on whether each chair would continue to be held by the same person. Few chairpersons actually have been removed, but notice has been served that the seniority system is no longer automatic, thereby reminding everyone that all committee assignments are party decisions. Thus, although party leaders no longer can control the votes of many members, the party system itself remains an important factor.

The continuing importance of parties in Congress became especially evident after the Republicans won control of Congress in 1994. During the first few months of the 104th Congress, the Republican leadership was able to maintain nearly unanimous support among party members on vote after vote as it sought to implement the GOP's legislative agenda. By the end of 1995, however, splits within the party began to surface over issues such as welfare reform and balancing the budget. This legislative struggle will be discussed further in Chapter 11.

The Weakening of Party Organization

> ➤ Why has the importance of parties in the American political system declined?
> ➤ What have the parties done to maintain their influence within government?

George Washington's warning against the "baneful effects of the spirit of party" was echoed by the representatives of social, economic, and political elites in many nations who saw their right to rule challenged by groups able to organize the collective energies and resources of the mass public.

Opposition to party politics was the basis for a number of the institutional reforms of the American political process promulgated at the turn of the twentieth century during the so-called Progressive Era. Many Progressive reformers were undoubtedly motivated by a sincere desire to rid politics of corruption and to improve the quality and efficiency of government in the United States. But simultaneously, from the perspective of middle- and upper-class Progressives and the financial, commercial, and industrial elites with which they were often associated, the weakening or elimination of party organization also meant that power would more readily be acquired and retained by the "best men," that is, those with wealth, position, and education.

Progressives instituted a long list of anti-party reforms. The introduction of nonpartisan local elections encouraged voters and candidates to become independent of party ties. The development of the primary election took away party leaders' control over nominations and greatly weakened party discipline. The extension of civil service systems (discussed further in Chapter 13) made it impossible for party leaders to hire and fire government workers and thus stripped the parties of armies of patronage workers who owed their government jobs to the party leaders and who could be counted upon to hand out leaflets, knock on doors, bring voters to the polls, and perform all the other tasks that helped the parties win elections. These reforms obviously did not destroy political parties as entities, but taken together, they did substantially weaken party organizations in the United States. After the turn of the century, the strength of American political parties gradually diminished. Between the two world wars, organization remained the major tool available to contending electoral forces, but in most areas of the country the "reformed" state and local parties that survived the Progressive Era gradually lost their organizational vitality and coherence, and they became less effective campaign tools. Again, Progressive reform did not eliminate the political party as an entity. Most areas of the nation continued to boast Democratic and Republican party groupings. But reform did mean the elimination of the permanent mass organizations that had been the parties' principal campaign weapons. In the new reformed legal and institutional environment of American politics, an environment that included merit systems (see Chapter 13), direct primaries, and nonpartisan elections (see Chapter 9), the chance that any group could construct and maintain an effective, large-scale organization was reduced.

Today's Democratic and Republican parties differ greatly from their predecessors. In recent decades, the Democrats and Republicans have become entrenched in distinct segments of the national governmental apparatus. The Democrats have a hold on federal social service, labor and regulatory agencies, and government bureaucracies and nonprofit organizations on the state and local levels that help administer national social programs. This entrenchment has its roots in Franklin D. Roosevelt's New Deal and Lyndon Johnson's Great Society programs, which expanded the size and institutional capacities of the national government's domestic agencies. These developments transformed the Democrats from a political force based upon state and local party machines into one grounded in the domestic bureaucracy.

In 1993, the Democrats sought to entrench themselves still further in the domestic state apparatus. The three chief vehicles for this effort were President Clinton's economic proposals, health care reform proposals, and political reform initiatives. Taken together, these proposals represented a bold effort to ensure continuing Democratic control of the government. Adoption of these proposals would have solidified the Democratic Party's institutional base in the bureaucracies of the executive branch while making it all the more difficult for Republicans to dislodge the Democrats through electoral methods. For these reasons, Republicans blocked Clinton's legislative proposals.

The Republicans, in turn, control the national security apparatus, sectors of the economy that benefit from military spending, and those segments of American society threatened by the welfare and regulatory state built by the Democrats. This was one of the major factors behind the efforts of the Republican-led 104th Congress to increase levels of defense spending while reducing domestic social spending. In essence, the Republicans sought to direct the flow of federal funds into agencies and institutions associated with their party while reducing the flow of funds into those sectors of the government in which the Democrats were entrenched.

To a considerable extent, the competitive entrenchment of Republicans and Democrats has replaced mass electoral mobilization as a means of securing power in the United States today. This is one reason why high levels of partisan conflict coexist with low rates of voter participation in contemporary American politics. To today's parties, traditional electoral politics is only one arena of political combat. In between elections, the Democrats and Republicans engage in institutional struggles whose outcome is every bit as important to them as the verdict at the ballot box. You will hear more about this in the next chapter.

Parties and Democracy

➤ Do parties help or hinder democracy?

Democracy and political parties arose together in the modern world. Without democracy, of course, a system of competing political parties never could have emerged. At the same time, without a system of competing political parties, democracy never could have flourished. Without a strong opposition, rulers would never have surrendered power, and without well-organized parties, ordinary people could never have acquired or used the right to vote. It is because of this strong historical association between democracy and political parties that the current weakness of American political parties is a matter of concern. Weak political parties are one reason behind the low levels of voter turnout in the United States. Weak political parties help powerful special interests to expand their influence—one reason that we worry so much about the corrupting influence of campaign contributions. In short, the weakness of American political parties saps the vitality of American democracy.

Summary

Political parties seek to control government by controlling its personnel. Elections are one means to this end. Thus, parties take shape from the electoral process.

Party organizations exist at every level of American government. The national party organizations are generally less important than the state and local party units. Each party's national committee and congressional campaign committees help to recruit candidates and raise money. The national conventions have, for the most part, lost their nominating functions, but still play an important role in determining party rules and party platforms.

The two-party system dominates U.S. politics. During the course of American history, the government has generally been dominated by one or the other party for long periods of time. This is generally followed by a period of realignment during which new groups attempt to seize power and the previously dominant party may be displaced by its rival. There have been five critical electoral realignments in American political history.

Today, on individual issues, the two parties differ little. In general, however, Democrats tend to be more liberal on issues and Republicans tend to be more conservative. Even though party affiliation means less to Americans than it once did, partisanship remains important. What ticket-splitting there is occurs mainly at the presidential level.

Third parties are short-lived for several reasons. They have limited electoral support, the tradition of the two-party system is strong, and a major party often adopts the platform of a third party. Single-member districts with two competing parties also discourage third parties.

Nominating and electing are the basic functions of parties. Parties are critical for getting out the vote, recruiting candidates, facilitating popular choice, and organizing the government. Parties also influence voting through the ties of party identification, particularly the strong ties formed with party activists. A variety of group characteristics can influence party identification, including race and ethnicity, gender, religion, class, ideology, and region.

The decline in party strength in contemporary America is one reason for the nation's low rates of voter turnout and for the growing strength of other political forces such as interest groups. Without strong parties, the continuing vitality of American democracy is open to question.

FOR FURTHER READING

Beck, Paul A., and Frank J. Sorauf. *Party Politics in America.* 7th ed. New York: HarperCollins, 1991.

Burnham, Walter Dean. *Critical Elections and the Mainsprings of American Politics.* New York: Norton, 1970.

Chambers, William N., and Walter Dean Burnham. *The American Party Systems: Stages of Political Development.* New York: Oxford University Press, 1975.

Edsall, Thomas Byrne, and Mary D. Edsall. *Chain Reaction: The Impact of Race, Rights, and Taxes on American Politics.* New York: Norton, 1993.

Goldman, Ralph. *The National Party Chairmen and Committees: Factionalism at the Top.* Armonk, NY: M. E. Sharpe, 1990.

Grimshaw, William J. *Bitter Fruit: Black Politics and the Chicago Machine, 1931–1991.* Chicago: University of Chicago Press, 1992.

Kayden, Xandra, and Eddie Mahe, Jr. *The Party Goes On: The Persistence of the Two-Party System in the United States.* New York: Basic Books, 1985.

Lawson, Kay, and Peter Merkl. *When Parties Fail: Emerging Alternative Organizations.* Princeton, NJ: Princeton University Press, 1988.

Milkis, Sidney. *The President and the Parties: The Transformation of the American Party System since the New Deal.* New York: Oxford University Press, 1993.

Phillips, Kevin. *Boiling Point: Democrats, Republicans, and the Decline of Middle Class Prosperity.* New York: Random House, 1993.

Sundquist, James. *Dynamics of the Party System.* Washington, DC: Brookings Institution, 1983.

Wattenberg, Martin. *The Decline of American Political Parties 1952–1988.* Cambridge, MA: Harvard University Press, 1990.

STUDY OUTLINE

1. In modern history, political parties have been the chief points of contact between governments and groups and forces in society. By organizing political parties, social forces attempt to gain some control over government policies and personnel.

What Are Political Parties?

1. Political parties as they are known today developed along with the expansion of suffrage, and actually took their shape from the electoral process.
2. Party organizations exist at virtually every level of American government—usually taking the form of committees made up of active party members.
3. Although national party conventions no longer have the power to nominate presidential candidates, they are still important in determining the party's rules and platform.
4. The national committee and the congressional campaign committees play important roles in recruiting candidates and raising money.

The Two-Party System in America

1. Historically, parties originate through either internal or external mobilization by those seeking to win governmental power.
2. The Democratic Party originated through a process of internal mobilization, as the Jeffersonian Party splintered into four factions in 1824, and Andrew Jackson emerged as the leader of one of these four groups.
3. The Republican Party grew through a process of external mobilization as antislavery groups formed a new party to oppose the 1854 Kansas-Nebraska Act.
4. The United States has experienced five realigning eras, which occur when the established political elite weak-

ens sufficiently to permit the creation of new coalitions of forces capable of capturing and holding the reins of government.

5. Despite the existence of some real philosophical differences between the Democratic and Republican parties, there is considerable overlap between them because each seeks to represent a wide range of interests.
6. American third parties have always represented social and economic protests ignored by the other parties, despite the fact that the United States is said to have a two-party system.

Functions of the Parties

1. Although parties perform a wide variety of functions, they are primarily involved in providing the candidates for office, encouraging citizens to vote, and facilitating mass electoral choice.
2. Individuals tend to form psychological ties with parties; these ties are called "party identification." This identification often follows demographic and regional lines.
3. Political parties help to organize Congress. Congressional leadership and the committee system are both products of the two-party system.

The Weakening of Party Organization

1. The anti-party reforms of the Progressive Era have served to weaken political parties throughout the twentieth century.
2. Rather than engaging in mass electoral competition, the weakened parties have competed by entrenching themselves in distinct segments of the national governmental apparatus.

Parties and Democracy

1. Democracy has always depended upon a strong party system.
2. The weakness of contemporary American political parties has strengthened interest groups, reduced voter turnout, and threatened the vitality of American democracy.

Practice Quiz

1. Which political party would celebrate its founders through a Jefferson-Jackson Day celebration?
   a. Democratic
   b. Republican
   c. Whig
   d. United We Stand
2. Which turn-of-the-century party enjoyed great success in reforming American politics?
   a. Progressive
   b. Democratic
   c. Socialist
   d. American Independent
3. Through which mechanism did Boss Tweed and other party leaders in the late nineteenth and early twentieth centuries maintain their control?
   a. civil service reform
   b. soft money contributions
   c. machine politics
   d. electoral reform
4. Political parties in America are organized on what level?
   a. national
   b. state
   c. county
   d. all of the above
5. Contemporary national party conventions are important because
   a. they decide who will be the party's presidential candidate.
   b. they determine the party's rules and platform.
   c. both a and b are correct.
   d. neither a nor b is correct.
6. Which party was founded as a political expression of the antislavery movement?
   a. American Independent
   b. Prohibition
   c. Republican
   d. Democratic
7. Historically, when do realignments occur?
   a. typically, every twenty years
   b. whenever a minority party takes over Congress
   c. when large numbers of voters permanently shift their support from one party to another
   d. in odd-numbered years
8. Party organization tends to
   a. discourage mass participation.
   b. make electoral choices more difficult.
   c. benefit the wealthier segments of society.
   d. benefit the poorer segments of society.

9. What was the name of the party that nominated George Wallace as its candidate for president in 1968?
   a. American Independent
   b. Socialist
   c. Democratic
   d. Antimasonic

10. What role do parties play in Congress?
   a. They select leaders, such as the Speaker of the House.
   b. They assign members to committees.
   c. Both a and b are correct.
   d. Parties play no role in Congress.

CRITICAL THINKING QUESTIONS

1. Describe the factors that have contributed to the overall weakening of political parties in America. How are parties weaker? How do they remain important? What are the advantages of a political system with weak political parties? What are the disadvantages?
2. Historically, third parties have developed in American history when certain issues or constituencies have been ignored by the existing parties. Considering the similarities and differences between the Democratic and Republican parties, where might a budding third party find a constituency? What issues might it adopt? Finally, what structural and ideological obstacles might that third party face?

KEY TERMS

caucus (political) a normally closed meeting of a political or legislative group to select candidates, plan strategy, or make decisions regarding legislative matters. (p. 265)

critical electoral realignment the point in history when a new party supplants the ruling party, becoming in turn the dominant political force. In the United States, this has tended to occur roughly every thirty years (pp. 276–77)

machines strong party organizations in late-nineteenth- and early-twentieth-century American cities. These machines were led by "bosses" who controlled party nominations and patronage. (p. 271)

majority party the party that holds the majority of legislative seats in either the House or the Senate. (p. 292)

minority party the party that holds a minority of legislative seats in either the House or the Senate. (p. 292)

multiple-member district an electorate that selects all candidates at large from the whole district; each voter is given the number of votes equivalent to the number of seats to be filled. (p. 281)

national convention a national party political institution that serves to nominate the party's presidential and vice presidential candidates, establish party rules, and write and ratify the party's platform. (p. 265)

nomination the process through which political parties select their candidates for election to public office. (p. 283)

party activists partisans who contribute time, energy, and effort to support their party and its candidates. (p. 289)

party identification an individual voter's psychological ties to one party or another. (p. 289)

platform a party document, written at a national convention, that contains party philosophy, principles, and positions on issues. (p. 267)

political parties organized groups that attempt to influence the government by electing their members to important government offices. (p. 264)

single-member district an electorate that is allowed to select only one representative from each district; the normal method of representation in the United States. (p. 281)

third parties parties that organize to compete against the two major American political parties. (p. 279)

9

Campaigns and Elections

* ★ Elections in America
  - What is the history of the suffrage in the United States? What factors influence how many voters participate?
  - What different types of elections are held in the United States? What rules determine who wins elections?
  - How does the government determine the boundaries of electoral districts? How is the ballot determined?
* ★ Election Campaigns
  - What are the steps in a successful election campaign?
* ★ Presidential Elections
  - How is the president elected?
  - What factors have the greatest impact on a general election campaign?
* ★ Money and Politics
  - How do candidates raise and spend campaign funds? How does the government regulate campaign spending? How does money affect how certain social groups achieve electoral success?
* ★ How Voters Decide
  - What are the primary influences on voters' decisions?
* ★ The Decline of Voting
  - Why is political participation relatively low in the United States? Have attempts to increase participation succeeded? Why or why not? What are the implications for democracy?

OVER THE PAST two centuries, elections have come to play a significant role in the political processes of most nations. The forms that elections take and the purposes they serve, however, vary greatly from nation to nation. The most important difference among national electoral systems is that some provide the opportunity for opposition while others do not. Democratic electoral systems, such as those that have evolved in the United States and western Europe, allow opposing forces to compete against and even to replace current office holders. Authoritarian electoral systems, by contrast, do not allow the defeat of those in power. In the authoritarian context, elections are used primarily to mobilize popular enthusiasm for the government, to provide an outlet for popular discontent, and to persuade foreigners that the regime is legitimate—i.e., that it has the support of the people. In the former Soviet Union, for example, citizens were required to vote even though no opposition to Communist Party candidates was allowed.

In democracies, elections can also serve as institutions of legitimation and as safety valves for social discontent. But beyond these functions, democratic elections facilitate popular influence, promote leadership accountability, and offer groups in society a measure of protection from the abuse of governmental power. Citizens exercise influence through elections by determining who should control the government. The chance to decide who will govern serves as an opportunity for ordinary citizens to make choices about the policies, programs, and directions of government action. In the United States, for example, recent Democratic and Republican candidates have differed significantly on issues of taxing, social spending, and governmental regulation. As American voters have chosen between the two parties' candidates, they have also made choices about these issues.

Elections promote leadership accountability because the threat of defeat at the polls exerts pressure on those in power to conduct themselves in a responsible manner and to take account of popular interests and wishes when they make their decisions. As James Madison observed in the *Federalist Papers*, elected leaders are "compelled to anticipate the moment when their power is to cease, when their exercise of it is to be reviewed, and when they must descend to the level from which they were raised, there forever to remain unless a faithful discharge of their trust shall have established their title to a renewal of it."[1] It is because of this need to anticipate the dissatisfaction of their constituents that elected officials constantly monitor public opinion polls as they decide what positions to take on policy issues.

Finally, the right to vote, or **suffrage**, can serve as an important source of protection for groups in American society. The passage of the 1965 Voting Rights Act, for example, enfranchised millions of African Americans in the South, paving the way for the election of thousands of new black public officials at the local, state, and national levels and ensuring that white politicians could no longer ignore the views and needs of African Americans. The Voting Rights Act was one of the chief spurs for the elimination of many overt forms of racial discrimination as well as for the diminution of racist rhetoric in American public life.

In this chapter, we shall examine the place of elections in American political life. We will first examine some of the formal aspects of electoral participation. Second, we will see how election campaigns are conducted in the United States. Then we will assess the various factors that influence voters' decisions. Finally, we will consider the impact of elections upon American government and politics.

Elections in America

- What is the history of the suffrage in the United States? What factors influence how many voters participate?
- What different types of elections are held in the United States? What rules determine who wins elections?
- How does the government determine the boundaries of electoral districts? How is the ballot determined?

In the United States, elections are held at regular intervals. National presidential elections take place every four years, on the first Tuesday in November; congressional elections are held every two years on the same Tuesday. (Congressional elections that do not coincide with a presidential election are sometimes called **midterm elections.**) Elections for state and local office also often coincide with national elections. Some states and municipalities, however, prefer to schedule their local elections for times that do not coincide with national contests to ensure that local results will not be affected by national trends.

In the American federal system, the responsibility for organizing elections rests largely with state and local governments. State laws specify how elections are to be administered, determine the boundaries of electoral districts, and specify candidate and voter qualifications. Elections are administered by state, county, and municipal election boards that are responsible for establishing and staffing polling places and verifying the eligibility of individuals who come to vote.

Voting Rights

In principle, states determine who is eligible to vote. During the nineteenth and early twentieth centuries, voter eligibility requirements often varied greatly from state to state. Some states openly abridged the right to vote on the basis of race; others did not. Some states imposed property restrictions on voting; others had no such restrictions. Most states mandated lengthy residency requirements, which meant that persons moving from one state to another sometimes lost their right to vote for as much as a year. In more recent years, however, constitutional amendments, federal statutes, and federal court decisions have limited states' discretion in the area of voting rights. Individual states may establish brief residency requirements, generally fifteen days, for record-keeping purposes. Beyond this, states have little or no power to regulate the suffrage.

Today in the United States, all native-born or naturalized citizens over the age of eighteen, with the exception of convicted felons, have the right to vote. During the colonial and early national periods of American history, the right to vote was generally restricted to white males over the age of twenty-one. Many states also limited voting to those who owned property or paid more than a specified amount of annual tax. Property and tax requirements began to be rescinded during the 1820s, however, and had generally disappeared by the end of the Civil War.

By the time of the Civil War, blacks had won the right to vote in most northern states. In the South, black voting rights were established by the Fifteenth Amendment, ratified in 1870, which prohibited denial of the right to vote on the basis of race. Despite the Fifteenth Amendment, the voting rights of African Americans were effectively rescinded during the 1880s by the states of the former Confederacy. During this period, the southern states created what was called the "Jim Crow" system of racial segregation. As part of this system, a variety of devices, such as **poll taxes** and literacy tests, were used to prevent virtually all blacks from voting. During the 1950s and 1960s, through the Civil Rights movement led by Dr. Martin Luther King, Jr., and

After passage of the Voting Rights Act of 1965, the national government intervened in areas where African Americans were denied the right to vote. As a result, thousands of new black voters were registered.

The quiet upstate New York town of Seneca Falls played host to what would later come to be known as the starting point of the modern women's movement. Convened in July 1848, and organized by activists Elizabeth Cady Stanton (who lived in Seneca Falls) and Lucretia Mott, the Seneca Falls Convention drew three hundred delegates to discuss and formulate plans to advance the political and social rights of women.

The centerpiece of the convention was its Declaration of Sentiments and Resolutions. Patterned after the Declaration of Independence, the Seneca Falls document declared, "We hold these truths to be self-evident: that all men and women are created equal," and "The history of mankind is a history of repeated injuries and usurpations on the part of man toward woman, having in direct object the establishment of an absolute tyranny over her." The most controversial provision of the declaration, nearly rejected as too radical, was the call for the right to vote for women. Although most of the delegates were women, about forty men participated, including the renowned abolitionist Frederick Douglass.

The link to the antislavery movement was not new. Stanton and Mott had attended the World Anti-slavery Convention in London in 1840, but had been denied delegate seats because of their sex. This rebuke helped precipitate the 1848 convention. The movements for abolition of slavery and women's rights were also closely linked with the temperance movement (because alcohol abuse was closely linked to male abuses of women). The convergence of the antislavery, temperance, and suffrage movements was reflected in the views and actions of other women's movement leaders, such as Susan B. Anthony.

The convention and its participants were subjected to widespread ridicule, but similar conventions were organized in other states, and in the same year, New York State passed the Married Women's Property Act in order to restore the right of a married woman to own property. Frustration with the general failure to win reforms in other states accelerated suffrage activism after the Civil War. In 1872, Anthony and several other women were arrested in Rochester, New York, for illegally registering and voting in that year's national election. (The men who

others, African Americans demanded the restoration of their voting rights. Their goal was accomplished through the enactment of the 1965 Voting Rights Act, which provided for the federal government to register voters in states that discriminated against minority citizens. The result was the reenfranchisement of southern blacks for the first time since the 1860s.

Women won the right to vote in 1920, with the adoption of the Nineteenth Amendment. This amendment resulted primarily from the activities of the women's suffrage movement, led by Elizabeth Cady Stanton, Susan B. Anthony, and Carrie Chapman Catt during the late nineteenth and early twentieth centuries. The "suffragettes," as they were called, held rallies, demonstrations, and protest marches for more than half a century before achieving their goal. The cause of women's suffrage was ultimately advanced by World War I. President Woodrow Wilson and members of Congress were convinced that women would be more likely to support the war effort if they were granted the right to vote. For this same reason, women were given the right to vote in Great Britain and Canada during the First World War.

allowed the women to register and vote were also indicted; Anthony paid their expenses, and eventually won presidential pardons for them.) At her trial, Judge Ward Hunt ordered the jury to find her guilty without deliberation. Yet Anthony was allowed to address the court, saying, "Your denial of my citizen's right to vote is the denial of my right of consent as one of the governed, the denial of my right of representation as one of the taxed, the denial of my right to a trial of my peers as an offender against the law."[1] Hunt assessed Anthony a fine of $100, but did not sentence her to jail. Anthony refused to pay the fine.

The following decade, suffragists used the occasion of the Constitution's centennial to protest the continued denial of their rights. For these women, the centennial represented "a century of injustice." The unveiling of the Statue of Liberty, depicting liberty as a woman, in New York Harbor in 1886 prompted women's rights advocates to call it "the greatest hypocrisy of the nineteenth century," in that "not one single woman throughout the length and breadth of the Land is as yet in possession of political Liberty."[2]

The climactic movement toward suffrage was formally launched in 1878 with the introduction of a proposed constitutional amendment in Congress. Parallel efforts were made in the states. The Nineteenth Amendment, granting women the right to vote, was finally adopted in 1920, after most of the movement's original leaders had died.

SOURCE: Miriam Gurko, *The Ladies of Seneca Falls: The Birth of the Women's Rights Movement* (New York: Macmillan, 1974).

[1]Jill Dupont, "Susan B. Anthony," New York Notes (Albany, NY: New York State Commission on the Bicentennial of the U.S. Constitution, 1988), p. 3.

[2]Dupont, "Susan B. Anthony," p. 4.

The most recent expansion of the suffrage in the United States took place in 1971, during the Vietnam War, when the Twenty-sixth Amendment was ratified, lowering the voting age from twenty-one to eighteen. Unlike black suffrage and women's suffrage, which came about in part because of the demands of groups that had been deprived of the right to vote, the Twenty-sixth Amendment was not a response to the demands of young people to be given the right to vote. Instead, many policy makers hoped that the right to vote would channel the disruptive protest activities of students involved in the anti–Vietnam War movement into peaceful participation at the ballot box.

Voter Participation

Although the United States has developed a system of universal suffrage, America's rate of voter participation, or **turnout**, is very low. Slightly more than 50 percent of those eligible participate in national presidential elections, while barely one-third of eligible voters take part in midterm congressional elections (see Figure 9.1). Turnout in state and local races that do not coincide with national contests is typically even lower. In European countries, by contrast, national voter turnout is usually between 80 and 90 percent.[2]

The difference between American and European levels of turnout has much to do with registration rules and party strength. In the United States, individuals who are eligible to vote must register with the state election board before they are actually allowed to vote. Registration requirements were introduced at the end of the nineteenth century in response to the demands of the Progressive movement. Progressives hoped to make voting more difficult both to reduce multiple voting and other forms of corruption and to discourage immigrant and working-class voters from going to the polls. When first introduced, registration was extremely difficult and, in some states, reduced voter turnout by as much as 50 percent.

Registration requirements particularly depress the participation of those with little education and low incomes because registration requires a greater

FIGURE 9.1

More Americans tend to vote in presidential election years than in years when only congressional and local elections are held.

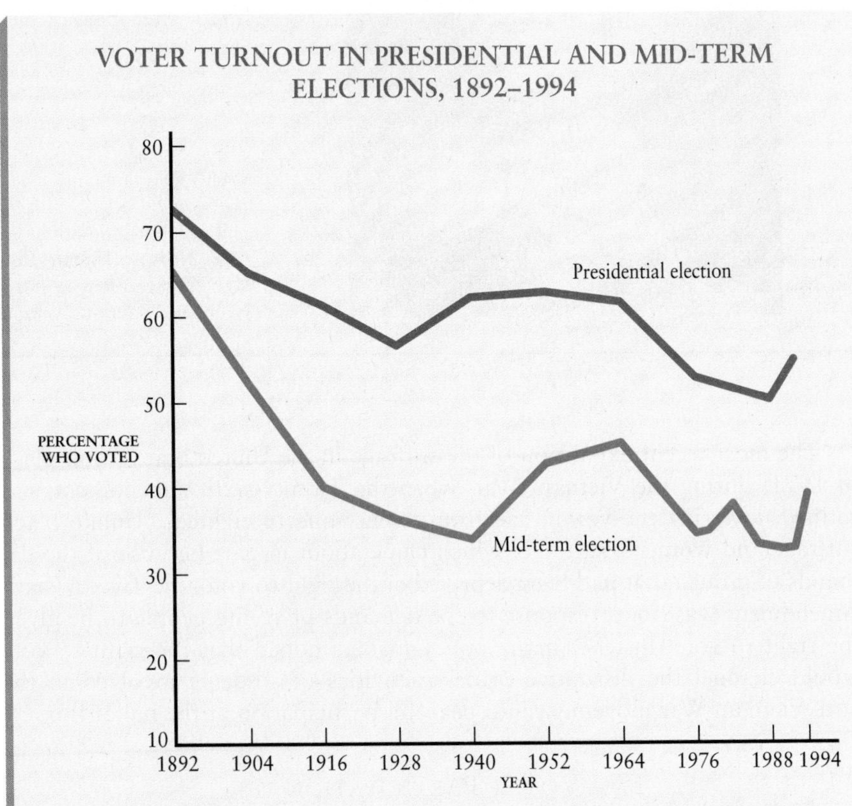

SOURCES: 1892–1958: Erik Austin and Jerome Clubb, *Political Facts of the United States since 1789* (New York: Columbia University Press, 1986), pp. 378–79; 1960–92: U.S. Bureau of the Census, *Statistical Abstract of the United States: 1992* (Washington, DC: Government Printing Office, 1992); 1994: U.S. Newswire, November 11, 1994.

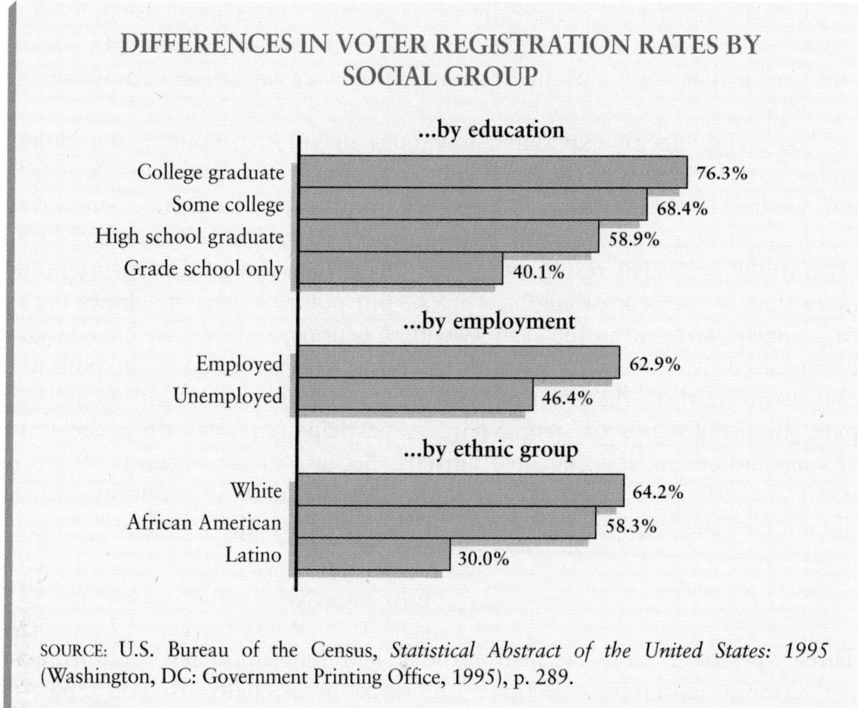

SOURCE: U.S. Bureau of the Census, *Statistical Abstract of the United States: 1995* (Washington, DC: Government Printing Office, 1995), p. 289.

FIGURE 9.2

The percentage of Americans who are registered to vote varies according to education level, employment status, and ethnic group.

degree of political involvement and interest than does the act of voting itself. To vote, a person need be concerned only with the particular election campaign at hand. Requiring individuals to register before the next election forces them to make a decision to participate on the basis of an abstract interest in the electoral process rather than a simple concern with a specific campaign. Such an abstract interest in electoral politics is largely a product of education. Those with relatively little education may become interested in political events once the issues of a particular campaign become salient, but by that time it may be too late to register. As a result, personal registration requirements not only diminish the size of the electorate but also tend to create an electorate that is, in the aggregate, better educated, higher in income and social status, and composed of fewer African Americans and other minorities than the citizenry as a whole (see Figure 9.2).

Over the years, voter registration restrictions have been modified somewhat to make registration easier. In most states, an eligible individual may register to vote simply by mailing a postcard to the state election board. In 1993, Congress approved and President Clinton signed the Motor Voter bill to ease voter registration by allowing individuals to register when they apply for driver's licenses, as well as in public assistance and military recruitment offices.[3] A similar bill was vetoed by President George Bush in 1992. Bush and other Republicans objected to the bill because they feared it would increase registration by poor and minority voters, who generally tend to support the Democrats. Experience suggests, however, that *any* registration rules, however liberal, tend to depress voting on the part of the poor and unedu-

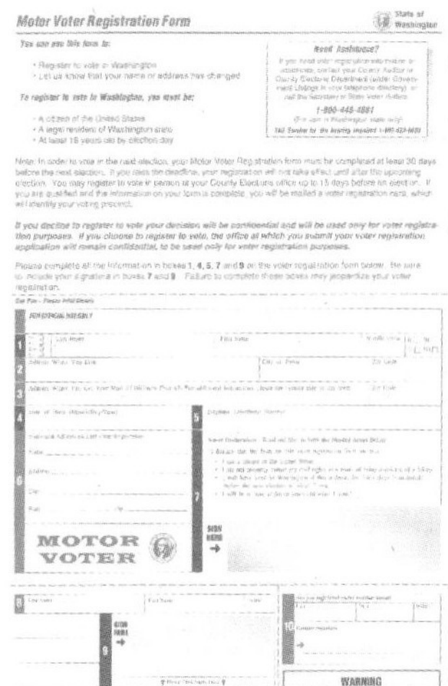
Motor Voter Registration Form

MOTOR VOTER

A Motor Voter registration form.

cated. In Europe, there is typically no registration burden on the individual voter; voter registration is handled automatically by the government. This is one reason that voter turnout rates in Europe are higher than those in the United States.

The second factor explaining low rates of voter turnout in the United States is the weakness of the American party system. As we saw in Chapter 8, during the nineteenth century, American political party machines employed hundreds of thousands of workers to organize and mobilize voters and bring them to the polls. The result was an extremely high rate of turnout, typically more than 90 percent of eligible voters.[4] But political party machines began to decline in strength in the early twentieth century and by now have largely disappeared. Without party workers to encourage them to go to the polls and even to bring them there if necessary, many eligible voters will not participate. In the absence of strong parties, participation rates drop the most among poorer and less-educated citizens. Because of the absence of strong political parties, the American electorate is smaller and skewed more toward the middle class than the population of all those potentially eligible to vote.

TYPES OF ELECTIONS

Three types of elections are held in the United States: primary elections, general elections, and runoff elections. Americans occasionally also participate in a fourth voting process, the referendum, but the referendum is not actually an election.

Primary elections are used to select each party's candidates for the general election. In the case of local and statewide offices, the winners of primary elections face one another as their parties' nominees in the general election. At the presidential level, however, primary elections are indirect; they are used to select state delegates to the national nominating conventions, at which the major party presidential candidates are chosen. America is one of the only nations in the world to use primary elections. In most countries, nominations are controlled by party officials, as they once were in the United States. The primary system was introduced at the turn of the century by Progressive reformers who hoped to weaken the power of party leaders by taking candidate nominations out of their hands.

Under the laws of some states, only registered members of a political party may vote in a primary election to select that party's candidates. This is called a **closed primary**. Other states allow all registered voters to decide on the day of the primary in which party's primary they will participate. This is called an **open primary**.

The primary is followed by the general election—the decisive electoral contest. The winner of the general election is elected to office for a specified term. In some states, however, mainly in the southeast, if no candidate wins an absolute majority in the primary, a runoff election is held before the general election. This situation is most likely to arise if there are more than two candidates, none of whom receives a majority of the votes cast. A runoff election is held between the two candidates who received the largest number of votes.

Some states also provide for referendum voting. The **referendum** process allows citizens to vote directly on proposed laws or other governmental actions. In recent years, voters in several states have voted to set limits on tax rates, to block state and local spending proposals, and to prohibit social services for illegal immigrants. Although it involves voting, a referendum is not an election. The election is an institution of representative government. Through an election, voters choose officials to act for them. The referendum, by contrast, is an institution of direct democracy; it allows voters to govern directly without intervention by government officials. The validity of referenda results, however, are subject to judicial action. If a court finds that a referendum outcome violates the state or national constitution, it can overturn the result. This happened in the case of a 1995 California referendum curtailing social services to illegal aliens.[5]

The Criteria for Winning

In some countries, to win a seat in the parliament or other governing body, a candidate must receive an absolute majority (50% + 1) of all the votes cast in the relevant district. This type of electoral system is called a **majority system** and, in the United States, is used in primary elections by some southern states. Majority systems usually include a provision for a runoff election between the two top candidates, because if the initial race draws several candidates, there is little chance that any one will receive a majority.

In other nations, candidates for office need not win an absolute majority of the votes cast to win an election. Instead, victory is awarded to the candidate who receives the most votes, regardless of the actual percentage this represents. A candidate receiving 50 percent, 30 percent, or 20 percent of the vote can win if no other candidate received more votes. This type of electoral system is called a **plurality system** and is used in virtually all general elections in the United States.

Most European nations employ a third type of electoral system, called **proportional representation**. Under proportional rules, competing political parties are awarded legislative seats in rough proportion to the percentage of the popular votes cast that each party won. A party that wins 30 percent of the vote will receive roughly 30 percent of the seats in the parliament or other representative body. In the United States, proportional representation is used by many states in presidential primary elections.

In general, proportional representation works to the advantage of smaller or weaker groups in society, whereas plurality and majority rules tend to help larger and more powerful forces. Proportional representation benefits smaller or weaker groups because it usually allows a party to win legislative seats with fewer votes than would be required under a majority or plurality system. In Europe, for example, a party that wins 10 percent of the national vote might win 10 percent of the parliamentary seats. In the United States, by contrast, a party that wins 10 percent of the vote would probably win no seats in Congress. Because they give small parties little chance of success, plurality and majority systems tend to reduce the number of competitive political parties. Proportional representation, on the other hand, tends to increase the

WHO WINS?

Majority System
Winner must receive a simple majority (50 percent plus one)
Example: formerly used in primary elections in the South

Plurality System
Winner is the candidate who receives the most votes, regardless of the percentage
Example: currently used in almost all general elections throughout the country

Proportional Representation
Winners are selected to a representative body in the proportion to the votes their party received
Example: used in New York City in the 1930s, resulting in several Communist seats on the City Council

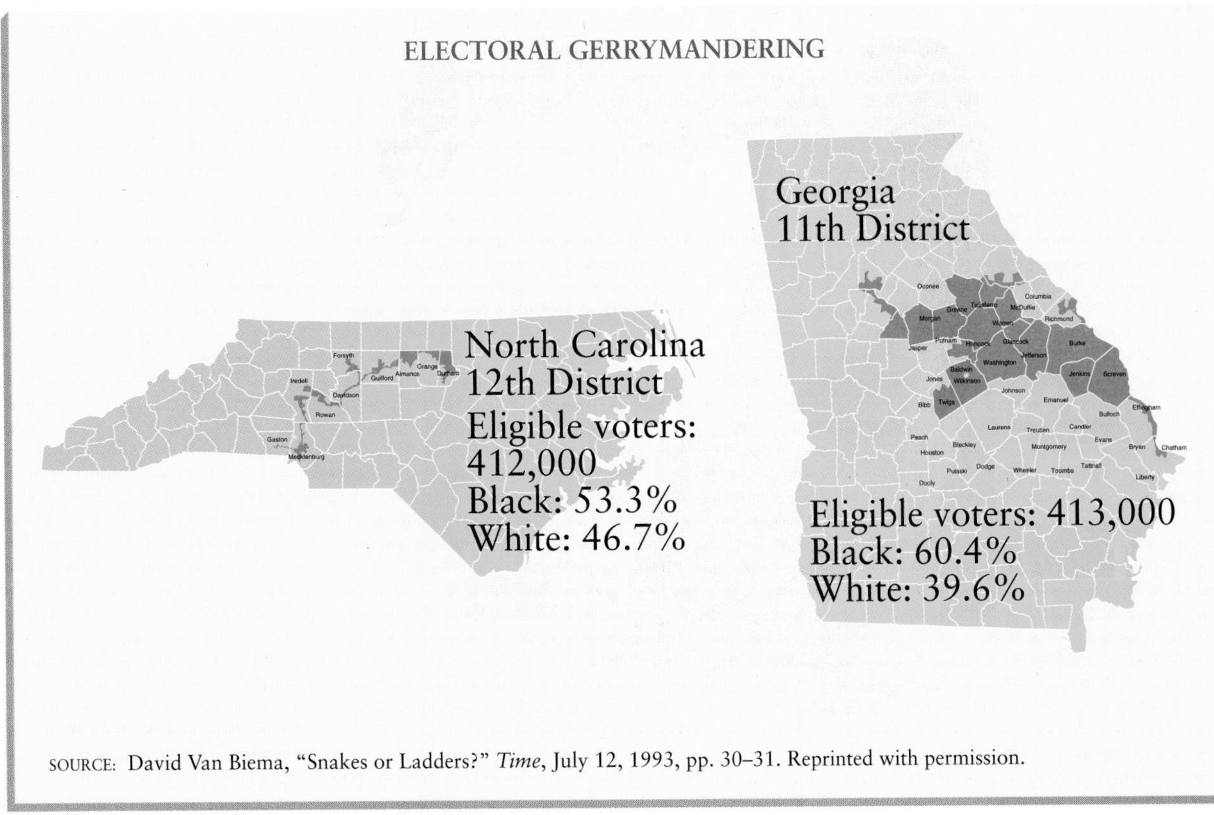

SOURCE: David Van Biema, "Snakes or Ladders?" *Time*, July 12, 1993, pp. 30–31. Reprinted with permission.

FIGURE 9.4

North Carolina's 12th Congressional District and Georgia's 11th Congressional District were drawn in unusual shapes in an attempt to create minority election districts and encourage the election of minority representatives to Congress. Both these districts have been ruled unconstitutional by the U.S. Supreme Court.

sional districts made up primarily of minority group members. This practice was intended to increase the number of African Americans elected to public office (see Figure 9.4). The Supreme Court has viewed this effort as constitutionally dubious, however. Beginning with the 1993 case of *Shaw v. Reno*, the Court has undermined efforts to create such **minority districts.**[8]

THE BALLOT

Prior to the 1890s, voters cast ballots according to political parties. Each party printed its own ballots, listed only its own candidates for each office, and employed party workers to distribute its ballots at the polls. Because only one party's candidates appeared on any ballot, it was very difficult for a voter to cast anything other than a straight party vote.

The advent of a new, neutral ballot represented a significant change in electoral procedure. The new ballot was prepared and administered by the state rather than the parties. Each ballot was identical and included the names of all candidates for office (see Figure 9.5). This ballot reform made it possible for voters to make their choices on the basis of the individual rather than the collective merits of a party's candidates. Because all candidates for the same office now appeared on the same ballot, voters were no longer forced to choose a straight party ticket. This gave rise to the phenomenon of split-ticket voting in American elections.

THE PARTY-COLUMN BALLOT (NOVEMBER 1996)

	Office	A DEMOCRATIC	B REPUBLICAN	C CONSERVATIVE	D INDEPENDENCE	E LIBERAL	F RIGHT TO LIFE	G FREEDOM	H NATURAL LAW
1	Electors for President and Vice President of the United States / Electores para Presidente y Vice-Presidente de los Estados Unidos	Bill Clinton and Al Gore 1A	Bob Dole and Jack Kemp 1B	Bob Dole and Jack Kemp 1C	Ross Perot and Pat Choate 1D	Bill Clinton and Al Gore 1E	Howard Phillips and Herbert W. Titus 1F	Bob Dole and Jack Kemp 1G	H NATURAL LAW: John Hagelin and Mike Tompkins 1H; I LIBERTARIAN: Harry Browne and Jo Jorgensen 1I; J SOCIALIST WORKERS SWP: James E. Harris and Laura Garza 1J; K WORKERS WORLD: Monica Gail Moorehead and Gloria La Riva 1K; L GREEN: Ralph Nader and Muriel K. Tillinghast 1L
14	Justices of the Supreme Court / Jueces de la Corte Suprema	Guy J. Mangano 14A	Guy J. Mangano 14B	Guy J. Mangano 14C		Guy J. Mangano 14E			
15		Gabriel M. Krausman 15A	Gabriel M. Krausman 15B	Gabriel M. Krausman 15C		Gabriel M. Krausman 15E			
16		Ruth E. Moskowitz 16A	Ruth E. Moskowitz 16B	Anthony A. LaBella, Jr. 16C		Ruth E. Moskowitz 16E			
17		Ronald J. Aiello 17A	Ronald J. Aiello 17B	Ronald J. Aiello 17C		Ronald J. Aiello 17E			
18		Francois A. Rivera 18A	Michael Forzano 18B	David Ironman 18C		Francois Rivera 18E			
19		Frank V. Ponterio 19A	Joseph P. Grancio 19B	Frank V. Ponterio 19C	Frank V. Ponterio 19D	Joseph P. Grancio 19E			
20		Frank J. Barbaro 20A	Frank J. Barbaro 20B	Robert Bressler 20C		Philip J. Kaplan 20E			
21		Deborah A. Dowling 21A	Charles A. Kuffner, Jr. 21B	Charles A. Kuffner, Jr. 21C		Charles A. Kuffner, Jr. 21E			
22	Surrogate / Juez de Testamentaria	Michael H. Feinberg 22A	Michael H. Feinberg 22B	Michael H. Feinberg 22C		Michael H. Feinberg 22E			
23	Judge of the Civil Court - County / Juez de la Corte Civil - Condado	Bernard Fuchs 23A	Bernard Fuchs 23B	John J. D'Emic 23C		Bernard Fuchs 23E			
24	Representative in Congress / Representante en Congreso	Charles E. Schumer 24A	Robert J. Verga 24B	Michael Masse 24C	Robert J. Verga 24D	Charles E. Schumer 24E		Robert J. Verga 24G	
25	State Senator / Senador Estatal	Marty Markowitz 25A	David Greene 25B	Clarence John 25C				David Greene 25G	
26	Member of Assembly / Miembro de la Asamblea	James F. Brennan 26A	Evan McNeeley 26B	Evan McNeeley 26C		James F. Brennan 26E			

PROPOSALS
PROPUESTAS

PROPOSAL NUMBER ONE, A PROPOSITION

THE CLEAN WATER/CLEAN AIR BOND ACT OF 1996

Shall chapter 412 of the laws of 1996 known as the clean water/clean air bond act of 1996, authorizing the creation of state debt to provide moneys for the preservation, enhancement, restoration, and improvement of the quality of the state's environment and natural resources in the amount of one billion seven hundred fifty million dollars ($1,750,000,000) be approved?

1 YES / SI ☐ NO ☐

PROPUESTA NUMERO UNO, UNA PROPUESTA

LA LEY DE BONOS PARA AGUA LIMPIA/AIRE LIMPIO DE 1996

¿Deberá aprobarse el capítulo 412 de las leyes de 1996, conocido como la ley de bonos para agua limpia/aire limpio de 1996, autorizando la creación de endeudamiento estatal a fin de generar fondos destinados a la conservación, renovación, restauración y mejora de la calidad del medio ambiente y recursos naturales del estado, por un importe de mil setecientos cincuenta millones de dolares ($1.750.000.000)?

PROPOSAL NUMBER TWO, A LOCAL QUESTION

A LOCAL LAW TO AMEND THE NEW YORK CITY CHARTER, IN RELATION TO TERM LIMITS AND STAGGERED TERMS

The proposed local law, entitled "A local law to amend the New York City Charter, in relation to term limits and staggered terms," would amend current Charter provisions, which prohibit the Mayor, Comptroller, Public Advocate, Borough Presidents and members of the City Council from serving more than two full consecutive terms, including at least one four-year term for Council members, after January 1, 1994. The proposed local law would prohibit those officials from serving more than three full consecutive terms or twelve consecutive years, whichever is greater, after January 1, 1994, except for members of the City Council first elected in the year 2003, who would be prohibited from serving more than ten consecutive years. Shall the proposed local law be approved?

2 YES / SI ☐ NO ☐

PROPUESTA NUMERO DOS, UNA PREGUNTA LOCAL

UNA LEY LOCAL PARA ENMENDAR LA CARTA CONSTITUTVIA DEL GOBIERNO DE LA CIUDAD DE NUEVA YORK, EN RELACION A LIMITES EN LA DURACION DE LOS CARGOS Y AL ESPACIAMIENTO EN EL EJERCICIO DE LOS CARGOS

La ley local propuesta, intitulada "Una ley local para enmendar la Carta Constitutvia del Gobierno de la Ciudad de Nueva York, en relación a límites en la duración de los cargos y al espaciamiento en el ejercicio de los cargos." La ley local propuesta enmendaría las disposiciones de la Carta Constitutiva actual, las cuales prohíben al alcalde, al contralor, al defensor público, a los presidentes de los condados y a los miembros del Concejo Municipal, ocupar sus cargos por más de dos períodos consecutivos completos, incluyendo por lo menos un período de cuatro años en el caso de los miembros del Concejo, después del 1 de Enero de 1994. La ley local propuesta prohibiría a dichos funcionarios ocupar sus cargos por más de tres períodos consecutivos completos o doce años consecutivos, lo que sea mayor, después del 1 de Enero de 1994, excepto los miembros del Concejo Municipal que sean electos por primera vez en el año 2003, a quienes se las prohibirá ocupar su cargo por más de diez años consecutivos. ¿Debería aprobarse la ley local propuesta?

FIGURE 9.5

The party-column ballot makes it easier for voters to choose candidates from only one party; each party's slate is listed in one column.

If a voter supports candidates from more than one party in the same election, he or she is said to be casting a **split-ticket vote**. Voters who support only one party's candidates are casting a **straight-ticket vote**. Straight-ticket voting occurs most often when a voter casts a ballot for a party's presidential candidate and then "automatically" votes for the remainder of that party's candidates. The result of this voting pattern is known as the **coattail effect**.

Prior to the reform of the ballot, it was not uncommon for an entire incumbent administration to be swept from office and replaced by an entirely new set of officials. In the absence of a real possibility of split-ticket voting, any desire on the part of the electorate for change could be expressed only as a vote against all candidates of the party in power. Because of this, there always existed the possibility, particularly at the state and local levels, that an insurgent slate committed to policy change could be swept into power. The party ballot thus increased the potential impact of elections upon the government's composition. Although this potential may not always have been realized, the party ballot at least increased the chance that electoral decisions could lead to policy changes. By contrast, because it permitted choice on the basis of candidates' individual appeals, ticket splitting led to increasingly divided partisan control of government.

THE ELECTORAL COLLEGE

In the early history of popular voting, nations often made use of indirect elections. In these elections, voters would choose the members of an intermediate body. These members would, in turn, select public officials. The assumption underlying such processes was that ordinary citizens were not really qualified to choose their leaders and could not be trusted to do so directly. The last vestige of this procedure in America is the **electoral college**, the group of electors who formally select the president and vice president of the United States.

When Americans go to the polls on election day, they are technically not voting directly for presidential candidates. Instead, voters within each state are choosing among slates of electors selected by each state's party leadership and pledged, if elected, to support that party's presidential candidate. In each state, the slate that wins casts all the state's electoral votes for its party's candidate. Each state is entitled to a number of electoral votes equal to the number of the state's senators and representatives combined, for a total of 535 electoral votes for the fifty states. Occasionally, an elector breaks his or her pledge and votes for the other party's candidate. For example, in 1976, when the Republicans carried the state of Washington, one Republican elector from that state refused to vote for Gerald Ford, the Republican presidential nominee. Many states have now enacted statutes formally binding electors to their pledges, but some constitutional authorities doubt whether such statutes are enforceable.

In each state, the electors whose slate has won proceed to the state's capital on the Monday following the second Wednesday in December and formally cast their ballots. These are sent to Washington, tallied by the Congress in January, and the name of the winner is formally announced. If no candidate receives a majority of all electoral votes, the names of the top three candidates would be submitted to the House, where each state would be able to cast one vote. Whether a state's vote would be decided by a majority, plurality, or some other fraction of the state's delegates would be determined under rules established by the House.

In 1800 and 1824, the electoral college failed to produce a majority for any candidate. In the election of 1800, Thomas Jefferson, the Jeffersonian Republican Party's presidential candidate, and Aaron Burr, that party's vice presidential candidate, received an equal number of votes in the electoral college, throwing the election into the House of Representatives. (The Constitution at that time made no distinction between presidential and vice presidential candidates, specifying only that the individual receiving a majority of electoral votes would be named president.) Some members of the Federalist Party in Congress suggested that they should seize the opportunity to damage the Republican cause by supporting Burr and denying Jefferson the presidency. Federalist leader Alexander Hamilton put a stop to this mischievous notion, however, and made certain that his party supported Jefferson. Hamilton's actions enraged Burr and helped lead to the infamous duel between the two men, in which Hamilton was killed. The Twelfth Amendment, ratified in 1804, was designed to prevent a repetition of such an inconclusive election by providing for separate electoral college votes for president and vice president.

In the 1824 election, four candidates—John Quincy Adams, Andrew Jackson, Henry Clay, and William H. Crawford—divided the electoral vote; no one of them received a majority. The House of Representatives eventually chose Adams over the others, even though Jackson had won more electoral and popular votes. After 1824, the two major political parties had begun to dominate presidential politics to such an extent that by December of each election year, only two candidates remained for the electors to choose between, thus ensuring that one would receive a majority. This freed the parties and the candidates from having to plan their campaigns to culminate in Congress, and Congress very quickly ceased to dominate the presidential selection process.

On all but two occasions since 1824, the electoral vote has simply ratified the nationwide popular vote. Since electoral votes are won on a state-by-state basis, it is mathematically possible for a candidate who receives a nationwide popular plurality to fail to carry states whose electoral votes would add up to a majority. Thus, in 1876, Rutherford B. Hayes was the winner in the electoral college despite receiving fewer popular votes than his rival, Samuel Tilden. In 1888, Grover Cleveland received more popular votes than Benjamin Harrison, but received fewer electoral votes.

The possibility that in some future election the electoral college will, once again, produce an outcome that is inconsistent with the popular vote has led to many calls for the abolition of this institution and the introduction of some form of direct popular election of the president. Ross Perot's 1992 candidacy, for example, at one point opened the possibility of a discrepancy between the popular and electoral totals, and even raised the specter of an election decided in the House of Representatives. Efforts to introduce such a reform, however, are usually blocked by political forces that believe they benefit from the present system. For example, minority groups that are influential in large urban states with many electoral votes feel that their voting strength would be diminished in a direct, nationwide, popular election. At the same time, some Republicans believe that their party's usual presidential strength in the South and the West gives them a distinct advantage in the electoral college. There is little doubt, however, that an election resulting in a discrepancy between the electoral and popular outcomes would create irresistible political pressure to eliminate the electoral college and introduce direct popular election of the president.

Election Campaigns

➤ What are the steps in a successful election campaign?

A **campaign** is an effort by political candidates and their supporters to win the backing of donors, political activists, and voters in their quest for political office. Campaigns precede every primary and general election. Because of the complexity of the campaign process, and because of the amount of money that candidates must raise, presidential campaigns usually begin almost two years before the November presidential elections. The campaign for any office consists of a number of steps (see Figure 9.6). Candidates must first organize groups of supporters who will help them raise funds and bring their name to the attention of the media and potential donors. This step is relatively easy for a candidate currently in the office. The current office-holder is called an **incumbent**. Incumbents usually are already well known and have little difficulty attracting supporters and contributors, unless of course they have been subject to damaging publicity while in office.

ADVISERS

The next step in a typical campaign involves recruiting advisers and creating a formal campaign organization (see Figure 9.7). Most candidates, especially for national or statewide office, will need a campaign manager, a media consultant, a pollster, a financial adviser, and a press spokesperson, as well as a

Bob Dole's campaign staff surrounds him before he goes on stage for a debate during the 1996 New Hampshire primary.

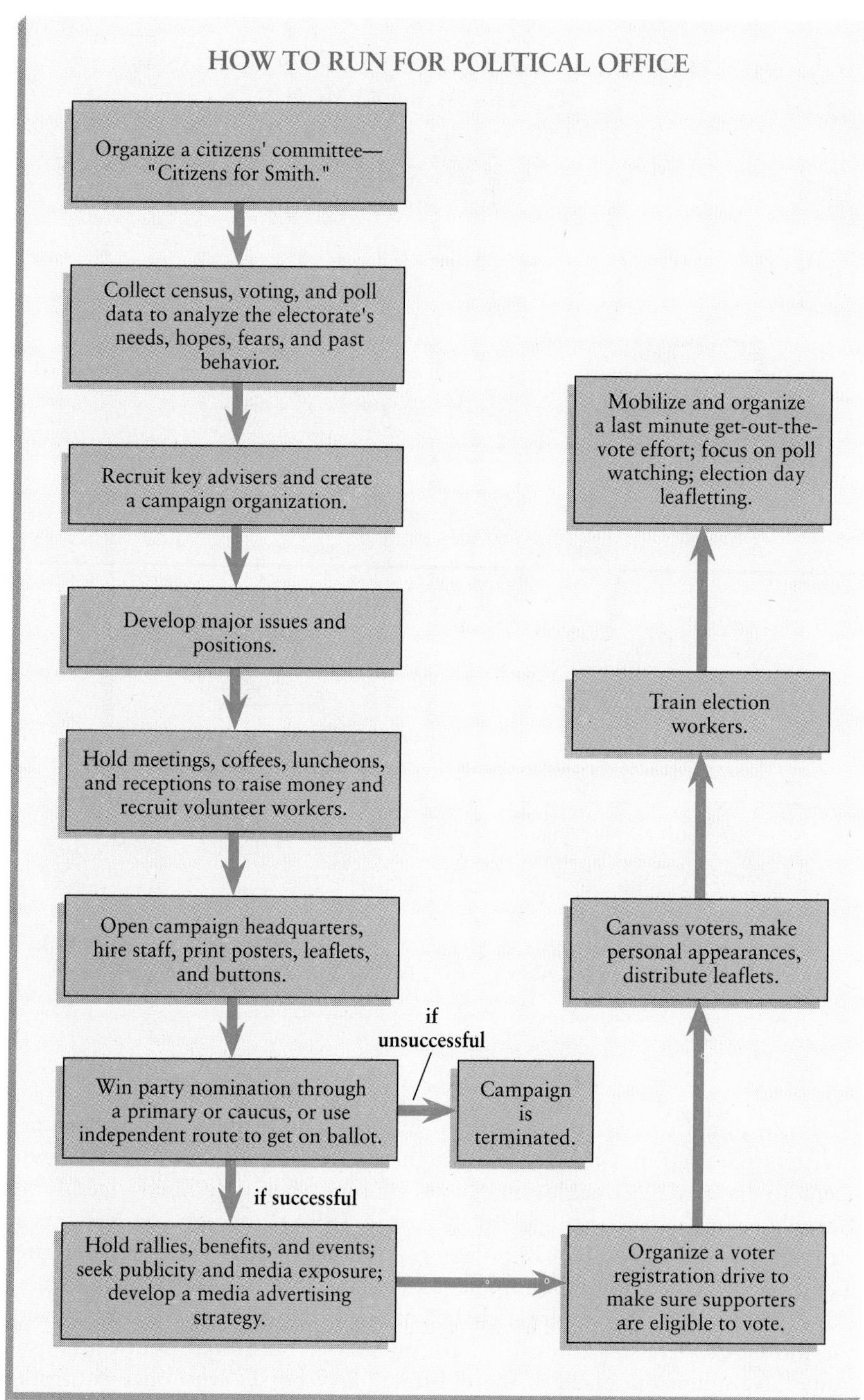

FIGURE 9.6

staff director to coordinate the activities of volunteer and paid workers. For a local campaign, candidates generally need hundreds of workers. State-level campaigns call for thousands of workers, and presidential campaigns require tens of thousands of workers throughout the nation.

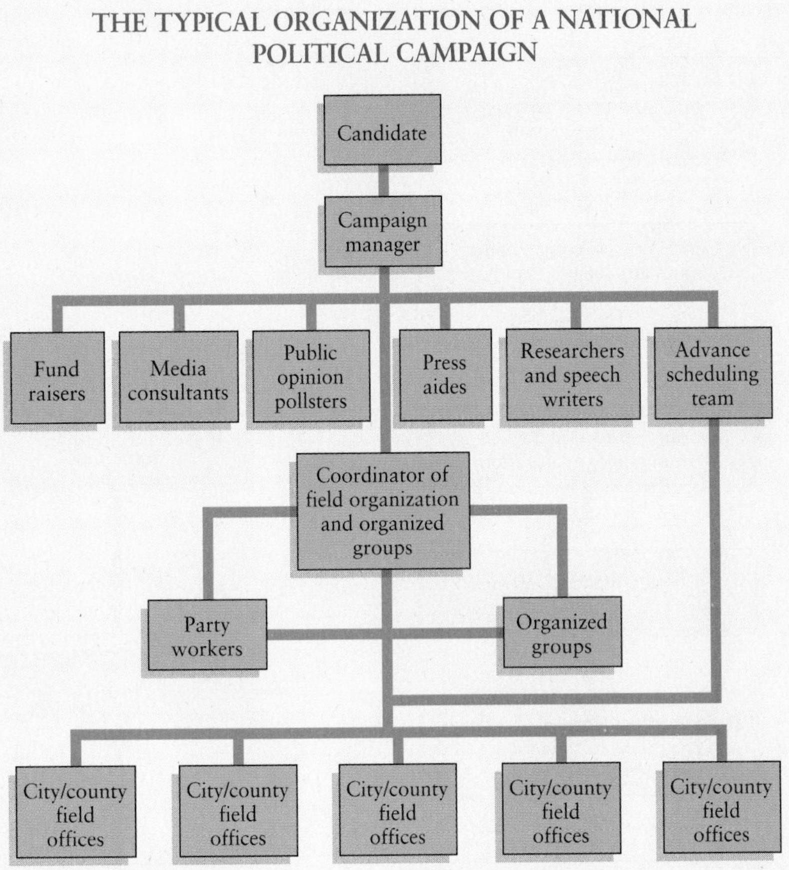

FIGURE 9.7

THE TYPICAL ORGANIZATION OF A NATIONAL POLITICAL CAMPAIGN

Candidate

Campaign manager

Fund raisers

Media consultants

Public opinion pollsters

Press aides

Researchers and speech writers

Advance scheduling team

Coordinator of field organization and organized groups

Party workers

Organized groups

City/county field offices

City/county field offices

City/county field offices

City/county field offices

City/county field offices

SOURCE: L. Sandy Maisel, *Parties and Elections in America*, 2nd ed. (New York: McGraw-Hill, 1993), p. 190. Copyright © 1993, McGraw-Hill. Used with permission.

Professional campaign workers, including the managers, consultants, and pollsters required in a modern campaign, prefer to work for candidates who seem to have a reasonable chance of winning. For individuals like James Carville, who helped manage Bill Clinton's 1992 campaign, or Republican strategists Roger Ailes and Bob Teeter, politics is a profession and repeated associations with winning campaigns are the route to professional success. Candidates seen as having little chance of winning often have difficulty hiring the most experienced professional consultants. Professional political consultants have taken the place of the old-time party bosses who once controlled political campaigns. Most consultants who direct campaigns specialize in politics, although some are drawn from the ranks of corporate advertising and may work with commercial clients in addition to politicians. Campaign consultants conduct public opinion polls, produce television commercials, organize direct-mail campaigns, and develop the issues and advertising messages the candidate will use to mobilize support.

AMERICAN POLITICAL CULTURE

Race and Representation

"No taxation without representation!" From the Boston Tea Party forward, the demand for political representation has been at the heart of American ideals of democratic governance. Every major advance of American democracy—Andrew Jackson's overthrow of the "King Caucus," the Fifteenth Amendment guaranteeing blacks the right to vote, the Nineteenth Amendment extending the right to vote to women—has also broadened the range of interests able to seek just representation. But what is "just" representation? In a political system based on majority rule, how can a minority be assured that its views will be listened to? And how can efforts to accommodate minorities be reconciled with the need to protect the no-less-important rights of majorities?

Tension between majorities and minorities over how to achieve fair representation in American government is as old as the Republic. Today Americans take for granted the compromises hammered out at the constitutional convention in Philadelphia. But it is important to realize that this solution to the problem of representation in the national legislature was a political compromise rather than the fulfillment of some ideal of perfect representation. In fact, every actual scheme of translating citizens' wishes into electoral outcomes distorts those wishes, emphasizing some and silencing others. It is in this context that we should understand contemporary debates about race and representation in America.

The century-long legacy of the abandonment of Reconstruction after the Civil War was the disenfranchisement of African Americans in the South. Finally, with the Voting Rights Act of 1965, the federal government took a major step to increase African Americans' electoral representation. The act's two major provisions prohibited states from denying anyone the right to vote on the basis of race, and required southern states to gain approval from the federal government before making any changes in voting procedures or electoral districts. The act's constitutionality was immediately challenged; in finding it constitutional in 1966, Supreme Court Chief Justice Earl Warren defended it but acknowledged the controversy over its intrusive means: "The Court has recognized that exceptional conditions can justify legislative measures not otherwise appropriate."[1]

Since 1965, the issue of how the federal government should protect the voting rights of African Americans has become more complex. The heart of the matter is that the more African Americans' voting power is concentrated in particular electoral districts, the less they are represented in other districts. Is a system that gives minorities a few token seats in the legislature, but denies them a significant role in affecting most elections, fair? No clear principles have emerged about what "fair" means when it comes to representation for minorities in America. Traditionalists argue that all concessions to racial-bloc voting threaten to fragment a system based on local, geographically distinct majorities. Critics of traditional voting methods argue that some form of proportional representation is the only fair way to give minorities an adequate voice in legislatures.

Current law exacerbates the widespread confusion. A 1982 amendment to the Voting Rights Act removed the need to prove deliberate discrimination in order to find a scheme of representation unfair, but also said that the law could not be read as guaranteeing a right to proportional representation. The Supreme Court, despite repeated rulings in voting rights cases, has yet to clarify the standards that should guide efforts to achieve just representation. Today it is clear what most Americans want: just representation, but also a move away from acknowledging race as a politically relevant fact. Can both be attained at the same time? Is the present widespread desire for color-blind representation a fulfillment, at last, of American ideals—or an abandonment by an arrogant majority of the push for equality?

[1]*South Carolina v. Katzenbach*, 383 U.S. 301 (1966).

Together with their advisers, candidates must begin serious fund-raising efforts at an early stage in the campaign. To have a reasonable chance of winning a seat in the House of Representatives, a candidate may need to raise more than $500,000. To win a Senate seat, a candidate may need ten times that much. We will look in more detail at the sources of political money later in this chapter.

POLLING

Another important element of a campaign is polling. To be competitive, a candidate must collect voting and poll data to assess the electorate's needs, hopes, fears, and past behavior. Polls are conducted throughout most political campaigns. Surveys of voter opinion provide the basic information that candidates and their staffs use to craft campaign strategies—i.e., to select issues, to assess their own strengths and weaknesses as well as those of the opposition, to check voter response to the campaign, and to measure the degree to which various constituent groups may be responsive to campaign appeals. The themes, issues, and messages that candidates present during a campaign are generally based upon polls and smaller face-to-face sessions with voters, called "focus groups." In the 1992 presidential campaign, Bill Clinton's emphasis on the economy, exemplified by the campaign staff's slogan "It's the economy, stupid," was based on the view that the economy was the chief concern among American voters. In preparation for the 1996 campaign, Clinton adopted a strategy of "triangulation" based upon consultant Richard Morris's interpretation of poll data. Morris advised Clinton that he would win the most votes by positioning himself between liberal Democrats and conservative Republicans, in a sense forming the apex of a triangle.[9] In recent years, pollsters have become central figures in most national campaigns and some have continued as advisers to their clients after they win the election. For example, Stanley Greenberg was Bill Clinton's chief pollster in the 1992 presidential campaign and was an influential adviser during the first two years of the Clinton presidency.

THE PRIMARIES

For many candidates, the next step in a campaign is the primary election. In the case of all offices but the presidency, state and local primary elections determine which candidates will receive the major parties' official nominations. Of course, candidates can run for office without the Democratic or Republican nomination. In most states, however, independent and third-party candidates must obtain many thousands of petition signatures to qualify for the general election ballot. This requirement alone discourages most independent and third-party bids. More important, most Americans are reluctant to vote for candidates other than those nominated by the two major parties. Thus most of the time, a major party nomination is a necessary condition for electoral success. For some lucky candidates, the primary election is *pro forma*. Some popular incumbents coast to victory without having to face a serious challenge. In most major races, however, candidates can expect to compete in a primary election.

Caucus chairperson Charles Richardson gathers ballots from Republican Party members in Runnells, Iowa, during the 1996 caucus.

There are essentially two types of primary contests: the personality clash and the ideological, or factional, struggle. In the first category are primaries that simply represent competing efforts by ambitious individuals to secure election to office. In 1994, for example, six Republicans vied for the Republican Party's nomination for governor of Tennessee. All six candidates claimed to be conservative, and they had similar positions on most issues. The race was eventually won by Bill Frist, who went on to victory in the November election. This type of primary can be very healthy for a political party because it can enhance interest in the campaign and can produce a nominee with the ability to win the general election.

The second type of primary—the ideological struggle—can have different consequences. Ideological struggles usually occur when one wing of a party decides that an incumbent is too willing to compromise or too moderate in his or her political views. For example, in 1992, President George Bush was challenged for the Republican presidential nomination by conservative columnist Pat Buchanan. Buchanan charged Bush with being too willing to compromise conservative principles. Such ideological challenges not only reveal rifts within a party coalition, but the friction and resentment they cause can undermine a party's general election chances. In 1968, for example, primary struggles between liberal and moderate Democrats left such a bitter taste that many liberals sat out the general election.

Ideological struggles can also produce candidates who are too liberal or too conservative to win the general election. Primary electorates are much smaller and tend to be ideologically more extreme than the general electorate: Democratic primary voters are somewhat more liberal than the general electorate, and Republican primary voters are typically more conservative than the general electorate. Thus, the winner of an intra-party ideological struggle may prove too extreme for the general election. In 1994, for example, arch-conservative Oliver North won the Virginia Republican senatorial primary over a moderate opponent, but was drubbed in the general election. Many moderate Republicans, including Virginia's other senator, John Warner, refused to support North.

Presidential Elections

- How is the president elected?
- What factors have the greatest impact on a general election campaign?

Although they also involve primary elections, the major party presidential nominations follow a pattern that is quite different from the nominating process employed for other political offices. In some years, particularly when an incumbent president is running for re-election, one party's nomination may not be contested. If, however, the Democratic or Republican presidential nomination *is* contested, candidates typically compete in primaries or presidential nominating caucuses in all fifty states, attempting to capture national convention delegates. Most states use primary elections to choose the delegates for national conventions. A few states use the **caucus**, a nominating process that begins with precinct-level meetings throughout the state. Some caucuses, called **open caucuses**, are open to anyone wishing to attend. Other states use **closed caucuses**, open only to registered party members. Citizens attending the caucuses typically elect delegates to statewide conventions at which delegates to the national party conventions are chosen.

The primaries and caucuses usually begin in February of a presidential election year and end in June (see Figure 9.8). The early ones are most important because they can help front-running candidates secure media attention and financial support. Gradually, the primary and caucus process has become "front loaded," with states vying with one another to increase their political influence by holding their nominating processes first. Traditionally, the New Hampshire primary and the Iowa caucuses are considered the most important of the early events, and candidates spend months courting voter support in these two states. A candidate who performs well in Iowa and New Hampshire will usually be able to secure support and better media coverage for subsequent races. A candidate who fares badly in these two states may be written off as a loser.

As noted in Chapter 8, the Democratic Party requires that state presidential primaries allocate delegates on the basis of **proportional representation**; Democratic candidates win delegates in rough proportion to their percentage of the primary vote. The Republican Party does not require proportional representation, but most states have now written proportional representation requirements into their election laws. A few states use the **winner-take-all system,** by which the candidate with the most votes wins all the party's delegates in that state.

When the primaries and caucuses are concluded, it is usually clear which candidates have won their parties' nominations. Yet one major step remains before the nomination is actually awarded: the national party convention.

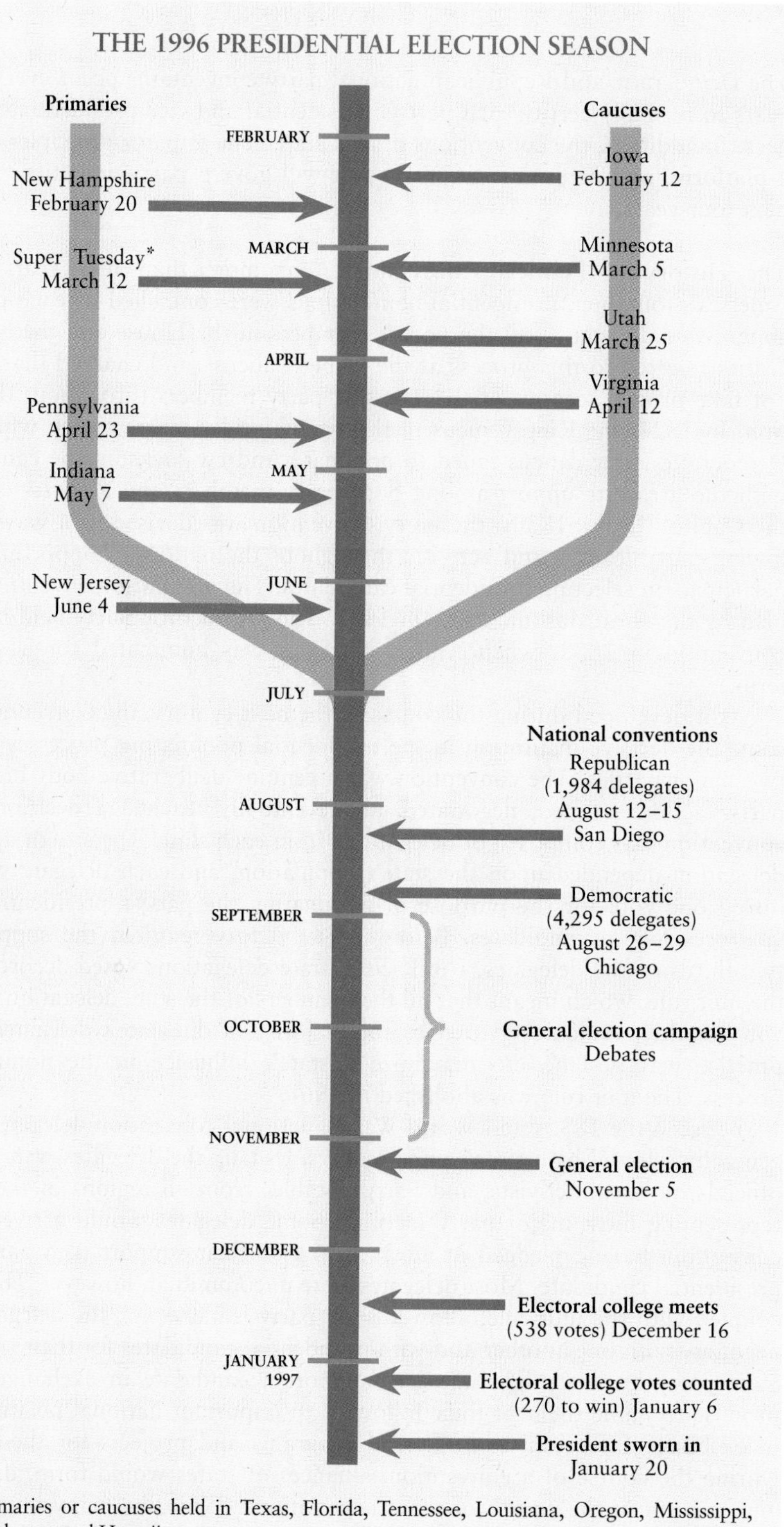
THE 1996 PRESIDENTIAL ELECTION SEASON
Primaries
Caucuses
FEBRUARY
Iowa
February 12
New Hampshire
February 20
MARCH
Minnesota
March 5
Super Tuesday*
March 12
Utah
March 25
APRIL
Virginia
April 12
Pennsylvania
April 23
Indiana
May 7
MAY
New Jersey
June 4
JUNE
JULY
National conventions
Republican
(1,984 delegates)
August 12–15
San Diego
AUGUST
Democratic
(4,295 delegates)
August 26–29
Chicago
SEPTEMBER
OCTOBER
General election campaign
Debates
NOVEMBER
General election
November 5
DECEMBER
Electoral college meets
(538 votes) December 16
JANUARY
1997
Electoral college votes counted
(270 to win) January 6
President sworn in
January 20
*Primaries or caucuses held in Texas, Florida, Tennessee, Louisiana, Oregon, Mississippi, Oklahoma, and Hawaii.

FIGURE 9.8

THE CONVENTION

The Democratic and Republican national party conventions occur every four years to formally certify each party's presidential and vice presidential nominees. In addition, the conventions draft a statement of party principles called a **platform,** and determine the rules that will govern party activities for the next four years.

The History of Political Conventions For more than fifty years after America's founding, presidential nominations were controlled by each party's congressional caucus—all the party's members in the House and the Senate. Critics referred to this process as the "King Caucus" and charged that it did not take proper account of the views of party members throughout the nation. In 1824, the King Caucus method came under severe attack when the Democratic Party caucus failed to nominate Andrew Jackson, the candidate with the greatest support among both party members and activists outside the Capitol. In the 1830s, the party convention was devised as a way of allowing party leaders and activists throughout the nation an opportunity to participate in selecting presidential candidates. The first party convention was held by the Anti-Masonic Party in 1831. The Democratic Party held its first convention in 1832, when Andrew Jackson was nominated for a second term.

As it developed during the course of the next century, the convention became the decisive institution in the presidential nominating processes of the two major parties. The convention was a genuine deliberative body in which party factions argued, negotiated, and eventually reached a decision. The convention was composed of delegations from each state. The size of a state's delegation depended upon the state's population, and each delegate was allowed one vote for the purpose of nominating the party's presidential and vice presidential candidates. Before 1936, victory required the support of two-thirds of the delegates. Until 1968, state delegations voted according to the **unit rule,** which meant that all the members of the state delegation would vote for the candidate favored by the majority of the state's delegates. This practice was designed to maximize a state's influence in the nominating process. The unit rule was abolished in 1968.

Between the 1830s and World War II, national convention delegates were generally selected by a state's party leaders. Usually the delegates were public officials, political activists, and party notables from all regions of the state, representing most major party factions. Some delegates would arrive at the convention having pledged in advance to give their support to a particular presidential candidate. Most delegates were uncommitted, however. This fact, coupled with the unit rule, allowed state party leaders (i.e., the delegates) to negotiate with one another and with presidential candidates for their support. State party leaders might agree to support a candidate in exchange for a promise to name them or their followers to important national positions, or in exchange for promises of federal programs and projects for their state. During the course of a convention, alliances of states would form, dissolve, and re-form in the course of tense negotiations. Typically, many votes were needed before the nomination could be decided. Often, deadlocks developed between the most powerful party factions, and state leaders would be forced to find a compromise, or "dark-horse," candidate. Among the more famous dark-horse nominees were James Polk in 1844 and Warren Harding in 1920. Although he was virtually unknown, Polk won the Democratic nomination when it became clear that none of the more established candidates could win. Similarly, Harding, another political unknown, won his nomination after the major candidates had fought one another to a standstill.

In its day, the convention was seen as a democratic reform. In later years, however, new generations of reformers came to view the convention as a symbol of rule by party leaders. The convention also strengthened the independence and power of the presidency, by taking the nominating process out of the hands of Congress.

Contemporary Party Conventions Whereas the traditional party convention was a deliberative assembly, the contemporary convention acts more to ratify than to determine the party's presidential and vice presidential nominations. Today, as we saw earlier in this chapter, the nomination is actually determined in a series of primary elections and local party caucuses held in virtually all fifty states during several months prior to the convention. These primaries and caucuses determine how each state's convention delegates will vote. Candidates now arrive at the convention knowing who has enough delegate support in hand to assure a victory in the first round of balloting. State party leaders no longer serve as power brokers, and the party's presidential and vice presidential choices are made relatively quickly.

Even though the party convention no longer controls presidential nominations, it still has a number of important tasks. The first of these is the adoption of party rules concerning such matters as convention delegate selection and future presidential primary elections. In 1972, for example, the Democratic convention accepted rules requiring convention delegates to be broadly representative of the party's membership in terms of race and gender. After those rules were passed, the convention refused to seat several state delegations that were deemed not to meet this standard.

Another important task for the convention is the drafting of a party platform—a statement of principles and pledges around which the delegates can unite. Although the two major parties' platforms tend to contain many similar principles and platitudes, differences between the two platforms can be significant. In recent years, for example, the Republican platform has advocated tax cuts and taken strong positions on such social issues as affirmative action and abortion. The Democratic platforms, on the other hand, have focused on the important of maintaining welfare and regulatory programs. A close reading of both parties' platforms can reveal some of the ideological differences between the parties.

Convention Delegates Today, convention **delegates** are generally political activists with strong positions on social and political issues. Generally, Republican delegates tend to be more conservative than Republican voters as a whole, whereas Democratic delegates tend to be more liberal than the majority of Democratic voters. In states such as Michigan and Iowa, local party caucuses choose many of the delegates who will actually attend the national convention. In most of the remaining states, primary elections determine how a state's delegation will vote, but the actual delegates are selected by state

Delegates at the 1996 Democratic National Convention cheered after Bill Clinton's acceptance speech.

party officials. Delegate votes won in primary elections are apportioned to candidates on the basis of proportional representation. Thus a candidate who received 30 percent of the vote in the California Democratic primary would receive roughly 30 percent of the state's delegate votes at the party's national convention.

As was mentioned earlier in this chapter, the Democratic Party requires that a state's convention delegation be representative of that state's Democratic electorate in terms of race, gender, and age. Republican delegates, by contrast, are more likely to be male and white. The Democrats also reserve slots for elected Democratic Party officials, called **superdelegates**. All the Democratic governors and about 80 percent of the party's members of Congress now attend the national convention as delegates.

Convention Procedure Each party convention lasts several days. The convention usually begins with the selection of party committees, including the credentials, rules, and platform committees, and the election of a temporary convention chairperson. This individual normally delivers a keynote address highlighting the party's appeals and concerns. After all the delegates have been seated by the credentials committee, a permanent chair is elected. This person presides over the presidential and vice presidential nominations, the adoption of a party platform, and any votes on rules that are proposed by the rules committee.

Although the actual presidential nomination is effectively decided before the convention, the names of a number of candidates are generally put in nomination and speeches made on their behalf at the convention. To be nominated is considered an honor, and ambitious politicians are eager for the media attention, however brief, that such a nomination brings.

All the nominating speeches, as well as speeches by party notables, are carefully scrutinized by the mass media, which report and analyze the major events of the convention. In the 1950s and 1960s, the television networks provided "gavel-to-gavel" coverage of the Democratic and Republican national conventions. Today, however, the major television networks carry convention highlights only. Because the parties are eager to receive as much media coverage as possible, they schedule convention events in order to reach large television audiences. The parties typically try to present the actual presidential nomination and the nominee's acceptance speech during prime viewing time, normally between 8:00 and 11:00 P.M. on a weeknight. Often, however, these plans are thwarted. In 1988, for example, Democratic candidate Michael Dukakis was not formally nominated until well after midnight; most television viewers had already gone to bed. Some analysts believed this hurt Dukakis's campaign. In other cases, nominating speeches and other convention addresses have used strident rhetoric that many television viewers have seen as ideologically extremist. In 1992, the Republican cause was damaged when several convention speakers called for "culture wars" against their liberal opponents. Similarly, in 1964, Republican presidential candidate Barry Goldwater's speech accepting his nomination seemed to defend political extremism. This speech helped to undermine Goldwater's electoral chances. Intensive media coverage of the national conventions has allowed voters an opportunity to see the ideological makeup of each party, as well as the differences between the two major parties.

After the nominating speeches are concluded, the voting begins. The names of the states are called alphabetically and the state delegation's vote reported by its chairperson. During this process, noisy and colorful demonstrations are staged in support of the nominees. When the nomination is formally decided, a lengthy demonstration ensues, with bands and colorful balloons celebrating the conclusion of the process. The party's vice presidential candidate is usually nominated the next day. This individual is almost always selected by the presidential nominee, and the choice is merely ratified by the convention. After the nominations have been settled and most other party business has been resolved, the presidential and vice presidential nominees deliver acceptance speeches. These speeches are opportunities for the nominees to begin their formal campaigns on a positive note, and the speeches are usually carefully crafted to make as much of an impression on the electorate as possible.

The General Election

For those candidates lucky enough to survive the nominating process, the last hurdle is the general election. There are essentially two types of general election in the United States today. The first type is the organizationally driven, labor-intensive election. In general, local elections and many congressional races fall into this category. Candidates campaign in such elections by recruiting large numbers of volunteer workers to hand out leaflets and organize rallies. The candidates make appearances at receptions, community group meetings, and local events, and even in shopping malls and on busy street corners. Generally, local and congressional campaigns depend less upon issues and policy proposals and more upon hard work designed to make the candidate more visible than his or her opponent.

Statewide campaigns, some congressional races, and, of course, the national presidential election fall into the second category: the media-driven, capital-intensive electoral campaign. This type of campaign requires vast amounts of money to fuel its efforts. These campaigns also make use of volunteers and organization and candidate appearances. The main technique of these more visible campaigns, however, is to use the broadcast media to present the electorate with themes and issues that will induce them to support one candidate over another. Extensive use of radio and television has become the hallmark of the modern statewide or national political campaign. One commonly used broadcast technique is the fifteen-, thirty-, or sixty-second television **spot advertisement**, which permits a candidate's message to be delivered to a target audience before uninterested or hostile viewers can tune it out. Examples of effective spot ads include George Bush's 1988 "Willie Horton" ad, which implied that Bush's opponent, Michael Dukakis, coddled criminals, and Lyndon Johnson's 1964 "daisy girl" ad, which suggested that his opponent, Barry Goldwater, would lead the United States into nuclear war. Television spot ads are used to establish candidate name recognition, to create a favorable image of the candidate and a negative image of the opponent, to link the candidate with desirable groups in the community, and to communicate the candidate's stands on selected issues. Media campaigns generally follow the trail outlined by a candidate's polls, emphasizing issues and personal characteristics that appear important in the poll data. (See Chapter 6 for a discussion of public opinion polling.)

The "daisy girl" from Lyndon Johnson's now-famous 1964 campaign commercial. As the little girl picked petals, she counted, "1–2–3. . . ." At the same time, the voice of an announcer ominously counted "10–9–8. . . ." When the announcer reached 0, a blinding nuclear explosion was shown, with President Lyndon Johnson saying, "These are the stakes: To make a world in which all of God's children can live or go into the dark. We must either love each other or we must die."

The broadcast media are so central to modern campaigns that most of a candidate's activities are tied to media strategies. Candidates' personal appearances are timed to generate maximum television and radio coverage; those candidates who already hold public office may use their official positions to generate media interest. For example, members of Congress running for re-election or for the presidency usually schedule hearings on some topic of interest with the hope of attracting the television cameras.

The 1992 presidential campaign introduced three new media techniques: the talk show interview, the "electronic town hall meeting," and the "infomercial." Candidates used television and radio interview programs to reach the large audiences drawn to this newly popular entertainment program format. Some of these programs allow audience members to telephone the show with questions, which gives candidates a chance to demonstrate that they are interested in the views of ordinary people. The **town meeting** format allows candidates the opportunity to appear in an auditorium-like setting and interact with ordinary citizens, thus underlining the candidates' concern with the views and needs of the voters. Moreover, both the talk show appearance and the town meeting allow candidates to deliver their messages to millions of Americans without the input of journalists or commentators who might criticize or question the candidates' assertions.

The **infomercial** is a lengthy presentation, often lasting thirty minutes. Although infomercials are designed to have the appearance of news programs, they are actually presentations of a candidate's views. Independent candidate Ross Perot made frequent use of infomercials during the 1992 presidential campaign.

The most dramatic use of the broadcast media in contemporary politics is the televised candidate debate. Televised presidential debates began with the famous 1960 Kennedy-Nixon clash. Today, both presidential and vice presidential candidates hold debates, as do candidates for statewide and even local offices. Debates allow candidates to reach voters who have not fully made up their minds about the election. Moreover, debates can increase the visibility of lesser-known candidates. In 1960, John F. Kennedy's strong performance in the presidential debate was a major factor in bringing about his victory over the much-better-known Richard Nixon.

THE 1996 ELECTION

In 1996, President Bill Clinton won a solid victory in the national presidential election to become the first Democratic president re-elected for a second term since Lyndon Johnson defeated Barry Goldwater in 1964, and the first to be re-elected for a second full term since Franklin Roosevelt's 1936 landslide. Clinton won 49 percent of the popular vote and carried 31 states, for a total of 379 electoral votes. Republican challenger Bob Dole won only 41 percent of the popular vote and carried 19 states, with 159 electoral votes. Reform Party candidate Ross Perot, who had won 19 percent of the popular vote in 1992, dropped to 8 percent in 1996.

Clinton ran well in traditionally Democratic constituencies. Voters with incomes below $30,000 supported Clinton by a margin of 56 to 33 percent. By contrast, those earning more than $75,000 gave Dole their support by a 50-to-42 percent margin. Eighty-three percent of African Americans voted for Clinton. Those voters who call themselves liberals gave Clinton 78 percent of their votes. Americans who said Medicare and Social Security were their major concerns gave Clinton 67 percent of their votes. Finally, as has been the case in most recent elections, the 1996 results showed a significant "gender gap": 54 percent of women voted for Clinton, but only 44 percent of men did so.[10]

Despite Clinton's solid victory, Democratic Senate and House candidates did not fare especially well in 1996. Republicans actually gained two Senate seats to give the GOP a 55-to-45 majority in the upper chamber. In House races, Democrats gained 8 seats, falling far short of the 19 that would have been needed to recapture control of the House of Representatives. Republicans will have a 237-to-205 House majority in the 105th Congress.

Poll data suggests that some voters deliberately split their tickets in order to prevent either political party from fully controlling the government. Ironically, many voters chose Clinton in part as a reaction to Newt Gingrich and the Republican-led 104th Congress. Having decided to vote for Clinton, however, some of these individuals voted for Republican congressional candidates because they feared that a Democratic president plus a Democratic Congress would mean the enactment of expensive new federal programs.[11] Nearly one in seven, or more than 6 million voters who supported Clinton simultaneously gave their vote to a Republican congressional candidate.

Against the backdrop of a nation at peace and a robust economy, ideal conditions for re-election, Clinton demonstrated once again that he is a polished, articulate, and vigorous campaigner, particularly in front of the television cameras. Republican nominee Bob Dole, on the other hand, although he

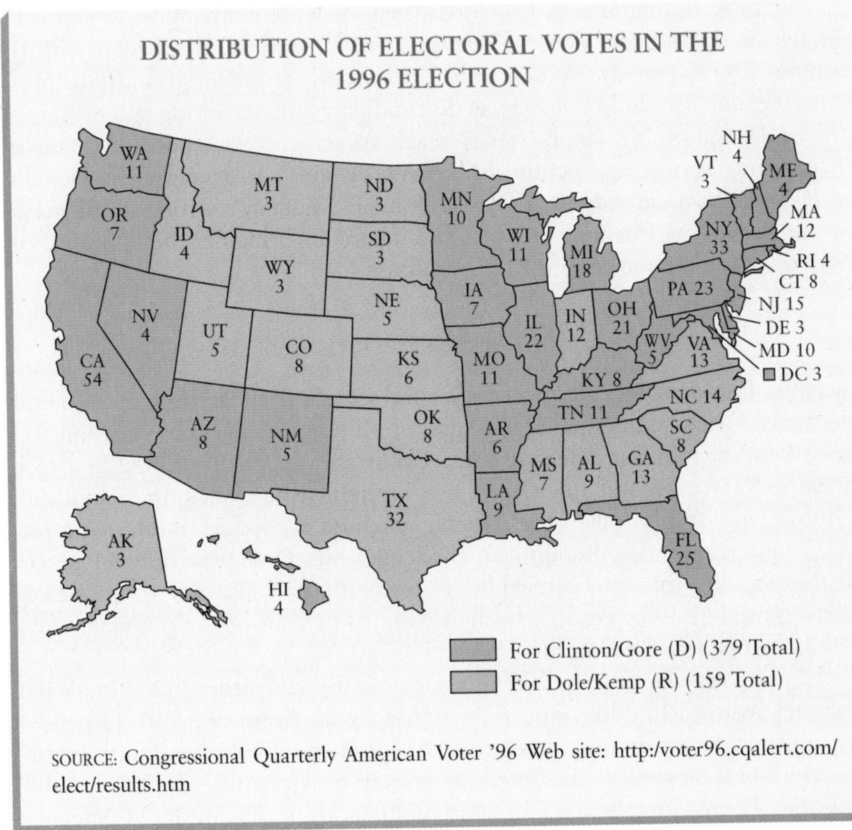

DISTRIBUTION OF ELECTORAL VOTES IN THE 1996 ELECTION

SOURCE: Congressional Quarterly American Voter '96 Web site: http:/voter96.cqalert.com/elect/results.htm

FIGURE 9.9

was an able and effective senator, seemed to lack the media savvy and public relations skills needed by a modern presidential candidate.

As recently as the summer of 1995, Clinton's chances for re-election had seemed poor. He had been widely blamed for the Democrats' loss of both houses of Congress in 1994 and had been forced to the sidelines for a while as the GOP legislative juggernaut pushed forward in 1995.[12] After the 1994 elections, however, Clinton and his advisers developed a strategy to bolster the president's political image. This strategy called for Clinton to move sharply to the political right to occupy a middle ground between liberal congressional Democrats and conservative congressional Republicans. Thus Clinton advocated a series of tax-cut initiatives (the "middle class bill of rights"), called for tough anti-crime measures, embraced the idea of voluntary school prayer, spoke out against sex and violence on television, dropped much of his opposition to Republican welfare reform proposals, and advocated "family values" in a series of public addresses.

Clinton's shift to the right outraged many of his liberal advisers. However, his strategy successfully robbed the Republicans of their most potent issues in the 1996 elections.[13] The 1995–96 budget battle in which congressional Republicans forced two partial shutdowns of federal agencies allowed Clinton to portray himself as a moderate, willing to compromise, while congressional Republicans were pilloried as militant radicals by the national media. "The most important event of 1995," said Democratic pollster Geoff Garin, "was that the Republicans vacated the center in a radical way, and President Clinton was very smart and very effective in filling the vacuum and occupying the center in American politics."[14]

★ Money and Politics

➤ How do candidates raise and spend campaign funds? How does the government regulate campaign spending? How does money affect how certain social groups achieve electoral success?

As we have just seen, modern national political campaigns are fueled by enormous amounts of money. In a national race, millions of dollars are spent on media time, as well as on public opinion polls and media consultants. In 1992, political candidates spent a total of more than $1 billion on election campaigns. The average winning candidate in a campaign for a seat in the House of Representatives spent more than $500,000; the average winner in a senatorial campaign spent $4 million.[15] The 1992 Democratic and Republican presidential candidates each received $55 million in public funds to run their campaigns, while independent candidate Ross Perot spent several million dollars of his own money to finance his presidential bid.[16] Each presidential candidate was also helped by tens of millions of dollars in so-called independent expenditures on the part of corporate and ideological political action committees (PACs). As long as such political expenditures are not formally coordinated with a candidate's campaign, they are considered to be constitutionally protected free speech and are not subject to legal limitation or even reporting requirements. Likewise, independent spending by political parties is also considered to be an expression of free speech.[17]

Federal Election Commission data suggest that approximately one-fourth of the private funds spent on political campaigns in the United States is raised through small, direct-mail contributions; about one-fourth is provided by large, individual gifts; and another fourth comes from contributions from PACs. The remaining fourth is drawn from the political parties and from candidates' personal or family resources.[18]

Direct mail serves both as a vehicle for communicating with voters and as a mechanism for raising funds. Direct mail fund raising efforts begin with the purchase or rental of computerized mailing lists of voters deemed likely to support the candidate because of their partisan ties, interests, or ideology. Candidates send out pamphlets, letters, and brochures describing their views and appealing for funds. Tens of millions of dollars are raised by national, state, and local candidates through direct mail each year, usually in $25 and $50 contributions.[19]

PACs are organizations established by corporations, labor unions, or interest groups to channel the contributions of their members into political campaigns. Under the terms of the 1971 Federal Elections Campaign Act, which governs campaign finance in the United States, PACs are permitted to make larger contributions to any given candidate than individuals are allowed to make (see Box 9.1). Individuals may donate a maximum of $1,000 to any single candidate, but a PAC may donate as much as $5,000 to each candidate. Moreover, allied or related PACs often coordinate their campaign contributions, greatly increasing the amount of money a candidate actually receives from the same interest group. As a result, PACs have become central to campaign finance in the United States. Many critics assert that PACs corrupt the political process by allowing corporations and other interests to influence politicians with large contributions. These critics call for reform of the campaign financing process. It is by no means clear, however, that PACs corrupt the political process any more than large, individual contributions.

The United States is one of the few advanced industrial nations that permit individual candidates to accept large private contributions from individual or corporate donors. Most mandate either public funding of campaigns or, as in the case of Britain, require that large private donations be made to political parties rather than to individual candidates. The logic of such a requirement is that a contribution that might seem very large to an individual candidate would weigh much less heavily if made to a national party. Thus, the chance that a donor could buy influence would be reduced.

On the basis of the Supreme Court's 1976 decision in *Buckley v. Valeo*, the right of individuals to spend their *own* money to campaign for office is a

BOX 9.1

FEDERAL CAMPAIGN FINANCE REGULATION

Campaign Contributions

No individual may contribute more than $1,000 to any one candidate in any single election. Individuals may contribute as much as $20,000 to a national party committee and up to $5,000 to a political action committee. Full disclosure is required by candidates of all contributions over $100. Candidates may not accept cash contributions over $100.

Political Action Committees

Any corporation, labor union, trade association, or other organization may establish a political action committee (PAC). PACs must contribute to the campaigns of at least five different candidates and may contribute as much as $5,000 per candidate in any given election.

Presidential Elections

Candidates in presidential primaries may receive federal matching funds if they raise at least $5,000 in each of twenty states. The money raised must come in contributions of $250 or less. The amount raised by candidates in this way is matched by the federal government, dollar for dollar, up to a limit of $5 million. In the general election, major-party candidates' campaigns are fully funded by the federal government. Candidates may spend no money beyond their federal funding. Independent groups may spend money on behalf of a candidate so long as their efforts are not directly tied to the official campaign. Minor-party candidates may get partial federal funding.

Federal Election Commission (FEC)

The six-member FEC supervises federal elections, collects and publicizes campaign finance records, and investigates violations of federal campaign finance law.

Bob Dole at a fund-raising event in New York City, part of a nationwide tour to raise money for his 1996 presidential campaign.

constitutionally protected matter of free speech and is not subject to limitation. Thus, extremely wealthy candidates often contribute millions of dollars to their own campaigns. Michael Huffington, for example, spent approximately $20 million of his own funds in an unsuccessful California Senate bid in 1994. As was noted above, "independent" spending is also free from regulation; private groups, political parties, and wealthy individuals may spend as much as they wish to help elect one candidate or defeat another, as long as these expenditures are not coordinated with any political campaign. Many business and ideological groups engage in such activities, but since they are not subject to reporting requirements, the full extent of independent spending is not known.

The Federal Elections Campaign Act also provides for public funding of presidential campaigns. As they seek a major party presidential nomination, candidates become eligible for public funds by raising at least $5,000 in individual contributions of $250 or less in each of twenty states. Candidates who reach this threshold may apply for federal funds to match, on a dollar-for-dollar basis, all individual contributions of $250 or less they receive. The funds are drawn from the Presidential Election Campaign Fund. Taxpayers can contribute $1 to this fund, at no additional cost to themselves, by checking a box on the first page of their federal income tax returns. Major party presidential candidates receive a lump sum (currently nearly $60 million) during the summer prior to the general election. They must meet all their general expenses from this money. Third-party candidates are only eligible for public funding if they received at least 5 percent of the vote in the previous presidential race. This stipulation effectively blocks pre-election funding for third-party or independent candidates, although a third party that wins more than 5 percent of the vote can receive public funding after the election. In 1980, John Anderson convinced banks to loan him money for an independent candidacy on the strength of poll data showing that he would receive more than 5 percent of the vote and thus would obtain public funds with which to repay the loans. Under current law, no candidate is required to accept public funding for either the nominating races or general presidential election. Candidates who do not accept public funding are not affected by any expenditure limits. Thus, in 1992 Ross Perot financed his own presidential bid and was not bound by the $55 million limit to which the Democratic and Republican candidates were held that year.

Over the past several years, a number of pieces of legislation have proposed additional restrictions on the private funding of campaigns. Political reform has been blocked, however, because the two major parties disagree over the form it should take. The Republicans have developed a very efficient direct-mail apparatus and would be willing to place limits on the role of PACs. The Democrats, by contrast, depend more heavily on PACs and fear that limiting their role would hurt the party's electoral chances.

Ellen Malcolm, president of EMILY's List, at a fund-raising event for the group.

The important role played by private funds in American politics affects the balance of power among contending social groups. Politicians need large amounts of money to campaign successfully for major offices. This fact inevitably ties their interests to the interests of the groups and forces that can provide this money. In a nation as large and diverse as the United States, to be sure, campaign contributors represent many different groups and often represent clashing interests. Business groups, labor groups, environmental groups, and pro-choice and right-to-life forces all contribute millions of dollars to political campaigns. Through such PACs as EMILY's List, women's groups contribute millions of dollars to women running for political office. One set of trade associations may contribute millions to win politicians' support for telecommunications reform, while another set may contribute just as much to block the same reform efforts. Insurance companies may contribute millions of dollars to Democrats to win their support for changes in the health care system, while physicians may contribute equal amounts to prevent the same changes from becoming law.

Despite this diversity of contributors, however, not all interests play a role in financing political campaigns. Only those interests that have a good deal of money to spend can make their interests known in this way. These interests are not monolithic, but they do not completely reflect the diversity of American society. The poor, the destitute, and the downtrodden also live in America and have an interest in the outcome of political campaigns. Who is to speak for them?

How Voters Decide

➤ What are the primary influences on voters' decisions?

Whatever the capacity of those with the money and power to influence the electoral process, it is the millions of individual decisions on election day that ultimately determine electoral outcomes. Sooner or later the choices of voters weigh more heavily than the schemes of campaign advisers or the leverage of interest groups.

Three types of factors influence voters' decisions at the polls: partisan loyalty, issue and policy concerns, and candidate characteristics.

PARTISAN LOYALTY

Many studies have shown that most Americans identify more or less strongly with one or the other of the two major political parties. Partisan loyalty was considerably stronger during the 1940s and 1950s than it is today. But even now most voters feel a certain sense of identification or kinship with the Democratic or Republican party. This sense of identification is often handed down from parents to children and is reinforced by social and cultural ties. Partisan identification predisposes voters in favor of their party's candidates and against those of the opposing party (see Figure 9.10). At the level of the presidential contest, issues and candidate personalities may become very important, although even here many Americans supported George Bush or Bill Clinton in the 1992 race only because of partisan loyalty. But partisanship is more likely to assert itself in the less-visible races, where issues and the candidates are not as well known. State legislative races, for example, are often decided by voters' party ties. Once formed, voters' partisan loyalties seldom change. Voters tend to keep their party affiliations unless some crisis causes them to reexamine the bases of their loyalties and to conclude that they have not given their support to the appropriate party. During these relatively infrequent periods of electoral change, millions of voters can change their party ties. For example, at the beginning of the New Deal era between 1932 and 1936, millions of former Republicans transferred their allegiance to Franklin Roosevelt and the Democrats.

FIGURE 9.10

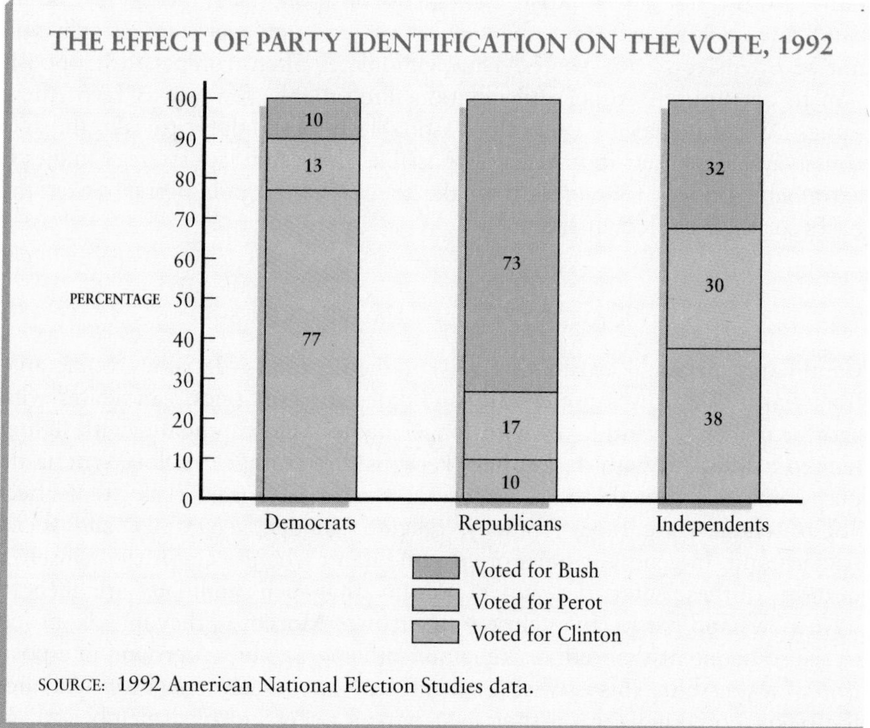

SOURCE: 1992 American National Election Studies data.

ISSUES

Issues and policy preferences are a second factor influencing voters' choices at the polls. Voters may cast their ballots for the candidate whose position on economic issues they believe to be closest to their own. Similarly, they may select the candidate who has what they believe to be the best record on foreign policy. Issues are more important in some races than others. If candidates actually "take issue" with one another, that is, articulate and publicize very different positions on important public questions, then voters are more likely to be able to identify and act upon whatever policy preferences they may have. The 1964 election, pitting conservative Republican Barry Goldwater against liberal Democrat Lyndon Johnson, was one in which each candidate vigorously promoted a perspective on the role of government and shape of national policy very different from the one asserted by his opponent. Voters elected Johnson, basing their choice on the issues. The 1980 and 1984 contests won by Ronald Reagan, the most conservative American president of the postwar period, were also very heavily issue oriented, with Reagan emphasizing tax policy, social policy, and foreign policy positions different from prior American governmental commitments. In response, many voters based their choices on issue and policy preferences. The 1992 election emphasized economic issues. Voters concerned with America's continuing economic recession and long-term economic prospects gave their support to Bill Clinton, who called for an end to Reaganomics. Efforts by Bush to inject other issues, such as "family values," into the race proved generally unsuccessful.

The ability of voters to make choices on the bases of issue or policy preferences is diminished, however, if competing candidates do not differ substantially or do not focus their campaigns on policy matters. Very often, candidates deliberately take the safe course and emphasize topics that will not be offensive to any voters. Thus, candidates often trumpet their opposition to corruption, crime, and inflation. Presumably, few voters favor these things. While it may be perfectly reasonable for candidates to take the safe course and remain as inoffensive as possible, this candidate strategy makes it extremely difficult for voters to make their issue or policy preferences the bases for their choices at the polls.

CANDIDATE CHARACTERISTICS

Candidates' personal attributes always influence voters' decisions. Some analysts claim that voters prefer tall candidates to short ones, candidates with shorter names to candidates with longer names, and candidates with lighter hair to candidates with darker hair. Perhaps these rather frivolous criteria do play some role. But the more important candidate characteristics that affect voters' choices are race, ethnicity, religion, gender, geography, and social background. In general, voters prefer candidates who are closer to themselves in terms of these categories. Voters presume that such candidates are likely to have views and perspectives close to their own. Moreover, they may be proud to see someone of their ethnic, religious, or geographic background in a position of leadership. This is why, for many years, politicians sought to "balance the ticket," making certain that their party's ticket included members of as many important groups as possible. In 1988, for example, Democratic presi-

Senator Carol Moseley-Braun, shown here meeting with shoppers at a mall in suburban Chicago during her election campaign, was elected with the overwhelming support of African American voters in Illinois. She was the first black woman elected to the U.S. Senate.

dential candidate and Massachusetts governor Michael Dukakis named Texas senator Lloyd Bentsen as his running mate to balance the ticket with a conservative southerner. George Bush, in turn, selected Dan Quayle to appeal to younger voters and ultra-conservatives.

Just as a candidate's personal characteristics may attract some voters, they may repel others. Many voters are prejudiced against candidates of certain ethnic, racial, or religious groups. And for many years voters were reluctant to support the political candidacies of women, although this appears to be changing.

Voters also pay attention to candidates' personality characteristics, such as "decisiveness," "honesty," and "vigor." In recent years, integrity has become a key election issue. During the 1992 campaign, George Bush accused Bill Clinton of seeking to mislead voters about his anti–Vietnam War activities and his efforts to avoid the draft during the 1960s. This, Bush said, revealed that Clinton lacked the integrity required of a president. Clinton, in turn, accused Bush of resorting to mudslinging because of his poor standing in the polls—an indication of Bush's own character deficiencies.

All candidates seek, through polling and other mechanisms, to determine the best image to project to the electorate. At the same time, the communications media—television in particular—exercise a good deal of control over how voters perceive candidates. During the 1992 campaign, as we saw earlier, the candidates developed a number of techniques designed to take control of the image-making process away from the media. Among the chief instruments of this "spin control" was the candidate talk-show appearance, used quite effectively by both Ross Perot and Bill Clinton.

The Decline of Voting

> ➤ Why is political participation relatively low in the United States? Have attempts to increase participation succeeded? Why or why not? What are the implications for democracy?

Despite the sound and fury of contemporary American politics, one very important fact stands out: participation in the American political process is abysmally low. Politicians in recent years have been locked in intense struggles. As we will see in Chapter 11, partisan division in Congress has reached its highest level of intensity since the nineteenth century. Nevertheless, millions of citizens have remained uninvolved. For every American who voted in the bitterly fought 1994 congressional races, for example, two stayed home.[20]

This lack of popular involvement is sometimes attributed to the shortcomings of American citizens—many millions do not go to the trouble of registering and voting. In actuality, however, low levels of popular participation in American politics are as much (or more) the fault of politicians as of voters. Even with America's personal registration rules, higher levels of political participation could be achieved if competing political forces made a serious effort to mobilize voters. Unfortunately, however, contending political forces in the United States have found ways of attacking their opponents that do not require them to engage in voter mobilization, and many prefer to use these methods than to endeavor to bring more voters to the polls. The low levels of popular mobilization that are typical of contemporary American politics are very much a function of the way that politics is conducted in the United States today.

For most of U.S. history, elections were the main arenas of political combat. In recent years, however, elections have become less effective as ways of resolving political conflicts in the United States. Today's political struggles are frequently waged elsewhere, and crucial policy choices tend to be made outside the electoral realm. Rather than engage voters directly, contending political forces rely on such weapons of institutional combat as congressional investigations, media revelations, and judicial proceedings. In contemporary America, electoral success often fails to confer the capacity to govern, and political forces, even if they lose at the polls or do not even compete in the electoral arena, have been able to exercise considerable power.

ELECTIONS AND DEMOCRACY

During the political struggles of the past decades, politicians sought to undermine the institution associated with their foes, disgrace one another on national television, force their competitors to resign from office, and in a number of cases, send their opponents to prison. Remarkably, one tactic that has not been so widely used is the mobilization of the electorate. Of course, Democrats and Republicans have contested each other and continue to contest each other in national elections. Voter turnout even inched up in 1992.

However, neither side has made much effort to mobilize *new* voters, to create strong local party organizations, or in general, to make full use of the electoral arena to defeat its enemies.

The 1993 Motor Voter bill was, at best, a very hesitant step in the direction of expanded voter participation. This act requires all states to allow voters to register by mail when they renew their driver's licenses (twenty-eight states already had similar mail-in procedures) and provides for the placement of voter registration forms in motor vehicle, public assistance, and military recruitment offices. This type of passive approach to registration still places the burden of action on the individual citizen and is not likely to result in many new voters, especially among the poor and uneducated. Since 1993, the National Voter Registration Act, as the Motor Voter bill is formally called, has added nearly 5 million new registrants to the voting rolls across the nation. Though this is a positive step, barely 10 percent of these new registrants have actually voted.[21] Mobilization requires more than the distribution of forms.[22]

It is certainly not true that politicians don't know how to mobilize new voters and expand electoral competition. Voter mobilization is hardly a mysterious process. It entails an investment of funds and organizational effort to register voters actively and bring them to the polls on election day. Occasionally, politicians demonstrate that they *do* know how to mobilize voters if they have a strong enough incentive. For example, a massive get-out-the-vote effort by Democrats to defeat neo-Nazi David Duke in the 1991 Louisiana gubernatorial election led to a voter turnout of over 80 percent of those eligible—twice the normal turnout level for a Louisiana election. And in the 1990s it was the GOP, through its alliance with conservative religious leaders, that made the more concerted effort to bring new voters into the electorate. This effort was limited in scope, but it played an important part in the Republican Party's capture of both houses of Congress in 1994. The GOP's

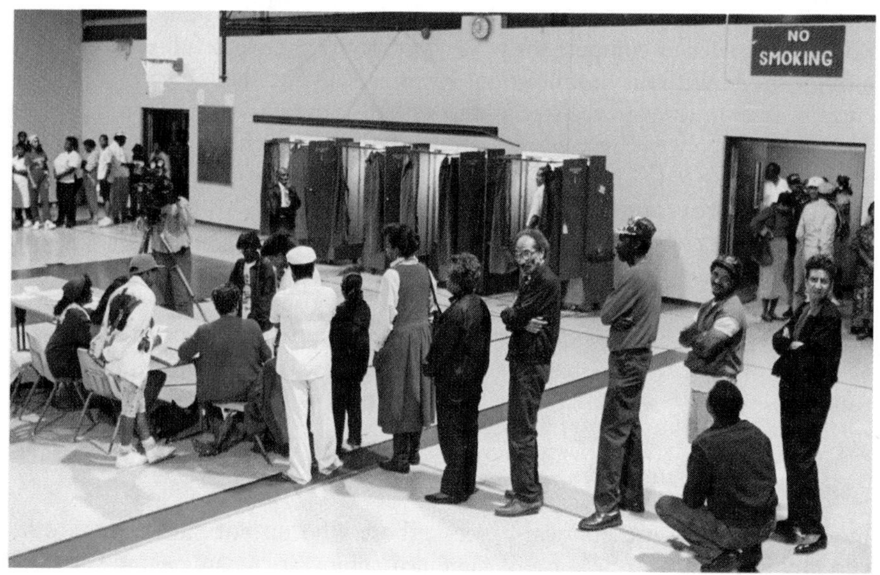

The 1991 gubernatorial race in Louisiana produced heavy voter turnout; many voters were mobilized by an anti–David Duke campaign.

gains from this limited strategy of mobilization demonstrate what could be achieved from a fuller mobilization of the national electorate.

How extraordinary, then, that politicians stop short of attempting to expand the electorate to overwhelm their foes in competitive elections. Why is this? A large part of the answer to this question is that the decline of political party organizations over the past several decades strengthened politicians in both camps who were linked with and supported by the middle and upper-middle classes. Recall from Chapter 8 that party organization is an especially important instrument for enhancing the political influence of groups at the bottom of the social hierarchy—groups whose major political resource is numbers. Parties allowed politicians to organize the energies of large numbers of individuals from the lower classes to counter the superior financial and institutional resources available to those from the middle and upper classes.

The decline of party organization that resulted, in large measure, from the efforts of upper- and middle-class "reformers" over the years has undermined politicians such as union officials and Democratic and Republican "machine" leaders who had a stake in popular mobilization, while it has strengthened politicians with an upper-middle- or upper-class base. Recall the effects of registration laws that were discussed earlier in this chapter. As a result of these reforms, today's Democratic and Republican parties are dominated by different segments of the American upper-middle class. For the most part, contemporary Republicans speak for business and professionals from the private sector, while Democratic politicians and political activists are drawn from and speak for upper-middle-class professionals in the public and not-for-profit sectors.

Both sides give lip service to the idea of fuller popular participation in political life. Politicians and their upper-middle-class constituents in both camps, however, have access to a variety of different political resources—the news media, the courts, universities, and interest groups, to say nothing of substantial financial resources. As a result, neither side has much need for or interest in political tactics that might, in effect, stir up trouble from below. Both sides prefer to compete for power without engaging in full-scale popular mobilization. Without mobilization drives that might encourage low-income citizens or minorities to register and to actually vote, the population that does vote tends to be wealthier, whiter, and better-educated than the population as a whole. Figure 9.11 shows the marked differences in voter turnout linked to ethnic group, education level, and employment status. This trend has created a political process whose class bias is so obvious and egregious that, if it continues, Americans may have to begin adding a qualifier when they describe their politics as democratic. Perhaps the terms "semi-democratic," "quasi-democratic," or "neo-democratic" are in order to describe a political process in which ordinary voters have as little influence as they do in contemporary America.

ELECTIONS AND EQUALITY

In a quasi-democratic political process, those who do not participate are inherently unequal. It is because of the quasi-democratic character of American

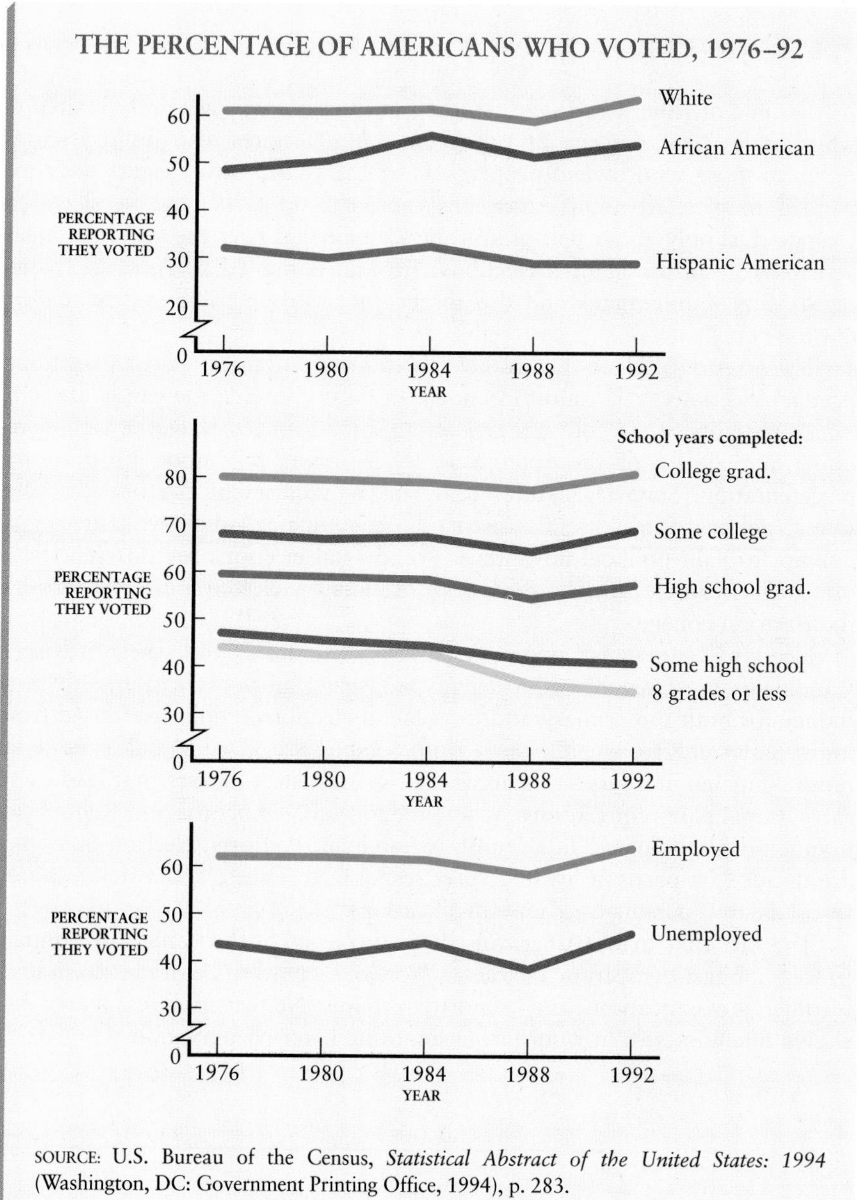

SOURCE: U.S. Bureau of the Census, *Statistical Abstract of the United States: 1994* (Washington, DC: Government Printing Office, 1994), p. 283.

FIGURE 9.11

Whether or not Americans are likely to vote depends in part upon their ethnic group, education level, and employment status.

politics that both political parties today focus more on the middle-class concerns of deficits and taxes and far less on the working-class concern of unemployment. Is it not because of these quasi-democratic politics that the two parties argue about how much to cut social programs to balance the budget while barely mentioning the various tax deductions enjoyed by upper-middle-income voters?

★ Summary

At the time of America's founding, the right to vote was generally limited to white males over the age of twenty-one. Many states also limited voting rights to those who owned property. Over the years, voting rights were expanded to give all adult Americans the right to participate in elections. Despite this, only about half of all American citizens over the age of eighteen actually vote in presidential elections. Turnout is limited by America's voter registration requirements and the absence of a strong party system to "get out the vote."

Three types of elections are held in the United States: general elections, primary elections, and runoff elections. In most contests, the candidate winning a plurality of the vote is the victor. In some contests, however, victory requires a majority of the votes cast, while others rely upon proportional representation. State legislatures draw the boundaries of electoral districts. Often, political forces use a redistricting technique called gerrymandering to attempt to gain political advantage. Presidential elections are different from other American electoral contests. The president is elected indirectly through the electoral college.

Election campaigns are directed by candidates and their advisers. Candidates must secure endorsements, construct an organization, and raise money for both the primary and the general elections. Funds are raised from individuals and from political action committees. Presidential candidates must campaign in a series of statewide primaries and caucuses that lead up to the national party conventions, where the formal Democratic and Republican nominations take place. In addition to candidates' efforts, election outcomes are decided by partisan loyalty, voter response to issues, and voter response to candidates' personalities and qualifications.

The fact that many Americans do not vote gives the American political process a quasi-democratic character. Nonvoters tend to be drawn from low-income, low-education, and minority groups. Neither political party has shown much interest in vigorously promoting voter participation.

FOR FURTHER READING

Black, Earl, and Merle Black. *The Vital South: How Presidents Are Elected.* Cambridge, MA: Harvard University Press, 1992.

Carmines, Edward G., and James Stimson. *Issue Evolution: The Racial Transformation of American Politics.* Princeton, NJ: Princeton University Press, 1988.

Fowler, Linda, and Robert D. McClure. *Political Ambition: Who Decides to Run for Congress.* New Haven, CT: Yale University Press, 1989.

Ginsberg, Benjamin, and Martin Shefter. *Politics by Other Means: Institutional Conflict and the Declining Significance of Elections in America.* New York: Basic Books, 1990.

Piven, Frances Fox, and Richard A. Cloward. *Why Americans Don't Vote.* New York: Pantheon, 1988.

Sorauf, Frank. *Inside Campaign Finance: Myths and Realities.* New Haven, CT: Yale University Press, 1992.

Tate, Katherine. *From Protest to Politics: The New Black Voters in American Elections.* Cambridge, MA: Harvard University Press, 1994.

Wilcox, Clyde. *God's Warriors: The Christian Right in Twentieth-Century America.* Baltimore: Johns Hopkins University Press, 1991.

Witt, Linda, Karen Paget, and Glenna Matthews. *Running as a Woman: Gender and Power in American Politics.* New York: Free Press, 1994.

STUDY OUTLINE

Elections in America

1. In Democratic systems, elections can be used to replace current office-holders as well as to serve as institutions of legitimation.
2. Elections also help to promote government accountability and serve as a source of protection for groups in society.
3. In the American federal system, the responsibility for organizing elections rests largely with state and local governments.
4. Throughout American history, there has been a progressive, if uneven, expansion of suffrage to groups such as African Americans, women, and youths.
5. Though the United States now has a system of universal suffrage, voter turnout continues to be low.
6. State legislators routinely seek to influence electoral outcomes by manipulating the organization of electoral districts.
7. Prior to the 1890s, voters cast ballots according to political parties. The advent of the neutral ballot allowed voters to choose individual candidates rather than a political party as a whole.
8. Americans do not vote directly for presidential candidates. Rather, they choose electors who are pledged to support a party's presidential candidate.

Election Campaigns

1. The first step in campaigning involves the organization of supporters to help the candidate raise funds and create public name recognition.
2. The next steps of campaigning involve hiring experts—campaign managers, media consultants, pollsters, etc.—to aid in developing issues and a message and communicating them to the public.
3. Because, most of the time, a major party nomination is necessary for electoral success, candidates must seek a party's nomination in primary elections.

Presidential Elections

1. Presidential candidates secure a party's nomination by running in state party primaries and caucuses.
2. Nominations of presidential candidates were first made in caucuses of a party's members of Congress. This system was replaced, in the 1830s, by nominating conventions, which were designed to be a more democratic, deliberative method of nominating candidates.
3. Contemporary conventions merely ratify a party's presidential and vice presidential nominations, although conventions still draft the party platform and adopt rules governing the party and its future conventions.
4. General elections in local races involve labor-intensive campaigns, whereas general elections in statewide and national campaigns are more capital-intensive.
5. In capital-intensive campaigns, the main technique is to use the broadcast media to present the electorate with themes and issues that will induce them to support one candidate rather than another.

Money and Politics

1. About one-fourth of campaign funds in the United States is raised through small direct mail contributions; one-fourth is provided by large gifts; one-fourth is provided by PACs; and the remainder is drawn from the political parties or candidates' personal resources.
2. Campaign finance is regulated by the Federal Elections Campaign Act of 1971.
3. The role played by private money in American politics affects the relative power of social groups. As a result, less-affluent groups have considerably less power in the political system.

How Voters Decide

1. Three factors influence voters' decisions at the polls: partisan loyalty, issues, and candidate characteristics.
2. Partisan loyalty predisposes voters in favor of their party's candidates and against those of the opposing party.
3. The impact of issues and policy preferences on electoral choice is diminished if competing candidates do not differ substantially or do not focus their campaigns on policy matters.
4. Candidates' attributes and personality characteristics always influence voters' decisions.
5. The salience of these three bases of electoral choice varies from contest to contest and from voter to voter.

The Decline of Voting

1. Participation in elections in the United States is low and relatively little effort has been made to mobilize voters because contending political forces rely less on elections to resolve political conflicts.
2. The Motor Voter bill was a hesitant step toward expanding voter participation.
3. The decline of political parties has strengthened the ties between elected leaders and members of the upper and middle classes, who tend to vote more regularly.
4. The quasi-democratic features of the American electoral system reveal its inherent inequality.

PRACTICE QUIZ

1. What is the most important different between democratic and authoritarian electoral systems?
   a. The latter do not allow the defeat of those in power.
   b. There are no elections in authoritarian systems.
   c. Democratic systems use elections as a safety valve for social discontent.
   d. Authoritarian elections are not organized by party.
2. The neutral ballot made it possible for voters to
   a. vote the party line.
   b. split-ticket vote.
   c. send clear mandates for policy change.
   d. both a and b
3. Which of the following best describes the electorate in the United States prior to the 1820s?
   a. landowning white males over the age of 21
   b. all white males
   c. all literate males
   d. "universal suffrage"
4. Which of the following negatively impacts voter turnout in the United States?
   a. registration requirements
   b. weak parties
   c. neither a nor b
   d. both a and b
5. What is the difference between an open and a closed primary?
   a. You must pay a poll tax to vote in a closed primary.
   b. Open primaries allow voters to split the ticket.
   c. In closed primaries, only registered members of a political party may vote to select that party's candidates.
   d. They are fundamentally the same thing.
6. What are the potential consequences of ideological struggles in primary contests?
   a. General election chances may be undermined.
   b. Party extremists may win the nomination.
   c. Typical party supporters may refuse to support the party's nominee.
   d. all of the above
7. What is the most fundamental change in national conventions in the twentieth century?
   a. They no longer nominate presidential candidates.
   b. Now party platforms are written at the convention.
   c. The participation of electoral officials in conventions has continued to decline.
   d. none of the above
8. Which of the following is not an example of a media technique introduced in the 1992 presidential campaign?
   a. the spot advertisement
   b. the town meeting
   c. the infomercial
   d. A, b, and c were all introduced in 1992.
9. In *Buckley v. Valeo*, the Supreme Court ruled that
   a. PAC donations to campaigns are constitutionally protected.
   b. The right of individuals to spend their own money to campaign is constitutionally protected.
   c. The political system is corrupt.
   d. The Federal Elections Campaign Act is unconstitutional.
10. Partisan loyalty
   a. is often handed down from parents to children.
   b. changes frequently.
   c. has little impact on electoral choice.
   d. is mandated in states with closed primaries.

CRITICAL THINKING QUESTIONS

1. Describe the expansion of suffrage in the United States since the founding era. Why might the government have denied participation to so many for so long? What forces have influenced the eventual expansion of voting rights? What impact has the expansion of suffrage had on political parties, elections, and governance in the United States?
2. What are the sources of campaign money in American politics? Why do candidates for public office need to raise so much money? How has the government sought to balance the competing ideals of free expression and equal representation in regard to campaign financing? Is this yet another example of a conflict between liberty and democracy?

KEY TERMS

benign gerrymandering attempts to draw district boundaries so as to create districts made up primarily of disadvantaged or underrepresented minorities. (p. 311)

campaign an effort by political candidates and their staffs to win the backing of donors, political activists, and voters in the quest for political office. (p. 316)

caucus (political) a normally closed meeting of a political or legislative group to select candidates, plan strategy, or make decisions regarding legislative matters. (p. 322)

closed caucus a presidential nominating caucus open only to registered party members. (p. 322)

closed primary a primary election in which voters can participate in the nomination of candidates, but only of the party in which they are enrolled for a period of time prior to primary day. (p. 308)

coattail effect the result of voters casting their ballot for president or governor and "automatically" voting for the remainder of the party's ticket. (p. 314)

delegates political activists selected to vote at a party's national convention. (p. 325)

electoral college the presidential electors from each state who meet after the popular election to cast ballots for president and vice president. (p. 314)

gerrymandering apportionment of voters in districts in such a way as to give unfair advantage to one political party. (p. 311)

incumbent a candidate running for a position that he or she already holds. (p. 316)

infomercial a lengthy campaign advertisement on television. (p. 328)

majority system a type of electoral system in which, to win a seat in the parliament or other representative body, a candidate must receive a majority of all the votes cast in the relevant district. (p. 309)

midterm elections congressional elections that do not coincide with a presidential election; also called *off-year elections*. (p. 303)

minority district a gerrymandered voting district that improves the chances of minority candidates by making selected minority groups the majority within the district. (p. 312)

open caucus a presidential nominating caucus open to anyone who wishes to attend. (p. 322)

open primary a primary election in which the voter can wait until the day of the primary to choose which party to enroll in to select candidates for the general election. (p. 308)

platform a party document, written at a national convention, that contains party philosophy, principles, and positions on issues. (p. 324)

plurality system a type of electoral system in which, to win a seat in the parliament or other representative body, a candidate need only receive the most votes in the election, not necessarily a majority of votes cast. (p. 309)

poll tax a state-imposed tax upon voters as a prerequisite for registration. Poll taxes were rendered unconstitutional in national elections by the Twenty-fourth Amendment, and in state elections by the Supreme Court in 1966. (p. 303)

primary elections elections used to select a party's candidate for the general election. (p. 308)

proportional representation a multiple-member district system that allows each political party representation in proportion to its percentage of the total vote. (p. 309)

referendum the practice of referring a measure proposed or passed by a legislature to the vote of the electorate for approval or rejection. (p. 309)

split-ticket voting the practice of casting ballots for the candidates of at least two different political parties in the same election. (p. 314)

spot advertisement a fifteen-, thirty-, or sixty-second television campaign commercial that permits a candidate's message to be delivered to a target audience. (p. 328)

straight-ticket voting the practice of casting ballots for candidates of only one party. (p. 314)

suffrage the right to vote; also called *franchise*. (p. 302)

superdelegate a convention delegate position, in Democratic conventions, reserved for party officials. (p. 326)

town meeting a format in which candidates meet with ordinary citizens. Allows candidates to deliver messages without the presence of journalists or commentators. (p. 328)

turnout the percentage of eligible individuals who actually vote. (p. 305)

unit rule the convention voting system under which a state delegation casts all of its votes for the candidate supported by the majority of the state's delegates. (p. 324)

winner-take-all system a system in which all of a state's presidential nominating delegates are awarded to the candidate who wins the most votes, while runners-up receive no delegates. (p. 322)

10

Groups and Interests

- ★ The Character of Interest Groups
  - Why do interest groups form?
  - What interests are represented by these groups?
  - What are the organizational components of interest groups?
  - What are the benefits of interest-group membership?
  - What are the characteristics of interest-group members?
- ★ The Proliferation of Groups
  - Why has the number of interest groups grown in recent years?
  - What is the "New Politics" movement?
- ★ Strategies: The Quest for Political Power
  - What are some of the strategies interest groups use to gain influence?
  - What are the purposes of these strategies?
- ★ Groups and Interests: The Dilemma
  - What are the problems involved in curbing the influence of interest groups?

In March 1995, about midway into the first one hundred days of the Republican 104th Congress, seven college students from Oregon met with Oregon senator Mark Hatfield, chairman of the powerful Senate Appropriations Committee, to persuade him to oppose cuts in the budget for student aid programs. Senator Hatfield, a long-standing member of the liberal wing of the Republican Party, cordially endorsed the students' goals but warned them that since the majority of Republicans in Congress were so strongly committed to the goals expressed in the Republican Contract with America and to the hundreds of billions of dollars of cuts that would be required to balance the federal budget by 2002, that the only way to protect the student aid program from complete elimination was to lobby mightily in favor of the program but to be ready to accept severe cuts in its funding. Few of the students' many sympathizers in Congress were going to be willing to go any farther than that.

Meanwhile, student rallies were held on a number of East Coast campuses. These efforts generated letters and telephone calls estimated in the thousands.[1] An entirely new group was formed, the National Association of Students in Higher Education (NASHE), to concentrate exclusively on student aid, supplementing the efforts of the established general student interest group, the United States Students Association, which was involved in a variety of policy issues apart from student aid, and which also had a reputation for being too liberal for the Republican majority in the House. As of mid-1995, NASHE had no members but was hopeful of building a foundation for itself by gaining the affiliation of already-existing campus groups and certain state-level student associations. Communication among the organizers and potential affiliates took place over the Internet. Could this be a modern version of the Committees of Correspondence that helped mobilize colonial opposition to British rule in the years prior to the Revolution? This comparison may be slightly exaggerated, especially since NASHE had still not gotten off the ground as Congress and the president were putting the final touches on the 1996 budget.

However, it is not an exaggeration to compare the 1995 student effort to citizen activities that had so impressed Alexis de Tocqueville in the 1830s. In Tocqueville's view, the genius of American democracy lay in "voluntary association." Tocqueville observed that Americans were not particularly civic-minded most of the time and were happy to go their individual ways seeking their fortunes as opportunity and imagination drove them. But, like the Minutemen of the Revolution, when a threat to their community or way of life was perceived, Americans mobilized into "voluntary associations" to engage in politics long enough to put things right. Tocqueville compared these American voluntary associations to the "permanent and compulsory associations" in European countries, which, like corporations, "centralize the direction of their forces as much as possible. . . ."[2] He saw the American version as superior in every way.

Thus our comparison is most appropriate. A few hundred college students, feeling the threat of discontinued federal assistance, set aside their books and laptop computers and formed a voluntary association to engage in politics long enough to put their demands on the government agenda. In Tocqueville's day, such a voluntary association would have focused on local and state governments. Today the focus of group activity includes the national government as well, because groups go wherever power is. The fact that the NASHE had not succeeded in organizing after nearly a year of trying does not negate the comparison—it makes it more realistic, demonstrating that in our time, and probably in the 1830s, it is simply not easy to get people to invest time and money into organization, even when ample threat or incentive is present.

The other side of Tocqueville's comparison did not stand the test of time. Even as Tocqueville wrote, there were already some "permanent associations" in the United States. The first such associations were probably the working people's associations, especially those of skilled workers, such as shoemakers, carpenters, bricklayers, etc. In Europe these associations were called guilds. The famous Carpenter Hall in Philadelphia was, after all, the meeting place of the guild, or trade association, of carpenters in the Philadelphia area. After the Civil War, the pace of group organization in America quickened. The first trade unions were formed—some of them offshoots of the guilds, and others formations of semi-skilled and unskilled workers. Farmers, despite their greater dispersion in the countryside, were quick to form highly concentrated interest groups in response to the commercialization of agriculture. Some were national associations open to all farmers, and others were "commodity associations," made up of producers of the same product—a corn association, a wheat association, and so on. Toward the end of the nineteenth century, associations of businesses were formed, largely in response to the threat they perceived from unions. These, too, were called trade associations.[3]

None of these groups were voluntary associations comparable to the Minutemen. These groups were formed as corporations, with every intention of being permanent and providing permanent services to their members. In politics they came to be called "pressure groups," "lobbies," or "interest groups," but politics was rarely the only service these groups were intended to perform. For many of these groups, politics was only an occasional activity—the occasion being a bill offered in a local, state, or federal legislature or a legal case that cut across the members' shared interests. Many of their shared interests were not political at all. But when politics did cut across their interests, these groups were prepared to address the issue; they did not have to start from scratch, the way the NASHE had to or perhaps the way the voluntary associations had to in the 1830s.

As long as freedom exists, groups like these will organize and attempt to exert their influence over the political process. And groups will form wherever power exists. It should therefore be no surprise that the most impressive growth in the number and scale of interest groups has been at the national level since the 1930s. But even as the growth of the national government leveled off in the 1970s and 1980s, and actually declined in the late 1980s and 1990s, the spread of interest groups continued. It is no longer just the expansion of the national government that spawns interest groups, but the *existence* of that government with all the power it possesses. As long as there is a powerful government in the United States, there will be a large network of interest groups around it.

During the 1992 national elections, more than four thousand special-interest groups contributed over $230 million to Democratic and Republican candidates. Many of the largest contributions came from industries whose members have extensive dealings with the federal government. Does this sea of special-interest money affect the behavior of our legislators? The answer seems to be that often it does. In June 1994, President Clinton, who previously had called for "relying less on black-tie dinners and more on brown-bag lunches" for fund raising, was criticized for hosting a $1,500-per-person black-tie dinner designed to raise $2 million for Democratic candidates.[4] The dinner, which organizers called "An American Celebration," included among its honorary co-chairs Dwayne O. Andreas, chairman of the board of the Archer Daniels Midland Company (ADM), a huge agricultural firm that is very dependent upon federal policy and very generous to both political parties. Andreas paid $100,000 for the privilege of being listed as a dinner co-chair, though he never actually attended the affair. A week later, ADM won a major political victory when the Environmental Protection Agency (EPA), with the urging of the White House, ruled that a substantial share of the gasoline sold in the United States by 1996 must contain corn-based ethanol. ADM controls 60 percent of America's ethanol production, and stood to gain millions of dollars from the EPA's decision.[5] The White House, of course, de-

Dwayne O. Andreas, chair of the Archer Daniels Midland company, is a major contributor to candidates of both major parties.

nied any connection between the contributions made by ADM and the favorable EPA ruling. (A federal appeals court struck down the EPA ruling in 1995.)

The framers of the American Constitution feared the power that could be wielded by organized interests. Yet they believed that interest groups thrived because of liberty—the freedom that all Americans enjoyed to organize and express their views. If the government were given the power to regulate or in any way to forbid efforts by organized interests to interfere in the political process, the government would in effect have the power to suppress liberty. The solution to this dilemma was presented by James Madison:

> Take in a greater variety of parties and interest [and] you make it less probable that a majority of the whole will have a common motive to invade the rights of other citizens. . . . [Hence the advantage] enjoyed by a large over a small republic.[6]

According to the Madisonian theory, a good constitution encourages multitudes of interests so that no single interest, which he called a "faction," can ever tyrannize the others. The basic assumption is that competition among interests will produce balance, with all the interests regulating each other.[7] Today, this Madisonian principle of regulation is called **pluralism.** According to pluralist theory, all interests are and should be free to compete for influence in the United States. Moreover, according to a pluralist doctrine, the outcome of this competition is compromise and moderation, since no group is likely to be able to achieve any of its goals without accommodating itself to some of the views of its many competitors.[8]

Marion Hammer, president of the National Rifle Association, speaking at its 1996 convention.

Tens of thousands of organized groups have formed in the United States, ranging from civic associations to huge nationwide groups like the National Rifle Association, whose chief cause is opposition to restrictions on gun ownership, or Common Cause, a public-interest group that advocates a variety of liberal political reforms. Despite the array of interest groups in American politics, however, we can be sure neither that all interests are represented equally nor that the results of this group competition are consistent with the common good. One criticism of interest-group pluralism is its class bias in favor of those with greater financial resources. As one critic put it, "The flaw in the pluralist heaven is that the heavenly chorus sings with a strong upper-class accent."[9] Another assumption of pluralism is that all groups have equal access to the political process and that achieving an outcome favorable to a particular group depends only upon that group's strength and resources, not upon biases inherent in the political system. But, as we shall see, group politics is a political format that has worked and continues to work more to the advantage of some types of interests than others.

In this chapter, we will examine some of the antecedents and consequences of interest-group politics in the United States. First, we will seek to understand the character of the interests promoted by interest groups. Second, we will assess the growth of interest-group activity in recent American political history, including the emergence of "public-interest" groups. Finally, we will review and evaluate the strategies that competing groups use in their struggle for influence.

The Character of Interest Groups

- ➤ Why do interest groups form?
- ➤ What interests are represented by these groups?
- ➤ What are the organizational components of interest groups?
- ➤ What are the benefits of interest-group membership?
- ➤ What are the characteristics of interest-group members?

Individuals form groups in order to increase the chance that their views will be heard and their interests treated favorably by the government. Interest groups are organized to influence governmental decisions. There are an enormous number of interest groups in the United States, and millions of Americans are members of one or more groups, at least to the extent of paying dues or attending an occasional meeting.

By representing the interests of such large numbers of people and encouraging political participation, organized groups can and do enhance American democracy. But because not all interests are represented equally, interest-group politics works to the advantage of some and the disadvantage of others.

What Interests Are Represented?

Business and Agricultural Groups Interest groups come in as many shapes and sizes as the interests they represent. When most people think about interest groups, they immediately think of groups with a direct economic interest in governmental actions. These groups are generally supported by groups of producers or manufacturers in a particular economic sector. Examples of this type of group include the National Petroleum Refiners Association and the American Farm Bureau Federation. At the same time that broadly representative groups such as these are active in Washington, specific companies, such as Shell Oil, International Business Machines, and General Motors, may be active on certain issues that are of particular concern to them.

President Bill Clinton greets members of the American Federation of State, County, and Municipal Employees.

Labor Groups Labor organizations are equally active lobbyists. The AFL-CIO, the United Mine Workers, and the Teamsters are all groups that lobby on behalf of organized labor. In recent years, groups have arisen to further the interests of public employees, the most significant among these being the American Federation of State, County, and Municipal Employees.

Professional Associations Professional lobbies like the American Bar Association and the American Medical Association have been particularly successful in furthering their members' interests in state and federal legislatures. Financial institutions, represented by organizations such as the American Bankers Association and the National Savings & Loan League, although often less visible than other lobbies, also play an important role in shaping legislative policy.

Public-Interest Groups Recent years have witnessed the growth of a powerful "public-interest" lobby purporting to represent interests whose concerns are not addressed by traditional lobbies. These groups have been most visible in the consumer protection and environmental policy areas, although public interest groups cover a broad range of issues. The National Resources Defense Council, the Union of Concerned Scientists, and Common Cause are all examples of public-interest groups.

Ideological Groups Closely related to and overlapping public-interest groups are ideological groups, organized in support of a particular political or philosophical perspective. People for the American Way, for example, promotes liberal values, whereas the Christian Coalition focuses on conservative social goals and the National Taxpayers Union campaigns to reduce the size of the federal government.

Public-Sector Groups The perceived need for representation on Capitol Hill has generated a public sector lobby in the past several years, including the National League of Cities and the "research" lobby. The latter group comprises think tanks and universities that have an interest in obtaining government funds for research and support, and it includes such institutions as Harvard University, the Brookings Institution, and the American Enterprise Institute. Indeed, universities have expanded their lobbying efforts even as they have reduced faculty positions and course offerings.[10]

ORGANIZATIONAL COMPONENTS

Ralph Nader founded an entire network of public-interest groups.

Although there are many interest groups, most share certain key organizational components. These include leadership, money, an agency or office, and members.

First, every group must have a leadership and decision-making structure. For some groups, this structure is very simple. For others, it can be quite elaborate and involve hundreds of local chapters that are melded into a national apparatus. Interest-group leadership is, in some respects, analogous to business leadership. Many interest groups are initially organized by political entrepreneurs with a strong commitment to a particular set of goals. Such entrepreneurs see the formation of a group as a means both for achieving those goals and for enhancing their own influence in the political process. Just as is true in the business world, however, successful groups often become bureaucratized; the initial entrepreneurial leadership is replaced by a paid professional staff. In the 1960s, for example, Ralph Nader led a loosely organized band of consumer advocates ("Nader's Raiders") in a crusade for product safety that resulted in the enactment of a number of pieces of legislation and numerous regulations, such as the requirement that all new cars be equipped with air bags. Today, Nader remains active in the consumer movement, and his ragtag band of raiders has been transformed into a well-organized and well-financed phalanx of interlocked groups, including Public Citizen, the Center for the Study of Responsive Law, and the Center for Science in the Public Interest, all led by professional staffs.

Members and supporters of the National Organization for Women regularly participate in rallies organized by the group. This rally was held on the Mall in Washington in 1995.

Second, every interest group must build a financial structure capable of sustaining an organization and funding the group's activities. Most interest groups rely on membership dues and voluntary contributions from sympathizers. Many also sell some ancillary services to members, such as insurance and vacation tours. Third, most groups establish an agency that actually carries out the group's tasks. This may be a research organization, a public relations office, or a lobbying office in Washington or a state capital.

Finally, all interest groups must attract and keep members. Somehow, groups must persuade individuals to invest the money, time, energy, or effort required to take part in the group's activities. Members play a larger role in some groups than in others. In **membership associations,** group members actually serve on committees and engage in projects. In the case of labor unions, members may march on picket lines, and in the case of political or ideological groups, members may participate in demonstrations and protests. In another set of groups, **"staff organizations,"** a professional staff conducts most of the group's activities; members are called upon only to pay dues and make other contributions. Among the well-known public-interest groups, some, such as the National Organization for Women (NOW), are membership groups, whereas others, such as Defenders of Wildlife and the Children's Defense Fund, are staff organizations.

The "Free Rider" Problem Whether they need individuals to volunteer or merely to write checks, both types of groups need to recruit and retain members. Yet many groups find this task difficult, even when it comes to recruiting members who agree strongly with the group's goals. Why? As economist

Mancur Olson explains, the benefits of a group's success are often broadly available and cannot be denied to nonmembers.[11] Such benefits can be called **collective goods.** This term is usually associated with certain government benefits, but it can also be applied to beneficial outcomes of interest-group activity. Following Olson's own example, suppose a number of private property owners live near a mosquito-infested swamp. Each owner wants this swamp cleared. But if one or a few of the owners were to clear the swamp alone, their actions would benefit all the other owners as well, without any effort on the part of those other owners. Each of the inactive owners would be a **free rider** on the efforts of the ones who cleared the swamp. Thus, there is a disincentive for any of the owners to undertake the job alone.

Since the number of concerned owners is small in this particular case, they might eventually be able to organize themselves to share the costs as well as enjoy the benefits of clearing the swamp. But suppose the numbers of interested people are increased. Suppose the common concern is not the neighborhood swamp but polluted air or groundwater involving thousands of residents in a region, or in fact millions of residents in a whole nation. National defense is the most obvious collective good whose benefits are shared by every resident, regardless of the taxes they pay or the support they provide. As the number of involved persons increases, or as the size of the group increases, the free rider phenomenon becomes more of a problem. Individuals do not have much incentive to become active members and supporters of a group that is already working more or less on their behalf. The group would no doubt be more influential if all concerned individuals were active members—if there were no free riders. But groups will not reduce their efforts just because free riders get the same benefits as dues-paying activists. In fact, groups may try even harder precisely because there are free riders, with the hope that the free riders will be encouraged to join in.

Why Join? Despite the free rider problem, interest groups offer numerous incentives to join. Most importantly, they make various "selective benefits" available only to group members. These benefits can be information-related, material, solidary, or purposive. Table 10.1 gives some examples of the range of benefits in each of these categories.

Informational benefits are the most widespread and important category of selective benefits offered to group members. Information is provided through conferences, training programs, and newsletters and other periodicals sent automatically to those who have paid membership dues.

Material benefits include anything that can be measured monetarily, such as special services, goods, and even money. A broad range of material benefits can be offered by groups to attract members. These benefits often include discount purchasing, shared advertising, and, perhaps most valuable of all, health and retirement insurance.

Another option identified on Table 10.1 is that of **solidary benefits.** The most notable of this class of benefits are the friendship and "networking" opportunities that membership provides. Another benefit that has become extremely important to many of the newer nonprofit and citizen groups is what has come to be called "consciousness raising." One example of this can be seen in the claims of many women's organizations that active participation

SELECTIVE BENEFITS OF INTEREST GROUP MEMBERSHIP

Category	Benefits
Informational benefits	Conferences
	Professional contacts
	Training programs
	Publications
	Coordination among organizations
	Research
	Legal help
	Professional codes
	Collective bargaining
Material benefits	Travel packages
	Insurance
	Discounts on consumer goods
Solidary benefits	Friendship
	Networking opportunities
Purposive benefits	Advocacy
	Representation before government
	Participation in public affairs

SOURCE: Adapted from Jack Walker, Jr., *Mobilizing Interest Groups in America: Patrons, Professions, and Social Movements* (Ann Arbor: University of Michigan Press, 1991), p. 86.

TABLE 10.1

conveys to each female member of the organization an enhanced sense of her own value and a stronger ability to advance individual as well as collective civil rights. A similar solidary or psychological benefit has been the mainstay of the appeal of group membership to discouraged and disillusioned African Americans since their emergence as a constitutionally free and equal people. An outward sign of the use of this kind of solidary benefit to attract members can be seen in the changes in self-designation that a group uses. Witness the progression of terminology that African Americans have used to refer to themselves since the Civil War: from "African," to "colored" (as seen in the name of the National Association for the Advancement of Colored People, founded in 1907), to "Negro," to "Negro American," to "black" (popularized with the founding of the more radical Student Nonviolent Coordinating Committee (SNCC) in the late 1960s), and, most recently, to "African American" (associated most personally with Jesse Jackson, who moved into national prominence with his famous chant, "I am somebody"). The widespread use of these various terms has been promoted by organizations seeking to attract new members through the solidary benefit of group identification.

African Americans lined up to join the NAACP during a membership drive in the 1940s.

A fourth type of benefit involves the appeal of the purpose of an interest group. The benefits of religious interest groups provide us with the best examples of such **purposive benefits.** The Protestant evangelical tradition of holding "revival" meetings to restore the faith is distinctly nonpolitical. "Render unto Caesar the things that are Caesar's" was the cry of the original

Christians to reassure the Romans that Christianity itself was nonpolitical. However, that very tradition of evangelism and revival has provided a foundation and an energy that can be funneled into effective political organizations whenever there is need to influence public policies of concern to religious interests. The so-called Christian Right is a powerful movement made up of a number of interest groups that offer virtually no material benefits to their members. The growth and success of these groups depends upon the religious identifications and affirmations of their members. Many such religiously based interest groups have arisen, especially at state and local levels, throughout American history. For example, both the abolition and the prohibition movements were driven by religious interest groups whose main attractions were non-material benefits.

Ideology itself, or the sharing of a commonly developed ideology, is another important non-material benefit. Many of the most successful interest groups of the past twenty years have been citizen groups or public-interest groups, whose members are brought together largely around shared ideological goals, including government reform, election and campaign reform, civil rights, economic equality, "family values," or even opposition to government itself.

The AARP and the Benefits of Membership One group that has been extremely successful in recruiting members and mobilizing them for political action is the American Association of Retired Persons (AARP). The AARP was founded in 1958 as a result of the efforts of a retired California high school principal, Ethel Percy Andrus, to find affordable health insurance for herself and for the thousands of members of the National Retired Teachers Association (NRTA). In 1955 she found an insurer who was willing to give NRTA members a low, group rate. In 1958, partly at the urging of the insurer (who found that insuring the elderly was quite profitable), Andrus founded the AARP. For the insurer it provided an expanded market; for Andrus it was a way to serve the ever-growing elderly population, whose problems and needs were expanding along with their numbers and their life expectancy.

A subscription to *Modern Maturity* is one of the selective benefits of membership in the AARP.

Today, the AARP is a large and powerful organization with an annual income of $382 million. In addition, the organization receives $86 million in federal grants. Its national headquarters in Washington, D.C., staffed by 1,750 full-time employees, is so large that it has its own zip code. Its monthly periodical, *Modern Maturity*, has a circulation larger than the combined circulations of *Time*, *Newsweek*, and *US News and World Report*.[12]

How did this large organization overcome the free rider problem and recruit 33 million older people as members? First, no other organization on earth has ever provided more successfully the selective benefits necessary to overcome the free rider problem. It helps that AARP began as an organization to provide affordable health insurance for aging members rather than as an organization to influence public policy. But that fact only strengthens the argument that members need short-term individual benefits if they are to invest effort in a longer-term and less concrete set of benefits. As the AARP evolved into a political interest group, its leadership also added more selective benefits for individual members. They provided guidance against consumer fraud, offered low-interest credit cards, evaluated and endorsed products that were deemed of best value to members, and provided auto insurance and a discounted mail-order pharmacy—all this and more to maintain member solidarity, even when the political goals of the leadership were of doubtful utility to the typical member. For example, during a Senate hearing in 1995, a senior, highly respected senator, Alan Simpson of Wyoming, charged that the AARP leadership had lobbied against the balanced budget amendment in 1994–95 despite general member opinion supporting the amendment.[13] An older but still more telling example was the AARP's successful lobbying for enactment of the catastrophic health-care bill for senior citizens in 1988, funded by a tax on wealthy retirees, who rebelled against the plan. According to the *Washington Post,* "the ensuing protest from some seniors was so intense that Congress repealed the law a year later."[14]

The political power of a group as large and well organized as the AARP is tremendous. AARP members can be counted on to protest whenever programs benefiting the elderly are threatened.

In a group as large as the AARP, members are bound to disagree on particular subjects, often creating serious factional disputes. And key policy makers like Senator Simpson no doubt attempt to play off one faction of the AARP against another. But the resources of the AARP are so extensive that its leadership has been able to mobilize itself for each issue of importance to the group. One of its most successful methods of mobilization for political action is the "telephone tree," with which AARP leaders can quickly mobilize thousands of members for and against proposals that affect Social Security, Medicare, and other questions of security for the aging. A "telephone tree" in each state enables the state AARP chair to phone all of the AARP district directors, who then can phone the presidents of the dozens of local chapters, who can call their local officers and individual members. Within twenty-four hours, thousands of individual AARP members can be contacting local, state, and national officials to express their opposition to proposed legislation.

It is no wonder that the AARP is respected and feared throughout Washington, D.C. But no matter how impressive a group's record of influence—and a reputation for power is almost as effective as power itself—no group can win all of the time. Moreover, a change of party control can change interest-group power drastically, as it did for the AARP and many other welfare-oriented groups when Republicans won control of Congress and the national agenda in November 1994 and sought across-the-board cuts in social spending.

The Characteristics of Members

Membership in interest groups is not randomly distributed in the population. People with higher incomes, higher levels of education, and management or professional occupations are much more likely to become members of groups than those who occupy the lower rungs on the socioeconomic ladder (see Figure 10.1).[15] Well-educated, upper-income business and professional people are more likely to have the time and the money and to have acquired through the educational process the concerns and skills needed to play a role in a group or association. Moreover, for business and professional people, group membership may provide personal contacts and access to information that can help advance their careers. At the same time, of course, corporate entities—businesses and the like—usually have ample resources to form or participate in groups that seek to advance their causes.

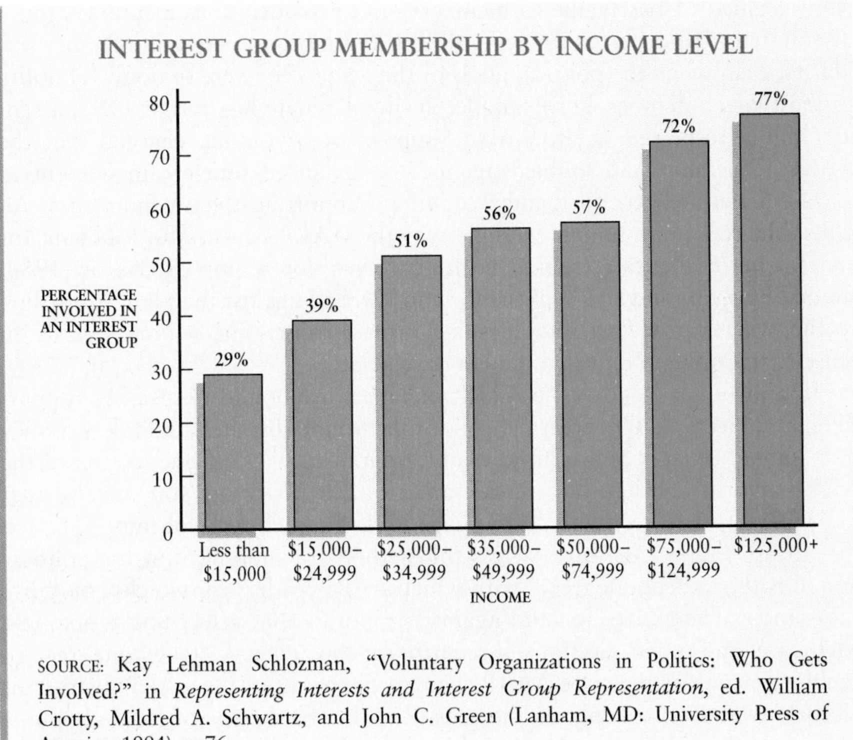

SOURCE: Kay Lehman Schlozman, "Voluntary Organizations in Politics: Who Gets Involved?" in *Representing Interests and Interest Group Representation*, ed. William Crotty, Mildred A. Schwartz, and John C. Green (Lanham, MD: University Press of America, 1994), p. 76.

FIGURE 10.1

The percentage of Americans who report that they are involved in an organization that takes a stand on political issues increases with income level.

The result is that interest-group politics in the United States tends to have a very pronounced upper-class bias. Certainly, there are many interest groups and political associations that have a working-class or lower-class membership—labor organizations or welfare-rights organizations, for example—but the great majority of interest groups and their members are drawn from the middle and upper-middle classes. In general, the "interests" served by interest groups are the interests of society's "haves." Even when interest groups take opposing positions on issues and policies, the conflicting positions they espouse usually reflect divisions among upper-income strata rather than conflicts between the upper and lower classes.

In general, to obtain adequate political representation, forces from the bottom rungs of the socioeconomic ladder must be organized on the massive scale associated with political parties. Parties can organize and mobilize the collective energies of large numbers of people who, as individuals, may have very limited resources. Interest groups, on the other hand, generally organize smaller numbers of the better-to-do. Thus, the relative importance of political parties and interest groups in American politics has far-ranging implications for the distribution of political power in the United States. As we saw in Chapter 8, political parties have declined in influence in recent years. Interest groups, on the other hand, as we shall see in the next section, have become much more numerous, more active, and more influential in American politics.

The Proliferation of Groups

> ➤ Why has the number of interest groups grown in recent years?
> ➤ What is the "New Politics" movement?

Over the past twenty-five years, there has been an enormous increase both in the number of interest groups seeking to play a role in the American political process and in the extent of their opportunity to influence that process. This explosion of interest-group activity has two basic origins—first, the expansion of the role of government during this period; and second, the coming of age of a new and dynamic set of political forces in the United States—a set of forces that have relied heavily on "public-interest" groups to advance their causes.

The Expansion of Government

Modern governments' extensive economic and social programs have powerful politicizing effects, often sparking the organization of new groups and interests. The activities of organized groups are usually viewed in terms of their effects upon governmental action. But interest-group activity is often as much a consequence as an antecedent of governmental programs. Even when national policies are initially responses to the appeals of pressure groups, government involvement in any area can be a powerful stimulus for political organization and action by those whose interests are affected. A *New York Times* report, for example, noted that during the 1970s, expanded federal regulation of the automobile, oil, gas, education, and health care industries impelled each of these interests to increase substantially its efforts to influence the government's behavior. These efforts, in turn, spurred the organization of other groups to augment or counter the activities of the first.[16] Similarly, federal social programs have occasionally sparked political organization and action on the part of clientele groups seeking to influence the distribution of benefits and, in turn, the organization of groups opposed to the programs or their cost. For example, federal programs and court decisions in such areas as abortion and school prayer were the stimuli for political action and organization by fundamentalist religious groups. Thus, the expansion of government in recent decades has also stimulated increased group activity and organization.

One contemporary example of a proposed government program that sparked intensive organization and political action by affected interests is the case of health care reform. Soon after his election, President Bill Clinton announced the formation of a health care task force charged with developing plans for a complete overhaul of the nation's medical care system. Claiming that the escalating cost of health care represented a national social and economic crisis, Clinton and other Democratic strategists also believed that the creation of a vast federal health care program would provide them with the opportunity to link major constituency groups to the Clinton administration and the Democratic Party for years to come.

In a television ad created by the Health Insurance Association of America, an organization opposed to Bill Clinton's health care reform plan, "Harry and Louise" express concerns about the plan (left). The Democratic National Committee countered with its own "Harry and Louise" ad supporting the plan (right).

While the health care plan was being formulated, major efforts were launched by various groups of physicians, hospitals, pharmaceutical and insurance companies, nurses, mental health professionals, and even chiropractors. Every group claimed to speak for the "public interest," although, curiously, each group's understanding of the public interest differed from the others in some significant detail.

The administration denounced all these special-interest activities. At one point, Clinton rejected a plea from the American Medical Association to be included in the health care reform planning process.[17] At the same time, however, the administration organized its own public relations campaign to sell health care reform to the public and to Congress. Clinton presumed (correctly) that congressional Republicans would bitterly oppose this major effort to expand the Democratic party's political base. Republicans did not accept the president's version of the public interest any more readily than he would have accepted the health care industry's corporate interests as the public interest.

THE NEW POLITICS MOVEMENT AND PUBLIC-INTEREST GROUPS

The second factor accounting for the explosion of interest-group activity in recent years has been the emergence of a new set of forces in American politics that can collectively be called the "New Politics" movement.

The **New Politics movement** is made up of upper-middle-class professionals and intellectuals for whom the Civil Rights and antiwar movements were formative experiences, just as the Great Depression and World War II had been for their parents. The crusade against racial discrimination and the Vietnam War led these young men and women to see themselves as a political force in opposition to the public policies and politicians associated with the nation's postwar regime. In more recent years, the forces of New Politics have focused their attention on such issues as environmental protection, women's rights, and nuclear disarmament.

Members of the New Politics movement constructed or strengthened public-interest groups such as Common Cause, the Sierra Club, the Environmental Defense Fund, Physicians for Social Responsibility, the National Organization for Women, and the various organizations formed by consumer activist Ralph Nader. Through these groups, New Politics forces were able to influence the media, Congress, and even the judiciary and enjoyed a remarkable degree of success during the late 1960s and early 1970s in securing the enactment of policies they favored. For example, opponents of the war in Vietnam ultimately succeeded in securing the withdrawal of American forces from that conflict, and through the War Powers Act, the Foreign Commitments Resolution, the Arms Export Control Act, and stricter scrutiny of the Central Intelligence Agency (CIA), they were able to impose limits on the president's ability to use American troops, intelligence operatives, and weapons to prop up anticommunist regimes abroad. New Politics activists also played a major role in securing the enactment of environmental, consumer, and occupational health and safety legislation.

New Politics groups sought to distinguish themselves from other interest groups—business groups, in particular—by styling themselves as **public-interest groups,** terminology which suggests that they served the general good rather than their own selfish interest. These groups' claims to represent *only* the public interest should be viewed with caution, however. Quite often, goals that are said to be in the general or public interest are also or indeed primarily in the particular interest of those who espouse them. For example, environmental controls and consumer regulations not only serve a general interest in air and water quality and public safety, they also represent a way of attacking and weakening the New Politics movement's political rivals, especially big business and organized labor, by imposing restrictions on the manner in which goods can be produced, on capital investment, and on the flow of federal resources to these interests.

Many groups regularly demonstrate at the U.S. Capitol building. Members of Greenpeace, an environmental group, are shown here protesting against proposed environmental deregulation.

Private groups have also succeeded in cloaking their particular interests in the mantle of the public interest by allying themselves with public-interest groups. One recent example is the case of cable television re-regulation. In 1987, Congress freed the cable television industry from price regulation by local governments. The result was a 61 percent increase in cable rates over the next three years. Public-interest groups, led by the Consumer Federation of America (CFA), lobbied for the enactment of federal regulations governing cable prices and policies. Their efforts, however, were defeated by the cable industry. Then, in 1991, consumer groups formed an alliance with the National Association of Broadcasters (NAB)—a powerful lobby group representing the television networks and local television stations. The NAB promised to support cable re-regulation in exchange for CFA support for a statutory provision that would require cable companies to pay local television stations for permission to transmit their programs. CBS president Laurence Tisch said that this provision would be worth one billion dollars to the broadcast industry. The NAB, in turn, mobilized the support of organized labor. Labor was willing to support the broadcasters because most television stations are unionized, whereas most cable companies are not. Gene Kimmelman, legislative director of the CFA, called the alliance with broadcasters "a deal with the devil that was not a bad deal."[18]

In 1992, the alliance of consumer groups, broadcasters, and organized labor was able to overcome the lobbying power of the cable owners to secure

THE CHRISTIAN COALITION

Issues involving morality have received increasing public attention in recent years, and many interest groups have sought to promote their vision of the proper role of government in areas where politics and morality collide. One of the most prominent of these interest groups is the Christian Coalition.

Founded by television evangelist and 1988 Republican presidential aspirant Pat Robertson in 1989, the Christian Coalition drew initial strength from Robertson's presidential campaign apparatus and from followers of his evangelical television program, *The 700 Club*. The Christian Coalition first pursued a narrow strategy, opposing abortion, pornography, and homosexuality, and supporting school prayer and other "pro-family" issues. According to the coalition's executive director, Ralph Reed, the organization's purpose is to "take back this country, one precinct at a time," in order to "see a country once again governed by Christians . . . and Christian values."[1]

Claiming about 1.7 million members, the coalition's strength derives mostly from evangelical Christians, who profess to have been "born again." Most of the leaders of the coalition are drawn from the Pentecostal sect. The largest Pentecostal church, the Assemblies of God, provided primary resources and personnel for Robertson's 1988 presidential bid.

The coalition has become an important force within the Republican Party, although it has some Democratic adherents as well. In 1992, incumbent presidential candidate George Bush gave coalition leaders and supporters control over the Republican Party platform in exchange for their support. The party's platform proved to be too extreme for many, however, and some analysts contended that the extremism demonstrated at the 1992 Republican National Convention contributed to Bush's defeat.

In an effort to broaden and soften the coalition's appeal, director Reed has pushed to widen and diversify the organization's concerns. In a 1993 interview, for example, Reed emphasized the importance of such issues as tax relief, increasing the standard income-tax deduction for children, a balanced budget amendment, and health care reform.[2] The organization is also paying more attention to such issues as crime and education. In addition, Reed has sought greater flexibility by encouraging the coalition to tone down its rhetoric and seek coalitions with other,

fice that he planned to end the military's ban on gay and lesbian soldiers. The Rev. Jerry Falwell, an evangelical leader, called upon viewers of his television program to dial a telephone number that would add their names to a petition urging Clinton to retain the ban on gays in the military. Within a few hours, 24,000 persons had called to support the petition.[43]

Grassroots lobbying campaigns have been so effective in recent years that a number of Washington consulting firms have begun to specialize in this area. Firms such as Bonner and Associates, for example, will work to generate grassroots telephone campaigns on behalf of or in opposition to important legislative proposals. Such efforts can be very expensive. Reportedly, one trade association recently paid the Bonner firm three million dollars to generate and sustain a grassroots effort to defeat a bill on the Senate floor.[44]

Has grassroots campaigning been overutilized? One story in the *New York Times* forces us to ask that question. Ten giant companies in the financial services, manufacturing, and high-tech industries began a grassroots campaign in 1992 and spent millions of dollars over the next three years to more mainstream conservative groups. Thus members have been advised to be less abrasive and less strident. Reed has also launched a campaign to broaden the group's support base, notably by seeking to recruit among religiously oriented blacks, Latinos, and Catholics. These tactics have met with limited success so far, but Reed is confident that many Americans share the views of the Christian Coalition. According to Reed, the coalition needed to broaden its appeal because "we have allowed ourselves to be ghettoized by a narrow band of issues like abortion, homosexual rights and prayer in school."[3]

At the local level, the Christian Coalition has labored to elect school board members and win control of local party organizations around the country. As many as a dozen state-level Republican Party organizations are now significantly influenced by coalition adherents. To the dismay of critics, coalition members have often won elections by fielding so-called stealth candidates who conceal their affiliation with the coalition until after winning election. This subterfuge was pursued because of the coalition's reputation for taking a narrow, extremist, and exclusionary approach to politics. Reed encountered some criticism for bragging about the success of the organization's stealth tactics.[4]

Despite these criticisms, the coalition's influence in the Republican Party is reflected by the fact that, in 1996, nearly all of the party's contenders for the presidency spoke at the coalition's annual conventions and took other actions to court the support of coalition members. Although its size may remain limited, the Christian Coalition has played the interest-group politics game with remarkable skill and sophistication.

SOURCE: Allen D. Hertzke, *Echoes of Discontent: Jesse Jackson, Pat Robertson, and the Resurgence of Populism* (Washington, DC: Congressional Quarterly Press, 1993).

[1] James M. Perry, "The Christian Coalition Crusades to Broaden Rightist Political Base," *Wall Street Journal*, July 19, 1994, p. 1.

[2] "Mobilizing the Christian Right," *Campaigns and Elections*, October/November 1993, pp. 33–36.

[3] Laurence I. Barrett, "Fighting for God and the Right Wing," *Time*, September 13, 1993, p. 58.

[4] Barrett, "Fighting for God," p. 58.

influence a decision in Congress to limit the ability of investors to sue for fraud. Retaining an expensive consulting firm, these corporations paid for the use of specialized computer software to persuade Congress that there was "an outpouring of popular support for the proposal." Thousands of letters from individuals flooded Capitol Hill. Many of those letters were written and sent by people who sincerely believed that investor lawsuits are often frivolous and should be curtailed. But much of the mail was phony, generated by the Washington-based campaign consultants; the letters came from people who had no strong feelings or even no opinion at all about the issue. More and more people, including leading members of Congress, are becoming quite skeptical of such methods, charging that these are not genuine grassroots campaigns but instead represent **"Astroturf lobbying"** (a play on the name of an artificial grass used on many sports fields). Such Astroturf campaigns have increased in frequency in recent years as members of Congress have grown more and more skeptical of Washington lobbyists and far more concerned about demonstrations of support for a particular issue by their constituents.

AMERICAN POLITICAL CULTURE

Losing Money Left and Right?

How did Coors do it? How did this large brewing company, which has annual sales of more than $1.5 billion, manage to provoke simultaneous calls for boycotts from opposite ends of the ideological spectrum—from gay and lesbian groups *and* from Christian and conservative groups? In the words of a Coors spokesperson, "We are caught between a rock and a hard place."[1] The case of the rival Coors boycotts reveals how intertwined politics, culture, and business are in American society.

The current boycott by gay and lesbian activist groups is due in part to the prominent role the Coors family has played in conservative politics. Jeffrey Coors, the nephew of the company's chairperson and brother of its chief executive officer, heads the Free Congress Foundation, a conservative group that opposes legislative efforts to define and protect the rights of homosexuals. But the gay and lesbian boycott can be traced back even further, to the 1980s, when Coors, because of its anti-union stance, was the object of a nationwide labor boycott. Many groups on the political left joined this labor boycott. Even after the labor boycott officially ended in 1987, many gay and lesbian activists refused to purchase Coors products. Despite efforts to win back their business by contributing money for AIDS research and gay community projects and conferences, Coors has remained an unpopular name in the gay community. Coors concedes it has suffered from the hostility of many gays and lesbians. "We can't tell you how much we've lost," says a Coors spokesperson, "but we know it has had an impact."

Against this background, in 1995 Coors became one of the first corporations in America to extend health care insurance and other benefits to the partners of its homosexual employees. Coors contends that this "domestic partners program" is not an attempt to win back gays and lesbians by supporting gay rights, but is instead a reflection of the company's commitment to providing equitable benefits for all its employees. Gay and lesbian groups have reacted cautiously to the company's efforts. "We are always pleased to see any company make a step in the right direction, but we have to be careful shoppers and look at the big picture," said a spokesperson for one gay rights group.

But some conservative and Christian groups have responded to Coors' policy with fury. A conservative Kansas minister trying to organize an anti-Coors campaign sent faxes to churches around the country: "The Coors family of hypocrites claim to fear God, but sponsor filthy fags!" The press secretary for Concerned Women of America, a conservative organization with more than 600,000 members, said that Coors' new domestic-partners program "legitimizes the homosexual lifestyle"—a policy anathema to the values of conservative Americans.

Can corporations like Coors avoid triggering controversies as they navigate the complex terrain of American political culture in the 1990s? Probably not. Americans are sharply divided over community moral standards, over the "right" and "wrong" of how people should live their lives. And in a capitalist economy, how people live depends in large part on the salary and benefits they derive from their jobs. Thus cultural arguments about the values that shape Americans' lives spill over, inevitably, into arguments about how corporations ought to behave.

[1] Quoted in Jay Mathews, "At Coors, A Brewing Dilemma over Gay Rights," *Washington Post,* September 16, 1995, p. A1, from which all quotations herein are taken.

But after the firms mentioned above spent millions of dollars and generated thousands of letters to members of Congress, they came to the somber conclusion that "it's more effective to have 100 letters from your district where constituents took the time to write and understand the issue," because "Congress is sophisticated enough to know the difference."[45]

Using Electoral Politics

Many interest groups decide that it is far more effective to elect the right legislators than to try to influence the incumbents through lobbying or through a changed or mobilized mass opinion. Interest groups can influence elections by two means: financial support funded through political action committees, and campaign activism.

Political Action Committees By far the most common electoral strategy employed by interest groups is that of giving financial support to the parties or to particular candidates. But such support can easily cross the threshold into outright bribery. Therefore, Congress has occasionally made an effort to regulate this strategy. Congress's most recent effort was the Federal Election Campaign Act of 1971 (amended in 1974). This act limits campaign contributions and requires that each candidate or campaign committee itemize the full name and address, occupation, and principal business of each person who contributes more than $100. These provisions have been effective up to a point, considering the rather large number of embarrassments, indictments, resignations, and criminal convictions in the aftermath of the Watergate scandal.

The Watergate scandal was triggered by the illegal entry of Republican workers into the office of the Democratic National Committee in the Watergate apartment building. But an investigation quickly revealed numerous violations of campaign finance laws, involving millions of dollars in unregistered cash from corporate executives to President Nixon's re-election committee. Many of these revelations were made by the famous Ervin Committee, whose official name and jurisdiction was the Senate Select Committee to Investigate the 1972 Presidential Campaign Activities.

Reaction to Watergate produced further legislation on campaign finance in 1974 and 1976, but the effect has been to restrict individual rather than interest-group campaign activity. Individuals may now contribute no more than $1,000 to any candidate for federal office in any primary or general election. A **political action committee** (PAC), however, can contribute $5,000, provided it contributes to at least five different federal candidates each year. Beyond this, the laws permit corporations, unions, and other interest groups to form PACs and to pay the costs of soliciting funds from private citizens for the PACs.

Electoral spending by interest groups has been increasing steadily despite the flurry of reform following Watergate. Table 10.3 presents a dramatic picture of the growth of PACs as the source of campaign contributions. The dollar amounts for each year reveal the growth in electoral spending. The number of PACs has also increased significantly—from 480 in 1972 to more

TABLE 10.3

PAC SPENDING, 1977–94

Years	Contributions
1977–78 (est.)	$ 77,800,000
1979–80	131,153,384
1981–82	190,173,539
1983–84	266,822,476
1985–86	339,954,416
1987–88	364,201,275
1989–90	372,100,000
1991–92	402,300,000
1993–94	387,400,000

SOURCE: Federal Election Commission.

than 4,000 in 1992 (see Figure 10.4). Although the reform legislation of the early and mid-1970s attempted to reduce the influence that special interests have over elections, the effect has been almost the exact opposite. Opportunities for legally influencing campaigns are now widespread.

GOPAC, a political action committee founded by Newt Gingrich, helped many Republicans get elected to Congress in 1994.

Given the enormous costs of television commercials, polls, computers, and other elements of the new political technology (see Chapter 9), most politicians are eager to receive PAC contributions and are at least willing to give a friendly hearing to the needs and interests of contributors. It is probably not the case that most politicians simply sell their services to the interests that fund their campaigns. But there is considerable evidence to support the contention that interest groups' campaign contributions do influence the overall pattern of political behavior in Congress and in the state legislatures. Recently, for example, a lawsuit brought to light documents recording the activities of the General Electric Company's political action committee over a ten-year period. The PAC donated hundreds of thousands of dollars to congressional and senatorial campaigns for individuals who were or could be "helpful" to the company. One House member was given money because company officials felt that his help in protecting a $20 million GE project "alone justifies supporting him."[46]

PACs provide more than just the financial support that individual candidates receive. Under present federal law, there is no restriction on the amount that individuals and interests can contribute directly to the parties for voter registration, grassroots organizing, and other party activities not directly linked to a particular candidate's campaign. Such contributions, called **soft money,** allow individuals and interest groups to circumvent restrictions on campaign contributions. Critics argue that soft money contributions allow wealthy donors to have unfair influence in the political process. Perhaps this potential does exist. However, soft money also provides the national and state parties with the means to engage in voter registration and turnout drives.

In 1993, President Clinton proposed legislation designed to diminish the impact of private contributions in political campaigns. Under the Clinton

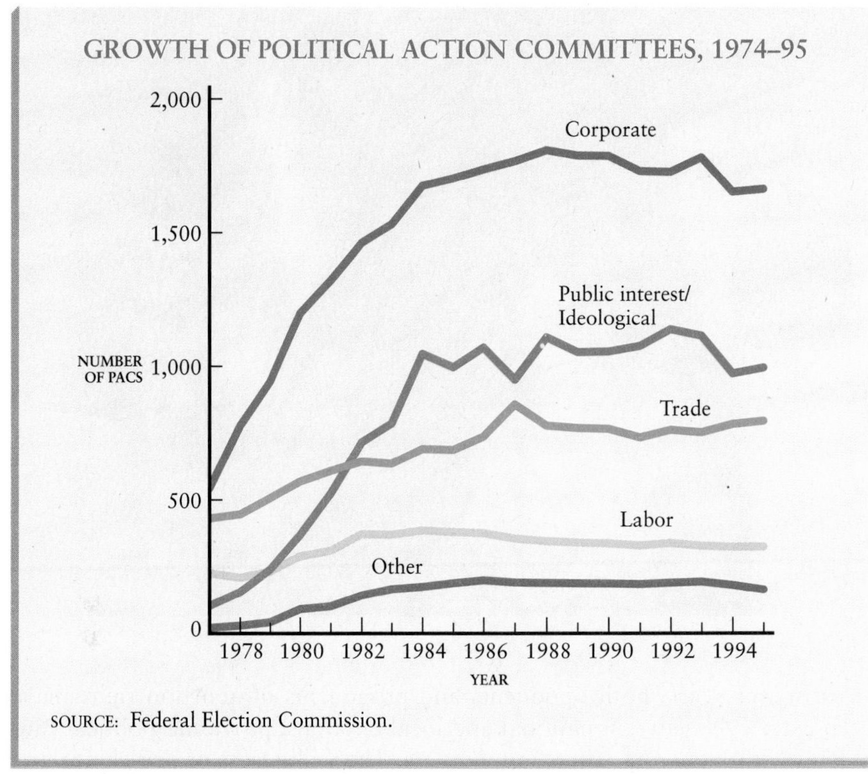

SOURCE: Federal Election Commission.

FIGURE 10.4

proposals, congressional candidates could voluntarily agree to spending limits that would, in turn, entitle them to public campaign funds. At the same time, contributions by individuals to political parties would be limited and contributions by PACs to campaigns would be curtailed. Clinton's proposal, however, was defeated in October 1994.

Forming PACs and contributing to the campaign coffers of candidates is basically a strategy of buying access. These patterns of giving draw most interest groups much closer to one or the other of the major parties.[47] Nevertheless, most PACs make it a policy to give at least some money to candidates of both parties because (1) this strategy provides a form of insurance in case a group's favorite candidate does not win; (2) a group can usually find a few sympathetic friends in either party; and (3) it helps a group maintain a public impression of nonpartisanship.

Campaign Activism Financial support is not the only way that organized groups seek influence through electoral politics. Sometimes, activism can be even more important than campaign contributions. For example, most American trade unions have been so strongly affiliated with the Democratic Party as to be presumed members. In some states, unions have provided virtually all of the members of the Democratic state organization. The powerful United Auto Workers union, for example, provided most of the workers for the Michigan Democratic Party's voter-turnout drives. African Americans have, at certain times and in certain places, been a mainstay of the Democratic Party organization.

The National Organization for Women actively supports female Democratic candidates for public office. NOW president Patricia Ireland (center) introduced Carol Moseley-Braun (at podium) at the NOW convention in 1992. Braun was later elected to the Senate.

In recent years, both opponents and proponents of abortion rights have been extremely active in national and local elections, providing political candidates with numerous campaign workers. The willingness of pro-choice and anti-abortion groups to work vigorously in election campaigns helps to explain why the issue of abortion is far more important politically than its salience in public opinion polls might suggest (see Chapter 6).

In 1992, activists on both sides campaigned hard for the election of congressional candidates who supported their positions. In House races, abortion rights activists, organized in such groups as the Planned Parenthood Federation and Voters for Choice, helped secure the election of a number of sympathetic new legislators. Some observers calculated that backers of abortion rights gained as many as twenty votes in the House of Representatives. At the same time, opponents of abortion, led by the National Right to Life Committee, were pleased to see Georgia Democratic senator Wyche Fowler defeated by his Republican opponent, Paul Coverdell, in a special runoff election. Fowler, a consistent supporter of abortion rights, had been vehemently opposed by anti-abortion forces.

Of course, abortion rights groups were especially pleased by the defeat of George Bush and the victory of Bill Clinton in the 1992 presidential contest. Since the late 1970s, Republican presidential strategy had used opposition to abortion as a way of attracting the allegiance of conservative Catholics and fundamentalist Protestants. To this end, President Bush had supported legislative restrictions on abortion, appointed federal judges known to be unfriendly to abortion, and signed a number of executive orders limiting abortion. These included the so-called gag rule prohibiting abortion counseling in federally funded family planning clinics. President Clinton, who had been strongly supported by abortion-rights forces, quickly rescinded the gag rule and other anti-abortion executive orders of the Bush administration. Abortion rights groups have pressed Clinton for the enactment of a "Freedom of Choice Act" that would outlaw most state restrictions on abortion.[48] After the Republicans won control of Congress in 1994, however, there was little chance that such legislation would be enacted.

One remarkable fact about the political activity of interest groups is how infrequently major interest groups have tried to form their own party. The fact that they have rarely done so is to a large extent attributable to the strength of the two-party tradition in the United States. But there is also a significant negative influence: the barriers erected by state laws regarding the formation of new political parties. As a consequence, significant interests such as "the working class," women, and African Americans have not been able to find clear expression in the electoral process. Their interests are always being adulterated by other interests within their chosen party. Yet this situation has a positive side: the two-party system has—unintentionally—softened social demarcations by cutting across classes, races, and other fundamental interests that deeply divide people. These interests are adulterated and softened, subduing what might otherwise become the kind of class conflict that we see so often in European history, where class, race, and ethnic interests have become radicalized when they are not forced to reconcile themselves with other interests in a broad political party.[49]

Using Bribery

The line between politics and corruption will always be difficult to draw. Most people will agree that it is better to seek power by currying favor than by using force or intimidation. When power is sought by outright purchase, however, the effect on the political system can be more demoralizing and disorienting than even the use of force.

The Washington bribery scandal Koreagate, which came to light in the late 1970s, is a case in point. Originating with Korean businessman Tong Sun Park, a web of legal and illegal favors was spun around at least two dozen members of the House and Senate. Donations went to at least three former member of Congress: $22,500 to Richard Hanna of California, and undisclosed amounts to Cornelius Gallagher of New Jersey and Otto Passman of Louisiana. The wife of Edwin Edwards, a congressman who later became governor of Louisiana, received $10,000. Other contributions included $4,650 to John Brademas of Indiana, the deputy House majority whip, and $4,000 to John McFall of California. Only a few indictments were ever handed down as a result of congressional committee and grand jury investigations, although suspicions of still more widespread and serious bribery efforts persisted. Yet, it cannot be proven that Park or the Korean government got much for their money. It may even be that Park was merely trying to buy access in illegal or suspicious ways rather than trying to pay bribes for specific favors.

Bribery is widespread in American society, but its true extent in national politics is unknown—and because of its nature is likely to remain unknown. Some say corruption from bribery is declining, and an occasional scandal like Watergate or Koreagate is proof to them that it is being exposed and rooted out. Others insist that such corruption is not declining, and they offer as evi-

INTEREST GROUP STRATEGIES

Going Public

Especially via advertising; also through boycotts, strikes, rallies, marches, and sit-ins, generating positive news coverage

Lobbying

Influencing the passage or defeat of legislation

Three types of lobbyists:

Amateur—loyal members of a group seeking passage of legislation that is currently under scrutiny

Paid—often lawyers or professionals without a personal interest in the legislation who are not full-time lobbyists

Staff—employed by a specific interest group full time for the express purpose of influencing or drafting legislation

Access

Development of close ties to decision makers on Capitol Hill

Litigation

Taking action through the courts, usually in one of three ways:

Filing suit against a specific government agency or program

Financing suits brought against the government by individuals

Filing companion briefs as *amicus curiae* (friend of the court) to existing court cases

Partisan Politics

Giving financial support to a particular party or candidate

Congress passed the Federal Election Campaign Act of 1971 to try to regulate this practice by limiting the amount of funding interest groups can contribute to campaigns

Bribery

Illegally buying the favor of public officials

Bribery is limited in the amount of influence it gains

BOX 10.1

dence the same examples! Although the dispute between optimists and pessimists cannot be resolved, a few general things can be said about bribery to keep the issue in a proper perspective.

First, bribery is probably used more often to sustain friends than to convert opposition. An offer of a bribe to a member of the opposition is extremely risky. The offer itself can be exposed, or it can be accepted with no intention of giving anything in return. The briber will certainly not bring suit for breach of contract.

Second, the offer of a bribe is frequently seen as evidence of weakness. Since bribery is risky, it tends to be used only when all other tactics have been tried and found wanting. Thus, the offer of a bribe can be counterproductive.

Third, bribery is only one of many forms of corruption, and corruption is not limited to the political realm. For example, department stores build into their prices a factor of at least 10 percent to cover losses from theft, and the Department of Commerce estimates that employees account for the major portion of inventory thefts.[50] One student of corruption in private industry estimates that theft, especially employee theft, accounts for 25 percent of all business losses.[51]

Fourth, bribery is probably limited to the narrowest of political issues: Who will get a bridge or the contract to build it? Who gets a tax break, and how much of one? How amicably and quickly can a case be settled before it gets to court or to a commission? The bigger the issue—the more public it is, the larger the number of participants, the broader its scope—the less likely it is that bribery will be employed as a strategy. With important issues, the stakes are big enough to make people want to use bribery, but they generally would not do it because there would be too many people to bribe, too much uncertainty, and too many advantages to be gained by the opposition from exposing the briber.

 Groups and Interests: The Dilemma

> ➤ What are the problems involved in curbing the influence of interest groups?

James Madison wrote that "liberty is to faction as air is to fire."[52] By this he meant that the organization and proliferation of interests was inevitable in a free society. To seek to place limits on the organization of interests, in Madison's view, would be to limit liberty itself. Madison believed that interests should be permitted to regulate themselves by competing with one another. So long as competition among interests was free, open, and vigorous, there would be some balance of power among them and no one interest would be able to dominate the political or governmental process.

There is considerable competition among organized groups in the United States. As we saw, cable television interests were recently defeated by an alliance of television networks and consumer groups after a fierce battle. Similarly, pro-choice and anti-abortion forces continue to be locked in a bitter struggle. Nevertheless, interest-group politics is not as free of bias as Madisonian theory might suggest. Though the weak and poor do occasionally become organized to assert their rights, interest-group politics is generally a form of political competition in which the wealthy and powerful are best able to engage.

Moreover, although groups sometimes organize to promote broad public concerns, interest groups more often represent relatively narrow, selfish interests. Small, self-interested groups can be organized much more easily than large and more diffuse collectives. For one thing, the members of a relatively small group—say, bankers or hunting enthusiasts—are usually able to recognize their shared interests and the need to pursue them in the political arena. Members of large and more diffuse groups—say, consumers or potential victims of firearms—often find it difficult to recognize their shared interests or the need to engage in collective action to achieve them.[53] This is why causes presented as public interests by their proponents often turn out, upon examination, to be private interests wrapped in a public mantle.

Thus, we have a dilemma to which there is no ideal answer. To regulate interest-group politics is, as Madison warned, to limit freedom and to expand governmental power. Not to regulate interest-group politics, on the other hand, may be to ignore equal justice. Those who believe that there are simple solutions to the issues of political life would do well to ponder this problem.

Summary

Interest groups are pervasive in America. James Madison predicted that special interest groups would proliferate in a free society, but that competition among them would lead to moderation and compromise. Today, this theory is called pluralism. Individuals join or form groups to enhance their influence. To succeed, groups need leadership, a financial base, and active members. Recruiting new members can be difficult because of the "free rider" problem. Interest groups overcome this problem by offering selective benefits to members only. These include information, material benefits, solidary benefits, or purposive benefits.

The number of interest groups in America has increased because of the expansion of the government into new areas. This increase has included not only economic interests, but also "public-interest" groups whose members do not seek economic gain. Both economic and public-interest groups seek influence through a variety of techniques.

Lobbying is the act of petitioning legislators. Lobbyists—individuals who receive some form of compensation for lobbying—are required to register with the House and Senate. In spite of an undeserved reputation for corruption, lobbyists serve a useful function, providing members of Congress with a vital flow of information.

Access is participation in government. Groups with access have less need for lobbying. Most groups build up access over time through great effort. They work years to get their members into positions of influence on congressional committees. Means of gaining access include corridoring in the bureaucracy, grassroots approaches, personnel-interchange approaches, and influence peddling.

Litigation sometimes serves interest groups when other strategies fail. Groups may bring suit on their own behalf, finance suits brought by individuals, or file amicus curiae briefs.

Going public is an effort to mobilize the widest and most favorable climate of opinion. Advertising is a common technique in this strategy. Other techniques are boycotts, strikes, rallies, and marches.

Groups engage in electoral politics either by embracing one of the major parties, usually through financial support, or through a nonpartisan strategy. Interest groups' campaign contributions now seem to be flowing into the coffers of candidates at a faster rate than ever before.

When all else fails, some groups try bribery. Although many believe bribery is widespread, it is nonetheless often a sign of weakness or an effort merely to sustain existing government support.

FOR FURTHER READING

Cigler, Allan J., and Burdett A. Loomis, eds. *Interest Group Politics.* Washington, DC: Congressional Quarterly Press, 1983.

Clawson, Dan, Alan Neustadtl, and Denise Scott. *Money Talks: Corporate PACs and Political Influence.* New York: Basic Books, 1992.

Costain, Anne. *Inviting Women's Rebellion: A Political Process Interpretation of the Women's Movement.* Baltimore, MD: Johns Hopkins University Press, 1992.

Day, Christine. *What Older Americans Think: Interest Groups and Aging Policy.* Princeton, NJ: Princeton University Press, 1990.

Goldfield, Michael. *The Decline of Organized Labor in the United States.* Chicago: University of Chicago Press, 1987.

Hansen, John Mark. *Gaining Access: Congress and the Farm Lobby, 1919–1981.* Chicago: University of Chicago Press, 1991.

Heinz, John P., Edward O. Laumann, Robert L. Nelson, and Robert H. Salisbury. *The Hollow Core: Private Interests in National Policy Making.* Cambridge, MA: Harvard University Press, 1993.

Lowi, Theodore J. *The End of Liberalism.* New York: Norton, 1979.

Moe, Terry M. *The Organization of Interests.* Chicago: University of Chicago Press, 1980.

Olson, Mancur, Jr. *The Logic of Collective Action: Public Goods and the Theory of Groups.* Cambridge, MA: Harvard University Press, 1971.

Olzak, Susan. *The Dynamics of Ethnic Competition and Conflict.* Stanford, CA: Stanford University Press, 1992.

Paige, Connie. *The Right-to-Lifers.* New York: Summit, 1983.

Petracca, Mark, ed. *The Politics of Interests: Interest Groups Transformed.* Boulder, CO: Westview, 1992.

Pope, Jacqueline. *Biting the Hand that Feeds Them: Women on Welfare at the Grass Roots Level.* New York: Praeger, 1989.

Schlozman, Kay Lehman, and John T. Tierney. *Organized Interests and American Democracy.* New York: Harper & Row, 1986.

Staggenborg, Suzanne. *The Pro-Choice Movement: Organization and Activism in the Abortion Conflict.* New York: Oxford University Press, 1991.

Truman, David. *The Governmental Process: Political Interests and Public Opinion.* New York: Knopf, 1951.

Vogel, David. *Fluctuating Fortunes.* New York: Basic Books, 1989.

STUDY OUTLINE

The Character of Interest Groups

1. An enormous number of diverse interest groups exists in the United States.
2. Most interest groups share key organizational components, such as mechanisms for member recruitment, financial and decision-making processes, and agencies that actually carry out group goals.
3. Interest-group politics in the United States tends to have a pronounced upper-class bias because of the characteristics of interest-group members.
4. Because of natural disincentives to join interest groups, groups offer material, solidary, and purposive benefits to entice people to join.

The Proliferation of Groups

1. The modern expansion of governmental economic and social programs has contributed to the enormous increase in the number of groups seeking to influence the American political system.
2. The second factor accounting for the explosion of interest-group activity in recent years was the emergence of a new set of forces in American politics: the New Politics movement.

Strategies: The Quest for Political Power

1. Lobbying is an effort by outsiders to influence Congress or government agencies by providing them with information about issues, giving them support, and even threatening them with retaliation.
2. Access is actual involvement and influence in the decision-making process.
3. Interest groups often turn to litigation when they lack access or feel they have insufficient influence over the formulation and implementation of public policy.
4. Going public is a strategy that attempts to mobilize the widest and most favorable climate of opinion.
5. Many groups use a nonpartisan strategy in electoral politics to avoid giving up access to one party by embracing the other.

6. Using bribery to purchase political power has a demoralizing and disorienting effect on the political system.

GROUPS AND INTERESTS: THE DILEMMA

1. The organization of private interests into groups to advance their own views is a necessary and intrinsic element of the liberty of citizens to pursue their private lives, and to express their views, individually and collectively.
2. The organization of private interests into groups is biased in favor of the wealthy and the powerful, who have superior knowledge, opportunity, and resources with which to organize.

PRACTICE QUIZ

1. The theory that competition among organized interests will produce balance with all the interests regulating one another is
   a. pluralism.
   b. elite power politics.
   c. democracy.
   d. socialism.
2. To overcome the free rider problem, groups
   a. provide general benefits.
   b. litigate.
   c. go public.
   d. provide selective benefits.
3. Politically organized religious groups often make use of
   a. material benefits.
   b. solidary benefits.
   c. purposive benefits.
   d. none of the above.
4. Which of the following best describes the reputation of the AARP in the Washington community?
   a. It is respected and feared.
   b. It is supported and well liked by all political forces.
   c. It is believed to be ineffective.
   d. It wins the political battles it fights.
5. Which types of interest groups are most often associated with the New Politics movement?
   a. public interest groups
   b. professional associations
   c. government groups
   d. labor groups
6. The military-industrial complex is an example of
   a. pluralism.
   b. public-interest politics.
   c. access politics.
   d. party politics.
7. "Corridoring" refers to
   a. lobbying the corridors of Congress.
   b. a litigation technique.
   c. lobbying the president and the White House staff.
   d. lobbying an executive agency.
8. In which of the following ways do interest groups use the courts to affect public policy?
   a. filing amicus briefs
   b. bringing suit itself
   c. financing those bringing suit
   d. all of the above
9. According to this text, what is the limit a PAC can contribute to a primary or general election campaign?
   a. $1,000
   b. $5,000
   c. $10,000
   d. $50,000
10. Which of the following is not an activity in which interest groups frequently engage?
   a. starting their own political party
   b. litigation
   c. lobbying
   d. contributing to campaigns

CRITICAL THINKING QUESTIONS

1. A dilemma is presented by the values of liberty and equality in regard to interest-group activity. On the one hand, individuals should have the liberty to organize themselves politically in order to express their views. On the other hand, there is a strong class bias in the politics of organized interests. How has the U.S. government sought to regulate group activity in order to balance these competing values? What else might government do to make group politics less biased? What are the potential consequences—both good and bad—of the actions you suggest?

2. Describe the different techniques of influence used by organized interests. When is one technique preferable to another? With the rise of the New Politics movement, different techniques are now used more frequently. Which ones? Why, do you think, are these techniques so well suited to New Politics?

KEY TERMS

access the actual involvement of interest groups in the decision-making process. (p. 366)

Astroturf lobbying a negative term used to describe group-directed and exaggerated grassroots lobbying. (p. 375)

capture an interest's acquisition of substantial influence over the government agency charged with regulating its activities. (p. 367)

collective goods benefits, sought by groups, that are broadly available and cannot be denied to nonmembers. (p. 354)

corridoring working to gain influence in an executive agency. (p. 366)

cross-lobbying a term to describe lobbyists lobbying one another. (p. 365)

free riders those who enjoy the benefits of collective goods but did not participate in acquiring them. (p. 354)

going public a strategy that attempts to mobilize the widest and most favorable climate of public opinion. (p. 372)

grassroots lobbying a lobbying campaign in which a group mobilizes its membership to contact government officials in support of the group's position. (p. 373)

institutional advertising advertising designed to create a positive image of an organization. (p. 373)

iron triangle the stable, cooperative relationship that often develops between a congressional committee, an administrative agency, and one or more supportive interest groups. (p. 366)

lobbying a strategy by which organized interests seek to influence the passage of legislation by exerting direct pressure on members of the legislature. (p. 362)

material benefits special goods, services, or money provided to members of groups to entice others to join. (p. 354)

membership associations organized groups in which members actually play a substantial role, sitting on committees and engaging in group projects. (p. 353)

military-industrial complex a concept coined by President Eisenhower, in which he referred to the threats to American democracy that may arise from too close a friendship between major corporations in the defense industry and the Pentagon. This is one example of the larger political phenomenon of the "iron triangle." (p. 368)

New Politics movement a political movement that began in the 1960s and 1970s, made up of professionals and intellectuals for whom the Civil Rights and antiwar movements were formative experiences. The New Politics movement strengthened public-interest groups. (p. 360)

pluralism the theory that all interests are and should be free to compete for influence in the government. The outcome of this competition is compromise and moderation. (p. 350)

political action committee (PAC) a private group that raises and distributes funds for use in election campaigns. (p. 377)

public-interest groups groups that claim they serve the general good rather than their own particular interest. (p. 361)

purposive benefits selective benefits of group membership that emphasize the purpose and accomplishments of the group. (p. 355)

reverse lobbying a strategy by which members of Congress bring pressure to bear on lobby groups to support particular courses of action. (p. 365)

soft money money contributed directly to political parties for voter registration and organization. (p. 378)

solidary benefits selective benefits of group membership that emphasize friendship, networking, and consciousness-raising. (p. 354)

staff organization a type of membership group in which a professional staff conducts most of the group's activities. (p. 353)

PART IV

Institutions

11

Congress

- ★ **Congress: Representing the American People**

  How does Congress represent the United States as a whole? In what ways is it not representative?

  In what specific ways do members of Congress act as agents for their constituencies?

  In what ways does the electoral system determine who is elected to Congress?

- ★ **The Organization of Congress**

  What are the basic building blocks of congressional organization? What is the role of each in forming legislation?

- ★ **Rules of Lawmaking: How a Bill Becomes a Law**

  How do the rules of congressional procedure influence the fate of legislation as well as determine the distribution of power in Congress?

- ★ **How Congress Decides**

  What sorts of influences inside and outside of government determine how members of Congress vote on legislation? How do these influences vary according to the type of issue?

- ★ **Beyond Legislation: Other Congressional Powers**

  Besides the power to pass legislation, what other powers allow Congress to influence the process of government?

- ★ **Power and Representation**

  What is the relationship between congressional power and congressional representation?

  What is the history of congressional power vis-à-vis the president?

  Can Congress be both representative and effective?

IF YOU WANT to find out what your congressional representative or senator has been doing lately, there are many ways to do so. You can watch your mailbox—most congressional offices send newsletters to constituents to report the office's activities. You can find your representative's home page on the World Wide Web. To get a sense of what is happening in Congress you can tune your television to C-SPAN; chances are that some congressional debate or committee hearing will be in progress. If you want to make your views known to your congressional representative, that is also pretty easy. You can send a postcard or a letter—the address of your representative can usually be found in the blue pages of your local telephone book. You can also call or fax his or her Washington office. The number isn't hard to get; consult your local phone book or call Washington, D.C., directory information.

Despite these many different ways people can learn about Congress and contact their representatives and senators, citizens regularly complain that Congress is "out of touch." In a 1990 poll, only 12 percent of Americans said they believed that congressional representatives "pay a good deal of attention to the people who elect them when deciding what to do in Congress." Eighty percent felt that members of Congress lost touch with their constituents soon after being elected. Congress is also the least trusted of America's national institutions.[1]

What is puzzling is that these feelings of distrust and alienation from Congress have grown stronger precisely as access to Congress and its members has increased. Most of the proceedings of Congress have been open to the public since the passage of numerous "sunshine reforms" in the 1970s; today Congress conducts very few secret hearings. Public opinion polls taken before Congress became more accessible and open showed higher levels of trust and a greater belief that citizens could influence their representatives' decisions. Why has trust in Congress dropped rather than increased as new forms of access and increased openness have been put into place?

In this chapter we shall try to understand the relationship between Congress and the American people. Congress is central to American democracy because it serves as the voice of the people and because it controls a formidable battery of powers that it uses to shape policies. To understand the pivotal role that Congress plays in American democracy, we will first examine the concept of representation, looking closely at what it means to say that Congress represents the American people. Next, we will discuss the legislative process, showing how Congress is organized and examining how Congress actually makes decisions. Finally, we will consider how representation is related to power: Does having representation mean having power?

Congress: Representing the American People

- How does Congress represent the United States as a whole? In what ways is it not representative?
- In what specific ways do members of Congress act as agents for their constituencies?
- In what ways does the electoral system determine who is elected to Congress?

Assemblies and the idea of representation have been around in one form or another for centuries. But until the eighteenth century—with the American and French revolutions—assemblies were usually means used by monarchs to gain or regain the support of local leaders. Eventually, regional lords and lesser barons, joined by the rising merchant classes, began to see the assembly as a place where they could state their case against the monarch, rather than merely receive his messages to take back to their regions. Through their efforts, the assembly was slowly converted from part of the monarch's regime to an institution that could be used against the monarchy and, later, used by the middle classes against the aristocracy. But the original function of the assembly—getting obedience through consent—never disappeared. It was simply joined by new functions. Once the assembly had evolved into a place where demands could be made, it became a "parliament"—a place where people could come together to talk. ("Parliament" is derived from the French *parler*—to talk.) The French and many other Europeans gave their national assemblies the name "parliament" because they felt that talk was the essential feature of these bodies. Although the U.S. Congress does not share that name, talk is still one of its essential ingredients, built into its very structure. Talk is facilitated by the fact that each member of the House and Senate is, in principle, equal to all the other members. Although the committee structure of Congress gives some members more power than others, a measure of equality in Congress exists by virtue of the fact that membership is determined entirely by election from districts defined as absolutely equal. Each member's primary responsibility is to the district, to his or her **constituency**, not to the congressional leadership, a party, or even Congress itself.

House and Senate: Differences in Representation

The framers of the Constitution provided for a **bicameral** legislature—that is, a legislative body consisting of two chambers. As we saw in Chapter 3, the framers intended each of these chambers, the House and Senate, to serve a different constituency. Members of the Senate, appointed by state legislatures for six-year terms, were to represent the elite members of society and to be more attuned to the interests of property than of population. Today, members of the House and Senate are elected directly by the people. The 435 members of the House are elected from districts apportioned according to population; the 100 members of the Senate are elected by state, with 2 senators from each. Senators continue to have much longer terms in office and usually represent much larger and more diverse constituencies than do their counterparts in the House (see Table 11.1).

The House and Senate play different roles in the legislative process. In essence, the Senate is the more deliberative of the two bodies—the forum in which any and all ideas can receive a thorough public airing. The House is the more centralized and organized of the two bodies—better equipped to

Table 11.1

DIFFERENCES BETWEEN THE HOUSE AND THE SENATE

	House	Senate
Minimum age of member	25 years	30 years
U.S. citizenship	at least 7 years	at least 9 years
Length of term	2 years	6 years
Number per state	Depends on population: 1 per 30,000 in 1789; now 1 per 550,000	2 per state
Constituency	Tends to be local	Both local and national

A detail from Samuel Morse's *The Old House of Representatives.* During the nineteenth century, Congress was the dominant branch of government.

play a routine role in the governmental process. In part, this difference stems from the different rules governing the two bodies. These rules give House leaders more control over the legislative process and provide for House members to specialize in certain legislative areas. The rules of the much-smaller Senate give its leadership relatively little power and discourage specialization.

Both formal and informal factors contribute to differences between the two chambers of Congress. Differences in the length of terms and requirements for holding office specified by the Constitution in turn generate differences in how members of each body develop their constituencies and exercise their powers of office. The result is that members of the House most effectively and frequently serve as the agents of well-organized local interests with specific legislative agendas—for instance, used-car dealers seeking relief from regulation, labor unions seeking more favorable legislation, or farmers looking for higher subsidies. The small size and relative homogeneity of their constituencies and the frequency with which they must seek re-election make House members more attuned to the legislative needs of local interest groups.

Senators, on the other hand, serve larger and more heterogeneous constituencies. As a result, they are somewhat better able than members of the House to serve as the agents for groups and interests organized on a statewide or national basis. Moreover, with longer terms in office, senators have the luxury of considering "new ideas" or seeking to bring together new coalitions of interests, rather than simply serving existing ones.

In recent years, the House has exhibited considerably more intense partisanship and ideological division than the Senate. Because of their diverse constituencies, senators are more inclined to seek compromise positions that will offend as few voters and interest groups as possible. Members of the House, in contrast, typically represent more homogeneous districts in which their own party is dominant. This situation has tended to make House members less inclined to seek compromises and more willing to stick to partisan and ideological guns than their counterparts in the Senate during the past several decades. This is one reason why the Senate took the lead in attempting to construct a compromise approach to health care reform during the summer of 1994, when ideological and partisan division in the House appeared to preclude any possibility of compromise. At one point, for example, Republican Whip Newt Gingrich called the Democrats' goal of universal health care coverage a recipe for a "police state."[2]

After the Republican triumph in the 1994 congressional election, Gingrich, now the Speaker of the House, showed little inclination to compromise with the Democrats. But as the 1996 elections approached, many Republicans feared being seen as a "do-nothing" Congress. In the summer of 1996, they compromised with the Democrats to raise the minimum wage and to pass modest health care reforms.[3]

Sociological vs. Agency Representation

We have become so accustomed to the idea of representative government that we tend to forget what a peculiar concept representation really is. A representative claims to act or speak for some other person or group. But how can one person be trusted to speak for another? How do we know that those who call themselves our representatives are actually speaking on our behalf, rather than simply pursuing their own interests?

There are two circumstances under which one person reasonably might be trusted to speak for another. The first of these occurs if the two individuals are so similar in background, character, interests, and perspectives that anything said by one would very likely reflect the views of the other as well. This principle is at the heart of what is sometimes called **sociological representation**—the sort of representation that takes place when representatives have the same racial, ethnic, religious, or educational backgrounds as their constituents. The assumption is that sociological similarity helps to promote good representation; thus, the composition of a properly constituted representative assembly should mirror the composition of society.

The second circumstance under which one person might be trusted to speak for another occurs if the two are formally bound together so that the representative is in some way accountable to those he or she purports to represent. If representatives can somehow be punished or held to account for failing to speak properly for their constituents, then we know they have an incentive to provide good representation even if their own personal backgrounds, views, and interests differ from those they represent. This principle is called **agency representation**—the sort of representation that takes place when constituents have the power to hire and fire their representatives.

Both sociological and agency representation play a role in the relationship between members of Congress and their constituencies.

The Social Composition of the U.S. Congress The extent to which the U.S. Congress is representative of the American people in a sociological sense can be seen by examining the distribution of important social characteristics in the House and Senate today. It comes as no surprise that the religious affiliations of members of both the House and Senate are overwhelmingly Protestant—the distribution is very close to the proportion in the population at large—although the Protestant category is composed of more than fifteen denominations. Catholics are the second largest category of religious affiliation, and Jews a much smaller third category.[4] Religious affiliations directly affect congressional debate on a limited range of issues where different moral views are at stake, such as abortion.

Statistics on ethnic or national background are difficult to get and generally unreliable. Individual members of Congress may make a point of their ethnic backgrounds, but an actual count has not been done. Occasionally, an issue like support for Israel or for the Greek community in Cyprus may activate members of Congress along religious or ethnic lines. But these exceptions actually underscore the essentially symbolic nature of these social characteristics.

African Americans, women, Hispanic Americans, and Asian Americans have increased their congressional representation somewhat in the past two decades (see Figure 11.1). In 1996, fifty-two women were elected to the House of Representatives (up from only twenty-nine in 1990). Nine women now serve in the Senate. As Tables 11.2 and 11.3 illustrate, the representation of women and minorities in Congress is still not comparable to their proportions in the general population. Since many important contemporary national

FIGURE 11.1

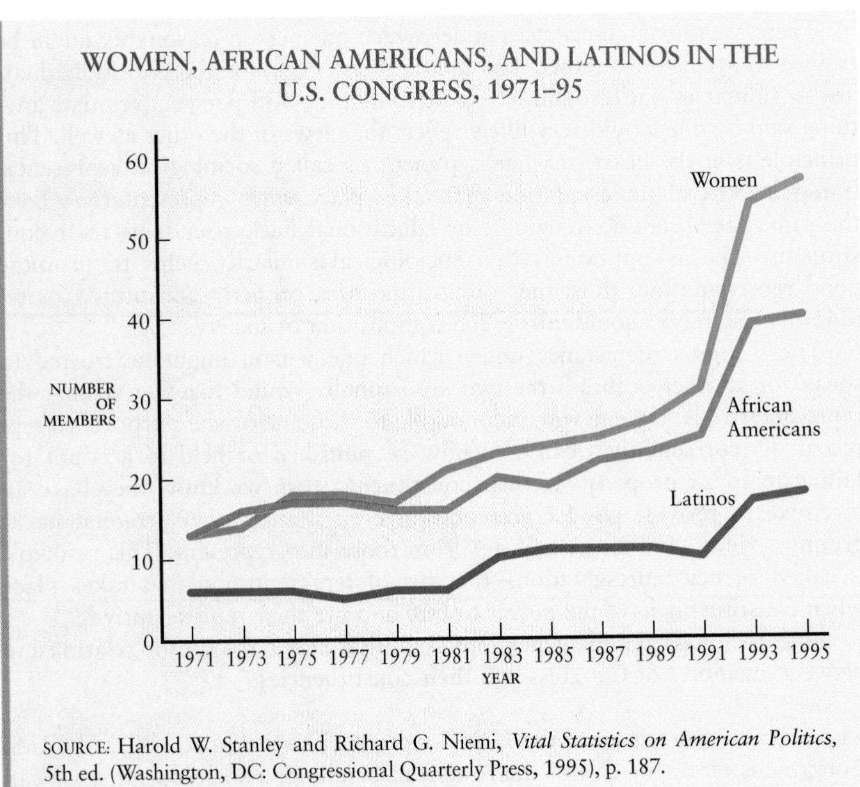

SOURCE: Harold W. Stanley and Richard G. Niemi, *Vital Statistics on American Politics*, 5th ed. (Washington, DC: Congressional Quarterly Press, 1995), p. 187.

REPRESENTATION OF WOMEN IN THE 105TH CONGRESS (1997–98)

House (52)

California: Lynn Woolsey, D; Nancy Pelosi, D; Anna G. Eshoo, D; Zoe Lofgren, D; Loretta Sanchez, D; Ellen Tauscher, D; Juanita McDonald, D; Jane Harman, D; Lucille Roybal-Allard, D; Maxine Waters, D

Colorado: Diana DeGette, D

Connecticut: Barbara B. Kennelly, D; Rosa DeLauro, D; Nancy L. Johnson, R

District of Columbia: Eleanor Holmes Norton, D*

Florida: Corrine Brown, D; Tillie Fowler, R; Karen L. Thurman, D; Carrie Meek, D; Ileana Ros-Lehtinen, R

Georgia: Cynthia McKinney, D

Hawaii: Patsy T. Mink, D

Idaho: Helen Chenoweth, R

Indiana: Julia Carson, D

Kentucky: Anne Northup, R

Maryland: Constance A. Morella, R

Michigan: Lynn Rivers, D; Debbie Stabenow, D; Carolyn Kilpatrick, D

Missouri: Karen McCarthy, D; Pat Danner, D; JoAnn Emerson, R

New Jersey: Marge Roukema, R

New York: Nydia M. Velázquez, D; Susan Molinari, R; Carolyn B. Maloney, D; Nita M. Lowey, D; Sue W. Kelly, R; Louise M. Slaughter, D; Carolyn McCarthy, D

North Carolina: Eva Clayton, D; Sue Myrick, R

Ohio: Marcy Kaptur, D; Deborah Pryce, R

Oregon: Elizabeth Furse, D; Darlene Hooley, D

Texas: Sheila Jackson-Lee, D; Eddie Bernice Johnson, D; Kay Granger, R

Washington: Linda Smith, R; Jennifer Dunn, R

Wyoming: Barbara Cubin, R

Senate (9)

California: Dianne Feinstein, D; Barbara Boxer, D

Illinois: Carol Moseley-Braun, D

Louisiana: Mary Landrieu, D

Maryland: Barbara A. Mikulski, D

Maine: Olympia J. Snowe, R; Susan Collins, R

Texas: Kay Bailey Hutchison, R

Washington: Patty Murray, D

*Non-voting delegate

SOURCE: National Women's Political Caucus Fact Sheet.

TABLE 11.2

issues do cut along racial and gender lines, a considerable amount of clamor for reform in the representative process is likely to continue until these groups are fully represented.

The occupational backgrounds of members of Congress have always been a matter of interest because so many issues cut along economic lines that are relevant to occupations and industries. The legal profession is the dominant career of most members of Congress prior to their election to Congress. Public service or politics is also a significant background. In addition, many members of Congress also have important ties to business and industry.[5] One composite portrait of a typical member of Congress has been that of "a middle-aged male lawyer whose father was of the professional or managerial class; a native-born 'white,' or—if he cannot avoid being an immigrant—a

TABLE 11.3

REPRESENTATION OF ETHNIC MINORITIES IN THE 105TH CONGRESS (1997–98)

Blacks

House (38)
Alabama: Earl F. Hilliard, D
California: Ronald V. Dellums, D; Julian C. Dixon, D; Maxine Waters, D
District of Columbia: Eleanor Holmes Norton, D*
Florida: Corrine Brown, D; Carrie Meek, D; Alcee L. Hastings, D
Georgia: Sanford Bishop, D; John Lewis, D; Cynthia McKinney, D
Illinois: Bobby L. Rush, D; Jesse Jackson, Jr., D; Danny Davis, D
Indiana: Julia Carson, D
Louisiana: William J. Jefferson, D
Maryland: Albert R. Wynn, D; Elijah Cummings, D
Michigan: John Conyers Jr., D; Carolyn Kilpatrick, D
Mississippi: Bennie Thompson, D
Missouri: William L. Clay, D
New Jersey: Donald M. Payne, D
New York: Floyd H. Flake, D; Edolphus Towns, D; Major R. Owens, D; Charles B. Rangel, D
North Carolina: Eva Clayton, D; Melvin Watt, D
Ohio: Louis Stokes, D
Oklahoma: J. C. Watts, R
Pennsylvania: Chaka Fattah, D
South Carolina: James E. Clyburn, D
Tennessee: Harold E. Ford, Jr., D
Texas: Sheila Jackson-Lee D; Eddie Bernice Johnson, D
Virginia: Robert C. Scott, D

Senate (1)
Illinois: Carol Moseley-Braun, D

Hispanics

House (20)
Arizona: Ed Pastor, D
California: Xavier Becerra, D; Matthew G. Martinez, D; Lucille Roybal-Allard, D; Esteban E. Torres, D; Loretta Sanchez, D
Florida: Ileana Ros-Lehtinen, R; Lincoln Diaz-Balart, R
Illinois: Luis V. Gutierrez, D
New Jersey: Robert Menendez, D
New Mexico: Bill Richardson, D
New York: Nydia M. Velázquez, D; Jose E. Serrano, D
Puerto Rico: Carlos Romero-Barcelo, D*
Texas: Henry B. Gonzalez, D; Henry Bonilla, R; Solomon P. Ortiz, D; Frank Tejeda, D; Ruben Hinojosa, D; Silvestre Reyes, D

Asians and Pacific Islanders

House (5)
American Samoa: Eni F. H. Faleomavaega, D*
California: Robert T. Matsui, D; Jay C. Kim, R
Guam: Robert A. Underwood, D*
Hawaii: Patsy T. Mink, D

Senate (2)
Hawaii: Daniel K. Inouye, D; Daniel K. Akaka, D

American Indian

Senate (1)
Colorado: Ben Nighthorse Campbell, R

*Non-voting delegate

product of northwestern or central Europe or Canada, rather than of eastern or southern Europe, Latin America, Africa or Asia."[6] This is not a portrait of the U.S. population. Congress is not a sociological microcosm of American society, and it probably can never become one. One obvious reason is that the skills and resources needed to achieve political success in the United States are much more likely to be found among well-educated and relatively well-to-do Americans than among members of minority groups and the poor. Take money, for example. As we saw in Chapter 9, successful congressional candidates must be able to raise hundreds of thousands of dollars to finance their campaigns. Poor people from the inner city are much less likely to be able to convince corporate political action committees to provide them with these funds.

Is Congress still able to legislate fairly or to take account of a diversity of views and interests if it is not a sociologically representative assembly? The task is certainly much more difficult. Yet there is reason to believe it can. Representatives, as we shall see shortly, can serve as the agents of their constituents, even if they do not precisely mirror their sociological attributes. Yet, sociological representation is a matter of some importance, even if it is not an absolute prerequisite for fair legislation on the part of members of the House and Senate. At the least, the social composition of a representative assembly is important for symbolic purposes—to demonstrate to groups in the population that they are taken seriously by the government. Concern about the proportion of women, African Americans, and ethnic minorities in Congress and elsewhere in government would exist whether or not these social characteristics influenced the outcomes of laws and policies. It is rare to find a social group whose members do not feel shortchanged if someone like themselves is not a member of the assembly. Thus, the symbolic composition of Congress is ultimately important for the political stability of the United States. If Congress is not representative symbolically, then its own authority and indeed that of the entire government would be reduced.[7]

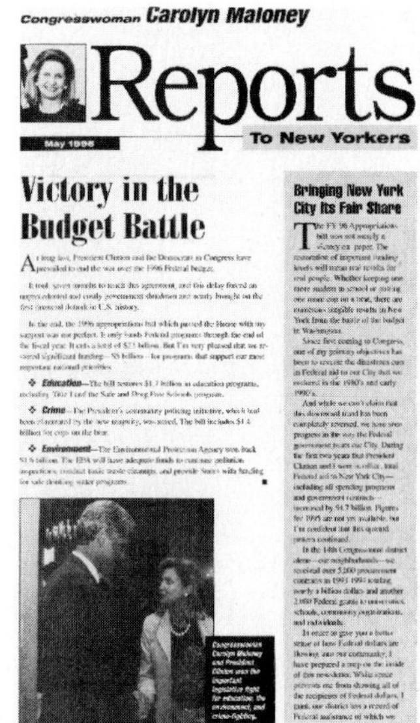

Congresswoman Carolyn Maloney

Reports To New Yorkers

May 1996

Victory in the Budget Battle

Bringing New York City Its Fair Share

Members of Congress can reach out to their constituents by mailing thousands of newsletters free of charge.

Representatives as Agents A good deal of evidence indicates that whether or not members of Congress share their constituents' sociological characteristics, they *do* work very hard to speak for their constituents' views and serve their constituents' interests in the governmental process. The idea of representative as agent is similar to the relationship of lawyer and client. True, the relationship between the member of Congress and as many as 550,000 "clients" in the district, or the senator and millions of "clients" in the state, is very different from that of the lawyer and client. But the criteria of performance are comparable. One expects at the very least that each representative will constantly be seeking to discover the interests of the constituency and will be speaking for those interests in Congress and in other centers of government.[8]

There is constant communication between constituents and congressional offices. For example, each year the House and Senate post offices handle nearly 100 million pieces of incoming mail, and in recent years, members of Congress have sent out nearly 400 million pieces of mail.[9]

The seriousness with which members of the House attempt to behave as representatives can be seen in the amount of time spent on behalf of their constituents. Well over a quarter of their time and nearly two-thirds of the time of their staff members is devoted to constituency service (called "case work"). This service is not merely a matter of writing and mailing letters. It includes talking to constituents, providing them with minor services, presenting special bills for them, and attempting to influence decisions by regulatory commissions on their behalf.[10]

Although no members of Congress are above constituency pressures (and they would not want to be), on many issues constituents do not have very strong views and representatives are free to act as they think best. Foreign policy issues often fall into this category. But in many districts there are two or three issues on which constituents have such pronounced opinions that representatives feel they have little freedom of choice. For example, representatives from wheat, cotton, or tobacco districts probably will not want to exercise a great deal of independence on relevant agricultural legislation. In the oil-rich states (such as Oklahoma, Texas, and California), senators and members of the House are likely to be leading advocates of oil interests. For one thing, they are probably fearful of voting against their district interests; for another, the districts are unlikely to have elected representatives who would *want* to vote against them.

The influence of constituencies is so pervasive that both parties have strongly embraced the informal rule that nothing should be done to endanger the re-election chances of any member. Party leaders obey this rule fairly consistently by not asking any member to vote in a way that might conflict with a district interest.

THE ELECTORAL CONNECTION

The sociological composition of Congress and the activities of representatives once they are in office are very much influenced by electoral considerations. Three factors related to the U.S. electoral system affect who gets elected and what they do once in office. The first set of issues concerns who decides to run for office and which candidates have an edge over others. The second issue is that of incumbency advantage. Finally, the way congressional district lines are drawn can greatly affect the outcome of an election. Let us examine more closely the impact that these considerations have on representation.

Voters' choices are restricted from the start by who decides to run for office. In the past, decisions about who would run for a particular elected office were made by local party officials. A person who had a record of service to the party, or who was owed a favor, or whose "turn" had come up might be nominated by party leaders for an office. Today, few party organizations have the power to slate candidates in that way. Instead, the decision to run for Congress is a more personal choice. One of the most important factors determining who runs for office is a candidate's individual ambition.[11] A potential candidate may also assess whether he or she can attract enough money to mount a credible campaign. The ability to raise money depends on connections with other politicians, interest groups, and national party organizations. In the past, the difficulty of raising campaign funds posed a disadvantage to female candidates. Since the 1980s, however, a number of powerful **political action committees** (PACs) have emerged to recruit women and fund their campaigns. The largest of them, EMILY's List, has become one of the most powerful fundraisers of all PACs. Recent research shows that money is no longer the barrier it once was to women running for office.[12]

Features distinctive to each congressional district also affect the field of candidates. Among them are the range of other political opportunities that may lure potential candidates away. In addition, the way the congressional district overlaps with state legislative boundaries may affect a candidate's decision to run. A state-level representative or senator who is considering running for the U.S. Congress is more likely to assess his or her prospects favorably if his or her state district coincides with the congressional district (because the voters will already know him or her). And for any candidate, decisions about running must be made early, because once money has been committed to already-declared candidates, it is harder for new candidates to break into a race. Thus, the outcome of a November election is partially determined many months earlier, when decisions to run are finalized.

Incumbency plays a very important role in the American electoral system and in the kind of representation citizens get in Washington. Once in office, members of Congress possess an array of tools that they can use to stack the deck in favor of their re-election. The most important of these is constituency service: taking care of the problems and requests of individual voters. Through such services and through regular newsletter mailings, the incumbent seeks to establish a "personal" relationship with his or her constituents. The success of this strategy is evident in the high rates of re-election for congressional incumbents: nearly 95 percent for House members and 86 percent for members of the Senate in recent years (see Figure 11.2).[13] It is also evident in what is called **sophomore surge**—the tendency for candidates to win a higher percentage of the vote when seeking future terms in office.

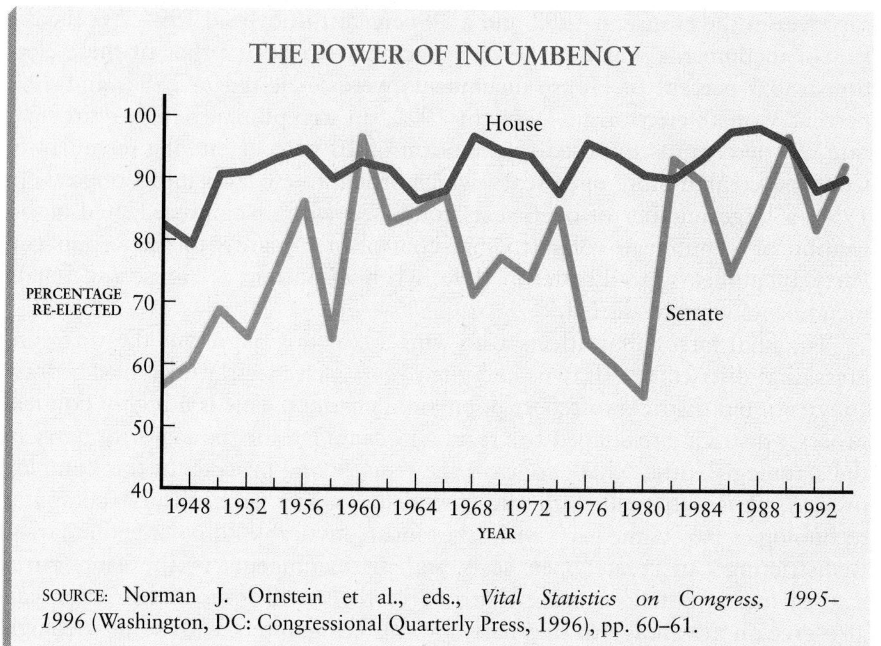

SOURCE: Norman J. Ornstein et al., eds., *Vital Statistics on Congress, 1995–1996* (Washington, DC: Congressional Quarterly Press, 1996), pp. 60–61.

FIGURE 11.2

Members of Congress who run for re-election have a very good chance of winning.

Incumbency can also help a candidate by scaring off potential challengers. In many races, potential candidates may decide not to run because they fear that the incumbent simply has too much money or is too well liked or too well known. Potentially strong challengers may also decide that a district's partisan leanings are too unfavorable. The experience of Republican representative Dan Miller in Florida is instructive. When Miller first ran in 1992, he faced five opponents in the Republican primary and a bruising campaign against his Democratic opponent in the general election. In the 1994 election, by contrast, Miller faced only nominal opposition in the Republican primary, winning 81 percent of the vote. In the general election, the strongest potential challenger from the Democratic Party decided not to run; the combination of the incumbency advantage with the strongly Republican leanings of the district gave the Democrats little chance of winning. Miller was re-elected without a challenge.[14]

The advantage of incumbency thus tends to preserve the status quo in Congress. This fact has implications for the social composition of Congress. For example, incumbency advantage makes it harder for women to increase their numbers in Congress because most incumbents are men. Women who run for open seats (for which there are no incumbents) are just as likely to win as male candidates.[15] Supporters of **term limits** argue that such limits are the only way to get new faces into Congress. They believe that incumbency advantage and the tendency of many legislators to view politics as a career mean that very little turnover will occur in Congress unless limits are imposed on the number of terms a legislator can serve.

But the tendency toward the status quo is not absolute. In recent years, political observers have suggested that the incumbency advantage may be declining. In the 1992 and 1994 elections, for example, voters expressed considerable anger and dissatisfaction with incumbents, producing a 25 percent turnover in the House in 1992 and a 20 percent turnover in 1994. Yet the defeat of incumbents was not the main factor at work in either of these elections; 88.3 percent of House incumbents were re-elected in 1992, and 90.2 percent won re-election in 1994. In 1992, an exceptionally high retirement rate (20 percent, as opposed to the norm of 10 percent) among members of Congress created more open seats, which brought new faces into Congress. In 1994, a large number of open seats combined with an unprecedented mobilization of Republican voters to shift control of Congress to the Republican Party. Incumbents fared better in 1996, when 95 percent of House and Senate incumbents were re-elected.[16]

The final factor that affects who wins a seat in Congress is the way congressional districts are drawn. Every ten years, state legislatures must redraw congressional districts to reflect population changes. This is a highly political process: districts are shaped to create an advantage for the majority party in the state legislature, which controls the redistricting process. In this complex process, those charged with drawing districts use sophisticated computer technologies to come up with the most favorable district boundaries. Redistricting can create open seats and pit incumbents of the same party against one another, ensuring that one of them will lose. Redistricting can also give an advantage to one party by clustering voters with some ideologi-

Representative Cynthia McKinney, a Democrat from Georgia, holds maps of her Congressional district (right) and the 6th District of Texas. In 1995, the Supreme Court held that McKinney's district, which was 64 percent African American, was unfairly based on race. No challenge was made to Texas's 6th District, which was predominantly white. McKinney handily won re-election in 1996 even though her district had been redrawn to include more white voters.

cal or sociological characteristics in a single district, or by separating those voters into two or more districts.

As we saw in Chapter 9, since the passage of the 1982 amendments to the 1964 Civil Rights Act, race has become a major—and controversial—consideration in drawing voting districts. These amendments, which encouraged the creation of districts in which members of racial minorities have decisive majorities, have greatly increased the number of minority representatives in Congress. After the 1991–92 redistricting, the number of predominantly minority districts doubled, rising from twenty-six to fifty-two. Among the most fervent supporters of the new minority districts were white Republicans, who used the opportunity to create more districts dominated by white Republican voters. These developments raise thorny questions about representation. Some analysts argue that the system may grant minorities greater sociological representation, but it has made it more difficult for minorities to win substantive policy goals. This was a common argument after the sweeping Republican victories in the 1994 congressional elections. Others dispute this argument, noting that the strong surge of Republican voters was more significant than any losses due to racial redistricting.[17]

In 1995, the Supreme Court limited racial redistricting in *Miller v. Johnson*, in which the Court stated that race could not be the predominant factor in creating electoral districts. Yet concerns about redistricting and representation have not disappeared. The distinction between race being a "predominant" factor and its being one factor among many is very hazy. Because the drawing of district boundaries affects incumbents as well as the field of candidates who decide to run for office, it continues to be a key battleground on which political parties fight about the meaning of representation.

Direct Patronage

As we saw in the preceding discussion, members of Congress often have an opportunity to provide direct benefits, or **patronage**, for their constituents. The most important of these opportunities for direct patronage is in legislation that has been described half-jokingly as the **pork barrel**. This type of legislation specifies a project to be funded or other authorizations, as well as the location of the project within a particular district. Many observers of Congress argue that pork-barrel bills are the only ones that some members are serious about moving toward actual passage, because they are seen as so important to members' re-election bids.

The building of dams is a classic example of pork-barrel spending.

A common form of pork barreling is the "earmark," the practice through which members of Congress insert into otherwise pork-free bills language that provides special benefits for their own constituents. For example, in 1991, Representative Paul Kanjorski (D-Pa.) was able to insert into a section of the Pentagon's budget two paragraphs earmarking $20 million to create "an advanced technology demonstration facility for environmental technology," and stipulating further that "these funds are to be provided only to the organization known as 'Earth Conservancy' in Hanover Township, Pennsylvania." This organization was not only in Kanjorski's district, but was also headed by his brother.[18]

Often, congressional leaders will use pork-barrel projects in exchange for votes on other matters. For example, while serving as Senate majority leader in 1957, Lyndon Johnson won crucial support for civil rights legislation by awarding water projects to Senators Margaret Chase Smith of Maine and Frank Church of Idaho. The most important rule of pork-barreling is that any member of Congress whose district receives a project as part of a bill must support all the other projects on the bill. This cuts across party and ideological lines. Thus, the same 1984 appropriations bill that was supported by conservative Republican senator Ted Stevens of Alaska because it provided funds for Blackhawk helicopters for the Alaska National Guard was also supported by liberal Democrat Ted Kennedy, who had won a provision for $2 million for a lighthouse at Nantucket.

In 1996, as part of the Republicans' Contract with America, Congress granted the president a **line-item veto**, which allows the president to eliminate such earmarks from bills presented to the White House for signature. Republican leaders were willing to risk giving such a powerful tool to a Democratic president because they calculated that, over the decades of Democratic congresses, the GOP had learned to live without much pork, while Democrats had become dependent upon pork to solidify their electoral support. Republican leaders also hoped that a future Republican president, wielding the line-item veto, would be able to further undermine Democratic political strength.

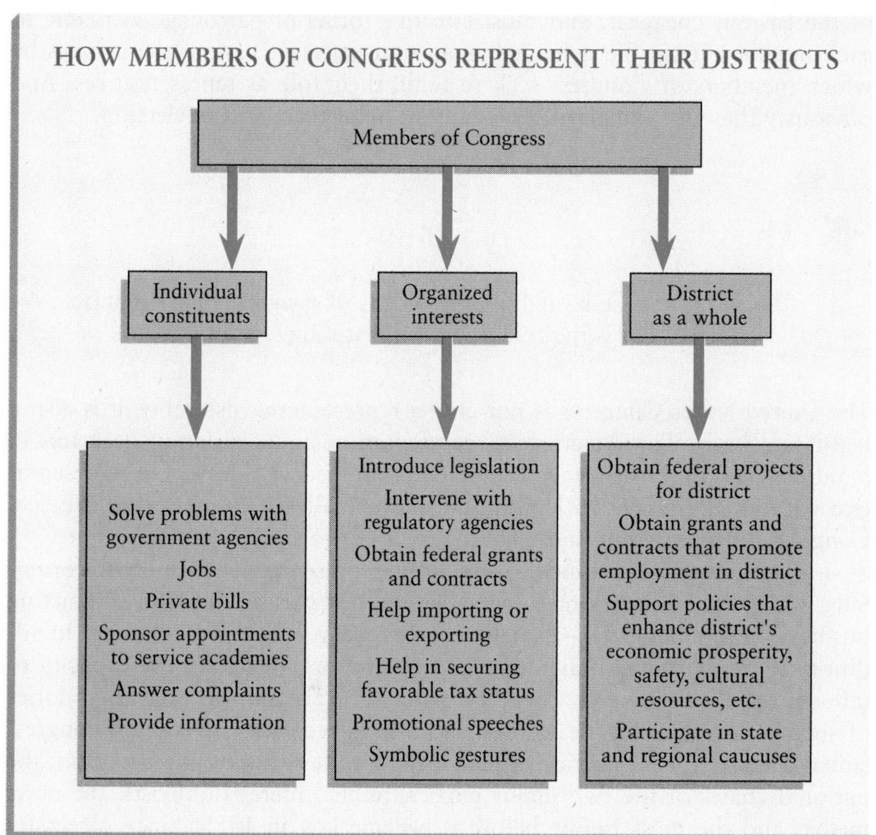

FIGURE 11.3

A limited amount of other direct patronage also exists (see Figure 11.3). One important form of this constituency service is intervention with federal administrative agencies on behalf of constituents. Members of the House and Senate and their staff members spend a great deal of time on the telephone and in administrative offices seeking to secure favorable treatment for constituents and supporters. A small but related form of patronage is getting an appointment to one of the military academies for the child of a constituent. Traditionally, these appointments are allocated one to a district.

A different form of patronage is the **private bill**—a proposal to grant some kind of relief, special privilege, or exemption to the person named in the bill. The private bill is a type of legislation, but it is distinguished from a public bill, which is supposed to deal with general rules and categories of behavior, people, and institutions. As many as 75 percent of all private bills introduced (and one-third of the ones that pass) are concerned with providing relief for foreign nationals who cannot get permanent visas to the United States because the immigration quota for their country is filled or because of something unusual about their particular situation.[19]

Private legislation is a congressional privilege that is often abused, but it is impossible to imagine members of Congress giving it up completely. It is one of the easiest, cheapest, and most effective forms of patronage available to each member. It can be defended as an indispensable part of the process by which members of Congress seek to fulfill their role as representatives. And obviously they like the privilege because it helps them win re-election.

The Organization of Congress

> ➤ What are the basic building blocks of congressional organization? What is the role of each in forming legislation?

The United States Congress is not only a representative assembly. It is also a legislative body. For Americans, representation and legislation go hand in hand. As we saw earlier, however, many parliamentary bodies are representative without the power to legislate. It is no small achievement that the U.S. Congress both represents *and* governs.

It is extraordinarily difficult for a large, representative assembly to formulate, enact, and implement laws. The internal complexities of conducting business within Congress—the legislative process—alone are daunting. In addition, there are many individuals and institutions that have the capacity to influence the legislative process. For example, legislation to raise the salaries of members of the House of Representatives received input from congressional leaders of both parties, special legislative task forces, the president, the national chairs of the two major parties, public interest lobbyists, the news media, and the mass public before it became law in 1989. Since successful legislation requires the confluence of so many distinct factors, it is little wonder that most of the thousands of bills considered by Congress each year are defeated long before they reach the president.

Before an idea or proposal can become a law, it must pass through a complex set of organizations and procedures in Congress. Collectively, these are called the policy-making process, or the legislative process. Understanding this process is central to understanding why some ideas and proposals eventually become law while most do not.

Over its more than two-hundred-year history, Congress has established procedures for creating a division of labor, setting an agenda, maintaining order through rules and procedures, and placing limits on debate and discussion. Still, congressional policy making often is an unwieldy process and the often torturous deliberation affects the kind of legislation that Congress ultimately produces. To win support for their ideas within this complex framework, sponsors of legislation must build compromises that accommodate a broad range of interests. As a consequence, it is far easier to pass bills that represent incremental change rather than comprehensive reform. In addition, legislation often resembles a Christmas tree—festooned with a variety of measures added on by individual congressional representatives. Although such measures may have little to do with the policy under consideration, they are needed to build majority support in Congress.

To exercise its power to make the law, Congress must first bring about something close to an organizational miracle. The building blocks of congressional organization include the political parties, the committee system, congressional staff, the caucuses, and the parliamentary rules of the House and Senate. Each of these factors plays a key role in the organization of Congress and in the process through which Congress formulates and enacts laws.

Party Leadership in the House and the Senate

Every two years, at the beginning of a new Congress, the members of each party gather to elect their House leaders. This gathering is traditionally called the **conference** (House Democrats call theirs the **caucus**). The elected leader of the majority party is later proposed to the whole House and is automatically elected to the position of **Speaker of the House**, with voting along straight party lines. The House majority conference or caucus then also elects a **majority leader**. The minority party goes through the same process and selects the **minority leader**. Both parties also elect whips to line up party members on important votes and to relay voting information to the leaders.

Next in line of importance for each party after the Speaker and majority or minority leader is its Committee on Committees (called the Steering and Policy Committee by the Democrats), whose tasks are to assign new legislators to committees and to deal with the requests of incumbent members for transfers from one committee to another. Currently, the Speaker serves as chair of the Republican Committee on Committees, while the minority leader chairs the Democratic Steering and Policy Committee. (The Republicans have a separate Policy Committee.) At one time, party leaders strictly controlled committee assignments, using them to enforce party discipline. Today, in principle, representatives receive the assignments they want. But assignments on the most important committees are often sought by several individuals, which gives the leadership an opportunity to cement alliances (and, perhaps, make enemies) as it resolves conflicting requests.

In 1994, Republican congressional candidates signed a "Contract with America," promoted by Newt Gingrich, which called for tax cuts, term limits, and a balanced budget amendment, among other things. The contract was initially popular with the electorate, which voted the Republicans into power in the House and Senate.

HOUSE AND SENATE LEADERSHIP IN THE 105TH CONGRESS*

The Senate

Republican Leadership
Majority Leader: Trent Lott (MS)
Majority Whip: Don Nickles (OK)
Chief Deputy Whip: Judd Gregg (NH)

Democratic Leadership
Minority Leader: Tom Daschle (SD)
Minority Whip: Wendell Ford (KY)
Chief Deputy Whip: John Breaux (LA)

The House

Republican Leadership
Speaker: Newt Gingrich (GA)
Majority Leader: Richard Armey (TX)
Majority Whip: Tom DeLay (TX)

Democratic Leadership
Minority Leader: Richard Gephardt (MO)
Minority Whip: David Bonior (MI)

*as of December 1, 1996.

Generally, representatives seek assignments that will allow them to influence decisions of special importance to their districts. Representatives from farm districts, for example, may request seats on the Agriculture Committee.[20] Seats on powerful committees such as Ways and Means, which is responsible for tax legislation, and Appropriations are especially popular.

Within the Senate, the president pro tempore exercises primarily ceremonial leadership. Usually, the majority party designates a member with the greatest seniority to serve in this capacity. Real power is in the hands of the majority leader and minority leader, each elected by party conference. Together they control the Senate's calendar, or agenda for legislation. In addition, the senators from each party elect a whip. Each party also elects a Policy Committee, which advises the leadership on legislative priorities.

The structure of majority party leadership in the House and the Senate is shown in Figures 11.4 and 11.5.

In addition to these tasks of organization, congressional party leaders may also seek to establish a legislative agenda. Since the New Deal, presidents have taken the lead in creating legislative agendas (this trend will be discussed in the next chapter). But in recent years congressional leaders, facing a White House controlled by the opposing party, have attempted to devise their own agendas. Democratic leaders of Congress sought to create a common Democratic perspective in 1981 when Ronald Reagan became president. The Republican Congress elected in 1994 expanded on this idea with its Contract with America. In both cases, the majority party leadership has sought to create a consensus among its congressional members around an overall vision to guide legislative activity and to make individual pieces of legislation part of a bigger picture that is distinct from the agenda of the president.

Congressional party leaders have used various strategies to construct such agendas and build consensus around them. Democratic leaders staged an annual Democratic Issues Conference to bring party members together to consider a common agenda. Ongoing task forces produced issue handbooks that highlighted the party's distinctive policy perspectives. These activities did not commit members to particular policies, but instead served to educate members, giving them a shared background on important issues.[21] But these efforts fell short of creating a common agenda. Committee and subcommittee chairs followed their own priorities, not those of the party leadership.

When Bill Clinton was elected president in 1992, Republicans followed a similar strategy, using an annual issues conference to promote a common Republican agenda in Congress. But the Contract with America went further in seeking party unity on policy. With much public fanfare Republican candidates signed the contract, promising to promote its objectives once they were elected. This device no doubt served to promote the unusual coherence and loyalty to the leadership agenda displayed by House Republicans in 1995.

THE COMMITTEE SYSTEM: THE CORE OF CONGRESS

The committee system is central to the operation of Congress. At each stage of the legislative process, Congress relies on committees and subcommittees to do the hard work of sorting through alternatives and writing legislation. There are several different kinds of congressional committees; these include

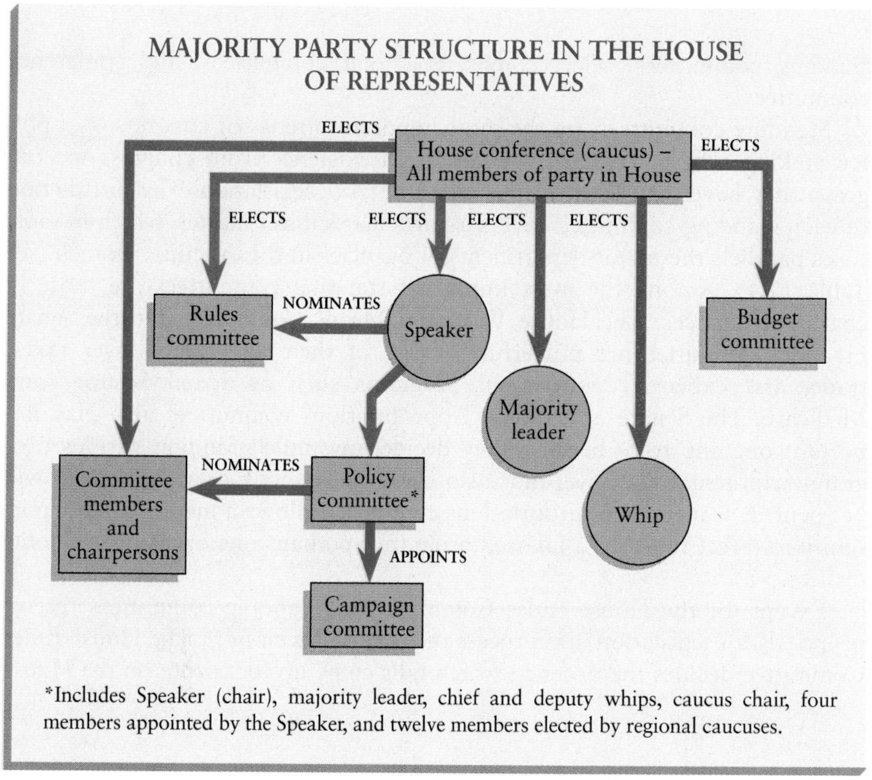

MAJORITY PARTY STRUCTURE IN THE HOUSE OF REPRESENTATIVES

House conference (caucus) – All members of party in House
ELECTS
ELECTS
ELECTS
ELECTS
ELECTS
ELECTS
Rules committee
NOMINATES
Speaker
Budget committee
Majority leader
Whip
Committee members and chairpersons
NOMINATES
Policy committee*
APPOINTS
Campaign committee

*Includes Speaker (chair), majority leader, chief and deputy whips, caucus chair, four members appointed by the Speaker, and twelve members elected by regional caucuses.

FIGURE 11.4

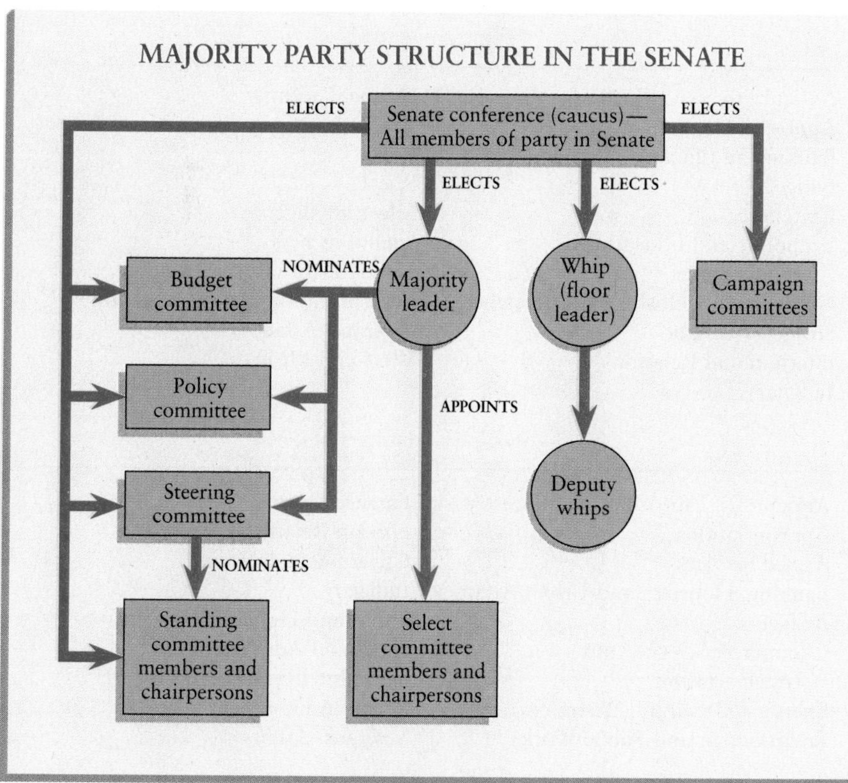

FIGURE 11.5

standing committees, select committees, joint committees, and conference committees.

Standing committees are the most important arenas of congressional policy making. These committees continue in existence from congress to congress; they have the power to propose and write legislation. The jurisdiction of each standing committee covers a particular subject matter, which in most cases parallels the major departments or agencies in the executive branch (see Table 11.4). Among the most important standing committees are those in charge of finances. The House Ways and Means Committee and the Senate Finance Committee are powerful because of their jurisdiction over taxes, trade, and expensive entitlement programs such as Social Security and Medicare. The Senate and House Appropriations committees also play important ongoing roles because they decide how much funding various programs will actually receive; they also determine exactly how the money will be spent. A seat on an appropriations committee allows a member the opportunity to direct funds to a favored program—perhaps one in his or her home district.

Except for the House Rules Committee, all standing committees receive proposals for legislation and process them into official bills. The House Rules Committee decides the order in which bills come up for a vote on the House

TABLE 11.4

PERMANENT COMMITTEES OF CONGRESS

House committees	
Agriculture	National Security
Appropriations	Resources
Banking and Financial Services	Rules
Budget	Science
Commerce	Select Intelligence
Economic and Educational Opportunities	Small Business
Government Reform and Oversight	Standards of Official Conduct
House Oversight	Transportation and Infrastructure
International Relations	Veterans' Affairs
Judiciary	Ways and Means

Senate committees	
Agriculture, Nutrition, and Forestry	Finance
Appropriations	Foreign Relations
Armed Services	Governmental Affairs
Banking, Housing, and Urban Affairs	Judiciary
Budget	Labor and Human Resources
Commerce, Science, and Transportation	Rules and Administration
Energy and Natural Resources	Select Intelligence
Environment and Public Works	Small Business
	Veterans' Affairs

floor and determines the specific rules that govern the length of debate and opportunity for amendments. The Senate, which has less formal organization and fewer rules, does not have a rules committee.

Select committees are usually not permanent and usually do not have the power to report legislation. (The House and Senate Select Intelligence committees are permanent, however, and do have the power to report legislation.) These committees may hold hearings and serve as focal points for the issues they are charged with considering. Congressional leaders form select committees when they want to take up issues that fall between the jurisdictions of existing committees, to highlight an issue, or to investigate a particular problem. Examples of select committees investigating political scandals include the Senate Watergate Committee of 1973, the committees set up in 1987 to investigate the Iran-Contra affair, and the Whitewater Committee of the 104th Congress. Select committees set up to highlight ongoing issues have included the House Select Committee on Hunger, established in 1984, and the House Select Narcotics Committee. A few select committees have remained in existence for many years, such as the select committees on aging; hunger; children, youth, and families; and narcotics abuse and control. In 1995, however, congressional Republicans abolished most of these select committees, both to streamline operations and to remove a forum used primarily by Democratic representatives and their allies.

Joint committees involve members from both the Senate and the House. There are four such committees: economic, taxation, library, and printing. These joint committees are permanent, but they do not have the power to report legislation. The Joint Economic Committee and the Joint Taxation Committee have often played important roles in collecting information and holding hearings on economic and financial issues.

Finally, **conference committees** are temporary committees whose members are appointed by the Speaker of the House and the presiding officer of the Senate. These committees are charged with reaching a compromise on legislation once it has been passed by the House and the Senate. Conference committees play an extremely important role in determining what laws are actually passed, because they must reconcile any differences in the legislation passed by the House and Senate.

Seats on the Senate Armed Services Committee, shown meeting here, are highly coveted.

Assignments to standing committees are made by a "committee on committees" appointed by the leadership of each party in each chamber of Congress. For the most part, these committees try to accommodate the requests of individual members for assignments. The decision about which committee seats to pursue is the most important choice an incoming member of Congress faces. Members are guided by different considerations in requesting committee assignments, but most prominent are serving constituent interests, making good public policy, and winning more influence in Congress.[22]

Within each committee, hierarchy is based on seniority. **Seniority** is determined by years of continuous service on a particular committee, not years of service in the House or Senate. In general, each committee is chaired by the most senior member of the majority party. But the principle of seniority is not absolute. Both Democrats and Republicans have violated it on occasion. At the start of the 104th Congress, House Republicans violated the principle of seniority in the selection of a number of key committee chairs.

Over the years, Congress has reformed its organizational structure and operating procedures. Most changes have been made to improve efficiency, but some reforms have also represented a response to political considerations. In the 1970s, for example, a series of reforms substantially altered the organization of power in Congress. Among the most important changes put into place at that time were an increase in the number of subcommittees; greater autonomy for subcommittee chairs; the opening of most committee deliberations to the public; and a system of multiple referral of bills, which allowed several committees to consider one bill at the same time. One of the driving impulses behind these reforms was an effort to reduce the power of committee chairs. In the past, committee chairs exercised considerable power; they determined hearing schedules, selected subcommittee members, and appointed committee staff. Some chairs used their power to block consideration of bills they opposed. Because of the seniority system, many of the key committees were chaired by southern Democrats who stymied liberal legislation throughout the 1960s and early 1970s. By enhancing subcommittee power and allowing more members to chair subcommittees and appoint subcommittee staff, the reforms undercut the power of committee chairs.

Yet the reforms of the 1970s created new problems for Congress. As a consequence of the reforms, power has become more fragmented, making it harder to reach agreement on legislation. With power dissipated over a large number of committees and subcommittees, members spend more time in unproductive "turf battles." In addition, as committees expanded in size, members found they had so many committee responsibilities that they had to run from meeting to meeting. Thus their ability to specialize in a particular policy area has diminished as their responsibilities have increased.[23] The Republican leadership of the 104th Congress sought to reverse the fragmentation of congressional power and concentrate more authority in the party leadership. One of the ways the House achieved this was by violating the principle of seniority in the selection of a number of committee chairs. This move tied committee chairs more closely to the leadership. In addition, the Republican leadership eliminated 25 of the House's 115 subcommittees and gave committee chairs more power over their subcommittees. The result was an unusually cohesive congressional majority, which pushed forward a common agenda. This unity came at a cost, however. Committees in the 104th Congress were far less likely to engage in deliberation, and the quickened pace of the legislative process meant that committee members often did not know the content of the bills they were considering.[24]

THE STAFF SYSTEM: STAFFERS AND AGENCIES

A congressional institution second in importance only to the committee system is the staff system. Every member of Congress employs a large number of staff members, whose tasks include handling constituency requests and, to a large and growing extent, dealing with legislative details and the activities of administrative agencies. Increasingly, staffers bear the primary responsibility for formulating and drafting proposals, organizing hearings, dealing with administrative agencies, and negotiating with lobbyists. Indeed, legislators typically deal with one another through staff, rather than through direct,

Representative Connie Morella meets with staff in her Capitol Hill office. Staffers typically perform routine office work and deal with requests from constituents, but some also help in developing new policy initiatives and drafting legislation.

personal contact. Representatives and senators together employ nearly eleven thousand staffers in their Washington and home offices. Today, staffers even develop policy ideas, draft legislation, and in some instances, have a good deal of influence over the legislative process.

In addition to the personal staffs of individual senators and representatives, Congress also employs roughly two thousand committee staffers. These individuals comprise the permanent staff, who stay attached to every House and Senate committee regardless of turnover in Congress and who are responsible for organizing and administering the committee's work, including research, scheduling, organizing hearings, and drafting legislation. Committee staffers can come to play key roles in the legislative process. One example of the importance of committee staffers is the so-called Gephardt health care reform bill, named for the then–House majority leader, Richard Gephardt of Missouri, and introduced in August 1994. Though the bill bore Gephardt's name, it was actually crafted by a small group of staff members of the House Ways and Means Committee. These aides, under the direction of David Abernathy, the staff's leading health care specialist, debated methods of cost control, service delivery, the role of the insurance industry, and the needs of patients, and listened to hundreds of lobbyists before drafting the complex Gephardt bill.[25]

As Figure 11.6 shows, the number of congressional staff members grew rapidly during the 1960s and 1970s, leveled off in the 1980s, and decreased dramatically in 1995. This sudden drop fulfilled the Republican congressional candidates' campaign promise to reduce the size of committee staffs.

Not only does Congress employ personal and committee staff, but it has also established **staff agencies** designed to provide the legislative branch with resources and expertise independent of the executive branch. These agencies enhance Congress's capacity to oversee administrative agencies and to evalu-

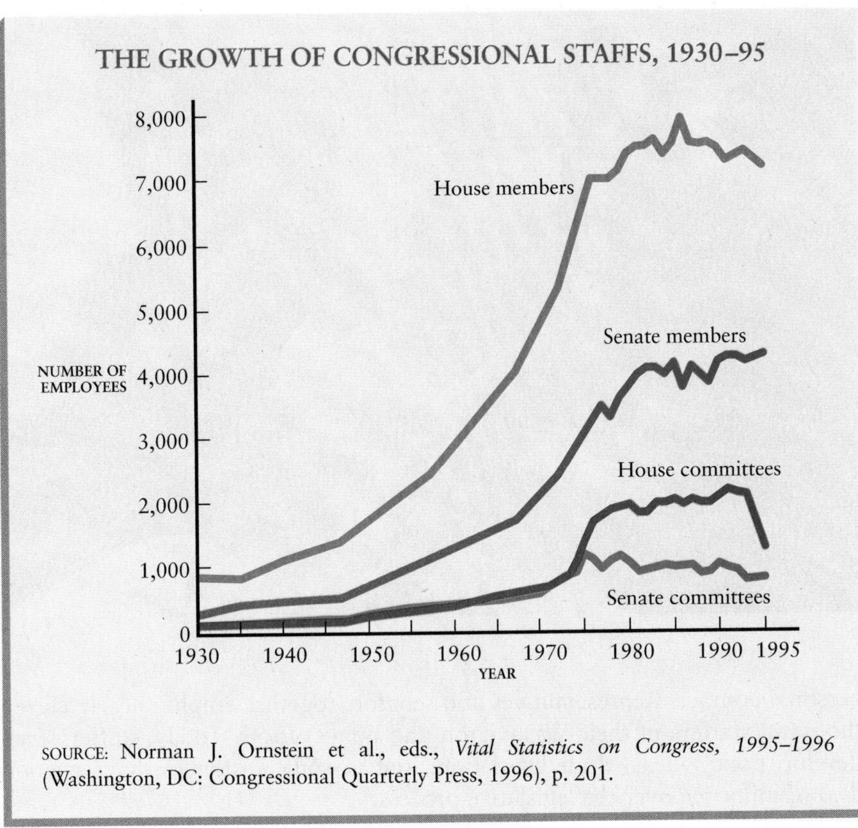

SOURCE: Norman J. Ornstein et al., eds., *Vital Statistics on Congress, 1995–1996* (Washington, DC: Congressional Quarterly Press, 1996), p. 201.

FIGURE 11.6

ate presidential programs and proposals. They include the Congressional Research Service, which performs research for legislators who wish to know the facts and competing arguments relevant to policy proposals or other legislative business; the General Accounting Office, through which Congress can investigate the financial and administrative affairs of any government agency or program; and the Congressional Budget Office, which assesses the economic implications and likely costs of proposed federal programs, such as health care reform proposals. A fourth agency, the Office of Technology Assessment, which provided Congress with analyses of scientific or technical issues, was abolished in 1995.

INFORMAL ORGANIZATION: THE CAUCUSES

In addition to the official organization of Congress, there also exists an unofficial organizational structure—the caucuses. **Caucuses** are groups of senators or representatives who share certain opinions, interests, or social characteristics. They include ideological caucuses such as the liberal Democratic Study Group, the conservative Democratic Forum (popularly known as the "boll weevils"), and the moderate Republican Wednesday Group. At the same time, there are a large number of caucuses composed of legislators representing particular economic or policy interests, such as the Travel and Tourism Caucus, the Steel Caucus, the Mushroom Caucus, and Concerned Senators for the Arts. Legislators who share common backgrounds or social characteristics have organized caucuses such as the Congressional Black Caucus, the Congressional Caucus for Women's Issues, and the Hispanic Caucus. All these caucuses seek to advance the interests of the groups they represent by promoting legislation, encouraging Congress to hold hearings, and pressing administrative agencies for favorable treatment. The Congressional Black Caucus, for example, which in 1996 included forty representatives and one senator, has played an active role in Congress since 1970.

Before the 104th Congress, many of the largest and most effective caucuses were registered as Legislative Service Organizations (LSOs). LSOs were allotted office space in congressional buildings and congressional members were allowed to transfer some of their own budgets to the LSO. Several of the most effective LSOs, including the Black Caucus, the Hispanic Caucus, and the Women's Caucus, were closely tied to the Democratic Party. One LSO, the Democratic Study Group (DSG), once employed eighteen full-time analysts to help congressional Democrats evaluate proposed and pending legislation. The Republican leadership of the 104th Congress took away the budgets, staffs, and offices of all LSOs, in part because of these LSOs' links to the Democrats.[26] But most caucuses continued their activities, and new ones were created after this change. Of course, some of the larger caucuses found it harder to coordinate their activities and provide information to their members after they lost their status as LSOs, but caucuses continue to be an important part of congressional organization.[27]

Rules of Lawmaking: How a Bill Becomes a Law

> ➤ How do the rules of congressional procedure influence the fate of legislation as well as determine the distribution of power in Congress?

The institutional structure of Congress is one key factor that helps to shape the legislative process. A second and equally important set of factors is the rules of congressional procedure. These rules govern everything from the introduction of a bill through its submission to the president for signing (see Figure 11.7). Not only do these regulations influence the fate of each and every bill, they also help to determine the distribution of power in the Congress.

Committee Deliberation

Even if a member of Congress, the White House, or a federal agency has spent months developing and drafting a piece of legislation, it does not become a bill until it is submitted officially by a senator or representative to the clerk of the House or Senate and referred to the appropriate committee for

FIGURE 11.7

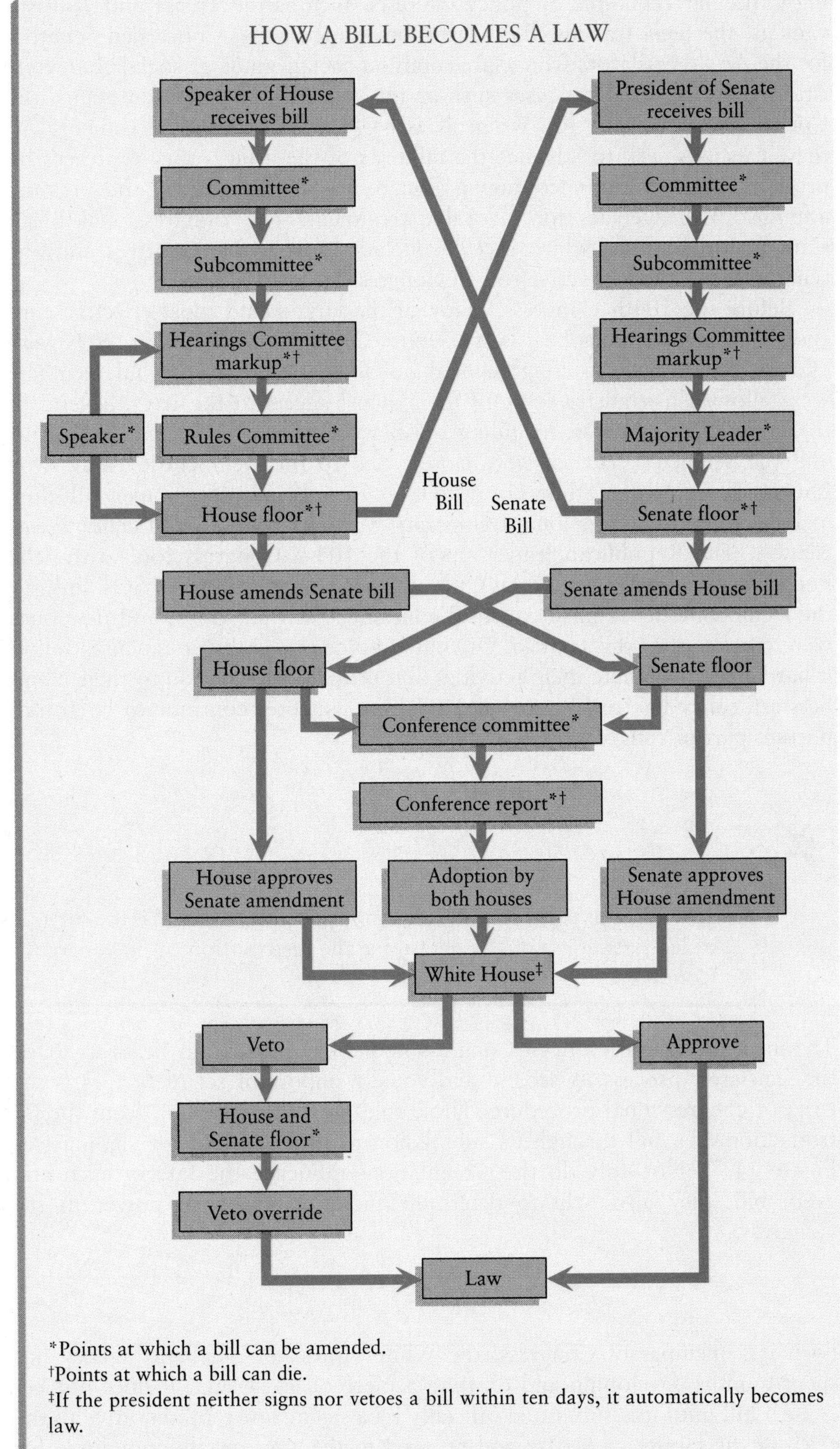

*Points at which a bill can be amended.
†Points at which a bill can die.
‡If the president neither signs nor vetoes a bill within ten days, it automatically becomes law.

deliberation. No floor action on any bill can take place until the committee with jurisdiction over it has taken all the time it needs to deliberate. During the course of its deliberations, the committee typically refers the bill to one of its subcommittees, which may hold hearings, listen to expert testimony, and amend the proposed legislation before referring it to the full committee for consideration. The full committee may accept the recommendation of the subcommittee or hold its own hearings and prepare its own amendments. Or, even more frequently, the committee and subcommittee may do little or nothing with a bill that has been submitted to them. Many bills are simply allowed to "die in committee" with little or no serious consideration given to them. Often, members of Congress introduce legislation that they neither expect nor desire to see enacted into law, merely to please a constituency group. These bills die a quick and painless death. Other pieces of legislation have ardent supporters and die in committee only after a long battle. But, in either case, most bills are never reported out of the committees to which they are assigned. In a typical congressional session, 95 percent of the roughly eight thousand bills introduced die in committee—an indication of the power of the congressional committee system.

The relative handful of bills that are reported out of committee must, in the House, pass one additional hurdle within the committee system—the Rules Committee. This powerful committee determines the rules that will govern action on the bill on the House floor. In particular, the Rules Committee allots the time for debate and decides to what extent amendments to the bill can be proposed from the floor. A bill's supporters generally prefer a **closed rule,** which puts severe limits on floor debate and amendments. Opponents of a bill usually prefer an **open rule,** which permits potentially damaging floor debate and makes it easier to add amendments that may cripple the bill or weaken its chances for passage. Thus, the outcome of the Rules Committee's deliberations can be extremely important and the committee's hearings can be an occasion for sharp conflict.

Debate

Party control of the agenda is reinforced by the rule giving the Speaker of the House and the president of the Senate the power of recognition during debate on a bill. Usually the chair knows the purpose for which a member intends to speak well in advance of the occasion. Spontaneous efforts to gain recognition are often foiled. For example, the Speaker may ask, "For what purpose does the member rise?" before deciding whether to grant recognition.

In the House, virtually all of the time allotted by the Rules Committee for debate on a given bill is controlled by the bill's sponsor and by its leading opponent. In almost every case, these two people are the committee chair and the ranking minority member of the committee that processed the bill—or those they designate. These two participants are, by rule and tradition, granted the power to allocate most of the debate time in small amounts to members who are seeking to speak for or against the measure. Preference in the allocation of time goes to the members of the committee whose jurisdiction covers the bill.

Senator Strom Thurmond of South Carolina leaving the Senate chamber after delivering a twenty-four-hour, nineteen-minute filibuster against a civil rights bill in 1957.

In the Senate, the leadership has much less control over floor debate. Indeed, the Senate is unique among the world's legislative bodies for its commitment to unlimited debate. Once given the floor, a senator may speak as long as he or she wishes. On a number of memorable occasions, senators have used this right to prevent action on legislation that they opposed. Through this tactic, called the **filibuster,** small minorities or even one individual in the Senate can force the majority to give in. During the 1950s and 1960s, for example, opponents of civil rights legislation often sought to block its passage by staging a filibuster. The votes of three-fifths of the Senate, or sixty votes, are needed to end a filibuster. This procedure is called **cloture.**

Whereas the filibuster was once an extraordinary tactic used only on rare occasions, in recent years it has been used increasingly often (see Figure 11.8). In 1994, the filibuster was used by Republicans and some Democrats to defeat legislation that would have prohibited employers from permanently replacing striking workers. Later, Republicans threatened to filibuster health care reform legislation. Some Democrats argued that Senate Republicans had begun to use the filibuster as a routine instrument of legislative obstructionism to make up for their minority status in Congress, and proposed rule changes that would make filibustering more difficult. One of the most senior Democrats in the Senate, however, former majority leader Robert Byrd of West Virginia, warned against limiting the filibuster, saying, "The minority can be right, and on many occasions in this country's history, the minority was right."[28] After the GOP won control of the Senate in 1994, many Democrats began to agree with Senator Byrd. They used the filibuster to block Republican initiatives on environmental and social policy. A Democratic-led filibuster in 1996, for example, halted Republican efforts to open up large areas of protected federal land in Utah for development.

FIGURE 11.8

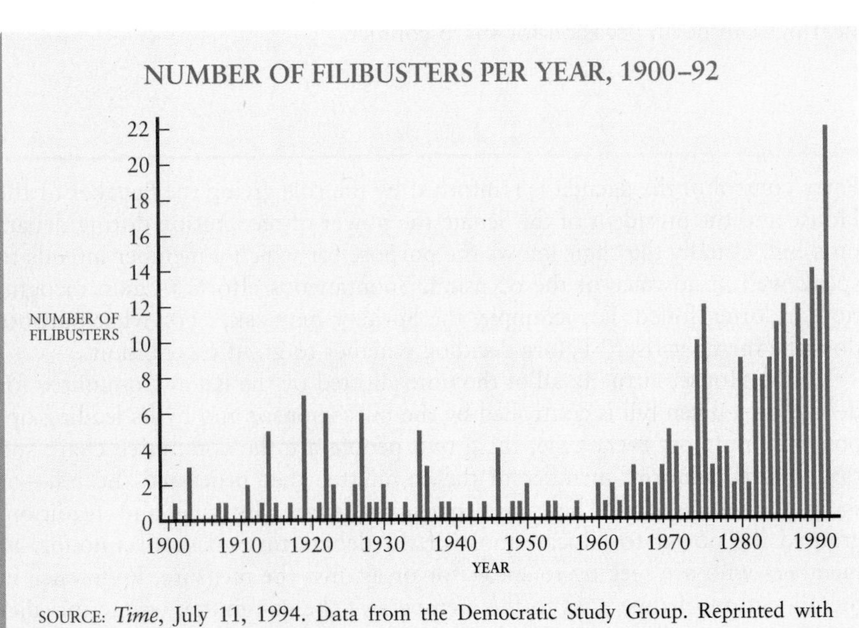

SOURCE: *Time*, July 11, 1994. Data from the Democratic Study Group. Reprinted with permission.

Although it is the best known, the filibuster is not the only technique used to block Senate debate. Under Senate rules, members have a virtually unlimited ability to propose amendments to a pending bill. Each amendment must be voted on before the bill can come to a final vote. The introduction of new amendments can only be stopped by unanimous consent. This, in effect, can permit a determined minority to filibuster-by-amendment, indefinitely delaying the passage of a bill. This tactic was briefly used by Republicans in 1994 to delay the administration's health care initiative. Senators can also place "holds," or stalling devices, on bills to delay debate. Senators place holds on bills when they fear that openly opposing them will be unpopular. Because holds are kept secret, the senators placing the holds do not have to take public responsibility for their actions. Such holds blocked bipartisan efforts to enact popular health insurance reforms for much of 1996.

Once a bill is debated on the floor of the House and the Senate, the leaders schedule it for a vote on the floor of each chamber. By this time, congressional leaders know what the vote will be; leaders do not bring legislation to the floor unless they are fairly certain it is going to pass. As a consequence, it is unusual for the leadership to lose a bill on the floor. On rare occasions, the last moments of the floor vote can be very dramatic, as each party's leadership puts its whip organization into action to make sure that wavering members vote with the party.

Conference Committee: Reconciling House and Senate Versions of Legislation

Getting a bill out of committee and through one of the houses of Congress is no guarantee that a bill will be enacted into law. Frequently, bills that began with similar provisions in both chambers emerge with little resemblance to each other. Alternatively, a bill may be passed by one chamber but undergo substantial revision in the other chamber. In such cases, a conference commit-

This conference committee is meeting to reconcile the differences between House and Senate versions of a budget bill.

tee composed of the senior members of the committees or subcommittees that initiated the bills may be required to iron out differences between the two pieces of legislation. Sometimes members or leaders will let objectionable provisions pass on the floor with the idea that they will get the change they want in conference. Usually, conference committees meet behind closed doors. Agreement requires a majority of each of the two delegations. Legislation that emerges successfully from a conference committee is more often a compromise than a clear victory of one set of forces over another.

When a bill comes out of conference, it faces one more hurdle. Before a bill can be sent to the president for signing, the House-Senate conference report must be approved on the floor of each chamber. Usually such approval is given quickly. Occasionally, however, a bill's opponents use this round of approval as one last opportunity to defeat a piece of legislation.

PRESIDENTIAL ACTION

Once adopted by the House and Senate, a bill goes to the president, who may choose to sign the bill into law or **veto** it. The veto is the president's constitutional power to reject a piece of legislation. To veto a bill, the president returns it unsigned within ten days to the house of Congress in which it originated. If Congress adjourns during the ten-day period, and the president has taken no action, the bill is also considered to be vetoed. This latter method is known as the **pocket veto.** The possibility of a presidential veto affects how willing members of Congress are to push for different pieces of legislation at different times. If they think a proposal is likely to be vetoed they might shelve it for a later time.

A presidential veto may be overridden by a two-thirds vote in both the House and Senate. A veto override says much about the support that a president can expect from Congress, and it can deliver a stinging blow to the executive branch. President George Bush used his veto power on forty-six occasions during his four years in office and in all but one instance was able to defeat or avoid a congressional override of his action. Bush's frequent resort to the veto power was one indicator of the struggle between the White House and the Congress over domestic and foreign policy that took place during his term. Similarly, President Clinton used the veto to block many Republican programs in 1995.

How Congress Decides

> ➤ What sorts of influences inside and outside of government determine how members of Congress vote on legislation? How do these influences vary according to the type of issue?

What determines the kinds of legislation that Congress ultimately produces? According to the most simple theories of representation, members of Congress would respond to the views of their constituents. In fact, the process of creating a legislative agenda, drawing up a list of possible measures, and deciding among them is a very complex process, in which a variety of influences from inside and outside government play important roles. External influences include a legislator's constituency and various interest groups. Influences from inside government include party leadership, congressional colleagues, and the president. Let us examine each of these influences individually and then consider how they interact to produce congressional policy decisions.

Constituency

Because members of Congress, for the most part, want to be re-elected, we would expect the views of their constituents to have a key influence on the decisions that legislators make. Yet constituency influence is not so straightforward. In fact, most constituents do not even know what policies their representatives support. The number of citizens who *do* pay attention to such matters—the attentive public—is usually very small. Nonetheless, members of Congress spend a lot of time worrying about what their constituents think, because these representatives realize that the choices they make may be scrutinized in a future election and used as ammunition by an opposing candidate. Because of this possibility, members of Congress try to anticipate their constituents' policy views.[29] Legislators are more likely to act in accordance with those views if they think that voters will take them into account during elections. In this way, constituents may affect congressional policy choices even when there is little direct evidence of their influence.

Representative John Conyers meets with constituents in his Capitol Hill office.

Interest Groups

Interest groups are another important external influence on the policies that Congress produces. When members of Congress are making voting decisions, those interest groups that have some connection to constituents in particular members' districts are most likely to be influential. For this reason, interest groups with the ability to mobilize followers in many congressional districts may be especially influential in Congress. The small-business lobby, for example, played an important role in defeating President Clinton's proposal for comprehensive health care reform in 1993–94. The mobilization of networks of small businesses across the country meant that virtually every member of Congress had to take their views into account. In recent years, Washington-based interest groups with little grassroots strength have recognized the importance of such locally generated activity. They have, accordingly, sought to simulate grassroots pressure, using a strategy that has been nicknamed "Astroturf lobbying." Such campaigns encourage constituents to sign form letters or postcards, which are then sent to congressional representatives. Sophisticated "grassroots" campaigns set up toll-free telephone numbers for a system in which simply reporting your name and address to the listening computer will generate a letter to your congressional representative. One Senate office estimated that such organized campaigns to demonstrate "grassroots" support account for two-thirds of the mail the office received. As such campaigns increase, however, they may become less influential, because members of Congress are aware of how rare actual constituent interest actually is.[30]

Members of the letter carriers' union lobby a member of Congress.

Interest groups also have substantial influence in setting the legislative agenda and in helping to craft specific language in legislation. Today, sophisticated lobbyists win influence by providing information about policies to busy members of Congress. As one lobbyist noted, "You can't get access without knowledge. . . . I can go in to see [former Energy and Commerce Committee chair] John Dingell, but if I have nothing to offer or nothing to say, he's not going to want to see me."[31] In recent years, interest groups have also begun to build broader coalitions and comprehensive campaigns around particular policy issues. These coalitions do not rise from the grass roots, but instead are put together by Washington lobbyists who launch comprehensive lobbying campaigns that combine stimulated grassroots activity with information and campaign funding for members of Congress. In the 104th Congress, the Republican leadership worked so closely with lobbyists that critics charged that the boundaries between lobbyists and legislators had been erased, and that lobbyists had become "adjunct staff to the Republican leadership."[32]

Party Discipline

In both the House and Senate, party leaders have a good deal of influence over the behavior of their party members. This influence, sometimes called "party discipline," was once so powerful that it dominated the lawmaking process. At the turn of the century, party leaders could often command the allegiance of more than 90 percent of their members. A vote on which 90 percent or more of the members of one party take one position while at least 90 percent of the members of the other party take the opposing position is called a **party vote.** At the beginning of the twentieth century, nearly half of all **roll-call votes** in the House of Representatives were party votes. Today, this type

AMERICAN POLITICAL CULTURE

The Values of Newt Gingrich

"America is an idea, the most idea-based civilization in history. To be an American is to embrace a set of values. . . ."[1] The writer of these words is Newt Gingrich, one of the most influential and important American politicians today. Gingrich, the fifty-four-year-old Speaker of the House, spearheaded the Republican takeover of Congress in 1994 in part by successfully casting the elections as a national referendum on "values." But what are the values that Newt Gingrich professes? Are those who embrace different values, or express ambivalence about them, not really Americans?

In his book *To Renew America,* Gingrich lists five values that "form the heart of [American] civilization."[2] They so deeply define an American identity, he says, that an immigrant who accepts them is as fully "American" as a Boston Brahmin whose ancestors arrived on the Mayflower. According to Gingrich, these core American values are, first, a common understanding of national identity and origin, an understanding based on religious faith: "In America, power comes from God to the individual and is loaned to the state."[3] The other American values according to Gingrich are an ethic of individual responsibility, a spirit of entrepreneurial free enterprise, the spirit of invention and discovery, and pragmatism and the concern for craft and excellence.

By portraying "the heart of our civilization" as agreement on certain values, Gingrich suggests that consensus is the normal mode of American life, and that conflict represents an aberration in that pattern. Such a "consensus model" was the dominant view of American historians in the 1950s and early 1960s, the years when Gingrich's intellectual orientation was formed and to which he constantly appeals as a high-water mark of American values: "If you want a sense of the personal values we should be communicating to children, get the Boy Scout or Girl Scout handbook. Or go and look at *Reader's Digest* and *The Saturday Evening Post* from around 1955."[4] The consensus model lost favor during the 1960s, first with the civil rights struggle in the South, and then with the disillusionment surrounding the Vietnam War. It is significant that Gingrich has little to say about this period as reflective of American values, although surely the mass political protests of that time drew deeply on a tradition of American idealism.

If "America is an idea," as Newt Gingrich says, and if that idea is represented by the values he professes, then are those with a different idea and different values not really Americans? Gingrich's argument about the values at the heart of American civilization will probably strike most of us as a somewhat accurate description of mainstream American beliefs over the centuries. But the mainstream, of course, is not the whole river. Dissenting views and beliefs have always had a place in American life. In fact, toleration for dissent and difference—for individual liberty and the individual's right to define his or her pursuit of happiness—is one of the proudest and most deeply held of American values. But celebrating certain "American" values runs the risk of turning difference into disloyalty, and politics from a civil struggle between honorably differing factions into a kind of holy war to preserve American culture. Such an impulse once drove Newt Gingrich to call President Clinton and his wife "the enemies of normal Americans." Are they? Or are they, and other political opponents of Newt Gingrich, as "normal" and "American" as he is, despite their different ideas?

[1] Newt Gingrich, *To Renew America* (New York: HarperCollins, 1995), p. 30. All quotations herein are taken from this book.

[2] p. 32.

[3] p. 34.

[4] p. 78.

of party-line voting is rare in Congress. It is, however, fairly common to find at least a majority of the Democrats opposing a majority of the Republicans on any given issue.

Typically, party unity is greater in the House than in the Senate. House rules grant greater procedural control of business to the majority party leaders, which gives them more influence over House members. In the Senate, however, the leadership has few sanctions over its members. Senate Minority Leader Tom Daschle once observed that a Senate leader seeking to influence other senators has as incentives "a bushel full of carrots and a few twigs."[33]

Party unity has increased in recent sessions of Congress as a result of the intense partisan struggles during the Reagan and Bush years (see Figure 11.9). Although straight party-line voting continued briefly in the 103rd Congress (1993–94) following Bill Clinton's election in 1992, the situation soon gave way to the many long-term factors working against party discipline in the United States.[34]

At the beginning of the first session of the 104th Congress, House Speaker Newt Gingrich was able to secure the support of virtually all House Republicans for elements of the GOP Contract with America (see Box 11.1). As the session wore on, however, party unity began to diminish, particularly over the issue of tax cuts. Gingrich had hoped to enact a substantial tax cut, but some other Republicans argued that any savings from cuts in federal spending should be applied to deficit reduction. In spite of such disagreements, however, party unity among Republicans in the House was impressive, particularly in light of the fact that Gingrich had at his disposal none of the sanctions that nineteenth-century Speakers used to maintain party discipline. Gingrich seemed able to command unity purely on the basis of ideology and personality.

FIGURE 11.9

The party unity score is the percentage of times that members voted with the majority of their party on votes on which a majority of one party voted against the majority of the other party.

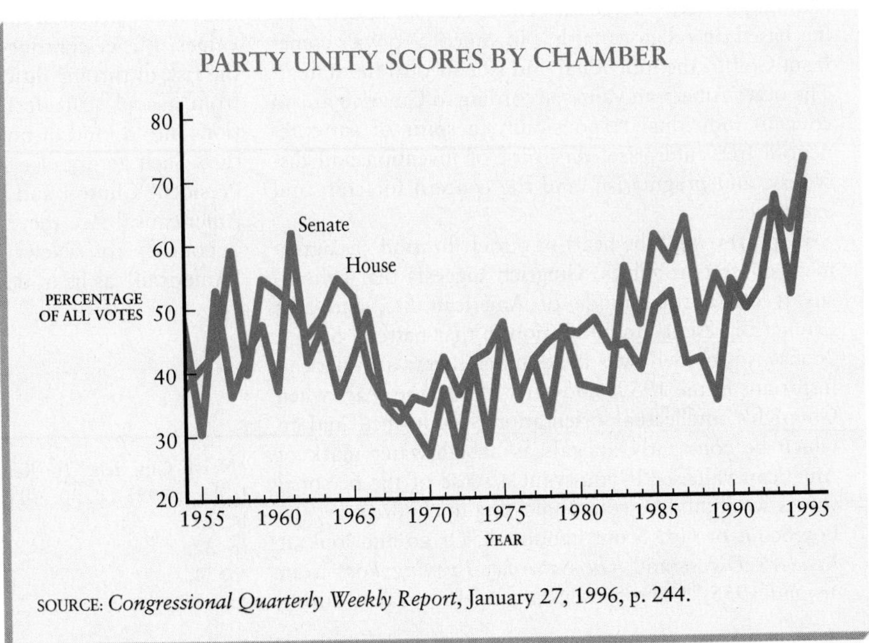

SOURCE: *Congressional Quarterly Weekly Report*, January 27, 1996, p. 244.

In the Senate, of course, efforts by Republican leaders to impose unity upon their members were never very successful. For example, a major piece of the Republican agenda in the first hundred days of the 104th Congress—the balanced budget amendment—was defeated, or at least deferred, by the vote of one powerful Republican senator, Mark Hatfield.

The GOP's full-scale offensive against agencies and programs that serve Democratic interests and constituencies initially produced high levels of Democratic party unity in both the House and Senate. By March 1995, how-

BOX 11.1

Ten bills that House Republicans pledged to introduce during the first one hundred days of a Republican-led 104th Congress

HOUSE REPUBLICANS' "CONTRACT WITH AMERICA"

1 **Fiscal Responsibility Act** would propose a constitutional amendment requiring the president to submit, and the Congress to pass, a balanced federal budget for each fiscal year; and would give the president a line-item veto over specific budgetary provisions in a bill passed by Congress.

2 **Taking Back Our Streets Act** would limit federal and state *habeas corpus* appeals; mandate minimum sentences for and victim restitution from those convicted of gun-related crimes; replace recently passed crime-prevention programs with block grants for local law-enforcement programs; relax rules for admission of evidence at criminal trials; and speed deportation procedures for aliens convicted of serious crimes.

3 **Personal Responsibility Act** would limit eligibility for the federal Aid to Families with Dependent Children (AFDC) program; deny AFDC benefits to teenage mothers; impose work requirements for those receiving AFDC benefits; and transfer much of the responsibility for social welfare programs to the states.

4 **Family Reinforcement Act** would grant tax credits for adoption and for care of elderly dependents and increase penalties for sexual offenses against children.

5 **American Dream Restoration Act** would grant tax credits for families with children; reduce taxes on some married couples; and expand uses for Individual Retirement Accounts (IRAs).

6 **National Security Restoration Act** would restrict participation of U.S. forces in United Nations peacekeeping activities; subject all funding for and participation in U.N. peacekeeping activities to congressional approval; and reinstate development of the "Star Wars" anti-ballistic missile defense system and other such systems.

7 **Senior Citizens' Equity Act** would double the income level beyond which Social Security benefits are reduced; reduce taxes on upper-income recipients of Social Security; and create tax benefits for the purchase of private long-term health care insurance.

8 **Job Creation and Wage Enhancement Act** would cut the capital gains tax; increase the estate tax exemption; and impose additional requirements for and restrictions on federal regulation.

9 **Common Sense Legal Reforms Act** would require the loser to pay the legal expenses of the winner in lawsuits filed in federal courts; reform product liability laws; and limit lawsuits by shareholders against companies whose stock they hold.

10 **Citizen Legislature Act** would propose a constitutional amendment to limit tenure of senators and representatives to a maximum of 12 years.

SOURCE: House Republican Conference, *Legislative Digest,* September 27, 1994.

ever, some conservative Democrats had begun to break ranks. Several Democratic representatives actually switched their affiliations to the Republican Party because, according to some, the Democratic Party was no longer interested in the views of its conservative members.

To some extent, party unity is based on ideology and background. Republican members of Congress are more likely than Democrats to be drawn from rural or suburban areas. Democrats are likely to be more liberal on economic and social questions than their Republican colleagues. These differences certainly help to explain roll-call divisions between the two parties. Ideology and background, however, are only part of the explanation of party unity. The other part has to do with party organization and leadership. Although party organization has weakened since the turn of the century, today's party leaders still have some resources at their disposal: (1) committee assignments, (2) access to the floor, (3) the whip system, (4) logrolling, and (5) the presidency. These resources are regularly used and are often effective in securing the support of party members.

Committee Assignments Leaders can create debts among members by helping them get favorable committee assignments. These assignments are made early in the congressional careers of most members and cannot be taken from them if they later balk at party discipline. Nevertheless, if the leadership goes out of its way to get the right assignment for a member, this effort is likely to create a bond of obligation that can be called upon without any other payments or favors. This is one reason the leadership worked so hard to give freshmen favorable assignments in the 104th Congress.

Access to the Floor The most important everyday resource available to the parties is control over access to the floor. With thousands of bills awaiting passage and most members clamoring for access in order to influence a bill or to publicize themselves, floor time is precious. In the Senate, the leadership allows ranking committee members to influence the allocation of floor time—who will speak for how long; in the House, the Speaker, as head of the majority party (in consultation with the minority leader), allocates large blocks of floor time. Thus, floor time is allocated in both houses of Congress by the majority and minority leaders. More importantly, the Speaker of the House and the majority leader in the Senate possess the power of recognition. Although this power may not appear to be substantial, it is a formidable authority and can be used to stymie a piece of legislation completely or to frustrate a member's attempts to speak on a particular issue. Because the power is significant, members of Congress usually attempt to stay on good terms with the Speaker and the majority leader in order to ensure that they will continue to be recognized.

Some House members, Republicans in particular, have also taken advantage of "special orders," under which members can address the floor after the close of business. These addresses are typically made to an empty chamber, but are usually carried live by C-SPAN, a cable television channel. Before 1995, when Democrats controlled the House floor, Republicans often were forced to use special orders to present their views effectively to national audiences. Representative Newt Gingrich, for example, launched a televised after-

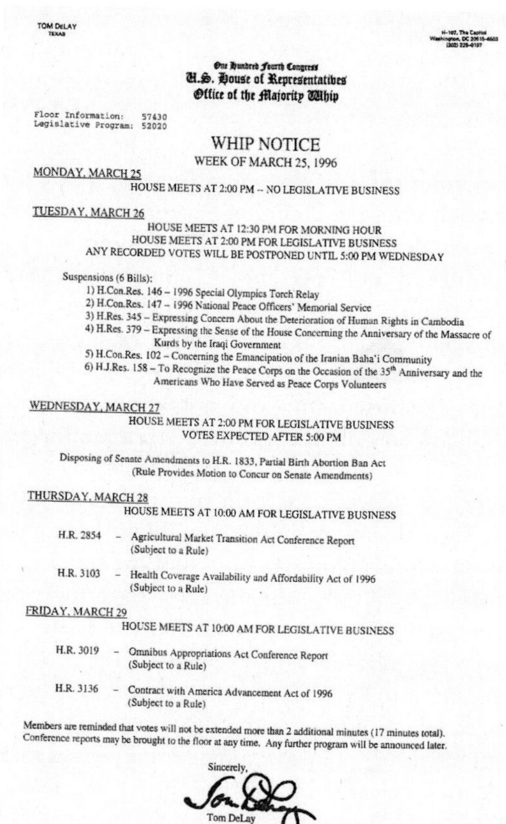

TOM DELAY
TEXAS

H-107, The Capitol
Washington, DC 20515-6503
(202) 225-0197

One Hundred Fourth Congress
U.S. House of Representatives
Office of the Majority Whip

Floor Information: 57430
Legislative Program: 52020

WHIP NOTICE

WEEK OF MARCH 25, 1996

MONDAY, MARCH 25

HOUSE MEETS AT 2:00 PM -- NO LEGISLATIVE BUSINESS

TUESDAY, MARCH 26

HOUSE MEETS AT 12:30 PM FOR MORNING HOUR
HOUSE MEETS AT 2:00 PM FOR LEGISLATIVE BUSINESS
ANY RECORDED VOTES WILL BE POSTPONED UNTIL 5:00 PM WEDNESDAY

Suspensions (6 Bills):

1) H.Con.Res. 146 – 1996 Special Olympics Torch Relay
2) H.Con.Res. 147 – 1996 National Peace Officers' Memorial Service
3) H.Res. 345 – Expressing Concern About the Deterioration of Human Rights in Cambodia
4) H.Res. 379 – Expressing the Sense of the House Concerning the Anniversary of the Massacre of Kurds by the Iraqi Government
5) H.Con.Res. 102 – Concerning the Emancipation of the Iranian Baha'i Community
6) H.J.Res. 158 – To Recognize the Peace Corps on the Occasion of the 35th Anniversary and the Americans Who Have Served as Peace Corps Volunteers

WEDNESDAY, MARCH 27

HOUSE MEETS AT 2:00 PM FOR LEGISLATIVE BUSINESS
VOTES EXPECTED AFTER 5:00 PM

Disposing of Senate Amendments to H.R. 1833, Partial Birth Abortion Ban Act
(Rule Provides Motion to Concur on Senate Amendments)

THURSDAY, MARCH 28

HOUSE MEETS AT 10:00 AM FOR LEGISLATIVE BUSINESS

H.R. 2854 – Agricultural Market Transition Act Conference Report
(Subject to a Rule)

H.R. 3103 – Health Coverage Availability and Affordability Act of 1996
(Subject to a Rule)

FRIDAY, MARCH 29

HOUSE MEETS AT 10:00 AM FOR LEGISLATIVE BUSINESS

H.R. 3019 – Omnibus Appropriations Act Conference Report
(Subject to a Rule)

H.R. 3136 – Contract with America Advancement Act of 1996
(Subject to a Rule)

Members are reminded that votes will not be extended more than 2 additional minutes (17 minutes total). Conference reports may be brought to the floor at any time. Any further program will be announced later.

Sincerely,

Tom DeLay
Majority Whip

A "whip notice" sent by House Majority Whip Tom DeLay to inform Republican members of the House of their leadership's agenda for that week.

hours attack on Democratic House Speaker Jim Wright in 1988 that ultimately led to Wright's resignation.

The Whip System Some influence accrues to party leaders through the **whip system,** which is primarily a communications network. Between twelve and twenty assistant and regional whips are selected to operate at the direction of the majority or minority leader and the whip. They take polls of all the members in order to learn their intentions on specific bills. This enables the leaders to know if they have enough support to allow a vote as well as whether the vote is so close that they need to put pressure on a few undecided members. Leaders also use the whip system to convey their wishes and plans to the members, but only in very close votes do they actually exert pressure on a member. In those instances, the Speaker or a lieutenant will go to a few party members who have indicated they will switch if their vote is essential. The whip system helps the leaders limit pressuring members to a few times per session.

The whip system helps maintain party unity in both houses of Congress, but it is particularly critical in the House of Representatives because of the large number of legislators whose positions and votes must be accounted for. The majority and minority whips and their assistants must be adept at inducing compromise among legislators who hold widely differing viewpoints. The whips' personal styles and their perception of their function significantly affect the development of legislative coalitions and influence the compromises that emerge.

Logrolling An agreement between two or more members of Congress who have nothing in common except the need for support is called **logrolling.** The agreement states, in effect, "You support me on bill X and I'll support you on another bill of your choice." Since party leaders are the center of the communications networks in the two chambers, they can help members create large logrolling coalitions. Hundreds of logrolling deals are made each year, and while there are no official record-keeping books, it would be a poor party leader whose whips did not know who owed what to whom. In some instances, logrolling produces strange alliances. A seemingly unlikely alliance emerged in Congress in June 1994, when 119 mainly conservative senators and representatives from oil-producing states met with President Clinton to suggest that they might be willing to support the president's health care proposals in exchange for his support for a number of tax breaks for the oil industry. Senator J. Bennett Johnston of Louisiana, a leader of the oil-state representatives, contended that the issues of health care and oil production were closely related since both "affected the long-term economic security of the nation." Ironically, the oil-producing groups that promoted this alliance are generally among the most conservative forces in the nation. When asked what he personally thought of the president's health care proposal, George Alcorn, a leading industry lobbyist involved in the logrolling effort, dismissed Clinton's plan as "socialized medicine." Good logrolling, it would seem, is not hampered by minor ideological concerns.[35]

The Presidency Of all the influences that maintain the clarity of party lines in Congress, the influence of the presidency is probably the most important. Indeed, the office is a touchstone of party discipline in Congress. Since the late 1940s, under President Harry Truman, presidents each year have identified a number of bills to be considered part of their administration's program. By the mid-1950s, both parties in Congress began to look to the president for these proposals, which became the most significant part of Congress's agenda. The president's support is a criterion for party loyalty, and party leaders are able to use it to rally some members.

WEIGHING DIVERSE INFLUENCES

Clearly, many different factors affect congressional decisions. But at various points in the decision-making process, some factors are likely to be more influential than others. For example, interest groups may be more effective at the committee stage, when their expertise is especially valued and their visibility is less obvious. Because committees play a key role in deciding what legislation actually reaches the floor of the House or Senate, interest groups can often put a halt to bills they dislike, or they can ensure that the options that do reach the floor are those that the group's members support.

Once legislation reaches the floor, and members of Congress are deciding among alternatives, constituent opinion will become more important. Legislators are also influenced very much by other legislators: many of their assessments about the substance and politics of legislation come from fellow members of Congress.

The influence of the external and internal forces described in the preceding section also varies according to the kind of issue being considered. On policies of great importance to powerful interest groups—farm subsidies, for example—those groups are likely to have considerable influence. On other issues, members of Congress may be less attentive to narrow interest groups and more willing to consider what they see as the general interest.

Finally, the mix of influences varies according to the historical moment. The 1994 electoral victory of Republicans allowed their party to control both houses of Congress for the first time in forty years. That fact, combined with an unusually assertive Republican leadership, meant that party leaders became especially important in decision making. The willingness of moderate Republicans to support measures they had once opposed indicated the unusual importance of party leadership in this period. As House Minority Leader Richard Gephardt put it, "When you've been in the desert 40 years, your instinct is to help Moses."[36]

Beyond Legislation: Other Congressional Powers

> ➤ Besides the power to pass legislation, what other powers allow Congress to influence the process of government?

In addition to the power to make the law, Congress has at its disposal an array of other instruments through which to influence the process of government. The Constitution gives the Senate the power to approve treaties and appointments. And Congress has a number of other powers through which it can share with the other branches the capacity to administer the laws.

Oversight

Oversight, as applied to Congress, refers not to something neglected, but to the effort to oversee or to supervise how legislation is carried out by the executive branch. Oversight is carried out by committees or subcommittees of the Senate or House, which conduct hearings and investigations in order to analyze and evaluate bureaucratic agencies and the effectiveness of their programs. Their purpose may be to locate inefficiencies or abuses of power, to explore the relationship between what an agency does and what a law intended, or to change or abolish a program. Most programs and agencies are subject to some oversight every year during the course of hearings on **appropriations,** that is, the funding of agencies and government programs.

Committees or subcommittees have the power to subpoena witnesses, take oaths, cross-examine, compel testimony, and bring criminal charges for contempt (refusing to cooperate) and perjury (lying). Hearings and investigations resemble each other in many ways, but they differ on one fundamental point. A hearing is usually held on a specific bill, and the questions asked there are usually intended to build a record with regard to that bill. In an investigation, the committee or subcommittee does not begin with a particular bill, but examines a broad area or problem and then concludes its investigation with one or more proposed bills. One example of an investigation is the congressional inquiry into the Reagan administration's shipment of arms to the government of Iran.

Advice and Consent: Special Senate Powers

The Constitution has given the Senate a special power, one that is not based on lawmaking. The president has the power to make treaties and to appoint top executive officers, ambassadors, and federal judges—but only "with the Advice and Consent of the Senate" (Article II, Section 2). For treaties, two-thirds of those present must concur; for appointments, a simple majority is required.

The power to approve or reject presidential requests also involves the power to set conditions. The Senate only occasionally exercises its power to reject treaties and appointments, and usually that is when opposite parties control the Senate and the White House. During the final two years of President Reagan's term, for example, Senate Democrats rejected Judge Robert Bork's Supreme Court nomination and gave clear indications that they would reject a second Reagan nominee, Judge Douglas Ginsburg, who withdrew his nomination before the Senate could act. These instances, however, actually underscore the restraint with which the Senate usually uses its power to reject presidential requests. For example, only nine judicial nominees have been rejected by the Senate during the past century, whereas hundreds have been approved.

Most presidents make every effort to take potential Senate opposition into account in treaty negotiations and will frequently resort to **executive agreements** with foreign powers instead of treaties. The Supreme Court has held that such agreements are equivalent to treaties, but they do not need Senate approval.[37] In the past, presidents sometimes concluded secret agreements without informing Congress of the agreements' contents, or even their existence. For example, American involvement in the Vietnam War grew in part out of a series of secret arrangements made between American presidents and the South Vietnamese during the 1950s and 1960s. Congress did not even learn of the existence of these agreements until 1969. In 1972, Congress passed the Case Act, which requires that the president inform Congress of any executive agreement within sixty days of its having been reached. This provides Congress with the opportunity to cancel agreements that it opposes. In addition, Congress can limit the president's ability to conduct foreign policy through executive agreement by refusing to appropriate the funds needed to implement an agreement. In this way, for example, executive agreements to provide American economic or military assistance to foreign governments can be modified or even canceled by Congress.

Power and Representation

- What is the relationship between congressional power and congressional representation?
- What is the history of congressional power vis-à-vis the president?
- Can Congress be both representative and effective?

Congressional power cannot be separated from congressional representation. Indeed, there is a reciprocal relationship between the two. Without its important governmental powers, Congress would be a very different sort of representative body. Americans might feel some sense of symbolic representation if they found that Congress contained members of their own race, religion, ethnic background, or social class. They might feel some sense of gratification if members of Congress tried to help them with their problems. But without its array of powers, Congress could do little to represent effectively the views and interests of its constituents. Power is necessary for effective congressional representation. At the same time, the power of Congress is ultimately a function of its capacity to effectively represent important groups and forces in American society. This can best be understood by looking at the relationship between Congress and the executive branch over the course of American history.

Because they feared both executive and legislative tyranny, the framers of the Constitution pitted Congress and the president against one another. But for more than one hundred years, the contest was unequal. During the first century of American government, Congress was the dominant institution. American foreign and domestic policy was formulated and implemented by Congress, and generally, the most powerful figures in American government were the Speaker of the House and the leaders of the Senate—not the president. The War of 1812 was planned and fought by Congress. The great sectional compromises prior to the Civil War were formulated in Congress, without much intervention from the executive branch. Even during the Civil War, a period of extraordinary presidential leadership, a joint congressional committee on the conduct of the war played a role in formulating war plans and campaign tactics, and even had a hand in the promotion of officers. After the Civil War, when President Andrew Johnson sought to interfere with congressional plans for Reconstruction, he was summarily impeached, saved from conviction by only one vote. Subsequent presidents understood the moral and did not attempt to thwart Congress.

This congressional pre-eminence began to diminish after the turn of the century, so that by the 1960s, the executive had become, at least temporarily, the dominant branch of American government. The major domestic policy initiatives of the twentieth century—Franklin Roosevelt's "New Deal," Harry Truman's "Fair Deal," John F. Kennedy's "New Frontier," and Lyndon Johnson's "Great Society"—all included some congressional involvement but were essentially developed, introduced, and implemented by the executive. In

The opening of the Senate impeachment of President Andrew Johnson on March 13, 1868. The articles of impeachment accused Johnson of failing to execute the laws passed by Congress.

the area of foreign policy, although Congress continued to be influential during the twentieth century, the focus of decision-making power clearly moved into the executive branch. The War of 1812 may have been a congressional war, but in the twentieth century, American entry into World War I, World War II, Korea, Vietnam, and a host of lesser conflicts was essentially a presidential—not a congressional—decision. What accounts for this decline of congressional power?

A key factor in understanding the power of any political institution, be it Congress, the executive, or the judiciary, is its representative character. If a political institution is able to link itself to important groups and forces in the society by serving their interests and meeting their needs, then these forces can generally be expected, in turn, to support that institution in its struggles with other agencies or against any public opposition to its programs. On the other hand, if a political institution is unable to link itself to a political constituency, then it may find itself without defenses if it comes under attack. During the nineteenth century, Congress—particularly the House of Representatives—was the most accessible and permeable institution of American government. Turnover in the House was rapid, and new groups and forces in American society generally found it easy to obtain access to the House and to find members of Congress to support their aims and interests. In other words, Congress was the most representative governmental institution. This led various groups in society to support Congress in its battles with the executive branch and the courts. For example, during the 1830s, many merchants and bankers found Congress very receptive to their interests and became a strong constituency for congressional power vis-à-vis what they called the "usurpations" of the executive branch under President Andrew Jackson, in particular his attack on the Bank of the United States, an institution that business interests saw as essential to their well-being.

During the twentieth century, the executive branch became far more accessible than Congress and important national political forces began more and more to turn to the executive with their problems.[38] To the extent that they found the executive to be hospitable to them, these forces began to support executive or presidential rather than congressional power. The critical juncture in the congressional-executive balance was the period of the New Deal. In the 1930s, President Franklin Delano Roosevelt succeeded, through major innovations in programs and policies, in linking a number of important social and political forces—organized labor, urban political machines, farmers, blacks, key sectors of American industry—to the executive branch. These forces were the beneficiaries of the programs developed by the Roosevelt administration and its successors. In turn, these forces formed a constituency for executive power.[39] The upshot was that during the Roosevelt era, powerful groups, forces, and interests in American society came to see the executive branch as more representative—as the agency most likely to be open to their demands. This perception helped greatly to enhance executive power at the expense of congressional power.

Thus, power and representation have been closely linked in congressional history. Congress was most powerful when it was most representative, least powerful when it was least accessible to important groups in society. In the last thirty years, there has been a good deal of resurgence of congressional power vis-à-vis the executive. This occurred primarily because Democratic-controlled Congresses sought to represent many important political forces, such as the civil rights, feminist, environmental, consumer, and peace movements, which in turn became constituencies for congressional power. The increased numbers of minorities and women in the Congress have also ensured that issues of special concern to these groups reached the congressional agenda (although it still does not guarantee that Congress will address their concerns). According to one study, women in the 101st Congress (1989–90) were responsible for 89 percent of the feminist legislation introduced in those years.[40] To increase their effectiveness, women, blacks, Latinos, and Asians in Congress have organized into caucuses, which can provide research and support to mobilize on issues that their members identify as important. The Congressional Black Caucus, for example, has presented its priorities through an alternative budget introduced into Congress. The Congressional Caucus for Women's Issues has consistently supported a number of bills to promote women's economic equality.[41]

A few of the fifty-seven women who served in the 104th Congress, who were responsible for introducing to Congress issues ranging from women's health to gun control. Shown here, from left to right, are Senators Nancy Kassebaum, Carol Moseley-Braun, Barbara Boxer, Barbara Mikulski, Kay Bailey Hutchison, Dianne Feinstein, and Patty Murray.

During the mid-1990s, Congress became more receptive to a variety of new conservative political forces, including groups on the social and religious right as well as more traditional economic conservatives. After Republicans won control of both houses in the 1994 elections, Congress took the lead in developing programs and policies supported by these groups. These efforts won Congress the support of conservative forces in its battles for power against a Democratic White House.

But the resurgence of congressional power and the opening of access to new interests has also sparked discontent. In fact, as Congress has become more powerful and its deliberations have become more open, the American public seems to feel less and less satisfied that Congress is effective and representative. How has this happened?

THE AARP: GRAY POWER

America's elderly population has been growing at an ever-increasing rate. Advances in health care and quality of life for the nation's senior citizens have meant longer, fuller lives. As this population and its resources have grown, so has its political power.

In recent decades, many of the government's most important, large-scale programs have been aimed at the elderly population. Such landmark programs as Social Security, designed to provide a national, guaranteed retirement pension program, and Medicare, which provides health care to millions of senior citizens, have consumed a greater percentage of federal resources. As a consequence, these "entitlement" programs have come under close scrutiny by budget cutters looking for a way to reduce federal spending.

Yet no important changes in such programs are likely to occur without the approval of the American Association of Retired Persons (AARP). Arguably the most powerful and feared interest group in the country, the AARP was founded in 1958, partly in response to the unwillingness of private insurance companies to offer insurance protection for the elderly (a need that was filled with the creation of Medicare in 1965). The AARP at first had relatively little involvement in politics, but by the 1970s, its growing membership base became more politicized as tightening budget pressures squeezed entitlement programs.

In recent years, the AARP has grown by leaps and bounds; it now claims 33 million members. In 1994, it generated $382 million in revenues. In addition, it received another $86 million in federal grants. Almost half of its operating money comes from the sale of various products and services to its members; advertising in its publications, including the magazine *Modern Maturity,* generates about 12 percent of the organization's revenues. Annual membership dues of $8 per year generate almost 40 percent of AARP revenues. AARP membership is attractive not only because of the low cost of membership, but also because members have access to a wide array of discounted services and programs, including insurance, a mail-order prescription drug supply, and mutual funds. The only requirement for joining is that members be at least 50 years old.

In part, the congressional reforms enacted in the 1970s actually did make Congress less effective and, ironically, more permeable to special interests. The fragmentation of power in Congress has made it harder for members to reach decisions. "Turf battles"—struggles over who should take charge of what—often take more congressional energy than deliberations over policy. The decentralization of power in Congress has made each member more of an independent operator. Members are now less willing to compromise and more eager to take positions that benefit them individually, even if they undermine possibilities for enacting policy. These circumstances have created a Congress that sometimes seems to spend endless hours in increasingly negative debates that do not produce results. The public, therefore, has come to view Congress as a group of privileged elites concerned only about their own prerogatives. The word "gridlock" seems to sum up the state of congressional decision making.

Ironically, the measures that sought to ensure more public access to Congress have actually increased the access of interest groups. Open committee meetings have made it possible for sophisticated interest groups to monitor and influence every aspect of developing legislation. The narrow perspective put forth by an interest group makes it difficult for members of Congress to keep their eyes on the big picture of what it wants to achieve. Hundreds of

The AARP's size and resources make it a powerful force in Washington politics, and one that few members of Congress have wanted to challenge. In addition, its vast membership base is composed of people who have a lifetime's accumulation of experience and knowledge that can be put to political purposes, and who also are more likely to have the time to devote to political activities precisely because many of them no longer work. Furthermore, although some elderly live on the edge of poverty, the average wealth of the elderly population is second only to that of the age group just below retirement age.

Yet the AARP's intensive and mostly effective lobbying efforts have come under political fire in recent years because the organization receives tax-exempt status by virtue of its status as a private social welfare organization. It thus pays no income taxes, and also receives federal grants and reduced postal rates. Critics in Congress have questioned whether the AARP should be engaged in political lobbying while receiving so many government benefits and breaks.

In 1995, legislation was introduced in Congress to prevent politically active groups such as the AARP from receiving federal grant money. In addition, both the Internal Revenue Service and the U.S. Postal Service have challenged some of the AARP's special breaks. Nevertheless, the movement of America's population patterns toward an ever-older society, combined with escalating pressures to reduce government spending and entitlement programs, all but guarantee that the AARP will continue to be a formidable force in Washington. Few elected officials can dismiss the weight of 33 million citizens.

SOURCE: Henry J. Pratt, *The Gray Lobby* (Chicago: University of Chicago Press, 1976).

amendments can undermine the overall thrust of legislation. Open meetings also deprive members of Congress of the political "cover" often necessary to make compromises. Worried that particular actions could be used against them in a future election, members of Congress have become very risk averse. In this sense, too much accountability can paralyze the institution.

The very strong role of the Republican congressional leadership elected in the 104th Congress only temporarily quieted complaints about congressional gridlock. Doubts about congressional effectiveness and representativeness remain. The congressional reforms of the 1970s were intended to distribute power more equally inside Congress in order to provide more equal representation to all constituents. But these reforms made it more difficult for members to build coalitions and for legislators to become experts in particular policy areas. The unanticipated, negative consequences of these reforms have highlighted the trade-off between representation and effectiveness in Congress.[42] Americans are becoming increasingly aware that greater individual access to Congress and more symbolic representation do not add up to more power. The results have increased public cynicism and apathy. Rebuilding public faith in Congress may require yet another round of institutional reform, as well as efforts to organize and mobilize broad social interests to achieve meaningful representation.

Summary

The U.S. Congress plays a vital role in American democracy. It is both the key national representative body and the focal point for decision making in Washington, D.C. Throughout American history, Congress has sought to combine representation and power as it made policy. In recent years, however, many Americans have become disillusioned with the ability of Congress to represent fairly and to exercise power responsibly.

Both sociological and agency representation play a role in the relationship between members of Congress and their constituencies. However, Congress is not fully representative because it is not a sociological microcosm of the United States. Members of Congress do seek to act as agents for their constituents by representing the views and interests of those constituents in the governmental process.

The activities of members of Congress are strongly influenced by electoral considerations. Who gets elected to Congress is influenced by who runs for office, the power of incumbency, and the way congressional districts are drawn. In order to assist their chances of re-election, members of Congress provide services and patronage to their constituents.

In order to make policy, Congress depends on a complex internal organization. Six basic dimensions of Congress affect the legislative process: (1) the parties, (2) the committees, (3) the staff, (4) the caucuses, (5) the rules, and (6) the presidency.

Since the Constitution provides only for a presiding officer in each house, some method had to be devised for conducting business. Parties quickly assumed the responsbility for this. In the House, the majority party elects a leader every two years. This individual becomes Speaker. In addition, a majority leader and a minority leader (from the minority party) and party whips are elected. Each party has a committee whose job it is to make committee assignments. Party structure in the Senate is similar, except that the vice president of the United States is the Senate president.

The committee system surpasses the party system in its importance in Congress. In the early nineteenth century, standing committees became a fundamental aspect of Congress. They have, for the most part, evolved to correspond to executive branch departments or programs and thus reflect and maintain the separation of powers.

Congress also establishes rules of procedure to guide policy making. The Senate has a tradition of unlimited debate, on which the various cloture rules it has passed have had little effect. Filibusters still occur. The rules of the House, on the other hand, restrict talk and support committees; deliberation is recognized as committee business. The House Rules Committee has the power to control debate and floor amendments. The rules prescribe the formal procedure through which bills become law. Generally, the parties control scheduling and agenda, but the committees determine action on the floor. Committees, seniority, and rules all limit the ability of members to represent their constituents. Yet, these factors enable Congress to maintain its role as a major participant in government.

Many different factors affect how Congress ultimately decides on legislation. Among the most important influences are constituency preferences, interest group pressures, and party discipline. Typically party discipline is stronger in the House than in the Senate. Parties have several means of maintaining discipline: (1) favorable committee assignments create obligations; (2) floor time in the debate on one bill can be allocated in exchange for a specific vote on another; (3) the whip system allows party leaders to assess support for a bill and convey their wishes to members; (4) party leaders can help members create large logrolling coalitions; and (5) the president can champion certain pieces of legislation and thereby muster support along party lines. In most cases, party leaders accept constituency obligations as a valid reason for voting against the party position.

Despite this complex organization aimed at promoting effective decision making, many Americans worry that Congress is unable to make important decisions. In addition, they charge that Congress is out of touch with the American people. The strong role of the Republican leadership in the 104th Congress temporarily reduced charges of congressional inaction, but ultimately, the 104th Congress passed very little legislation. As a result, dissatisfaction with congressional effectiveness and representativeness has not subsided.

FOR FURTHER READING

Berg, John C., *Class, Gender, Race, and Power in the U.S. Congress.* Boulder, CO: Westview, 1994.

Burrell, Barbara C., *A Woman's Place Is in the House: Campaigning for Congress in the Feminist Era.* Ann Arbor: University of Michigan Press, 1994.

Cook, Elizabeth Adell, Sue Thomas, and Clyde Wilcox, eds. *The Year of the Woman: Myth and Reality.* Boulder, CO: Westview, 1994.

Davidson, Roger H., ed. *The Postreform Congress.* New York: St. Martin's, 1991.

Dodd, Lawrence, and Bruce I. Oppenheimer, eds. *Congress Reconsidered.* 5th ed. Washington, DC: Congressional Quarterly Press, 1993.

Fenno, Richard F. *Congressmen in Committees.* Boston: Little, Brown, 1973.

Fenno, Richard F. *Homestyle: House Members in Their Districts.* Boston: Little, Brown, 1978.

Fiorina, Morris. *Congress: Keystone of the Washington Establishment.* 2nd ed. New Haven, CT: Yale University Press, 1989.

Fowler, Linda, and Robert McClure. *Political Ambition: Who Decides to Run for Congress?* New Haven, CT: Yale University Press, 1989.

Light, Paul. *Forging Legislation.* New York: Norton, 1991.

Mayhew, David R. *Congress: The Electoral Connection.* New Haven, CT: Yale University Press, 1974.

Sinclair, Barbara. *The Transformation of the U.S. Senate.* Baltimore: Johns Hopkins University Press, 1989.

Smith, Steven S., and Christopher Deering. *Committees in Congress.* 2nd ed. Washington, DC: Congressional Quarterly Press, 1990.

Thomas, Sue. *How Women Legislate.* New York: Oxford University Press, 1994.

STUDY OUTLINE

Congress: Representing the American People

1. The House and Senate play different roles in the legislative process. The Senate is more deliberative, whereas the House is characterized by greater centralization and organization.
2. House members are more attuned to localized narrow interests in society, whereas senators are more able than House members to represent statewide or national interests.
3. In recent years, the House has exhibited more partisanship and ideological division than the Senate.
4. Congress is not fully representative because it is not a sociological microcosm of American society.

successful effort to reduce the federal budget deficit in American history, cutting it by a third in his first two budgets. He had staked his presidency on the passage of two global trade accords and had won. He had, with Vice President Al Gore, launched a remarkably thorough plan to "reinvent government," streamlining federal regulations and procurement practices and reducing by more than a quarter of a million the number of federal employees. He had done all this with minimal increases in taxes—fewer than 2 percent of Americans paid higher taxes because of the tax increases in the 1993 budget. And Clinton's expansion of the earned-income tax credit, intended to lift working Americans out of poverty, increased tax subsidies to the almost 15 million full-time workers who already were eligible, and expanded eligibility for an additional 4.5 million full-time workers in 1995. He was, as he had sought to be, the very model of the modern successful president, a self-styled "New Democrat," a master of the bully pulpit and high-tech communications, a skillful communicator, and a powerful legislative leader. And yet, only a year later, he was widely seen as a weak, crippled figure. Was this the beginning of the end of his presidency? But wait.

Congress dominated 1995 with the aggressive, Republican majorities in the House and the Senate, driven by the Contract with America. Newt Gingrich became the most powerful Speaker of the House since the early part of the twentieth century. The Republican Party in the House was united behind Gingrich as no party had been united since 1900. One Republican bill after another was passed in the House; many of these bills were large and ambitious. But most of the ambitious legislation was compromised or delayed in the Senate or the White House, not only because the Senate was a more moderate legislative body, but also because President Clinton had begun to make good on his threat to veto any legislation containing items he opposed. And Clinton kept his promise, even when the lack of an approved budget and the failure to raise the congressionally set limit on the federal debt closed down the federal government altogether.

By January 1996, as a weary 104th Congress reassembled for its second session, it was clear in the polls and among the pundits and professional politicians that Clinton had regained the upper hand. The Republicans, preoccupied with the nomination of a presidential candidate to run against Clinton, virtually declared a moratorium on legislative activity in Congress for the first two months of the session. Furthermore, they were becoming resigned to the prospect of having to seek another mandate from the people in November before they could make further progress on their once-ambitious agenda. President Clinton appeared once again to be the "Comeback Kid." But more important to our story, the presidency was back, battered but still the center of government in the United States.

The modern American presidency is the most powerful democratically elected political office in the world. But it is also one of the most frustrating and vulnerable. The very forces that can catapult a relative political unknown like Bill Clinton into the presidency can, once he is in office, rob him of much of his power and leave him responding to, rather than shaping, events. The president, more than any member of Congress, represents and articulates the will of the people. But the people's will can be a fickle and unreliable political resource—as Bill Clinton and all of his recent predecessors have learned.

All of this points to the dual nature of the presidency: with power comes vulnerability. The framers, wanting "energy in the Executive," provided for a single-headed office with an electoral base independent of Congress. But by giving the presidency no explicit powers independent of Congress, the framers forced each president to provide that energy by asserting powers beyond the Constitution itself. Thus a tug of war between formal constitutional provisions for a president who is little more than chief clerk and a theory of necessity favoring a real chief executive has persisted for over two centuries. But it was not until Franklin Roosevelt that the tug of war seemed to have been won for the chief executive presidency, because after FDR, as we shall see, every president has been strong, whether committed to the strong presidency or not. FDR presided over a revolution in government. In response to major events—the Great Depression and World War II—FDR oversaw the greatest expansion in the size, activity, and personnel of the national government in American history. But this revolution in government was not the only revolution that had occurred. FDR was also central to a revolution in the *presidency*, which quickly followed the revolution in government. The strong presidency and a new system of presidential government became institutionalized after 1937. Our task is to explain how and why this occurred. Why did the presidency not only become stronger but also displace Congress as the center, in a new system that we call presidential government? Why did that strong presidency become the center of a new, mass popular democracy with a single, national constituency? And why, as the power of the presidency has increased, have popular expectations of presidential performance increased at an even faster rate?

Our focus in the first three parts of this chapter is to explore the resources of presidential power, which we will divide into three categories: constitutional, institutional, and political. But resources alone are not power—they must be converted to power. We will thus conclude by looking at how modern presidents have converted these resources of power into real presidential power, replacing congressional government with presidential government.

The Constitutional Powers of the Presidency

- What powers does the Constitution provide to the president as head of state? Have presidents used these powers to make the presidency too powerful or even imperial?
- What powers does the Constitution provide to the president as head of government?

Article II of the Constitution, which establishes the presidency, does not solve the dilemma of power. Although Article II has been called "the most loosely drawn chapter of the Constitution,"[1] the framers were neither indecisive nor confused. They held profoundly conflicting views of the executive branch, and Article II was probably the best compromise they could make. The formulation the framers agreed upon is magnificent in its ambiguity: "The executive Power shall be vested in a President of the United States of America" (Article II, Section 1, first sentence). The meaning of "executive power," however, is not defined except indirectly in the very last sentence of Section 3, which provides that the president "shall take Care that the Laws be faithfully executed."[2]

One very important conclusion can be drawn from these two provisions: The office of the president was to be an office of **delegated powers.** Since, as we have already seen, all of the powers of the national government are defined as powers of Congress and are incorporated into Article I, Section 8, then the "executive power" of Article II, Section 3, must be understood to be defined as the power to execute faithfully the laws *as they are adopted by Congress*. This does not doom the presidency to weakness. Presumably, Congress can pass laws delegating almost any of its powers to the president. But presidents are not free to discover sources of executive power completely independent of the laws as passed by Congress. In 1890, the Supreme Court did hold that the president could be bold and expansive in the inferences he drew from the Constitution as to "the rights, duties and obligations" of the presidency, but the powers of the president would have to come from that Constitution and laws, not from some independent or absolute idea of executive power.[3]

Immediately following the first sentence of Section 1, Article II defines the manner in which the president is to be chosen. This is a very odd sequence, but it does say something about the struggle the delegates were having over how to provide great power of action or energy to the executive and at the same time to balance that power with limitations. The struggle was between those delegates who wanted the president to be selected by, and thus responsible to, Congress and those delegates who preferred that the president be elected directly by the people. Direct popular election would create a more independent and more powerful presidency. With the adoption of a scheme of indirect election through an electoral college in which the electors would be selected by the state legislatures (and close elections would be resolved in the House of Representatives), the framers hoped to achieve a "republican" solution: a strong president responsible to state and national legislators rather than directly to the electorate. This indirect method of electing the president probably did dampen the power of most presidents in the nineteenth century. This conclusion is supported by the fact that, as we shall see below, presidential power increased as the president developed a closer and more direct relationship to a mass electorate.

The heart of presidential power as defined by the Constitution is found in Sections 2 and 3, where the several clauses define the presidency in two dimensions: the president as head of state and the president as head of government. Although these will be given separate treatment here, the presidency can be understood only by the combination of the two.

THE PRESIDENT AS HEAD OF STATE: SOME IMPERIAL QUALITIES

The constitutional position of the president as head of state is defined by three constitutional provisions, which are the source of some of the most important powers on which presidents can draw. The areas can be classified as follows:

1. *Military.* Article II, Section 2, provides for the power as "Commander in Chief of the Army and Navy of the United States, and of the Militia of the several States, when called in to the actual Service of the United States."
2. *Judicial.* Article II, Section 2, also provides the power to "grant Reprieves and Pardons for Offences against the United States, except in Cases of Impeachment."
3. *Diplomatic.* Article II, Section 3, provides the power to "receive Ambassadors and other public Ministers."

Even though the presidency is an office of delegated powers, for a century and a half after the founding, many feared that the president's power could become dictatorial. This political cartoon criticized President Andrew Jackson's use of the veto power.

Military First, the position of commander in chief makes the president the highest military authority in the United States, with control of the entire defense establishment. No American president, however, would dare put on a military uniform for a state function—not even a former general like Eisenhower—even though the president is the highest military officer in war and in peace. The president is also head of the secret intelligence hierarchy, which includes not only the Central Intelligence Agency (CIA) but also the National Security Council (NSC), the National Security Agency (NSA), the Federal Bureau of Investigation (FBI), and a host of less well-known but very powerful international and domestic security agencies. But of course, care must be taken not to conclude too much from this—as some presidents have done. Although Article II, Section 1, does state that all the executive power is vested in the president, and Section 2 does provide that the president shall be commander in chief of all armed forces, including state militias, these impressive provisions must be read in the context of Article I, wherein seven of the eighteen clauses of Section 8 provide particular military and foreign policy powers to Congress, including the power to declare wars for which presidents are responsible. Presidents have tried to evade this at their peril. In full awareness of the woe visited upon President Lyndon Johnson for evading and misleading Congress at the outset of the Vietnam War, President Bush sought explicit congressional authorization for the Gulf War in January 1991.

Judicial The presidential power to grant reprieves, pardons, and amnesties involves the power of life and death over all individuals who may be a threat to the security of the United States. Presidents may use this power on behalf of a particular individual, as did Gerald Ford when he pardoned Richard Nixon in 1974 "for all offenses against the United States which he . . . has committed or may have committed." Or they may use it on a large scale, as did President Andrew Johnson in 1868, when he gave full amnesty to all southerners who had participated in the "Late Rebellion," and President Carter in 1977, when he declared an amnesty for all the draft evaders of the Vietnam War. This power of life and death over others helped elevate the president to the level of earlier conquerors and kings by establishing him as the person before whom supplicants might come to make their pleas for mercy.

Diplomatic When President Washington received Edmond Genêt ("Citizen Genêt") as the formal emissary of the revolutionary government of France in 1793 and had his cabinet officers and Congress back his decision, he established a greatly expanded interpretation of the power to "receive

President Richard Nixon improved relations with China in 1972 by using his power to recognize foreign governments. Nixon's visit to China was an important diplomatic event.

Ambassadors and other public Ministers," extending it to the power to "recognize" other countries. That power gives the president the almost unconditional authority to review the claims of any new ruling groups to determine if they indeed control the territory and population of their country, so that they can commit it to treaties and other agreements. Critics may have questioned the wisdom of President Nixon's recognition of the People's Republic of China and of President Carter's recognition of the Sandinista government in Nicaragua. But they did not question the president's authority to make such decisions. Because the breakup of the Soviet bloc was generally perceived as a positive event, no one criticized President Bush for his quick recognition of the several former Soviet and Yugoslav republics as soon as they declared themselves independent states.

The Imperial Presidency? Have presidents used these three constitutional powers—military, judicial, and diplomatic—to make the presidency too powerful, indeed "imperial?"[4] Debate over the answer to this question has produced an unusual lineup, with presidents and the Supreme Court on one side and Congress on the other. In 1936, the Supreme Court supported the expansive view of the presidency by holding that Congress may delegate a degree of discretion to the president in foreign affairs that might violate the separation of powers if it were in a domestic arena.[5] The Supreme Court also upheld the president's power to use executive agreements to conduct foreign policy.[6] An **executive agreement** is exactly like a treaty because it is a contract between two countries, but an executive agreement does not require a two-thirds vote of approval by the Senate. Ordinarily, executive agreements are used to carry out commitments already made in treaties, or to arrange for matters well below the level of policy. But when presidents have found it expedient to use an executive agreement in place of a treaty, the Court has gone along. This verges on an imperial power.

Many recent presidents have even gone beyond formal executive agreements to engage in what amounts to unilateral action. They may seek formal congressional authorization, as in 1964 when President Lyndon Johnson con-

President Lyndon B. Johnson pressured Congress to pass the Gulf of Tonkin resolution, which he quickly signed into law. Johnson interpreted the measure as a congressional declaration of war and used it as justification for escalating America's involvement in Vietnam.

vinced Congress to adopt the Gulf of Tonkin Resolution authorizing him to expand the American military presence in Vietnam. Johnson interpreted the resolution as a delegation of discretion to use any and all national resources according to his own judgment. Others may not even bother with the authorization but merely assume it, as President Nixon did when he claimed to need no congressional authorization to continue or to expand the Vietnam War.

These presidential claims and actions led to a congressional reaction, however. In 1973, Congress passed the **War Powers Act** over President Nixon's veto. This resolution asserted that the president could send American troops into action abroad only in the event of a declaration of war or other statutory authorization by Congress, or if American troops were attacked or directly endangered. This was an obvious effort to revive the principle that the presidency is an office of delegated powers—that is, powers granted by Congress—and that there is no blanket prerogative.

Nevertheless, this resolution has not prevented presidents from using force when they have deemed it necessary (see Table 12.1). President Reagan took at least four military actions that could be seen as violations of the War Powers Resolution. The first was the 1983 stationing of troops in Beirut. Although their original purpose had been to remain neutral while lending support to United Nations peace efforts, President Reagan redefined their mission as one of supporting President Amin Gemeyal's government in Lebanon, thereby taking sides and putting American troops at risk, which ul-

TABLE 12.1

PRESIDENTIAL ACTIONS TAKEN IN VIOLATION OF THE WAR POWERS ACT

President	Presidential action	Date of action
Ford	sent troops into Cambodia to rescue crew of the *Mayaguez,* which had been captured by Cambodian forces	May 1975
Carter	sent troops into Iran in failed attempt to rescue American hostages	May 1980
Reagan	stationed troops in Beirut with redefined mission of supporting the Lebanese government; 230 troops died	October 1983
Reagan	sent troops to invade Grenada, with ostensible purpose of rescuing American students	October 1983
Reagan	diverted profits from illegal arms sales to Iran to finance (illegally) the Contra rebels in Nicaragua	1985–86
Reagan	ordered surprise bombing of Libya by U.S. planes overflying several European countries	April 1986
Bush	ordered military invasion of Panama, ending in arrest of Panamanian president Manuel Noriega	December 1989
Bush	stationed U.S. troops in Somalia to restore order and protect food deliveries	1992–93
Clinton	ordered launch of 23 Tomahawk missiles against Iraqi intelligence headquarters	June 1993
Clinton	ordered military intervention in Haiti	September 1994

timately led to the killing of 230 American soldiers. The second action was the 1983 Grenada invasion, which again introduced American armed forces into situations where "imminent involvement in hostilities is clearly indicated . . ." without consulting Congress. The third was the 1986 surprise bombing of Libya in response to the alleged participation of the Libyan government in international terrorism. The fourth was the diversion of profits from arms sales to Iran to finance the Contra rebels (who were seeking to overthrow the communist-led government) in Nicaragua, as revealed in November 1986. These experiences were not lost on President Bush. He disregarded Congress in the invasion of Panama but was fortunate in bringing the affair to a successful conclusion quite quickly. In contrast, once he saw that the situation in Kuwait in 1990 was tending toward protracted military involvement, he submitted the issue to Congress.

Although President Clinton had appeared at first to be reluctant to take bold international initiatives, he did not hesitate to use direct action when events seemed to threaten his own position or his view of the national interest. Clinton did not seek congressional approval for ordering a missile launch against Iraqi intelligence headquarters in mid-1993. Dramatic as it was, the White House declared it to be a retaliation for an attack against the United States itself—Iraqi intelligence agents had allegedly plotted to assassinate former president George Bush. Clinton's ordering of military intervention in Haiti in September 1994 to overthrow Haiti's military regime would surely have brought loud calls in Congress for invocation of the War Powers Act if a single shot had been fired during the intervention. Fortunately for Clinton, his emissaries were able to persuade Haiti's military rulers to step down and allow the restoration of civilian rule before any military action occurred. Finally, Clinton's series of unilateral actions in Bosnia dramatically tested his independence from Congress. First, Clinton unilaterally approved the use of American planes to bomb Serbian strategic positions in the late summer of 1995 (which pressured the Serbs to participate in peace negotiations with Croats and Bosnian Muslims). Second, to make the peace negotiations succeed, Clinton unilaterally pledged the American military to monitor the implementation of the agreement, including committing twenty thousand U.S. troops to monitor the agreement on the ground. With U.S. forces already in Bosnia, all Congress could do was pass a resolution in December 1995, after a long debate, to authorize financial support for the troops but also to disapprove of Clinton's actions and to demand further reporting to Congress in the future.

Perhaps more important than any of these cases of unilateral presidential action is presidential involvement in secret diplomacy. One important example is the Reagan administration's secret negotiation with Iran for the release of American hostages in return for arms sales. Former secretary of defense Caspar Weinberger warned President Reagan that arms transfers were almost certainly illegal under the Arms Export Control Act.[7] President Reagan responded, "Well, the American people would never forgive me if I failed to get these hostages out over this legal question." And as to his potential violation of an act of Congress, the President quipped, "Visiting hours are on Thursday."[8] Democrats in Congress were up in arms when this diplomacy was exposed. But they were hardly in a better position when their own president, nearly ten years later, conducted extensive secret diplomacy in Bosnia through his personal emissary, Richard Holbrooke.[9] What emerges from cases like these is a clear sense that although Congress can and does limit presidential discretion, no piece of legislation can end the struggle over presidential power. Whenever the president is willing to take the political risk, Congress will almost certainly have to acquiesce. This principle is virtually lodged in the Constitution.

The Domestic Presidency: The President as Head of Government

The constitutional basis of the domestic presidency also has three parts. And here again, although real power grows out of the combination of the parts, the analysis is greatly aided by examining the parts separately:

1. *Executive.* The "executive power" is vested in the president by Article II, Section 1, to see that all the laws are faithfully executed (Section 3), and to appoint, remove, and supervise all executive officers and to appoint all federal judges (Article II, Section 2).
2. *Military.* This power is derived from Article IV, Section 4, which stipulates that the president has the power to protect every state "against Invasion; and . . . against domestic Violence."
3. *Legislative.* The president is given the power under various provisions to participate effectively and authoritatively in the legislative process.

Executive Power The most important basis of the president's power as chief executive is to be found in Article II, Section 3, which stipulates that the president must see that all the laws are faithfully executed, and Section 2, which provides that the president will appoint, remove, and supervise all executive officers, and appoint all federal judges. The power to appoint the principal executive officers and to require each of them to report to the president on subjects relating to the duties of their departments makes the president the true chief executive officer (CEO) of the nation. In this manner, the Constitution focuses executive power and legal responsibility upon the president. The famous sign on President Truman's desk, "The buck stops here," was not merely an assertion of Truman's personal sense of responsibility but was in fact recognition by him of the legal and constitutional responsibility of the president. The president is subject to some limitations, because the appointment of all such officers, including ambassadors, ministers, and federal judges, is subject to a majority approval by the Senate. But these appointments are at the discretion of the president, and the loyalty and the responsibility of each appointment are presumed to be directed toward the president. Although the United States has no cabinet in the parliamentary sense of a collective decision-making body or board of directors with collective responsibilities (discussed later in this chapter), the Constitution nevertheless recognizes departments with department heads, and that recognition establishes the lines of legal responsibility up and down the executive hierarchy, culminating in the presidency (see Figure 12.1).

FIGURE 12.1

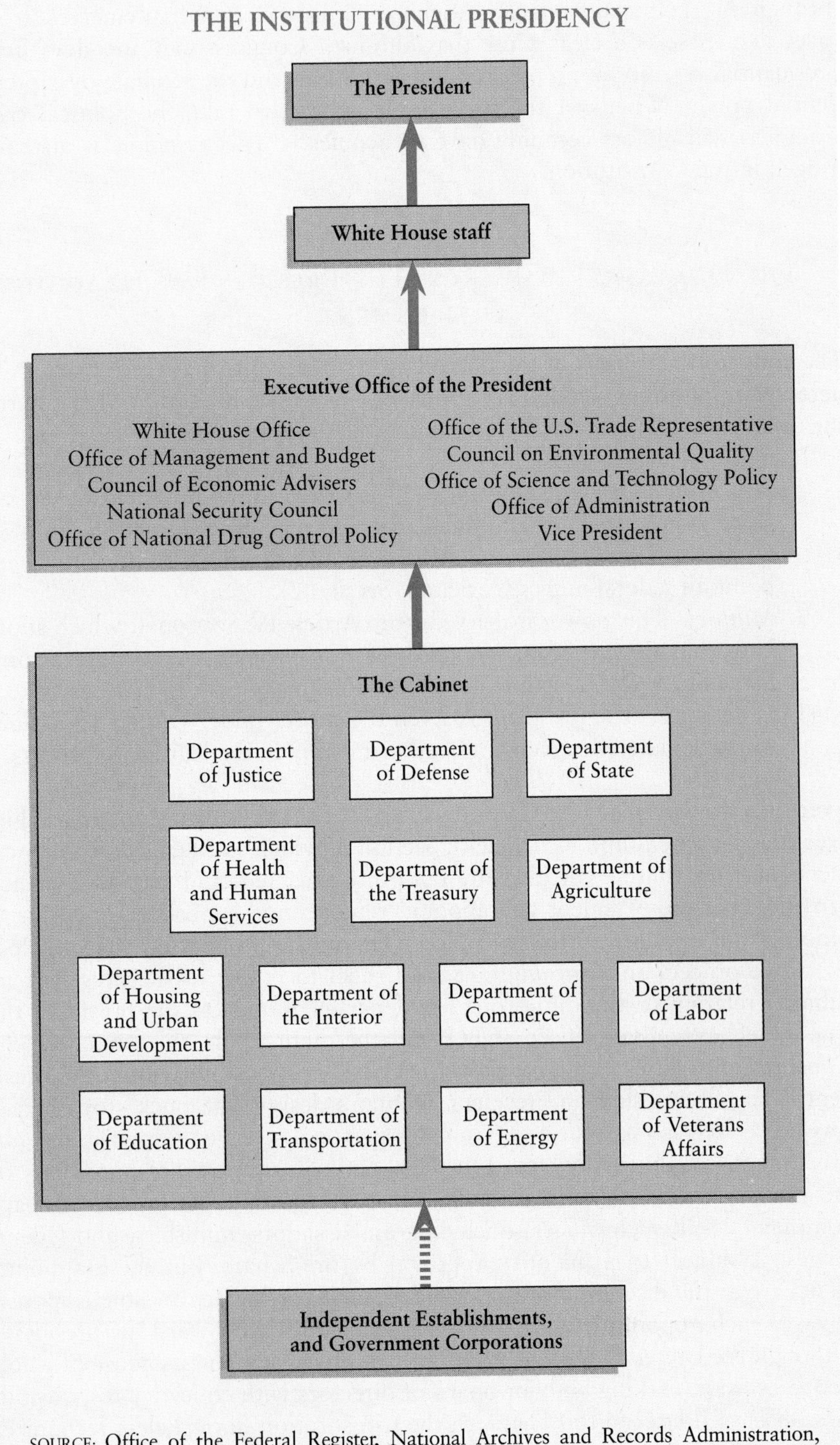

SOURCE: Office of the Federal Register, National Archives and Records Administration, *The United States Government Manual, 1995–96* (Washington, DC: Government Printing Office, 1995), p. 22.

Military Sources of Domestic Presidential Power Although Article IV, Section 4, provides that the "United States shall [protect] every State . . . against Invasion . . . and . . . domestic Violence," Congress has made this an explicit presidential power through statutes directing the president as commander in chief to discharge these obligations.[10] The Constitution restrains the president's use of domestic force by providing that a state legislature (or governor when the legislature is not in session) must request federal troops before the president can send them into the state to provide public order. Yet, this proviso is not absolute. First, presidents are not obligated to deploy national troops merely because the state legislature or governor makes such a request. And more important, the president may deploy troops in a state or city without a specific request from the state legislature or governor if the president considers it necessary in order to maintain an essential national service, in order to enforce a federal judicial order, or in order to protect federally guaranteed civil rights.

One historic example of the unilateral use of presidential power to protect the states against domestic disorder, even when the states don't request it, was the decision by President Dwight Eisenhower in 1957 to send troops into Little Rock, Arkansas, literally against the wishes of the state of Arkansas, to enforce court orders to integrate Little Rock's Central High School. The governor of Arkansas, Orval Faubus, had actually posted the Arkansas National Guard at the entrance of Central High School to prevent the court-ordered admission of nine black students. After an effort to negotiate with Governor Faubus failed, President Eisenhower reluctantly sent a thousand paratroopers to Little Rock, who stood watch while the black students took their places in the all-white classrooms. This case makes quite clear that the president does not have to wait for a request by a state legislature or governor before acting as a domestic commander in chief.[11]

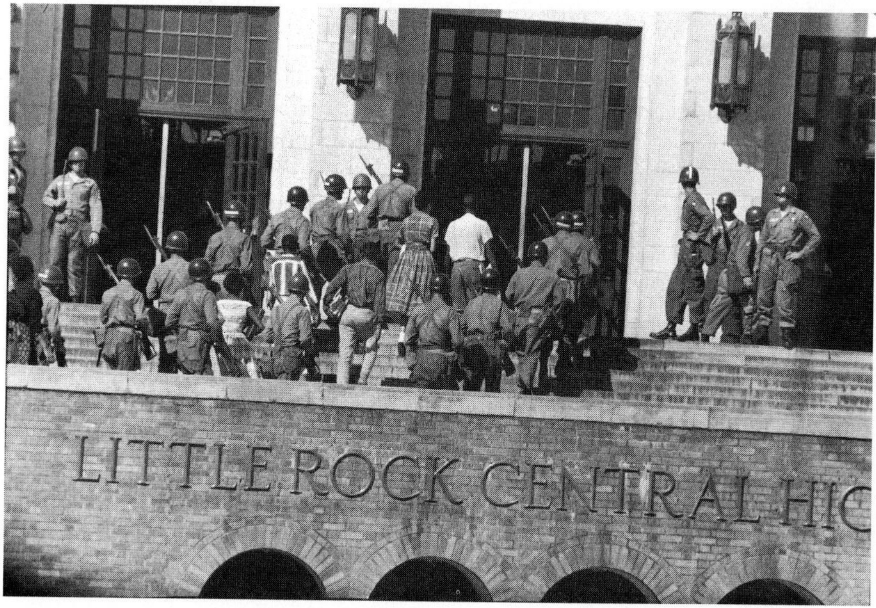

In 1957, Arkansas governor Orval Faubus ignored a federal court order and used the state's National Guard to prevent nine black students from attending Little Rock's Central High School. President Dwight Eisenhower was forced to send a thousand soldiers to protect the black students. The troops stayed for the entire school year.

However, in most instances of domestic disorder—whether from human or from natural causes—presidents tend to exercise unilateral power by declaring a "state of emergency," thereby making available federal grants, insurance, and direct assistance. In 1992, in the aftermath of the devastating riots in Los Angeles and the hurricanes in Florida, American troops were very much in evidence, sent in by the president, but in the role more of Good Samaritans than of military police.

The President's Legislative Power The president plays a role not only in the administration of government but also in the legislative process. Two constitutional provisions are the primary sources of the president's power in the legislative arena. The first of these is the provision in Article II, Section 3, providing that the president "shall from time to time give to the Congress Information of the State of the Union, and recommend to their Consideration such Measures as he shall judge necessary and expedient." The second of the president's legislative powers is of course the veto power assigned by Article I, Section 7.[12]

The first of these powers does not at first appear to be of any great import. It is a mere obligation on the part of the president to make recommendations for Congress's consideration. But as political and social conditions began to favor an increasingly prominent role for presidents, each president, especially since Franklin Delano Roosevelt, began to rely upon this provision to become the primary initiator of proposals for legislative action in Congress and the principal source for public awareness of national issues, as well as the most important single individual participant in legislative decisions. Few today doubt that the president and the executive branch together are the primary source for many important congressional actions.[13]

The **veto** power is the president's constitutional power to turn down acts of Congress (see Figure 12.2). This power alone makes the president the most important single legislative leader.[14] No bill vetoed by the president can become law unless both the House and Senate override the veto by a two-thirds vote. In the case of a **pocket veto,** Congress does not even have the option of overriding the veto, but must reintroduce the bill in the next session. A pocket veto can occur when the president is presented with a bill during the last ten days of a legislative session. Usually, if a president does not sign a bill within ten days, it automatically becomes law. But this is true only while Congress is in session. If a president chooses not to sign a bill presented within the last ten days that Congress is in session, then the ten-day limit does not expire until Congress is out of session, and instead of becoming law, the bill is vetoed.

Figure 12.3 reveals the widely different use presidents have made of their veto power. Use of the veto varies according to the political situation that each president confronts. Franklin D. Roosevelt, even with his own party in control of Congress, used the veto power extensively as an exercise of presidential leadership. As we shall see later in this chapter, FDR's time in office (1933–45) established the presidency as the center of the national government. Harry S. Truman (1945–53) and Dwight D. Eisenhower (1953–61) faced Congresses controlled by the opposition party and used the veto power vigorously to confront their opponents. During Bill Clinton's first two years

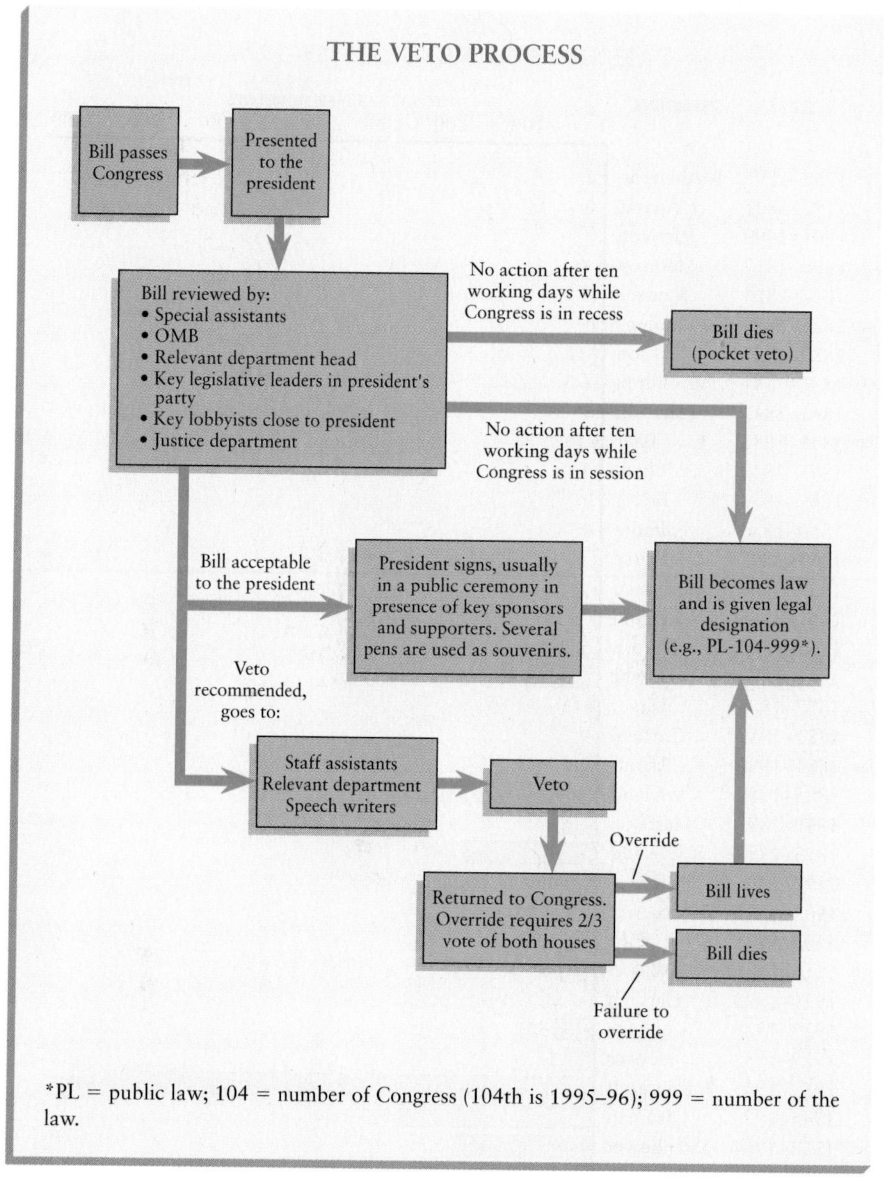

FIGURE 12.2

in office, when Democrats controlled both houses of Congress, he vetoed no bills. Following the congressional elections of 1994, however, Clinton confronted a Republican-controlled Congress with a definite agenda, and he too began to use his veto power more vigorously. In the process, Clinton recaptured the national spotlight that had seemingly shifted to the Speaker of the House, Newt Gingrich.

Although not explicitly stated as such, the Constitution also provides the president with the power of initiative. To "initiate" means to originate, and in government that can mean power. The framers of the Constitution clearly saw this as one of the keys to executive power. The president as an individual is able to initiate decisive action, whereas Congress, as a relatively large as-

FIGURE 12.3

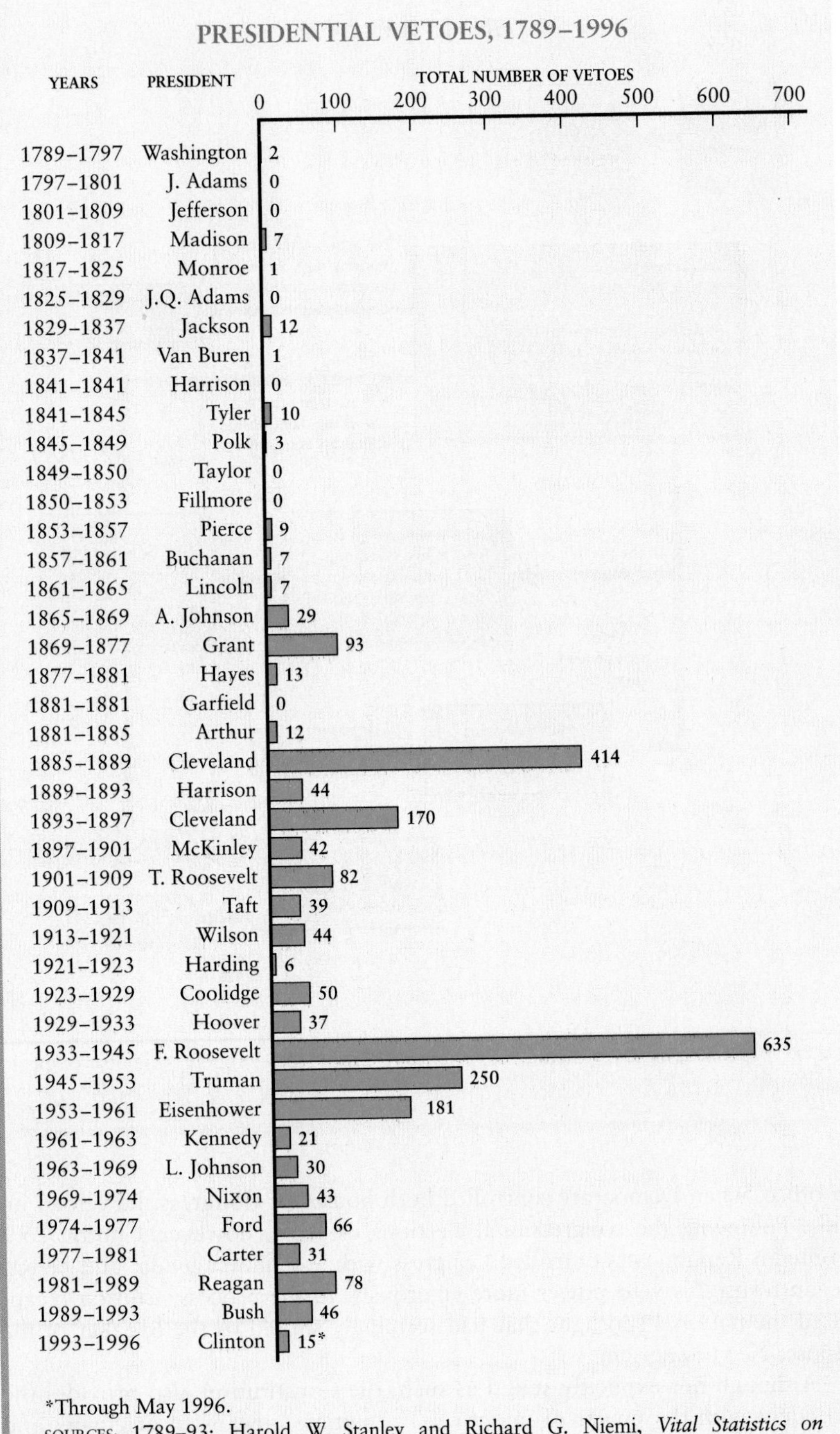

*Through May 1996.

SOURCES: 1789–93: Harold W. Stanley and Richard G. Niemi, *Vital Statistics on American Politics*, 3rd ed. (Washington, DC: Congressional Quarterly Press, 1994), Table 8–13, p. 278; 1993–96: *Congressional Quarterly Weekly Report*, vol. 54, no. 1 (January 6, 1996), p. 10; vol. 54, no. 19 (May 11, 1996), p. 1342; and vol. 54, no. 21 (May 25, 1996), p. 1504.

sembly, must deliberate and debate before it can act. Initiative also implies the ability to formulate proposals for important policies. There is power in this, too.

★ Institutional Resources of Presidential Power

- ➤ What institutional resources does the president use to manage the executive branch?
- ➤ Which of these resources have presidents increasingly relied on?

Constitutional sources of power are not the only resources available to the president. Presidents have at their disposal a variety of other formal and informal resources that have important implications for their ability to govern. Indeed, without these other resources, presidents would lack the ability—the tools of management and public mobilization—to make much use of the power and responsibility given to them by Congress. Let us first consider the president's formal institutional resources and then, in the section following, turn to the more informal political resources that affect a president's capacity to govern, in particular the president's base of popular support.

Patronage as a Tool of Management

The first tool of management available to most presidents is a form of **patronage**—the choice of high-level political appointees. These appointments allow the president to fill top management positions with individuals who will attempt to carry out the president's agenda. But the president must appoint individuals who have experience and interest in the programs that they are to administer and who share the president's goals with respect to these programs. At the same time, presidents use the appointment process to build links to powerful political and economic constituencies by giving representation to important state political party organizations, the business community, organized labor, the scientific and university communities, organized agriculture, and certain large and well-organized religious groups.

When President Clinton took office in 1993, there were about four thousand political appointments that could be made "at the pleasure of the president."[15] About half of these are very attractive "plums," with salaries ranging from $60,000 to $120,000 a year (in 1995). In fact, the general directory of these appointments, *Policy and Supporting Positions*, is commonly referred to in Washington as the "Plum Book."[16] At the top are approximately 1,500 White House and Senior Executive Service (SES) positions. More than 2,000 others are categorized as "Schedule C" positions, defined as "position[s] of a confidential or policy determining character . . . to which appointments may be made without examination by [the Office of Personnel Management].[17] Other emergency and transitional appointments can also be made at the president's discretion. Obviously, four thousand appointments are far too many for a president to make personally. But all presidents are particularly attentive to as many as 1,500 of the higher-level appointments.[18]

Over the past several decades, the character of these top-level appointments has changed. Up until the 1970s, modern presidents showed a distinct preference for outsiders—men (and a very few women) whose experience prior to top presidential appointment had been outside government altogether and outside the campaign organization of the president as well. Few top appointees had any significant experience in the administrative processes of the agencies they were to be responsible for managing. Presidents tended to draw their top appointees from among business executives, state governors, and interest-group leaders, with an occasional former senator, member of Congress, or university professor. Many appointees barely knew the president before they were chosen, few had a long working relationship with the president, and still fewer had any working relationship with other members of the president's administration.

Beginning in the 1970s, however, the background of appointees began to show more national government and Washington administrative experience. President Carter, despite his claim to being an outsider to Washington, drew liberally from among people who had served Presidents Lyndon Johnson and John Kennedy in the 1960s. President Reagan drew from the Nixon administration, President Bush appointed a still higher percentage of Washington insiders, and President Clinton established a similar pattern. Bush's preference for appointees with national government experience could be attributed to the fact that he himself was an insider with long and varied experience in Washington. Clinton's preference for choosing people with Washington experience has been attributed to his determination to be a strong and active president. His appointees have included former and serving members of Congress as well as members of previous administrations, and they, along with the former governors, mayors, campaign officials, and other public officials tell a story of Clinton's genuine commitment to the value and effectiveness of experience in public office as a qualification for high appointment in his administration. It seems ironic that these very presidents, as well as the candidates who ran against them, have virtually all campaigned *against* Washington insiders and "the Beltway elite."[19]

THE CABINET

In the American system of government, the **Cabinet** is the traditional but informal designation for the heads of all the major federal government departments. The Cabinet has no constitutional status. Unlike in England and many other parliamentary countries, where the cabinet *is* the government, the American Cabinet is not a collective body. It meets but makes no decisions as a group. Each appointment must be approved by the Senate, but Cabinet members are not responsible to the Senate or to Congress at large. Cabinet appointments help build party and popular support, but the Cabinet is not a party organ. The Cabinet is made up of directors, but is not a true board of directors.

Why don't real cabinets serve collectively as a board of directors? After all, we speak collectively of the Bush administration or the Clinton administration. And we call it a Cabinet, and all its members (with an occasional exception) are members of the same party, which will be subjected to the

President Bill Clinton and members of his Cabinet in 1993—the most diverse Cabinet in presidential history.

judgment of the electorate after four years. Why, then, have we never developed a cabinet with a concept of collective responsibility—a cabinet with members who share the president's political responsibilities and help diffuse and divert some of the heavy burden of the president's personal responsibilities? The explanation lies deep in the American system of national politics, which catches the cabinet and each member of it in a web of three basic interacting forces:

1. Each presidential candidate must build a winning electoral coalition, state by state. Winning primaries and collecting delegates for the party convention and then building a coalition to win the general election requires that the candidate build a direct, personal relationship with the public. Expectations of national government performance come to focus *personally* on the candidate, who must as president produce or give the appearance of making things happen. The responsibilities of office are personal and immediate, and the president is under too much personal pressure once the nomination is won to stop and create a viable Cabinet. In fact, by the time a president is inaugurated, it is too late to create a true cabinet government. Presidents don't even know personally some of their appointees, and many appointees don't know each other.
2. Cabinet members have their own constituencies and are usually selected by the president because of the support they can bring with them. But these constituencies do not automatically transfer to the president, and they may at times be at odds with the president. For the

same reason, it is extremely difficult to remove a Cabinet member or other high-level official.

3. Each Cabinet member heads a department that is a large bureaucracy with a momentum of its own. Career administrators consider political executives birds of passage. Often they see an order from a political executive as being in conflict with the judgment and expectations of their profession. Thus, career administrators do not easily fall into line with each new administration. Cabinet members often face a choice between giving loyalty to the president or gaining the loyalty of their own departments.

Aware of this web of forces, the president tends to develop a burning impatience with and a mild distrust of Cabinet members; to make the Cabinet a rubber stamp for actions already decided on; and to demand results, or the appearance of results, more immediately and more frequently than most department heads can provide. Since Cabinet appointees generally have not shared political careers with the president or with each other, and since they may meet literally for the first time after their selection, the formation of an effective governing group out of this motley collection of appointments is unlikely. While President Clinton's insistence on a Cabinet diverse enough to resemble American society could be considered an act of political wisdom, it virtually guaranteed that few of his appointees had ever spent much time working together or even knew the policy positions or beliefs of the other appointees.[20]

Some presidents have relied more heavily on an "inner Cabinet," the **National Security Council** (NSC). The NSC, established by law in 1947, is composed of the president, the vice president, the secretaries of state, defense, and the treasury, the attorney general, and other officials invited by the president. It has its own staff of foreign-policy specialists run by the special assistant to the president for national security affairs. Table 12.2 suggests that for these highest appointments, presidents turn to people from outside Washington, usually long-time associates. A counterpart, the Domestic Council, was created by law in 1970, but no specific members were designated for it. President Clinton hit upon his own version of the Domestic Council, called the National Economic Council, which shares competing functions with the Council of Economic Advisers.

Presidents have obviously been uneven and unpredictable in their reliance on the NSC and other subcabinet bodies, because executive management is inherently a personal matter. Despite all the personal variations, however, one generalization can be made: Presidents have increasingly preferred the White House staff instead of the cabinet as their means of managing the gigantic executive branch.

THE WHITE HOUSE STAFF

The **White House staff** is composed mainly of analysts and advisers.[21] Although many of the top White House staff members are given the title "special assistant" for a particular task or sector, the types of judgments they are expected to make and the kinds of advice they are supposed to give are a good deal broader and more generally political than those coming from the

TABLE 12.2

The inner Cabinet comprises the four Cabinet posts that legally make up the National Security Council.

BACKGROUNDS OF APPOINTEES TO INNER CABINET, 1961–94

Secretary of State
William Rogers (RMN) Law practice, attorney general
Henry Kissinger (RMN-GF) Professor
Cyrus Vance (JC) International law, department of defense official
Edmund Muskie (JC) Senator
Alexander Haig (RR) General, assistant to the president, NATO command
George Shultz (RR) Professor, secretary of treasury (RMN), corporate executive
James Baker (GB) Texas corporate law, chief of staff, secretary of treasury (RR)
Warren M. Christopher (BC) Corporate law, department of state official

Secretary of the Treasury
David Kennedy (RMN) Banking and finance
John Connally (RMN) Governor, law practice
George Shultz (RMN) Professor, head of OMB
William Simon (RMN-GF) Securities and investments
Michael Blumenthal (JC) Corporate executive
William Miller (JC) Corporate executive, Federal Reserve Board
Donald Regan (RR) Securities executive
James Baker (RR) Texas corporate law, chief of staff
Nicholas Brady (RR-GB) Investment banker
Lloyd M. Bentsen (BC) Financier, senator
Robert M. Rubin (BC) Financier

Secretary of Defense
Melvin Laird (RMN) Congressman
Elliot Richardson (RMN) State lieutenant governor, secretary of HEW
James Schlesinger (RMN-GF) Professor, science administrator, head of CIA
Donald Rumsfeld (GF) congressman, NATO official
Harold Brown (JC) Air Force secretary, college president
Caspar Weinberger (RR) Secretary of HEW (RMN), head of OMB, corporate official
Frank Carlucci (RR) Career government official
Richard Cheney (GB) Congressman, chief of staff (GF)
Les Aspin (BC) Congressman, chair, House Armed Services Committee
William J. Perry (BC) Career government official

Attorney General
John Mitchell (RMN) Law practice, securities adviser
Richard Kleindienst (RMN) Law practice
Elliot Richardson (RMN) State official, lieutenant governor, secretary of defense (RMN)
William Saxbe (RMN-GF) Senator, state attorney general
Edward Levi (GF) Law professor, college president
Griffin Bell (JC) Law practice
Benjamin Civiletti (JC) Law practice
William French Smith (RR) Lawyer, adviser to president
Edwin Meese (RR) Lawyer, aide to president
Richard Thornburgh (RR-GB) Governor, lawyer
Janet Reno (BC) Dade County (Miami) Prosecutor

RMN=Richard M. Nixon; GF=Gerald Ford; JC=Jimmy Carter; RR=Ronald Reagan; GB=George Bush; BC=Bill Clinton.

SOURCES: *Congress and the Nation,* vol. 4 (Washington DC: Congressional Quarterly, 1977), pp. 1107–11; *Who's Who in American Politics* (New York: Bowker, 1973, 1977); and *Who's Who in America* (Chicago: Marquis, various years).

Executive Office of the President or from the cabinet departments. The members of the White House staff also tend to be more closely associated with the president than other presidentially appointed officials (see Table 12.3).

From an informal group of fewer than a dozen people (popularly called the **Kitchen Cabinet**), and no more than four dozen at the height of the domestic Roosevelt presidency in 1937, the White House staff has grown substantially with each successive president (see Figure 12.4).[22] Richard Nixon employed 550 people in 1972. President Carter, who found so many of the requirements of presidential power distasteful, and who publicly vowed to keep his staff small and decentralized, built an even larger and more centralized staff. President Clinton promised during the campaign to reduce the White House staff by 25 percent, but there is no indication he sustained this effort. A large White House staff has become essential.

The biggest variation among presidential management practices lies not in the size of the White House staff but in its organization. President Reagan went to the extreme in delegating important management powers to his chief of staff, and he elevated his budget director to an unprecedented level of power in *policy* making rather than merely *budget* making. President Bush centralized his staff even more under chief of staff John Sununu. At the same time, Bush continued to deal directly with his cabinet heads, the press, and key members of Congress. President Clinton showed a definite preference for competition among equals in his cabinet and among senior White House officials, obviously liking competition and conflict among staff members, for which FDR's staff was also famous. But the troubles Clinton has had in turning this conflict and competition into coherent policies and well-articulated

TABLE 12.3

APPOINTEES WHO HAD A CLOSE ASSOCIATION WITH THE PRESIDENT PRIOR TO SELECTION (1961–94)

Appointees in	All	Democrats	Republicans
Inner Cabinet* (State, Defense, Treasury, Attorney General)	35%	29%	39%
Outer Cabinet (all other cabinet posts)	20%	11%	26%
Executive Office of the President (EOP)	38%	50%	31%
White House Staff	64%	81%	49%

*This generally refers to the top four Cabinet posts that legally make up the National Security Council (see Table 12.2).

SOURCE: James W. Riddlesperger and James D. King, "Presidential Appointments to the Cabinet, Executive Office, and White House Staff," *Presidential Studies Quarterly* 16, no. 4 (1986), pp. 696–97. Courtesy of the Center for the Study of the Presidency. This is a new table extending the data from 1985 to 1994, provided courtesy of the authors. Our thanks to Professors Riddlesperger and King.

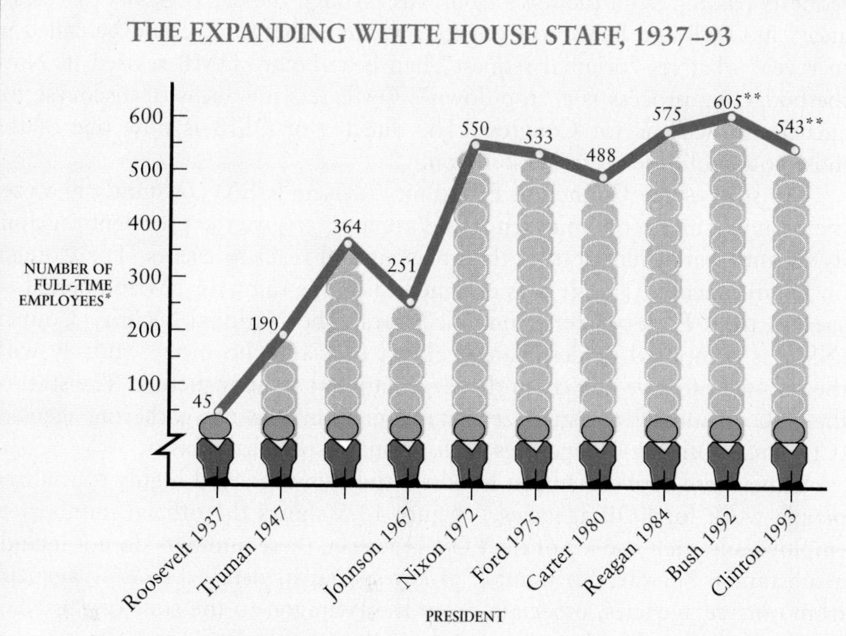

*These figures do not include the employees temporarily detailed to the White House from outside agencies (about 50–75 in 1992 and 1993).

†The vice president employs more than 20 people, and there are at least 100 people on the staff of the National Security Council. These people work in the White House and the Executive Office buildings, but are not included in these totals, except where noted.

‡These figures include the staffs of the Office of the President, the Executive Residence, and the Office of the Vice President.

SOURCES: 1937–84: Thomas E. Cronin, "The Swelling of the Presidency: Can Anyone Reverse the Tide?" in *American Government: Readings and Cases*, 8th ed., ed. Peter Woll (Boston: Little, Brown, 1984), p. 347; 1992–93: provided by the Office of Management and Budget and the White House.

FIGURE 12.4

messages suggests that he might have done better to emulate his immediate predecessors in their preference for hierarchy and centralization.[23]

THE EXECUTIVE OFFICE OF THE PRESIDENT

The development of the White House staff can be appreciated only in its relation to the still-larger **Executive Office of the President** (EOP). Created in 1939, the EOP is a major part of what is often called the "institutional presidency"—the permanent agencies that perform defined management tasks for the president. The most important and the largest EOP agency is the Office of Management and Budget (OMB). Its roles in preparing the national budget, designing the president's program, reporting on agency activities, and overseeing regulatory proposals make OMB personnel part of virtually every conceivable presidential responsibility. The status and power of the OMB has grown in importance with each successive president. The process of budgeting at one time was a "bottom-up" procedure, with expenditure and program requests passing from the lowest bureaus through the departments to "clearance" in OMB and hence to Congress, where each agency could be called in to reveal what its "original request" had been before OMB revised it. Now the budgeting process is a "top-down"; OMB sets the terms of discourse for agencies as well as for Congress. The director of OMB is now one of the most powerful officials in Washington.

The staff of the Council of Economic Advisers (CEA) constantly analyzes the economy and economic trends and attempts to give the president the ability to anticipate events rather than to wait and react to events. The Council on Environmental Quality was designed to do the same for environmental issues as the CEA does for economic issues. The National Security Council (NSC) is composed of designated cabinet officials who meet regularly with the president to give advice on the large national security picture. The staff of the NSC assimilates and analyzes data from all intelligence-gathering agencies (CIA, etc.). Other EOP agencies perform more specialized tasks.

Somewhere between fifteen hundred and two thousand highly specialized people work for EOP agencies.[24] Figure 12.5 shows the official numbers of employees in each agency of the EOP. However, these numbers do not include a substantial but variable number of key specialists detailed to EOP agencies from outside agencies, especially from the Pentagon to the staff of the NSC. The importance of each agency in the EOP varies according to the personal orientations of each president. For example, the NSC staff was of immense importance under President Nixon, especially because it served essentially as the personal staff of presidential assistant Henry Kissinger. But it was of less importance to President Bush, who looked outside the EOP altogether for military policy matters, much more to the Joint Chiefs of Staff and its chair, General Colin Powell.

The Vice Presidency

The vice presidency is a constitutional anomaly even though the office was created along with the presidency by the Constitution. The vice president exists for two purposes only: to succeed the president in case of death, resignation, or incapacitation and to preside over the Senate, casting a tie-breaking vote when necessary.[25]

The main value of the vice presidency as a political resource for the president is electoral. Traditionally, a presidential candidate's most important rule for the choice of a running mate is that he or she bring the support of at least one state (preferably a large one) not otherwise likely to support the ticket. Another rule holds that the vice presidential nominee should provide some regional balance and, wherever possible, some balance among various ideological or ethnic subsections of the party. It is very doubtful that John Kennedy would have won in 1960 without his vice presidential candidate, Lyndon Johnson, and the contribution Johnson made to winning in Texas. It is equally doubtful that Jimmy Carter would have been elected if his running mate had not been someone like Walter Mondale from Minnesota. The emphasis, however, has recently shifted away from geographical to ideological balance. In 1980, Ronald Reagan probably could have carried Texas without George Bush as his running mate; nonetheless, Reagan selected him because

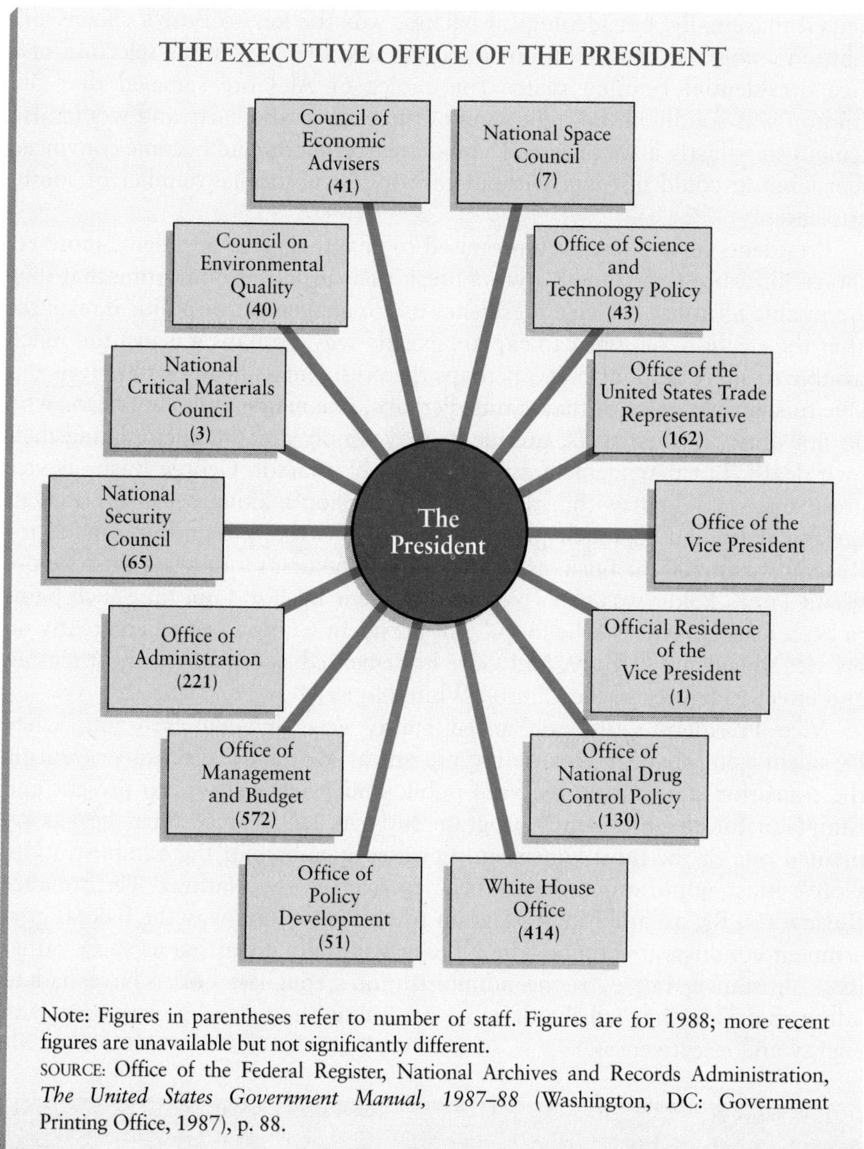

Note: Figures in parentheses refer to number of staff. Figures are for 1988; more recent figures are unavailable but not significantly different.

SOURCE: Office of the Federal Register, National Archives and Records Administration, *The United States Government Manual, 1987–88* (Washington, DC: Government Printing Office, 1987), p. 88.

FIGURE 12.5

he needed someone like Bush from the moderate mainstream of the party to help unite the party; Bush's second-place finish in the primaries also made him an attractive candidate who would help Reagan reunify the party. In 1988, both presidential candidates went for ideological balance. Democrat Michael Dukakis, a Massachusetts liberal, selected as his running mate Senator Lloyd Bentsen, whose record put him at the opposite, conservative extreme of the party. Since Republican Bush was not fully embraced by the conservative wing of his party, despite his eight years of loyal service to President Reagan, he chose arch-conservative Indiana Senator J. Danforth Quayle as his running mate. Quayle's youth and midwestern roots may have helped marginally, but ideological balance was the key to Bush's choice. Bill Clinton combined considerations of region and ideology in his selection of a vice presidential running mate. The choice of Al Gore signaled that Bill Clinton was solidly in the right wing of the Democratic Party and would also remain steadfastly a southerner. Democratic strategists had become convinced that Clinton could not win without carrying a substantial number of southern states.

Presidents have constantly promised to give their vice presidents more responsibility, but they almost always break their promises, indicating that they are unable to utilize the vice presidency as a management or political resource after the election. No one can explain exactly why. Perhaps it is just too much trouble to share responsibility. Perhaps the president as head of state feels unable to share any part of that status. Perhaps, like many adult Americans who do not draw up their wills, presidents may simply dread contemplating their own death. But management style is certainly a factor. George Bush, as vice president, was "kept within the loop" of decision making because President Reagan delegated so much power. A copy of virtually everything made for Reagan was made for Bush, especially during the first term, when Bush's close friend James Baker was chief of staff. President Bush did not take such pains to keep Dan Quayle "in the loop," but President Clinton has relied greatly on his vice president, Al Gore, and Gore has emerged as one of the most trusted and effective figures in the Clinton White House.

Vice President Gore's enhanced status was signaled early on, when President Clinton kept him visibly present at all public appearances during the transition and during the vital public and private efforts to present and campaign for the president's program early in 1993. Since then, he has remained one of the most consistently praised members of the administration. Gore's most important task has been to oversee the National Performance Review (NPR), an ambitious program to "reinvent" the way the federal government conducts its affairs. The NPR was initially dismissed as show rather than substance, but even the administration's toughest critics have had to admit that Gore has led the drive to streamline the federal government with energy and effectiveness.

Vice President Al Gore promoted his plan to "reinvent" government on David Letterman's television show, where he railed against the government's procurement requirements, which even specified the number of pieces into which a government ashtray may shatter.

take things slowly."[26] If the 1996 campaign was an accurate sign, Clinton planned a moderate course for his second term.

Party as a Presidential Resource

Although on the decline, the president's party is far from insignificant as a political resource (see also Chapter 8). Figure 12.6 dramatically demonstrates the point with a forty-one-year history of the presidential "batting average" in Congress—the percentage of winning roll-call votes in Congress on bills publicly supported by the president. Note, for example, that President Eisenhower's "batting average" started out with a very impressive .900 but declined to .700 by the end of his first term and to little more than half his starting point by the end of his administration. The single most important explanation of this decline was Eisenhower's loss of a Republican Party majority in Congress after 1954, the recapture of some seats in 1956, although short of a majority, and then a significant loss of seats to the Democrats after the election of 1958.

The presidential batting average went back up and stayed consistently higher through the Kennedy and Johnson years, mainly because these two presidents enjoyed Democratic Party majorities in the Senate and in the House. Even so, Johnson's batting average in the House dropped significantly during his last two years, following a very large loss of Democratic seats in

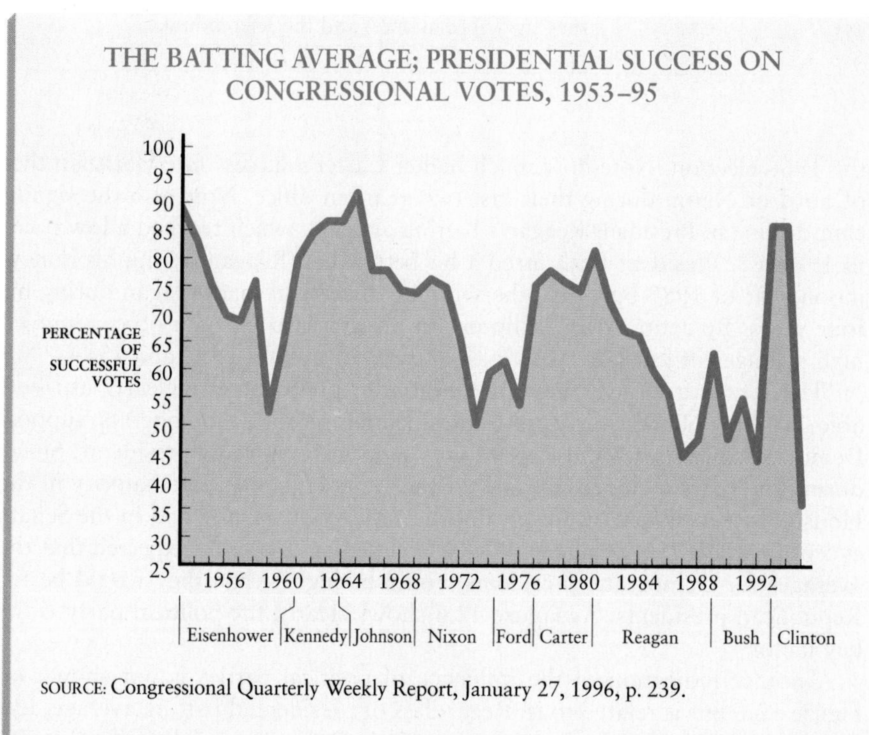

SOURCE: Congressional Quarterly Weekly Report, January 27, 1996, p. 239.

FIGURE 12.6

The presidential "batting average" is the percentage of votes on which the president took a position and that position was successful.

The Populist Party of the late nineteenth century was the first third party to seriously challenge the dominance of the Republican and Democratic parties. More significantly, the populist movement from which the party arose was in every sense a grassroots movement, made up of average working people, that profoundly altered the course of American politics.

The Populists were composed of farmers and residents of small towns, mostly from the South, the Midwest, and the far West, who valued the agrarian life that was buffeted by harsh economic forces and was fast being eclipsed in America by the growth of urban areas and the rise of industrialization. Despite their loathing for corporate power and urban, monied interests, poor farmers sought alliances with two disparate and disaffected groups: urban workers and southern blacks. This alliance of America's downtrodden and underpaid workers emerged, according to historian Eric F. Goldman, "bursting up from the bottom [of society]."[1]

Meeting in 1892 in Omaha, Nebraska, the Populist Party (also called the People's Party) adopted a platform that shook much of the American establishment. Central to populist doctrine was the idea that the country was divided into producers and nonproducers. Producers were Americans who worked with their hands to create products and commodities that generated wealth. Because of their importance, producers (i.e., average workers) should exercise national political control, the Populists said. Nonproducers, such as bankers and financiers, were those who simply manipulated the wealth generated by producers; their power should be curtailed. To that end, the Populists proposed such radical ideas as the progressive income tax, federal ownership of public services such as the railroads and the telephone and telegraph systems, low interest government-backed loan programs for farmers, free coinage of silver, and such procedural reforms as the secret ballot, direct election of U.S. senators, and the initiative (the ability to turn an elected official out of office by a special vote) and the referendum.

the 1966 election. Note how much higher Carter's success rate was than that of Ford or Nixon during their last two years in office. Note also the significant decline in President Reagan's batting average, which reached a low point in 1987–88. President Bush fared a bit better than Reagan during his honeymoon year of 1989 but was otherwise less successful than Reagan during his four years. By contrast, Bill Clinton, in his first two years in office, enjoyed high averages of legislative success—86 percent in both 1993 and 1994.

The low batting averages for Republican presidents are clearly attributable to the political party as a presidential resource. Democrats support Democratic presidents and Republicans support Republican presidents. Since, during the years included in Figure 12.6, Democrats held the majority in the House of Representatives for all but the 1952–54 Congress and in the Senate except for the 1952–54 and 1980–86 Congresses, it is to be expected that the averages for Democratic presidents would be higher than they would be for Republican presidents. As Figure 12.6 shows clearly, the political party is the key factor.

Another indication of the influence of political parties is not shown on Figure 12.6 but is related to it: Regardless of presidential batting average, legislative output was at a record low in 1995. Only eighty-eight bills were en-

In the 1892 elections, Populists elected five U.S. senators, ten members of the House of Representatives, three state governors, and over fifteen hundred state and local officials around the country. Populist presidential candidate James B. Weaver won electoral votes from six states and took over 8 percent of the popular vote. But Populist thunder was stolen in 1896 by the Democratic Party, which adopted a free-silver platform and nominated for the presidency a young, fiery Populist midwesterner, William Jennings Bryan. Most Populists accepted a union with the Democrats, but Bryan failed to stir eastern urban workers, and he lost to Republican William McKinley.

In areas where Populists gained control, they succeeded in enacting meaningful reforms. In North Carolina, for example, a Populist-Republican coalition increased funding for public schools and advanced several economic reforms. Kansas Populists reformed banking and railroad regulations. Yet the failure of the altruistic effort by the Populists and Bryan to attract significant urban worker support doomed the movement, especially since the nation was shifting from a rural to an urban base.

This grassroots people's movement was prescient in its platform, in that most of the Populists' "radical" proposals eventually became law. The Populist effort to unite poor white farmers and urban workers with poor black farmers cost Populists key southern support. Nevertheless, populist efforts to unite poor whites and blacks reflected a nobility of sentiment not to be seen again until the Civil Rights movement of the 1950s and 1960s.

SOURCE: Lawrence Goodwyn, *The Populist Movement in America: A Short History of Agrarian Revolt in America* (New York: Oxford University Press, 1978).

[1]Eric F. Goldman, "A Least Common Denominator," in *Populism,* ed. Theodore Saloutos (New York: Holt, Rinehart, and Winston, 1968), p. 9.

acted during the entire session—the lowest legislative output since 1933, when the Twentieth Amendment abolished the "lame duck" session and moved the starting date of congressional sessions from March to early January (and thus cut two entire months off the length of the Congress that was in session at the time). This low output in 1995 was not due solely to the fact that Washington was in a state of **divided government** (the situation in which one party controls the White House and the other party controls Congress). When government is divided with Democrats controlling Congress and Republicans controlling the White House (as was the case during the George Bush administration, for example), legislative output remains relatively high. But when divided government puts the Republicans in control of Congress, as in 1995, legislative output drops tremendously.[27]

At the same time, party has its limitations as a resource. The more unified the president's party is behind legislative requests from the White House, the more unified the opposition party is also likely to be. Unless the president's party majority is very large, appeals must also be made to the opposition to make up for the inevitable defectors within the ranks of the president's own party. Consequently, the president often poses as being above partisanship in order to win "bipartisan" support in Congress. But in pursuing a bipartisan strategy, a president cannot concentrate solely on building the party loyalty and party discipline that would maximize the value of the party's support in Congress. This is a dilemma for all presidents, particularly those faced with an opposition-controlled Congress. For example, although President Clinton enjoyed clear Democratic majorities in the House and the Senate during the first two years of his presidency, he had to move carefully because the Republicans were so close to 100 percent in opposition to him that a few Democratic defectors could beat him. Clinton won the Senate vote on the deficit-reduction plan by a margin of 50 to 49, with Vice President Gore having to cast the tie-breaking vote in late June 1993. Clinton lost on his $16 billion stimulus package because he could not muster four Republican votes to break a Republican filibuster in the Senate. And he lost his fight against the renewal of the Hyde amendment (forbidding Medicaid reimbursement for abortions) because many House Democrats joined the Republicans to pass it. Partisan opposition in Congress proved so strong that Clinton was unable even to bring the centerpieces of his legislative agenda—health care and welfare reform—to votes during the years in which he enjoyed majorities in Congress. This helps explain the paradox of Clinton's legislative scorecard: high batting averages but failures on key issues.

Groups as a Presidential Resource

The classic case in modern times of groups as a resource for the presidency is the Roosevelt or New Deal coalition.[28] The New Deal coalition was composed of an inconsistent, indeed contradictory, set of interests. Some of these interests were not organized interest groups, but were regional interests, such as southern whites, or residents of large cities in the industrial Northeast and Midwest, or blacks who later succeeded in organizing as an interest group. In addition to these sectional interests that were drawn to the New Deal, there were several large, self-consciously organized interest groups. The most important in the New Deal coalition were organized labor, agriculture, and the financial community.[29] All of the parts were held together by a judicious use of patronage—not merely patronage in jobs but patronage in policies. Many of the groups were permitted virtually to write their own legislation. In exchange, the groups supported President Roosevelt and his successors in their battles with opposing politicians.

Republican presidents have had their group coalition base also. The most important segments of organized business have tended to support Republican presidents. They have most often been joined by upper-income groups, as well as by some ethnic groups. In recent years, Republican presidents have expanded their interest coalition base. President Reagan, for example, won the support of traditionally Democratic southern white and northern blue-collar voters. This expanded base of support served him well in his struggles with Congress. When the Reagan/Republican coalition began to loosen toward the end of the Bush administration, the astute Bill Clinton was quick to sense it. His 1992 campaign succeeded in part because he brought back together many of the original interests that had made up the New Deal coalition. But he attempted to go even beyond those interests by holding an unprecedented "economic summit" in Little Rock, Arkansas, less than a

President Bill Clinton and Vice President Al Gore meet with auto executives from General Motors, Ford, and Chrysler. During his first term, Clinton courted big business in order to solidify his electoral base.

month after his election. It was a very public meeting of some three hundred bankers, corporate executives, interest-group representatives, prominent economists, and a sprinkling of average citizens—with Clinton himself presiding for almost the entire forty-eight hours of speech-making and serious discussion. It was indeed an extraordinary effort to expand the president's coalition base.

Presidential Use of the Media

While the media have grown increasingly important during presidential campaigns (see Chapter 9), their importance is even greater during a president's term in office. Twentieth-century presidents have sought a more direct relationship with the public and have used the media to achieve this end. Modern presidents have learned that they can use their relationship with the media to mobilize popular support for their programs and to attempt to force Congress to follow their lead.

The president is able to take full advantage of access to the communications media mainly because of the legal and constitutional bases of initiative. In the media, reporting on what is new sells newspapers. The president has at hand the thousands of policy proposals that come up to the White House through the administrative agencies; these can be fed to the media as newsworthy initiatives. Consequently, virtually all newspapers and television networks habitually look to the White House as the chief source of news about public policy. They tend to assign one of their most skillful reporters to the White House "beat." And since news is money, they need the president as much as the president needs them in order to meet their mutual need to make news. Presidents have successfully gotten from Congress significant additions to their staff to take care of press releases and other forms of communication. In this manner, the formal and the informal aspects of initiative tend to reinforce each other: The formal resources put the president at the center of policy formulation; this becomes the center of gravity for all buyers and sellers of news, which in turn requires the president to provide easy access to this news. Members of Congress, especially senators, are also key sources of news. But Congress is an anarchy of sources. The White House has more control over what and when, which is what political initiative is all about.

Presidential personalities make a difference in how these informal factors are used. Different presidents use the media in quite different ways. One of the first presidents to use the media was Theodore Roosevelt, who referred to the presidency as a "bully pulpit" because its visibility allowed him to preach to the nation and bring popular pressure to bear against his opponents in Congress. But the first president to try to reach the public directly through the media was Franklin Roosevelt. During the 1930s, FDR used radio broadcasts known as "fireside chats," press conferences, speeches, and movie newsreels to rally support for his New Deal programs and, later, to build popular support for American rearmament in the face of the growing danger in Europe and the Far East. FDR also cultivated strong relationships with national news correspondents to ensure favorable publicity for his programs. FDR's efforts to reach out to the American people and mobilize their support were among the factors that made him one of the strongest presidents in American history. His appeals to the American people allowed FDR to "reach over the heads" of congressional opponents and force them to follow his lead because their constituents demanded it.

Teddy Roosevelt used the presidency as a "bully pulpit" to promote his vision of America.

The press conference as an institution probably got its start in the 1930s, when Franklin Roosevelt gave several a month. But his press conferences were not recorded or broadcast "live," and direct quotes were not permitted. The model we know today got its start with Eisenhower and was put into final form by Kennedy. Since 1961, the presidential press conference has been a distinctive institution, available whenever the president wants to dominate the news. Between 300 and 400 certified reporters attend and file their accounts within minutes of the concluding words, "Thank you, Mr. President." But despite the importance of the press conference, its value to each president has varied. Although the average from Kennedy through Carter was about two press conferences a month, Johnson dropped virtually out of sight for almost half of 1965 when Vietnam was warming up, and so did Nixon for over five months in 1973 during the Watergate hearings. Moreover, Johnson and Ford preferred to call impromptu press conferences with only a few minutes' notice. President Reagan single-handedly brought the average down by holding only seven press conferences during his entire first year in office and only sporadically thereafter. In great contrast, President Bush held more conferences during his first seventeen months than Reagan held in eight years. Bush also shifted them from elaborate prime-time television affairs in the ornate East Room to less formal gatherings in the White House briefing room. Fewer reporters and more time for follow-up questions permitted media representatives to "concentrate on information for their stories, rather than getting attention for themselves."[30] President Clinton has tended to take both Reagan and Bush approaches, combining Reagan's high profile—elaborate press conferences and prime-time broadcasts—with the more personal one-on-one approach generally preferred by Bush. But thanks to Ross Perot, there

During the 1992 presidential campaign, Bill Clinton appeared on MTV to court the votes of young Americans. Clinton answered questions about his vision for America but also about his personal life, including whether he would inhale if he smoked marijuana and what type of underwear he wears (boxers).

is now a third approach, for which President Clinton has shown a certain aptitude: the informal and basically nonpolitical talk shows, such as those of Larry King and Oprah Winfrey. Such an informal approach has its risks, however: President Clinton is widely perceived as lacking the gravity a president is expected to possess. It is hard to argue with this conclusion when one considers that he is the first president to have answered a question (on MTV) about what kind of underwear he wears.

Of course, in addition to the presidential press conference there are other routes from the White House to news prominence.[31] For example, President Nixon preferred direct television addresses, and President Carter tried to make initiatives more homey with a television adaptation of President Roosevelt's "fireside chats." President Reagan made unusually good use of prime-time television addresses and also instituted more informal but regular Saturday afternoon radio broadcasts, a tradition that President Clinton has continued.

Public Opinion

Most Americans feel that presidents should follow public opinion. Interestingly, however, many of the most successful presidents have been public opinion leaders rather than followers.

In 1963, President John Kennedy signed a nuclear test ban treaty with the Soviet Union, even though public opinion polls seemed to show that most Americans thought the treaty was a bad idea. Kennedy believed that the treaty served the national interest and that most Americans did not know enough about the issue at stake to have fixed views on the topic. He assured his nervous advisers that, since most Americans lacked strong views on the topic, they would assume that the president's actions were correct. Kennedy was right: After he signed the treaty, polls showed that most Americans supported his decision.

President George Bush used the same logic during the Persian Gulf crisis that followed the Iraqi invasion of Kuwait. At the time, opinion was divided both within Congress and among the broader public. Congressional leaders tried to constrain the president's ability to use forces in combat, urging him instead to rely on diplomacy and economic sanctions to compel Iraq's withdrawal. Congressional criticism, especially televised Senate hearings, helped erode Bush's popular standing and almost undermined his power to act. In January 1991, however, Bush sought and narrowly received congressional approval to use force against Iraq. The overwhelming success of the American military effort produced a surge of popular support for Bush; his approval rating rose to over 90 percent.

Presidents who devote too much of their time to the vicissitudes of public opinion polls often discover that they are several steps behind shifts in opinion, for polls tell politicians what the public wanted yesterday, not what it will think tomorrow. This was certainly President Clinton's experience in 1993–94 with the issue of health care reform. Administration polls continually showed public support for the president's policy initiatives—until opponents of his efforts began getting their own message through. Using several highly effective media campaigns, Clinton's opponents convinced millions of Americans that the president's program was too complex and that it would reduce access to health care. The president was left promoting an unpopular program.

Bill Clinton relied heavily on public opinion in formulating and presenting many of his administration's programs. Several members of his staff, including David Gergen and George Stephanopoulos, were hired specifically to shape and influence public opinion. Clinton was heavily criticized for hiring Gergen, who had previously worked in the same capacity for Ronald Reagan. This crossover raised important questions about the integrity of "spinmeisters" such as Gergen, who seem to care more about the influence they have with the public than about the policies they are hired to promote.

Politicians are generally better off if they try to do what they believe is best and then hope that the public will come to agree with them. Most politicians, however, are afraid to use such a simple approach.

Mass Popularity as a Resource (and a Liability)

In addition to utilizing the media and public opinion polls, recent presidents, particularly Bill Clinton, have reached out directly to the American public to gain its approval. President Clinton's enormously high public profile, as is indicated by the number of public appearances he makes (see Figure 12.7), is only the most recent dramatic expression of the presidency as a "permanent campaign" for re-election. A study by political scientist Charles O. Jones shows that President Clinton engaged in campaign-like activity throughout

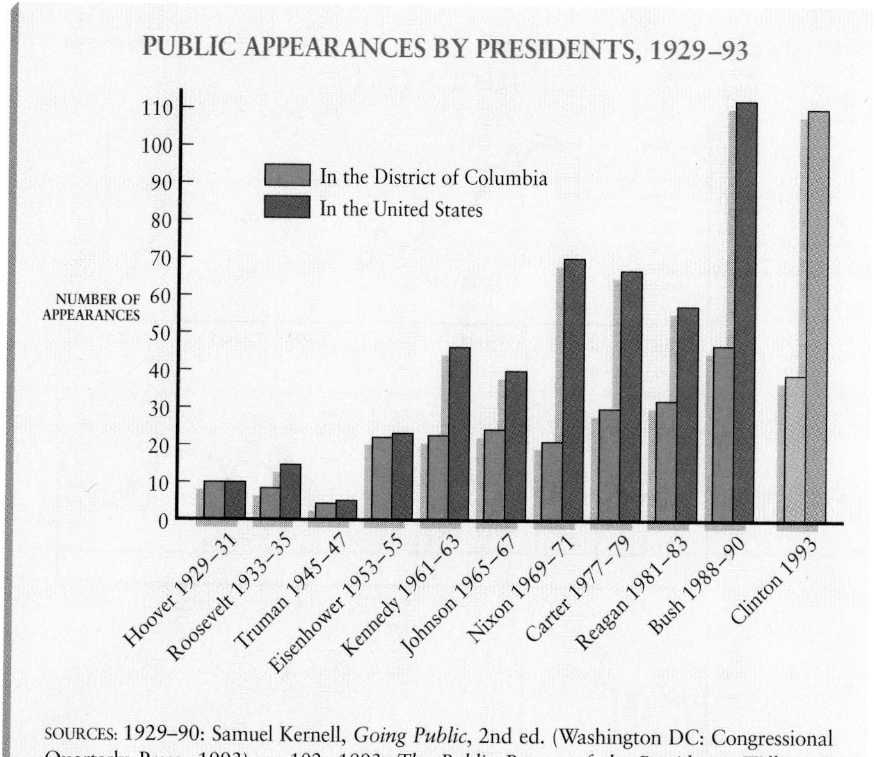

SOURCES: 1929–90: Samuel Kernell, *Going Public*, 2nd ed. (Washington DC: Congressional Quarterly Press, 1993), p. 102; 1993: *The Public Papers of the Presidents: William J. Clinton*, 1993, Books 1 and 2. (Washington, DC: Government Printing Office, 1994).

FIGURE 12.7

President Bill Clinton made as many or more public appearances in his first year in office than any of his predecessors made in their first three years in office.

his presidency, and is proving to be the most-traveled American president in history. In his first twenty months in office, he made 203 appearances outside of Washington, compared with 178 for George Bush and 58 for Ronald Reagan. Clinton's tendency to go around rather than through party organizations is reflected in the fact that while Presidents Bush and Reagan devoted about 25 percent of their appearances to party functions, Clinton's comparable figure is only 8 percent.[32]

Even with the help of all other institutional and political resources, successful presidents have to be able to mobilize mass opinion in their favor in order to keep Congress in line. But as we shall see, each president tends to *use up* mass resources. Virtually everyone is aware that presidents are constantly making appeals to the public over the heads of Congress and the Washington community. But the mass public does not turn out to be made up of fools. The American people react to presidential actions rather than mere speeches or other image-making devices.

The public's sensitivity to presidential actions can be seen in the tendency of all presidents to lose popular support. Despite the twists and turns shown on Figure 12.8, the percentage of positive responses to "Do you approve of the way the president is handling his job?" starts out at a level significantly higher than the percentage of votes the president got in the previous national

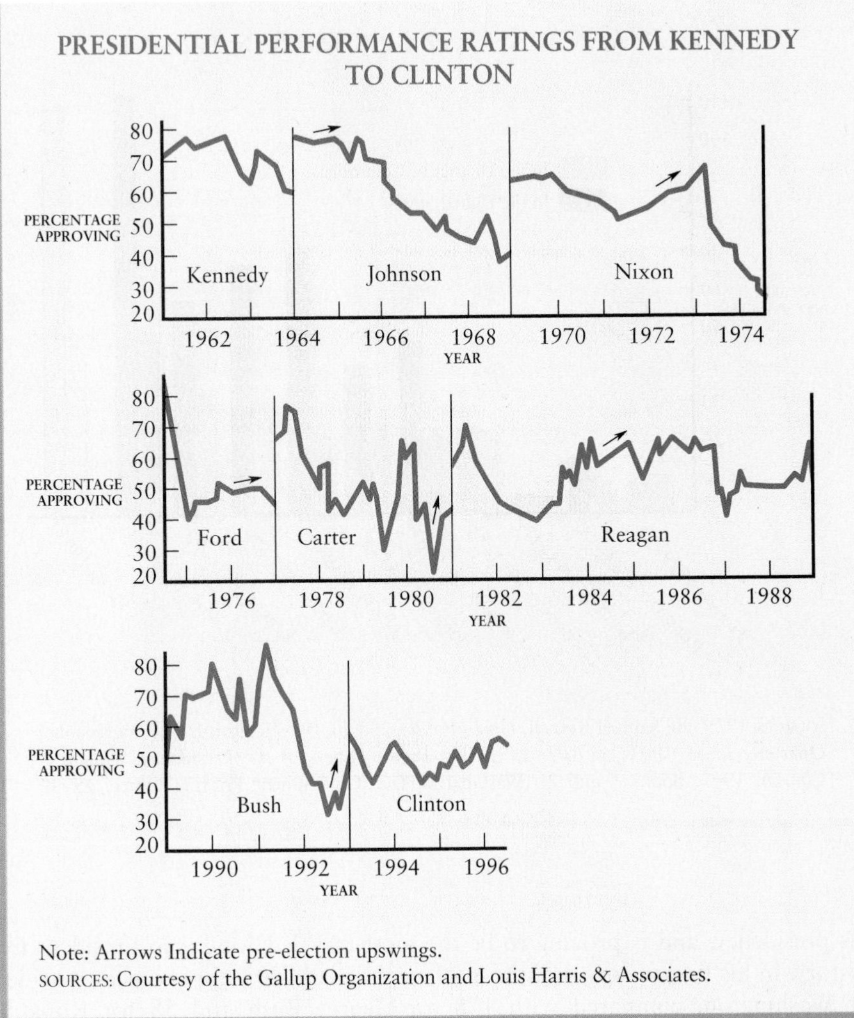

FIGURE 12.8

In presidential performance rating polls, respondents are asked, "Do you approve of the way the president is handling his job?" This graph shows the percentage of positive responses.

election and then declines over the next four years. Though the shape of the line differs, the destination is the same.

This general downward tendency is to be expected if American voters are rational, inasmuch as almost any action taken by the president can be divisive, with some voters approving and other voters disapproving. Take, for example, the enormous drop in President Ford's initially high approval rating in 1974 following his decision to pardon President Nixon. President Carter took a similar beating in April 1979, despite his already low ratings, after gas rationing was imposed throughout the country. President Reagan's approval history shows one of the biggest drops in the history of approval rating questions (15 percentage points) following revelation late in 1986 that his national security staff had been involved in selling arms to Iran. President Bush took similar losses in several instances, especially in 1990 following his breach of promise on "no new taxes." And President Clinton's ratings dropped from an initial 57 percent to 49 percent in April 1993, largely in response to his domestic package of tax increases and spending cuts.[33] After

AMERICAN POLITICAL CULTURE

Harry S. Truman

Harry S. Truman, the thirty-third president of the United States, is as close to a folk hero as exists among modern presidents. Truman is often held up as a rebuke to today's politicians, a genuine, plain-spoken man whose favorite sayings—"The buck stops here" and "If you can't stand the heat, you better get out of the kitchen"—bespoke a personal integrity largely vanished from the field of politics. But the truth is far more complex. Truman, like any other person who rises to be president, was a consummate politician: shrewd, calculating, and self-interested. But he believed that politics could be a noble calling and that it was not dishonorable to further one's own ambition, if one did not lose sight of the true end of politics—the common good.

Love of politics was in Truman's blood. He grew up in Independence, Missouri, an avid reader of history. Among his family's favorite annual events were the Democratic picnics every August at Lone Jack, Missouri. The Truman family would arrive in a wagon laden with food and settle down for hours of listening to orations from politicians and would-be politicians. In the summer of 1900, when Truman was sixteen years old, his father took him to the Democratic National Convention in Kansas City, at which William Jennings Bryan, the candidate of the common man, was renominated to run against William McKinley. The half-hour of tumultuous cheering after Bryan was chosen was one of the most stirring things young Truman had ever witnessed.[1]

But Truman did not sentimentalize politics. In a letter he wrote as a young man he said, "Politics sure is the ruination of many a good man. . . . To succeed politically he must be an egoist or a fool or a ward boss tool."[2] (Ironically, the greatest obstacle Truman faced later in his career was the widespread perception that he was merely a "ward boss tool.") He entered politics in 1922 as a candidate for county judge, or administrator, picked by the powerful Kansas City political machine headed by Tom Pendergast. From the beginning, Truman combined two seemingly contradictory motives: loyalty to the Democratic Pendergast machine (and later on, as a senator, also to Franklin Roosevelt and the New Deal), with personal integrity and devotion to public service. In 1939, after FBI investigations exposed massive voting and financial fraud by Pendergast and many of his lieutenants, Truman wryly observed in a letter to his wife, "Looks like everybody got rich in Jackson County but me."[3]

Truman's combination of political loyalty and rectitude was one that many in his time did not believe, and one that many today cannot understand. When he assumed the presidency after the death of Franklin Roosevelt in April 1945, he portrayed himself as the executor of Roosevelt's programs. But despite his deep and evident loyalty to the memory of FDR, he was too savvy a politician to let it threaten his own term in office. He mistrusted the Cabinet he had inherited from Roosevelt: "There was not a man on the list who would talk frankly at a Cabinet meeting! The honest ones were afraid to and the others wanted to fool me anyhow."[4] Within four months, all but two members of Roosevelt's Cabinet had been replaced.

Truman was an intelligent, savvy man, not afraid to take steps he deemed necessary for his political ends. But he was never merely a politician in the commonest and worst sense of the word. A scholar speaking at a 1995 conference honoring the fiftieth anniversary of the Truman presidency deftly summed up Harry S. Truman's feelings about his life's work: "He was proud to be a politician. Imagine that."[5]

[1]David McCullough, *Truman* (New York: Simon & Schuster, 1992), p. 63.
[2]Quoted in ibid., pp. 89–90.
[3]Quoted in ibid., p. 240.
[4]Quoted in William E. Leuchtenberg, *In the Shadow of FDR: Harry Truman to Bill Clinton,* 2nd ed. revised (Ithaca, N.Y.: Cornell University Press, 1993), pp. 14–15.
[5]Betty Houchin Winfield, quoted in Charlotte Grimes, "This Politician Was Very Proud of What He Did," *St. Louis Post-Dispatch,* April 13, 1995, p. 5B.

rises and falls that largely reflected the changing fortunes of his ambitious agenda, the president's approval rating in January 1995 stood at the same level, 49 percent. By the end of 1995, Clinton's ratings had climbed to 51 percent, but by the end of February 1996 they were back down toward his 1995 average of 48–49 percent approval.

The general downward tendency in approval ratings is interrupted at times by upward "blips." Table 12.4 puts these blips under the microscope, revealing that although Americans respond negatively to most *domestic* issues, they consistently respond positively to *international* actions or events associated with the president. Analysts call this reaction the "rallying effect."

This rallying effect explains why President Reagan's approval ratings between 1983 and 1986 moved upward when the experience of his predecessors would have led us to expect them to go downward (as was shown on Figure 12.8). This was largely in response to a series of international events beginning in September 1983: the Soviets shot down a South Korean airliner, 2,000 marines were sent to Lebanon, a terrorist attack killed 230 of those marines, and Grenada was successfully invaded. President Reagan's performance began to drop toward the end of 1986, when serious arms reduction negotiations reduced his ability to "go it alone" and to choose international events at will to associate with.

Figure 12.9 demonstrates in more detail the same pattern with President Bush. No president had ever enjoyed such consistently high ratings so far into his term. But note the remarkable sequence of international events, as shown by the annotations on Figure 12.9. Each of these is what the late Republican

FIGURE 12.9

Respondents to this poll were asked, "Do you approve of the way George Bush is handling his job?" The graph shows the percentage of positive responses.

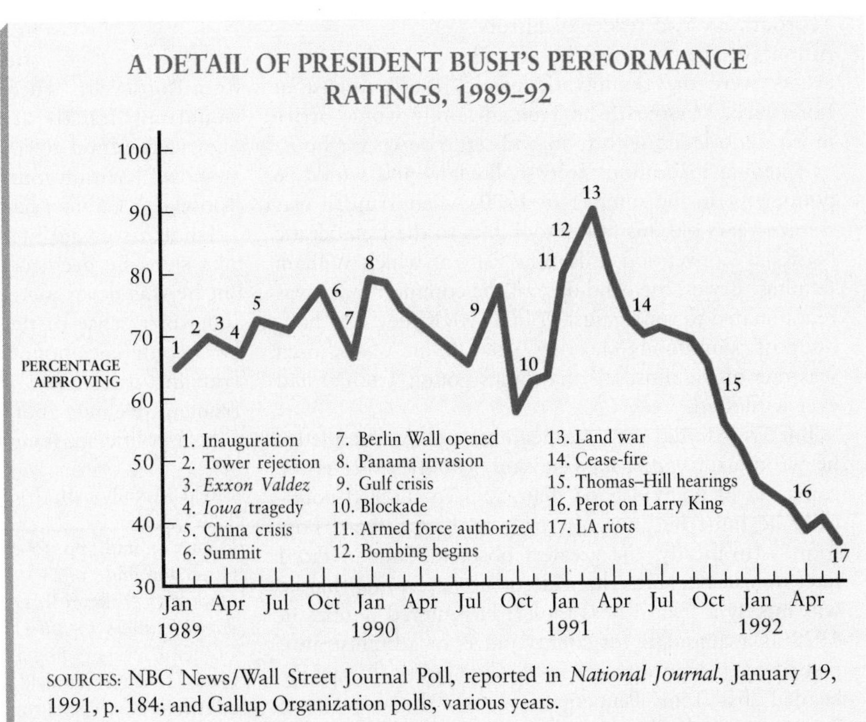

SOURCES: NBC News/Wall Street Journal Poll, reported in *National Journal*, January 19, 1991, p. 184; and Gallup Organization polls, various years.

TABLE 12.4

THE PRESIDENT IN THE EYES OF THE PUBLIC—A HISTORY OF INTERNATIONAL EVENTS AND POPULAR REACTION

Presidential action at issue	Percentage of sample group who approved of presidential actions: Before the action	After the action
Nixon announces Vietnam withdrawal plan	October 1969 53%	November 1969 68%
Nixon's trip to China	December 1971 49%	February 1972 56%
Vietnam peace agreement	December 1972 53%	January 1973 67%
Mayaguez incident	May 1975 40%	June 1975 51%
Camp David summit on the Middle East	September 1978 42%	September 1978 56%
American hostage crisis in Iran; Iranian assets frozen	November 1979 32%	December 1979 61%
Hostage rescue attempts	April 1980 39%	April 1980 43%
Korean airliner shot down by Soviets	September 1983 45%	September 1983 55%
Terrorist attack on U.S. Marine barracks in Lebanon, killing 230; Successful invasion of Grenada	October 1983 48%	November 1983 56%
TWA airliner hijacked by Shiites	June 1985 63%	July 1985 63%
U.S. bombs Libya	March 1986 63%	April 1986 69%
Tiananmen Square demonstrations	April 1989 60%	June 1989 74%
Authorization for use of armed forces against Iraq; Beginning of war	October 1990 57%	January 1991 91%
Cruise missile attack on Iraqi intelligence headquarters	June 1993 39%	June 1993 50%
Entry of U.S. troops into Haiti	September 1994 34%	September 1994 45%

SOURCE: Courtesy of Roper Opinion Research Center, Storrs, CT, and the Harris Poll, September 22, 1994. A more detailed examination of 1989–92 is given in Figure 12.9.

Party chair Lee Atwater called a "political jackpot." But, having reached a historic high of 91 percent approval in January 1991, Bush's ratings plunged to among the lowest for any president in recent history.

Why? Surely the persistent recession hurt him, but economists disagreed on just how grave the recession was; some were asserting in 1993 that the recession had ended in 1991, well before the 1992 presidential campaign ever began. Ross Perot's candidacy could well have hurt President Bush. But here again, many analysts argued in 1992 and continued to argue in 1993 that Perot had taken away votes about equally from both candidates, not from Bush alone. What is most striking about the period of Bush's decline in 1991 and 1992 is the absence of international events associated with the president after the Gulf War. President Bush had a reputation for dealing face-to-face with heads of state throughout the world, using personal diplomacy to very good effect in putting together the U.N.-sponsored coalition in the Gulf War. But it is quite probable that the very success of Bush's personal diplomacy contributed to his political undoing in the last eighteen months of his term.

Perhaps a more fundamental reason for Bush's approval decline was the collapse of the Soviet Union and the end of the cold war. Without the implacable Soviet presence, the condition for strong "rallying effects" may have been permanently weakened. Bush did not get the expected credit for the foreign events that occurred in 1992. And the same applies to Clinton. There was virtually no rallying effect during 1994, despite several front-page international events such as the passage of the North American Free Trade Agreement and the General Agreement on Tariffs and Trade, the military actions in Haiti and Somalia, and some normally valuable state visits to key foreign capitals. Presidents will continue to travel and to associate themselves with international events for political purposes, hoping to get the "foreign policy fix" that cold-war presidents so often used to boost flagging approval scores. But the days of "the fix" may be over. With the end of the cold war, the rise and decline of presidents' approval ratings—and thus, to a great extent, of presidents themselves—may depend less on the ability to capture the world's and the nation's attention in international affairs than on the ability to navigate through the ceaseless currents of domestic politics.

There is nothing inherently wrong with the rallying effect, and Americans should probably be commended for their collective rationality and be encouraged to continue to rally to the president in response to important international events. But it is not a healthy situation in a democracy for a president to have to decide *between* popularity and diplomacy.

The Rise of Presidential Government

- What relationship between the president and Congress did the framers of the Constitution intend? What factors allowed this relationship to endure for so long?
- When, why, and how did presidential government become an established fact of American politics?

Most of the real power of the modern presidency comes from powers granted by the Constitution and the laws made by Congress delegating powers to the president.[34] Thus, any person properly elected and sworn in as president will possess almost all of the power held by the strongest of presidents in American history. Even a "lame duck" president still possesses all of the power of the office. For example, during the weeks after his electoral defeat in 1992, President Bush committed troops to Somalia and conducted a series of air strikes against Iraq.

The presidency has become a genuinely democratic institution, and its mass popular base is respected by Congress and by all of the social forces and organized interests that seek to influence the national government. But we must recognize an extremely important fact about the presidency: The popular base of the presidency is important less because it gives the president power, and more because it gives the president *consent to use* all of the power already vested in the presidency by the Constitution and by Congress. The other formal and informal resources lodged in the presidency—the resources we have studied throughout this chapter—are just that: resources. But resources are not power; they must be converted into power. This process—the conversion of the resources of the presidency into the power that twentieth-century American presidents wield—took more than a century to develop in the United States.

The Legislative Epoch, 1800–1933

In 1885, an obscure political science professor named Woodrow Wilson entitled his general textbook *Congressional Government* because American government was just that, "congressional government." This characterization seemed to fly in the face of the separation of powers principle that the three separate branches were and ought to be equal. Nevertheless, there is ample evidence that Wilson's description of the national government was consistent not only with nineteenth-century reality but also with the intentions of the framers. Within the system of three separate and competing powers, the clear intent of the Constitution was for *legislative supremacy*.

The strongest evidence of original intent is the fact that the powers of the national government were not placed in a separate article of the Constitution, but were instead listed in Article I, the legislative article. Madison had laid it out explicitly in *The Federalist* No. 51: "In republican government, the legislative authority necessarily predominates."[35] The first decade of the new government was unique precisely because it was first; everything was precedent making, and nothing was secure. It was a state-building decade in which relations between president and Congress were more cooperative than they would be at any time thereafter.

Before the Republic was a decade old, Congress began to develop a strong organization, including its own elected leadership, the first standing committees, and the party hierarchies. By the second term of President Thomas Jefferson (1805), the executive branch was beginning to play the secondary role anticipated by the Constitution. The quality of presidential performance and then of presidential personality and character declined accordingly. The president during this era was seen by some observers as little more than America's "chief clerk." It was said of President James Madison, who had been principal author of the Constitution, that he knew everything about government except how to govern. Indeed, most historians agree that after Jefferson and until the beginning of the twentieth century, Presidents Jackson and Lincoln were the only exceptions to what had been the rule of weak presidents, and those two exceptions can be explained, since one was a war hero and founder of the Democratic Party and the other was a wartime president and first leader of the newly founded Republican Party.

One of the reasons that so few great men became presidents in the nineteenth century is that there was only occasional room for greatness in such a weak office.[36] The national government of that period was not a particularly powerful entity. Another reason for the weak presidency of the nineteenth century is that during this period the presidency was not closely linked to major national political and social forces. Indeed, there were few important *national* political or social forces to which presidents could have linked themselves even if they had wanted to. Federalism had taken very good care of this by fragmenting political interests and diverting the energies of interest groups toward the state and local levels of government, where most key decisions were being made.

The presidency was strengthened somewhat in the 1830s with the introduction of the national convention system of nominating presidential candidates. Until then, presidential candidates had been nominated by their party's congressional delegates. This was the **caucus** system of nominating candidates, and it was derisively called "King Caucus" because any candidate for president had to be beholden to the party's leaders in Congress in order to get the party's nomination and the support of the party's congressional delegation in the presidential election. The national nominating convention arose outside Congress in order to provide some representation for a party's voters who lived in districts where they weren't numerous enough to elect a member of Congress. The political party in each state made its own provisions for selecting delegates to attend the presidential nominating convention, and in virtually all states the selection was dominated by the party leaders (called "bosses" by the opposition party). Only in recent decades have state laws intervened to regularize the selection process and to provide (in all but a few instances) for open election of delegates. The convention system quickly became the most popular method of nominating candidates for all elective offices and remained so until well into the twentieth century, when it succumbed to the criticism that it was a nondemocratic method dominated by a few leaders in a "smoke-filled room." But in the nineteenth century, it was seen as a victory for democracy against the congressional elite. And the national convention gave the presidency a base of power independent of Congress.

This additional independence did not immediately transform the presidency into the office we recognize today because the parties disappeared back into their states and Congress once the national election was over. But the national convention did begin to open the presidency to larger social forces and newly organized interests in society. In other words, it gave the presidency a mass popular base that would eventually support and demand increased presidential power. Improvements in telephone, telegraph, and other forms of mass communication allowed individuals to share their complaints and allowed national leaders—especially presidents and presidential candidates—to reach out directly to people to ally themselves with, and even sometimes to create, popular groups and forces. Eventually, though more slowly, the presidential selection process began to be further democratized, with the adoption of primary elections through which millions of ordinary citizens were given an opportunity to take part in the presidential nominating process by popular selection of convention delegates.

But despite political and social conditions favoring the enhancement of the presidency, the development of presidential government as we know it today did not mature until the middle of the twentieth century. For a long period, even as the national government began to grow, Congress was careful to keep tight reins on the president's power. The real turning point in the history of American national government came during the administration of Franklin Delano Roosevelt. The New Deal was a response to political forces that had been gathering national strength and focus for fifty years. What is remarkable is not that they gathered but that they took so long to gain influence in Washington—and even then it took the Great Depression to bring about the new national government.

The New Deal and the Presidency

The "First Hundred Days" of the Roosevelt administration in 1933 had no parallel in U.S. history. But this period was only the beginning. The policies proposed by President Roosevelt and adopted by Congress during the first thousand days of his administration so changed the size and character of the national government that they constitute a moment in American history equivalent to the Founding or to the Civil War. The president's constitutional obligation to see "that the Laws be faithfully executed" became, during Roosevelt's presidency, virtually a responsibility to make the laws as well as to execute them.

Franklin Delano Roosevelt signing the Social Security bill of 1935, one of the most significant pieces of legislation to come out of the New Deal.

New Programs Expand the Role of National Government Many of the New Deal programs were extensions of the traditional national government approach, which was described already in Chapter 4 (see especially Table 4.1). But the New Deal went well beyond the traditional approach, adopting types of policies never before tried on a large scale by the national government; it began intervening into economic life in ways that had hitherto been reserved to the states. In other words, the national government discovered that it, too, had "the power" to directly regulate individuals as well as provide roads and other services.

Delegation of Power The most important constitutional effect of Congress's actions during the New Deal was the enhancement of presidential power. Most major acts of Congress in this period involved significant exercises of control over the economy. But few programs specified the actual controls to be used. Instead, Congress authorized the president, or, in some cases, a new agency—to determine what the controls would be. Some of the new agencies were independent commissions responsible to Congress. But most of the new agencies and programs of the New Deal were placed in the executive branch directly under presidential authority.

Technically, this form of congressional act is called the "delegation of power." In theory, the delegation of power works as follows: (1) Congress recognizes a problem; (2) Congress acknowledges that it has neither the time nor the expertise to deal with the problem; and (3) Congress therefore sets the basic policies and then delegates to an agency the power to "fill in the details." But in practice, Congress was delegating not merely the power to "fill in the details," but actual and real policy-making powers, that is, real legislative powers, to the executive branch.

No modern government can avoid the delegation of significant legislative powers to the executive branch. But the fact remains that this delegation produced a fundamental shift in the American constitutional framework. During the 1930s, the growth of the national government through acts delegating legislative power tilted the American national structure away from a Congress-centered government toward a president-centered government.[37] Congress continues to be the constitutional source of policy, and Congress can rescind these delegations of power or restrict them with later amendments, committee oversight, or budget cuts. But we can say that presidential government has become an established fact of American life.

★ Summary

The foundations for presidential government were laid in the Constitution, which provides for a unitary executive who is head of state as well as head of government. The first section of this chapter reviewed the powers of each: the head of state with its military, judicial, and diplomatic powers; the head of government with its executive, military, and legislative powers.

The second section of this chapter focused on the president's institutional and political resources. The cabinet, the other top appointments, the White House staff, and the Executive Office of the President are some of the impressive institutional resources of presidential power. The president's political party, the supportive group coalitions, and access to the media and, through that, access to the millions of Americans who make up the general public are formidable political resources that can be used to bolster a president's power. But these resources are not cost- or risk-free. A direct relationship with the mass public is the president's most potent modern resource, but it is also the most problematic.

The final section of this chapter traced the rise of modern presidential government after the much longer period of congressional dominance. There is no mystery in the shift to government centered on the presidency. Congress built the modern presidency by delegating to it not only the power to implement the vast new programs of the 1930s but also by delegating its own legislative power to make the policies themselves. Presidential government is now an established fact of American politics.

FOR FURTHER READING

Barber, James David. *The Presidential Character.* Englewood Cliffs, NJ: Prentice-Hall, 1985.

Drew, Elizabeth. *On the Edge: The Clinton Presidency.* New York: Simon & Schuster, 1994.

Hart, John. *The Presidential Branch: From Washington to Clinton.* Chatham, NJ: Chatham House, 1995.

Hinckley, Barbara, and Paul Brace. *Follow the Leader: Opinion Polls and Modern Presidents.* New York: Basic Books, 1992.

Kernell, Samuel. *Going Public: New Strategies of Presi-*

dential Leadership. Washington, DC: Congressional Quarterly Press, 1986.

Lowi, Theodore J. *The Personal President: Power Invested, Promise Unfulfilled.* Ithaca, NY: Cornell University Press, 1985.

Milkis, Sidney M. *The President and the Parties: The Transformation of the American Party System since the New Deal.* New York: Oxford University Press, 1993.

Nelson, Michael, ed. *The Presidency and the Political System.* 4th ed. Washington, DC: Congressional Quarterly Press, 1994.

Neustadt, Richard E. *Presidential Power: The Politics of Leadership from Roosevelt to Reagan.* Rev. ed. New York: Free Press, 1990.

Pfiffner, James P. *The Modern Presidency.* New York: St. Martin's, 1994.

Skowronek, Stephen. *The Politics Presidents Make: Presidential Leadership from John Adams to George Bush.* Cambridge, MA: Harvard University Press, 1993.

Spitzer, Robert. *The Presidential Veto: Touchstone of the American Presidency.* Albany, NY: SUNY Press, 1988.

Tulis, Jeffrey. *The Rhetorical Presidency.* Princeton, NJ: Princeton University Press, 1987.

Watson, Richard A., and Norman Thomas. *The Politics of the Presidency.* Washington, DC: Congressional Quarterly Press, 1988.

STUDY OUTLINE

The Constitutional Powers of the Presidency

1. The president as head of state is defined by three constitutional provisions—military, judicial, and diplomatic—that are the source of some of the most important powers on which the president can draw.
2. The position of commander in chief makes the president the highest military authority in the United States, with control of the entire military establishment.
3. The presidential power to grant reprieves, pardons, and amnesties allows the president to choose freedom or confinement, and even life or death for all individuals who have violated, or are suspected of having violated, federal laws, including people who directly threaten the security of the United States.
4. The power to receive representatives of foreign countries allows the president almost unconditional authority to determine whether a new ruling group can indeed commit its country to treaties and other agreements.
5. The president's role as head of government rests on a constitutional foundation consisting of three principal sources: executive power, domestic military authority, and legislative power.
6. The Constitution delegated to the president, as commander in chief, the obligation to protect every state against invasion and domestic violence.
7. The president's legislative power consists of the obligation to make recommendations for consideration by Congress and the ability to veto legislation.

Institutional Resources of Presidential Power

1. Presidents have at their disposal a variety of institutional resources—such as the power to fill high-level political positions—that directly affect a president's ability to govern.
2. Presidents increasingly have preferred the White House staff to the cabinet as a tool for managing the gigantic executive branch.
3. The White House staff, which is composed primarily of analysts and advisers, has grown from an informal group of fewer than a dozen people to a new presidential bureaucracy.
4. The Executive Office of the President, often called the institutional presidency, is larger than the White House staff, and comprises the president's permanent management agencies.

Political Resources of Presidential Power

1. The president also has political resources upon which to draw in exercising the powers of office.
2. Presidents often use their electoral victories to increase their power by claiming the election was a mandate for a certain course of action.
3. Although its traditional influence is on the decline, the president's party is still significant as a means of achieving legislative success.
4. Interest groups and coalitions supportive of the president's agenda are also a dependable resource for presidential government.
5. Over the past half-century, the American executive branch has harnessed mass popularity successfully as a political resource.

The Rise of Presidential Government

1. American government was dominated by Congress between 1800 and 1933; during that time the executive

office played the secondary role anticipated by the framers of the Constitution.

2. During the New Deal, Congress shifted the balance in favor of the executive office by delegating vast discretionary power to the president for the implementation of policy.
3. Many New Deal programs expanded the traditional role of national government by allowing it to intervene in economic life in ways that previously had been reserved to the states.
4. Presidential power was enhanced by the New Deal's placement of new agencies and programs in the executive branch directly under presidential authority.

PRACTICE QUIZ

1. Which article of the Constitution established the presidency?
   a. Article I
   b. Article II
   c. Article III
   d. none of the above
2. Which of the following does not represent a classification of a constitutional provision designating the president as head of state?
   a. legislative
   b. military
   c. judicial
   d. diplomatic
3. Which of the following does not require the advice and consent of the Senate?
   a. an executive agreement
   b. a treaty
   c. Supreme Court nominations
   d. All of the above require the advice and consent of the Senate.
4. Which of the following terms has been used to describe the presidency as it has used constitutional and other powers to make itself more powerful?
   a. "the delegated presidency"
   b. "the imperial presidency"
   c. "the personal presidency"
   d. "the pre-emptive presidency"
5. By what process can Congress reject a presidential veto?
   a. veto override
   b. pocket veto
   c. executive delegation
   d. impeachment
6. Which of the following describes the presidential foreign policy advisory council composed of the president; the vice president; the secretaries of state, defense, and the treasury; the attorney general; and others?
   a. the "Inner Cabinet"
   b. the National Security Council
   c. both a and b
   d. neither a nor b
7. The Office of Management and Budget is part of
   a. the Executive Office of the President.
   b. the White House staff.
   c. the Kitchen Cabinet.
   d. both a and b.
8. In what book did Woodrow Wilson describe American government in 1885?
   a. *A Separated System*
   b. *Checks and Balances*
   c. *Presidential Government*
   d. *Congressional Government*
9. Which twentieth-century presidency transformed the American system of government from a Congress-centered to a president-centered system?
   a. Woodrow Wilson's
   b. Franklin Roosevelt's
   c. Richard Nixon's
   d. Jimmy Carter's
10. How many people work for agencies within the Executive Office of the President?
    a. 25 to 50
    b. 700 to 1,000
    c. 1,500 to 2,000
    d. 4,500 to 5,000

CRITICAL THINKING QUESTIONS

1. At times, the Congress has been the dominant branch of government. At other times, the presidency has predominated. Describe the changes in the relationship between the presidency and the Congress throughout American history. What factors contributed to the dominance of Congress? What factors contributed to the resurgence of the presidency? Which branch of government dominates now? Why do you think so?

2. Presidents have constitutional, institutional, and political sources of power. Which of the three do you think most accounts for the powers of the presidency? Is it, in fact, possible to discern among these the true source of presidential power? Select a president and discuss the ways in which that particular president used each source of power to succeed in the presidency.

KEY TERMS

Cabinet the secretaries, or chief administrators, of the major departments of the federal government. Cabinet secretaries are appointed by the president with the consent of the Senate. (p. 458)

caucus (political) a normally closed meeting of a political or legislative group to select candidates, plan strategy, or make decisions regarding legislative matters. (p. 484)

delegated powers constitutional powers that are assigned to one governmental agency but that are exercised by another agency with the express permission of the first. (p. 446)

divided government the condition in American government wherein the presidency is controlled by one party while the opposing party controls one or both houses of Congress. (p. 471)

executive agreement an agreement, made between the president and another country, that has the force of a treaty but does not require the Senate's "advice and consent." (p. 448)

Executive Office of the President (EOP) the permanent agencies that perform defined management tasks for the president. Created in 1939, the EOP includes the Office of Management and Budget, the Council of Economic Advisers, the National Security Council, and other agencies. (p. 463)

Kitchen Cabinet an informal group of advisers to whom the president turns for counsel and guidance. Members of the official Cabinet may or may not also be members of the Kitchen Cabinet. (p. 462)

mandate a claim by a victorious candidate that the electorate has given him or her special authority to carry out promises made during the campaign. (p. 468)

National Security Council (NSC) a presidential foreign policy advisory council composed of the president; the vice president; the secretaries of state, defense, and the treasury; the attorney general; and other officials invited by the president. The NSC has a staff of foreign-policy specialists. (p. 460)

patronage resources available to higher officials, usually opportunities to make partisan appointments to offices and to confer grants, licenses, or special favors to supporters. (p. 457)

pocket veto a presidential veto that is automatically triggered if the president does not act on a given piece of legislation passed during the final ten days of a legislative session. (p. 454)

veto the president's constitutional power to turn down acts of Congress. A presidential veto may be overridden by a two-thirds vote of each house of Congress. (p. 454)

War Powers Resolution a resolution of Congress that the president can send troops into action abroad only by authorization of Congress, or if American troops are already under attack or serious threat. (p. 449)

White House staff analysts and advisers to the president, often given the title "special assistant." (p. 460)

13

Bureaucracy in a Democracy

★ Bureaucracy and Bureaucrats

Why do bureaucracies exist? Why are they needed?

Has the federal bureaucracy grown too large?

What roles do government bureaucrats perform? What types of access do citizens have to the bureaucracy?

Is the federal bureaucracy representative?

★ The Organization of the Executive Branch

What are the agencies that make up the executive branch?

How can one classify these agencies according to their missions?

★ Can the Bureaucracy Be Reduced?

What methods have been used to reduce the size and the role of the federal bureaucracy?

How effective can efforts to reduce the bureaucracy be?

★ Can Bureaucracy Be Controlled?

How can bureaucracy and democracy coexist? What popular controls over the bureaucracy exist?

How do the president and Congress manage and oversee the bureaucracy?

What is the most effective means to guarantee a responsible bureaucracy?

The "real world" that college students are told they are preparing for is largely a world of work—of earning a living by collaborating in the production of goods and services for which other people are willing to pay. For most students, college is an opportunity to improve their employment prospects. And with the exception of a few who will own and operate small businesses or independent medical or law practices or who will be self-supporting artists or musicians, college graduates will go from a bachelor's, graduate, or professional degree directly to salaried employment in a private company or a public organization of a hundred or more employees. In other words, most college graduates will work for somebody else. The source of income for most will be a salary, which will come from an employer who makes the job possible.

That job will typically consist of a set of responsibilities and tasks defined by the employer to meet the needs of the organization. Specific assignments come from the employee's immediate superior. Often a new employee's real work begins after weeks or months of on-the-job training. This is true even for many who have advanced degrees or significant experience, because the organization—whether a private company or a government agency—will need to accustom the new employee to the special way the organization operates. To gain maximum efficiency, the employer provides a salary sufficient to get each employee to contribute precisely to the mission of the organization—whether the output of the organization is computers, television programs, welfare services, or environmental protection regulations. The organization has a mission defined by its output, and all of the jobs within that organization are defined to serve that mission.

In the course of a career, the average person will make two or three job changes. But with the exception of the few who will have enough capital to form a private practice or establish an independently owned company, the job changes will be from one position to another—one with more responsibility and higher pay—within one relatively large organization or from one large organization to another. For most people this will be the very definition of a career—moving upward, step by step, to higher levels of responsibility in return for higher salary and more privileges. Success in one's career is typically defined by the size of one's salary and other benefits, by titles that convey the level of responsibility one holds, and by certain additional titles and prizes that convey recognition for meritorious contributions.

Turn now to Table 13.1, which identifies the basic characteristics of bureaucracy. These characteristics are found in virtually *all* organizations, whether public or private, military or religious, for profit or nonprofit, pro-

TABLE 13.1

THE SIX PRIMARY CHARACTERISTICS OF BUREAUCRACY

Characteristic	Explanation
Division of labor	Workers are specialized. Each worker develops a skill in a particular job and performs the job routinely and repetitively, thereby increasing productivity.
Allocation of functions	Each task is assigned. No one makes a whole product; each worker depends on the output of other workers.
Allocation of responsibility	Each task becomes a personal responsibility—a contractual obligation. No task can be changed without permission.
Supervision	Some workers are assigned the special task of watching over other workers rather than contributing directly to the creation of the product. Each supervisor watches over a few workers (a situation known as span of control), and communications between workers or between levels move in a prescribed fashion (known as chain of command).
Purchase of full-time employment	The organization controls all the time the worker is on the job, so each worker can be assigned and held to a task. Some part-time and contracted work is tolerated, but it is held to a minimum.
Identification of career within the organization	Workers come to identify with the organization as a way of life. Seniority, pension rights, and promotions are geared to this relationship.

ducers of goods or providers of services. Most organizations are bureaucracies, and most of their employees are bureaucrats.

But if bureaucracy is so common in the workplace, why have "bureaucracy" and "bureaucrat" become such negative words? Why has "bureaucracy" come to mean only government, when in fact it is a universal phenomenon? Why do we call government activity we don't like "bureaucracy" and government activity we approve of "administration"? Why do we reserve the term "bureaucrat" for people whose work we don't like when as a matter of fact most of us are or will be bureaucrats ourselves?

These questions require some serious reflection. We have to clarify what we mean by "bureaucracy" before we can understand the nature and character of the executive branch of the U.S. government. That will be the first task of this chapter. Then we will be able to look at the agencies of the executive branch with some objectivity, in order to gain a broader understanding of government itself while maintaining the capacity to criticize the things about it that deserve criticism. This will lead us to the question posed in the final section of the chapter: Can bureaucracy and democracy coexist? Can bureaucracy be made accountable to the political branches of the government—the president and Congress—and, through them, to the people?

Bureaucracy and Bureaucrats

- Why do bureaucracies exist? Why are they needed?
- Has the federal bureaucracy grown too large?
- What roles do government bureaucrats perform? What types of access do citizens have to the bureaucracy?
- Is the federal bureaucracy representative?

Bureaucracy is nothing more nor less than a form of organization, as defined by the attributes on Table 13.1. To gain some objectivity, and to appreciate the universality of bureaucracy, let us take the word and break it into its two main parts—*bureau* and *cracy. Bureau,* a French word, can mean either "office" or "desk." *Cracy* is the Greek word for "rule" or "form of rule." For example, "democracy" means rule by the people *(demos),* a form of government in which the people prevail. "Theocracy" refers to rule by clergy or churches. "Gerontocracy" would describe a system ruled by the elders of the community. Putting *bureau* and *cracy* back together produces a very interesting definition: **Bureaucracy** is a form of rule by offices and desks. Each member of an organization has an office, meaning a place as well as a set of responsibilities. That is, each "office" comprises a set of tasks that are specialized to the needs of the organization, and the person holding that office (or position) performs those specialized tasks. Specialization and repetition are essential to the efficiency of any organization. Therefore, when an organization is inefficient, it is almost certainly because it is not bureaucratized enough!

Since it is absolutely essential for any large organization to be run as efficiently as possible, organizations from every part of social life have made major contributions to the advancement of bureaucracy. For example, one of the most widely used terms for a member of an organization is not "bureaucrat" but "clerk." It may come as something of a surprise that the origin of the world "clerk" is "cleric," which indicates that religious organizations, especially the Roman Catholic Church, have made major contributions to the advancement of bureaucracy, or what we now call "organization theory" or "management science." The Roman Catholic Church was also instrumental in the development of budgeting and accounting, without which no large organization, private or public, would be able to sustain itself.

Armies have also been great innovators in the advancement of bureaucracy. The use of the terms "line" and "staff" in organizations comes from military usage, indicating a strict specialization of function between the line units, which deal with the enemy, and the staff units, which support the line units. This distinction is just the beginning of the tremendous specialization of functions in any large military organization.

This line/staff distinction has spread to all sorts of organizations beyond the military. Private corporations have in some areas been even more inventive in the advancement of the principles of bureaucracy. The formal process of projecting goals and ways to meet them, something we call "planning," came not from governments but from large corporations. The five-year plan that came to be associated with the Soviet Union and other socialist bureaucracies was something that the communists borrowed from the capitalists. Industrial giants like the Ford Motor Company were the first organizations to prove that efficiency could be gained by careful study of every task until it could be reduced to its narrowest, most specialized, and most repetitive movements in order to "fine-tune" production for maximum output. Later on, when many reformers began to argue that governments should be run more like businesses, this efficiency and specialization is precisely what they meant: that government should be *more* bureaucratized.

The movie *Brazil* portrayed a stereotypical view of bureaucracy: a large, impersonal, and threatening organization.

In reality, government bureaucracy performs many important tasks. For example, government bureaucrats in the Federal Emergency Management Agency (left) coordinate relief efforts to areas devastated by natural disasters. These soldiers (right), for instance, were sent to Florida to work in areas damaged by a hurricane.

The Size of the Federal Service

In his State of the Union address to Congress on January 23, 1996, President Bill Clinton declared that "the era of big government is over." With his reelection campaign looming, Clinton was capitalizing on popular sentiment that the federal government had grown too large. Despite fears of bureaucratic growth getting out of hand, however, the federal service has hardly grown at all during the past twenty-five years; it reached its peak postwar level in 1968 with 2.9 million civilian employees plus an additional 3.6 million military personnel (a figure swollen by Vietnam). The number of civilian federal employees has since remained close to that figure. (In 1993, it was 3,012,839.[1])

The growth of the federal service is even less imposing when placed in the context of the total work force and when compared to the size of state and local public employment. Figure 13.1 indicates that, since 1950, the ratio of federal employment to the total work force has been steady, and in fact has *declined* slightly in the past fifteen years. In 1950, there were 4.3 million state and local civil service employees (about 6.5 percent of the country's work force). In 1978, there were 12.7 million (nearly 15 percent of the work force), and the ratio remained about the same for the ensuing decade. Federal employment, in contrast, exceeded 5 percent of the work force only during World War II (not shown), and almost all of that momentary growth was military. After the demobilization, which continued until 1950 (as shown in Figure 13.1), the federal service has tended to grow at a rate that keeps pace with the economy and society. That is demonstrated by the lower line on Figure 13.1, which shows a constant relation between federal civilian employment and the size of the U.S. work force. Variations in federal employment since 1946 have been in the military and are directly related to war and the cold war (as shown by the top line on Figure 13.1).

Another useful comparison is to be found in Figure 13.2. Although the dollar increase in federal spending shown by the bars looks impressive, the trend line indicating the relation of federal spending to the Gross Domestic Product (GDP) has moved in thirty-five years from 18 percent to 21 percent—which suggests that the national government has grown just a bit more than necessary to keep pace with the growth of the economy.

In sum, the national government is indeed "very large," but it has not been growing any faster than the economy or the society. The same is roughly true of the growth pattern of state and local public personnel. Bureaucracy keeps pace with society, despite people's seeming dislike for it, because the control towers, the prisons, the Social Security system, and other essential elements cannot be operated without bureaucracy. The United States certainly could not have conducted a successful war in the Persian Gulf without a gigantic military bureaucracy.

FIGURE 13.1

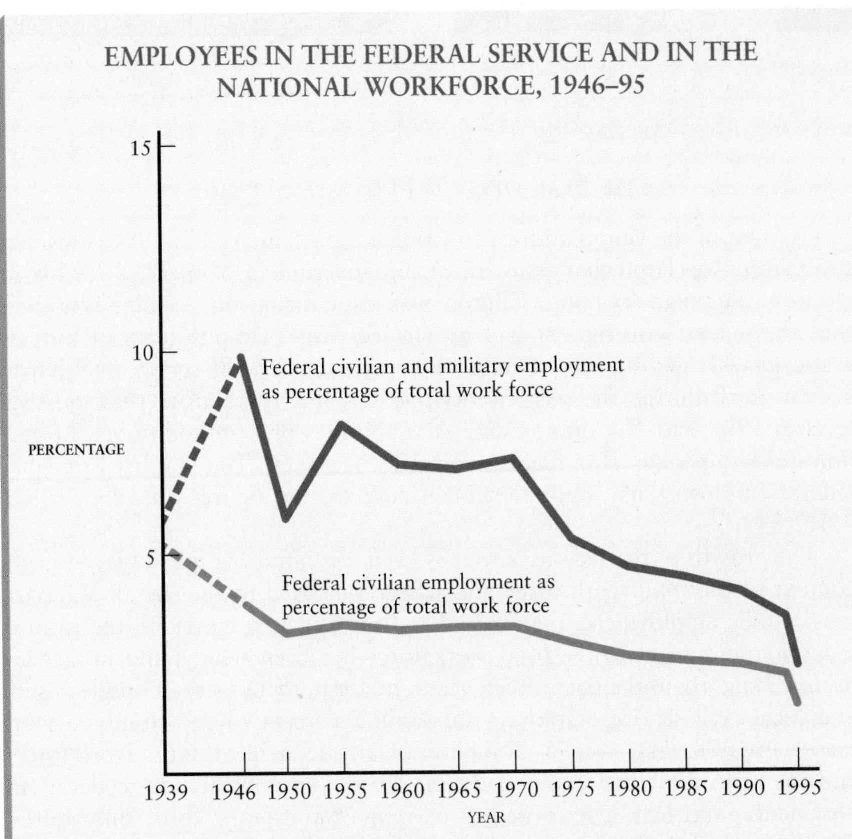

SOURCES: Tax Foundation, *Facts & Figures on Government Finance, 1990* (Baltimore, MD: Johns Hopkins University Press, 1990), pp. 22 and 44; Office of Management and Budget, *Budget of the United States Government, FY 1996, Historical Tables* (Washington, DC: Government Printing Office, 1995), p. 245; and U.S. Department of Labor, Bureau of Labor Statistics, *Employment and Earnings* (monthly).

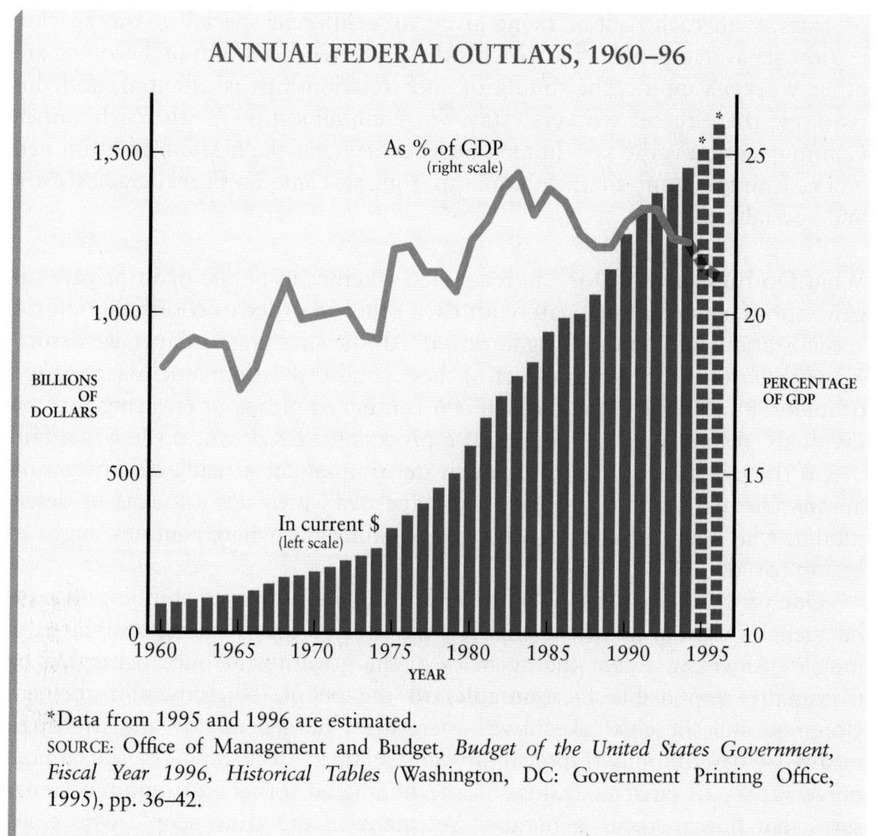

*Data from 1995 and 1996 are estimated.

SOURCE: Office of Management and Budget, *Budget of the United States Government, Fiscal Year 1996, Historical Tables* (Washington, DC: Government Printing Office, 1995), pp. 36–42.

FIGURE 13.2

Although the federal executive branch is large and complex, everything about it is commonplace. Bureaucracies are commonplace because they touch so many aspects of daily life. Government bureaucracies implement the decisions made by the political process. Bureaucracies are full of routine because that assures the regular delivery of the services and ensures that each agency fulfills its mandate. Public bureaucracies are powerful because legislatures and chief executives, and indeed the people, delegate to them vast power to make sure a particular job is done—enabling citizens to be more free to pursue their private ends. And for the same reason, bureaucracies are a threat to freedom, because their size, their momentum, and the interests of the civil servants themselves in keeping their jobs impel bureaucracies and bureaucrats to resist any change of direction.

BUREAUCRATS

"Government by offices and desks" conveys to most people a picture of hundreds of office workers shuffling millions of pieces of paper. There is a lot of truth in that image, but we have to look more closely at what papers are being shuffled and why. More than seventy years ago, an astute observer defined bureaucracy as "continuous routine business."[2] As we saw at the beginning of this chapter, almost any organization succeeds by reducing its work to routines, with each routine being given to a different specialist. But specialization separates people from each other; one worker's output becomes another worker's input. The timing of such relationships is essential, and this requires that these workers stay in communication with each other. Communication is the key. In fact, bureaucracy was the first information network. Routine came first; voluminous routine came as bureaucracies grew and specialized.

What Do Bureaucrats Do? Bureaucrats, whether in public or in private organizations, first communicate with each other in order to coordinate all the specializations within their organization. All the shuffling of paper we associate with bureaucracy is a product of the second task of bureaucrats: the need to maintain a "**paper trail,**" which is a routinized means of ensuring that individuals' responsibilities are met. If a process breaks down, if there is a failure, if there is a loss of profit in a private company or a rising dissatisfaction among clients of public agencies, the paper trail provides a means of determining who was responsible, who was at fault, and where routines ought to be improved.

One of the major reasons why there may be more paper shuffling in public agencies than in private agencies is the need to establish responsibility. As long as Americans want the agencies in the government bureaucracy to be maximally responsible (**accountable**) to the people—directly and through Congress and the chief executive—there must be dependable and thorough means of determining responsibility and blame. "Red tape" is the almost universal cry of citizens against all the numbered forms and required signatures that bureaucracies generate.[3] Yet many of the same people who complain about red tape are the first to demand subpoenas requiring delivery of every conceivable document that may have some bearing on an alleged error of an agency or of individuals in an agency. What if the issue is the tragic explosion of the *Challenger* space shuttle or a gigantic overrun of expenditures for a new missile system for the Air Force? The bureaucrats in the National Aeronautics and Space Administration (NASA) or in the Air Force are required to create the record by which their own performances will later be judged.[4] And since Americans are more fearful of public bureaucracies and are therefore more likely to demand their accountability, public bureaucracies are likely to produce a great deal more paper than private bureaucracies.

Buried in red tape? This Food and Drug Administration reviewer now works on a laptop computer. The FDA is striving to computerize its operations and reduce agency review time.

Those first two activities of bureaucrats—communicating with each other and keeping copies of all those communications to maintain a paper trail—add up to a third: **implementation,** that is, implementing the objectives of the organization as laid down by its board of directors (if a private company) or by law (if a public agency). In government, the "bosses" are ultimately the legislature and the elected chief executive.

When the bosses—Congress, in particular, when it is making the law—are clear in their instructions to bureaucrats, implementation is a fairly straightforward process. Bureaucrats translate the law into specific routines for each of the employees of an agency. But what happens to routine administrative implementation when there are several bosses who disagree as to what the instructions ought to be? This requires yet a fourth job for bureaucrats: **interpretation.** Interpretation is a form of implementation, in that the bureaucrats still have to carry out what they believe to be the intentions of their superiors. But when bureaucrats have to interpret a law before implementing it, they are in effect engaging in *lawmaking*. Congress often deliberately delegates to an administrative agency the responsibility of lawmaking. Members of Congress often conclude that some area of industry needs regulating or some area of the environment needs protection, but they are unwilling or unable to specify just how that should be done. In such situations, Congress delegates to the appropriate agency a broad authority within which the bureaucrats have to make law. This creates constitutional tensions, because broad delegations from Congress to an agency to make law would appear to be a violation of the separation of powers. Yet in the past sixty years, the Supreme Court has rarely invoked the principle of the separation of powers to declare that Congress went too far in delegating to an agency the power to make law. And in no instance since 1935 has the Supreme Court declared an important act of Congress unconstitutional on these grounds.[5] Thus, when people criticize "bureaucrats" for overstepping their power or for behaving irresponsibly, they should actually refocus their criticism away from bureaucracy and toward the inadequate job Congress and the president do in providing appropriate instructions to and limitations on the work of bureaucrats. One could say that the primary purpose of the "rule of law" is to draft legislation that provides clear directions to administrators. If a person has a grudge against bureaucracy, the remedy, if there is one, will be found in Congress. (We return to this at the end of the chapter.)

In sum, government bureaucrats do essentially the same things that bureaucrats in large private organizations do, and neither type deserves the disrespect embodied in the term "bureaucrat." But because of the authoritative, coercive nature of government, far more constraints are imposed on public bureaucrats than on private bureaucrats, even when their jobs are the same. Public bureaucrats are required to maintain a far more thorough paper trail. Public bureaucrats are also subject to a great deal more access from the public. Newspaper reporters, for example, have access to public bureaucrats that they could never hope to get with private bureaucrats. Public access has been vastly facilitated in the past thirty years; the adoption of the Freedom of Information Act (FOIA) in 1966 gave ordinary citizens the right of access to agency files and agency data to determine whether derogatory information exists in the file about the citizens themselves and to learn about what the agency is doing in general.

Michael Ravnitsky with some of the 900 FBI files he has requested under the Freedom of Information Act.

And finally, citizens are given far more opportunities to participate in the decision-making processes of public agencies. There are limits of time, money, and expertise to this kind of access, but it does exist, and it occupies a great deal of the time of mid-level and senior public bureaucrats. This public exposure and access serves a purpose, but it also cuts down significantly on the efficiency of public bureaucrats. Thus, much of the lower efficiency of public agencies can be attributed to the political, judicial, legal, and publicity restraints put on public bureaucrats.

The Merit System: How to Become a Bureaucrat In return for all these inconveniences, public bureaucrats are rewarded in part with greater job security than their counterparts in most private organizations enjoy. More than a century ago, the federal government attempted to imitate business by passing

Early in the history of the United States, the selection of those few employees hired by the government was based on competence and nonpartisanship. But beginning with the presidency of Andrew Jackson, the selection of government employees became partisan, with Jackson and subsequent presidents basing job decisions primarily on a person's party loyalty and his or her record of past political service. This practice, dubbed "the spoils system," degraded the quality and efficiency of government service to such an extent that in 1853 Congress instituted an examination system for departmental clerks. Yet the effort to improve and professionalize the governmental service requirements for the growing ranks of non-elective employees won little support until after the Civil War.

At the state and local levels, the awarding of government jobs to political friends was widespread. Indeed, it was a primary means by which local political organizations built their political bases of strength. Such patronage practices still exist to a limited extent in state and local governments. At the national level, however, the patronage system was broken with the Pendleton (Civil Service Reform) Act of 1883.

The drive toward merit-based civil service was led by a member of Congress from Rhode Island, Thomas Jenckes, who proposed a set of competitive examinations (a system used by the military) as the basis for selecting government employees. In addition, he proposed that government employees be allowed to maintain their jobs as long as they performed satisfactorily; they would not need to fear the loss of their job at the whim of a political leader.

This system was proposed as a way to enhance the government's performance and to stem the growing tide of office-seekers whose demands diverted time and effort away from the task of governing. A merit-based system, argued reformers, would improve government efficiency by emphasizing skill over political connections and by ending the frequent replacement of employees each time a new election was held; it would also encourage the brightest and ablest young workers to join the federal service. In addition, the spoils system was morally corrupting in the eyes of reformers. As one noted, "the theory which regards places in the public service as prizes to be distributed after an election, like plunder after a battle . . . necessarily ruins the self-respect of public employees,

the Civil Service Act of 1883, which was followed by almost universal adoption of equivalent laws in state and local governments. These laws required that appointees to public office be qualified for the job to which they are appointed. This policy came to be called the **merit system;** its ideal was not merely to put an end to political appointments under the "spoils system" but also to require adequate preparation for every job by holding competitive examinations through which the very best candidates were to be hired.

As a further safeguard against political interference (and to compensate for the lower-than-average pay given to public employees), merit system employees—genuine civil servants—were given a form of tenure: legal protection against being fired without a show of cause. Reasonable people may disagree about the value of job tenure and how far it should extend in the civil service, but the justifiable objective of tenure—cleansing bureaucracy of political interference while upgrading performance—cannot be disputed.

Who Are the Bureaucrats? To what extent does the American bureaucracy look like the American people? To what extent is it a microcosm of American society? Civil servants are not average Americans, but they are, in some re-

. . . prostitutes elections into a desperate strife for personal profit, and degrades the national character by lowering the moral tone and standard of the country."[1]

Although the spoils system provided benefits to the winning political party, victorious presidents buckled under the weight of having to select so many employees. By the early 1880s, presidents filled up to two hundred thousand federal jobs with political friends and supporters. In 1881, President James Garfield wrote that "my day is frittered away with the personal seeking of people when it ought to be given to the great problems which concern the whole country."[2] Similar problems plagued members of Congress. Senator Henry Cabot Lodge complained that "the system of patronage . . . has converted Congress into a machine for the division of offices, for which it was never intended."[3] Ironically, the final political push that resulted in the enactment of civil service reform occurred when a frustrated office-seeker tracked down President James Garfield in a Baltimore train station and shot him in 1881.

The enactment of civil service reform did not need the connection between patronage and politics. Even today, presidents and members of Congress award jobs to the political faithful. But with a federal bureaucracy of nearly three million employees, the number of politically appointed jobs amounts to a small percentage of the total—in the case of those appointed by the president, for example, to only a few thousand.

The change to the merit system was one applauded by most. But it had at least one unanticipated and probably undesirable consequence, in that it deprived political parties of a key resource—jobs—used to build party strength and support. Thus, civil service reform hastened the decline of political parties.

SOURCE: Leonard D. White, *The Republican Era* (New York: Free Press, 1958).

[1] Leonard D. White, *The Republican Era* (New York: Free Press, 1958), p. 298.

[2] Ibid., p. 6.

[3] Ibid., p. 300.

spects, what most Americans would like to be and what most Americans would like the rest of the world to believe about them. As one expert appraisal put it, "While the popular image of the civil service is one of acres of clerks processing mountains of forms, in fact the activities and structure of the [federal civilian] workforce . . . now resemble those of a research-and-development company."[6] Nearly 65 percent of permanent civilian white-collar federal workers have had some college education; over 35 percent have a bachelor's degree or higher; about 7 percent have a master's degree; and about 2 percent have a Ph.D. This compares quite favorably with the general population. According to the 1990 census, for example, 13 percent of all persons 25 years or older held a bachelor's degree, and 7 percent held a graduate or professional degree. Moreover, the infusion of technological skills into the federal civil service has occurred far faster and to a far greater extent than in the American workforce at large. For example, the number of engineers in the federal civil service increased by more than 50 percent between the early 1970s and the early 1990s; the number of computer specialists increased by more than 600 percent. Not counting occupations within the U.S. Postal Service, the occupational groups in the government that are expanding fastest today are legal and legal-related occupations, medical and other health groups, biological sciences, and social sciences.[7]

The image projected by the composition of the federal civil service is not quite as positive when we turn to an examination of its social characteristics other than education and training. This is precisely because, in the matter of the representation of women and minorities, the federal service resembles the workforce at large: women and minorities are not represented in the workforce in proportion to their representation in the population at large. But even so, the federal civil service is making more progress toward equal representation than is the case in the national workforce at large. For example, in 1965, women constituted 34 percent of the federal civilian workforce. But by 1985, women had moved up to 41 percent of the workforce, and by 1990, to 43 percent.[8] In 1965, African Americans constituted 13 percent of the federal civilian workforce; as of 1993, they constituted 16.8 percent. This compares to 10.5 percent in the civilian labor force at large (see Figure 13.3). Thus, blacks might even be said to be "over-represented" in the federal bureaucracy.[9] The same is not the case for Hispanics, Asian Americans, and Native Americans, who tend to be slightly under-represented in the federal civil service.

This picture of the civil service changes in an interesting way when federal employees are broken down according to salary, or "GS level."[10] As Figure 13.4 shows, each minority group is over-represented in the lowest pay cate-

FIGURE 13.3

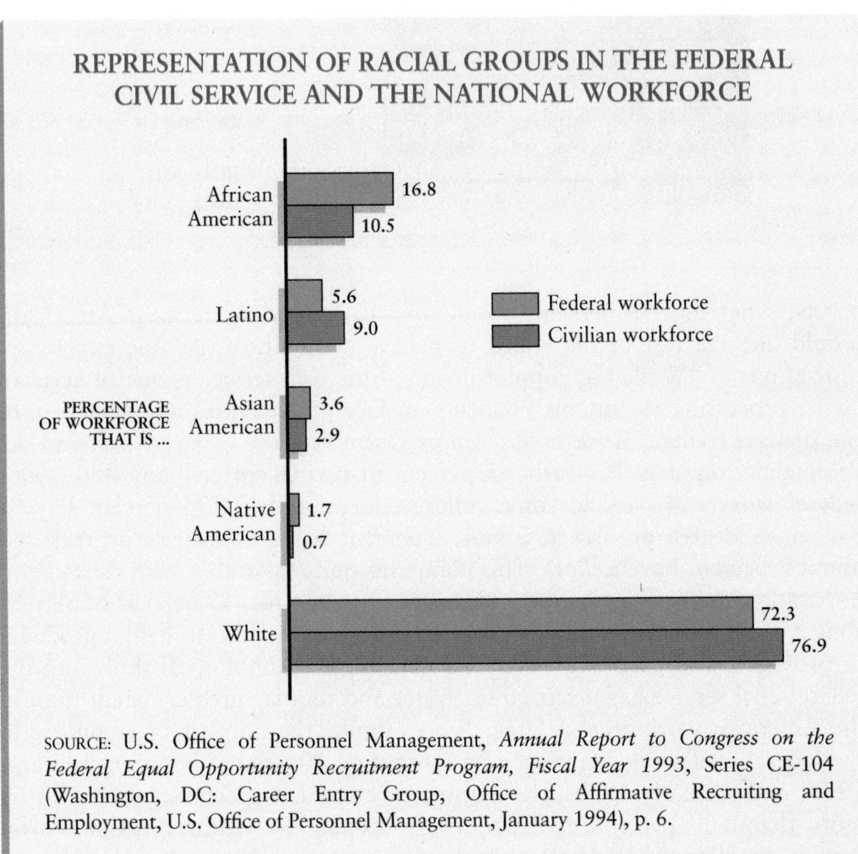

SOURCE: U.S. Office of Personnel Management, *Annual Report to Congress on the Federal Equal Opportunity Recruitment Program, Fiscal Year 1993*, Series CE-104 (Washington, DC: Career Entry Group, Office of Affirmative Recruiting and Employment, U.S. Office of Personnel Management, January 1994), p. 6.

FIGURE 13.4

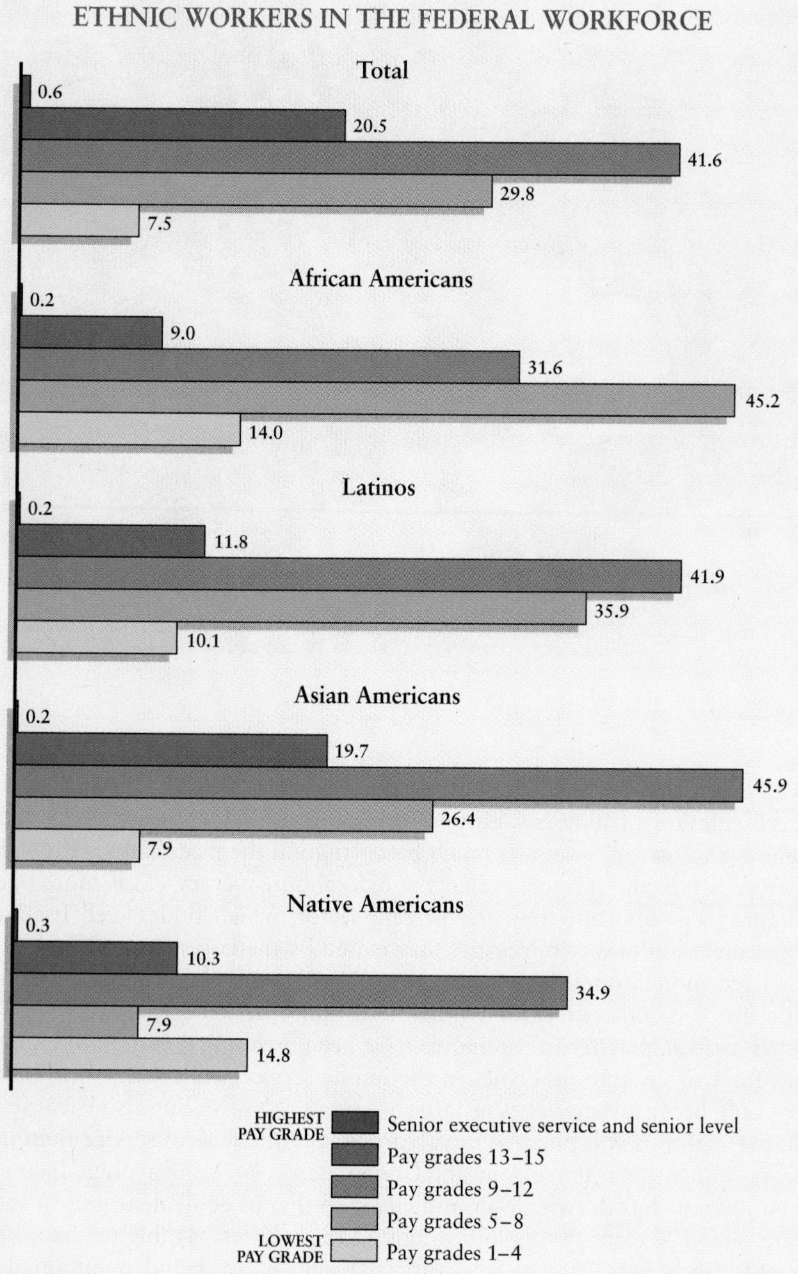

ETHNIC WORKERS IN THE FEDERAL WORKFORCE

	Total	African Americans	Latinos	Asian Americans	Native Americans
Senior executive service and senior level (HIGHEST PAY GRADE)	0.6	0.2	0.2	0.2	0.3
Pay grades 13–15	20.5	9.0	11.8	19.7	10.3
Pay grades 9–12	41.6	31.6	41.9	45.9	34.9
Pay grades 5–8	29.8	45.2	35.9	26.4	7.9
Pay grades 1–4 (LOWEST PAY GRADE)	7.5	14.0	10.1	7.9	14.8

SOURCE: U.S. Office of Personnel Management, *Annual Report to Congress on the Federal Equal Opportunity Recruitment Program, Fiscal Year 1993*, Series CE-104 (Washington, DC: Career Entry Group, Office of Affirmative Recruiting and Employment, U.S. Office of Personnel Management, January 1994), pp. 12, 15, 18, 21.

Most of the low-ranking IRS employees who process tax forms by hand are women, predominantly from minority groups.

gories, but this success drops off as the pay scale goes up. Nevertheless, the representation of minority groups in the highest categories—GS 15 and the Senior Executive Service—is much better than in the past. Thus, although the picture is mixed, "it appears that the federal bureaucracy . . . is more open to minority employment than the private sector, which bodes well for an improvement in the way minorities are treated by the government."[11]

Even though opportunities at the very highest levels of public administration are still constricted for women and minorities, the "glass ceilings" and other artificial barriers of prejudice have been breaking down, and opportunities for women and minorities in the public service will continue to improve, not only because Americans at large are more receptive but also because affirmative action is still pursued more earnestly in the federal service than in any other occupational universe in the United States. Even the average income for civil servants has drawn closer and closer to that of equivalent jobs in the private sector—except for a rigid ceiling on the salaries payable to top administrators (including Cabinet-level officials), which is set and maintained by a long tradition that civil servants should receive salaries no higher than those received by senators and members of the House.[12]

During his campaign for the presidency, Bill Clinton expressed his desire for an administration that "looked like America"; he wanted to improve the administration's sociological representation. One appraisal of Clinton's Cabinet choices concluded that "Clinton succeeded . . . in naming a cabinet that is probably more diverse in background than any in history. His choice of six women, four blacks, and two Hispanics to 23 top-tier posts eclipsed

Jimmy Carter's previous standard for slighting white males."[13] Clinton's sub-Cabinet appointments were also deemed a success, in a statistical sense, in terms of his goal of appointing top officials who "look like America." Clinton's efforts significantly delayed the complete staffing of his administration—an indication of the difficulty of changing the composition of the federal bureaucracy. Making the bureaucracy truly look like America will require decades and will happen only when American values truly embrace such a goal. Even so, turning around an institution comprising nearly 3 million civilian and 1.5 million military employees is akin to turning around a large battleship with a few dozen oars.

 The Organization of the Executive Branch

- What are the agencies that make up the executive branch?
- How can one classify these agencies according to their missions?

Departments, agencies, and bureaus are the operating parts of the bureaucratic whole. Figure 13.5 is an organizational chart of one of the largest and most important federal departments, the Department of Agriculture. Its organization is typical of most federal agencies. At the top is the head of the department, who in the United States is called the "secretary" of the department.[14] Below the secretary and the deputy secretary is a second tier of "undersecretaries" who have management responsibilities for one or more operating agencies, shown in the smaller print directly below each undersecretary. Those operating agencies are the third tier of the department, yet they are the highest level of responsibility for the actual programs around which the entire department is organized. This third tier is generally called the "bureau level." Each bureau-level agency is usually operating under a statute, adopted by Congress, that set up the program and gave the agency its authority and jurisdiction. The names of these bureau-level agencies are often quite well known to the public—the Forest Service and the Agricultural Research Service, for example. These are the so-called line agencies, or agencies that deal directly with the public. (Recall the military origin of the term "line agency," discussed earlier in this chapter.) Sometimes these agencies are officially called "bureaus," as in the Federal Bureau of Investigation (FBI), which is a part of the third tier of the Department of Justice. But "bureau" is also the conventional term for this level of administrative agency, even though many agencies or their supporters have preferred over the years to adopt a more palatable designation, such as "service" or "administration." Each bureau is, of course, subdivided into still other units, known as divisions, offices, or units—all are parts of the bureaucratic hierarchy.

In the Department of Agriculture there is still another tier, occupied by three assistant secretaries. Two of those assistant secretaries—those in charge of congressional relations and administration—have responsibilities that cut across all of the other bureaus. These assistant secretaries provide services and internal controls for the entire department. (The third, the assistant secretary for marketing and regulatory services, is responsible for three line

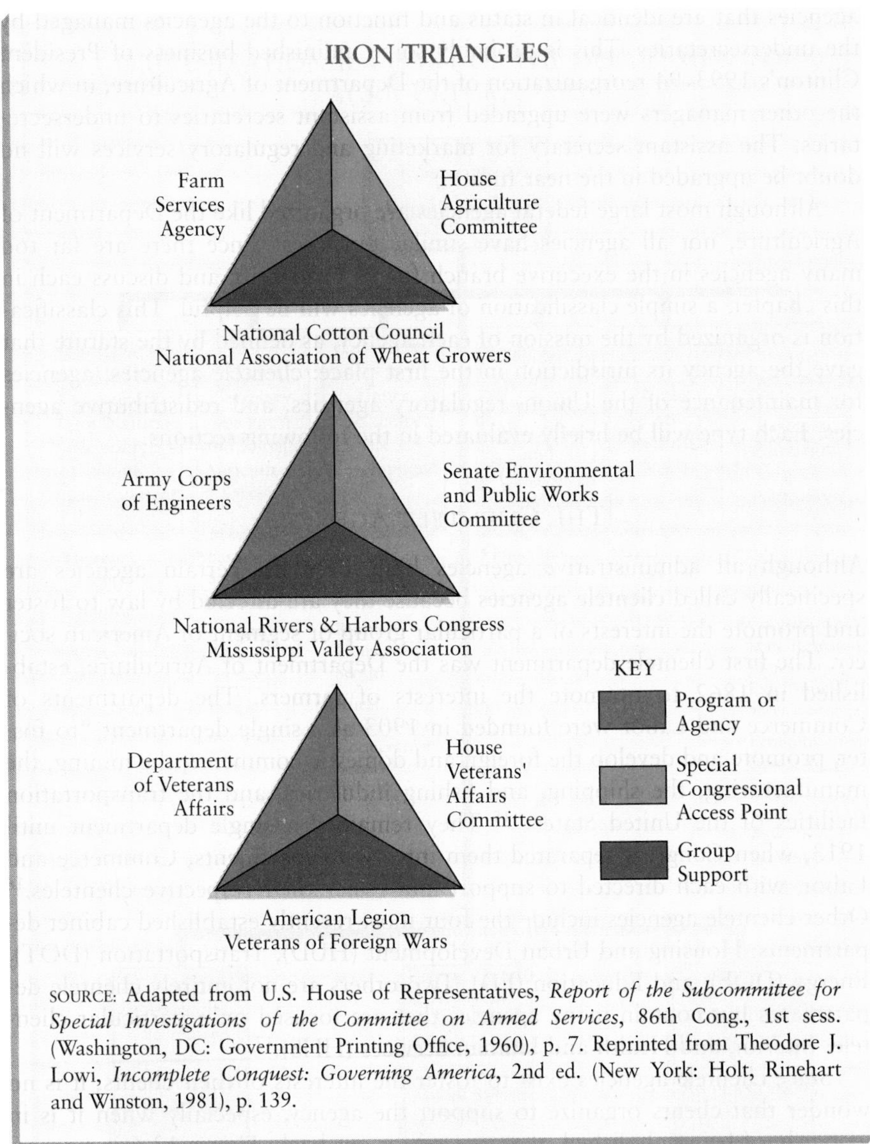

SOURCE: Adapted from U.S. House of Representatives, *Report of the Subcommittee for Special Investigations of the Committee on Armed Services*, 86th Cong., 1st sess. (Washington, DC: Government Printing Office, 1960), p. 7. Reprinted from Theodore J. Lowi, *Incomplete Conquest: Governing America*, 2nd ed. (New York: Holt, Rinehart and Winston, 1981), p. 139.

FIGURE 13.6

by the end of the Reagan administration in 1988, the Department of Education and the Department of Energy were still very much alive. Another eight years later they still had not been eliminated. Even though the "revolutionary" Republican 104th Congress pledged to kill these two departments as well as a third, the Department of Commerce, they did not fulfill this pledge. In fact the House Republicans in 1995 called for the elimination of nearly three hundred programs but succeeded in killing only thirty. For the rest, they had to be content with "squeezing budgets without eliminating functions . . . to deliver on every promise ever made with less and less money."[18]

Unless a president or congressional committee wants to drop everything else and concentrate entirely on eliminating one or two departments, the constituency of a clientele department is too strong to be battled on a part-time basis. The supportive constituency of the Department of Education includes the departments of education in all fifty states, all the school boards and school systems in the thousands of counties and cities across the country, the major unions of secondary school teachers, and a large proportion of the teachers' colleges in the country. One of the most formidable lobbies in the United States is the National Education Association (NEA), which has a chapter in every state in the country. It was the NEA and its access to President Carter that led to the creation of the Department of Education in the first place. The constituency supporting the Department of Energy incudes the major utilities and other power-generating industries, the major research universities, and the several states that produce oil and gas or that are home to atomic energy or other power plants that produce large amounts of energy.

President Clinton addressing the 1996 convention of the National Education Association. The teachers' lobby is an important constituency for the Democratic Party.

Another factor that adds to the endurance of the clientele agencies is the fact that a large proportion of their employees work far from Washington, D.C. People may still believe that most federal bureaucrats live and work in the District of Columbia, but in fact nearly 90 percent of federal employees work elsewhere in the country, and a substantial number work abroad. The presence of so many federal employees in local areas works to the particular advantage of clientele agencies, because these employees are able to establish friendly and mutually supportive relationships with local businesses and other organized groups looking for help from the clientele departments. This adds weight to the third corner of the iron triangle, which is usually ready to come to the aid of the department or agencies in trouble.[19]

Agencies for Maintenance of the Union

One of the remarkable features of American federalism is that the most vital agencies for the maintenance of the Union are located in state and local governments—namely, the police. But some agencies vital to maintaining national integration do exist in the national government, and they can be grouped for convenience into three categories: (1) agencies for control of the sources of federal government revenue, (2) agencies for control of conduct defined as a threat to internal national security, and (3) agencies for defending American security from external threats. The departments of greatest concern in these three areas are, respectively, Treasury, Justice, and Defense and State.

Revenue Agencies One of the first actions of Congress under President George Washington was to create the Department of the Treasury, and probably its oldest function is the collection of taxes on imports, called tariffs. Now housed in the United States Customs Service, federal customs agents are located at every U.S. seaport and international airport to oversee the collection of tariffs. But far and away the most important of the **revenue agencies** is the Internal Revenue Service (IRS). The Customs Service and the IRS are two of at least twelve bureaus within the Treasury Department. The IRS will be our single case study in this section.

The IRS is not unresponsive to political influences, especially given the fact that it must maintain cooperative relationships with the two oldest and most important congressional committees, the House Ways and Means Committee and the Senate Finance Committee. Nevertheless, the political patterns of the IRS are virtually the opposite of those of a clientele agency. As one expert put it, "probably no organization in the country, public or private, creates as much clientele *dis*favor as the Internal Revenue Service. The very nature of its work brings it into an adversary relationship with vast numbers of Americans every year."[20] Yet despite the many complaints about the IRS, it appears to have been evenhanded in its administration of the "tax code," since surprisingly few scandals have soiled its record.

Although thousands upon thousands of influential corporations and wealthy individuals have a strong and active interest in American tax policy, key taxation decision are not governed by iron triangles. They are in fact set by agreements between the president, the Treasury Department, and the leading members of the two tax committees in Congress. External influence is not spread throughout the fifty states, but instead is much more centralized in the majority political party, a few key figures in Congress, and a handful of professional lobbyists. Suspicions of unfair exemptions and of favoritism are widespread, and they do exist, but these exemptions come largely from Congress, *not* from the IRS itself.

Agencies for Internal Security As long as the country is not in a state of insurrection, most of the task of maintaining the Union takes the form of legal work, and the primary responsibility for that lies in the Department of Justice. It is indeed a luxury, and rare in the world, when national unity can be maintained by routines of civil law with an army of lawyers, instead of martial law imposed by a real army with guns.

The largest and most important unit of the Justice Department is the Criminal Division. Lawyers in the Criminal Division represent the United States government when it is the plaintiff enforcing the federal criminal laws, except for those cases (about 25 percent) specifically assigned to other divisions or agencies. Criminal litigation is handled by U.S. attorneys, who are appointed by the president. There is one U.S. attorney in each of the ninety-four federal judicial districts; he or she supervises the work of a number of assistant U.S. attorneys.

J. Edgar Hoover built the FBI into one of the most famous and most feared government agencies in American history.

The Civil Division of the Justice Department deals with litigation in which the United States is the defendant being sued for injury and damages allegedly inflicted by a government official. The missions of the other divisions of the Justice Department—Antitrust, Civil Rights, Environment and Natural Resources, and Tax—are described by their names.

The best known bureau of the Justice Department is the Federal Bureau of Investigation (FBI). The FBI handles no litigation but instead serves as the principal information-gathering agency for the department and for the president. Established in 1908, the FBI expanded and advanced in stature during the 1920s and 1930s under the direction of J. Edgar Hoover. Although it is only one of the many bureaus and divisions in the Department of Justice, and although it officially has no higher status than any of the others, it is politically the most significant.

Despite its professionalism and its fierce pride in its autonomy, the FBI has not been unresponsive to the partisan commitments of Democratic and

Republican administrations. Although the FBI has always achieved its best publicity from the spectacular apprehension of famous criminals, such as John Dillinger, George "Machine Gun" Kelly, and Bonnie and Clyde,[21] it has followed the president's direction in focusing on particular crime problems. Thus it has infiltrated Nazi and Mafia organizations; it operates the vast loyalty and security investigation programs covering all federal employees since the Truman presidency; it monitored and infiltrated the Ku Klux Klan and the Civil Rights movement in the 1950s and 1960s; and it has infiltrated radical political groups and extreme religious cults and survivalist militias in the 1980s and 1990s.

Agencies for External National Security Two departments occupy center stage in maintaining national security: the departments of State and Defense. Since they will be the major players in our chapter on foreign policy, we will only look briefly at their organizational structure and general political tendencies in this section.

Although diplomacy is generally considered the primary task of the State Department, diplomatic missions are only one of its organizational dimensions. As of 1996, the State Department comprised nineteen bureau-level units, each under the direction of an undersecretary or an assistant secretary. Six of these are geographic or regional bureaus concerned with all problems within a defined region of the world; nine are "functional" bureaus, handling such things as economic and business affairs, intelligence and research, and international organizations. Four are bureaus of internal affairs, which handle such areas as security, finance and management, and legal issues.

These bureaus support the responsibilities of the elite of foreign affairs, the foreign service officers (FSOs), who staff U.S. embassies around the world and who hold almost all of the most powerful positions in the department below the rank of ambassador.[22] The ambassadorial positions, especially the plum positions in the major capitals of the world, are filled by political appointees, many of whom get their positions by having been important donors to the victorious presidential campaign.

Despite the importance of the State Department in foreign affairs, fewer than 20 percent of all U.S. government employees working abroad are directly under its authority. By far the largest number of career government professionals working abroad are under the authority of the Defense Department.

The creation of the Department of Defense by legislation between 1947 and 1949 was an effort to unify the two historic military departments, the War Department and the Navy Department, and to integrate them with a new department, the Air Force. Real unification, however, did not occur. The Defense Department simply added more pluralism to an already pluralistic national security establishment.

The American military, following worldwide military tradition, is organized according to a "chain of command"—a tight hierarchy of clear responsibility and rank, made clearer by uniforms, special insignia, and detailed organizational charts and rules of order and etiquette. The "line agencies" in the Department of Defense are the military commands, distributed geographically by divisions and fleets to deal with current or potential enemies. The

Storm over the ATF

The conflict between public power and private interest can be seen clearly in the activities of what has come to be the most unpopular agency of the 1990s: the Bureau of Alcohol, Tobacco, and Firearms (ATF). Charged with regulating the trade and use of liquor, cigarettes, and guns—three products especially dear to many Americans—the ATF carries out its mandate in an atmosphere of mistrust, violence, and accusations of misconduct. In 1995 such accusations resulted in congressional hearings into ATF operations and the validity of the charges against it.

Congressional investigations of the ATF are not new; as a consequence of investigations in 1979, Congress cut the agency's budget and prohibited it from computerizing its records (a prohibition that still stands).

The recent charges against the ATF arise in part from its involvement in the standoff at the Branch Davidian compound in Waco, Texas. The siege began on February 28, 1993, when, as part of a firearms investigation, ATF agents tried to serve a search warrant at the compound of a small religious community called the Branch Davidians. The heavily armed Davidians resisted the warrant, and in the ensuing shootout, four ATF agents and six Davidians were killed. (The FBI then took over the case, and was responsible for launching the tear-gas attack two months later that led to the fiery deaths of about eighty Davidians.) Critics charged that the ATF ignored warnings that the Davidians would respond to a show of force with violence and that the agency planned the operation, in which seventy armed agents took part, without informing senior officials who were supposed to oversee ATF activities. A subsequent Treasury Department review assailed the ATF for inaccurate information, poor plans, and subsequent lies by ATF officials to deflect blame onto subordinates.

At congressional hearings in the fall of 1995, senior ATF officials defended the agency by saying that it had made and was continuing to make significant reforms. But because of its front-line police and regulatory functions, especially on the hot-button issue of gun control, the ATF is likely to remain at the center of a storm of controversy, regardless of how it manages its affairs. The growing divide between American conservatives and liberals on the question of gun ownership only magnifies the activities of the ATF. The National Rifle Association (NRA) has trained its sights on the ATF, and works methodically to publicize every allegation of ATF misconduct. Interestingly, observers note that the NRA does not want to abolish the ATF, for fear that the agency's gun-control functions would be taken over by the Secret Service and the FBI, which have sophisticated computer systems. Instead, in the words of one official, the NRA wants "a cowed and chastened ATF."[1] To that end, it has launched savage attacks on the agency, including a notorious 1995 fund-raising letter likening federal agents to Nazi storm troopers, which prompted former president George Bush to renounce his lifetime membership in the NRA.

The firestorm surrounding the ATF may have already radicalized some Americans. Timothy McVeigh, the man accused of the bombing of a federal office building in Oklahoma City, is said to have been driven to the deed by his rage over the Waco tragedy. And according to police officers, members of one paramilitary group, the Michigan Militia, "have been found with the names and addresses of ATF agents, as well as the addresses of their children's schools."[2] The spread of violence and the polarization of public opinion have put the ATF at the center of a storm—but its very functions create that storm. As long as there are laws concerning guns, alcohol, tobacco, or any other goods that are wanted by substantial numbers of people but are considered immoral or dangerous by others, there will be federal agencies that must apply and enforce those laws—and life-and-death disputes will play themselves out, on the boundary between private life and public order.

[1] Quoted in John Mintz, "A Way of Life for ATF: Fending Off Gun Lobby Efforts to Kill It," *Washington Post*, July 24, 1995, p. A4.

[2] Ibid.

"staff agencies," such as logistics, intelligence, personnel, research and development, quartermaster, and engineering, exist to serve the "line agencies." At the top of the military chain of command are chiefs of staff (called chief of naval operations in the Navy, and commandant in the Marines). These chiefs of staff also constitute the membership of the Joint Chiefs of Staff—the center of military policy and management. The chair of the Joint Chiefs of Staff is appointed by the president, with consent of the Senate, for a term of two years that can be extended for another term. The president selects the chair from among the chiefs of the three principal armed service departments (Army, Navy, and Air Force), and in practice, the job rotates among the chiefs of those three departments. (The commandant of the Marine Corps is a member of the Joint Chiefs of Staff, but the Marine Corps is not a separate department—it is part of the Navy Department.)

Within the Department of Defense, the professionalized military has to compete with a second administrative system: the civilian system. In addition to there being civilian employees throughout the department, the heads of the respective departments of the Army, Navy, and Air Force are also civilians, appointed by the president. The primary job of the civilian secretaries of these departments is a staff job—that of supplying personnel and procuring equipment. As one military reporter put it, a secretary of the Navy can be responsible for the development of a missile-launching submarine costing billions of dollars but has little to say on whether the submarine is needed or how it should be used.[23]

This structure—two career systems plus three departments within the Department of Defense—when combined with two similar career systems in the State Department and the several important independent agencies that also have a hand in U.S. foreign policy, has produced rampant pluralism in the politics of U.S. external national security. There is no better example of this extreme pluralism than that which was revealed in the Iran-Contra affair of the late 1980s, in which the ability to bypass other agencies and routines enabled "rogues" and "loose cannons" on the National Security Council staff to draw the United States into embarrassing inconsistencies of policy with several countries.

Yet matters could be worse if the U.S. military looked upon itself as an institution equal to and independent of civilian authority. A brief glance at the historic problem of civil-military relations in Latin America or even in Europe will remind Americans of their good luck in having a military that stresses subordination to civilian political authority. For example, American military commanders cooperated completely after World War II when Congress reduced the Army's personnel level from 3.5 million to 400,000 troops, with equivalent cuts in Air Force and Navy strength. Nor did the American military display any public opposition when President Truman fired the great military hero General Douglas MacArthur for his insubordination during the Korean War.

America's primary political problem with its military has not been the historic one of how to keep the military out of politics (which is a perennial problem in many of the world's countries), but how to keep politics out of the military. In the heat of the 1992 presidential campaign, for example, President Bush made a stop in Fort Worth, Texas, where he announced his approval of the sale to Taiwan of up to 150 new F-16 fighter planes. It was no coincidence that the manufacture of military planes is an important part of the Fort Worth economy; Bush's decision saved an estimated 11,000 jobs. Bush's later decision to sell F-15 fighter planes to Saudi Arabia violated his own policy against the proliferation of high-tech weapons, but promised to save jobs in the St. Louis economy. Bush broke his reduced-spending pledge in Michigan, where "$9 billion in pork went out the window in one campaign week" with his renewal of M-1 tank production. As one senior member of the Senate Armed Services Committee asserted, "We already have more tanks than we will ever need."[24] President Clinton's long list of proposed military base closings, a major part of his budget-cutting drive for 1993, caused a firestorm of opposition even within his own party, including a number of members of Congress who were otherwise prominently in favor of significant reductions in the Pentagon budget.

Politicians' emphasis on jobs rather than on strategy and policy when dealing with military funding is a clear signal of the use of the military for political purposes. The 1995 Republican commitment to increase the amount of defense spending, coupled with President Clinton's willingness to cooperate by seeking an additional $25 billion increase in the Pentagon budget for 1995, had more to do with the domestic pressures of employment in defense and defense industries than with military necessity in the post–cold war era. President Eisenhower's warning about the "military-industrial complex" deserves to be kept in mind here (see Chapter 10). The iron triangle of defense plays clientele agency politics inside the establishment that is responsible for the security of the entire nation.

The Regulatory Agencies

In this section, we will look at regulatory agencies as an administrative phenomenon. We will discuss regulatory *policies* in later chapters.

The United States has no "Department of Regulation" but has many **regulatory agencies**. Some of these are bureaus within departments, such as the Food and Drug Administration (FDA) in the Department of Health and Human Services, the Occupational Safety and Health Administration (OSHA) in the Department of Labor, and the Animal and Plant Health Inspection Service (APHIS) in the Department of Agriculture. Other regulatory agencies are independent regulatory commissions, such as the Federal Communications Commission (FCC) and the Environmental Protection Agency (EPA). But whether departmental or independent, an agency or commission is regulatory if Congress delegates to it relatively broad powers over a sector of the economy or a type of commercial activity and authorizes it to make rules restricting the conduct of people and businesses within that jurisdiction. Rules made by regulatory agencies have the force and effect of law. And when these agencies make decisions or issue orders settling disputes between parties or between the government and a party, they are acting like courts.

Agencies for Redistribution

Fiscal (or monetary) agencies and welfare agencies seem at first to be too far apart to belong to the same category, but they are related in a very special

Regulatory agencies have a strong presence in the lives of all Americans. For instance, the foods we eat are subject to myriad regulations from federal, state, and local agencies.

way. Both types are responsible for the transfer of hundreds of billions of dollars annually between the public and the private spheres. Through such transfers, these agencies influence how people and corporations spend and invest trillions of dollars each year. We call these types of agencies **redistributive agencies** because they influence the amount of money in the economy and because they directly influence who has money, who has credit, and whether people will want to invest or save their money rather than spend it.

Fiscal and Monetary Agencies The best term for government activity affecting or relating to money is **fiscal policy.** The *fisc* was the Roman imperial treasury; "fiscal" can refer to anything and everything having to do with public finance. However, we in the United States choose to make a further distinction, reserving "fiscal" for taxing and spending policies and using "monetary" for policies having to do with banks, credit, and currency. Yet a third term, "welfare," deserves to be treated as an equal member of this redistributive category.[25]

The administration of fiscal policy occurs primarily in the Treasury Department. It is no contradiction to include the Treasury here as well as with the agencies for maintenance of the Union. This duplication indicates two things: first, that the Treasury is a complex department that performs more than one function of government; and second, that traditional controls have had to adapt to modern economic conditions and new technologies.

Today, in addition to collecting income, corporate, and other taxes, the Treasury is also responsible for managing the enormous national debt—$4.64 trillion in 1994, a figure that grows by $250–$300 billion each year. (The national debt was a mere $914 billion in 1980.) Debt is not simply something the country owes; it is something a country has to manage and administer. The debt is also a fiscal instrument in the hands of the federal government that can be used—through manipulation of the interest rate and through the buying and selling of government bonds—to slow down or to speed up the activity of the entire national economy, as well as to defend the value of the dollar in international trade.

The Treasury Department is also responsible for printing the U.S. currency, but currency represents only a tiny proportion of the entire money economy. Most of the trillions of dollars used in the transactions of the private and public sectors of the U.S. economy exist in computerized accounts, not in currency.

Another important fiscal agency (although for technical reasons it is called an agency of monetary policy) is the **Federal Reserve System,** which is headed by the Federal Reserve Board. The Federal Reserve System (called simply the Fed) has authority over the interest rates and lending activities of the nation's most important banks. Congress established the Fed in 1913 as a clearing house responsible for adjusting the supply of money and credit to the needs of commerce and industry in different regions of the country. The Fed is also responsible for ensuring that banks do not overextend themselves, a policy that guards against a chain of bank failures during a sudden economic scare, such as occurred in 1929. The Federal Reserve Board directs the operations of the twelve district Federal Reserve Banks, which are essentially "bankers' banks," serving the monetary needs of the hundreds of member banks in the national banking system.[26]

Welfare Agencies Welfare agencies seem at first glance to be just another set of clientele agencies, with dependent people as their clientele. But there is a big difference between welfare agencies and other clientele agencies: Welfare agencies operate under laws that discriminate between rich and poor, old and young. Access to welfare agencies is restricted to those individuals who fall within particular legally defined categories. Those who fall outside the relevant legal category would not be entitled to access even if they were to seek it. In contrast, people come under the jurisdiction of traditional clientele agencies (such as the Department of Agriculture) either through self-selection or by coincidence. Access to a genuine clientele agency is open to almost anyone.

The most important and expensive of the welfare programs are the insurance programs, traditionally called Social Security, to which all employed persons contribute through taxes during their working years and from which they receive benefits as a matter of right when in need.[27] Two other programs come closer to the popular understanding of welfare—Aid to Families with Dependent Children (AFDC) and Supplemental Security Income (SSI). No contributions are required for access to these programs, each of which is **means-tested**—that is, applicants for benefits must demonstrate that their total annual cash earnings fall below the officially defined poverty line.

There is a third category of welfare, called "in-kind programs," which includes food stamps and Medicaid. These two programs are also means-tested; people who fall below the minimum income qualify for the noncash benefits of food stamps and the noncash Medicaid services of hospitals and doctors. Cash is involved in the Medicaid program, but it does not go directly to the person receiving benefits; the government pays the doctor or hospital directly for the services rendered. Another welfare program with very large fiscal significance is Medicare, a health insurance program for the elderly, which is not means-tested.

There is no single government department responsible for all of the programs that comprise the "Social Security system" or the "welfare state." The largest of all the agencies in this field is the Social Security Administration (SSA), an independent federal agency that manages Social Security, Medicare, and SSI. The Department of Health and Human Services administers the AFDC and Medicaid programs. The Department of Agriculture is responsible for the food stamp program.

The entire welfare system is in trouble today. Welfare state programs redistribute a measurable amount of wealth from those who work to those who do not and from the young to the elderly. Since these programs were started, the redistribution of wealth has become legitimate in the United States, and even popular. But during the sixty-year history of the welfare state, the ratio of those in the workforce (being taxed) to those outside the workforce (dependent on assistance) has dropped from 18:1 to 4:1. It is therefore no wonder that a Democratic candidate for president in 1992 could campaign successfully on a pledge "to end welfare as we know it." In 1994, President Bill Clinton proposed reforming welfare to a "two years and you're out" policy, which would require that AFDC recipients born after 1971 find work within two years of accepting AFDC support for themselves and their children. The Republican Congress took a much more radical step in 1995: the Senate passed a bill to terminate entitlement programs for the poor and "devolve" all federal funding for such programs to the states, to use at their discretion. This convinced President Clinton that the time had finally come "to end welfare as we know it," and in 1996 he signed into law an even more radical bill to eliminate the federal guarantee of cash assistance to the needy, to authorize the states to run their own welfare programs, to put a lifetime limit of five years on benefits paid to any family, and to require work within two years of receipt of welfare assistance. Accountability in welfare agencies will be the key domestic political issue of the coming years.

Can the Bureaucracy Be Reduced?

- What methods have been used to reduce the size and the role of the federal bureaucracy?
- How effective can efforts to reduce the bureaucracy be?

Some Americans would argue that bureaucracy is always too big and that it always should be reduced. In the 1990s Americans seem particularly enthusiastic about reducing (or to use the popular contemporary word, "downsizing") the federal bureaucracy. This downsizing could be achieved in at least three ways: termination, devolution, or privatization.

Termination

The only *certain* way to reduce the size of the bureaucracy is to eliminate programs. Variations in the levels of federal personnel and expenditures (as was shown on Figures 13.1 and 13.2) demonstrate the futility of trying to make permanent cuts in existing agencies. Most agencies have a supportive constituency that will fight to reinstate any cuts that are made. Termination is the only way to ensure an agency's reduction and it is a rare occurrence, even with the Reagan and Bush administrations, both of which proclaimed a strong commitment to the reduction of the national government. In fact, not a single national government agency or program was terminated during the twelve years of Reagan and Bush.

The Republican 104th Congress was even more committed than Reagan and Bush to the termination of programs. Newt Gingrich, Speaker of the House, took Congress by storm with his promises of a virtual revolution in government. But when the dust had settled at the end of the first session of the Gingrich-led Congress there had been no significant progress toward downsizing through termination of agencies and programs.[28] This lack of success is not the product of a flaw in the character of Republicans. As antagonistic as Americans may be toward bureaucracy in general, they grow attached to the services being rendered and protections being offered by particular bureaucratic agencies; that is, they fiercely defend their favorite agencies while perceiving no inconsistency between that defense and their antagonistic attitude toward the bureaucratic phenomenon in general. A good case in point is the agonizing problem of closing military bases in the wake of the end of the cold war, when the United States no longer needs so many bases. Since every base is in some congressional member's constituency, it proved impossible for Congress to decide to close any of them. Consequently, between 1988 and 1990, Congress established a Defense Base Closure and Realignment Commission to decide on base closings, taking the matter out of Congress's hands altogether.[29] And even so, the process has been slow and agonizing.

Selecting locations for military bases is a classic example of clientele agency politics. As a result, the process of closing bases has been difficult. Members of Congress used to try to overturn decisions to close bases in their districts. Because that is no longer possible, members of Congress such as Senator Diane Feinstein of California have sought to convert military bases for other government purposes. Critics say this isn't reducing bureaucracy, just shifting it around.

Devolution

The next best approach to genuine reduction of the size of the bureaucracy is **devolution**—downsizing the federal bureaucracy by delegating the implementation of programs to state and local governments. In some instances this may amount to genuine termination of certain programs, such as AFDC and Medicaid, because some states will choose not to have the program at all, if the federal laws provide that much discretion to the states. In fact, many people favor devolution precisely because they see it as a politically safer way to terminate programs. But the problem that arises with devolution is that programs that were once uniform across the country (because they were the national government's responsibility) can become highly variable, with some states providing benefits not available in other states. To a point, variation can be considered one of the virtues of federalism. But there are dangers inherent in large variations and inequalities in the provision of services and benefits in a democracy. For example, since the Food and Drug Administration (FDA) has been under attack in recent years, could the problem be solved by devolving its regulatory tasks to the states? Would people care if drugs would require "caution" labels in some states and not in others? Would Americans want each state to set its own air and water pollution control policies without regard to the fact that pollution flows across state boundaries? Devolution, as attractive as it may be, is not an approach that can be applied across the board without analyzing carefully the nature of the program and of the problems it is designed to solve. Even the capacity of states to handle "devolved" programs will vary. According to the Brookings Institution, the level of state and local government employment varies from state to state—from a low of 400 per 10,000 residents in some states to a high of 700 per 10,000 in others. "Such administrative diversity is bound to mediate the course and consequences of any substantial devolution of federal responsibility; no one-size-fits-all devolution [from federal to state and local government] can work."[30]

Privatization

Privatization seems like a synonym for termination, but that is true only at the extreme. Most of what is called "privatization" is not termination at all but the provision of government goods and services by private contractors under direct government supervision. Except for top-secret strategic materials, virtually all of the production of military hardware, from boats to bullets, is done on a privatized basis by private contractors. Billions of dollars of research services are bought under contract by governments; these private contractors are universities as well as ordinary industrial corporations and private "think tanks." **Privatization** simply means that a formerly public activity is picked up under contract by a private company or companies. But such programs are still very much government programs; they are paid for by government and supervised by government. Privatization downsizes the government only in that the workers providing the service are no longer counted as part of the government bureaucracy.

None of this analysis and criticism is intended to discourage efforts to downsize the government bureaucracies. But in the process of trying to downsize the government, two fundamental points ought to be kept clearly in mind. First, the federal bureaucracy is here to stay, and even if so-called revolutionary campaigns to downsize the government are completely successful, they will not reduce the federal bureaucracy by very much. Second, government must therefore concentrate on a much older but now much more pressing problem: how to make the bureaucracy that exists more compatible with the democracy the American people desire.

Can Bureaucracy Be Controlled?

- How can bureaucracy and democracy coexist? What popular controls over the bureaucracy exist?
- How do the president and Congress manage and oversee the bureaucracy?
- What is the most effective means to guarantee a responsible bureaucracy?

The title of this chapter, "Bureaucracy in a Democracy," is intended to convey the sense that the two are contradictory.[31] Americans cannot live with bureaucracy, but they also cannot live without it. The task is neither to retreat from bureaucracy nor to attack it, but to take advantage of its strengths while making it more accountable to the demands of democratic politics and representative government. This task will be the focus of the remainder of this chapter.

Two hundred years, millions of employees, and trillions of dollars after the Founding, we must return to James Madison's observation, "You must first enable the government to control the governed; and in the next place oblige it to control itself."[32] Today the problem is the same, only now the process has a name: administrative accountability. **Accountability** implies that there is some higher authority by which the actions of the bureaucracy will be guided and judged. The highest authority in a democracy is *demos*—the people—and the guidance for bureaucratic action is the popular will. But that ideal of accountability must be translated into practical terms by the president and Congress. (The federal courts translate as well; they will be discussed in the next chapter.)

THE PRESIDENT AS CHIEF EXECUTIVE

In 1937, President Franklin Roosevelt's Committee on Administrative Management gave official sanction to an idea that had been growing increasingly urgent: "The president needs help." The national government had grown rapidly during the preceding twenty-five years, but the structures and procedures necessary to manage the burgeoning executive branch had not yet been established. The response to the call for "help" for the president initially took the form of three management policies: (1) All communications and decisions that related to executive policy decisions must pass through the White House; (2) In order to cope with such a flow, the White House must have adequate staffs of specialists in research, analysis, legislative and legal writing, and public affairs; and (3) The White House must have additional staff to follow through on presidential decisions—to ensure that those decisions are made, communicated to Congress, and carried out by the appropriate agency.

Making the Managerial Presidency Establishing a management capacity for the presidency began in earnest with FDR, but it did not stop there.[33] The story of the modern presidency can be told largely as a series of responses to the plea for managerial help. Indeed, each expansion of the national government into new policies and programs in the twentieth century has been accompanied by a parallel expansion of the president's management authority. This pattern began even before FDR's presidency, with the policy innovations of President Woodrow Wilson between 1913 and 1920. Congress responded to Wilson's policies with the 1921 Budget and Accounting Act, which turned over the prime legislative power of budgeting to the White House. Each successive president has continued this pattern, creating what we now know as the "managerial presidency."

Presidents John Kennedy and Lyndon Johnson were committed both to government expansion and to management expansion, in the spirit of their party's hero, FDR. President Nixon also strengthened and enlarged the managerial presidency, but for somewhat different reasons. He sought the strongest possible managerial hand because he had to assume that the overwhelming majority of federal employees had sympathies with the Democratic Party, which had controlled the White House and had sponsored governmental growth for twenty-eight of the previous thirty-six years.[34]

President Jimmy Carter was probably more preoccupied with administrative reform and reorganization than any other president in this century. His reorganization of the civil service will long be recognized as one of the most significant contributions of his presidency. The Civil Service Reform Act of 1978 was the first major revamping of the federal civil service since its creation in 1883. The 1978 act abolished the century-old Civil Service Commission (CSC) and replaced it with three agencies, each designed to handle one of the CSC's functions on the theory that the competing demands of these functions had given the CSC an "identity crisis." The Merit Systems Protection Board (MSPB) was created to defend competitive merit recruitment and promotion from political encroachment. A separate Federal Labor Relations Authority (FLRA) was set up to administer collective bargaining and individual personnel grievances. The third new agency, the Office of Personnel Management (OPM), was created to manage recruiting, testing, training, and the retirement system. The Senior Executive Service was also created at this time to recognize and foster "public management" as a profession and to facilitate the movement of top, "supergrade" career officials across agencies and departments.[35]

Carter also tried to impose a stringent budgetary process on all executive agencies. Called "zero-base budgeting," it was a method of budgeting from the bottom up, wherein each agency was required to rejustify its entire mission rather than merely its next year's request. Zero-base budgeting did not succeed, but the effort was not lost on President Reagan. Although Reagan gave the impression of being a laid-back president, he actually centralized management to an unprecedented degree. From Carter's "bottom-up" approach, Reagan went to a "top-down" approach whereby the initial bud-

President Clinton and Vice President Gore promised that their "reinventing government" plan would make the bureaucracy more efficient and save the taxpayers over $100 billion, as well as reduce the reams of federal rules and regulations shown behind them here.

getary decisions would be made in the White House and the agencies would be required to fit within those decisions. This process converted the Office of Management and Budget (OMB) into an agency of policy determination and presidential management.[36] President Bush took Reagan's centralization strategy even further in using the White House staff instead of Cabinet secretaries for managing the executive branch.[37]

President Clinton engaged in the most systematic effort to "change the way the government does business," a phrase he used often to describe the goal of his National Performance Review (NPR), one of the most important administrative reform efforts of the twentieth century. In September 1993, he launched the NPR, based on a set of 384 proposals drafted by a panel headed by Vice President Al Gore. The avowed goal of the NPR was to "reinvent government"—to make the federal bureaucracy more efficient, accountable, and effective. But this is little more than new language for the same management goal held by each of his predecessors.

Virtually all observers agree that the NPR has made substantial progress. Its goals include savings of more than $100 billion over five years, in large part by cutting the federal workforce by 12 percent (or more than 270,000 jobs) by the end of 1999. The NPR has also focused on cutting red tape, streamlining procurement (how the government purchases goods and services), improving the coordination of federal management, and simplifying federal rules. For instance, the OMB abolished the notorious ten-thousand-page Federal Personnel Manual and the Standard Form 171, the government's lengthy job application form. Another example is even more revealing of the nature of the NPR's work: The Defense Department's method for reimbursing its employees' travel expenses used to take seventeen steps and two months; an employee-designed reform encouraged by the NPR streamlined this to a four-step, computer-based procedure taking less than fifteen minutes, with an anticipated savings of $1 billion over five years.

One potentially significant weakness of the NPR noted by critics is that it has no strategy for dealing with congressional opposition to certain bureaucratic reforms. Donald Kettl, a respected reform advocate, warned that "virtually no reform that really matters can be achieved without at least implicit congressional support. The NPR has not yet developed a full strategy for winning that support."[38] One consequence, for instance, is that in 1994 Congress voted to exempt the Department of Veterans Affairs from the personnel reductions imposed by the NPR, a development that could make attainment of the NPR's goals impossible. A good way to fight such congressional actions is with publicity, but it is a troubling sign for the NPR's long-term prospects (and for President Clinton's standing) that national polls say two-thirds of Americans either have never heard of the NPR or believe the federal government is continuing to grow.[39]

The overall accomplishment of President Clinton and the NPR has certainly been respectable, even in the eyes of the Republican opposition. But despite this accomplishment and the optimism about further reform, a certain humility is in order when we think about "reinventing" the federal civil service. To make incremental changes in bureaucracies, even valuable ones, is possible; to change the very nature of bureaucracy is not.

The Problem of Management Control by the White House Staff The cabinet's historic failure to perform as a board of directors (see Chapter 12), and the inability of any other agency to perform that function have left a management vacuum in the U.S. government. OMB has met part of the need, and indeed the management power of the director of OMB seems to increase with each new president. But the need for executive management control goes far beyond what even the boldest of OMB directors can achieve. The White House staff has filled this vacuum to a certain extent precisely because, in the past thirty years, the "special assistants to the president" have been given relatively specialized jurisdictions over one or more departments or strategic issues. These staffers have additional power and credibility beyond their access to the president because they also have access to confidential information. Since information is the most important bureaucratic resource, White House staff members gain management power by having access to the CIA for international intelligence and the FBI and Treasury for knowledge about the personal life of every government official (since each government employee has to go through a rigorous FBI security clearance procedure prior to being appointed and promoted).

Responsible bureaucracy, however, is not going to come simply from more presidential power, more administrative staff, and more management control. All this was inadequate to the task of keeping the National Security Council staff from seizing the initiative to run its own policies toward Iran and Nicaragua for at least two years (1985–86) after Congress had explicitly re-

In 1987, Oliver North, an aide to President Reagan's National Security Council, testified before a joint congressional committee investigating the Iran-Contra affair. Such congressional investigations are a classic example of oversight.

stricted activities toward Nicaragua and the president had forbidden negotiations with Iran. The Tower Commission, appointed to investigate the Iran-Contra affair, concluded that although there was nothing fundamentally wrong with the institutions involved in foreign-policy making—the Department of State, the Department of Defense, the White House, and Congress—there had been a "flawed process," "a failure of responsibility," and a thinness of the president's personal engagement in the issues. The Tower Commission found that "at no time did [Reagan] insist upon accountability and performance review."[40]

No particular management style is guaranteed to work. Each White House management innovation, from one president to the next, shows only the inadequacy of the approaches of previous presidents. And as the White House and the Executive Office of the President grow, the management bureaucracy itself becomes a management problem. Something more and different is obviously needed.

Congress and Responsible Bureaucracy

Congress is constitutionally essential to responsible bureaucracy because ultimately the key to bureaucratic responsibility is legislation. When a law is passed and its intent is clear, the accountability for implementation of that law is also clear. Then the president knows what to "faithfully execute," and the responsible agency understands what is expected of it. But when Congress enacts vague legislation, agencies must resort to their own interpretations. The president and the federal courts often step in to tell agencies what the legislation intended. And so do the most intensely interested groups. Yet when everybody, from president to courts to interest groups, gets involved in the actual interpretation of legislative intent, to whom and to what is the agency accountable? Even when the agency wants to behave responsibly, how shall accountability be accomplished?

Congress's answer is **oversight.** The more power Congress has delegated to the executive, the more it has sought to re-involve itself in directing the interpretation of laws through committee and subcommittee oversight of each agency. The standing committee system in Congress is well-suited for oversight, inasmuch as most of the congressional committees and subcommittees have jurisdictions roughly parallel to one or more departments and agencies, and members of Congress who sit on these committees can develop expertise equal to that of the bureaucrats. Appropriations committees as well as authorization committees have oversight powers—as do their respective subcommittees. In addition to these, the Government Reform and Oversight Committee in the House and the Governmental Affairs Committee in the Senate have oversight powers not limited by departmental jurisdiction.

The best indication of Congress's oversight efforts is the use of public hearings, before which bureaucrats and other witnesses are summoned to discuss and defend agency budgets and past decisions. The data drawn from systematic studies of congressional committee and subcommittee hearings and meetings show quite dramatically that Congress has tried through oversight to keep pace with the expansion of the executive branch. Between 1950 and 1980, for example, the annual number of committee and subcommittee meetings in the House of Representatives rose steadily from 3,210 to 7,022; in the Senate, the number of such meetings rose from 2,607 to 4,265 (in 1975–76). Beginning in 1980 in the House and 1978 in the Senate, the number of committee and subcommittee hearings and meetings slowly began to decline, reaching 4,222 in the House and 2,597 in the Senate by the mid-1980s. This pattern of rise and decline in committee and subcommittee oversight activity strongly suggests that congressional vigilance toward the executive branch is responsive more to long-term growth in government than to yearly activity or to partisan considerations.[41]

Oversight can also be carried out by individual members of Congress. Such inquiries addressed to bureaucrats are considered standard congressional "case work" and can turn up significant questions of public responsibility even when the motivation is only to meet the demand of an individual constituent. Oversight also takes place through communications between congressional staff and agency staff. The number of congressional staff has been enlarged tremendously since the Legislative Reorganization Act of 1946, and the legislative staff, especially the staff of the committees, is just as professionalized and specialized as the staff of executive agencies. In addition, Congress has created for itself three large agencies whose obligations are to engage in constant research on problems taking place in or confronted by the executive branch. These are the General Accounting Office (GAO), the Congressional Research Service (CRS), and the Congressional Budget Office (CBO). Each of these agencies is designed to give Congress information independent of the information it can get directly from the executive branch through hearings and other communications.[42] Another source of information for oversight is direct from citizens through the Freedom of Information Act (FOIA; discussed earlier in this chapter). Nevertheless, the information gained by citizens through FOIA can be effective only through the institution-

In a public hearing before a House subcommittee, Kimberly Bergalis, who contracted AIDS from her dentist and later died from the disease, urged the subcommittee to enact legislation to make AIDS testing mandatory for health care workers.

alized channels of congressional committees and, on a few occasions, through public-interest litigation in the federal courts.

In the final analysis, the best approach to maintaining accountability is for Congress to spend more time clarifying its legislative intent and less time on oversight activity. If Congress's intent in making laws were clearer, Congress could then afford to defer far more to presidential management to maintain bureaucratic accountability. Bureaucrats are more responsive to clear legislative guidance than to anything else, but when Congress and the president are at odds about interpretation, bureaucrats can evade responsibility by playing off one branch against another.

Bureaucracy is here to stay. No reinvention of government or radical decentralization of power or substantial budget-cutting from reductions in personnel can alter the basic fact of bureaucracy or resolve the problem of reconciling bureaucracy with democracy. As is true of all complex social and political problems, the solution to the conflict between bureaucracy and democracy lies in a sober awareness of the nature of the problem.

★ Summary

Bureaucracy is a universal form of organization, found in businesses, churches, foundations, and universities, as well as in the public sphere. All essential government services and regulations are carried out by bureaucracies—specifically, by administrative agencies. Bureaucrats are appointed to their offices based on the "merit system." Federal bureaucrats are generally better-educated than the U.S. population as a whole. Women and African Americans are also well represented, although they tend to be concentrated at the lower pay levels.

The agencies of the executive branch can be grouped into four categories: (1) clientele agencies, (2) agencies for maintaining the Union, (3) regulatory agencies, and (4) agencies for redistribution. All of these agencies are alike in that they are all bureaucratic. These agencies differ in the way they are organized, in the way they participate in the political process, and in their levels of responsiveness to political authority. In recent years, attempts have been made to reduce or "downsize" the bureaucracy by termination, devolution, and privatization. Although these efforts are popular with the American people, they cannot reduce the size of the federal bureaucracy by much.

The executive and the legislative branches do the toughest job any government is called upon to do: making the bureaucracy accountable to the people. Democratizing bureaucracy is the unending task of politics in a democracy.

FOR FURTHER READING

Arnold, Peri E. *Making the Managerial Presidency: Comprehensive Organization Planning*. Princeton: Princeton University Press, 1986.

Fesler, James W., and Donald F. Kettl. *The Politics of the Administrative Process*. Chatham, NJ: Chatham House, 1991.

Skowronek, Stephen. *Building a New American State: The Expansion of National Administrative Capacities, 1877–1920*. New York: Cambridge University Press, 1982.

Wildavsky, Aaron. *The New Politics of the Budget Process*. 2nd ed. New York: HarperCollins, 1992.

Wilson, James Q. *Bureaucracy: What Government Agencies Do and Why They Do It*. New York: Basic Books, 1989.

Wood, Dan B. *Bureaucratic Dynamics: The Role of Bureaucracy in a Democracy*. Boulder, CO: Westview, 1994.

STUDY OUTLINE

Bureaucracy and Bureaucrats

1. Bureaucracy is simply a form of organization. Specialization and repetition are essential to the efficiency of any organization.
2. Despite fears of bureaucratic growth, the federal service has grown little during the past twenty-five years. The national government is large, but the federal service has not been growing any faster than the economy or the society.
3. Bureaucratic communication leaves a paper trail which, although unpopular, provides a means of holding bureaucrats responsible and accountable.
4. Because statutes and executive orders often provide only vague instructions, one important job of the bureaucrat is to interpret the intentions of Congress and the president prior to implementation of orders.
5. The lower efficiency of public agencies can be attributed to the added constraints put on them, as compared to those put on private agencies.
6. Through civil service reform, national and state governments have attempted to reduce political interference in public bureaucracy by granting certain public bureaucrats legal protection against being fired without a show of cause.
7. In terms of the hiring of various demographic groups, the federal civil service—like the rest of society—has problems, but it has been improving.

The Organization of the Executive Branch

1. One type of executive agency—the clientele agency—exists to foster the interests of a specific group in society. In turn, that group works to support its agency when it is in jeopardy.
2. America's chief revenue agency, the Internal Revenue Service, engenders hostility rather than clientele support among groups and individual citizens. For the most part, American tax-policy making is centralized; agreements are struck between the president, the Treasury Department, and the leading members of the two tax committees in Congress.
3. Political considerations have frequently had an impact both on agencies for internal security and on agencies for external national security.
4. Regulatory agencies in the United States are given the authority to regulate various industries; these agencies often act like courts when making decisions or settling disputes.
5. Agencies of redistribution influence the amount of money in the economy and directly influence who has money, who has credit, and whether people will want to invest or spend.

Can the Bureaucracy Be Reduced?

1. The bureaucracy can be reduced in three ways: termination, devolution, and privatization.

Can Bureaucracy Be Controlled?

1. Each expansion of the national government in the twentieth century has been accompanied by a parallel expansion of presidential management authority, but the expansion of presidential power cannot guarantee responsible bureaucracy.
2. Although Congress attempts to control the bureaucracy through oversight, a more effective way to ensure accountability may be to clarify legislative intent.

PRACTICE QUIZ

1. Which of the following best describes the growth of the federal service in the past twenty-five years?
   a. rampant, exponential growth
   b. little growth at all
   c. decrease in the total number of federal employees.
   d. vast, compared to the growth of the economy and the society
2. A means by which bureaucrats are regularly held accountable is
   a. media scrutiny.
   b. presidential site visits.
   c. the paper trail.
   d. none of the above
3. What task must bureaucrats perform if Congress charges them with enforcing a law through explicit directions?
   a. implementation
   b. interpretation
   c. lawmaking
   d. quasi-judicial decision making
4. Which of the following was *not* a component of the 1978 civil service reforms?
   a. the merit system
   b. a type of tenure system
   c. a spoils system
   d. All of the above were associated with the 1978 civil service reforms.
5. Which of the following terms best characterizes the representation of African Americans in the federal workforce?
   a. over-representation
   b. under-representation
   c. nonexistent
   d. bifurcated
6. Which of the following is a way in which the bureaucracy might be reduced?
   a. devolution
   b. termination
   c. privatization
   d. all of the above
7. Which of the following is *not* an example of a clientele agency?
   a. Department of Justice
   b. Department of Commerce
   c. Department of Agriculture
   d. Department of Housing and Urban Development
8. What explains the FBI's political significance as compared to the other divisions and bureaus within the Department of Justice?
   a. the FBI's higher legal status
   b. the leadership of J. Edgar Hoover in the 1920s and 1930s
   c. the FBI's clientele nature
   d. the FBI's relationship to the CIA
9. Which president warned of the military-industrial complex?
   a. Franklin Roosevelt
   b. John Kennedy
   c. Dwight Eisenhower
   d. Richard Nixon
10. Which president instituted the stringent budgetary process known as "zero-base budgeting"?
    a. Richard Nixon
    b. Lyndon Johnson
    c. Jimmy Carter
    d. Ronald Reagan

CRITICAL THINKING QUESTIONS

1. Often the efficiency of public bureaucracies is judged in terms of the efficiency of private business and other organizations. In many instances, government has been expected to do things that businesses in the marketplace have chosen not to do or have found unprofitable. Might the tasks that government is asked to perform be more prone to inefficiency? Think about the ways in which business might be able to perform some tasks that government currently performs. Would business necessarily perform these tasks more efficiently? Should efficiency be the only priority in the public enterprise?
2. Describe the ways in which the public controls its bureaucracy. How much and what kind of control should the public exercise? Through elected officials—i.e., the president and the Congress—the public can achieve some control over the bureaucracy. What are the relative advantages and disadvantages of presidential and congressional control of the bureaucracy?

KEY TERMS

accountability the obligation to justify the discharge of duties in the fulfillment of responsibilities to a person or persons in higher authority, and to be answerable to that authority for failing to fulfill the assigned duties and responsibilities. (p. 498)

bureaucracy the complex structure of offices, tasks, rules, and principles of organization that are employed by all large-scale institutions to coordinate effectively the work of their personnel. (p. 493)

clientele agencies departments or bureaus of government whose mission is to promote, serve, or represent a particular interest or a particular segment or geographical area of the country. (p. 507)

devolution a policy to remove a program from one level of government by delegating it or passing it down to a lower level of government, such as from the national government to the state and local governments. (p. 519)

Federal Reserve System (Fed) a system of twelve Federal Reserve Banks that facilitates exchanges of cash, checks, and credit; regulates member banks; and uses monetary policies to fight inflation and deflation. (p. 516)

fiscal policy the use of taxing, monetary, and spending powers to manipulate the economy. (p. 515)

implementation the efforts of departments and agencies to translate laws into specific bureaucratic routines. (p. 498)

interpretation the process wherein bureaucrats implement ambiguous statutes, requiring agencies to make educated guesses as to what Congress or higher administrative authorities intended. (p. 498)

iron triangle the stable, cooperative relationships that often develop between a congressional committee, an administrative agency, and one or more supportive interest groups. Not all of these relationships are triangular, but the iron triangle is the most typical. (p. 507)

means testing a procedure by which potential beneficiaries of a public assistance program establish their eligibility by demonstrating a genuine need for the assistance. (p. 516)

merit system a product of civil service reform, in which appointees to positions in public bureaucracies must objectively be deemed qualified for the position. (p. 500)

oversight the effort by Congress, through hearings, investigations, and other techniques, to exercise control over the activities of executive agencies. (p. 524)

paper trail written accounts by which the process of decision making and the participants in a decision can, if desired, be later reconstructed. Often called *red tape.* (p. 498)

privatization removing all or part of a program from the public sector to the private sector. (p. 519)

redistributive agencies a general category of agencies including fiscal agencies, monetary agencies, and welfare agencies, whose net effect is to shift large aggregates of wealth from rich to poor, young to old, etc. (p. 515))

regulatory agencies departments, bureaus, or independent agencies whose primary mission is to impose limits, restrictions, or other obligations on the conduct of individuals or companies in the private sector. (p. 514)

revenue agencies agencies responsible for collecting taxes. Examples include the Internal Revenue Service for income taxes, the U.S. Customs Service for tariffs and other taxes on imported goods, and the Bureau of Alcohol, Tobacco, and Firearms for collection of taxes on the sales of those particular products. (p. 507)

14

The Federal Courts

★ The Legal System

Within what broad categories of law do cases arise?
How is the U.S. court system structured?

★ Federal Jurisdiction

What is the importance of the federal court system?
What factors play a role in the appointment of federal judges?
What shapes the flow of cases through the Supreme Court?

★ The Power of the Supreme Court: Judicial Review

What is the basis for the Supreme Court's power of judicial review?
How does the power of judicial review make the Supreme Court a lawmaking body?
How does a case reach the Supreme Court? Once accepted, how does a case proceed?
What factors influence the judicial philosophy of the Supreme Court?

★ Judicial Power and Politics

How has the power of the federal courts been limited throughout much of American history?
How have the role and power of the federal courts been transformed over the last fifty years?
How has the increase in the Supreme Court's power changed its role in the political process?

IN RECENT YEARS, colleges and universities have seen a flood of civil and criminal litigation. Faculty members denied promotion or tenure have brought suits charging that their school's action was biased. Although the most familiar bias complaints involve allegations of discrimination against women or African Americans, it is becoming increasingly common for white male professors to charge that they, too, are the victims of prejudice. In one recent case, for example, a white male job applicant sued the College of Charleston in South Carolina, alleging that he had been denied a tenure-track position in the college's religious studies department because he was a devout Christian. The college denied the allegation, asserting that it had offered the position to the best-qualified person from among nearly three hundred applicants—this individual happened to be Jewish. The judge who heard the case ruled in favor of the college.[1] In another recent federal court case, a Duke University professor charged that he had been denied tenure simply because his department wished to fire a black professor and feared that it would be charged with racial bias if it did not also fire a white professor. This case has not yet been fully resolved.[2]

In other instances, students may become involved in legal disputes. During the 1960s, of course, litigation initiated by African American students compelled many all-white universities in the South, such as the University of

Mississippi and the University of Alabama, to admit black students. More recently, the battle for integration has broadened to include issues of gender as well as race. In 1994 and 1996, for example, the Supreme Court ordered the Citadel and the Virginia Military Institute, both all-male military colleges, to accept women who wished to attend. The Court reasoned that since these colleges were supported by public funds, they were prohibited by federal civil rights law from discriminating on the basis of gender in their admissions policies.[3]

Gender has also been the issue in a number of court cases arising from Title IX of the federal Higher Education Act. Title IX, among other things, requires colleges and universities to spend substantially equal amounts of money on men's and women's athletic programs. This requirement was resisted by a number of universities until female athletes began to secure federal court orders compelling schools to comply with the law. One university that has taken Title IX seriously is the University of Connecticut, which saw its men's and women's basketball teams ranked first in the nation in 1995.

In 1995, a student group at the University of Virginia scored a dramatic legal victory before the U.S. Supreme Court. The university had refused to provide support from the student activities fund for *Wide Awake,* a magazine published by a Christian student group. Although other student publications received subsidies from the activities fund, university policy prohibited grants to religious groups. Ronald Rosenberger, a Virginia undergraduate and an editor of the magazine, and his fellow editors filed suit in federal court charging, among other things, that the university's refusal to fund their magazine because of its religious focus violated their First Amendment right to freedom of speech. A federal district court ruled in favor of the university on the grounds that funding for a religious newspaper by a state university would violate the Constitution's prohibition against government support for religion. Rosenberger and his colleagues appealed, but lost again when the district court's decision was affirmed by the Fourth Circuit Court of Appeals, which said that the Constitution mandated a strict separation of church and state. Undeterred, the student editors appealed the circuit court's decision to the Supreme Court. In June 1995, the Supreme Court ruled in favor of the student group, holding that the university's policies amounted to state support for some ideas but not others. This, said the Court, represented a fundamental violation of the First Amendment.[4] The *Rosenberger* decision represents a potential loosening of the Court's long-standing opposition to any government support for religious groups or ideas, and it demonstrates how much influence can be exerted by a determined group of students.

Still another area of litigation pits students against faculty members and faculty against their universities: sexual harassment. Over the past several years, most schools have adopted rules and administrative procedures designed to protect students from inappropriate sexual overtures on the part of faculty and staff members. Until recently, students who were the victims of such harassment were often discouraged from making complaints. Today, however, most schools encourage students to bring complaints to administrative and faculty committees that investigate and punish violations of sexual conduct rules. Procedures for bringing charges are now widely publicized on most campuses. As a result, sexual harassment complaints have become more common at many schools.

Some college faculty members have charged that the rules governing sexual harassment are vaguely drawn and that the committees charged with investigating complaints are often biased against the accused. Several professors found guilty by college officials of harassment have filed suit in the federal courts to have these findings reversed. In one recent case that arose at the University of New Hampshire, for example, an English professor was disciplined and suspended because of sexual references he allegedly made during his class lectures. In 1994, a federal judge, asserting that the professor's comments fell well within the area of speech protected by the First Amendment, ordered the university to reinstate the professor and pay him nearly a quarter of a million dollars in back pay, damages, and legal fees.[5]

This sea of litigation is hardly unique to academe. University students and faculty are no more litigious than other Americans. Every year nearly twenty-five million cases are tried in American courts and one American in every nine is directly involved in litigation. Cases can arise from disputes between citizens, from efforts by government agencies to punish wrongdoing, or from citizens' efforts to prove that a right provided them by law has been infringed upon as a result of government action—or inaction. Many critics of the U.S. legal system assert that Americans have become much too litigious (ready to use the courts for all purposes), and perhaps that is true. But the heavy use that Americans make of the courts is also an indication of the extent of conflict in American society. And given the existence of social conflict, it is far better that Americans seek to settle their differences through the courts rather than by fighting or feuding.

Some critics contend that American society has become too litigious, citing an increase in the number of "frivolous lawsuits" filed each year, such as the one filed by this homeless man against the Morristown Public Library, which had ejected him for offensive personal hygiene.

In this chapter, we will first examine the legal system, including the types of cases that the federal courts consider and the types of law with which they deal. Second, we will assess the organization and structure of the federal court system as well as the flow of cases through the courts. Third, we will consider judicial review and how it makes the Supreme Court a "lawmaking body." We will also examine the procedures of and influences on the Supreme Court. Finally, we will analyze the role and power of the federal courts in the American political process, looking in particular at the growth of judicial power in the United States.

The framers of the American Constitution called the Supreme Court the "least dangerous branch" of American government. Today, it is not unusual to hear friends *and* foes of the Court refer to it as the "imperial judiciary."[6] Before we can understand this transformation and its consequences, however, we must look in some detail at America's judicial process.

The Legal System

> ➤ Within what broad categories of law do cases arise?
> ➤ How is the U.S. court system structured?

Originally, a "court" was the place where a sovereign ruled—where the king and his entourage governed. Settling disputes between citizens was part of governing. According to the Bible, King Solomon had to settle the dispute between two women over which of them was the mother of the child both claimed. Judging is the settling of disputes, a function that was slowly separated from the king and the king's court and made into a separate institution of government. Courts have taken over from kings the power to settle controversies by hearing the facts on both sides and deciding which side possesses the greater merit. But since judges are not kings, they must have a basis for their authority. That basis in the United States is the Constitution and the law. Courts decide cases by hearing the facts on both sides of a dispute and applying the relevant law or principle to the facts.

CASES AND THE LAW

Court cases in the United States proceed under three broad categories of law: criminal law, civil law, and public law (see Table 14.1).

Cases of **criminal law** are those in which the government charges an individual with violating a statute that has been enacted to protect the public

TABLE 14.1

TYPES OF LAWS AND DISPUTES

Type of law	Type of case or dispute	Form of case
Criminal law	Cases arising out of actions that violate laws protecting the health, safety, and morals of the community. The government is always the plaintiff.	*U.S. (or state) v. Jones* *Jones v. U.S. (or state),* if Jones lost and is appealing
Civil law	"Private law," involving disputes between citizens or between government and citizen where no crime is alleged. Two general types are contract and tort. *Contract cases* are disputes that arise over voluntary actions. *Tort cases* are disputes that arise out of obligations inherent in social life. Negligence and slander are examples of torts.	*Smith v. Jones* *New York v. Jones* *U.S. v. Jones* *Jones v. New York*
Public law	All cases where the powers of government or the rights of citizens are involved. The government is the defendant. *Constitutional law* involves judicial review of the basis of a government's action in relation to specific clauses of the Constitution as interpreted in Supreme Court cases. *Administrative law* involves disputes over the statutory authority, jurisdiction, or procedures of administrative agencies.	*Jones v. U.S. (or state)* *In re Jones* *Smith v. Jones,* if a license or statute is at issue in their private dispute

health, safety, morals, or welfare. In criminal cases, the government is always the **plaintiff** (the party that brings charges) and alleges that a criminal violation has been committed by a named **defendant.** Most criminal cases arise in state and municipal courts and involve matters ranging from traffic offenses through robbery and murder. Another large and growing body of federal criminal law deals with such matters as tax evasion, mail fraud, and the sale of narcotics. Defendants found guilty of criminal violations may be fined or sent to prison.

The case of *California v. Simpson* was a case of criminal law.

Cases of **civil law** involve disputes among individuals or between individuals and the government where no criminal violation is charged. Unlike criminal cases, the losers in civil cases cannot be fined or sent to prison, although they may be required to pay monetary damages for their actions. In a civil case, the one who brings a complaint is the plaintiff and the one against whom the complaint is brought is the defendant. The two most common types of civil cases involve contracts and torts. In a typical contract case, an individual or corporation charges that it has suffered because of another's violation of a specific agreement between the two. For example, the Smith Manufacturing Corporation may charge that Jones Distributors failed to honor an agreement to deliver raw materials at a specified time, causing Smith to lose business. Smith asks the court to order Jones to compensate it for the damage allegedly suffered. In a typical tort case, one individual charges that he or she has been injured by another's negligence or malfeasance. Medical malpractice suits are one example of tort cases.

In deciding civil cases, courts apply statutes (laws) and legal **precedent** (prior decisions). State and federal statutes, for example, often govern the conditions under which contracts are and are not legally binding. Jones Distributors might argue that it was not obliged to fulfill its contract with the Smith Corporation because actions by Smith, such as the failure to make promised payments, constituted fraud under state law. Attorneys for a physician being sued for malpractice, on the other hand, may search for prior instances in which courts ruled that actions similar to those of their client did not constitute negligence. Such precedents are applied under the doctrine of ***stare decisis,*** a Latin phrase meaning "let the decision stand."

A case becomes a matter of the third category, **public law,** when a plaintiff or defendant in a civil or criminal case seeks to show that their case involves the powers of government or rights of citizens as defined under the Constitution or by statute. One major form of public law is constitutional law, under which a court will examine the government's actions to see if they conform to the Constitution as it has been interpreted by the judiciary. Thus, what began as an ordinary criminal case may enter the realm of public law if a defendant claims that his or her constitutional rights were violated by the police. Another important arena of public law is administrative law, which involves disputes over the jurisdiction, procedures, or authority of administrative agencies. Under this type of law, civil litigation between an individual and the government may become a matter of public law if the individual asserts that the government is violating a statute or abusing its power under the Constitution. For example, land owners have asserted that federal and state restrictions on land use constitute violations of the Fifth Amendment's restrictions on the government's ability to confiscate private property. Recently, the

Supreme Court has been very sympathetic to such claims, which effectively transform an ordinary civil dispute into a major issue of public law.

Most of the important Supreme Court cases we will examine in this chapter involve judgments concerning the constitutional or statutory basis of the actions of government agencies. As we shall see, it is in this arena of public law that the Supreme Court's decisions can have significant consequences for American politics and society.

TYPES OF COURTS

In the United States, systems of courts have been established both by the federal government and by the governments of the individual states. Both systems have several levels, as shown in Figure 14.1. More than 99 percent of all court cases in the United States are heard in state courts. The overwhelming majority of criminal cases, for example, involve violations of state laws prohibiting such actions as murder, robbery, fraud, theft, and assault. If such a case is brought to trial, it will be heard in a state **trial court**, in front of a judge and sometimes a jury, who will determine whether the defendant violated state law. If the defendant is convicted, he or she may appeal the conviction to a higher court, such as a state **appellate court**, and from there to a state's **supreme court.** Similarly, in civil cases, most litigation is brought in the courts established by the state in which the activity in question took place. For example, a patient bringing suit against a physician for malpractice would file the suit in the appropriate court in the state where the alleged malpractice occurred. The judge hearing the case would apply state law and state

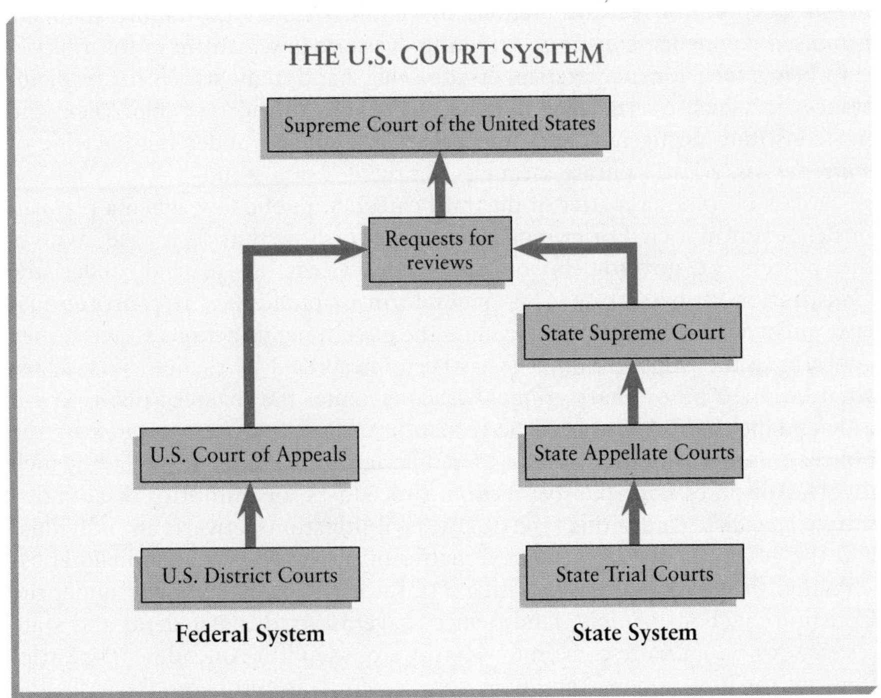

FIGURE 14.1

The state and federal court systems parallel each other until they reach the Supreme Court.

precedent to the matter at hand. (It should be noted that in both criminal and civil matters, most cases are settled before trial through negotiated agreements between the parties. In criminal cases these agreements are called **plea bargains.**)

Although each state has its own set of laws, these laws have much in common from state to state. Murder and robbery, obviously, are illegal in all states, although the range of possible punishments for those crimes varies from state to state. Some states, for example, provide for capital punishment (the death penalty) for murder and other serious offenses; other states do not. As we saw in Chapter 4, however, some acts that are criminal offenses in one state may be legal in another state. Prostitution, for example, is legal in some Nevada counties, although it is outlawed in all other states. Considerable similarity among the states is also found in the realm of civil law. In the case of contract law, most states have adopted the **Uniform Commercial Code** in order to reduce interstate differences. In areas such as family law, however, which covers such matters as divorce and child custody arrangements, state laws vary greatly.

Cases are heard in the federal courts if they involve federal laws, treaties with other nations, or the U.S. Constitution; these areas are the official **jurisdiction** of the federal courts. In addition, any case in which the U.S. government is a party is heard in the federal courts. If, for example, an individual is charged with violating a federal criminal statute, such as evading the payment of income taxes, charges would be brought before a federal judge by a federal prosecutor. Civil cases involving the citizens of more than one state and in which more than fifty thousand dollars is at stake may be heard in either the federal or the state courts, usually depending upon the preference of the plaintiff.

Federal courts serve another purpose in addition to trying cases within their jurisdiction: that of hearing appeals from state-level courts. Individuals found guilty of breaking a state criminal law, for example, can appeal their convictions to a federal court by raising a constitutional issue and asking a federal court to determine whether the state's actions were consistent with the requirements of the U.S. Constitution. An appellant might assert, for example, that the state court denied him or her the right to counsel, imposed excessive bail, or otherwise denied the appellant **due process.** Under such circumstances, an appellant can ask the federal court to overturn his or her conviction. Federal courts are not obligated to accept such appeals and will do so only if they feel that the issues raised have considerable merit and if the appellant has exhausted all possible remedies within the state courts. (This procedure is discussed in more detail later in this chapter.) The decisions of state supreme courts may also be appealed to the U.S. Supreme Court if the state court's decision has conflicted with prior U.S. Supreme Court rulings or has raised some important question of federal law. Such appeals are accepted by the U.S. Supreme Court at its discretion.

Although the federal courts hear only a small fraction of all the civil and criminal cases decided each year in the United States, their decisions are extremely important. It is in the federal courts that the Constitution and federal laws that govern all Americans are interpreted and their meaning and significance established. Moreover, it is in the federal courts that the powers and limitations of the increasingly powerful national government are tested. Finally, through their power to review the decisions of the state courts, it is ultimately the federal courts that dominate the American judicial system.

Federal Jurisdiction

- What is the importance of the federal court system?
- What factors play a role in the appointment of federal judges?
- What shapes the flow of cases through the Supreme Court?

Of all the cases heard in the United States in 1993, federal district courts (the lowest federal level) received 274,000. Although this number is up substantially from the 87,000 cases heard in 1961, it still constitutes under 1 percent of the judiciary's business. The federal courts of appeal listened to 49,770 cases in 1993, and the U.S. Supreme Court reviewed 7,245 in its 1992–93 term. Only 83 cases were given full-dress Supreme Court review (the nine justices actually sitting *en banc*—in full court—and hearing the lawyers argue the case).[7]

THE LOWER FEDERAL COURTS

Most of the cases of original federal jurisdiction are handled by the federal district courts. Courts of **original jurisdiction** are the courts that are responsible for discovering the facts in a controversy and creating the record upon which a judgment is based. Although the Constitution gives the Supreme Court original jurisdiction in several types of cases, such as those affecting ambassadors and those in which a state is one of the parties, most original jurisdiction goes to the lowest courts—the trial courts. (In courts that have appellate jurisdiction, judges receive cases after the factual record is established by the trial court. Ordinarily, new facts cannot be presented before appellate courts.)

There are eighty-nine district courts in the fifty states, plus one in the District of Columbia and one in Puerto Rico, and three territorial courts. These courts are staffed by 610 federal district judges. District judges are assigned to district courts according to the workload; the busiest of these courts may have as many as twenty-eight judges. Only one judge is assigned to each case, except where statutes provide for three-judge courts to deal with special issues. The routines and procedures of the federal district courts are essentially the same as those of the lower state courts, except that federal procedural requirements tend to be stricter. States, for example, do not have to provide a grand jury, a twelve-member trial jury, or a unanimous jury verdict. Federal courts must provide all these things.

THE APPELLATE COURTS

Roughly 10 percent of all lower court and federal agency cases are accepted for review by the federal appeals courts and by the Supreme Court in its capacity as an appellate court. The country is divided into twelve judicial circuits, each of which has a U.S. Court of Appeals. Every state, the District of Columbia, and each of the territories is assigned to the circuit in the continental United States that is closest to it.

Except for cases selected for review by the Supreme Court, decisions made by the appeals courts are final. Because of this finality, certain safeguards have been built into the system. The most important is the provision of more than one judge for every appeals case. Each court of appeals has from six to twenty-eight permanent judgeships, depending on the workload of the circuit. Although normally three judges hear appealed cases, in some instances a larger number of judges sit together *en banc*.

Another safeguard is provided by the assignment of a Supreme Court justice as the circuit justice for each of the twelve circuits. Since the creation of the appeals court in 1891, the circuit justice's primary duty has been to review appeals arising in the circuit in order to expedite Supreme Court action. The most frequent and best-known action of circuit justices is that of reviewing requests for stays of execution when the full Court is unable to do so—primarily during the summer, when the Court is in recess.

The Supreme Court building in Washington, D.C.

The Supreme Court

The Supreme Court is America's highest court. Article III of the Constitution vests "the judicial power of the United States" in the Supreme Court, and this court is supreme in fact as well as form. The Supreme Court is made up of a chief justice and eight associate justices. The **chief justice** presides over the Court's public sessions and conferences. In the Court's actual deliberations and decisions, however, the chief justice has no more authority than his colleagues. Each justice casts one vote. To some extent, the influence of the chief justice is a function of his or her own leadership ability. Some chief justices, such as the late Earl Warren, have been able to lead the court in a new direction. In other instances, forceful associate justices, such as the late Felix Frankfurter, are the dominant figures on the Court.

The members of the Supreme Court in 1996 (from left to right): Antonin Scalia, Ruth Bader Ginsburg, John Paul Stevens, David Souter, Chief Justice William Rehnquist, Clarence Thomas, Sandra Day O'Connor, Stephen Breyer, and Anthony Kennedy.

The Constitution does not specify the number of justices that should sit on the Supreme Court; Congress has the authority to change the Court's size. In the early nineteenth century, there were six Supreme Court justices; later there were seven. Congress set the number of justices at nine in 1869, and the Court has remained that size ever since. In 1937, President Franklin D. Roosevelt, infuriated by several Supreme Court decisions that struck down New Deal programs, asked Congress to enlarge the Court so that he could add a few sympathetic justices to the bench. Although Congress balked at Roosevelt's "Court packing" plan, the Court gave in to FDR's pressure and began to take a more favorable view of his policy initiatives. The president, in turn, dropped his efforts to enlarge the Court. The Court's surrender to FDR came to be known as "the switch in time that saved nine."

How Judges Are Appointed

Federal judges are appointed by the president and are generally selected from among the more prominent or politically active members of the legal profession. Many federal judges previously served as state court judges or state or local prosecutors. In an informal nominating process, candidates for vacancies on the U.S. District Court are generally suggested to the president by a U.S. senator from the president's own party who represents the state in which the vacancy has occurred. Senators often see such a nomination as a way to reward important allies and contributors in their states. If the state has no senator from the president's party, the governor or members of the state's House delegation may make suggestions. In general, presidents endeavor to appoint judges who possess legal experience and good character and whose partisan and ideological views are similar to the president's own. During the presidencies of Ronald Reagan and George Bush, most federal judicial appointees were conservative Republicans. Bush established an advisory committee to screen judicial nominees in order to make certain that their legal and political philosophies were sufficiently conservative. Bill Clinton's appointees to the federal bench, on the other hand, have tended to be liberal Democrats. Clinton has also made a major effort to appoint women and African Americans to the federal courts. Nearly half of his nominees have been drawn from these groups.

Once the president has formally nominated an individual, the nominee must be considered by the Senate Judiciary Committee and confirmed by a majority vote in the full Senate. Before the president makes a formal nomination, however, the senators from the candidate's own state must indicate that they support the nominee. This is an informal but seldom violated practice called **senatorial courtesy.** Because the Senate will rarely approve a nominee opposed by a senator from his or her own state, the president will usually not bother to present such a nomination to the Senate. Through this arrangement, senators are able to exercise veto power over appointments to the federal bench in their own states. In recent years, the Senate Judiciary Committee has also sought to signal the president when it has had qualms about a judicial nomination. After the Republicans won control of the Senate in 1994, for example, Judiciary Committee Chair Orrin Hatch of Utah let President Clinton know that he considered two of Clinton's nominees to be too liberal. The president withdrew the nominations.

Federal appeals court nominations follow much the same pattern. Since appeals court judges preside over jurisdictions that include several states, however, senators do not have as strong a role in proposing potential candidates. Instead, potential appeals court candidates are generally suggested to the president by the Justice Department or by important members of the administration. The senators from the nominee's own state are still consulted before the president will formally act.

If political factors play an important role in the selection of district and appellate court judges, they are decisive when it comes to Supreme Court appointments. Because the high court has so much influence over American law and politics, virtually all presidents have made an effort to select justices who share their own political philosophies. Presidents Ronald Reagan and George Bush, for example, appointed five justices whom they believed to have conservative perspectives: Justices Sandra Day O'Connor, Antonin Scalia, Anthony Kennedy, David Souter, and Clarence Thomas. Reagan also elevated William Rehnquist to the position of chief justice. Reagan and Bush sought appointees who believed in reducing government intervention in the economy and who supported the moral positions taken by the Republican Party in recent years, particularly opposition to abortion. However, not all the Reagan and Bush appointees have fulfilled their sponsors' expectations. Bush appointee David Souter, for example, has been attacked by conservatives as a turncoat for his decisions on school prayer and abortion rights. Nevertheless, through their appointments, Reagan and Bush were able to create a far more conservative Supreme Court. For his part, President Bill Clinton has endeavored to appoint liberal justices. Clinton named Ruth Bader Ginsburg and Stephen Breyer to the Court, hoping to counteract the influence of the Reagan and Bush appointees. (Table 14.2 shows information about the current Supreme Court justices.)

TABLE 14.2

SUPREME COURT JUSTICES, 1996
(IN ORDER OF SENIORITY)

Name	Year of birth	Prior experience	Appointed by	Year of appointment
William H. Rehnquist *Chief Justice*	1924	Assistant Attorney General	Nixon*	1972
John Paul Stevens	1920	Federal Judge	Ford	1975
Sandra Day O'Connor	1930	State Judge	Reagan	1981
Antonin Scalia	1936	Law Professor, Federal Judge	Reagan	1986
Anthony Kennedy	1936	Federal Judge	Reagan	1988
David Souter	1939	Federal Judge	Bush	1990
Clarence Thomas	1948	Federal Judge	Bush	1991
Ruth Bader Ginsburg	1933	Federal Judge	Clinton	1993
Stephen Breyer	1938	Federal Judge	Clinton	1994

*Appointed chief justice by Reagan in 1986.

In recent years, Supreme Court nominations have come to involve intense partisan struggle. Typically, after the president has named a nominee, interest groups opposed to the nomination have mobilized opposition in the media, the public, and the Senate. When President Bush proposed conservative judge Clarence Thomas for the Court, for example, liberal groups launched a campaign to discredit Thomas. After extensive research into his background, opponents of the nomination were able to produce evidence suggesting that Thomas had sexually harassed a former subordinate, Anita Hill. Thomas denied the charge. After contentious Senate Judiciary Committee hearings, highlighted by testimony from both Thomas and Hill, Thomas narrowly won confirmation.

Likewise, conservative interest groups carefully scrutinized Bill Clinton's liberal nominees, hoping to find information about them that would sabotage their appointments. During his two opportunities to name Supreme Court justices, Clinton was compelled to drop several potential appointees because of information unearthed by political opponents.

These struggles over judicial appointments indicate the growing intensity of partisan struggle in the United States today. They also indicate how much importance competing political forces attach to Supreme Court appointments. Because these contending forces see the outcome as critical, they are willing to engage in a fierce struggle when Supreme Court appointments are at stake.

Controlling the Flow of Cases

In addition to the judges themselves, three other agencies or groups play an important role in shaping the flow of cases through the federal courts: the solicitor general, the Federal Bureau of Investigation, and federal law clerks.

The Solicitor General If any single person has greater influence than individual judges over the federal courts, it is the **solicitor general** of the United States. The solicitor general is the third-ranking official in the Justice Department (below the attorney general and the deputy attorney general) but is the top government lawyer in virtually all cases before the Supreme Court where the government is a party. The solicitor general has the greatest control over the flow of cases; his or her actions are not reviewed by any higher authority in the executive branch. More than half the Supreme Court's total work load consists of cases under the direct charge of the solicitor general.

The solicitor general exercises especially strong influence by screening cases before any agency of the federal government can appeal them to the Supreme Court; indeed, the justices rely on the solicitor general to "screen out undeserving litigation and furnish them with an agenda to government cases that deserve serious consideration."[8] Typically, more requests for appeals are rejected than are accepted by the solicitor general. Agency heads may lobby the president or otherwise try to circumvent the solicitor general, and a few of the independent agencies have a statutory right to make direct appeals, but these are almost inevitably doomed to ***per curiam*** rejection—rejection through a brief, unsigned opinion by the whole Court—if the solicitor general refuses to participate. Congress has given only a few agencies, includ-

In testimony before the Senate Judiciary Committee, Anita Hill alleged that Supreme Court nominee Clarence Thomas had sexually harassed her. Hill's testimony brought nationwide attention to the nomination hearings. The Senate subsequently approved Thomas by the narrowest ratification margin in history, 52 to 48.

ing the Federal Communications Commission, the Federal Maritime Commission, and in some cases, the Department of Agriculture (even though it is not an independent agency), the right to appeal directly to the Supreme Court without going through the solicitor general.

The solicitor general can enter a case even when the federal government is not a direct litigant by writing an ***amicus curiae*** ("friend of the court") brief. A "friend of the court" is not a direct party to a case but has a vital interest in its outcome. Thus, when the government has such an interest, the solicitor general can file as *amicus curiae,* or a federal court can invite such a brief because it wants an opinion in writing. The solicitor general also has the power to invite others to enter cases as *amici curiae.*

In addition to exercising substantial control over the flow of cases, the solicitor general can shape the arguments used before the federal courts. Indeed, the Supreme Court tends to give special attention to the way the solicitor general characterizes the issues. The solicitor general is the person appearing most frequently before the Court and, theoretically at least, is the most disinterested. The credibility of the solicitor general is not hurt when several times each year he or she comes to the Court to withdraw a case with the admission that the government has made an error.

The solicitor general's sway over the flow of cases does not, however, entirely overshadow the influence of the other agencies and divisions in the Department of Justice. The solicitor general is counsel for the major divisions in the department, including the Antitrust, Tax, Civil Rights, and Criminal divisions. Their activities generate a great part of the solicitor general's agenda. This is particularly true of the Criminal Division, whose cases are appealed every day. These cases are generated by initiatives taken by the United States Attorneys and the district judges before whom they practice.

AMERICAN POLITICAL CULTURE

"Our One Supreme Court": The Common-Law Court Movement

"I am a private party and not a subject of the United States nor subject to its jurisdiction, as it has no constitutional jurisdiction except in the District of Columbia and its possessions." With this statement, uttered in a common-law court, you can declare yourself a "freeman" and remove yourself from the duty to file income taxes, to obtain a driver's license, or indeed to be bound by any state or federal laws. Or so proponents of the common-law court movement argue.

The common-law movement arose in the West about twenty years ago. As environmental agents, sheriffs, IRS agents, and other government officials sought to foreclose or impose tax liens on property or investigate incidents of illegal hunting, many westerners felt the government had turned against them. One result was the common-law court movement.

Proponents trace the notion of common-law courts back to documents they believe are part of a western cultural tradition of individual liberty and sovereignty: the Bible, the Magna Carta, the U.S. Constitution, and certain state constitutions. So-called freemen begin with an idea that all Americans believe—that ultimate sovereignty rests in the hands of the people—but from this idea they draw a radical conclusion: that they can, as individuals, choose to repudiate all the powers of government. Freemen assert that the present forms of government in the United States, both state and national, are illegitimate and tyrannical; they often argue that the Constitution has been suspended since President Roosevelt declared emergency powers in 1933. Freemen portray themselves as committed to restoring American democracy and constitutional government.

Over the last twenty years the common-law movement has spread across the country. Today, thousands of Americans who consider themselves freemen meet in self-styled courts in places like Arlington, Texas; Columbus, Ohio; Franklin, Delaware; and Roundup, Montana. In a typical court, often called "Our One Supreme Court," a jury of twelve men is chosen (the common-law movement discourages women from playing public roles). The jury is very important: jurors do not merely decide a case, they also act as judge and lawyers, asking questions, maintaining order, calling for documents, deliberating openly, and rendering a verdict.

Two kinds of cases heard in common-law courts are actions for "quiet title for person" and for "quiet title." A person claiming "quiet title for person" makes a statement like the one quoted at the beginning of this essay. With the jury's decision, the plaintiff is recognized as a freeman, no longer subject to the jurisdiction of the federal or state governments—even to the extent of rejecting ZIP codes and 911 emergency service. In a case for "quiet title," a plaintiff comes before the court to claim ownership of a plot of land, after having filed a public notice announcing the claim. Banks, corporations, and the government—the usual "owners" of the land in question—do not appear in "court" to contest the claim. In the absence of any contestation, the jury typically awards such plots of land to anyone who claims them.

Is there any common sense in the common-law movement? The logic of the common-law court movement is essentially anarchistic, as a common-law enthusiast makes plain: "Common law says the people have all the rights and the government can do nothing to infringe on the rights of the people."[1] Since most government action, by its very nature, represents a balance and compromise among the rights of groups or individuals, the logical conclusion is that there is very little of anything that government *can* do. Common-law advocates would enthusiastically endorse such a view. But in practice it would return us not to a once-upon-a-time America of small government and civic virtue, but to a land with no functioning governments at all, in which citizens would play out a radical version of self-reliance.

[1] Gene Schroder, quoted in Eileen Dempsey and Jim Woods, "Outside the System: An Uncommon Approach on Common Law," *Columbus Dispatch*, September 10, 1995, p. 1A.

The FBI Another important influence on the flow of cases through the federal appellate judiciary comes from the Federal Bureau of Investigation (FBI), one of the bureaus of the Department of Justice. Its work provides data for numerous government cases against businesses, individual citizens, and state and local government officials. Its data are the most vital source of material for cases in the areas of national security and organized crime.

The FBI also has the important function of linking the Justice Department very closely to cases being brought by state and local government officials. Since the FBI has a long history of cooperation with state and local police forces, the solicitor general often joins (as *amicus curiae*) appeals involving state criminal cases.

Law Clerks Every federal judge employs law clerks to research legal issues and assist with the preparation of opinions. Each Supreme Court justice is assigned four clerks. The clerks are almost always honors graduates of the nation's most prestigious law schools. A clerkship with a Supreme Court justice is a great honor and generally indicates that the fortunate individual is likely to reach the very top of the legal profession. The work of the Supreme Court clerks is a closely guarded secret, but it is likely that some justices rely heavily upon their clerks for advice in writing opinions and in deciding whether an individual case ought to be heard by the Court. It is often rumored that certain opinions were actually written by a clerk rather than a justice. Although such rumors are difficult to substantiate, it is clear that at the end of long judicial careers, justices such as William O. Douglas and Thurgood Marshall had become so infirm that they were compelled to rely on the judgments of their law clerks.

Law clerks play an important role in the Supreme Court justices' decisions to accept cases, in researching the backgrounds of cases that are accepted, and in drafting opinions. Here, Chief Justice Rehnquist meets with his law clerks.

The Power of the Supreme Court: Judicial Review

- What is the basis for the Supreme Court's power of judicial review?
- How does the power of judicial review make the Supreme Court a lawmaking body?
- How does a case reach the Supreme Court? Once accepted, how does a case proceed?
- What factors influence the judicial philosophy of the Supreme Court?

One of the most important powers of the Supreme Court is the power of **judicial review**—the authority and the obligation to review any lower court decision where a substantial issue of public law is involved. The disputes can be over the constitutionality of federal or state laws, over the propriety or constitutionality of the court procedures followed, or over whether public officers are exceeding their authority. The Supreme Court's power of judicial review has come to mean review not only of lower court decisions but also of state legislation and acts of Congress. For this reason, if for no other, the Supreme Court is more than a judicial agency—it is a major lawmaking body.

The Supreme Court's power of judicial review over lower court decisions has never been at issue. Nor has there been any serious quibble over the power of the federal courts to review administrative agencies in order to determine whether their actions and decisions are within the powers delegated to them by Congress. There has, however, been a great deal of controversy occasioned by the Supreme Court's efforts to review acts of Congress and the decisions of state courts and legislatures.

Chief Justice John Marshall established the Supreme Court's power to rule on the constitutionality of federal and state laws.

Judicial Review of Acts of Congress

Since the Constitution does not give the Supreme Court the power of judicial review of congressional enactments, the Court's exercise of it is something of a usurpation. It is not known whether the framers of the Constitution opposed judicial review, but "if they intended to provide for it in the Constitution, they did so in a most obscure fashion."[9] Disputes over the intentions of the framers were settled in 1803 in the case of *Marbury v. Madison.*[10] Although Congress and the president have often been at odds with the Court, its legal power to review acts of Congress has not been seriously questioned since 1803 (see Box 14.1). One reason is that judicial power has been accepted as natural, if not intended. Another reason is that the Supreme Court has rarely reviewed the constitutionality of acts of Congress, especially in the past fifty years. When such acts do come up for review, the Court makes a self-conscious effort to give them an interpretation that will make them constitutional.

Judicial Review of State Actions

The power of the Supreme Court to review state legislation or other state action and to determine its constitutionality is neither granted by the

MARBURY V. MADISON

The 1803 Supreme Court decision handed down in *Marbury v. Madison* established the power of the Court to review acts of Congress. The case arose over a suit filed by William Marbury and seven other people against Secretary of State James Madison to require him to approve their appointments as justices of the peace. These had been last-minute ("midnight judges") appointments of outgoing president John Adams. Chief Justice John Marshall held that although Marbury and the others were entitled to their appointments, the Supreme Court had no power to order Madison to deliver them, because the relevant section of the first Judiciary Act of 1789 was unconstitutional—giving the courts powers not intended by Article III of the Constitution.

Marshall reasoned that constitutions are framed to serve as the "fundamental and paramount law of the nation." Thus, he argued, with respect to the legislative action of Congress, the Constitution is a "superior . . . law, unchangeable by ordinary means." He concluded that an act of Congress that contradicts the Constitution must be judged void.

As to the question of whether the Court was empowered to rule on the constitutionality of legislative action, Marshall responded emphatically that it is "the province and duty of the judicial department to say what the law is." Since the Constitution is the supreme law of the land, he reasoned, it is clearly within the realm of the Court's responsibility to rule on the constitutionality of legislative acts and treaties. This principle has held sway ever since.

SOURCES: Gerald Gunther, *Constitutional Law* (Mineola, NY: Fountain Press, 1980), pp. 9–11; and *Marbury v. Madison,* 1 Cr. 137 (1803).

BOX 14.1

Constitution nor inherent in the federal system. But the logic of the **supremacy clause** of Article VI of the Constitution, which declares it and laws made under its authority to be the supreme law of the land, is very strong. Furthermore, in the Judiciary Act of 1789, Congress conferred on the Supreme Court the power to reverse state constitutions and laws whenever they are clearly in conflict with the U.S. Constitution, federal laws, or treaties.[11] This power gives the Supreme Court appellate jurisdiction over all of the millions of cases handled by American courts each year.

The supremacy clause of the Constitution not only established the federal Constitution, statutes, and treaties as the "supreme law of the land," but also provided that "the Judges in every State shall be bound thereby, any Thing in the Constitution or Laws of the State to the Contrary notwithstanding." Under this authority, the Supreme Court has frequently overturned state constitutional provisions or statutes and state court decisions it deems to contravene rights or privileges guaranteed under the federal Constitution or federal statutes.

The civil rights area abounds with examples of state laws that were overturned because the statutes violated guarantees of due process and equal protection contained in the Fourteenth Amendment to the Constitution. For example, in the 1954 case of *Brown v. Board of Education*, the Court overturned statutes from Kansas, South Carolina, Virginia, and Delaware that either required or permitted segregated public schools, on the basis that such

The Supreme Court has the power to overturn state laws. In 1996, the Supreme Court found unconstitutional a Rhode Island law that had prohibited the advertising of prices of alcoholic beverages. The Court claimed that the Rhode Island law had violated the First Amendment right of free speech.

statutes denied black schoolchildren equal protection of the law. In 1967, in *Loving v. Virginia,* the Court invalidated a Virginia statute prohibiting interracial marriages.[12]

State statutes in other subject matter areas are equally subject to challenge. In *Griswold v. Connecticut,* the Court invalidated a Connecticut statute prohibiting the general distribution of contraceptives to married couples on the basis that the statute violated the couples' rights to marital privacy.[13] In *Brandenburg v. Ohio,* the Court overturned an Ohio statute forbidding any person from urging criminal acts as a means of inducing political reform or from joining any association that advocated such activities on the grounds that the statute punished "mere advocacy" and therefore violated the free speech provisions of the Constitution.[14]

JUDICIAL REVIEW AND LAWMAKING

When courts of original jurisdiction apply existing statutes or past cases directly to citizens, the effect is the same as legislation. Lawyers study judicial decisions in order to discover underlying principles, and they advise their clients accordingly. Often the process is nothing more than reasoning by analogy: the facts in a particular case are so close to those in one or more previous cases that the same decision should be handed down. Such judge-made law is called common law.

The appellate courts, however, are in another realm. Their rulings can be considered laws, but they are laws governing the behavior only of the judiciary. They influence citizens' conduct only because, in the words of Justice Oliver Wendell Holmes, who served on the Supreme Court from 1900 to 1932, lawyers make "prophecies of what the courts will do in fact."[15]

The written opinion of an appellate court is about halfway between common law and statutory law. It is judge-made and draws heavily on the precedents of previous cases. But it tries to articulate the rule of law controlling the case in question and future cases like it. In this respect, it is like a statute. But it differs from a statute in that a statute addresses itself to the future conduct of citizens, whereas a written opinion addresses itself mainly to the willingness or ability of courts in the future to take cases and render favorable opinions. Decisions by appellate courts affect citizens by giving them a cause of action or by taking it away from them. That is, they open or close access to the courts.

A specific case may help clarify the distinction. Before the Second World War, one of the most insidious forms of racial discrimination was the "restrictive covenant," a clause in a contract whereby the purchasers of a house agreed that if they later decided to sell it, they would sell only to a Caucasian. When a test case finally reached the Supreme Court in 1948, the Court ruled unanimously that citizens had a right to discriminate with restrictive covenants in their sales contracts but that the courts could not enforce these contracts. Its argument was that enforcement would constitute violation of the Fourteenth Amendment provision that no state shall "deny to any person within its jurisdiction equal protection under the law."[16] The Court was thereby predicting what it would and would not do in future cases of this sort. Most states have now enacted statutes that forbid homeowners to place such covenants in sales contracts.

Gideon v. Wainwright extends the point. When the Supreme Court ordered a new trial for Clarence Earl Gideon because he had been denied the right to legal counsel,[17] it said to all trial judges and prosecutors that henceforth they would be wasting their time if they cut corners in trials of indigent defendants. It also invited thousands of prisoners to appeal their convictions. (See Chapter 5 for a further discussion of this case.)

Many areas of civil law have been constructed in the same way—by judicial messages to other judges, some of which are codified eventually into legislative enactments. An example of great concern to employees and employers is that of liability for injuries sustained at work. Courts have sided with employees so often that it has become virtually useless for employers to fight injury cases. It has become "the law" that employers are liable for such injuries, without regard to negligence. But the law in this instance is simply a series of messages to lawyers that they should advise their corporate clients not to appeal injury decisions.

The appellate courts cannot decide what behavior will henceforth be a crime. They cannot directly prevent the police from forcing confessions or intimidating witnesses. In other words, they cannot directly change the behavior of citizens or eliminate abuses of power. What they can do, however, is make it easier for mistreated persons to gain redress.

In redressing wrongs, the appellate courts—and even the Supreme Court itself—often call for a radical change in legal principle. Changes in race relations, for example, would probably have taken a great deal longer if the Supreme Court had not rendered the 1954 decision *Brown v. Board of Education* that redefined the rights of African Americans.

Similarly, the Supreme Court interpreted the doctrine of the separation of church and state so as to alter significantly the practice of religion in public institutions. For example, in a 1962 case, *Engel v. Vitale,* the Court declared that a once widely observed ritual—the recitation of a prayer by students in a public school—was unconstitutional under the establishment clause of the First Amendment. Almost all the dramatic changes in the treatment of criminals and of persons accused of crimes have been made by the appellate courts, especially the Supreme Court. The Supreme Court brought about a veritable revolution in the criminal process with three cases over less than five years: *Gideon v. Wainwright,* in 1963, was just discussed. *Escobedo v. Illinois,* in 1964, gave suspects the right to remain silent and the right to have counsel present during questioning. But the *Escobedo* decision left confusions that allowed differing decisions to be made by lower courts. In *Miranda v. Arizona,* in 1966, the Supreme Court cleared up these confusions by setting forth what is known as the ***Miranda* rule:** arrested people have the right to remain silent, the right to be informed that anything they say can be held against them, and the right to counsel before and during police interrogation (see Chapter 5).[18]

One of the most significant changes brought about by the Supreme Court was the revolution in legislative representation unleashed by the 1962 case of *Baker v. Carr.*[19] In this landmark case, the Supreme Court held that it could no longer avoid reviewing complaints about the apportionment of seats in state legislatures. Following that decision, the federal courts went on to force reapportionment of all state, county, and local legislatures in the country.

How Cases Reach the Supreme Court

Given the millions of disputes that arise every year, the job of the Supreme Court would be impossible if it were not able to control the flow of cases and its own case load. Its original jurisdiction is only a minor problem. The original jurisdiction includes (1) cases between the United States and one of the fifty states, (2) cases between two or more states, (3) cases involving foreign ambassadors or other ministers, and (4) cases brought by one state against citizens of another state or against a foreign country. The most important of these cases are disputes between states over land, water, or old debts. Generally, the Supreme Court deals with these cases by appointing a "special master," usually a retired judge, to actually hear the case and present a report. The Supreme Court then allows the states involved in the dispute to present arguments for or against the master's opinion.[20]

Rules of Access Over the years, the courts have developed specific rules that govern which cases within their jurisdiction they will and will not hear. In order to have access to the courts, cases must meet certain criteria. These rules of access can be broken down into three major categories: case or controversy, standing, and mootness.

Article III of the Constitution and Supreme Court decisions define judicial power as extending only to "cases and controversies." This means that the case before a court must be an actual controversy, not a hypothetical one, with two truly adversarial parties. The courts have interpreted this language to mean that they do not have the power to render advisory opinions to legislatures or agencies about the constitutionality of proposed laws or regulations. Furthermore, even after a law is enacted, the courts will generally refuse to consider its constitutionality until it is actually applied.

Parties to a case must also have **standing,** that is, they must show that they have a substantial stake in the outcome of the case. The traditional requirement for standing has been to show injury to oneself; that injury can be personal, economic, or even aesthetic, for example. In order for a group or class of people to have standing (as in class action suits), each member must show specific injury. This means that a general interest in the environment, for instance, does not provide a group with sufficient basis for standing.

The Supreme Court also uses a third criterion in determining whether it will hear a case: that of **mootness.** In theory, this requirement disqualifies cases that are brought too late—after the relevant facts have changed or the problem has been resolved by other means. The criterion of mootness, however, is subject to the discretion of the courts, which have begun to relax the rules of mootness, particularly in cases where a situation that has been resolved is likely to come up again. In the abortion case *Roe v. Wade,* for example, the Supreme Court rejected the lower court's argument that because the pregnancy had already come to term, the case was moot. The Court agreed to hear the case because no pregnancy was likely to outlast the lengthy appeals process.

Putting aside the formal criteria, the Supreme Court is most likely to accept cases that involve conflicting decisions by the federal circuit courts, cases that present important questions of civil rights or civil liberties, and cases in which the federal government is the appellant. Ultimately, however, the question of which cases to accept can come down to the preferences and priorities of the justices. If a group of justices believes that the Court should intervene in a particular area of policy or politics, they are likely to look for a case or cases that will serve as vehicles for judicial intervention. For many years, for example, the Court was not interested in considering challenges to affirmative action or other programs designed to provide particular benefits to minorities. In recent years, however, several of the Court's more conservative justices have been eager to push back the limits of affirmative action and racial preference, and have therefore accepted a number of cases that would allow them to do so. In 1995, the Court's decisions in *Adarand Constructors v. Pena, Missouri v. Jenkins,* and *Miller v. Johnson* placed new restrictions on federal affirmative action programs, school desegregation efforts, and attempts to increase minority representation in Congress through the creation of "minority districts" (see Chapter 9).[21] Similarly, because some justices have felt that the Court had gone too far in the past in restricting public support for religious ideas, the Court accepted the case of *Rosenberger v. University of Virginia,* which was discussed at the beginning of this chapter. This case served as a vehicle through which a group of justices could assert a new set of rules allowing a closer relationship between church and state.

Writs Decisions handed down by lower courts can reach the Supreme Court in one of two ways: through a writ of *certiorari,* or, in the case of convicted state prisoners, through a writ of *habeas corpus.* A writ is a court document conveying an order of some sort. In recent years, an effort has been made to give the Court more discretion regarding the cases it chooses to hear. Before 1988, the Supreme Court was obligated to review cases on what was called a writ of appeal. This has since been eliminated, and the Court now has virtually complete discretion over what cases it will hear.

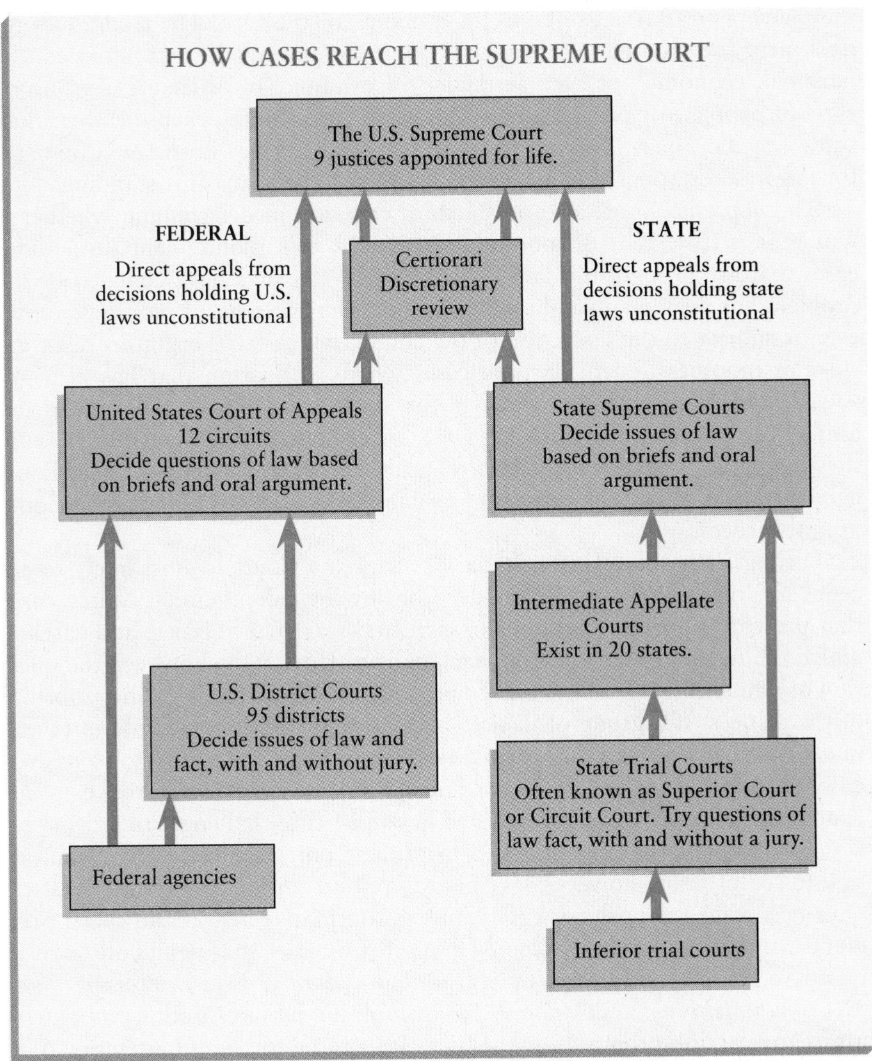

FIGURE 14.2

Most cases reach the Supreme Court through the **writ of *certiorari*,** which is granted whenever four of the nine justices agree to review a case. The Supreme Court was once so inundated with appeals that in 1925 Congress enacted laws giving it some control over its case load with the power to issue writs of *certiorari*. Rule 10 of the Supreme Court's own rules of procedure defines *certiorari* as "not a matter of right, but of sound judicial discretion . . . granted only where there are special and important reasons therefor." The reasons provided for in Rule 10 are

1. Where a state has made a decision that conflicts with previous Supreme Court decisions;
2. Where a state court has come up with an entirely new federal question;
3. Where one court of appeals has rendered a decision in conflict with another;

4. Where there are other inconsistent rulings between two or more courts or states; and
5. Where a single court of appeals has sanctioned too great a departure by a lower court from normal judicial proceedings (a reason rarely given).

The **writ of *habeas corpus*** is a fundamental safeguard of individual rights (see Box 14.2). Its historical purpose is to enable an accused person to challenge arbitrary detention and to force an open trial before a judge. But in

BOX 14.2

HABEAS CORPUS

A writ of *habeas corpus* is an order issued by a court directing the release of an individual in custody. This writ is obtained by filing a petition alleging that the detention of the individual is improper for reasons specific to each case, from allegations that the person in custody is not the person who committed the crime to allegations that technical errors have denied the accused certain constitutional rights. Petitions for writs of *habeas corpus* may take many forms. Petitions may be filed by an attorney on behalf of an individual in custody, but they are as frequently filed by the person in custody. In fact, most jails and prisons have at least one "jailhouse lawyer"—an inmate who spends the majority of his or her time preparing petitions for writs of *habeas corpus* for other inmates. If a court decides the petition should be granted, it will issue a writ of *habeas corpus* (order of release) citing the reasons set forth in the petition. A petition for a writ of *habeas corpus* generally takes the following form:

John Jones
v.
People of the State
of North Carolina

John Jones respectfully states that:

1. He is imprisoned at the Doe County Jail in Doe, North Carolina.
2. He has been imprisoned by Jane Smith, Sheriff of Doe County, North Carolina.
3. He has been imprisoned as the result of a conviction of theft entered in Doe County on January 1, 1988.
4. This imprisonment is illegal because the court failed to provide John Jones with assistance of counsel.
5. John Jones has not previously applied for a writ of *habeas corpus* (or, if a previous writ has been filed, the circumstances under which the writ was filed are stated here).
6. John Jones has not filed an appeal (or if an appeal has been filed, the disposition of the appeal is stated here).

Accordingly, John Jones asks that a writ of *habeas corpus* directed to Jane Smith, Sheriff of Doe County, be issued inquiring into the propriety of this imprisonment and ordering his release from custody, pursuant to law.

1867, Congress's distrust of southern courts led it to confer on federal courts the authority to issue writs of *habeas corpus* to prisoners already tried or being tried in state courts of proper jurisdiction, where the constitutional rights of the prisoner were possibly being violated. This writ gives state prisoners a second channel toward Supreme Court review in case their direct appeal from the highest state court fails. The writ of *habeas corpus* is discretionary; that is, the Court can decide which cases to review.

Lobbying for Access: Interests and the Court At the same time that the Court exercises discretion over which cases it will review, groups and forces in society often seek to persuade the justices to listen to their problems. Interest groups use several different strategies to get the Court's attention. Lawyers representing these groups try to choose the proper client and the proper case, so that the issues in question are most dramatically and appropriately portrayed. They also have to pick the right district or jurisdiction in which to bring the case. Sometimes they even have to wait for an appropriate political climate.

Group litigants have to plan carefully when to use and when to avoid publicity. They must also attempt to develop a proper record at the trial court level, one that includes some constitutional arguments and even, when possible, errors on the part of the trial court. One of the most effective litigation strategies used in getting cases accepted for review by the appellate courts is bringing the same type of suit in more than one circuit (i.e., developing a "pattern of cases"), in the hope that inconsistent treatment by two different courts will improve the chance of a Supreme Court review.

The Supreme Court is open to outside political influence. Interest groups lobby the Court formally by filing amicus curiae briefs, and informally through public opinion. In 1989, members of the National Organization for Women and the National Abortion Rights Action League gathered while the Court met to rule on *Webster v. Reproductive Health Services*, an important abortion rights case.

Congress will sometimes provide interest groups with legislation designed to facilitate their use of litigation. One important recent example is the 1990 Americans with Disabilities Act (ADA), enacted after intense lobbying by public interest and advocacy groups. The ADA, in conjunction with the 1991 Civil Rights Act, opens the way for disabled individuals to make effective use of the courts to press their interests.

The two most notable users of the pattern of cases strategy in recent years have been the National Association for the Advancement of Colored People (NAACP) and the American Civil Liberties Union (ACLU). For many years, the NAACP (and its Defense Fund—now a separate group) has worked through local chapters and with many individuals to encourage litigation on issues of racial discrimination and segregation. Sometimes it distributes petitions to be signed by parents and filed with local school boards and courts, deliberately sowing the seeds of future litigation. The NAACP and the ACLU often encourage private parties to bring suit and then join the suit as *amici curiae.*

One illustration of an interest group employing a carefully crafted litigation strategy to pursue its goals through the judiciary was the Texas-based effort to establish a right to free public school education for children of illegal aliens. The issue arose in 1977 when the Texas state legislature, responding to a sudden public backlash against illegal immigration from Mexico, enacted a law permitting school districts to charge undocumented children hefty tuition for the privilege of attending public school. A public-interest law organization, the Mexican-American Legal Defense Fund, prepared to challenge the law in court after determining that public opposition precluded any chance of persuading the legislature to change its own law.

Part of the defense fund's litigation strategy was to bring a lawsuit in the northern section of Texas, far from the Mexican border, where illegal immigration would be at a minimum. Thus, in Tyler, Texas, where the complaint was initially filed, the trial court found only sixty undocumented alien students in a school district composed of 16,000. This strategy effectively contradicted the state's argument that the Texas law was necessary to reduce the burdens on educational resources created by masses of incoming aliens. Another useful litigation tactic was to select plaintiffs who, although illegal aliens, were nevertheless clearly planning to remain in Texas even without free public education for their children. Thus, all of the plaintiffs came from families that had already lived in Tyler for several years and included at least one child who was an American citizen by virtue of birth in the United States. By emphasizing the stability of such families, the defense fund argued convincingly that the Texas law would not motivate families to return to the poverty in Mexico from which they had fled, but would more likely result in the creation of a subclass of illiterate people who would add to the state's unemployment and crime rates. Five years after the lawsuit on behalf of the Tyler children began, the U.S. Supreme Court in the case of *Plyler v. Doe* held that the Texas law was unconstitutional under the equal protection clause of the Fourteenth Amendment.[22]

In many states, it is considered unethical and illegal for attorneys to engage in "fomenting and soliciting legal business in which they are not parties and have no pecuniary right or liability." The NAACP was sued by the state of Virginia in the late 1950s in an attempt to restrict or eliminate its efforts to influence the pattern of cases. The Supreme Court reviewed the case in 1963, recognized that the strategy was being utilized, and held that it was protected by the First and Fourteenth Amendments, just as other forms of speech and petition are protected.[23]

Thus, many pathbreaking cases are eventually granted *certiorari* because continued refusal to review one or more of them would amount to a rule of law just as much as if the courts had handed down a written opinion. In this sense, the flow of cases, especially the pattern of significant cases, influences the behavior of the appellate judiciary.

THE SUPREME COURT'S PROCEDURES

The Supreme Court's decision to accept a case is the beginning of what can be a lengthy and complex process (see Figure 14.3). First, the attorneys on both sides must prepare **briefs**—written documents that may be several hundred pages long in which the attorneys explain why the Court should rule in favor of their client. Briefs are filled with referrals to precedents specifically chosen to show that other courts have frequently ruled in the same way that the Supreme Court is being asked to rule. The attorneys for both sides muster the most compelling precedents they can in support of their arguments.

As the attorneys prepare their briefs, they often ask sympathetic interest groups for their help. Groups are asked to file *amicus curiae* briefs that sup-

FIGURE 14.3

In addition to the individual justices who make up the Supreme Court, various groups and factors also may influence the Court's decision on any given case.

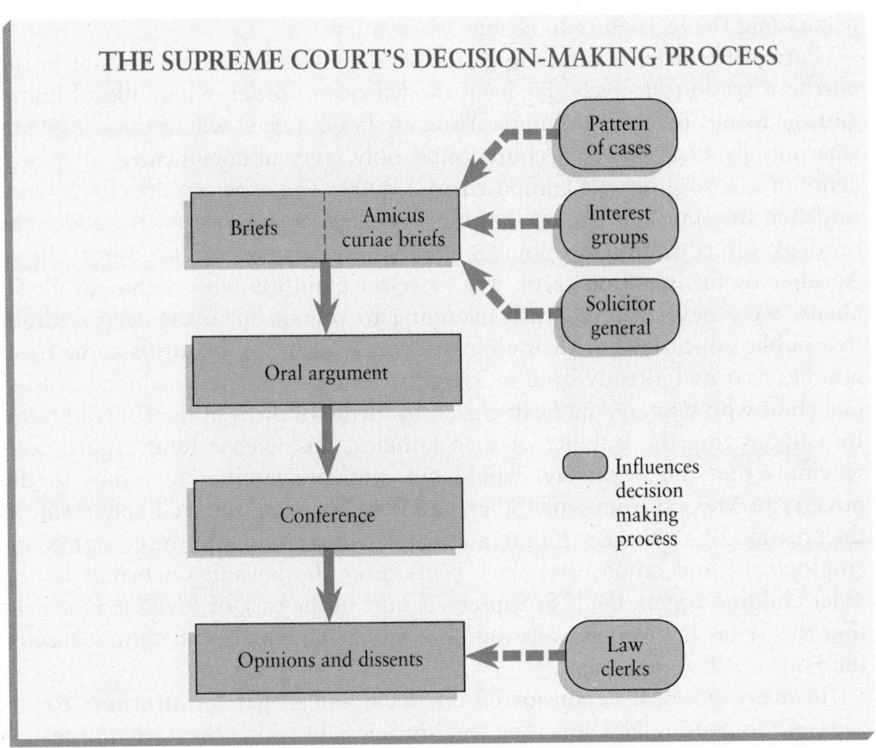

port the claims of one or the other litigant. In a case involving separation of church and state, for example, liberal groups such as the ACLU and Citizens for the American Way are likely to be asked to file *amicus* briefs in support of strict separation, whereas conservative religious groups are likely to file *amicus* briefs advocating increased public support for religious ideas. Often, dozens of briefs will be filed on each side of a major case. *Amicus* filings are one of the primary methods used by interest groups to lobby the Court. By filing these briefs, groups indicate to the Court where their group stands and signal to the justices that they believe the case to be an important one.

The next stage of a case is **oral argument,** in which attorneys for both sides appear before the Court to present their positions and answer the justices' questions. Each attorney has only a half hour to present his or her case, and this time includes interruptions for questions. Certain members of the Court, such as Justice Antonin Scalia, are known to interrupt attorneys dozens of times. Others, such as Justice Clarence Thomas, seldom ask questions. For an attorney, the opportunity to argue a case before the Supreme Court is a singular honor and a mark of professional distinction. It can also be a harrowing experience, as justices break into a carefully prepared presentation to ask pointed questions. Oral argument can be very important to the outcome of a case. It allows justices to better understand the heart of the case and to raise questions that might not have been addressed in the opposing side's briefs. It is not uncommon for justices to go beyond the strictly legal issues and ask opposing counsel to discuss the implications of the case for the Court and the nation at large.

This 1935 photo is the only known photograph of the Supreme Court hearing oral arguments.

Following oral argument, the Court discusses the case in its Wednesday or Friday conference. The chief justice presides over the conference and speaks first; the other justices follow in order of seniority. The Court's conference is secret, and no outsiders are permitted to attend. The justices discuss the case and eventually reach a decision on the basis of a majority vote. If the Court is divided, a number of votes may be taken before a final decision is reached. As the case is discussed, justices may try to influence or change one another's opinions. At times, this may result in compromise decisions. On the current Court, for example, several justices, including Rehnquist, Scalia, and Thomas, are known to favor overturning the 1973 *Roe v. Wade* decision that prohibited the states from outlawing abortions. Other justices, including Souter, Breyer, and Ginsburg, are known to oppose such a course of action. This division has resulted in several compromise decisions, in which the Court has allowed some state restriction of abortion but has not permitted states to outlaw abortion altogether.

Opinion Writing After a decision has been reached, one of the members of the majority is assigned to write the **opinion.** This assignment is made by the chief justice, or by the most senior justice in the majority if the chief justice is on the losing side. The assignment of the opinion can make a significant difference to the interpretation of a decision. Every opinion of the Supreme Court sets a major precedent for future cases throughout the judicial system. Lawyers and judges in the lower courts will examine the opinion carefully to ascertain the Supreme Court's meaning. Differences in wording and emphasis

THE NAACP: USING THE LAW TO GET JUSTICE

Part of the white segregationist backlash that spread throughout the American South in the late 1800s and early 1900s was the enactment of the laws that mandated residential segregation by race. In the city of Louisville, Kentucky, the city council passed such an ordinance in 1914 in order to make sure that African Americans would not move into white-only portions of the city. This legal expression of racial hatred came under legal attack by a newly formed organization that had decided to devote its limited resources toward seeking legal remedies to racial discrimination.

The National Association for the Advancement of Colored People (NAACP) filed suit against Louisville's law. After they lost their case in state courts, the NAACP appealed the case to the Supreme Court. In 1917, the court struck down the segregationist law as a clear violation of the Fourteenth Amendment and of federal law granting blacks the same rights as whites to buy, sell, and own property.[1] The NAACP's suit had struck down its first Jim Crow law.

By 1929, the NAACP had argued five cases before the Supreme Court, but its still-meager resources limited its ability to seek justice. But about this time, the fund of a wealthy philanthropist, Charles Garland, granted the organization $100,000 to conduct "a large-scale, widespread, dramatic campaign to give the Southern Negro his constitutional rights, his political and civil equality."[2] The NAACP drew up a detailed plan for challenging legalized segregation. Drawing on the brilliant legal skills of Charles Houston and his student from Howard University Law School, Thurgood Marshall, the group planned to attack the "separate but equal" doctrine established by *Plessy v. Ferguson* by first showing that facilities set aside for blacks were almost never equal. Their second step was to challenge the separate but equal doctrine directly as inconsistent with the principles embodied in the Constitution.

In the meantime, the NAACP challenged the legality of "kangaroo" trials that were used to convict innocent blacks, some of whom were sentenced to death by all-white juries without benefit of legal advice or a proper defense. In 1944, after three decades of lawsuits by the NAACP, the Supreme Court declared the southern "white

can have important implications for future litigation. Once the majority opinion is drafted, it is circulated to the other justices. Some members of the majority may decide that they cannot accept all the language of the opinion and therefore write "concurring" opinions that support the decision but offer a somewhat different rationale or emphasis. In assigning an opinion, serious thought must be given to the impression the case will make on lawyers and on the public, as well as to the probability that one justice's opinion will be more widely accepted than another's.

One of the more dramatic instances of this tactical consideration occurred in 1944, when Chief Justice Harlan F. Stone chose Justice Felix Frankfurter to write the opinion in the "white primary" case *Smith v. Allwright.* The chief justice believed that this sensitive case, which overturned the southern practice of prohibiting black participation in nominating primaries, required the efforts of the most brilliant and scholarly jurist on the Court. But the day after Stone made the assignment, Justice Robert H. Jackson wrote a letter to Stone urging a change of assignment. In his letter, Jackson argued that primary" elections unconstitutional. Two years later, the NAACP won its first case against segregation in transportation when the Court struck down racial restrictions affecting buses. The NAACP also won victories on behalf of blacks seeking admission to state law schools.

A legal milestone was finally reached in 1954, when the Supreme Court unanimously overturned *Plessy v. Ferguson* and the principle of separate-but-equal, ordering segregated schools to begin the process of integration in *Brown v. Board of Education of Topeka, Kansas.*

Thurgood Marshall, who led the legal charge in the *Brown* case, argued 32 civil rights cases for the NAACP, winning nearly all of them. In 1962, Marshall was appointed to the U.S court of appeals by President Kennedy. Five years later, he was elevated by President Johnson to the very court in which he had won so many battles for African Americans. As the first black to serve on the Supreme Court, Marshall continued to argue that, despite many legal victories, the structures of American society still protected racism.

Along with Marshall, many argue that racism was and is deeply embedded in the fabric of society. Indeed, the original Constitution not only acknowledged but condoned the subjugation of blacks through slavery. Even so, the NAACP was able to use the constitutional framework through the judicial branch to wipe away the most offensive structures of racism in America. The process took many decades, and it continues to the present.

SOURCE: Richard Kluger, *Simple Justice* (New York: Vintage, 1975).

[1] *Buchanan v. Warley,* 245 U.S. 60 (1917). The other cases discussed herein *are Smith v. Allwright,* 321 U.S. 649 (1944); *Plessy v. Ferguson,* 3 S.Ct. 18 (1896); *Morgan v. Virginia,* 328 U.S. 373 (1946); and *Brown v. Board of Education of Topeka, Kansas,* 74 S.Ct. 686 (1954).

[2] Richard Kluger, *Simple Justice* (New York: Vintage, 1975), p. 132.

Frankfurter, a foreign-born Jew from New England, would not win the South with his opinion, regardless of its brilliance. Stone accepted the advice and substituted Justice Stanley Reed, an American-born Protestant from Kentucky and a southern Democrat in good standing.[24]

Oliver Wendell Holmes, Jr., the "great dissenter."

Dissent Justices who disagree with the majority decision of the Court may choose to publicize the character of their disagreement in the form of a **dissenting opinion.** Dissents can be used to express irritation with an outcome or to signal to defeated political forces in the nation that their position is supported by at least some members of the Court. Ironically, the most dependable way an individual justice can exercise a direct and clear influence on the Court is to write a dissent. Because there is no need to please a majority, dissenting opinions can be more eloquent and less guarded than majority opinions. Some of the greatest writing in the history of the Court is found in dissents, and some of the most famous justices, such as Oliver Wendell Holmes, Louis D. Brandeis, and William O. Douglas, were notable dissenters.

In the single 1952–53 Court term, Douglas wrote thirty-five dissenting opinions. In the 1958–59 term, he wrote eleven dissents. During the latter term, Justices Frankfurter and Harlan wrote thirteen and nine dissents, respectively.

Dissent plays a special role in the work and impact of the Court because it amounts to an appeal to lawyers all over the country to keep bringing cases of the sort at issue. Therefore, an effective dissent influences the flow of cases through the Court as well as the arguments that will be used by lawyers in later cases. Even more important, dissent emphasizes the fact that, although the Court speaks with a single opinion, it is the opinion only of the majority—and one day the majority might go the other way.

EXPLAINING SUPREME COURT DECISIONS

The Supreme Court explains its decisions in terms of law and precedent. But although law and precedent do have an effect upon the Court's deliberations and eventual decisions, it is the Supreme Court that decides what laws actually mean and what importance precedent will actually have. Throughout its history, the Court has shaped and reshaped the law. In the late nineteenth and early twentieth centuries, for example, the Supreme Court held that the Constitution, law, and precedent permitted racial segregation in the United States. Beginning in the late 1950s, however, the Court found that the Constitution prohibited segregation on the basis of race and indicated that the use of racial categories in legislation was always suspect. By the 1970s and 1980s, the Court once again held that the Constitution permitted the use of racial categories—when such categories were needed to help members of minority groups achieve full participation in American society. In the 1990s, the Court began to retreat from this position, too, indicating that governmental efforts to provide extra help to racial minorities could represent an unconstitutional infringement upon the rights of the majority.

Although it is not the only relevant factor, the prime explanation for these movements is shifts in judicial philosophy. These shifts, in turn, result from changes in the Court's composition as justices retire and are replaced by new justices who, as we saw earlier, tend to share the philosophical outlook of the president who appointed them.

Activism and Restraint One element of judicial philosophy is the issue of activism versus restraint. Over the years, some justices have believed that courts should interpret the Constitution according to the stated intentions of its framers and defer to the views of Congress when interpreting federal statutes. The late justice Felix Frankfurter, for example, advocated judicial deference to legislative bodies and avoidance of the "political thicket," in which the Court would entangle itself by deciding questions that were essentially political rather than legal in character. Advocates of **judicial restraint** are sometimes called "strict constructionists," because they look strictly to the words of the Constitution in interpreting its meaning.

The alternative to restraint is **judicial activism.** Activist judges such as the former chief justice Earl Warren and two of the leading members of his court, Justices Hugo Black and William O. Douglas, believed that the Court should go beyond the words of the Constitution or a statute to consider the broader societal implications of its decisions. Activist judges sometimes strike out in new directions, promulgating new interpretations or inventing new legal and constitutional concepts when they believe these to be socially desirable. For example, Justice Harry Blackmun's decision in *Roe v. Wade* was based upon a constitutional right to privacy that is not found in the words of the Constitution. Blackmun and the other members of the majority in the *Roe* case argued that the right to privacy was implied by other constitutional provisions. In this instance of judicial activism, the Court knew the result it wanted to achieve and was not afraid to make the law conform to the desired outcome.

Harry Blackmun, author of the Supreme Court's decision in *Roe v. Wade*.

Political Ideology The second component of judicial philosophy is political ideology. The liberal or conservative outlooks of justices play an important role in their decisions. Indeed, the philosophy of activism versus restraint is, to a large extent, a smokescreen for political ideology. For the most part, liberal judges have been activists, willing to use the law to achieve social and political change, whereas conservatives have been associated with judicial restraint. Interestingly, however, in recent years some conservative justices who have long called for restraint have actually become activists in seeking to undo some of the work of liberal jurists over the past three decades.

From the 1950s to the 1980s, the Supreme Court took an activist role in such areas as civil rights, civil liberties, abortion, voting rights, and police procedures. For example, the Supreme Court was more responsible than any other governmental institution for breaking down America's system of racial segregation. The Supreme Court virtually prohibited states from interfering with the right of a woman to seek an abortion and sharply curtailed state restrictions on voting rights. And it was the Supreme Court that placed restrictions on the behavior of local police and prosecutors in criminal cases. In a series of decisions between 1989 and 1995, however, the conservative justices appointed by Reagan and Bush were able to swing the Court to a more conservative position on civil rights, affirmative action, abortion rights, property rights, criminal procedure, voting rights, desegregation, and the power of the national government.

Yet the efforts by Reagan and Bush to reshape the federal judiciary were not fully successful. Often in American history, judges have surprised and disappointed the presidents who named them to the bench. Justice Souter, for example, has been far less conservative than President Bush and the Republicans who supported Souter's appointment thought he would be. Likewise, Justices O'Connor and Kennedy have disappointed conservatives by opposing limitations on abortion.

Nevertheless, with a combined total of twelve years in office, Reagan and Bush were also able to exercise a good deal of influence on the composition of the federal district and appellate courts. By the end of Bush's term, he and Reagan together had appointed nearly half of all federal judges. Thus, whatever impact Reagan and Bush ultimately have on the Supreme Court, their appointments will certainly influence the temperament and behavior of the district and circuit courts for years to come.

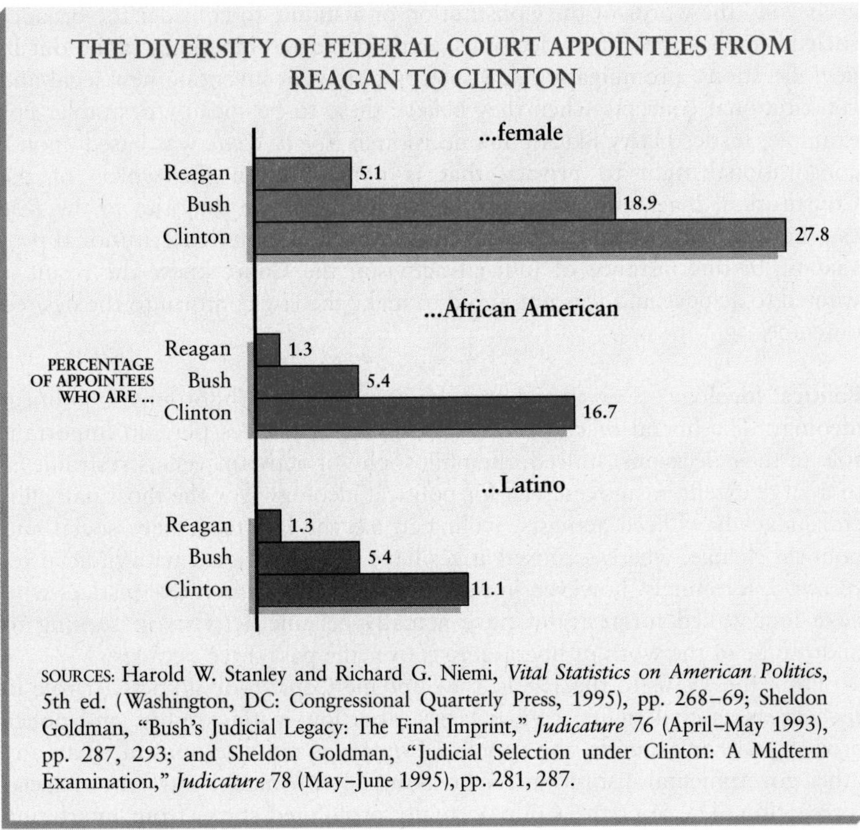

SOURCES: Harold W. Stanley and Richard G. Niemi, *Vital Statistics on American Politics*, 5th ed. (Washington, DC: Congressional Quarterly Press, 1995), pp. 268–69; Sheldon Goldman, "Bush's Judicial Legacy: The Final Imprint," *Judicature* 76 (April–May 1993), pp. 287, 293; and Sheldon Goldman, "Judicial Selection under Clinton: A Midterm Examination," *Judicature* 78 (May–June 1995), pp. 281, 287.

FIGURE 14.4

President Clinton promised to appoint more liberal jurists to the district and appellate courts, as well as to increase the number of women and minorities serving on the federal bench. During his first two years in office, Clinton held to this promise; more than 60 percent of his 128 judicial nominees were women or members of minority groups (see Figure 14.4).[25] A large number of judicial vacancies remained unfilled, however, when the Republicans took control of Congress at the end of 1994. Soon after the election, Senator Orrin Hatch of Utah, the new chair of the Senate Judiciary Committee, which confirms judicial nominations, indicated his intention to oppose any nominee whom he deemed to be too liberal. This prompted the Clinton White House to withdraw some nominations and to search for district and appellate nominees who would be more acceptable to the Republicans.[26]

The political struggles of the 1980s and 1990s amply illustrate the importance of judicial ideology. Is abortion a fundamental right or a criminal activity? How much separation must there be between church and state? Does the use of the Voting Rights Act to increase minority representation constitute a violation of the rights of whites? The answers to these and many other questions cannot be found in the words of the Constitution. They must be located, instead, in the hearts of the judges who interpret that text.

Judicial Power and Politics

- How has the power of the federal courts been limited throughout much of American history?
- How have the role and power of the federal courts been transformed over the last fifty years?
- How has the increase in the Supreme Court's power changed its role in the political process?

One of the most important institutional changes to occur in the United States during the past half-century has been the striking transformation of the role and power of the federal courts, and of the Supreme Court in particular. Understanding how this transformation came about is the key to understanding the contemporary role of the courts in America.

Traditional Limitations on the Federal Courts

For much of American history, the power of the federal courts was subject to five limitations.[27] First, courts were constrained by judicial rules of standing that limited access to the bench. Claimants who simply disagreed with governmental action or inaction could not obtain access. Access to the courts was limited to individuals who could show that they were particularly affected by the government's behavior in some area. This limitation on access to the courts diminished the judiciary's capacity to forge links with important political and social forces.

Second, courts were traditionally limited in the character of the relief they could provide. In general, courts acted only to offer relief or assistance to individuals and not to broad social classes, again inhibiting the formation of alliances between the courts and important social forces. Third, courts lacked enforcement powers of their own and were compelled to rely upon executive or state agencies to ensure compliance with their edicts. If the executive or state agencies were unwilling to assist the courts, judicial enactments could go unheeded, as when President Andrew Jackson declined to enforce Chief Justice John Marshall's 1832 order to the state of Georgia to release two missionaries it had arrested on Cherokee lands. Marshall asserted that the state had no right to enter the Cherokee lands without their assent.[28] Jackson is reputed to have said, "John Marshall has made his decision, now let him enforce it."

Fourth, federal judges are, of course, appointed by the president (with the consent of the Senate). As a result, the president and Congress can shape the composition of the federal courts and ultimately, perhaps, the character of judicial decisions. Finally, Congress has the power to change both the size and jurisdiction of the Supreme Court and other federal courts. In many areas, federal courts obtain their jurisdiction not from the Constitution but from congressional statutes. On a number of occasions, Congress has threatened to take matters out of the Court's hands when it was unhappy with the Court's policies.[29] For example, on one memorable occasion, presidential and congressional threats to expand the size of the Supreme Court—Franklin Roosevelt's "court packing" plan—encouraged the justices to drop their opposition to New Deal programs.

As a result of these five limitations on judicial power, through much of their history the chief function of the federal courts was to provide judicial support for executive agencies and to legitimate acts of Congress by declaring them to be consistent with constitutional principles. Only on rare occasions have the federal courts actually dared to challenge Congress or the executive branch.[30]

TWO JUDICIAL REVOLUTIONS

Since the Second World War, however, the role of the federal judiciary has been strengthened and expanded. There have actually been two judicial revolutions in the United States since World War II. The first and most visible of these was the substantive revolution in judicial policy. As we saw earlier in this chapter and in Chapter 5, in policy areas, including school desegregation, legislative apportionment, and criminal procedure, as well as obscenity, abortion, and voting rights, the Supreme Court was at the forefront of a series of sweeping changes in the role of the U.S. government, and ultimately, in the character of American society.[31]

Outside the Los Angeles federal courthouse, women suffering the effects of defective silicone breast implants protested Dow Chemical's failure to pay the settlement of a class action suit. Federal courts have been the site of numerous class action suits in recent decades.

But at the same time that the courts were introducing important policy innovations, they were also bringing about a second, less visible revolution. During the 1960s and 1970s, the Supreme Court and other federal courts instituted a series of changes in judicial procedures that fundamentally expanded the power of the courts in the United States. First, the federal courts liberalized the concept of standing to permit almost any group that seeks to challenge the actions of an administrative agency to bring its case before the federal bench. In 1971, for example, the Supreme Court ruled that public interest groups could use the National Environmental Policy Act to challenge the actions of federal agencies by claiming that the agencies' activities might have adverse environmental consequences.[32]

Congress helped to make it even easier for groups dissatisfied with government policies to bring their cases to the courts by adopting Section 1,983 of the U.S. Code, which permits the practice of "fee shifting." Section 1,983 allows citizens who successfully bring a suit against a public official for violating their constitutional rights to collect their attorneys' fees and costs from the government. Thus, Section 1,983 encourages individuals and groups to bring their problems to the courts rather than to Congress or the executive branch. These changes have given the courts a far greater role in the administrative process than ever before. Many federal judges are concerned that federal legislation in areas such as health care reform would create new rights and entitlements that would give rise to a deluge of court cases. "Any time you create a new right, you create a host of disputes and claims," warned Barbara Rothstein, chief judge of the federal district court in Seattle, Washington.[33]

Second, the federal courts broadened the scope of relief to permit themselves to act on behalf of broad categories or classes of persons in "class action" cases, rather than just on behalf of individuals.[34] A **class action suit** is a procedural device that permits large numbers of persons with common interests to join together under a representative party to bring or defend a lawsuit. One example of a class action suit is the case of *In re Agent Orange Product Liability Litigation,* in which a federal judge in New York certified Vietnam War veterans as a class with standing to sue a manufacturer of herbicides for damages allegedly incurred from exposure to the defendant's product while in Vietnam.[35] The class potentially numbered in the tens of thousands.

Federal Judge W. Arthur Garrity implemented the desegregation of the Boston public school system through a series of controversial court decisions.

Third, the federal courts began to employ so-called structural remedies, in effect retaining jurisdiction of cases until the court's mandate had actually been implemented to its satisfaction.[36] The best-known of these instances was Federal Judge W. Arthur Garrity's effort to operate the Boston school system from his bench in order to ensure its desegregation. Between 1974 and 1985, Judge Garrity issued fourteen decisions relating to different aspects of the Boston school desegregation plan that had been developed under his authority and put into effect under his supervision.[37] In another recent case, Federal Judge Leonard B. Sand imposed fines that would have forced the city of Yonkers, New York, into bankruptcy if it had refused to accept his plan to build public housing in white neighborhoods. After several days of fines, the city gave in to the judge's ruling.

Through these three judicial mechanisms, the federal courts paved the way for an unprecedented expansion of national judicial power. In essence, liberalization of the rules of standing and expansion of the scope of judicial relief drew the federal courts into linkages with important social interests and classes, while the introduction of structural remedies enhanced the courts' ability to serve these constituencies. Thus, during the 1960s and 1970s, the power of the federal courts expanded in the same way the power of the executive expanded during the 1930s—through links with constituencies, such as civil rights, consumer, environmental, and feminist groups, that staunchly defended the Supreme Court in its battles with Congress, the executive, or other interest groups.

The Reagan and Bush administrations sought to end the relationship between the Court and liberal political forces. As we saw earlier, the conservative judges appointed by these Republican presidents modified the Court's position in areas such as abortion, affirmative action, and judicial procedure, though not as completely as some conservatives had hoped. Interestingly, however, the current Court has not been eager to surrender the expanded powers carved out by earlier, liberal Courts. In a number of decisions during the 1980s and 1990s, the Court was willing to make use of its expanded powers on behalf of interests it favored.[38]

In the important 1992 case of *Lujan v. Defenders of Wildlife,* the Court seemed to retreat to a conception of standing more restrictive than that affirmed by liberal activist jurists.[39] Rather than representing an example of judicial restraint, however, the *Lujan* case was actually a direct judicial challenge to congressional power. The case involved an effort by an environmental group, the Defenders of Wildlife, to make use of the 1973 Endangered Species Act to block the expenditure of federal funds being used by the governments of Egypt and Sri Lanka for public works projects. Environmentalists charged that the projects threatened the habitats of several endangered species of birds and, therefore, that the expenditure of federal funds to support the projects violated the 1973 act. The Interior Department claimed that the act affected only domestic projects.[40]

The Endangered Species Act, like a number of other pieces of liberal environmental and consumer legislation enacted by Congress, encourages citizen suits—suits by activist groups not directly harmed by the action in question—to challenge government policies they deem to be inconsistent with the act. Justice Scalia, however, writing for the Court's majority in the *Lujan* decision, reasserted a more traditional conception of standing, requiring those bringing suit against a government policy to show that the policy is likely to cause *them* direct and imminent injury.

Had Scalia stopped at this point, the case might have been seen as an example of judicial restraint. But Scalia went on to question the validity of any statutory provision for citizen suits. Such legislative provisions, according to Justice Scalia, violate Article III of the Constitution, which limits the federal courts to consideration of actual "cases and controversies." This interpretation would strip Congress of its capacity to promote the enforcement of regulatory statutes by encouraging activist groups not directly affected or injured to be on the lookout for violations that could provide the basis for lawsuits. This enforcement mechanism—which conservatives liken to bounty hunting—was an extremely important congressional instrument and played a prominent part in the enforcement of such pieces of legislation as the 1990 Americans with Disabilities Act. Thus, the *Lujan* case offers an example of judicial activism rather than of judicial restraint; even the most conservative justices are reluctant to surrender the powers now wielded by the Court.

The Judiciary: Liberty and Democracy

In the original conception of the framers, the judiciary was to be the institution that would protect individual liberty from the government. As we saw in Chapter 3, the framers believed that in a democracy the great danger was what they termed "tyranny of the majority"—the possibility that a popular majority, "united or actuated by some common impulse or passion," would "trample on the rules of justice."[41] The framers hoped that the courts would protect liberty from the potential excesses of democracy. And for most of American history, this was precisely the role played by the federal courts. The courts' most important decisions were those that protected the freedoms—to speak, worship, publish, vote, and attend school—of groups and individuals whose political views, religious beliefs, or racial or ethnic background made them unpopular.

In recent years, however, the courts have been changing their role in the political process. Rather than serve simply as a bastion of individual liberty against the excessive power of the majority, the judiciary has tried to play an active role in helping groups and forces in American society bring about social and political change in the fight for equality. In a sense, the judiciary has entered the political process and has begun to behave more like the democratic institutions whose sometimes misdirected impulses toward tyranny the courts were supposed to keep in check. This change poses a basic dilemma for students of American government. If the courts have become simply one more part of the democratic political process, then who is left to protect the liberty of individuals?

 Summary

Millions of cases come to trial every year in the United States. The great majority—nearly 99 percent—are tried in state and local courts. The types of law are common law, civil law, criminal law, and public law.

Three kinds of cases fall under federal jurisdiction: (1) civil cases involving citizens from different states, (2) civil cases where a federal agency is seeking to enforce federal laws that provide for civil penalties, and (3) cases involving federal criminal statutes or where state criminal cases have been made issues of public law. Judicial power extends only to cases and controversies. Litigants must have standing to sue, and courts neither hand down opinions on hypothetical issues nor take the initiative.

The organization of the federal judiciary provides for original jurisdiction in the federal district courts, the U.S. Court of Claims, the U.S. Tax Court, the Customs Court, and federal regulatory agencies.

Each district court is in one of the twelve appellate districts, called circuits, presided over by a court of appeals. Appellate courts admit no new evidence; their rulings are based solely on the records of the court proceedings or agency hearings that led to the original decision. Appeals court rulings are final unless the Supreme Court chooses to review them. The Supreme Court has some original jurisdiction, but its major job is to review lower court decisions involving substantial issues of public law.

Federal judges are appointed by the president subject to confirmation by the Senate. Presidents generally attempt to select judges whose political philosophy is similar to their own. Over time, presidents have been able to exert a great deal of influence over the federal courts through their appointments.

There is no explicit constitutional authority for the Supreme Court to review acts of Congress. Nonetheless, the 1803 case of *Marbury v. Madison* established the Court's right to review congressional acts. The supremacy clause of Article VI and the Judiciary Act of 1789 give the Court the power to review state constitutions and laws.

Both appellate and Supreme Court decisions, including the decision not to review a case, make law. The impact of such law usually favors the status quo. Yet, many revolutionary changes in the law have come about through appellate court and Supreme Court rulings—in the criminal process, in apportionment, and in civil rights. Judge-made law is like a statute in that it articulates the law as it relates to future controversies. It differs from a statute in that it is intended to guide judges rather than the citizenry in general.

Most cases reach the Supreme Court through a writ of *certiorari* or a writ of *habeas corpus*. Once the Court has accepted a case, attorneys for both sides prepare briefs and seek *amicus curiae* briefs from sympathetic groups. Cases are presented to the Court in oral argument, are discussed by the justices during the Court's conference, and are decided by a majority vote of the justices. The Court's opinion is written by a member of the majority. Members of the minority may write dissenting opinions, while other members of the majority may write concurring opinions.

The influence of the individual member of the Supreme Court is limited. Writing the majority opinion for a case is an opportunity for a justice to influence the judiciary. But the need to frame an opinion in such a way as to develop majority support on the Court may limit such opportunities. Dissenting opinions can have more impact than the majority opinion; they stimulate a continued flow of cases around that issue. The solicitor general is the most important single influence outside the Court itself because he or she controls the flow of cases brought by the Justice Department and also shapes the argument in those cases. But the flow of cases is a force in itself, which the Department of Justice cannot entirely control. Social problems give rise to similar cases that ultimately must be adjudicated and appealed. Some interest groups try to develop such case patterns as a means of gaining power through the courts.

In recent years, the importance of the federal judiciary—the Supreme Court in particular—has increased substantially as the courts have developed new tools of judicial power and forged alliances with important forces in American society.

FOR FURTHER READING

Abraham, Henry. *The Judicial Process*. 6th ed. New York: Oxford University Press, 1993.

Bryner, Gary, and Dennis L. Thompson. *The Constitution and the Regulation of Society*. Provo, UT: Brigham Young University, 1988.

Davis, Sue. *Justice Rehnquist and the Constitution*. Princeton: Princeton University Press, 1989.

Graber, Mark A. *Transforming Free Speech: The Ambiguous Legacy of Civil Libertarianism*. Berkeley: University of California Press, 1991.

Kahn, Ronald. *The Supreme Court and Constitutional Theory, 1953–1993*. Lawrence: University Press of Kansas, 1994.

McCann, Michael W. *Rights at Work*. Chicago: University of Chicago Press, 1994.

Mezey, Susan G. *No Longer Disabled: The Federal Courts and the Politics of Social Security Disability*. New York: Greenwood, 1988.

O'Brien, David M. *Storm Center: The Supreme Court in American Politics*. 4th ed. New York: Norton, 1996.

Rosenberg, Gerald. *The Hollow Hope: Can Courts Bring about Social Change?* Chicago: University of Chicago Press, 1991.

Rubin, Eva. *Abortion, Politics and the Courts*. Westport, CT: Greenwood Press, 1982.

Silverstein, Mark. *Judicious Choices: The New Politics of Supreme Court Confirmations*. New York: Norton, 1994.

STUDY OUTLINE

THE LEGAL SYSTEM

1. Court cases in the United States proceed under three categories of law: criminal, civil, and public.
2. In the area of criminal law, either a state government or the federal government is the plaintiff who alleges that someone has committed a crime.
3. Civil cases are those between individuals or between individuals and the government in which no criminal violation is charged. In deciding these cases, courts apply statutes and legal precedent.
4. Public law involves questions of whether the government has the constitutional or statutory authority to take action.
5. By far, most cases are heard by state courts.
6. Cases are heard in federal courts if the U.S. government is a party in the case or the case involves federal statutes, treaties with other nations, or the U.S. Constitution.
7. Although the federal courts hear only a fraction of all the cases decided every year in the United States, federal court decisions are extremely important.

Federal Jurisdiction

1. The eighty-nine federal district courts are trial courts of original jurisdiction and their cases are, in form, indistinguishable from cases in the state trial courts.
2. The twelve U.S. courts of appeals review and render decisions in approximately 10 percent of all lower-court and agency cases.
3. Federal judges are appointed by the president and confirmed by a majority vote of the full Senate.
4. The Supreme Court is the highest court in the country and has the power and the obligation to review any lower court decision involving a substantial issue of public law, state legislation, or act of Congress.
5. The Constitution does not specify the number of justices that should sit on the Supreme Court, although since 1869 there have been nine—one chief justice and eight associate justices.
6. The solicitor general can influence the Court by screening cases before they reach the Supreme Court, submitting *amicus* briefs, and shaping the arguments used before the Court.

The Power of the Supreme Court: Judicial Review

1. The Supreme Court's power to review acts of Congress, although accepted as natural and rarely challenged, is not specifically granted by the Constitution.
2. The Supreme Court's power to review state action or legislation derives from the Constitution's supremacy clause, although it is neither granted specifically by the Constitution nor inherent in the federal system.
3. Appeals of lower court decisions can reach the Supreme Court in one of two ways: through a writ of *certiorari,* or, in the case of convicted state prisoners, through a writ of *habeas corpus.*
4. Over the years, courts have developed specific rules that govern which cases within their jurisdiction they hear. These rules of access can be broken down into three categories: case or controversy, standing, and mootness.
5. Groups and forces in society attempt to influence justices' rulings on particular issues.
6. After filing written arguments, or briefs, attorneys present oral argument to the Supreme Court. After oral argument, the justices discuss the case and vote on a final decision.
7. The Supreme Court always explains its decisions in terms of law and precedent.
8. Despite the rule of precedent, the Court often reshapes law. Such changes in the interpretation of law can be explained, in part, by changes in the judicial philosophy of activism versus restraint and by changes in political ideology.

Judicial Power and Politics

1. For much of American history, the power of the federal courts was subject to five limitations: standing, the limited relief courts could provide, the lack of enforcement powers, political appointment, and the power of Congress to change the size and jurisdiction of federal courts.
2. The role of the federal judiciary has been strengthened since World War II by two judicial revolutions. The first revolution was a substantive revolution in several policy areas. The second revolution involved changes in judicial procedures that lessened traditional limitations on the courts.

Practice Quiz

1. Which of the following is a brief submitted to the Supreme Court by someone other than one of the parties in the case?
   a. *amicus curiae*
   b. *habeas corpus*
   c. solicitor general
   d. *ex post* brief
2. By what term is the practice of the courts to uphold precedent known?
   a. *certiorari*
   b. *stare decisis*
   c. rule of four
   d. senatorial courtesy
3. Which government official is responsible for arguing the federal government's position in cases before the Supreme Court?
   a. the vice president
   b. the attorney general
   c. the U.S. district attorney
   d. the solicitor general

4. Which of the following helps to explain the expanded power of the judiciary since World War II?
   a. changes in judicial procedure
   b. changes in judicial policy areas
   c. Neither a nor b is correct.
   d. Both a and b are correct.

5. What is the name for the body of law that involves disputes between private parties?
   a. civil law
   b. privacy law
   c. household law
   d. common law

6. Under what authority is the number of Supreme Court justices decided?
   a. the president
   b. the chief justice
   c. Congress
   d. the Constitution

7. Which of the following does not influence the flow of cases heard by the Supreme Court?
   a. the Supreme Court itself
   b. the solicitor general
   c. the attorney general
   d. the FBI

8. Which of the following cases involved the "right to privacy?"
   a. *Griswold v. Connecticut*
   b. *Brown v. Board of Education*
   c. *Schneckloth v. Bustamante*
   d. *Marbury v. Madison*

9. Which of the following Supreme Court cases from the 1960s involved the rights of criminal suspects?
   a. *Gideon v. Wainwright*
   b. *Miranda v. Arizona*
   c. *Escobedo v. Illinois*
   d. all of the above

10. Where do most trials in America take place?
   a. state and local courts
   b. appellate courts
   c. federal courts
   d. the Supreme Court

CRITICAL THINKING QUESTIONS

1. Judicial philosophies of activism and restraint are often confused with the political ideologies of liberalism and conservatism in the courts. What do you think the roots of this confusion are? To what extent is the common understanding correct? To what extent is it incorrect? Are there ways in which conservatives have been or could be activists in the courts? Are there ways in which liberals have exercised or could exercise judicial restraint?

2. In many ways, courts are expected to be apolitical institutions of government. In what ways are courts, judges, and justices shielded from politics and political pressure? In what ways are they vulnerable to political pressure? Are the courts an appropriate place for politics? What is the danger of having too much or too little political accountability in judicial decision making?

KEY TERMS

amicus curiae literally, "friend of the court"; individuals or groups who are not parties to a lawsuit but who seek to assist the Supreme Court in reaching a decision by presenting additional briefs. (p. 543)

appellate court a court that hears the appeals of trial court decisions. (p. 536)

briefs written documents in which attorneys explain, using case precedents, why the court should find in favor of their client. (p. 556)

chief justice justice on the Supreme Court who presides over the Court's public sessions. (p. 539)

civil law a system of jurisprudence, including private law and governmental actions, to settle disputes that do not involve criminal penalties. (p. 535)

class action suit a legal action by which a group or class of individuals with common interests can file a suit on behalf of everyone who shares that interest. (p. 564)

criminal law the branch of law that deals with disputes

or actions involving criminal penalties (as opposed to civil law); it regulates the conduct of individuals, defines crimes, and provides punishment for criminal acts. (p. 534)

defendant the one against whom a complaint is brought in a criminal or civil case. (p. 535)

dissenting opinion a decision written by a justice in the minority in a particular case in which the justice wishes to express his or her reasoning in the case. (p. 559)

due process of law the right of every citizen against arbitrary action by national or state governments. (p. 537)

judicial activism judicial philosophy that posits that the Court should go beyond the words of the Constitution or a statute to consider the broader societal implications of its decisions. (p. 560)

judicial restraint judicial philosophy whose adherents refuse to go beyond the clear words of the Constitution in interpreting its meaning. (p. 560)

judicial review the power of the courts to declare actions of the legislative and executive branches invalid or unconstitutional. The Supreme Court asserted this power in *Marbury v. Madison.* (p. 546)

jurisdiction the sphere of a court's power and authority. (p. 537)

***Miranda* rule** the requirement, articulated by the Supreme Court in *Miranda v. Arizona,* that persons under arrest must be informed prior to police interrogation of their rights to remain silent and to have the benefit of legal counsel. (p. 550)

mootness a criterion used by courts to screen cases that no longer require resolution. (p. 551)

opinion the written explanation of the Supreme Court's decision in a particular case. (p. 557)

oral argument stage in Supreme Court procedure in which attorneys for both sides appear before the Court to present their positions and answer questions posed by justices. (p. 557)

original jurisdiction the authority to initially consider a case. Distinguished from *appellate jurisdiction*, which is the authority to hear appeals from a lower court's decision. (p. 538)

per curiam decision by an appellate court, without a written opinion, that refuses to review the decision of a lower court; amounts to a reaffirmation of the lower court's opinion. (p. 542)

plaintiff the individual or organization who brings a complaint in court. (p. 535)

plea bargains negotiated agreements in criminal cases in which a defendant agrees to plead guilty in return for the state's agreement to reduce the severity of the criminal charge the defendant is facing. (p. 537)

precedents prior cases whose principles are used by judges as the bases for their decisions in present cases. (p. 535)

public law cases in private law, civil law, or criminal law in which one party to the dispute argues that a license is unfair, a law is inequitable or unconstitutional, or an agency has acted unfairly, violated a procedure, or gone beyond its jurisdiction. (p. 535)

senatorial courtesy the practice whereby the president, before formally nominating a person for a federal judgeship, seeks the indication that senators from the candidate's own state support the nomination. (p. 540)

solicitor general the top government lawyer in all cases before the Supreme Court where the government is a party. (p. 542)

standing the right of an individual or organization to initiate a court case. (p. 550)

stare decisis literally, "let the decision stand." The doctrine that a previous decision by a court applies as a precedent in similar cases until that decision is overruled. (p. 535)

supremacy clause Article VI of the Constitution, which states that laws passed by the national government and all treaties are the supreme law of the land and superior to all laws adopted by any state or any subdivision. (p. 547)

supreme court the highest court in a particular state or in the United States. This court primarily serves an appellate function. (p. 536)

trial court the first court to hear a criminal or civil case. (p. 536)

Uniform Commercial Code code used in many states in the area of contract law to reduce interstate differences in judicial decisions. (p. 537)

writ of *certiorari* a decision of at least four of the nine Supreme Court justices to review a decision of a lower court; from the Latin "to make more certain." (p. 552)

writ of *habeas corpus* a court order that the individual in custody be brought into court and shown the cause for detention. *Habeas corpus* is guaranteed by the Constitution and can be suspended only in cases of rebellion or invasion. (p. 553)

15

State and Local Governments

★ The Changing Role of State Governments

In what ways have the states been laboratories of democracy?

How effective are state governments in serving a broad public interest?

What new public policy roles have the states assumed?

What are the negative consequences of the changing role of state governments?

★ Local Government and American Democracy

In what ways are local governments creatures of state government? How have different forms of local government sought to gain autonomy and independence?

What are the two basic types of city government? What are the implications of each for representation and democracy?

How did the differences in size and resources among local governments develop? What are the implications of these differences for democracy?

What are the problems of big cities in the federal system? How has the relationship between the cities and the national government changed over time? What strategies have been proposed to revive American cities?

IN 1995, ten thousand students in New York State took to the streets to protest Governor George Pataki's proposal to cut funding for and to raise tuition at New York's two university systems, the State University of New York (SUNY) and the City University of New York (CUNY). The governor argued that the state could no longer afford to subsidize the education of its young people at the rate it once did; moreover, he wanted to ease the tax burden on New York State residents. Critics of Pataki's plan charged that, compared to other states, New York was not doing very much to support its university system or to subsidize its students. They pointed to other state university systems where students paid less and the state subsidized more. For example, in 1995, students at the University of Maryland at College Park paid $2,270 per year in tuition; the state added a $9,298 subsidy. Under Pataki's plan, a $3,500 annual tuition payment for students attending a SUNY college would be subsidized by $4,318 from the state.[1] Such differences in the cost of public university education are an inherent part of public higher education in the United States because it is up to the states to create and finance public universities.

States are responsible for many such decisions about spending and taxing that affect the lives of and opportunities open to the residents of each state. Localities, too, make decisions that determine the quality and scope of public services. For most of the twentieth century, New York City offered its residents public welfare benefits that had no equal in the nation. These benefits included public hospitals, libraries, and free university education. Other cities, especially those in the Sun Belt, opted to keep their tax rates low and to offer far less in the way of public services.

These differences highlight a central feature of the way American democracy operates. States and localities can—and do—make very different decisions about the amount of taxes individuals and businesses should pay and what kinds of public services the government should provide in return. The ability of states and localities to make such decisions about taxing and spending and to operate their own programs is key to a meaningful **federalism.** But the same differences also raise important questions about the ideals of democracy and equality.

Because state and local governments have such important responsibilities in the American political system, the quality of American democracy as a whole depends on how democracy is practiced at the lower levels of government. If the policy choices made in states and localities are to be perceived as having **legitimacy,** the political process through which such choices are made must ensure that all voices are heard. Thus, to understand how American democracy really works, we must know how representative the country's state and local political systems are. Do all citizens have equal access to state and local politics? How do different political institutions in states and localities affect which voices ring loudest in state politics?

The different decisions that states and localities make also present substantial challenges to the ideal of equality. What kinds of inequalities should be tolerated as legitimate choices made through local democratic processes? Which inequalities do Americans, as a nation, find unacceptable? Over the course of American history, this question has been answered in different ways. For example, for over a century after the Civil War, the decision to legalize or forbid racial segregation was left to the states. After the 1960s, however, as Americans decided that this arrangement was not consistent with their national ideals, the national government intervened to prevent states from enacting discriminatory laws. Thus, changing national assessments of the kind and degree of inequality that the nation will tolerate are a key factor in limiting or expanding the scope of state and local decision making.

This chapter examines the vitality of democracy in states and localities, showing how changing views about equality have promoted important changes in state and local governments. The first section of the chapter traces the evolution of state governments, showing why they were viewed as unrepresentative and incapable only fifty years ago and how they have reclaimed a more central role today. The second section examines local government. It pays particular attention to the special role that cities have played in the development of American democracy and explores why U.S. cities have become so troubled in recent years.

The Changing Role of State Governments

- In what ways have the states been laboratories of democracy?
- How effective are state governments in serving a broad public interest?
- What new public policy roles have the states assumed?
- What are the negative consequences of the changing role of state governments?

For a century and a half after the Founding, the energy and initiative in American politics and policy lay with the states. In the 1930s, however, as we saw in Chapter 4, much of the action shifted to the federal level when Franklin Roosevelt's New Deal staked out new areas of concern for the federal government in social policy and economic regulation. By the 1960s, when President Lyndon Johnson launched the Great Society, many Americans viewed the states as political backwaters with unfair political systems and corrupt governments.

But the growth of national policies ultimately made state governments stronger, not weaker. The important role that states played in administering many federal programs strengthened state administrative capacities. With the political reforms of the 1960s and 1970s and the successes of the 1960s Civil Rights movement in ending the political exclusion of African Americans in the South, state government was poised for a comeback. Since the 1970s, federal policy has devolved more power to the states in three different stages of "New Federalism" (see Chapter 4). The decline in public confidence in the federal government since the 1970s has persuaded many citizens that the states should be given more leeway to solve problems in their own ways.

Laboratories of Democracy?

In 1932, Supreme Court justice Louis Brandeis praised the states as **laboratories of democracy.**[2] By this he meant that states could experiment with many different policies as they searched for the best ways to meet the needs of their citizens. At the close of the Progressive Era, when Brandeis used that phrase, states had indeed been experimenting with policies as a wave of reform movements swept across the country. Reformers hoped above all to make politics less corrupt; many state legislators and governors were "in the pockets" of big money interests. For example, during the early years of the twentieth century, the Southern Pacific Railroad controlled California state politics.

Women played a particularly important role in these state-level reforms. In every state, women's organizations became active in politics, pushing for social reforms that would rid state and local government of corruption. Although women did not yet have the vote in many states, they saw themselves as a voice for morality in the political sphere. They sought to implement policies that paid special attention to the needs of women and children. Among the reforms they initiated in many states were child labor laws, educational reform, maternal and child health programs, and "mothers' pensions" (a forerunner of programs such as Aid to Families with Dependent Children—what we typically call "welfare.")[3]

Despite two decades of innovation, however, the states were not able to maintain the momentum of reform. When the Great Depression hit in 1929, states turned to the federal government for help. President Roosevelt's New Deal launched a burst of government activity in which Washington quickly overshadowed the states. But it was not only federal activism that pushed states to the sidelines after the 1930s, it was also the failure of states to provide equal representation for their citizens and to operate effective governments. By the 1950s and 1960s, the problems with state government had become so glaring that some critics contended that the era of the states was over.[4]

Protected by new federal laws, black Americans living in southern states began to vote in large numbers during the 1960s.

Who Is Represented in State Politics?

The biggest argument against the states before the 1960s was that the southern states were not full democracies. They denied African American citizens the most fundamental civil and political rights. Since the turn of the century and the establishment of Jim Crow legislation, black citizens had been segregated, prevented from voting, and effectively barred from other forms of political participation. In many states in the Southwest, Mexican Americans faced similar barriers. In some states, such as Texas, many Mexican Americans were segregated into separate schools and made to use separate public facilities. They were also prevented from voting.[5] In many of these states, poor whites did not participate in politics either. Although they were not formally barred from participating, the poor were rarely mobilized to participate in politics. Rates of participation by minorities and the poor in many southern elections were extremely low (see Chapter 9).

As the Civil Rights movement gained ground in the 1950s and 1960s, these state practices were caught in the national spotlight. Southern governors, such as Orval Faubus in Arkansas and George Wallace in Alabama, became famous across the country for defying federal court orders to integrate their public schools and universities. In 1963, when George Wallace gave his inaugural address as governor of Alabama, he declared, "I say segregation now, segregation tomorrow, segregation forever."[6] Southern politicians defended segregation and the political exclusion of black citizens by claiming states' rights.

Legalized racial exclusion and very low rates of voter participation occurred primarily in southern states, but states across the nation shared another political problem: State legislatures did not provide equal representation to all citizens. In the House of Representatives, seats are reallocated, or reapportioned, every ten years to reflect population changes; legislative districts are redrawn, or **redistricted**, as a result. Most states, however, were not changing their own district lines as their populations shifted. In 1960, for example, a number of states had not reapportioned their legislatures for fifty years. As a result, the size of the population in each district could vary dramatically. Before reform in Tennessee, for example, the district with the smallest population contained only 2,340 people, whereas the district with the largest population held 42,298.[7] Yet each district could only elect one representative to the state legislature. The result was that rural interests were greatly overrepresented in many state legislatures. Cities, which had grown tremendously in the first half of the twentieth century, did not get their fair share of representation.[8]

In the 1960s, states finally began to provide equal representation for all citizens. The Civil Rights movement changed the southern states forever. With the passage of the 1964 Civil Rights Act and the 1965 Voting Rights Act, African Americans in the South became full citizens. Segregated public facilities were outlawed and black citizens in the South were allowed to vote. Voting began to increase almost immediately. In Mississippi, where only 6.7 percent of the black population had been registered to vote in 1964, 59.8 percent of the black population had registered by 1967.[9]

The Civil Rights movement also inspired a similar drive for civil and political rights among Mexican Americans. Political movements in the 1960s and 1970s successfully asserted the political rights of Mexican Americans and challenged policies of segregation. The extension of the provisions of the Voting Rights Act to Mexican Americans in the Southwest in 1975 furthered their quest for political inclusion.[10]

In addition to these movements for political inclusion, two Supreme Court cases in the 1960s transformed representation in state legislatures across the country. In 1962, the Court ruled in *Baker v. Carr* that the federal courts had jurisdiction over the ways in which states drew their legislative districts. Two years later, in *Reynolds v. Sims*, the Court ruled in favor of "one person, one vote," which meant that the states would have to reapportion their legislatures so that every district held the same number of people."[11]

This "reapportionment revolution" spurred important changes in state politics. As states redrew legislative districts and held elections in the 1960s and 1970s, rural representation declined and legislators from cities and suburbs took their place. These changes meant that a small group of rural interests could no longer dominate politics in most states. As a result, states became more attentive to the problems of metropolitan areas than they had been when rural interests held sway.

The democratization of state politics changed the profile of state legislators, as Figure 15.1 indicates. In 1980, there were 310 black legislators in state governments; by 1995 the number of black legislators had grown to 555.[12] Even by 1995, however, only one African American had been elected governor: Douglas Wilder of Virginia. Latino representation in state politics also increased. In 1985, there were 101 state legislators of Latino background; by 1995, the number had grown to 176.[13]

The number of women in state legislatures and in other state political offices also increased greatly from the 1960s to the present. In 1995, 20.7 percent of state legislators were women, a five-fold increase since 1969. Women also held 26 percent of statewide elective offices in 1995, up from 10 percent in 1975. Ella Grasso of Connecticut became the first woman elected as governor in her own right in 1974. Still, by 1995, only 13 women had ever served as state governors.[14]

As women and minorities won increasing numbers of seats in state legislatures, they have mobilized to make their presence felt. Black and Latino

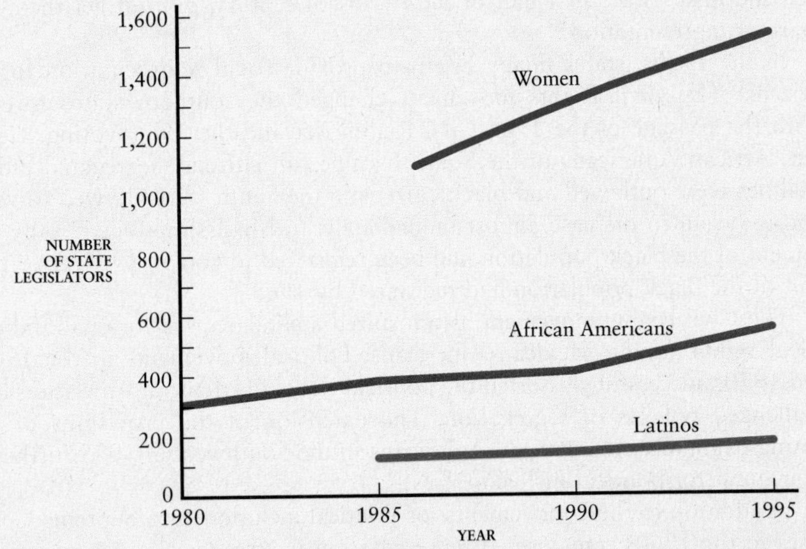

*Data for Latino legislators unavailable prior to 1985.

SOURCES: U.S. Bureau of the Census, *Statistical Abstract of the United States: 1995* (Washington, DC: Government Printing Office, 1995), pp. 285, 287; Harold W. Stanley and Richard G. Niemi, *Vital Statistics on American Politics*, 5th ed. (Washington, DC: Congressional Quarterly Press, 1995), pp. 372–73; Sara E. Rix, ed., *The American Woman, 1987–88: A Report in Depth* (New York: Norton, 1987), p. 313; Rix, ed., *The American Woman, 1990–91: A Status Report* (New York: Norton, 1990), p. 387; Cynthia Costello and Anne J. Stone, eds., *The American Woman 1994–95: Women and Health* (New York: Norton, 1994), p. 350; and Cynthia Costello and Barbara Kivimae Krimgold, eds., *The American Woman: 1996–97: Women and Work* (New York: Norton, 1996), p. 338.

FIGURE 15.1

caucuses are active in state legislatures, as are women's caucuses. The purpose of these caucuses is to provide a forum for discussing and advocating on behalf of the specific interests that women and minorities have on policies such as social programs and affirmative action.

Thus, over the past thirty years or so, state governments have come a long way. Systems of representation are now fairer, and groups that once had little voice in state politics have made important gains in representation.

How Effective Is State Government?

Unfair systems of political representation were not the only problems to be found in the states. In the past, most state governments were also poorly equipped to design and administer policy. Many of the basic institutions of state politics allowed a few powerful interests to dominate politics. As a result, state governments often served narrow private interests instead of the broader public interest.

In order for the states to serve the public most effectively, many state con-

State legislatures, such as the Texas House of Representatives (pictured here), have seen a large increase in the number of women elected to office.

stitutions needed to be reformed to provide a framework for modern government. The national Constitution is a brief statement of principles that has served well for over two hundred years, but the state constitutions were very different. They tended to be long, complicated documents written in obscure language that often served to protect special interests. For example, until 1974 the Louisiana Constitution contained some 236,000 words, almost half the length of *Gone with the Wind*.[15] Since the 1970s, many states have reformed their constitutions, making them shorter and clearer—more like the national Constitution.

State legislatures and executive branches were also too weak to serve as guardians of the public interest. State legislatures were notorious for their unprofessional conduct. The legislatures met infrequently and, when they did meet, critics charged that they cared more about private interests than the public interest. The former governor of North Carolina, Terry Sanford, charged that many state legislatures were in the pockets of important business interests: "In Montana, Anaconda Copper [a mining company] exercised disproportionate influence; in Illinois and Florida, the race tracks; in Wyoming, the cattlemen's association; in Louisiana, the oil companies; and in Connecticut, the drug industry and the insurance companies."[16]

Governor Jimmy Davis of Louisiana.

Governors had few powers and were ill prepared to take the lead as policy makers. Many governors were insiders in narrow political cliques or colorful figures who had little experience in governing. For example, Louisiana twice elected Jimmy Davis as governor (in 1944 and again in 1960). Known as a "hillbilly singer," Davis rode a horse up the steps of the capitol building when he was inaugurated; four years later he sang his farewell address to the legislature. Even those governors who were better prepared to take office lacked the powers necessary to govern effectively. Many governors could not control the executive agencies of state government. The heads of many state administrative agencies were elected, not appointed by the governor. As a result, they had little loyalty to the governor, who was just one executive among many.[17] These arrangements made it difficult to have any accountability in state government.

Reforms in state legislatures and executive branches have greatly strengthened the policy-making capacities of states in recent years. Legislatures in all but seven states now meet every year. Many states still limit the number of days per year that the legislature may be in session, but these limits are routinely overcome by calling special sessions. State legislators have higher salaries than in the past, as well as more money to hire staff. These changes have allowed the state legislatures to function more effectively as policy-making bodies. These reforms have also encouraged a broader range of citizens to run for the legislature. Thirty years ago, the typical state legislator was a lawyer or real estate agent who treated his or her legislative seat as a part-time job. But with higher salaries and greater staff support, representatives are now drawn from many other backgrounds (although lawyer continues to be the most common occupation). Increasingly, these legislators view politics as a career. These changes have combined to create what political scientists call a "professional legislature."[18]

Governors, too, are now more equipped to be effective policymakers. Political scientists rank the strength of governors along several dimensions: strong governors can remain in office for several terms; they have the power to appoint many state officials; they have authority over the state budget; and they have the power to veto laws or parts of laws that the legislature sends them. Among the states in which governors have strong institutional powers are Hawaii, Iowa, Maryland, New York, New Jersey, Ohio, Pennsylvania, Tennessee, and West Virginia. States in which governors have the weakest institutional powers include North Carolina, South Carolina, and Vermont.[19]

Governor Tommy Thompson signed groundbreaking legislation changing the welfare system in Wisconsin in 1996. Thompson had been one of the leaders among governors calling for more state control over the welfare system.

One important power that forty-three state governors have is the **line-item veto**, which allows the governor to strike out parts of bills that the legislature passes. In this way, the governor exercises significant power over the legislature and can play a strong role in determining the final shape of legislation. Wisconsin has an unusually strong version of the line-item veto. In 1987, when Republican governor Tommy Thompson disagreed with the Democratic state legislature about the level of welfare benefits in an appropriations bill that had been passed, he vetoed two digits and a decimal point from the benefit formula, effectively reducing benefits by 6 percent![20]

Reforms in state administrative agencies reinforce many governors' new powers and make states more accountable. The old patronage system, in which governors and legislators appointed administrative personnel, is less important because increasing numbers of employees are now covered by civil service systems (discussed in Chapter 13). By 1980, 75 percent of all full-time state employees were covered by some sort of merit system.[21] In addition, states reorganized their executive branches to reduce the number of agencies and to promote accountability.

All of these reforms have made state governments far more responsive and effective than they were in the past. Yet there remains room for improvement. Many governors are still weaker than their legislatures and remain unable to control the state administrative agencies. Moreover, as we shall see below, the reforms of the last thirty years have generated new problems that raise questions about the representativeness and effectiveness of state government.

What Do States Do?

As states opened up their systems of representation and strengthened their political institutions, they also began to do more for their citizens. The traditional areas of policy that states oversee are education, transportation, health care, and welfare. But even though the states controlled these policies, until recently, local governments (counties and cities) footed much of the bill. Over the past two decades, however, states have begun to shoulder a greater share of the financing for many programs. They have also taken on a greater range of activities.

Figure 15.2 shows how the average state budget was allocated in 1994. Education has traditionally been and remains the biggest expenditure in the states, although its share of state budgets has shrunk. Some areas of policy have grown larger and more expensive over time. Two policy areas that have experienced very fast growth in recent years are corrections (i.e., prisons and parole), and health care. Annual state expenditures for corrections mushroomed from $4.4 billion in 1980 to more than $20 billion in 1992 as rates of incarceration soared.[22] Rising health care costs made Medicaid, the federal state program that serves the poor and many elderly people, the fastest-growing part of state budgets in the 1980s and 1990s. State budgets also reflect the new activities that states have taken on. Areas in which states are now much more active than in the past include economic development and environmental regulation.[23]

In order to manage these new responsibilities, many states have had to overhaul their revenue systems, expanding existing tax sources and imposing new taxes. The primary sources of state tax revenue today are general sales

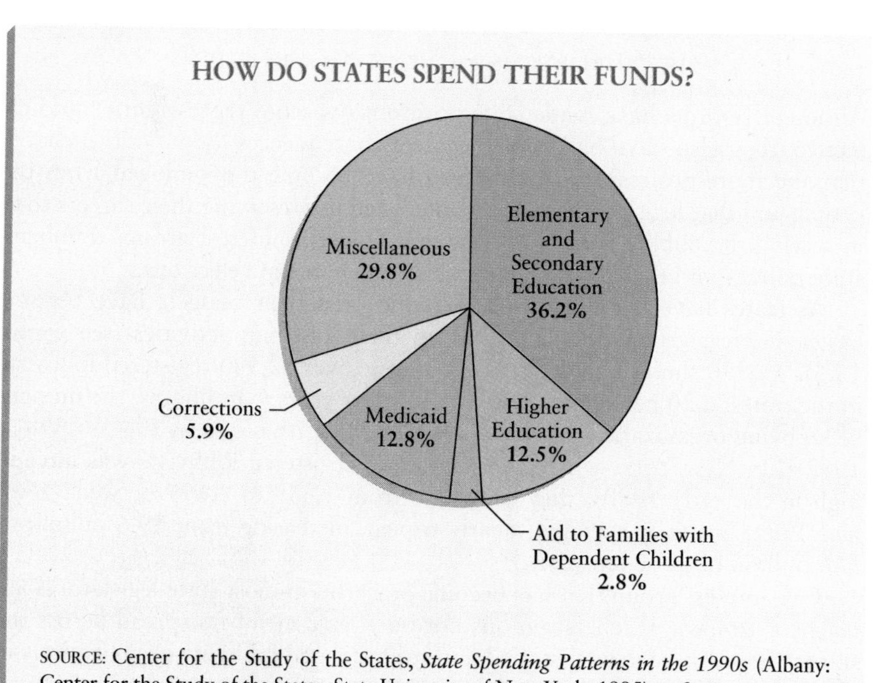

SOURCE: Center for the Study of the States, *State Spending Patterns in the 1990s* (Albany: Center for the Study of the States, State University of New York, 1995), p. 3.

FIGURE 15.2

In fiscal year 1994, the average state spent nearly half of its annual budget on education.

taxes, personal income taxes, sales and excise taxes, corporate income taxes, and severance taxes, which are imposed on natural resources such as coal and oil.[24] The greatest percentage of states' revenue comes from sales taxes, which provided 49 percent of state tax revenues in 1990, and individual income taxes, which provided 32 percent of state tax revenues. States vary considerably in the amount and type of taxes they impose. For example, seven states (Alaska, Florida, Nevada, South Dakota, Texas, Washington, and Wyoming) have no personal income tax. Four (Nevada, Texas, Washington, and Wyoming) have no corporate income tax.[25]

In 1996, the Florida Lottery Department proposed selling lottery tickets through vending machines in airports, malls, and other public locations in order to boost ticket sales and state revenues.

In their search for new sources of revenue in the 1980s, many states instituted lotteries and imposed sales taxes on newly legalized gambling activities. But lotteries and legalized gambling are controversial sources of revenue. Many citizens disapprove of gambling and fear it will spawn other unsavory activities in the state. Other critics object to lotteries because they see them as a form of regressive taxation—because lower-income people tend to spend more of their income on lottery tickets than higher-income people do.[26]

Many commentators praise the states because they are required by law to balance their budgets every year (except in Vermont). In fact, states often keep separate capital budgets to pay off long-term expenditures. To raise the funds for such expenditures, states issue bonds—interest-bearing certificates of debt bought and sold in national financial markets. But state debt is considerably smaller than the federal deficit: in 1990–91, 79 percent of the debt owed by all levels of government in the United States was owed by the federal government, 13 percent was owed by local governments, and 8 percent was owed by state governments.[27]

New Problems in State Government

A lobbyist for the Virginia Education Association confers with members of the Virginia House over a bill to provide more retirement money for state teachers.

Although reforms have made state governments more representative and effective, they also have had some negative consequences. Some critics charge that the more-professional legislatures have become too removed from the people and that legislators are more interested in preserving their careers than in serving the public. Some also fear that powerful interest groups dominate state politics and that money matters too much in state elections.

As states have taken on more activities and their budgets have become larger, interest groups have stepped up their lobbying activities (see Figure 15.3). A 1990 survey showed that there were over 42,500 registered lobbyists in the states, a 20 percent increase in only four years.[28] In Illinois, the number of lobbying organizations nearly tripled, growing from 390 in 1982 to 998 in 1992.[29] In New York, where the number of registered lobbyists was already high in the early 1980s, they only rose from 1,659 to 1,699 between 1982 and 1992, but their spending nearly tripled, increasing from $9.6 million to $26 million in those ten years.[30]

One interest group that has become powerful in most state legislatures are teachers' unions. Teachers' unions not only have members spread across the states, they also have well-staffed and sophisticated lobbying organizations in the state capitals. In addition, businesses from every sector of the economy

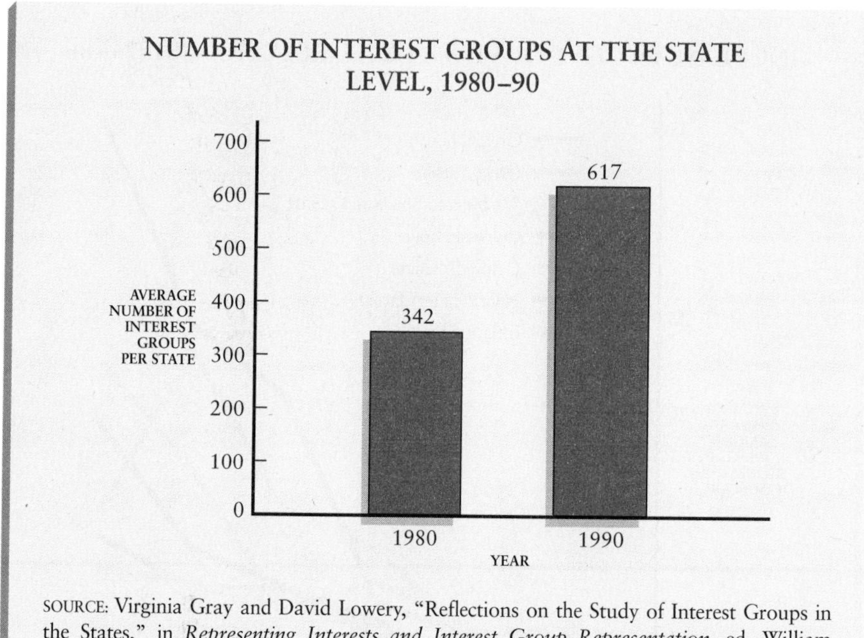

SOURCE: Virginia Gray and David Lowery, "Reflections on the Study of Interest Groups in the States," in *Representing Interests and Interest Group Representation*, ed. William Crotty, Mildred A. Schwartz, and John C. Green (Lanham, MD: University Press of America, 1994), p. 64.

FIGURE 15.3

now find it important to have lobbyists to protect their interests. Not having a lobbyist can lead to trouble. In Florida, for example, legislators looking for a new revenue source decided to impose a new sales tax on dry cleaning, a business that did not have a lobbyist to defend its interest in Tallahassee. After the tax passed, dry cleaners quickly hired a lobbyist![31]

The growing importance of interest groups in the legislative process is evident in the influence that interest groups have over legislative agendas. One Illinois lawmaker who took office in 1992 recalled that he was warned during his freshman orientation that "out of all the time [he would serve] in the legislature, [he] would probably think of only four bills on [his] own. The rest would be handed to [him] by special interests."[32]

As the power of interest groups has increased, so has the importance of money in state elections. The cost of state election campaigns has risen dramatically in recent years (see Figure 15.4). A closely contested state legislative race in California can cost $1 million. Costs are lower in other states, but they are still much higher than they were in the past. As a result, candidates have had to search for more and more funding sources. As at the national level, political action committees (PACs) now play an important role in financing state-level elections, too.

Growing dissatisfaction with these new features of state government has fueled the movement to limit the number of terms that state legislators and state executive branch officials can serve. Although the Supreme Court ruled in 1995 that terms limits for U.S. congressional representatives are unconstitutional, states may decide whether to adopt such limits for state offices. By

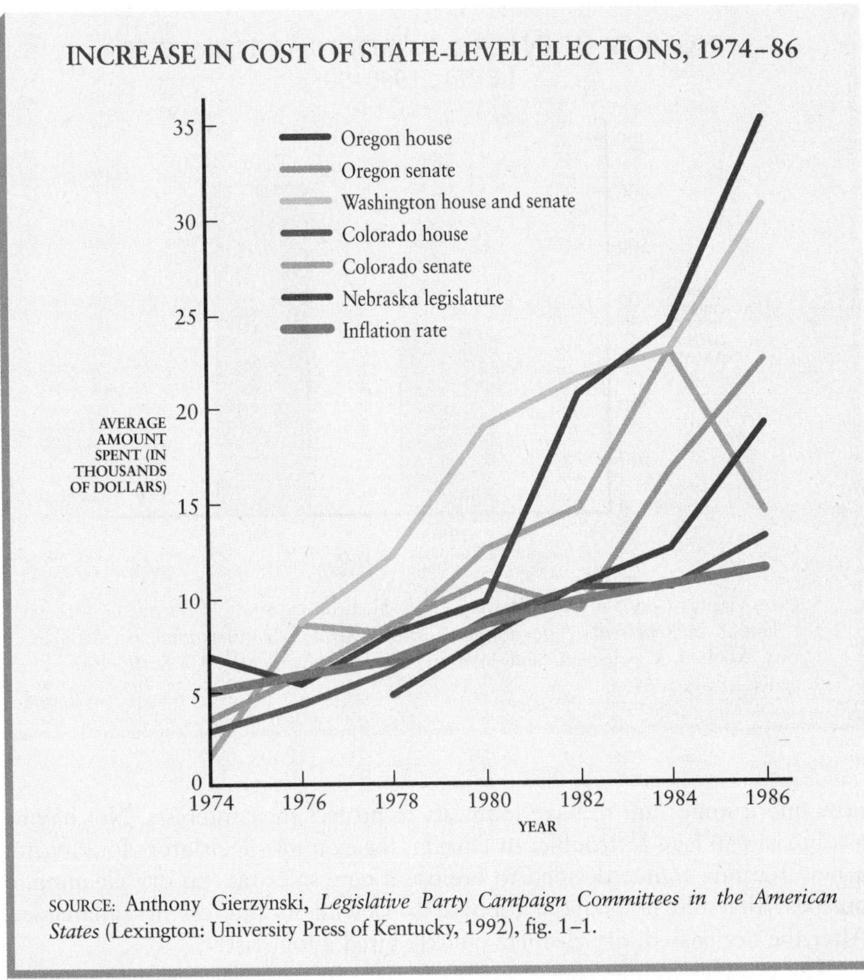

SOURCE: Anthony Gierzynski, *Legislative Party Campaign Committees in the American States* (Lexington: University Press of Kentucky, 1992), fig. 1-1.

FIGURE 15.4

1994, fifteen states had adopted term limits for state elected officials. Although the provisions vary by state, the most common limitation restricts service to eight years in a particular legislative chamber. Critics of term limits argue that such limits are not necessary because there has been considerable turnover in legislatures without these limits. For example, between 1979 and 1989, more than 72 percent of state legislators had left office. Because most of these limits have been in effect for only a few years, it is too early to tell what impact they will have on state politics. However, many observers predict that they will weaken state legislatures. Some minority group members fear that term limits will hurt minorities by taking away the seniority advantage that some representatives from minority districts have enjoyed.[33]

On the other side of the coin, critics claim that some of the traditional tools for promoting citizen access to policy making in the states have been misused. Many states, especially those in the West and Southwest, allow citi-

Opponents of Proposition 209, known as the California Civil Rights Initiative by its supporters, staged a protest at the state capitol. In 1996, California voters approved the measure, which prohibits the use of race and gender preferences in state hiring, contracting, and education.

zens to propose policies directly through the use of the **referendum** and the **initiative.** In recent years, as the use of these tools has increased dramatically, new questions have emerged. The first is whether the initiative and referendum processes are really tools for grassroots democracy. Many of the most important initiatives are now placed on the ballot by powerful interest groups, not by individuals associated with a grassroots movement. These interest groups pay workers to gather signatures. Although there is nothing illegal about this activity, it stands in contrast to the popular control of politics that the initiative was supposed to ensure. The frequent use of the initiative raises a second problem as well. When many important policy decisions are made in this way, the legislature's policy-making powers are undermined. Policy making by initiative does not promote compromise or allow consideration of how the proposed policy interacts with other desirable policies.[34]

Many of the new conditions that now characterize state politics—such as the increase in lobbying and interest-group activity—also affect the federal government. But the negative impact on democracy may be more severe in state politics, where a smaller number of key interest groups can more easily dominate politics. Some states have strong regulations governing interest groups and PACs, but others impose virtually no limits on money in politics.[35] In addition, as we saw in Chapter 4, the economic competition among states makes it difficult for them to act as the guarantors of equality. Thus, even though states have become more representative and more administratively capable, there are several features inherent to the states that limit their ability to ensure a broadly representative democracy and to promote equality. As we will see in the next section, such problems are even greater at the local level.

Local Government and American Democracy

- In what ways are local governments creatures of state government? How have different forms of local government sought to gain autonomy and independence?
- What are the two basic types of city government? What are the implications of each for representation and democracy?
- How did the differences in size and resources among local governments develop? What are the implications of these differences for democracy?
- What are the problems of big cities in the federal system? How has the relationship between the cities and the national government changed over time? What strategies have been proposed to revive American cities?

Local government occupies a peculiar but very important place in the American system. In fact, the status of American local government is probably unique in world experience.

Local governments became administratively important in the early years of the Republic because the states possessed little administrative capability and relied on local governments to implement the laws of the state. Many local governments had a long colonial history and had been in existence before the state governments were formed. Local government was an alternative to a statewide bureaucracy.

New England town meetings, such as this one in Strafford, Vermont, have been idealized as an institution of American democracy. In reality, the number of towns with this form of government is declining and those that retain it are often dominated by political activists and interest groups.

The states created two forms of local government: territorial and corporate. The basic territorial unit is the county; every resident of the state is also a resident of a county (except in Rhode Island and Connecticut, which do not have county governments). Traditionally, counties existed only for handling state obligations, whether these were administrative, legislative, or judicial, whether the job was building roads or collecting state taxes, or catching bootleggers.

The second, or corporate unit, is the city, town, or village. These are called "corporate" because each holds an actual corporate charter granted it by the state government; they are formed (incorporated) by residents of an area as these residents discover that because of their proximity, their common problems can be more effectively and more cheaply dealt with cooperatively. Not everyone lives in a city or a town; many rural areas are unincorporated.

Although cities, especially larger cities, develop unique political and governmental personalities, they are nevertheless like the counties in being units of state administration. We associate police forces, fire fighting companies, and public health and zoning agencies with the very essence of local government. But all of those functions and agencies are operating under *state* laws. The state legislature and courts allow cities to adapt state laws to local needs, and out of that discretion cities can develop their own political personalities. But they remain under state authority. In 1868, this principle was confirmed in a famous ruling known as Dillon's Rule. Judge John F. Dillon of Iowa ruled that state legislatures were supreme over cities. Legislatures could, in his words, ". . . sweep from existence all of the municipal corporations of the state, and the corporations could not prevent it."[36]

In fact, state governments did not do away with cities; instead, they gave them more power and autonomy. The most important means of giving cities independence was **home rule.** Beginning in Missouri in 1875, the states began to change their constitutions to permit cities (and eventually a few counties) of a certain size and urban density to frame and adopt local charters. By the beginning of the twentieth century, home rule had been adopted in many of the states. Gradually the provisions of home rule were extended to give cities the right of ordinary corporations to change their government structures, to hold property, to sue and be sued, and most importantly, they guaranteed that state legislatures would not pass legislation concerning the "local affairs, property, and government" of cities except by laws of statewide application. This final provision was a guarantee within the state constitution that no city would be subjected to special legislation imposed on that city alone by the state legislature. As part of this movement, many states began to allow cities to make basic laws for themselves rather than leaving cities to administer laws passed by the state legislature. Cities were given the power to make their own laws (called **ordinances**) to regulate slaughterhouses, to regulate and establish public transportation services and facilities, to regulate local markets and trade centers, to set quality and safety standards for the construction of apartments and other private buildings, and to set rules and standards for fire prevention.

Cities, towns, and villages are called "general purpose governments" because of the variety of local functions they perform. There is another kind of local government, called a **special district,** that is only charged with a few functions and often just a single function. Examples of special districts include water districts, housing districts, park districts, and transportation districts. Special districts usually cut across city and town boundaries. State legislatures must approve the creation of special districts and grant them authority to tax and to issue bonds.

Special districts have several advantages. They make it possible to provide services to a broader area than is covered by traditional cities and towns, since districts can overlap other local boundaries. They also can provide local services that might otherwise be hard to finance, given taxing and debt limitations that the states impose on general purpose governments. Illinois has more local governments than any other state, in part because the Illinois state constitution severely limited the amount of debt that cities could incur. To deal with these limits, many special districts were created; those around Chicago include the Mosquito Abatement District, the Forest Preserve District, the Metropolitan Sanitary District, the Cook County Health and Hospital Governing Commission, the Regional Transportation Authority, and the Chicago Regional Port District.[37]

After such powers were delegated from state governments to local governments, it was inevitable that people would come to the conclusion that cities constituted a third level of sovereignty, and that some cities, such as New York City, were the constitutional equal of a state. But these conclusions are distinctly untrue. There are only two levels of sovereignty in the United States: the national government and the state government. Local governments, important as they have become in this urban nation, remain exactly what they have always been: creatures of state government.

Representation in Urban Politics

Cities hold a special place in the development of American democracy, for it was in cities that the great masses of immigrants became American citizens. City government served as the introduction to democracy and provided access to power for many immigrant groups in the United States. Cities were also the places where social reformers in the early part of the twentieth century tested their ideas about how to improve government.

Two basic types of city government have predominated in the United States. Each has had different implications for how citizens were represented. In **machine cities,** politics were dominated by party organizations that controlled nominations for office and mobilized voters in favor of particular candidates. Most machine cities were located in the Northeast and the Midwest, where large immigrant populations settled. The heyday of the political machine was in the early part of this century before the New Deal. But even after the New Deal, machine politics thrived in a number of cities including Chicago, Pittsburgh, and Albany.[38] **Reform cities,** on the other hand, adopted a variety of political reforms that reduced the role of political parties in local politics. Reform cities are disproportionately located in the Southwest and the West. Many medium-sized cities and suburban municipalities across the United States adopted similar reforms.

The city politics to which many immigrants were introduced in the early years of this century were run by political machines. Machines traditionally won support by offering **patronage,** divisible rewards such as jobs or contracts on city projects. The classic urban machine was a tightly run organization with precinct captains, ward leaders, and citywide leaders. Those who worked for the organization were often rewarded with city jobs, many of which required little work. Loyalty to the organization was paramount. Furthermore, political machines were not open organizations that anybody could join. Former federal judge Abner Mikva told of volunteering to work in Chicago politics in the 1950s and being asked, "Who sent you?" When he replied that nobody had sent him, the reply was "We don't want nobody nobody sent!"[39]

Different interpretations have been offered about what machine politics meant for American democracy and for the immigrant groups who came to U.S. cities between the 1850s and the early 1900s. Most political analysts initially condemned machines as antidemocratic and corrupt. They said that machines served the interests of powerful businesses and did not help the working people who voted for them.[40] Later scholars took a different approach, however. They saw machines as important tools for helping immigrants become integrated into American politics. Many political machines sponsored drives to encourage immigrants to become citizens, to register, and to vote. Seen this way, the precinct captain was a friendly face who helped his fellow immigrants connect with the political system and gain access to public

This Thomas Nast cartoon hailed the triumph of democratic politics and reform over "Boss" Tweed's corrupt New York City political machine.

jobs and other benefits that machines controlled.[41] Yet even though machines performed these functions at times, this view romanticizes machine politics. In fact, machines did not have enough benefits to spread around to truly benefit immigrant groups in general. The Irish quickly monopolized political power in cities when they arrived in the 1840s and 1850s. The ethnic groups that came after them—Italians, Jews, and Eastern Europeans—were far less likely to control urban politics. These later groups received some benefits from machines, but much of what they got was only symbolic recognition, such as the parades and ethnic holidays that were an essential part of life in machine cities.

Members of racial minorities were at the bottom of the ladder in machine cities. In some cities, African Americans received patronage but usually on terms that were not as favorable as those of white ethnic groups. In Chicago, African Americans were organized into a "submachine" that controlled the votes in the six black wards on the south side of the city. This concentrated vote gave African Americans more political clout in Chicago than in any other big city before the 1960s. But the jobs and other benefits that blacks received through their participation in Chicago's machine politics were inferior to those received by white ethnics. Although African Americans were rewarded with city jobs, these tended to be low-paying positions, such as porters and janitors.[42]

in how cities are governed and to increase the benefits that minorities get from city government.[49]

The questions about the relationship between representation, power, and "who gets what" from government are some of the most fundamental questions about democracy. In the next sections, we will examine more closely what it means to win power in cities today and why cities seem so hard to govern.

AMERICAN DEMOCRACY AND LOCAL POLITICAL BOUNDARIES

Local governments vary greatly in size, population, and resources. Such differences mean that local governments do not all have the same ability to meet the needs of their citizens. How did localities become so different in the United States and what does it mean for American democracy? To answer this question we must examine how local governments are formed and what determines who lives in which communities. What we will see is that Americans have created communities that separate people by race and by class.

Among the most important factors that shape localities are laws about annexation and incorporation.[50] Because state governments set the laws that govern annexation and incorporation, they vary from state to state. In the states in the Northeast and Midwest, it is generally hard for a big city to annex surrounding territory. Since the turn of the century, suburbs in these states have resisted being taken over by neighboring cities. Brookline, Massachusetts, became the first suburb to declare its autonomy when it resisted being annexed to Boston in 1874. In the Sun Belt, especially in Texas, state law makes it easier for big cities to annex neighboring territory. Thus Houston grew from 160 square miles in 1950 to 539.9 square miles in 1990 by annexing much of its surrounding territory (see Figure 15.6). Annexation allows big cities to capture the benefits of the growth that occurs in their suburbs. In general, cities that can annex easily have stronger tax bases than older, smaller cities that have not been above to capture growth on their fringes.

In most states, citizens who want to form a separate jurisdiction by incorporating find it easy to do so. Once they have formed a separate jurisdiction, they can shape its character by using the powers of zoning to determine what kinds of people can live and what kinds of businesses can operate within their borders.[51] For example, by limiting the number of apartment buildings or by ruling that houses must be located on large lots, local governments can ensure that poorer people will not be able to live in their communities.

These features of American local political organization, often praised as the essence of American democracy, provide powerful incentives for well-off citizens to form separate political jurisdictions, thus shielding themselves from the economic costs and political dangers of the less well-off. In the racially and ethnically diverse context of American society, the impulse to separate is also driven by racial and ethnic antipathies, leading to what sociologists Douglas Massey and Nancy Denton have called "American apartheid."[52] In a study examining why new local jurisdictions formed after World War II, political scientist Nancy Burns found three main reasons: citi-

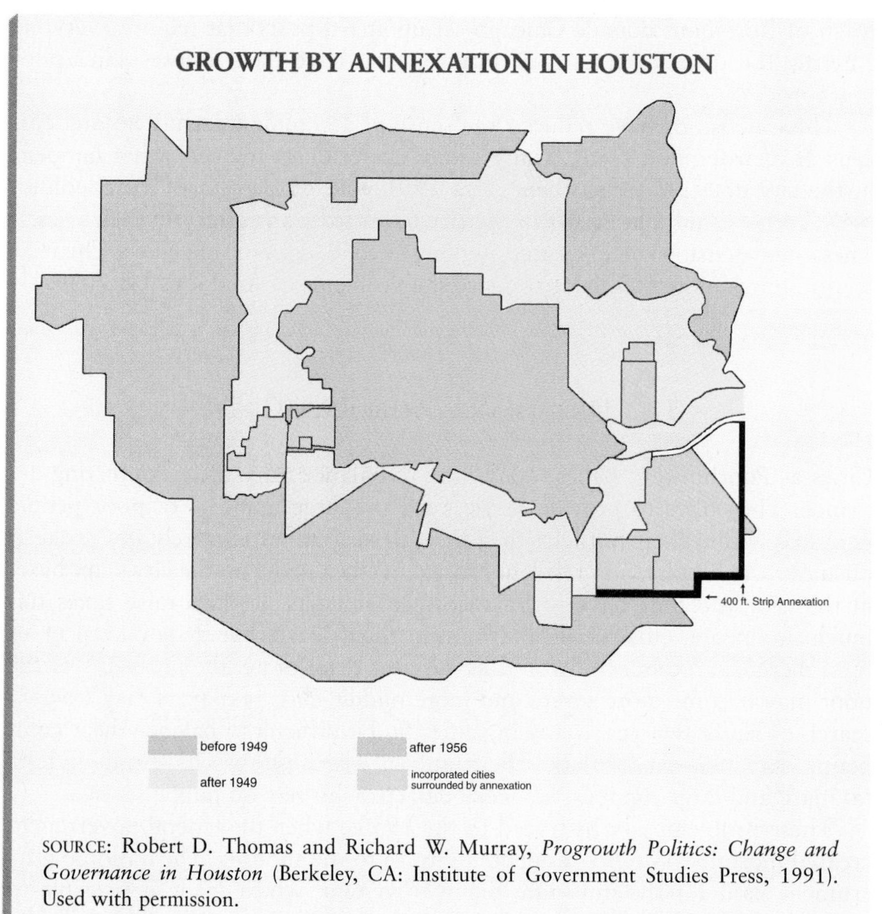

SOURCE: Robert D. Thomas and Richard W. Murray, *Progrowth Politics: Change and Governance in Houston* (Berkeley, CA: Institute of Government Studies Press, 1991). Used with permission.

FIGURE 15.6

Over the course of the twentieth century, annexation was the primary means by which a number of southern and western cities, such as Houston, expanded their populations, economies, and political clout. Houston more than tripled in size as the result of two major annexations in 1949 and 1956.

zens wanted to obtain better services, to pay lower taxes, and to avoid integration.[53] Local government boundaries became a way to enforce racial and class divisions.

As Americans have grown fearful of crime and other urban problems, they have tried to make the boundaries between local governments—especially the boundaries between cities and suburbs—stronger. This form of politics is called "defensive localism"; evidence of it can be seen in many different ways, some symbolic, others very real.[54] In the past, suburbs sought status by identifying with the city that spawned them; now they want to emphasize their differences. Some suburbs go so far as to change their names so they no longer are identified with the nearby city. East Paterson, New Jersey (a suburb of Paterson) and East Detroit, Michigan (a suburb of Detroit), changed their names to Elmwood Park and Erin Heights, respectively, so that they would no longer be identified as closely with the city.[55] The desire for safety and distance from the city has also led to the creation of gated cities. These homogenous communities restrict access to residents and their guests. Some older towns have tried to create the advantages of gated cities. The

Many communities are now "gated," allowing access only to residents.

town of Rosemont outside Chicago set up guard posts that require everyone entering the town to state their business and have their license plates photographed.[56]

These divisions have reduced the sense of a common destiny among citizens of metropolitan areas. Many suburban residents say that what happens in the city does not affect them. In a 1991 poll, 51 percent of metropolitan New Yorkers said that events in the city had hardly any effect on their lives.[57] These new divisions have created important challenges for big cities. The next section looks more closely at some of the problems of America's big cities.

THE DILEMMA OF AMERICAN CITIES

Cities as Poorhouses Cities today have to balance three often conflicting demands. They have to provide services for the large numbers of poor people who live within their borders; they have to keep taxes relatively low to keep businesses and taxpaying residents (who together make up the city's **tax base**) in the city, and they have to balance their budgets. If cities raise taxes too much, taxpaying citizens and businesses might leave, but if they keep taxes (and therefore revenues) low and let services deteriorate, the problems of the poor may become more severe and more middle-class taxpayers may leave in search of better services. Many big cities find it difficult to balance these competing demands—and balance their budgets—because they have a dwindling tax base and large numbers of needy citizens who rely on public services.

These problems can be traced to the 1950s, when the federal government created incentives for city residents to move to the suburbs. The national government paid for the interstate highway system, which made it possible to live outside the city and commute in for work. Low-interest loans insured by the Federal Housing Administration (FHA) allowed many working-class people to buy their own homes for the first time in American history. But these same policies hurt cities. New highways often cut through existing neighborhoods, displacing families and destroying the fabric of the community. Minority communities were often the hardest hit.

Residents who lived in urban areas that banks and insurance companies had "redlined" found it nearly impossible to obtain loans, mortgages, and insurance. In recent years, challenges to the practice of redlining have spurred inner city investments by banks.

Housing policies were also administered in a racially discriminatory way until the late 1960s. Lending guidelines greatly favored suburbs over cities: some banks **"redlined"** whole areas of cities, marking those areas that were considered "unsuitable" for loans. Regardless of an individual's credit history, he or she could not receive a loan for housing in a redlined area. The historian Kenneth T. Jackson has shown that the FHA used explicit racial criteria in determining how housing loans would be distributed.[58] A study by the American Friends Service Committee in 1955 estimated that between 1935 and 1950, less than 2 percent of the housing financed with federal mortgage assistance was open to African Americans.[59] Added to these problems with private housing was the nature of public housing. Only the very poor could qualify for public housing, which was built by local governments (although financed by the federal government) and was racially segregated. Many of these public housing projects became "warehouses for the poor." Very few suburbs built public housing.[60]

These policies meant that cities contained a greater proportion of a metropolitan area's poor population than the suburbs. In the 1970s and 1980s, businesses began to follow middle- and upper-middle-class white citizens leaving the city for the suburbs. And, as the growing black and Latino middle class took advantage of the new housing opportunities open to them in the 1970s and 1980s, they too began to leave cities. These emigrations have left cities with needy populations and a precarious tax base with which to address the problems of their citizens.

These problems make it difficult to govern cities. When the first generation of minority mayors came to power in the 1970s, they promised to make life better for their poorest constituents. But, confronted with forces beyond their control, these mayors were not able to make life substantially better for the urban poor. In many cities, governing has become even more difficult with the arrival of new immigrants. In recent years, cities have experienced the greatest influx of immigrants since the first decades of the twentieth century. Many of these immigrants have started businesses and helped to revive deteriorating neighborhoods. But their arrival has also created new burdens on city governments. For example, cities often provide public services in many languages in order to serve the needs of non-English-speaking residents. In many cities, multiracial coalitions have become hard to sustain as different groups fight for shares of the shrinking pie.

The Federal Government and the Cities Until the 1980s, the federal government provided extra financial assistance to cities that helped them balance the competing claims on their budgets. National politicians paid attention to cities because they were politically important: urban party organizations provided votes that could make or break a presidential election. Mayor Richard J. Daley of Chicago delivered votes that were critical to President John F. Kennedy's narrow win in 1960.[61]

In the era of "marble cake federalism" in the 1960s (see Chapter 4), the federal government created many new programs to assist cities and their poor residents. To underscore the importance of cities and the ongoing commitment of the federal government to assist them, President Lyndon Johnson created the Department of Housing and Urban Development (HUD) in 1965. Although many urban programs were altered during the 1970s, the federal government continued to acknowledge its responsibility for cities by providing substantial financial assistance in the form of grants and loan programs. The U.S. Conference of Mayors and the National League of Cities, interest groups that had access to the president and to Congress, played a large role in winning this federal assistance.

By the 1980s, however, cities had become far less important in national politics. President Ronald Reagan successfully pushed for deep cuts in federal aid to cities. The only programs that Reagan totally eliminated during the 1980s were those that particularly benefited local governments. For example, in 1981 Congress terminated the Comprehensive Employment and Training Act, which cities had used (unofficially) to bolster the ranks of their employees. By 1988, Urban Development Action Grants, a major urban development program, lost their funding entirely. The area of social policy most severely cut during the 1980s was housing assistance, which disproportion-

COMMUNITY GROUPS

Revitalizing poor urban neighborhoods poses difficult challenges for national and local policy makers. As middle-class residents move to the suburbs, the neighborhoods they leave behind often become poorer and more dilapidated. A cycle of decline can set in, making it difficult to provide safe and attractive neighborhoods for low-income residents. By the late 1970s, some urban neighborhoods, such as the South Bronx in New York City, were so littered with abandoned and burned-out buildings that they became national symbols for urban decline.

In the 1980s, however, community-based organizations in many cities took the lead in finding solutions for poor neighborhoods. Guarding against arsonists and working with city governments, such groups have rehabilitated existing housing and, assisted by several federal programs, have built affordable housing for people with low and moderate incomes. Through these activities, community organizations have revived many areas once believed to be hopeless.

Some community development groups grew out of the determination of residents to save their homes. For example, the Banana Kelly Community Improvement Association in the Bronx was formed in 1977, when residents of a curved section of Kelly Street (hence "banana") in the Bronx prevented their building from being demolished and fought for loans to rehabilitate their housing. Adopting the slogan "Don't Move, Improve," the Banana Kelly residents cleaned up their street and patrolled it themselves to make it safer. Small successes multiplied over time as the organization sought to improve nearby housing. By 1995, Banana Kelly managed fifty-two buildings and had real estate holdings estimated to be worth more than $50 million.[1]

Other community development groups are church-based organizations. One such group, East Brooklyn Congregations, was formed in 1978 by a group of ministers in the East New York section of Brooklyn. An area traditionally populated by poor immigrants and minorities, East New York was littered with many abandoned buildings and empty lots by the early 1980s. The East Brooklyn Congregations proposed something quite new to revitalize the community: build low-cost suburban-style housing for low- and moderate-income residents in

ately benefited cities.[62] In all, grants for city governments were cut some 46 percent between 1980 and 1990. In the average large city, 22 percent of city expenditures were covered by federal aid in 1980; by 1989, federal aid covered only 6 percent of those expenditures (see also Table 4.3, p. 126).[63]

Cities did not do much better even after Bill Clinton was elected as the first Democratic president in twelve years. Many mayors hoped that Clinton would support increased federal assistance for cities. But as Congress became more concerned about limiting government spending, the president's initiatives were rejected. Although some new programs were created to assist cities during the Clinton administration, on the whole, the federal government avoided a return to the higher levels of urban assistance it provided in the 1960s and 1970s.

This new approach of the national government toward cities has been called by some "fend-for-yourself federalism." It leaves cities more on their own to provide services to their diverse residents, keep taxes from getting too high, and keep their cities fiscally sound.

the city. Called "Nehemiah Homes" after the biblical prophet who rebuilt Jerusalem, the project built 2,300 homes with fences and small yards in a neighborhood once strewn with rubble and abandoned buildings.

Finding the money to finance such projects is not easy and these organizations have had to patch together diverse sources of funds. One important source has been the low-income-housing tax credit, which provides a tax break to corporations that invest in low-income housing. Community development groups have also benefited from the Community Reinvestment Act (CRA), a federal program that requires banks to invest in the neighborhoods in which they do business. During the 1980s, as federal funds for housing declined, community groups became adept at using the CRA to induce banks to finance local development projects. In addition, community development organizations receive assistance from local public-private partnerships in many cities and from two national organizations, the Local Initiatives Support Corporation and the Enterprise Foundation. These organizations provide loans, grants, and technical assistance for community development.

Despite the many successes of community development organizations, their ability to revitalize poor neighborhoods has been limited. The difficulty in securing funds has limited the scope of their activities and the abilities of community groups vary greatly between different cities and neighborhoods. Moreover, when local community development groups have sought to move beyond housing to economic development, their efforts have been less successful. Access to jobs remains a persistent problem that community development organizations have not been able to address. Nonetheless, successes such as those of Banana Kelly and East Brooklyn Congregations may be the first steps in reclaiming neighborhoods that once seemed beyond hope.

[1] Lis Harris, "Banana Kelly's Toughest Fight," *New Yorker,* July 24, 1995, p. 34.

The Future of Cities

American cities face an uncertain future. Three developments in recent years, however, suggest ways to strengthen cities and make life better for urban residents. The first is a growing interest in **regionalism.** Rather than seeing cities and suburbs as competitors, a regional approach to politics and policy tries to look at what each can gain by cooperation. The most far-reaching form of regionalism actually consolidates city and county governments into a single government, a move that can expand the resource base of the city. Some cities that have merged with counties include Nashville, Tennessee; Indianapolis, Indiana; and Jacksonville, Florida. But such consolidations are rare; five out of six attempts at consolidation fail because the individual governments and their residents want to remain separate. Suburban residents may not want to lose their autonomy, and city residents may fear that they, too, would lose power if city and county were merged. Racial issues are often involved in assessments of whether or not to merge. In 1993, the newly elected black mayor of Memphis, W. W. Herenton, proposed that the city and county consolidate. The mayor wanted to recapture the taxes of the businesses and residents that had been leaving the city for the surrounding county. But when black city officials and white officials in the suburbs opposed the plan, the mayor was forced to drop the idea.[64]

Despite the friction between cities and suburbs, some organizations have been created to promote regional dialogues. Most metropolitan areas have "councils of governments," which were created in the 1960s to provide a forum for the different governments to discuss common problems such as pollution and transportation. In most cases, these organizations are very weak and have no power to force member governments to cooperate. Some metropolitan areas take the idea of regionalism further. Minneapolis–St. Paul has a regional agreement for sharing part of the region's tax base; this agreement reduces competition for economic development among the different governments of the region. In Portland, Oregon, the Metropolitan Service District has important powers over land use, transportation planning, and environmental issues. As an elected body, it is the closest thing to regional government in the United States.[65]

A second strategy that many cities have adopted is to "reinvent" local government to make it more efficient. In many big cities, pragmatic new mayors have sought to improve management and "downsize" city governments. These mayors have tried to reduce the cost of services in cities by tough negotiations with municipal unions. Philadelphia Mayor Edward Rendell is often cited as an example of this new breed of mayor. When Rendell took office in 1992, Philadelphia was near bankruptcy. By holding down the wages of city workers and privatizing some city services, Rendell succeeded in stabilizing city finances. But Rendell himself notes the limits of such actions: they have not prevented business and residents from leaving the city. Rendell likens his situation to doctors in an emergency room with a patient who has both cancer and a bullet wound: "What we have done with the help of the city council and the business community, is to take care of the bullet wound problem. . . . Now we have to cure the cancer—the erosion of the tax base of the city of Philadelphia, crime and violence and the whole panoply of crippling social problems that have literally been dumped on our cities."[66]

A third strategy for reviving cities depends upon community organizations.[67] Many poor neighborhoods have local organizations that seek to involve local citizens in improving the community. These organizations have taken the lead in building housing in poor neighborhoods since the 1980s. Areas that many thought would never revive are now filled with low-cost housing due to the efforts of such groups. Many of these groups are church-based organizations that have strong roots in the community. One example is the East Brooklyn Congregations, which built a large section of low-cost housing in Brooklyn, New York. With the leadership of charismatic ministers such as Johnny Ray Youngblood, the East Brooklyn Congregations has reinvigorated a declining community.[68]

The work of such organizations revives the spirit of community involvement that Americans cherish. Yet these organizations do not have the resources to solve the problems of poor neighborhoods on their own. They have relied on financial assistance and support from city, state, and federal governments for their efforts to be successful.

AMERICAN POLITICAL CULTURE

Building from the Ground Up

Communities Organized for Public Service (COPS) in San Antonio, Texas, is one of the most powerful and effective community organizations in the country. COPS started in 1973, when a young organizer named Ernesto Cortes began knocking on doors in San Antonio's poor Hispanic communities. Cortes had recently been trained as a community organizer by the Industrial Areas Foundation, an organization founded by Saul Alinsky, a community organizer in Chicago during the 1930s and 1940s. The Alinsky style of organizing relies on small meetings in which organizers learn the problems of the community and identify leaders who will help unite people to address these problems. Cortes found valuable organizational and financial assistance in San Antonio's Catholic parishes, which became important components of the COPS organization.

A "bottom-up" strategy was essential to COPS's early success in attracting members.[1] The organization focused on issues that residents identified as most important in their daily lives, such as drainage problems, poor roads, and the absence of sidewalks—all of which reflected the neglect of Mexican American neighborhoods by the city government. COPS initially won citywide attention by launching large-scale and highly publicized protests. For example, COPS organized hundreds of community residents to disrupt business at a major bank by having them exchange pennies for dollars and dollars for pennies all day. While this disruption was occurring, COPS leaders met with city officials to discuss an alternative city budget that would provide additional resources to poor Hispanic neighborhoods. This combination of protest and negotiation proved successful: the city began to shift more resources to parts of the city it had neglected in the past.

These early successes helped the organization grow, as community residents saw the positive results of their participation. Due to its successful strategies, COPS has gained substantial influence over the distribution of federal community development funds in San Antonio. By organizing its members to attend public hearings on how the funds should be spent, COPS ensures that city council members take its concerns into account. COPS members prepare for such hearings by holding meetings to identify economic development projects that they believe are important to their communities. In recent years, COPS has launched major projects to improve public schools and to provide quality job training. Through all these activities, COPS has become a power to be reckoned with in San Antonio, and the once-neglected Hispanic neighborhoods of the city have benefited from improved infrastructure and public services.

In the early 1980s, Cortes and other organizers from the Industrial Areas Foundation began to build a similar grassroots organization in the predominantly black neighborhood of east San Antonio. These efforts gave rise to a multiracial organization, the Metro Alliance. Today, COPS and the Metro Alliance cooperate on issues important to both organizations, such as education and job training.

COPS and the Metro Alliance continue to emphasize grassroots initiative and involvement. They do not take on direct administrative responsibility for projects; instead they create new agencies to handle such activities.[2] This approach leaves the organizations free to concentrate on building neighborhood leadership and organizing community members to define and take action on their common problems.

[1] Joseph D. Sekul, "Communities Organized for Public Service: Citizen Power and Public Policy in San Antonio," *The Politics of San Antonio*, ed. David R. Johnson, John A. Booth, and Richard J. Harris (Lincoln: University of Nebraska Press, 1983), p. 176.

[2] Mark Warren, "Social Capital and Community Empowerment: Religion and Political Organization in the Texas Industrial Areas Foundation," (Ph.D. Diss., Department of Sociology, Harvard University, 1995), p. 68.

★ Summary

This chapter examined the place of state and cities in the federal system. We saw that although the states were praised as laboratories of democracy, and although localities have been considered the cornerstone of democracy in the United States, states and localities both restricted participation and favored some interest over others. Moreover, the organization of power and the poor quality of administrative institutions at the state and local level often meant that these governments were not capable of carrying out the wishes of their citizens. Nor did states provide equal representation for all citizens. Rural areas were overrepresented in state legislatures, and in southern states, African Americans were barred from participating in politics. In many Southwestern states Mexican Americans were also denied the right to participate.

Beginning in the 1960s, states began to open up their political systems and reform their administrations. This paved the way for a revival of states and raised new arguments about transferring more authority to the states.

The final section of the chapter examined local government. It showed how cities in the Northeast and the Midwest integrated new immigrants into the American political system in machine politics. In the Southwest, reform governments limited political participation and created cities that were governed by small groups of elites. The American practice of forming new localities has helped to reinforce social divisions; local boundaries often separate citizens by race and income. Large cities have been disadvantaged because the poorest citizens generally concentrate in cities, not in suburbs. This means that mayors face the difficult task of balancing their budgets, restraining tax increases, and providing services to the poor. Although the federal government once provided cities substantial financial assistance, cities are increasingly left on their own to manage this difficult situation.

Americans often tend to think of the governments that are closest to the people—such as states and localities—as the most democratic. This chapter has shown, however, that state and local governments have often been the least democratic part of the American political system. Important reforms in recent years have made these governments more open and responsive to all citizens. But new developments in state and local politics—such as the growing number of lobbyists in state capitols—suggest that the struggle to defend openness and democracy will continue in the future.

FOR FURTHER READING

Burns, Nancy. *The Formation of American Local Governments: Private Values in Public Institutions.* New York: Oxford University Press, 1994.

Fuchs, Ester R. *Mayors and Money: Fiscal Policy in New York and Chicago.* Chicago: University of Chicago Press, 1992.

Gray, Virginia, and Herbert Jacob, eds. *Politics in the American States: A Comparative Analysis.* 6th ed. Washington, DC: Congressional Quarterly Press, 1996.

Montejano, David. *Anglos and Mexicans in the Making of Texas, 1836–1986.* Austin: University of Texas Press, 1986.

Pinderhughes, Dianne M. *Race and Ethnicity in Chicago Politics.* Urbana: University of Illinois Press, 1987.

Rosenthal, Alan. *The Third House: Lobbyists and Lobbying in the States.* Washington, DC: Congressional Quarterly Press, 1993.

STUDY OUTLINE

The Changing Role of State Governments

1. During the Progressive Era, states were considered laboratories of democracy in which policies of reform movements, many led by women's organizations, were cultivated in state government.
2. In the 1930s, the federal government reasserted itself, both because of the crisis of the Great Depression and because of the failures of states to provide fair representation and effective governance to their citizens.
3. African Americans in the southern states and Mexican Americans in the southwestern states were segregated and faced barriers to voting.
4. The Civil Rights movement provided a spotlight on political and social abuses in southern states.
5. In the 1960s, states began to provide more equal participation for citizens. Federal laws such as the 1964 Civil Rights Act and the 1965 Voting Rights Act, as well as Supreme Court cases, gave the federal government jurisdiction over state reapportionment and forced state governments to become more representative.
6. In addition to problems of representation, states also could not administer policy well. Long, unwieldy constitutions and unprofessional and weak political institutions stood as barriers to effective state governance.
7. Reforms have made state legislatures more professional and governors more effective policy makers. These reforms, in addition to various other administrative reforms, have made state governments more effective than they had been in the past.
8. Increased professionalism and increased activity of state governments have attracted interest groups who frequently lobby state officials and contribute money to campaigns for state office.

Local Government and American Democracy

1. There are two forms of local government in the United States: territorial and corporate. Counties are examples of territorial units, while cities are corporate units. Both counties and cities are units of state administration.
2. Although city governments are under state government authority, states have sought to give cities more power and autonomy. Despite their high level of autonomy, cities are not sovereign; they remain creatures of state government.
3. In the early twentieth century, reformers sought to "clean up" the corruption of urban politics by instituting changes in election practices and civil service reform in an effort to weaken urban machines.
4. Changes in the demographic composition of urban areas in the 1970s and 1980s led to increased minority representation in city government.
5. For many years, national politicians paid particular attention to the problems of cities in order to garner the electoral support of urban party organizations. By the 1980s, however, cities had become far less important politically.

PRACTICE QUIZ

1. The overall effect of the growth of national policies has been
   a. to weaken state government.
   b. to strengthen state government.
   c. to provide uniform laws in the nation.
   d. to make the states more diverse culturally.
2. During the Progressive Era, the primary role of women in state politics involved
   a. the election of more women to statewide office.
   b. seeking the adoption of programs that would assist their husbands.
   c. pushing for social reforms to rid state and local governments of corruption and to help children.
   d. no interest in state politics at all.
3. As a result of the "reapportionment revolution" by which states drew new legislative districts for elected offices,
   a. rural representation declined and legislators from cities and suburbs took their place.
   b. fewer African Americans, Latinos, and women were elected to statewide offices.
   c. state governments became less representative of their populations.
   d. none of the above.
4. Which of the following contributed to the ineffectiveness of state government?
   a. massive amounts of lobbying of state officials
   b. the commerce clause
   c. long and obscure state constitutions
   d. none of the above
5. Which of the following does not represent a trend in state government?
   a. There are increased numbers of groups lobbying state legislatures.

b. State governments have had to shoulder more of the burden of financing public policies.
c. The states have not had to raise more revenue in order to balance their budgets.
d. State legislatures have become more representative.

6. Home rule began in the late nineteenth century as an effort by state governments to give more authority to
a. governors.
b. state legislatures.
c. cities.
d. the federal government.

7. Which of the following is *not* true about machine cities?
a. They were dominated by strong party organizations.
b. They occurred mostly in the Northeast and the Midwest.
c. They were known for patronage and corruption.
d. They disappeared after the New Deal.

8. New local jurisdictions are formed to
a. obtain better services.
b. pay lower taxes.
c. avoid racial integration.
d. all of the above.

9. Which of the following best describes the relationship of the federal government to the cities?
a. Since the 1940s, the federal government has ignored urban areas.
b. National politicians were very interested in urban politics from the New Deal until the 1980s.
c. Cities have done much better under the Clinton administration than they had in the previous twelve years.
d. Both b and c are correct.

10. Which of the following has *not* been utilized as a means of strengthening cities?
a. promoting the common interests of suburbs and cities through regional cooperation
b. downsizing city government to make it more efficient and less costly
c. encouraging business through tax incentives to hire only residents of inner cities
d. creating organizations that seek to improve the community and involve local citizens

CRITICAL THINKING QUESTIONS

1. In what ways do state governments share the same problems with the national government? Are state governments more or less democratic than the national government? Why?
2. From machine politics to the politics of annexation and incorporation, in what ways have the politics of immigration, ethnicity, and race affected urban government? How are the issues of race and ethnicity interwoven with the dilemmas currently facing American cities?

KEY TERMS

at-large system the system of electing city council members based on a constituency of the entire city rather than specified subdivisions of the city. This system was used in reform cities in order to get the "best" candidates. (p. 590)

civil service reform reform adopted in cities, as well as in the federal government, to ensure the hiring and firing of government employees based on merit. This was an effort to discourage patronage. (p. 590)

district system a system of electing city council members from a number of local districts, rather than from the city as a whole. This system was widely adopted in cities during the 1970s and 1980s to ensure minority representation on city councils. (p. 591)

federalism a system of government in which power is divided, by a constitution, between a central government and regional governments. (p. 574)

home rule power delegated by the state to a local unit of government to manage its own affairs. (p. 587)

initiative procedure in twenty-three states that allows citizens to place policy proposals on the ballot, usually after gathering a specified number of signatures on a petition. (p. 585)

laboratories of democracy a phrase applied to the states, referring to their ability to experiment with a wide range of policies. This ability to experiment is viewed as a strength of the American system of federalism. (p. 575)

legitimacy popular acceptance of a government and its decisions. (p. 574)

line-item veto the power of the executive to veto specific provisions (lines) of a bill passed by the legislature. (p. 580)

machine cities cities in which politics was dominated by party organizations that controlled nominations for office and mobilized party voters. (p. 588)

ordinances legislative acts of a local legislature or municipal commission. Puts the force of law under city charter but is a lower order of law than a statute of the national or state legislature. (p. 587)

patronage the resources available to higher officials, usually opportunities to make partisan appointments to offices and to confer grants, licenses, or special favors to supporters. (p. 588)

redistricting the process of redrawing election districts and redistributing legislative representatives. This happens every ten years to reflect shifts in population or in response to legal challenges to existing districts. (p. 576)

redlining racially discriminatory housing policy by which people living in a certain geographic location were systematically denied mortgage loans. (p. 594)

referendum the practice of referring a measure proposed or passed by a legislature to the vote of the electorate for approval or rejection. (p. 585)

reform cities cities that adopted a variety of reforms in order to reduce the role of political parties and increase the role of experts in local politics. (p. 588)

regionalism the idea that all the different towns and cities in a metropolitan area constitute a single region. Rather than seeing cities and suburbs as competitors, this perspective views the different parts of the metropolitan area as interdependent. (p. 597)

special district a form of local government that usually cuts across city and town boundaries and is charged with a few very specific functions. (p. 587)

tax base the property and income within a political jurisdiction, such as a city or a state, that can be taxed. (p. 594)

PART V

★

Policy

16

Government and the Economy

★ Techniques of Control

What categories of techniques of control does the government use to form public policy? What are some examples of each?

★ Substantive Uses of Public Policy

What is the impact of federalism on public policy?

How is the national government fundamental in promoting a national market economy?

What influences government adoption of regulatory policies?

What forms of economic policy help encourage a capitalist economy?

★ Reflections on the Role of Government

How does public policy balance liberty, equality, and democracy?

GOVERNMENTS in America have always played a role in the economy. Unlike with most other countries, we must use "governments" in the plural in referring to the United States because of federalism, but that should not mask the importance of government itself and of the many public policies that have promoted and regulated the American economy. Both the state and national governments have maintained public order and in so doing have enabled individuals and companies to function in a capitalist economy that has encouraged both private ownership and public intervention in ways that have sustained massive economic growth. Yet, although economic growth is a goal that everyone can agree on, the public policies designed to achieve this goal are open to debate. Take inflation, for example. **Inflation,** which is a consistent increase in the general level of prices, is a problem every administration—Democratic or Republican, pro-government or anti-government—must confront with timely and appropriate policies. Everyone agrees that inflation is caused by too many dollars chasing too few goods, a situation that increases prices at a rate higher than wage increases or productivity increases. But people can disagree intensely about what particular anti-inflationary policy is in fact the most timely and most appropriate. This makes the problem of inflation a good introduction to the public policy phenomenon.

Toward the end of the Vietnam War, inflationary pressures began to mount because President Johnson had committed the United States to guns *and* butter—that is, to increased military expenditure without cutting domestic expenditure or raising taxes to pay for it. Despite efforts by Congress and President Nixon in 1970 to control inflation by trying to regulate wage, price, rent, and interest increases, and despite President Carter's efforts to control the inflationary effect of the "oil crisis" with tariffs, quotas, and a regulatory tax on gasoline to discourage consumption, and despite President Carter's additional effort to reduce consumer spending by adopting a **fiscal policy** of raising Social Security taxes, inflation continued to approach record-high levels.

When President Reagan came into office in 1981, he replaced the oil import restrictions and President Carter's tax increases with an almost opposite policy—a general tax cut—intended to encourage corporations to invest more and produce more, which would thereby cut inflation by increasing the abundance of goods. But inflationary pressures were showing no signs of relaxing until President Reagan succeeded in getting the **Federal Reserve Board** to lower interest rates in order to encourage further investment. (High interest rates discourage borrowing for investment and consumption.)

For whatever combination of reasons, the inflation rate did in fact begin to drop during the 1980s. By 1993 and the accession of President Clinton, inflation rates had been so low for so long that the government was able to relax the vigil on inflation and turn its attention toward policies that might increase the rate of economic growth. (As a general rule, Republicans are more sensitive to inflation, while Democrats are quicker to worry about general economic growth.) One of President Clinton's earliest successes was convincing Alan Greenspan, chair of the Federal Reserve Board, that some new spending for an economic stimulus would not "overheat" the economy to such an extent that the Federal Reserve would have to jump back in and raise interest rates. But despite Greenspan's approval, the Republicans in Congress, along with a few conservative Democrats, forced President Clinton to reduce his stimulus package severely from the requested $16 billion (itself a modest figure) to a minuscule figure below $1 billion. Inflation rates continued to run relatively low, toward 2 and 3 percent per year, compared to the double-digit inflation rates of the 1970s.

No one can guess whether inflation or unemployment will be the policy priority of the future, but we can say confidently that no government will stand by and let rampant inflation excessively influence the economy. Government acts such as increasing interest rates, restricting imports, or cutting taxes are called public policies. **Public policy** can be defined simply as an officially expressed purpose or intention backed by a sanction, which can be a reward or a punishment. Thus, a public policy can be a law, a rule, a statute, an edict, a regulation, or an order. Today, the term "public policy" is the term of preference, probably because it conveys more of an impression of flexibility and compassion than other terms. But the citizen, especially the student of political science, should never forget that the words "policy" and "police" have common origins. Both derive from *polis* and *polity*, which refer to the political community. Consequently, it must be clearly understood that all public policies are coercive, even when they are motivated by the best and most beneficent of intentions. Because public policies are coercive, many people wrongly conclude that all public policies—all government—should be opposed. For us, the coercive element in public policy should instill not absolute opposition but a healthy respect for the risks as well as the good that may be inherent in any public policy.

The job of this chapter and of the succeeding three chapters is to step beyond the *politics* and the *institutions* to look at the *purposes* of government—the public policies. This chapter will focus on policies toward the economy; Chapter 17 will cover social and welfare policies; Chapter 18 will look at civil rights policies; and Chapter 19 will concentrate on foreign policies and international affairs. The first section of this chapter will provide an introduction to public policy. It is a simple inventory of the "techniques of control," the tools available to any government to encourage or coerce its citizens to obey. The second section of this chapter will examine how these techniques are used in actual policies to influence the domestic economy. These policies have been organized into three categories: (1) policies to protect public order and private property; (2) policies that control or influence the free market; and (3) policies that are designed to defend and enhance the vitality of America's capitalist economy. This chapter ends where Chapter 17 begins, on issues involving the welfare state. Since welfare policies require taxes, they are both economic as well as social policies, and thus they will be discussed both in this chapter and the next.

Techniques of Control

➤ What categories of techniques of control does the government use to form public policy? What are some examples of each?

Techniques of control are to policy makers what tools are to a carpenter. There is a limited number of techniques; with each there is a logic and a limit; and there is an accumulation of experience that helps us to understand when a certain technique is likely to work. There is no unanimous agreement on techniques, just as carpenters will disagree about the best tool for a task. But we offer here a workable elementary handbook of techniques that will be useful for analyzing the policies we will examine in this and succeeding chapters.

Table 16.1 lists some important techniques of control available to policy makers. These techniques can be grouped into three categories—promotional, regulatory, and redistributive techniques—and the specifics of each will be discussed and explained in this section.

Promotional Techniques

Promotional techniques are the carrots of public policy. Their purpose is to encourage people to do something they might not otherwise do or to get people to do more of what they are already doing. Sometimes the purpose is merely to compensate people for something done in the past. Promotional techniques can be classified into at least three separate types—subsidies, contracts, and licenses.

Subsidies **Subsidies** are simply government grants of cash or other valuable commodities, such as land. Although subsidies are often denounced as "giveaways," they have played a fundamental role in the history of government in

TECHNIQUES OF PUBLIC CONTROL

Types of techniques	Techniques	Definitions and examples
Promotional techniques	Subsidies and grants of cash, land, etc.	"Patronage" is the promotion of private activity through what recipients consider "benefits" (example: in the nineteenth century the government encouraged westward settlement by granting land to those who went west)
	Contracts	Agreements with individuals or firms in the "private sector" to purchase goods or services
	Licenses	Unconditional permission to do something that is otherwise illegal (franchise, permit)
Regulatory techniques	Criminal penalties	Heavy fines or imprisonment, loss of citizenship
	Civil penalties	Less onerous fines, probation, public exposure, restitution
	Administrative regulations	Setting interest rates, maintaining standards of health and safety, investigating and publicizing wrongdoing
	Subsidies, contracts, and licenses	Regulatory techniques when certain conditions are attached (example: the government refuses to award a contract to firms that show no evidence of affirmative action in hiring)
	Regulatory taxes	Taxes that keep consumption or production down (liquor, gas, cigarette taxes)
	Expropriation	"Eminent domain"—the power to take private property for public use
Redistributive techniques	Taxes	Altering the redistribution of money by changing taxes or tax rules
	Budgeting and spending through subsidies and contracts	Deficit spending to pump money into the economy when it needs a boost; creating a budget surplus by cutting spending or increasing taxes to discourage consumption in inflationary times
	Fiscal use of credit and interest (monetary techniques)	Changing interest rates to affect both demand for money and consumption (example: the Federal Reserve Board raises interest rates to slow economic growth and ward off inflation)

TABLE 16.1

the United States. Subsidies were the dominant form of public policy of the national government and the state and local governments throughout the nineteenth century. They continue to be an important category of public policy at all levels of government. The first planning document ever written for the national government, Alexander Hamilton's *Report on Manufactures*, was based almost entirely on Hamilton's assumption that American industry could be encouraged by federal subsidies and that these were not only desirable but constitutional.

Between 1851 and 1871, railroad companies were given more than two hundred million acres of public land by the federal government. The railroads then sold the land at low prices to attract settlers to build along their lines.

The thrust of Hamilton's plan was not lost on later policy makers. Subsidies in the form of land grants were given to farmers and to railroad companies to encourage western settlement. Substantial cash subsidies have traditionally been given to commercial shipbuilders to help build the commercial fleet and to guarantee the use of the ships as military personnel carriers in time of war. Policies using the subsidy technique have continued to be plentiful in the twentieth century, even during the 1990s when there was widespread public and official hostility toward subsidies. For example, through 1994, the total annual value of subsidies to industry alone was estimated at \$53 billion, based on relatively conservative Congressional Budget Office (CBO) figures.[1] Crop subsidies alone, implemented by the Department of Agriculture, amount to about \$6 billion annually.

Subsidies have always been a technique favored by politicians because subsidies can be treated as "benefits" that can be spread widely in response to many demands that might otherwise produce profound political conflict. Subsidies can, in other words, be used to buy off the opposition.

Another secret of the popularity of subsidies is that those who receive the benefits do not perceive the controls inherent in them. In the first place, most of the resources available for subsidies come from taxation. (In the nineteenth century, there was a lot of public land to distribute, but that is no longer the case.) Second, the effect of any subsidy has to be measured somewhat indirectly in terms of what people *would be doing* if the subsidy had not been available. For example, many thousands of people settled in lands west of the Mississippi only because land subsidies were available. Hundreds of research laboratories exist in universities and corporations only because certain types of research subsidies from the government are available. And finally, once subsidies exist, the threat of their removal becomes a very significant technique of control.

Contracting Like any corporation, a government agency must purchase goods and services by contract. The law requires open bidding for a substantial proportion of these contracts because government contracts are extremely valuable to businesses in the private sector and because the opportunities and incentives for abuse are very great. But contracting is more than a method of buying goods and services. Contracting is also an important technique of policy because government agencies are often authorized to use their **contracting power** as a means of encouraging corporations to improve themselves, as a means of helping to build up whole sectors of the economy, and as a means of encouraging certain desirable goals or behavior, such as equal employment opportunity. For example, the infant airline industry of the 1930s was nurtured by the national government's lucrative contracts to carry airmail. A more recent example is the use of government contracting to encourage industries, universities, and other organizations to engage in research and development.

The contracting power was of great significance for the Reagan and Bush administrations because of their commitment to "privatization." A president who wants to restore as much government as possible to the private sector

Vice President Al Gore at an unveiling of a model of a new spacecraft developed by Lockheed Martin. The national government's contract with Lockheed Martin called for spending close to $1 billion on the spacecraft's development.

may seek to terminate a government program and leave the activity to private companies to pick up. That would be true privatization. But in most instances, true privatization is neither sought nor achieved. Instead, the government program is transferred to a private company to provide the service *under a contract with the government*, paid for by the government, and supervised by a government agency. In this case, privatization is only a euphemism.

Government-by-contract has been around for a long time, and has always been seen by business as a major source of economic opportunity. In the Pentagon alone, nearly $94 billion was spent in 1994 on contracts with the twenty top defense companies in the United States and abroad. The top company, in terms of the value of its defense contracts, was Lockheed Martin, whose revenues from those defense contracts amounted to $14.4 billion. This represented nearly 63 percent of Lockheed Martin's total annual revenues. McDonnell Douglas came in second with slightly over $9 billion in 1994. Revenues from defense contracts represented nearly 64 percent of their total annual revenues.[2]

Licensing A **license** is a privilege granted by a government to do something that it otherwise considers to be illegal. For example, state laws make practicing medicine or driving a taxi illegal without a license. The states then create a board of doctors and a "hack bureau" to grant licenses for the practice of medicine or for the operation of a cab to all persons who have met the particular qualifications specified in the statute or by the agency. Like subsidies and contracting, licensing has two sides. One is the giveaway side, making the license a desirable object of patronage. The other side of licensing is the control or regulatory side, which will be discussed next.

Regulatory Techniques

If promotional techniques are the carrots of public policy, **regulatory techniques** can be considered the sticks. **Regulation** comes in several forms, but every regulatory technique shares a common trait: direct government control of conduct. The conduct may be regulated because people feel it is harmful to others, or threatens to be, such as drunk driving or false advertising. Or the conduct may be regulated because people think it's immoral, whether it is harming anybody or not, such as prostitution, gambling, or drinking. Because there are many forms of regulation, we have subdivided them here: (1) police regulation, through civil and criminal penalties, (2) administrative regulation, and (3) regulatory taxation.

Police Regulation "Police regulation" is not a technical term, but we use it for this category because these techniques come closest to the traditional exercise of **police power**—a power traditionally reserved to the states. After a person's arrest and conviction, these techniques are administered by courts and, where necessary, penal institutions. They are regulatory techniques.

Civil penalties usually refer to fines or some other form of material restitution (such as public service) as a sanction for violating civil laws or such common law principles as negligence. Civil penalties can range from a $5 fine for a parking violation to a more onerous penalty for late payment of income taxes to the much more onerous penalties for violating antitrust laws against unfair competition or environmental protection laws against pollution. **Criminal penalties** usually refer to imprisonment but can also involve heavy fines and the loss of certain civil rights and liberties, such as the right to vote or the freedom of speech.

Administrative Regulation Police regulation addresses conduct considered immoral. In order to eliminate such conduct, strict laws have been passed and severe sanctions enacted. But what about conduct that is not considered morally wrong but that may have harmful consequences? For example, there is nothing morally wrong with radio or television broadcasting. But broadcasting on a particular frequency or channel is regulated by government because there would be virtual chaos if everybody could broadcast on any frequency at any time.

"Radio Ron" of Berkeley, California, has battled with the Federal Communications Commission (FCC) over its regulation of the radio broadcast spectrum.

This kind of conduct is thought of less as *policed* conduct and more as *regulated* conduct. When conduct is said to be regulated, the purpose is rarely to eliminate the conduct but rather to influence it toward more appropriate channels, toward more appropriate locations, or toward certain qualified types of persons, all for the purpose of minimizing injuries or inconveniences. This type of regulation is sometimes called **administrative regulation** because the controls are given over to civilian agencies rather than to the police. Each regulatory agency has extensive powers to keep a sector of the economy under surveillance and also has powers to make rules dealing with the behavior of individual companies and people. But these administrative agencies have fewer powers of punishment than the police and the courts have, and the administrative agencies generally rely on the courts to issue orders enforcing the rules and decisions made by the agencies.

Sometimes a government will adopt administrative regulation if an economic activity is considered so important that it is not to be entrusted to competition among several companies in the private sector. This is the rationale for the regulation of local or regional power companies. A single company, traditionally called a "utility," is given an exclusive license (or franchise) to offer these services, but since the one company is made a legal **monopoly** and is protected from competition by other companies, the government gives an administrative agency the power to regulate the quality of the services rendered, the rates charged for those services, and the margin of profit that the company is permitted to make.

At other times, administrative regulation is the chosen technique because the legislature decides that the economy needs protection from itself—that is, it may set up a regulatory agency to protect companies from destructive or predatory competition, on the assumption that economic competition is not always its own solution. This is the rationale behind the Federal Trade Commission, which has the responsibility of watching over such practices as price discrimination or pooling agreements between two or more companies when their purpose is to eliminate competitors.

Table 16.1 listed subsidies, contracting, and licensing twice, as examples of both promotional and regulatory policies, because although these techniques can be used as strictly promotional policies, they can also be used as techniques of administrative regulation. It all depends on whether the law sets serious conditions on eligibility for the subsidy, license, or contract. To put it another way, the threat of losing a valuable subsidy, license, or contract can be used by the government to improve compliance with the goals of regulation. For example, the threat of removal of the subsidies called "federal aid to education" has had a very significant influence on the willingness of schools to cooperate in the desegregation of their student bodies and faculties. For another example, social welfare subsidies (benefits) can be lowered to encourage or force people to take low-paying jobs, or they can be increased to placate people when they are engaging in political protest.[3]

Like subsidies and licensing, government contracting can be an entirely different kind of technique of control when the contract or its denial is used as a reward or punishment to gain obedience in a regulatory program. For example, Presidents Kennedy and Johnson used their considerable power to influence the employment practices of all the corporations seeking contracts from the national government to provide goods or services. Both Kennedy and Johnson issued executive orders, administered by the Office of Federal Contract Compliance in the Department of Labor, to prohibit discrimination by firms receiving government contracts.[4] The value of these contracts to many private corporations was so great that they were quite willing to alter if not eliminate racial discrimination in employment practices if that was the only way to qualify for government contracts. For the same reason, many companies include in their employment ads the statement "We are an equal opportunity employer."

Regulatory Taxation Taxation is generally understood to be a fiscal technique, and it will be discussed as such later in this chapter. But in many instances, the primary purpose of a tax is not to raise revenue but to discourage or eliminate an activity altogether by making it too expensive for most people. Such taxes are called **regulatory taxes.** For example, since the end of Prohibition, although there has been no penalty for the production or sale of alcoholic beverages, the alcohol industry has not been free from regulation. First, all alcoholic beverages have to be licensed, allowing only those companies that are "bonded" to put their product on the market. Beyond that, federal and state taxes on alcohol are made disproportionately high, on the theory that, in addition to the revenue gained, less alcohol will be consumed.

Americans may see a great deal more regulation by taxation in the future, for at least the following reasons. First, it is a kind of hidden regulation, acceptable to people who in principle are against regulation. Second, it permits a certain amount of choice. For example, a heavy tax on gasoline or on smokestack and chemical industries (called an "effluent tax") will encourage drivers and these companies to regulate their own activities by permitting them to decide how much pollution they can afford. Third, advocates of regulatory taxation believe it to be more efficient than other forms of regulation, requiring less bureaucracy and less supervision.

Taxes on cigarettes raise about $11 billion annually for federal, state, and local governments. Although these taxes are effective revenue generators, they can also be effective in discouraging smoking. These tobacco farmers are protesting a proposed cigarette tax increase, because it would likely lower demand for cigarettes even further.

Expropriation Seizing private property for a public use, or **expropriation,** is a widely used technique of control in the United States, especially in land-use regulation. Almost all public works, from highways to parks to government office buildings, involve the forceful taking of some private property in order to assemble sufficient land and the correct distribution of land for the necessary construction. The vast Interstate Highway Program required expropriation of thousands of narrow strips of private land. Urban redevelopment projects often require city governments to use the powers of seizure in the service of private developers, who actually build the urban projects on the land that would be far too expensive if purchased on the open market. Private utilities that supply electricity and gas to individual subscribers are given powers to take private property whenever a new facility or a right-of-way is needed.

We generally call the power to expropriate **eminent domain,** a power that is recognized as inherent in any government. The Fifth Amendment of the U.S. Constitution surrounds this expropriation power with important safeguards against abuse, so that government agencies in the United States are not permitted to use that power except through a strict due process, and they must offer "fair market value" for the land sought.[5]

Forcing individuals to work for a public purpose is another form of expropriation. The draft of young men for the armed forces, court orders to strikers to return to work, and sentences for convicted felons to do community service are examples of the regular use of expropriation in the United States.

Redistributive Techniques

Redistributive techniques (also called macroeconomic techniques) are usually of two types—fiscal and monetary—but they have a common purpose: to control people by manipulating the entire economy rather than by regulating people directly. (*Macroeconomic* refers to the economy as a system.) Whereas

THE LABOR MOVEMENT

The movement to organize America's workers into unions grew out of the rise of industrialization and the appalling working conditions faced by the average worker. Low wages, long hours, hazardous conditions, the exploitation of child labor, and a lack of job security were typical experiences for the working American in the nineteenth and twentieth centuries.

The first modern unions were trade unions whose membership was usually limited to skilled workers in particular occupations. The Knights of Labor was one of the first such unions. Formed in 1869 as an organization of garment workers, it peaked in the late 1880s with a successful strike against railroad interests. But the union rapidly declined in the 1890s because of an economic downturn and opposition from large corporations. In 1886, the American Federation of Labor (AFL) was formed. Its leader, Samuel Gompers, kept the union's membership limited to those in the skilled craft trades, excluding industrial workers who lacked particular trade skills. The AFL's membership grew, and it succeeded in winning higher wages, shorter hours, safer and cleaner working conditions, job security, protections for women and children workers, and the right to bargain collectively. But the AFL's relative political conservatism, its rejection of socialist members, and its exclusion of unskilled workers encouraged the emergence of more radical groups, such as the Industrial Workers of the World (IWW).

The IWW was formed in 1905 by miners, lumberjacks, dockworkers, farmworkers and others, mostly from the West. Unlike the AFL, the IWW embraced both skilled and unskilled workers. It rejected the capitalist wage system and viewed business leaders as the enemies of workers. The "Wobblies," as they were called, advocated the formation of "one big union." In addition to strikes, a tactic used by the AFL and other unions, the IWW called for illegal actions, such as sabotage, when necessary. The high point of IWW strength was 1912, when it won a strike at a textile plant in Massachusetts. The most visible and charismatic socialist leader was Eugene V. Debs, but Debs had parted ways with the more radical IWW around the time of IWW's founding, in 1905. Debs formed the Socialist Party of America, which between 1904 and 1908 was the only important socialist party in the United States.

American fears of socialism pushed the national gov-

regulatory techniques focus on individual conduct—"Walking on the grass is not permitted," or "Membership in a union may not be used to deny employment, nor may a worker be fired for promoting union membership"—redistributive techniques seek to control conduct more indirectly by altering the conditions of conduct or manipulating the environment of conduct.

Fiscal Techniques Fiscal techniques of control are the government's taxing and spending powers. Personal and corporate income taxes, which raise most of the U.S. government's revenues, are the most prominent examples. While the direct purpose of an income tax is to raise revenue, each tax has a different impact on the economy, and government can plan for that impact. For example, although the main reason favoring a significant increase in the Social Security tax (which is an income tax) under President Jimmy Carter was to keep Social Security solvent, a big reason for it in the minds of many legislators was that it would reduce inflation by shrinking the amount of money people had in their hands to buy more goods and services.

ernment toward a crackdown on all socialist leaders for speaking out against American involvement in World War I. In 1918, most of them, including Debs, were sent to prison on charges of sedition. Despite the rejection of the socialist unionism, changes in industrialization increased the number of unskilled industrial workers, most of whom were still excluded from the powerful AFL. In 1934 and 1935, some AFL leaders pressed the organization to form industrial unions, which would combine all workers in a single industry under one union, instead of separating them by trades. When the increasingly conservative AFL leaders refused, the reformers bolted the organization and formed the Congress of Industrial Organizations (CIO) in 1937. The CIO achieved a major organizing victory by winning the right to establish an industrial union in the steel industry in 1937. That same year, it succeeded in organizing at General Motors and Chrysler. The fiercely anti-union Ford Motor company yielded in 1940. By the start of World War II, the CIO claimed 5 million members, compared to the AFL's 4.6 million.

These union victories came at a high price, as most business leaders fought unionization with intimidation, violence, and mass firings of employees suspected of engaging in union activities. The AFL and the CIO were able to win major improvements in working conditions and security that helped millions of workers enter the middle class. In 1955, the AFL and CIO merged to form the AFL-CIO. In recent decades, as workers have shifted from blue-collar occupations (physical labor) to white-collar occupations (office work), unionism has declined. Nevertheless, the union movement continues to address the working conditions of many Americans.

SOURCE: Michael Goldfield, *The Decline of Organized Labor in the United States* (Chicago: University of Chicago Press, 1987).

Likewise, President Clinton's commitment in his 1992 campaign to a "middle-class tax cut" was motivated by the goal of encouraging economic growth through increased consumption. Soon after the election, upon learning that the deficit would be far larger than had been earlier reported to him, he confessed he would have to break his promise of such a tax cut. Nevertheless, the idea of a middle-class tax cut is an example of a fiscal policy aimed at increased consumption, because of the theory that people in middle-income brackets tend to spend a high proportion of unexpected earnings or windfalls, rather than saving or investing them.[6]

Monetary Techniques **Monetary techniques** also seek to influence conduct by manipulating the entire economy through the supply or availability of money. The Federal Reserve System (the Fed) can adopt what is called a "hard money policy" by increasing the interest rate it charges member banks (called the discount rate). In 1980, when inflation was at a historic high, the Fed permitted interest rates to reach a high of nearly 20 percent, in an attempt to rein inflation in. During the 1991 recession, however, the Fed permitted interest rates to drop well below 10 percent, hoping this would encourage people to borrow more to buy houses, etc. Another monetary policy is one of increasing or decreasing the **reserve requirement,** which sets the actual proportion of deposited money that a bank must keep "on demand" as it makes all the rest of the deposits available as new loans.[7] A third important technique used by the Fed is **open market operations**—the buying and selling of Treasury securities to absorb excess dollars or to release more dollars into the economy. The Fed will be discussed in greater detail later in this chapter.

Spending Power as Fiscal Policy Perhaps the most important redistributive technique of all is the most familiar one: the "spending power," which is a combination of subsidies and contracts. These techniques can be used for policy goals far beyond the goods and services bought and the individual conduct regulated. This is why subsidies and contracting show up yet again on Table 16.1, as techniques of fiscal policy.

Agricultural subsidies are one example of the national government's use of its purchasing power as a fiscal or redistributive technique. And since the 1930s, the federal government has attempted to raise and to stabilize the prices of several important agricultural products, such as corn and wheat, by authorizing the Department of Agriculture to buy enormous amounts of these commodities if prices on the market fall below a fixed level.

Government has developed a historic stake in money, credit, and agriculture, just as it has in major public works and regulation—all seen as essential conditions of a stable and growing economy.

Substantive Uses of Public Policy

- What is the impact of federalism on public policy?
- How is the national government fundamental in promoting a national market economy?
- What influences government adoption of regulatory policies?
- What forms of economic policy help encourage a capitalist economy?

We now come to the examination of how the techniques of control just examined are employed to implement public policies. But before we can do that we have to do something that would not be necessary if this textbook were on, say, the government of England or of France. We have to re-introduce federalism, because so much of the effort by government in America to influence the economy is carried out by the states.

FEDERALISM AND PUBLIC POLICY

Most public policies in American history have been policies adopted by the state legislatures, not by Congress. Table 16.2 shows that, during the first century and a half of U.S. history, the national government simply did far less

TABLE 16.2

PUBLIC POLICIES IN THE UNITED STATES, 1800–1933

National government policies (domestic)	State government policies	Local government policies
Internal improvements	Property laws (including slavery)	Adaptation of state laws to local conditions ("variances")
Subsidies	Estate and inheritance laws	Public works
Tariffs	Commerce laws	Contracts for public works
Public lands disposal	Banking and credit laws	Licensing of public accommodations
Patents	Corporate laws	Assessible improvements
Currency	Insurance laws	Basic public services
	Family laws	
	Morals laws	
	Public health laws	
	Education laws	
	General penal laws	
	Eminent domain laws	
	Construction codes	
	Land-use laws	
	Water and mineral laws	
	Criminal procedure laws	
	Electoral and political parties laws	
	Local government laws	
	Civil service laws	
	Occupations and professions laws	

governing than the state governments did. Furthermore, a closer look at the "national" column in Table 16.2 reveals that all of the policies adopted by the national government during that time were promotional policies (defined in the preceding section of this chapter). In the American federal system, there is no national police force; there is almost no national criminal law; there is no national common law; there are no national property laws, no national marriage laws, no national laws concerning the practice of law, medicine, or accounting; there are no national estate laws (although there are national estate taxes); and there are no national divorce or custody laws. Except for a few federal laws dealing with interstate crimes and crimes in the federal territories, there are few national laws on anything except promoting commerce. It is no wonder that foreigners tend to refer to America as a "commercial republic."

The list of national laws shown in Table 16.2 began slowly to grow just before the First World War with the establishment (by constitutional amendment) of the power to adopt a national income tax, the establishment of the Federal Reserve System, and the addition of a few more interstate commerce rules. Still, there was no *significant* increase in the policies that make up the national column until 1933. Even as the national government grew during the 1930s, the states continued to adopt and implement the same kinds of public policies that they had always adopted and implemented. In other words the national government grew, but it did not grow at the expense of the states.

The current widespread skepticism in the United States against the national government and its tremendous expansion over the past fifty years has some basis: It is definitely time to re-evaluate many established federal programs, to abolish some of them and turn others over to the state and local governments. But the current uproar about "returning power to the states" hides the truth about public policy in the United States. The federal courts, beginning in the 1950s, did begin to restrict the powers of the states to use law to separate the races, to treat men differently from women, etc. (see Chapters 5 and 18). But the courts did not *remove* those powers from the states, nor did the court seek to transfer any of those state powers from the states to the national government. The national government has become much bigger since the 1930s, but this was added growth, not a transfer of powers. Federalism is still alive and well.

MAKING AND MAINTAINING A NATIONAL MARKET ECONOMY

Valuable as the states have been in developing public policies to promote a market economy, their separate boundaries, their separate laws, and their separate traditions have also been a barrier to those enterprises seeking to expand beyond local markets. In fact, the protectionism of some states against others was precisely why America's first constitution, the Articles of Confederation, was ultimately considered a failure and in need of replacement. Giving Congress the powers of Article I, Section 8, enabled the national government to provide a system of roads, canals, and communications that would foster a regional and ultimately a national market. In *Gibbons v. Ogden*, one of the most important cases the Supreme Court has ever handed down, the states were told in no uncertain terms that they could not pass laws that would tend to interrupt or otherwise burden the free flow of commerce among the states.[8] In the twentieth century, one of the major reasons why Congress began to adopt national business regulatory policies was that the regulated companies themselves felt burdened by the inconsistencies among the states. These companies often preferred a single, national regulatory authority, no matter how burdensome, because they would have consistency throughout the United States and could thereby treat the nation as a single market.[9] Table 16.3 provides a historical overview of regulation in our federal system.

Promoting the Market During the nineteenth century, the national government was almost exclusively a promoter of markets. National roads and canals were built to tie states and regions together. National tariff policies promoted domestic markets by restricting imported goods; a tax on an import raised its price and weakened its ability to compete with similar domes-

FEDERALISM AND THE REGULATION OF THE U.S. ECONOMY

	National government and economic regulation	State governments and economic regulation
Nineteenth century		
Pre–Civil War Post–Civil War	Fugitive slaves Railroads Interstate trusts and monopolies	Property ownership Monopolies Price discrimination Contracts and their enforcement Apprenticeship Professional licensing Compulsory education Public utilities Banking Slaves (in southern states) Agricultural markets Oil and gas extraction Coal mines
Twentieth century		
Pre-1933	Unfair trade practices National banks Impure food and drugs	All the nineteenth-century policies (except slavery) plus—
Post-1933	Stock markets Agricultural markets Trade unions Coal mines Telecommunications Natural gas transport Atomic energy Equal employment and other civil rights Environment Consumer product safety	Child labor Working conditions Equal employment opportunity Equal education opportunity TV cable access Local land use (zoning) Land conservation Building construction standards

TABLE 16.3

tic products. The national government also heavily subsidized the railroad system. Until the 1840s, railroads were thought to be of limited commercial value. But between 1850 and 1872, Congress granted over 100 million acres of public domain land to railroad interests, and state and local governments pitched in an estimated $280 million in cash and credit. Before the end of the century, 35,000 miles of track existed—almost half the world's total.

In the twentieth century, traditional promotional techniques were expanded and some new ones were invented. For example, a great proportion of the promotional activities of the national government are now done indirectly through **categorical grants** (see Chapter 4). The national government

In addition to land on which to lay tracks, railroad companies were provided financial aid by federal, state, and local governments to construct the railroads.

offers grants to states on condition that the state (or local) government undertake a particular activity. Thus, in order to use motor transportation to improve national markets, a 900,000-mile national highway system was built during the 1930s, based on a formula whereby the national government would pay 50 percent of the cost if the state would provide the other 50 percent. Over twenty years, beginning in the late 1950s, the federal government constructed nearly 45,000 miles of interstate highways. This was brought about through a program whereby the national government agreed to pay 90 percent of the construction costs on the condition that each state provide for 10 percent of the costs of any portion of a highway built within its boundaries.[10] There are similar examples of U.S. government promotional policy in each of the country's major industrial sectors.

The promotional policies of the national government since the mid-nineteenth century have been strongly supported by both of the major political parties. Today, Republicans oppose national government growth as a matter of principle and ideology, and for good reason: many of these policies are nothing more than payoffs for influential members of Congress, interest groups, and favored constituencies. But Republicans have created promotional policies, too. In any case, the narrowly conceived "pork-barrel" policies should not discredit the importance of promotional policies in American history, without which a genuine national economy would have taken much longer to develop.

Regulating the Market As the American economy prospered throughout the nineteenth century, some companies grew so large that they were recognized as possessing "market power." This meant that they were powerful enough to eliminate competitors and to impose conditions on consumers rather than cater to consumer demand. The growth of billion-dollar corporations led to collusion among companies to control prices, much to the dismay of smaller

AMERICAN POLITICAL CULTURE

Downsizing

From 1989 through 1995, while American business profits skyrocketed, companies began to cut their personnel levels at alarming rates; layoffs announced during these years totaled three million jobs lost.[1] Some of the massive reductions at individual corporations were staggering. For example, General Motors announced in 1991 that it would eliminate 70,000 people from its workforce. In 1993, IBM said it would cut 63,000 jobs. And at the end of 1995, AT&T, despite its good financial health and rising profits, made the shocking announcement that it would slash 40,000 jobs—13 percent of its total workforce—by the end of 1998. AT&T announced these cuts in a year that saw American businesses earn record profits, a year in which the Dow Jones industrial average (which measures the strength of the stock market) rose above the 5,000 mark, gaining over a third in value.

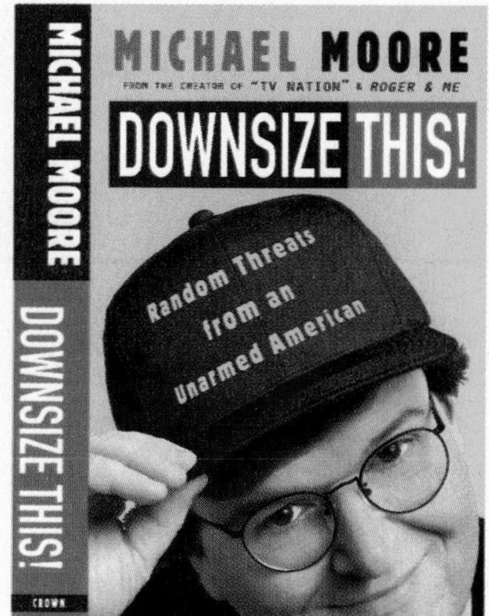

"Downsizing" in the midst of prosperity is one of the most troubling stories of American capitalism at the end of the twentieth century. Most economists agree on the underlying explanation: a new era of global competition. But that is little solace to the millions of Americans who have lost their jobs, especially when economists disagree about whether downsizing will ensure the competitiveness of U.S. businesses in the world market. And in a time when Americans have spoken strongly in favor of "smaller government" (even if they are not sure what they want cut), it is plain that government has neither the resources nor the mandate to do much to alter the present balance of profits and layoffs. Even liberal economists such as Robert Reich, President Clinton's secretary of labor, concede that "in the future the Federal Government will have a more modest role in safeguarding the economic security of Americans."[2]

What if we look at downsizing not as an economic problem, but a cultural one? Indeed some economists argue that the recent downsizing trend has been fueled more by ideology and the corporate version of "keeping up with the Joneses" than by economic necessity. One economist calls downsizing "addictive," less a rationally conceived plan than "the habit of choice for a generation of managers."[3] Another notes, "When companies run into problems, they downsize as a matter of course," even if downsizing is not necessarily the right solution to their problems.[4]

In the early 1960s, President John F. Kennedy, arguing for a tax cut and the importance of a sound economy to the nation, said that a rising tide lifts all boats. His was an optimistic view that reflected a sense that economic prosperity was justified if it benefited the entire nation. In the 1990s this view seems to have evolved into a less communal, more individualistic perspective. Today many would argue, especially with regard to economics, that there is no "communal good," just the maximization of individual goods. For better or worse, the new American bargain with capitalism seems to be this: let the rising tide lift most of the boats, and if some of the crew get thrown overboard to lighten the load, may I not be one of those unfortunate people. This may be sound economics—but is it sound politics?

[1]Based on a study by Challenger, Gray & Christmas, cited in Bob Herbert, "Firing Their Customers," *New York Times,* December 29, 1995, p. A11.

[2]Robert B. Reich, "How to Avoid These Layoffs?" *New York Times,* January 4, 1996, p. A21.

[3]Quoted in David Francis, "What Does a Company Do After Downsizing?" *Christian Science Monitor,* October 20, 1995, p. 8.

[4]Francis, "What Does a Company Do?" p. 8.

In 1906, Congress passed the New Meat Inspection Act, which required that all meat intended for interstate commerce meet federal health standards. This photo shows a Chicago slaughterhouse immediately following the passage of the act.

businesses and ordinary consumers. Moreover, the expanding economy was more mechanized and this involved greater dangers to employees as well as to consumers.

Small businesses, laborers, farmers, and consumers all began to clamor for protective regulation. Although the states had been regulating businesses in one way or another all along, interest groups turned toward Washington as economic problems appeared to be beyond the reach of the individual state governments. If markets were national, there would have to be national regulation.[11]

The first national regulatory policy was the Interstate Commerce Act of 1887, which created the first national independent regulatory commission, the Interstate Commerce Commission (ICC), designed to control the monopolistic practices of the railroads. Two years later, the Sherman Antitrust Act extended regulatory power to cover all monopolistic practices, including "trusts" or any other agreement between companies to eliminate competition. These were strengthened in 1914 with the enactment of the Federal Trade Act (creating the Federal Trade Commission, or FTC) and the Clayton Act. The only significant addition of national regulatory policy beyond regulation of interstate trade, however, was the establishment of the Federal Reserve System in 1913, which was given powers to regulate the banking industry along with its general monetary powers.

The modern epoch of comprehensive national regulation began in the 1930s. Most of the regulatory programs of the 1930s were established to regulate the conduct of companies within specifically designated sectors of

American industry. For example, the jurisdiction of one agency was the securities industry; the jurisdiction of another was the radio (and eventually television) industry. Another was banking. Another was coal mining; still another was agriculture. When Congress turned once again toward regulatory policies in the 1970s, it became still more bold, moving beyond the effort to regulate specific sectors of industry toward regulating some aspect of the entire economy. The scope or jurisdiction of such agencies as the Occupational Safety and Health Administration (OSHA), the Consumer Product Safety Commission (CPSC), and the Environmental Protection Agency (EPA) is as broad and as wide as the entire economy, indeed the entire society. This is why both defenders and critics of these 1970s programs have agreed to distinguish them from the New Deal agencies by calling the 1970s programs "new regulation" and "social regulation." This is a reasonable distinction as long as we do not forget the fact that all of these agencies are regulatory in that they use regulatory techniques to control some aspect of the conduct of individuals or companies. Another important area of social regulation is civil rights; this will be discussed in Chapter 18.

An official from the Consumer Product Safety Commission demonstrates the potential danger of some types of baby cribs. In areas of consumer safety, the national government regularly plays a protective role.

Deregulation Today, so-called conservatives, as represented by Newt Gingrich and Bob Dole, are in principle opposed to government intervention in the economy.[12] They see government not as part of the solution, but as part of the problem. They adamantly oppose intervention by techniques of promoting commerce and are even more opposed to intervention through techniques of regulation. They believe that markets would be bigger and healthier if not regulated at all.

The **deregulation** movement actually began under Presidents Ford and Carter. Their accomplishments include the Securities Act Amendment of 1975, the Railroad Revitalization Act of 1976, the Airline Deregulation Act of 1978, the Staggers Rail Deregulation Act of 1980, the Depository Institution Deregulation and Monetary Control Act of 1980, and the Motor Carrier Act of 1980.

President Reagan's approach to deregulation is a good lesson in the relationship between executive management and legislative authority. Reagan almost immediately provided for an average 20 percent cut in the budgets of all the regulatory agencies. Although this cutback did not have any significant effect on the total budget of the federal government, because the regulatory agencies are not very large, it certainly required severe reductions in the agencies' staff and therefore severe reductions in the level and vigor of regulatory activity by the federal government.

Reagan's second approach to deregulation by management was his appointment of agency board members who were not in sympathy with the regulatory mission of the specific agency. In fact, some of the members of these commissions were genuinely hostile to the mission of their agency.[13] Another important approach President Reagan took to the task of changing the direction of regulation was "presidential oversight." One of his first actions after taking office was Executive Order 12291, issued February 17, 1981, which gave the Office of Management and Budget (OMB) the authority to review all proposals by all executive branch agencies for new regulations to be applied to companies or people within their jurisdiction. By this means,

President Reagan succeeded in reducing the total number of regulations issued by federal agencies to such an extent that the number of pages in the *Federal Register* dropped from 87,000 in 1980 to 49,600 in 1987.[14] Although Presidents Bush and Clinton also favored deregulation as a principle, the number of pages crept up steadily after 1987, reaching 69,680 by 1993. Still, this was significantly fewer than there had been in 1980.

In 1993, President Clinton and Vice President Al Gore criticized the vast number of federal regulations, pointing especially to regulations on purchasing everything from aspirin to insect repellent as "outrageous" rules that wasted taxpayers' money. Despite the president's rhetoric, it has been the Republicans who have sought most vigorously to cut the number of regulations.

The election of 1994 reminded everyone in Washington that the antiregulation spirit had been revived. The Republicans' "Contract with America" had promised restrictions on federal regulation, and several bills were introduced at the very outset of the 104th Congress. Telecommunications laws were to be revised downward. Pollution control and endangered species laws were to be overhauled to reduce the amount of regulation in the environmental area. Perhaps of greater importance were two bills that aimed to impose a regulatory oversight process even more strict than that set up by President Reagan. These bills, if adopted, would impose a strict assessment process on every regulatory rule proposed by an administrative agency. Most probably, this would reduce still further the number of pages in the *Federal Register*.

Yet, as potent as the 1995 deregulation proposals were, the Republican Congress did not propose that any regulatory programs be terminated. Considering the Republicans' 1994 campaign rhetoric about government being too large, the lack of proposals to eliminate regulations produced some frustrated responses from the strongest supporters of deregulation. For example, the distinguished British magazine the *Economist*, one of the most radically free-market libertarian publications, observed that

> by squeezing budgets without eliminating functions, the Republicans are asking the government to deliver on every promise ever made with less and less money. This "less of the same" approach is a congressional staple. . . . However, squeezing is politically easier than choosing; which is why, since the Reagan years, Congress has been doing almost exclusively the former, when it needs to be doing the latter.[15]

Except for finally fulfilling Reagan's wish to abolish the Interstate Commerce Commission, the Republicans in Congress do not seem to be seriously committed to terminating any major regulatory program or activity. (They do favor termination of the Commerce Department, but there are almost no regulatory programs in that department, and they do not suggest that Commerce's activities be terminated—only that they be redistributed to other departments.)

There are several reasons why the national government gets into, out of, and back into regulatory policies.[16] In some instances, the government is responding to public opinion. Table 16.4 gives an interesting history of American attitudes toward regulation, support for which has modestly but noticeably increased since the late 1980s. Political opinion is particularly pronounced on specific issues. For example, one poll in mid-1992 found that more than 60 percent of those questioned supported increased regulation of guns and alcohol.[17] Another 1992 poll found that despite the country's many economic problems, Americans favored more environmental regulation even if forced to choose between environment and economic growth.[18] On certain

ATTITUDES TOWARD GOVERNMENT REGULATION, 1948–93

	1948	1952	1962	1974	1978	1979	1980	1987	1993
Too much	35%	49%	13%	28%	43%	47%	54%	38%	37%
Right amount	27	29	27	38	23	23	19	32	30
Not enough, need more	23	7	29	24	25	24	19	23	28

SOURCES: Figures for 1948, 1952, 1962, 1978, 1979, and 1980 are from various national polls as reported in Seymour Martin Lipset and William Schneider, *The Confidence Gap* (New York: Free Press, 1983), pp. 222–28. Reprinted by permission. Figures for 1974 are an average of Harris polls between 1974 and 1977, during which there was "no clear trend." Figures for 1987 are based on *Wall Street Journal* polls. Figures for 1993 are based on Gallup polls. Allowances should be made for different ways in which the questions were asked.

TABLE 16.4

moral issues, such as abortion, drug dealing, and pornography, Americans tend to support even higher levels of regulation, in the form of abortion laws, stiffer prison sentences for convicted drug dealers and users, and limits on free speech over the Internet for items considered obscene or pornographic.

Other waves of government regulation are more political in origin. The president may owe to an interest group or a sector of the economy a particular debt that can best be met by adding or subtracting a regulatory policy.[19] A third reason is morality. A number of examples have already been given of federal and state regulations aimed at "criminalizing" conduct deemed immoral—taxes on alcohol and tobacco products, for example. Moreover, there are signs that *more* morals-based regulation may be forthcoming, because morality is perhaps the strongest motivation regarding regulations on abortion, drug sales, AIDS testing, smoking in public, labeling foods, etc. Efficiency is a fourth reason for changes in regulation of the marketplace, because competition usually forces companies to be more efficient. For example, although many Americans believe that competition happens naturally when companies are left alone, they have also historically supported "antitrust" regulation to force certain companies to be more competitive by prohibiting them from eliminating their competition through acquisition or collusive deals to control prices. A fifth reason for regulation is pure and simple convenience. Americans are quick to say "there ought to be a law" when people, places, or things stand in their way or add to their risk of injury. Most of the time it is difficult to draw a clear line between regulations aimed at eliminating injuries and inconveniences, and regulations aimed at reducing the risk of such injuries and inconveniences. But these are practical matters, and regulations vary according to how many people feel a regulation will have the desired practical consequences. Finally, a sixth reason for regulation is equity, such as when a government program seeks to reduce racial discrimination in the workplace (see Chapter 18).

Conservatives argue that deregulation would make businesses more efficient and competitive, while liberals argue that some regulation is necessary to reduce the risk that unfettered competition creates.

As a general rule, conservatives tend to favor more regulation for moral reasons; liberals favor increased regulations for instrumental reasons, such as to reduce risk or to gain equity. But both favor regulation some of the time. With all of these reasons for regulating, it is quite unlikely that any president will significantly reduce the level of government regulation for long. There will be cycles of regulation and deregulation because legislatures and administrators are responsive to changes in attitudes and sentiments about what needs regulating and by how much. But it is truly unlikely that the overall amount of state and national government regulation in the United States will be significantly reduced.

MAINTAINING A CAPITALIST ECONOMY

Government and capitalism are not inherent foes; they depend on each other. American businesses have flourished because of the expanding markets that federal government promotional and regulatory policies helped to foster. The study of government policies toward our capitalist economy will thus enrich our understanding of capitalism.

The Constitution provides that Congress shall have the power

> To lay and collect Taxes, . . . to pay the Debts and provide for the common Defence and general Welfare; . . . To borrow Money; . . . To coin Money [and] regulate the Value thereof. . . .

These clauses of Article I, Section 8, are the constitutional sources of the fiscal and monetary policies of the national government. Nothing is said, however, about *how* these powers can be used, although the way they are used shapes the economy. Most of the policies in the history of the United States have been distinctly capitalistic, that is, they have aimed at promoting investment and ownership by individuals and corporations in the private sector. That was true even during the first half of the nineteenth century, before anyone had a firm understanding of what capitalism was really all about.[20]

Monetary Policies As mentioned earlier in this chapter, monetary techniques manipulate the growth of the entire economy by controlling the availability of money to banks. With a very few exceptions, banks in the United States are privately owned and locally operated. Until well into the twentieth century, banks were regulated, if at all, by state legislatures. Each bank was granted a charter, giving it permission to make loans, hold deposits, and make investments within that state. Although more than 25,000 banks continue to be state-chartered banks, they are less important than they used to be in the overall financial picture, as the most important banks now are members of the federal banking system.

But banks did not become the core of American capitalism without intense political controversy. The Federalist majority in Congress, led by Alexander Hamilton, did in fact establish a Bank of the United States in 1791, but it was vigorously opposed by agrarian interests led by Thomas Jefferson, based on the fear that the interests of urban, industrial capitalism would dominate such a bank. The Bank of the United States was terminated during the administration of Andrew Jackson, but the fear of a central, public bank still existed eight decades later, when Congress in 1913 established an institution—the **Federal Reserve System** (the Fed)—to integrate private banks into a single system. Yet even the Fed was not permitted to become a central bank. The Fed is a banker's bank. It charters national banks and regulates them in important respects.[21] The major advantage of belonging to the federal system is that each member bank can borrow money from the Fed, using as collateral the notes on loans already held by the bank. This enables banks to fund their loan operations continually, as long as there is demand for new loans. This ability of a member bank to borrow money from the Fed is a profoundly important monetary policy.

The Fed charges interest, called a **discount rate**, on its loans to member banks. By changing the discount rate it charges on loans to banks all across the country, the Fed can have a powerful effect on inflation and economic growth. If the Fed significantly decreases the discount rate, it can give a boost to a sagging economy. If the Fed raises discount rates, it can slow down expansion of the economy, because the higher discount rate pushes up the interest rates charged by leading private banks to their customers.

Recent activities of the Fed are indicative of the availability of these monetary powers and the willingness of Fed officials to use them. After a decade of high rates of inflation in the 1970s, the Fed began to raise interest rates to combat inflation. Interest rates remained unusually high for several years during the 1980s. As the inflation rate gradually dropped, the Fed lowered interest rates. When President Clinton took office in 1993, interest rates were quite low. When the national economy began to grow again, in 1994, the Fed felt that inflation might again become a threat, and the Federal Reserve Board once again raised interest rates. By 1995, there had been seven Fed rate in-

the richest Americans) was growing during the years before truly progressive income taxation was implemented—from a gap of 37.9 percentage points in 1910 to a gap of 45.9 percentage points twenty years later, just before the stock market crash of 1929 and the beginning of the Great Depression. The gap continued to grow for another six years, until the mid-1930s, when a genuine progressive income tax was adopted by Congress. During the next forty years, the gap between the poorest and the richest was reduced from a high of 47.6 percentage points to around 36 percentage points, where it remained until 1980. After 1980 the gap began slowly to spread again. What happened?

First, most of the taxes in the United States are regressive taxes—such as Social Security taxes, state sales taxes, many federal excise taxes, and tariffs—and these taxes tend to neutralize the redistributive impact of the federal and state progressive income taxes. Second, the redistribution of wealth is not the only policy objective of the income tax. A secondary (and for many people, the primary) objective is the encouragement of the capitalist economy by rewarding investment. The tax laws allow individuals or companies to deduct from their taxable income any money they can justify as an investment or a "business expense"; this gives an incentive to individuals and companies to spend money to expand their production, their advertising, or their staff, and reduces the income taxes businesses have to pay. These kinds of deductions are called incentives or "equity" by those who support them. Others call them "loopholes." The tax laws of the 1980s actually closed a number of important loopholes in U.S. tax laws. But others still exist—on home mortgages and on business expenses, for example—and others will return, because there is a strong consensus among members of Congress, both Democrats and Republicans, that businesses often need such incentives. The differences between the two parties focus largely on which incentives are justifiable.[23]

Finally, the tax reform laws of 1981 and 1986 significantly reduced the progressiveness of the federal income tax. Drastic rate reductions were instituted in 1986, and as of 1995, there were five tax brackets, ranging from a 15 percent tax on those in the lowest income bracket to 39.6 percent on those in the highest income bracket. Prior to the 1980s, the highest tax brackets sometimes were taxed at a rate of 90 percent on the last $1 million of taxable income earned in a given year. The lower tax rates introduced in the 1980s sharply reduced the redistributive impact of federal income taxation.

All the signs suggest that the gap between rich and poor will continue to spread, even if slowly. The persistence of large annual deficits in the national government's budget severely limited the ability of either party to tax or to spend in any manner that might favor the lower income brackets. Both parties have committed themselves to cutting expenditures that favor the lower brackets—especially welfare and medical assistance programs. In addition, the agenda of the Republicans in Congress includes plans not only to avoid new taxes, but to cut taxes in ways that encourage economic growth—by cutting taxes on those in the upper income brackets, who are most likely to invest and therefore to foster economic growth. Meanwhile, Social Security taxes—the most regressive taxes of all—remain high and are likely to be increased.[24]

Controversies over taxation policy will always exist. Those who favor a less progressive tax argue that people with low incomes will not benefit from *any* taxing system if it discourages the wealthy from taking risks with investments. These people believe that an expanding economy is never regressive, because "a rising tide lifts all boats." This was the argument put forth by former 1996 presidential candidate (and millionaire) Steve Forbes, who proposed that the United States abolish the current tax structure and adopt a "flat tax," which would tax all income at the same rate. Those on the opposite side of that argument see a quite different story. They argue that it is precisely because of progressive income taxation during the twentieth century that the gap between the income received by the lowest fifth of the population and the highest fifth of the population shrank between 1929 and 1970. They also argue that there is now cause for concern because the gap between the lowest fifth and the highest fifth has grown once again since 1970.

In every presidential election year, both Democrats and Republicans try to woo voters with pledges of tax cuts. In 1996, President Clinton resurrected his "middle-class tax cut," and former senator Bob Dole proposed a fifteen percent general income tax cut and a fifty percent cut in the capital gains tax (which would benefit those with higher incomes). Given the growing disparities in income shown by Table 16.5, such proposals increase the possibility that America is moving closer to the Marxist hypothesis that, under capitalism, the rich get richer and the poor get poorer. If some of these tax cuts are adopted, the gap between rich and poor will in fact grow, unless redistributive *spending* is substantially increased.

Government Spending Modern monetary, fiscal, and tax policies are not the only techniques for influencing the economy and redistributing wealth. Government's spending power is another. President Franklin Roosevelt's practical instincts led him to this conclusion. He seemed to recognize from the beginning of the New Deal that, although money spent on roads, farms, parks, and art would accomplish good things and would put some people back

Tax policy is often an issue in presidential campaigns. In 1996, Bob Dole promised a 15 percent tax cut to all Americans as part of his economic plan. However, many voters doubted that Dole could implement tax cuts without further increasing the federal deficit.

to work, the more important reason for government spending was not the specific projects but the total amount of money that the government spends on *all* projects.

If people were unemployed and couldn't buy anything, and if companies were pessimistic and would neither invest nor hire, then government spending to consume, to invest, and to hire would be a net gain for the economy. In order to achieve this spending without raising taxes, the government would run a budget deficit, borrowing money to cover the gap between revenue and spending.[25] Then along came the great British economist John Maynard Keynes to give Roosevelt theoretical justification for what he was doing. Keynes argued that governments are a significant economic force and they can use their power to make up for the imperfections of the capitalist system. Fiscal techniques, he argued, ought to be used as part of a "counter-cyclical" policy, in which, on the one hand, spending would be significantly increased to fight deflationary sides of the business cycle, and, on the other hand, spending would be cut and tax rates would be kept high to produce budget surpluses, to fight the inflationary side of the business cycle.[26]

At least three serious weaknesses in the Keynesian approach to fiscal policy were exposed during the 1970s. First, although public spending can supplement private spending to produce higher demand and thereby stimulate the economy, there is no guarantee that the public money will be spent on things that help produce higher productivity, higher employment, and prosperity. Public expenditure can merely inflate the economy.

Second, governments may not be able to increase spending quickly enough to reverse declining employment or a pessimistic psychology among consumers and investors. New public works take time, arriving perhaps too late to boost the economy, perhaps just in time to inflate it.

Third, a very large and growing proportion of the annual federal budget is mandated or, in the words of the Office of Management and Budget (OMB), "relatively uncontrollable." Interest payments on the national debt, for example, are determined by the actual size of the national debt. Legislation has mandated payment rates for such programs as retirement under Social Security, retirement for federal employees, unemployment assistance, Medicare, and farm price supports. These payments increase with the cost of living; they increase as the average age of the population goes up; they increase as national and world agricultural surpluses go up. In 1970, 64 percent of the total federal budget was made up of these **uncontrollables**; in 1975, 72.8 percent fell into that category; and by 1990, around 75 percent was in the uncontrollable category. This means that the national government now has very little flexibility to increase or decrease spending to counteract fluctuations in the business cycle.

Perhaps the most important lesson to be learned from the Keynesian epoch of fiscal policy is more political than economic: government spending as a fiscal policy works fairly well when deliberate deficit spending is used to stop a recession and to speed up the recovery period, but it does not work very well in fighting against inflation, because elected politicians are politically unable to make the drastic expenditure cuts necessary to balance the budget, much less to produce a budgetary surplus.

The Welfare State as Fiscal Policy It is inevitable that we conclude a discussion of economic policies with a glance at the welfare state. Although most of the discussion of the welfare state is reserved for the next chapter (on social policies), we have to recognize that the foremost principle of welfare policy, a principle even more important than the need for a safety net for the dependent, is fiscal policy: to contribute to the stability of the economy by combatting the highs and lows of the business cycle. Despite the increasing inflexibility of welfare spending as fiscal policy, other elements of the welfare state continue to fulfill this fiscal principle. For example, when the economy is declining and more people are losing their jobs or are retiring early, the government's welfare spending increases automatically (because more people are receiving payments). On the other side, as the economy heats up and more money chasing fewer goods produces inflation, the automatic increase in Social Security and Medicare taxes (because there is more income to tax) restrains excess consumer activity. That is sound fiscal policy. The political and social aspects of the welfare state carry over into the next chapter.

Reflections on the Role of Government

➤ How does public policy balance liberty, equality, and democracy?

With the exception of a few radical anarchists, all the people want some public policies some of the time. And there is no way to predict what policies will be adopted, expanded, de-emphasized, or terminated. But whatever happens, at least two points can be stated with some confidence.

First, nothing about public policy is natural, inherent, or divine. Policies will always reflect the interests of those with influence. Second, above and beyond the political realities, important moral and ethical principles are involved, because each policy decision affects the balance between citizens' liberties and government's power. All of the really important policies—including virtually all the examples in Chapters 16–19—are seen by their supporters as necessary, as a condition for their own liberty and safety. But this only confirms our assertion that *liberty depends upon control,* even as liberty is threatened by control. My individual liberty depends upon the restraints of all other persons who might affect my actions. Although most of society's restraints are self-imposed—we call that civility, without which no society can work—many restraints are governmentally imposed. What would private property be worth without governmental restraints against trespass? What would freedom of contract be worth without laws making breach of contract more expensive than observance? The study of public policies is simply one more way of exploring the shifting balance between freedom and power. Good government is not created and maintained by establishing one position for all time between citizens' liberties and governmental control. The requirements of liberty are not constant. Policies must be designed and redesigned to meet new challenges.

★ Summary

The study of public policy is necessary for the understanding of government in action—how government seeks to control the population through promotional and coercive means. *Policy* is the purposive and deliberate aspect of government in action. But if a policy is to come anywhere near to obtaining its stated goal (public order, clean air, stable prices, equal employment opportunity), it must be backed up by sanctions, that is, by some ability to reward or punish people and to implement or administer those sanctions. These are the "techniques of control," which fall into three categories: promotional techniques, regulatory techniques, and redistributive techniques.

Promotional techniques are thought to be the carrots of public policy. Government subsidies, government contracts, and licensing are examples of incentives available to government to get people to do things they might not otherwise do, or to do more of what they are already doing. This chapter examined how promotional techniques are used to promote and maintain the national market economy.

Regulatory techniques seek to control conduct by imposing restrictions and obligations directly on individuals. Although many people complain about regulatory policies, the purpose of most such policies is to benefit the economy by imposing restrictions on companies thought to be engaging in activities harmful to the economy. For example, antitrust policies are intended to benefit economic competition by restricting monopolistic practices. Less popular regulatory policies seek to protect the consumer even if the regulation is an intervention into the economy that reduces competition or efficiency. Laws requiring companies to reduce air and water pollution, laws keeping new drugs off the market, and laws requiring the full labeling of the contents of foods and drugs are examples of such regulatory policies.

Redistributive techniques fall into two groups: fiscal and monetary policies. The government uses redistributive techniques to influence the entire economy, largely in a capitalistic direction. Currency, banks, and credit are heavily shaped by national monetary policies. Taxation, the most important fiscal policy, exists for far more than raising revenue. Taxation is a redistributive policy, which can be either progressive (with higher taxes for upper than for lower incomes) or regressive (applying one rate to all and therefore taking a higher percentage tax from the lowest brackets). Various exemptions, deductions, and investment credits are written into taxes to encourage desired behavior, such as more investment or more saving versus more consumption.

This chapter concluded with a look at welfare policy, because it is an important fiscal policy. Welfare as a social policy will be treated in the next chapter.

FOR FURTHER READING

Breyer, Stephen G., and Richard B. Stewart. *Administrative Law and Regulatory Policy: Problems, Text, and Cases*, 3rd ed. Boston, MA: Little, Brown, 1992.

Cochran, Clarke E., Lawrence C. Mayer, T. R. Curr, and N. Joseph Cayer. *American Public Policy—An Introduction,* 4th ed. New York: St. Martin's, 1993.

Derthick, Martha, and Paul Quirk. *The Politics of Deregulation.* Washington, DC: Brookings Institution, 1985.

Drew, Elizabeth. *On the Edge: The Clinton Presidency.* New York: Simon & Schuster, 1994.

Greider, William. *Secrets of the Temple: How the Federal Reserve Runs the Country.* New York: Simon & Schuster, 1987.

Heilbroner, Robert. *The Nature and Logic of Capitalism.* New York: Norton, 1985.

Krugman, Paul. *Peddling Prosperity: Economic Sense and Nonsense in the Age of Diminished Expectations.* New York: Norton, 1994.

Levi, Margaret. *Of Rule and Revenue.* Berkeley: University of California Press, 1988.

Sanders, M. Elizabeth. *The Regulation of Natural Gas.* Philadelphia: Temple University Press, 1981.

STUDY OUTLINE

1. Public policy is an officially expressed intention backed by a sanction, which can be a reward or a punishment.

Techniques of Control

1. Promotional techniques, which can promote private activity through unconditional benefits, are the carrots of public policy. Promotional techniques can be classified into three categories: subsidies, contracts, and licenses.
2. Regulatory techniques come in several forms—police regulation, administrative regulation, regulatory taxation, and expropriation—but share the common trait of direct government control of conduct.
3. Redistributive techniques usually take one of two forms, but their common purpose is to control people by manipulating the entire economy rather than by regulating people directly. Redistributive techniques include both fiscal and monetary techniques.
4. The government's spending power may be the most important fiscal technique since it can be used for policy goals beyond the goods and services bought and the individual conduct regulated.

Substantive Uses of Public Policy

1. Most public policies in American history have been policies adopted by state legislatures rather than Congress. As the federal government grew stronger, it did not grow at the expense of state power.
2. The national government has been absolutely fundamental in promoting national markets, which it has accomplished through various patronage techniques of control.
3. Initially, government attempts to regulate the market focused on organizing agencies to regulate a specialized sector, but more recent efforts by Congress turned toward regulating some aspect of the entire economy.
4. Deregulation was one of the techniques used by President Reagan to decrease government intervention in the economy.
5. Politics, morality, efficiency, convenience, risk reduction, and equity are just some of the reasons why government gets into, out of, and back into regulatory policies.
6. Most monetary policies affecting banks, credit, and insurance are aimed at encouraging a maximum of property ownership and a maximum of capital investment by individuals and corporations in the private sector.
7. Although the primary purpose of the income tax is to raise revenue, reduction of the disparities of wealth between the lowest and highest income brackets and encouragement of the capitalist economy are two important secondary objectives.
8. The national government attempts to use its spending power and its significant economic force to influence the economy, redistribute wealth, and make up for the imperfections of the capitalist system.
9. Welfare policy is, in part, designed to contribute to the stability of the economy by cutting down on the extreme fluctuations of the business cycle.

PRACTICE QUIZ

1. A tax that places a greater burden on those who are better able to afford it is called
   a. regressive.
   b. progressive.
   c. a flat tax.
   d. voodoo economics.
2. Which of the following is not a category of the techniques of public control?
   a. promotional
   b. apportioning
   c. regulatory
   d. redistributive
3. Licenses are examples of
   a. promotional techniques.
   b. regulatory techniques.
   c. redistributive techniques.
   d. all of the above
4. A situation in which the government attempts to affect the economy through taxing and spending is an example of
   a. an expropriation policy.
   b. a monetary policy.
   c. a fiscal policy.
   d. eminent domain.
5. Which political body has adopted most of the public policies in American history?
   a. Congress
   b. the presidency
   c. the Supreme Court
   d. state legislatures
6. In which of the following cases did the Supreme Court say that states could not pass laws that would tend to interrupt the free flow of commerce among the states?
   a. *Marbury v. Madison*
   b. *Pollock v. Farmers' Loan and Trust Company*
   c. *Schechter Poultry Company v. United States*
   d. *Gibbons v. Ogden*
7. Which major political party has supported the promotional policies of the national government since the mid-nineteenth century?
   a. the Democrats
   b. the Republicans
   c. both the Democrats and the Republicans
   d. neither the Democrats nor the Republicans
8. Which of the following is not a reason that government forms and changes regulatory policies?
   a. public opinion
   b. politics
   c. morality
   d. budget surplus
9. The theories of which economist were used to help justify the spending activity of the New Deal?
   a. John Maynard Keynes
   b. Milton Friedman
   c. Karl Marx
   d. Arthur Laffer
10. Which of the following institutions is responsible for monetary policies such as loaning member banks money?
    a. Federal Deposit Insurance Corporation
    b. Bank of the United States
    c. Federal Reserve System
    d. Internal Revenue Service

CRITICAL THINKING QUESTIONS

1. Describe the relative utility of several techniques of government control. In what instances might one expect the government to use each technique? How have these techniques been used in the past? Think about a specific instance of government intervention in the U.S. economy since the New Deal. What technique of control was used? What other techniques might have been used?
2. One of the chief functions of government is the collection of revenue. Describe the system of taxation used by the United States national government. What are the multiple goals of tax policy in America? How else might some of these goals be achieved? In what ways is the tax system in the United States progressive? In what ways is it regressive? How might recent calls for a "flat tax" change not only the tax system itself but also the goals the system seeks to achieve?

KEY TERMS

administrative regulation rules made by regulatory agencies and commissions. (p. 613)

categorical grants congressional grants given to states and localities on the condition that expenditures be limited to a problem or group specified by the law. (p. 621)

civil penalties regulatory techniques in which fines or another form of material restitution is imposed for violating civil laws or common law principles, such as negligence. (p. 613)

contracting power the power of government to set conditions on companies seeking to sell goods or services to government agencies. (p. 611)

criminal penalties regulatory techniques in which imprisonment or heavy fines and the loss of certain civil rights and liberties are imposed. (p. 613)

deregulation a policy of reducing or eliminating regulatory restraints on the conduct of individuals or private institutions. (p. 625)

discount rate the interest rate charged by the Federal Reserve System when commercial banks borrow in order to expand their lending operations; an effective tool of monetary policy. (p. 629)

eminent domain the right of government to take private property for public use. (p. 615)

expropriation confiscation of property with or without compensation. (p. 615)

Federal Reserve Board the governing board of the Federal Reserve System, comprised of a chair and six other members, all appointed by the president with the consent of the Senate. (p. 608)

Federal Reserve System (Fed) a system of twelve Federal Reserve Banks that facilitates exchanges of cash, checks, and credit; regulates member banks; and uses monetary policies to fight inflation and deflation. (p. 629)

fiscal policy the use of taxing, monetary, and spending powers to manipulate the economy. (p. 608)

inflation a consistent increase in the general level of prices. (p. 607)

license permission to engage in some activity that is otherwise illegal, such as hunting or practicing medicine. (p. 612)

monetary techniques efforts to regulate the economy through manipulation of the supply of money and credit. America's most powerful institution in the area of monetary policy is the Federal Reserve Board. (p. 617)

monopoly the existence of a single firm in a market that controls all the goods and services of that market; absence of competition. (p. 614)

open market operations method by which the Open Market Committee of the Federal Reserve System buys and sells government securities, etc., to help finance government operations and to loosen or tighten the total amount of money circulating in the economy. (p. 618)

police power power reserved to the state to regulate the health, safety, and morals of citizens. (p. 613)

policy of redistribution a policy whose objective is to tax or spend in such a way as to reduce the disparities of wealth between the lowest and the highest income brackets. (p. 631)

progressive/regressive taxation taxation that hits the upper income brackets more heavily (progressive) or the lower income brackets more heavily (regressive). (pp. 630–31)

promotional techniques techniques that encourage people to do something they might not otherwise do or to continue an action or behavior. Three types of promotional techniques are subsidies, contracts, and licenses. (p. 609)

public policy a law, rule, statute, or edict that expresses the government's goals and provides for rewards and punishments to promote their attainment. (p. 608)

redistributive techniques techniques—fiscal or monetary—designed to control people by manipulating the entire economy rather than by regulating people directly. (p. 615)

regulation a technique of control in which the government adopts rules imposing restrictions on the conduct of private citizens. (p. 613)

regulatory tax a tax whose primary purpose is not to raise revenue but to influence conduct: e.g., a heavy tax on gasoline to discourage recreational driving. (p. 615)

regulatory techniques techniques that government uses to control the conduct of the people. (p. 613)

reserve requirement the amount of liquid assets and ready cash that banks are required to hold to meet depositors' demands for their money. (p. 618)

subsidies government grants of cash or other valuable commodities such as land to individuals or organizations; used to promote activities desired by the government, to reward political support, or to buy off political opposition. (p. 609)

uncontrollables budgetary items that are beyond the control of budgetary committees and can only be controlled by substantive legislative action in Congress. Some uncontrollables are beyond the power of Congress, because the terms of payments are set in contracts, such as interest on the debt. (p. 634)

17

Social Policy

The Welfare State

What type of welfare system existed before the creation of the welfare state in the 1930s?

What are some important examples of contributory and noncontributory welfare programs?

What two major welfare programs were created in 1965? What were the long-term effects of these programs?

Has welfare reform been successful? Why or why not?

Who Gets What from Social Policy?

Which groups receive the most benefits from social policies? Which groups receive the fewest?

How effectively does social policy reach the groups that are most likely to be poor?

Breaking the Cycle of Poverty

What policies are aimed at helping the poor break out of poverty? Which policies have been most successful?

The Welfare State and American Values

How has the formation of social policy reflected the debate over liberty, equality, and democracy?

IN 1994, the Republican Party, as part of its "Contract with America," vowed to scale back the growth of the welfare system. Yet by 1996, they had enacted very little of their ambitious agenda. As we saw in Chapter 10, when Americans saw that their government benefits might be reduced, they protested vigorously. Among those who protested were student groups angry about the proposed cuts in funding for educational loans.

In fact, despite the Republican rhetoric of 1994, very few Americans favor abolishing the network of government benefits called the welfare state. Americans are genuinely committed to a free society and the free competitive economy that goes with it. But Americans are also committed to other values besides free economic competition, such as some form of economic equality. Because some of these values are inconsistent with each other, there is always going to be something of a struggle in American politics between economic liberty and economic equality.

If there is one widely shared American ideal, it is the belief in **equality of opportunity:** the freedom to use whatever talents and wealth one has to reach one's fullest potential. This ideal is enshrined in the Declaration of Independence:

> We hold these truths to be self-evident, that all men are created equal, that they are endowed by their Creator with certain unalienable Rights, that among these are Life, Liberty, and the pursuit of Happiness.

What Thomas Jefferson, the Declaration's author, meant is that all individuals have the right to pursue happiness, in fact, an *equal* right to pursue happiness—or as we put it today, an equal opportunity.

But however much we may admire it, the ideal of equal opportunity raises questions and poses problems. First, and most important, equality of opportunity inevitably means *in*equality of results or outcomes. One of the obvious reasons for this is inequalities in talent. But in the real world, talent is not the only differentiating factor. Another explanation is past inequality—the inequality of past generations visited upon the present one. This is generally called social class, or the class system. Inequality may result from poverty; lacking money for food may lead to inadequate nutrition, which may in turn explain reduced talent and reduced energies to compete. Educational opportunities also are limited by past inequalities. Since the quality of one's education and the status of one's school contribute to success, inadequate education is a tremendous disadvantage when looking for a job or a promotion. All of these factors make up social class, and social class shapes opportunity and success, regardless of talent.

Finally, there is prejudice pure and simple. This includes racial and religious bias, ethnocentrism, and traditionalist attitudes toward the roles of women. Some of these prejudices are caused by the class system, because social class separates people, and their ignorance of each other breeds anxiety and stereotyping.

As observed in Chapter 16, there is a great divide in America between rich and poor. However, one must be careful when making this statement. In the first place, overall economic growth has been so great during the twentieth century that the share received by the lowest income brackets is a much larger aggregate amount than it was one hundred years ago, even if their percentage of the total has not improved. Second, many of the individuals who occupy the lowest income brackets don't remain there for long.

But here's the rub: Although it is true that the composition of the lowest bracket is quite fluid in the United States, with a lot of people entering at the bottom and escaping after short periods of time, it is also true that the people in the bottom brackets are disproportionately composed of members of groups who have been deprived of opportunities to pursue their interests and their happiness. And it is undeniably true as well that in today's America, millions of people are born, live, and will die in poverty, and may realistically expect their children to do the same.

For example, although many African Americans have improved their economic situations over the past few decades, *as a group* African Americans remain economically deprived. In 1993, the per capita income for white Americans was $16,800, but the per capita income for blacks was close to $7,000 less, just $9,863. In 1993, one-seventh of the U.S. population—39 million people—lived in what the government defines as poverty (for a family of four, an income of about $14,800). Looked at according to race, the figures were strikingly different: 12.2 percent of all whites lived below the

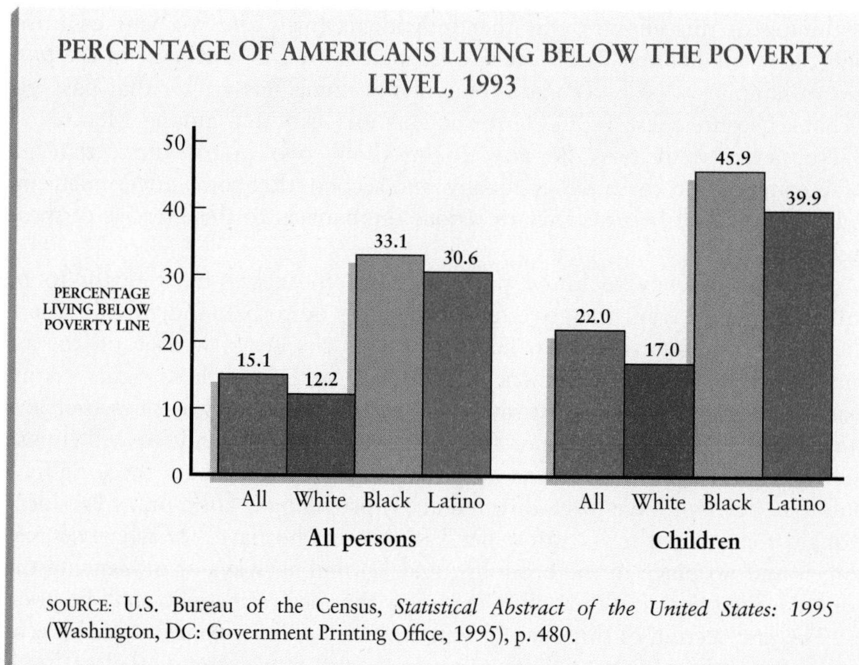

SOURCE: U.S. Bureau of the Census, *Statistical Abstract of the United States: 1995* (Washington, DC: Government Printing Office, 1995), p. 480.

FIGURE 17.1

poverty level, but 33.1 percent of all African Americans—one-third—lived in poverty. In the case of children, the disparities are even more glaring (see Figure 17.1). More than one-fifth of all children in America, 22.0 percent, lived in poverty in 1993, but when broken down by race the numbers reveal that while one in six white children lives in poverty, almost half of all black children, 45.9 percent, live in officially defined poverty. These inequalities of distribution apply not only to blacks but also to Latinos. In 1993, for example, 30.6 percent of all Latinos—and 39.9 percent of Latino children—lived in poverty.[1]

Even for members of minority groups who are "making it," inequalities seem to plague them in occupations all the way up the ladder. For example, African American males in professional and technical jobs earned income on average nearly 30 percent less than whites in comparable jobs. African Americans in managerial, administrative, and sales positions earned only 65 percent of the incomes of white males in those same positions, and African Americans in skilled trades earned about 70 percent of what whites earned. Similar inequalities are evident between men and women in the labor force. In 1991, families headed by a single female earned an income of less than 59 percent of those headed by a single male.[2] At the upper end of the economic ladder, inequalities persist: a 1990 study of chief executives of America's 1,000 largest publicly held corporations found that out of a total of 986 chief executives, only two were women.[3] Economic disparities between men and women at the high and low ends of the employment ladder has led to the feminist movement's demand of "equal pay for equal work."

Let us now return to Thomas Jefferson and the Declaration of Independence. The main point of the passage from the Declaration quoted at the beginning of this chapter was that individuals (men *and* women) have the right, the "unalienable" right, not to happiness itself, but at least to the *pursuit* of happiness. Now let's add the sentence immediately after that passage: "That to secure these rights, Governments are instituted among Men. . . ." There never seemed to be any doubt about two points: first, that all Americans shared these rights equally, and second, that some government involvement would be necessary to reduce the barriers to the exercise of these rights.

There is no way to know precisely when the government ought to be called upon and what the government ought to do to help individuals secure the right to pursue their own happiness. This chapter is written on the assumption that *some* government involvement "to secure these rights" is inevitable, necessary, and constitutional. But this in no way implies that any *particular* policy is inevitable or that the government has made or will choose the right policies. We recognize only that, in trying "to secure these rights," public policy will have to be directed at (1) providing a floor, or, as President Ronald Reagan put it, a "safety net," for those who have, for whatever reason, found no place in the economy, and (2) finding ways of influencing the conduct, the rules, and the values in society that determine who shall be poor.

The first section of this chapter will deal with policies concerned with economic inequality. Most of these come under the conventional label of "welfare policy" or "the welfare state." The second section will deal with other social policies that are important but that fall outside the category of what is usually meant by "welfare." In the third section, we will look at policies aimed at permanently changing the status of America's poorest citizens. And last, we will consider how the welfare state in America reflects (or does not reflect) the values of liberty, equality, and democracy.

The Welfare State

- ➤ What type of welfare system existed before the creation of the welfare state in the 1930s?
- ➤ What are some important examples of contributory and noncontributory welfare programs?
- ➤ What two major welfare programs were created in 1965? What were the long-term effects of these programs?
- ➤ Has welfare reform been successful? Why or why not?

For much of American history, local governments and private charities were in charge of caring for the poor. During the 1930s, when this largely private system of charity collapsed in the face of widespread economic destitution, the federal government created the beginnings of an American welfare state. The idea of the welfare state was new; it meant that the national government would oversee programs designed to promote economic security for all Americans—not just for the poor. The American system of social welfare comprises many different policies enacted over the years since the Great Depression. Because each program is governed by distinct rules, the kind and level of assistance available varies widely.

The History of the Welfare System

There has always been a welfare system in America. But until 1935, it was almost entirely private, composed of an extensive system of voluntary philanthropy through churches and other religious groups, ethnic and fraternal societies, communities and neighborhoods, and philanthropically inclined rich individuals. Most often it was called "charity," and although it was private and voluntary, it was thought of as a public obligation.

There were great variations in the generosity of charity from town to town, but one thing seems to have been universal: the tradition of distinguishing between two classes of poverty—the "deserving poor" and the "undeserving poor." The deserving poor were the widows and orphans and others rendered dependent by some misfortune, such as the death or serious injury of the family's breadwinner in the course of honest labor. The undeserving poor were able-bodied persons unwilling to work, transients new to the community, and others of whom, for various reasons, the community did not approve. This private charity was a very subjective matter; the givers and their agents spent a great deal of time and resources examining the qualifications, both economic and moral, of the seekers of charity.

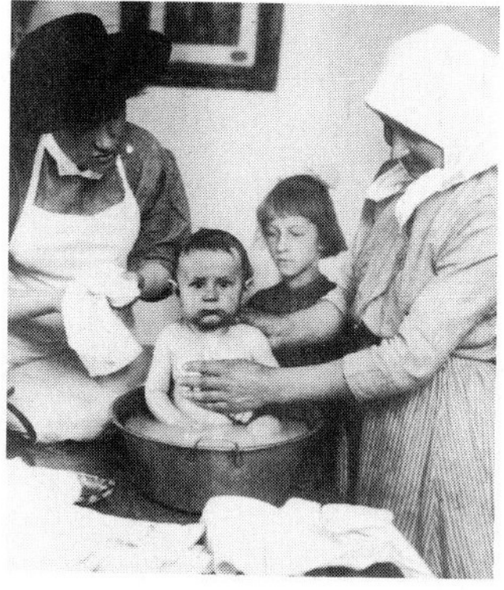

Chicago's Hull House was one of the most famous settlement houses in the early twentieth century. There, social workers instructed the poor in proper methods of hygiene and child rearing.

Much of the private charity was given in cash, called "outdoor relief." But because of fears that outdoor relief spawned poverty rather than relieving or preventing it, many communities set up settlement houses and other "indoor relief" institutions. Some of America's most dedicated and unselfish citizens worked in the settlement houses, and their work made a significant contribution to the development of the field of social work.

A still larger institution of indoor relief was the police station, where many of America's poor sought temporary shelter. But even in the severest weather, the homeless could not stay in police stations for many nights without being jailed as vagrants.[4] Indeed, the settlement houses and the police departments were not all that different in their approaches, since social workers in those days tended to consider "all social case work [to be] mental hygiene."[5] And even though not all social workers were budding psychiatrists, "it was true that they focused on counseling and other preventive techniques, obscuring and even ignoring larger structural problems."[6]

The severe limitations on financing faced by private charitable organizations and settlement houses slowly produced a movement by many groups toward public assumption of some of these charitable or welfare functions. Workers' compensation laws were enacted in a few states, for example, but the effect of such laws was limited because they benefited only workers injured on the job, and of them, only those who worked for certain types of companies. A more important effort, one that led more directly to the modern welfare state, was public aid to mothers with dependent children. Beginning in Illinois in 1911, the movement for mother's pensions spread to include forty states by 1926. Initially, such aid was viewed as simply an inexpensive alternative to providing "indoor relief" to mothers and their children. Moreover, applicants not only had to pass a rigorous means test, but also had to prove that they were deserving, because the laws provided that assistance would be provided only to individuals who were deemed to be "physically, mentally, and morally fit." In most states, a mother was deemed unfit if her children were illegitimate.[7]

In effect, these criteria proved to be racially discriminatory. Many African Americans in the South and ethnic immigrants in the North were denied benefits on the grounds of "moral unfitness." Furthermore, local governments were allowed to decide whether to establish such pension programs. In the South, many counties with large numbers of African American women refused to implement assistance programs.

In the early days of the Depression, much of the available assistance for the destitute was provided by private groups, through projects such as this soup kitchen in New York City.

Despite the spread of state government programs to assume some of the obligation to relieve the poor, the private sector remained dominant until the 1930s. Even as late as 1928, only 11.6 percent of all relief granted in fifteen of the largest cities came from public funds.[8] Nevertheless, the various state and local public experiences provided guidance and precedents for the national government's welfare system, once it was developed.

The traditional approach, dominated by the private sector with its severe distinction between deserving and undeserving poor, crumbled in 1929 before the stark reality of the Great Depression. During the Depression, misfortune became so widespread and private wealth shrank so drastically that private charity was out of the question and the distinction between deserving and undeserving became impossible to draw. Around 20 percent of the workforce immediately became unemployed; this figure grew as the Depression stretched into years. Moreover, few of these individuals had any monetary resources or any family farm upon which to fall back. Banks failed, wiping out the savings of millions who had been prudent enough or fortunate enough to have any savings at all. Thousands of businesses failed as well, throwing middle-class Americans onto the bread lines along with unemployed laborers, dispossessed farmers, and those who had never worked in any capacity whatsoever. The Great Depression proved to Americans that poverty could be a result of imperfections in the economic system as well as of individual irresponsibility. It also forced Americans to alter drastically their standards regarding who was deserving and who was not.

Once poverty and dependency were accepted as problems inherent in the economic system, a large-scale public policy approach was not far away. By the time the Roosevelt administration took office in 1933, the question was not whether there was to be a public welfare system, but how generous or restrictive that system would be.

Foundations of the Welfare State

If the welfare state were truly a state, its founding would be the Social Security Act of 1935. This act created two separate categories of welfare: contributory and noncontributory. Table 17.1 lists the key programs in each of these categories, with the year of their enactment and the most recent figures on the number of Americans they benefit and their cost to the federal government.

Contributory Programs The category of welfare programs that are financed by taxation can justifiably be called "forced savings"; these programs force working Americans to set aside a portion of their current earnings to provide income and benefits during their retirement years. These **contributory programs** are what most people have in mind when they refer to **Social Security**

PUBLIC WELFARE PROGRAMS

Type of program	Year enacted	Number of recipients in 1995 (in millions)	Federal outlays in 1995 (in billions)
Contributory (Insurance) System			
Old Age, Survivors, and Disability Insurance	1935	43.3	$334.2
Medicare	1965	37.1	$173.3
Unemployment Compensation	1935	8.9	$23.9
Noncontributory (Public Assistance) System			
Medicaid	1965	36.4	$96.4
Food Stamps	1964	27.2	$25.7
Aid to Families with Dependent Children*	1935	5.1	$16.9
Supplemental Security Income (cash assistance for aged, blind, disabled)	1974	6.3	$28.2
Housing Assistance to low-income families	1937	NA	$23.3
School Lunch Program	1946	37.3	$7.6
Training and employment program	1982	NA	$3.7
Temporary Assistance to Needy Families	1996	NA	NA

NA = Not available.
*Terminated in 1996.
SOURCE: Office of Management and Budget, *Budget of the United States Government, Fiscal Year 1995* (Washington, DC: Government Printing Office, 1995), Historical Tables, pp. 176, 217–19; Mid-session Review of the 1995 Budget, pp. 27–28.

TABLE 17.1

or social insurance. Under the original contributory program, old-age insurance, the employer and the employee were each required to pay equal amounts, which in 1937 were set at 1 percent of the first $3,000 of wages, to be deducted from the paycheck of each employee and matched by the same amount from the employer. This percentage has increased over the years; the contribution is now 7.65 percent subdivided as follows: 6.20 percent on the first $62,700 of income for Social Security benefits, plus 1.45 percent on all earnings for Medicare.[9]

Social Security may seem to be a rather conservative approach to welfare. In effect, the Social Security tax, as a forced saving, sends a message that people cannot be trusted to save voluntarily in order to take care of their own needs. But in another sense, it is quite radical. Social Security is not real insurance; workers' contributions do not accumulate in a personal account, like they would in an annuity. Consequently, contributors do not receive benefits in proportion to their own contributions, and this means that there is a redistribution of wealth occurring. In brief, Social Security mildly redistributes wealth from higher- to lower-income people, and it quite significantly redistributes wealth from younger workers to older retirees.

Congress increased Social Security benefits every two or three years during the 1950s and 1960s. The biggest single expansion in contributory programs since 1935 was the establishment in 1965 of **Medicare,** which provides substantial medical services to elderly persons who are already eligible to receive old-age, survivors', and disability insurance under the original Social Security system. In 1972, Congress decided to end the grind of biennial legislation to increase benefits by establishing **indexing,** whereby benefits paid out under contributory programs would be modified annually by **cost of living adjustments** (COLAs) designed to increase benefits to keep up with the rate of inflation. But, of course, Social Security taxes (contributions) also increased after almost every benefit increase. This made Social Security, in the words of one observer, "a politically ideal program. It bridged partisan conflict by providing liberal benefits under conservative financial auspices."[10] In other words, conservatives could more readily yield to the demands of the well-organized and ever-growing constituency of elderly voters if benefit increases were automatic; liberals could cement conservative support by agreeing to finance the increased benefits through increases in the regressive Social Security tax rather than out of the general revenues coming from the more progressive income tax. (See Chapter 16 for a discussion of regressive and progressive taxes.)

Noncontributory Programs Programs to which beneficiaries do not have to contribute—**noncontributory programs**—are also known as "public assistance programs," or, derisively, as "welfare." Until 1996, the most important noncontributory program was **Aid to Families with Dependent Children** (AFDC, originally called Aid to Dependent Children, or ADC), which was founded in 1935 by the original Social Security Act. In 1996, Congress abolished AFDC and replaced it with the Temporary Assistance to Needy Families (TANF) block grant. Eligibility for public assistance is determined by **means testing,** a procedure that requires applicants to show a financial need for assistance. Between 1935 and 1965, the government created programs to provide housing assistance, school lunches, and food stamps to other needy Americans.

The federally funded school lunch program provides nutritious lunches for needy children. In many schools in poor neighborhoods, a majority of the students rely on the school lunch program.

As with contributory programs, the noncontributory public assistance programs also made their most significant advances in the 1960s and 1970s. The largest single category of expansion was the establishment in 1965 of **Medicaid,** a program that provides extended medical services to all low-income persons who have already established eligibility through means testing under AFDC or TANF. Noncontributory programs underwent another major transformation in the 1970s in the level of benefits they provide. Besides being means tested, noncontributory programs are federal rather than national; grants-in-aid are provided by the national government to the states as incentives to establish the programs (see Chapter 4). Thus, from the beginning there were considerable disparities in benefits from state to state. The national government sought to rectify the disparities in levels of old-age benefits in 1974 by creating the **Supplemental Security Income** (SSI) program to augment benefits for the aged, blind, and disabled. SSI provides uniform minimum benefits across the entire nation and includes mandatory COLAs. States are allowed to be more generous if they wish, but no state is permitted to provide benefits below the minimum level set by the national government. As a result, twenty-five states increased their own SSI benefits to the mandated level.

The AFDC program was also administered by the states, as is the new TANF program, and, like the old-age benefits just discussed, benefit levels vary widely from state to state (see Figure 17.2). For example, although the median national "standard of need" for a family of three was $542 per month (55 percent of the poverty-line income) in 1994, the states' monthly AFDC benefits varied from $120 in Mississippi to $923 in Alaska.[11]

The number of people receiving AFDC benefits expanded in the 1970s, in part because new welfare programs had been established in the mid-1960s: Medicaid (discussed earlier) and **food stamps**, which are coupons that can be exchanged for food at most grocery stores. These programs provide what are called **in-kind benefits**—noncash goods and services that would otherwise have to be paid for in cash by the beneficiary. In addition to simply adding on the cost of medical services and food to the level of benefits given to AFDC recipients, the possibility of receiving Medicaid benefits provided an incentive for poor Americans to establish their eligibility for AFDC, which would also establish their eligibility to receive Medicaid. At the same time, the govern-

FIGURE 17.2

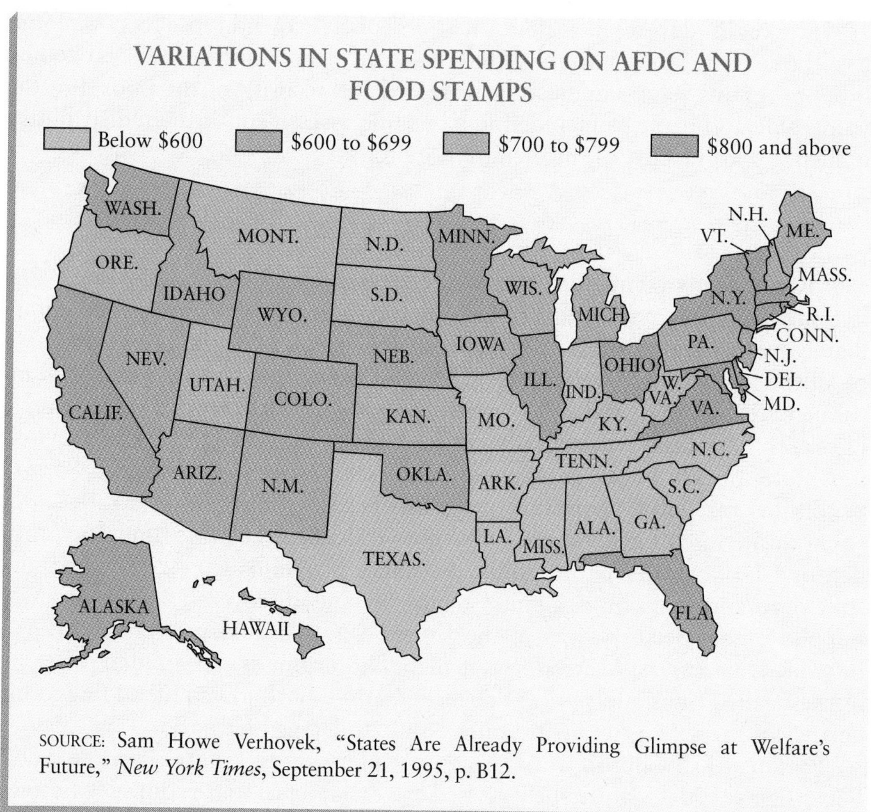

SOURCE: Sam Howe Verhovek, "States Are Already Providing Glimpse at Welfare's Future," *New York Times*, September 21, 1995, p. B12.

ment significantly expanded its publicity efforts to encourage the dependent unemployed to establish their eligibility for these various programs.

Another, more complex reason for the growth of AFDC in the 1970s was that it became more difficult for the government to terminate people's AFDC benefits for lack of eligibility. In the 1970 case of *Goldberg v. Kelly*, the Supreme Court held that the financial benefits of AFDC could not be revoked without due process—i.e., a hearing at which evidence is presented, etc.[12] This ruling inaugurated the concept of the **entitlement**, a class of government benefits with a status similar to that of property (which, according to the Fourteenth Amendment, cannot be taken from people "without due process of law"). *Goldberg v. Kelly* did not provide that the beneficiary had a "right" to government benefits; it provided that once a person's eligibility for AFDC was established, and as long as the program was still in effect, that person could not be denied benefits without due process. The decision left open the possibility that Congress could terminate the program and its benefits by passing a piece of legislation. If the welfare benefit were truly a property right, Congress would have no authority to deny it by a mere majority vote.

Thus the establishment of in-kind benefit programs and the legal obstacles involved in terminating benefits contributed to the growth of the welfare state. But it is important to note that real federal spending on AFDC itself did not rise after the mid-1970s. Unlike Social Security, AFDC was not indexed to inflation; without cost of living adjustments, the value of AFDC benefits fell by more than one-third during the past twenty years. Moreover, the largest noncontributory welfare program, Medicaid (as shown by Table 17.1), actually devotes less than one-third of its expenditures to poor families; the rest goes to the disabled and the elderly in nursing homes.[13] Together, these programs have significantly increased the security of the poor and the vulnerable and must be included in a genuine assessment of the redistributive influence and the cost of the welfare state today.

WELFARE REFORM

The Republicans controlling the White House and the Senate in the 1980s initially had welfare reform very high on their agenda. They proceeded immediately, with the cooperation of many Democrats, to cut the rate of increase of all the major social welfare programs, including the contributory social insurance programs and the noncontributory, "need-based" programs. However, very little was actually cut in either type of program, and the welfare state quickly began to expand again (see Figure 17.3). After 1984, expenditures for public assistance programs began to increase at a rate about equal to the rate of general economic growth (called the gross domestic product, or GDP). Moreover, no public assistance programs were terminated, despite Republican railings against them. Having discovered how extremely popular Social Security was in the United States, President Ronald Reagan thought it necessary to make frequent public promises not to alter what he himself called the "safety net." President George Bush joined in, adding to his defense of the safety net his promise of a "kinder, gentler nation."

President Bill Clinton was elected on a platform of "putting people first," but deficit realities significantly revised the meaning of that promise. Clinton's

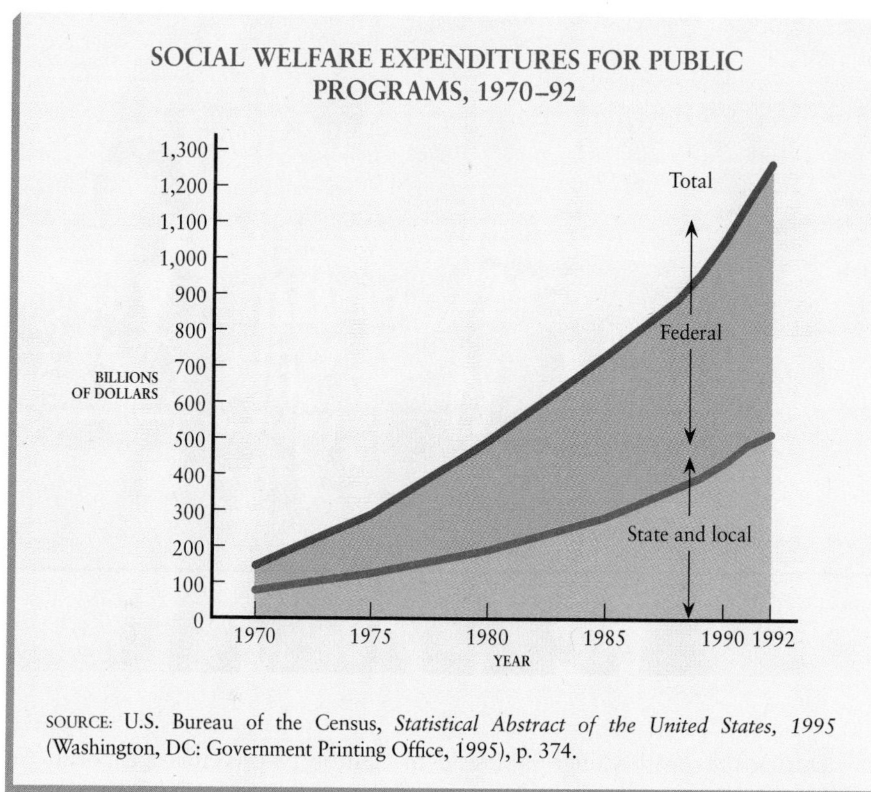

SOURCE: U.S. Bureau of the Census, *Statistical Abstract of the United States, 1995* (Washington, DC: Government Printing Office, 1995), p. 374.

FIGURE 17.3

most positive achievement in the welfare field was his 1994 increase in the Earned Income Tax Credit, by which working parents whose annual income falls below approximately $25,000 can file through their income tax returns for an income supplement of up to $2,500. Yet aside from this one benefit increase, Clinton's campaign to "end welfare as we know it" had led to no new, concrete policies by 1995. By 1994, Clinton had proposed a new welfare plan that would have required four hundred thousand welfare recipients to find jobs by 2000 and would have limited benefits to two years for those who refused to work or to join job-training programs. But the 1994 Republican congressional triumph moved President Clinton to the periphery of policy making, especially in welfare and other social policy matters. His reform proposal died.

The Republicans brought with them their "Contract with America," which included a promise to introduce a bill to "reduce illegitimacy, control welfare spending, and reduce welfare dependence." The Republican welfare bill was far more radical than anything Clinton had in mind: removing the federal guarantee of assistance, forcing 1.5 million welfare recipients to work by 2000, denying public aid to legal immigrants who are not citizens, and granting states wide discretion in administering welfare programs. In fact, the Republican plan would return full discretion and implementation to the states, eliminating the national standards referred to earlier. The Republicans would achieve this by replacing the existing welfare programs with direct-to-the-state cash programs, called block grants.

During President Clinton's first term, members of Congress unveiled a variety of proposals for reforming welfare. Republicans were ultimately successful when the president signed reforms they had initiated in 1996.

During the 104th Congress, President Clinton twice vetoed proposals for welfare reform, arguing that they would harm children. However, in August 1996, the president signed a third bill similar to the previous proposals. This major reform of welfare abolished AFDC and replaced the federal guarantee of assistance to the poor with block grants to the states through the new **Temporary Assistance to Needy Families** (TANF) program. This program allows states to deny assistance to legal immigrants and requires the head of each family receiving welfare to work within two years or lose assistance. The legislation also establishes a lifetime limit of five years on the receipt of assistance. This dramatic reform raised many new questions about whether there would be enough jobs for welfare recipients, whether the block grant would provide adequate funds in the future, and whether states would be able to administer the new program effectively. These concerns suggest that the 1996 law may not mark the end of welfare reform but may be a prelude to a round of future reforms.

Who Gets What from Social Policy?

- Which groups receive the most benefits from social policies? Which groups receive the fewest?
- How effectively does social policy reach the groups that are most likely to be poor?

The two categories of social policy—contributory and noncontributory—generally serve different groups of people. We can understand much about the

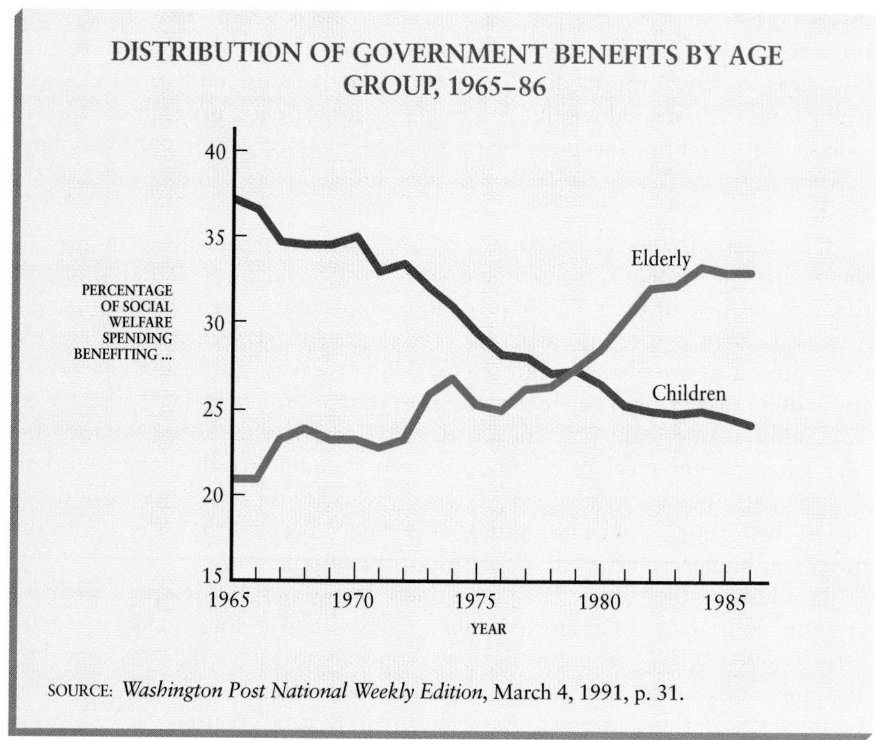

SOURCE: *Washington Post National Weekly Edition*, March 4, 1991, p. 31.

FIGURE 17.4

development of social policy by examining which constituencies benefit from different policies.

The strongest and most generous programs are those in which the beneficiaries are widely perceived as deserving of assistance and also are politically powerful. Because Americans prize work, constituencies who have "earned" their benefits in some way or those who cannot work because of a disability are usually seen as most deserving of government assistance. Politically powerful constituencies are those who vote as a group, lobby effectively, and mobilize to protect the programs from which they benefit.

When we study social policies from a group perspective, we can see that the elderly and the middle class receive the most benefits from the government's social policies and that children and the working poor receive the fewest (see Figure 17.4). In addition, America's social policies do little to change the fact that minorities and women are more likely to be poor than white Americans and men.

THE ELDERLY

The elderly are the beneficiaries of the two strongest and most generous social policies: old-age pensions (what we call Social Security) and Medicare (medical care for the elderly). As these programs have grown, they have provided most elderly Americans with economic security and have dramatically reduced the poverty rate among the elderly. In 1959, before very many people over the age of sixty-five received social insurance, the poverty rate for the elderly was 35 percent; by 1992, it had dropped to 12.9 percent.[14] Because of this progress, many people call Social Security the most effective anti-poverty program in the United States.[15] This does not mean that the elderly are rich, however; in 1992, the median income of elderly households was $13,959, well below the national median income. The aim of these programs is to provide security and prevent poverty, rather than to assist people once they have become poor. And they succeeded in preventing poverty among most of the aged.

One reason that Social Security and Medicare are politically strong is that the elderly are widely seen as a deserving population. They are not expected to work because of their age. Moreover, both programs are contributory, and a work history is a requirement for receiving a Social Security pension. But these programs are also strong because they serve a constituency that has become quite powerful. The elderly are a very large group: in 1992, there were 32.3 million Americans over the age of sixty-five. Because Social Security and Medicare are **universal programs**, they are available to all former workers and their spouses over the age of sixty-five, whether they are poor or not. The size of this group is of such political importance because the elderly turn out to vote in higher numbers than the rest of the population.

In addition, the elderly have developed strong and sophisticated lobbying organizations that can influence policy making and mobilize elderly Americans to defend these programs against proposals to cut them. One important and influential organization that defends the interests of old people in Washington is the American Association of Retired Persons (AARP). The AARP had 32 million members in 1994, amounting to one-fifth of all voters. It also has a sophisticated lobbying organization in Washington, which employs 28 lobbyists and a staff of 165 policy analysts.[16] (See Chapter 10 for more discussion of the AARP's lobbying efforts.) Although the AARP is the

Senior citizens vigorously protested cuts in Medicare that were proposed by the Republican Congress in 1995. Fearing negative political repercussions, Congress retreated from its efforts to overhaul the Medicare system.

largest and the strongest organization of the elderly, other groups, such as the National Council of Senior Citizens, to which many retired union members belong, also lobby Congress on behalf of the elderly.

When Congress considers changes in programs that affect the elderly, these lobbying groups pay close attention. They mobilize their supporters and work with legislators to block changes they believe will hurt the elderly. Because of the tremendous political strength of the elderly, Social Security has been nicknamed the "third rail of American politics: touch it and you die."[17] In 1995, the power of the elderly lobby appeared on the wane as congressional Republicans proposed significant changes in Medicare. Ultimately, however, Congress dropped these proposals in the face of public disapproval—much of it stimulated by senior citizens' organizations.

The Middle Class

Americans don't usually think of the middle class as benefiting from social policies, but government action promotes the social welfare of the middle class in a variety of ways. First, medical care and pensions for the elderly help the middle class by relieving them of the burden of caring for elderly relatives. Before these programs existed, old people were more likely to live with and depend financially upon their adult children. Many middle-class families whose parents and grandparents are in nursing homes rely on Medicaid to pay nursing-home bills.

In addition, the middle class benefits from what some analysts call the **"shadow welfare state."**[18] These are the social benefits that private employers offer to their workers: medical insurance and pensions, for example. The federal government subsidizes such benefits by not taxing the payments that employers and employees make for health insurance and pensions. These **tax expenditures,** as they are called, are an important way in which the federal government helps ensure the social welfare of the middle class. (Such programs are called "tax expenditures" because the federal government helps finance them through the tax system rather than by direct spending.) Another key tax expenditure that helps the middle class is the tax exemption on mortgage interest payments: taxpayers can deduct the amount they have paid in interest on a mortgage from the income they report on their tax return. By not taxing these payments, the government makes homeownership less expensive.

People often don't think of these tax expenditures as part of social policy because they are not as visible as the programs that provide direct payments or services to beneficiaries. But tax expenditures represent a significant federal investment: They cost the national treasury some $300 billion a year and make it easier and less expensive for working Americans to obtain health care, save for retirement, and buy homes. These programs are very popular with the middle class and Congress rarely considers reducing them. On the few occasions when public officials have tried to limit these programs—with proposals to limit the amount of mortgage interest that can be deducted, for example—they have quickly retreated. These programs are simply too popular among Americans whose power comes from their numbers at the polling booth.

It is an ironic axiom of American politics that those in society who are most in need—the poor, the disaffected, the uneducated—are also least likely to benefit from the rewards society has to offer. Some believe that this is simply just deserts: people who are poor simply do not work hard enough. Yet major changes in the economy and in society often wreak havoc for people who lose jobs or cannot find work because factories close, because the skills they possess are no longer in demand, or because other broad shifts occur in the national economic system.

After the end of World War II, many southern blacks were driven from agriculture by the rise of mechanization and the continuing burden of racism. By the millions, African Americans moved to northern cities in the 1940s and 1950s in search of jobs and enhanced opportunities. Yet many found only poverty and hardship. In desperation, the urban poor sought government assistance, leading to a dramatic rise in the number of urban residents who received government aid. In 1960, for example, 745,000 American families received assistance from AFDC; the total cost of the program was less than $1 billion. By 1972, three million families were receiving AFDC aid, at a cost of $6 billion. Concurrently, the Johnson administration was expanding its efforts to assist the poor, the Civil Rights movement was accelerating, and unrest was growing in American cities.

Even though welfare rolls were growing, those who worked with the poor realized that as many as half of those eligible for government assistance were not receiving it, and that many of those getting aid were actually receiving less than they were entitled to under the law. In an effort to improve the conditions of the poor (with the ultimate goal of ending poverty), a small group of welfare activists formed the National Welfare Rights Organization (NWRO). It sought to educate and mobilize poor people around the country by launching "welfare rights" information campaigns, gaining help from local leaders in urban ghettos, and by organizing marches, demonstrations, and other activities designed to draw attention to and improve the plight of the nation's poor. Some of the group's organizers sought to cultivate disruptive activities

THE WORKING POOR

People who are working but are poor or are just above the poverty line receive only limited assistance from government social programs. This is somewhat surprising, given that Americans value work so highly. But the working poor are typically employed in jobs that do not provide pensions or health care; often they are renters because they cannot afford to buy homes. This means they cannot benefit from the shadow welfare state that subsidizes the social benefits enjoyed by most middle-class Americans. At the same time, however, they cannot get assistance through programs such as Medicaid and TANF, which are largely restricted to the nonworking poor.

Two government programs do assist the working poor: the Earned Income Tax Credit (EITC) and food stamps. The EITC was implemented in 1976 to provide poor workers some relief from increases in the taxes that pay for Social Security. As it has expanded, the EITC has provided a modest wage supplement for the working poor, allowing them to catch up on utility bills or pay for children's clothing. Poor workers can also receive food stamps. These two programs help supplement the income of poor workers, but they offer as the most effective way to dramatize the issue, and to precipitate a crisis among welfare agencies in hopes of bringing about a genuine restructuring of American welfare.

In 1966, organizers staged a "Walk for Adequate Welfare" from Cleveland to Columbus, Ohio. An initial march of forty people ballooned to several thousand by the end of the march, with comparable demonstrations springing up in more than fifteen American cities. In 1967, a formal founding convention was held. By year's end, NWRO claimed 5,000 members. As its membership grew, important concessions were won by poor people around the country. NWRO membership peaked at 22,500 in 1969.

The gains won by NWRO efforts proved to be short-lived. Most importantly, the NWRO failed to attract and retain more members. This problem arose in large measure from the inherent problem of organizing and mobilizing those on the margins of society. The immediate incentive for poor people to become involved was the prospect of improved benefits. Yet when better benefits were obtained, some members dropped out. Of greater significance was the fact that the tide of urban unrest that swept the cities in the mid-1960s began to subside by the end of the decade. As it did, so, too, did the anger that fueled the NWRO's activities. Further, the NWRO began to turn its limited resources and energies away from local organizing and recruiting. But the NWRO lacked the resources and skills to be effective in Washington, D.C., and by turning away from organizing activities in cities around the country, it cut itself off from its primary base of support. Thus, the experiment to organize and politicize the poor ended with the NWRO's dissolution in 1973.

SOURCE: Frances Fox Piven and Richard A. Cloward, *Poor People's Movements: Why They Succeed, How They Fail* (New York: Pantheon, 1977).

only modest support. Because the wages of less-educated workers have declined significantly over the past fifteen years and minimum wages have not kept pace with inflation, the problems of the working poor remain acute.

Even though the working poor may be seen as deserving, they are not politically powerful because they are not organized. There is no equivalent to the AARP for the poor. Nonetheless, because work is highly valued in American society, politicians find it difficult to cut the few social programs that help the working poor. In the 104th Congress, efforts to cut the EITC were defeated by coalitions of Democrats and moderate Republicans, although Congress did place new restrictions on food stamps and reduced the level of spending.

The Nonworking Poor

The only nonworking, able-bodied poor people who receive federal cash assistance are parents who are caring for children. The primary source of cash assistance for these families was AFDC and now is the state-run TANF program, but they also rely on food stamps and Medicaid. Able-bodied adults who are not caring for children are not eligible for federal assistance other than food stamps. Many states provide small amounts of cash assistance to such individuals through programs called "general assistance," but in the past decade, many states have abolished or greatly reduced their general assistance programs in an effort to encourage these adults to work. Thus, the primary reason the federal government provides any assistance to able-bodied adults is because they are caring for children. Although Americans don't like to subsidize adults who are not working, they do not want to harm children.

AFDC was the most unpopular social spending program, and as a result, spending on it declined over the past two decades. Under the TANF block grants, spending will likely fall further. Because AFDC benefits did not rise to keep pace with inflation, the real value of these benefits dropped by one-third in the past two decades. Welfare recipients have little political power to resist cuts in their benefits. In the late 1960s and early 1970s, the short-lived National Welfare Rights Organization sought to represent the interests of welfare recipients. But it proved difficult to keep the organization operating because its members and its constituents had few resources and were difficult to organize.[19] Because welfare recipients are widely viewed as undeserving, and because they are not politically organized, they have played little part in recent debates about welfare.

MINORITIES, WOMEN, AND CHILDREN

We saw at the beginning of this chapter that minorities, women, and children are disproportionately poor. Much of this poverty is the result of disadvantages that stem from the position of these groups in the labor market. As we saw from the statistics in the introduction to this chapter, African Americans and Latinos tend to be economically less well off than the rest of the American population. Much of this economic inequality stems from the fact that minority workers tend to have low-wage jobs. Minorities are also more likely to become unemployed and to remain unemployed for longer periods of time than are white Americans. African Americans, for example, typically have experienced twice as much unemployment than other Americans have. The combination of low-wage jobs and unemployment often means that minorities are less likely to have jobs that give them access to the shadow welfare state. They are more likely to fall into the precarious categories of the working poor or the nonworking poor.

A former recipient of welfare, this mother of three successfully fought to receive a long overdue child-support payment from her ex-husband. Now the owner of a residential contracting business, she wants to start a company to hunt "deadbeat dads."

In the past several decades, policy analysts have begun to talk about the "feminization of poverty," or the fact that women are more likely to be poor than men are. This problem is particularly acute for single mothers, who are more than twice as likely to fall below the poverty line than the average American (see Figure 17.5). When the Social Security Act was passed in 1935, the main programs for poor women were Aid to Dependent Children (ADC) and survivors' insurance for widows. The framers of the act believed that ADC would gradually disappear as more women became eligible for survivors' insurance. The social model behind the Social Security Act was that of a male breadwinner with a wife and children. Women were not expected to work, and if a woman's husband died, ADC or survivors' insurance would

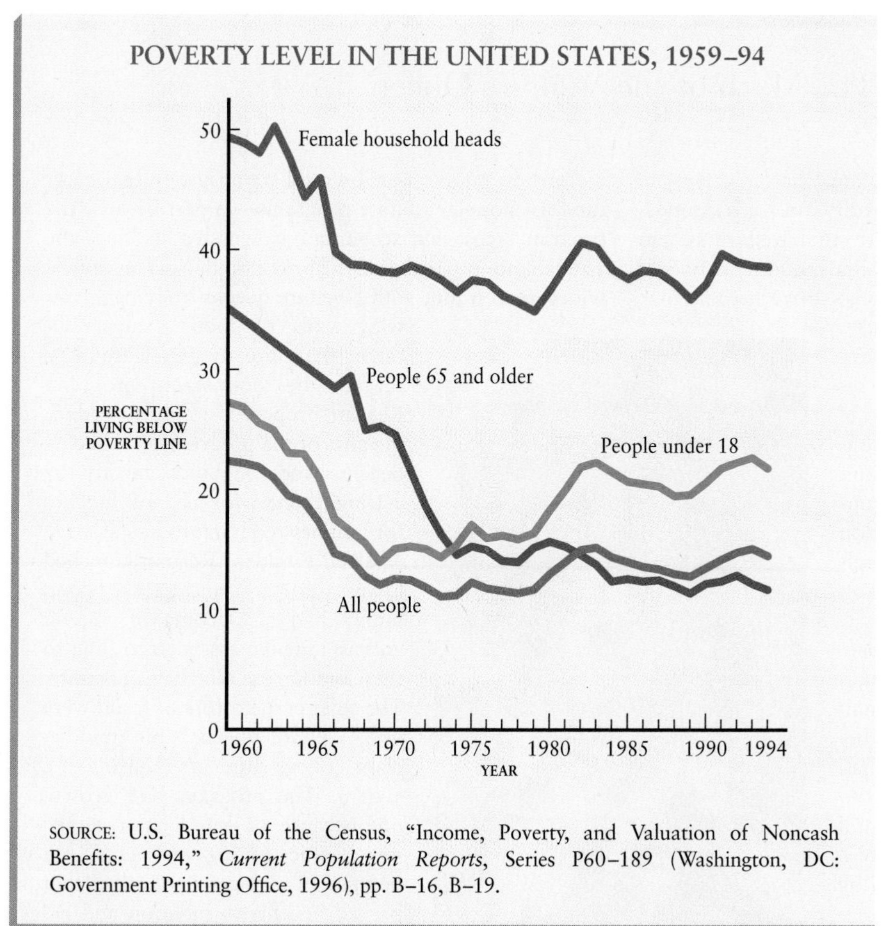

SOURCE: U.S. Bureau of the Census, "Income, Poverty, and Valuation of Noncash Benefits: 1994," *Current Population Reports*, Series P60–189 (Washington, DC: Government Printing Office, 1996), pp. B–16, B–19.

FIGURE 17.5

help her stay at home and raise her children. The framers of Social Security did not envision today's large number of single women heading families. At the same time, they did not envision that so many women with children would also be working. This combination of changes helped make AFDC (the successor program to ADC) more controversial. Many people ask, Why shouldn't welfare recipients work, if the majority of women who are not on welfare work?

The need to combine work and childcare is a problem for most single parents. This problem is more acute for single mothers than for single fathers, because on average, women still earn less than men, and because working creates new expenses such as childcare and transportation costs. Many women working in low-wage jobs do not receive health insurance as a benefit of their jobs; they must pay the cost of such insurance themselves. As a result, many poor women found that once they were working, the expenses of childcare, transportation, insurance, etc. left them with less cash per month than they would have received if they had not worked and had instead collected AFDC and Medicaid benefits. These women concluded that it was not "worth it" for them to leave AFDC and work. Some states have begun experimenting with

The Myth of the Welfare Queen

When Ronald Reagan ran for president in 1976, he expressed his disdain for a supposedly wasteful and ineffectual welfare system with the story of the brazen "welfare queen" who got rich by bilking the system and who drove her Cadillac to pick up her welfare checks. Reagan failed in his 1976 presidential bid, but the anecdote, repeated hundreds of times over the succeeding years, captured the public imagination, helped propel him to the presidency in 1980, and contributed to rising public indignation about supposedly widespread welfare abuse. Where did Reagan's anecdote come from?

Reagan based his famous anecdote on the story of Linda Taylor, a forty-nine-year-old Chicago woman who made headlines in 1976 because of accusations that she had committed massive welfare fraud to amass furs, jewelry, a Cadillac, and several other cars, and a portfolio of stocks and bonds, all financed by more than $150,000 a year in welfare benefits. Taylor was accused of using more than 20 aliases, addresses, and telephone numbers, along with more than 30 wigs, to apply for and receive multiple benefits in every possible category of public assistance: welfare payments, rent subsidies, medical reimbursement, food stamps, transportation allowances, child care expenses, and survivors' benefits (she was alleged to have had a number of husbands, including several who had died). To add to the picture of incompetence on the part of welfare bureaucrats, Taylor was discovered not by them but by suspicious police detectives after she filed a fraudulent burglary report. In 1977, Taylor was found guilty of welfare fraud and perjury, but for far less than the earlier lurid accusations—she was convicted of using two aliases to collect 23 public aid checks worth $8,000. Just as Taylor herself was scarcely a typical example of a welfare recipient, the crimes of which she was convicted were far less than those of which she had been accused.

When Ronald Reagan took office in 1981, he made the attack on welfare one of his first priorities. One of his earliest targets was the food stamp program, one of the least popular welfare programs—in part because the program's cost and scope had grown steadily since the 1960s, and in part because of the popular perception of widespread fraud, with "welfare queens" buying steaks with wads of food stamps. But rather than directly attack fraud or revamp the food stamp program, Reagan proposed simply to reduce the cost of the program by reducing benefits and eligibility, mostly by cutting money for school lunches for families receiving food stamps.

When President Reagan launched his assault, the typical food stamp family had an income of $3,900 and no tangible assets, according to the Community Nutrition Institute. The chief perpetrators of fraud were not "welfare queens" but middle-class college students abusing the system. The program had grown, not because of fraud or a ruined work ethic among recipients, but because of changes in the law that pegged benefits to inflation and because of poor economic conditions in the late 1970s. "The short explanation for the program's growth is that it works," said one advocate in 1981.[1]

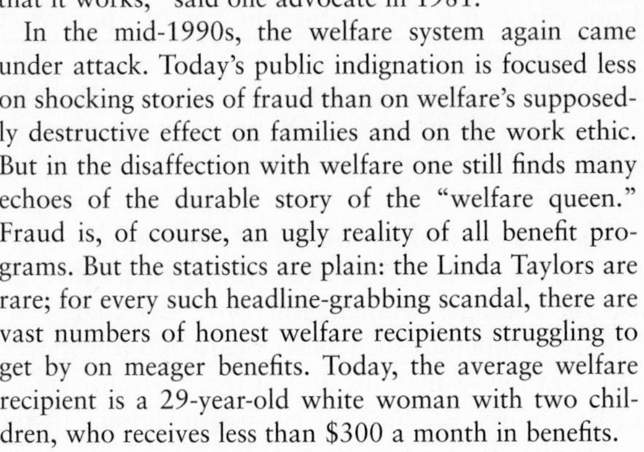

In the mid-1990s, the welfare system again came under attack. Today's public indignation is focused less on shocking stories of fraud than on welfare's supposedly destructive effect on families and on the work ethic. But in the disaffection with welfare one still finds many echoes of the durable story of the "welfare queen." Fraud is, of course, an ugly reality of all benefit programs. But the statistics are plain: the Linda Taylors are rare; for every such headline-grabbing scandal, there are vast numbers of honest welfare recipients struggling to get by on meager benefits. Today, the average welfare recipient is a 29-year-old white woman with two children, who receives less than $300 a month in benefits.

[1] Nancy Amidei, quoted in Steven V. Roberts, "Food Stamps Program: How It Grew and How Reagan Wants to Cut It Back," *New York Times,* April 4, 1981, p. A11.

programs to encourage women to work by allowing them to keep some of their welfare benefits even when they are working. Although Americans want individuals to be self-sufficient, research suggests that single mothers with low-wage jobs are likely to need continuing assistance to make ends meet.[20]

One of the most troubling issues related to American social policy is the number of American children who live in poverty. The rate of child poverty in 1993 was 22.0 percent—nearly 6 percent higher than that of the population as a whole. These high rates of poverty stem in part from the design of American social policies. Because these policies do not generously assist able-bodied adults who aren't working, and because these policies offer little help to the working poor, the children of these adults are likely to be poor as well.

As child poverty has grown, several lobbying groups have emerged to represent children's interests; the most well-known of these is the Children's Defense Fund. But even with a sophisticated lobbying operation, poor children do not have much political power. Although their numbers are large, children do not vote and therefore cannot wield much political power.[21]

Breaking the Cycle of Poverty

- What policies are aimed at helping the poor break out of poverty?
- Which policies have been most successful?

Poverty is a cycle. Many individuals break out of it, but they have to overcome heavy odds. Although many policies may aim at breaking the cycle and others have a beneficial effect on the redistribution of opportunities, four types of policies stand out as most significant: education policies, employment policies, health policies, and housing policies.

Education Policies

Those who understand American federalism from Chapter 4 already are aware that most of the education of the American people is provided by the public policies of state and local governments. What may be less appreciated is the fact that these education policies—especially the policy of universal compulsory public education—are the most important single force in the distribution and redistribution of opportunity in America.

Compared to state and local efforts, the role of national education policy pales in comparison. With but three exceptions, the national government did not involve itself at all in education for the first century of its existence as an independent republic (see Table 17.2). The first two of these exceptions were actually prior to the Constitution—the Land Ordinance of 1785 and the Northwest Ordinance of 1787. These provided for a survey of all the public lands in the Northwest Territory and required that four sections of the thirty-six sections in each township be reserved for public schools and their maintenance. It was not until 1862, with adoption of the Morrill Act, that Congress took a third step, establishing the land-grant colleges and universities. Later in the nineteenth century, more federal programs were created for the educa-

GROWTH OF THE WELFARE STATE

	Welfare	Education	Health and housing
State era (1789–1935)	Private and local charity State child labor laws State unemployment and injury compensation State mothers' pensions	Northwest Ordinance of 1787 (federal) Local academies Local public schools State compulsory education laws Federal Morrill Act of 1862 for land-grant colleges	Local public health ordinances
Federal era (1935–present)	Federal Social Security System Disability insurance VISTA, OEO* Supplemental Security Income Cost of living adjustment (indexing)	GI Bill National Defense Education Act of 1958 Elementary and Secondary Education Act of 1965 School desegregation Head Start	Public housing Hospital construction School lunch program Food stamps Medicare Medicaid

*VISTA = Volunteers in Service to America; OEO = Office of Economic Opportunity

Table 17.2

tion of farmers and other rural residents. But the most important national education policies have come only since World War II: the GI Bill of Rights of 1944, the National Defense Education Act (NDEA) of 1958, the Elementary and Secondary Education Act of 1965 (ESEA), and various youth and adult vocational training acts since 1958. Note, however, that since the GI Bill was aimed almost entirely at post-secondary schooling, the national government did not really enter the field of elementary education until after 1957.[22]

What finally brought the national government into elementary education was embarrassment over the fact that the Soviet Union had beaten the United States into space with the launching of Sputnik. The national policy under NDEA was aimed specifically at improving education in science and mathematics. General federal aid for education did not come until ESEA in 1965, which allocated funds to school districts with substantial numbers of children from families who were unemployed or earning less than $2,000 a year. By the early 1970s, federal expenditures for elementary and secondary education were running over $4 billion per year, and rose to a peak in 1980 at $4.8 billion.[23] Cuts by the Reagan administration of over 10 percent were substantial but not anywhere near the administration's goals. President Bush vowed time after time to be the "education president," and the Democratic majority in

Congress was more than ready to help him. In truth, however, all of Bush's plans for improving elementary and secondary education depended on private financing or on state and local governments.

President Clinton's education program had a more national and public orientation, as might be expected of a Democratic president. It included more federal aid for preschool programs for needy children, national education standards coupled with teachers' incentives, and, at the post-secondary level, scholarships for minorities and an ambitious national service program available to all students to earn credit toward college tuition. Clinton's most concrete achievement in education policy was the Improving America's Schools Act of 1994, also known as Goals 2000, which aimed to reverse federal policies dating back to the 1960s that set lower academic standards for schools in poorer school districts than for those in wealthier ones. Goals 2000, in keeping with the rest of Clinton's education agenda, set uniform national standards for educational achievement from the wealthiest to the poorest school districts, and committed $400 million in federal funds to help establish these standards. The logic of the old system was that it was unfair to expect disadvantaged children to have to perform at the same level as children from wealthier backgrounds. But the result, not surprisingly, was to discourage children in poor school districts from achieving academic excellence. President Clinton's education secretary, Richard Riley, assessed the consequences in a 1994 speech: "About the fastest way I know to create an unthinking, angry 18-year-old who is spiritually numb and heading down the road to violence is to give that young person a watered-down curriculum from first grade on."[24]

Employment and Training Programs

Considering the importance that Americans attach to work and the high value they place on education, it is somewhat surprising that the United

President Clinton often visits schools to highlight the importance of improving education. His "Goals 2000" program aimed to establish standards for academic achievement.

States does not have a strong system for employment and job training. Such programs have two goals. One is to prepare entry-level workers for new jobs or to retrain workers whose jobs have disappeared. A second goal is to provide public jobs during economic downturns when sufficient private employment is not available. Since the 1930s, the American employment and training systems have fared poorly in terms of expenditures, stability, and results.[25]

The first public employment programs were launched during the New Deal. These programs were created to use the power of the federal government to get people back to work again. An "alphabet soup" of federal programs sought to employ those who did not have jobs: the Civilian Conservation Corps (CCC) put young men to work on environmental projects in rural areas; and the Works Progress Administration (WPA) employed many different kinds of workers, from writers and artists to manual laborers. In the despairing circumstances of the Great Depression, these public employment programs enjoyed widespread support. But by the end of the 1930s, questions about corruption and inefficiency in employment programs reduced support for them.

Not until the 1960s did the federal government try again. This time, as part of the War on Poverty, government programs were designed to train and retrain workers, primarily the poor, rather than to provide them with public employment. For the most part, the results of these programs were disappointing. It proved very difficult to design effective training policies in the federal system; lack of coordination and poor administration plagued the Great Society training programs. Concern about such administrative problems led Congress to combine funds for all the different training programs into a single block grant in 1973, via the Comprehensive Employment and

During the Depression, the WPA program put unemployed people to work on a wide range of public projects, from construction to the arts.

Training Act (CETA). In doing this, Congress hoped that more local flexibility would create more effective programs.

CETA expanded greatly and, as unemployment rose sharply during the 1970s, became primarily a public-service employment program. The federal government provided state and local governments funds to create jobs for the unemployed. At its peak, CETA had a budget of more than $10 billion and provided jobs for nearly 739,000 workers—12 percent of the nation's unemployed. But complaints soon arose that CETA was providing jobs primarily to people who were the most job-ready and was doing little for the most disadvantaged. This practice of selecting the most well-prepared as participants—called "creaming"—has been a persistent problem with other job-training programs as well. Critics also charged that localities were simply using CETA money to perform tasks they would have paid for out of their own funds if federal money had not been available. Congress abolished CETA in 1981, making it one of the only federal programs totally eliminated in the past twenty or so years.[26]

But job training has remained a popular idea, and in 1982, Congress created a new program that supported local efforts at job training. The Job Training Partnership Act (JTPA) became the primary federal program supporting job training. In addition to retraining adult workers, JTPA provides funding for summer jobs for youth. President Clinton placed an especially high value on creating a strong system of job training. Clinton's program made use of tax credits and direct subsidies to employers to set up apprentice-training jobs for young people and was to be part of a more ambitious national system that was called "life-long learning." It was inspired by training programs that exist in some European countries, and it coupled national initiatives with community organizations and administration. Yet Clinton's initiatives in job training remained small, as budgetary pressures and congressional skepticism limited his legislative achievements. Nevertheless, as the American economy changes and many corporations transfer operations out of the country or downsize their workforces, the need for retraining has become more pressing. Such training is particularly important for the three-quarters of American workers who have not finished four years of college. Enhancing the ability of the federal government to assist American workers, who face increasing economic insecurity, is one of the most important challenges confronting policy makers today.

Health Policies

Until recent decades, no government in the United States—national, state, or local—concerned itself directly with individual health. But public responsibility was always accepted for *public* health. After New York City's newly created Board of Health was credited with holding down a cholera epidemic in 1867, most states followed with the creation of statewide public health agencies. Within a decade, the results were obvious. Between 1884 and 1894, for example, Massachusetts's rate of infant mortality dropped from 161.3 per 1,000 to 141.4 per 1,000.[27] Reductions in mortality rates during the late nineteenth century may be the most significant contribution ever made by government to human welfare.

President Clinton presents a pen to Jeanne White after signing the Ryan White Reauthorization Act in 1996. Named after White's young son, who died of AIDS, the act provided federal funds for AIDS research.

The U.S. Public Health Service (USPHS) has been in existence since 1798 but was a small part of public health policy until after World War II. Established in 1937, but little noticed for twenty years, was the National Institutes of Health (NIH), an agency within the USPHS created to do biomedical research. Between 1950 and 1989, NIH expenditures by the national government increased from $160 million to $7.1 billion—two-thirds of the nation's entire expenditure on health research. NIH research on the link between smoking and disease led to one of the most visible public health campaigns in American history. Today, NIH's focus has turned to cancer and acquired immunodeficiency syndrome (AIDS). As with smoking, this work on AIDS has resulted in massive public health education as well as new products and regulations.

Other, more recent commitments to the improvement of public health are the numerous laws aimed at cleaning up and defending the environment (including the creation in 1970 of the Environmental Protection Agency) and laws attempting to improve the health and safety of consumer products (regulated by the Consumer Product Safety Commission, created in 1972). Health policies aimed directly at the poor include Medicaid and nutritional programs, particularly food stamps and the school lunch program.

During the early 1980s, the Reagan administration succeeded in cutting Medicaid by stiffening the eligibility requirements; Congress cooperated further by cutting the rate of increase in Medicaid. Public assistance to state and local governments was cut by 20 percent. But before Reagan's second term was over, most of the health budget, as with welfare, began to receive increased appropriations.

In the fiscal year 1995 budget, federal grants to states for Medicaid totaled $96.4 billion, up from $70 billion in 1992 and $40 billion in 1990. Federal programs for AIDS research, treatment, prevention, and income support had a budget of $11.8 billion in 1995, a major increase over five years from the $2.9 billion spent in 1990.[28] President Clinton also put greater emphasis on AIDS by appointing an "AIDS czar" to coordinate federal AIDS policy, and by giving this position Cabinet status. However, the position has been a difficult balancing act between advocates, health care professionals, and the realities of government finances.

President Clinton's major attempt to reshape federal health policy, and the boldest policy initiative of his administration, was his effort to reform America's health care system. In September 1993, Clinton announced a plan with two key objectives: to limit the rising costs of the American health care system (1991 per capita health spending in America, $2,932, was 83 percent higher than in 21 other industrialized nations)[29] and to provide universal health insurance coverage for all Americans (almost 40 million Americans lack health insurance). Clinton's plan at first garnered enormous public support and seemed likely to win congressional approval in some form. But the plan, which entailed a major expansion of federal administration of the health care system, gradually lost momentum as resistance to it took root among those who feared changes in a system that worked well for them. Although Clinton had pledged to make health care the centerpiece of his 1994 legislative agenda, no health care bill even came up for a full congressional vote that year. The president's failure on health care was judged by many to be one of the chief causes of the Republican landslide in the 1994 congressional elections.

Housing Policies

Through public housing for low-income families, which originated in 1937 with the Wagner-Steagall National Housing Act, and subsidized private housing after 1950, the percent of American families living in overcrowded conditions was reduced from 20 percent in 1940 to 9 percent in 1970. Federal policies made an even greater contribution to reducing "substandard" housing, defined by the U.S. Census Bureau as dilapidated houses without hot running water and without some other plumbing. In 1940, almost 50 percent of American households lived in substandard housing. By 1950, this had been reduced to 35 percent; by 1975, to 8 percent.[30] Urban redevelopment programs and rent-supplement programs have helped in a small way to give low-income families access to better neighborhoods and, through that, to better schools and working conditions.

Housing programs were heavily opposed by the Reagan administration, which succeeded in reducing housing benefits by 15 percent and in cutting the number of newly assisted households from an annual average of 300,000 in the late 1970s to 100,000 by 1984.[31] President Bush reversed both, concluding his administration with a $25 billion authorization for housing programs in his 1991 budget. Bush's secretary of Housing and Urban Development (HUD), Jack Kemp, received a great deal of credit for cleaning up a major scandal inherited from Reagan, but the most important legacy he passed on to President Clinton and his first HUD secretary, Henry Cisneros, was $7 billion in unspent authorization, about $3 billion of which was earmarked for housing.[32] Since Cisneros is a former mayor (of San Antonio) and Clinton is a former governor, the country's mayors and governors greeted the Clinton administration with optimism about a more cooperative federalism.

The Clinton administration showed a strong ideological commitment to encouraging housing policies and combatting homelessness. For instance, in 1994, HUD launched a comprehensive plan to increase emergency shelter availability, access to transitional and rehabilitative services, and the amount of affordable permanent housing. Federal appropriations nearly doubled in 1995, to $1.7 billion. The fundamental constraint on efforts to assist the homeless, estimated by HUD to number 600,000 "absolute homeless" (those lacking an address, a phone, and a job), is budgetary: There is simply not enough money available in the current political climate to manage federal housing and homeless policies in the way the administration wishes.

The Welfare State and American Values

➤ How has the formation of social policy reflected the debate over liberty, equality, and democracy?

The development of social policy in the United States reflects the tensions between the values of liberty, equality, and democracy. Until the 1930s, the federal government did very little in the domain of social policy. The country's major social policy was free public education, which was established by the states and administered locally. Americans placed especially strong emphasis on education because an educated citizenry was seen as an essential component of a strong democracy.[33] Given the strength of these beliefs, it is not surprising that free public education was available in the United States well before European nations established public education systems.

Other public social policies, established from the 1930s on, have stirred up much more controversy. Liberals often argue that more generous social policies are needed if America is to truly ensure equality of opportunity. Some liberals have argued that the government needs to go beyond simply providing opportunity and should ensure more equal conditions, especially where children are concerned. Conservative critics, on the other hand, often argue that social policies that offer income support take the ideal of equality too far and, in the process, do for individuals what they should be doing for themselves. From this perspective, social policies make the government too big, and big government is seen as a fundamental threat to Americans' liberties.

Yet conservatives do not agree about how best to achieve a balance between the ideals of liberty, equality, and democracy. Two different conservative perspectives can be distinguished. The **libertarian** view holds that government social policy interferes with society too much and, in the process, has created more problems than it has solved.[34] Many libertarians believe that the mere existence of social policies is an infringement on individual liberties: the government forces some citizens to pay taxes for the benefit of other citizens. The most extreme policy prescription that emerges from this perspective advocates the elimination of all social policies. For example, political scientist Charles Murray has proposed eliminating all social programs except temporary unemployment insurance. In his view, such a move would both enhance the freedom of all Americans and improve society, because individuals would recover their individual initiative if they had to take care of themselves.[35] A less sweeping approach would reduce social programs to a bare minimum or make them temporary.

Other conservatives see things differently. They want to use the power of the government to enforce certain standards of behavior among beneficiaries of government social programs. Many people with these views call themselves **new paternalists.**[36] They believe that government social programs have not forced recipients to behave responsibly. They reject the idea that social programs should simply be abandoned, because they fear the consequences for our democracy. New paternalists do not believe that individuals will behave more responsibly if government programs are withdrawn; instead they fear that social disorder will simply continue. In their view, such disorder will inevitably undermine a healthy democracy, and the primary role of government social policy should be to restore the social order.

Some of the measures supported by new paternalists are also backed by many liberals. These include requiring work in exchange for welfare benefits and compelling absent parents (usually fathers) to make child support payments to the families they have abandoned. Many people from varying political perspectives applauded in 1995 when the federal government tracked down and arrested a prominent investment banker who had fled from state to state in order to avoid paying child support.[37] Other measures are more controversial. For example, some states have enacted reforms denying additional welfare benefits to women who bear a child while on welfare. Liberals charge that such measures violate a most basic individual liberty: the right to have children.[38] New paternalists argue that infringement of individual liberties is simply the price that beneficiaries of government programs have to pay in return for receiving public support.

Conservatives share the view that the primary problems that many social policies address are not economic in origin but instead stem from individual deficiencies. If people behaved more responsibly—if they saved for their retirement, if they did not have children they can't afford to support—there would be little need for government social policy. Liberals, in contrast, believe that the root of many social problems is economic. They believe that opportunities for economic success are not equally available to all Americans and that it is the government's responsibility to open opportunities for all. Thus liberals are far more likely than conservatives to believe that the ideal of equality compels the state to provide social programs. But, like conservatives, liberals do not all agree: some liberals place a greater emphasis on achieving equality as a *result:* others believe that government should do all it can to provide opportunity but that it should not go beyond providing opportunity.

Some liberals who believe that the government should do more to promote equal outcomes have argued that social benefits should be provided as a right of citizenship and that all Americans should be entitled to a basic standard of living. At particular historical moments, there have been social move-

Although the 1996 welfare reform bill passed in Congress by a large margin of votes, many advocates for women and the disadvantaged believed that the new measure would harm poor families.

ments arguing in favor of such approaches to social policy in the United States, but views arguing in favor of equality of result have always been disadvantaged in the American political system. The idea of "social rights," prevalent in many European nations, has no counterpart in American politics. Moreover, the Supreme Court repeatedly refused to acknowledge social or economic rights in the 1960s and 1970s, even as it was making strong efforts to ensure political and civil rights.[39]

Most liberals, then, argue that the aim of social policy should be to provide equality of opportunity. They believe that it is particularly important to ensure that all children have an equal chance to succeed. The sharpest liberal criticism of current social policy has been directed at its failure to address the growth of child poverty. This criticism stems from the belief that poor children have far less opportunity to succeed than the children of the well-off and that such inequalities are incompatible with fundamental American ideals. Liberals also believe that the government has an important role in creating opportunities for adults. President Clinton has argued that new policies are needed to help workers adapt to changes in the economy. In his vision, social policy should seek to reduce inequalities and open opportunities for individuals who are trying to help themselves by working or seeking education and training. This view borrows some of the conservative emphasis on responsible individual behavior but combines it with attention to the ideal of equality.

Where do average Americans fit in all these debates? Americans are often said to be philosophical conservatives and operational liberals.[40] When asked about government social policy in the abstract, they say they disapprove of activist government—a decidedly conservative view. But when they must evaluate particular programs, Americans generally express support—a more liberal perspective. Some programs, of course, are preferred over others. Policies in which the recipients are regarded as deserving, such as programs for the elderly, receive more support than those that assist working-age people. Programs that have a reputation for effectiveness and programs that require people to help themselves through work are also viewed favorably.[41]

In sum, most Americans take a pragmatic approach to social welfare policies: they favor programs that work, and they want to reform those that seem not to work. By rejecting the policy extremes, Americans signal their awareness of the tensions that social policies generate among their most deeply held values of liberty, equality, and democracy. Political debates about social policy connect most closely with the public when they consider which mix of policies represents the appropriate balance among these three ideals, rather than when they ask the public to choose among them.

★ Summary

The capitalist system is the most productive type of economy on earth, but it is not perfect. Poverty amidst plenty continues. Many policies have emerged to deal with these imperfections. This chapter discussed the welfare state and gave an account of how Americans came to recognize extremes of poverty and dependency and how Congress then attempted to reduce these extremes with policies that moderately redistribute opportunity.

The first section of this chapter examined the development of social policies. These policies—and the political conflicts surrounding them—underscore the fact that Americans hold multiple ideals. Americans are truly committed to individual liberty, but they also support equality of opportunity.

Welfare state policies are subdivided into several categories. First there are the contributory programs. Virtually all employed persons are required to contribute a portion of their wages into welfare trust funds, and later on, when they retire or are disabled, they have a right, or entitlement, to draw upon those contributions. Another category of welfare is composed of noncontributory programs, also called "public assistance." These programs provide benefits for people who can demonstrate need by passing a "means test." Assistance from contributory and noncontributory programs can involve either cash benefits or in-kind benefits.

Contributory and noncontributory programs generally serve different groups of people. The elderly, who are widely viewed as deserving of benefits, receive the most comprehensive and generous social programs. The middle class benefits from the "shadow welfare state," which consists of benefits offered through their jobs but supported by federal tax breaks. There are few social programs to support the working poor because many noncontributory social programs, such as Medicaid and the new Temporary Assistance to Needy Families block grant, are reserved for the nonworking poor.

The last section of the chapter considered the tensions between the welfare state and American values. Social policies represent a balance among the ideals of liberty, democracy, and equality. Although political debates often frame the issues surrounding social policies in terms that emphasize one value over others, most Americans tend to take a pragmatic perspective that strikes a balance among these core political ideals.

FOR FURTHER READING

Gutman, Amy. *Democratic Education.* Princeton, NJ: Princeton University Press, 1987.

Katz, Michael. *In the Shadow of the Poorhouse: A Social History of Welfare in America.* New York: Basic Books, 1986.

Katznelson, Ira, and Margaret Weir. *Schooling for All: Race, Class, and the Democratic Ideal.* New York: Basic Books, 1985.

Light, Paul. *Artful Work: The Politics of Social Security Reform.* New York: Random House, 1985.

Marmor, Theodore R., Jerry L. Mashaw, and Phillip L. Harvey. *America's Misunderstood Welfare State.* New York: Basic Books, 1990.

Murray, Charles. *Losing Ground: American Social Policy, 1950–1980.* New York: Basic Books, 1984.

Orfield, Gary, and Carole Ashkinaze. *The Closing Door: Conservative Policy and Black Opportunity.* Chicago: University of Chicago Press, 1991.

Patterson, James T. *America's Struggle against Poverty, 1900–1994.* Cambridge, MA: Harvard University Press, 1994.

Piven, Frances Fox, and Richard A. Cloward. *Regulating the Poor.* New York: Pantheon, 1971.

Schwarz, John E. *America's Hidden Success: A Reassessment of Twenty Years of Public Policy.* New York: Norton, 1988.

Weir, Margaret, Ann Orloff, and Theda Skocpol. *The Politics of Social Policy in the United States.* Princeton, NJ: Princeton University Press, 1988.

STUDY OUTLINE

1. Equality of opportunity, a widely shared American ideal, was enshrined by Thomas Jefferson in the Declaration of Independence. But there remain problems associated with this ideal.
2. The lowest income brackets are disproportionately composed of members of groups who have been deprived of opportunities.

THE WELFARE STATE

1. Prior to 1935, the welfare system in America was composed of private groups rather than government. State governments gradually assumed some of the obligation to relieve the poor.
2. The founding of the welfare state can be dated to the Social Security Act of 1935; this act provided for both contributory and noncontributory welfare programs.
3. Contributory programs—such as Social Security and unemployment compensation—provide "forced savings" for individuals who, as a consequence of making a contribution, can receive program benefits at a later time.
4. Noncontributory programs—such as food stamps and Temporary Assistance to Needy Families (TANF)—provide assistance to people based on demonstrated need rather than any contribution they may have made.

WHO GETS WHAT FROM SOCIAL POLICY?

1. The elderly are the beneficiaries of generous social policies in part because they are perceived as being a deserving population and because they have become a strong interest group.
2. The middle class benefits from social policies in many ways; one way is through the use of tax expenditures, which provide that certain payments made by employers and employees are not taxed by the government.
3. People who are working but are still poor receive limited assistance from government social programs. Although they may be seen as deserving, they receive

only limited assistance because they lack organization and political power.

4. Medicaid and TANF are programs aimed at the able-bodied, nonworking poor, but they only receive assistance if they are parents caring for children. The unpopularity of such programs has prompted efforts to decrease spending in recent years.

Breaking the Cycle of Poverty

1. Education, employment, health, and housing policies are four ways to break the cycle of poverty and redistribute opportunities.
2. The education policies of state and local governments are the most important single force in the distribution and redistribution of opportunity in America.
3. Employment and job training programs have not been a consistent goal of the modern welfare state.
4. Although states also took the early lead in the arena of public health policy, the federal government began to adopt policies in the early 1900s to protect citizens from the effects of pollution and other health hazards.
5. Federal housing policy consists of many pork-barrel programs, but it also represents a commitment to improving the conditions and opportunities of the poor.

The Welfare State and American Values

1. The development of social policy in the United States reflects the tensions between the values of liberty, equality, and democracy. Various conservative and liberal perspectives attempt to reconcile these tensions with differing views on social policy. Each of these approaches seems out of step, however, with the more pragmatic view held by most Americans.

PRACTICE QUIZ

1. Which of the following is *not* an example of a contributory program?
   a. Social Security
   b. Medicare
   c. food stamps
   d. All of the above are examples of contributory programs.
2. Approximately what proportion of the United States population lives in what the government defines as poverty?
   a. 1/10
   b. 1/7
   c. 1/4
   d. 1/100
3. Prior to 1935, the private welfare system in the United States made a distinction between
   a. contributory and noncontributory programs.
   b. citizens and recent immigrants.
   c. the deserving poor and the undeserving poor.
   d. religious and secular assistance.
4. America's welfare state was constructed initially in response to
   a. World War II.
   b. political reforms of the Progressive era.
   c. the Great Depression.
   d. the growth of the military-industrial complex.
5. Which of the following are examples of in-kind benefits?
   a. Medicaid and food stamps
   b. Social Security payments and cost of living adjustments
   c. Medicare and unemployment compensation
   d. none of the above
6. Which of the following Supreme Court cases provided due process protections for AFDC recipients?
   a. *Goldberg v. Kelly*
   b. *Bakke v. Board of Regents*
   c. *Brown v. Board of Education*
   d. *INS v. Chadha*
7. Which of the following was President Clinton's initiative in welfare policy?
   a. the Personal Responsibility Act
   b. the "Safety Net" Act
   c. expanding most noncontributory programs
   d. expanding the Earned Income Tax Credit
8. In terms of receiving benefits of social policies, what distinguishes the elderly from the working poor?
   a. The elderly are perceived as deserving, whereas the working poor are not.
   b. There is no significant difference between these two groups.
   c. The elderly are more organized and more politically powerful than are the working poor.
   d. The elderly are less organized and less politically powerful than are the working poor.

9. Who are the chief beneficiaries of the "shadow welfare state"?
   a. the rich
   b. the nonworking poor
   c. the working poor
   d. the middle class

10. Which of the following is *not* aimed at breaking the cycle of poverty?
    a. drug policies
    b. education policies
    c. employment training programs
    d. health policies

CRITICAL THINKING QUESTIONS

1. Two factors that seem to influence a particular group's ability to get what it wants from social policy are a) the perception that the group is deserving, and b) the political organization and power of the group. In some ways, it is easy to take each of these factors as an independent ingredient of social policy success. But each factor could be seen as having an impact on the other. Select a group and discuss its relative success or failure in social policy. How might the perception of a group as deserving of assistance (and the assistance it receives) help that group become organized and politically powerful? How might organization and political power help shape public opinion favorably toward the group you selected?

2. Describe the changes over time in the welfare state in the United States. What factors led to the expansion of governmental power (both state and national) over social policy? What factors might lead to a decrease of governmental activity in social policy? How do you think social policy in the United States will change in the future? Which of today's political forces and debates will be important in shaping the social policies of the future?

KEY TERMS

Aid to Families with Dependent Children (AFDC) federal funds, administered by the states, for children living with parents or relatives who fall below state standards of need. Replaced in 1996 by TANF. (p. 648)

contributory programs social programs financed in whole or in part by taxation or other mandatory contributions by their present or future recipients. The most important example is Social Security, which is financed by a payroll tax. (p. 646)

cost of living adjustments (COLAs) changes made to the level of benefits of a government program based on the rate of inflation. (p. 648)

entitlement eligibility for benefits by virtue of a category of benefits defined by legislation. (p. 650)

equality of opportunity a widely shared American ideal that all people have the freedom to use whatever talents and wealth they have to reach their fullest potential. (p. 641)

food stamps coupons that can be exchanged for food at most grocery stores; the largest in-kind benefits program. (p. 649)

indexing periodic process of adjusting social benefits or wages to account for increases in the cost of living. (p. 648)

in-kind benefits goods and services provided to needy individuals and families by the federal government. (p. 649)

libertarian the political philosophy that is skeptical of any government intervention as a potential threat against individual liberty; libertarians believe that government has caused more problems that it has solved. (p. 668)

means-testing a procedure by which potetential beneficiaries of a public assistance program establish their eligibility by demonstrating a genuine need for the assistance. (p. 648)

Medicaid a federally financed, state-operated program providing medical services to low-income people. (p. 648)

Medicare a form of national health insurance for the elderly and the disabled. (p. 648)

new paternalists conservatives who believe that social

policy can be used to enforce certain standards of behavior among beneficiaries. (p. 669)

noncontributory programs social programs that provide assistance to people based on demonstrated need rather than any contribution they have made. (p. 648)

shadow welfare state social benefits that private employers offer to their workers, such as medical insurance and pensions. (p. 655)

Social Security a contributory welfare program into which working Americans contribute a percentage of their wages, and from which they receive cash benefits after retirement. (p. 646)

Supplemental Security Income (SSI) a program providing a minimum monthly income to people who pass a "means test" and who are sixty-five or older, blind, or disabled. Financed from general revenues rather than from Social Security contributions. (p. 649)

tax expenditures government subsidies provided to employers and employees through tax deductions for amounts spent on health insurance and other benefits; these represent one way the government helps to ensure the social welfare of the middle class. (p. 655)

Temporary Assistance to Needy Families (TANF) a federal block grant that replaced the AFDC program in 1996. (p. 652)

universal programs programs available to everyone in a certain category; these programs are not "means tested." (p. 654)

18

Civil Rights Policy

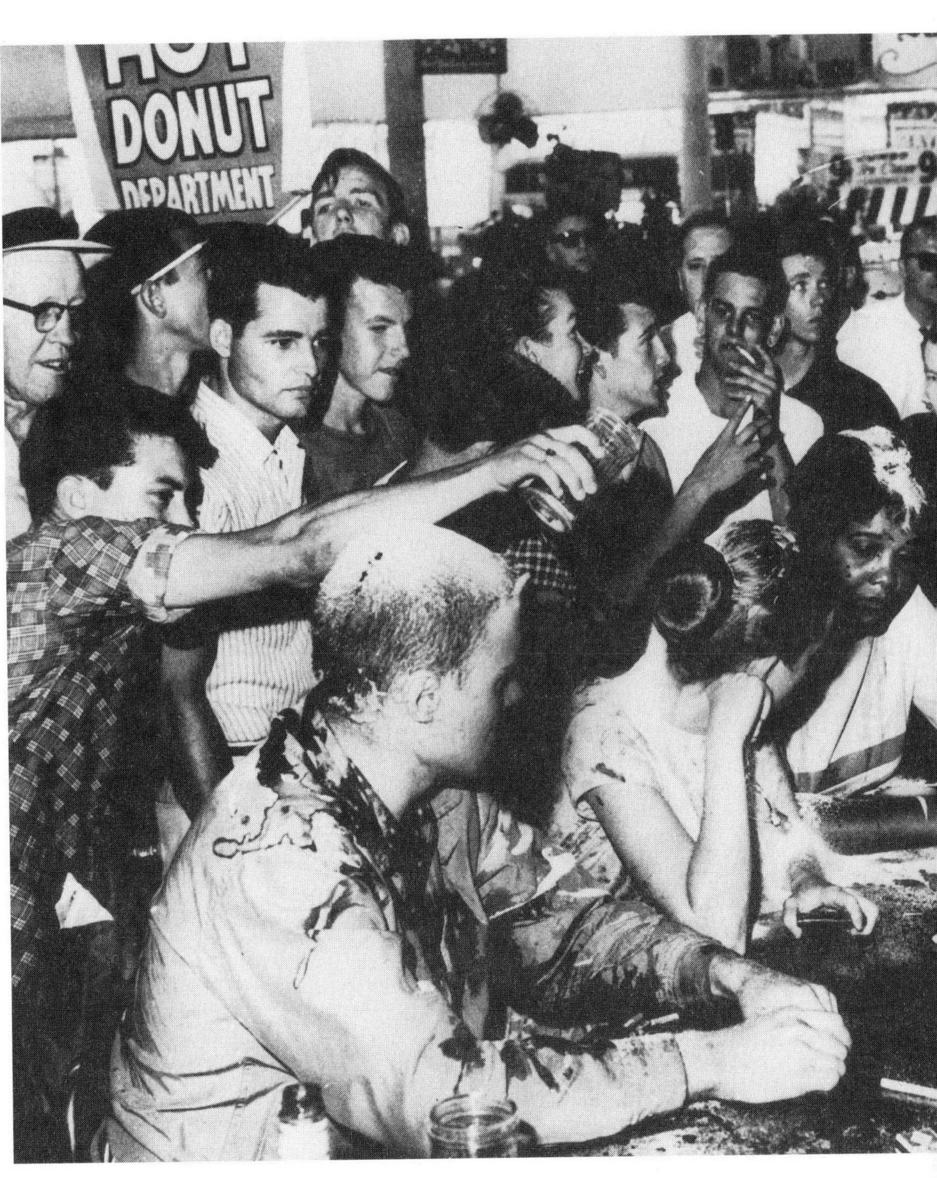

★ Civil Rights

What is the legal basis for civil rights?

How has the equal protection clause historically been enforced?

What is the critical Supreme Court ruling in the battle for equal protection?

How has Congress tried to make equal protection a reality?

In what areas did the civil rights acts seek to provide equal access and protection?

★ The Universalization of Civil Rights

What groups were spurred by the provision of the Civil Rights Act of 1964 outlawing discrimination in employment practices based on race, religion, and sex to seek broader protection under the law?

What is the politics of the universalization of civil rights?

★ Affirmative Action

What is the basis for affirmative action? What forms does it take?

How does affirmative action contribute to the polarization of the politics of civil rights?

IN 1960, four black students from North Carolina A&T made history: The four freshmen sat down at Woolworth's whites-only lunch counter in Greensboro, North Carolina, challenging the policies of segregation that kept blacks and whites in separate public and private accommodations across the South. Day after day the students sat at the counter, ignoring the taunts of onlookers, determined to break the system of segregation. Their actions and those of many other students, clergy members, and ordinary citizens finally did abolish such practices as separate white and black park benches, water fountains, and waiting rooms; the end of segregation meant opening access to public and private institutions on equal terms to all. But the victories of the Civil Rights movement did not come cheaply: many marchers, freedom riders, and sit-in participants were beaten; some were murdered.

Today, the Greensboro lunch counter is a part of history, on display at the Smithsonian Institution in Washington, D.C. Many goals of the Civil Rights movement that aroused such controversy in 1960 are now widely accepted as the proper expression of the American commitment to equal rights. But the question of what is meant by "equal rights" is hardly settled. While most Americans reject the idea that government should create equal outcomes for its citizens, they do widely endorse government action to prohibit public and private discrimination and they support the idea of equality of opportunity. However, even this concept is elusive. When past denial of rights creates unequal starting points for some groups, should government take additional steps to ensure equal opportunity? What kinds of groups should be specially protected against discrimination? Should the disabled receive special protection? Should gays and lesbians? Finally, what kinds of steps are acceptable to remedy discrimination, and who should bear the costs? These questions are at the heart of contemporary debates over civil rights.

Consider the role of race in university admissions. During the 1970s, in an effort to boost minority enrollment, many universities began to consider an applicant's racial background in their admissions decisions. The University of California (U.C.) system was at the forefront of this process. In 1995, however, the regents of the U.C. system voted to abandon race-based admissions practices. Governor Pete Wilson of California argued that affirmative action trampled on individual rights by admitting unqualified students and denying admission to qualified students. Supporters contended that taking race into account in admissions decisions does not mean accepting unqualified students. Instead, they argued, it means expanding acceptance criteria to include other considerations in addition to grades and test scores. In any event, they argued, merit (defined as test scores) has never been the sole criterion for admission at many universities. Private universities, for example, have long admitted substantial numbers of "legacies"—children of alumni who donate money to the institution—with little attention to grades and test scores. The president of the University of California defended affirmative action in broader public terms: "We are a public institution in the most demographically diverse state in the union. Our affirmative action and other diversity programs more than any other single factor have helped us prepare California for its future . . ."[1]

What is the proper government action here? How can broad public goals be weighed against individual rights? Is there an individual right to admission to a public university based on test scores and grades? Are twenty-five years of affirmative action sufficient to remedy past inequalities based on race? Why should individuals today be required to pay a price for past discrimination?

In the United States, the history of slavery and legalized racial discrimination against African Americans coexists uneasily with a strong tradition of individual liberty. Indeed, for much of our history Americans have struggled to reconcile such exclusionary racial practices with our notions of individual rights. With the adoption of the Fourteenth Amendment in 1868, civil rights became part of the Constitution, guaranteed to each citizen through "equal protection of the laws." These words launched a century of political movements and legal efforts to press for racial equality. The African American quest for civil rights in turn inspired many other groups, including members of other racial and ethnic groups, women, the disabled, and gays and lesbians, to seek new laws and constitutional guarantees of their civil rights.

In this chapter we will examine the legal developments and political movements that have expanded the scope of civil rights since the Fourteenth Amendment was adopted in 1868. We begin with the establishment of legal segregation in the South and the Civil Rights movement that overthrew it. Next, we trace the broad impact that civil rights legislation has had on American life. We then explore how other groups, including women, Native Americans, Latinos, the disabled, and gays and lesbians, formed movements to win active protection of their rights as well. Finally, we examine the development of affirmative action and the controversies surrounding it.

Civil Rights

> ➤ What is the legal basis for civil rights?
> ➤ How has the equal protection clause historically been enforced?
> ➤ What is the critical Supreme Court ruling in the battle for equal protection?
> ➤ How has Congress tried to make equal protection a reality?
> ➤ In what areas did the civil rights acts seek to provide equal access and protection?

Congress passed the Fourteenth Amendment and the states ratified it in the aftermath of the Civil War. Together with the Thirteenth Amendment, which abolished slavery, and the Fifteenth Amendment, which guaranteed voting rights for black men, it seemed to provide a guarantee of civil rights for the newly freed black slaves. But the general language of the Fourteenth Amendment meant that its support for civil rights could be far-reaching. The very simplicity of the "equal protection clause" of the Fourteenth Amendment left it open to interpretation:

> No State shall make or enforce any law which shall . . . deny to any person within its jurisdiction the equal protection of the laws.

But in the very first Fourteenth Amendment case to come before the Supreme Court, the majority gave it a distinct meaning:

> . . . it is not difficult to give meaning to this clause ["the equal protection of the laws"]. The existence of laws in the States . . . which discriminated with gross injustice and hardship against [Negroes] as a class, was the evil to be remedied by this clause, and by it such laws are forbidden.[2]

Beyond that, contemporaries of the Fourteenth Amendment understood well that private persons offering conveyances, accommodations, or places of amusement to the public incurred certain public obligations to offer them to one and all—in other words, these are *public* accommodations, such that arbitrary discrimination in their use would amount to denial of equal protection of the laws—unless a government took action to overcome the discrimination.[3] This puts governments under obligation to take positive actions to extend to each citizen the opportunities and resources necessary to their proper enjoyment of freedom. A skeptic once observed that "the law, in its majestic equality, forbids the rich as well as the poor to sleep under bridges, to beg in the streets, and to steal bread."[4] The purpose of civil rights principles and laws is to use government in such a way as to give equality a more substantive meaning than that.

Discrimination refers to the use of any unreasonable and unjust criterion of exclusion. Of course, all laws discriminate, including some people while excluding others; but some discrimination is considered unreasonable. For example, it is considered reasonable to use age as a criterion for legal drinking, excluding all persons younger than twenty-one. But is age a reasonable distinction when seventy (or sixty-five or sixty) is selected as the age for compulsory retirement? In the mid-1970s, Congress answered this question by making old age a new civil right; compulsory retirement at seventy is now an unlawful, unreasonable, discriminatory use of age.

PLESSY V. FERGUSON: "SEPARATE BUT EQUAL"

Following its initial decisions making "equal protection" a civil right, the Supreme Court turned conservative, no more ready to enforce the civil rights aspects of the Fourteenth Amendment than it was to enforce the civil liberties provisions. The Court declared the Civil Rights Act of 1875 unconstitutional on the grounds that the act sought to protect blacks against discrimination by *private* businesses, while the Fourteenth Amendment, according to the Court's interpretation, was intended to protect individuals from discrimination only against actions by *public* officials of state and local governments.

In 1896, the Court went still further, in the infamous case of *Plessy v. Ferguson*, by upholding a Louisiana statute that *required* segregation of the races on trolleys and other public carriers (and by implication in all public facilities, including schools). Plessy, a man defined as "one-eighth black," had violated a Louisiana law that provided for "equal but separate accommodations" on trains and a $25 fine for any white passenger who sat in a car reserved for blacks or any black passenger who sat in a car reserved for whites. The Supreme Court held that the Fourteenth Amendment's "equal protection of the laws" was not violated by racial distinction as long as the facilities were equal, thus establishing the "separate but equal" rule that prevailed through the mid-twentieth century. People generally pretended that segre-

Separate *and equal*? This 1941 photograph of a school for black students in rural Georgia shows the unequal conditions that African Americans faced in schools and other public accommodations.

gated accommodations were equal as long as some accommodation for blacks existed. The Court said that although "the object of the [Fourteenth] Amendment was undoubtedly to enforce the absolute equality of the two races before the law, . . . it could not have intended to abolish distinctions based on color, or to enforce social, as distinguished from political, equality, or a commingling of the two races upon terms unsatisfactory to either."[5] What the Court was saying in effect was that the use of race as a criterion of exclusion in public matters was not unreasonable.

Racial Discrimination after World War II

The shame of discrimination against black military personnel during World War II, plus revelation of Nazi racial atrocities, moved President Harry S. Truman finally to bring the problem to the White House and national attention, with the appointment in 1946 of the President's Commission on Civil Rights. In 1948, the commission submitted its report, *To Secure These Rights,* which laid bare the extent of the problem of racial discrimination and its consequences. The report also revealed the success of experiments with racial integration in the armed forces during World War II to demonstrate to southern society that it had nothing to fear. But the committee recognized that the national government had no clear constitutional authority to pass and implement civil rights legislation. The committee proposed tying civil rights legislation to the commerce power, although it was clear that discrimination was not itself part of the flow of interstate commerce.[6] The committee even suggested using the treaty power as a source of constitutional authority for civil rights legislation.[7]

As for the Supreme Court, it had begun to change its position on racial discrimination before World War II by being stricter about the criterion of equal facilities in the "separate but equal" rule. In 1938, for example, the Court rejected Missouri's policy of paying the tuition of qualified blacks to out-of-state law schools rather than admitting them to the University of Missouri Law School.[8]

After the war, modest progress resumed. In 1950, the Court rejected Texas's claim that its new "law school for Negroes" afforded education equal to that of the all-white University of Texas Law School. Without confronting the "separate but equal" principle itself, the Court's decision anticipated its future civil rights rulings by opening the question of whether *any* segregated facility could be truly equal.[9]

But the Supreme Court, in ordering the admission of blacks to all-white state law schools, did not directly confront the "separate but equal" rule because the Court needed only to recognize the absence of any *equal* law school for blacks. The same was true in 1944, when the Supreme Court struck down the southern practice of "white primaries," which legally excluded blacks from participation in the nominating process. Here the Court simply recognized that primaries could no longer be regarded as the private affairs of the parties but were an integral aspect of the electoral process. This made parties "an agency of the State," and therefore any practice of discrimination against blacks was "state action within the meaning of the Fifteenth Amendment."[10] The most important pre-1954 decision was probably *Shelley v. Kraemer,* in which the Court ruled against the widespread practice of "restrictive covenants," whereby the seller of a home added a clause to the sales contract requiring the buyer to agree not to sell the home later to any non-Caucasian, non-Christian, etc. The Court ruled that although private persons could sign such restrictive covenants, they could not be judicially enforced since the Fourteenth Amendment prohibits any organ of the state, including the courts, from denying equal protection of its laws.[11]

Although none of those pre-1954 cases confronted "separate but equal" and the principle of racial discrimination as such, they were extremely significant to black leaders in the 1940s and gave them encouragement enough to believe that there was at last an opportunity and enough legal precedent to change the constitutional framework itself. Much of this legal work was done by the Legal Defense and Educational Fund of the National Association for the Advancement of Colored People (NAACP). Formed in 1909 to fight discrimination against black people, the NAACP was the most important civil rights organization during the first half of the twentieth century. It set up its Legal Defense Fund to support an ongoing challenge to the legal edifice of segregation. Until the late 1940s, lawyers working for the Legal Defense Fund had concentrated on winning small victories within that framework. Then, in 1948, the Legal Defense Fund upgraded its approach by simultaneously filing suits in different federal districts and through each level of schooling from unequal provision of kindergarten for blacks to unequal sports and science facilities in all-black high schools. After nearly two years of these mostly successful equalization suits, the lawyers decided the time was ripe to confront the "separate but equal" rule head on, but they felt they needed some heavier artillery to lead the attack. Their choice to lead this attack was Thurgood Marshall, who had been fighting, and often winning, equalization suits since the early 1930s. Marshall was pessimistic about the readiness of the Supreme Court for a full confrontation with segregation itself and the constitutional principle sustaining it. But the unwillingness of Congress after the 1948 election to consider fair employment legislation seems to have convinced Marshall that the courts were the only hope.

The Supreme Court must have come to the same conclusion because, during the four years following 1948, there emerged a clear impression that the Court was willing to take more civil rights cases on appeal. Yet, this was no guarantee that the Court would reverse *on principle* the separate but equal precedent of *Plessy v. Ferguson*. All through 1951 and 1952, as cases were winding slowly through the lower-court litigation maze, there were intense discussions and disagreements among NAACP lawyers as to whether a full-scale assault on *Plessy* was good strategy or whether it might not be better to continue with specific cases alleging unequal treatment and demanding relief with a Court-imposed policy of equalization.[12] But for some lawyers like Marshall, these kinds of victories could amount to a defeat. South Carolina, for example, under the leadership of Governor James F. Byrnes, a former Supreme Court justice, had undertaken a strategy of equalization of school services on a large scale in order to satisfy the *Plessy* rule and to head off or render moot litigation against the principle of separate but equal.

In the fall of 1952, the Court had on its docket cases from Kansas, South Carolina, Virginia, Delaware, and the District of Columbia challenging the constitutionality of school segregation. Of these, the Kansas case became the chosen one. It seemed to be ahead of the pack in its district court, and it had the special advantage of being located in a state outside the Deep South.[13]

A nine-year-old Linda Brown in 1952.

Oliver Brown, the father of three girls, lived "across the tracks" in a low-income, racially mixed Topeka neighborhood. Every school-day morning, Linda Brown took the school bus to the Monroe School for black children about a mile away. In September 1950, Oliver Brown took Linda to the all-white Sumner School, which was closer to home, to enter her into the third grade in defiance of state law and local segregation rules. When they were refused, Brown took his case to the NAACP, and soon thereafter ***Brown v. Board of Education*** was born. In mid-1953, the Court announced that the several cases on their way up would be re-argued within a set of questions having to do with the intent of the Fourteenth Amendment. Almost exactly a year later, the Court responded to those questions in one of the most important decisions in its history.

In deciding the *Brown* case, the Court, to the surprise of many, basically rejected as inconclusive all the learned arguments about the intent and the history of the Fourteenth Amendment and committed itself to considering only the consequences of segregation:

> Does segregation of children in public schools solely on the basis of race, even though the physical facilities and other "tangible" factors may be equal, deprive the children of the minority group of equal educational opportunities? We believe that it does. . . . We conclude that in the field of public education the doctrine of "separate but equal" has no place. Separate educational facilities are inherently unequal.[14]

The *Brown* decision altered the constitutional framework in two fundamental respects. First, after *Brown,* the states no longer had the power to use race as a criterion of discrimination in law. Second, the national government from then on had the power (and eventually the obligation) to intervene with strict regulatory policies against the discriminatory actions of state or local governments, school boards, employers, and many others in the private sector (see Chapter 16).

Civil Rights after *Brown v. Board of Education*

Brown v. Board of Education withdrew all constitutional authority to use race as a criterion of exclusion, and it signaled more clearly the Court's determination to use the **strict scrutiny** test in cases related to racial discrimination. This meant that the burden of proof would fall on the government—not on the challengers—to show that the law in question *was* constitutional.[15] Although the use of strict scrutiny in cases relating to racial discrimination would give an advantage to those attacking racial discrimination, the historic decision in *Brown v. Board of Education* was merely a small opening move. First, the Court ruling "to admit to public schools on a racially nondiscriminatory basis with all deliberate speed," which came a year later,[16] was directly binding only on the five school boards that had been defendants in the cases appealed to the Supreme Court. Rather than fall into line, as most parties do when a new judicial principle is handed down, most states refused to cooperate until sued, and many ingenious schemes were employed to delay obedience (such as paying the tuition for white students to attend newly created "private" academies). Second, even as southern school boards began to cooperate by eliminating their legally enforced (**de jure**) school segregation, there remained extensive actual (**de facto**) school segregation in the North as well as in the South, as a consequence of racially segregated housing that could not be reached by the 1954–55 *Brown* principles. Third, discrimination in employment, public accommodations, juries, voting, and other areas of social and economic activity were not directly touched by *Brown.*

A decade of frustration following *Brown* made it fairly obvious to all that adjudication alone would not succeed. The goal of "equal protection" required positive, or affirmative, action by Congress and by administrative agencies. And given massive southern resistance and a generally negative national public opinion toward racial integration, progress would not be made through courts, Congress, or federal agencies without intense, well-organized support. Table 18.1 shows the increase in civil rights demonstrations for voting rights and public accommodations during the fourteen years following *Brown.* It shows that organized civil rights demonstrations began to mount

TABLE 18.1

PEACEFUL CIVIL RIGHTS DEMONSTRATIONS, 1954–68

Year	Total	For public accommodations	For voting
1954	0	0	0
1955	0	0	0
1956	18	6	0
1957	44	9	0
1958	19	8	0
1959	7	11	0
1960	173	127	0
1961	198	122	0
1962	77	44	0
1963	272	140	1
1964	271	93	12
1965	387	21	128
1966	171	15	32
1967	93	3	3
1968	97	2	0

NOTE: This table is drawn from a search of the *New York Times Index* for all references to civil rights demonstrations during the years the table covers. The table should be taken simply as indicative, for the data—news stories in a single paper—are very crude. The classification of the incident as peaceful or violent and the subject area of the demonstration are inferred from the entry in the *Index,* usually the headline from the story. The two subcategories reported here—public accommodations and voting—do not sum to the total because demonstrations dealing with a variety of other issues (e.g., education, employment, police brutality) are included in the total.

SOURCE: Jonathan D. Casper, *The Politics of Civil Liberties* (New York: Harper & Row, 1972), p. 90.

Hundreds of thousands of demonstrators gathered in the March on Washington in March 1963 to demand civil rights for African Americans.

slowly but surely after *Brown v. Board of Education.* By the 1960s, the many organizations that made up the Civil Rights movement had accumulated experience and built networks capable of launching massive direct-action campaigns against southern segregationists. The Southern Christian Leadership Conference, the Student Nonviolent Coordinating Committee, and many other organizations had built a movement that stretched across the South. The movement used the media to attract nationwide attention and support. In the massive March on Washington in 1963, the Reverend Martin Luther King, Jr., staked out the movement's moral claims in his famous "I Have a Dream" speech. The image of protesters being beaten, attacked by police dogs, and set upon with fire hoses did much to win broad sympathy for the cause of black civil rights and to discredit state and local governments in the South. In this way, the movement created intense pressure for a reluctant federal government to take more assertive steps to defend black civil rights.

Political action and congressional action culminated in a series of stunning majorities in congressional votes for enactment of fundamental new civil rights laws. An important insight to be drawn from Table 18.1 is that the constitutional action by the Supreme Court in 1954–55 actually *produced* the Civil Rights movement as it came to be known in the late 1950s. Adding Table 18.2 to Table 18.1 reveals still another insight into the political relationships among the three branches of the national government: Just as *political* agitation to expand rights followed the Court's formal recognition of their existence, so did greatly expanded *judicial* action follow the success of political action in Congress. Table 18.2 confirms this by showing the enormous jump in NAACP-sponsored civil rights cases brought in the courts. The

ACTIVITY OF NAACP LEGAL DEFENSE AND EDUCATIONAL FUND (LDF), 1963–67

Year	Individuals defended by the LDF	Cases on LDF docket
1963	4,200	107
1964	10,400	145
1965	17,000	225
1966	14,000	375
1967	13,000	420

SOURCE: Data from *Report 66,* published in 1967 by the NAACP Legal Defense and Educational Fund. Reprinted from Jonathan D. Casper, *The Politics of Civil Liberties* (New York: Harper & Row, 1972), p. 91. Reprinted by permission of the NAACP Legal Defense and Educational Fund, Inc.

TABLE 18.2

number of actual cases brought by the Legal Defense Fund of the NAACP actually continued to go up at a significant rate even as the number of individuals defended by these cases dropped. This suggests how strongly the NAACP was interested in using the cases to advance the principles of civil rights rather than to improve the prospects of individual black litigants.

School Desegregation, Phase One Although the District of Columbia and some of the school districts in the border states began to respond almost immediately to court-ordered desegregation, the states of the Deep South responded with a carefully planned delaying tactic commonly called "massive resistance" by the more demagogic southern leaders and "nullification" and "interposition" by the centrists. Either way, southern politicians stood shoulder-to-shoulder to declare that the Supreme Court's decisions and orders were without effect. The legislatures in these states enacted statutes ordering school districts to maintain segregated schools and state superintendents to terminate state funding wherever there was racial mixing in the classroom. Some southern states violated their own long traditions of local school autonomy by centralizing public school authority under the governor or the state board of education and by giving states the power to close the schools and to provide alternative private schooling wherever local school boards might be tending to obey the Supreme Court.

Most of these plans of "massive resistance" were tested in the federal courts and were struck down as unconstitutional.[17] But southern resistance was not confined to legislation. For example, in Arkansas in 1957, Governor Orval Faubus mobilized the Arkansas National Guard to intercede against enforcement of a federal court order to integrate Central High School of Little Rock, and President Eisenhower was forced to deploy U.S. troops and literally place the city under martial law. The Supreme Court considered the Little Rock confrontation so historically important that the opinion it rendered in that case was not only agreed to unanimously but was, unprecedentedly, signed personally by each and every one of the justices.[18] The end of massive resistance, however, became simply the beginning of still another southern strategy, "pupil placement" laws, which authorized school districts to place each pupil in a school according to a whole variety of academic, personal, and psychological considerations, never mentioning race at all. This put the burden of transferring to an all-white school on the nonwhite children and their parents, making it almost impossible for a single court order to cover a whole district, let alone a whole state. This delayed desegregation a while longer.[19]

As new devices were invented by the southern states to avoid desegregation, the federal courts followed with cases and decisions quashing them. Ten years after *Brown,* fewer than 1 percent of black school-age children in the Deep South were attending schools with whites.[20] It had become unmistakably clear well before that time that the federal courts could not do the job alone. The first modern effort to legislate in the field of civil rights was made in 1957, but the law contained only a federal guarantee of voting rights, without any powers of enforcement, although it did create the Civil Rights Commission to study abuses. Much more important legislation for civil rights followed, especially the Civil Rights Act of 1964. It is important to observe here the mutual dependence of the courts and legislatures—not only do the legislatures need constitutional authority to act, but the courts need legislative and political assistance, through the power of the purse and the power to organize administrative agencies to implement court orders, and through the focusing of political support. Consequently, even as the U.S. Congress finally moved into the field of school desegregation (and other areas of "equal protection"), the courts continued to exercise their powers, not only by placing court orders against recalcitrant school districts, but also by extending and reinterpreting aspects of the "equal protection" clause to support legislative and administrative actions (see Figure 18.1).

Resistance to school desegregation in the South during the 1950s was dramatized by events at Little Rock Central High School in 1957, when an angry mob of white students prevented black students from entering the school. As a result, the federal government sent troops to protect the black students and to uphold the desegregation plan.

FIGURE 18.1

Political action and government action spurred each others to produce dramatic changes in American civil rights policies.

CAUSE AND EFFECT IN THE CIVIL RIGHTS MOVEMENT

Judicial and Legal Action	Political Action
1954 *Brown* v. *Board of Education*	
1955 *Brown* II—Implementation of *Brown* I	**1955** Montgomery Bus Boycott
1956 Federal courts order school integration, especially one ordering Autherine Lucy admitted to University of Alabama, with Governor Wallace officially protesting	
1957 Civil Rights Act creating Civil Rights Commission; President Eisenhower sends paratroops to Little Rock, Arkansas, to enforce integration of Central High School	**1957** Southern Christian Leadership Conference (SCLC) formed, with Martin Luther King, Jr., as president
1960 First substantive Civil Rights Act, primarily voting rights	**1960** Student Nonviolent Coordinating Committee formed to organize protests, sit-ins, freedom rides
1961 Interstate Commerce Commission orders desegregation on all buses, trains, and in terminals	
1961 JFK favors executive action over civil rights legislation	
1963 JFK shifts, supports strong civil rights law; assassination; LBJ asserts strong support for civil rights	**1963** Nonviolent demonstrations in Birmingham, Alabama, lead to King's arrest and his "Letter from the Birmingham Jail"
	1963 March on Washington
1964 Congress passes historic Civil Rights Act covering voting, employment, public accommodations, education	
1965 Voting Rights Act	**1965** King announces drive to register 3 million blacks in the South
1966 War on Poverty in full swing	Movement dissipates: part toward litigation, part toward Community Action Programs, part toward war protest, part toward more militant "Black Power" actions

The Civil Rights Acts The right to equal protection of the laws could be established and, to a certain extent, implemented by the courts. But after a decade of very frustrating efforts, the courts and Congress ultimately came to the conclusion that the federal courts alone were not adequate to the task of changing the social rules, and that legislation and administrative action would be needed.

Table 18.3 (pp. 690–91) provides an overview of the efforts made by Congress to use its legislative powers to help make equal protection of the laws a reality. As this table indicates, three civil rights acts were passed during the first decade after the 1954 Supreme Court decision in *Brown v. Board of Education.* But these acts were of only marginal importance. The first two, in 1957 and 1960, established that the Fourteenth Amendment of the Constitution, adopted almost a century earlier, could no longer be disregarded, particularly with regard to voting. The third, the Equal Pay Act of 1963, was more important, but it was concerned with women, did not touch the question of racial discrimination, and had no enforcement mechanisms.

By far the most important piece of legislation passed by Congress concerning equal opportunity was the Civil Rights Act of 1964. It not only put some teeth in the voting rights provisions of the 1957 and 1960 acts but also went far beyond voting to attack discrimination in public accommodations, segregation in the schools, and at long last, the discriminatory conduct of employers in hiring, promoting, and laying off their employees. Discrimination against women was also included, extending the important 1963 provisions. The 1964 act seemed bold at the time, but it was enacted ten years after the Supreme Court had declared racial discrimination "inherently unequal" under the Fifth and Fourteenth amendments. And it was enacted long after blacks had demonstrated that discrimination was no longer acceptable. The choice in 1964 was not between congressional action or inaction but between legal action and expanded violence.

In 1993, after the Denny's restaurant chain was charged with racial discrimination, Denny's restaurants were boycotted by protesters such as these from the Labor Black Struggle League.

Public Accommodations After the passage of the 1964 Civil Rights Act, public accommodations quickly removed some of the most visible forms of racial discrimination. Signs defining "colored" and "white" restrooms, water fountains, waiting rooms, and seating arrangements were removed and a host of other practices that relegated black people to separate and inferior arrangements were ended. In addition, the federal government filed more than 400 antidiscrimination suits in federal courts against hotels, restaurants, taverns, gas stations, and other "public accommodations" under Title II.

Many aspects of legalized racial segregation—such as separate Bibles in the courtroom—seem like ancient history today. But the issue of racial discrimination in public settings is by no means over. In 1993, six African American Secret Service agents filed charges against the Denny's restaurant chain for failing to serve them; white Secret Service agents at a nearby table had received prompt service. Similar charges citing discriminatory service at Denny's restaurants surfaced across the country. Faced with evidence of a pattern of systematic discrimination and numerous lawsuits, Denny's paid $45 million in damages to plaintiffs in Maryland and California in what is said to be the largest settlement ever in a public accommodation case.[21] The Denny's

TABLE 18.3

THE KEY PROVISIONS OF FEDERAL CIVIL RIGHTS LAWS, 1957–91	
Civil Rights Act of 1957	Established the Commission on Civil Rights to monitor civil rights progress. Elevated the importance of the Civil Rights Division of the Department of Justice, headed by an assistant attorney general. Made it a federal crime to attempt to intimidate a voter or to prevent a person from voting.
Civil Rights Act of 1960	Increased the sanction against obstruction of voting or of court orders enforcing the vote. Established federal power to appoint referees to register voters wherever a "pattern or practice" of discrimination was found by a federal court.
Equal Pay Act of 1963	Banned wage discrimination on the basis of sex in jobs requiring equal skill, effort, and responsibility. Exceptions involved employee pay differentials based on factors other than sex, such as merit or seniority.
Civil Rights Act of 1964	*Voting:* Title I made attainment of a sixth-grade education (in English) a presumption to literacy. *Public accommodations:* Title II barred discrimination in any commercial lodging of more than five rooms for transient guests and in any service station, restaurant, theater, or commercial conveyance. *Public schools:* Title IV empowered the attorney general to sue for desegregation whenever he or she found a segregation complaint meritorious. Title VI authorized the withholding of federal aid from segregated schools. *Private employment:* Title VII outlawed discrimination in a variety of employment practices on the basis of race, religion, and sex (sex added for the first time in an area other than wage discrimination). Established the Equal Employment Opportunity Commission (EEOC) to enforce the law but required it to defer enforcement to state or local agencies for sixty days following each complaint.
Voting Rights Act of 1965	*Voting rights only:* Empowered the attorney general, with the Civil Service Commission, to appoint voting examiners to replace local registrars wherever he or she found fewer than 50 percent of the persons of voting age had voted in the 1964 presidential election and to suspend all literacy tests where they were used as a tool of discrimination.

case shows how effective the Civil Rights Act of 1964 can be in challenging racial discrimination. In addition to the settlement, the chain vowed to expand employment and management opportunities for minorities in Denny's restaurants. Other forms of racial discrimination in public accommodations are harder to challenge, however. For example, there is considerable evidence that taxicabs often refuse to pick up black passengers.[22] Such practices may be common, but they are difficult to prove and remedy through the law.

THE KEY PROVISIONS OF FEDERAL CIVIL RIGHTS LAWS, 1957–91 *(continued)*

Civil Rights Act of 1968	*Open housing:* Made it a crime to refuse to sell or rent a dwelling on the basis of race or religion, if a bona fide offer had been made, or to discriminate in advertising or in the terms and conditions of sale or rental. Administered by the Department of Housing and Urban Development, but the burden of proof is on the complainant, who must seek local remedies first, where they exist.
Amendments of 1970 to 1965 Voting Rights Act	Extended 1965 act and included some districts in northern states.
Equal Employment Opportunity Act of 1972	Increased coverage of the Civil Rights Act of 1964 to include public-sector employees. Gave EEOC authority to bring suit against persons engaging in "patterns or practice" of employment discrimination.
Amendments of 1975 to 1965 Voting Rights Act	Extended 1965 act and broadened antidiscrimination measures to include protection for language minorities (e.g., Latinos, Native Americans).
Amendments of 1978 to 1964 Civil Rights Act	Prohibited discrimination in employment on the basis of pregnancy or related disabilities. Required that pregnancy or related medical conditions be treated as disabilities eligible for medical and liability insurance.
Amendments of 1982 to 1965 Voting Rights Act	Extended 1965 act and strengthened antidiscrimination measures by requiring only proof of *effect* of discrimination, not *intent* to discriminate.
Americans with Disabilities Act of 1990	Extended to people with disabilities protection from discrimination in employment and public accommodations similar to the protection given to women and racial, religious, and ethnic minorities by the 1964 Civil Rights Act. Required that public transportation systems, other public services, and telecommunications systems be accessible to those with disabilities.
Civil Rights Act of 1991	Reversed several Court decisions, beginning with *Wards Cove v. Atonio* (1989), that had made it harder for women and minorities to seek compensation for job discrimination. It put back on the employer the burden of proof to show that a discriminatory policy was a business necessity.

School Desegregation The 1964 Civil Rights Act also declared discrimination by private employers and state governments (school boards, etc.) illegal, then went further to provide for administrative agencies to help the courts implement these laws. Title IV of the act, for example, authorized the executive branch, through the Justice Department, to implement federal court orders to desegregate schools, and to do so without having to wait for individual parents to bring complaints. Title VI of the act vastly strengthened the role of the executive branch and the credibility of court orders by providing that federal grants-in-aid to state and local governments for education must be withheld from any school system practicing racial segregation. Title VI became the most effective weapon for desegregating schools outside the South, because the situation in northern communities was more subtle and difficult to reach. In the South, the problem was segregation by law coupled with overt resistance to the national government's efforts to change the situation. In contrast, outside the South, segregated facilities were the outcome of hundreds of thousands of housing choices made by individuals and families. Once racial residential patterns emerged, racial homogeneity, property values, and neighborhood schools and churches were defended by realtors, neighborhood organizations, and the like. Thus, in order to eliminate discrimination nationwide, the 1964 Civil Rights Act (1) gave the president through the Office for Civil Rights of the Justice Department the power to withhold federal education grants,[23] and (2) gave the attorney general of the United States the power to initiate suits (rather than having to await complaints) wherever there was a "pattern or practice" of discrimination.[24]

In the decade following the 1964 Civil Rights Act, the Justice Department brought legal action against more than five hundred school districts. During the same period, administrative agencies filed actions against six hundred school districts, threatening to suspend federal aid to education unless real desegregation steps were taken.

Busing One step taken toward desegregation was busing children from poor urban school districts to wealthier suburban ones. In 1971, the Supreme Court held that state-imposed desegregation could be brought about by busing children across school districts, even where relatively long distances were involved:

> If school authorities fail in their affirmative obligations judicial authority may be invoked. Once a right and a violation have been shown, the scope of a district court's equitable powers to remedy past wrongs is broad. . . . Bus transportation [is] a normal and accepted tool of educational policy.[25]

But the decision went beyond that, adding that under certain limited circumstances even racial quotas could be used as the "starting point in shaping a remedy to correct past constitutional violations," and that pairing or grouping of schools and reorganizing school attendance zones would also be acceptable.

Three years later, however, this principle was severely restricted when the Supreme Court determined that only cities found guilty of deliberate and de jure racial segregation would have to desegregate their schools.[26] This ruling had the effect of exempting most northern states and cities from busing because school segregation in northern cities is generally de facto segregation that follows from segregated housing and from thousands of acts of private discrimination against blacks and other minorities.

Detroit and Boston provide the best illustrations of the agonizing problem of making further progress in civil rights in the schools under the constitutional framework established by these decisions. Following the lead of the Supreme Court, a federal district court and a federal court of appeals had found that Detroit had engaged in deliberate segregation and that, since Detroit schools were overwhelmingly black, the only way to provide a remedy was to bus students between Detroit and the white suburbs beyond the Detroit city boundaries. The Supreme Court had previously approved a similar "interdistrict" integration plan for Charlotte, North Carolina, but it refused to do so for Detroit. Although Detroit's segregation had been deliberate, the city and suburban boundary lines had not been drawn deliberately to separate the races. Therefore, the remedy had to take place within Detroit. That same year, and no doubt influenced by the Detroit decision as well as by President Nixon, Congress amended Title VI of the 1964 Civil Rights Act, reducing the authority of the federal government to withhold monetary assistance only in instances of proven, de jure, state-government-imposed segregation. This action was extremely significant in taking the heat off most northern school districts.

In 1974, opposition to busing necessitated a police escort for buses carrying black students in Boston.

In Boston, school authorities were found guilty of deliberately building school facilities and drawing school districts "to increase racial segregation." After vain efforts by Boston school authorities to draw up an acceptable plan to remedy the segregation, federal Judge W. Arthur Garrity ordered an elaborate desegregation plan of his own involving busing between the all-black neighborhood of Roxbury and the nearby white, working-class community of South Boston. Opponents of this plan were organized and eventually took the case to the Supreme Court, where *certiorari* (the Court's device for accepting appeals; see Chapter 14) was denied; this had the effect of approving Judge Garrity's order. The city's schools were so segregated and uncooperative that even the conservative Nixon administration had already initiated a punitive cutoff of funds. But many liberals also criticized Judge Garrity's plan as being badly conceived, because it involved two neighboring communities with a history of tension and mutual resentment. The plan worked well at the elementary school level but proved so explosive at the high school level that it generated a continuing crisis for the city of Boston and for the whole nation over court-ordered, federally directed desegregation in the North.[27]

Court-ordered busing divided Boston's black and white communities. In 1976, a mob of protesters outside the Boston federal courthouse sought to impale this innocent black bystander, a lawyer on his way to his office. This Pulitzer Prize–winning photograph shows the tension and conflict resulting from the struggle for equal rights for African Americans.

Additional progress in the desegregation of schools is likely to be extremely slow unless the Supreme Court decides to permit federal action against de facto segregation and against the varieties of private schools and academies that have sprung up for the purpose of avoiding integration. The prospects for further school integration diminished with a Supreme Court decision handed down on January 15, 1991. The opinion, written for the Court by Chief Justice William Rehnquist, held that lower federal courts could end supervision of local school boards if those boards could show compliance "in good faith" with court orders to desegregate and could show that "vestiges of past discrimination" had been eliminated "to the extent practicable."[28] It is not necessarily easy for a school board to prove that the new standard has been met, but this was the first time since *Brown* and the 1964 Civil Rights Act that the Court had opened the door at all to retreat.

That door was opened further by a 1995 decision in which the Court ruled that the remedies being applied in Kansas City, Missouri, were improper.[29] In accordance with a lower court ruling, the state was pouring additional funding into salaries and remedial programs for Kansas City schools, which had a history of segregation. The aim of the spending was to improve student performance and to attract white students from the suburbs into the city schools. The Supreme Court declared the interdistrict goal improper and reiterated its earlier ruling that states can free themselves of court orders by showing a good faith effort. This decision indicated the Court's new willingness to end desegregation plans even when predominantly minority schools continue to lag significantly behind white suburban schools.

Outlawing Discrimination in Employment Despite the agonizingly slow progress of school desegregation, there was some progress made in other areas of civil rights during the 1960s and 1970s. Voting rights were established and fairly quickly began to revolutionize southern politics. Service on juries was no longer denied to minorities. But progress in the right to participate in politics and government dramatized the relative lack of progress in the economic domain, and it was in this area that battles over civil rights were increasingly fought.

The federal courts and the Justice Department entered this area through Title VII of the Civil Rights Act of 1964, which outlawed job discrimination by all private and public employers, including governmental agencies (such as fire and police departments), that employed more than fifteen workers. We have already seen that the Supreme Court gave "interstate commerce" such a broad definition that Congress had the constitutional authority to cover discrimination by virtually any local employers.[30] Title VII makes it unlawful to discriminate in employment on the basis of color, religion, sex, or national origin, as well as race.

Title VII delegated some of the powers to enforce fair employment practices to the Justice Department's Civil Rights Division and others to a new agency created in the 1964 act, the Equal Employment Opportunity Commission (EEOC). By executive order, these agencies had the power of the national government to revoke public contracts for goods and services and to refuse to engage in contracts for goods and services with any private company that could not guarantee that its rules for hiring, promotion, and firing were nondiscriminatory. Executive orders in 1965, 1967, and 1969 by Presidents Johnson and Nixon extended and reaffirmed nondiscrimination practices in employment and promotion in the federal government service. And in 1972, President Nixon and a Democratic Congress cooperated to strengthen the EEOC by giving it authority to initiate suits rather than wait for grievances.

But one problem with Title VII was that the complaining party had to show that deliberate discrimination was the cause of the failure to get a job or a training opportunity. Rarely does an employer explicitly admit discrimination on the basis of race, sex, or any other illegal reason. Recognizing the rarity of such an admission, the courts have allowed aggrieved parties (the plaintiffs) to make their case if they can show that an employer's hiring practices had the *effect* of exclusion. A leading case in 1971 involved a "class action" by several black employees in North Carolina attempting to show with statistical evidence that blacks had been relegated to only one department in the Duke Power Company, which involved the least desirable, manual-labor jobs, and that they had been kept out of contention for the better jobs because the employer had added attainment of a high school education and the passing of specially prepared aptitude tests as qualifications for higher jobs. The Supreme Court held that although the statistical evidence did not prove intentional discrimination, and although the requirements were race-neutral in appearance, their effects were sufficient to shift the burden of justification to the employer to show that the requirements were a "business necessity" that bore "a demonstrable relationship to successful performance."[31] The ruling in this case was subsequently applied to other hiring, promotion, and training programs.[32]

Voting Rights Although 1964 was the *most* important year for civil rights legislation, it was not the only important year. In 1965, Congress significantly strengthened legislation protecting voting rights by barring literacy and other tests as a condition for voting in six southern states,[33] by setting criminal penalties for interference with efforts to vote, and by providing for the replacement of local registrars with federally appointed registrars in counties designated by the attorney general as significantly resistant to registering eligible blacks to vote. The right to vote was further strengthened with ratification in 1964 of the Twenty-fourth Amendment, which abolished the poll tax, and in 1975 with legislation permanently outlawing literacy tests in all fifty states and mandating bilingual ballots or oral assistance for Spanish, Chinese, Japanese, Koreans, Native Americans, and Eskimos.

In the long run, the laws extending and protecting voting rights could prove to be the most effective of all the great civil rights legislation, because the progress in black political participation produced by these acts has altered the shape of American politics. In 1965, in the seven states of the Old Confederacy covered by the Voting Rights Act, 29.3 percent of the eligible black residents were registered to vote, compared to 73.4 percent of the white residents (see Table 18.4). Mississippi was the extreme case, with 6.7 percent black and 69.9 percent white registration. In 1967, a mere two years after implementation of the voting rights laws, 52.1 percent of the eligible blacks in the seven states were registered, comparing favorably to 79.5 percent of

REGISTRATION BY RACE AND STATE IN SOUTHERN STATES COVERED BY THE VOTING RIGHTS ACT

	Before the act*			After the act* 1971–72		
	White	Black	Gap†	White	Black	Gap†
Alabama	69.2%	19.3%	49.9%	80.7%	57.1%	23.6%
Georgia	62.6	27.4	35.2	70.6	67.8	2.8
Louisiana	80.5	31.6	48.9	80.0	59.1	20.9
Mississippi	69.9	6.7	63.2	71.6	62.2	9.4
North Carolina	96.8	46.8	50.0	62.2	46.3	15.9
South Carolina	75.7	37.3	38.4	51.2	48.0	3.2
Virginia	61.1	38.3	22.8	61.2	54.0	7.2
TOTAL	73.4	29.3	44.1	67.8	56.6	11.2

*Available registration data as of March 1965 and 1971–72.
†The gap is the percentage point difference between white and black registration rates.
SOURCE: U.S. Commission on Civil Rights, *Political Participation* (1968), Appendix VII: Voter Education Project, Attachment to Press Release, October 3, 1972.

TABLE 18.4

A student volunteer oversees an older woman registering to vote in Mississippi following passage of the Voting Rights Act in 1965. The percentage of African Americans registered to vote in Mississippi increased from about 7 percent in 1965 to more than 62 percent in 1972.

the eligible whites, a gap of 27.4 points. By 1972, the gap between black and white registration in the seven states was only 11.2 points, and in Mississippi the gap had been reduced to 9.4 points. At one time, white leaders in Mississippi attempted to dilute the influence of this growing black vote by gerrymandering districts to ensure that no blacks would be elected to Congress. But the black voters changed Mississippi before Mississippi could change them. In 1988, 11 percent of all elected officials in Mississippi were black. This was up one full percentage point from 1987 and closely approximates the size of the national black electorate, which at the time was just over 11 percent of the American voting-age population. Mississippi's blacks had made significant gains (as was true in other Deep South states) as elected state and local representatives, and Mississippi was one of only eight states in the country in which a black judge presided over the highest state court. (Four of the eight were Deep South states.)[34]

Housing The Civil Rights Act of 1964 did not address housing, but in 1968, Congress passed another civil rights act specifically to outlaw housing discrimination. Called the Fair Housing Act, the law prohibited discrimination in the sale or rental of most housing—eventually covering nearly all the nation's housing. Housing was among the most controversial of discrimination issues because of deeply entrenched patterns of residential segregation across the United States. Such segregation was not simply a product of individual choice. Local housing authorities deliberately segregated public housing, and federal guidelines had sanctioned discrimination in Federal Housing Administration mortgage lending, effectively preventing blacks from joining the exodus to the suburbs in the 1950s and 1960s. Nonetheless, Congress had been reluctant to tackle housing discrimination, fearing the tremendous controversy it could arouse. But, just as the housing legislation was being considered in April 1968, Martin Luther King, Jr., was assassinated; this tragedy brought the measure unexpected support in Congress.

Although it pronounced sweeping goals, the Fair Housing Act had little effect on housing segregation because its enforcement mechanisms were so weak. Individuals believing they had been discriminated against had to file suit themselves. The burden was on the individual to prove that housing discrimination had occurred, even though such discrimination is often subtle and difficult to document. Although local fair-housing groups emerged to assist individuals in their court claims, the procedures for proving discrimination proved a formidable barrier to effective change. These procedures were not altered until 1988, when Congress passed the Fair Housing Amendments Act. This new law put more teeth in the enforcement procedures and allowed the Department of Housing and Urban Development (HUD) to initiate legal action in cases of discrimination. With vigorous use, these provisions may prove more successful than past efforts at combatting housing discrimination.[35]

Other avenues for challenging residential segregation also had mixed success. HUD tried briefly in the early 1970s to create racially "open communities" by withholding federal funds to suburbs that refused to accept subsidized housing. Confronted with charges of "forced integration" and bitter local protests, however, the administration quickly backed down. Efforts to prohibit discrimination in lending have been somewhat more promising. Several laws passed in the 1970s required banks to report information about their mortgage lending patterns, making it more difficult for them to engage in **redlining**, the practice of refusing to lend to entire neighborhoods. The 1977 Community Reinvestment Act required banks to lend in neighborhoods in which they do business. Through vigorous use of this act, many neighborhood organizations have reached agreements with banks that have significantly increased investment in some poor neighborhoods.

The Universalization of Civil Rights

- What groups were spurred by the provision of the Civil Rights Act of 1964 outlawing discrimination in employment practices based on race, religion, and sex to seek broader protection under the law?
- What is the politics of the universalization of civil rights?

Even before equal employment laws began to have a positive effect on the economic situation of blacks, something far more dramatic began happening—the universalization of civil rights. The right not to be discriminated against was being successfully claimed by the other groups listed in Title VII of the 1964 Civil Rights Act—those defined by sex, religion, or national origin—and eventually by still other groups defined by age or sexual preference. This universalization of civil rights has become the new frontier of the civil rights struggle, and women have emerged with the greatest prominence in this new struggle. The effort to define and end gender discrimination in employment has led to the historic joining of women's rights to the civil rights cause.

As gender discrimination began to be seen as an important civil rights issue, other groups arose demanding recognition and active protection of their civil rights. Under Title VII, any group or individual can try, and in fact is encouraged to try, to convert goals and grievances into questions of rights and of the deprivation of those rights. A plaintiff must only establish that his or her membership in a group is an unreasonable basis for discrimination—i.e., that it cannot be proven to be a "job-related" or otherwise clearly reasonable and relevant decision. In America today, the list of individuals and groups claiming illegal discrimination is lengthy.

Women and Gender Discrimination

Title VII provided a valuable tool for the growing women's movement in the 1960s and 1970s. In fact, in many ways the law fostered the growth of the women's movement. The first major campaign of the National Organization for Women (NOW) involved picketing the Equal Employment Opportunity Commission for its refusal to ban sex-segregated employment advertisements. NOW also sued the *New York Times* for continuing to publish such ads after the passage of Title VII. Another organization, the Women's Equity Action League (WEAL), pursued legal action on a wide range of sex discrimination issues, filing lawsuits against law schools and medical schools for discriminatory admission policies, for example.

Building on these victories and the growth of the women's movement, feminist activists sought an "Equal Rights Amendment" (ERA) to the Constitution. The proposed amendment was short: its substantive passage stated that "equality of rights under the law shall not be denied or abridged by the United States or by any State on account of sex." The amendment's supporters believed that such a sweeping guarantee of equal rights was a

Even though the Equal Rights Amendment seemed a simple declaration of equal opportunity for women, opposition both inside and outside the women's movement prevented its passage.

The Violence against Women Act

Each year in the United States, women are the targets of more than half a million sexual assaults, among them 170,000 rapes and 140,000 attempted rapes.[1] This is more than three times the number actually reported to police, a discrepancy that many experts attribute to the reluctance on the part of many women to file formal charges. Everyone agrees that rape and sexual assault represent not just a tragedy for each victim, but a terrible problem for American society. But are rape and other forms of sexual assault also violations of civil rights? Or is the new federal law that defines them as such, the 1994 Violence against Women Act, an excessive broadening of the meaning of "civil rights," one that waters down more traditional understandings of civil rights?

Proponents of the act, prominent among them President Clinton and the National Organization for Women (NOW), argue that rape and sexual assault against women are hate crimes, just as lynching was once a common hate crime against blacks. They argue that just as lynching served to intimidate all blacks in a community, rape and other crimes of violence against individual women serve to intimidate all women. The Violence against Women Act, which gives the victims of sexual assault the right to sue for damages in federal court, draws on federal antilynching laws, which effectively ended the practice by defining it as a violation of civil rights and, consequently, as a violation of federal law.

Skeptics, however, maintain that the Violence against Women Act distorts the notion of "civil rights." They note that lynchings occurred with the wide, if usually tacit, support of whole communities; such wide participation in effect legitimized lynching, turning it from a solitary crime into an act of political oppression. But the situation with rape and other sexual assaults is different, skeptics say. Rape, though it may be statistically too frequent, is never legitimized and supported by a whole community. Thus, skeptics see little basis for finding a political significance in rape. Many of them assert that proponents of the Violence against Women Act realize this, and are driven by more narrowly political calculations. Such critics charge that the act will erode local jurisdiction over law and order and inundate federal courts with cases.

By early 1995, however, only one case had been brought under the act. It was filed by a young student at Virginia Tech, who claims she was raped during her first month at the school by two members of the school's football team, and that the university did not take her complaint seriously. The woman, Christy Brzonkala (she has chosen to release her name to publicize the case), initially brought a confidential university disciplinary complaint against the two men, but the university dismissed the complaint against one of the men for lack of evidence. The other man, who admitted having sex with the woman but maintained that it had been consensual, received a year's suspension. Just before football season, however, Virginia Tech officials canceled this suspension and cleared him to play. When she heard this, Brzonkala withdrew from the university.

For the two athletes named in the case, who maintain their innocence, and for Virginia Tech, which maintains that it handled the situation properly, the Violence against Women Act represents a form of harassment over matters already resolved. But Christy Brzonkala says that the law is appropriate, because her rape was part of a pattern of misbehavior at Virginia Tech, a pattern in which a female student matters less to the university than a gifted and potentially valuable male athlete. Brzonkala's suit seeks $8.3 million from Virginia Tech and the two young men—a figure chosen because it represents the amount the university's football team received for playing in the 1995 Sugar Bowl.

[1]Data are from the 1995 National Crime Victimization Survey, a federal government survey that each year interviews more than 100,000 Americans aged 12 or older.

necessary tool for ending all discrimination against women and for making gender roles more equal. Opponents charged that it would be socially disruptive and would introduce changes—such as coed restrooms—that most Americans did not want. The amendment easily passed Congress in 1972 and won quick approval in many state legislatures, but it fell three states short of the thirty-eight needed to ratify the amendment by the 1982 deadline for its ratification.[36]

Despite the failure of the ERA, gender discrimination expanded dramatically as an area of civil rights law. In the 1970s, the conservative Burger Court helped to establish gender discrimination as a major and highly visible civil rights issue. Although the Burger Court refused to treat gender discrimination as the equivalent of racial discrimination,[37] it did make it easier for plaintiffs to file and win suits on the basis of gender discrimination by applying an "intermediate" level of review to these cases.[38] This **intermediate scrutiny** is midway between traditional rules of evidence, which put the burden of proof on the plaintiff, and the doctrine of strict scrutiny, which requires the defendant to show not only that a particular classification is reasonable but also that there is a need or compelling interest for it. Intermediate scrutiny shifts the burden of proof partially onto the defendant, rather than leaving it entirely on the plaintiff. The use of this intermediate level of scrutiny emerged as an important force in the battle against gender discrimination in numerous cases, such as *Mississippi University for Women v. Hogan*, the first such case in which Justice Sandra Day O'Connor played a critical role.[39] Recently, Justice Ruth Bader Ginsburg has even suggested that the question of whether gender should be treated like race had not yet been decided.[40] The future direction of the Court on gender discrimination may well be toward an even broader definition and application of civil rights with regard to women. It is ironic, as one traces the rise of gender discrimination as an area of judicial concern and intervention, that the major steps forward were taken not by the supposedly liberal Warren Court, but by a chief justice appointed by a Republican, President Richard Nixon, and continued by justices such as Sandra Day O'Connor, who was appointed by another Republican, President Ronald Reagan.

College athletics programs have been affected by gender discrimination battles. In recent years, colleges and universities have added more women's sports programs to comply with government orders.

One major step was taken in 1992, when the Court decided in *Franklin v. Gwinnett County Public Schools* that violations of Title IX of the 1972 Education Act could be remedied with monetary damages.[41] Title IX forbade gender discrimination in education, but it initially sparked little litigation because of its weak enforcement provisions. The Court's 1992 ruling that monetary damages could be awarded for gender discrimination opened the door for more legal action in the area of education. The greatest impact has been in the areas of sexual harassment—the subject of the *Franklin* case—and in equal treatment of women's athletic programs. The potential for monetary damages has made universities and public schools take the problem of sexual harassment more seriously. Colleges and universities have also started to pay more attention to women's athletic programs. In the two years after the *Franklin* case, complaints to the Education Department's Office for Civil Rights about unequal treatment of women's athletic programs nearly tripled. In several high-profile legal cases, some prominent universities have been ordered to create more women's sports programs; many other colleges and universities have begun to add more women's programs in order to avoid potential litigation.[42]

The development of gender discrimination as an important part of the civil rights struggle has coincided with the rise of women's politics as a discrete movement in American politics. As with the struggle for racial equality, the relationship between changes in government policies and political action suggests that changes in government policies to a great degree produce political action. Today, the existence of a powerful women's movement derives in large measure from the enactment of Title VII of the Civil Rights Act of 1964 and from the Burger Court's vital steps in applying that law to protect women. The recognition of women's civil rights has become an issue that in many ways transcends the usual distinctions of American political debate. In the heavily partisan debate over the federal crime bill enacted in 1994, for instance, the section of the bill that enjoyed the widest support was the Violence Against Women Act, whose most important feature is that it defines gender-biased violent crimes as a matter of civil rights, and creates a civil rights remedy for women who have been the victims of such crimes. Women may now file civil as well as criminal suits against their assailants, which means that they are no longer solely dependent on prosecutors to defend them against violent crime.

Latinos and Asian Americans

Although the Civil Rights Act of 1964 outlawed discrimination on the basis of national origin, limited English proficiency barred many Asian Americans and Latinos from full participation in American life. Two developments in the 1970s, however, established rights for language minorities. In 1974, the Supreme Court ruled in *Lau v. Nichols,* a suit filed on behalf of Chinese students in San Francisco, that school districts have to provide education for students whose English is limited.[43] It did not mandate bilingual education but it established a duty to provide instruction that the students could understand. A year later, as we saw earlier in this chapter, the 1975 amendments to the Voting Rights Act permanently outlawed literacy tests in all fifty states and mandated bilingual ballots or oral assistance for those who spoke Spanish, Chinese, Japanese, Korean, Native American languages, or Eskimo languages.

Asian Americans and Latinos have also been concerned about the impact of immigration laws on their civil rights. Many Asian American and Latino organizations opposed the Immigration Reform and Control Act of 1986 because it imposed sanctions on employers who hire undocumented workers. Such sanctions, they feared, would lead employers to discriminate against Latinos and Asian Americans. These suspicions were confirmed in a 1990 report by the General Accounting Office that found employer sanctions had created a "widespread pattern of discrimination" against Latinos and other people who appear foreign.[44] Latinos and Asian Americans have established organizations modeled on the NAACP's Legal Defense Fund, such as the Mexican-American Legal Defense Fund (MALDEF) and the Asian Law Caucus, to monitor and challenge such discrimination. These groups have increasingly turned their attention to the rights of legal and illegal immigrants, as anti-immigrant sentiment has grown in recent years.

NATIVE AMERICANS

As a language minority, Native Americans were affected by the 1975 amendments to the Voting Rights Act and the *Lau* decision. The *Lau* decision established the right of Native Americans to be taught in their own languages. This marked quite a change from the boarding schools once run by the Bureau of Indian Affairs, at which members of Indian tribes had been forbidden to speak their own languages. In addition to these language-related issues, Native Americans have sought to expand their rights on the basis of their sovereign status. Since the 1920s and 1930s, Native American tribes have sued the federal government for illegally seizing land, seeking monetary reparations and land as damages. Both types of damages have been awarded in such suits, but only in small amounts. Native American tribes have been more successful in winning federal recognition of their sovereignty. Sovereign status has, in turn, allowed them to exercise greater self-determination. Most significant economically was a 1987 Supreme Court decision that freed Native American tribes from most state regulations prohibiting gambling. The establishment of casino gambling on Native American lands has brought a substantial flow of new income into desperately poor reservations.

DISABLED AMERICANS

Over the last two decades, Americans with disabilities have actively sought and secured legislation guaranteeing their equal rights.

The concept of rights for the disabled began to emerge in the 1970s as the civil rights model spread to other groups. The seed was planted in a little-noticed provision of the 1973 Rehabilitation Act, which outlawed discrimination against individuals on the basis of disabilities. As in many other cases, the law itself helped give rise to the movement demanding rights for the handicapped.[45] Modeling itself on the NAACP's Legal Defense Fund, the disability movement founded a Disability Rights Education and Defense Fund to press their legal claims. The movement achieved its greatest success with the passage of the Americans with Disabilities Act of 1990, which guarantees equal employment rights and access to public businesses for the disabled. Claims of discrimination in violation of this act are considered by the Equal Employment Opportunity Commission. The impact of the law has been far-reaching, as businesses and public facilities have installed ramps, elevators, and other devices to meet the act's requirements.[46] Five years after its passage, however, concerns about the act's costs began to emerge, as did doubts about whether it truly was assisting people with severe disabilities.

GAYS AND LESBIANS

In less than thirty years, the gay and lesbian movement has become one of the largest civil rights movements in contemporary America. Beginning with street protests in the 1960s, the movement has grown into a well-financed and sophisticated lobby. The Human Rights Campaign Fund is the primary national political action committee (PAC) focused on gay rights; it provides campaign financing and volunteers to work for candidates endorsed by the group. The movement has also formed legal rights organizations, including the Lambda Legal Defense and Education Fund.

Gay and lesbian rights drew national attention in 1993, when President Bill Clinton confronted the question of whether gays should be allowed to serve in the military. As a candidate, Clinton had said he favored lifting the ban on homosexuals in the military. The issue set off a huge controversy in the first months of Clinton's presidency. After nearly a year of deliberation, the administration enunciated a compromise: their "Don't ask, Don't tell" policy. This policy allows gays and lesbians to serve in the military so long as they do not openly proclaim their sexual orientation or engage in homosexual activity. The administration maintained that the ruling would protect gays and lesbians against witch-hunting investigations, but many gay and lesbian advocates expressed disappointment, charging the president with reneging on his campaign promise.

But until 1996, there was no Supreme Court ruling or national legislation explicitly protecting gays and lesbians from discrimination. The first gay rights case that the Court decided, *Bowers v. Hardwick*, ruled against a right to privacy that would protect consensual homosexual activity.[47] After the *Bowers* decision, the gay and lesbian rights movement sought suitable legal cases to test the constitutionality of discrimination against gays and lesbians, much as the black Civil Rights movement did in the late 1940s and 1950s. As one advocate put it, "lesbians and gay men are looking for their *Brown v. Board of Education*."[48] Among the cases tested were those stemming from local ordinances restricting gay rights (including the right to marry), job discrimination, and family law issues such as adoption and parental rights. In 1996, the Supreme Court, in *Romer v. Evans*, explicitly extended fundamental civil rights protections to gays and lesbians, by declaring unconstitutional a 1992 amendment to the Colorado state constitution that prohibited local governments from passing ordinances to protect gay rights.[49] The decision's forceful language highlighted the connection between gay rights and civil rights as it declared discrimination against gay people unconstitutional.

Affirmative Action

- What is the basis for affirmative action? What forms does it take?
- How does affirmative action contribute to the polarization of the politics of civil rights?

Not only has the politics of rights spread to increasing numbers of groups in American society since the 1960s, it has also expanded its goal. The relatively narrow goal of equalizing opportunity by eliminating discriminatory barriers developed toward the far broader goal of **affirmative action**—compensatory action to overcome the consequences of past discrimination. An affirmative action policy tends to involve two novel approaches: (1) positive or benign discrimination in which race or some other status is actually taken into ac-

On June 27, 1969, police raided a gay bar called the Stonewall in the Greenwich Village section of New York City. Unlike in countless other such raids, many of the gay patrons of the Stonewall refused to run from the police. Instead, they fought the police, throwing bricks and loose change. The unrest escalated, continuing into the next day. For the first time, large numbers of gays and lesbians were willing to publicly acknowledge their homosexuality, openly challenging police practices and state laws they considered discriminatory and oppressive.

This impromptu riot, labeled "the Stonewall uprising," marked the beginning of the modern gay rights movement. It came in the midst of widespread social unrest throughout the United States when African Americans, women, and others were seeking to redefine their civil rights.

The controversial effort to extend and protect the civil rights of gays and lesbians encountered substantial roadblocks because of deep religious and moral traditions which define homosexual activity as immoral and unnatural. Thus the initial emphasis in the gay rights movement was to win greater tolerance from a society that had long refused to publicly acknowledge, much less discuss, the durability and persistence of gay life. In recent years, the gay rights movement has taken a more directly political approach. It has sought to elect gays to public office, to eliminate discrimination in employment and housing, to step up prosecution of hate crimes against gays, and to win legal recognition of same-sex marriages. Much of this political activity has focused on winning the inclusion of sexual orientation as a category covered by existing antidiscrimination law. Today, employers and educational institutions are forbidden from discriminating on the basis of race, sex, religion, or physical disability. Gay rights activists have worked to prohibit discrimination based on sexual orientation as well.

These efforts have led critics to charge that the gay rights movement is attempting to win preferential treatment under the law, or even formal approval of the homosexual lifestyle. Gay rights advocates respond that their purpose is to end improper discrimination against gays, not to grant them special protections or recognition. The idea that gay persons might be fired from a job or evicted from an apartment solely because they are gay is the sort of discriminatory treatment that they believe the

count, but for compensatory action rather than mistreatment; and (2) compensatory action to favor members of the disadvantaged group who themselves may never have been the victims of discrimination. Quotas may be but are not necessarily involved in affirmative action policies.

President Lyndon Johnson put the case emotionally in 1965: "You do not take a person who, for years, has been hobbled by chains . . . and then say you are free to compete with all the others, and still just believe that you have been completely fair.[50] Johnson attempted to inaugurate affirmative action by executive orders directing agency heads and personnel officers to pursue vigorously a policy of minority employment in the federal civil service and in companies doing business with the national government. But affirmative action did not become a prominent goal of the national government until the 1970s.

Affirmative action also took the form of efforts by the agencies in the Department of Health, Education, and Welfare to shift their focus from "desegregation" to "integration."[51] Federal agencies—sometimes with court orders and sometimes without them—required school districts to present plans law should prosecute. A more controversial area involves the question of whether gay couples should be able to adopt children, share medical insurance coverage, or have marriages legally recognized by states.

Some cities around the country have extended such antidiscrimination protections to gays. The mayor of the city of Ithaca, New York, announced in 1995 that he would recognize gay marriages (even though the declaration was not legally binding). Yet other areas have enacted regulations specifically barring any laws to protect homosexuals. In 1992, for example, Colorado voters approved an amendment to the state constitution, spearheaded by conservative religious groups, forbidding the state and local governments from enacting laws that protect homosexuals from discrimination. Although the measure was declared unconstitutional by the Supreme Court, it reflected a backlash against gay rights felt in many parts of the country.[1]

The gay rights movement has even affected presidential politics. During the 1992 presidential campaign, Bill Clinton announced that, if elected, he would end the ban on gays in the military. When he attempted to follow through on his promise in 1993, he encountered stiff opposition, which ultimately resulted in the "Don't ask, don't tell" policy (which means that gays in the military would not be prosecuted as long as they did not openly proclaim or practice their homosexuality). In 1995, Republican presidential candidate Bob Dole solicited and accepted a campaign contribution from a Republican gay group, the Log Cabin society. Yet when he was criticized by conservatives in his party for accepting the money, he returned the contribution.

The uniquely personal and controversial nature of homosexuality suggests that the advocates and opponents of gay rights will continue to fight with ever-greater intensity in the coming years.

SOURCE: David E. Newton, *Gay and Lesbian Rights: A Reference Handbook* (Santa Barbara, CA: ABC-CLIO, 1994).

[1] *Romer v. Evans,* 116 S.Ct. 1620 (1996).

for busing children across district lines, for pairing schools, for closing certain schools, and for redistributing faculties as well as students, under pain of loss of grants-in-aid from the federal government. The guidelines issued for such plans literally constituted preferential treatment to compensate for past discrimination, and without this legislatively assisted approach to court integration orders, there would certainly not have been the dramatic increase in black children attending integrated classes. The yellow school bus became a symbol of hope for many and a signal of defeat for others.

Affirmative action was also initiated in the area of employment opportunity. The Equal Employment Opportunity Commission often has required plans whereby employers must attempt to increase the number of their minority employees, and the office of Federal Contract Compliance in the Department of Labor has used the threat of contract revocation for the same purpose.

As the affirmative action movement spread, it also began to divide civil rights activists and their supporters. The whole issue of qualification versus minority preference was addressed formally by the Supreme Court in the case

Allan Bakke at his graduation ceremony from the medical school of the University of California at Davis.

of Allan Bakke. Bakke, a white male with no minority affiliation, brought suit against the University of California at Davis Medical School on the grounds that in denying him admission the school had discriminated against him on the basis of his race (that year the school had reserved 16 of 100 available slots for minority applicants). He argued that his grades and test scores had ranked him well above many students who had been accepted at the school and that the only possible explanation for his rejection was that those others accepted were black or Latino while he was white. In 1978, Bakke won his case before the Supreme Court and was admitted to the medical school, but he did not succeed in getting affirmative action declared unconstitutional. The Court rejected the procedures at the University of California because its medical school had used both a quota *and* a separate admissions system for minorities. The Court agreed with Bakke's argument that racial categorizations are suspect categories that place a severe burden of proof on those using them to show a "compelling public purpose." The Court went on to say that achieving "a diverse student body" was such a public purpose, but the method of a rigid quota of student slots assigned on the basis of race was incompatible with the equal protection clause. Thus, the Court permitted universities (and presumably other schools, training programs, and hiring authorities) to continue to take minority status into consideration, but limited severely the use of quotas to situations in which (1) previous discrimination had been shown, and (2) it was used more as a guideline for social diversity than as a mathematically defined ratio.[52]

For nearly a decade after *Bakke*, the Supreme Court was tentative and permissive about efforts by corporations and governments to experiment with affirmative action programs in employment.[53] But in 1989, the Court returned to the Bakke position that any "rigid numerical quota" is suspect. In *Wards Cove v. Atonio*, the Court backed away further from affirmative action by easing the way for employers to prefer white males, holding that the burden of proof of unlawful discrimination should be shifted from the defendant (the employer) to the plaintiff (the person claiming to be the victim of discrimination).[54] This decision virtually overruled the Court's prior holding.[55] That same year, the Court ruled that any affirmative action program already approved by federal courts could be subsequently challenged by white males who allege that the program discriminates against them.[56]

Presidential support for affirmative action was declining at the same time. Ronald Reagan became "the first president in the post–World War II period to reverse this trend of an increasingly active government role in . . . redressing the consequences of past discrimination." Under Reagan, the budgets and staff of key civil rights agencies were cut to the bone.[57] Busing was opposed. Government cases against school segregation, housing discrimination, and job discrimination dropped to a fraction of the cases brought under previous administrations.[58] And, although federal court decisions have upheld the use of statistics on the effect of discrimination as a basis for Justice Department initiatives in filing suits to open opportunities for minorities, the Justice Department under President Reagan virtually terminated such suits, focusing instead on individual cases where intent to discriminate could be proven.[59]

President Bush continued in the Reagan direction. He vetoed the Civil Rights Act of 1990 as a "quota bill" (although he accepted essentially the same bill in 1991). But most importantly, he "relentlessly" appointed known social conservatives to the federal courts "with the same energy that Ronald Reagan did."[60] And his single appointment to the Supreme Court, Clarence Thomas, who replaced civil rights advocate Thurgood Marshall, has been an opponent of anything that has to do with affirmative action.

But in 1991, after a lengthy battle with the White House, Congress enacted a piece of legislation designed to undo the effects of the decisions limiting affirmative action. Under the terms of the Civil Rights Act of 1991, the burden of proof in employment discrimination cases was shifted back to employers. In addition, the act made it more difficult to mount later challenges to consent decrees in affirmative action cases. Despite Congress's actions, however, the federal judiciary will have the last word as cases under the new law reach the courts. In a 5-to-4 decision in 1993, the Supreme Court ruled that employees had to prove their employers intended discrimination, again placing the burden of proof on employees.[61]

All of these efforts by the executive, legislative, and judicial branches to shape the meaning of affirmative action today tend to center on a key issue: What is the appropriate level of review in affirmative action cases—that is, on whom should the burden of proof be placed, the plaintiff or the defendant? Currently, the law of the land is best expressed by the decision in *Richmond v. Croson* that the plaintiff bears the burden of proof (see also Chapter 14).[62]

In 1994 the Clinton administration made a significant change in the federal government's attitude toward affirmative action efforts. A white schoolteacher in New Jersey had brought a suit against her school district charging that her layoff was racially motivated, since a black colleague who had been hired the same day as she had been was not laid off. Under President Bush, the Justice Department had filed a brief on her behalf in 1989, but in 1994 the Clinton administration formally reversed course in a new brief, saying that the previous position had been mistaken and supporting the school district's right to make such distinctions based on race as long as it did not involve the use of quotas. "The interest of the United States is [in] integrating the work force," declared the assistant attorney general for civil rights in the Clinton administration.[63]

In 1995, the Supreme Court's ruling in *Adarand Constructors v. Pena* further weakened affirmative action. This decision stated that race-based policies, such as preferences given by the government to minority contractors, must survive strict scrutiny, placing the burden on the government to show that such affirmative action programs serve a compelling government interest and are narrowly tailored to address identifiable past discrimination.[64] President Clinton responded to the *Adarand* decision by ordering a review of all government affirmative action policies and practices. Although many observers suspected that the president would use the review as an opportunity to back away from affirmative action, the conclusions of the task force largely defended existing policies. Reflecting the influence of the Supreme Court's decision in *Adarand*, President Clinton acknowledged that some government policies would need to change. But on the whole, the review found that most affirmative action policies were fair and did not "unduly burden nonbeneficiaries."[65]

Affirmative action efforts have contributed to the polarization of the politics of civil rights. At the risk of grievous oversimplification, we can divide the sides by two labels: liberals and conservatives.[66] The conservatives' argument against affirmative action can be reduced to two major points. The first is that rights in the American tradition are *individual* rights, and affirmative action violates this concept by concerning itself with "group rights," an idea said to be alien to the American tradition. The second point has to do with quotas. Conservatives would argue that the Constitution is "color blind," and that any discrimination, even if it is called positive or benign discrimination, ultimately violates the equal protection clause.

The liberal side agrees that rights ultimately come down to individuals, but argues that, since the essence of discrimination is the use of unreasonable and unjust criteria of exclusion to deprive *an entire group* of access to something valuable the society has to offer, then the phenomenon of discrimination itself has to be attacked on a group basis. Liberals can also use Supreme Court history to support their side, because the first definitive interpretation of the Fourteenth Amendment by the Court in 1873 stated explicitly that

> [t]he existence of laws in the state where the newly emancipated Negroes resided, which discriminated with gross injustice and hardship against them *as a class*, was the evil to be remedied by this clause [emphasis added].[67]

Liberals also have a response to the other conservative argument concerning quotas. The liberal response is that the Supreme Court has already accepted ratios—a form of quota—that are admitted as evidence to prove a "pattern of practice of discrimination" sufficient to reverse the burden of proof—to obligate the employer to show that there was *not* an intent to discriminate. Liberals can also argue that benign quotas have often been used by Americans both to compensate for some bad action in the past or to provide some desired distribution of social characteristics—sometimes called diversity. For example, a long and respected policy in the United States is that of "veteran's preference," on the basis of which the government automatically adds a certain number of points on civil service examinations to persons who have served the country in the armed forces. The justification is that ex-soldiers deserve compensation for having made sacrifices for the good of the country. And the goal of social diversity has justified "positive discrimination," especially in higher education, the very institution where the conservatives have most adamantly argued against positive quotas for blacks and women. For example, all of the Ivy League schools and many other private colleges and universities regularly and consistently reserve admissions places for some students whose qualifications in a strict academic sense are below those of others who are not admitted. These schools not only recruit students from minority groups, but they set aside places for the children of loyal alumni and of their own faculty, even when, in a pure competition solely and exclusively based on test scores and high school records, many of those same children would not have been admitted. These practices are not conclusive justification in themselves, but they certainly underscore the liberal argument that affirmative or compensatory action for minorities who have been unjustly treated in the past is not alien to American experience.

Many University of California students actively defended affirmative action programs, which came under fire during the 1996 debate over the California Civil Rights Initiative. The initiative, which passed as a statewide referendum, prohibits state or local governments from using race or gender as a basis in hiring, education, or contracting.

Although the problems of rights in America are agonizing, they can be looked at optimistically. The United States has a long way to go before it constructs a truly just, "equally protected" society. But it also has come very far

AMERICANS' OPINIONS ON CIVIL RIGHTS LAWS			
	Total	Whites	Blacks
Yes	38%	33%	70%
No	58	62	26
No opinion	4	5	4

SOURCE: George Gallup, Jr., *The Gallup Poll: Public Opinion 1993* (Wilmington, DE: Scholarly Resources, 1994), p. 178.

TABLE 18.5

Responses to the question "Do you think new civil rights laws are needed to reduce discrimination against blacks, or not?"

in a relatively short time. Groups pressing for equality have been able to use government to change a variety of discriminatory practices. The federal government has become an active partner in ensuring civil rights and political equality. All explicit de jure barriers to minorities have been dismantled. Many de facto barriers have also been dismantled, and thousands upon thousands of new opportunities have been opened. Perhaps the greatest promise, however, is in fact the rise of the "politics of rights." The American people are now accustomed to interest groups—conservative and liberal—who call themselves "public interest groups" and accept the efforts of such groups to translate their goals in vigorous and eloquent statements about their rights to their goals. Few people now fear that such a politics of rights will produce violence. Deep and fundamental differences have polarized many Americans (see Table 18.5), but political and governmental institutions have proven themselves capable of maintaining balances between them. This kind of balancing can be done without violence so long as everyone recognizes that policy choices, even about rights, cannot be absolute.

Finally, the most important contribution to be made by the politics of rights is probably to the American conscience. Whatever compromises have to be made in order to govern without violence, Americans cannot afford to be satisfied. Injustices do exist. We cannot eliminate them all, but we must maintain our sense of shame for the injustices that persist. This is precisely why the constitutional framework is so important in the real world and not just in theory. It establishes a context of rights, defined both as limits on the power of the government (civil liberties) and as rightful claims to particular opportunities or benefits (civil rights). Without that framework, rights would remain in the world of abstract philosophy; with that framework, in the United States, they remain now as they did two hundred years ago, as real causes of action.

★ Summary

The constitutional basis of civil rights is the "equal protection" clause. This clause imposes a positive obligation on government to advance civil rights, and its original motivation seems to have been to eliminate the gross injustices suffered by "the newly emancipated Negroes . . . as a class." Civil rights call for the expansion of governmental power rather than restraints upon it. This expanded power allows the government to take an active role in promoting equality. But there was little advancement in the interpretation or application of the "equal protection" clause until after World War II. The major breakthrough came in 1954 with *Brown v. Board of Education,* and advancements came in fits and starts during the succeeding ten years.

After 1964, Congress finally supported the federal courts with effective civil rights legislation that outlawed a number of discriminatory practices in the private sector and provided for the withholding of federal grants-in-aid to any local government, school, or private employer as a sanction to help enforce the civil rights laws. From that point, civil rights developed in two ways. First, the definition of civil rights was expanded to include victims of discrimination other than blacks. Second, the definition of civil rights became increasingly positive; affirmative action has become an official term. Judicial decisions, congressional statutes, and administrative agency actions all have moved beyond the original goal of eliminating discrimination toward creating new opportunities for minorities and, in some areas, compensating today's minorities for the consequences of discriminatory actions not directly against them but against members of their group in the past. Because compensatory civil rights action has sometimes relied upon quotas, there has been intense debate over the constitutionality as well as the desirability of affirmative action.

The story has not ended and is not likely to end. The politics of rights will remain an important part of American political discourse.

FOR FURTHER READING

Baer, Judith A. *Equality under the Constitution: Reclaiming the Fourteenth Amendment.* Ithaca, NY: Cornell University Press, 1983.

Garrow, David J. *Bearing the Cross: Martin Luther King and the Southern Christian Leadership Conference: A Personal Portrait.* New York: Morrow, 1986.

Glendon, Mary Ann. *Rights Talk: The Impoverishment of Political Discourse.* New York: Free Press, 1991.

Greenberg, Jack. *Crusaders in the Courts: How a Dedicated Band of Lawyers Fought for the Civil Rights Revolution.* New York: Basic Books, 1994.

Massey, Douglas S., and Nancy A. Denton. *American Apartheid: Segregation and the Making of the Underclass.* Cambridge, MA: Harvard University Press, 1993.

Nava, Michael. *Created Equal: Why Gay Rights Matter to America.* New York: St. Martin's, 1994.

Rosenberg, Gerald N. *The Hollow Hope: Can Courts Bring About Social Change?* Chicago: University of Chicago Press, 1991.

Thernstrom, Abigail M. *Whose Votes Count? Affirmative Action and Minority Voting Rights.* Cambridge, MA: Harvard University Press, 1987.

STUDY OUTLINE

CIVIL RIGHTS

1. From 1896 until the end of World War II, the Supreme Court held that the Fourteenth Amendment's equal protection clause was not violated by racial distinction as long as the facilities were equal.
2. After World War II, the Supreme Court began to under-

mine the separate but equal doctrine, eventually declaring it unconstitutional in *Brown v. Board of Education.*

3. The *Brown* decision marked the beginning of a difficult battle for equal protection in education, employment, housing, voting, and other areas of social and economic activity.
4. The first phase of school desegregation was met with such massive resistance in the South that, ten years after *Brown,* fewer than 1 percent of black children in the South were attending schools with whites.
5. In 1971, the Supreme Court held that state-imposed desegregation could be brought about by busing children across school districts.
6. Title VII of the Civil Rights Act of 1964 outlawed job discrimination by all private and public employers, including governmental agencies, that employed more than fifteen workers.
7. In 1965, Congress significantly strengthened legislation protecting voting rights by barring literacy and other tests as a condition for voting in southern states. In the long run, the laws extending and protecting voting rights could prove to be the most effective of all civil rights legislation, because increased political participation by minorities has altered the shape of American politics.

The Universalization of Civil Rights

1. The protections won by the African American civil rights movement spilled over to protect other groups as well, including women, Latinos, Asian Americans, Native Americans, disabled Americans, and gays and lesbians.

Affirmative Action

1. By seeking to provide compensatory action to overcome the consequences of past discrimination, affirmative action represents the expansion of the goals of groups championing minority rights.
2. Affirmative action has been a controversial policy. Opponents charge that affirmative action creates group rights and establishes quotas, both of which are inimical to the American tradition. Proponents of affirmative action argue that the long history of group discrimination makes affirmative action necessary and that efforts to compensate for some bad action in the past are well within the federal government's purview.

PRACTICE QUIZ

1. When did civil rights become part of the Constitution?
   a. in 1789 at the Founding
   b. with the adoption of the Fourteenth Amendment in 1868
   c. with the adoption of the Nineteenth Amendment in 1920
   d. in the 1954 *Brown v. Board of Education* case

2. The Supreme Court declared the Civil Rights Act of 1875 unconstitutional because
   a. the Fourteenth Amendment had yet to be adopted.
   b. it sought to protect blacks against discrimination by private businesses.
   c. it sought to protect blacks against discrimination by state governments.
   d. The 1875 Civil Rights Act was not ruled unconstitutional.

3. Which president brought discrimination to national attention with the President's Commission on Civil Rights?
   a. President Harry Truman
   b. President John Kennedy
   c. President Richard Nixon
   d. President Ronald Reagan

4. Which of the following organizations established a Legal Defense Fund to challenge segregation?
   a. the Association of American Trial Lawyers
   b. the National Association for the Advancement of Colored People
   c. the Student Nonviolent Coordinating Committee
   d. the Southern Christian Leadership Council

5. Which of the following made discrimination by private employers and state governments illegal?
   a. the Fourteenth Amendment
   b. *Brown v. Board of Education*
   c. the 1964 Civil Rights Act
   d. *Bakke v. Board of Regents*

6. In what way does the struggle for gender equality most resemble the struggle for racial equality?
   a. There has been very little political action in realizing the goal.

b. Changes in government policies to a great degree produced political action.
c. The Supreme Court has not ruled on the issue.
d. No legislation has passed adopting the aims of the movement.

7. Which of the following measures outlawed literacy tests and mandated bilingual ballots for voters who did not speak English?
a. the 1964 Civil Rights Act
b. *Smith v. Allwright*
c. *Lau v. Nichols*
d. the 1975 amendments to the Voting Rights Act

8. Which of the following civil rights measures dealt with access to public businesses and accommodations?
a. the 1990 Americans with Disabilities Act
b. the 1964 Civil Rights Act
c. neither a nor b
d. both a and b

9. Which of the following cases represents the *Brown v. Board of Education* case for lesbians and gay men?
a. *Bowers v. Hardwick*
b. *Lau v. Nichols*
c. *Romer v. Evans*
d. There has not been a Supreme Court ruling explicitly protecting gays and lesbians from discrimination.

10. In what case did the Supreme Court find that "rigid quotas" are incompatible with the equal protection clause of the Fourteenth Amendment?
a. *Bakke v. Board of Regents*
b. *Brown v. Board of Education*
c. *United States v. Nixon*
d. *Immigration and Naturalization Service v. Chadha*

CRITICAL THINKING QUESTIONS

1. Supporters of affirmative action argue that it is intended not only to compensate for past discrimination, but also to level an uneven playing field in which discrimination still exists. What do you think? To what extent do we have a society free from discrimination? What is the impact of affirmative action on society today? What alternatives to affirmative action policies exist?

2. Describe the changes in American society between the *Plessy v. Ferguson* and the *Brown v. Board of Education* decisions. Using this as an example, explain how changes in society can lead to changes in civil rights policy or other types of government policy. How might changes in society have predicted the changes in civil rights policy in America since the *Brown* case? How might the changes in civil rights policy have changed American society?

KEY TERMS

affirmative action government policies or programs that seek to redress past injustices against specified groups by making special efforts to provide members of these groups with access to educational and employment opportunities. (p. 703)

Brown v. Board of Education the 1954 Supreme Court decision that struck down the "separate but equal" doctrine as fundamentally unequal. This case eliminated state power to use race as a criterion of discrimination in law and provided the national government with the power to intervene by exercising strict regulatory policies against discriminatory actions. (p. 683)

de facto literally, "by fact"; practices that occur even when there is no legal enforcement, such as school segregation in much of the United States today. (p. 684)

de jure literally, "by law"; legally enforced practices, such as school segregation in the South before the 1960s. (p. 684)

discrimination the use of any unreasonable and unjust criterion of exclusion. (p. 679)

intermediate scrutiny test, used by the Supreme Court in gender discrimination cases, which places the burden of proof partially on the government and partially on the challengers to show that the law in question is constitutional. (p. 700)

redlining a practice in which banks refuse to make loans to people living in a certain geographic location. (p. 697)

strict scrutiny test, used by the Supreme Court in racial discrimination cases and other cases involving civil liberties and civil rights, which places the burden of proof on the government rather than on the challengers to show that the law in question is constitutional. (p. 683)

19

Foreign Policy and Democracy

★ The Players: The Makers and Shapers of Foreign Policy

What institutions make up the foreign policy establishment?

What groups help shape foreign policy? Among these players, which are most influential?

★ The Setting: A World of Nation-States

What is the international setting within which the United States pursues its foreign policy?

★ The Values in American Foreign Policy

What values guided the traditional system of foreign policy?

What are the legacies of the traditional system?

When and why did the traditional system of foreign policy end?

What new values guided U.S. foreign policy after World War II?

★ The Instruments of Modern American Foreign Policy

What are the six primary instruments of modern American foreign policy?

How does each instrument reflect a balance between the values of the traditional system of foreign policy and the values of cold war politics?

★ Roles Nations Play

What four traditional foreign policy roles has the United States adopted throughout its history?

Since the end of World War II, how has the role of the United States in world affairs evolved?

★ Making Foreign Policy in a Democracy

What institution best serves as the "vital middle" between the American people and the president in forming successful foreign policy?

EVER SINCE George Washington, in his farewell address, warned the American people "to have . . . as little political connection as possible" with foreign nations and to "steer clear of permanent alliances," Americans have been distrustful of foreign policy. Despite this distrust, the United States has been forced to pursue its national interests in the world, even if this has meant fighting a war. As a result of its foreign entanglements, the United States emerged as a world power, but not without maintaining some misgivings about foreign policy. As Alexis de Tocqueville noted in the 1830s, democracies lack the best qualities for the successful pursuit of foreign policy goals:

> Foreign policies demand scarcely any of those qualities which are peculiar to a democracy; they require, on the contrary, the perfect use of almost all those in which it is deficient. . . . A democracy can only with great difficulty regulate the details of an important undertaking, persevere in a fixed design, and work out its execution in spite of serious obstacles. It cannot combine its measures with secrecy or await their consequences with patience.[1]

The fear of foreign entanglements and the secrecy necessary to make foreign policy work formed the basis of American distrust. In some cases involving national security or fighting certain evils in the world, intervention and even cooperation with other nations was justified in the eyes of the public. Americans even learned to tolerate secrecy in the conduct of diplomacy to prevent war. But the Vietnam War shifted American sentiments back toward distrust. In 1971, the *New York Times* began publishing the "Pentagon Papers," excerpts from a secret Defense Department study of U.S. involvement in Vietnam. The Pentagon Papers revealed that U.S. officials had lied through the media to the American public about the country's entry into the war. The publication of the Pentagon Papers is but one example of how, as the American people learned more about their government, their distrust grew. And, as some elected officials discovered, the American people are a powerful force.

The American people can make or break any foreign policy. American public opinion can, as de Tocqueville warned, create barriers so that officials cannot "persevere in a fixed design . . . "; the American people can also rally to a national appeal in a way that gives greater strength to an international commitment and greater capacity to sustain that commitment—as with foreign aid, or, for that matter, the Vietnam War. It is now almost forgotten that most Americans, prior to the revelations in the Pentagon Papers, actually supported the Vietnam War substantially and consistently, despite the unusually active antiwar movement and an increasingly hostile press.[2]

This extraordinary power of the American people is impressive, but it does have an ugly side: The power of the American people and their quick responsiveness to international events associated with the president (the "rallying effect" discussed in Chapter 12) force presidents and other foreign policy makers to engage in deceit. In order to manipulate the public into supporting foreign policies, high-ranking officials have on occasion actually conspired to give false or misleading information to the American public. The Pentagon Papers are perhaps the most well-known example of such foreign policy deception. Two other, more recent, examples will illustrate the point further: the Iran-Contra scandal from the Republican administration of Ronald Reagan and the Iran-Bosnia deal from the Democratic administration of Bill Clinton.

In 1986, it was revealed that the Reagan administration had furnished weapons to Iran, through Israeli intermediaries, in exchange for Iranian influence with Muslim fundamentalists holding several Americans hostage in Lebanon. This action was contrary to Reagan's popular promise that he would not compromise with terrorists. At the same time, it was also revealed that the weapons had actually been *sold* to Iran, in violation of U.S. law, by private intermediaries at an enormous profit. The profits from these sales had been diverted to finance the guerrilla activities of the Contras, a group fighting against the socialist regime in Nicaragua. This financing was also illegal; Congress had placed severe restrictions on aid to the Contras at least four times between 1982 and 1985. The strongest wording was enacted in 1984, barring all Contra funding "for the purpose or which would have the effect of supporting, directly or indirectly, military or paramilitary operations in Nicaragua by any nation, group, organization, movement, or individual." When the Iran-Contra affair was revealed to the public, several mid-level staff members stepped forward to accept the blame and to defend President Reagan. They argued that the president was unaware of their actions; as for the illegal diversion of profits to the Contras, the spokesperson for the president simply argued that, despite the broad wording of the legislation, it did not apply to the covert activities of the National Security Council.[3]

Although the Iran-Bosnia deal was not such a full-scale scandal, it illustrates the extent to which policy makers seek to protect themselves from the American public. Furthermore, the consequences of Iran-Bosnia may be far more significant than those of Iran-Contra, because of Bosnia's location in post–cold war Europe and because the probability of expansion and escalation of the conflict was higher in Bosnia. (Leaders remember, even if people don't, that World War I started in Sarajevo.) In September 1991, the United Nations imposed an arms embargo on the nations of the former Yugoslavia who had gone to war against each other in their struggle for territory and recognition as new nation-states. The embargo favored one faction, the Bosnian Serbs, because their allies in Serbia had inherited a substantial share of weaponry from the military of the former Yugoslav regime. President George Bush had fully supported the embargo and had objected strenuously when a plane loaded with Iranian arms landed in a sector controlled by the Bosnian Muslims. During his 1992 campaign, Bill Clinton had denounced President Bush and had called for the use of "whatever it takes to stop the slaughter" in Bosnia. And early in his presidency, Clinton had advocated a policy of "lift and strike"—lifting the embargo and launching American air strikes, despite strong objections from European countries. But Clinton quickly backed away from that position to the Bush position of support for the embargo. Meanwhile, Republicans in Congress, led by Senator Bob Dole, argued vehemently that the embargo should be lifted in order to create an even playing field (the Bosnian Serbs were overwhelming the Croats and the Bosnian Muslims).

By March 1994, the Clinton administration had begun to recognize that the only way to gain an even playing field and to make some kind of cease-fire possible was for the Bosnian Muslims and the Croatians to gain a few victories over the Serbs. The following month, when Croatian president Franjo Tudjman asked the American ambassador, Peter Galbraith, what the Clinton administration's response would be if he established a "pipeline" of arms from Iran to Bosnia, Galbraith's response—which had been carefully worked out the night before "at the highest levels" (meaning with President Clinton himself)—was that he, the ambassador, had "no instructions." This amounted to a tacit acceptance, an agreement to "look the other way," and Iran opened up a large flow of arms to Bosnia's Muslim government. Thus armed, the Croatians and the Bosnians won enough victories over the Serbs to bring all three factions to the bargaining table in Dayton, Ohio, where

President Clinton's personal emissary was able to work out an agreement that gave the Bosnian Serbs, the Croatians, and the Bosnian Muslims some hope of peace and that gave President Clinton some credit as an international mover and shaker. The cease-fire worked out in Dayton was followed in September 1996 with an election. Although few viewed the election as a big step toward democracy in the former Yugoslavia, the cease-fire enabled some Bosnians to return to a somewhat normal life.

Yet the price of this peace was a new Iranian presence in the Balkan Peninsula, a presence that constitutes an important threat to American and allied military forces in the region, and that also becomes a factor in European affairs. The Clinton administration's secrecy and the indirect way in which the Iran-Bosnia affair was conducted kept a large number of valuable advisers "out of the loop"—unable to offer advice to the president. It also kept American and European publics in the dark. Had Americans and Europeans known of the impending involvement of Iran in the Balkans, their anti-Iran sentiments might well have reversed European opposition to Clinton's "lift and strike" policy as an approach to peace in the former Yugoslavia. Some may call this double dealing hypocrisy; more important is the fact that it was secrecy, born of fear of exposure to public judgment.[4]

This leaves us with a dilemma. The American people possess an uncommon influence on what their government does, even in foreign policy. But people can make mistakes and bad decisions. In domestic policy situations a bad decision can be written off as one of the acceptable costs of democracy: bad decisions merely produce 20 or 30 percent cost overruns in a public project, or the collapse of a bridge, or the tearing down of public housing projects after only a decade of use. But a mistake in foreign policy can result in a war, and in modern warfare, most victories are achieved at great cost.

This chapter has no solution to the many foreign policy issues the United States confronts. Nonetheless, because the conduct of foreign policy is so complex and because there are particular problems facing a democracy such as the United States as it formulates and puts into effect particular foreign policies, a well-balanced analysis of foreign policy problems is essential. Such an analysis must treat at least five dimensions of foreign policy, which will make up the five main sections of this chapter:

1. *Players.* Who makes and shapes foreign policy in the United States?
2. *Setting.* What is the world within which the United States pursues its foreign policies?
3. *Values.* What does the United States want? What are its national interests, if any? What counts as success?
4. *Instruments.* What tools are available for the conduct of foreign policy? What institutions, administrative arrangements, laws, and programs have been established in order to enable the government to pursue America's national interests?
5. *Roles.* How does the United States behave in world politics? Are its roles consistent with its values?

An examination of these five dimensions provides a lens for looking at democracy itself. We conclude this chapter by asking, "Who *should* make foreign policy in a democracy?"

The Players: The Makers and Shapers of Foreign Policy

- What institutions make up the foreign policy establishment?
- What groups help shape foreign policy? Among these players, which are most influential?

Although the power of the American people over foreign policy is impossible to overestimate, "the people" should not be given all the credit or all the blame for actual policies and their outcomes. As in domestic policy, foreign policy making is a highly pluralistic arena. First there are the official players, those who comprise the "foreign policy establishment"; these players and the agencies they head can be called the actual "makers" of foreign policy. But there are other major players, less official but still influential. We call these the "shapers."

Who Makes Foreign Policy?

The President Although many foreign policy decisions can be made without so much as the president's fingerprint on them, these decisions must be made and implemented in the name of the president. In both of the stories told in the introductory section, Iran-Contra and Iran-Bosnia, much of the action took place far from the White House and was hidden from the president. But those decisions and actions were taken to further a goal that the president wanted. That all foreign policies come from the president is a necessity in making any foreign policy. All heads of state must have some confidence that each head of state has enough power and stability to negotiate, to make agreements, and to keep those agreements.

The Bureaucracy The major foreign policy players in the bureaucracy are the secretaries of the departments of State, Defense, and the Treasury; the Joint Chiefs of Staff (JCOS), especially the chair of the JCOS; and the director of the Central Intelligence Agency (CIA). A separate unit in the bureaucracy comprised of these people and a few others is the National Security Council (NSC), whose main purpose is to iron out the differences among the key players and to integrate their positions in order to confirm or reinforce a decision the president wants to make in foreign policy or military policy. In the Clinton administration, the secretary of Commerce has also become an increasingly important foreign policy maker, with the rise and spread of economic globalization. Clinton's first secretary of Commerce, Ron Brown, was not the first to be active in promoting world trade, but he may well have been the most vigorous and successful up to now.

In addition to these top cabinet-level officials, key lower-level staff members have policy-making influence as strong as that of the Cabinet secretaries—some may occasionally exceed Cabinet influence. These include the two or three specialized national security advisers in the White House, the staff of the NSC (headed by the national security adviser), and a few other

President Clinton announcing the extension of most-favored-nation status to China in 1996. The debate over China's status involved Congress, interest groups concerned about issues ranging from human rights to foreign trade, and the media, although, as in most matters of foreign policy, the president had the most important role in the debate.

career bureaucrats in the departments of State and Defense whose influence varies according to their specialty and to the foreign policy issue at hand.

Congress In foreign policy making, Congress has to be subdivided into three parts. The first part is the Senate. For most of American history, the Senate was the only important congressional foreign policy player because of its constitutional role in reviewing and approving treaties. The treaty power is still the primary entrée of the Senate into foreign policy making. But since World War II and the continual involvement of the United States in international security and foreign aid, Congress as a whole has become a major foreign policy maker because most modern foreign policies require financing, which requires both the House of Representatives and the Senate. Congress has also become increasingly involved in foreign policy making because of the increasing use by the president of **executive agreements** to conduct foreign policy. Executive agreements have the force of treaties but do not require prior approval by the Senate. They can, however, be revoked by action of both chambers of Congress.

The third congressional player is the foreign policy and military policy committees: in the Senate these are the Foreign Relations Committee and the Armed Services Committee; in the House, these are the International Affairs Committee and the Armed Services Committee. Usually, a few members of these committees who have spent years specializing in foreign affairs become trusted members of the foreign policy establishment and are actually makers rather than mere shapers of foreign policy. In fact, several members of Congress have left to become key foreign affairs Cabinet members.[5]

WHO SHAPES FOREIGN POLICY?

The shapers of foreign policy are the non-official, informal players, but they are typically people or groups that have great influence in the making of foreign policy. Of course, the influence of any given group varies according to the party and the ideology that is dominant at a given moment.

Interest Groups Far and away the most important category of nonofficial player is the interest group—that is, the interest groups to whom one or more foreign policy issues are of long-standing and vital relevance. The type of interest group with the reputation for the most influence is the economic interest group. Yet the myths about their influence far outnumber and outweigh the realities. The actual influence of organized economic interest groups in foreign policy varies enormously from issue to issue and year to year. Most of these groups are "single-issue" groups and are therefore most active when their particular issue is on the agenda. On many of the broader and more sustained policy issues, such as the **North American Free Trade Agreement** (NAFTA) or the general question of American involvement in international trade, the larger interest groups, sometimes called "peak associations," find it difficult to maintain tight enough control of their many members to speak with a single voice. The most systematic study of international trade policies and their interest groups concluded that the leaders of these large, economic interest groups spend more time maintaining consensus among their members than they do actually lobbying Congress or pressuring major players in the executive branch.[6] The more successful economic interest groups, in terms of influencing foreign policy, are the narrower, single-issue groups such as the tobacco industry, which over the years has successfully kept American foreign policy from putting heavy restrictions on international trade in and advertising of tobacco products, and the computer hardware and software industries, which have successfully hardened the American attitude toward Chinese piracy of intellectual property rights.

Another type of interest group with a well-founded reputation for influence in foreign policy is made up of people with strong attachments and identifications to their country of national origin. The interest group with the reputation for greatest influence is American Jews, whose family and emotional ties to Israel make them one of the most alert and potentially one of

Jewish-American groups such as the Coalition for Jewish Concerns, shown demonstrating outside the United Nations in New York City, are vocal on policy matters concerning the Middle East.

the most active interest groups in the whole field of foreign policy. But note once again how narrowly specialized that interest is—it focuses almost entirely and exclusively on policies toward Israel. Similarly, Americans of Irish heritage, despite having resided in the United States for two, three, or four generations, still maintain a vigilance about American policies toward Ireland and Northern Ireland; many even contribute to the activities of the Irish Republican Army. Many other ethnic and national interest groups wield similar influence over American foreign policy.

A third type of interest group, one with a reputation that has been growing in the past two decades, is the human rights interest group. Such groups are made up of people who, instead of having self-serving economic or ethnic interests in foreign policy, are genuinely concerned for the welfare and treatment of people throughout the world—particularly those who suffer under harsh political regimes. A relatively small but often quite influential example is Amnesty International, whose exposés of human rights abuses have altered the practices of many regimes around the world.

A related type of group with a fast-growing influence is the ecological or environmental group, sometimes called the "greens." Groups of this nature often depend more on demonstrations than on the usual forms and strategies of influence in Washington—lobbying and using electoral politics, for example. Demonstrations in strategically located areas can have significant influence on American foreign policy. One good example of this is the opposition that relatively small environmental protection groups in the United States raised against American contracts to buy electrical power from the Canadian province of Quebec: The group opposed the ecological effect of the enlarged hydroelectric power dams that were going to have to be built in order to accommodate American demands.[7]

The Media Here again, myth may outweigh truth about media influence in foreign policy. The most important element of the policy influence of the media is the speed and scale with which the media can spread political communications. In that factor alone, the media's influence is growing—more news reaches more people faster, and people's reaction times are therefore shorter. When we combine this ability to communicate faster with the "feedback" medium of public opinion polling, it becomes clear how the media have become so influential—they enable the American people to reach the president and the other official makers of foreign policy.[8]

There is one other aspect of media influence to consider. Many unhappy politicians complain bitterly of "media bias." The complaint most often heard is that journalists have a liberal (anti-Republican) bias. Although this general complaint has never been adequately documented, one aspect of media bias has been shown. Using survey evidence, Michael Robinson demonstrated that reliance on television as a source of news gave people negative attitudes toward public policies and especially toward government and public officials.[9] Robinson called this attitude "videomalaise." A later study found, in addition, that "television news in particular has an inherent bias toward reporting negative and critical information. In other words, 'videomalaise' [is] as much a product of the medium as of the message."[10] One probable influence of the media on foreign as well as domestic policy has been to make the American people far more cynical and skeptical than they would otherwise have been. Beyond that, however, the influence of any medium of communication or any one influential journalist or news program varies from case to case.

Putting It Together

What can we say about who really makes American foreign policy? First, except for the president, the influence of players and shapers varies from case to case—this is a good reason to look with some care at each example of foreign policy in this chapter. Second, since the one constant influence is the centrality of the president in foreign policy making, it is best to evaluate other actors and factors as they interact with the president.[11] Third, the reason influence varies from case to case is that each case arises under different conditions and with vastly different time constraints: for issues that arise and are resolved quickly, the opportunity for influence is limited. Fourth, foreign policy experts will usually disagree about the level of influence any player or type of player has on policy making.

But just to get started, let's make a few tentative generalizations and then put them to the test with the substance and experience reported in the remainder of this chapter. First, when an important foreign policy decision has to be made under conditions of crisis—where "time is of the essence"—the influence of the presidency is at its strongest. Second, under those time constraints, access to the decision is limited almost exclusively to the narrowest definition of the "foreign policy establishment." The arena for participation is tiny; any discussion at all is limited to the officially and constitutionally designated players. To put this another way, in a crisis, the foreign policy establishment works as it is supposed to.[12] As time becomes less restricted, even when the decision to be made is of great importance, the arena of participation expands to include more government players and more nonofficial, informal players—the most concerned interest groups and the most important journalists. In other words, the arena becomes more pluralistic, and therefore less distinguishable from the politics of domestic policy making. Third, because there are so many other countries with power and interests on any given issue, there are severe limits on the choices the United States can make. As one author concludes, in foreign affairs, "policy takes precedence over politics."[13] Thus, even though foreign policy making in noncrisis situations may more closely resemble the pluralistic politics of domestic policy making, foreign policy making is still a narrower arena with fewer participants.

The Setting: A World of Nation-States

➤ What is the international setting within which the United States pursues its foreign policy?

A nation is a population of individuals bound to each other by a common past, a common language, or other cultural ties that draw these individuals together and distinguish them from other peoples. When such a nation has sufficient self-consciousness to organize itself also into a political entity, it is generally referred to as a **nation-state.** But why form a nation-state? As Hans Morgenthau, one of the most eminent students of the nation-state, noted, "The most elementary function of the nation-state is the defense of the life of its citizens and of their civilization. A political organization that is no longer able to defend these values . . . must yield, either through peaceful transformation or violent destruction, to one capable of that defense."[14]

For at least two centuries, nation-states have effectively defended their populations, and the attraction to forming nation-states does not seem to have waned as a third century approaches. There were 54 nation-states at the beginning of the twentieth century. In 1945, when the United Nations (UN) was founded, there were 67, of which 51 were UN charter members. By the end of 1994, the total number of UN member states stood at 184.

Yet the profusion of nation-states presents a paradox: They arise out of a concern for self-defense, but they tend to draw each other into war. Why? As people form themselves into nation-states as a means of defense, they become unified only by isolating themselves from other nations. By doing so, each nation deprives itself of information about the motives and interests of other nations. Modern means of transportation and communication have made the world smaller but not better acquainted. Mutual ignorance has tended to breed hostility because each nation-state conducts its foreign policy on the assumption that every country will pursue its interests at the expense of others.

The national purpose or national interest of the nation-state is said to be the maintenance of its **sovereignty.** Sovereignty can be defined as respect by other nations for the claim by a government that it has conquered its territory and is the sole authority over its population.

Obviously, no nation-state is completely sovereign. In 1973, even the most powerful nation-states were brutally reminded of the fragility of their sovereignty when the Organization of Petroleum Exporting Countries (OPEC) adopted a common foreign policy to control the price of oil on the world market, and the price of oil quadrupled. The fragility of sovereignty was also shown when Iraq occupied Kuwait in 1990 and then had its own sovereignty violated by a large UN military force.

The power of a nation-state can be measured roughly according to the number and size of its **clients,** states that have the capacity to carry out their own foreign policy most of the time, but that still depend upon the interests of one or more of the major powers.[15] By that standard, the United States is the greatest **nation-state,** but it is not the only one. For most of this century, the Soviet Union was virtually America's equal; the Russian Republic will probably regain much of its status by early in the twenty-first century. The People's Republic of China, Japan, and the oil-rich Arab states are also powerful nation-states.

The Values in American Foreign Policy

➤ What values guided the traditional system of foreign policy?
➤ What are the legacies of the traditional system?
➤ When and why did the traditional system of foreign policy end?
➤ What new values guided U.S. foreign policy after World War II?

When President Washington was preparing to leave office in 1796, he crafted with great care, and with the help of Alexander Hamilton and James Madison, a farewell address that is one of the most memorable documents in American history. We have already had occasion to look at a portion of Washington's farewell address, because in it he gave some stern warnings against political parties (see Chapter 8). But Washington's greater concern was to warn the nation against foreign influence:

> History and experience prove that foreign influence is one of the most baneful foes of republican government. . . . The great rule of conduct for us in regard to foreign nations is, in extending our commercial relations to have with them as little *political* connection as possible. So far as we have already formed engagements let them be fulfilled with perfect good faith. Here let us stop. . . . There can be no greater error than to expect or calculate upon real favors from nation to nation. . . . Trust to temporary alliances for extraordinary emergencies, [but in all other instances] steer clear of permanent alliances with any portion of the foreign world. . . . Such an attachment of a small or weak toward a great and powerful nation dooms the former to be the satellite of the latter [emphasis in original.][16]

With the exception of a few leaders such as Thomas Jefferson and Thomas Paine, who were eager to take sides with the French against all others, Washington was probably expressing sentiments shared by most Americans. In fact, during most of the nineteenth century, American foreign policy was to a large extent no foreign policy. But Americans were never isolationist, if isolationism means the refusal to have any associations with the outside world. Americans were eager for trade and for treaties and contracts facilitating trade. Americans were also expansionists, but their vision of expansionism was limited to filling up the North American continent only (see Figure 19.1).

Three familiar historical factors help explain why Washington's sentiments became the tradition and the source of American foreign policy values. The first was the deep anti-statist ideology shared by most Americans in the nineteenth century and into the twentieth century. Although we witness widespread anti-statism today, in the form of calls for tax cuts, deregulation, privatization, and other efforts to "get the government off our backs," such sentiments were far more intense in the past, when many Americans opposed foreign entanglements, a professional military, and secret diplomacy. The second factor was federalism. The third was the position of the United States in the world as a client state. Most nineteenth-century Americans recognized that if the United States became entangled in foreign affairs, national power would naturally grow at the expense of the states, and so would the presi-

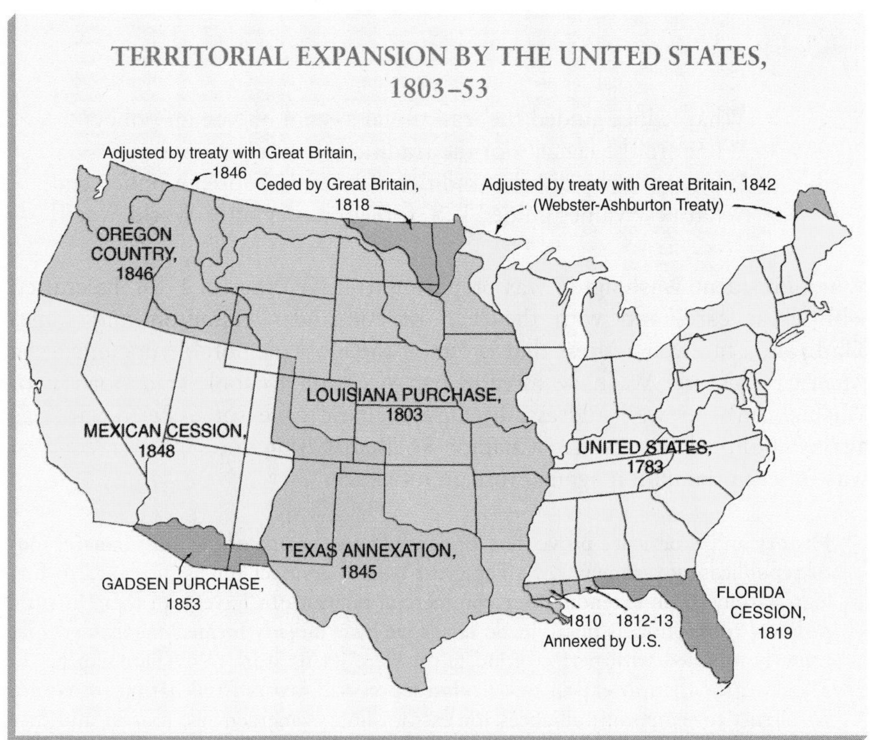

FIGURE 19.1
America's foreign policy during the nineteenth century was primarily focused on territorial expansion, as the nation sought to fuel its growing economy with land and natural resources.

dency at the expense of Congress. Why? Because foreign policy meant having a professional diplomatic corps, professional armed forces with a general staff—and secrets. This meant professionalism, elitism, and remoteness from citizens. Being a client state gave us the luxury of being able to keep our foreign policy to a minimum. Moreover, maintaining American sovereignty was in the interest of the European powers because it prevented any one of them from gaining an advantage over the others in the Western Hemisphere.

LEGACIES OF THE TRADITIONAL SYSTEM

Two identifiable legacies flowed from the long tradition based on anti-statism, federalism, and client status. One is the intermingling of domestic and foreign policy institutions. The second is unilateralism—America's willingness to go it alone. Each of these reveals a great deal about the values behind today's conduct of foreign policy.

Intermingling of Domestic and Foreign Policy Because the major European powers once policed the world, American political leaders could treat foreign policy as a mere extension of domestic policy. The tariff is the best example. A tax on one category of imported goods as a favor to interests in one section of the country would directly cause friction elsewhere in the country. But the demands of those adversely affected could be met without directly compromising the original tariff, by adding a tariff to still other goods that would placate those who were complaining about the original tariff. In this manner,

Congress was continually adding and adjusting tariffs on more and more classes of commodities.

An important aspect of the treatment of foreign affairs as an extension of domestic policy was amateurism. Unlike many other countries, Americans refused to develop a tradition of a separate foreign service composed of professional people who spent much of their adult lives in foreign countries, learning foreign languages, absorbing foreign cultures, and developing a sympathy for foreign points of view. Instead, Americans have tended to be highly suspicious of any American diplomat or entrepreneur who spoke sympathetically of any foreign viewpoints.[17] No systematic progress was made to create a professional diplomatic corps until after the passage of the Foreign Service Act of 1946.

Unilateralism Unilateralism, not isolationism, was the American posture toward the world until the middle of the twentieth century. Isolationism means trying to cut off contacts with the outside, to be a self-sufficient fortress. America was never isolationist; it preferred **unilateralism**, or "going it alone." Americans have always been more likely to rally around the president in support of direct action rather than for a sustained, diplomatic involvement.

The Great Leap—Thirty Years Late

The traditional era of U.S. foreign policy came to an end with World War I for several important reasons. First, the "balance of power" system[18] that had kept the major European powers from world war for a hundred years had collapsed.[19] In fact, the great powers themselves had collapsed internally. The most devastating of all wars up to that time had ruined their economies, their empires, and, in most cases, their political systems. Second, the United States was no longer a client state but in fact one of the great powers. Third, as we saw in earlier chapters, the United States was soon to shed its traditional domestic system of federalism with its national government of almost pure promotional policy. Thus, virtually all the conditions that contributed to the traditional system of American foreign policy had disappeared. Yet there was no discernible change in America's approach to foreign policy in the period between World War I and World War II. After World War I, as one foreign policy analyst put it, "the United States withdrew once more into its insularity. Since America was unwilling to use its power, that power, for purposes of foreign policy, did not really exist."[20]

The Great Leap in foreign policy was finally made thirty years after conditions demanded it and only then after another world war, to which America's post–World War I behavior had undoubtedly contributed. This is not said with the intent merely to criticize—for who knows how different the world would have been if America had been more engaged in world affairs during the interwar years. The observation is made to emphasize the strength of the traditional pattern, so strong as to resist change in the face of compelling conditions.

Pressure for a new tradition came into direct conflict with the old. The new tradition required foreign entanglements; the old tradition feared them deeply. The new tradition required diplomacy; the old distrusted it. The new

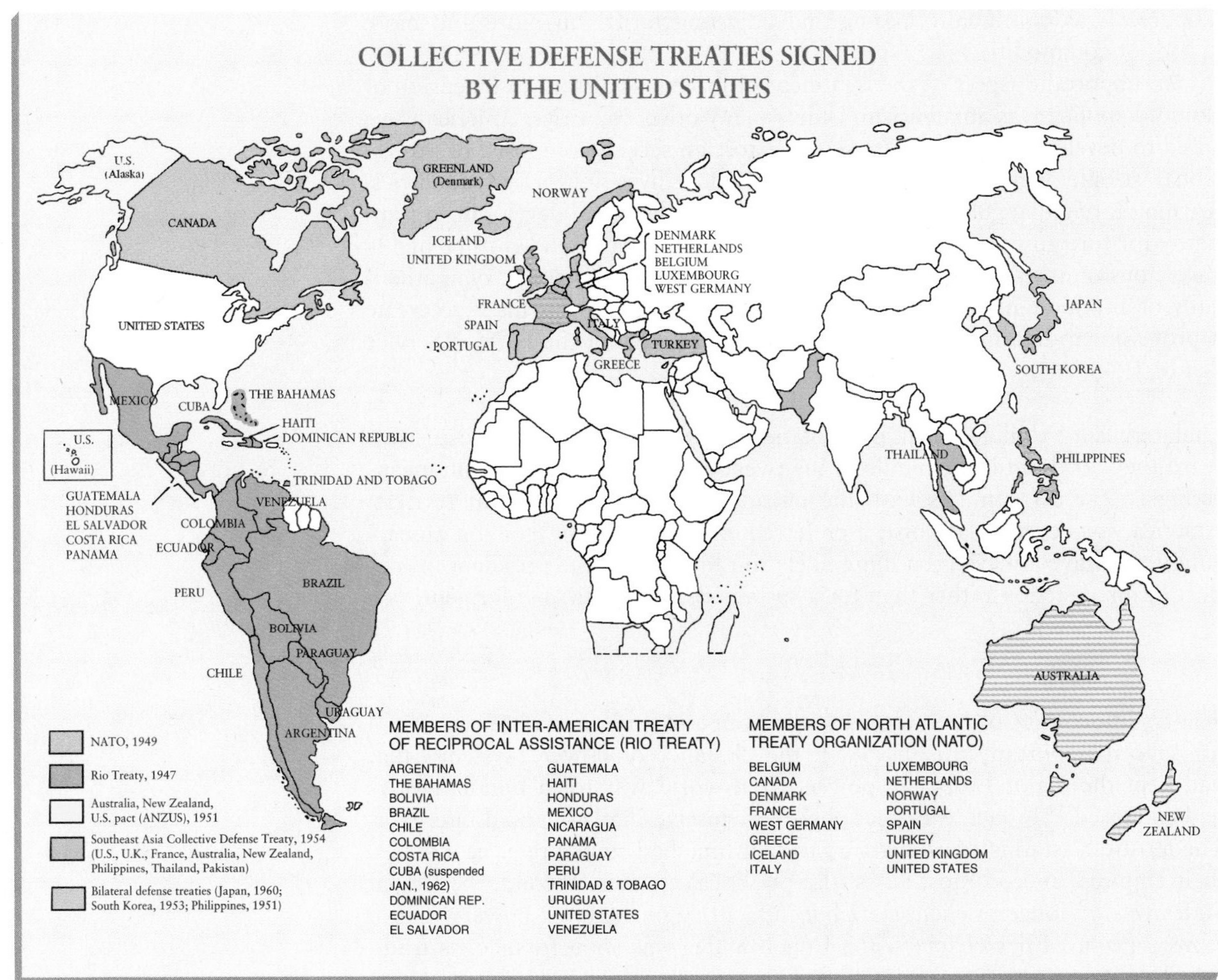

FIGURE 19.2

tradition required acceptance of antagonistic political systems; the old embraced democracy and was aloof from all else.

The values of the new tradition were all apparent during the **cold war.** Instead of unilateralism, the United States pursued **multilateralism,** entering into treaties with other nations to achieve its foreign policy goals (see Figure 19.2). The most notable of these treaties is that which formed the **North Atlantic Treaty Organization** (NATO) in 1948, which allied the United States, Canada, and most of western Europe. With its NATO allies, the United States practiced a two-pronged policy in dealing with its rival, the Soviet Union: **containment** and deterrence. Fearing that the Soviet Union was bent on world domination, the United States fought wars in Korea and Vietnam to "contain" Soviet power. And in order to deter a direct attack against itself or its NATO allies, the United States developed a multi-billion-dollar nuclear arsenal capable of destroying the Soviet Union many times over.

The primary instruments of foreign policy in the new, post–World War II tradition can also be seen as six case studies in the balancing of the old tradition against the demands for a new tradition. Each is a dramatic illustration of how traditional values shaped the instruments we would use to fashion our new place in the world as the leading imperial power.

The Instruments of Modern American Foreign Policy

> ➤ What are the six primary instruments of modern American foreign policy?
> ➤ How does each instrument reflect a balance between the values of the traditional system of foreign policy and the values of cold war politics?

Any nation-state has at hand certain instruments, or tools, to use in implementing its foreign policy. An instrument is neutral, capable of serving many goals. There have been many instruments of American foreign policy, and we can deal here only with those instruments we deem to be most important in the modern epoch: diplomacy, the United Nations, the international monetary structure, economic aid, collective security, and military deterrence. Each of these instruments will be evaluated in this section for its utility in the conduct of American foreign policy, and each will be assessed in light of the history and development of American values.

Diplomacy

We begin this treatment of instruments with diplomacy because it is the instrument to which all other instruments should be subordinated, although they seldom are. **Diplomacy** is the representation of a government to other foreign governments. Its purpose is to promote national values or interests by peaceful means. According to Hans Morgenthau, "a diplomacy that ends in war has failed in its primary objective."[21]

The first effort to create a modern diplomatic service in the United States was made through the Rogers Act of 1924, which established the initial framework for a professional foreign service staff. But it took World War II and the Foreign Service Act of 1946 to forge the foreign service into a fully professional diplomatic corps.

Diplomacy, by its very nature, is overshadowed by spectacular international events, dramatic initiatives, and meetings among heads of state or their direct personal representatives. The traditional American distrust of diplomacy continues today, albeit in weaker form. Impatience with or downright distrust of diplomacy has been built not only into all the other instruments of foreign policy but also into the modern presidential system itself.[22] So much personal responsibility has been heaped upon the presidency that it is difficult for presidents to entrust any of their authority or responsibility in foreign policy to professional diplomats in the State Department and other bureaucracies. And the American practice of appointing political friends and campaign donors to major ambassadorial positions does not inspire trust. During his first year in office, President Bush named 87 ambassadorial appointees, 48 of whom were important political contributors. President Clinton appointed even fewer professional diplomats to ambassadorships than either President Reagan or President Bush.[23]

Electoral politics is not the only kind of politics affecting the nature and timing of ambassadorial appointments. The Republican chair of the Senate Foreign Relations Committee, Jesse Helms, blocked eighteen of President Clinton's ambassadorial nominations for most of the 1995 congressional session, demanding that Clinton agree to merge three independent foreign policy agencies with the State Department. Although Helms did not win everything he demanded from President Clinton, he did gain some important concessions in return for his approval of the ambassadors during the last days before Congress recessed in December 1995.[24]

Distrust of diplomacy has also produced a tendency among all recent presidents to turn frequently to military and civilian personnel outside the State Department to take on a special diplomatic role as direct personal representatives of the president. As discouraging as it is to those who have dedicated their careers to foreign service to have political hacks appointed over their heads, it is probably even more discouraging when they are displaced from a foreign policy issue as soon as relations with the country they are posted in begin to heat up. When a special personal representative is sent abroad to represent the president, that envoy holds a status higher than that of the local ambassador, and the embassy becomes the envoy's temporary residence and base of operation. Despite the impressive professionalization of the American foreign service—with advanced training, competitive exams, language requirements, and career commitment—this practice of displacing career ambassadors with political appointees and with special personal presidential representatives continues. For instance, when President Clinton sought in 1994 to make a final diplomatic attempt to persuade Haiti's military dictator to relinquish power to the country's freely elected president before dispatching U.S. military forces to the island, he sent a team of three personal representatives—former president Jimmy Carter, Senator Sam Nunn, and former chairman of the Joint Chiefs of Staff Colin Powell.

Senator Sam Nunn, former president Jimmy Carter, President Bill Clinton, and Chair of the Joint Chiefs of Staff Colin Powell conferred over U.S. policy toward Haiti.

The significance of diplomacy and its vulnerability to domestic politics may be better appreciated as we proceed to the other instruments. Diplomacy was an instrument more or less imposed on Americans as the prevailing method of dealing among nation-states in the nineteenth century. The other instruments to be identified and assessed below are instruments that Americans self-consciously crafted for themselves to take care of their own chosen place in the world affairs of the second half of the twentieth century. They are, therefore, more reflective of American culture and values than is diplomacy.

THE UNITED NATIONS

The utility of the **United Nations** (UN) to the United States as an instrument of foreign policy can too easily be underestimated. During the first decade or more after its founding in 1945, the United Nations was a direct servant of

American interests. The most spectacular example of the use of the United Nations as an instrument of American foreign policy was the official UN authorization and sponsorship of intervention in Korea with an international "peacekeeping force" in 1950. Thanks to the Soviet boycott of the United Nations at that time, which deprived the USSR of its ability to use its veto in the Security Council of the UN, the United States was able to conduct the Korean War under the auspices of the United Nations.

The United States provided 40 percent of the UN budget in 1946 (its first full year of operation) and 28.1 percent of the $1.1 billion UN budget in 1994–95.[25] Many Americans feel that the United Nations does not give good value for the investment. But any evaluation of the United Nations must take into account the purpose for which the United States sought to create it: to achieve **power without diplomacy.** After World War II, when the United States could no longer remain aloof from foreign policy, the nation's leaders sought to use our power to create an international structure that could be run with a minimum of regular diplomatic involvement—so that Americans could return to their normal domestic pursuits. As one constitutional scholar characterized our Founding in 1787, so we could say of our effort to found the United Nations—we sought to create "a machine that would go of itself."[26]

The UN may have gained a new lease on life in the post–cold war era, first with its performance in the Gulf War and then with its role in Somalia. Although President Bush's immediate reaction to Iraq's invasion of Kuwait was unilateral, he quickly turned to the UN for sponsorship. The UN General Assembly initially adopted resolutions condemning the invasion and approving the full blockade of Iraq. Once the blockade was seen as having failed to achieve the unconditional withdrawal demanded by the UN, the General Assembly adopted further resolutions authorizing the twenty-nine-nation coalition to use force if, by January 15, 1991, the resolutions were not observed. The Gulf War victory was a genuine UN victory. The cost of the operation was estimated at $61.1 billion. First authorized by the U.S. Congress, actual U.S. outlays were offset by pledges from the other participants—the largest shares coming from Saudi Arabia ($15.6 billion), Kuwait ($16 billion), Japan ($10 billion), and Germany ($6.5 billion). The final U.S. costs were estimated at a maximum of $8 billion.[27]

Whether or not the UN is able to maintain its central position in future border and trade disputes, demands for self-determination, and other provocations to war depends entirely upon the character of each dispute. The Gulf War was a special case because it was a clear instance of invasion of one country by another that also threatened the control of oil, which is of vital interest to the industrial countries of the world. But in the case of Somalia, although the conflict violated the world's conscience, it did not threaten vital national interests outside the country's region. The United States had propped up Somalia's government for years for purely cold war purposes, but abandoned its dictatorial regime in 1990 and left it to a chaotic civil war involving many warlords, tribal leaders, and gangs of marauding youths. Late in 1992, thousands of American soldiers under UN sponsorship were dispatched with almost no advance preparation of the public for a limited military intervention to make the country safe enough for humanitarian aid. One expert on diplomatic affairs characterized the operation as the affirmation of an important principle (and possibly a new UN precedent): "Once a country utterly loses its ability to govern itself, it also loses its claim to sovereignty and should become a ward of the United Nations."[28]

But Somalia also suggests how fragile the American commitment to such "wars of conscience" can be. After a bloody firefight in October 1993, in which more than a dozen American soldiers were killed and some of their bodies dragged through the streets of Mogadishu—scenes that shocked American television viewers—President Clinton announced his intention to withdraw all American forces from Somalia. That withdrawal was completed on March 31, 1994.

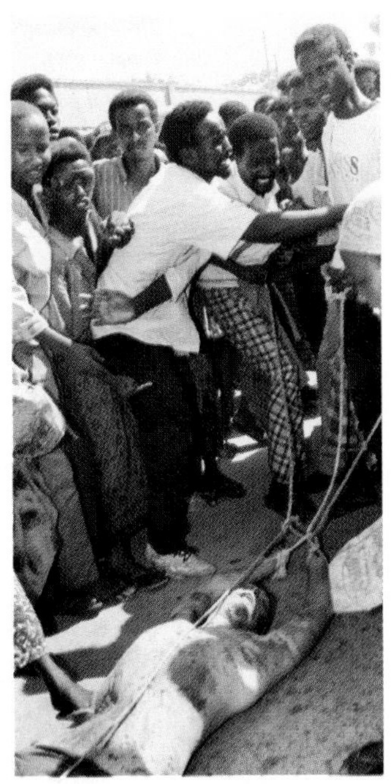

The body of an American soldier was dragged through the streets of Mogadishu, Somalia.

Somalia was the first conflict for which UN troops were brought in for strictly humanitarian purposes. The next was in the former Yugoslavia. When Yugoslavia's communist regime collapsed in the early 1990s, the country broke apart into historically ethnically distinct regions. In one of these, Bosnia, a fierce war broke out between Muslims, Croatians, and Serbians. From the outset, all outside parties urged peace, and United Nations troops were deployed to create "safe havens" in several Bosnian cities and towns. Yet despite his campaign criticism of President Bush for not doing more to stop the bloodshed in Bosnia, President Clinton was also unable to muster enough support for a more active policy. Faced with resistance from NATO allies and from Russia, and with the unwillingness of the American people to risk the lives of U.S. soldiers over an issue not vital to U.S. interests, Clinton gave up his stern warnings and accepted the outcome: the international community's failure to prevent Serbs from waging a war of aggression and "ethnic cleansing."

Not until November 1995, after still another year of frustration and with UN peacekeeping troops in increasingly serious danger from both sides in the Yugoslav civil war, was President Clinton able to achieve a ceasefire and a peace agreement in Dayton, Ohio, among the heads of the warring factions.

UN troops in Bosnia were stationed there for humanitarian purposes.

Despite the difficulty of restoring peace, the UN and its peacekeeping troops did an extraordinary job in the former Yugoslavia, dealing both with the intransigence of the warring parties and with the disagreement among the European powers about how to deal with a vicious and destructive civil war in their own neighborhood. This and other recent UN interventions show the promise and the limits of the UN as an instrument of foreign policy in the post–cold war era. Although the United States can no longer control UN decisions, as it could in the UN's early days, the UN continues to function as a useful instrument of American foreign policy.[29]

The International Monetary Structure

Fear of a repeat of the economic devastation that followed World War I brought the United States together with its allies (except the USSR) to Bretton Woods, New Hampshire, in 1944 to create a new international economic structure for the postwar world. The result was two institutions: the International Bank for Reconstruction and Development (commonly called the World Bank) and the International Monetary Fund.

The World Bank was set up to finance long-term capital. Leading nations took on the obligation of contributing funds to enable the World Bank to make loans to capital-hungry countries. (The U.S. quota has been about one-third of the total.)

The **International Monetary Fund** (IMF) was set up to provide for the short-term flow of money. After the war, the dollar, instead of gold, was the chief means by which the currencies of one country would be "changed into" currencies of another country for purposes of making international transactions. To permit debtor countries with no international balances to make purchases and investments, the IMF was set up to lend dollars or other appropriate currencies to needy member countries to help them overcome temporary trade deficits. For many years after World War II, the IMF, along with U.S. foreign aid, in effect constituted the only international medium of exchange.

During the past decade, the IMF has returned to a position of enhanced importance through its efforts to reform some of the largest debtor nations, particularly those in the Third World, to bring them more fully into the global capitalist economy. The IMF succeeded in defusing the Third World "debt bomb," as it was often called in the early 1980s. (Ironically, as Table 19.1 shows, today the world's largest debtor is the United States.) The power of the IMF to set conditions on the loans it makes and to work with major private banks to refinance ("roll over") existing debt seems to have had a positive effect. For example, on August 20, 1982, Mexico announced that it would quit trying to repay its international debt, for the time being. This also meant no more borrowing. Exactly ten years later, in August of 1992, "the Latin American debt saga [was], more or less, over. . . . Nowhere are the celebrations of life after debt bigger than on Wall Street. The reemerging markets of Latin America had become hot business."[30] This modest but substantial reentry of Latin American countries into the world market is not due altogether to efforts of the IMF or the World Bank. But they helped pave the way for a trickle, then a flow, if not a flood, of Wall Street investment in Mexico and other countries. In December 1994, however, the value of the Mexican peso declined severely against the dollar. The peso's collapse threw the Mexican economy into crisis and shook investors and markets around the

TABLE 19.1

THE WORLD'S LEADING DEBTOR NATIONS IN 1991 (IN BILLIONS OF DOLLARS)

Nation	Debt	Nation	Debt
United States	$3,683	China	$67
Mexico	105	Argentina	63
Brazil	98	South Korea	55
Indonesia	76	Turkey	53
India	72	Greece	44

SOURCES: U.S. Bureau of the Census, *Statistical Abstract of the United States, 1993* (Washington, DC: Government Printing Office, 1993), p. 292; Organization for Economic Cooperation and Development (OECD), *Financing and External Debt of Developing Countries, 1992* (Paris, OECD, 1993).

world. After years of seemingly steady reform and progress, the Mexican crisis of 1994–95 was a sober reminder of the uncertainties of debt, reform, and development in the Third World.

In the early 1990s, Russia and thirteen other former Soviet republics were invited to join the IMF and the World Bank with the expectation of receiving $10.5 billion from these two agencies, primarily for a ruble-stabilization fund. Each republic was to get a permanent IMF representative, and the IMF increased its staff by at least 10 percent to provide the expertise necessary to cope with the problems of these emerging capitalist economies.[31]

Economic Aid

Commitment to rebuilding war-torn countries came as early as commitment to the basic postwar international monetary structure. This is the way President Franklin Roosevelt put the case in a press conference in November 1942, less than one year after the United States entered World War II:

> Sure, we are going to rehabilitate [other nations after the war]. Why? . . . Not only from the humanitarian point of view . . . but from the viewpoint of our own pocketbooks, and our safety from future war.[32]

The particular form and timing for enacting American foreign aid was heavily influenced by Great Britain's sudden decision in 1947 that it would no longer be able to maintain its commitments to Greece and Turkey (full proof that America would now have to *have* clients rather than *be* one). Within three weeks of that announcement, President Truman recommended a $400 million direct aid program for Greece and Turkey, and by mid-May of 1947, Congress approved it. Since President Truman had placed the Greece-Turkey action within the larger context of a commitment to help rebuild and defend all countries the world over, wherever the leadership wished to develop democratic systems or to ward off communism, the Greek-Turkish aid was followed quickly by the historically unprecedented program that came to be known as the Marshall Plan, named in honor of Secretary of State (and former five-star general) George C. Marshall.[33]

The **Marshall Plan**—officially known as the European Recovery Program (ERP)—was essential for the rebuilding of war-torn Europe. By 1952, the United States had spent over $34 billion for the relief, reconstruction, and economic recovery of Western Europe. The emphasis was shifted in 1951, with passage of the Mutual Security Act, to building up European military capacity. Of the $48 billion appropriated between 1952 and 1961, over half went for military assistance, the rest for continuing economic aid. Over those years, the geographic emphasis of U.S. aid also shifted, toward South Korea, Taiwan, the Philippines, Vietnam, Iran, Greece, and Turkey—that is, toward the rim of communism. In the 1960s, the emphasis shifted once again, toward what became known as the Third World. From 1962 to 1975, over $100 billion was sent, mainly to Latin America for economic assistance. Other countries of Africa and Asia were also brought in.[34]

Many critics have argued that foreign aid is really aid for political and economic elites, not for the people. Although this is to a large extent true, it

Between 1948 and 1951, the European Recovery Program, popularly known as the Marshall Plan, spent billions of dollars rebuilding Western Europe. This Berlin site was reconstructed as an office building and shopping center.

needs to be understood in a broader context. If a country's leaders oppose distributing food or any other form of assistance to its people, there is little the United States, or any aid organization, can do, short of terminating the assistance. Goods have to be exchanged across national borders before they can reach the people who need them. Needy people would probably be worse off if the United States cut off aid altogether. The lines of international communication must be kept open. That is why diplomacy exists, and foreign aid can facilitate diplomacy, just as diplomacy is necessary to help get foreign aid where it is most needed.

Another important criticism of U.S. foreign aid policy is that it has not been tied closely enough to U.S. diplomacy. The original Marshall Plan was set up as an independent program outside the State Department and had its own separate missions in each participating country. Essentially, "ERP became a Second State Department."[35] This did not change until the program was reorganized as the Agency for International Development (AID) in the early 1960s. Meanwhile, the Defense Department has always had principal jurisdiction over that substantial proportion of economic aid that goes to military assistance. The Department of Agriculture administers the commodity aid programs, such as Food for Peace. Each department has in effect been able to conduct its own foreign policy, leaving many foreign diplomats to ask, "Who's in charge here?"

That brings us back to the history of U.S. efforts to balance traditional values with the modern needs of world leadership. Economic assistance is an instrument of American foreign policy, but it has been less effective than it might have been because of the inability of American politics to overcome its traditional opposition to foreign entanglements and build a unified foreign policy—something that the older nation-states would call a foreign ministry. We have undoubtedly made progress, but foreigners still often wonder who is in charge.

COLLECTIVE SECURITY

In 1947, most Americans hoped that the United States could meet its world obligations through the United Nations and economic structures alone. But most foreign policy makers recognized that it was a vain hope even as they were permitting and encouraging Americans to believe it. They had anticipated the need for military entanglements at the time of drafting the original UN Charter by insisting upon language that recognized the right of all nations to provide for their mutual defense independently of the United Nations. And almost immediately after enactment of the Marshall Plan, the White House and a parade of State and Defense Department officials followed up with an urgent request to the Senate to ratify and to Congress to finance mutual defense alliances.

At first quite reluctant to approve treaties providing for national security alliances, the Senate ultimately agreed with the executive branch. The first collective security agreement was the Rio Treaty (ratified by the Senate in September 1947), which created the Organization of American States (OAS). This was the model treaty, anticipating all succeeding collective security treaties by providing that an armed attack against any of its members "shall be considered as an attack against all the American States," including the United States. A more significant break with U.S. tradition against peacetime entanglements came with the North Atlantic Treaty (signed in April 1949), which created the North Atlantic Treaty Organization (NATO). ANZUS, a treaty tying Australia and New Zealand to the United States, was signed in September 1951. Three years later, the Southeast Asia Treaty created the Southeast Asia Treaty Organization (SEATO).

In addition to these **multilateral treaties,** the United States entered into a number of **bilateral treaties**—treaties between two countries. As one author has observed, the United States has been a *producer* of security while most of its allies have been *consumers* of security.[36] Figure 19.3 demonstrates that the United States has consistently devoted a greater percentage of its gross domestic product (GDP) to defense than have its NATO allies and Japan.

This pattern has continued in the post–cold war era, and its best illustration is in the Persian Gulf War, where the United States provided the initiative, the leadership, and most of the armed forces, even though its allies were obliged to reimburse over 90 percent of the cost.

It is difficult to evaluate collective security and its treaties, because the purpose of collective security as an instrument of foreign policy is prevention, and success of this kind has to be measured according to what did *not* happen. The critics have argued that U.S. collective security treaties posed a threat of encirclement to the Soviet Union, forcing it to produce its own collective security, particularly the Warsaw Pact[37] Nevertheless, no one can deny the counterargument that the world has enjoyed more than fifty years without world war.

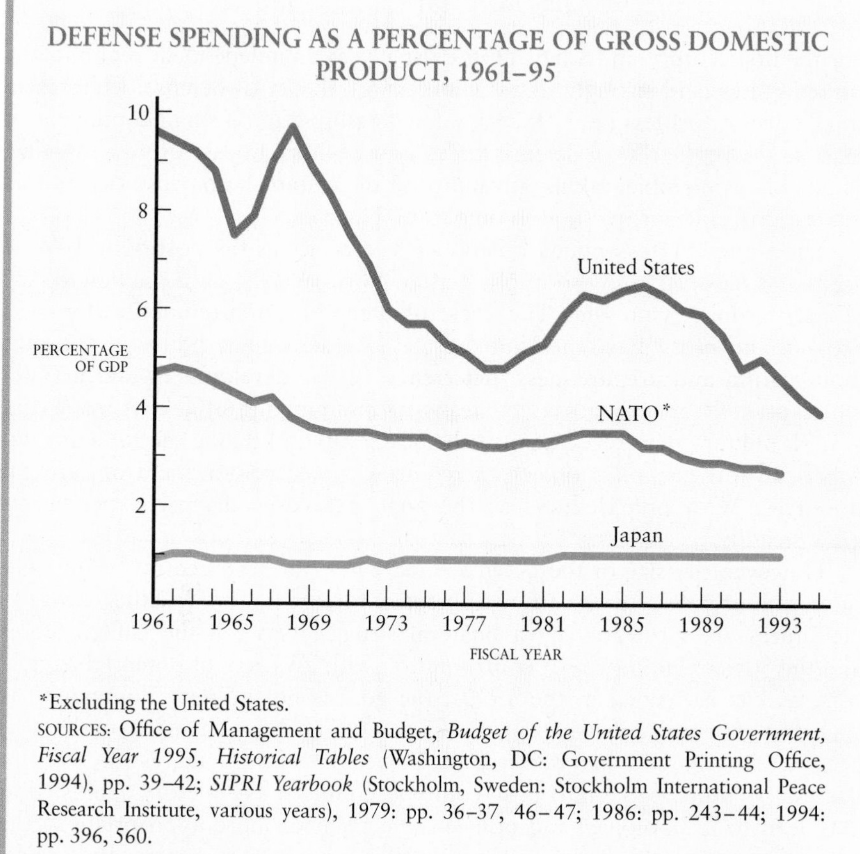

*Excluding the United States.

SOURCES: Office of Management and Budget, *Budget of the United States Government, Fiscal Year 1995, Historical Tables* (Washington, DC: Government Printing Office, 1994), pp. 39–42; *SIPRI Yearbook* (Stockholm, Sweden: Stockholm International Peace Research Institute, various years), 1979: pp. 36–37, 46–47; 1986: pp. 243–44; 1994: pp. 396, 560.

FIGURE 19.3

Although the Soviet Union has collapsed, Russia has emerged from a period of confusion and consolidation signaling its determination to play once again an active role in regional and world politics. The challenge for the United States and NATO in coming years will be how to broaden membership in the alliance to include the nations of Eastern Europe and some of the former Soviet republics without antagonizing Russia, which might see such an expansion of NATO as a new era of encirclement. The Partnership for Peace has served as a loosely defined first step toward full membership for these nations, which want NATO's protection against possible Russian expansionism.

NATO's ability to assist in implementing the uncertain peace in the Bosnian civil war will be a genuine test of the viability of NATO and collective security in general, now that the cold war is over. NATO and the other mutual security organizations throughout the world are likely to survive. But these organizations are going to be less like military alliances and more like economic associations to advance technology, reduce trade barriers, and protect the world environment. Another form of collective security may well have emerged from the 1991 Persian Gulf War, with nations forming temporary coalitions under UN sponsorship to check a particularly aggressive nation.

Military Deterrence

For the first century and a half of its existence as an independent republic, the United States held strongly to a "Minuteman" theory of defense: Maintain a small corps of professional officers, a few flagships, and a small contingent of marines; leave the rest of defense to the state militias. In case of war, mobilize as quickly as possible, taking advantage of the country's immense size and its separation from Europe to gain time to mobilize.

The United States applied this policy as recently as the post–World War I years and was beginning to apply it after World War II, until the new policy of preparedness won out. The cycle of demobilization-remobilization was broken, and in its place the United States adopted a new policy of constant mobilization and preparedness: **deterrence**, or the development and maintenance of military strength as a means of discouraging attack. After World War II, military deterrence against the Soviet Union became the fundamental American foreign policy objective, requiring a vast commitment of national resources. With preparedness as the goal, peacetime defense expenditures grew steadily.

However, the size of the defense budget has not been central to the consideration of deterrence as an instrument of foreign policy. Whether arms expenditures are motivated by a bilateral struggle between the United States and the Soviet Union or by a confrontation with a variety of potential aggressors, as has happened in the 1990s, the goal is not military dominance as such but *deterrence from any attack at all.* The Iraqi invasion of Kuwait proved that whatever had deterred the Soviet Union from aggression was not necessarily translatable into post–cold war conflicts. The victory against Iraq may lead to technologies and policies of deterrence more appropriate to the post–cold war world. But deterrence is still the name of the game, and the re-

Thousands of nuclear arms, such as this Titan missile housed in a silo in the Midwest, were built by the United States as part of its policy of deterrence against the Soviet Union.

sumption and escalation of arms sales throughout the world, and especially in the Middle East since the Gulf War, suggest that the United States and other powers will have a real struggle to make deterrence work. There continues to be a kind of "arms race," but that race now tends to be not for quantitative but for technologically qualitative superiority.

For over a century after Napoleon brought to the world the first mass citizen armies, military capacity in the Western world was measured quantitatively. Technology was, of course, always important. Technological superiority helped to make possible the domination of the Western powers over their non-Western colonies and the domination of small U.S. armed contingents over Native Americans. But it was probably not until World War II that technology became the key to the military's value as an instrument of foreign policy. From then on, the technological tail began to wag the military dog. And it is not merely a question of adding technology by giving each soldier an automatic weapon and an electronic communications device. Technology means a policy of planned technological innovation. Probably the most important outcome of the Persian Gulf War, especially from the military point of view, is that most of this expensive technology—laser-guided bombs, cruise missiles, satellite reconnaissance, computerized coordination of battles—worked as well as its supporters had claimed. This will likely enhance the credibility of using military technology as the primary deterrent in the world.

The policy of planned technological innovation is called research and development (R&D). R&D is certainly not limited to national defense. American industries spend billions of dollars on R&D annually, and many nonmilitary agencies of the federal government engage in some R&D. But nowhere is R&D such a high priority as in the modern American military establishment. The U.S. government and private industry together spend about $150 billion a year on R&D "covering everything from mapping the human genome to exploring the frontiers of physics. That is about 3 percent of America's gross domestic product, and about the same percentage that Japan and Germany spend."[38] But there the similarity ends. Germany and Japan devote almost all of their R&D to civilian projects; the United States spends about 40 percent of its R&D on military projects. This amounted to $47.8 billion in 1992, up from $18.4 billion in 1980.[39] There is an additional "hidden" R&D military budget in the private manufacture of military hardware. It is difficult to determine just where R&D ends and manufacturing begins; nevertheless, it is certain that R&D takes a significant bite of each private defense production contract.

The end of the cold war raised public expectations for a "peace dividend" at last, after nearly a decade of the largest peacetime defense budget increases in U.S. history. Many defense experts, liberal and conservative, feared what they called a budget "free-fall," not only because deterrence was still needed but also because severe and abrupt cuts could endanger private industry in many friendly foreign countries as well as in the United States.

The Persian Gulf War brought both points dramatically into focus. First, the Iraqi invasion of Kuwait revealed the size, strength, and advanced modern technological base not only of the Iraqi armed forces but of other countries, Arab and non-Arab, including the capability, then or soon, to make atomic weapons and other weapons of massive destructive power. Moreover, the demand for advanced weaponry was intensifying. The decisive victory of the United States and its allies in the Gulf War, far from discouraging the international arms trade, gave it fresh impetus. Following the Gulf War victory, *Newsweek* reported that "industry reps quickly realized that foreign customers would now be beating a path to their doors, seeking to buy the winning weaponry." The Soviet Union at one time led the list of major world arms sellers, and Russia and several other republics of the former Soviet Union have continued to make international arms sales, particularly since now there are "no ideological limitations" in the competition for customers.[40] The United States now leads the list of military weapons exporters, followed by Russia, France, Great Britain, and China. Thus, some shrinkage of defense expenditure has been desirable, but Democrats and Republicans alike agree that this reduction must be guided by the continuing need to maintain U.S. and allied credibility as a deterrent to post–cold war arms races.

As to the second point, domestic pressures join international demands to fuel post–cold war defense spending. Each cut in military production and each closing of a military base or plant translates into a significant loss of jobs. Moreover, the conversion of defense industries to domestic uses is not a problem faced by the United States alone. Figure 19.4 conveys a dramatic

FIGURE 19.4

This is a summary of an elaborate diagram of at least seventy-five separate parts that go into the F-16.

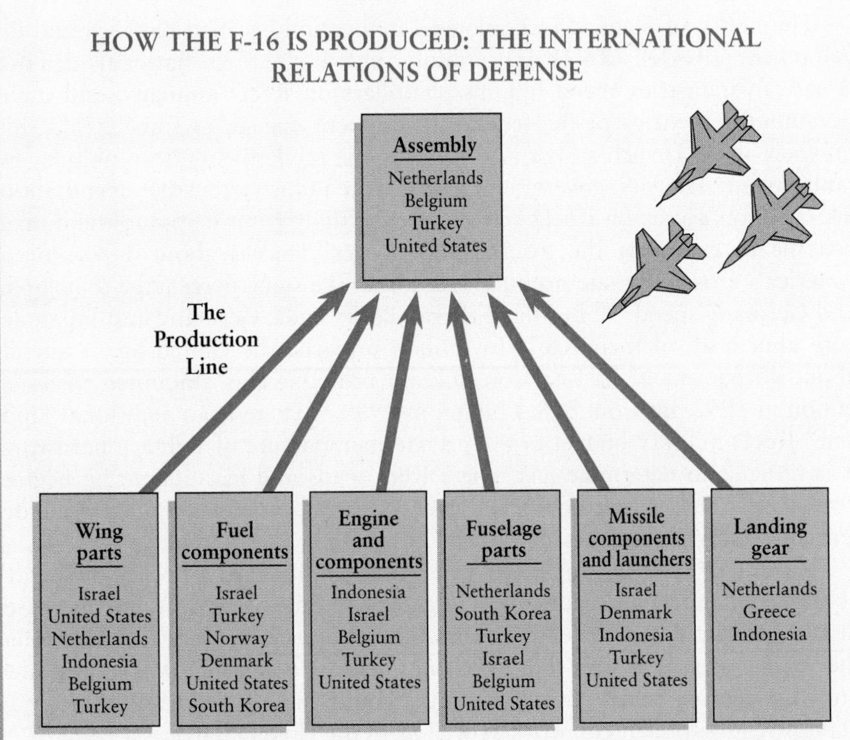

SOURCE: U.S. Congress, Office of Technology Assessment, *Arming Our Allies: Cooperation and Competition in Defense Technology*, Series OTA-ICS-449 (Washington, DC: Government Printing Office, May 1990), pp. 42–43. Information provided by the primary manufacturer, General Dynamics Corporation.

picture of the "international relations" of the production of one single weapons system, the F-16 fighter airplane.

All of this suggests that the threat of the arms race and international conflicts persists even in the post–cold war era. It also suggests that the United States is an important part of the problem as well as the most essential part of the solution. The only real hope for a significant reduction in the international demand for arms will come from changes in the general political and economic environment. But such changes do not happen spontaneously. On the international level, genuine reduction in the demand for arms will require diplomacy; try as we might, power without diplomacy can never be a permanent solution. And this must in turn be accompanied by economic growth, not only in the United States but everywhere.

★ Roles Nations Play

- What four traditional foreign policy roles has the United States adopted throughout its history?
- Since the end of World War II, how has the role of the United States in world affairs evolved?

Although each president has hundreds of small foreign fires to fight and can choose whichever instruments of policy best fit each particular situation, the primary foreign policy problem any president faces is choosing an overall role for the country in foreign affairs. Roles help us to define a situation in order to control the element of surprise in international relations. Surprise is in fact the most dangerous aspect of international relations, especially in a world made smaller and more fragile by advances in and the proliferation of military technology.

Choosing a Role

The problem of choosing a role can be understood by identifying a limited number of roles played by nation-states in the past. Four such roles will be drawn from history—the Napoleonic, the Holy Alliance, the balance-of-power, and the economic expansionist roles. Although the definitions given here will be exaggerations of the real world, they do capture in broad outline the basic choices available.

The Napoleonic Role The **Napoleonic Role** takes its name from the role played by post-revolutionary France under Napoleon. The French at that time felt not only that their new democratic system of government was the best on earth but also that France would not be safe until democracy was adopted universally. If this meant intervention into the internal affairs of France's neighbors, and if that meant warlike reactions, then so be it. President Woodrow Wilson expressed a similar viewpoint when he supported the U.S. declaration of war in 1917 with his argument that "the world must be made safe for democracy." Obviously such a position can be adopted by any powerful nation as a rationalization for intervening at its convenience in

Former Panamanian dictator Manuel Noriega was ousted by the U.S. military in 1989.

the internal affairs of another country. But it can also be sincerely espoused, and in the United States it has from time to time enjoyed broad popular consensus. We played the Napoleonic role most recently in ousting Philippine dictator Ferdinand Marcos (February 1986), Panamanian leader Manuel Noriega (December 1989), the Sandinista government of Nicaragua (February 1990), and the military rulers of Haiti (September 1994).

The Holy Alliance Role The concept of the **Holy Alliance Role** emerged out of the defeat of Napoleon and the agreement by the leaders of Great Britain, Russia, Austria, and Prussia to preserve the social order against *all* revolution, including democratic revolution, at whatever cost. (Post-Napoleonic France also joined it.) The Holy Alliance made use of every kind of political instrument available—including political suppression, espionage, sabotage, and outright military intervention—to keep existing governments in power. The Holy Alliance role is comparable to the Napoleonic role in that each operates on the assumption that intervention into the internal affairs of other countries is justified for the maintenance of peace. But Napoleonic intervention is motivated by fear of dictatorship, and it can accept and even encourage revolution. In contrast, Holy Alliance intervention is antagonistic to any form of political change, even when this means supporting an existing dictatorship.[41] Because the Holy Alliance role became more important after the cold war ended, illustrations of this role will be given later in the chapter.

The Balance-of-Power Role The **balance-of-power role** is basically an effort by the major powers to play off against each other so that no great power or combination of great and lesser powers can impose conditions on others. The most relevant example of the use of this strategy is found in the nineteenth century, especially the latter half. The feature of the balance-of-power role that is most distinct from the two previously identified roles is that this role accepts the political system of each country, asking no questions except whether the country will join an alliance and will use its resources to ensure that each country will respect the borders and interests of all the others.[42]

The Economic Expansionist Role The **economic expansionist role,** also called the capitalist role, shares with the balance-of-power role the attitude that the political system or ideology of a country is irrelevant; the only question is whether a country has anything to buy or sell and whether its entrepreneurs, corporations, and government agencies will honor their contracts. Governments and their armies are occasionally drawn into economic expansionist relationships in order to establish, reopen, or expand trade relationships, and to keep the lines of commerce open. But the role is political, too. The point can be made that the economic expansionist role was the role consistently played by the United States in Latin and Central America, until the cold war (perhaps in the 1960s and beyond) pushed us toward the Holy Alliance role with most of those countries.

Like arms control, however, economic expansion does not happen spontaneously. In the past, economic expansion owed a great deal to military backing, because contracts do not enforce themselves, trade deficits are not paid automatically, and new regimes do not always honor the commitments made by regimes they replace. The only way to expand economic relationships is through diplomacy.

Roles for America Today

Although "making the world safe for democracy" was used to justify the U.S. entry into World War I, it was taken more seriously after World War II, when at last the United States was willing to play a more sustained part in world affairs. The Napoleonic role was most suited to America's view of the postwar world. To create the world's ruling regimes in the American image would indeed give Americans the opportunity to return to their private pursuits, for if all or even most of the world's countries were governed by democratic constitutions, there would be no more war, since no democracy would ever attack another democracy—or so it has been assumed.[43]

Making the World Safe for Democracy The emergence of the Soviet Union as a superpower was the overwhelming influence on American foreign policy thinking in the post–World War II era. The distribution of power in the world was "bipolar," and Americans saw the world separated in two, with an "iron curtain" dividing the communist world from the free world. Immediately after the war, America's foreign policy goal had been "pro-democracy," a Napoleonic role dominated by the Marshall Plan and the genuine hope for a democratic world. This quickly shifted toward a Holy Alliance role, with "containment" as the primary foreign policy criterion.[44] Containment was fundamentally a Holy Alliance concept. According to foreign-policy expert Richard Barnet, during the 1950s and 1960s, "the United States used its military or paramilitary power on an average of once every eighteen months either to prevent a government deemed undesirable from coming to power or to overthrow a revolutionary or reformist government considered inimical to America's interests."[45] Although Barnet did not refer to Holy Alliance, his description fits the model perfectly.

During the 1970s, the United States played the Holy Alliance role less frequently, not so much because of the outcome of the Vietnam War as because of the emergence of a multipolar world. In 1972, the United States accepted (and later recognized) the communist government of the People's Republic of China and broke forever its pure bipolar, cold war view of world power distribution. Other powers became politically important as well, including Japan, the European Economic Community (now the European Union), India, and, depending on their own resolve, the countries making up the Organization of Petroleum Exporting Countries (OPEC). The United States experimented with all four of the previously identified roles, depending on which was appropriate to a specific region of the world. In the Middle East, America tended to play an almost classic balance-of-power role, by appearing sometimes cool in its relations with Israel and by playing off one Arab country against another. The United States has been able to do this despite the fact that every country in the Middle East recognizes that for cultural, domestic, and geostrategic reasons, the United States has always considered Israel as its

FREE SPEECH AND THE VIETNAM WAR

The relative political calm of the 1950s gave way to a turbulent, frenetic, and anti–status quo political environment in the 1960s. This dramatic political change was sparked by a variety of concerns, including poverty, racial discrimination, and, especially, America's growing involvement in the Vietnam War. College campuses became hotbeds of protest and discontent, and the University of California at Berkeley, long known for student agitation, was among the first places to register that discontent. The Berkeley campus was the birthplace of what came to be known as the "free speech movement."

In the early 1960s, politicized Berkeley students launched a series of protests, demonstrations, marches, sit-ins, and other activities intended to draw attention to several causes, including the Civil Rights movement, nuclear disarmament, and the fight against a nationwide anti-communist movement. These protests were held both on and off campus, and followed the nonviolent style used by civil rights activists in the South. The formerly strict campus rules against political activities had been loosened at Berkeley, but students continued to push for greater freedom of expression. In the face of what it saw as improper student organization of social and political protest from the campus, the university administration imposed restrictions on certain on-campus activities, expelled some students, and called in police forces to maintain campus order.

In 1964, student leaders at Berkeley formed the Free Speech Movement. Within a few months, they won their effort to get the university to roll back its restrictions on political speech and other lawful political activities. Yet the movement was less about the particular question of free speech on campus as it was an umbrella organization encompassing a wide array of protest activities. Increasingly mistrustful of authority figures at the university and in the country at large, the Free Speech Movement's adherents sought to extend the classroom into the street and bring the street into the classroom. By the spring of 1965, as America began to escalate its military involvement in Vietnam, students began to lodge protests against the war and against the military draft that supported it. A new group, Students for a Democratic Society (SDS), epitomized the new political

most durable and important ally in the region and has unwaveringly committed itself to Israel's survival in a very hostile environment. President Nixon introduced balance-of-power considerations in the Far East by "playing the China card." In other parts of the world, particularly in Latin America, we tended to hold to the Holy Alliance and Napoleonic roles.

This multipolar phase ended after 1989, with the collapse of the Soviet Union and the end of the cold war. Soon thereafter the Warsaw Pact collapsed too, ending armed confrontation in Europe. With almost equal suddenness, the popular demand for "self-determination" produced several new nation-states and the demand for still more. On the one hand, it was indeed good to witness the re-emergence of some twenty-five major nationalities after anywhere from forty-five to seventy-five years of suppression. On the other hand, policy makers with a sense of history are aware that this new world order bears a strong resemblance to the world of 1914. Then, the trend was known as "Balkanization." Balkanization meant nationhood and self-determination, but it also meant war. The Soviet Union after World War I and Yugoslavia after World War II kept more than twenty nationalities from mak-

movement that sought to accelerate political and social change in the United States.

As America's involvement in Vietnam increased, so too did student agitation and protest. The antiwar movement spread to many college campuses and became both more vocal and more radicalized. President Lyndon Johnson came under particular attack for his Vietnam policies. Johnson continued to assure the country that the U.S. military was winning the war, but when Americans learned that Johnson had not been honest with the public about what turned out to be a military and political quagmire, American sentiment began to turn against the war. In 1967 and 1968, disaffected students worked intensively to dislodge Johnson by supporting the peace candidacy of Democratic senator Eugene McCarthy. Rising support for McCarthy helped persuade Johnson not to seek re-election in 1968.

The election of Richard Nixon to the presidency in 1968 did not put an end to the war, and antiwar activities intensified across the country. Those activities peaked with Nixon's invasion of Cambodia in 1970, which prompted tumultuous student reaction on campuses everywhere. The student cause was further dramatized when four students at Kent State University in Ohio were shot and killed by National Guard troops during a protest against the invasion of Cambodia.

By 1972, American military involvement had been significantly cut, and a year later, American involvement in Vietnam effectively ended. The eclipsing war also meant an eclipsing student movement. Student activism and protests encompassing such issues as the environment, women's rights, and civil rights continued, but the degree and intensity of student activism seen in the 1960s would not appear again. In the words of Berkeley faculty member Nathan Glazer, the Free Speech Movement "stands at the beginning of the student rebellion in this country."

SOURCE: David Lance Goines, *The Free Speech Movement* (Berkeley, CA: Ten Speed Press, 1993).

ing war against each other for several decades. In 1989 and the years that followed, the world was caught unprepared for the dangers of a new disorder that the re-emergence of these nationalities produced.

It should also be emphasized that the demand for nationhood emerged with new vigor in many other parts of the world—the Middle East, South and Southeast Asia, and South Africa. Perhaps we are seeing worldwide Balkanization; we should not overlook the re-emergence of the spirit of nationhood among ethnic minorities in Canada and the United States.

Making the World Safe for Democracy and Markets The abrupt end of the cold war unleashed another dynamic factor, the globalization of markets; one could call it the globalization of capitalism. This is good news, but it has its problematic side because the free market can disrupt nationhood. Although the globalization of markets is enormously productive, countries like to enjoy its benefits while attempting at the same time to prevent international economic influences from affecting local jobs, local families, and established class and tribal relationships.

This struggle between capitalism and nationhood produces a new kind of bipolarity in the world. The old world order was shaped by *external bipolarity*—of West versus East. This seems to have been replaced by *internal bipolarity,* wherein each country is struggling to make its own hard policy choices to preserve its cultural uniqueness while competing effectively in the global marketplace.

Approval of the North American Free Trade Agreement (NAFTA) serves as the best example of this struggle within the United States. NAFTA was supported by a majority of Democrats and Republicans on the grounds that a freer, global market was in America's national interest. But even as NAFTA was being embraced by large bipartisan majorities in Congress, three important factions were rising to fight it. Former presidential candidate Pat Buchanan led a large segment of conservative Americans to fight NAFTA because, he argued, communities and families would be threatened by job losses and by competition from legal and illegal immigrant workers. Another large faction, led by Ross Perot, opposed NAFTA largely on the theory that American companies would move their operations to Mexico, where labor costs are lower. Organized labor also joined the fight against NAFTA.

The battle over NAFTA is just one example of the "internal bipolarity" that is coming to the fore around the world. As *New York Times* foreign affairs columnist Thomas Friedman put it, ". . . now that the free market is triumphing on a global basis, the most interesting conflicts are between the winners and losers within countries. It is these internal battles that will increasingly shape international affairs."[46] To take his observation a step fur-

Many labor groups in the United States, such as this electrical workers' union, opposed the passage of NAFTA and lobbied Congress against its passage.

ther, the losers within countries will be those who focus only on local concerns—local interests and local traditions—and who will almost always lean toward protectionism and isolationism in foreign affairs. The following is an excerpt from an important presidential campaign speech by Pat Buchanan a few weeks before the 1996 New Hampshire primary:

> I've gone around this country, and I've seen what happens when company towns become ghost towns. These working people, who agree with us on so many cultural and social issues, they're wondering why we're selling them down the river.[47]

Buchanan repeated and strengthened this theme all during his presidential primary campaign:

> When go-go global capitalism is uprooting entire communities and families, I ask conservatives what it is we are trying to conserve. ["Good" capitalists and "bad" capitalists] are part of the same market morality that will cannibalize all other sensibilities if we don't retain strong common values and strong organizations that can keep it in check.[48]

The global market is here to stay and American values have changed enough to incorporate it, despite the toll it may take on community and family tradition. Meanwhile, many of the elements of foreign policy created during the cold war still exist because they turned out to be good adjustments to the modern era. The Marshall Plan and the various forms of international economic aid that succeeded it continue to this day. Although appropriations for foreign aid have been shrinking, only a small minority of members of the Senate and the House favor the outright abolition of foreign aid programs. NATO and other collective security arrangements continue, as do some aspects of containment, even though there is no longer a Soviet Union, because collective security arrangements have, as we shall see, proven useful in dealing with new democracies and other nations seeking to join the global market. Even though the former Soviet Union is now more often an ally than an adversary, the United States still quite frequently uses unilateral and multilateral means of keeping civil wars contained within their own borders, so that conflict does not spread into neighboring states. America is practicing a new form of containment, but one that is based on the values and institutions of cold war containment.

Another traditional value that has been updated and given fresh application is the American commitment to "making the world safe for democracy." By this, Woodrow Wilson and eventually all Americans intended that we would fight foreign wars only to keep violent conflicts and corrupting foreign influences away from our shores. That particular value has been refashioned to mean "making the world safe for democracy and markets," which requires that American policy look more closely at and act more directly upon the domestic institutions of other countries, so that there will be more trade outlets as well as more stable and less warlike regimes. This, too, is a modern application of an older faith—the belief that democracies may compete economically with each other but will never go to war against each other. The question remains, however, what are the implications of internal bipolarity for the role the United States is going to play in the post–cold war world?

The Holy Alliance Role in the Post–Cold War Era At first glance, it appears that America finally got what it wanted—a world that would run itself well enough without need for much U.S. foreign policy. But we have obviously been betrayed by events. U.S. foreign policy roles and priorities have not been shuffled very much, if at all. In fact, the Holy Alliance role seems to be more prominent than ever. There is, of course, one big difference—the absence of the Soviet Union and the current willingness of Russia to support rather than oppose American policies. During the cold war era, the purpose of the Holy Alliance role was to keep regimes in power as long as they did not espouse Soviet foreign policy goals. In the post–cold war world, the purpose of the Holy Alliance role is still to keep regimes in power, but only as long as they maintain general stability, keep their nationalities contained within their own borders, and encourage their economies to attain some level of participation in the global market.

Perhaps the first indication of post–cold war American foreign policy was President Bush's conciliatory approach to the dictatorial regime of the People's Republic of China following its brutal military suppression of the democratic student movement in Tiananmen Square in June 1989. Not only did the dictator Deng Xiaoping receive America's most ardent public embrace, China received the coveted most favored nation (MFN) trade status despite repeated efforts by Congress to deny it until China reformed.[49] President Clinton continued this approach, renewing China's MFN status each year despite China's embarrassing rebuff to American efforts to win some concessions on human rights. The president declared his desire to decouple China's MFN status from its human rights record, arguing that economic growth provided the only effective means to bring about political reform in a country as large and as powerful as China.

Iraq offers probably the most meaningful example of the practice of the Holy Alliance role because the U.S. approach to Iraq's invasion of Kuwait was a genuine "concert of nations" approach. The concert in this case was the twenty-nine-nation alliance, under UN sponsorship, that removed Iraq's army from Kuwait. After the alliance victory, President Bush initially took a Napoleonic position, urging the people of Iraq to "take matters into their own hands" and to force Hussein to "step aside." But once the uprisings began, President Bush backed away, thus revealing that the real intent had been to leave the existing military and party dictatorship in power, with or without Hussein.

The abortive U.S. intervention in Somalia, launched by President Bush in the last months of 1992 and continued briefly by President Clinton, shows a similar pattern. When the initial U.S. goal—to end the famine by restoring law and order—proved inadequate in the face of Somalia's political disintegration, Clinton chose to withdraw American soldiers rather than broaden their mission. The Holy Alliance role cannot succeed when there is no order left to restore.

The U.S. policy toward Bosnia is a clear case of playing the Holy Alliance role. At first, the United States deferred to the European nations when a violent civil war erupted following Croatia and Bosnia-Hertzegovina's declarations of independence as separate nation-states. When Europe failed to address the problem adequately, the United States and the United Kingdom

A Holy Alliance? Representatives from Russia, Germany, Bosnia-Herzegovina, Croatia, Serbia, France, the United Kingdom, and the United States met in Dayton, Ohio, in November 1995 to broker a peace settlement for Bosnia.

developed a joint peace plan for the warring factions: this, too, failed to end the violence. Finally, in 1995, the United States brushed aside the mantles of humanitarian aid and third-party negotiating and took a more direct approach. Our surprise 1995 bombing of Bosnian Serb military locations finally drove the three warring factions to the negotiating table in Dayton, Ohio; this meeting produced a narrow but momentarily effective armistice. But what emerged out of that process was a new alliance of twenty-five nations, acting "in concert" to separate the factions by recognized boundary lines. The aim of these policies was to prevent the spread of violence across international borders into neighboring countries. Although one-third of the sixty thousand occupying troops and virtually all of the navy and air force troops in Bosnia are American, twenty-four other nations have a physical presence in the field, all in order to maintain the status quo. Almost everything about this operation, including the geographical location, is an acting out of the traditional Holy Alliance role.

The International Arms Trade Another indication of America's post–cold war role is the new arms race—that is, the international market in military products—and the growing importance of the Holy Alliance role in America's effort to produce a "new world order." The primary incentive in the international sale of military products is to keep the American defense industry alive and prosperous in the face of cuts in the defense budget. The United States today is the world's biggest producer and exporter of advanced weaponry. In 1993, for instance, 73 percent of new arms deals in the Third World came from America, and the value of American arms sales to Third World nations totalled $14.8 billion.[50] Many other countries also manufacture military materials, and a tremendous proportion of their military goods are for export. These countries are Brazil (over 80 percent for export); Italy (62 percent);

Israel (47 percent); Spain (41 percent); the United Kingdom (40 percent); and Sweden (24 percent).[51] This means that each of these economies has a heavy stake in the international arms market. It also means that the United States and Russia in particular have a double stake in the maintenance of that market, because they profit not only from their own exports but from royalties they earn on the exports of the other countries, since most of the weapons and weapons components that these smaller countries manufacture are under license from the United States or Russia.[52]

Until 1991, Iraq was the biggest importer of military goods. Between 1983 and 1988, the U.S. Arms Control and Disarmament Agency could identify $40 billion worth of arms bought by Iraq on the international market. And Iraq will almost certainly return in the near future to major status as a purchaser. Meanwhile, the largest importers today are Saudi Arabia ($26 billion imported during the same five years), India ($15 billion during the same period), Syria ($13 billion), and Iran ($12 billion).[53]

Fighter planes, produced in the United Kingdom, but bound for Saudi Arabia. Saudi Arabia is currently the world's largest importer of arms.

Why are these countries buying so much advanced military material? In some instances there are actual arms races. Just as the United States and the Soviet Union used weaponry as a deterrent against each other, so smaller, neighboring countries use their weaponry as a deterrent against one another. The value of weapons importation for these countries can be seen in the regular use the United States and the United Nations make of restrictions and embargoes on weapons as sanctions against "misbehaving" countries.

Another reason is that many of the most despotic regimes view a big military presence as an essential means of maintaining control of their own populations. And all too often, the United States has cooperated in this aspect of the arms trade, even encouraging it as part of its Holy Alliance role. Supporting existing regimes was a key aspect of the original Holy Alliance of the nineteenth century, and it remains a key aspect of it in the post–cold war world today. The United States will never wholly approve of despotic regimes and is rarely even comfortable with benevolent but undemocratic ones. But America finds itself supporting distasteful regimes because it likes world stability more than it dislikes undemocratic regimes. And this attitude makes the Holy Alliance role a lot easier to play, because it is an attitude with which our European allies are historically comfortable.

A Holy Alliance role will never relieve the United States of the need for diplomacy, however. In fact, diplomacy becomes all the more important because despotic regimes eventually fail and in the process attempt to thrust their problems on their neighbors. The dissolution of Yugoslavia and the struggles of a concert of nations to stop the genocidal ethnic struggle there testify to the limits of the Holy Alliance role. The painstaking efforts of the Clinton administration to reach a diplomatic settlement with North Korea over its efforts to develop nuclear weapons also testify to the continuing importance of diplomacy. This is not to argue that war is never justifiable or that peace can always be achieved through discussions among professional diplomats or purchased by compromise or appeasement. It is only to argue that there are severe limits on how often a country like the United States can engage in Holy Alliances. When leaders in a democracy engage in unilateral or multilateral direct action, with or without military force, they must have overwhelming justification. In all instances, the political should dominate the military. That is what diplomacy is all about. In 1952, the distinguished military career of General Douglas MacArthur was abruptly terminated when President Truman dismissed him for insubordination. At issue was MacArthur's unwillingness to allow the military in Korea to be subordinated to politicians and diplomats. MacArthur's argument was "In war, there is no substitute for victory."[54] But he was overlooking the prior question and therefore missed the very point that should guide any foreign policy: Is there a substitute for war?

Making Foreign Policy in a Democracy

> ➤ What institution best serves as the "vital middle" between the American people and the president in forming successful foreign policy?

The American people seem to have joined the modern world. They fairly consistently give the president their support in representing America abroad. They have, by and large, accepted new or revised values in response to new world conditions that are beyond America's capacity to control. In fact, Americans no longer seem to suffer from the illusion that America is omnipotent and that some government official or political party must be at fault when things go wrong. The last time the illusion of American omnipotence was brutally expressed was in the early 1950s, when McCarthyites called for the heads of those "traitors who lost China,"—as though China was ever ours to lose.[55]

America is indeed more mature than it once was. Few Americans were aroused to action in response to Pat Buchanan's eloquent appeals in his 1996 presidential campaign to rise up against the new global economic reality. Many Americans will suffer from globalization, but for the most part they are ready to cope with the uncertainties of global anarchy while maintaining optimism about America's eventual success.

Nevertheless, the good news about America's optimistic posture toward the new world does not vanquish the nagging doubts about the capacity of democracies in foreign affairs. The American people are too large and diffuse a nation to participate in making foreign policy in any truly democratic way. A people, even a free and mature people, can at best set limits, or broadly defined national interests within which policy makers and policy shapers can operate. A people can constrain power but cannot guide or direct the powerful.

If the whole American people is too broad to conduct foreign policy, the American presidency is too narrow. We need a "vital middle" player to form foreign policy in our democracy. This "vital middle" is in fact provided by the Constitution. Foreign policy was always supposed to involve the president *and* Congress, and, now that the cold war has ended, no time is more appropriate to revive that principle. During the cold war, a genuine foreign policy debate was carried out in Congress about once every decade. Each time it happened, it was a great moment of renewal of the Constitution and redirection and revitalization of public policy. The "Cooper/Church" debate

AMERICAN POLITICAL CULTURE

The End of the Vietnam War?

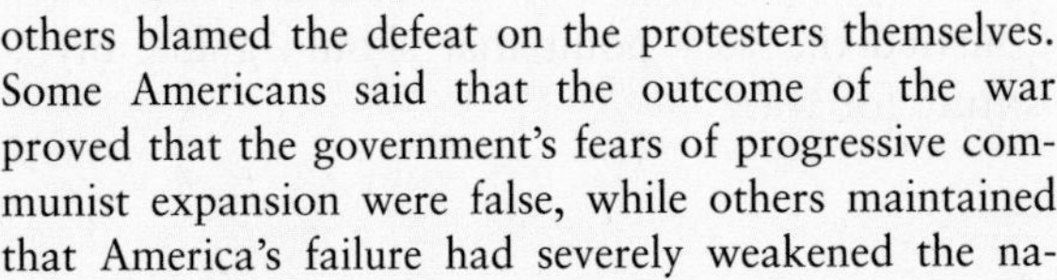

"This moment offers us the opportunity to bind up our own wounds. . . . Whatever divided us before, let us consign to the past. Let this moment, in the words of Scripture, 'Be a time to heal, and a time to build.'"[1] "Today will forever be known by America's veterans as Black Tuesday."[2] Both of these statements, the first by President Bill Clinton and the second by a group of veterans and relatives of American soldiers still missing from the Vietnam War, refer to President Clinton's decision to normalize relations between the United States and Vietnam. The sharply differing statements indicate the deep divisions that remain among many Americans who lived during the war.

Today it is hard to recapture the passions that Vietnam aroused in the 1960s. Vietnam was the defining national event for an entire generation of Americans. To those who supported the war, it was an honorable attempt to preserve the liberty of an ally, South Vietnam, and a vital step in resisting the encroachment of communist tyranny around the globe. To its opponents, the war, with its carpet bombing, defoliation, and destruction of villages, was an American crime against the people of Vietnam. Millions of young people grew up detesting the military establishment that fought in the war; many came to believe that their own nation was evil. Draft-card burnings, expressions of support for the North Vietnamese, and denunciations of America were common occurrences on college campuses across the country. At an antiwar demonstration at Kent State University in Ohio in 1970, four young people were killed by ill-trained National Guard troops. For one side, the victims were martyrs; for the other, they deserved little sympathy.

In 1973, the last American combat forces withdrew from South Vietnam; two years later, Saigon fell and the war ended. But the end of the war did not end the recriminations. The defeat prompted some Americans to say that the antiwar protesters had been right, while others blamed the defeat on the protesters themselves. Some Americans said that the outcome of the war proved that the government's fears of progressive communist expansion were false, while others maintained that America's failure had severely weakened the nation's international standing and encouraged Soviet adventurism elsewhere in the world. Thus the aftermath of the war kept alive the bitterness between two divided camps of Americans and led to two very different understandings of the "lessons" of Vietnam.

By 1995, the Clinton administration felt that enough time had passed to normalize relations. This decision was strongly influenced by economic rather than moral considerations: American business interests were too important to continue being shut out of such a large market. The time had come, President Clinton said, to let go of the past and turn to the present. Not all agree with him. The passions of the Vietnam War will continue to burn for some Americans, especially for those who served, for those who lost family members, and for the more than eight hundred thousand Vietnamese refugees who now live in the United States. Yet even among some Vietnamese Americans there is the sense that the normalization of relations is long overdue. As one man, now a newspaper columnist in California, noted, "Thank God we are at the end of the road. This should have happened in 1945 [when Japanese occupation ended and trouble with French colonial power resumed]. It's all been so unnecessary. What a waste of life. What a tragedy it has all been."[3]

[1] Transcript of President Clinton's announcement, *New York Times,* July 12, 1995, p. A9.

[2] Alison Mitchell, "U.S. Grants Full Ties to Hanoi; Time for Healing, Clinton Says," *New York Times,* July 12, 1995, p. A8.

[3] T. T. Nhu, quoted in Seth Mydans, "For Many of Those Who Fled Vietnam, a Day of Sadness, Anger and Hope," *New York Times,* July 12, 1995, p. A9.

in 1970 over the continuation of military activity in Cambodia did very little to alter the course of the Vietnam War, but in focusing on the constitutionality of the war and the legality of the U.S. incursion into Cambodia, the debate revived the strength of constitutionalism in the United States and brought America to its senses about the difference between democracy and tyranny. Almost exactly twenty years later, the Persian Gulf War did the same thing. Anticipating opposition in Congress, President Bush sought and got UN support and multilateral cooperation. When he took the issue to Congress in January 1991, he was supported by a narrow margin, but he got from the debate an enlightened and guided support that no opinion poll could have provided. Success in the Gulf War brought Bush a 90 percent popular approval rating. But that was not the true measure of his political base; Congress was.

The end of the cold war has opened Congress to opportunities in foreign policy debates that it has not had since before the Great Depression. During the cold war, because the United States had to remain mobilized and secretive most of the time, it could not afford a substantial and public congressional role in foreign policy. But now, without the imminent threat of atomic holocaust, genuine crises are rare. Thus even important foreign policy issues permit time for debate and deliberation, which allows Congress to play its legitimate role.

During the cold war, following as it did a world war and a long domestic economic crisis, Congress developed what one expert has called "a culture of deference"—a bipartisan culture of defeat that can be summed up by a maxim shared by most influential members of the House and Senate: "We shouldn't make foreign policy."[56] But this doesn't make sense anymore. The end of the cold war did not just liberate the republics of the former Soviet Union and Eastern Europe to embrace democracy; it liberated all legislatures of the world to get involved in foreign affairs. Foreign policy making in the United States will remain the president's domain. But public deliberation and debate, in an ongoing search for the national interest, is the domain of Congress. Congress is the vital middle between a hopeless isolationist rejection of foreign policy altogether and an equally hopeless delegation of total power to the chief executive.

★ Summary

This chapter began by raising some dilemmas about forming foreign policy in a democracy like the United States. Skepticism about foreign entanglements and the secrecy surrounding many foreign policy issues form the basis of these dilemmas. Although we cannot provide solutions to the foreign policy issues that the United States faces, we can provide a well-balanced analysis of the problems of foreign policy. This analysis is based on the five basic dimensions of foreign policy: the players, the setting, the values, the instruments, and the roles.

The first section of this chapter looked at the players in foreign policy: the makers and the shapers. The influence of institutions and groups varies from case to case, with the important exception of the president. Since the president is central to all foreign policy, it is best to assess how other actors interact with the president. In most instances, this interaction involves only the narrowest element of the foreign policy establishment. The American people have an opportunity to influence foreign policy, but primarily through Congress or interest groups.

Foreign policy is also guided by developments within the international system. The United States operates as a nation-state in a world of nation-states whose ignorance of each other breeds distrust and hostility. The purpose of foreign policy is to defend national sovereignty against other nation-states that are conducting their foreign policy for the same purpose.

The next section, on values, traced the history of American values that had a particular relevance to American perspectives on the outside world. We found that the American fear of a big government applied to foreign as well as domestic governmental powers. The Founders and the active public of the Founding period all recognized that foreign policy was special, that the national government had special powers in its dealings with foreigners, and that presidential supremacy was justified in the conduct of foreign affairs. The only way to avoid the big national government and presidential supremacy was to avoid the foreign entanglements that made foreign policy, diplomacy, secrecy, and presidential discretion necessary. Americans held on to their "anti-statist" tradition until World War II, long after world conditions cried out for American involvement. And even as we became involved in world affairs, we held on tightly to the legacies of 150 years of tradition: the intermingling of domestic and foreign policy institutions, and unilateralism, the tendency to "go it alone" when confronted with foreign conflicts.

We then looked at the instruments—that is, the tools—of American foreign policy. These are the basic statutes and the institutions by which foreign policy has been conducted since World War II: diplomacy, the United Nations, the international monetary structure, economic aid, collective security, and military deterrence. Although Republicans and Democrats look at the world somewhat differently, and although each president has tried to impose a distinctive flavor on foreign policy, they have all made use of these basic instruments, and that has given foreign policies a certain continuity. When Congress created these instruments after World War II, the old tradition was still so strong that it moved Congress to try to create instruments that would do their international work with a minimum of diplomacy—a minimum of human involvement. This is what we called power without diplomacy.

The next section concentrated on the role or roles the president and Congress have sought to play in the world. To help simplify the tremendous variety of tactics and strategies that foreign policy leaders can select, we narrowed the field down to four categories of roles nations play, suggesting that there is a certain amount of consistency and stability in the conduct of a nation-state in its dealings with other nation-states. These were labeled according to actual roles that diplomatic historians have identified in the history of major Western nation-states: The Napoleonic, Holy Alliance, balance-of-power, and economic expansionist roles. We also attempted to identify and assess the role of the United States in the post–cold war era, essentially the Holy Alliance role. But whatever its advantages may be, the Holy Alliance approach will never allow the United States to conduct foreign policy without diplomacy. America is tied inextricably to the perils and ambiguities of international relationships, and diplomacy is still the monarch of all available instruments of foreign policy.

We concluded by returning to the dilemma we raised in the chapter's introduction: In a democracy like the United States, who should make foreign policy? The chapter provided numerous case studies to seek an answer to this question. We believe that between the extremes of isolationism and total power resting with the president resides a middle ground where the American people can express their will through the members of Congress. The national interest can be defined only through debate and deliberation, which we hope will serve as the foundations for the formation of foreign policy in the American democracy.

FOR FURTHER READING

Crabb, Cecil V., and Kevin V. Mulcahy. *Presidents and Foreign Policymaking: From FDR to Reagan.* Baton Rouge: Louisiana State University Press, 1986.

Gilpin, Robert. *The Political Economy of International Relations.* Princeton, NJ: Princeton University Press, 1987.

Graubard, Stephen, ed. "The Exit from Communism." *Daedalus* 121, no. 2 (spring 1992).

Graubard, Stephen, ed. "The Quest for World Order." *Daedalus* 124, no. 3 (summer 1995).

Greenfield, Liah. *Nationalism: Five Roads to Modernity.* Cambridge, MA: Harvard University Press, 1993.

Keller, William W. *Arm in Arm: The Political Economy of the Global Arms Race.* New York: Basic Books, 1995.

Kennan, George F. *Around the Cragged Hill: A Personal and Political Philosophy.* New York: Norton, 1993.

Kennedy, Paul M. *The Rise and Fall of the Great Powers: Economic Change and Military Conflict from 1500 to 2000.* New York: Random House, 1987.

LaFeber, Walter. *The American Age: United States Foreign Policy at Home and Abroad since 1750.* New York: Norton, 1989.

Smist, Frank J., Jr. *Congress Oversees the U.S. Intelligence Community, 1947–1994.* 2nd ed. Knoxville: University of Tennessee Press, 1994.

U.S. Congress. *Report of the Congressional Committees Investigating the Iran-Contra Affair.* New York: Random House, 1988.

Wirls, Daniel. *Buildup: The Politics of Defense in the Reagan Era.* Ithaca, NY: Cornell University Press, 1992.

STUDY OUTLINE

1. Traditionally, Americans have been skeptical and distrustful of foreign policy.
2. Public opinion can have a determinative impact on the success or failure of foreign policy. Consequently, politicians often engage in deceit in order to curry the public's favor.

The Players: The Makers and Shapers of Foreign Policy

1. All foreign policy decisions must be made and implemented in the name of the president.
2. The key players in foreign policy in the bureaucracy are the secretaries of State, Defense, and Treasury; the Joint Chiefs of Staff (especially the chair); and the Director of the Central Intelligence Agency.
3. Although the Senate traditionally has more foreign policy power than the House, since World War II, the House and the Senate have both been important players in foreign policy.
4. Many types of interest groups help shape American foreign policy. These groups include economic interest groups, ethnic or national interest groups, and human rights interest groups.
5. The media serve to communicate issues and policies to the American people, and to communicate the public's opinions back to the president. One definite influence of television on foreign policy has been to make the

American people more cynical and skeptical than they otherwise would have been.

6. Individual or group influence in foreign policy varies from case to case and from situation to situation.

The Setting: A World of Nation-States

1. Sovereignty is a continuum that has new, small, and relatively weak nation-states at one end, major powers at the other end, and somewhat wealthy and strong nation-states not always able to pursue their own foreign policy in between.

The Values in American Foreign Policy

1. The intermingling of domestic and foreign policy institutions and unilateralism are the two identifiable legacies of our traditional system of maintaining sovereignty.
2. The intermingling of domestic and foreign policy institutions was originally possible because the major European powers policed the world.
3. Traditionally, unilateralism, the desire to go it alone, was the American posture toward the world.
4. Although the traditional era of American foreign policy came to an end with World War I, there was no discernible change in approach to such policy until after World War II.

The Instruments of Modern American Foreign Policy

1. Diplomacy is the representation of a government to other foreign governments, and it is the foreign policy instrument to which all other instruments must be subordinated.
2. The United Nations is an instrument whose usefulness to American foreign policy can too easily be underestimated.
3. The international monetary structure, which consists of the World Bank and the International Monetary Fund, was created to avoid the economic devastation that followed World War I.
4. Economic aid has been important as an instrument of American foreign policy, but it was put together as a balance between traditional values and the modern needs of a great, imperial power.
5. After World War II, the United States recognized the importance of collective security, and subsequently entered into multilateral collective security treaties and other bilateral treaties.
6. World War II broke the American cycle of demobilization-remobilization, and led to a new policy of military preparedness.

Roles Nations Play

1. There are four roles available to a nation in the conduct of its foreign policy: the Napoleonic Role, the Holy Alliance role, the balance-of-power role, and the economic expansionist role.
2. Although the United States played the Napoleonic role during the postwar era and then switched to the Holy Alliance role, the United States is now beginning to adopt all four roles, playing whichever one is appropriate to a particular region and set of circumstances.

Practice Quiz

1. Who noted that a democracy such as the United States lacked the qualities best suited for successful foreign policies?
   a. George Washington
   b. Alexis de Tocqueville
   c. Woodrow Wilson
   d. Ronald Reagan
2. Which of the following signifies an instance in which the United States government was deceitful in the pursuit of foreign policy goals?
   a. the Pentagon Papers
   b. Iran-Contra
   c. Iran-Bosnia
   d. all of the above
3. Which of the following congressional committees is not a player in foreign policy?
   a. Senate Foreign Relations Committee
   b. Senate Armed Services Committee
   c. House Armed Services Committee
   d. House Foreign Relations Committee
4. The one conclusive way in which the media affects American foreign policy is by
   a. supporting liberal positions.
   b. always being "anti-administration."
   c. causing "videomalaise."
   d. being more skeptical about Republican administrations than Democratic ones.

5. In the twentieth century, the number of nation-states
   a. has decreased greatly.
   b. has increased greatly.
   c. has remained the same.
   d. increased somewhat, but has declined steadily since World War II.

6. Which of the following terms best describes the American posture toward the world prior to the middle of the twentieth century?
   a. interventionist
   b. isolationist
   c. unilateralist
   d. none of the above

7. The United Nations' activity in Somalia and the former Yugoslavia point to a new role for the UN. Which of the following best describes that new role?
   a. humanitarian
   b. power without diplomacy
   c. arms broker
   d. "safe havens"

8. Which of the following are important international economic institutions created after World War II?
   a. the Federal Reserve
   b. the World Bank
   c. the International Monetary Fund
   d. Both b and c are correct.

9. Which of the following terms describes the idea that the development and maintenance of military strength discourages attack?
   a. deterrence
   b. containment
   c. "minuteman" theory of defense
   d. detente

10. Which of the following best describes the action taken against Iraq after its invasion of Kuwait?
    a. unilateral action by the United States
    b. bilateral action by the United States and Saudi Arabia
    c. a genuine "concert of nations"
    d. "Napoleonic censure"

CRITICAL THINKING QUESTIONS

1. In previous chapters we have learned about the political nature of most of the key players in American foreign policy. How might politics (in addition to democracy) impede the effectiveness of the United States in the international arena? Can you think of an instance in which the United States was hampered by domestic politics?

2. What is the proper balance between governmental effectiveness in international politics and the public's "right to know"? Surely, for tactical reasons the government should be able to keep some activities secret. But given the potential for abuse of governmental secrecy, how might the public hold the government accountable while preserving for the United States the tactical advantage of secrecy?

KEY TERMS

balance-of-power role the strategy whereby many countries form alliances with one or more other countries in order to counterbalance the behavior of other, usually more powerful, nation-states. (p. 742)

bilateral treaties treaties made between two nations. (p. 736)

client state a nation-state dependent upon a more powerful nation-state, but which still has enough power and resources to conduct its own foreign policy up to a point. (p. 724)

cold war the period of struggle between the United States and the former Soviet Union between the late 1940s and about 1990. (p. 728)

containment the policy used by the United States during the cold war to restrict the expansion of communism and limit the influence of the Soviet Union. (p. 728)

deterrence the development and maintenance of military strength as a means of discouraging attack. (p. 738)

diplomacy the representation of a government to other foreign governments. (p. 729)

economic expansionist role the strategy often pursued by capitalist countries to adopt foreign policies that will maximize the success of domestic corporations in their dealings with other countries. (p. 742)

executive agreement an agreement, made between the president and another country, that has the force of a treaty but does not require the Senate's "advice and consent." (p. 720)

Holy Alliance role a strategy pursued by a superpower to prevent any change in the existing distribution of power among nation-states, even if this requires intervention into the internal affairs of another country in order to keep a ruler from being overturned. (p. 742)

International Monetary Fund (IMF) an institution established in 1944 at Bretton Woods, New Hampshire, which provides loans and facilitates international monetary exchange. (p. 733)

Marshall Plan the U.S. European Recovery Plan, in which over $34 billion was spent for the relief, reconstruction, and economic recovery of Western Europe after World War II. (p. 734)

multilateralism a foreign policy that seeks to encourage the involvement of several nation-states in coordinated action, usually in relation to a common adversary, with terms and conditions usually specified in a multi-country treaty. (p. 728)

multilateral treaties treaties among more than two nations. (p. 736)

Napoleonic role a strategy pursued by a powerful nation to prevent aggressive actions against themselves by improving the internal state of affairs of a particular country, even if this means encouraging revolution in that country. (p. 741)

nation-state a political entity consisting of a people with some common cultural experience (nation) who also share a common political authority (state), recognized by other sovereignties (nation-states). (p. 724)

North Atlantic Treaty Organization (NATO) a treaty organization, comprising the United States, Canada, and most of western Europe, formed in 1948 to counter the perceived threat from the Soviet Union. (p. 721)

power without diplomacy a post–World War II foreign policy in which the goal was to use American power to create an international structure that could be run with a minimum of regular diplomatic involvement. (p. 731)

sovereignty supreme and independent political authority. (p. 724)

unilateralism a foreign policy that seeks to avoid international alliances, entanglements, and permanent commitments in favor of independence, neutrality, and freedom of action. (p. 727)

United Nations an organization of nations founded in 1945 to serve as a channel for negotiation and a means of settling international disputes peaceably. The UN has had frequent successes in providing a forum for negotiation and on some occasions a means of preventing international conflicts from spreading. On a number of occasions, the UN has been a convenient cover for U.S. foreign policy goals. (p. 730)

Appendix

The Declaration of Independence

In Congress, July 4, 1776

The unanimous Declaration of the thirteen united States of America,

When in the Course of human events, it becomes necessary for one people to dissolve the political bands which have connected them with another, and to assume among the powers of the earth, the separate and equal station to which the Laws of Nature and of Nature's God entitle them, a decent respect to the opinions of mankind requires that they should declare the causes which impel them to the separation.

We hold these truths to be self-evident, that all men are created equal, that they are endowed by their Creator with certain unalienable Rights, that among these are Life, Liberty and the pursuit of Happiness.—That to secure these rights, Governments are instituted among Men, deriving their just powers from the consent of the governed. —That whenever any Form of Government becomes destructive of these ends, it is the Right of the People to alter or to abolish it, and to institute new Government, laying its foundation on such principles and organizing its powers in such form, as to them shall seem most likely to effect their Safety and Happiness. Prudence, indeed, will dictate that Governments long established should not be changed for light and transient causes; and accordingly all experience hath shewn, that mankind are more disposed to suffer, while evils are sufferable, than to right themselves by abolishing the forms to which they are accustomed. But when a long train of abuses and usurpations, pursuing invariably the same Object evinces a design to reduce them under absolute Despotism, it is their right, it is their duty, to throw off such Government, and to provide new Guards for their future security.—Such has been the patient sufferance of these Colonies; and such is now the necessity which constrains them to alter their former Systems of Government. The history of the present King of Great Britain is a history of repeated injuries and usurpations, all having in direct object the establishment of an absolute Tyranny over these States. To prove this, let Facts be submitted to a candid world.

He has refused his Assent to Laws, the most wholesome and necessary for the public good.

He has forbidden his Governors to pass Laws of immediate and pressing importance, unless suspended in their operation till his Assent should be obtained; and when so suspended, he has utterly neglected to attend to them.

He has refused to pass other Laws for the accommodation of large districts of people, unless those people would relinquish the right of Representation in the Legislature, a right inestimable to them and formidable to tyrants only.

He has called together legislative bodies at places unusual, uncomfortable, and distant from the depository of their public Records, for the sole purpose of fatiguing them into compliance with his measures.

He has dissolved Representative Houses repeatedly, for opposing with manly firmness his invasions on the rights of the people.

He has refused for a long time, after such dissolutions, to cause others to be elected; whereby the Legislative powers, incapable of Annihilation, have returned to the People at large for their exercise; the State remaining in the mean time exposed to all the dangers of invasion from without, and convulsions within.

He has endeavoured to prevent the population of these States; for that purpose obstructing the Laws for Naturalization of Foreigners; refusing to pass others to encourage their migrations hither, and raising the conditions of new Appropriations of Lands.

He has obstructed the Administration of Justice, by refusing his Assent to Laws for establishing Judiciary powers.

He has made Judges dependent on his Will alone, for the tenure of their offices, and the amount and payment of their salaries.

He has erected a multitude of New Offices, and sent hither swarms of Officers to harrass our people, and eat out their substance.

He has kept among us, in times of peace, Standing Armies without the Consent of our legislatures.

He has affected to render the Military independent of and superior to the Civil power.

He has combined with others to subject us to a jurisdiction foreign to our constitution, and unacknowledged by our laws; giving his Assent to their Acts of pretended Legislation:

For Quartering large bodies of armed troops among us:

For protecting them, by a mock Trial, from punishment for any Murders which they should commit on the Inhabitants of these States:

For cutting off our Trade with all parts of the world:

For imposing Taxes on us without our Consent:

For depriving us in many cases, of the benefits of Trial by Jury:

For transporting us beyond Seas to be tried for pretended offences:

For abolishing the free System of English Laws in a neighboring Province, establishing therein an Arbitrary government, and enlarging its Boundaries so as to render it at once an example and fit instrument for introducing the same absolute rule into these Colonies:

For taking away our Charters, abolishing our most valuable Laws, and altering fundamentally the Forms of our Governments:

For suspending our own Legislatures, and declaring themselves invested with power to legislate for us in all cases whatsoever.

He has abdicated Government here, by declaring us out of his Protection and waging War against us.

He has plundered our seas, ravaged our Coasts, burnt our towns, and destroyed the lives of our people.

He is at this time transporting large Armies of foreign Mercenaries to compleat the works of death, desolation and tyranny, already begun with circumstances of Cruelty & perfidy scarcely paralleled in the most barbarous ages, and totally unworthy the Head of a civilized nation.

He has constrained our fellow Citizens taken Captive on the high Seas to bear Arms against their Country, to become the executioners of their friends and Brethren, or to fall themselves by their Hands.

He has excited domestic insurrections amongst us, and has endeavoured to bring on the inhabitants of our frontiers, the merciless Indian Savages, whose known rule of warfare, is an undistinguished destruction of all ages, sexes and conditions.

In every stage of these Oppressions We have Petitioned for Redress in the most humble terms: Our repeated Petitions have been answered only by repeated injury. A Prince whose character is thus marked by every act which may define a Tyrant, is unfit to be the ruler of a free people.

Nor have We been wanting in attentions to our Brittish brethren. We have warned them from time to time of attempts by their legislature to extend an unwarrantable jurisdiction over us. We have reminded them of the circumstances of our emigration and settlement here. We have appealed to their native justice and magnanimity, and we have conjured them by the ties of our common kindred to disavow these usurpations, which, would inevitably interrupt our connections and correspondence. They too have been deaf to the voice of justice and of consanguinity. We must, therefore, acquiesce in the necessity, which denounces our Separation, and hold them, as we hold the rest of mankind, Enemies in War, in Peace Friends.

We, Therefore, the Representatives of the United States of America, in General Congress, Assembled, appealing to the Supreme Judge of the world for the rectitude of our intentions, do, in the Name, and by Authority of the good People of these Colonies, solemnly publish and declare, That these United Colonies are, and of Right ought to be Free and Independent States; that they are Absolved from all Allegiance to the British Crown, and that all political connection between them and the State of Great Britain, is and ought to be totally dissolved; and that as Free and Independent States, they have full Power to levy War, conclude Peace, contract Alliances, establish Commerce, and to do all other Acts and Things which Independent States may of right do. And for the support of this Declaration, with a firm reliance on the protection of divine Providence, we mutually pledge to each other our Lives, our Fortunes and our sacred Honor.

The foregoing Declaration was, by order of Congress, engrossed, and signed by the following members:

John Hancock

NEW HAMPSHIRE
Josiah Bartlett
William Whipple
Matthew Thornton

MASSACHUSETTS BAY
Samuel Adams
John Adams
Robert Treat Paine
Elbridge Gerry

RHODE ISLAND
Stephen Hopkins
William Ellery

CONNECTICUT
Roger Sherman
Samuel Huntington
William Williams
Oliver Wolcott

NEW YORK
William Floyd
Philip Livingston
Francis Lewis
Lewis Morris

NEW JERSEY
Richard Stockton
John Witherspoon
Francis Hopkinson
John Hart
Abraham Clark

PENNSYLVANIA
Robert Morris
Benjamin Rush
Benjamin Franklin
John Morton
George Clymer
James Smith
George Taylor
James Wilson
George Ross

DELAWARE
Caesar Rodney
George Read
Thomas M'Kean

MARYLAND
Samuel Chase
William Paca
Thomas Stone
Charles Carroll,
of Carrollton

VIRGINIA
George Wythe
Richard Henry Lee
Thomas Jefferson
Benjamin Harrison
Thomas Nelson, Jr.
Francis Lightfoot Lee
Carter Braxton

NORTH CAROLINA
William Hooper
Joseph Hewes
John Penn

SOUTH CAROLINA
Edward Rutledge
Thomas Heyward, Jr.
Thomas Lynch, Jr.
Arthur Middleton

GEORGIA
Button Gwinnett
Lyman Hall
George Walton

Resolved, That copies of the Declaration be sent to the several assemblies, conventions, and committees, or councils of safety, and to the several commanding officers of the continental troops; that it be proclaimed in each of the United States, at the head of the army.

The Articles of Confederation

Agreed to by Congress November 15, 1777;
ratified and in force March 1, 1781

To all whom these Presents shall come, we the undersigned Delegates of the States affixed to our Names, send greeting. Whereas the Delegates of the United States of America, in Congress assembled, did, on the fifteenth day of November, in the Year of Our Lord One thousand Seven Hundred and Seventy seven, and in the Second Year of the Independence of America, agree to certain articles of Confederation and perpetual Union between the States of Newhampshire, Massachusetts-bay, Rhodeisland and Providence Plantations, Connecticut, New-York, New-Jersey, Pennsylvania, Delaware, Maryland, Virginia, North-Carolina, South-Carolina and Georgia in the words following, viz. "Articles of Confederation and perpetual Union between the states of Newhampshire, Massachusetts-bay, Rhodeisland and Providence Plantations, Connecticut, New-York, New-Jersey, Pennsylvania, Delaware, Maryland, Virginia, North-Carolina, South-Carolina and Georgia.

Art. I. The Stile of this confederacy shall be "The United States of America."

Art. II. Each state retains its sovereignty, freedom and independence, and every Power, Jurisdiction and right, which is not by this confederation expressly delegated to the United States, in Congress assembled.

Art. III. The said states hereby severally enter into a firm league of friendship with each other, for their common defence, the security of their Liberties, and their mutual and general welfare, binding themselves to assist each other, against all force offered to, or attacks made upon them, or any of them, on account of religion, sovereignty, trade, or any other pretence whatever.

Art. IV. The better to secure and perpetuate mutual friendship and intercourse among the people of the different states in this union, the free inhabitants of each of these states, paupers, vagabonds and fugitives from Justice excepted, shall be entitled to all privileges and immunities of free citizens in the several states; and the people of each state shall have free ingress and regress to and from any other state, and shall enjoy therein all the privileges of trade and commerce, subject to the same duties, impositions and restrictions as the inhabitants thereof respectively, provided that such restriction shall not extend so far as to prevent the removal of property imported into any state, to any other state, of which the Owner is an inhabitant; provided also that no imposition, duties or restriction shall be laid by any state, on the property of the united states, or either of them.

If any Person guilty of, or charged with treason, felony, or other high misdemeanor in any state, shall flee from Justice, and be found in any of the united states, he shall, upon demand of the Governor or executive power, of the state from which he fled, be delivered up and removed to the state having jurisdiction of his offence.

Full faith and credit shall be given in each of these states to the records, acts and judicial proceedings of the courts and magistrates of every other state.

Art. V. For the more convenient management of the general interests of the united states, delegates shall be annually appointed in such manner as the legislature of each state shall direct, to meet in Congress on the first Monday in November, in every year, with a power reserved to each state, to recall its delegates, or any of them, at any time within the year, and to send others in their stead, for the remainder of the Year.

No state shall be represented in Congress by less than two, nor by more than seven Members; and no person shall be capable of being a delegate for more than three years in any term of six years; nor shall any person, being a delegate, be capable of holding any office under the united states, for which he, or another for his benefit receives any salary, fees or emolument of any kind.

Each state shall maintain its own delegates in a meeting of the states, and while they act as members of the committee of the states.

In determining questions in the united states, in Congress assembled, each state shall have one vote.

Freedom of speech and debate in Congress shall not be

impeached or questioned in any Court, or place out of Congress, and the members of congress shall be protected in their persons from arrests and imprisonments, during the time of their going to and from, and attendance on congress, except for treason, felony, or breach of the peace.

Art. VI. No state without the Consent of the united states in congress assembled, shall send any embassy to, or receive any embassy from, or enter into any conference, agreement, or alliance or treaty with any King, prince or state; nor shall any person holding any office or profit or trust under the united states, or any of them, accept of any present, emolument, office or title of any kind whatever from any king, prince or foreign state; nor shall the united states in congress assembled, or any of them, grant any title of nobility.

No two or more states shall enter into any treaty, confederation or alliance whatever between them, without the consent of the united states in congress assembled, specifying accurately the purposes for which the same is to be entered into, and how long it shall continue.

No state shall lay any imposts or duties, which may interfere with any stipulations in treaties, entered into by the united states in congress assembled, with any king, prince or state, in pursuance of any treaties already proposed by congress, to the courts of France and Spain.

No vessels of war shall be kept up in time of peace by any state, except such number only, as shall be deemed necessary by the united states in congress assembled, for the defence of such state, or its trade; nor shall any body of forces be kept up by any state, in time of peace, except such number only, as in the judgment of the united states, in congress assembled, shall be deemed requisite to garrison the forts necessary for the defence of such state; but every state shall always keep up a well regulated and disciplined militia, sufficiently armed and accoutred, and shall provide and constantly have ready for use, in public stores, a due number of field pieces and tents, and a proper quantity of arms, ammunition and camp equipage.

No state shall engage in any war without the consent of the united states in congress assembled, unless such state be actually invaded by enemies, or shall have received certain advice of a resolution being formed by some nation of Indians to invade such state, and the danger is so imminent as not to admit of a delay, till the united states in congress asssembled can be consulted; nor shall any state grant commissions to any ships or vessels of war, nor letters of marque or reprisal, except it be after a declaration of war by the united states in congress assembled, and then only against the kingdom or state and the subjects thereof, against which war has been so declared, and under such regulations as shall be established by the united states in congress assembled, unless such state be infested by pirates; in which case vessels of war may be fitted out for that occasion, and kept so long as the danger shall continue, or until the united states in congress assembled shall determine otherwise.

Art. VII. When land-forces are raised by any state for the common defence, all officers of or under the rank of colonel, shall be appointed by the legislature of each state respectively, by whom such forces shall be raised, or in such manner as such state shall direct, and all vacancies shall be filled up by the state which first made the appointment.

Art. VIII. All charges of war, and all other expences that shall be incurred for the common defence or general welfare, and allowed by the united states in congress assembled, shall be defrayed out of a common treasury, which shall be supplied by the several states in proportion to the value of all land within each state, granted to or surveyed for any Person, as such land and the buildings and improvements thereon shall be estimated according to such mode as the united states in congress assembled, shall from time to time direct and appoint.

The taxes for paying that proportion shall be laid and levied by the authority and direction of the legislatures of the several states within the time agreed upon by the united states in congress assembled.

Art. IX. The united states in congress assembled, shall have the sole and exclusive right and power of determining on peace and war, except in the cases mentioned in the sixth article—of sending and receiving ambassadors—entering into treaties and alliances, provided that no treaty of commerce shall be made whereby the legislative power of the respective states shall be restrained from imposing such imposts and duties on foreigners, as their own people are subjected to, or from prohibiting the exportation of any species of goods or commodities whatsoever—of establishing rules for deciding in all cases, what captures on land or water shall be legal, and in what manner prizes taken by land or naval forces in the service of the united states shall be divided or appropriated—of granting letters of marque and reprisal in times of peace—appointing courts for the trial of piracies and felonies committed on the high seas and establishing courts for receiving and determining finally appeals in all cases of captures, provided that no member of congress shall be appointed a judge of any of the said courts.

The united states in congress assembled shall also be the last resort on appeal in all disputes and differences now subsisting or that hereafter may arise between two or more states concerning boundary, jurisdiction or any other cause whatever; which authority shall always be exercised in the manner following. Whenever the legislative or executive authority or lawful agent of any state in controversy with another shall present a petition to congress stating the matter in question and praying for a hearing, notice thereof shall be given by order of congress to the legislative or executive authority of the other state in controversy, and a day assigned for the appearance of the parties by their lawful agents, who shall then be directed to appoint by joint consent, commissioners or judges to constitute a court for hearing and determining the matter in question: but if they cannot agree, congress shall name three persons out of each of the united states, and from the list of such persons each party shall alternately strike out one, the petitioners beginning, until the number shall be reduced to thirteen; and from that number not less than seven, nor more than nine names as congress shall direct, shall in the presence of congress be drawn out by lot, and the persons whose names shall be so drawn or any five of them, shall be commissioners or judges, to hear and finally determine the controversy, so always as a major part of the judges who shall hear the cause shall agree in the determination: and if either party shall neglect to attend at the day appointed, without shewing reasons, which congress shall judge sufficient, or being present shall refuse to strike, the congress shall proceed to nominate three persons out of each state, and the secretary of congress shall strike in behalf of such party absent or refusing; and the judgment and sentence of the court to be appointed, in the manner before prescribed, shall be final and conclusive; and if any of the parties shall refuse to submit to the authority of such court, or to appear to defend their claim or cause, the court shall nevertheless proceed to pronounce sentence, or judgment, which shall in like manner be final and decisive, the judgment or sentence and other proceedings being in either case transmitted to congress, and lodged among the acts of congress for the security of the parties concerned: provided that every commissioner, before he sits in judgment, shall take an oath to be administered by one of the judges of the supreme or superior court of the state, where the cause shall be tried, "well and truly to hear and determine the matter in question, according to the best of his judgment, without favour, affection or hope of reward:" provided also, that no state shall be deprived of territory for the benefit of the united states.

All controversies concerning the private right of soil claimed under different grants of two or more states, whose jurisdictions as they may respect such lands, and the states which passed such grants are adjusted, the said grants or either of them being at the same time claimed to have originated antecedent to such settlement of jurisdiction, shall on the petition of either party to the congress of the united states, be finally determined as near as may be in the same manner as is before prescribed for deciding disputes respecting territorial jurisdiction between different states.

The united states in congress assembled shall also have the sole and exclusive right and power of regulating the alloy and value of coin struck by their own authority, or by that of the respective states—fixing the standard of weights and measures throughout the united states—regulating the trade and managing all affairs with the Indians, not members of any of the states, provided that the legislative right of any state within its own limits be not infringed or violated—establishing and regulating post-offices from one state to another, throughout all the united states, and exacting such postage on the papers passing thro' the same as may be requisite to defray the expences of the said office—appointing all officers of the land forces, in the service of the united states, excepting regimental officers—appointing all the officers of the naval forces, and commissioning all officers whatever in the service of the united states—making rules for the government and regulation of the said land and naval forces, and directing their operations.

The united states in congress assembled shall have authority to appoint a committee, to sit in the recess of congress, to be denominated "A Committee of the States," and to consist of one delegate from each state; and to appoint such other committees and civil officers as may be necessary for managing the general affairs of the united states under their direction—to appoint one of their number to preside, provided that no person be allowed to serve in the office of president more than one year in any term of three years; to ascertain the necessary sums of Money to be raised for the service of the united states, and to appropriate and apply the same for defraying the public expenses—to borrow money, or emit bills on the credit of the united states, transmitting every half year to the respective states an account of the sums of money so borrowed or emitted,—to build and equip a navy—to agree upon the number of land forces, and to make requisitions from each state for its quota, in proportion to the number of white inhabitants in such state; which requisition shall be binding, and thereupon the legislature of each state shall appoint the regimental officers, raise the men and cloath, arm and equip then in a soldier like manner, at the expense of the united states; and the officers and men so cloathed, armed and equipped shall march to the place appointed, and within the time agreed on by the united states in congress assembled: But if the united states in congress assembled shall, on consideration of circumstances judge proper that any state should not raise men, or should raise a smaller number than its quota, and that any other state should raise a greater number of men than the quota thereof, such extra number shall be raised, officered, cloathed, armed and equipped in the same manner as the quota of such state, unless the legislature of such state shall judge that such extra number cannot be safely spared out of the same, in which case they shall raise officer, cloath, arm and equip as many of such extra number as they judge can be safely spared. And the officers and men so cloathed, armed and equipped, shall march to the place appointed, and within the time agreed on by the united states in congress assembled.

The united states in congress assembled shall never engage in a war, nor grant letters of marque and reprisal in time of peace, nor enter into any treaties or alliances, nor coin money, nor regulate the value thereof, nor ascertain the sums and expenses necessary for the defence and welfare of the united states, or any of them, nor emit bills, nor borrow money on the credit of the united states, nor appropriate money, nor agree upon the number of vessels of war, to be built or purchased, or the number of land or sea forces to be raised, nor appoint a commander in chief of the army or navy, unless nine states assent to the same: nor shall a question on any other point, except for adjourning from day to day be determined, unless by the votes of a majority of the united states in congress assembled.

The congress of the united states shall have power to adjourn to any time within the year, and to any place within the united states, so that no period of adjournment be for a longer duration than the space of six Months, and shall publish the Journal of their proceedings monthly, except such parts thereof relating to treaties, alliances or military operations, as in their judgment require secrecy; and the yeas and nays of the delegates of each state on any question shall be entered on the Journal, when it is desired by any delegate; and the delegates of a state, or any of them, at his or their request shall be furnished with a transcript of the said Journal, except such parts as are above excepted, to lay before the legislatures of the several states.

Art. X. The committee of the states, or any nine of them, shall be authorised to execute, in the recess of congress, such of the powers of congress as the united states in congress assembled, by the consent of nine states, shall from time to time think expedient to vest them with; provided that no power be delegated to the said committee, for the exercise of which, by the articles of confederation, the voice of nine states in the congress of the united states assembled is requisite.

Art. XI. Canada acceding to this confederation, and joining in the measures of the united states, shall be admitted into, and entitled to all the advantages of this union: but no other colony shall be admitted into the same, unless such admission be agreed to by nine states.

Art. XII. All bills of credit emitted, monies borrowed and debts contracted by, or under the authority of congress, before the assembling of the united states, in pursuance of the present confederation, shall be deemed and considered as a charge against the united states, for payment and satisfaction whereof the said united states and the public faith are hereby solemnly pledged.

Art. XIII. Every state shall abide by the determinations of the united states in congress assembled, on all questions which by this confederation are submitted to them. And the Articles of this confederation shall be inviolably observed by every state, and the union shall be perpetual; nor shall any alteration at any time hereafter be made in any of them; unless such alteration be agreed to in a congress of the united states, and be afterwards confirmed by the legislatures of every state.

And Whereas it hath pleased the Great Governor of the World to incline the hearts of the legislatures we respectively represent in congress, to approve of, and to authorize us to ratify the said articles of confederation and perpetual union. Know Ye that we the undersigned delegates, by virtue of the power and authority to us given for that purpose, do by these presents, in the name and in behalf of our respective constituents, fully and entirely ratify and confirm each and every of the said articles of confederation and perpetual union, and all and singular the matters and things therein contained: And we do further solemnly plight and engage the faith of our respective constituents, that they shall abide by the determinations of the united states in congress assembled, on all questions, which by the said confederation are submitted to them. And that the articles thereof shall be inviolably observed by the states we respectively represent, and that the union shall be perpetual. In Witness whereof we have hereunto set our hands in Congress. Done at Philadelphia in the state of Pennsylvania the ninth day of July, in the Year of our Lord one Thousand seven Hundred and Seventy-eight, and in the third year of the independence of America.

The Constitution of the United States of America

[PREAMBLE]

We the People of the United States, in Order to form a more perfect Union, establish Justice, insure domestic Tranquility, provide for the common defence, promote the general Welfare, and secure the Blessings of Liberty to ourselves and our Posterity, do ordain and establish this Constitution for the United States of America.

ARTICLE I

Section 1

[LEGISLATIVE POWERS]

All legislative Powers herein granted shall be vested in a Congress of the United States, which shall consist of a Senate and House of Representatives.

Section 2

[HOUSE OF REPRESENTATIVES, HOW CONSTITUTED, POWER OF IMPEACHMENT]

The House of Representatives shall be composed of Members chosen every second Year by the People of the several States, and the Electors in each State shall have the Qualifications requisite for Electors of the most numerous Branch of the State Legislature.

No Person shall be a Representative who shall not have attained to the Age of twenty five Years, and been seven Years a Citizen of the United States, and who shall not, when elected, be an Inhabitant of that State in which he shall be chosen.

Representatives and *direct Taxes*[1] shall be apportioned among the several States which may be included within this Union, according to their respective Numbers, *which shall be determined by adding to the whole Number of free Persons, including those bound to Service for a Term of Years,* and excluding Indians not taxed, *three fifths of all other Persons.*[2] The actual Enumeration shall be made within three Years after the first Meeting of the Congress of the United States, and within every subsequent Term of ten Years, in such Manner as they shall by Law direct. The Number of Representatives shall not exceed one for every thirty Thousand, but each State shall have at Least one Representative; *and until such enumeration shall be made, the State of New Hampshire shall be entitled to chuse three, Massachusetts eight, Rhode-Island and Providence Plantations one, Connecticut five, New-York six, New Jersey four, Pennsylvania eight, Delaware one, Maryland six, Virginia ten, North Carolina five, South Carolina five, and Georgia three.*[3]

When vacancies happen in the Representation from any State, the Executive Authority thereof shall issue Writs of Election to fill such Vacancies.

The House of Representatives shall chuse their Speaker and other Officers; and shall have the sole Power of Impeachment.

Section 3

[THE SENATE, HOW CONSTITUTED, IMPEACHMENT TRIALS]

The Senate of the United States shall be composed of two Senators from each State, *chosen by the Legislature thereof,*[4] for six Years; and each Senator shall have one Vote.

[1]Modified by Sixteenth Amendment.

[2]Modified by Fourteenth Amendment.

[3]Temporary provision.

[4]Modified by Seventeenth Amendment.

Immediately after they shall be assembled in Consequence of the first Election, they shall be divided as equally as may be into three Classes. The Seats of the Senators of the first Class shall be vacated at the Expiration of the second Year, of the second Class at the Expiration of the fourth Year, and of the third Class at the Expiration of the sixth Year, so that one third may be chosen every second Year; *and if Vacancies happen by Resignation, or otherwise, during the Recess of the Legislature of any State, the Executive thereof may make temporary Appointments until the next Meeting of the Legislature, which shall then fill such Vacancies.*[5]

No Person shall be a Senator who shall not have attained to the Age of thirty Years, and been nine Years a Citizen of the United States, and who shall not, when elected, be an Inhabitant of that State for which he shall be chosen.

The Vice President of the United States shall be President of the Senate, but shall have no Vote, unless they be equally divided.

The Senate shall chuse their other Officers, and also a President pro tempore, in the Absence of the Vice President, or when he shall exercise the Office of President of the United States.

The Senate shall have the sole Power to try all Impeachments. When sitting for that Purpose, they shall be on Oath or Affirmation. When the President of the United States is tried, the Chief Justice shall preside: And no Person shall be convicted without the Concurrence of two thirds of the Members present.

Judgment in Cases of Impeachment shall not extend further than to removal from Office, and disqualification to hold and enjoy any Office of honor, Trust or Profit under the United States: but the Party convicted shall nevertheless be liable and subject to Indictment, Trial, Judgment and Punishment, according to Law.

Section 4

[ELECTION OF SENATORS AND REPRESENTATIVES]

The Times, Places and Manner of holding Elections for Senators and Representatives, shall be prescribed in each State by the Legislature thereof; but the Congress may at any time by Law make or alter such Regulations, except as to the Places of chusing Senators.

The Congress shall assemble at least once in every Year, and such Meeting shall be on the first Monday in December, unless they shall by Law appoint a different Day.[6]

Section 5

[QUORUM, JOURNALS, MEETINGS, ADJOURNMENTS]

Each House shall be the Judge of the Elections, Returns and Qualifications of its own Members, and a Majority of each shall constitute a Quorum to do Business; but a smaller Number may adjourn from day to day, and may be authorized to compel the Attendance of absent Members, in such Manner, and under such Penalties as each House may provide.

Each House may determine the Rules of its Proceedings, punish its Members for disorderly Behaviour, and, with the Concurrence of two thirds, expel a Member.

Each House shall keep a Journal of its Proceedings, and from time to time publish the same, excepting such Parts as may in their Judgment require Secrecy; and the Yeas and Nays of the Members of either House on any questions shall, at the Desire of one fifth of those Present, be entered on the Journal.

Neither House, during the Session of Congress, shall, without the Consent of the other, adjourn for more than three days, nor to any other Place than that in which the two Houses shall be sitting.

Section 6

[COMPENSATION, PRIVILEGES, DISABILITIES]

The Senators and Representatives shall receive a Compensation for their Services, to be ascertained by Law, and paid out of the Treasury of the United States. They shall in all Cases, except Treason, Felony and Breach of the Peace, be privileged from Arrest during their Attendance at the Session of their respective Houses, and in going to and returning from the same; and for any Speech or Debate in either House, they shall not be questioned in any other Place.

No Senator or Representative shall, during the Time for which he was elected, be appointed to any civil Office under the Authority of the United States, which shall have been created, or the Emoluments whereof shall have been encreased during such time; and no Person holding any Office under the United States, shall be a Member of either House during his Continuance in Office.

Section 7

[PROCEDURE IN PASSING BILLS AND RESOLUTIONS]

All Bills for raising Revenue shall originate in the House of Representatives; but the Senate may propose or concur with Amendments as on other Bills.

Every Bill which shall have passed the House of Representatives and the Senate, shall, before it become a Law, be presented to the President of the United States: If he approve he shall sign it, but if not he shall return it, with his Objections to that House in which it shall have originated, who shall enter the Objections at large on their

[5]Modified by Seventeenth Amendment.

[6]Modified by Twentieth Amendment.

Journal, and proceed to reconsider it. If after such Reconsideration two thirds of that House shall agree to pass the Bill, it shall be sent, together with the Objections, to the other House, by which it shall likewise be reconsidered, and if approved by two thirds of that House, it shall become a Law. But in all such Cases the Votes of both Houses shall be determined by yeas and Nays, and the Names of the Persons voting for and against the Bill shall be entered on the Journal of each House respectively. If any Bill shall not be returned by the President within ten Days (Sundays excepted) after it shall have been presented to him, the Same shall be a Law, in like Manner as if he had signed it, unless the Congress by their Adjournment prevent its Return, in which Case it shall not be a Law.

Every Order, Resolution, or Vote to which the Concurrence of the Senate and House of Representatives may be necessary (except on a question of Adjournment) shall be presented to the President of the United States; and before the Same shall take Effect, shall be approved by him, or being disapproved by him, shall be repassed by two thirds of the Senate and House of Representatives, according to the Rules and Limitations prescribed in the Case of a Bill.

Section 8

[POWERS OF CONGRESS]

The Congress shall have Power

To lay and collect Taxes, Duties, Imposts and Excises, to pay the Debts and provide for the common Defence and general Welfare of the United States; but all Duties, Imposts and Excises shall be uniform throughout the United States;

To borrow Money on the credit of the United States;

To regulate Commerce with foreign Nations, and among the several States, and with the Indian Tribes;

To establish an uniform Rule of Naturalization, and uniform Laws on the subject of Bankruptcies throughout the United States;

To coin Money, regulate the Value thereof, and of foreign Coin, and fix the Standard of Weights and Measures;

To provide for the Punishment of counterfeiting the Securities and current Coin of the United States;

To establish Post Offices and post Roads;

To promote the Progress of Science and useful Arts, by securing for limited Times to Authors and Inventors the exclusive Right to their respective Writings and Discoveries;

To constitute Tribunals inferior to the supreme Court;

To define and punish Piracies and Felonies committed on the high Seas, and Offences against the Law of Nations;

To declare War, grant Letters of Marque and Reprisal, and make Rules concerning Captures on Land and Water;

To raise and support Armies, but no Appropriation of Money to that Use shall be for a longer Term than two Years;

To provide and maintain a Navy;

To make Rules for the Government and Regulation of the land and naval Forces;

To provide for calling forth the Militia to execute the Laws of the Union, suppress Insurrections and repel Invasions;

To provide for organizing, arming, and disciplining, the Militia, and for governing such Part of them as may be employed in the Service of the United States, reserving to the States respectively, the Appointment of the Officers, and the Authority of training the Militia according to the discipline prescribed by Congress;

To exercise exclusive Legislation in all Cases whatsoever, over such District (not exceeding ten Miles square) as may, by Cession of particular States, and the Acceptance of Congress, become the Seat of the Government of the United States, and to exercise like Authority over all Places purchased by the Consent of the Legislature of the State in which the Same shall be, for the Erection of Forts, Magazines, Arsenals, dock-Yards, and other needful Buildings;—And

To make all Laws which shall be necessary and proper for carrying into Execution the foregoing Powers, and all other Powers vested by this Constitution in the Government of the United States, or in any Department or Officer thereof.

Section 9

[SOME RESTRICTIONS ON FEDERAL POWER]

The Migration or Importation of such Persons as any of the States now existing shall think proper to admit, shall not be prohibited by the Congress prior to the Year one thousand eight hundred and eight, but a Tax or duty may be imposed on such Importation, not exceeding ten dollars for each Person.[7]

The Privilege of the Writ of Habeas Corpus shall not be suspended, unless when in Cases of Rebellion or Invasion the public Safety may require it.

No Bill of Attainder or ex post facto Law shall be passed.

No Capitation, or other direct, Tax shall be laid, unless in Proportion to the Census or Enumeration herein before directed to be taken.[8]

No Tax or Duty shall be laid on Articles exported from any State.

No Preference shall be given by any Regulation of Commerce or Revenue to the Ports of one State over those of another; nor shall Vessels bound to, or from, one State, be obliged to enter, clear, or pay Duties in another.

[7]Temporary provision.

[8]Modified by Sixteenth Amendment.

No Money shall be drawn from the Treasury, but in Consequence of Appropriations made by Law; and a regular Statement and Account of the Receipts and Expenditures of all public Money shall be published from time to time.

No Title of Nobility shall be granted by the United States: And no Person holding any Office of Profit or Trust under them, shall, without the Consent of the Congress, accept of any present, Emolument, Office, or Title, of any kind whatever, from any King, Prince, or foreign State.

Section 10

[RESTRICTIONS UPON POWERS OF STATES]

No State shall enter into any Treaty, Alliance, or Confederation; grant Letters of Marque and Reprisal; coin Money; emit Bills of Credit; make any Thing but gold and silver Coin a Tender in Payment of Debts; pass any Bill of Attainder, ex post facto Law, or Law impairing the Obligation of Contracts, or grant any Title of Nobility.

No State shall, without the Consent of the Congress, lay any Imposts or Duties on Imports or Exports, except what may be absolutely necessary for executing it's inspection Laws: and the net Produce of all Duties and Imposts, laid by any State on Imports or Exports, shall be for the Use of the Treasury of the United States; and all such Laws shall be subject to the Revision and Controul of the Congress.

No State shall, without the Consent of Congress, lay any Duty of Tonnage, keep Troops, or Ships of War in time of Peace, enter into any Agreement or Compact with another State, or with a foreign Power, or engage in War, unless actually invaded, or in such imminent Danger as will not admit of delay.

Article II

Section 1

[EXECUTIVE POWER, ELECTION, QUALIFICATIONS OF THE PRESIDENT]

The executive Power shall be vested in a President of the United States of America. *He shall hold his Office during the Term of four Years, and, together with the Vice President, chosen for the same Term, be elected, as follows*[9]

Each State shall appoint, in such Manner as the Legislature thereof may direct, a Number of Electors, equal to the whole Number of Senators and Representatives to which the State may be entitled in the Congress: but no Senator or Representative, or Person holding an Office of Trust or Profit under the United States, shall be appointed an Elector.

The electors shall meet in their respective States, and vote by ballot for two Persons, of whom one at least shall not be an Inhabitant of the same State with themselves. And they shall make a List of all the Persons voted for, and of the Number of Votes for each; which List they shall sign and certify, and transmit sealed to the Seat of the Government of the United States, directed to the President of the Senate. The President of the Senate shall, in the Presence of the Senate and House of Representatives, open all the Certificates, and the Votes shall then be counted. The Person having the greatest Number of Votes shall be the President, if such Number be a Majority of the whole Number of Electors appointed; and if there be more than one who have such Majority, and have an equal Number of Votes, then the House of Representatives shall immediately chuse by Ballot one of them for President; and if no Person have a Majority, then from the five highest on the List the said House shall in like Manner chuse the President. But in chusing the President, the Votes shall be taken by States, the Representation from each State having one Vote; A quorum for this Purpose shall consist of a Member or Members from two thirds of the States, and a Majority of all the States shall be necessary to a Choice. In every Case, after the Choice of the President, the person having the greatest Number of Votes of the Electors shall be the Vice President. But if there should remain two or more who have equal Votes, the Senate shall chuse from them by Ballot the Vice President.[10]

The Congress may determine the Time of chusing the Electors, and the Day on which they shall give their Votes; which Day shall be the same throughout the United States.

No Person except a natural born Citizen, or a Citizen of the United States, at the time of the Adoption of this Constitution, shall be eligible to the Office of President; neither shall any Person be eligible to that Office who shall not have attained to the Age of thirty five Years, and been fourteen Years a Resident within the United States.

In Case of the Removal of the President from Office, or his Death, Resignation, or Inability to discharge the Powers and Duties of the said Office, the Same shall devolve on the Vice President, and the Congress may by Law provide for the Case of Removal, Death, Resignation or Inability, both of the President and Vice President, declaring what Officer shall then act as President, and such Officer shall act accordingly, until the Disability be removed, or a President shall be elected.

The President shall, at stated Times, receive for his Services, a Compensation, which shall neither be increased nor diminished during the Period for which he shall have been elected, and he shall not receive within that Period any other Emolument from the United States, or any of them.

[9]Number of terms limited to two by Twenty-second Amendment.

[10]Modified by Twelfth and Twentieth Amendments.

Before he enter on the Execution of his Office, he shall take the following Oath or Affirmation:—"I do solemnly swear (or affirm) that I will faithfully execute the Office of President of the United States, and will to the best of my Ability, preserve, protect and defend the Constitution of the United States."

Section 2

[POWERS OF THE PRESIDENT]

The President shall be Commander in Chief of the Army and Navy of the United States, and of the Militia of the several States, when called into the actual Service of the United States; he may require the Opinion, in writing, of the principal Officer in each of the executive Departments, upon any Subject relating to the Duties of their respective Offices, and he shall have Power to grant Reprieves and Pardons for Offences against the United States, except in Cases of Impeachment.

He shall have Power, by and with the Advice and Consent of the Senate, to make Treaties, provided two thirds of the Senators present concur; and he shall nominate, and by and with the Advice and Consent of the Senate, shall appoint Ambassadors, other public Ministers and Consuls, Judges of the supreme Court, and all other Officers of the United States, whose Appointments are not herein otherwise provided for, and which shall be established by Law: but the Congress may by Law vest the Appointment of such inferior Officers, as they think proper, in the President alone, in the Courts of Law, or in the Heads of Departments.

The President shall have Power to fill up all Vacancies that may happen during the Recess of the Senate, by granting Commissions which shall expire at the End of their next Session.

Section 3

[POWERS AND DUTIES OF THE PRESIDENT]

He shall from time to time give to the Congress Information of the State of the Union, and recommend to their Consideration such Measures as he shall judge necessary and expedient; he may, on extraordinary Occasions, convene both Houses, or either of them, and in Case of Disagreement between them, with Respect to the Time of Adjournment, he may adjourn them to such Time as he shall think proper; he shall receive Ambassadors and other public Ministers; he shall take Care that the Laws be faithfully executed, and shall Commission all the Officers of the United States.

Section 4

[IMPEACHMENT]

The President, Vice President and all civil Officers of the United States, shall be removed from Office on Impeachment for, and Conviction of, Treason, Bribery, or other high Crimes and Misdemeanors.

ARTICLE III

Section 1

[JUDICIAL POWER, TENURE OF OFFICE]

The judicial Power of the United States, shall be vested in one supreme Court, and in such inferior Courts as the Congress may from time to time ordain and establish. The Judges, both of the supreme and inferior Courts, shall hold their Offices during good Behaviour, and shall, at stated Times, receive for their Services, a Compensation, which shall not be diminished during their Continuance in Office.

Section 2

[JURISDICTION]

The judicial Power shall extend to all Cases, in Law and Equity, arising under this Constitution, the Laws of the United States, and Treaties made, or which shall be made, under their Authority;—to all Cases affecting Ambassadors, other public Ministers and Consuls;—to all Cases of admiralty and maritime Jurisdiction;—to Controversies to which the United States shall be a Party;—to Controversies between two or more States;—*between a State and Citizens of another State;*—between Citizens of different States,—between Citizens of the same State claiming Lands under Grants of different States, *and between a State,* or the Citizens thereof, *and foreign States, Citizens or Subjects.*[11]

In all Cases affecting Ambassadors, other public Ministers and Consuls, and those in which a State shall be Party, the supreme Court shall have original Jurisdiction. In all the other Cases before mentioned, the supreme Court shall have appellate Jurisdiction, both as to Law and Fact, with such Exceptions, and under such Regulations as the Congress shall make.

The Trial of all Crimes, except in Cases of Impeachment, shall be by Jury; and such Trial shall be held in the State where the said Crimes shall have been committed; but when not committed within any State, the Trial shall be at such Place or Places as the Congress may by Law have directed.

Section 3

[TREASON, PROOF, AND PUNISHMENT]

Treason against the United States, shall consist only in levying War against them, or in adhering to their Enemies, giving them Aid and Comfort. No Person shall be con-

[11]Modified by Eleventh Amendment.

victed of Treason unless on the Testimony of two Witnesses to the same overt Act, or on Confession in open Court.

The Congress shall have Power to declare the Punishment of Treason, but no Attainder of Treason shall work Corruption of Blood, or Forfeiture except during the Life of the Person attainted.

ARTICLE IV

Section 1

[FAITH AND CREDIT AMONG STATES]

Full Faith and Credit shall be given in each State to the public Acts, Records, and judicial Proceedings of every other State. And the Congress may by general Laws prescribe the Manner in which such Acts, Records and Proceedings shall be proved, and the Effect thereof.

Section 2

[PRIVILEGES AND IMMUNITIES, FUGITIVES]

The Citizens of each State shall be entitled to all Privileges and Immunities of Citizens in the several States.

A Person charged in any State with Treason, Felony or other Crime, who shall flee from Justice, and be found in another State, shall on Demand of the executive Authority of the State from which he fled, be delivered up, to be removed to the State having Jurisdiction of the Crime.

No person held to Service or Labour in one State, under the Laws thereof, escaping into another, shall, in Consequence of any Law or Regulation therein, be discharged from such Service or Labour, but shall be delivered up on Claim of the Party to whom such Service or Labour may be due.[12]

Section 3

[ADMISSION OF NEW STATES]

New States may be admitted by the Congress into this Union; but no new State shall be formed or erected within the Jurisdiction of any other State; nor any State be formed by the Junction of two or more States, or Parts of States, without the Consent of the Legislatures of the States concerned as well as of the Congress.

The Congress shall have Power to dispose of and make all needful Rules and Regulations respecting the Territory or other Property belonging to the United States; and nothing in this Constitution shall be so construed as to Prejudice any Claims of the United States, or of any particular State.

Section 4

[GUARANTEE OF REPUBLICAN GOVERNMENT]

The United States shall guarantee to every State in this Union a Republican Form of Government, and shall protect each of them against Invasion; and on Application of the Legislature, or of the Executive (when the Legislature cannot be convened), against domestic Violence.

ARTICLE V

[AMENDMENT OF THE CONSTITUTION]

The Congress, whenever two thirds of both Houses shall deem it necessary, shall propose Amendments to this Constitution, or, on the Application of the Legislatures of two thirds of the several States, shall call a Convention for proposing Amendments, which, in either Case, shall be valid to all Intents and Purposes, as Part of this Constitution, when ratified by the Legislatures of three fourths of the several States, or by Conventions in three fourths thereof, as the one or the other Mode of Ratification may be proposed by the Congress; *Provided that no Amendment which may be made prior to the Year One thousand eight hundred and eight shall in any Manner affect the first and fourth Clauses in the Ninth Section of the first Article;*[13] and that no State, without its Consent, shall be deprived of its equal Suffrage in the Senate.

ARTICLE VI

[DEBTS, SUPREMACY, OATH]

All Debts contracted and Engagements entered into, before the Adoption of this Constitution, shall be as valid against the United States under this Constitution, as under the Confederation.

This Constitution, and the Laws of the United States which shall be made in Pursuance thereof; and all Treaties made, or which shall be made, under the Authority of the United States, shall be the supreme Law of the Land; and the Judges in every State shall be bound thereby, any Thing in the Constitution or Laws of any State to the Contrary notwithstanding.

The Senators and Representatives before mentioned, and the Members of the several State Legislatures, and all executive and judicial Officers, both of the United States and of the several States, shall be bound by Oath or Affirmation, to support this Constitution; but no religious Test shall be required as a Qualification to any Office or public Trust under the United States.

[12] Repealed by the Thirteenth Amendment.

[13] Temporary provision.

Article VII

[RATIFICATION AND ESTABLISHMENT]

The Ratification of the Conventions of nine States, shall be sufficient for the Establishment of this Constitution between the States so ratifying the Same.[14]

Done in Convention by the Unanimous Consent of the States present the Seventeenth Day of September in the Year of our Lord one thousand seven hundred and Eighty seven and of the Independence of the United States of America the Twelfth. *In Witness* whereof We have hereunto subscribed our Names,

G:° WASHINGTON—
Presidt. and deputy from Virginia

NEW HAMPSHIRE
John Langdon
Nicholas Gilman

MASSACHUSETTS
Nathaniel Gorham
Rufus King

CONNECTICUT
Wm. Saml. Johnson
Roger Sherman

NEW YORK
Alexander Hamilton

NEW JERSEY
Wil: Livingston
David Brearley
Wm. Paterson
Jona: Dayton

PENNSYLVANIA
B Franklin
Thomas Mifflin
Robt. Morris
Geo. Clymer
Thos. FitzSimons
Jared Ingersoll
James Wilson
Gouv Morris

DELAWARE
Geo: Read
Gunning Bedford jun
John Dickinson
Richard Bassett
Jaco: Broom

MARYLAND
James McHenry
Dan of St Thos. Jenifer
Danl. Carroll

VIRGINIA
John Blair—
James Madison Jr.

NORTH CAROLINA
Wm. Blount
Richd. Dobbs Spaight
Hu Williamson

SOUTH CAROLINA
J. Rutledge
Charles Cotesworth Pinckney
Charles Pinckney
Pierce Butler

GEORGIA
William Few
Abr Baldwin

[14]The Constitution was submitted on September 17, 1787, by the Constitutional Convention, was ratified by the conventions of several states at various dates up to May 29, 1790, and became effective on March 4, 1789.

Amendments to the Constitution

Proposed by Congress and Ratified by the Legislatures of the Several States, Pursuant to Article V of the Original Constitution.

Amendments I-X, known as the Bill of Rights, were proposed by Congress on September 25, 1789, and ratified on December 15, 1791.

AMENDMENT I

[FREEDOM OF RELIGION, OF SPEECH, AND OF THE PRESS]

Congress shall make no law respecting an establishment of religion, or prohibiting the free exercise thereof; or abridging the freedom of speech, or of the press; or the right of the people peaceably to assemble, and to petition the Government for a redress of grievances.

AMENDMENT II

[RIGHT TO KEEP AND BEAR ARMS]

A well regulated Militia, being necessary to the security of a free State, the right of the people to keep and bear Arms, shall not be infringed.

AMENDMENT III

[QUARTERING OF SOLDIERS]

No Soldier shall, in time of peace be quartered in any house, without the consent of the Owner, nor in time of war, but in a manner to be prescribed by law.

AMENDMENT IV

[SECURITY FROM UNWARRANTABLE SEARCH AND SEIZURE]

The right of the people to be secure in their persons, houses, papers, and effects, against unreasonable searches and seizures, shall not be violated, and no Warrants shall issue, but upon probable cause, supported by Oath or affirmation, and particularly describing the place to be searched, and the persons or things to be seized.

AMENDMENT V

[RIGHTS OF ACCUSED PERSONS IN CRIMINAL PROCEEDINGS]

No person shall be held to answer for a capital, or otherwise infamous crime, unless on a presentment or indictment of a Grand Jury, except in cases arising in the land or naval forces, or in the Militia, when in actual service in time of War or in public danger; nor shall any person be subject for the same offence to be twice put in jeopardy of life or limb; nor shall be compelled in any criminal case to be a witness against himself, nor be deprived of life, liberty, or property, without due process of law; nor shall private property be taken for public use, without just compensation.

AMENDMENT VI

[RIGHT TO SPEEDY TRIAL, WITNESSES, ETC.]

In all criminal prosecutions, the accused shall enjoy the right to a speedy and public trial, by an impartial jury of the State and district wherein the crime shall have been committed, which district shall have been previously ascertained by law, and to be informed of the nature and cause of the accusation; to be confronted with the witnesses against him; to have compulsory process for obtaining witnesses in his favor, and to have the Assistance of Counsel for his defence.

Amendment VII

[TRIAL BY JURY IN CIVIL CASES]

In suits at common law, where the value in controversy shall exceed twenty dollars, the right of trial by jury shall be preserved, and no fact tried by a jury, shall be otherwise reexamined in any Court of the United States, than according to the rules of the common law.

Amendment VIII

[BAILS, FINES, PUNISHMENTS]

Excessive bail shall not be required, nor excessive fines imposed, nor cruel and unusual punishments inflicted.

Amendment IX

[RESERVATION OF RIGHTS OF PEOPLE]

The enumeration in the Constitution, of certain rights, shall not be construed to deny or disparage others retained by the people.

Amendment X

[POWERS RESERVED TO STATES OR PEOPLE]

The powers not delegated to the United States by the Constitution, nor prohibited by it to the States, are reserved to the States respectively, or to the people.

Amendment XI

[Proposed by Congress on March 4, 1794; declared ratified on January 8, 1798.]

[RESTRICTION OF JUDICIAL POWER]

The Judicial power of the United States shall not be construed to extend to any suit in law or equity, commenced or prosecuted against one of the United States by Citizens of another State, or by Citizens or Subjects of any Foreign State.

Amendment XII

[Proposed by Congress on December 9, 1803; declared ratified on September 25, 1804.]

[ELECTION OF PRESIDENT AND VICE PRESIDENT]

The Electors shall meet in their respective states and vote by ballot for President and Vice-President, one of whom, at least, shall not be an inhabitant of the same state with themselves; they shall name in their ballots the person voted for as President, and in distinct ballots the person voted for as Vice-President, and they shall make distinct lists of all persons voted for as President, and of all persons voted for as Vice-President, and of the number of votes for each, which lists they shall sign and certify, and transmit sealed to the seat of the government of the United States, directed to the President of the Senate;—the President of the Senate shall, in presence of the Senate and House of Representatives, open all the certificates and the votes shall then be counted;—The person having the greatest number of votes for President, shall be the President, if such number be a majority of the whole number of Electors appointed; and if no person have such majority, then from the persons having the highest numbers not exceeding three on the list of those voted for as President, the House of Representatives shall choose immediately, by ballot, the President. But in choosing the President, the votes shall be taken by states, the representation from each state having one vote; a quorum for this purpose shall consist of a member or members from two-thirds of the states, and a majority of all the states shall be necessary to a choice. And if the House of Representatives shall not choose a President whenever the right of choice shall devolve upon them, before the fourth day of March next following, then the Vice-President shall act as President, as in the case of the death or other constitutional disability of the President.—The person having the greatest number of votes as Vice-President, shall be the Vice-President, if such number be a majority of the whole number of Electors appointed, and if no person have a majority, then from the two highest numbers on the list, the Senate shall choose the Vice-President; a quorum for the purpose shall consist of two-thirds of the whole number of Senators, and a majority of the whole number shall be necessary to a choice. But no person constitutionally ineligible to the office of President shall be eligible to that of Vice-President of the United States.

Amendment XIII

[Proposed by Congress on January 31, 1865; declared ratified on December 18, 1865.]

Section 1

[ABOLITION OF SLAVERY]

Neither slavery nor involuntary servitude, except as a punishment for crime whereof the party shall have been duly convicted, shall exist within the United States, or any place subject to their jurisdiction.

Section 2

[POWER TO ENFORCE THIS ARTICLE]

Congress shall have power to enforce this article by appropriate legislation.

AMENDMENT XIV

[Proposed by Congress on June 13, 1866, declared ratified on July 28, 1868.]

Section 1

[CITIZENSHIP RIGHTS NOT TO BE ABRIDGED BY STATES]

All persons born or naturalized in the United States, and subject to the jurisdiction thereof, are citizens of the United States and of the State wherein they reside. No State shall make or enforce any law which shall abridge the privileges or immunities of citizens of the United States; nor shall any State deprive any person of life, liberty, or property, without due process of law; nor deny to any person within its jurisdiction the equal protection of the laws.

Section 2

[APPORTIONMENT OF REPRESENTATIVES IN CONGRESS]

Representatives shall be apportioned among the several States according to their respective numbers, counting the whole number of persons in each State, excluding Indians not taxed. But when the right to vote at any election for the choice of electors for President and Vice-President of the United States, Representatives in Congress, the Executive and Judicial officers of a State, or the members of the Legislature thereof, is denied to any of the male inhabitants of such State, being twenty-one years of age, and citizens of the United States, or in any way abridged, except for participation in rebellion, or other crime, the basis of representation therein shall be reduced in the proportion which the number of such male citizens shall bear to the whole number of male citizens twenty-one years of age in such State.

Section 3

[PERSONS DISQUALIFIED FROM HOLDING OFFICE]

No person shall be a Senator or Representative in Congress, or elector of President and Vice-President, or hold any office, civil or military, under the United States, or under any State, who, having previously taken an oath, as a member of Congress, or as an officer of the United States, or as a member of any State legislature, or as an executive or judicial officer of any State, to support the Constitution of the United States, shall have engaged in insurrection or rebellion against the same, or given aid or comfort to the enemies thereof. But Congress may by a vote of two-thirds of each House, remove such disability.

Section 4

[WHAT PUBLIC DEBTS ARE VALID]

The validity of the public debt of the United States, authorized by law, including debts incurred for payment of pensions and bounties for services in suppressing insurrection or rebellion, shall not be questioned. But neither the United States nor any State shall assume or pay any debt or obligation incurred in aid of insurrection or rebellion against the United States, or any claim for the loss or emancipation of any slave; but all such debts, obligations and claims shall be held illegal and void.

Section 5

[POWER TO ENFORCE THIS ARTICLE]

The Congress shall have power to enforce, by appropriate legislation, the provisions of this article.

AMENDMENT XV

[Proposed by Congress on February 26, 1869; declared ratified on March 30, 1870.]

Section 1

[NEGRO SUFFRAGE]

The right of citizens of the United States to vote shall not be denied or abridged by the United States or by any State on account of race, color, or previous condition of servitude.

Section 2

[POWER TO ENFORCE THIS ARTICLE]

The Congress shall have power to enforce this article by appropriate legislation.

AMENDMENT XVI

[Proposed by Congress on July 2, 1909; declared ratified on February 25, 1913.]

[AUTHORIZING INCOME TAXES]

The Congress shall have power to lay and collect taxes on incomes, from whatever source derived, without apportionment among the several States, and without regard to any census or enumeration.

Amendment XVII

[Proposed by Congress on May 13, 1912; declared ratified on May 31, 1913.]

[POPULAR ELECTION OF SENATORS]

The Senate of the United States shall be composed of two Senators from each State, elected by the people thereof, for six years; and each Senator shall have one vote. The electors in each State shall have the qualifications requisite for electors of the most numerous branch of the State legislatures.

When vacancies happen in the representation of any State in the Senate, the executive authority of such State shall issue writs of election to fill such vacancies: *Provided,* That the legislature of any State may empower the executive thereof to make temporary appointments until the people fill the vacancies by election as the legislature may direct.

This amendment shall not be so construed as to affect the election or term of any Senator chosen before it becomes valid as part of the Constitution.

Amendment XVIII

[Proposed by Congress December 18, 1917; declared ratified on January 29, 1919.]

Section 1

[NATIONAL LIQUOR PROHIBITION]

After one year from the ratification of this article the manufacture, sale, or transportation of intoxicating liquors within, the importation thereof into, or the exportation thereof from the United States and all territory subject to the jurisdiction thereof for beverage purposes is hereby prohibited.

Section 2

[POWER TO ENFORCE THIS ARTICLE]

The Congress and the several States shall have concurrent power to enforce this article by appropriate legislation.

Section 3

[RATIFICATION WITHIN SEVEN YEARS]

This article shall be inoperative unless it shall have been ratified as an amendment to the Constitution by the legislatures of the several States, as provided in the Constitution, within seven years from the date of the submission hereof to the States by the Congress.[1]

Amendment XIX

[Proposed by Congress on June 4, 1919; declared ratified on August 26, 1920.]

[WOMAN SUFFRAGE]

The right of citizens of the United States to vote shall not be denied or abridged by the United States or by any State on account of sex.

Congress shall have power to enforce this article by appropriate legislation.

Amendment XX

[Proposed by Congress on March 2, 1932; declared ratified on February 6, 1933.]

Section 1

[TERMS OF OFFICE]

The terms of the President and Vice President shall end at noon on the 20th day of January, and the terms of Senators and Representatives at noon on the 3d day of January, of the years in which such terms would have ended if this article had not been ratified; and the terms of their successors shall then begin.

Section 2

[TIME OF CONVENING CONGRESS]

The Congress shall assemble at least once in every year, and such meeting shall begin at noon on the 3d day of January, unless they shall by law appoint a different day.

Section 3

[DEATH OF PRESIDENT-ELECT]

If, at the time fixed for the beginning of the term of the President, the President elect shall have died, the Vice President elect shall become President. If a President shall not have been chosen before the time fixed for the beginning of his term, or if the President elect shall have failed to qualify, then the Vice President elect shall act as President until a President shall have qualified; and the Congress may by law provide for the case wherein neither

[1]Repealed by the Twenty-first Amendment

a President elect nor a Vice President elect shall have qualified, declaring who shall then act as President, or the manner in which one who is to act shall be selected, and such person shall act accordingly until a President or Vice President shall have qualified.

Section 4

[ELECTION OF THE PRESIDENT]

The Congress may by law provide for the case of the death of any of the persons from whom the House of Representatives may choose a President whenever the right of choice shall have devolved upon them, and for the case of the death of any of the persons from whom the Senate may choose a Vice President whenever the right of choice shall have devolved upon them.

Section 5

[AMENDMENT TAKES EFFECT]

Sections 1 and 2 shall take effect on the 15th day of October following the ratification of this article.

Section 6

[RATIFICATION WITHIN SEVEN YEARS]

This article shall be inoperative unless it shall have been ratified as an amendment to the Constitution by the legislatures of three-fourths of the several States within seven years from the date of its submission.

AMENDMENT XXI

[Proposed by Congress on February 20, 1933; declared ratified on December 5, 1933.]

Section 1

[NATIONAL LIQUOR PROHIBITION REPEALED]

The eighteenth article of amendment to the Constitution of the United States is hereby repealed.

Section 2

[TRANSPORTATION OF LIQUOR INTO "DRY" STATES]

The transportation or importation into any State, Territory, or Possession of the United States for delivery or use therein of intoxicating liquors, in violation of the laws thereof, is hereby prohibited.

Section 3

[RATIFICATION WITHIN SEVEN YEARS]

This article shall be inoperative unless it shall have been ratified as an amendment to the Constitution by conventions in the several States, as provided in the Constitution, within seven years from the date of the submission hereof to the States by the Congress.

AMENDMENT XXII

[Proposed by Congress on March 21, 1947; declared ratified on February 27, 1951.]

Section 1

[TENURE OF PRESIDENT LIMITED]

No person shall be elected to the office of President more than twice, and no person who has held the office of President or acted as President, for more than two years of a term to which some other person was elected President shall be elected to the office of the President more than once. But this Article shall not apply to any person holding the office of President when this Article was proposed by the Congress, and shall not prevent any person who may be holding the office of President, or acting as President, during the term within which this Article becomes operative from holding the office of President or acting as President during the remainder of such term.

Section 2

[RATIFICATION WITHIN SEVEN YEARS]

This article shall be inoperative unless it shall have been ratified as an amendment to the Constitution by the legislatures of three-fourths of the several States within seven years from the date of its submission to the States by the Congress.

AMENDMENT XXIII

[Proposed by Congress on June 16, 1960; declared ratified on March 29, 1961.]

Section 1

[ELECTORAL COLLEGE VOTES FOR THE DISTRICT OF COLUMBIA]

The District constituting the seat of Government of the United States shall appoint in such manner as the Congress may direct:

A number of electors of President and Vice President equal to the whole number of Senators and Representatives in Congress to which the District would be entitled if it were a State, but in no event more than the least populous State; they shall be in addition to those appointed by the States, but they shall be considered, for the purposes of the election of President and Vice President, to be electors appointed by a State; and they shall meet in the District and perform such duties as provided by the twelfth article of amendment.

Section 2

[POWER TO ENFORCE THIS ARTICLE]

The Congress shall have power to enforce this article by appropriate legislation.

AMENDMENT XXIV

[Proposed by Congress on August 27, 1962; declared ratified on January 23, 1964.]

Section 1

[ANTI-POLL TAX]

The right of citizens of the United States to vote in any primary or other election for President or Vice President, for electors for President or Vice President, or for Senator or Representative of Congress, shall not be denied or abridged by the United States or any State by reason of failure to pay any poll tax or other tax.

Section 2

[POWER TO ENFORCE THIS ARTICLE]

The Congress shall have power to enforce this article by appropriate legislation.

AMENDMENT XXV

[Proposed by Congress on July 6, 1965; declared ratified on February 10, 1967.]

Section 1

[VICE PRESIDENT TO BECOME PRESIDENT]

In case of the removal of the President from office or his death or resignation, the Vice President shall become President.

Section 2

[CHOICE OF A NEW VICE PRESIDENT]

Whenever there is a vacancy in the office of the Vice President, the President shall nominate a Vice President who shall take the office upon confirmation by a majority vote of both houses of Congress.

Section 3

[PRESIDENT MAY DECLARE OWN DISABILITY]

Whenever the President transmits to the President pro tempore of the Senate and the Speaker of the House of Representatives his written declaration that he is unable to discharge the powers and duties of his office, and until he transmits to them a written declaration to the contrary, such powers and duties shall be discharged by the Vice President as Acting President.

Section 4

[ALTERNATE PROCEDURES TO DECLARE AND TO END PRESIDENTIAL DISABILITY]

Whenever the Vice President and a majority of either the principal officers of the executive departments, or of such other body as Congress may by law provide, transmit to the President pro tempore of the Senate and the Speaker of the House of Representatives their written declaration that the President is unable to discharge the powers and duties of his office, the Vice President shall immediately assume the powers and duties of the office as Acting President.

Thereafter, when the President transmits to the President pro tempore of the Senate and the Speaker of the House of Representatives his written declaration that no inability exists, he shall resume the powers and duties of his office unless the Vice President and a majority of either the principal officers of the executive department, or of such other body as Congress may by law provide, transmit within four days to the President pro tempore of the Senate and the Speaker of the House of Representatives their written declaration that the President is unable to discharge the powers and duties of his office. Thereupon Congress shall decide the issue, assembling within forty eight hours for that purpose if not in session. If the Congress, within twenty one days after receipt of the latter written declaration, or, if Congress is not in session, within twenty one days after Congress is required to assemble, determines by two-thirds vote of both Houses that the President is unable to discharge the powers and duties of his office, the Vice President shall continue to discharge the same as Acting President; otherwise, the President shall resume the powers and duties of his office.

Amendment XXVI

[Proposed by Congress on March 23, 1971; declared ratified on July 1, 1971.]

Section 1

[EIGHTEEN-YEAR-OLD VOTE]

The right of citizens of the United States, who are eighteen years of age or older, to vote shall not be denied or abridged by the United States or by any State on account of age.

Section 2

[POWER TO ENFORCE THIS ARTICLE]

The Congress shall have power to enforce this article by appropriate legislation.

Amendment XXVII

[Proposed by Congress on September 25, 1789; declared ratified on May 8, 1992.]

[CONGRESS CANNOT RAISE ITS OWN PAY]

No law varying the compensation for the services of the Senators and Representatives, shall take effect, until an election of representatives shall have intervened.

The Federalist Papers

No. 10: Madison

Among the numerous advantages promised by a well constructed Union, none deserves to be more accurately developed than its tendency to break and control the violence of faction. The friend of popular governments never finds himself so much alarmed for their character and fate, as when he contemplates their propensity to this dangerous vice. He will not fail therefore to set a due value on any plan which, without violating the principles to which he is attached, provides a proper cure for it. The instability, injustice, and confusion introduced into the public councils have, in truth, been the mortal diseases under which popular governments have everywhere perished, as they continue to be the favorite and fruitful topics from which the adversaries to liberty derive their most specious declamations. The valuable improvements made by the American constitutions on the popular models, both ancient and modern, cannot certainly be too much admired; but it would be an unwarrantable partiality to contend that they have as effectually obviated the danger on this side, as was wished and expected. Complaints are everywhere heard from our most considerate and virtuous citizens, equally the friends of public and private faith and of public and personal liberty, that our governments are too unstable, that the public good is disregarded in the conflicts of rival parties, and that measures are too often decided, not according to the rules of justice and the rights of the minor party, but by the superior force of an interested and overbearing majority. However anxiously we may wish that these complaints had no foundation, the evidence of known facts will not permit us to deny that they are in some degree true. It will be found, indeed, on a candid review of our situation, that some of the distresses under which we labor have been erroneously charged on the operation of our governments; but it will be found, at the same time, that other causes will not alone account for many of our heaviest misfortunes; and, particularly, for that prevailing and increasing distrust of public engagements and alarm for private rights which are echoed from one end of the continent to the other. These must be chiefly, if not wholly, effects of the unsteadiness and injustice with which a factious spirit has tainted our public administration.

By a faction I understand a number of citizens, whether amounting to a majority or minority of the whole, who are united and actuated by some common impulse of passion, or of interest, adverse to the rights of other citizens, or to the permanent and aggregate interests of the community.

There are two methods of curing the mischiefs of faction: the one, by removing its causes; the other, by controlling its effects.

There are again two methods of removing the causes of faction: the one, by destroying the liberty which is essential to its existence; the other, by giving to every citizen the same opinions, the same passions, and the same interests.

It could never be more truly said than of the first remedy, that it is worse than the disease. Liberty is to faction what air is to fire, an aliment without which it instantly expires. But it could not be a less folly to abolish liberty, which is essential to political life, because it nourishes faction, than it would be to wish the annihilation of air, which is essential to animal life, because it imparts to fire its destructive agency.

The second expedient is as impracticable, as the first would be unwise. As long as the reason of man continues fallible, and he is at liberty to exercise it, different opinions will be formed. As long as the connection subsists between his reason and his self-love, his opinions and his passions will have a reciprocal influence on each other; and the former will be objects to which the latter will attach themselves. The diversity in the faculties of men, from which the rights of property originate, is not less an insuperable obstacle to a uniformity of interests. The protection of these faculties is the first object of Government. From the protection of different and unequal faculties of acquiring property, the possession of different degrees and kinds of property immediately results; and from the influence of these on the sentiments and views of the respective proprietors, ensues a division of the society into different interests and parties.

The latent causes of faction are thus sown in the nature of man; and we see them everywhere brought into different degrees of activity, according to the different circumstances of civil society. A zeal for different opinions concerning religion, concerning Government, and many other points, as well of speculation as of practice; an attachment to different leaders ambitiously contending for pre-eminence and power; or to persons of other descriptions whose fortunes have been interesting to the human passions, have in turn divided mankind into parties, inflamed them with mutual animosity, and rendered them much more disposed to vex and oppress each other, than to co-operate for their common good. So strong is this propensity of mankind to fall into mutual animosities, that where no substantial occasion presents itself, the most frivolous and fanciful distinctions have been sufficient to kindle their unfriendly passions, and excite their most violent conflicts. But the most common and durable source of factions has been the various and unequal distribution of property. Those who hold and those who are without property have ever formed distinct interests in society. Those who are creditors, and those who are debtors, fall under a like discrimination. A landed interest, a manufacturing interest, a mercantile interest, a moneyed interest, with many lesser interests, grow up of necessity in civilized nations, and divide them into different classes, actuated by different sentiments and views. The regulation of these various and interfering interests forms the principal task of modern Legislation, and involves the spirit of party and faction in the necessary and ordinary operations of Government.

No man is allowed to be judge in his own cause, because his interest would certainly bias his judgment and, not improbably, corrupt his integrity. With equal, nay with greater reason, a body of men are unfit to be both judges and parties at the same time; yet what are many of the most important acts of legislation but so many judicial determinations, not indeed concerning the rights of single persons, but concerning the rights of large bodies of citizens; and what are the different classes of legislators but advocates and parties to the causes which they determine? Is a law proposed concerning private debts? It is a question to which the creditors are parties on one side and the debtors on the other. Justice ought to hold the balance between them. Yet the parties are, and must be, themselves the judges; and the most numerous party, or in other words, the most powerful faction must be expected to prevail. Shall domestic manufacturers be encouraged, and in what degree, by restrictions on foreign manufacturers? are questions which would be differently decided by the landed and the manufacturing classes, and probably by neither with a sole regard to justice and the public good. The apportionment of taxes on the various descriptions of property is an act which seems to require the most exact impartiality; yet there is, perhaps, no legislative act in which greater opportunity and temptation are given to a predominant party to trample on the rules of justice. Every shilling with which they overburden the inferior number is a shilling saved to their own pockets.

It is in vain to say that enlightened statesmen will be able to adjust these clashing interests and render them all subservient to the public good. Enlightened statesmen will not always be at the helm. Nor, in many cases, can such an adjustment be made at all without taking into view indirect and remote considerations, which will rarely prevail over the immediate interest which one party may find in disregarding the rights of another or the good of the whole.

The inference to which we are brought is that the *causes* of faction cannot be removed and that relief is only to be sought in the means of controlling its *effects*.

If a faction consists of less than a majority, relief is supplied by the republican principle, which enables the majority to defeat its sinister views by regular vote. It may clog the administration, it may convulse the society; but it will be unable to execute and mask its violence under the forms of the Constitution. When a majority is included in a faction, the form of popular government, on the other hand, enables it to sacrifice to its ruling passion or interest both the public good and the rights of other citizens. To secure the public good and private rights against the danger of such a faction, and at the same time to preserve the spirit and the form of popular government, is then the great object to which our enquiries are directed. Let me add that it is the great desideratum by which alone this form of government can be rescued from the opprobrium under which it has so long labored and be recommended to the esteem and adoption of mankind.

By what means is this object attainable? Evidently by one of two only. Either the existence of the same passion or interest in a majority at the same time must be prevented, or the majority, having such co-existent passion or interest, must be rendered, by their number and local situation, unable to concert and carry into effect schemes of oppression. If the impulse and the opportunity be suffered to coincide, we well know that neither moral nor religious motives can be relied on as an adequate control. They are not found to be such on the injustice and violence of individuals, and lose their efficacy in proportion to the number combined together, that is, in proportion as their efficacy becomes needful.

From this view of the subject it may be concluded that a pure Democracy, by which I mean a Society consisting of a small number of citizens, who assemble and administer the Government in person, can admit of no cure for the mischiefs of faction. A common passion or interest will, in almost every case, be felt by a majority of the whole; a communication and concert results from the form of Government itself; and there is nothing to check the inducements to sacrifice the weaker party or an obnoxious individual. Hence it is that such Democracies have ever been spectacles of turbulence and contention; have ever been found incompatible with personal security or the rights of property; and have in general been as short in their lives as they have been violent in their deaths. Theoretic politicians, who have patronized this species of Government, have erroneously supposed that by reducing mankind to a perfect equality in their political rights, they would at the same time be perfectly equalized and assimilated in their possessions, their opinions, and their passions.

A Republic, by which I mean a Government in which the scheme of representation takes place, opens a different prospect and promises the cure for which we are seeking. Let us examine the points in which it varies from pure Democracy, and we shall comprehend both the nature of the cure and the efficacy which it must derive from the Union.

The two great points of difference between a Democracy and a Republic are: first, the delegation of the Government, in the latter, to a small number of citizens elected by the rest; secondly, the greater number of citizens and greater sphere of country over which the latter may be extended.

The effect of the first difference is, on the one hand, to refine and enlarge the public views by passing them through the medium of a chosen body of citizens, whose wisdom may best discern the true interest of their country and whose patriotism and love of justice will be least likely to sacrifice it to temporary or partial considerations. Under such a regulation it may well happen that the public voice, pronounced by the representatives of the people, will be more consonant to the public good than if pronounced by the people themselves, convened for the purpose. On the other hand, the effect may be inverted. Men of factious tempers, of local prejudices, or of sinister designs, may, by intrigue, by corruption, or by other means, first obtain the suffrages, and then betray the interests of the people. The question resulting is, whether small or extensive Republics are most favorable to the election of proper guardians of the public weal; and it is clearly decided in favor of the latter by two obvious considerations.

In the first place it is to be remarked that however small the Republic may be, the Representatives must be raised to a certain number in order to guard against the cabals of a few; and that however large it may be they must be limited to a certain number in order to guard against the confusion of a multitude. Hence, the number of Representatives in the two cases not being in proportion to that of the Constituents, and being proportionally greatest in the small Republic, it follows that if the proportion of fit characters be not less in the large than in the small Republic, the former will present a greater option, and consequently a greater probability of a fit choice.

In the next place, as each Representative will be chosen by a greater number of citizens in the large than in the small Republic, it will be more difficult for unworthy candidates to practise with success the vicious arts by which elections are too often carried; and the suffrages of the people being more free, will be more likely to centre on men who possess the most attractive merit and the most diffusive and established characters.

It must be confessed that in this, as in most other cases, there is a mean, on both sides of which inconveniencies will be found to lie. By enlarging too much the number of electors, you render the representative too little acquainted with all their local circumstances and lesser interests; as by reducing it too much, you render him unduly attached to these, and too little fit to comprehend and pursue great and national objects. The Federal Constitution forms a happy combination in this respect; the great and aggregate interests being referred to the national, the local and particular to the State legislatures.

The other point of difference is the greater number of citizens and extent of territory which may be brought within the compass of Republican than of Democratic Government; and it is this circumstance principally which renders factious combinations less to be dreaded in the former than in the latter. The smaller the society, the fewer probably will be the distinct parties and interests composing it; the fewer the distinct parties and interests, the more frequently will a majority be found of the same party; and the smaller the number of individuals composing a majority, and the smaller the compass within which they are placed, the more easily will they concert and execute their plans of oppression. Extend the sphere and you take in a greater variety of parties and interests; you make it less probable that a majority of the whole will have a common motive to invade the rights of other citizens; or if such a common motive exists, it will be more difficult for all who feel it to discover their own strength and to act in unison with each other. Besides other impediments, it may be remarked, that where there is a consciousness of unjust or dishonorable purposes, communication is always checked by distrust in proportion to the number whose concurrence is necessary.

Hence, it clearly appears that the same advantage which a Republic has over a Democracy in controlling the effects of faction is enjoyed by a large over a small republic—is enjoyed by the Union over the States composing it. Does this advantage consist in the substitution of representatives whose enlightened views and virtuous sentiments render them superior to local prejudices and to schemes of injustice? It will not be denied that the representation of the Union will be most likely to possess these requisite endowments. Does it consist in the greater security afforded by a greater variety of parties, against the event of any one party being able to outnumber and oppress the rest? In an equal degree does the increased variety of parties comprised within the Union increase this security? Does it, in fine, consist in the greater obstacles opposed to the concert and accomplishment of the secret wishes of an unjust and interested majority? Here again the extent of the Union gives it the most palpable advantage.

The influence of factious leaders may kindle a flame within their particular States but will be unable to spread a general conflagration through the other States: a religious sect may degenerate into a political faction in a part of the Confederacy; but the variety of sects dispersed over the entire face of it must secure the national Councils against any danger from that source: a rage for paper money, for an abolition of debts, for an equal division of property, or for any other improper or wicked project, will be less apt to pervade the whole body of the Union than a particular member of it; in the same proportion as such a malady is more likely to taint a particular county or district than an entire State.

In the extent and proper structure of the Union, therefore, we behold a republican remedy for the diseases most incident to Republican Government. And according to the degree of pleasure and pride we feel in being republicans ought to be our zeal in cherishing the spirit and supporting the character of federalist.

PUBLIUS

No. 51: Madison

To what expedient, then, shall we finally resort, for maintaining in practice the necessary partition of power among the several departments as laid down in the constitution? The only answer that can be given is that as all these exterior provisions are found to be inadequate the defect must be supplied, by so contriving the interior structure of the government as that its several constituent parts may, by their mutual relations, be the means of keeping each other in their proper places. Without presuming to undertake a full development of this important idea I will hazard a few general observations which may perhaps place it in a clearer light, and enable us to form a more correct judgment of the principles and structure of the government planned by the convention.

In order to lay a due foundation for that separate and distinct exercise of the different powers of government, which to a certain extent is admitted on all hands to be essential to the preservation of liberty, it is evident that each department should have a will of its own; and consequently should be so constituted that the members of each should have as little agency as possible in the appointment of the members of the others. Were this principle rigorously adhered to, it would require that all the appointments for the supreme executive, legislative, and judiciary magistracies should be drawn from the same fountain of authority, the people, through channels having no communication whatever with one another. Perhaps such a plan of constructing the several departments would be less difficult in practice than it may in contemplation appear. Some difficulties, however, and some additional expense would attend the execution of it. Some deviations, therefore, from the principle must be admitted. In the constitution of the judiciary department in particular, it might be inexpedient to insist rigorously on the principle: first, because peculiar qualifications being essential in the members, the primary consideration ought to be to select that mode of choice which best secures these qualifications; second, because the permanent tenure by which the appointments are held in that department must soon destroy all sense of dependence on the authority conferring them.

It is equally evident that the members of each department should be as little dependent as possible on those of the others for the emoluments annexed to their offices. Were the executive magistrate, or the judges, not independent of the legislature in this particular, their independence in every other would be merely nominal.

But the great security against a gradual concentration of the several powers in the same department consists in giving to those who administer each department the necessary constitutional means and personal motives to resist encroachments of the others. The provision for defence must in this, as in all other cases, be made commensurate to the danger of attack. Ambition must be made to counteract ambition. The interest of the man must be connected with the constitutional rights of the place. It may be a reflection on human nature that such devices should be necessary to control the abuses of government. But what is government itself but the greatest of all reflections on human nature? If men were angels, no government would be necessary. If angels were to govern men, neither external nor internal controls on government would be necessary. In framing a government which is to be administered by men over men, the great difficulty lies in this: You must first enable the government to control the governed; and in the next place oblige it to control itself. A dependence on the people is, no doubt, the primary control on the government; but experience has taught mankind the necessity of auxiliary precautions.

This policy of supplying, by opposite and rival interests, the defect of better motives, might be traced through the whole system of human affairs, private as well as public. We see it particularly displayed in all the subordinate distributions of power, where the constant aim is to divide and arrange the several offices in such a manner as that each may be a check on the other; that the private interest of every individual may be a sentinel over the public rights. These inventions of prudence cannot be less requisite in the distribution of the supreme powers of the State.

But it is not possible to give to each department an equal power of self-defense. In republican government, the legislative authority necessarily predominates. The remedy for this inconveniency is to divide the legislature into different branches; and to render them, by different modes of election and different principles of action, as little connected with each other as the nature of their common functions and their common dependence on the society will admit. It may even be necessary to guard against dangerous encroachments by still further precautions. As the weight of the legislative authority requires that it should be thus divided, the weakness of the executive may require, on the other hand, that it should be fortified. An absolute negative on the legislature appears, at first view, to be the natural defense with which the executive magistrate should be armed. But perhaps it would be neither altogether safe nor alone sufficient. On ordinary occasions it might not be exerted with the requisite firmness, and on extraordinary occasions it might be perfidiously abused. May not this defect of an absolute negative be supplied by some qualified connection between this weaker branch of the stronger department, by which the latter may be led to support the constitutional rights of the former, without being too much detached from the rights of its own department?

If the principles on which these observations are founded be just, as I persuade myself they are, and they be applied as a criterion to the several State constitutions, and to the federal Constitution, it will be found that if the latter does not perfectly correspond with them, the former are infinitely less able to bear such a test.

There are, moreover, two considerations particularly applicable to the federal system of America, which place that system in a very interesting point of view.

First. In a single republic, all the power surrendered by the people is submitted to the administration of a single government; and usurpations are guarded against by a division of the government into distinct and separate departments. In the compound republic of America, the power surrendered by the people is first divided between two distinct governments, and then the portion allotted to each subdivided among distinct and separate departments. Hence a double security arises to the rights of the people. The different governments will control each other, at the same time that each will be controlled by itself.

Second. It is of great importance in a republic not only to guard the society against the oppression of its rulers, but to guard one part of the society against the injustice of the other part. Different interests necessarily exist in different classes of citizens. If a majority be united by a common interest, the rights of the minority will be insecure. There are but two methods of providing against this evil: The one by creating a will in the community independent of the majority—that is, of the society itself; the other, by comprehending in the society so many separate descriptions of citizens as will render an unjust combination of a majority of the whole very improbable, if not impracticable. The first method prevails in all governments possessing an hereditary or self-appointed authority. This, at best, is but a precarious security; because a power independent of the society may as well espouse the unjust views of the major as the rightful interests of the minor party, and may possibly be turned against both parties. The second method will be exemplified in the federal republic of the United States. Whilst all authority in it will be derived from and dependent on the society, the society itself will be broken into so many parts, interests and classes of citizens, that the rights of individuals, or of the minority, will be in little danger from interested combinations of the majority. In a free government the security for civil rights must be the same as that for religious rights. It consists in the one case in the multiplicity of interests, and in the other in the multiplicity of sects. The degree of security in both cases will depend on the number of interests and sects; and this may be presumed to depend on the extent of country and number of people comprehended under the same government. This view of the subject must particularly recommend a proper federal system to all the sincere and considerate friends of republican government: Since it shows that in exact proportion as the territory of the Union may be formed into more circumscribed Confederacies, or States, oppressive combinations of a majority will be facilitated; the best security, under the republican form, for the rights of every class of citizens, will be diminished; and consequently the stability and independence of some member of the government, the only other security, must be proportionally increased. Justice is the end of government. It is the end of civil society. It ever has been and ever will be pursued until it be obtained, or until liberty be lost in the pursuit. In a society under the forms of which the stronger faction can readily unite and oppress the weaker, anarchy may as truly be said to reign as in a state of nature, where the weaker individual is not secured against the violence of the stronger: And as, in the latter state, even the stronger individuals are prompted, by the uncertainty of their condition, to submit to a government which may protect the weak as well as themselves: So, in the former state, will the more powerful factions or parties be gradually induced, by a like motive, to wish for a government which will protect all parties, the weaker as well as the more powerful. It can be little doubted that if the State of Rhode Island was separated from the Confederacy and left to itself, the insecurity of rights under the popular form of government within such narrow limits would be displayed by such reiterated oppressions of factious majorities that some power altogether independent of the people would soon be called for by the voice of the very factions whose misrule had proved the necessity of it. In the extended republic of the United States, and among the great variety of interests, parties, and sects which it embraces, a coalition of a majority of the whole society could seldom take place on any other principles than those of justice and the general good; and there being thus less danger to a minor from the will of the major party, there must be less pretext, also, to provide for the security of the former, by introducing into the government a will not dependent on the latter, or, in other words, a will independent of the society itself. It is no less certain than it is important, notwithstanding the contrary opinions which have been entertained, that the larger the society, provided it lie within a practicable sphere, the more duly capable it will be of self-government. And happily for the *republican cause,* the practicable sphere may be carried to a very great extent by a judicious modification and mixture of the *federal principle.*

PUBLIUS

Presidents and Vice Presidents

	President	Vice President
1	George Washington (Federalist 1789)	John Adams (Federalist 1789)
2	John Adams (Federalist 1797)	Thomas Jefferson (Dem.-Rep. 1797)
3	Thomas Jefferson (Dem.-Rep. 1801)	Aaron Burr (Dem.-Rep. 1801) George Clinton (Dem.-Rep. 1805)
4	James Madison (Dem.-Rep. 1809)	George Clinton (Dem.-Rep. 1809) Elbridge Gerry (Dem.-Rep. 1813)
5	James Monroe (Dem.-Rep. 1817)	Daniel D. Tompkins (Dem.-Rep. 1817)
6	John Quincy Adams (Dem.-Rep. 1825)	John C. Calhoun (Dem.-Rep. 1825)
7	Andrew Jackson (Democratic 1829)	John C. Calhoun (Democratic 1829) Martin Van Buren (Democratic 1833)
8	Martin Van Buren (Democratic 1837)	Richard M. Johnson (Democratic 1837)
9	William H. Harrison (Whig 1841)	John Tyler (Whig 1841)
10	John Tyler (Whig and Democratic 1841)	
11	James K. Polk (Democratic 1845)	George M. Dallas (Democratic 1845)
12	Zachary Taylor (Whig 1849)	Millard Fillmore (Whig 1849)
13	Millard Fillmore (Whig 1850)	

	President	Vice President
14	Franklin Pierce (Democratic 1853)	William R. D. King (Democratic 1853)
15	James Buchanan (Democratic 1857)	John C. Breckinridge (Democratic 1857)
16	Abraham Lincoln (Republican 1861)	Hannibal Hamlin (Republican 1861) Andrew Johnson (Unionist 1865)
17	Andrew Johnson (Unionist 1865)	
18	Ulysses S. Grant (Republican 1869)	Schuyler Colfax (Republican 1869) Henry Wilson (Republican 1873)
19	Rutherford B. Hayes (Republican 1877)	William A. Wheeler (Republican 1877)
20	James A. Garfield (Republican 1881)	Chester A. Arthur (Republican 1881)
21	Chester A. Arthur (Republican 1881)	
22	Grover Cleveland (Democratic 1885)	Thomas A. Hendricks (Democratic 1885)
23	Benjamin Harrison (Republican 1889)	Levi P. Morton (Republican 1889)
24	Grover Cleveland (Democratic 1893)	Adlai E. Stevenson (Democratic 1893)
25	William McKinley (Republican 1897)	Garret A. Hobart (Republican 1897) Theodore Roosevelt (Republican 1901)
26	Theodore Roosevelt (Republican 1901)	Charles W. Fairbanks (Republican 1905)

	President	Vice President
27	William H. Taft (Republican 1909)	James S. Sherman (Republican 1909)
28	Woodrow Wilson (Democratic 1913)	Thomas R. Marshall (Democratic 1913)
29	Warren G. Harding (Republican 1921)	Calvin Coolidge (Republican 1921)
30	Calvin Coolidge (Republican 1923)	Charles G. Dawes (Republican 1925)
31	Herbert Hoover (Republican 1929)	Charles Curtis (Republican 1929)
32	Franklin D. Roosevelt (Democratic 1933)	John Nance Garner (Democratic 1933) Henry A. Wallace (Democratic 1941) Harry S. Truman (Democratic 1945)
33.	Harry S. Truman (Democratic 1945)	Alben W. Barkley (Democratic 1949)
34.	Dwight D. Eisenhower (Republican 1953)	Richard M. Nixon (Republican 1953)

	President	Vice President
35	John F. Kennedy (Democratic 1961)	Lyndon B. Johnson (Democratic 1961)
36	Lyndon B. Johnson (Democratic 1963)	Hubert H. Humphrey (Democratic 1965)
37	Richard M. Nixon (Republican 1969)	Spiro T. Agnew (Republican 1969) Gerald R. Ford (Republican 1973)
38	Gerald R. Ford (Republican 1974)	Nelson Rockefeller (Republican 1974)
39	James E. Carter (Democratic 1977)	Walter Mondale (Democratic 1977)
40	Ronald Reagan (Republican 1981)	George H. W. Bush (Republican 1981)
41	George H. W. Bush (Republican 1989)	J. Danforth Quayle (Republican 1989)
42	William J. Clinton (Democrat 1993)	Albert Gore, Jr. (Democrat 1993)

IMMIGRATION TO THE UNITED STATES BY PLACE OF ORIGIN, 1820–1989

Region and Country of Last Residence[1]	1820	1821–30	1831–40	1841–50	1851–60	1861–70	1871–80	1881–90	1891-1900	1901–10
All countries	8,385	143,439	599,125	1,713,251	2,598,214	2,314,824	2,812,191	5,246,613	3,687,564	8,795,386
Europe	7,690	98,797	495,681	1,597,442	2,452,577	2,065,141	1,271,925	4,735,484	3,555,352	8,056,040
Austria-Hungary	—[2]	—[2]	—[2]	—[2]	—[2]	7,800	72,969	353,719	592,707[23]	2,145,266[23]
Austria	—[2]	—[2]	—[2]	—[2]	—[2]	7,124[3]	63,009	226,038	234,081[3]	668,209[3]
Hungary	—[2]	—[2]	—[2]	—[2]	—[2]	484[3]	9.960	127,681	181,288[3]	808,511[3]
Belgium	1	27	22	5,074	4,738	6,734	7,221	20,177	18,167	41,635
Czechoslovakia	—[4]	—[4]	—[4]	—[4]	—[4]	—[4]	—[4]	—[4]	—[4]	—[4]
Denmark	20	169	1,063	539	3,749	17,094	31,771	88,132	50,231	65,285
France	371	8,497	45,575	77,262	76,358	35,986	72,206	50,464	30,770	73,379
Germany	968	6,761	152,454	434,626	951,667	787,468	718,182	1,452,970	505,152[23]	341,498[23]
Greece	—	20	49	16	31	72	210	2,308	15,979	167,519
Ireland[5]	3,614	50,724	207,381	780,719	914,119	435,778	436,871	655,482	388,416	339,065
Italy	30	409	2,253	1,870	9,231	11,725	55,759	307,309	651,893	2,045,877
Netherlands	49	1,078	1,412	8,251	10,789	9,102	16,541	53,701	26,758	48,262
Norway-Sweden	3	91	1,201	13,903	20,931	109,298	211,245	568,362	321,281	440,039
Norway	—[6]	—[6]	—[6]	—[6]	—[6]	—[6]	95,323	176,586	95,015	190,505
Sweden	—[6]	—[6]	—[6]	—[6]	—[6]	—[6]	115,922	391,776	226,266	249,534
Poland	5	16	369	105	1,164	2,027	12,970	51,806	96,720[23]	—[23]
Portugal	35	145	829	550	1,055	2,658	14,082	16,978	27,508	69,149
Romania	—[7]	—[7]	—[7]	—[7]	—[7]	—[7]	11[7]	6,348	12,750	53,008
Soviet Union	14	75	277	551	457	2,512	39,284	213,282	505,290[23]	1,597,306[23]
Spain	139	2,477	2,125	2,209	9,298	6,697	5,266	4,419	8,731	27,935
Switzerland	31	3,226	4,821	4,644	25,011	23,286	28,293	81,988	31,179	43,922
United Kingdom[5, 8]	2,410	25,079	75,810	267,044	423,974	606,896	548,043	807,357	271,538	525,950
Yugoslavia	—[9]	—[9]	—[9]	—[9]	—[9]	—[9]	—[9]	—[9]	—[9]	—[9]
Other Europe	—	3	40	79	5	8	1,001	682	282	39,945
Asia	6	30	55	141	41,538	64,759	124,160	69,942	74,862	323,543
China[10]	1	2	8	35	41,397	64,301	123,201	61,711	14,799	20,605
Hong Kong	—[11]	—[11]	—[11]	—[11]	—[11]	—[11]	—[11]	—[11]	—[11]	—[11]
India	1	8	39	36	43	69	163	269	68	4,713
Iran	—[12]	—[12]	—[12]	—[12]	—[12]	—[12]	—[12]	—[12]	—[12]	—[12]
Israel	—[13]	—[13]	—[13]	—[13]	—[13]	—[13]	—[13]	—[13]	—[13]	—[13]
Japan	—[14]	—[14]	—[14]	—[14]	—[14]	186	149	2,270	25,942	129,797
Korea	—[15]	—[15]	—[15]	—[15]	—[15]	—[15]	—[15]	—[15]	—[15]	—[15]

Philippines	—[16]	—[16]	—[16]	—[16]	—[16]	—[16]	—[16]	—[16]	—[16]	—[16]
Turkey	1	20	7	59	83	131	404	3,782	30,425	157,369
Vietnam	—[11]	—[11]	—[11]	—[11]	—[11]	—[11]	—[11]	—[11]	—[11]	—[11]
Other Asia	3	—	1	11	15	72	243	1,910	3,628	11,059
America	387	11,564	33,424	62,469	74,720	166,607	404,044	426,967	38,972	361,888
Canada & Newfoundland[17, 18]	209	2,277	13,624	41,723	59,309	153,878	383,640	393,304	3,311	179,226
Mexico[18]	1	4,817	6,599	3,271	3,078	2,191	5,162	1,913[19]	971[19]	49,642
Caribbean	164	3,834	12,301	13,528	10,660	9,046	13,957	29,042	33,066	107,548
Cuba	—[12]	—[12]	—[12]	—[12]	—[12]	—[12]	—[12]	—[12]	—[12]	—[12]
Dominican Republic	—[20]	—[20]	—[20]	—[20]	—[20]	—[20]	—[20]	—[20]	—[20]	—[20]
Jamaica	—[21]	—[21]	—[21]	—[21]	—[21]	—[21]	—[21]	—[21]	—[20]	—[20]
Haiti	—[20]	—[20]	—[20]	—[20]	—[20]	—[20]	—[20]	—[20]	—[21]	—[21]
Other Caribbean	164	3,834	12,301	13,528	10,660	9,046	13,957	29,042	33,066	107,548
Central America	2	105	44	368	449	95	157	404	549	8,192
El Salvador	—[20]	—[20]	—[20]	—[20]	—[20]	—[20]	—[20]	—[20]	—[20]	—[20]
Other Central America	2	105	44	368	449	95	157	404	549	8,192
South America	11	531	856	3,579	1,224	1,397	1,128	2,304	1,075	17,280
Argentina	—[20]	—[20]	—[20]	—[20]	—[20]	—[20]	—[20]	—[20]	—[20]	—[20]
Columbia	—[20]	—[20]	—[20]	—[20]	—[20]	—[20]	—[20]	—[20]	—[20]	—[20]
Ecuador	—[20]	—[20]	—[20]	—[20]	—[20]	—[20]	—[20]	—[20]	—[20]	—[20]
Other South America	11	531	856	3,579	1,224	1,397	1,128	2,304	1,075	17,280
Other America	—[22]	—[22]	—[22]	—[22]	—[22]	—[22]	—[22]	—[22]	—[22]	—[22]
Africa	1	16	54	55	210	312	358	857	350	7,368
Oceania	1	2	9	29	158	214	10,914	12,574	3,965	13,024
Not specified[22]	300	33,030	69,902	53,115	29,011	17,791	790	789	14,063	33,523[25]

[1]Data for years prior to 1906 relate to country whence alien came; data from 1906–79 and 1984–89 are for country of last permanent residence; and data for 1980–83 refer to country of birth. Because of changes in boundaries, changes in lists of countries, and lack of data for specified countries for various peirods, data for certain countries, especially for the total period 1820–1989, are not comparable throughout. Data for specified countries are included with countries to which they belonged prior to World War I. [2]Data for Austria and Hungary not reported until 1861. [3]Data for Austria and Hungary not reported separately for all years during the period. [4]No data available for Czechoslovakia until 1920.

[5]Prior to 1926, data for Northern Ireland included in Ireland.

[6]Data for Norway and Sweden not reported separately until 1871.

[7]No data available for Romania until 1880.

[8]Since 1925, data for United Kingdom refer to England, Scotland, Wales, and Northern Ireland.

[9]In 1920, a separate enumeration was made for the Kingdom of Serbs, Croats, and Slovenes. Since 1922, the Serb, Croat, and Slovene Kingdom recorded as Yugoslavia.

[10]Beginning in 1957, China includes Taiwan.

[11]Data not reported separately until 1952.

[12]Data not reported separately until 1925.

[13]Data not reported separately until 1949.

[14]No data available for Japan until 1861.

IMMIGRATION TO THE UNITED STATES BY PLACE OF ORIGIN, 1820–1989 (continued)

Region and Country of Last Residence[1]	1911–20	1921–30	1931–40	1941–50	1951–60	1961–70	1971–80	1981–89	Total 180 Years 1820–1989
All countries	5,735,811	4,107,209	528,431	1,035,039	2,515,479	3,321,677	4,493,314	5,801,579	55,457,531
Europe	4,321,887	2,463,194	347,566	621,147	1,325,727	1,123,492	800,368	637,524	36,977,034
Austria-Hungary	896,342[23]	63,548	11,424	28,329	103,743	26,022	16,028	20,152	4,338,049
Austria	453,649	32,868	3,563[24]	24,860[24]	67,106	20,621	9,478	14,566	1,825,172[3]
Hungary	442,693	30,680	7,861	3,469	36,637	5,401	6,550	5,586	1,666,801[3]
Belgium	33,746	15,846	4,817	12,189	18,575	9,192	5,329	6,239	209,729
Czechoslovakia	3,426[4]	102,194	14,393	8,347	918	3,273	6,023	6,649	145,223
Denmark	41,983	32,430	2,559	5,393	10,984	9,201	4,439	4,696	369,738
France	61,897	49,610	12,623	38,809	51,121	45,237	25,069	28,088	783,322
Germany	143,945[23]	412,202	114,058[24]	226,578[24]	477,765	190,796	74,414	79,809	7,071,313
Greece	184,201	51,084	9,119	8,973	47,608	85,969	92,369	34,490	700,017
Ireland[5]	146,181	211,234	10,973	19,789	48,362	32,966	11,490	22,229	4,715,393
Italy	1,109,524	455,315	68,028	57,661	185,491	214,111	129,368	51,008	5,356,862
Netherlands	43,718	26,948	7,150	14,860	52,277	30,606	10,492	10,723	372,717
Norway-Sweden	161,469	165,780	8,700	20,765	44,632	32,600	10,472	13,252	2,144,024
Norway	66,395	68,531	4,740	10,100	22,935	15,484	3,941	3,612	800,672[6]
Sweden	95,074	97,249	3,960	10,665	21,697	17,116	6,531	9,640	1,283,097[6]
Poland	4,813[23]	227,734	17,026	7,571	9,985	53,539	37,234	64,888	597,972
Portugal	89,732	29,994	3,329	7,423	19,588	76,065	101,710	36,365	497,195
Romania	13,311	67,646	3,871	1,076	1,039	2,531	12,393	27,361	201,345
Soviet Union	921,201[23]	61,742	1,370	571	671	2,465	38,961	42,898	3,428,927
Spain	68,611	28,958	3,258	2,898	7,894	44,659	39,141	17,689	282,404
Switzerland	23,091	29,676	5,512	10,547	17,675	18,453	8,235	7,561	358,151
United Kingdom[5, 8]	341,408	339,570	31,572	139,306	202,824	213,822	137,374	140,119	5,100,096
Yugoslavia	1,888[9]	49,064	5,835	1,576	8,225	20,381	30,540	15,984	133,493
Other Europe	31,400	42,619	11,949	8,486	16,350	11,604	9,287	7,324	181,064
Asia	247,236	112,059	16,595	37,028	153,249	427,642	1,588,178	2,416,278	5,697,301
China[10]	21,278	29,907	4,928	16,709	9,657	34,764	124,326	306,108	873,737
Hong Kong	—[11]	—[11]	—[11]	—[11]	15,541[11]	75,007	113,467	83,848	287,863[11]
India	2,082	1,886	496	1,761	1,973	27,189	164,134	221,977	426,907
Iran	—[12]	241[12]	195	1,380	3,388	10,339	45,136	101,267	161,946[12]
Israel	—[13]	—[13]	—[13]	476[13]	25,476	29,602	37,713	38,367	131,634[13]
Japan	83,837	33,462	1,948	1,555	46,250	39,988	49,775	40,654	455,813[14]
Korea	—[15]	—[15]	—[15]	107[15]	6,231	34,526	267,638	302,782	611,284[15]

Philippines	—[16]	—[16]	528	4,691	19,307	98,376	354,987	477,485	955,374[16]
Turkey	134,066	33,824	1,065	798	3,519	10,142	13,399	20,028	409,122
Vietnam	—[11]	—[11]	—[11]	—[11]	335[11]	4,340	172,820	266,027	443,522[11]
Other Asia	5,973	12,739	7,435	9,551	21,572	63,369	244,783	557,735	940,099
America	1,143,671	1,516,716	160,037	354,804	996,944	1,716,374	1,982,735	2,564,698	12,017,021
Canada & Newfoundland[17, 18]	742,185	924,515	108,527	171,718	377,952	413,310	169,939	132,296	4,270,943
Mexico[18]	219,004	459,287	22,319	60,589	299,811	453,937	640,294	975,657	3,208,543
Caribbean	123,424	74,899	15,502	49,725	123,091	470,213	741,126	759,416	2,590,542
Cuba	—[12]	15,901[12]	9,571	26,313	78,948	208,536	264,863	135,142	739,274[12]
Dominican Republic	—[20]	—[20]	1,150[20]	5,627	9,897	93,292	148,135	209,899	468,000[20]
Haiti	—[20]	—[20]	191[20]	911	4,442	34,499	56,335	118,510	214,888[20]
Jamaica	—[21]	—[21]	—[21]	—[21]	8,869[21]	74,906	137,577	184,481	405,833[21]
Other Caribbean	123,424	58,998	4,590	16,874	20,935[21]	58,980	134,216	111,384	762,547
Central America	17,159	15,769	5,861	21,665	44,751	101,330	134,640	321,845	673,385
El Salvador	—[20]	—[20]	673[20]	5,132	5,895	14,992	34,436	133,938	195,066[20]
Other Central America	17,159	15,769	5,188	16,533	38,856	86,338	100,204	187,907	478,319
South America	41,899	42,215	7,803	21,831	91,628	257,954	295,741	375,026	1,163,482
Argentina	—[20]	—[20]	1,349[20]	3,338	19,486	49,721	29,897	21,374	125,165[20]
Columbia	—[20]	—[20]	1,223[20]	3,858	18.048	72,028	77,347	99,066	271,570[20]
Ecuador	—[20]	—[20]	337[20]	2,417	9,841	36,780	50,077	43,841	143,293[20]
Other South America	41,899	42,215	4,894	12,218	44,253	99,425	138,420	210,745	623,454
Other America	—[22]	31[22]	25	29,276	59,711	19,630	995	458	110,126
Africa	8,443	6,286	1,750	7,367	14,092	28,954	80,779	144,096	301,348
Oceania	13,427	8,726	2,483	14,551	12,976	25,122	41,242	38,401	197,818
Not specified[22]	1,147	228	—	142	12,491	93	12	582	267,009

[15]Data not reported separately until 1948. [16]Prior to 1934, Philippines recorded as insular travel.
[17]Prior to 1920, Canada and Newfoundland recorded as British North America. From 1820–98, figures include all British North America possessions.
[18]Land arrivals not completely enumerated until 1908. [19]No data available for Mexico from 1886–93. [20]Data not reported separately until 1932.
[21]Data for Jamaica not collected until 1953. In prior years, consolidated under British West Indies, which is included in "Other Caribbean."
[22] "Other America" included in countries "Not specified" until 1925.
[23]From 1899–1919, data for Poland included in Austria-Hungary, Germany and the Soviet Union.
[24]From 1938–45, data for Austria included in Germany. [25]Includes 32,897 persons returning in 1906 to their homes in the United States.
— represents zero

NOTE: From 1820–67, figures represent alien passengers arrrived at seaports; from 1868–91 and 1895–97, immigrant aliens arrived; from 1892–94 and 1898–1989, immigrant aliens admitted for permanent residence. From 1892–1903, aliens entering by cabin class were not counted as immigrants. Land arrivals were not completely enumerated until 1908. For this table, fiscal year 1843 covers 9 months ending September 1843; fiscal years 1832 and 1850 cover 15 months ending December 31 of the respective years; and fiscal year 1868 covers 6 months ending June 30, 1868.

SOURCE: U.S. Immigration and Naturalization Service, 1991.

Glossary of Key Terms

access the actual involvement of interest groups in the decision-making process.

accountability the obligation to justify the discharge of duties in the fulfillment of responsibilities to a person or persons in higher authority, and to be answerable to that authority for failing to fulfill the assigned duties and responsibilities.

administrative regulation rules made by ***regulatory agencies*** and commissions.

affirmative action government policies or programs that seek to redress past injustices against specified groups by making special efforts to provide members of these groups with access to educational and employment opportunities.

agencies of socialization social institutions, including families and schools, that help to shape individuals' basic political beliefs and values.

agency representation the type of representation by which representatives are held accountable to their ***constituency*** if they fail to represent that constituency. This is the incentive for good representation when the personal backgrounds, views, and interests of the representative differ from those of his or her constituency.

Aid to Families with Dependent Children (AFDC) federal funds, administered by the states, for children living with parents or relatives who fall below state standards of need.

amicus curiae literally, "friend of the court"; individuals or groups who are not parties to a lawsuit but who seek to assist the Supreme Court in reaching a decision by presenting additional ***briefs.***

Antifederalists those who favored strong state governments and a weak national government and who were opponents of the constitution proposed at the American Constitutional Convention of 1787.

appellate court a court that hears the appeals of ***trial court*** decisions.

appropriations the amounts of money approved by Congress in statutes (bills) that each unit or agency of government can spend.

Articles of Confederation America's first written constitution, adopted by the Continental Congress in 1777, and which served as the basis for America's national government until 1789.

Astroturf lobbying a negative term used to describe group-directed and exaggerated ***grassroots lobbying.***

at-large system the system of electing city council members based on a constituency of the entire city rather than specified subdivisions of the city. This system was used in ***reform cities*** in order to get the "best" candidates. Compare with ***district system.***

authoritarian government a system of rule in which the government recognizes no formal limits but may nevertheless be restrained by the power of other social institutions.

autocracy a form of government in which a single individual—a king, queen, or dictator—rules.

balance of power role The strategy whereby many countries form alliances with one or more other countries in order to counterbalance the behavior of other, usually more powerful, ***nation-states.***

bandwagon effect a situation wherein reports of voter or delegate opinion can influence the actual outcome of an election or a nominating convention.

benign gerrymandering attempts to draw district boundaries so as to create districts made up primarily of disadvantaged or underrepresented minorities.

bicameral having a legislative assembly composed of two chambers or houses; opposite of ***unicameral.***

bilateral treaties treaties made between two nations. Contrast with ***multilateral treaties.***

Bill of Rights the first ten amendments to the U.S. Constitution, ratified in 1791; they ensure certain rights and liberties to the people.

black nationalism a movement that supported total separatism for African Americans, supporting goals that ranged from economic independence to emigration back to Africa.

block grants federal ***grants-in-aid*** that allow states considerable discretion in how the funds should be spent.

briefs written documents in which attorneys explain, using case precedents, why the court should find in favor of their client.

Brown v. Board of Education the 1954 Supreme Court decision that struck down the "separate but equal" doctrine as fundamentally unequal. This case eliminated state power to use race as a criterion of ***discrimination*** in law and provided the national government with the power to intervene by exercising strict regulatory policies against discriminatory actions.

burden of proof obligation of the prosecution (the government) in criminal cases to demonstrate the guilt of the defendant "beyond a reasonable doubt"; in civil cases the burden is on the plaintiff to prove his or her case by "a preponderance of the evidence"—a less difficult standard of proof.

bureaucracy the complex structure of offices, tasks, rules, and principles of organization that are employed by all large-scale institutions to coordinate the work of their personnel.

Cabinet the secretaries, or chief administrators, of the major departments of the federal government. Cabinet secretaries are appointed by the president with the consent of the Senate.

campaign an effort by political candidates and their staffs to win the backing of donors, political activists, and voters in the quest for political office.

capture an interest's acquisition of substantial influence over the government agency charged with regulating its activities.

categorical grants congressional grants given to states and localities on the condition that expenditures be limited to a problem or group specified by the law.

caucus (congressional) an association of members of Congress based on party, interest, or social group such as gender or race.

caucus (political) a normally closed meeting of a political or legislative group to select candidates, plan strategy, or make decisions regarding legislative matters.

checks and balances mechanisms through which each branch of government is able to participate in and influence the activities of the other branches. Major examples include the presidential ***veto*** power over congressional legislation, the power of the Senate to approve presidential appointments, and ***judicial review*** of congressional enactments.

chief justice justice on the Supreme Court who presides over the Court's public sessions.

civil law a system of jurisprudence, including private law and governmental actions, to settle disputes that do not involve ***criminal penalties.*** Compare with ***criminal law.***

civil liberties areas of personal freedom with which governments are constrained from interfering.

civil penalties ***regulatory techniques*** in which fines or another form of material restitution is imposed for violating civil laws or common law principles, such as negligence.

civil rights legal or moral claims that citizens are entitled to make upon the government.

civil service reform reform adopted in cities, as well as in the federal government, to ensure the hiring and firing of government employees based on merit. This was an effort to discourage ***patronage.***

class action suit a legal action by which a group or class of individuals with common interests can file a suit on behalf of everyone who shares that interest.

clientele agencies departments or bureaus of government whose mission is to promote, serve, or represent a particular interest or a particular segment or geographical area of the country.

client state a ***nation-state*** dependent upon a more powerful nation-state, but which still has enough power and resources to conduct its own foreign policy up to a point.

closed caucus a presidential nominating caucus open only to registered party members.

closed primary a primary election in which voters can participate in the nomination of candidates, but only of the party in which they are enrolled for a period of time prior to primary day. Compare with ***open primary.***

closed rule a provision by the House Rules Committee limiting or prohibiting the introduction of amendments during debate. Compare with ***open rule.***

cloture a rule allowing a majority of two-thirds or three-fifths of the members in a legislative body to set a time limit on debate over a given bill.

coattail effect the result of voters casting their ballot for president or governor and "automatically" voting for the remainder of the party's ticket.

cold war the period of struggle between the United States and the former Soviet Union between the late 1940s and 1990.

collective goods benefits, sought by groups, that are broadly available and cannot be denied to nonmembers.

commerce clause Article I, Section 8, of the Constitution, which delegates to Congress the power to "regulate commerce with foreign nations, and among the several States and with the Indian tribes." This clause was interpreted by the Supreme Court in favor of national power over the economy.

conference a gathering of House Republicans every two years to elect their House leaders. Democrats call their gathering the *caucus*.

conference committee a joint committee created to work out a compromise on House and Senate versions of a piece of legislation.

conservative today this term refers to those who generally support the social and economic status quo and are suspicious of efforts to introduce new political formulae and economic arrangements. Conservatives believe that a large and powerful government poses a threat to citizens' freedom.

constituency the district comprising the area from which an official is elected.

constitutional government a system of rule in which formal and effective limits are placed on the powers of the government.

containment the policy used by the United States during the ***cold war*** to restrict the expansion of communism and limit the influence of the Soviet Union.

contracting power the power of government to set conditions on companies seeking to sell goods or services to government agencies.

contributory programs social programs financed in whole or in part by taxation or other mandatory contributions by their present or future recipients. The most important example is Social Security, which is financed by a payroll tax.

cooperative federalism a type of federalism existing since the New Deal era in which ***grants-in-aid*** have been used strategically to encourage states and localities (without commanding them) to pursue nationally defined goals. Also known as *intergovernmental cooperation.*

cooptation the strategy of bringing an individual into a group by joint action of the members of that group, usually in order to reduce or eliminate the individual's opposition.

corridoring working to gain influence in an executive agency.

cost of living adjustments (COLAs) changes made to the level of benefits of a government program based on the rate of ***inflation.***

criminal law the branch of law that deals with disputes or actions involving ***criminal penalties*** (as opposed to ***civil law***); it regulates the conduct of individuals, defines crimes, and provides punishment for criminal acts.

criminal penalties regulatory techniques in which imprisonment or heavy fines and the loss of certain civil rights and liberties are imposed.

critical electoral realignment the point in history when a new party supplants the ruling party, becoming in turn the dominant political force. In the United States, this has tended to occur roughly every thirty years.

cross-lobbying a term to describe lobbyists ***lobbying*** one another.

de facto literally, "by fact"; practices that occur even when there is no legal enforcement, such as school segregation in much of the United States today.

defendant the one against whom a complaint is brought in a criminal or civil case.

de jure literally, "by law"; legally enforced practices, such as school segregation in the South before the 1960s.

delegated powers constitutional powers assigned to one governmental agency but that are exercised by another agency with the express permission of the first.

delegates political activists selected to vote at a party's ***national convention.***

democracy a system of rule that permits citizens to play a significant part in the governmental process, usually through the election of key public officials.

deregulation a policy of reducing or eliminating regulatory restraints on the conduct of individuals or private institutions.

deterrence the development and maintenance of military strength as a means of discouraging attack.

devolution a policy to remove a program from one level of government by delegating it or passing it down to a lower level of government, such as from the national government to the state and local governments.

diplomacy the representation of a government to other foreign governments.

direct-action politics a form of politics, such as civil disobedience or revolutionary action, that takes place outside formal channels.

direct democracy a system of rule that permits citizens to vote directly on laws and policies.

discount rate the interest rate charged by the ***Federal Reserve System*** when commercial banks borrow in order to expand their lending operations; an effective tool of monetary policy.

discrimination the use of any unreasonable and unjust criterion of exclusion.

dissenting opinion a decision written by a justice in the minority in a particular case in which the justice wishes to express his or her reasoning in the case.

district system a system of electing city council members from a number of local districts, rather than from the city as a whole. This system was widely adopted in cities during the 1970s and 1980s to ensure minority representation on city councils. Compare with ***at-large system.***

divided government the condition in American government wherein the presidency is controlled by one party while the opposing party controls one or both houses of Congress.

double jeopardy the Fifth Amendment right providing that no person can be tried twice for the same crime.

dual federalism the system of government that prevailed in the United States from 1789 to 1937, in which most fundamental governmental powers were shared between the federal and state governments.

due process of law the right of every citizen against arbitrary action by national or state governments.

economic expansionist role the strategy often pursued by capitalist countries to adopt foreign policies that will maximize the success of domestic corporations in their dealings with other countries.

elastic clause Article I, Section 8, of the Constitution (also known as the necessary and proper clause), which enumerates the powers of Congress and provides Congress with the authority to make all laws "necessary and proper" to carry them out.

electoral college the presidential electors from each state who meet after the popular election to cast ballots for president and vice president.

eminent domain the right of government to take private property for public use.

entitlement eligibility for benefits by virtue of a category of benefits defined by legislation.

equality of opportunity a widely shared American ideal that all people should have the freedom to use whatever talents and wealth they have to reach their fullest potential.

equal time rule the requirement that broadcasters provide candidates for the same political office an equal opportunity to communicate their messages to the public.

establishment clause the First Amendment clause that says that "Congress shall make no law respecting an establishment of religion." This clause means that a "wall of separation" exists between church and state.

exclusionary rule the ability of courts to exclude evidence obtained in violation of the Fourth Amendment.

executive agreement an agreement, made between the president and another country, that has the force of a treaty but does not require the Senate's "advice and consent."

Executive Office of the President (EOP) the permanent agencies that perform defined management tasks for the president. Created in 1939, the EOP includes the Office of Management and Budget, the Council of Economic Advisers, the National Security Council, and other agencies.

expressed powers specific powers granted to Congress under Article I, Section 8, of the Constitution.

expropriation confiscation of property with or without compensation.

fairness doctrine a Federal Communications Commission (FCC) requirement for broadcasters who air programs on controversial issues to provide time for opposing views. The FCC ceased enforcing this doctrine in 1985.

federalism a system of government in which power is divided, by a constitution, between a central government and regional governments.

Federalist Papers a series of essays written by James Madison, Alexander Hamilton, and John Jay supporting the ratification of the Constitution.

Federalists those who favored a strong national government and supported the constitution proposed at the American Constitutional Convention of 1787.

Federal Reserve Board the governing board of the ***Federal Reserve System,*** comprised of a chair and six other members, all appointed by the president with the consent of the Senate.

Federal Reserve System (Fed) a system of twelve Federal Reserve Banks, that facilitates exchanges of cash, checks, and credit; regulates member banks; and uses monetary policies to fight inflation and deflation.

fighting words speech that directly incites damaging conduct.

filibuster a tactic used by members of the Senate to prevent action on legislation they oppose by continuously holding the floor and speaking until the majority backs down. Once given the floor, senators have unlimited time to speak, and it requires a vote of three-fifths of the Senate to end a filibuster.

fiscal policy the use of taxing, monetary, and spending powers to manipulate the economy.

food stamps coupons that can be exchanged for food at most grocery stores; the largest ***in-kind benefits*** program.

formula grants ***grants-in-aid*** in which a formula is used to determine the amount of federal funds a state or local government will receive.

free exercise clause the First Amendment clause that protects a citizen's right to believe and practice whatever religion he or she chooses.

free riders those who enjoy the benefits of collective goods but did not participate in acquiring them.

gender gap a distinctive pattern of male and female voting that became important in the 1980s.

gerrymandering apportionment of voters in districts in such a way as to give unfair advantage to one political party.

going public a strategy that attempts to mobilize the widest and most favorable climate of opinion.

government institutions and procedures through which a territory and its people are ruled.

grants-in-aid programs through which Congress provides money to state and local governments on the condition that the funds be employed for purposes defined by the federal government.

grassroots lobbying a ***lobbying*** campaign in which a group mobilizes its membership to contact government officials in support of the group's position.

Great Compromise agreement reached at the Constitutional Convention of 1787 that gave each state an equal number of senators regardless of its population, but linked representation in the House of Representatives to population.

habeas corpus a court order demanding that an individual in custody be brought into court and shown the cause for detention. *Habeas corpus* is guaranteed by the Constitution and can be suspended only in cases of rebellion or invasion.

Holy Alliance role a strategy pursued by a superpower to prevent any change in the existing distribution of power among ***nation-states,*** even if this requires intervention into the internal affairs of another country in order to keep a ruler from being overturned.

home rule power delegated by the state to a local unit of government to manage its own affairs.

homesteading a national policy that permitted people to gain ownership of property by occupying public or unclaimed lands, living on the land for a specified period of time, and making certain minimal improvements on that land. Also known as *squatting*.

ideology the combined doctrines, assertions, and intentions of a social or political group that justify its behavior.

illusion of saliency the impression conveyed by polls that something is important to the public when actually it is not.

implementation the efforts of departments and agencies to translate laws into specific bureaucratic routines.

implied powers doctrine support for powers derived from the "necessary and proper" clause of Article I, Section 8, of the Constitution. Such powers are not specifically expressed, but are implied through the expansive interpretation of delegated powers.

incumbency holding a political office for which one is running.

incumbent a candidate running for a position that he or she already holds.

indexing periodic process of adjusting welfare payments or wages to account for increases in the cost of living.

inflation a consistent increase in the general level of prices.

infomercial a lengthy campaign advertisement on television.

initiative procedure in twenty-three states that allows citizens to place policy proposals on the ballot, usually after gathering a specified number of signatures on a petition.

in-kind benefits goods and services provided to needy individuals and families by the federal government.

institutional advertising advertising designed to create a positive image of an organization.

intergovernmental lobbying efforts by organizations representing state and local governments to influence national government policy making (examples include the National Governors' Association and the U.S. Conference of Mayors).

intermediate scrutiny test, used by the Supreme Court in gender discrimination cases, which places the burden of proof partially on the government and partially on the challengers to show that the law in question is constitutional.

International Monetary Fund (IMF) an institution established in 1944 at Bretton Woods, New Hampshire, which provides loans and facilitates international monetary exchange.

interpretation the process wherein bureaucrats implement ambiguous statutes, requiring agencies to make educated guesses as to what Congress or higher administrative authorities intended.

iron triangle the stable, cooperative relationships that often develop between a congressional committee, an administrative agency, and one or more supportive interest groups. Not all of these relationships are triangular, but the iron triangle is the most typical.

joint committee a legislative committee formed of members of both the House and the Senate.

judicial activism judicial philosophy that posits that the Court should go beyond the words of the Constitution or a statute to consider the broader societal implications of its decisions.

judicial restraint judicial philosophy whose adherents refuse to go beyond the clear words of the Constitution in interpreting its meaning.

judicial review the power of the courts to declare actions of the legislative and executive branches invalid or unconstitutional. The Supreme Court asserted this power in *Marbury v. Madison.*

jurisdiction the sphere of a court's power and authority.

Kitchen Cabinet an informal group of advisers to whom the president turns for counsel and guidance. Members of the official cabinet may or may not also be members of the Kitchen Cabinet.

laboratories of democracy a phrase applied to the states, referring to their ability to experiment with a wide range of policies. This ability to experiment is viewed as a strength of the American system of federalism.

legitimacy popular acceptance of a government and its decisions.

***Lemon* test** a rule articulated in *Lemon v. Kurtzman* that government action toward religion is permissible if it is secular in purpose, does not lead to "excessive entanglement" with religion, and neither promotes nor inhibits the practice of religion.

libel a written statement made in "reckless disregard of the truth" that is considered damaging to a victim because it is "malicious, scandalous, and defamatory."

liberal a liberal today generally supports political and social reform; extensive governmental intervention in the economy; the expansion of federal social services; more vigorous efforts on behalf of the poor, minorities, and women; and greater concern for consumers and the environment.

libertarian the political philosophy that is skeptical of any government intervention as a potential threat against individual liberty; libertarians believe that government has caused more problems than it has solved.

liberty freedom from governmental control.

license permission to engage in some activity that is otherwise illegal, such as hunting or practicing medicine.

limited government a government whose powers are defined and limited by a constitution.

line-item veto the power of the executive to ***veto*** specific provisions (lines) of a bill passed by the legislature.

lobbying a strategy by which organized interests seek to influence the passage of legislation by exerting direct pressure on members of the legislature.

logrolling a legislative practice wherein reciprocal agreements are made between legislators, usually in voting for or against a bill. In contrast to bargaining, parties to logrolling have nothing in common but their desire to exchange support.

machine cities cities in which politics was dominated by party organizations that controlled nominations for office and mobilized party voters.

machines strong party organizations in late-nineteenth- and early twentieth-century American cities. These machines were led by "bosses" who controlled party nominations and patronage.

majority leader the elected leader of the ***majority party*** in the House of Representatives or in the Senate. In the House, the majority leader is subordinate in the party hierarchy to the ***Speaker.***

majority party the party that holds the majority of legislative seats in either the House or the Senate.

majority system a type of electoral system in which, to win a seat in the parliament or other representative body, a candidate must receive a majority of all the votes cast in the relevant district. Compare ***plurality system.***

mandate a claim by a victorious candidate that the electorate has given him or her special authority to carry out promises made during the campaign.

marketplace of ideas the public forum in which beliefs and ideas are exchanged and compete.

Marshall Plan the U.S. European Recovery Plan, in which over $34 billion was spent for the relief, reconstruction, and economic recovery of Western Europe after World War II.

material benefits special goods, services, or money provided to members of groups to entice others to join.

means testing a procedure by which potential beneficiaries of a public assistance program establish their eligibility by demonstrating a genuine need for the assistance.

Medicaid a federally financed, state-operated program providing medical services to low-income people.

Medicare a form of national health insurance for the elderly and for the disabled.

membership associations organized groups in which members actually play a substantial role, sitting on committees and engaging in group projects.

merit system a product of civil service reform, in which appointees to positions in public bureaucracies must objectively be deemed qualified for the position.

midterm elections congressional elections that do not coincide with a presidential election; also called *off-year elections.*

military-industrial complex a concept coined by President Eisenhower, in which he referred to the threats to American democracy that may arise from too close a friendship between major corporations in the defense industry and the Pentagon. This is one example of the larger political phenomenon of the *iron triangle.*

minority district a ***gerrymandered*** voting district that improves the chances of minority candidates by making selected minority groups the majority within the district.

minority leader the elected leader of the ***minority party*** in the House or Senate.

minority party the party that holds a minority of legislative seats in either the House or the Senate.

***Miranda* rule** the requirement, articulated by the Supreme Court in *Miranda v. Arizona,* that persons under arrest must be informed prior to police interrogation of their rights to remain silent and to have the benefit of legal counsel.

monetary techniques efforts to regulate the economy through manipulation of the supply of money and credit. America's most powerful institution in the area of monetary policy is the ***Federal Reserve Board.***

monopoly the existence of a single firm in a market that controls all the goods and services of that market.; absence of competition.

mootness a criterion used by courts to screen cases that no longer require resolution.

multilateralism a foreign policy that seeks to encourage the involvement of several ***nation-states*** in coordinated action, usually in relation to a common adversary, with terms and conditions usually specified in a multi-country treaty.

multilateral treaties treaties among more than two nations.

multiple-member district an electorate that selects all candidates at large from the whole district; each voter is given the number of votes equivalent to the number of seats to be filled. Compare ***single-member district.***

Napoleonic role a strategy pursued by a powerful nation to prevent aggressive actions against themselves by improving the internal state of affairs of a particular country, even if this means encouraging revolution in that country.

national convention a national party political institution that serves to nominate the party's presidential and vice presidential candidates, establish party rules, and write and ratify the party's ***platform.***

nationalism the widely held belief that the people who occupy the same territory have something in common, and that they are a single community.

National Security Council (NSC) a presidential foreign policy advisory council composed of the president; the vice president; the secretaries of state, defense, and the treasury; the attorney general; and other officials invited by the president. The NSC has a staff of foreign-policy specialists.

nation-state a political entity consisting of a people with some common cultural experience (nation) who also share a common political authority (state) recognized by other sovereignties (nation-states).

nativism a nineteenth-century anti-immigrant movement based on fears of immigrants' Catholicism, potential radicalism, and race. Nativism also refers to a general antagonism toward immigration.

necessary and proper clause from Article I, Section 8, of the Constitution, it provides Congress with the authority to make all laws "necessary and proper" to carry out its expressed powers.

New Federalism attempts by Presidents Nixon and Reagan to return power to the states through ***block grants.***

New Jersey Plan a framework for the Constitution, introduced by William Paterson, which called for equal state representation in the national legislature regardless of population.

new paternalists conservatives who believe that social policy can be used to enforce certain standards of behavior among beneficiaries.

New Politics movement political movement that began in the 1960s and 1970s, made up of professionals and intellectuals for whom the Civil Rights and antiwar movements were formative experiences. The New Politics movement strengthened ***public-interest groups.***

news enclave population subgroups that receive most of their political information from sources other than the major national news media.

nomination the process through which political parties select their candidates for election to public office.

noncontributory programs social programs that provide assistance to people based on demonstrated need rather than any contribution they have made.

North Atlantic Treaty Organization (NATO) a treaty organization, comprising the United States, Canada, and most of western Europe, formed in 1948 to counter the perceived threat from the Soviet Union.

oligarchy a form of government in which a small group—landowners, military officers, or wealthy merchants—controls most of the governing decisions.

open caucus a presidential nominating caucus open to anyone who wishes to attend.

open market operations method by which the Open Market Committee of the ***Federal Reserve System*** buys and sells government securities, etc., to help finance government operations and to loosen or tighten the total amount of money circulating in the economy.

open primary a primary election in which the voter can wait until the day of the primary to choose which party to enroll in to select candidates for the general election.

open rule a provision by the House Rules Committee that permits floor debate and the addition of new amendments to a bill.

opinion the written explanation of the Supreme Court's decision in a particular case.

oral argument stage in Supreme Court procedure in which attorneys for both sides appear before the Court to present their positions and answer questions posed by justices.

ordinances legislative acts of a local legislature or municipal commission. Puts the force of law under city charter but is a lower order of law than a statute of the national or state legislature.

original jurisdiction the authority to initially consider a case. Distinguished from *appellate jurisdiction,* which is the authority to hear appeals from a lower court's decision.

oversight the effort by Congress, through hearings, investigations, and other techniques, to exercise control over the activities of executive agencies.

paper trail written accounts by which the process of decision making and the participants in a decision can, if desired, be later reconstructed. Often called *red tape*.

party activists partisans who contribute time, energy, and effort to support their party and its candidates.

party identification an individual voter's psychological ties to one party or another.

party vote a ***roll-call vote*** in the House or Senate in which at least 90 percent of the members of one party take a particular position and are opposed by at least 90 percent of the members of the other party. Party votes are rare today, although they were fairly common in the nineteenth century.

patronage the resources available to higher officials, usually opportunities to make partisan appointments to offices and to confer grants, licenses, or special favors to supporters.

per curiam decision by an ***appellate court,*** without a written opinion, that refuses to review the decision of a lower court; amounts to a reaffirmation of the lower court's opinion.

plaintiff the individual or organization who brings a complaint in court.

platform a party document, written at a national convention, that contains party philosophy, principles, and positions on issues.

plea bargains negotiated agreements in criminal cases in which a defendant agrees to plead guilty in return for the state's agreement to reduce the severity of the criminal charge the defendant is facing.

pluralism the theory that all interests are and should be free to compete for influence in the government. The outcome of this competition is compromise and moderation.

plurality system a type of electoral system in which, to win a seat in the parliament or other representative body, a candidate need only receive the most votes in the election, not necessarily a majority of votes cast. Compare ***majority system.***

pocket veto a presidential ***veto*** that is automatically triggered if the president does not act on a given piece of legislation passed during the final ten days of a legislative session.

police power power reserved to the state to regulate the health, safety, and morals of its citizens.

policy of redistribution a policy whose objective is to tax or spend in such a way as to reduce the disparities of wealth between the lowest and the highest income brackets.

political action committee (PAC) a private group that raises and distributes funds for use in election campaigns.

political culture broadly shared values, beliefs, and attitudes about how the government should function. American political culture emphasizes the values of liberty, equality, and democracy.

political machines local party organizations that control urban politics by mobilizing voters to elect the machines' candidates.

political parties organized groups that attempt to influence the government by electing their members to important government offices.

political socialization the induction of individuals into the political culture; learning how to accept authority; learning what is legitimate and what is not.

politics conflict over the leadership, structure, and policies of governments.

poll tax a state-imposed tax upon voters as a prerequisite to registration. Poll taxes were rendered unconstitutional in national elections by the Twenty-fourth Amendment and in state elections by the Supreme Court in 1966.

pork barrel appropriations made by legislative bodies for local projects that are often not needed but that are created so that local representatives can win re-election in their home districts.

power influence over a government's leadership, organization, or policies.

power without diplomacy a post–World War II foreign policy in which the goal was to use American power to create an international structure that could be run with a minimum of regular diplomatic involvement.

precedents prior cases whose principles are used by judges as the bases for their decisions in present cases.

preemption the principle that allows the national government to override state or local actions in certain policy areas.

preferred freedoms doctrine see ***strict scrutiny.***

primary elections elections used to select a party's candidate for the general election.

prior restraint an effort by a governmental agency to block the publication of material it deems libelous or harmful in some other way; censorship. In the United States, the courts forbid prior restraint except under the most extraordinary circumstances.

private bill a proposal in Congress to provide a specific person with some kind of relief, such as a special exemption from immigration quotas.

privatization removing all or part of a program from the public sector to the private sector.

procedural liberties restraints on how the government is supposed to act; for example, citizens are guaranteed the ***due process of law.***

progressive/regressive taxation taxation that hits the upper income brackets more heavily (progressive) or the lower income brackets more heavily (regressive).

project grants grant programs in which state and local governments submit proposals to federal agencies and for which funding is provided on a competitive basis.

promotional techniques techniques that encourage people to do something they might not otherwise do or to continue an action or behavior. Three types of promotional techniques are subsidies, contracts, and licenses.

proportional representation a ***multiple-member district*** system that allows each political party representation in proportion to its percentage of the total vote. Compare with ***winner-take-all system.***

public-interest groups groups that claim they serve the general good rather than their own particular interest.

public law cases in private law, civil law, or criminal law in which one party to the dispute argues that a license is unfair, a law is inequitable or unconstitutional, or an agency has acted unfairly, violated a procedure, or gone beyond its jurisdiction.

public opinion citizen's attitudes about political issues, personalities, institutions, and events.

public opinion polls scientific instruments for measuring public opinion.

public policy a law, rule, statute, or edict that expresses the government's goals and provides for rewards and punishments to promote their attainment.

purposive benefits selective benefits of group membership that emphasize the purpose and accomplishments of the group.

redistributive agencies a general category of agencies including fiscal agencies, monetary agencies, and welfare agencies, whose net effect is to shift large aggregates of wealth from rich to poor, young to old, etc.

redistributive programs economic policies designed to control the economy through taxing and spending, with the goal of benefiting the poor.

redistributive techniques techniques, fiscal or monetary, designed to control people by manipulating the entire economy rather than by regulating people directly.

redistricting the process of redrawing election districts and redistributing legislative representatives. This happens every ten years to reflect shifts in population or in response to legal challenges to existing districts.

redlining a practice in which banks refuse to make loans to people living in a certain geographic location.

referendum the practice of referring a measure proposed or passed by a legislature to the vote of the electorate for approval or rejection.

reform cities cities that adopted a variety of reforms in order to reduce the role of political parties and increase the role of experts in local politics.

regionalism the idea that all the different towns and cities in a metropolitan area constitute a single region. Rather than seeing cities and suburbs as competitors, this perspective views the different parts of the metropolitan area as interdependent.

regulated federalism a form of federalism in which Congress imposes legislation on states and localities, requiring them to meet national standards.

regulation a technique of control in which the government adopts rules imposing restrictions on the conduct of private citizens.

regulatory agencies departments, bureaus, or independent agencies whose primary mission is to impose limits, restrictions, or other obligations on the conduct of individuals or companies in the private sector.

regulatory tax a tax whose primary purpose is not to raise revenue but to influence conduct: e.g., a heavy tax on gasoline to discourage recreational driving.

regulatory techniques techniques that government uses to control the conduct of the people.

representative democracy/republic a system of government in which the populace selects representatives, who play a significant role in governmental decision making.

reserved powers powers, derived from the Tenth Amendment to the Constitution, that are not specifically delegated to the national government or denied to the states.

reserve requirement the amount of liquid assets and ready cash that banks are required to hold to meet depositors' demands for their money.

revenue agencies agencies responsible for collecting taxes. Examples include the Internal Revenue Service for income taxes, the U.S. Customs Service for tariffs and other taxes on imported goods, and the Bureau of Alcohol, Tobacco, and Firearms for collection of taxes on the sales of those particular products.

reverse lobbying a strategy by which members of Congress bring pressure to bear on lobby groups to support particular courses of action.

right of rebuttal a Federal Communications Commission regulation giving individuals the right to have the opportunity to respond to personal attacks made on a radio or television broadcast.

roll-call vote a vote in which each legislator's yes or no vote is recorded as the clerk calls the names of the members alphabetically.

salient interests attitudes and views that are important to the individual holding them.

sample a small group selected by researchers to represent the most important characteristics of an entire population.

select committee a (usually) temporary legislative committee set up to highlight or investigate a particular issue or address an issue not within the jurisdiction of existing committees. Compare ***standing committee.***

selective incorporation the process by which different protections in the Bill of Rights were incorporated into the Fourteenth Amendment, thus guaranteeing citizens protection from state as well as national government.

senatorial courtesy the practice whereby the president, before formally nominating a person for a federal judgeship, seeks the indication that senators from the candidate's own state support the nomination.

seniority priority or status ranking given to an individual on the basis of length of continuous service on a committee in Congress.

separation of powers the division of governmental power among several institutions that must cooperate in decision making.

shadow welfare state social benefits that private employers offer to their workers, such as medical insurance and pensions.

single-member district an electorate that is allowed to select only one representative from each district; the normal method of representation in the United States. Compare with ***multiple-member district.***

slander an oral statement, made in "reckless disregard of the truth," which is considered damaging to the victim because it is "malicious, scandalous, and defamatory."

Social Security a contributory welfare program into which working Americans contribute a percentage of their wages, and from which they receive cash benefits after retirement.

sociological representation a type of representation in which representatives have the same racial, ethnic, religious, or educational backgrounds as their constituents. It is based on the principle that if two individuals are similar in background, character, interests, and perspectives, then one could correctly represent the other's views.

soft money money contributed directly to political parties for voter registration and organization.

solicitor general the top government lawyer in all cases before the Supreme Court where the government is a party.

solidary benefits selective benefits of group membership that emphasize friendship, networking, and consciousness-raising.

sophomore surge the tendency for candidates to win a higher percentage of the vote after one term in office.

sovereignty supreme and independent political authority.

Speaker of the House the chief presiding officer of the House of Representatives. The Speaker is elected at the beginning of every Congress on a straight ***party vote.*** The Speaker is the most important party and House leader, and can influence the legislative agenda, the fate of individual pieces of legislation, and members' positions within the House.

special district a form of local government that usually cuts across city and town boundaries and is charged with a few very specific functions.

speech-plus speech accompanied by conduct such as sit-ins, picketing, and demonstrations; protection of this form of speech under the First Amendment is conditional, and restrictions imposed by state or local authorities are acceptable if properly balanced by considerations of public order.

split-ticket voting the practice of casting ballots for the candidates of at least two different political parties in the same election. Compare with ***straight-ticket voting.***

spot advertisement a fifteen-, thirty-, or sixty-second television campaign commercial that permits a candidate's message to be delivered to a target audience.

staff agency an agency responsible for maintaining the bureaucracy, with responsibilities such as purchasing, budgeting, personnel management, and planning.

staff organization a type of membership group in which a professional staff conducts most of the group's activities.

standing the right of an individual or organization to initiate a court case.

standing committee a permanent committee with the power to propose and write legislation that covers a particular subject such as finance or appropriations. Compare ***select committee.***

stare decisis literally "let the decision stand." The doctrine that a previous decision by a court applies as a precedent in similar cases until that decision is overruled.

states' rights the principle that the states should oppose the increasing authority of the national government. This principle was most popular in the period before the Civil War.

straight-ticket voting the practice of casting ballots for candidates of only one party. Compare with ***split-ticket voting.***

strict scrutiny test, used by Supreme Court in racial discrimination cases and other cases involving civil liberties and civil rights, which places the burden of proof on the government rather than on the challengers to show that the law in question is constitutional.

subsidies governmental grants of cash or other valuable commodities such as land to individuals or organizations; used to promote activities desired by the government, to reward political support, or to buy off political opposition.

substantive liberties restraints on what the government shall and shall not have the power to do.

suffrage the right to vote; also called *franchise.*

superdelegate convention delegate position, in Democratic conventions, reserved for party officials.

Supplemental Security Income (SSI) a program providing a minimum monthly income to people who pass a ***means test*** and who are sixty-five or older, blind, or disabled. Financed from general revenues rather than from Social Security contributions.

supremacy clause Article VI of the Constitution, which states that laws passed by the national government and all treaties are the supreme law of the land and superior to all laws adopted by any state or any subdivision.

supreme court the highest court in a particular state or in the United States. This court primarily serves an appellate function.

tax base the property and income within a political jurisdiction, such as a city or a state, that can be taxed.

tax expenditures government subsidies provided to employers and employees through tax deductions for amounts spent on health insurance and other benefits; these represent one way the government helps to ensure the social welfare of the middle class.

Temporary Assistance to Needy Families (TANF) a federal block grant that replaced the ***AFDC*** program in 1996.

term limits legally prescribed limits on the number of terms an elected official can serve.

third parties parties that organize to compete against the two major American political parties.

Three-fifths Compromise the agreement reached at the Constitutional Convention of 1787 that stipulated that for purposes of the apportionment of congressional seats, every slave would be counted as three-fifths of a person.

totalitarian government a system of rule in which the government recognizes no formal limits on its power and seeks to absorb or eliminate other social institutions that might challenge it.

town meeting a format in which candidates meet with ordinary citizens. Allows candidates to deliver messages without the presence of journalists or commentators.

trial court the first court to hear a criminal or civil case.

turnout the percentage of eligible individuals who actually vote.

tyranny oppressive and unjust government that employs cruel and unjust use of power and authority.

uncontrollables budgetary items that are beyond the control of budgetary committees and can only be controlled by substantive legislative action in Congress. Some uncontrollables are beyond the power of Congress, because the terms of payment are set in contracts, such as interest on the debt.

unfunded mandates regulations or conditions for receiving grants that impose costs on state and local governments for which they are not reimbursed by the federal government.

Uniform Commercial Code code used in many states in the area of contract law to reduce interstate differences in judicial decisions.

unilateralism a foreign policy that seeks to avoid international alliances, entanglements, and permanent commitments in favor of independence, neutrality, and freedom of action.

United Nations the organization of nations founded in 1945 to serve as a channel for negotiation, and a means of settling international disputes peaceably. The UN has had frequent successes in providing a forum for negotiation and on some occasions a means of preventing international conflicts from spreading. On a number of occasions, the UN has been a convenient cover for U.S. foreign policy goals.

unit rule the convention voting system under which a state delegation casts all of its votes for the candidate supported by the majority of the state's delegates.

universal programs programs available to everyone in a certain category; these programs are not ***means tested.***

veto the president's constitutional power to turn down acts of Congress. A presidential veto may be overridden by a two-thirds vote of each house of Congress.

Virginia Plan a framework for the Constitution, introduced by Edmund Randolph, which called for representation in the national legislature based upon the population of each state.

War Powers Resolution a resolution of Congress that the president can send troops into action abroad only by authorization of Congress, or if American troops are already under attack or serious threat.

whip system a communications network in each house of Congress; whips take polls of the membership in order to learn their intentions on specific legislative issues and to assist the majority and minority leaders in various tasks.

White House staff analysts and advisers to the president, often given the title "special assistant."

winner-take-all system a system in which all of a state's presidential nominating delegates are awarded to the candidate who wins the most votes, while runners-up receive no delegates. Compare with ***proportional representation.***

writ of *certiorari* a decision of at least four of the nine Supreme Court justices to review a decision of a lower court; from the Latin "to make more certain."

writ of *habeas corpus* a court order that the individual in custody be brought into court and shown the cause for detention. *Habeas corpus* is guaranteed by the Constitution and can be suspended only in cases of rebellion or invasion.

Endnotes

Chapter 1

1. E. J. Dionne, Jr., "The Timidity Budget," *Washington Post,* February 7, 1995, p. A19.

2. Charles Peters, "Tilting at Windmills," *Washington Monthly,* June 1995, p. 4.

3. See Eugen Weber, *Peasants into Frenchmen: The Modernization of Rural France, 1870–1914* (Stanford, CA: Stanford University Press, 1976), chap. 5.

4. See V. O. Key, *Politics, Parties, and Pressure Groups* (New York: Crowell, 1964), p. 201.

5. Harold Lasswell, *Politics: Who Gets What, When, How* (New York: Meridian Books, 1958).

6. Herbert McClosky and John Zaller, *The American Ethos: Public Attitudes toward Capitalism and Democracy* (Cambridge, MA: Harvard University Press, 1984), p. 19.

7. J. R. Pole, *The Pursuit of Equality in American History* (Berkeley: University of California Press, 1978), p. 3.

8. See Judith N. Shklar, *American Citizenship: The Quest for Inclusion* (Cambridge, MA: Harvard University Press, 1991).

9. Cindy Skrzycki, "OSHA Abandons Rules Effort on Repetitive Injury," *Washington Post,* June 13, 1995, p. D1.

10. See Rogers M. Smith, *Liberalism and American Constitutional Law* (Cambridge, MA: Harvard University Press, 1985), chap. 6.

11. The case was *San Antonio Independent School District v. Rodriguez,* 411 U.S. 1 (1973). See the discussion in Smith, *Liberalism and American Constitutional Law,* pp. 163–64.

12. See the discussion in Eileen McDonagh, "Gender Political Change," in *New Perspectives on American Politics,* ed. Lawrence C. Dodd and Calvin Jillson (Washington, DC: Congressional Quarterly Press, 1994), pp. 58–73. The argument for moving women's issues into the public sphere is made by Jean Bethke Elshtain, *Public Man, Private Woman* (Princeton, NJ: Princeton University Press, 1981).

13. On current differences in wealth, see Keith Bradsher, "Gap in Wealth in U.S. Called Widest in West," *New York Times,* April 17, 1995, p. A1; on income inequality, see Gary Burtless and Timothy Smeeding, "America's Tide Lifting the Yachts, Swamping the Rowboats," *Washington Post,* June 25, 1995, p. C3.

14. Kevin Phillips, *The Politics of Rich and Poor: Wealth and the American Electorate in the Reagan Aftermath* (New York: Random House, 1994); and Thomas Byrne Edsall, *The New Politics of Inequality* (New York: Norton, 1984).

15. Kevin Phillips, *Arrogant Capital: Washington, Wall Street, and the Frustration of American Politics* (Boston: Little, Brown, 1994).

Chapter 2

1. Scott Jaschick, "A Valuable Tool or Bias in Reverse?" *Chronicle of Higher Education,* April 28, 1995, pp. A14–A16. The case involving the Maryland scholarships was *Podberesky v. Kirwan,* 38 F.3rd 147 (4th Cir. 1994).

2. *Hopwood v. Texas,* 21 F.3d 603 (1996). In 1996, the Supreme Court declined to hear the *Hopwood* case, leaving in doubt the future of affirmative action in university admissions.

3. Richard Sandomir, "Brown University Held to Be Biased on Female Sports," *New York Times,* March 30, 1995, p. 1. On the broader use of Title IX to address sexual harassment in schools, see Tamar Lewin, "Students Use Law on Discrimination in Sex-Abuse Suits," *New York Times,* June 26, 1995, p. 1. The court case was *Cohen v. Brown University,* 879 F.Supp 185 (D.R.I. 1995).

4. *Rosenberger v. Rector and Visitors of the Unversity of Virginia,* 115 S.Ct. 2510 (1995).

5. Although we discuss each of these groups separately, it is important to note that these identities are not mutually exclusive. Members of different racial and ethnic groups also have class, gender, and religious allegiances. At times these overlapping affinities make it easier to reach consensus in politics because it means that individuals have cross-cutting identities; they can see much in common with many different people. In other cases, however, a single identity, such as race, can determine so much about a person's life that it draws a sharp line of difference.

6. Richard A. Easterlin, "Economic and Social Characteristics of the Immigrants," *Immigration,* ed. Richard A. Easterlin, David Ward, William S. Bernard, and Reed Ueda (Cambridge, MA: Harvard University Press, 1982), pp. 16–17.

7. John Higham, *Strangers in the Land: Patterns of American Nativism, 1860–1925* (New Brunswick, NJ: Rutgers University Press, 1988).

8. John Higham, *Strangers in the Land,* p. 95

9. It is important to note, however, that many European immigrants did not stay in the United States. Half of the southern Italians and over two-thirds of some groups from Eastern Europe who came to the United States between 1990 and 1910 returned home. See Richard Oestreicher, "Urban Working-Class Political Behavior and Theories of American Electoral Behavior," *Journal of American History* 74 (March 1988), p. 1274. On naturalization and citizenship, see Reed Ueda, "Naturalization and Citizenship," *Immigration,* ed. Easterlin et al., pp. 106–54.

10. Reed Ueda, "Naturalization and Citizenship," p. 118.

11. Nathan Glazer and Daniel P. Moynihan, *Beyond the Melting Pot* (Cambridge, MA: MIT Press, 1970), pp. 301–10.

12. August Meier and Elliot Rudwick, *From Plantation to Ghetto* (New York: Hill and Wang, 1976), pp. 184–88.

13. Meier and Rudwick, in *From Plantation to Ghetto,* note that behind the scenes Washington was more powerful and stood up some for political rights (p. 122). It is not always so easy to distinguish many kinds of self-help from nationalism. In fact, Wilson Jeremiah Moses identifies Washington with "technocratic black nationalism." See Wilson Jeremiah Moses, *The Golden Age of Black Nationalism, 1850–1925* (New York: Oxford University Press), p. 28.

14. On black nationalist thought, see Moses, *The Golden Age of Black Nationalism.*

15. On the growth of black political power and the more limited progress on social and economic change in the South after the Civil Rights movement, see James W. Button, *Blacks and Social Change: The Impact of the Civil Rights Movement in Southern Communities* (Princeton, NJ: Princeton University Press, 1993).

16. Quoted in Ronald Takaki, *A Different Mirror: A History of Multicultural America* (Boston: Little, Brown, 1993), p. 410.

17. See William Julius Wilson, *The Truly Disadvantaged: The Inner City, the Underclass, and Public Policy* (Chicago: University of Chicago Press, 1987); and Douglas Massey and Nancy Denton, *American Apartheid: Segregation and the Making of the American Underclass* (Cambridge, MA: Harvard University Press, 1993).

18. See Michael C. Dawson, *Behind the Mule: Race and Class in African-American Politics* (Princeton, NJ: Princeton University Press, 1994), chaps. 5 and 6.

19. Ibid.

20. New Mexico had a different history because not many Anglos settled there initially. ("Anglo" is the term for a non-Hispanic white generally of European background.) Mexican Americans had considerable power in territorial legislatures between 1865 and 1912. See Lawrence H. Fuchs, *The American Kaleidoscope* (Hanover, NH: University Press of New England, 1990), pp. 239–40.

21. On La Raza Unida Party, see "La Raza Unida Party and the Chicano Student Movement in California," in *Latinos in the American Political System,* ed. F. Chris Garcia (Notre Dame, IN: University of Notre Dame Press, 1988), pp. 213–35.

22. Glazer and Moynihan, *Beyond the Melting Pot,* p. 101.

23. U.S. House of Representatives, Committee on the Judiciary, Hearings on the Immigration and Nationality Act, 104th Cong., 1st sess. (May 1995), Serial no. 1, p. 596.

24. Rochelle L. Stanfield, "Cracking El Sistema," *National Journal,* June 1, 1991, pp. 1284–87.

25. *United States v. Wong Kim Ark,* 169 U.S. 649 (1898).

26. Only 1,428 Chinese were let in to the United States between 1944 and 1952. See Takaki, *A Different Mirror,* p. 387.

27. U.S. House of Representatives, Committee on the Judiciary, *Immigration and Nationality Act,* 10th ed. (May 1995), 104th Cong., 1st sess.; Serial no. 1, p. 596.

28. Ibid.

29. Jane Gross, "Diversity Hinders Asians' Power in the U.S.," *New York Times,* June 25, 1989, p. A22.

30. See Timothy P. Fong, *The First Suburban Chinatown* (Philadelphia: Temple University Press, 1994), pp. 153–56. Fong points out a persistent split among foreign-born and American-born Chinese.

31. Not all Indian tribes agreed with this, including the Navajos. See Takaki, *A Different Mirror,* pp. 238–45.

32. On the resurgence of Indian political activity, see Stephen Cornell, *The Return of the Native: American Indian Political Resurgence* (New York: Oxford University Press, 1990); and Dee Brown, *Bury My Heart at Wounded Knee* (New York: Holt, 1971).

33. Dirk Johnson, "Economic Pulse: Indian Country; Economies Come to Life on Indian Reservations," *New York Times,* July 3, 1994, p. 1.

34. On the Knights of Labor, see Leon Fink, *Workingmen's Democracy: The Knights of Labor and American Politics* (Urbana: University of Illinois Press, 1985).

35. Clay Chandler, "It's Getting Awfully Crowded in the Middle," *Washington Post,* December 18, 1994, p. H1.

36. See Edward N. Wolff, *Top Heavy: A Study of Increasing Inequality of Wealth in America* (New York: Twentieth Century Fund, 1995).

37. Cited in Benjamin DeMott, *The Imperial Middle: Why Americans Can't Think Straight about Class* (New York: Morrow, 1990), pp. 9–10.

38. On politics and women, see Paula Baker, "The Domestication of Politics: Women and American Political Society, 1780–1920," *American Historical Review* 89 (June 1984), pp. 620–47. On women's separate sphere, see Sheila M. Rothman, *Woman's Proper Place* (New York: Basic Books, 1978).

39. See Jo Freeman, *The Politics of Women's Liberation* (New York: Longman, 1975), p. 53; and Cynthia Harrison, *On Account of Sex* (Berkeley: University of California Press, 1988), chaps. 7 and 8.

40. See Jane Mansbridge, *Why We Lost the ERA* (Chicago: University of Chicago Press, 1984).

41. "Fact Sheet: The Gender Gap," Center for the American Woman and Politics, Eagleton Institute of Politics, Rutgers University, August 1994.

42. See Thomas B. Edsall, "Pollsters View Gender Gap as Political Fixture," *Washington Post,* August 15, 1995, p. A11.

43. Richard L. Berke, "Defections among Men to G.O.P. Helped Insure Rout of Democrats," *New York Times,* November 11, 1994, p. A1.

44. "Fact Sheet: Women in Elective Office," Center for the American Woman and Politics, Eagleton Institute of Politics, Rutgers University, May 1, 1995.

45. David S. Broder, "Key to Women's Political Parity: Running," *Washington Post,* September 8, 1994, p. A17.

46. "The Impact of Women in Public Office: Findings at a Glance," Center for the American Woman and Politics (New Brunswick, NJ: Rutgers University, n.d.).

47. Gwen Ifill, "The Louisiana Election; Female Lawmakers Wrestle with New Public Attitudes on 'Women's' Issues," *New York Times,* November 18, 1991, p. B7.

48. Samuel P. Huntington, *American Politics and the Promise of Disharmony* (Cambridge, MA: Harvard University Press, 1981), pp. 14–15.

49. A. James Reichley, *Religion in American Public Life* (Washington, DC: Brookings Institution Press, 1985), p. 186.

50. *Engel v. Vitale,* 370 U.S. 421 (1962); *Abington School District v. Schempp,* 374 U.S. 203 (1963); *Roe v. Wade*, 410 U.S. 113 (1973).

51. See Reichley, *Religion in American Public Life,* pp. 319–27.

52. David von Drehle, "Life of the Grand Old Party; Energized Coalition Enters Another Political Phase," *Washington Post,* August 14, 1994, p. A1.

53. See *Shaw v. Reno,* 509 U.S. 113 (1993), and *Miller v. Johnson,* 115 S.Ct. 2475 (1995).

54. Robert D. Putnam, "Bowling Alone: America's Declining Social Capital," *Journal of Democracy* 6 (January 1995), pp. 65–78.

55. See Christopher Lasch, *The Revolt of the Elites and the Betrayal of American Democracy* (New York: Norton, 1995). The idea of the 'secession of the rich' comes from Robert Reich, *The Work of Nations* (New York: Knopf, 1991), chaps. 23 and 24.

Chapter 3

1. Herbert Storing, *What the Antifederalists Were For* (Chicago: University of Chicago Press, 1981).

2. The social makeup of colonial America and some of the social conflicts that divided colonial society are discussed in Jackson Turner Main, *The Social Structure of Revolutionary America* (Princeton, NJ: Princeton University Press, 1965).

3. George B. Tindall and David E. Shi, *America: A Narrative History,* 3rd ed. (New York: Norton, 1992), p. 194.

4. For a discussion of events leading up to the Revolution, see Charles M. Andrews, *The Colonial Background of the American Revolution* (New Haven, CT: Yale University Press, 1924).

5. See Carl Becker, *The Declaration of Independence* (New York: Knopf, 1942).

6. See Merrill Jensen, *The Articles of Confederation* (Madison: University of Wisconsin Press, 1970).

7. Reported in Samuel E. Morrison, Henry Steele Commager, and William Leuchtenberg, *The Growth of the American Republic,* vol. 1 (New York: Oxford University Press, 1969), p. 244.

8. Quoted in Morrison et al., *The Growth of the American Republic,* vol. 1, p. 242.

9. Charles A. Beard, *An Economic Interpretation of the Constitution of the United States* (New York: Macmillan, 1913).

10. Madison's notes along with the somewhat less complete records kept by several other participants in the convention are available in a four-volume set. See Max Farrand, ed., *The Records of the Federal Convention of 1787,* 4 vols., rev. ed. (New Haven, CT: Yale University Press, 1966).

11. Farrand, ed., *The Records of the Federal Convention of 1787,* vol. 1, p. 476.

12. Farrand, ed., *The Records of the Federal Convention of 1787,* vol. 2, p. 10.

13. E. M. Earle, ed., *The Federalist* (New York: Modern Library, 1937), No. 71.

14. Earle, ed., *The Federalist,* No. 62.

15. Earle, ed., *The Federalist,* No. 70.

16. Max Farrand, *The Framing of the Constitution of the United States* (New Haven, CT: Yale University Press, 1962), p. 49.

17. Richard E. Neustadt, *Presidential Power* (New York: Wiley, 1960), p. 33.

18. Melancton Smith, quoted in Storing, *What the Anti-Federalists Were For,* p. 17.

19. "Essays of Brutus," No. 1, in Herbert Storing, ed., *The Complete Anti-Federalist* (Chicago: University of Chicago Press, 1981).

20. Earle, ed., *The Federalist*, No. 57.

21. "Essays of Brutus," No. 15, in Storing, ed., *The Complete Anti-Federalist.*

22. Earle, ed., *The Federalist*, No. 10.

23. Earle, ed., *The Federalist*, No. 10.

24. "Essays of Brutus," No. 7, in Storing, ed., *The Complete Anti-Federalist.*

25. "Essays of Brutus," No. 6, in Storing, ed., *The Complete Anti-Federalist.*

26. Storing, *What the Anti-Federalists Were For*, p. 28.

27. Earle, ed., *The Federalist,* No. 51.

28. Quoted in Storing, *What the Anti-Federalists Were For,* p. 30.

29. Observation by Colonel George Mason, delegate from Virginia, early during the convention period. Quoted in Farrand, ed., *The Records of the Federal Convention of 1787,* vol. 1, p. 202–3.

30. Clinton Rossiter, ed., *The Federalist Papers* (New York: New American Library, 1961), No. 43, p. 278.

31. See Marcia Lee, "The Equal Rights Amendment—Public Policy by Means of a Constitutional Amendment," in *The Politics of Policy-Making in America,* ed. David Caputo (San Francisco: Freeman, 1977); Jane Mansbridge, *Why We Lost the ERA* (Chicago: University of Chicago Press, 1986); and Donald Mathews and Jane Sherron DeHart, *Sex, Gender, and the Politics of the ERA* (New York: Oxford University Press, 1990).

32. The Fourteenth Amendment is included in this table as well as in Table 3.4 because it seeks not only to define citizenship but *seems* to intend also that this definition of citizenship included, along with the right to vote, all the rights of the Bill of Rights, regardless of the state in which the citizen resided. A great deal more will be said about this in Chapter 5.

33. Earle, ed., *The Federalist*, No. 10.

Chapter 4

1. Andre Henderson, "Cruise Control," *Governing*, February 1995, p. 39. Unemployment benefit figures are from U.S. House of Representatives, Committee on Ways and Means, *Where Your Money Goes: America's Entitlements: The 1994–95 Green Book* (Washington, DC: Brassey's, 1994), p. 276.

2. For a good treatment of the contrast between national political stability and social instability, see Samuel P. Huntington, *Political Order in Changing Societies* (New Haven, CT: Yale University Press, 1968), chap. 2.

3. *McCulloch v. Maryland*, 4 Wheaton 316 (1819).

4. *Gibbons v. Ogden*, 9 Wheaton 1 (1824).

5. The Sherman Antitrust Act, adopted in 1890, for example, was enacted not to restrict commerce, but rather to protect it from monopolies, or trusts, so as to prevent unfair trade practices, and to enable the market again to become self-regulating. Moreover, the Supreme Court sought to uphold liberty of contract to protect businesses. For example, in *Lochner v. New York*, 198 U.S. 45 (1905), the Court invalidated a New York law regulating the sanitary conditions and hours of labor of bakers on the grounds that the law interfered with liberty of contract.

6. The key case in this process of expanding the power of the national government is generally considered to be *NLRB v. Jones & Laughlin Steel Corporation*, 301 U.S. 1 (1937), in which the Supreme Court approved federal regulation of the workplace and thereby virtually eliminated interstate commerce as a limit on national government's power.

7. *U.S. v. Darby Lumber Co.*, 312 U.S. 100 (1941).

8. W. John Moore, "Pleading the 10th," *National Journal*, July 29, 1995, p. 1940.

9. *Seminole Indian Tribe v. Florida*, 116 S.Ct. 1114 (1996).

10. *United States v. Lopez*, 115 S.Ct. 1624 (1995).

11. A good discussion of the constitutional position of local governments is in York Willbern, *The Withering Away of the City* (Bloomington: Indiana University Press, 1971). For more on the structure and theory of federalism, see Thomas R. Dye, *American Federalism: Competition among Governments* (Lexington, MA: Lexington Books, 1990), chap. 1; and Martha Derthick, "Up-to-Date in Kansas City: Reflections on American Federalism" (the 1992 John Gaus Lecture), *PS: Political Science & Politics* 25 (December 1992), pp. 671–75.

12. See the poll reported in Guy Gugliotta, "Scaling Down the American Dream," *Washington Post*, April 19, 1995, p. A21.

13. Kenneth T. Palmer, "The Evolution of Grant Policies," in *The Changing Politics of Federal Grants*, by Lawrence D. Brown, James W. Fossett, and Kenneth T. Palmer (Washington, DC: Brookings, 1984) p. 15.

14. Palmer, "The Evolution of Grant Policies," p. 6.

15. Morton Grozdins, *The American System*, ed. Daniel J. Elazar (Chicago: Rand McNally, 1966).

16. On the problems with the states, see Terry Sanford, *Storm Over the States* (New York: McGraw-Hill, 1967).

17. James L. Sundquist with David W. Davis, *Making Federalism Work* (Washington, DC: Brookings, 1969), p. 271.

18. See Don Kettl, *The Regulation of American Federalism* (Baton Rouge: Louisiana State University Press, 1983). George Wallace was mistrusted by the architects of the War on Poverty because he was a strong proponent of racial segregation. He believed in "states' rights," which meant that states, not the federal government, should decide what liberty and equality meant.

19. See Advisory Commission on Intergovernmental Relations, *Federal Regulation of State and Local Governments: The Mixed Record of the 1980s* (Washington, DC: Advisory Commission on Intergovernmental Relations, July 1993).

20. Advisory Commission on Intergovernmental Relations, *Federal Regulation of State and Local Governments,* p. iii.

21. Ann Devroy and Helen Dewar, "Hailing Bipartisanship, Clinton Signs Bill to Restrict Unfunded Mandates," *Washington Post*, March 23, 1995, p. A10.

22. Quoted in Timothy Conlon, *New Federalism: Intergovernmental Reform from Nixon to Reagan* (Washington, DC: Brookings, 1988), p. 25.

23. For the emergence of complaints about federal categorical grants, see Palmer, "The Evolution of Grant Policies," pp. 17–18. On the governors' efforts to gain more control over federal grants after the 1994 congressional elections, see Dan Balz, "GOP Governors Eager to Do Things Their Way," *Washington Post*, November 22, 1994, p. A4.

24. Advisory Commission on Intergovernmental Relations, *Federal Regulation of State and Local Governments*, p. 51.

25. Dan Balz, "Governors Press Congress for Power to Manage Programs at State Level," *Washington Post*, December 11, 1994, p. A6; Robert Pear, "Attention Is Turning Governors' Heads: But Some Still Worry that Congress Will Shift Burden to the States," *New York Times*, January 30, 1995, p. A14.

26. Robert Frank, "Proposed Block Grants Seem Unlikely to Cure Management Problems," *Wall Street Journal*, May 1, 1995, p. 1.

27. Judith Havemann, "Scholars Question Whether Welfare Shift Is Reform," *Washington Post*, April 20, 1995, p. A8.

28. Malcolm Gladwell, "Proposed Education Cuts Protested in New York," *Washington Post*, March 25, 1995, p. A4.

29. On the NGA, see Larry Sabato, *Goodbye to Good-time Charlie: The American Governorship Transformed*, 2nd ed. (Washington, DC: Congressional Quarterly Press, 1983), pp. 175–79.

30. Charles H. Levine and James A. Thurber, "Reagan and the Intergovernmental Lobby: Iron Triangles, Cozy Subsystems, and Political Conflict," *Interest Group Politics*, 2nd ed., ed. Allan J. Cigler and Burdett A. Loomis (Washington, DC: Congressional Quarterly Press, 1986), chap. 11.

31. U.S. Committee on Federalism and National Purpose, *To Form a More Perfect Union* (Washington, DC: National Conference on Social Welfare, 1985). See also the discussion in Paul E. Peterson, *The Price of Federalism* (Washington, DC: Brookings, 1995), esp. chap. 8.

32. Sam Howe Verhovek, "Twice as Difficult to Be Twice as Nice," *New York Times*, March 25, 1995, p. 6.

33. Malcolm Gladwell, "In States' Experiments, a Cutting Contest," *Washington Post*, March 10, 1995, p. A1.

34. Guy Gugliotta, "Scaling Down the American Dream," *Washington Post*, April 19, 1995, p. 21; Albert R. Hunt, "Politics and People: Federalism Debate Is as much about Power as about Principle," *Wall Street Journal*, January 19, 1995, p. 19.

Chapter 5

1. *Madsen v. Women's Health Center,* 114 S.Ct. 2516 (1994).

2. Clinton Rossiter, ed., *The Federalist Papers* (New York: Mentor, 1961), No. 84, p. 513.

3. Rossiter, ed., *The Federalist Papers,* No. 84, p. 513.

4. Clinton Rossiter, *1787: The Grand Convention* (New York: Norton, 1987), p. 302.

5. Rossiter, *1787,* p. 303. Rossiter also reports that "in 1941 the States of Connecticut, Massachusetts and Georgia celebrated the sesquicentennial of the Bill of Rights by giving their hitherto withheld and unneeded assent."

6. Let there be no confusion about the words "liberty" and "freedom." They are synonymous and interchangeable. "Freedom" comes from the German, *Freiheit.* "Liberty" is from the French, *liberté.* Although people sometimes try to make them appear to be different, both of them have equal concern with the absence of restraints on individual choices of action.

7. For some recent scholarship on the Bill of Rights and its development, see Geoffrey Stone, Richard Epstein, and Cass Sunstein, eds., *The Bill of Rights and the Modern State* (Chicago: University of Chicago Press, 1992); and Michael J. Meyer and William A. Parent, eds., *The Constitution of Rights* (Ithaca, NY: Cornell University Press, 1992).

8. *Barron v. Baltimore,* 7 Peters 243, 246 (1833).

9. The Fourteenth Amendment also seems designed to introduce civil rights. The final clause of the all-important Section 1 provides that no state can "deny to any person within its jurisdiction the equal protection of the laws." It is not unreasonable to conclude that the purpose of this provision was to obligate the state governments as well as the national government to take *positive* actions to protect citizens from arbitrary and discriminatory actions, at least those based on race. This will be explored in the separate chapter on civil rights.

10. For example, *The Slaughterhouse Cases,* 16 Wallace 36 (1883).

11. *Chicago, Burlington and Quincy Railroad Company v. Chicago,* 166 U.S. 226 (1897).

12. *Gitlow v. New York,* 268 U.S. 652 (1925).

13. *Near v. Minnesota,* 283 U.S. 697 (1931); *Hague v. C.I.O.,* 307 U.S. 496 (1939).

14. *Palko v. Connecticut,* 302 U.S. 319 (1937).

15. All of these were implicitly included in the *Palko* case as "not incorporated" into the Fourteenth Amendment as limitations on the powers of the states.

16. There is one interesting exception, which involves the Sixth Amendment right to public trial. In the 1948 case *In re Oliver,* 33 U.S. 257, the right to public trial was, in effect, incorporated as part of the Fourteenth Amendment. However, the issue in that case was put more generally as "due process," and public trial itself was not actually mentioned in so many words. Later opinions, such as *Duncan v. Louisiana,* 391 U.S. 145 (1968), cited the *Oliver* case as the precedent for more explicit incorporation of public trials as part of the Fourteenth Amendment.

17. Alfred H. Kelly, Winfred A. Harbison, and Herman Belz, *The American Constitution: Its Origins and Development,* 6th ed. (New York: Norton, 1983), p. 647. We refer to only eight amendments because the first eight amendments are the true Bill of Rights. The Ninth Amendment confirms that the enumeration of rights in the Constitution is not supposed to mean that other rights cannot be added later. And the Tenth Amendment, as observed earlier, reassures the states that the powers not delegated to the national government (and not explicitly prohibited to the states) are reserved to the states or the people.

18. For a lively and readable treatment of the possibilities of restricting provisions of the Bill of Rights, without actually reversing prior decisions, see David G. Savage, *Turning Right: The Making of the Rehnquist Supreme Court* (New York: Wiley 1992). For an indication that the Supreme Court in the 1990s may in fact be moving toward more restrictions on the Bill of Rights, see Richard Lacayo, "The Soul of a New Majority," *Time,* July 10, 1995, pp. 46–48.

19. *Abington School District v. Schempp,* 374 U.S. 203 (1963).

20. *Engel v. Vitale,* 370 U.S. 421 (1962).

21. *Wallace v. Jaffree,* 472 U.S. 38 (1985).

22. *Lynch v. Donnelly,* 465 U.S. 668 (1984).

23. *Lemon v. Kurtzman,* 403 U.S. 602 (1971). The *Lemon* test is still good law, but as recently as the 1994 Court term, four justices have urged that the *Lemon* test be abandoned. Here is a settled area of law that may soon become unsettled.

24. *West Virginia State Board of Education v. Barnette,* 319 U.S. 624 (1943). The case it reversed was *Minersville School District v. Gobitus,* 310 U.S. 586 (1940).

25. *Employment Division, Department of Human Resources of Oregon v. Smith,* 494 U.S. 872 (1990).

26. *Wisconsin v. Yoder,* 406 U.S. 205 (1972).

27. Facts of the case reported in Laurie Goodstein, "The Separation that Divides: The Nation's Schools Are Becoming a Battle Ground on Church-State Relations," *Washington Post National Weekly Edition,* July 24–30, 1995, p. 31; and "Appeals Court in Bauchman Case Finds No Grounds for Contempt," press release, National Committee for Public Education and Religious Liberty, February 6, 1996.

28. The text of President Clinton's Memorandum on Religion in the Schools was printed in full in the *New York Times,* July 13, 1995, p. B10.

29. *U.S. v. Carolene Products Company,* 304 U.S. 144 (1938), note 4. Although this doctrine was laid out only in a footnote, it was being applied to a piece of state legislation through the Fourteenth Amendment and was concerned more with civil rights for minorities under the equal protection clause. This footnote is one of the Court's most important doctrines. See Alfred H. Kelly, Winfred A. Harbison, and Herman Belz, *The American Constitution: Its Origins and Development,* 7th ed. (New York: Norton, 1991), Vol. 2, pp. 519–23.

30. *Schenk v. U.S.,* 249 U.S. 47 (1919).

31. *Brandenburg v. Ohio,* 395 U.S. 444 (1969).

32. *Stromberg v. California,* 283 U.S. 359 (1931).

33. *Texas v. Johnson,* 488 U.S. 884 (1989).

34. *United States v. Eichman,* 496 U.S. 310 (1990).

35. For a good general discussion of "speech plus," see Louis Fisher, *American Constitutional Law* (New York: McGraw-Hill, 1990), pp. 544–46. The case upholding the buffer zone against the abortion protesters is *Madsen v. Women's Health Center,* 114 S.Ct. 2516 (1994).

36. See Fisher, *American Constitutional Law,* pp. 1249–51; *United States v. Rumely,* 345 U.S. 41 (1953); and *United States v. Harris,* 347 U.S. 612 (1954).

37. *New York Times v. Sullivan,* 376 U.S. 254 (1964).

38. *Masson v. New Yorker Magazine,* 111 S.Ct. 2419 (1991).

39. *Hustler Magazine v. Falwell,* 108 S.Ct. 876 (1988).

40. *Roth v. US,* 354 U.S. 476 (1957).

41. Concurring opinion in *Jacobellis v. Ohio,* 378 U.S. 184 (1964).

42. *Miller v. California,* 413 U.S. 15 (1973).

43. See, for example, "Are Movies and Music Killing America's Soul?" *Time,* June 12, 1995.

44. Wray Herbert, "Is Porn Un-American?" *U.S. News and World Report,* July 3, 1995, pp. 51–54.

45. Philip Elmer-Dewitt, "Fire Storm on the Computer Nets," *Time,* July 24, 1995, p. 57.

46. *Chaplinsky v. State of New Hampshire,* 315 U.S. 568 (1942).

47. *Dennis v. United States,* 341 U.S. 494 (1951), which upheld the infamous Smith Act of 1940, which provided criminal penalties for those who "willfully and knowingly conspire to teach and advocate the forceful and violent overthrow and destruction of the government."

48. "The Penn File: An Update," *Wall Street Journal,* April 11, 1994, p. A14.

49. *Meritor Savings Bank, FBD v. Vinson,* 477 U.S. 57 (1986).

50. Charles Fried, "The New First Amendment Jurisprudence: A Threat to Liberty," in *The Bill of Rights and the Modern State,* ed. Stone, Epstein, and Sunstein, p. 249.

51. *Broadcasting Company v. Acting Attorney General,* 405 U.S. 1000 (1972).

52. *Board of Trustees of the State University of New York v. Fox,* 109 S.Ct. 3028 (1989).

53. *City Council v. Taxpayers for Vincent,* 466 U.S. 789 (1984).

54. *Posadas de Puerto Rico Associates v. Tourism Company of Puerto Rico,* 479 U.S. 328 (1986).

55. Fisher, *American Constitutional Law,* p. 546.

56. *Bigelow v. Virginia,* 421 U.S. 809 (1975).

57. *Virginia State Board of Pharmacy v. Virginia Citizens Consumer Council,* 425 U.S. 748 (1976). Later cases restored the rights of lawyers to advertise their services.

58. *United States v. Miller,* 307 U.S. 174 (1939). A good, albeit brief, treatment of this will be found in Edward Corwin and J. W. Peltason, *Corwin & Peltason's Understanding the Constitution,* 13th ed. (Fort Worth, TX: Harcourt Brace, 1994), pp. 248–49.

59. The Supreme Court itself provides an intriguing suggestion for a criterion to distinguish between appropriate and inappropriate regulation of the right to bear arms. In 1939 the Supreme Court upheld a federal law making it a crime to ship sawed-off shotguns in interstate commerce, on the grounds that such weapons had no reasonable relationship "to the preservation or efficiency of a well-regulated militia." *U.S. v. Miller,* 307 U.S. 174 (1939).

60. See Corwin and Peltason, *Understanding the Constitution,* pp. 283–86.

61. *In re Winship,* 397 U.S. 361 (1970). An outstanding treatment of due process in issues involving the Fourth through Seventh amendments will be found in Fisher, *American Constitutional Law,* chap. 13.

62. *Horton v. California,* 496 U.S. 128 (1990).

63. *Mapp v. Ohio,* 367 U.S. 643 (1961). Although Ms. Mapp went free in this case, she was later convicted in New York on narcotics trafficking charges and served nine years of a twenty-year sentence.

64. Corwin and Peltason, *Understanding the Constitution,* p. 266.

65. For a good discussion of the issue, see Fisher, *American Constitutional, Law,* pp. 884–89.

66. Corwin and Peltason, *Understanding the Constitution,* p. 286.

67. *Miranda v. Arizona,* 348 U.S. 436 (1966).

68. *Berman v. Parker,* 348 U.S. 26 (1954). For a thorough analysis of the case see Benjamin Ginsberg, "*Berman v. Parker:* Congress, the Court, and the Public Purpose," *Polity* 4 (1971), pp. 48–75. For a later application of the case that suggests that "just compensation"—defined as something approximating market value—is about all a property owner can hope for protection against a public taking of property, see Theodore Lowi et al., *Poliscide: Big Government, Big Science, Lilliputian Politics,* 2nd ed. (Lanham, MD: University Press of America, 1990), pp. 267–70.

69. *Gideon v. Wainwright,* 372 U.S. 335 (1963). For a full account of the story of the trial and release of Clarence Earl Gideon, see Anthony Lewis, *Gideon's Trumpet* (New York: Random House, 1964). See also David O'Brien, *Storm Center,* 2nd ed. (New York: Norton, 1990).

70. For further discussion of these issues, see Corwin and Peltason, *Understanding the Constitution,* pp. 319–23.

71. *Congressional Quarterly Weekly Report,* October 21, 1995, p. 3212.

72. *Furman v. Georgia,* 408 U.S. 238 (1972).

73. *Gregg v. Georgia,* 428 U.S. 153 (1976).

74. *Minersville School District v. Gobitis,* 310 U.S. 586 (1940).

75. *West Virginia State Board of Education v. Barnette,* 319 U.S. 624 (1943).

76. *West Virginia State Board of Education v. Barnette.*

77. *NAACP v. Alabama ex rel. Patterson,* 357 U.S. 449 (1958).

78. *Griswold v. Connecticut,* 381 U.S. 479 (1965).

79. *Griswold v. Connecticut,* concurring opinion. In 1972, the Court extended the privacy right to unmarried women: *Eisenstadt v. Baird,* 405 U.S. 438 (1972).

80. *Roe v. Wade,* 410 U.S. 113 (1973).

81. See Paul Brest and Sanford Stevinson, *Processes of Constitutional Decision-Making: Cases and Materials,* 2nd ed. (Boston: Little, Brown, 1983), p. 660.

82. *Baker v. Carr,* 369 U.S. 186 (1962).

83. *Engle v. Vitale,* 370 U.S. 421 (1962), and the series of cases following on that case.

84. *Webster v. Reproductive Health Services,* 109 S.Ct. 3040 (1989), which upheld a Missouri law that restricted the use of public medical facilities for abortion. The decision opened the way for other states to limit the availability of abortion.

85. *Planned Parenthood of Southeastern Pennsylvania v. Casey,* 112 S.Ct. 2791 (1992).

86. Gayle Binion, "Undue Burden? Government Now Has Wide Latitude to Restrict Abortions," *Santa Barbara News-Press*, July 5, 1992, p. A13.

87. *Bowers v. Hardwick,* 478 U.S. 186 (1986).

88. The dissenters were quoting an earlier case, *Olmstead v. United States,* 27 U.S. 438 (1928), to emphasize the nature of their disagreement with the majority in the *Bowers* case.

Chapter 6

1. Alexander Astin et al., "The American Freshman: National Norms for Fall 1994," Cooperative Institutional Research Program of the American Council on Education and the Higher Education Research Institute of the University of California at Los Angeles, 1994.

2. Quoted in the *Tampa Tribune*, January 9, 1995, p. 1.

3. "UC Protest Rally Planned," *San Francisco Examiner*, July 23, 1995.

4. For a discussion of the political beliefs of Americans, see Harry Holloway and John George, *Public Opinion* (New York: St. Martin's, 1986). See also Paul R. Abramson, *Political Attitudes in America* (San Francisco: Freeman, 1983).

5. See Louis Hartz, *The Liberal Tradition in America* (New York: Harcourt, Brace, 1955).

6. Ben Gose, "Penn to Replace Controversial Speech Code; Will No Longer Punish Students for Insults," *Chronicle of Higher Education,* June 29, 1994, p. A30.

7. See Angus Campbell et al., *The American Voter* (New York: Wiley, 1960), p. 147.

8. Richard Morin, "Poll Reflects Division over Simpson Case," *Washington Post*, October 8, 1995, p. A31.

9. "Middle-Class Views in Black and White," *Washington Post*, October 9, 1995, p. A22.

10. For data see Rutgers University, Eagleton Institute of Politics, Center for the American Woman in Politics, "Sex Differences in Voter Turnout," August 1994.

11. Pamela Johnston Conover, "The Role of Social Groups in Political Thinking," *British Journal of Political Science* 18 (1988), pp. 51–78.

12. See Michael C. Dawson, "Structure and Ideology: The Shaping of Black Public Opinion," paper presented to the 1995 annual meeting of the Midwest Political Science Association, Chicago, Illinois, April 7–9, 1995. See also Michael C. Dawson, *Behind the Mule: Race, Class, and African American Politics* (Princeton, NJ: Princeton University Press, 1994).

13. Testimony of Dr. Mason Wright, Jr., chair of the National Housing Conference on Black Power, in *Housing Legislation of 1967: Hearings before the Subcommittee on Housing and Urban Affairs of the Committee on Banking and Currency* (Washington, DC: Government Printing Office, 1967), p. 865.

14. Harry L. Gracey, "Learning the Student Role: Kindergarten as Academic Boot Camp," in *The Quality of Life in America,* ed. A. David Hill (New York: Holt, 1973), p. 261.

15. U.S. Senate, Committee on the Judiciary, *Hearings before the Subcommittee on Constitutional Amendments on S.J. Res. 8, S.J. Res. 14, and S.J. Res. 78 Relating to Lowering the Voting Age to 18,* May 14, 15, and 16, 1968 (Washington DC: Government Printing Office, 1968), p. 12.

16. James Carney, "Playing by the Numbers," *Time,* April 11, 1994, p. 40.

17. David Broder, "White House Takes on Harry and Louise," *Washington Post,* July 8, 1994, p. A11

18. See Gillian Peele, *Revival and Reaction* (Oxford, U.K.: Clarendon, 1985). Also see Connie Paige, *The Right-to-Lifers* (New York: Summit, 1983).

19. See David Vogel, "The Power of Business in America: A Reappraisal," *British Journal of Political Science* 13 (January 1983), pp. 19–44.

20. See David Vogel, "The Public Interest Movement and the American Reform Tradition," *Political Science Quarterly* 96 (Winter 1980), pp. 607–27.

21. Jason DeParle, "The Clinton Welfare Bill Begins Trek in Congress," *New York Times,* July 15, 1994, p. 1.

22. Joe Queenan, "Birth of a Notion," *Washington Post,* September 20, 1992, p. C1.

23. Dawson, *Behind the Mule.*

24. Michael Kagay and Janet Elder, "Numbers Are No Problem for Pollsters, Words Are," *New York Times*, August 9, 1992, p. E6.

25. See Richard Morin, "Is Bush's Bounce a Boom or a Bust?" *Washington Post National Weekly Edition*, August 31–September 6, 1992, p. 37.

26. See Thomas E. Mann and Gary Orren, eds., *Media Polls in American Politics* (Washington, DC: Brookings, 1992).

27. For an excellent and reflective discussion by a journalist, see Richard Morin, "Clinton Slide in Survey Shows Perils of Polling," *Washington Post*, August 29, 1992, p. A6.

28. See Michael Traugott, "The Impact of Media Polls on the Public," in *Media Polls in American Politics*, Mann and Orren, ed., pp. 125–49.

29. For a fuller discussion of the uses of polling and the role of public opinion in American politics, see Benjamin Ginsberg, *The Captive Public* (New York: Basic Books, 1986).

30. Benjamin I. Page and Robert Y. Shapiro, "Effects of Public Opinion on Policy," *American Political Science Review* 77 (March 1983), pp. 175–90.

Chapter 7

1. Howard Kurtz, "A Trash Course in Free Speech; College Newspapers Pitched in Protests," *Washington Post,* July 29, 1993, p. C1.

2. Richard Daigle, "Collegiate Censorship by Theft," *Atlanta Journal and Constitution,* March 6, 1994, p. F1.

3. Daigle, "Collegiate Censorship by Theft."

4. Benjamin Ginsberg and Martin Shefter, *Politics by Other Means* (New York: Basic Books, 1990), p. 24.

5. Anthony Lewis, "Words Matter," *New York Times*, May 5, 1995, p. A31.

6. U.S. Bureau of the Census, *Statistical Abstract of the United States: 1994* (Washington, DC: Department of Commerce, 1994), pp. 567, 576.

7. See Leo Bogart, "Newspapers in Transition," *Wilson Quarterly*, special issue, 1982; and Richard Harwood, "The Golden Age of Press Diversity," *Washington Post*, July 22, 1994, p. A23.

8. See Benjamin Ginsberg, *The Captive Public* (New York: Basic Books, 1986).

9. Michael Dawson, "Structure and Ideology: The Shaping of Black Public Opinion," paper presented to the 1995 meeting of the Midwest Political Science Association, Chicago, Illinois, April 7, 1995.

10. Carla Robbins, "To Some, Soldier is a Hero for Refusing to Obey an Order," *Wall Street Journal*, January 24, 1996, p. 1.

11. *Red Lion Broadcasting Company v. FCC*, 395 U.S. 367 (1969).

12. *Near v. Minnesota*, 283 U.S. 697 (1931).

13. *New York Times v. U.S.*, 403 U.S. 731 (1971).

14. *Cable News Network v. Noriega*, 111 S.Ct. 451 (1990); *Turner Broadcasting System v. Federal Communications Commission*, 114 S.Ct. 2445 (1994).

15. *New York Times v. Sullivan*, 376 U.S. 254 (1964).

16. *Masson v. New Yorker Magazine*, 111 S.Ct. 2419 (1991).

17. See the discussions in Gary Paul Gates, *Air Time* (New York: Harper & Row, 1978); Edward Jay Epstein, *News from Nowhere* (New York: Random House, 1973); Michael Parenti, *Inventing Reality* (New York: St. Martin's, 1986); Herbert Gans, *Deciding What's News* (New York: Vintage, 1980); and W. Lance Bennett, *News: The Politics of Illusion* (New York: Longman, 1986).

18. See Edith Efron, *The News Twisters* (Los Angeles: Nash Publishing, 1971).

19. Michael Kinsley, "Bias and Baloney," *Washington Post*, November 26, 1992, p. A29; John H. Fund, "Why Clinton Shouldn't Be Steamed at Talk Radio," *Wall Street Journal*, July 7, 1994, p. A12.

20. Kinsley, "Bias and Baloney."

21. L. Brent Bozell III, "TV Viewers Await Universal Coverage," *Wall Street Journal*, August 23, 1994, p. A12.

22. See Peter Canellos, "Manipulating the Messengers," *Boston Globe*, November 26, 1995, p. A21.

23. See Tom Burnes, "The Organization of Public Opinion," in *Mass Communication and Society*, ed. James Curran (Beverly Hills, CA: Sage, 1979), pp. 44–230. See also David Altheide, *Creating Reality* (Beverly Hills, CA: Sage, 1976).

24. David Garrow, *Protest at Selma* (New Haven, CT: Yale University Press, 1978).

25. Garrow, *Protest at Selma.*

26. See Todd Gitlin, *The Whole World Is Watching* (Berkeley, CA: University of California Press, 1980).

27. Quoted in George Brown Tindall and David E. Shi, *America: A Narrative History*, 4th ed. (New York: Norton, 1996), p. 1429.

28. See Carl Bernstein, "The Idiot Culture," *New Republic*, June 8, 1992, pp. 22–28.

29. Howard Kurtz, "Media Pounce on Troubles as Pendulum Swings Again," *Washington Post*, February 1, 1993, p. 1.

30. Johanna Newman, *Lights, Camera, War* (New York: St. Martin's, 1996).

31. Alan Otten, "TV News Drops Kid-Glove Coverage of Election, Trading Staged Sound Bites for Hard Analysis," *Wall Street Journal*, October 12, 1992, p. A12.

32. See Ann Devroy, "TV Public Puts Clinton on Defensive," *Washington Post*, February 11, 1993, p. 1. See also Howard Kurtz, "Inaugurating a Talk Show Presidency," *Washington Post*, February 12, 1993, p. A4.

33. See, for example, Howard Kurtz, "Networks Stressed the Negative in Comments about Bush, Study Finds," *Washington Post*, November 15, 1992, p. A7. See also Howard Kurtz, "Republicans and Some Journalists Say Media Tend to Boost Clinton, Bash Bush," *Washington Post*, September 1, 1992, p. A7.

34. Howard Kurtz, "The Media and the Fiske Report," *Washington Post*, July 3, 1994, p. A4.

35. See Martin Linsky, *Impact: How the Press Affects Federal Policymaking* (New York: Norton, 1986).

Chapter 8

1. Agence France Presse wire service report, December 20, 1994.

2. Pan Xiaozhu, Xinhua News Agency report, July 30, 1994.

3. Reuters wire service report, February 11, 1995.

4. UPI wire service report, January 24, 1995.

5. Quoted in Peter Applebome, "Collegians Standing Up for Education," *Houston Chronicle*, March 30, 1995, p. A20.

6. Quoted in Applebome, "Collegians Standing Up."

7. See Richard Hofstadter, *The Idea of a Party System* (Berkeley: University of California Press, 1969).

8. See Harold Gosnell, *Machine Politics Chicago Model*, rev. ed. (Chicago: University of Chicago Press, 1968).

9. David Von Drehle and Thomas B. Edsall, "Life of the Grand Old Party: Energized Coalition Enters Another Political Phase," *Washington Post*, August 14, 1994, p. 1.

10. See Walter Dean Burnham, *Critical Elections and the Mainsprings of American Electoral Politics* (New York: Norton, 1970). See also James L. Sundquist, *Dynamics of the Party System* (Washington, DC: Brookings, 1983).

11. Benjamin Ginsberg, *The Consequences of Consent* (New York: Random House, 1982), chap. 4.

12. For a discussion of third parties in the United States, see Daniel Mazmanian, *Third Parties in Presidential Election* (Washington, DC: Brookings, 1974).

Daniel Mazmanian, *Third Parties in Presidential Election* (Washington, DC: Brookings, 1974).

13. See Maurice Duverger, *Political Parties* (New York: Wiley, 1954).

14. Gosnell, *Machine Politics*, chap. 4.

15. Stanley Kelley, Jr., Richard E. Ayres, and William G.

Bowen, "Registration and Voting: Putting First Things First," *American Political Science Review* 61 (June 1967), pp. 359–70.

16. David H. Fischer, *The Revolution of American Conservatism* (New York: Harper & Row, 1965), p. 93.

17. Fischer, *The Revolution of American Conservatism*, p. 109.

18. Henry Jones Ford, *The Rise and Growth of American Politics* (New York: Da Capo Press, 1967 reprint of the 1898 edition), chap. 9.

19. Ford, *The Rise and Growth of American Politics*, p. 125.

20. Ford, *The Rise and Growth of American Politics*, p. 125.

21. Ford, *The Rise and Growth of American Politics*, p. 126.

22. V. O. Key, *Southern Politics* (New York: Random House, 1949), chap. 14.

23. Key, *Southern Politics*.

24. Duverger, *Political Parties*, p. 426.

25. Duverger, *Political Parties*, chap 1.

Chapter 9

1. Clinton Rossiter, ed., *The Federalist Papers* (New York: New American Library, 1961), No. 57, p. 352.

2. Robert Jackman, "Political Institutions and Voter Turnout in the Democracies," *American Political Science Review* 81 (June 1987), p. 420.

3. Helen Dewar, " 'Motor Voter' Agreement Is Reached," *Washington Post*, April 28, 1993, p. A6.

4. Erik Austin and Jerome Chubb, *Political Facts of the United States since 1789* (New York: Columbia University Press, 1986), pp. 378–79.

5. *League of United Latin American Citizens v. Wilson*, CV-94-7569 (C.D. Calif.), 1995.

6. *Gray v. Sanders*, 372 U.S. 368 (1963); *Wesberry v. Sanders*, 376 U.S. 1 (1964); *Reynolds v. Sims*, 377 U.S. 533 (1964).

7. *Thornburg v. Gingles*, 478 U.S. 613 (1986).

8. *Shaw v. Reno*, 509 U.S. 113 (1993).

9. Mary McGrory, "The Lost Leader," *Washington Post*, October 26, 1995, p. A2.

10. Data are drawn from exit poll results reported in the *Washington Post*, November 6, 1996, p. B7.

11. See David Broder, "Parceling Out Power to Both Parties," *Washington Post*, November 6, 1996, p. B1.

12. Jon Healey, "Declining Fortunes: President's Leadership Role Eclipsed by Vigor and Unity of GOP Majority," *Congressional Quarterly Weekly Report*, Vol. 54, No. 4 (January 27, 1996), pp. 193–98.

13. Elizabeth Drew, *Showdown: The Struggle Between the Gingrich Congress and the Clinton White House* (New York: Simon & Schuster, 1996).

14. John F. Harris, "Clinton Had Ingredients for Victory a Year Ago," *Washington Post*, November 4, 1996, p. 1.

15. Federal Election Commission (FEC) reports.

16. FEC reports.

17. *Buckley v. Valeo*, 424 U.S. 1 (1976); *Colorado Republican Party v. Federal Election Commission*, 64 U.S.L.W. 4663 (1996.)

18. FEC reports.

19. FEC reports.

20. *Congressionial Research Report* 95–237, Government Information Access Company Newsletter Database, January 1, 1996.

21. See, for example, John Kennedy, "Will Florida's Drive Yield Turnout?" *Fort Lauderdale Sun-Sentinal*, December 18, 1995, p. 1A.

22. For an excellent discussion see Steven J. Rosenstone and John Mark Hansen, *Mobilization, Participation, and Democracy in America* (New York: Macmillan, 1993), chap. 8.

Chapter 10

1. Jim Zook, "Students Get a Crash Course in Lobbying Against Cuts to Federal Aid," *Chronicle of Higher Education*, March 31, 1995, p. A25.

2. Alexis de Tocqueville, *Democracy in America* (New York: Random House, 1955), vol. 1, chap. 12; vol. 2, chap. 5.

3. A good brief history of these relatively permanent associations that came to be called "interest groups" can be found in V. O. Key, *Politics, Parties, and Pressure Groups*, 2nd ed. (New York: Crowell, 1947).

4. Michael Wines, "Clinton under Attack on Big Contributions," *New York Times*, June 22 1994, p. 1.

5. Timothy Noah, "EPA Came Through for Archer Daniels Midland Soon after Andreas's Role at Presidential Dinner," *Wall Street Journal*, July 6, 1994, p. A20.

6. Clinton Rossiter, ed., *The Federalist Papers* (New York: New American Library, 1961), No. 10, p. 83.

7. Rossiter, ed., *Federalist Papers*, No. 10.

8. The best statement of the pluralist view is in David Truman, *The Governmental Process* (New York: Knopf, 1951), chap. 2.

9. E. E. Schattschneider, *The Semisovereign People* (New York: Holt, Rinehart, and Winston, 1960), p. 35.

10. Betsy Wagner and David Bowermaster, "B.S. Economics," *Washington Monthly*, November 1992, pp. 19–21.

11. Mancur Olson, *The Logic of Collective Action* (Cambridge, MA: Harvard University Press, 1965).

12. Timothy Penny and Steven Schier, *Payment Due: A Nation in Debt, A Generation in Trouble* (Boulder, CO: Westview, 1996), pp. 64–65.

13. Robert Pear, "Senator Challenges the Practices of a Retirees' Association," *New York Times*, June 14, 1995, p. A14.

14. David S. Hilzenrath, "AARP: Non-Profit or 'Big' Profit?" *Washington Post National Weekly Edition*, June 5–11, 1995, pp. 10–11.

15. Kay Lehman Schlozman and John T. Tierney, *Organized Interests and American Democracy* (New York: Harper & Row, 1986), p. 60.

16. John Herbers, "Special Interests Gaining Power as Voter Disillusionment Grows," *New York Times*, November 14, 1978.

17. Robert Pear, "White House Shuns Bigger A.M.A. Voice in Health Changes," *New York Times*, March 5, 1993, p. 1.

18. Mike Mills, "Bush Asks for a Sign of Loyalty; Congress Changes the Channel," *Congressional Quarterly Weekly Report,* October 10, 1992, pp. 3147–49.

19. See Benjamin Ginsberg, *The Captive Public* (New York: Basic Books, 1986), chap. 4. See also David Vogel, "The Public Interest Movement and the American Reform Tradition," *Political Science Quarterly* 95 (winter 1980), pp. 607–27.

20. For discussions of lobbying, see Allan J. Cigler and Burdett A. Loomis, eds., *Interest Group Politics* (Washington, DC: Congressional Quarterly Press, 1983). See also Jeffrey M. Berry, *Lobbying for the People* (Princeton, NJ: Princeton University Press, 1977).

21. "The Swarming Lobbyists," *Time,* August 7, 1978, p. 15.

22. Jacob Weisberg, "Springtime for Lobbyists," *New Republic,* February 1, 1993, pp. 33–41.

23. Michael Weisskopf, "Health Care Lobbies Lobby Each Other," *Washington Post,* March 1, 1994, p. A8.

24. Gregory B. Wilson, "A Congressional Lobbying Effort against the U.S. Chamber of Commerce," unpublished research paper, Johns Hopkins University, 1994.

25. Michael Weisskopf, "Lobbyists Rally around Their Own Cause: Clinton Move to Eliminate Tax Break Sparks Intense Hill Campaign," *Washington Post,* May 14, 1993, p. A16.

26. Phil Kuntz, "Ticket to a Better Image?" *Congressional Quarterly Weekly Report,* May 7, 1994, p. 1105.

27. See especially Marver Bernstein, *Regulating Business by Independent Commission* (Princeton, NJ: Princeton University Press, 1955). See also George J. Stigler, "The Theory of Economic Regulation," *Bell Journal of Economics and Management Science* 2 (1971), pp. 3–21.

28. Quoted in John E. Chubb, *Interest Groups and the Bureaucracy: The Politics of Energy* (Stanford, CA: Stanford University Press, 1983).

29. John P. Heinz, Edward O. Laumann, Robert L. Nelson, and Robert H. Salisbury, *The Hollow Core: Private Interests in National Policy Making* (Cambridge, MA: Harvard University Press, 1993), p. 96. See also Schlozman and Tierney, *Organized Interests and American Democracy,* chap. 13.

30. The famous and prophetic movie *The China Syndrome* portrayed some dramatic moments at a public hearing involving an administrative agency's decision to build or expand an atomic energy plant.

31. For further information on these advisory councils, see James W. Fesler and Donald F. Kettl, *The Politics of the Administrative Process* (Chatham, NJ: Chatham House, 1991), pp. 192–207; and David Rosenbloom, *Public Administration: Understanding Management, Politics, and Law in the Public Sector* (New York: Random House, 1986), pp. 68–72.

32. Fesler and Kettl, *The Politics of the Administrative Process,* pp. 68–69.

33. U.S. Congress, House of Representatives, *Report of the Subcommittee for Special Investigations of the Committee on Armed Services,* 96th Cong. 1st sess. (Washington, DC: Government Printing Office, 1960), p. 7.

34. Thomas Ricks, "With Cold War Over, the Military-Industrial Complex Is Dissolving," *Wall Street Journal,* May 20, 1993, p. 1.

35. William Raspberry, "Why Did Ron Brown Become a Target?" *Washington Post,* January 20, 1993, p. A21.

36. *Griswold v. Connecticut,* 85 S.Ct. 1678 (1965) *Eisenstadt v. Baird,* 405 U.S. 438 (1972); *Roe v. Wade,* 93 S.Ct. 705 (1973).

37. *Webster v. Reproductive Health Services,* 109 S.Ct. 3040 (1989).

38. *Brown v. Board of Education of Topeka, Kansas,* 74 S.Ct. 686 (1954).

39. See, for example, *Duke Power Co. v. Carolina Environmental Study Group,* 438 U.S. 59 (1978).

40. E. Pendleton Herring, *Group Representation before Congress* (New York: McGraw-Hill, 1936).

41. Ann Devroy, "Gay Rights Leaders Meet President in Oval Office: White House Tries to Play Down Session," *Washington Post,* April 17, 1993, p. 1.

42. Michael Weisskopf and Steven Mufson, "Lobbyists in Full Swing on Tax Plan," *Washington Post,* February 17, 1993, p. 1.

43. Michael Weisskopf, "Energized by Pulpit or Passion, the Public Is Calling," *Washington Post,* February 1, 1993, p. 1.

44. Stephen Engelberg, "A New Breed of Hired Hands Cultivates Grass-Roots Anger," *New York Times,* March 17, 1993, p. A1.

45. Jane Fritsch, "The Grass Roots, Just a Free Phone Call Away," *New York Times,* June 23, 1995, pp. A1 and A22.

46. See Charles Babcock, "GE Files Offer Rare View of What PACs Seek to Buy on Capitol Hill," *Washington Post,* June 1, 1993. p. A10.

47. For more on this pattern of giving and the outcomes in access and party affiliation, see Thomas Ferguson, *Follow the Gold* (Chicago: University of Chicago Press, 1995).

48. Julie Rovner, "Mixed Results on Both Sides Keep Spotlight on Abortion," *Congressional Quarterly Weekly Report,* November 7, 1992, pp. 3591–92.

49. Some Americans and even more Europeans would stress only the negative aspect of the softening and adulterating effect of the two-party system on class and other basic subdivisions of society. For a discussion of how the working class was divided and softened, with native workers joining the Democratic Party and new immigrant workers becoming Republicans, see Gwendolyn Mink, *Old Labor and New Immigrants in American Political Development: Union, Party, and State, 1875–1920* (Ithaca, NY: Cornell University Press, 1986).

50. Reported in "The Game Where Nobody Loses but Everybody Loses," *Forbes,* April 16, 1979, pp. 55–63.

51. Mark Lipman, *Stealing* (New York: Harper Magazine Press, 1970).

52. Rossiter, ed., *The Federalist Papers,* No. 10.

53. Olson, *The Logic of Collective Action.*

Chapter 11

1. Herb Asher and Mike Barr, "Popular Support for Congress and Its Members," and Karlyn Borman and Everett Carll Ladd, "Public Opinion toward Congress: A Historical Look," in *Congress, the Press, and the Public,* ed. Thomas E. Mann and Norman J. Ornstein (Washington DC: American Enterprise Institute and Brookings Institution, 1994), pp. 34, 51, 53.

2. Robin Toner, "Senate Now Has Main Role on Health," *New York Times,* August 15, 1994, p. A11.

3. Donna Cassata, "Finale Expected to Be Short, But Not Necessarily Sweet," *Congressional Quarterly Weekly Report,* August 31, 1996, p. 2418.

4. For data on religious affiliations of the members of the 104th Congress, see *Congressional Quarterly Weekly Report,* November 12, 1994.

5. For data on occupational backgrounds of the members of the 104th Congress, see *Congressional Quarterly Weekly Report,* November 12, 1994.

6. Marian D. Irish and James Prothro, *The Politics of American Democracy,* 5th ed. (Englewood Cliffs, NJ: Prentice-Hall, 1971), p. 352.

7. For a discussion, see Benjamin Ginsberg, *The Consequences of Consent* (New York: Random House, 1982), chap. 1.

8. For some interesting empirical evidence, see Angus Campbell, Philip Converse, Warren Miller, and Donald Stokes, *Elections and the Political Order* (New York: Wiley, 1966), chap. 11.

9. Congressional Quarterly, *Guide to the Congress of the United States,* 2nd ed. (Washington, DC: Congressional Quarterly Press, 1976), p. 588.

10. John S. Saloma, *Congress and the New Politics* (Boston: Little, Brown, 1969), pp. 184–85. A 1977 official report using less detailed categories came up with almost the same impression of Congress's workload. Commission on Administrative Review, *Administrative Reorganization and Legislative Management,* House Doc. #95-232 (September 28, 1977), vol. 2, especially pp. 17–19.

11. See Linda Fowler and Robert McClure, *Political Ambition: Who Decides to Run for Congress* (New Haven: Yale University Press, 1989); and Alan Erhenhalt, *The United States of Ambition* (New York: Times Books, 1991).

12. See Barbara C. Burrell, *A Woman's Place Is in the House: Campaigning for Congress in the Feminist Era* (Ann Arbor: University of Michigan Press, 1994), chap. 6; and the essays in Elizabeth Adell Cook, Sue Thomas, and Clyde Wilcox, eds., *The Year of the Woman: Myths and Realities* (Boulder, CO: Westview, 1994).

13. Norman J. Ornstein, Thomas E. Mann, and Michael J. Malbin, *Vital Statistics on Congress 1995–1996* (Washington, DC: Congressional Quarterly Press 1996), pp. 60–61; Robert S. Erickson and Gerald C. Wright, "Voters, Candidates, and Issues in Congressional Elections," in *Congress Reconsidered,* 5th ed., ed. Lawrence C. Dodd and Bruce I. Oppenheimer (Washington DC: Congressional Quarterly Press, 1993), p. 99; John R. Alford and David W. Brady, "Personal and Partisan Advantage in U.S. Congressional Elections, 1846–1990," in *Congress Reconsidered* ed. Dodd and Oppenheimer, pp. 141–57.

14. Kevin Merida, "The 2nd Time Is Easy; Many House Freshmen Have Secured Seats," *Washington Post,* October 18, 1994, p. A1.

15. See Burrell, *A Woman's Place Is in the House;* and David Broder, "Key to Women's Political Parity: Running," *Washington Post,* September 8, 1994, p. A17.

16. Based on author's tabulations.

17. "Did Redistricting Sink the Democrats?" *National Journal,* December 17, 1994, p. 2984.

18. Tim Weiner, "Sending Money to Home District: Earmarking and the Pork Barrel," *New York Times,* July 13, 1994, p. 1.

19. Congressional Quarterly, *Guide to the Congress of the United States,* pp. 229–310.

20. Richard Fenno, Jr., *Home Style: House Members in Their Districts* (Boston: Little, Brown, 1978).

21. On the agenda activities of the Democratic leadership, see Paul S. Herrnson and Kelly D. Patterson, "Toward a More Programmatic Democratic Party? Agenda-Setting and Coalition-Building in the House of Representatives," *Polity* 27 (summer 1995) pp. 607–28.

22. Richard C. Fenno, *Congressmen in Committees* (Boston: Little, Brown, 1973), p. 1; Richard L. Hall, "Participation, Abdication, and Representation in Congressional Committees," in *Congress Reconsidered,* ed. Dodd and Oppenheimer, p. 164.

23. See Thomas E. Mann and Norman J. Ornstein, *Renewing Congress: A First Report of the Renewing Congress Project* (Washington, DC: American Enterprise Institute and Brookings Institution, 1992). See also the essays in Roger H. Davidson, ed., *The Postreform Congress* (New York: St. Martin's, 1992).

24. Adam Clymer, "The House: Battlefield of Short-Tempered Partisanship," *New York Times,* July 16, 1995, p. 14; David S. Broder, "At 6 Months, House GOP Juggernaut Still Cohesive," *Washington Post,* July 17, 1995, p. A1.

25. Robert Pear, "With Long Hours and Little Fanfare, Staff Members Crafted a Health Bill," *New York Times,* August 6, 1994, p. 7.

26. Kenneth Cooper, "GOP Moves to Restrict Office Funds," *Washington Post,* December 7, 1994, p. 1.

27. Susan Webb Hammond, "Congressional Caucuses in the 104th Congress," in *Congress Reconsidered,* 6th ed., ed. Lawrence C. Dodd and Bruce I. Oppenheimer (Washington, DC: Congressional Quarterly Press, forthcoming).

28. Richard Sammon, "Panel Backs Senate Changes, But Fights Loom for Floor," *Congressional Quarterly Weekly Report,* June 18, 1994, pp. 1575–76.

29. See John W. Kingdon, *Congressmen's Voting Decisions* (New York: Harper and Row, 1973), chap. 3; and R. Douglas Arnold, *The Logic of Congressional Action* (New Haven, CT: Yale University Press, 1990).

30. Jane Fritsch, "The Grass Roots, Just a Free Phone Call Away," *New York Times,* June 23, 1995, p. A1.

31. Daniel Franklin, "Tommy Boggs and the Death of Health Care Reform," *Washington Monthly,* April 1995, p. 36.

32. Peter H. Stone, "Follow the Leaders," *National Journal,* June 24, 1995, p. 1641.

33. Holly Idelson, "Signs Point to Greater Loyalty on Both Sides of the Aisle," *Congressional Quarterly Weekly Report,* December 19, 1992, p. 3849.

34. David Broder, "Hill Democrats Vote as One: New Era of Unity or Short-term Honeymoon?" *Washington Post,* March 14, 1993, p. A1. See also Adam Clymer, "All Aboard: Clinton's Plan Gets Moving," *New York Times,* March 21, 1993, sec. 4, p. 1.

35. Allen R. Meyerson, "Oil-Patch Congressmen Seek Deal With Clinton," *New York Times,* June 14, 1994, p. D2.

36. David Broder, "At 6 Months, House GOP Juggernaut still Cohesive," *Washington Post,* July 17, 1995, p. A1.

37. *U.S. v. Pink,* 315 U.S. 203 (1942). For a good discussion

of the problem, see James W. Davis, *The American Presidency* (New York: Harper & Row, 1987), chap. 8.

38. See Samuel Huntington, "Congressional Responses to the Twentieth Century," in *Congress and America's Future,* ed. David Truman (Englewood Cliffs, NJ: Prentice Hall, 1965), chap. 1.

39. See Thomas Ferguson, "From Normalcy to New Deal: Industrial Structure, Party Competition and American Public Policy in the Great Depression," *International Organization 038* (winter 1984), pp. 42–94.

40. Burrell, *A Woman's Place Is in the House,* p. 163.

41. On the Congressional Black Caucus budget, see John C. Berg, *Class, Gender, Race, and Power in the U.S. Congress* (Boulder, CO: Westview, 1994). On the Congressional Caucus for Women's Issues, see Burrell, *A Woman's Place Is in the House,* chap. 8; and Susan Gluck Mezey, "Increasing the Number of Women in Office: Does It Matter?" in *The Year of the Woman,* ed. Cook, Thomas, and Wilcox, chap. 14.

42. See Kenneth A. Shepsle, "Representation and Governance: The Great Legislative Trade-off," *Political Science Quarterly* 103:3 (1988), pp. 461–84.

Chapter 12

1. E. S. Corwin, *The President: Office and Powers,* 3rd rev. ed. (New York: New York University Press, 1957), p. 2.

2. Article II, Section 3. There is a Section 4, but all it does is define impeachment.

3. *In re Neagle,* 135 U.S. 1 (1890). Neagle, a deputy U.S. marshal, had been authorized by the president to protect a Supreme Court justice whose life had been threatened by an angry litigant. When the litigant attempted to carry out his threat, Neagle shot and killed him. Neagle was then arrested by the local authorities and tried for murder. His defense was that his act was "done in pursuance of a law of the United States." Although the law was not an act of Congress, the Supreme Court declared that it was an executive order of the president, and the protection of a federal judge was a reasonable extension of the president's power to "take care that the laws be faithfully executed."

4. Arthur Schlesinger, Jr., *The Imperial Presidency* (Boston: Houghton Mifflin, 1973).

5. *U.S. v. Curtiss-Wright Corp.,* 299 U.S. 304 (1936). In 1934, Congress passed a joint resolution authorizing the president to prohibit the sale of military supplies to Bolivia and Paraguay, who were at war, if the president determined that the prohibition would contribute to peace between the two countries. When prosecuted for violating the embargo order by President Roosevelt, the defendants argued that Congress could not constitutionally delegate such broad discretion to the president. The Supreme Court disagreed. Previously, however, the Court had rejected the National Industrial Recovery Act precisely because Congress had delegated too much discretion to the president in a domestic policy. See *Schechter Poultry Corp. v. U.S.,* 295 U.S. 495 (1936).

6. In *United States v. Pink,* 315 U.S. 203 (1942), the Supreme Court confirmed that an executive agreement is the legal equivalent of a treaty, despite the absence of Senate approval. This case approved the executive agreement that was used to establish diplomatic relations with the Soviet Union in 1933. An executive agreement, not a treaty, was used in 1940 to exchange "fifty over-age destroyers" for ninety-nine-year leases on some important military bases.

7. This federal law restricts the export of American weapons, allowing such exports only "to friendly countries solely for internal security" and "legitimate self-defense."

8. Murray Waas and Craig Unger, "Annals of Government. In the Loop: Bush's Secret Mission," *New Yorker,* November 2, 1992, p. 73.

9. Roger Cohen, "Taming the Bullies of Bosnia," *New York Times Magazine,* December 17, 1995, pp. 58ff.

10. These statutes are contained mainly in Title 10 of the United States Code, Sections 331, 332, and 333.

11. The best study covering all aspects of the domestic use of the military is that of Adam Yarmolinsky, *The Military Establishment* (New York: Harper & Row, 1971). Probably the most famous instance of a president's unilateral use of the power to protect a state "against domestic violence" was in dealing with the Pullman Strike of 1894. The famous Supreme Court case that ensued was *In re Debs,* 158 U.S. 564 (1895).

12. There is a third source of presidential power implied from the provision for "faithful execution of the laws." This is the president's power to impound funds—that is, to refuse to spend money Congress has appropriated for certain purposes. One author referred to this as a "retroactive veto power" (Robert E. Goosetree, "The Power of the President to Impound Appropriated Funds," *American University Law Review,* January 1962). This impoundment power was used freely and to considerable effect by many modern presidents, and Congress occasionally delegated such power to the president by statute. But in reaction to the Watergate scandal, Congress adopted the Budget and Impoundment Control Act of 1974 and designed this act to circumscribe the president's ability to impound funds by requiring that the president must spend all appropriated funds unless both houses of Congress consent to an impoundment within forty-five days of a presidential request. Therefore, since 1974, the use of impoundment has declined significantly. Presidents have either had to bite their tongues and accept unwanted appropriations or had to revert to the older and more dependable but politically limited method of vetoing the entire bill. The line-item veto enacted by Congress in 1996, if it is not overturned by the Supreme Court, will greatly increase the president's ability to use the veto to shape legislation.

13. For a different perspective, see William F. Grover, *The President as Prisoner: A Structural Critique of the Carter and Reagan Years* (Albany: State University of New York Press, 1989).

14. For more on the veto, see Chapter 11 and Robert J. Spitzer, *The Presidential Veto: Touchstone of the American Presidency* (Albany: State University of New York Press, 1988).

15. All of these positions are exempted from the competitive civil service requirements. Some may have to meet a qualification standard as set by law or by an agency head, but they are otherwise discretionary and do not have to meet the general legal standards of the Office of Personnel Management.

16. Committee on Post Office and Civil Service, House of Representatives, *United States Government, Policy and Supporting Positions* (Washington, DC: Government Printing Office, 1992).

17. *Policy and Supporting Positions,* p. v.

18. James P. Pfiffner, "Political Appointees and Career Executives: The Democracy-Bureaucracy Nexus," in *Agenda for Excellence: Public Service in America,* ed. Patricia Ingraham and Donald Kettl (Chatham, NJ: Chatham House, 1992), pp. 48–50.

19. The "Beltway" is Interstate Highway 495, a circular bypass that surrounds Washington, D.C., and its environs. Symbolically, the Beltway marks the informal boundaries of the center of national power.

20. *New York Times,* December 23, 1992, p. 1.

21. A substantial portion of this section is taken from Theodore J. Lowi, *The Personal President* (Ithaca, NY: Cornell University Press, 1985), pp. 141–50.

22. All the figures since 1967, and probably 1957, are understated, because additional White House staff members were on "detail" service from the military and other departments (some secretly assigned) and are not counted here because they were not on the White House payroll.

23. See Donna K. H. Walters, "The Disarray at the White House Proves Clinton Wouldn't Last as a Fortune 500 CEO," *Plain Dealer,* July 10, 1994, p. 1C; and Paul Richter, "The Battle for Washington: Leon Panetta's Burden," *Los Angeles Times Sunday Magazine,* January 8, 1995, p. 16.

24. The actual number is difficult to estimate because, as with White House staff, some EOP personnel, especially in national security work, are detailed to EOP from outside agencies.

25. Article I, Section 3, provides that "The Vice-President . . . shall be President of the Senate, but shall have no Vote, unless they be equally divided." This is the only vote the vice president is allowed.

26. Quoted in Ann Devroy, "Clinton Reciprocates Perot's Criticism—The President Questions Why Texan Has Not Endorsed Plan," *Washington Post,* April 2, 1993, p. A7.

27. *Congressional Quarterly Weekly Report,* Vol. 54, no. 1 (1996), p. 7.

28. A wider range of group phenomena was covered in Chapter 10. In that chapter the focus was on the influence of groups *upon* the government and its policy-making processes. Here our concern is more with the relationship of groups to the presidency and the extent to which groups and coalitions of groups become a dependable resource for presidential government.

29. For a more detailed review of the New Deal coalition in comparison with later coalitions, see Thomas Ferguson and Joel Rogers, *Right Turn: The Decline of the Democrats and the Future of American Politics* (New York: Hill & Wang, 1986), chap. 2. For updates on the group basis of presidential politics, see Thomas Ferguson, "Money and Politics," in *Handbooks to the Modern Worlds—the United States,* vol. 2, ed. Godfrey Hodgson (New York: Facts on File, 1992), pp. 1060–84; and Lucius J. Barker, ed., "Black Electoral Politics," *National Political Science Review,* vol. 2 (New Brunswick, NJ: Transaction Publishers, 1990).

30. David Broder, "Some Newsworthy Presidential CPR," *Washington Post National Weekly Edition,* June 4–10, 1990, p. 4.

31. See George Edwards III, *At the Margins—Presidential Leadership of Congress* (New Haven, CT: Yale University Press, 1989), chap. 7; and Robert Locander, "The President and the News Media," in *Dimensions of the Modern Presidency,* ed. Edward Kearney (St. Louis: Forum Press, 1981), pp. 49–52.

32. Study cited in Ann Devroy, "Despite Panetta Pep Talk, White House Aides See Daunting Task," *Washington Post,* January 8, 1995, p. A4.

33. For data on the regularity of the loss of presidential support following domestic policy actions, see Theodore J. Lowi, *Incomplete Conquest: Governing America,* 2nd ed. (New York: Holt, Rinehart and Winston, 1981), pp. 310–17; and Raymond Tatalovich and Byron W. Daynes, *Presidential Power in the United States* (Monterey, CA: Brooks/Cole Publishing Co., 1984), pp. 102–6.

34. This very useful distinction between pow*er* and pow*ers* is inspired by Richard Neustadt, *Presidential Power* (New York: Wiley, 1960), p. 28.

35. E. M. Earle, ed., *The Federalist Papers* (New York: Modern Library, 1937), No. 51.

36. For related appraisals, see Jeffrey Tulis, *The Rhetorical Presidency* (Princeton, NJ: Princeton University Press, 1988); Stephen Skowronek, *The Politics Presidents Make: Leadership from John Adams to George Bush* (Cambridge: Harvard University Press, 1993); and Robert Spitzer, *President and Congress: Executive Hegemony at the Crossroads of American Government* (New York: McGraw-Hill, 1993).

37. The Supreme Court did in fact disapprove broad delegations of legislative power by declaring the National Industrial Recovery Act of 1933 unconstitutional on the grounds that Congress did not accompany the broad delegations with sufficient standards or guidelines for presidential discretion (*Panama Refining Co. v. Ryan*, 293 U.S. 388[1935], and *Schechter Poultry Corp. v. United States*, 295 U.S. 495 [1935]). The Supreme Court has never reversed those two decisions, but it has also never really followed them. Thus, broad delegations of legislative power from Congress to the executive branch can be presumed to be constitutional.

Chapter 13

1. *Facts and Figures on Government Finance, 1994* (Washington, DC: Tax Foundation, 1994), p. 77.

2. Arnold Brecht and Comstock Glaser, *The Art and Techniques of Administration in German Ministries* (Cambridge, MA: Harvard University Press, 1940), p. 6.

3. "Red tape" actually refers to the traditional practice of tying up bundles of bureaucratic records before storing them somewhere.

4. The presidential commission that investigated the *Challenger* tragedy was able to pinpoint a single technical failure on the basis of the evidence—the paper trail—assembled. Analysts of the tragedy concluded that "the decision to launch the *Challenger* was flawed. Those who made the decision were unaware of the recent history of [technical] problems. . . . If the decision-makers had known all the facts it is highly unlikely that they would have decided to launch [the shuttle] on January

28, 1986." See Barbara S. Romzek and Melvin Dubnick, "Accountability in the Public Sector: Lessons from the *Challenger* Tragedy," in *Current Issues in Public Administration,* 5th ed., ed. Frederick S. Lane (New York: St. Martin's, 1994), pp. 158–59.

5. The last truly important act of Congress to be declared unconstitutional on these grounds was the National Industrial Recovery Act, which the Supreme Court invalidated in 1935, in two historic cases: *Schechter Poultry Corp. v. United States,* 295 U.S. 495 (1935), and *Panama Refining Co. v. Ryan,* 293 U.S. 388 (1935).

6. Charles H. Levine and Rosslyn S. Kleeman, "The Quiet Crisis in the American Public Service," in *Agenda for Excellence: Public Service in America,* ed. Patricia Ingraham and Donald Kettl (Chatham, NJ: Chatham House, 1992), p. 214.

7. Levine and Kleeman, "The Quiet Crisis," p. 214.

8. Levine and Kleeman, "The Quiet Crisis," p. 209.

9. Figures cited in Paula D. McClain and Joseph Stewart, Jr., *"Can't We All Get Along?" Racial and Ethnic Minorities in American Politics* (Boulder, CO: Westview, 1995), pp. 102–5.

10. "GS" refers to the general schedule, or chart, of salary levels for all federal civil service employees.

11. McClain and Stewart *"Can't We All Get Along,"* p. 105.

12. As of 1995, salaries for GS-15 federal employees in Washington, D.C., could range between $71,664 and $93,166; salaries for the Senior Executive Service could range between $108,200 and $148,400. Office of Personnel Management, *Pay Structure of Federal Civil Service* (Washington, DC: Government Printing Office, annually).

13. Joel D. Aberbach, "The Federal Executive under Clinton," in *The Clinton Presidency: First Appraisals,* ed. Colin Campbell and Bert Rockman (Chatham, NJ: Chatham House, 1996), pp. 163–76.

14. There are historical reasons why American cabinet-level administrators are called "secretaries." During the Second Continental Congress and the subsequent confederal government, standing committees were formed to deal with executive functions related to foreign affairs, military and maritime issues, and public financing. The heads of those committees were called "secretaries" because their primary task was to handle all correspondence and documentation related to their areas of responsibility.

15. 32 Stat. 825; 15 U.S.C. 1501.

16. See Theodore J. Lowi, *The End of Liberalism* (New York: Norton, 1979), pp. 78–84.

17. As with the Interior Department, there are other departments that are placed under different classifications but that possess a few clientele agencies, even though the entire department is not a clientele department.

18. "The Republican Congress—The Evolution of a Revolution," *Economist,* November 4, 1995, pp. 23–25.

19. For a good story on the difficulty of abolishing a clientele agency, see David E. Sanger, "GOP Finds Commerce Department Is Hard to Uproot," *New York Times,* September 19, 1995, p. 1.

20. George E. Berkley, *The Craft of Public Administration* (Boston: Allyn & Bacon, 1975), p. 417. Emphasis added.

21. See William Keller, *The Liberals and J. Edgar Hoover* (Princeton, NJ: Princeton University Press, 1989). See also Victor Navasky, *Kennedy Justice* (New York: Atheneum, 1971), chap. 2 and p. 8.

22. For more detail, consult John E. Harr, *The Professional Diplomat* (Princeton, NJ: Princeton University Press, 1972), p. 11; and Nicholas Horrock, "The CIA Has Neighbors in the 'Intelligence Community,'" *New York Times,* June 29, 1975, sec. 4, p. 2. See also Roger Hilsman, *The Politics of Policy Making in Defense and Foreign Affairs,* 3rd ed. (Englewood Cliffs, NJ: Prentice Hall, 1993).

23. John W. Finney, "Service Secretaries Have the Title but Little Else," *New York Times,* July 24, 1973, p. 4. See also Adam Yarmolinsky, *The Military Establishment* (New York: Harper & Row, 1971), p. 17.

24. William Safire, "Bush's Gamble," *New York Times Magazine,* October 18, 1992, p. 60.

25. See Paul Peterson, *The Price of Federalism* (Washington, DC: Brookings, 1995) for a recent argument that "redistribution" is the distinctive function of the national government in the American federal system.

26. For an excellent political analysis of the Fed, see Donald Kettl, *Leadership at the Fed* (New Haven, CT: Yale University Press, 1986).

27. These are called "insurance" because the Social Security tax is a kind of premium; however, the programs are not fully self-sustaining, and people do not receive benefits in proportion to the size of their premiums.

28. A thorough review of the first session of the 104th Congress will be found in "Republican's Hopes for 1996 Lie in Unfinished Business," *Congressional Quarterly Weekly Report,* January 6, 1996, pp. 6–18.

29. Public Law 101-510, Title XXIX, Sections 2,901 and 2,902 of Part A (Defense Base Closure and Realignment Commission).

30. Donald F. Kettl and John I. DiIulio, *Fine Print,* Center for Public Management Report no. 95-1 (Washington, DC: Brookings Institution, 1995).

31. The title was inspired by a book by Charles Hyneman, *Bureaucracy in a Democracy* (New York: Harper, 1950). For a more recent effort to describe the federal bureaucracy and to provide some guidelines for improvement, see Patricia W. Ingraham and Donald F. Kettl, eds., *Agenda for Excellence: Public Service in America* (Chatham, NJ: Chatham House, 1992).

32. Clinton Rossiter, ed., *The Federalist Papers* (New York: New American Library, 1961), No. 51, p. 322.

33. The title of this section was inspired by Peri Arnold, *Making the Managerial Presidency* (Princeton, NJ: Princeton University Press, 1986).

34. See Richard Nathan, *The Plot that Failed: Nixon and the Administrative Presidency* (New York: Wiley, 1975), pp. 68–76.

35. For more details and evaluations, see David Rosenbloom, *Public Administration* (New York: Random House, 1986), pp. 186–221; Levine and Kleeman, "The Quiet Crisis"; and Patricia Ingraham and David Rosenbloom, "The State of Merit in the Federal Government," *Agenda for Excellence,* ed. Ingraham and Kettl.

36. Lester Salamon and Alan Abramson, "Governance: The Politics of Retrenchment," in *The Reagan Record,* ed. John Palmer and Isabel Sawhill (Cambridge, MA: Ballinger, 1984), p. 40.

37. Colin Campbell, "The White House and the Presidency under the 'Let's Deal' President," in *The Bush Presidency: First*

Appraisals, ed. Colin Campbell and Bert A. Rockman (Chatham, NJ: Chatham House, 1991), pp. 185–222.

38. Quoted in Stephen Barr, "Midterm Exam for 'Reinvention'; Study Cites 'Impressive Results' But Calls for Strategy to Win Congressional Support," *Washington Post*, August 19, 1994, p. A25.

39. There are many other examples of the difficulty of succeeding at administrative reform, especially in the public opinion vacuum that appears to surround this area. One fascinating case study involves the General Services Administration (GSA), one of the most notoriously unwieldy bureaucracies. See Faye Fiore, "Exec's Baptism of Fire in D.C.; GSA Chief Roger Johnson Reflects on Frustrating First Year that Made Him Yearn for Home," *Los Angeles Times*, July 14, 1994, p. A1.

40. Quoted in I. M. Destler, "Reagan and the World: An 'Awesome Stubbornness,'" in *The Reagan Legacy: Promise and Performance*, ed. Charles O. Jones (Chatham House, 1988), pp. 244 and 257. The source of the quote is *Report of the President's Special Review Board*, (Washington, DC: Government Printing Office, 1987).

41. Data from Norman Ornstein et al., *Vital Statistics on Congress, 1987–1988* (Washington, DC: Congressional Quarterly Press, 1987), pp. 161–62. See also Lawrence Dodd and Richard Schott, *Congress and the Administrative State* (New York: Wiley, 1979), p. 169. For a valuable and skeptical assessment of legislature oversight of administrations, see James W. Fesler and Donald F. Kettl, *The Politics of the Administrative Process* (Chatham, NJ: Chatham House, 1991), chap. 11.

42. The Office of Technology Assessment (OTA) was a fourth research agency serving Congress until 1995. It was one of the first agencies scheduled for elimination by the 104th Congress. Until 1983, Congress had still another tool of legislative oversight: the legislative veto. Each agency operating under such provisions was obliged to submit to Congress every proposed decision or rule, which would then lie before both chambers for thirty to sixty days. If Congress took no action by one-house or two-house resolution explicitly to veto the proposed measure during the prescribed period, it became law. The legislative veto was declared unconstitutional by the Supreme Court in 1983 on the grounds that it violated the separation of powers—the resolutions Congress passed to exercise its veto were not subject to presidential veto, as required by the Constitution. See *Immigration and Naturalization Service v. Chadha*, 462 U.S. 919 (1983).

Chapter 14

1. Carolyn J. Mooney, "Judge Finds No Anti-Christian Bias in Tenure Case," *Chronicle of Higher Education*, February 17, 1995, p. A18.

2. Peter Appelbome, "Goal Unmet, Duke Reveals Perils in Effort to Increase Black Faculty," *New York Times*, September 19, 1993, p. A1.

3. See Mike Clary, "The Citadel Surrenders Its All-Male Tradition," *Los Angeles Times*, August 13, 1995, p. A1; and *United States v. Virginia*, 94-1941 (1996).

4. *Rosenberger v. University of Virginia*, 94-329 (1995).

5. Richard Bernstein, "Guilty If Charged," *New York Review of Books*, January 13, 1994, p. 11.

6. See Richard Neely, *How Courts Govern America* (New Haven, CT: Yale University Press, 1981).

7. U.S. Bureau of the Census, *Statistical Abstract of the United States* (Washington, DC: Government Printing Office, 1995).

8. Robert Scigliano, *The Supreme Court and the Presidency* (New York: Free Press, 1971), p. 162. For an interesting critique of the solicitor general's role during the Reagan administration, see Lincoln Caplan, "Annals of the Law," *New Yorker*, August 17, 1987, pp. 30–62.

9. C. Herman Pritchett, *The American Constitution* (New York: McGraw-Hill, 1959), p. 138.

10. *Marbury v. Madison*, 1 Cr. 137 (1803).

11. This review power was affirmed by the Supreme Court in *Martin v. Hunter's Lessee*, 1 Wheat. 304 (1816).

12. *Brown v. Board of Education*, 347 U.S. 483 (1954); *Loving v. Virginia*, 388 U.S. 1 (1967).

13. *Griswold v. Connecticut*, 381 U.S. 479 (1965).

14. *Brandenburg v. Ohio*, 395 U.S. 444 (1969).

15. Oliver Wendell Holmes, Jr., "The Path of the Law," *Harvard Law Review* 10 (1897), p. 457.

16. *Shelley v. Kraemer*, 334 U.S. 1 (1948).

17. *Gideon v. Wainwright*, 372 U.S. 335 (1963).

18. *Engel v. Vitale*, 370 U.S. 421 (1962); *Gideon v. Wainwright*, 372 U.S. 335 (1963); *Escobedo v. Illinois*, 378 U.S. 478 (1964); and *Miranda v. Arizona*, 384 U.S. 436 (1966).

19. *Baker v. Carr*, 369 U.S. 186 (1962).

20. Walter F. Murphy, "The Supreme Court of the United States," in *Encyclopedia of the American Judicial System*, ed. Robert J. Janosik (New York: Scribner's, 1987).

21. *Adarand Constructors v. Pena*, 115 S.Ct. 2097 (1995); *Missouri v. Jenkins*, 115 S.Ct. 2573 (1995); *Miller v. Johnson*, 115 S.Ct. 2475 (1995).

22. *Plyler v. Doe*, 457 U.S. 202 (1982).

23. *NAACP v. Button*, 371 U.S. 415 (1963). The quotation is from the opinion in this case.

24. *Smith v. Allwright*, 321 U.S. 649 (1944).

25. *Chicago Daily Law Bulletin*, October 5, 1994.

26. R. W. Apple, Jr., "A Divided Government Remains, and With It the Prospect of Further Combat," *New York Times*, November 7, 1996, p. B6.

27. For limits on judicial power, see Alexander Bickel, *The Least Dangerous Branch* (Indianapolis, IN: Bobbs-Merrill, 1962).

28. *Worcester v. Georgia*, 6 Pet. 515 (1832).

29. See Walter Murphy, *Congress and the Court* (Chicago: University of Chicago Press, 1962).

30. Robert Dahl, "The Supreme Court and National Policy Making," *Journal of Public Law* 6 (1958), p. 279.

31. Martin Shapiro, "The Supreme Court: From Warren to Burger," in *The New American Political System*, ed. Anthony King (Washington, DC: American Enterprise Institute, 1978).

32. *Citizens to Preserve Overton Park v. Volpe*, 401 U.S. 402 (1971).

33. Toni Locy, "Bracing for Health Care's Caseload," *Washington Post*, August 22, 1994, p. A15.

34. See "Developments in the Law—Class Actions," *Harvard Law Review* 89 (1976), p. 1318.

35. *In re Agent Orange Product Liability Litigation,* 100 F.R.D. 718 (D.C.N.Y. 1983).

36. See Donald Horowitz, *The Courts and Social Policy* (Washington, DC: Brookings Institution, 1977).

37. *Moran v. McDonough,* 540 F. 2nd 527 (1 Cir., 1976; *cert. denied* 429 U.S. 1042 [1977]).

38. Mark Silverstein and Benjamin Ginsberg, "The Supreme Court and the New Politics of Judicial Power," *Political Science Quarterly* 102 (fall 1987), pp. 371–88.

39. *Lujan v. Defenders of Wildlife,* 112 S.Ct. 2130 (1992).

40. Linda Greenhouse, "Court Limits Legal Standing in Suits," *New York Times,* June 13, 1992, p. 12.

41. Clinton Rossiter, ed., *The Federalist Papers* (New York: New American Library, 1961), No. 10, p. 78.

Chapter 15

1. See Malcolm Gladwell, "Proposed Education Cuts Protested in New York," *Washington Post,* March 25, 1995, p. A4.

2. Dissenting opinion, *New State Ice Co. v. Liebmann,* 285 U.S. 262 (1932).

3. See Theda Skocpol, *Protecting Soldiers and Mothers: The Political Origins of Social Policy in the United States* (Cambridge, MA: Harvard University Press, 1992), chap. 8.

4. See the criticisms of the states in Terry Sanford, *Storm over the States* (New York: McGraw-Hill, 1967), chaps. 2 and 3.

5. David Montejano, *Anglos and Mexicans in the Making of Texas, 1836-1986* (Austin: University of Texas Press, 1986), chap. 10.

6. Quoted in Dan T. Carter, *The Politics of Rage: George Wallace, the Origins of the New Conservatism, and the Transformation of American Politics* (New York: Simon and Schuster, 1995), p. 109.

7. Anne O'M. Bowman and Richard C. Kearney, *The Resurgence of the States* (Englewood Cliffs, NJ: Prentice Hall, 1986), p. 17.

8. See Grant McConnell, *Private Power and American Democracy* (New York: Vintage Books, 1966), pp. 172–73.

9. See Frank R. Parker, *Black Votes Count* (Chapel Hill: University of North Carolina Press, 1990), p. 31. Parker's book shows, however, that registration was not enough, because Mississippi used a variety of techniques to dilute black voting strength.

10. David Montejano, *Anglos and Mexicans,* chaps. 12 and 13.

11. *Baker v. Carr,* 369 U.S. 186 (1962); *Reynolds v. Sims,* 377 U.S. 533 (1964).

12. Calculated by authors from U.S. Bureau of the Census, *Statistical Abstract of the United States, 1995* (Washington, DC: Government Printing Office, 1995), p. 287; and Harold W. Stanley and Richard G. Niemi, *Vital Statistics on American Politics,* 5th ed. (Washington, DC: Congressional Quarterly Press, 1995), pp. 372–73.

13. Authors' interviews with officials at the National Association of Latino Elected and Appointed Officials, Washington, DC, and U.S. Department of Commerce, *Statistical Abstract of the United States, 1995,* p. 287.

14. "Women in Elective Office, 1995," and "Statewide Elective Executive Women 1995," Center for the American Woman and Politics, Eagleton Institute of Politics, Rutgers University. Four of these thirteen women were elected governors as surrogates for their husbands who had died or were not eligible to run for re-election. The first of these, Nellie Taylor Ross, a Democrat, became governor of Wyoming in 1925.

15. Terry Sanford, *Storm over the States,* p. 29. The constitution that Louisiana adopted in 1974, which is still in effect, contains 51,448 words, still long in comparison with those of other states.

16. See Sanford, *Storm over the States,* p. 33.

17. Larry Sabato, *Goodbye to Goodtime Charlie: The American Governorship Transformed,* 2nd ed. (Washington, DC: Congressional Quarterly Press, 1983), p. 63.

18. See William Pound, "State Legislative Careers: Twenty-Five Years of Reform," in *Changing Patterns in State Legislative Careers,* ed. Gary D. Moncrief and Joel A. Thompson (Ann Arbor: University of Michigan Press, 1992), pp. 9–21.

19. Thad Beyle, "Governors: The Middlemen and Women in Our Political System," in *Politics in the American States: A Comparative Analysis,* 6th ed., ed. Virginia Gray and Herbert Jacob (Washington DC: Congressional Quarterly Press, 1996), p. 237.

20. William T. Gormley, Jr., "Accountability Battles in State Politics," in *The State of the States,* 2nd ed., ed. Carl E. Van Horn (Washington, DC: Congressional Quarterly Press, 1993), p. 182. See also the discussion of the veto by former Wisconsin house speaker Tom Loftus, in Loftus, *The Art of Legislative Politics* (Washington DC: Congressional Quarterly Press, 1994) pp. 70–75.

21. Richard C. Elling, "Bureaucracy: Maligned but Essential," in *Politics in the American States,* 6th ed., ed. Gray and Jacob (Washington, DC: Congressional Quarterly Press, 1996), p. 298.

22. *The Book of the States, 1994–95,* Vol. 30 (Lexington, KY: Council of State Governments, 1994) table 6.10.

23. See the essays in R. Scott Fosler, ed., *The New Economic Role of the American States* (New York: Oxford University Press, 1988).

24. See Richard F. Winters, "The Politics of Taxing and Spending," in *Politics in the American States,* 6th ed., ed. Gray and Jacob, pp. 328–29.

25. *The Book of the States, 1992–93,* Vol. 28 (Lexington, KY: Council of State Governments, 1993), table 6.29.

26. See Susan B. Hansen, "The Politics of Taxing and Spending," in *Politics in the American States: A Comparative Analysis,* 5th ed., ed. Virginia Gray, Herbert Jacob, and Robert B. Albritton (Glenview, IL: Scott Foresman/Little, Brown, 1990), pp. 345–46; and Richard F. Winters, "The Politics of Taxing and Spending," in *Politics in the American States,* 6th ed., ed. Gray and Jacob, p. 336.

27. *The Book of the States, 1992–93,* Vol. 28, p. 369.

28. Alan Rosenthal, *The Third House: Lobbyists and Lobbying in the States* (Washington DC: Congressional Quarterly Press, 1993), p. 4.

29. Craig A. Roberts and Paul Kleppner, *Almanac of Illinois Politics, 1994* (Springfield, IL: Sangamon State University, 1994), pp. 406–7.

30. David Louis Cingranelli, "Lobbying in New York," in *Governing New York State,* 3rd ed., ed. Jeffrey M. Stonecash, John Kenneth White, and Peter W. Colby (Albany: State University of New York Press, 1994), p. 181.

31. Rosenthal, *The Third House,* p. 4.

32. Jennifer Halperin, "Rookies Accustomed to Riding the Bench," *Illinois Issues,* May 14, 1994, p. 14.

33. *The Book of the States, 1994–95,* Vol. 30; see also David H. Everson, "'Natural' Term Limits in Illinois," in *State Government,* ed. Thad L. Beyle (Washington, DC: Congressional Quarterly Press, 1994), pp. 29–30.

34. On the use of the initiative see Thomas E. Cronin, *Direct Democracy: The Politics of Initiative, Referendum, and Recall* (Cambridge, MA: Harvard University Press, 1989). For proposals to reform the initiative process in California see Elisabeth R. Gerber, "Reforming the California Initiative Process: A Proposal to Increase Flexibility and Legislative Accountability," and John Ferejohn, "Reforming the Initiative Process," in *Constitutional Reform in California: Making State Government More Effective and Responsive,* ed. Bruce E. Cain and Roger G. Noll (Berkeley: Institute of Governmental Studies Press, University of California, 1995), pp. 291–312 and 313–25.

35. See Gareth Cook, "Devolution Chic," *Washington Monthly,* April 1995, pp. 13–14; and Sam Howe Verhovek, "With Power Shift, State Lawmakers See New Demands," *New York Times,* September 24, 1995, p. A1.

36. *City of Clinton v. Cedar Rapids and Missouri River Railroad Co.,* 24 Iowa 455, 475 (1868). On the constitutional position of local government see York Wilbern, *The Withering Away of the City* (Bloomington: Indiana University Press, 1971).

37. See Ester R. Fuchs, *Mayors and Money: Fiscal Policy in New York and Chicago* (Chicago: University of Chicago Press, 1992), pp. 192–202.

38. See Steven P. Erie, *Rainbow's End: Irish-Americans and the Dilemmas of Urban Machine Politics, 1840–1985* (Berkeley: University of California Press, 1988), chap. 4.

39. See Milton Rakove, *We Don't Want Nobody Nobody Sent: An Oral History of the Daley Years* (Bloomington: Indiana University Press, 1979), p. 318.

40. Erie, *Rainbow's End,* p. 4.

41. For the classic statement about machines serving latent functions of integration, see Robert K. Merton, "The Latent Functions of the Machine," in *Urban Government: A Reader in Politics and Government,* ed. Edward Banfield (Glencoe, IL: Free Press, 1961), pp. 180–90.

42. See Ira Katznelson, *Black Men, White Cities* (Chicago: University of Chicago Press, 1973), chap. 6. See also Dianne Pinderhughes, *Race and Ethnicity in Chicago Politics* (Urbana: University of Illinois Press, 1987).

43. Amy Bridges, *Morning Glories* (Princeton, NJ: Princeton University Press, forthcoming), manuscript pp. 127A, 185; Luis Fraga, "Domination through Democratic Means: Nonpartisan Slating Groups in City Electoral Politics," *Urban Affairs Quarterly,* Vol. 23, no. 4, pp. 528–55.

44. Thomas A. Baylis, "Leadership Change in Contemporary San Antonio," in *The Politics of San Antonio,* ed. David R. Johnson, John A. Booth, and Richard J. Harris (Lincoln: University of Nebraska Press, 1983), pp. 95–113.

45. Figures from Linda Williams, "Black Political Progress in the 1980s: The Electoral Arena," in *The New Black Politics,* 2nd ed., ed. Michael B. Preston, Lenneal J. Henderson, Jr., and Paul L. Puryear (New York: Longman, 1987) p. 120; and the National Conference of Black Mayors.

46. Paul Kleppner, *Chicago Divided: The Making of a Black Mayor* (DeKalb: Northern Illinois University Press, 1985), p. 149; Michael B. Preston, "The Election of Harold Washington: An Examination of the SES Model in the 1983 Chicago Mayoral Election," in *The New Black Politics,* ed. Preston, Henderson, and Puryear.

47. David Montejano, *Anglos and Mexicans,* chap. 12; on La Raza Unida Party see Carlos Munoz, Jr., and Mario Barrers, "La Raza Unida Party and the Chicano Student Movement in California," in *Latinos and the Political System,* ed. F. Chris Garcia (Notre Dame, IN: University of Notre Dame, 1988), chap. 11.

48. Figures from authors' interviews with officials of the National Association of Latino Elected and Appointed Officials, Washington, DC.

49. Rufus P. Browning, Dale Rogers Marshall, and David H. Tabb, *Protest Is Not Enough* (Berkeley: University of California Press, 1984); see also the essays in Rufus P. Browning, Dale Rogers Marshall, and David H. Tabb, eds., *Racial Politics in American Cities* (New York: Longman, 1990).

50. See Richard Briffault, "Our Localism: Part I—The Structure of Local Government Law," *Columbia Law Review,* Vol. 90, no. 1 (January 1990), pp. 72–85.

51. Edwin S. Mills, "Nonurban Policies as Urban Policies," *Urban Studies* 24 (1987), pp. 562–63; Michael N. Danielson, *The Politics of Exclusion* (New York: Columbia University Press, 1976), chap. 2.

52. Douglas Massey and Nancy Denton, *American Apartheid* (Cambridge, MA: Harvard University Press, 1993).

53. Nancy Burns, *The Formation of American Local Governments: Private Values in Public Institutions* (New York: Oxford University Press, 1994).

54. On the idea of defensive localism see Margaret Weir, "Poverty, Social Rights, and the Politics of Place in the United States," in *European Social Policy: Between Fragmentation and Integration,* ed. Stephan Leibfried and Paul Pierson (Washington, DC: Brookings Institution, 1995), chap. 10.

55. Kenneth T. Jackson, *Crabgrass Frontier: The Suburbanization of the United States* (New York: Oxford University Press, 1985), p. 273.

56. On the development of "private" local governments more generally, see Evan McKenzie, *Privatopia: Homeowner Associations and the Rise of Residential Private Government* (New Haven: Yale University Press, 1994). The case of Rosemont was reported on "All Things Considered," National Public Radio, June 19, 1995.

57. The results of this poll were reported in Elizabeth Kolbert, "Region around New York See Ties to City Faltering," *New York Times,* December 1, 1991, p. 1; and William Glaberson, "For

Many in the New York Region, the City is Ignored and Irrelevant," *New York Times,* January 2, 1992, p. 1.

58. Jackson, *Crabgrass Frontier,* pp. 207–15; and Desmond King, *Separate and Unequal: Black Americans and the U.S. Federal Government* (Oxford, U.K.: Oxford University Press, 1995), pp. 189–99.

59. King, *Separate and Unequal,* p. 193; and Mark I. Gelfand, *A Nation of Cities: The Federal Government and Urban America* (New York: Oxford University Press, 1975), p. 221. This estimate comes from a study critical of equal opportunity in housing, conducted by the American Friends Service Committee. See Jackson, *Crabgrass Frontier*, p. 209, on the difficulties in determining the exact extent of discrimination in FHA housing.

60. An excellent case study of the development of public housing in Chicago is Arnold R. Hirsch, *Making the Second Ghetto* (New York: Cambridge University Press, 1983).

61. On urban party organizations in the Democratic Party see David R. Mayhew, *Placing Parties in American Politics,* (Princeton, NJ: Princeton University Press, 1986) p. 325.

62. On housing policy see Paul Pierson, *Dismantling the Welfare State? Reagan, Thatcher, and the Politics of Retrenchment* (New York: Cambridge University Press, 1994), pp. 87–95.

63. See Demetrios Caraley, "Washington Abandons the Cities," *Political Science Quarterly,* vol. 107, no. 1 (Spring 1992), p. 8; Carol O'Cleireacain, "Cities' Role in the Metropolitan Economy and the Federal Structure," *Interwoven Destinies: Cities and the Nation,* ed. Henry G. Cisneros (New York: Norton, 1993), chap. 7.

64. Ronald Smothers, "City Seeks to Grow by Disappearing," *New York Times,* October 18, 1993, p. 10; Patti Patterson, "Herenton to Rethink His City-County Merger Plan," *Commercial Appeal,* December 10, 1993, p. A1.

65. Eileen Shanahan, "Going It Jointly: Regional Solutions for Local Problems," *Governing* 4 (August 1991), pp. 70–76.

66. Quoted in Neal R. Peirce, "Is Deregulation Enough? Lessons from Florida and Philadelphia," in *Deregulating the Public Service,* ed. John J. DiIulio (Washington DC: Brookings Institution, 1994), pp. 129–55.

67. For an overview of the activities of community organizations see Mitchell Sviridoff, "The Seeds of Urban Revival," *Public Interest* 114 (Winter 1994), pp. 82–103; and Paul C. Brophy, "Emerging Approaches to Community Development," in *Interwoven Destinies,* ed. Cisneros, chap. 9.

68. Jim Sleeper, *The Closest of Strangers* (New York: Norton, 1990), pp. 153–57.

Chapter 16

1. Robert Shapiro, *Cut and Invest: A Budget Strategy for the New Economy* (Washington, DC: Progressive Policy Institute, 1995), p. 15.

2. "The Arms Industry—Markets and Maginot Lines," *Economist,* October 28, 1995, pp. 23–25.

3. For an evaluation of the policy of withholding subsidies to carry out desegregation laws, see Gary Orfield, *Must We Bus?* (Washington, DC: Brookings Institution, 1978). For an evaluation of the use of subsidies to encourage work or to calm political unrest, see Frances Fox Piven and Richard Cloward, *Regulating the Poor: The Functions of Public Welfare* (New York: Random House, 1971).

4. For an evaluation of Kennedy's use of this kind of executive power, see Carl M. Brauer, *John F. Kennedy and the Second Reconstruction* (New York: Columbia University Press, 1977), especially chap. 3.

5. For an evaluation of the politics of eminent domain, see Theodore J. Lowi and Benjamin Ginsberg, *Poliscide* (New York: Macmillan, 1976), p. 235 and *passim,* and especially chaps. 11 and 12, written by Julia and Thomas Vitullo-Martin.

6. For a fascinating behind-the-scenes look at how and why President Clinton abandoned his campaign commitment to tax cuts and economic stimulus, and instead accepted the fiscal conservatism advocated by the Federal Reserve and its chairman, Alan Greenspan, see Bob Woodward, *The Agenda: Inside the Clinton White House* (New York: Simon & Schuster, 1994).

7. In 1989, President Bush proposed to Congress a significant increase in the legal reserve requirement for savings & loan companies (S&Ls), which are simply banks by another name. This would of course have an anti-inflationary effect, but it was not really a monetary policy because it was virtually forced on President Bush as a means of preventing these banks from engaging in the reckless investment activity of the previous decade, which had forced many into bankruptcy, eventually costing the American people $300 to $500 billion. Thus, in this case, the raising of the S&L reserve requirement was more an example of a regulatory policy. On the other hand, President Clinton's 1993 plan to relax certain banking regulations to help small businesses would be considered a monetary policy.

8. *Gibbons v. Ogden,* 9 Wheaton 1 (1824). This case was reaffirmed sixty years later even when the states were attempting to defend their own citizens from discriminatory charges by railroads for services rendered within their own state. The Supreme Court argued that the route of an interstate railroad could not be subdivided into its separate state segments for purposes of regulation. See *Wabash, St Louis and Pacific Railway Co. v. Illinois,* 118 U.S. 557 (1886).

9. Compare with Gabriel Kolko, *The Triumph of Conservatism* (New York: Free Press, 1963), chap. 6.

10. The act of 1955 officially designated the interstate highways as the National System of Interstate and Defense Highways. It was indirectly a major part of President Eisenhower's defense program. But it was just as obviously a "pork barrel" policy as any rivers and harbors legislation.

11. For an account of the relationship between mechanization and law, see Lawrence Friedman, *A History of American Law* (New York: Simon & Schuster, 1973), pp. 409–29.

12. Actually, this point of view is better understood as nineteenth-century liberalism, or free-market liberalism, following the theories of Adam Smith. However, after the New Deal appropriated "liberal" for their pro-government point of view, the Republican anti-government wing got tagged with the "conservative" label. With Reagan, the label took on more popular connotations, while "liberal" became stigmatized as the "L-word."

13. For a good evaluation of Reagan's efforts, see Kenneth J. Meier, *Regulation: Politics, Bureaucracy, and Economics* (New

York: St. Martin's, 1985), chaps. 4, 6, and 8; and George Eads and Michael Fix, "Regulatory Policy," in *The Reagan Experiment*, ed. John L. Palmer and Isabel Sawhill (Washington, DC: Urban Institute Press, 1982), chap. 5.

14. The *Federal Register* is the daily publication of all official acts of Congress, the president, and the administrative agencies. A law or executive order is not legally binding until published in the *Federal Register.*

15. "The Republican Congress—The Evolution of a Revolution," *Economist,* November 4, 1995, pp. 23–25.

16. For an excellent treatment of "why regulate," with a somewhat different listing of reasons, see Alan Stone, *Regulation and Its Alternatives* (Washington, DC: Congressional Quarterly Press, 1982), chaps. 3–5.

17. Gordon Black poll, press release, The Gordon Black Corporation, Rochester, NY, May 1992.

18. Roper poll, reported in Faye Rice, "Next Steps for the Environment," *Fortune,* October 19, 1992, p. 98.

19. See, for example, Martha Derthick and Paul Quirk, *The Politics of Deregulation* (Washington, DC: Brookings Institution, 1985), pp. 33–34.

20. The word "capitalism" did not come into common usage, according to the *Oxford English Dictionary,* until 1854. Words like "capital" and "capitalist" were around earlier, but the concept of capitalism as an economic system really came to the forefront with the writings of Karl Marx.

21. Banks today can choose between a state or a national charter. Under the state system, they are less stringently regulated and avoid the fees charged to members of the Fed. But they also miss out on the advantages of belonging to the Federal Reserve System.

22. The U.S. government imposed an income tax during the Civil War that remained in effect until 1872. In 1894, Congress enacted a modest 2 percent tax upon all incomes over $4,000. This $4,000 exemption was in fact fairly high, excluding all working-class people. But in 1895, the Supreme Court declared it unconstitutional, citing the provision of Article I, Section 9, that any direct tax would have to be proportional to the population in each state. See *Pollock v. Farmers' Loan and Trust Company,* 158 U.S. 601 (1895). In 1913, the Sixteenth Amendment was ratified, effectively reversing the *Pollock* case.

23. For a systematic account of the role of government in providing incentives and inducements to business, see C. E. Lindblom, *Politics and Markets* (New York: Basic Books, 1977), chap. 13. For a detailed account of the dramatic Reagan tax cuts and reforms, see Jeffrey Birnbaum and Alan Murray, *Showdown at Gucci Gulch—Lawmakers, Lobbyists, and the Unlikely Triumph of Tax Reform* (New York: Random House, 1987).

24. For further background, see David E. Rosenbaum, "Cutting the Deficit Overshadows Clinton's Promise to Cut Taxes," *New York Times,* January 12, 1993, p. A1; and "Clinton Weighing Freeze or New Tax on Social Security," *New York Times,* January 31, 1993, p. A1.

25. There is an ironic twist here. In the 1932 presidential election campaign, Roosevelt actually berated Hoover for being a big spender and producing budget deficits. Roosevelt promised to balance the budget!

26. John Maynard Keynes, *The General Theory of Employment Interest and Money* (New York: Harcourt Brace, 1936).

Chapter 17

1. Bureau of the Census, *Statistical Abstract of the United States 1995* (Washington, DC: Government Printing Office, 1995), pp. 479–80.

2. Bureau of the Census, *Current Population Reports,* Series P-60, no. 180 (Washington, DC: Government Printing Office, 1992), table 13.

3. "The Corporate Elite: The Chief Executives of the 1000 Most Valuable Publicly Held U.S. Companies," *Business Week,* October 19, 1990, p. 55.

4. A good source of pre-1930s welfare history is James T. Patterson, *America's Struggle against Poverty, 1900–1994* (Cambridge: Harvard University Press, 1994), chap. 2.

5. Quoted in Patterson, *America's Struggle against Poverty,* p. 26.

6. Patterson, *America's Struggle against Poverty*, p. 26

7. Patterson, *America's Struggle against Poverty*, p. 27

8. This figure is based on a WPA study by Ann E. Geddes, reported in Merle Fainsod et al., *Government and the American Economy,* 3rd. ed. (New York: Norton, 1959), p. 769.

9. The figures cited are for 1996.

10. Edward J. Harpham, "Fiscal Crisis and the Politics of Social Security Reform," in *The Attack on the Welfare State*, ed. Anthony Champagne and Edward Harpham (Prospect Heights, IL: Waveland, 1984), p. 13.

11. Sam Howe Verhovek, "States Are already Providing Glimpses at Welfare's Future," *New York Times*, September 21, 1995, pp. A1, B12.

12. *Goldberg v. Kelly*, 397 U.S. 254 (1970).

13. See U.S. House of Representatives, Committee on Ways and Means, *Where Your Money Goes: The 1995–95 Green Book* (Washington, DC: Brassey's, 1994), pp. 325, 802.

14. U.S. House of Representatives, Committee on Ways and Means, *Overview of Entitlement Programs 1994 Green Book* (Washington, DC: Government Printing Office, 1994), p. 859.

15. See, for example, Theodore R. Marmor, Jerry L. Mashaw, and Philip L. Harvey, *America's Misunderstood Welfare State* (New York: Basic Books, 1990), p. 156.

16. Burdett A. Loomis and Allen J. Cigler, "Introduction: The Changing Nature of Interest Group Politics," in *Interest Group Politics,* 4th ed., ed. Burdett A. Loomis and Allan J. Cigler (Washington, DC: Congressional Quarterly Press, 1995), p. 12.

17. See, for example, Senator Bob Kerrey's remarks quoted in David S. Broder, "Deficit Doomsday," *Washington Post,* August 7, 1994, p. C9.

18. See Beth Stevens, "Blurring the Boundaries: How the Federal Government Has Influenced Welfare Benefits in the Private Sector," in *The Politics of Social Policy in the United States,* ed. Margaret Weir, Ann Orloff, and Theda Skocpol (Princeton, NJ: Princeton University Press, 1988), pp. 122–48.

19. Frances Fox Piven and Richard Cloward, *Poor People's Movements* (New York: Pantheon, 1977), chap. 5.

20. See Christopher Jencks and Kathryn Edin, "Do Poor Women Have the Right to Bear Children?" *American Prospect* 20 (winter 1995), pp. 43–52.

21. For an argument that children should be given the vote, see Paul E. Petersen, "An Immodest Proposal," *Daedalus* 121 (fall 1992), pp. 151–74.

22. There were a couple of minor precedents. One was the Smith-Hughes Act of 1917, which made federal funds available to the states for vocational education at the elementary and secondary levels. Second, the Lanham Act of 1940 made federal funds available to schools in "federally impacted areas," that is, areas with an unusually large number of government employees and/or where the local tax base was reduced by large amounts of government-owned property.

23. Office of Management and Budget, *Budget of the United States Government, Fiscal Year 1982* (Washington, DC: Government Printing Office, 1981), p. 427.

24. Quoted in Rochelle L. Stanfield, "Education: An A for Effort—and Acheivement," *National Journal,* October 22, 1994, p. 2485.

25. For an analysis of employment and training initiatives since the 1930s, see Margaret Weir, *Politics and Jobs* (Princeton, NJ: Princeton University Press, 1992).

26. On CETA, see Donald C. Baumer and Carl E. Van Horn, *The Politics of Unemployment* (Washington, DC: Congressional Quarterly Press, 1985).

27. Morton Keller, *Affairs of State: Public Life in Nineteenth Century America* (Cambridge, MA: Belknap Press of Harvard University Press, 1977), p. 500.

28. Office of Management and Budget, *Budget of the United States Government* (Washington, DC: Government Printing Office, 1990, 1992, 1994).

29. U.N. Development Program, Organization for Economic Cooperation and Development, cited in Paul Spector, "Failure, by the Numbers," *New York Times,* September 24, 1994.

30. John E. Schwarz, *America's Hidden Success,* 2nd ed. (New York: Norton, 1988), pp. 41–42.

31. For more details, see John L. Palmer and Isabel V. Sawhill, eds., *The Reagan Record* (Cambridge, MA: Ballinger, 1984), Appendix C, pp. 363–79.

32. Guy Gugliotta, "Cisneros: Bringing a Touch of the Cities to HUD," *Washington Post National Weekly Edition,* January 18–24, 1993, pp. 11–12.

33. On the relationship between education and democracy in the United States, see Ira Katznelson and Margaret Weir, *Schooling for All: Race, Class, and the Democratic Ideal* (New York: Basic Books, 1985).

34. For a description of these different views among conservatives, see David Frum, *Dead Right* (New York: Basic Books, 1994).

35. See, for example, Charles Murray, *Losing Ground* (New York: Basic Books, 1984).

36. See, for example, Lawrence Mead, *Beyond Entitlement: The Social Obligations of Citizenship* (New York: Free Press, 1986).

37. See James C. McKinley, Jr., "Father Faces U.S. Charges over Support," *New York Times,* August 9, 1995, p. B1.

38. Jencks and Edin, "Do Poor Women Have the Right to Bear Children?"

39. See Elizabeth Bussiere, "The Failure of Constitutional Welfare Rights in the Warren Court," *Political Science Quarterly* 109 (winter 1994), pp. 105–31.

40. See L. Free and Hadley Cantril, *The Political Beliefs of Americans* (New York: Simon and Schuster, 1968).

41. See Fay Lomax Cook and Edith Barrett, *Support for the American Welfare State* (New York: Columbia University Press, 1992), and Hugh Heclo, "The Political Foundations of Antipoverty Policy," in *Fighting Poverty: What Works and What Doesn't,* ed. Sheldon H. Danziger and Daniel H. Weinberg (Cambridge, MA: Harvard University Press, 1986), pp. 312–40.

Chapter 18

1. William Booth, "U of Calif. Ends Racial Preferences," *Washington Post,* July 21, 1995, p. A1.

2. The *Slaughterhouse Cases,* 16 Wallace 36 (1873).

3. See *Civil Rights Cases,* 109 U.S. 3 (1883).

4. Anatole France, *Le lys rouge* (1894), chap. 7.

5. *Plessy v. Ferguson,* 163 U.S. 537 (1896).

6. The prospect of a Fair Employment Practices law tied to the commerce power produced the Dixiecrat break with the Democratic Party in 1948. The Democratic Party organization of the States of the Old Confederacy seceded from the national party and nominated its own candidate, the then-Democratic governor of South Carolina, Strom Thurmond, who is now a Republican senator. This almost cost President Truman the election.

7. This was based on the provision in Article VI of the Constitution that "all treaties made, . . . under the authority of the United States," shall be the "supreme law of the land." The committee recognized that if the U.S. Senate ratified the Human Rights Covenant of the United Nations—a treaty—then that power could be used as the constitutional umbrella for effective civil rights legislation. The Supreme Court had recognized in *Missouri v. Holland,* 252 U.S. 416 (1920), that a treaty could enlarge federal power at the expense of the states.

8. *Missouri ex rel. Gaines v. Canada,* 305 U.S. 337 (1938).

9. *Sweatt v. Painter,* 339 U.S. 629 (1950).

10. *Smith v. Allwright,* 321 U.S. 649 (1944).

11. *Shelley v. Kraemer,* 334 U.S. 1 (1948).

12. Kermit L. Hall, *The Magic Mirror: Law in American History* (New York: Oxford University Press, 1989), pp. 322–24. See also Richard Kluger, *Simple Justice* (New York: Random House, Vintage Edition, 1977), pp. 530–37.

13. The District of Columbia case came up too, but since the District of Columbia is not a state, this case did not directly involve the Fourteenth Amendment and its "equal protection" clause. It confronted the Court on the same grounds, however—that segregation is inherently unequal. Its victory in effect was "incorporation in reverse," with equal protection moving from the Fourteenth Amendment to become part of the Bill of Rights. See *Bolling v. Sharpe,* 347 U.S. 497 (1954).

14. *Brown v. Board of Education of Topeka, Kansas,* 347 U.S. 483 (1954).

15. The Supreme Court first declared that race was a suspect classification requiring strict scrutiny in the decision *Korematsu v. United States,* 323 U.S. 214 (1944). In this case, the Court upheld President Roosevelt's executive order of 1941 allowing the

military to exclude persons of Japanese ancestry from the West Coast and to place them in internment camps. It is one of the few cases in which classification based on race survived strict scrutiny.

16. *Brown v. Board of Education of Topeka, Kansas,* 349 U.S. 294 (1955), often referred to as *Brown II.*

17. The two most important cases were *Cooper v. Aaron,* 358 U.S. 1 (1958), which required Little Rock, Arkansas, to desegregate; and *Griffin v. Prince Edward County School Board,* 377 U.S. 218 (1964), which forced all the schools of that Virginia county to reopen after five years of closing to avoid desegregation.

18. In *Cooper,* the Supreme Court ordered immediate compliance with the lower court's desegregation order and went beyond that with a stern warning that it is "emphatically the province and duty of the judicial department to say what the law is."

19. *Shuttlesworth v. Birmingham Board of Education,* 358 U.S. 101 (1958), upheld a "pupil placement" plan purporting to assign pupils on various bases, with no mention of race. This case interpreted *Brown* to mean that school districts must stop explicit racial discrimination but were under no obligation to take positive steps to desegregate. For a while black parents were doomed to case-by-case approaches.

20. For good treatments of that long stretch of the struggle of the federal courts to integrate the schools, see Paul Brest and Sanford Levinson, *Processes of Constitutional Decision-Making: Cases and Materials,* 2nd ed. (Boston: Little, Brown, 1983), pp. 471–80; and Alfred Kelly et al., *The American Constitution: Its Origins and Development,* 6th ed. (New York: Norton, 1983), pp. 610–16.

21. Pierre Thomas, "Denny's to Settle Bias Cases," *Washington Post,* May 24, 1994, p. A1.

22. See Hamil Harris, "For Blacks, Cabs Can Be Hard to Get," *Washington Post,* July 21, 1994, p. J1.

23. For a thorough analysis of the Office for Civil Rights, see Jeremy Rabkin, "Office for Civil Rights," in *The Politics of Regulation,* ed. James Q. Wilson (New York: Basic Books, 1980).

24. This was an accepted way of using quotas or ratios to determine statistically that blacks or other minorities were being excluded from schools or jobs, and then on the basis of that statistical evidence to authorize the Justice Department to bring suits in individual cases and in "class action" suits as well. In most segregated situations outside the South, it is virtually impossible to identify and document an intent to discriminate.

25. *Swann v. Charlotte-Mecklenberg Board of Education,* 402 U.S. 1 (1971).

26. *Milliken v. Bradley,* 418 U.S. 717 (1974).

27. For a good evaluation of the Boston effort, see Gary Orfield, *Must We Bus? Segregated Schools and National Policy* (Washington: Brookings Institution, 1978), pp. 144–46. See also Bob Woodward and Scott Armstrong, *The Brethren: Inside the Supreme Court* (New York: Simon and Schuster, 1979), pp. 426–27; and J. Anthony Lukas, *Common Ground* (New York: Random House, 1986).

28. *Board of Education v. Dowell,* 498 U.S. 237 (1991).

29. *Missouri v. Jenkins,* 115 S.Ct. 2038 (1995).

30. See especially *Katzenbach v. McClung,* 379 U.S. 294 (1964). Almost immediately after passage of the Civil Rights Act of 1964, a case was brought challenging the validity of Title II, which covered discrimination in public accommodations. Ollie's Barbecue was a neighborhood restaurant in Birmingham, Alabama. It was located eleven blocks away from an interstate highway and even farther from railroad and bus stations. Its table service was for whites only; there was only a take-out service for blacks. The Supreme Court agreed that Ollie's was strictly an intrastate restaurant, but since a substantial proportion of its food and other supplies were bought from companies outside the state of Alabama, there was a sufficient connection to interstate commerce; therefore, racial discrimination at such restaurants would "impose commercial burdens of national magnitude upon interstate commerce." Although this case involved Title II, it had direct bearing on the constitutionality of Title VII.

31. *Griggs v. Duke Power Company,* 401 U.S. 24 (1971). See also Allan Sindler, *Bakke, DeFunis, and Minority Admissions* (New York: Longman, 1978), pp. 180–89.

32. For a good treatment of these issues, see Charles O. Gregory and Harold A. Katz, *Labor and the Law* (New York: Norton, 1979), chap. 17.

33. In 1970, this act was amended to outlaw for five years literacy tests as a condition for voting in all states.

34. Joint Center for Political Studies, *Black Elected Officials: A National Roster—1988* (Washington, DC: Joint Center for Political Studies Press, 1988), pp. 9–10. For a comprehensive analysis and evaluation of the Voting Rights Act, see Bernard Grofman and Chandler Davidson, eds., *Controversies in Minority Voting: The Voting Rights Act in Perspective* (Washington, DC: Brookings Institution, 1992).

35. See Douglas S. Massey and Nancy A. Denton, *American Apartheid: Segregation and the Making of the Underclass* (Cambridge, MA: Harvard University Press, 1993), chap. 7.

36. See Jane J. Mansbridge, *Why We Lost the ERA* (Chicago: University of Chicago Press, 1986); and Gilbert Steiner, *Constitutional Inequality* (Washington, DC: Brookings Institution, 1985).

37. See *Frontiero v. Richardson,* 411 U.S. 677 (1973).

38. See *Craig v. Boren,* 423 U.S. 1047 (1976).

39. See *Mississippi University for Women v. Hogan,* 454 U.S. 962 (1982), which upheld the use of the Fourteenth Amendment in gender discrimination cases. Justice Sandra Day O'Connor wrote the opinion in this 5-to-4 decision, declaring that gender discrimination against men was illegal.

40. See her opinion in *J.E.B. v. Alabama,* 114 S.Ct. 1419 (1994), which prohibited pre-emptory jury challenges based on the gender of a prospective juror.

41. *Franklin v. Gwinnett County Public Schools,* 503 U.S. 60 (1992).

42. Jennifer Halperin, "Women Step Up to Bat," *Illinois Issues* 21 (September 1995), pp. 11–14.

43. *Lau v. Nichols,* 414 U.S. 563 (1974).

44. Dick Kirschten, "Not Black and White," *National Journal,* March 2, 1991, p. 497.

45. See the discussion in Robert A. Katzmann, *Institutional Disability: The Saga of Transportation Policy for the Disabled* (Washington, DC: Brookings Institution, 1986).

46. For example, after pressure from the Justice Department, one of the nation's largest rental-car companies agreed to make special hand-controls available to any customer requesting them. See "Avis Agrees to Equip Cars for Disabled," *Los Angeles Times,* September 2, 1994, p. D1.

47. *Bowers v. Hardwick,* 478 U.S. 186 (1986).

48. Quoted in Joan Biskupic, "Gay Rights Activists Seek a Supreme Court Test Case," *Washington Post,* December 19, 1993, p. A1.

49. *Romer v. Evans,* 116 S.Ct. 1620 (1996).

50. From Lyndon B. Johnson, *The Vantage Point* (New York: Holt, Rinehart, and Winston, 1971), p. 166.

51. The Department of Health, Education, and Welfare (HEW) was the cabinet department charged with administering most federal social programs. In 1980, when education programs were transferred to the newly created Department of Education, HEW was renamed the Department of Health and Human Services.

52. *Regents of the University of California v. Bakke,* 438 U.S. 265 (1978).

53. See, for example, *United Steelworkers v. Weber,* 443 U.S. 193 (1979); and *Fullilove v. Klutznick,* 100 S.Ct. 2758 (1980).

54. *Ward's Cove v. Atonio,* 109 S.Ct. 2115 (1989).

55. *Griggs v. Duke Power Company,* 401 U.S. 24 (1971).

56. *Martin v. Wilks,* 109 S.Ct. 2180 (1989). In this case, some white firefighters in Birmingham challenged a consent decree mandating goals for hiring and promoting blacks. This was an affirmative action plan that had been worked out between the employer and aggrieved black employees and had been accepted by a federal court. Such agreements become "consent decrees" and are subject to enforcement. Chief Justice Rehnquist held that the white firefighters could challenge the legality of such programs, even though they had not been parties to the original litigation.

57. D. Lee Bawden and John L. Palmer, "Social Policy," in *The Reagan Record,* ed. John L. Palmer and Isabel V. Sawhill (Cambridge, MA: Ballinger, 1984), p. 201. See also E. W. Kelley, *Policy and Politics in the U.S.* (Philadelphia: Temple University Press, 1987), p. 269; and Harold Seidman and Robert Gilmour, *Politics, Position and Power,* 4th ed. (New York: Oxford University Press, 1986), pp. 130–35.

58. Bawden and Palmer, "Social Policy," p. 206.

59. Bawden and Palmer, "Social Policy," p. 206.

60. An observation by Nan Aron of the Liberal Alliance for Justice, quoted in Ruth Marcus, "Using the Bench to Bolster a Conservative Team," *Washington Post National Weekly Edition,* February 25–March 3, 1991, p. 31.

61. *St. Mary's Honor Center v. Hicks,* 113 S.Ct. 2742 (1993).

62. *City of Richmond v. J. A. Croson Co.,* 109 S.Ct. 706 (1989). For a ringing expression of the opposing view, see Justice Thurgood Marshall's dissent in this case.

63. "Layoffs Based on Race Only Are Backed by Justice Department," *Los Angeles Times,* September 7, 1994, p. A4. In 1995, however, the Court cast a skeptical eye on one of the federal government's affirmative action efforts—granting racial preferences in federal contracting—although the Court's opinion avoided the larger question of the constitutionality of all affirmative action programs.

64. *Adarand Constructors v. Pena,* 115 S.Ct. 2097 (1995).

65. Ann Devroy, "Clinton Study Backs Affirmative Action," *Washington Post,* July 19, 1995, p. A1.

66. There are still many genuine racists in America, but with the exception of a lunatic fringe, made up of neo-Nazis and members of the Ku Klux Klan, most racists are too ashamed or embarrassed to take part in normal political discourse. They are not included in either category here.

67. *Slaughterhouse Cases,* 16 Wallace 36 (1873).

Chapter 19

1. Alexis de Tocqueville, *Democracy in America,* Trans. Phillips Bradley (New York: Vintage 1945; original published 1835), Vol. 1, p. 243.

2. Bruce Russett, "Doves, Hawks, and U.S. Public Opinion," *Political Science Quarterly* 105, no. 4 (winter 1990–91), pp. 515–38. See also David W. Levy, *The Debate over Vietnam* (Baltimore, MD: Johns Hopkins University Press, 1991), pp. 95–98, 111, and 159.

3. Robert Spitzer, *President and Congress: Executive Hegemony at the Crossroads of American Government* (New York: McGraw-Hill, 1993), p. 226; see also pp. 220–32. See also Theodore Lowi, "Doin' the Cincinnati — Or, What Is There about the White House that Makes Its Occupants Do Bad Things?" in *National Political Science Review* 1 (1989), pp. 91–95.

4. The best and most highly readable account of the Iran-Bosnia affair will be found in Mark Danner, "Hypocrisy in Action: What's the Real Iran-Bosnia Scandal?" *New Yorker,* May 13, 1996, pp. 7–8.

5. Under President Bush, for example, Dick Cheney left the House to become secretary of defense; under President Clinton, Senator Lloyd Bentsen and Representative Les Aspin left Congress to become the secretaries of the treasury and defense, respectively.

6. Raymond A. Bauer, Ithiel de Sola Pool, and Lewis Anthony Dexter, *American Business and Public Policy: The Politics of Foreign Trade,* 2nd ed. (Chicago: Aldine-Atherton, 1972).

7. Brenda Holzinger, "Power Politics: Public Policy, Federalism, and Hydroelectric Power," unpublished Ph.D. dissertation, Cornell University, 1997.

8. For further discussion of the vulnerability of modern presidents to the people through the media, see Theodore Lowi, *The Personal President: Power Invested, Promise Unfulfilled* (Ithaca, NY: Cornell University Press, 1985); Jeffrey K. Tulis, *The Rhetorical Presidency* (Princeton, NJ: Princeton University Press, 1987); Samuel Kernell, *Going Public: New Strategies of Presidential Leadership* (Washington, DC: CQ Press, 1986); Richard Rose, *The Postmodern President: The White House Meets the World* (Chatham, NJ: Chatham House, 1988); and George C. Edwards, *The Public Presidency: The Pursuit of Popular Support* (New York: St. Martin's, 1983).

9. Michael J. Robinson, "Public Affairs Television and the Growth of Political Malaise: The Case of 'TV Selling of the Pentagon,'" *American Political Science Review* 70, no. 2 (June 1976), p. 425.

10. Seymour Martin Lipset and William Schneider, *The Confidence Gap: Business, Labor, and Government in the Public Mind* (New York: Free Press, 1983), p. 405.

11. A very good brief outline of the centrality of the president

in foreign policy will be found in Paul E. Peterson, "The President's Dominance in Foreign Policy Making," *Political Science Quarterly* 109, no. 2 (summer 1994), pp. 215, 234.

12. One confirmation of this will be found in Theodore Lowi, *The End of Liberalism,* 2nd ed. (New York: Norton, 1979), pp. 127–30; another will be found in Stephen Krasner, "Are Bureaucracies Important?" *Foreign Policy* 7 (summer 1972), pp. 159–79. However, it should be added that Krasner was writing his article in disagreement with Graham T. Allison, "Conceptual Models and the Cuban Missile Crisis," *American Political Science Review* 63, no. 3 (September 1969), pp. 689–718.

13. Peterson, "The President's Dominance in Foreign Policy," p. 232.

14. Hans J. Morgenthau, *The Purpose of American Politics* (New York: Knopf, 1960), pp. 169–70.

15. At least one nation-state in the middle of the continuum, Switzerland, is not a client state. Switzerland's sovereignty is well guarded by most other states in order to maintain at least one country where diplomacy and business can take place no matter how chaotic international relations may be. But most of the nation-states in this middle category are best understood as client states.

16. A full version of the text of the farewell address, along with a discussion of the contribution to it made by Hamilton and Madison, will be found in Daniel J. Boorstin, ed., *An American Primer* (Chicago: University of Chicago Press, 1966), vol. 1, pp. 192–210. This editing is by Richard B. Morris.

17. E. E. Schattschneider, *Politics, Pressures, and the Tariff* (Englewood Cliffs, NJ: Prentice-Hall, 1935).

18. "Balance of power" was the primary foreign policy role played by the major European powers during the nineteenth century, and it is a role available to the United States in contemporary foreign affairs, a role occasionally adopted but not on a world scale. This is the third of the four roles identified and discussed later in this chapter.

19. The best analysis of what he calls the "100 years' peace" will be found in Karl Polanyi, *The Great Transformation* (New York: Rinehart, 1944; Beacon paperback edition, 1957), pp. 5ff.

20. John G. Stoessinger, *Crusaders and Pragmatists: Movers of Modern American Foreign Policy* (New York: Norton, 1985), pp. 21, 34.

21. Hans Morgenthau, *Politics among Nations,* 2nd ed. (New York: Knopf, 1956), p. 505.

22. See Lowi, *The Personal President,* pp. 167–69.

23. Dick Kirschten, "Life Jacket, Anyone?" *National Journal* 26 (June 25, 1994), p. 1501.

24. "Senate Slashes Agency Budgets, Confirms Eighteen Ambassadors," *Congressional Quarterly,* December 16, 1995, p. 3821.

25. In 1994, the next four biggest contributors were Japan (11.9 percent), Germany (8.6 percent), Russia (6.4 percent), and France (5.7 percent). These figures do not include many specific UN operations and organizations, nor the U.S. contributions to these programs. See the *Statesman's Yearbook, 1994–95* (London: Macmillan, 1994), p. 6; and the *1995 Information Please Almanac* (Boston: Houghton Mifflin, 1994), pp. 73, 299.

26. Michael Kammen, *A Machine That Would Go of Itself: The Constitution in American Culture* (New York: Alfred A. Knopf, 1986).

27. There was, in fact, an angry dispute over a "surplus" of at least \$2.2 billion, on the basis of which Japan and others demanded a rebate. *Report of the Secretary of Defense to the President and Congress* (Washington, DC: Government Printing Office, 1992), p. 26.

28. Strobe Talbott, "America Abroad," *Time,* December 14, 1992, p. 35.

29. Not all American policy makers agree that the UN is a worthy instrument of American foreign policy. The UN is on the verge of bankruptcy, no thanks to the United States, which owes the UN nearly \$1.5 billion in dues. For a review, see Barbara Crossette, "U.N., Facing Bankruptcy, Plans to Cut Payroll by Ten Percent," *New York Times,* February 6, 1996, p. A3.

30. "Falling in Love Again," *Economist,* August 22, 1992, p. 63.

31. "IMF: Sleeve-Rolling Time," *Economist,* May 2, 1992, pp. 98–99.

32. Quoted in John Lewis Gaddis, *The United States and the Origins of the Cold War* (New York: Columbia University Press, 1972), p. 21.

33. The best account of the decision and its purposes will be found in Joseph Jones, *The Fifteen Weeks* (New York: Viking, 1955).

34. Robert A. Pastor, *Congress and the Politics of U.S. Foreign Economic Policy* (Berkeley: University of California Press, 1980), pp. 256–80.

35. Quoted in Lowi, *The End of Liberalism,* 2nd ed., p. 162.

36. George Quester, *The Continuing Problem of International Politics* (Hinsdale, IL: Dryden Press, 1974), p. 229.

37. The Warsaw Pact was signed in 1955 by the Soviet Union, the German Democratic Republic (East Germany), Poland, Hungary, Czechoslovakia, Romania, Bulgaria, and Albania. Albania later dropped out. The Warsaw Pact was terminated in 1991.

38. Michael Lubell, "Getting the Right Mix on R&D," *New York Times,* December 27, 1992, sec. 3, p. 11.

39. The R&D budget totals include the Department of Defense, Department of Energy (military related), and the National Aeronautics and Space Administration. See *Statistical Abstract of the United States: 1990,* pp. 331, 584.

40. "Arms for Sale," *Newsweek,* April 8, 1991, pp. 22–27.

41. For a thorough and instructive exposition of the original Holy Alliance pattern, see Paul M. Kennedy, *The Rise and Fall of the Great Powers: Economic Change and Military Conflict from 1500 to 2000* (New York: Random House, 1987), pp. 159–60. And for a comparison of the Holy Alliance role with the balance-of-power role, to be discussed next, see Polanyi, *The Great Transformation,* pp. 5–11 and 259–62.

42. Felix Gilbert et al., *The Norton History of Modern Europe* (New York: Norton, 1971), pp. 1222–24.

43. For a summary of the entire literature about the "democratic peace," see Henry S. Farber and Joanne Gowa, "Politics and Peace," *International Security* 20, no. 2 (fall 1995), pp. 123–46. See also Jack Levi, "Domestic Politics and War," *Journal of Interdisciplinary History* 18, no. 4 (spring 1988), pp. 653–73.

44. The original theory of containment was articulated by former ambassador and scholar George Kennan in a famous article published under the pseudonym Mr. X, "The Sources of Soviet Conduct," *Foreign Affairs* 25 (1947), p. 556.

45. Richard Barnet, "Reflections," *New Yorker,* March 9, 1987, p. 82.

46. Thomas L. Friedman, "14 Big Macs Later . . . ," *New York Times,* December 31, 1995, sec. 4, p. 9.

47. The speech was given in LaFayette, Louisiana, December 18, 1995, quoted in the *New York Times,* "Buchanan: In His Own Words," December 31, 1995, p. 20.

48. Paul Ruffins, "Strange Bedfellows: Pat Buchanan's Arguments Might Well Have Been Written by the AFL-CIO," *Washington Post National Weekly Edition,* March 11–17, 1996, p. 23.

49. The 1974 Trade Act provides that nonmarket—namely communist—countries will not receive the MFN trade concessions enjoyed by the United States's best customers unless the president waives the restriction.

50. Two sales to wealthy but vulnerable Middle East nations accounted for 80 percent of this total: Saudi Arabia paid $9.5 billion for 72 F-15 jet fighters from McDonnell Douglas, and Kuwait paid $2.2 billion for 256 M1-A2 tanks from General Dynamics. See "Look Who's Dominating the Arms Trade," *New York Times,* August 20, 1994, p. A22.

51. See U.S. Congress, Office of Technology Assessment, *Global Arms Trade* (Washington, DC: Government Printing Office, June 1991).

52. The license is a sale to a foreign company by, for example, a U.S. company, of the right to manufacture one of its products. This is subject to approval by the departments of Defense and State.

53. See U.S. Congress, Office of Technology Assessment, *Global Arms Trade,* pp. 4–7.

54. Address, joint meeting of Congress, April 10, 1951.

55. See Denis Brogan, "The Illusion of American Omnipotence," *Harper's,* December 1952, p. 21.

56. Stephen R. Weissman, *A Culture of Deference* (New York: Basic Books, 1995), p. 17.

Illustration Credits

2, 7, 18, 24, 33 (top), 36, 42, 56, 57, 68, 100 (both), 110, 116, 119, 128, 131, 134, 136, 142, 152, 157 (both), 159, 168, 169, 171 (top), 174, 179, 186, 194, 195, 207, 212, 215, 230, 239, 242, 244, 246, 249, 250, 252, 253 (bottom), 255, 270, 281, 283, 285, 286, 287, 291, 300, 316, 321, 326, 333, 346, 349, 350, 351, 352, 353, 361, 368, 372, 376, 378, 380, 390, 403, 407, 418, 432, 435, 459, 475, 490, 495 (left), 498, 499, 504, 509, 512, 518, 522, 524, 525, 530, 544, 554, 561, 564, 565, 572, 580, 582 (both), 585, 586, 590 (bottom), 593 (bottom), 594, 597, 612, 613, 615, 625, 626, 630, 633, 640, 646, 648, 652, 654, 658, 660, 666, 670, 676, 683, 685, 687, 689, 708, 720, 721, 730, 732 (bottom), 738, 742, 749, 750 AP/Wide World Photos; **10 (center)** Hulton Deutsch/Corbis; **10 (right), 30, 32, 40, 120, 205, 355** Library of Congress/Corbis; **10 (left)** National Portrait Gallery, London; **11** From the Art Collection of The Boatmen's National Bank of St. Louis; **12, 49, 53, 59, 171 (bottom), 208, 209, 219, 269, 272, 303, 339, 448 (both), 448, 485, 510, 559 (both), 576, 617, 624, 663, 693 (top), 698, 706, 735, 752** UPI/Corbis-Bettmann; **15, 73, 78, 83, 92, 97, 253 (top), 305, 319, 394, 447, 471, 501, 543, 546, 611, 657, 664, 680** Corbis-Bettmann; **19** Lyndon Baines Johnson Library/Corbis; **29** Culver Pictures; **31** Chicago Historical Society; **33 (bottom)** Bettmann/Corbis; **35, 47, 81, 274** Library of Congress; **39** © B. Daemmrich/The Image Works; **44, 275, 311, 589, 622** The Granger Collection, New York; **52, 122, 163, 193, 337, 423, 442, 467, 473, 495 (right), 535** Reuters/Corbis-Bettmann; **77** The Historic New Orleans Collection, #1975.93.2; **86** National Museum of American Art, Washington, D.C./Art Resource, NY; **91** Eastern National Park and Monument Association/Corbis; **94** Courtesy, American Antiquarian Society; **96** Rare Books and Manuscripts Division, The New York Public Library, Astor, Lenox and Tilden Foundations; **104** The Library Company of Philadelphia; **114** Collection of the New-York Historical Society; **124** PEMCO Webster and Stevens Collection, Museum of History and Industry, Seattle/Corbis; **125** Billy E. Barnes/Stock, Boston; **135** Philip Gould/Corbis; **151** Eunice Harris/Photo Researchers, Inc.; **153** © Karim Shamsi-Basha/SYGMA; **160** 1996 Response Telemedia Inc.; **161** Time Picture Service; **166** Nik Wheeler/Corbis; **173** Collection of the Supreme Court of the United States; **191** Dan Habib/Impact Visuals; **211** By Permission of Bob Gorrell and Creators Syndicate; **226** © 1996 Time Inc. New Media. All rights reserved.; **231** © 1996 The Washington Post. Reprinted with permission. Other articles reprinted by courtesies of The Boston Globe, Pioneer Press, Star Tribune, Detroit Free Press and The New York Times; **232** Courtesy The City Sun; **235 (both)** From the Collection of the Minnesota Historical Society; **237** Stock Montage, Inc.; **243** © 1963 Charles Moore/Black Star; **248** Courtesy Extreme Studios. YOUNGBLOOD STRIKEFILE™ is trademark and copyright © 1993 Rob Liefeld, all rights reserved.; **260** Dan Lamont/Corbis; **267, 364, 404, 411, 413, 419, 421, 422, 705** © Paul S. Conklin; **284, 474** Brown Brothers; **290** Courtesy Brett Morgen; **312 (both)** Copyright 1993 Time, Inc. Reprinted by permission.; **328** LBJ Library Collection, Austin, TX; **334** © Cynthia Carris/Impact Visuals; **356** Courtesy Alen MacWeeney and Modern Maturity; **357** UPI, Washington; **360 (right)** Courtesy of the Democratic National Committee; **360 (left)** Courtesy of the Health Insurance Association of America; **373** © 1996 Flip Schulke; **375** © Rick Reinhard/Impact Visuals 1993; **433** Copyright Max Hirshfeld; **453** © 1957 Burt Glinn/Magnum Photos, Inc.; **466** Photo by Alan F. Singer © CBS 1995; **479** Courtesy of the Truman Library, Independence, MO; **494** Photofest; **515** Courtesy IMC Global Inc.; **533** New Jersey Newsphotos; **539** Collection, The Supreme Court of the United States, courtesy The Supreme Court Historical Society. Photo by Richard Strauss, Smithsonian Institution; **539** Joe Sohms/Corbis; **545** © 1986, Ken Heinen; **548** © Providence Journal-Bulletin Photo; **557** Photo by Erich Solomon; **579 (bottom)** Courtesy Louisiana State Archives, John B. Gasquet Collection; **579 (top)** Photograph by the Texas House of Representatives Photography Department; **590 (top)** Photo by Patrick Downs. Copyright, 1995, Los Angeles Times. Reprinted by permission.; **593 (top)** Based on map from *Progrowth Politics: Change and Governance in Houston*, by Robert D. Thomas and Richard W. Murray, IGS Press, University of California at Berkeley, 1991; **599** Courtesy of the Express-News collection, the Institute of Texan cultures; **606** © 1994 Jerome Friar, Impact Visuals; **623** Courtesy Crown Publishers; **628** © 1995 Paul Duginski; **645** Chicago Historical Society (ICHi-20216).; **693 (bottom)** Stanley J. Forman, Pulitzer Prize 1977; **696** Magnum Photos Inc. © 1960 Eve Arnold; **699** © Daily Press Inc.; **700** Phil Schermeister/Corbis; **702** Harvey Finkle/Impact Visuals; **714, 746** Joseph Sohm/Chromo Sohm Inc./Corbis; **732 (top)** P. Watson/Toronto Star; **745** University Archives. The Bancroft Library. University of California, Berkeley.

Answer Key

Chapter 1	Chapter 4	Chapter 7	Chapter 10	Chapter 13
1. d	1. b	1. d	1. a	1. b
2. b	2. c	2. b	2. d	2. c
3. c	3. d	3. c	3. c	3. a
4. c	4. b	4. c	4. a	4. c
5. c	5. b	5. d	5. a	5. a
6. a	6. c	6. a	6. c	6. d
7. d	7. a	7. d	7. d	7. a
8. c	8. d	8. d	8. d	8. b
9. a	9. c	9. d	9. b	9. c
10. a	10. b	10. a	10. a	10. c

Chapter 2	Chapter 5	Chapter 8	Chapter 11	Chapter 14
1. b	1. a	1. a	1. b	1. a
2. d	2. c	2. a	2. d	2. b
3. a	3. c	3. c	3. c	3. d
4. a	4. a	4. d	4. c	4. d
5. c	5. d	5. b	5. a	5. a
6. d	6. d	6. c	6. c	6. c
7. d	7. b	7. c	7. b	7. c
8. a	8. d	8. d	8. b	8. a
9. b	9. a	9. a	9. a	9. d
10. b	10. c	10. c	10. c	10. b

Chapter 3	Chapter 6	Chapter 9	Chapter 12	Chapter 15
1. b	1. c	1. a	1. b	1. b
2. b	2. a	2. b	2. a	2. c
3. b	3. d	3. a	3. a	3. a
4. d	4. c	4. d	4. b	4. c
5. c	5. d	5. c	5. a	5. c
6. c	6. a	6. d	6. c	6. c
7. d	7. c	7. a	7. a	7. d
8. d	8. c	8. a	8. d	8. c
9. d	9. a	9. b	9. b	9. b
10. a	10. a	10. a	10. c	10. c

Chapter 16

1. b
2. b
3. a
4. c
5. d
6. d
7. c
8. d
9. a
10. c

Chapter 17

1. c
2. b
3. c
4. c
5. a
6. a
7. d
8. c
9. d
10. a

Chapter 18

1. b
2. b
3. a
4. b
5. c
6. b
7. d
8. d
9. d
10. a

Chapter 19

1. b
2. d
3. d
4. c
5. b
6. c
7. a
8. d
9. a
10. c

Index

Numbers in *italics* refer to tables and illustrations.